THE OXFORD HANDBOOK OF

DANCE AND
WELLBEING

THE OXFORD HANDBOOK OF

DANCE AND WELLBEING

Edited by

VICKY KARKOU, SUE OLIVER,

and

SOPHIA LYCOURIS

OXFORD

UNIVERSITY PRESS

Oxford University Press is a department of the University of Oxford. It furthers
the University's objective of excellence in research, scholarship, and education
by publishing worldwide. Oxford is a registered trade mark of Oxford University
Press in the UK and certain other countries.

Published in the United States of America by Oxford University Press
198 Madison Avenue, New York, NY 10016, United States of America.

Library of Congress Cataloging-in-Publication Data
Names: Karkou, Vicky, editor. | Oliver, Sue, 1952– editor. | Lycouris, Sophia, 1961– editor.
Title: The Oxford handbook of dance and wellbeing / edited by Vicky Karkou,
Sue Oliver and Sophia Lycouris.
Other titles: Handbook of dance and wellbeing
Description: New York, NY : Oxford University Press, 2017.
Identifiers: LCCN 2016050561 | ISBN 9780199949298 (hardback) | ISBN 9780197526330 (paperback) |
ISBN 9780190655112 (epub)
Subjects: LCSH: Dance—Psychological aspects. | Dance—Social aspects. | Dance—Physiological
aspects. | Dance therapy. | Well-being. | BISAC: MUSIC / Genres & Styles / Dance.
Classification: LCC GV1588.5 .O84 2017 | DDC 792.8—dc23
LC record available at https://lccn.loc.gov/2016050561

The image used for the cover of the book is created by Professor Raymond MacDonald and it is titled:
"Dance in the Sun then Head to water"; used with permission.

Devoted to our life and dance partners for supporting us in the making of this book.

CONTENTS

PART II: DANCE WITHIN PERFORMATIVE CONTEXTS

PART III: DANCE IN EDUCATION

PART V: DANCE IN HEALTHCARE CONTEXTS

FOREWORD

PROFESSOR RAYMOND MACDONALD

Reid School of Music, Edinburgh College of Art,
University of Edinburgh, UK

DANCE presents beautiful and complex ambiguities. As an elemental mode of expression it has the potential to communicate ideas and emotions that are profound, timeless, and universal. Importantly, as embodied movement, dance opens up a limitless landscape of interpretative possibilities, and this ambiguity of meaning is one of the primary reasons why dance is a powerful communicative medium. Regardless of the specific idea or emotion a choreographer wishes to convey, a dancer, and subsequently the viewer, interprets meaning with reference to a dynamic and constantly evolving stream of variables such as culture, personality, expectations, previous experience, and so on. Ambiguity is celebrated within aesthetic epistemologies, and beauty and meaning are constructed along an infinite number of dimensions. Dance is therefore a powerful, unique, and separate channel of communication and, given these features, the potential links to health and wellbeing are emphatic and clear.

However, within healthcare epistemologies, ambiguity has a more controversial place, not least because in this context goals are to enhance wellbeing, alleviate suffering, and ameliorate pain and distress by accurately predicting the effects of specific interventions. Therefore, with time and resources in demand like never before, researchers working in this area seek to reduce uncertainty to further knowledge about how interventions can be developed and delivered. In contributing to the growing body of knowledge that seeks not only to understand the health benefits of dance, but also to shed light on the mechanisms that underpin these developments, this book is both a celebration of, and desire to reduce, ambiguity.

A wealth of approaches innovatively, systematically, and concisely investigate how embodied movement can be used for healthcare purposes, and this book celebrates both the beauty of dance and its potential for positive effects. Of course, beauty is a controversial word. In the arts, narrow constructions of beauty can inhibit participants' expression or reduce confidence. Nonetheless, beauty can also be conceptual, intellectual, unconscious, and manifested in oblique ways, and this is implied and explored within many of the chapters.

Beauty can also be evident in virtuosic performances, where mesmerizing technique and craft are on display for all to see. However, virtuosity is an overrated virtue, and the debilitating expectations of craft-based virtuosity can be particularly stifling in music and dance. When a baby, in a display of innate creative virtuosity, first explores a musical instrument or responds rhythmically to music, the aim is adventure and discovery. It is a search for newness, for creative expression and for human connection. The desire to communicate and to collaborate in music and movement is universal. Self-expression through movement is not only a quest for self and a desire for expression, but fulfils a need to be connected and feel part of something beyond the boundaries of our body. Creative collaboration is fundamental to music and dance and these features are implied in all the interventions presented.

One challenge for researchers is to develop an evidence base to support the use of these interventions for health and wellbeing purposes. This text demonstrates how the field has moved beyond a reliance on randomised controlled trials and draws evidence from multiple sources including qualitative, quantitative, experimental, anecdotal, neurological, discursive, and so on. What is crucial is that we are able to differentiate between these different types of evidence, while at the same time allowing them to coexist.

'And those who were seen dancing were thought to be insane by those who could not hear the music.' This epithet—of unknown provenance, but possibly (or fancifully) by Nietzsche—not only highlights the subjective nature of mental health but also subtlety signifies the inextricable link between dancing and music. From Elvis Presley's scandalizing gyrations, to the percussive polyrhythms of Will Gaines' tap shoes; from the balletic performances of Evelyn Glennie, to the choreographed feet-stamp and drags and hand-claps of Michael Jackson's dancers in 'Thriller', where music ends and dance begins is often beautifully ambiguous. Moreover, dance shares some fundamental features with music. It is universal—all societies use music and dance for a vast array of social purposes—and it is accessible and social—everybody can dance. Like music, dance is a creative and a particularly potent form of collaborative creativity. Therefore, it is a universally accessible form of collaborative creativity, quintessentially social, and inextricably linked to families, cultures, and educational systems. It is therefore an excellent medium to study in terms of its benefits on health and wellbeing.

Dance, and all artistic endeavours, have issues of 'self' and 'other' as core themes. As suggested previously, artistic expression is often constructed as both an expression of individual identity and also as a form of collaborative creativity that celebrates the importance collectivism. One theme that emerges from this book is the concept of identity and the potential for dance to bring about positive changes. Constructions of the self focus upon a fluid, constantly evolving, and socially constructed view of personality. However, personality, self, and identity are contested terms (MacDonald et al. 2017). For example, are is a finite number of stable enduring building blocks of personality, neurologically determined, identified as traits and constituted by our genetic inheritance that predict our behaviour? Or are we individually so unique, so phenomenologically idiosyncratic, that to understand personality effectively we have to explore subjective experience? If so, are attempts at population generalization essentially futile? Maybe it makes no sense to think of identity residing within the mind at all, but rather constituted in the language that we use on a day-to-day basis. Alternatively, is the driving force of the self the universal and psychodynamic unconscious motivations of existence that if expressed unaltered lead to our annihilation? These are just some of the approaches to personality, and they produce infinite options when searching for explanations of behaviour.

In endeavouring to understand dance interventions in healthcare contexts, this book makes a bold and innovative step in pulling together a multidisciplinary group of leading international scholars who tackle issues of identity in different yet related ways. The chapters present an overarching view of research highlighting the ambiguities of relating and living in a complex contemporary world. The complexities of relating and the contrasting priorities of the individual versus the group have engaged generations of thinkers. Kierkegaard's reflections on his own identity and relationships was, he believed, transfigured by divine governance into universal significance, and he viewed himself as a 'singular universal' (Lane 2010). Divine governance or not, the father of existentialism did signal that no matter how personal and intimate our psychological journeys, there are commonalities in the ambiguities of relating that resonate universality.

The book does not present comprehensive structures of personality but rather the chapters open up multiple seams, narrow and endlessly deep—multiple seams of personality dilemmas. These dilemmas are interrogated and problematized in such a way that we are invited to speculate on the nature of personality and whether or not we engage with its implications there is no escape from the Faustian *Gretchenfrage* (the big question) of the context. What is personality? While Nietzsche's answer to the original *Grechenfrage* question was 'God is dead', he did view dance as an almost sacred pastime, stating, in *Thus Spoke Zarathustra* (1891): 'I would believe only in a God that knows how to dance'. Nietzsche danced daily, saying that it was his 'only kind of piety', his 'divine service'. Moreover, he was well known to be a proponent of the arts, with dance being his particular favourite. This was partly due to his belief in 'life-affirmation', in which he not only encouraged artistic pursuits such as dancing but, conversely, invited us to question all activities that drain life's vast but finite energy from us. 'We should consider every day lost on which we have not danced at least once'. So, was Nietzsche really a bit of a groover? It has to be said that from an evidence-based perspective we are not sure exactly whether he danced every day or what his precise pronouncements were on dancing, but there is no doubt that he placed immense importance on artistic endeavours and, in particular, was an advocate for the positive effects of dancing.

One of life's fundamental challenges, which dance facilitates, is how to develop, negotiate and maintain intimacy. There are, of course, many barriers to intimacy: the need to ensure that vulnerabilities are not exposed, and that personal space is preserved and not threatened. Issues of vulnerability and intimacy are tied up with how we relate to the world, and these ambiguities of relating begin at birth in the cooing and babbling that takes place between a parent and a baby. There is considerable evidence to suggest that these interactions are musical, rhythmical, and dance-like. Everybody has a social and biological guarantee of musicianship—not a vague utopian ideal, but the conclusion drawn by scientists researching the foundations of human behaviour (MacDonald et al. 2012). Before we communicate by using language, music plays a fundamental role in the earliest and most important bonding relationship of our life: that with our parents. We sing before we can talk, and we dance before we can walk. These interactions are improvisatory and ambiguous (MacDonald and Wilson 2016)—improvisatory in the sense that improvisation is defined as a spontaneous, creative, and social unfolding of communication. Therefore, not only are we all musical, and not only are we all dancers, but we are all improvisers. Life's beautiful and ambiguous journey is one long improvisation.

References

Lane, K. H. (2010). *Kierkegaard and the Concept of Religious Authorship*. Tübingen: Mohr Siebeck.

MacDonald, R. A. R., Kreutz, G., and Mitchell, L. A. (eds.) (2012). *Music, Health and Wellbeing*. Oxford: Oxford University Press.

MacDonald, R. A. R., Miell, D., and Hargreaves, D. J. (eds.) (2017). *The Handbook of Musical Identities*. Oxford: Oxford University Press.

MacDonald, R. A. R. and Wilson, G. B. (2016). 'Billy Connolly, Daniel Barenboim, Willie Wonka, Jazz Bastards and the universality of improvisation', in G. Lewis and B. Piekut (eds.). *The Oxford Handbook of Critical Improvisation Studies*. New York, NY: Oxford University Press, pp. 103–21.

Nietzsche, F. (1891). *Thus Spoke Zarathustra: A Book for All and None*. Chemnitz: Ernst Schmeitzner.

Foreword

....

SHARON CHAIKLIN, BC-DMT
Past President, American Dance Therapy Association,
Columbia, MD, USA

THE scope of this large tome is beyond the usual. It is clearly a reference book to which one can go for numerous reasons such as to gather information, to question, to rethink, and to stimulate new possibilities. The co-editors have made use of their many years of experience in dance, research, therapy, and teaching to formulate the vast scope that dance brings to the newly developing areas called 'wellbeing'. They have called upon a large network of practitioners from several countries to offer their unique perspectives on a wide range of subjects that nevertheless focuses on movement, the body, and dance in relation to the ideas of aspects of wellbeing.

The nature of dance itself is naturally therapeutic as it makes use of the totality of the human being: the physical self, the creative self, the expressive self, and the emotional self. By examining it in more detail to discover how it may be used more purposefully in multiple settings is a fruitful endeavour. This is certainly accomplished in many chapters offered under the categories of the body, performance, education, community, and health. The authors describe how each of their areas of expertise is used to enable growth and self-satisfaction. Some make use of various forms of research in describing the results while others are more of a narrative. However, all have a point of view which pinpoints an aspect of the work which leads to the idea of wellbeing.

Wellbeing is developing as an idea in many fields, such as public policy, psychology, psychiatry, and physical and mental health. It is generally described as satisfaction with life as long as basic needs are met economically, if one has health and strong personal relationships and there is a sense of purpose and accomplishment that sustains one in daily life. Each of the authors has examined, through the lens of their practice, how the use of their knowledge and skills make use of dance in its many forms, and the possible implications that provide depth to their work in meeting one or more aspects of the above description of wellbeing.

My own experiences as a performer and long-time practitioner of dance therapy in mental-health settings, as well as teaching my profession in graduate schools and workshops internationally, resonate with many of the ideas and possibilities set forth within the many chapters. Some of them stimulated new thinking about areas less familiar to me. It would be my assumption that even those who are knowledgeable in the art of dance, will find much to hold their interest as they explore the work of others in related but different areas.

It has been a vast task to gather so much information into one handbook, for which the editors are to be commended. It not only their vision but their openness to many unusual possibilities that may be beneficial to the reader. What makes this book of particular value is that there is recognition that words do not always do service to the topic of movement. Movement is an ephemeral art form that cannot be recorded on a piece of paper satisfactorily. In recognition of this, the editors have therefore gathered a large array of videos connected to the various chapters, which are then made accessible. To see what the author is describing adds a whole new dimension to understanding and learning. To my knowledge, this is a powerful addition that has not been available before.

The understanding of all that dance has to offer has been slow in acceptance among the many systems that provide multi-services to people of all ages and many needs. In some countries it has been suspect, as the body is usually disconnected from the thinking self and is not thought to provide more than functional or sexual use. In others, dance might be more acceptable as part of the culture but not yet integrated as offering more in-depth personal resources for a variety of needs. For those who believe in its incredible possibilities in providing aid for such problems as learning disabilities, depression, social isolation, chronic pain, and a multitude of other issues that cry out for attention, we are patiently hoping that the larger world will soon understand the power of dance. This addition to the literature will offer the opportunity for others to learn what dance has to offer and therefore include it as an idea whose time has come.

EDITORS

....

Vicky Karkou, PhD, is Professor of Dance, Arts and Wellbeing at Edge Hill University, Ormskirk, UK. She is a qualified researcher, educator, dance teacher, and dance movement psychotherapist, having worked with vulnerable children and adults in schools, voluntary organizations, and the NHS. Her main research and teaching area is in the arts for wellbeing. She has an honorary doctorate of medicine from Riga Stradins University in recognition of her contribution to the development of arts therapies training in Latvia. She is well published in national and international journals, and is the co-editor for the international journal *Body, Movement and Dance in Psychotherapy*. She travels extensively as a speaker at conferences and educational programmes around the world and as a consultant in those fields.

Sue Oliver, PhD, M.Ed., BA, PGCE, Cert. Dance in Ed., is a freelance dance tutor and researcher. Based in Scotland, she left her post as senior teacher and dance tutor for her local education authority to concentrate on her research in creative dance and wellbeing, focusing on children, adolescents, and latterly older adults, including seated movement to music in daycare settings. Current projects include dance for people with Parkinson's disease, and community-based choreographic projects.

Sophia Lycouris, PhD, is Reader in Interdisciplinary Choreography at the University of Edinburgh, Edinburgh College of Art, with responsibility for Interdisciplinary Creative Practices, Masters and PhD programmes. Her research specialism is in haptic experiments.

Contributors

Thania Acarón, PhD (University of Aberdeen), MEd (New York University), DMP, is a performer, choreographer, and dance movement therapist from Puerto Rico, and is currently based in Scotland and Wales. She obtained her PhD on the role of dance in violence prevention, and is currently working as a performing arts lecturer at University of Wales Trinity Saint David. Thania offers international workshops on movement, wellbeing, and interdisciplinary, practice and is co-artistic director of Orphaned Limbs Collective. <http://www.thania.info>; <http://www.orphanedlimbs.com>

Beatrice Allegranti, PhD, is Reader in Dance Movement Psychotherapy and Director of the Centre for Arts Therapies Research at the University of Roehampton. She is Senior Registered Dance Movement Psychotherapist and Clinical Supervisor, ADMPUK. Her international experience encompasses choreography and film-making, as well as clinical practice and supervision. Her clinical experience spans UK NHS work in adult mental health, dementia, special needs, autism, and training staff in dementia units to engage with service users through kinaesthetic empathy in treatment. Beatrice's feminist research investigates the boundaries and politics of moving bodies in performance, psychotherapeutic, and scientific contexts. She is passionate about the power of the arts as a vehicle for not just showing, but of 'knowing', giving us a way to understand the complexity of human experiences in a multilayered and creative way. She has numerous publications.

Abdulazeem Alotaibi, PhD (Queen Margaret University, Edinburgh), is head of physical education and kinaesiology at Qassim University, Alqassim, Saudia Arabia, and has an MSc in kinaesiology. His special interest is in movement therapy with children who have mild learning difficulties.

Diane Amans is a freelance dance artist, lecturer, and consultant offering professional development, arts and health projects, evaluation, and mentoring. She is course tutor on the annual Introduction to Community Dance Practice summer school organized by People Dancing: Foundation for Community Dance, and runs a similar course for the Japan Contemporary Dance Network in Osaka. In the UK she delivers training and follow-up mentoring for dance artists, volunteers, and activity leaders working with groups in a range of settings around the country. Her published work spans dance in communities and arts and health sectors, including dance with older people. She is a 2014 Winston Churchill Fellow, and has worked with community dance practitioners in Australia and New Zealand.

Foteini Athanasiadou, MSc, RDMP, has worked as a primary school teacher in Anatolia College, Greece, for three years. She has been involved in NGO activities, working with deprived children with emotional difficulties on a voluntary base. She has also worked with dementia suffers, children on the autistic spectrum, and adults on the autistic spectrum as a dance movement psychotherapy student.

Zoë Avstreih, PhD, is Professor Emeritus (Naropa University), the Founder and Director of the Center for the Study of Authentic Movement, a Board Certified dance/movement therapist (American Dance Therapy Association), a licensed professional counsellor in Colorado, and a licensed psychoanalyst and creative arts therapist in New York State. Currently, she devotes her professional time to offering retreats and training opportunities for mature individuals to immerse in the practice of Authentic Movement for personal and professional development. A pioneer in the development of Authentic Movement, she lectures and teaches internationally and has published widely in the field.

Gonzalo Bacigalupe, EdD (University of Massachusetts at Amherst), MPH (Harvard University), is Professor of the Master of Science in Family Therapy Program and the PhD in the Department of Counseling and School Psychology, College of Education and Human Development at the University of Massachusetts in Boston. He is a Visiting Senior Researcher at the National Research Center for Integrated Management of Natural Disasters, and Visiting Professor at the Catholic University of Valparaiso in Chile. He is a representative of the APA International Relations in Psychology Committee, and is member of several editorial boards and co-editor of *Psicoperspectivas*, an open-source Chilean psychology journal dedicated to the interface of the individual with society.

Jane Bacon is Professor of Dance, Performance, and Somatics at the University of Chichester, and has a private practice as a Jungian analyst, focusing trainer, and Authentic Movement practitioner. She teaches Authentic Movement, and is co-director of the Choreographic Lab and co-editor of the journal *Choreographic Practices*. Her key interest is in creative processes—artistic, psychological, and spiritual approaches such as 'focusing', 'active imagination', and 'mindfulness'. Her work is widely published.

Fiona Bannon, PhD, is Chair of Dance in Higher Education in the UK, and is based at the University of Leeds, working with students exploring collaborative practice, choreography, research methods, and improvisation. Her main work with doctoral researchers touches on investigations of varied arts practice as research. Her current research includes the preparation of a manuscript, 'Approaching collaborative practices: ethical considerations in performance and dance'. She is part of the team currently exploring the relaunch of World Dance Alliance-Europe.

Nancy Beardall, PhD, BC-DMT, LMHC, CMA, is Dance/Movement Therapy Coordinator in the Graduate School of Arts and Sciences at Lesley University, Cambridge, Massachusetts. As a dance/movement therapist, consultant, Certified

Movement Analyst, and educator, her work has focused on dance, dance/movement therapy, and cognitive, social/emotional, and relational development using dance/movement therapy and the expressive arts in the public schools. Her community-building programmes through the expressive arts have involved students, parents, and community members. She is a co-author of *Marking Connections: Building Community and Gender Dialogue in Secondary Schools*. She is active in the American Dance Therapy Association, and currently serves on the Approval Committee, Educator's Committee, and ADTA Standards Task Force.

Bettina Bläsing, PhD, is a post-doctoral researcher and responsible investigator at the Center of Excellence Cognitive Interaction Technology (CITEC) at Bielefeld University, Germany. Her academic background is in biology, leading to work as a scientific editor and science journalist for various newspapers. As scientific coordinator at Leipzig University she conducted postdoctoral work in Leipzig before joining the Neurocognition and at Bielefeld University, Germany. Her main research interests are mental representations of body, movement, and space, the control and learning of complex movements and manual actions, and expertise in dance.

Jan Bolwell is a choreographer, dance educator, performer, and playwright. She is Director of Wellington's Crows Feet Dance Collective, a community dance company for mature women. Since its inception in 1999 she has created twenty-five works for the company, including 'The Armed Man' in commemoration of World War I, and 'Hākari: The Dinner Party', which examines the lives of ten iconic historic and contemporary women from Asia and the Pacific. She has also written and performed in five plays, all of which have toured extensively throughout New Zealand. Jan works as a tertiary dance educator. She writes education resources for the Royal New Zealand Ballet, and is an adviser to Te Kura, New Zealand's national distance education school.

Iris Bräuninger, PhD (University of Tübingen), MA (Laban Centre/City University London), completed her dance studies (TELOS Dance Theatre) in Stuttgart. She is a certified psychotherapist (ECP), registered senior dance therapist, supervisor (BTD, ADMTE), and KMP notator. She worked as a postdoctoral researcher at the University of Deusto, Spain. She is a lecturer and tutor at the DMT Master Program at the Universidad Autonoma Barcelona, Spain. She has published numerous articles and two books. Iris has more than twenty years of clinical practice in hospital and psychotherapeutic settings, and was formerly a researcher and deputy head of the Dance Movement, Music and Physio Therapy Department, Psychiatric University Hospital, Zürich. She is currently affiliated to the University of Applied Sciences of Special Needs Education, Zürich.

Jo Bungay-Orr, MSc (Queen Margaret University), studied dance from the age of three at the Susan Robinson School of Ballet, and completed her training at the Royal Ballet School. She worked and performed as a professional ballet dancer under her maiden name, Bungay, primarily with the Scottish Ballet, before embarking on her studies in dance movement psychotherapy. Jo has mainly worked with children in mainstream schools, but also has experience with adult mental health groups in Glasgow. She now lives with her husband in Scotland, where they provide support to vulnerable young people who are leaving care.

Ramsay Burt, PhD, is Professor of Dance at De Montfort University, Leicester, UK. His publications include aspects of gender, race, and modernity. In 2013–14, with Professor Christy Adair, he undertook a two-year funded research project in British Dance and the African Diaspora which culminated in an exhibition at the International Slavery Museum in Liverpool. With Susan Foster, he is founder editor of *Discourses in Dance*. Since 2008 he has been a regular visiting teacher at PARTS in Brussels.

Luis Calmeiro, PhD, MSc, is a lecturer in sport and exercise psychology at Abertay University, Dundee. His research focuses on stress, cognitive appraisals, coping mechanisms when performing under pressure, and the study of health-related behavioural and psychosocial correlates of physical activity and wellbeing. He maintains a number of national and international collaborations, and his work has been published in peer-reviewed journals in the areas of sport and exercise psychology and public health.

Chan Nga Shan is a dancer, dance instructor, choreographer, and dance movement psychotherapist. After graduating from the Hong Kong Academy for Performing Arts, She began her career by working in different media with different artists, including visual arts, films, site-specific dance, musical and theatrical performances, and international commercial events with renowned brands. As a dancer, she has always been fascinated with the power of movements, and began her journey to discover the knowledge of dance movement psychotherapy. Her main area of interest is in non-pharmaceutical interventions for mental illness. She has worked with adults showing symptoms of schizophrenia, dementia, and autism, and with children with special needs. Shan is recently volunteering in Kenya and China, providing DMP sessions for children suffering from HIV and children who have had traumatic experiences.

Athiná Copteros, PhD, MSc, is a registered dance movement psychotherapist having completed her MSc at Queen Margaret University, Edinburgh. She has recently completed her doctoral studies at Rhodes University, Grahamstown, South Africa. Her work currently focuses on the relationality between people and ecology and the role that body and movement can play in healing the split within and between ourselves, each other and our environment. Coming from a country with a history of colonialism and apartheid, social justice is critical to her work, and involves a focus on creating effective agency. Her PhD with a transdisciplinary group of researchers explores ways of working within transdisciplinary complex social–ecological systems using DMP.

Joan Davis is a certified BMC® practitioner, an Authentic Movement practitioner, and a Hakomi Sensorimotor Trauma Psychotherapist based in Wicklow, Ireland. She pioneered contemporary dance in Ireland in the 1970s and 1980s, and has experimented with collaborative art as a professional artist and therapist. She has authored two books on Authentic Movement and performance, and has developed and taught somatic practice for many years. In 2012 she began Origins, a three-year somatically based training programme, approved by ISMETA, of the human developmental and evolutionary process from preconception to standing.

Louise Douse, PhD, is a Lecturer in Dance at the University of Bedfordshire, specializing in dance and technology, on which she has presented papers at several international conferences. She is Secretary of the Laban Guild in the UK, and continues to develop her research in the area of movement analysis and optimal experience. Louise has also recently been granted funding from her institution for research in the area of, and motivation in, student learning, with the aim of developing an interactive digital tool for skill development and personal goal setting.

Kim Dunphy, PhD, has worked as a dance educator and therapist in a range of settings, including community groups, schools, hospitals, and disability services. She has lectured on dance education at Deakin and Melbourne Universities, and on dance movement therapy at RMIT University. She is a partner in Making Dance Matter, a consultancy which contributes to evidence for the efficacy of dance-movement and other expressive arts therapies. Her PhD thesis (Deakin University, Melbourne) investigated 'The role of participatory arts in social change in East Timor'.

Mark Edward, PhD, is a performance artist, dance maker, and educator. He has worked for Rambert Dance Company and Senza Tempo Dance Theatre, and with Penny Arcade in her seminal work *Bad Reputations*. His principle research areas include gender, sexuality, ageing, and wellbeing in performance. He has published in scholarly and non-academic books and journals in these areas. At the core of his investigations is the idea of self in research, or, as he puts it, 'mesearch'. Mark was awarded a PhD in 2016 for his mesearching into ageing in dance and drag queen performance cultures. He continues to deliver his mesearch at various conferences throughout the world, and creates work for various companies and arts organizations.

Barbara Erber, MSc (Dance Movement Psychotherapy), also holds a Diploma in Integrative Bodywork. She first trained in various forms of music therapy. Illnesses in her teens and early twenties led her on a profound healing journey, which inspired a passionate discovery of psychotherapy and the world of the body and movement. She has been working with traumatized adults and children in various settings, focusing on the relationship between trauma and physical symptoms. Her life and work are profoundly influenced by the discipline of Authentic Movement. She recently embarked on a PhD, studying how fear of self-expression is processed in Authentic Movement.

Paola Esposito, PhD (Brookes University), MA (Goldsmiths College), is an Early Career Research and Teaching Fellow in Medical Anthropology at the Institute of Social and Cultural Anthropology, University of Oxford. Her main research interest is the social articulation of the lived body through performative and therapeutic practices. She is currently working on integrating visual and graphic methods in the teaching and learning of Medical Anthropology.

Anita Forsblom, PhD, is a music therapist, supervisor, dance/movement therapist, and Fellow of the Bonny Method of Guided Imagery and music, granted by the Association for Music and Imagery (USA). She is a private practitioner of music therapy and dance/movement therapy in Finland, and is interested in people's experiences of music listening, and therapy processes in music therapy and dance movement therapy.

Carolyn Fresquez received an MSc in Dance Movement Psychotherapy (DMP) from Queen Margaret University in Edinburgh, Scotland, and is a registered member of the Association for Dance Movement Psychotherapy, United Kingdom (ADMP UK). She received her undergraduate degree in Creative Studies, Literature from the University of California, Santa Barbara. She believes strongly in a mind–body connection, in movement's capacity for transformation, and in the power of a therapeutic relationship. She has experience working with a variety of people and clients in many different artistic, therapeutic, and educational capacities. She lives with her family in Albuquerque, New Mexico.

Thomas Fuchs, MD, PhD, is a psychiatrist and philosopher, and Jaspers Professor and head of the section 'Phenomenological Psychopathology and Psychotherapy' at the Department of Psychiatry in Heidelberg, Chairman of the Section 'Philosophical Foundations of Psychiatry' of the German Psychiatric Association (DGPPN), and Fellow of the Marsilius-Kolleg (Centre for Advanced Interdisciplinary Studies) at the University of Heidelberg. His major research areas are phenomenological psychopathology, psychology and psychotherapy; coherence and disorders of self-experience, phenomenology and cognitive neuroscience, and history and ethics of medicine and psychiatry.

Doran George, PhD (UCLA), has published extensively on somatic training in late-twentieth-century contemporary dance. He trained at the European Dance Development Center (NL). He has secured public and other funding (for example, Arts Council of England, British Council) for choreography that interrogates the construction of (trans)gender, queer, and disabled identities. He also applies dance in non-arts contexts; for example, in residency with the Alzheimer's Association. He produces academic and professional symposia and conferences, while in universities, art colleges, and professional dance, and teaches critical and studio courses in dance, performance, and cultural studies.

June Gersten Roberts, is a senior lecturer in dance at Edge Hill University, Liverpool, where she teaches dance theory and choreography. Her dance videos and tactile installations explore sensory experiences, closely observing texture, skin, and incidental movement. She works across the disciplines of video, dance, writing and textile arts, exploring the haptic image, body and touch. Collaborative projects with dancers and visual artists include performances, videos and installations created for galleries, hospitals, libraries and museums.

Nancy Goldov, PsyD, BC-DMT, is a psychologist and board-certified dance/ movement therapist, in Seattle, Washington. She provides dance/movement therapy, psychoanalytic psychotherapy, Eye Movement Desensitization and Reprocessing, and neuropsychological testing to adults. Her dissertation research, on the effects of medical dance/movement therapy on body image in women with breast cancer was supported, in part, by a grant from the Marian Chace Foundation of the American Dance Therapy Association. She is the Washington State Public Education Coordinator for the American Psychological Association, and is also a dancer and musician.

Marie-Helene Grosbras, PhD, holds the research chair of Laboratoire de Neurosciences Cognitives at Aix Marseille University. Her research interests include the relationships between the control of action and the control of perception, with a particular interest in social perception. More precisely, she studies how the brain mechanisms involved in those processes can change as a function of experience, brain damage, or development. She uses a variety of psychophysics and brain-imaging techniques in healthy humans (functional magnetic resonance imaging, electroencephalography, and non-invasive brain stimulation).

Judith Lynne Hanna, PhD (Columbia), is an affiliate research scientist in the Department of Anthropology at the University of Maryland, College Park, USA, and a consultant in the arts, education, health, public policy, and the United States Constitution's First Amendment protection of speech, including dance. See www.judithhanna for publications on dance and the body, within performative contexts, in education, and in the community. As a dancer, anthropologist, and critic, she examines dance in its many manifestations and in diverse locations internationally. Her work has been published widely in thirteen countries and in several languages.

Erika Hansen, EdD (Counselling Psychology), has focused on military sexual trauma and predictive variables of PTSD among victims and perpetrators. She is a case manager in the CDCR prison population, and has worked in the mental health field as a crisis counsellor, detox counsellor, case manager, resident assistant, mentor, intake worker, and domestic violence crisis counsellor. She focuses on building relationships with safety, using existential, social construction approaches aimed to empower the clients with emphasizing their human potential

Heather Hill, PhD, is a dance movement therapist and professional member of the Dance-Movement Therapy Association of Australia. Much of her work is with people living with dementia, in the role of consultant in dementia care, offering experiential/embodied training in person-centred care practice. She continues to work as a dance movement therapist and teacher. She has published extensively and contributed several chapters to books in the fields of nursing, dementia, and dance movement therapy, as well as authoring her own.

Michael Huxley, PhD, is Reader in Dance at De Montfort University, Leicester, UK. His work has been widely published in books and journals, and his published research has been on early modern dance and dance history. He has been a senior member of various boards, committees, and teams, and is currently Director of De Montfort University's

Centre for Interdisciplinary Research in Dance. His most recent publication is *The Dancer's World 1920–1945: Modern Dancers and Their Practices Reconsidered*.

Lindesay M. C. Irvine, PhD, MSc, BA, FHEA, RNT, RGN, is a senior lecturer in nursing at Queen Margaret University, Edinburgh. Her main academic interests are in how and why people learn and change through education, along with a continuing enthusiasm for helping people achieve the best they can by facilitating their learning. She supervises and facilitates students at all levels of study, and is particularly interested in using person-centred approaches as a means of engaging students in developing their own learning with relevance to their professional practice or learning contexts.

Corinne Jola, PhD, is a lecturer in psychology at Abertay University, Dundee, Scotland, and is a trained choreographer (MA, Laban Trinity College, London), dancer (IWANSON, School of Contemporary Dance, Munich), and cognitive neuroscientist (PhD, University of Zurich), and has held a number of post-doctoral posts in the field of arts, especially interdisciplinary approaches. She has published extensively, and has collaborated and trained with the dance company EG|PC in Amsterdam. Her own artistic installations and choreographic work was presented across the UK and in Switzerland, and her teaching spans the intersection of dance and science to artists across Europe (for example, Impulse Tanz Festival, Vienna, Tanzfabrik, Berlin, and FAA, Bataville in France).

Julie Joseph, MSc (Queen Margaret University), is Chief Executive of Common Thread, a Scottish company offering therapeutic residential care and education to some of the country's most vulnerable young people. She has worked with adolescents for more than fifteen years, and as a movement psychotherapist she works with young people within the care sector and secondary schools. Her work is strongly influenced by attachment and trauma models. She is presently engaged in her PhD study, which focuses on the effect of dance movement psychotherapy on adolescents with symptoms of moderate depression.

Toshiharu Kasai is a professor and the director of Master course of Clinical Psychology, Sapporo Gakuin University, Japan. He is also a Certified Dance Therapist and Vice president of Japan Dance Therapy Association. As a Butoh dancer he is known as Itto Morita of Butoh GooSayTen, performing around the world since 1980s.

Rosie Kay trained at London Contemporary Dance School, and after a career as a performer formed the Rosie Kay Dance Company in 2004. She has created award-winning theatre work that includes 'Soldiers: The Body Is The Frontline' (2010 + 2015), based on extensive research with military, which toured the UK and internationally, 'Sluts of Possession' (2013), in collaboration with the Pitt Rivers Museum, 'There is Hope' (2012), exploring religion, and 'Double Points: K', in collaboration with Emio Greco|PC. Site-specific works include 'Haining Dreaming' (2013), 'The Great Train Dance' (2011), on the Severn Valley Railway, and 'Ballet on the Buses'. Kay was the first Leverhulme Artist in Residence at the School of Anthropology and Museum Ethnography,

University of Oxford, and is a former Rayne Foundation Fellow and Associate Artist of DanceXchange, Birmingham.

Janna Kelbel, Master Student at the University of Heidelberg, Department of Psychology, Heidelberg, Germany.

Anna Kenrick trained at the Northern School of Contemporary Dance, Leeds, after which she worked with the Education Team at The Place, London. In 2002 she joined the Ludus Dance Company, where she worked as both a dancer and teacher. She performed in the tours of 'Perfecting Eugene', 'Trapped', and 'Zygote', as well as working with choreographers Rosie Kay, Filip Van Huffel, and Hannah Gillgren. She joined YDance in 2007 as Project Director for the Free To Dance project, and has choreographed a number of pieces for Project Y, YDance's National Youth Dance Company.

Anna Fiona Keogh is a dance movement psychotherapist, researcher, and Laban-based creative dance teacher in Dublin, Ireland. She works in private practice and in a variety of settings with people of all ages and diverse needs. She is influenced by movement and dance forms such as Authentic Movement, butoh, contact improvisation and tango, and is particularly interested in exploring the relationship between mindfulness practice and movement.

Ann Kipling Brown, PhD, is Professor Emerita of the University of Regina, having worked for many years in the arts education programme in the Faculty of Education. She works extensively in dance education, focusing on assisting children, youth, and adults in finding passion and personal expression in dance. Her research and teaching include dance pedagogy, curriculum development, dance creation, and movement notation. In her professional and community service Ann has served on many committees—provincial, national and international—that focus on the research and role of the arts/dance in community, education, and professional programmes. She also has been involved in hosting provincial and international dance and arts education conferences.

Sabine C. Koch, PhD, MA, BC-DMT, is a psychologist and dance/movement therapist, and a researcher and lecturer at the University of Heidelberg and the University of Alanus in Alfter. She is a specialist in Kestenberg Movement Profiling (KMP), movement analysis, and dance/movement therapy, and her current work includes 'Embodiment: The Influence of Movement on Affect, Attitudes and Cognition', and a national research project on 'Language of Movement and Dance' (BMBF). She has worked with children, and with depressed, psychotic, autistic, psychosomatic, elderly, trauma and dissociative identity disorder patients. Her research interests include embodiment, personality, social psychology, observational methods, psycholinguistics, non-verbal communication, gender, health psychology, phenomenology, body psychotherapy, movement analysis, and creative arts therapies.

Astrid Kolter, Dipl. Psych. (University of Marburg), is a dance/movement therapist (Institute of Frankfurt, 2014). She is a dance teacher, and was a research assistant on the project Body Language of Movement and Dance (University of Heidelberg, 2009–11).

Monika Konold is a certificated music therapist and physiotherapist, living and working in Germany.

Periklis Ktonas, PhD, is Professor Emeritus at the University of Houston, and a senior researcher on biomedical engineering applications with the Department of Psychiatry, University of Athens Medical School. He has conducted several funded research activities, many of which have focused on the development of methodologies for the accurate and efficient analysis of bioelectrical signals, in particular the electroencephalogram (EEG), with clinical applications in neurology and psychiatry. He has been an Associate Editor of the *IEEE Transactions on Biomedical Engineering* and chair of the IEEE EMBS Technical Committee on Neuroengineering. He received the IEEE Third Millenium Medal for his contributions to biomedical engineering.

Kristo Kaarlo Matias Kulju, PhD, is a dance/movement therapist who studied dance and somatics at ISLO. He is currently working as a private practitioner of dance/movement therapy in Finland.

Petra Kuppers, PhD, teaches performance studies and disability studies at the University of Michigan. She is a disability culture activist and a community performance artist. She also teaches at Goddard College's Low Residency MFA in Interdisciplinary Arts, and leads The Olimpias, a performance research collective (<http://www.olimpias.org>). Her *Disability Culture and Community Performance: Find a Strange and Twisted Shape* (2011/2013) explores The Olimpias' arts-based research methods, and won the Sally Banes Prize of the American Society for Theatre Research. Her work has been widely published, and her most recent book is *Studying Disability Arts and Culture: An Introduction* (2014). The Olimpias, of which she is the artistic director is an artists' collective founded in Wales in 1996 during work with mental health system survivors.

Carolyn Lappin was educated at Glasgow University, and began working in the arts at the Citizens' Theatre. From 1984 until 2001 she worked with Scottish Youth Theatre as General Manager, also managing the Old Athenaeum Theatre in central Glasgow. She has also been Administrator for Winged Horse Touring Productions, IPB Productions, and Spontaneous Combustions, and was Chair of the Independent Theatre Council in Scotland from 1996 to 1998, and a member of the UK ITC Board of Directors. She is a mentor for the Federation of Scottish Theatre Step-Up scheme, and a member of the Advisory Board of Conflux. She joined YDance (Scottish Youth Dance) in 2002.

Christina Larek attended the University of Hildesheim, where she studied physical education and German to become a primary-school and secondary-school teacher. Since her early youth she has danced ballet, modern dance, and Latin/standard. Since 2008 she has worked as a professional teacher with pupils of various ages in northern Germany.

Outi Leinonen, MSc (Sports Science), trained in dance from childhood, within a variety of groups, and has performed and competed in Finland and internationally. As a dance teacher she has worked in youth camps in Finland, Brazil, Germany, and Croatia.

Currently, she is teaching in the Christian Dance School of Jyväskylä and dancing in the Campuksen Koonto Dance Team of yje University of Jyväskylä. Her Master's thesis was a research project at the Department of Music, University of Jyväskylä, entitled 'Movement analysis of depressed and non-depressed persons expressing emotions through spontaneous movement to music.'

Susan Loman, MA, BC-DMT, NCC, KMP analyst, is Director of the Dance/Movement Therapy and Counselling Program, and professor and associate chair of the Department of Applied Psychology, Antioch University New England. She has been co-editor of the *American Journal of Dance Therapy*, and has served on numerous boards, including as chair of the ADTA Education Committee. She is a co-author of the book *The Meaning of Movement: Developmental and Clinical Perspectives of the Kestenberg Movement Profile*, and is the author of numerous articles, chapters, and books on the Kestenberg Movement Profile and dance/movement therapy. She teaches her specialities at Antioch and throughout the United States, and has taught in Germany, The Netherlands, Italy, England, Scotland, South Korea, Argentina, and Switzerland. In 2014 she was awarded the Lifetime Achievement Award from the American Dance Therapy Association.

Elizabeth Loughlin, MA, B. Litt Hons Performing Arts, BA Dip. Social Studies, Dip. Dance Movt Th. (IDTIA), is a dance therapist and social worker. She is a professional member of the Dance Therapy Association of Australia, and works as part of the health-care team in the Parent–Infant Research Institute (PIRI) set within the Australian public hospital system. Her mother–infant dance therapy and her former dance therapy with girls and women with Turner syndrome have been regularly presented at national and international health conferences, and her dance therapy and social work is published in dance therapy, health, social work, and medical publications. She has a continuing private studio dance practice, and is lecturer and supervisor in the International Dance Therapy Institute of Australia.

Geoff Luck, PhD (Keele University), has worked at the Department of Music of the University of Jyväskylä, Finland, and latterly as an Assistant Professor. In 2008 he was awarded a five-year Academy of Finland Research Fellowship to study the kinematics and dynamics of musical communication. This interdisciplinary project incorporated elements of biomechanics, psychology, and neuroscience to examine the role of body movement in both rhythmic and expressive musical communication. During his tenure in Jyväskylä, he carried out an extensive range of human-centred scientific studies on a range of topics, and has published more than fifty scientific works. A large proportion of his research has focused on quantifying, classifying, and predicting music-related behaviour using a wide range of statistical techniques.

Alexia Margariti, PhD (University of Peloponnese and University of Athens Medical School), is a teacher of dance, a dance therapist, and past President of the Greek Association of Dance Therapists. She studied at the State School of Dance in Athens, and at the Sorbonne, France, where she obtained a Maitrise de Danse. She has worked at several institutions in Greece with psychiatric populations, children with special needs, drug addicts, and other special groups. Her research interests involve quantification of body movement and neurophysiological parameters in dance therapy.

Mariam Mchitarian, RN, MSc, is a dance/movement psychotherapist who currently works at the Ministry of Health in the Republic of Cyprus. In private practice she is actively involved with dance movement therapy of patients with chronic disease. She studied nursing in Larissa, Greece, and qualified with distinction in 2007. Apart from her nursing duties, she participated in the survey of coronary heart disease in Paphos district, and as speaker in health sciences and medical conferences in Cyprus. She is mainly interested in medical dance movement psychotherapy, and especially the role of dance movement psychotherapy in cardiac rehabilitation and other chronic diseases.

Joseph A. Moutiris, MD, PhD, MSc, FESC, is Associate Director of Cardiology in Nicosia and Paphos General Hospitals, Cyprus, and external lecturer in the University of Nicosia. His special scientific interests include prevention of coronary heart disease. He was the coordinator of the Cyprus Survey of Coronary Heart Disease and of the Paphos Heart Study, the results of which were announced at the 2006 WCC/ESC Congress of Cardiology and the 2010 EuroPrevent Meeting. He is actively involved in teaching medical students trainees in cardiology and other health professionals. He is a member of the board of the Society of Cardiology, and is the coordinator of training in cardiology in Cyprus. He is a reviewer of medical journals, and is the author of a significant number of papers and articles.

Sue Mullane, PhD (Deakin University, Melbourne), BEd, Grad. Dip. Special Education, Grad. Dip. Movement Dance, M.Ed. (dance therapy research), is a partner in Making Dance Matter, a consultancy that seeks to contribute to evidence for the efficacy of dance-movement and other expressive arts therapies. She is a professional member of the Dance Movement Therapy Association of Australasia (DTAA), and is also a primary/special-education teacher who works as a dance-movement specialist in a large special needs school in Melbourne. She has a particular interest in the relationship of dance movement therapy to the education curriculum and in the assessment of dance with special-needs students.

Andrea Olsen is a Professor of Dance and has held the John C. Elder Professorship in Environmental Studies at Middlebury College in Vermont. She is the author of a triad of books: *The Place of Dance, Body and Earth*, and *Bodystories* in collaboration with Caryn McHose, and she performs and teaches internationally.

Tally Palmer is Professor and Director of the Unilever Centre for Environmental Water Quality, Institute for Water Research, Rhodes University, South Africa.

Heidrun Panhofer PhD (University of Hertfordshire), MA (Dance Movement Psychotherapy, London City University), created the Master and Postgraduate Programme of Dance Movement Therapy at the Department of Psychology, Universitat Autònoma de Barcelona, Spain, and has coordinated it since 2003. Originally Austrian, she edited the first book on dance movement therapy in Spanish—*El cuerpo* *en psicoterapia: La teoría y práctica de la Danza Movimiento Terapia (The Body in Psychotherapy: Theory and Practice of Dance Movement Therapy)*—and has published extensively on DMT skills, embodiment approaches, supervision in DMT, and so on. Formerly President of the Spanish Association for Dance Movement Therapy (ADMTE), she lectures in DMT at universities and institutes in Spain, France, Italy, Portugal, and Austria, and her clinical practice includes group and individual work with children, adolescents, and adults in special educational institutions, different psychiatric settings, and in private practice in the UK, Germany, and Spain.

Thomas Paparrigopoulos, PhD, is Associate Professor of Psychiatry at the Department of Psychiatry of the University of Athens Medical School. His clinical and research activities have focused mainly on sleep medicine, alcoholism, psychoneuroendocrinology, neuropsychiatry, disaster psychiatry, and clinical studies in psychiatry. He is member of several Greek, European, and international medical societies, and is co-chair of the WPA section on psychiatry and sleep/wakefulness disorders. He is currently heads the Inpatient Alcohol Detoxification Clinic, the ATHENA Outpatient Detoxification Service, and the Neuropsychiatry Unit at the First Psychiatric Clinic of the Department of Psychiatry, University of Athens Medical School, at Eginition Hospital, and is co-director of the Sleep Study Unit at the same hospital. He is the author or co-author of numerous publications.

Helen Payne, PhD (London), is a professor at the University of Hertfordshire and is principal supervisor for a number of PhD candidates in arts psychotherapies, health, and education. She is an accredited psychotherapist with the United Kingdom Council for Psychotherapy, and is a senior registered dance movement psychotherapist with the Association for Dance Movement Psychotherapy/DMP UK. Her publications include numerous peer-reviewed articles and books. She has led funded and non-funded research projects, and leads a University spin-out Pathways2Wellbeing delivering services using the BodyMind Approach™ for patients in primary health care. She is founding editor-in-chief for the international, peer-reviewed journal *Body, Movement and Dance in Psychotherapy*.

Marcia Plevin is a choreographer, professional dancer, and dance movement therapist, BC-DMT, American counsellor, NCC, and Italian psychologist. She is affiliated as a teacher and supervisor with the Institute of Expressive Psychotherapy, Bologna, the Institute Inspirees of Creative Education, Beijing, Bilgi University, Istanbul, and APID, the Italian association for dance movement therapists. She was co-founder of Creative Movement method Garcia-Plevin, and has taught Authentic Movement throughout Europe for more than twenty years.

Frank Pollick, PhD, is Professor of Psychology at the University of Glasgow, and has previously worked as a research fellow at Advanced Telecommunications Research (ATR) in Kyoto, Japan. His research explores how we experience the sights and sounds of human actions. This includes using behavioural experiments to understand the boundaries of human perception, and brain imaging experiments to understand how brain systems process audio and visual information. He is interested in how experience and development influence the ability to understand actions, and has studied brain mechanisms of action recognition in dancers, drummers, and individuals on the autism spectrum.

Cynthia Pratt is Professor of Dance at Butler University Indianapolis, as well as being a dancer, teacher, and choreographer whose work often reflects her continued interest in dance as both an aesthetic art form and as a catalyst for community building. She received her MFA from Temple University, and is a Certified Movement Analyst through the Laban/Bartenieff Institute for Movement studies in New York City. For the past two decades she has been the Guest Choreographer in Residence for Dance Kaleidoscope, Indiana's premier modern dance company, and has had set works throughout the United States and abroad.

Marko Punkanen, PhD, is a music therapist, dance/movement therapist, and trauma psychotherapist who currently works as a music/dance-movement/psychotherapist and supervisor in private practice. He is actively involved with music therapy and dance/movement therapy training. Previously, he was a researcher in the Finnish Centre of Excellence in Interdisciplinary Music Research at the University of Jyväskylä. He was part of the research team which investigated the perception and preferences of emotions in music of depressed patients and the efficacy of improvisational, individual music therapy for depression.

Matthew Reason is Professor of Theatre and Performance at York St John University, UK. His research engages with theatre and dance audiences, theatre for children, performance documentation, and photography. His publications include *Documentation, Disappearance and the Representation of Live Performance* (2006) and *The Young Audience: Exploring and Enhancing Children's Experiences of Theatre* (2010), and he co-edited, with Dee Reynolds, *Kinesthetic Empathy in Creative and Cultural Contexts* (2012).

Maralia Reca, PhD (Psychology, Palermo University, Buenos Aires), BC-DMT, is a certified dance/movement therapist (American Dance Therapy Association) and a lecturer at Caece University, Buenos Aires, where she founded and directed postgraduate training in dance/movement therapy, as she had also done in San Juan. Formerly, she was a professional dancer at Manhattan Festival Ballet and the Martha Graham School of Contemporary Dance, New York, where she studied DMT. She presents regularly at conferences, teaches abroad, and has much published work. She was elected President of the Argentinean Association of Dance Therapy in 2011.

André Luiz Teixeira Reis, PhD (University of Bristol), MEd (University of Brasilia), is a lecturer and researcher at the University of Brasilia. He graduated in physical education, and later attained his Master's degree and PhD, using capoeira—the Brazilian dance-art-form—as the subject of his studies on health and well-being.

Taira Restar, MA, RSMT, is a somatic movement therapist and coach. She offers international workshops in wellbeing.

Emma Roberts is a movement and drama therapist and certified 5RHYTHMS® teacher, and is currently teaching 5Rhythms internationally. She also works as a freelance movement director in theatre. Her previous work includes movement and drama therapy in mental health, adults with autism, vulnerable families dealing with trauma, bereavement, addiction, abuse, and teenage parenting. Additionally, she has worked as a trainer and actor in public and corporate settings as well as in film, television, and theatre, including as a director and movement specialist for Still Point Theatre.

Suvi Saarikallio, PhD, works as an Academy of Finland Research Fellow at the Department of Music, University of Jyväskylä. Her research focuses on the psychosocial aspects of musical behaviour, including mood and emotion, personality, adolescent development, and wellbeing. She is an internationally acknowledged expert, particularly in research on music as emotional self-regulation, and has presented invited lectures and published articles in international peer-reviewed journals.

Heribert Sattel is Scientific Assistant at Klinikum Rechts der Isar, Munich, Germany.

Claire Schaub-Moore, PhD, CPsychol, AFBPsS, MA DMP, is a Professor of psychology, a chartered psychologist, a counselling psychologist, an Associate fellow of the British Psychological Society, Psychologische Psychotherapeutin, and a dance and movement psychotherapist, group therapist, traumatherapist, and supervisor. Currently, she works with children, adolescents, and adults in her practice, and as a supervisor for various institutions within the social and health welfare system. She teaches in HE in Germany, England, and Austria, and has taught trauma-pedagogics and therapy for several years. She has also published her research work.

Ilene A. Serlin, PhD, BC-DMT, is a licensed psychologist and registered dance/movement therapist in practice in San Francisco and Marin county. She is the past President of the San Francisco Psychological Association, a Fellow of the American Psychological Association, and a past President of the Division of Humanistic Psychology. She has taught at Saybrook University, Lesley University, UCLA, the NY Gestalt Institute, and the C. G. Jung Institute in Zurich. She is the editor of *Whole Person Healthcare* (2007) and the author of much published work. She serves on the editorial boards of *PsycCritiques*, the *American Journal of Dance Therapy*, the *Journal of Humanistic Psychology, Arts and Health: An International Journal of Research, Policy and Practice*, the *Journal of Applied Arts and Health*, and *The Humanistic Psychologist*.

Sherry B. Shapiro, EdD, is Professor Emeritus of Dance and past director of Women's Studies at Meredith College, Raleigh, North Carolina. She has served in state, national, and international organizations, presented nationally and internationally, and is the author or editor of four books. She has been a recipient of a Fulbright Scholarship and Fulbright Specialist, and has received awards for research and artistic work, as well as her work as a dance educator. She has served as a project coordinator for a programme in peace education research developed as a joint effort between North Carolina and the University of Haifa, Israel, and served for six years as the Research Officer for Dance and The Child International.

Allison Singer, PhD, is currently lecturer in Applied Theatre and programme leader for the MA in Applied Theatre and Intervention at the University of Leeds. She is a dance movement psychotherapist, dramatherapist, dance anthropologist and ethnomusicologist. Central to her work is the integration of applied anthropological approaches and arts psychotherapy practice, and the use of a multi-modal approach in arts psychotherapies. Her clinical work includes work with people with profound and complex learning difficulties, elderly people, refugees, and internally displaced children and their families. She has numerous publications, and has presented her research widely. She has led and taught on several drama therapy and dance movement psychotherapy programmes in the UK.

Laura Hope Steckler, PhD, CPsychol, RSMT, is a clinical and somatic psychologist, body psychotherapist, somatic movement therapist, and mindfulness instructor. She trained with body psychotherapy pioneer Ilana Rubenfeld, who integrated the Alexander technique and Feldenkrais method with gestalt psychotherapy. She has danced professionally, and has extensive experience with various movement and somatic disciplines and their use in clinical work. She has a deep and abiding interest in the mind–body connection and how movement can be used to facilitate wholeness and wellbeing.

Jayne Stevens is Principal Lecturer in Dance at De Montfort University, Leicester. Her roles within the University have included Head of Dance (until 2016) and Head of Pedagogic Research in the Centre for Excellence in Performance Arts (2005–09). In 2000 she was awarded a National Teaching Fellowship in recognition of individual excellence and innovation in teaching. She is an editorial board member of the journals *Research in Dance Education* and *Journal of Dance and Somatic Practices*. Her current research encompasses creative practices and pedagogy, dance and spirituality, the history of community and participatory dance, employability and the creative industries.

Marcus Stueck, PhD, is scientific head of interdisciplinary scientific projects on Biodanza and health at the University of Leizig, researching the immunological, endocrinological, physiological, and psychological effects of Biodanza in adults and children. He is also Professor for Educational Psychology in Riga, Professor of Psychology, Leading Scientist, at the University of Applied Science, Saxony (DPFA), and Director of the Institute of Biodanza Research Leipzig (IBR BIONET).

Haodan Tan is a PhD student in human–computer interaction design programming at the School of Informatics, Indiana University. Previously, she obtained her MSc (Psychology, University of Glasgow) and MDes (Hong Kong Polytechnic University). With an interdisciplinary background, her research interests lie in the social and cultural aspects of computing, with an emphasis on the emotional and aesthetic experiences. More specifically, her work includes understanding people's emotional attachments with objects through the lens of heritage perspective, and the implication for HCI and interaction design.

Marietta L. van der Linden PhD (Bioengineering, Strathclyde University, Glasgow) is a senior research fellow at the School of Health Sciences, Queen Margaret University,

Edinburgh, and has an MSc in Human Movement Sciences (VU Amsterdam). She has a special interest in exercise and assistive technology interventions for people with long-term neurological conditions such as cerebral palsy and multiple sclerosis.

Mati Vargas-Gibson, MA (History, Northeastern University, Boston), MA (Fine Arts, Illinois University), has danced ballet, folk, flamenco, and belly dance since an early age. She is an accredited 5Rhythms™ teacher and a member of the International 5Rhythms Teacher's Association, currently teaching regularly in United States and Mexico. Her interests lie in body–mind techniques, and she has complemented her learning and experiences with other body awareness methods, such as SoulMotion™, Feldenkrais™, Authentic Movement™, process work, gestalt movement therapy, yoga, pilates, sufi whirling, ecstatic dance, and ritual trance dance. She is interested in using music as medicine to support the dance and then presencing the unique way each dancer's spirit reacts.

Grigoris Vaslamatzis, MD, is a physician and Professor of Psychiatry at Athens University Medical School (Eginition Hospital). He is a training member of the Hellenic Society of Psychoanalytic Psychotherapy, where he acted as a President 1998–2002 and 2009–13. From 2001 to 2012 was Director of the Department of Psychoanalytic Psychotherapy of Athens University Medical School, and since 2011 he has been Director of the Psychotherapy Centre, the Director of the Department of Personality Disorders, and Director of the Unit of Group Analytic Psychotherapy. He is a Fellow of the American Academy of Psychoanalysis and Dynamic Psychiatry, and a member of the editorial board of *Psychoanalytic Psychotherapy*. He is the editor of four psychoanalytic books, and his work is widely published in international journals.

Alejandra Villegas, PhD, is Director of the Biodanza schools in Leipzig and Riga. Stemming from her work in Argentina and Spain, she produced the first PhD on Biodanza, at the University of Leipzig, researching the psychological effects of Biodanza. She has participated in many Biodanza research projects, and is the author of several scientific publications.

Hilda Wengrower, PhD, is a dance movement therapist and counsellor. She is a lecturer in the Academic College for Society and Arts, Israel, and head of the dance movement therapy section of the Israeli Association of Arts Therapies. She has co-edited and authored work on dance, creative processes, intergroup conflict, clinical aspects of dance movement therapy, artistic methods for research, and principles and methods of arts therapies in non-clinical settings. She is also a journal editor. She teaches and supervises internationally, and retains an active private practice in Jerusalem.

Sarena Wolfaard, BA (Hons), is an accredited 5Rhythms® teacher, which has taken her to Finland, Scotland, and South Africa. She is an Open Floor International Teacher, studying process-oriented psychotherapy, and works in private practice with individuals, incorporating elements from 5Rhythms® and Open Floor International with psychotherapy. As a co-founder of Handspring Publishing, she works with researchers and prominent teachers in manual therapy, bodywork, and movement. She is a member of the International 5Rhythms Teacher's Association, the Complementary Therapy Association, and the Fascia Research Society, and is a UKCP trainee member.

Ania Zubala, PhD, is a psychologist who trained in psychodynamic and arts psychotherapies. She has worked in clinical roles with adults experiencing mental ill-health in Scotland, and is dedicated to improving clinical practice by advancing research in the area of psychotherapy and non-pharmaceutical interventions. Following a research bursary award from Queen Margaret University, Edinburgh, she has been exploring the value of arts psychotherapies in the treatment of adult depression in the UK. This work concluded with a PhD and a number of publications in peer-reviewed journals. Her research focuses on evidence-based interventions to enhance psychological wellbeing of diverse populations, and she is currently a postdoctoral researcher with the Scottish Improvement Science Collaborating Centre at the University of Dundee.

ABOUT THE COMPANION WEBSITE

www.oup.com/us/ohdw

Oxford University Press has created a password-protected website to accompany *The Oxford Handbook of Dance and Wellbeing*. Video content on the site illustrates concepts discussed throughout the *Handbook* by both academics and practitioners. Examples available online are indicated with ▶

Username:	Password:
Music5	Book1745

....

INTRODUCTION

....

VICKY KARKOU, SUE OLIVER,
AND SOPHIA LYCOURIS

DANCE—from the work of the baby kicking his/her legs with excitement when the adult sings a song, to the work of a professional ballet dancer who skilfully performs multiple pirouettes on stage—regards the body as the main agent for creative and artistic engagement. From the breath of an improviser to the contraction and release movement of a contemporary dancer, the body is present, rising, falling, expanding, shrinking, advancing, and retreating, often sensing the inner self, connecting with the environment, living and dying. The body is currently receiving renewed attention from neuroscientists that shifts our understanding of its relationship with the mind. Instead of being treated as inferior to the mind, body and mind as seen as interlinked and interconnected; the body and mind are one. Research studies in neuroscience, for example, provide evidence for the biological basis of thoughts and feelings, and links between the body and cognition and the body and emotions (Schore 1994; Damasio 2000, 2005). The Cartesian split is questioned, giving way to terms such as 'embodied emotion' and 'embodied cognition'. The discovery of mirror neurons in the brain (Rizzolatti et al. 1996; Gazzola et al. 2006) and their links with empathy, and kinaesthetic empathy in particular, also takes a central place in contemporary debates; how we interact with others, what we see and what we experience while we exist in the world are all important and deeply imprinted in our brains and bodies. Finally, the plasticity of the brain, and thus a lifelong ability for humans to make new synaptic connections (Edelman 1987), is another interesting area of work that encourages us to think of humans as being in a state of ongoing change, and in a constant interaction with the environment—an environment we shape, and one that also shapes us. In response to these discoveries, a rippling effect has been created in a number of other fields such as psychology, psychotherapy, education, community practice, and the arts. New ways of thinking have emerged that place the body, movement, and dance in a much more central place than what they had previously, and with renewed significance for wellbeing. However, so far there have been no attempts to examine this topic in a comprehensive manner.

Even less attention has been placed in *dance* and its contribution for wellbeing. Dance—a form of art that is often associated with children, women, or gay people—has suffered from hegemonic notions that attach negative references to this form of art (Polhemus 1998; Meekums 2000; Karkou 2012). Because of this, dance—perceived as insubstantial, frivolous, or even dirty—has received much less attention.

Furthermore, as an embodied art form, the discussion around dance through the written word, and in this case through a book, offers inherent challenges and perpetuates the Cartesian superiority of thought (and 'word') over matter (in this case, 'body'). Books that cover the topic of dance are therefore relatively few. In addition, a range of dance styles from modern and contemporary dance to Biodanza and 5Rhythms and from improvisatory practices and Authentic Movement to Butoh and Capoeira have hardly ever been seen together in one publication. Even more unusual is to bring professional, educational, and community dance practices alongside contributions from the field of dance movement psychotherapy. Finally, the topic of dance as an agent of health and wellbeing that goes beyond popular connections of dance with joy has only recently received some attention (e.g. Beecher 2005; Burkhudt and Rhodes 2012). The scope for exploring this topic further is very wide.

Turning to the concept of wellbeing, there is an overall consensus that health and wellbeing are closely connected with a complex network of interrelated factors (Harris and Hastings 2005). Furthermore, the World Health Organisation (2006) defines health as 'a state of complete physical, mental, and social wellbeing and not merely the absence of disease or infirmity' (p. 1).

Interestingly, in recently years the concept of 'wellbeing' is gaining increasing popularity. Governments in Europe, for example, argue that the economic wealth of a country is not a sufficient measure to capture growth. Following governmental intervention, the Office for National Statistics (ONS) in the UK has recently, and since 2011, begun to measure wellbeing, offering a loose definition of the term, associating it with how people, neighbourhoods, and countries are doing beyond Gross Domestic Product (GDP), the traditional measure of economic growth. Based on a national debate (Office of National Statistics 2011), the same source proposes ten 'measureable' dimensions:

1. Personal wellbeing.
2. Our relationships.
3. Health.
4. What we do.
5. Where we live.
6. The natural environment.
7. Personal finance.
8. The economy.
9. Education and skills.
10. Governance.

These have been turned into quantifiable measures which are now used not only in the UK but in the whole of Europe, if not beyond. The sceptics amongst us may think that these measures have been introduced at an interesting time in order to shift attention away from the economic crisis. However, for those of us who have an interest in dance (and the arts more generally) and wellbeing, the new measures and associated policies bring to the foreground the discussion on wellbeing, and personal wellbeing in particular—an area that has been traditionally neglected.

Of course, we cannot disconnect economic growth from measures of wellbeing; comparing wellbeing measures across European countries, for example—the countries at the top of the ladder in terms of scores of wellbeing measures—tend to be places such as Finland and Denmark: countries with high GDP. Still, this shift of attention to wellbeing and a presentation of this concept as a complex construct affected by multiple factors are indeed very welcomed and offer a good foundation for further explorations of the topic of dance and wellbeing, and this is indeed what we are trying to do in this book.

We have therefore invited contributors to discuss the underlying principles of their work, question given assumptions, and add to existing theoretical and practical knowledge on the topic. In all cases we have offered our understanding of the concept of wellbeing as a complex concept which involves the interplay between physical, psychological, social, and spiritual aspects. We have invited them to comment on this definition, redefine it, or focus on one aspect of wellbeing as it is relevant to their own work.

Furthermore, this book looks at diverse types of dance and related movement practices aspiring to contribute towards understanding their impact on wellbeing, offer new understanding of existing practices, and support the development of new ways of working. In particular, the book aims to:

1. Explore useful ideas, while critically considering existing concepts and models with which different forms of dance and movement make contributions towards wellbeing.
2. Bring together and discuss diverse research-based dance and movement examples for their input to wellbeing.
3. Create a space where sufficient exchange is enabled, different views of wellbeing are explored, professional borders are expanded, and improvement of current and future practice can be considered.

The research components of the book are kept intentionally broad to include quantitative, qualitative, and arts-based research, and thus to cover diverse discourses, methodologies, and perspectives that will add to the development of a complete picture about the topic. Therefore, objective observations, felt experiences, and artistic explorations are all equally valued as being able to make an important contribution to wellbeing from different perspectives. Different perspectives are also encouraged through bringing together dance and movement practitioners, community artists, teachers, health professionals, psychologists, and psychotherapists from around the world. In all cases, contributors have anchored their input on the particular way in which they view dance and movement as impacting on wellbeing. Their inputs are organized within five parts, all of which are seen as framing contexts to which contributors to this book have been invited to respond:

A. Dance and the Body. The body is seen as the smallest 'context'; contributors are invited to discuss this topic either through an objective or subjective stance. Neuroscientific, physiological, anatomical, somatic, philosophical, and spiritual perspectives are included.

B. Dance within Performative Contexts. In this part the emphasis is on dance as an art form, including processes of creation and modes of presentation in both conventional, and less conventional, settings. It includes chapters on therapeutic or transformative performance on stage, but also performances in urban communities, derelict old buildings, or selected locations in the countryside.

C. Dance in Education. Dance within primary (mainstream and special schools), secondary, and tertiary education is explored for its potential effect on wellbeing as it impacts learning. Topics on policy, theory, practice, and research are covered.

D. Dance in the Community. This part places a particular emphasis on the sociological, anthropological, and political aspects of dance as they impact wellbeing, covering a diversity of styles, perspectives, types of participation, and participating groups.

E. Dance within Healthcare Contexts. This last part deals with the use of dance within health, including work taking place in primary, secondary, and tertiary care as well as public health.

As a way of helping the reader to synthesize these diverse views, in each of the introductions to these parts we identify overlapping practices, clarify themes, and highlight contradictions or paradoxes. Furthermore, as editors we ask questions attempting to stimulate thinking and generate debate, and thus support readers to process the material presented.

We hope that the supplementary video material available on the companion website adds another layer to this unique book, offering opportunities to understand and process information in a way that is not available in other texts dealing with dance. It offers the opportunity for an engagement with the topic which is not based simply on words. For a book on dance, this online accompaniment becomes crucial.

Finally, as editors we ask you, the readers, to approach this text not only as an academic publication. Since we argue for the value of an embodied cognition and an embodied emotion, we ask you to play with the idea of engaging with this text as embodied beings, and to respond to the text through your emotive selves. We hope this way of approaching this text will stimulate you and offer alternative understandings of what is a very complex and multilayered topic.

References

Burkhurdt, J. and Rhodes, J, (2012). *Dance Active: Commissioning Dance or Health and Well-being: Guidance and Resources for Commissioners*. <http://www.pdsw.org.uk/assets/Uploads/Breathe-Commissioning-Dance-for-Health-Wellbeing-Guide-for-Commissioners-by-Jan-Burkhardt-2012.pdf>

Beecher, O. (2005). *The Dance Experience and Sense of Being: Therapeutic Application and Modern Dance*. PhD thesis, University of Limerick.

Damasio, A. (2000). *The Feeling of What Happens: Body and Emotion in the Making of Consciousness*. London: Harvest Books.

Damasio, A. (2005). *Descartes' Error: Emotion, Reason, and the Human Brain*. London: Penguin.

Edelman, G. (1987). *Neural Darwinism: The Theory of Neuronal Group Selection*. New York, NY: Basic Books.

Gazzola, V., Aziz-Zadeh, L., and Keysers, C. (2006). 'Empathy and the somatotopic auditory mirror system in humans', *Current Biology*, 16: 1824–9.

Harris, A. and Hastings, N. (2005). *Working the System: Creating a State of Wellbeing*. Edinburgh: Scottish Council Foundation.

Karkou, V. (2012). 'Aspects of theory and practice in dance movement psychotherapy: Similarities and differences from music therapy', in R. MacDonald, G. Kreutz, and L. Mitchell (eds.), *Music, Health and Wellbeing*. Oxford: Oxford University Press, pp. 213–29.

Meekums, B. (2000). *Creative Group Therapy for Women Survivors of Child Sexual Abuse: An Introduction for Social Work and Health Professionals: Speaking the Unspeakable*. Philadelphia, PA: Jessica Kingsley.

Office of National Statistics (ONS) (2011). *Measuring National Well-being: A Discussion Paper on Domains and Measures*. <http://www.ons.gov.uk/ons/rel/wellbeing/measuring-national-well-being/discussion-paper-on-domains-and-measures/measuring-national-well-being---discussion-paper-on-domains-and-measures.html>

Polhemus, T. (1998). 'Dance, gender and culture', in A. Carter (ed.), *The Routledge Dance Studies Reader*. London: Routledge, pp. 171–9.

Rizzolatti, G., Fadiga, L., Gallese, V., and Fogassi, L. (1996). 'Premotor cortex and the recognition of motor actions', *Cognitive Brain Research*, 3: 131–41.

Schore, A. (1994) *Affect Regulation and the Origin of the Self*. Mahwah, NJ: Lawrence Erlbaum Associates.

World Health Organization (WHO) (2006). *Constitution of the World Health Organization: Basic Documents*, 45th edn., Supplement.

PART I

DANCE AND THE BODY

INTRODUCTION TO PART 1

VICKY KARKOU AND SUE OLIVER

THIS first part intends to set the scene in its rightful home: the body. As such, it treats the body as the primary 'location' of dance where wellbeing, measured or felt, can be found. Chapters refer to neuroscientific, physiological, psychological, philosophical, and spiritual approaches to movement and dance and reflect a continuum from objective to subjective experiences and from scientific reasoning to transpersonal discourses. In all cases, contributions are brought together to reflect multiple and, we would hope, coherent ways in which dance can contribute to wellbeing.

Jola and Calmeiro begin this part with a very comprehensive overview of research-based explanations of the 'feel-good effect' of participating in dance. Biochemical, neuronal, and psychosocial mechanisms are explored and explained, rooting the reader to the scientific basis of the contribution of dance to wellbeing. A critique of the quality of current research is also offered identifying areas where our scientific knowledge is still limited and areas where further research can take place.

A more in-depth discussion of neurocognitive research in particular is explored in Chapters 2 and 3, reflecting the increased interest of neuroscience on dance and embodiment in general. Bettina Bläsing, from Germany, is the author of Chapter 2, which discusses the impact of dance on the brain. Different technologies used in these studies are presented and key findings are discussed, while the limitations of both available technologies and research designs are acknowledged. The text, clear and informative, provides a useful overview of a research area that can be highly jargonistic and, for this reason, potentially inaccessible to lay readers.

Chapter 3, by Grosbas, Reason, Tan, Kay, and Pollick, involves results from a particular brain study: a large multicentred study in the UK called 'Watching Dance' and funded by the Arts and Humanities Research Council. The chapter offers a very insightful perspective of how brain scans can be used to offer an understanding of what happens to the brain when one views dance (contemporary dance in particular in this case), and how qualitative data can explain, complement, and enhance findings from these brain scans to improve our understanding of the impact of dance on wellbeing.

In Chapter 4, neuroscientific and neurocognitive perspectives give way to physiological insights. Biodanza—a form of dance more often found as a community-based practice for adults—is modified to address the needs of kindergarten and primary-school children. The authors, Stück and Villegas, from Germany and Brazil respectively, argue that there are potential benefits of this practice for children. They review and present study results that suggest that Biodanza for children can have a direct impact on hormones, and as a consequence in the capacity of these children to self-regulate. Although the studies referred to are small and the designs naturalistic and pragmatic, some interesting trends are apparent that may be relevant not only for Biodanza but also for other forms of dance.

In Chapter 5, Judith Hanna indeed acknowledges the impact of dance on physiology, linking scientific evidence with anthropological perspectives and shifting our attention from one type of dance to diverse forms: dance for fitness, cultural dance, and educational, professional, and amateur dance as treatment. The impact of these diverse types of dance on stress is explored, creating a bridge between different types of dance and different types of perspectives.

Chapters 6, 7, 8, and 9 are all written by therapists. Panhofer and Avstreih are dance-movement therapists, Steckler is a Body Psychotherapist and a dancer, and Bacon is a choreographer and Jungian analyst. As a result, all four chapters bring a different perspective in this part that address philosophical considerations (Panhofer) and highlight dance techniques that can be used within a therapeutic context (Steckler) or explore spiritual dimensions (Bacon and Avstreih).

For example, Heidrun Panhofer—the leader of the Catalan dance movement therapy programme in Barcelona—discusses the concept of body memory and proposes a shift away from the Cartesian split though the introduction of 'thinking in movement'. Drawing from her own empirical research, she claims that through the use of movement, different types of information can be accessed that can be useful not only for therapy, and Dance Movement Psychotherapy in particular, but also for supervision.

Similarly, Laura Steckler, an American practitioner based in Scotland, discusses the value of diverse uses of movement and dance activities within Body Psychotherapy—a form of psychotherapy stemming from Wilhelm Reich. Drawing from choreographic practices and Butoh, her choices are underpinned with psychotherapeutic theory and are illustrated through clinical vignettes.

Authentic movement—a practice developed in the 1950s by movement therapist Mary Starks Whitehouse (1999) and based on the theories of C. G. Jung (1961)—is explored in Chapter 8 by Jane Bacon, a dancer and Jungian analyst from the UK. Jane argues that this practice, with its inner focus, can encourage people to a level of authenticity which can make a valuable contribution to the therapeutic transformation of trauma and thus to the development of wellbeing.

Similarly, in Chapter 9, Zoe Avstreih, a dance/movement therapist from the USA, argues that this inner focus can also create direct links with a sense of embodied spirituality, connecting with what she calls the 'sacred'. She also argues that authentic movement can potentially facilitate the development of a therapeutic thread between the self, the community, and the life in all its mystery.

This part ends with Chapter 10 by Andrea Olsen, a somatic dance practitioner also from the USA, who encourages the reader to engage with the text in an active way—one that moves beyond a simple reading. Scientific distance and objectivity are here challenged to the core, inviting us, the readers, to not simply engage with the text cognitively, but to also bring our body into the experience and engage as whole human beings. Moving beyond our usual ways of relating to our bodies, and through a series of experiential tasks, Olsen invites us to increase our awareness of our anatomy and reconnect with our bodies and the environment around us. This chapter also includes references to some beautifully created video material, completing the first 'bouquet' of perspectives covered in this book, and available with the online version.

References

Jung, C. G. (1961). *Memories, Dreams, Reflections*. New York, NY: Random House.

Whitehouse, M. S. (1999). 'C. G. Jung and dance therapy: Two major principles', in P. Pallaro (ed.) (1979), *Authentic Movement: Essays by Mary Starks Whitehouse, Janet Adler and Joan Chodorow*. London: Jessica Kingsley Publishers, pp. 73–105.

CHAPTER 1

THE DANCING QUEEN

Explanatory Mechanisms of the 'Feel-Good Effect'
in Dance

CORINNE JOLA AND LUIS CALMEIRO

INTRODUCTION

OVER the last decade, an increasing number of research publications have shown evidence for positive effects of dance participation on individuals' health and wellbeing across a large spectrum of age groups and societies (Gardner et al. 2008; Keogh et al. 2009; O'Neill et al. 2011). Beyond improvements in physical fitness and cognitive abilities, the positive effects include a strengthening of group coherence, an increasing willingness to help others, and an improvement of successful rehabilitation (Quiroga Murcia et al. 2010), as well as accident prevention (Fernandez-Arguelles et al. 2015); to name just a few. The rise in empirical investigations into the benefits of dance is surprising: dance is still frequently stigmatized as a low-level leisurely activity on the one hand (e.g. Walker 2010) and as an unhealthy profession on the other hand (e.g. Koutedakis and Sharp 1999). Moreover, dance professionals were socially and intellectually denounced well into the twentieth century (Garfola 2010). Based on such myths, many sceptics do not even consider dance as a profession per se.

However, with an emphasis on dance as a form of physical activity and the surge to find solutions to reduce obesity and other health-related issues that are based on the populations' increasing physical inactivity, dance offers great opportunities. Notably, dance is a very popular joyful activity to do as well as to watch. It is second only to football as the most commonly offered physical activity in UK schools' physical education curriculum. In addition, school links to clubs showed the biggest increase for dance since 2008 (Quick et al. 2010). Nevertheless, for a successful implementation of dance interventions it is important that dance overcomes the stigmas attached to it—predominantly those regarding age, class, race, gender, level of physical activity, and appearance.

According to Lansley and Early (2011, p. 12), ageism is the most critical prejudice in dance, as it affects dance hardest and often remains unvoiced. Due to physical and psychological demands, dancers' careers are understood to be extremely short (e.g. Wanke et al. 2012). However, recent trends provide encouragement that performing dance is possible at a higher age (e.g. Pina Bausch, Sylvie Guillem, Carlos Acosta, Tamara Rojo, Steve Paxton, Jane Dudley, Julyen Hamilton; see also Figure 1.1). Furthermore, with mature dancers becoming increasingly present, the possibilities when defining goals and designing appropriate training schedules for dancers at different levels and stages are more tangible.

Another poignant misconception of and in dance is related to the intensity and level of physical activity. With so many different dance styles, the physical demands are almost impossible to summarize, and dance-specific knowledge is required to recognize the demands on dancers' bodies (Wanke et al. 2012). Notably, while the cardiovascular and muscular efforts dance demands may be discredited by some, professional dancers are expected to have a mind-set of 'never giving up' which poses risks for their health and wellbeing.

Clearly, professional dance expertise is a highly trained skill achieved through a huge amount of deliberate practice (Ericsson 2008). However, recent research conducted at top UK universities (e.g. Trinity Laban, Royal Holloway) provided evidence that

FIGURE 1.1. An elderly couple dancing, by Rebecca Leith (© C. Jola and L. Calmeiro). Dance is not restricted to age, gender, or physical appearances, and dance intervention benefits can be found over a wide age-range. In fact, while age as an indicator of physical maturity should be taken into consideration for the outline of appropriate training, encouragement is plentiful that performing and enjoying dance is possible at a higher age, and that training can start late.

tailored high-intensity training programmes should include resting periods for optimal dance performance and injury prevention and focus on quality, not quantity (Wyon 2010). The importance of rest periods for consolidation processes of general complex motor (Rieth et al. 2010) and cognitive tasks (Mercer 2014) is an established fact. It is thus important that pauses in dance practice are credited. Wyon (2010), for example, suggested that a rehearsal can end early, particularly when the desired quality is achieved. For most professional and vocational dancers, however, this is not common practice.

De facto, it is often the case that insights that go against existing cultural practices are particularly slow in being implemented. This is true for dance with its prejudices and expectations, as well as for science with its established empirical standards. For example, while the amount of research on the physical, psychological, and neuronal processes linked to dance increased tremendously over the last decade, the predominantly reductionist scientific approach has often failed to capture the complexity of dance (Jola, Grosbras, and Pollick 2011; Jola 2016) and interpretations need to be handled carefully. We argue that with a better understanding of the underlying physical, neuronal, and psychological mechanisms of dance, more substantial critiques of existing practices and better targeted propositions for novel approaches in support of health and wellbeing in dance are possible—even if some of these scientists may not have initially set out to target those aspects (e.g. Cross et al. 2014).

In general, physical activity has been associated with a variety of health benefits, including a sense of feeling good (Haskell et al. 2007; Penedo and Dahn 2005; Warburton et al. 2006). This 'feel-good effect' associated with physical activity is linked to physiological as well as psychological effects (Ekkekakis 2003; Hyde et al. 2011). Notably, positive effects through dance participation can be expected to go beyond physical health, since dance in its optimal form combines physical activity with cognitive, social, psychological (including emotional), spiritual, and creative processes (e.g. Burkhardt and Rhodes 2012; Siddall 2010). Indeed, dance participants reported beneficial effects on all of these factors (Quiroga Murcia et al. 2010) with a more positive-activated (e.g. feel happy, elated, energetic, euphoric) as well as a more positive-deactivated (e.g. feel released, relaxed, calm) feeling after dancing. Furthermore, quantitative studies found positive effects of recreational dance interventions on physical and psychosocial health and wellbeing in children and adolescents (Burkhardt and Brennan 2012), as well as in the older population (Connolly and Redding 2010).

While there is considerable consensus in what pertains to the health and wellbeing benefits of physical activities in general, the research concerning the explanatory mechanisms of such benefits is less conclusive. This chapter thus aims at initiating a pathway towards a more comprehensive understanding of the underlying mechanisms of the benefits of dance as a special form of physical activity. We emphasize the physical activity component of dance to the detriment of other, nonetheless relevant, components (e.g. Christensen and Jola 2015; Jola 2016) because of (a) the contemporary political relevance of viewing dance as a physical activity and (b) the need to understand mechanisms of health and wellbeing that underpin the physical aspects of dance.

We argue that a better understanding of the complexity and interaction of these explanatory mechanisms will provide substantial support for the successful continuation of dance participation with a focus on health and wellbeing. This is particularly important, since dance also entails considerable health and wellbeing risks (e.g. Padham and Aujla 2014) in addition to the high risk of dance-specific physical injuries (e.g. Russell 2013). In the professional, vocational, and sometimes recreational sectors, high incidences of injuries, fatigue, and psychosocial pressures are common, potentially related with distorted eating habits prevalent in ballet dance (e.g. Aalten 2007; Macleod 1998), continuous practice despite serious injuries (e.g. Nordin-Bates et al. 2011), and drug misuse (Sekulic et al. 2010), respectively. According to some authors, the most prevalent risk factors are of cultural and aesthetic origin (see Aalten 2007; Wanke et al. 2012). For example, ballet dance defies gravity and the anatomy of the human body, causing stress on the dancer's body and mind (see also Wyon et al. 2011). Thus, concerns about professional and vocational dancers' health and wellbeing are understandably high and its potential effects on the recreational sector should not be ignored. The aim is therefore to sensitize the reader to the characteristic effects of dance practice that allow a more informed understanding of often contradicting findings. Each section can be read independently.

Explanatory Mechanisms

Among the various hypotheses advanced to explain a relationship between physical activity and wellbeing in dance, we emphasize the biochemical, neuronal, and psychosocial mechanisms. Notably, while some of the explanatory mechanisms in relation to dance have been studied extensively (e.g. psychosocial effects of dance movement therapy or self-perception, functional brain changes), others have received little attention (e.g. structural brain changes, neurohumoral and serotonin (5-HT)/dopamine (DA) responses; but see Quiroga Murcia et al. 2009). Hence, for those cases where no specific reference to dance is available, we report from a general physical activity/exercise perspective and discuss potential links to dance practice to stimulate further research.

Biochemical Mechanisms

The Endorphin Hypothesis

Endorphins such as β-endorphins, encephalins, and dynophin are hormones that have an important role in the regulation of pain perception and feelings of euphoria. Due to its analgesic effects, these opioid peptides can mediate psychological benefits of physical activity; it has been suggested that the increase of circulatory endorphins—particularly β-endorphins—observed during physical activities is responsible for the 'runner's high' so often reported by regular joggers (Marieb 2012).

Presently, evidence for the increase of plasma-level endorphins exists in relation to the increasing effort demands of the activity in anaerobic exercise (e.g. Schwarz and Kindermann 1992), aerobic dance (Pierce et al. 1993), and the interactivity of the movements with music (Tarr et al. 2014). Whether the anaerobic threshold is reached in dancing or not is dependent on the dance style (Angioi et al. 2011; Liiv et al. 2014; Wyon et al. 2011). Also, not music listening per se, but the creation of music and interaction with music, was shown to determine endorphin release (Dunbar et al. 2012). For example, interactive musical feedback during a repetitive machine supported workout was found to enhance the individuals' mood compared to passive music listening (Fritz et al. 2013). In addition, Tarr et al. (2014) proposed that agency and/or group co-ordination are necessary for music-induced endorphin levels to rise. These findings support the notion that during dance practice, live music should be preferred over recorded music and that dancers release more endorphins—even when the dancers may not reach the anaerobic threshold—when a communicative interaction between performers and the musician is present.

It is less clear, however, whether the feeling of 'high' after performing could be induced by endorphins. To our knowledge, only one study addressed the endorphin response specifically to dance (Pierce et al. 1993), showing an increase of circulating endorphins after forty-five minutes of aerobic dance. However, the endorphins are unlikely to be directly responsible for the 'feel-good effect' in dance as well as other physical activities: although blood concentration of endorphins is generally increased during exercise, its effects on mood states are questionable. Researchers have failed to demonstrate that endorphins are able to pass through the blood–brain barrier to act on the brain centres responsible for the regulation of mood (Boecker et al. 2008; Buckworth et al. 2013; O'Neal et al. 2000). However, Boecker et al. (2008) were the first to show in vivo evidence in human participants that sustained physical exercise resulted in release of endogenous opioids (within the central nervous system) in the fronto-limbic regions of the brain (see Figure 1.3), responsible for affective modulation. More importantly, such increased opioid activity was associated with the euphoric sensation characteristic of the 'runner's high'. Further investigations are required into studying how mood in recreational and professional dancers may depend on endogenous opioid levels. Although these are associated with wellbeing as discussed, it may also explain the possible 'exercise addiction' observed in injured professional and recreational dancers (Nordin-Bates et al. 2011) and athletes alike (Boecker et al. 2008), who continue their training regardless of the harmful consequences to their health. Nevertheless, it appears that the feeling of 'high', particularly experienced after performance, is more likely related to cortisol levels.

Dance and Cortisol Response

As represented in Figure 1.2, the hypothalamic–pituitary–adrenal (HPA) axis regulates the stress response of an organism, ultimately through the liberation of a number of hormones such as cortisol. Exercise has been shown to influence the HPA system that regulates stress responses. While 'acute' exercise activates this system, adaptation to repeated

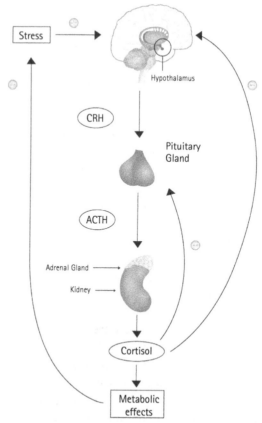

FIGURE 1.2. The hypothalamic–pituitary–adrenal system, by Rebecca Leith. (© This figure is adapted by Jola and Calmeiro from S. Hiller-Sturmhöfel and A. Bartke (1998), 'The endocrine system: an overview', *Alcohol Health and Research World*, 22(3): 153–64, PubMed 15706790.) The hypothalamic-pituitary-adrenal (HPA) axis that regulates the stress response of an organism through the production of the hormone corticotropin releasing factor (CRF) in the pituitary gland is illustrated. CRF liberates the adrenocorticotropic hormone (ACTH); and in turn, the ACTH acts on the adrenal glands, liberating a number of hormones into the blood stream, including mineralocorticoids (mainly aldosterone) and glucocorticoids (such as cortisone, corticosterone, and, most importantly in humans, cortisol). A small fraction of these glucocorticoids remains 'free' in the blood stream (that is, unbounded to chemical substances) and is eventually diffused to the saliva (Rohleder et al. 2007). The main goal of the HPA system is to prepare the organism for an efficient 'fight or flight' response to a stressor and to protect against long-term stress. An excessive activation of this system induces biochemical alterations, which interfere with the functioning of brain structures that regulate the emotional states, such as the amygdala, the hippocampus, and the nucleus accumbens (O'Neal et al. 2000). Therefore, low levels of cortisol are a biomarker of good health (Miller et al. 2009).

bouts of exercise ('chronic' exercise) attenuates the effects of acute exercise regardless of its intensity; therefore, repeated exercise results in decrease HPA activation (Buckworth et al. 2013). Hence, as a form of physical activity, regular dance can have a beneficial impact on wellbeing through the regulation of the HPA axis activation.

Although exercise is a physical strain that can activate the HPA axis, particularly in episodes of intense physical exertion (Davies and Few 1973; McMurray et al. 1996; Tremblay et al. 2005), the psychological demands of the stimuli can activate the HPA axis more strongly than the physical demands (Berndt at al. 2012; Rohleder et al. 2007).

Increases in positive affect and decreases in salivary cortisol concentrations were found in a sample of Tango Argentino dancers (Quiroga Murcia et al. 2009). Specifically, regular dancing (with partner and music) resulted in lower levels of cortisol than dancing with a partner without music. In addition, music also had an influence on the neurohumoral responses to dance as significant decreases were observed in tango dancing with music but without a partner. Conversely, elevated cortisol levels were also found in competitive ballroom dancing (Rohleder et al. 2007) and dance students during short solo performances (Quested et al. 2011). Notably, these changes were shown to occur due to the social-evaluative threat associated with the competitive nature of the tasks rather than the physical exertion required. Berndt et al. (2012) argue that professional dancers are subject to a variety of stressors that may result in acute increased cortisol responses that when repeated over a long period of time (i.e. chronic stress exposure) can lead to loss of quality of life associated to increased stress sensitivity, pain, and fatigue.

Quested et al. (2011) argue that the positive effect of dance on wellbeing can be due to fulfilment of individuals' basic psychological needs; that is, the need to feel competent, in control of our own behaviour, and socially connected with others (Ryan and Deci 2000). Quested et al. (2011) found evidence that low levels of satisfaction of dancers' basic psychological needs may result in prolonged or repeated cortisol elevation, which can have negative consequences on long-term wellbeing (Burns 2006). Dancers who reported higher basic psychological needs satisfaction had lower cortisol responses and reduced levels of anxiety. In addition, Rohleder et al. (2007) demonstrated lower cortisol levels in group formation dancers in comparison to individual couple dancers, which the authors attributed to the social support experienced during the group dancing. These results demonstrate that the psychological satisfaction is crucial for dancers' health and wellbeing—potentially more so than the type or level of physical exertion while dancing.

Brain Neurotransmitters

Whether physical, social, or psychological the causes for the benefits of physical activity on wellbeing, there is a documented association between physical activity and exercise with an enhancement of the transmission of brain chemical neurotransmitters—specifically DA, norepinephrine (NE), and 5-HT (Hyde et al. 2011). Notably, the study of changes in brain neurotransmitters following exercise relies primarily on animal models (Dishman 1997).

DA has an important role in initiating and controlling movement (Meeusen and De Meirleir 1995). Habitually physically active animals have an enhanced brain DA synthesis (Foley and Fleshner 2008) and DA metabolism in the brain as a whole (Chaouloff 1989) or in specific regions (see Figure 1.3) such as the midbrain, hippocampus, striatum, and hypothalamus (Davis and Bailey 1997). Exercise affects the dopaminergic system as

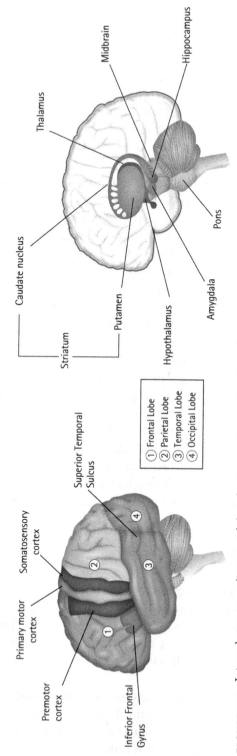

FIGURE 1.3. Internal structures (image right) and outer cortical surface from the lateral (side) view (image left), by Rebecca Leith (© C. Jola and L. Calmeiro). Indicated are (image left) the four main lobes of the cortex (outer layer of neural tissue—grey matter/cell bodies), areas considered part of the mirror neuron network (primary motor cortex, the inferior frontal gyrus, the inferior and superior parietal lobe, the superior temporal sulcus, and the somatosensory cortex), and (image right) internal structures associated with relevant biochemical mechanisms.

suggested by the association between fatigue and reductions of DA synthesis and metabolism in the brain stem and midbrain. Furthermore, when brain DA levels are maintained, fatigue is delayed.

Notably, DA is also one of the regulators of appetite (Abizaid 2009). Therefore, the increased dopaminergic activity after the intense physical exertion associated with professional dance practice could explain the experience of dancers in suppression of their appetite (Crabtree et al. 2014). In combination with aesthetic or schedule enforced diets (e.g. Aalten 2007; Koutedakis and Jamurtas 2004), these exercise-induced appetite suppressions can lead to detrimental effects on the individual's health that have not yet been systematically researched (Howe et al. 2014).

Moreover, empirical studies that specifically target dancers' nutritional needs are to this day marginal but much needed. For example, Brown and Wyon (2014a) showed evidence that dancers' positive mood is significantly linked to their nutrition behaviour and blood sugar—i.e. glucose levels. The authors' also showed that attempts to educate dancers on the nutritional needs, potentially in the form of supplements, are important (Brown and Wyon 2014b). Clearly, more field studies are needed to gain a better understanding of the specific needs and problematic issues related to changes in biochemical mechanisms and nutritional modifiers of the 'feel-good effect' (such as increased proneness to injury due to inadequate diet; see Wanke et al. 2012).

NE is a major modulator of neural activity in the brain (Dunn and Dishman 1991) and the primary brain site for its production is the locus coeruleus, located in the pons (Buckworth et al. 2013; see Figure 1.3). Noradrenergic responses regulate autonomic arousal, attention vigilance, and neuroendocrine responses to stress (Dishman 1997), including those associated with anxiety and depression (Soares et al. 1999). Studies suggest that chronic physical activity alters brain levels of NE and its major metabolites in regions of the brain known to be involved in integrating behavioural and endocrine responses to stressors other than exercise (Dishman 1997; Sothmann and Kastello 1997). Research also suggests that in physically active animals there was less NE depletion or higher synthesis rates during exposure to controllable and uncontrollable stressors when compared with sedentary animals (Dunn et al. 1996). Furthermore, research also suggests the role of exercise in increasing brain NE activity in conditions of chronic hypoadrenergic activity (Sothmann and Kastello 1997) by providing 'psychopharmacological evidence consistent with an anti-depressant effect of physical activity' (Dishman 1997: 67). In fact, chronic activity-wheel running protected against the depletion of NE in face of stressors (e.g. uncontrollable foot-shock) in sedentary animals (Dishman et al. 1993; Dishman et al. 1997; Soares et al. 1999).

5-HT neurons are distributed to all areas of the central nervous system. Activity of 5-HT neurons is associated with pain, fatigue, appetite, sleep, and corticosteroid activity (Dunn and Dishman 1991). Levels of 5-HT or its metabolite, 5-hydroxyindoleacetic acid (5-HIAA), in the cerebrospinal fluid and urine are below normal during depressive episodes in humans (Landers and Arent 2001). Although research that focused on the effects of exercise on the serotonergic system has generated mixed results (Dunn and

Dishman 1991), there is some evidence that exercise increases brain 5-HT synthesis and metabolism (Chaouloff 1989; Davis and Bailey 1997). Analysis of regional differences in 5-HT and 5-HIAA following ninety minutes of treadmill running showed increases of both substances in the midbrain, hippocampus, and striatum (Davis and Bailey 1997; see Figure 1.3). Such increases are thought to be facilitated by improved concentration of free tryptophan levels in the blood after exercise, which stimulates tryptophan entry in the brain for 5-HT synthesis (Chaouloff 1997; Meeusen and De Meirleir 1995). Chaouloff (1997) showed that one hour of treadmill running resulted in increased brain tryptophan concentration accompanied by a small but significant increase in 5-HIAA, indicative of increased 5-HT synthesis and turnover.

In addition to the focus on brain monoamines in animal models, studies of the presumed anxiolytic effects of exercise focused on increased locomotion, which reflects an adaptive motivational state indicating reduced behavioural inhibition (e.g. few approaches to the centre of the open field, freezing) (Dishman 1997). Fearful locomotion is regulated through reciprocal inhibition between gamma aminobutyric acid (GABA) and DA transmission within the corpus striatum (Dishman et al. 1996). The corpus striatum is a set of nuclei located in the forebrain, responsible for the coordination of slow sustained body movements and inhibition of unnecessary movement patterns. Consistent with the suggestion that exercise has an anxiolytic effect in rats, Dishman et al. (1996) observed that chronic activity-wheel running increased locomotion during open field behaviour and decreased the density of $GABA_A$ receptors in the corpus striatum subsequent to increased GABA concentration.

Animal studies have showed that environmental manipulations, such as exercise, induced biochemical changes that have been found to mediate the antidepressive benefits observed by pharmacological treatments (Remington 2009). However, studies with humans are limited for technical and ethical reasons, making measurement of brain neurotransmitters difficult. For example, in a rare study performed with humans, Wang et al. (2000) did not detect any changes in DA striatal release after thirty minutes of vigorous aerobic exercise on the treadmill. The authors attributed this failure to corroborate the research with animal studies to the poor sensitivity of the method used to detect low levels of DA increase. Therefore, studies focus mainly on peripheral levels of these catecholamines. Plasma levels of NE and DA were found to be increased after both moderate and intense bouts of physical exercise (Winter et al. 2007). Jeong et al. (2005) have identified increases in plasma 5-HT concentration and decreases in DA concentration in adolescents with mild depression following twelve weeks of dance movement therapy (DMT).

In summary, because monoamines contribute to the adjustment of the activity of the thalamus and limbic system (see Figure 1.3), responsible for the regulation of mood states and emotional functioning (Buckworth et al. 2013), the possibility that exercise may stimulate production and release of monoamines in the brain may justify the preventive and therapeutic role of exercise (Biddle and Mutrie 2008) and, by extension, dance.

NEURONAL MECHANISMS

Background Dance and the Brain

As Figure 1.3 illustrates, the outer surface of the brain is divided into four main lobes. These lobes entail formations called gyri and sulci, which are used to identify the lobes. In analogy to landscape, the gyri and sulci would be the 'hills' and 'valleys', respectively. En gross, the different lobes are found to process different types of information. For example, the occipital lobe processes visual information, the temporal lobe auditory information, the parietal lobe spatial and physical properties, and thinking has been located in the frontal lobe. The more inferior structures are considered to process emotional information. While there is good reason to assume a close relationship between functional processes and the underlying neuronal architectures, to assume such a distinct modular structure of the human brain is a tremendous simplification. The cognitive and perceptual processes are complex, depend on several parts of the brain, and are inevitably interlinked, leading to a network of activity across the brain when conducting a task. In the case of dance, it is important to understand that the brain's activity spans across an extended network of areas involved in the processing of multiple sensory, motor, cognitive, and emotional functions.

These diverse ranges of functions are 'orchestrated' in the grey matter—the outer layers of the cortical surface, consisting of nerve cells. The underlying white matter contains connections between nerve cells, mostly myelinated axons. Here, our main interest is in how a dancer's brain adapts to its demands and how this may explain some of the effects on health and wellbeing.

Adaptations to environmental inputs as well as internal modulations are an intrinsic property of the human brain (Pascual-Leone et al. 2005). Novel techniques, such as magnet resonance imaging (MRI), electroencephalography (EEG), or near-infrared spectroscopy (NIRS), allow assessing such neuroplasticity non-invasively, in form of changes in brain function (activity of grey matter in response to particular stimuli or tasks) and the brain's architecture (structural anatomy of grey matter and white matter). Notably, however, each method has its particular limits. For example, measuring brain activity during large whole body movements presents a challenge due to movement artefacts. Moreover, the narrow space in an MRI scanner poses an undeniable adversity when aiming to study activity in response to dance.

Other restrictions are the spatial and temporal resolutions of each method (Logothetis 2008). The vast amount of neuroscientific studies on dance published over the last ten years has predominantly looked at functional brain processes in the domain of perception and cognition in response to dance practice without considering accompanying structural differences (Blaesing et al. 2012; Sevdalis and Keller 2011). Direct links between functional and structural changes in 'motor training-induced neuroplasticity' (Bezzola et al. 2012) have as yet received limited attention. Notably, in particular for health and wellbeing (Bolandzadeh et al. 2012) as well as brain changes based on learning and expertise (Fields 2010), the white matter structure is nonetheless important.

Nevertheless, studies that acknowledge dance in its full complexity (i.e. high ecological validity) as an audio-visual stimulus that contains multiple sensory practices impacting on vision, audition, touch, and somatosensory processes have increased in number. This led to an even stronger presence of dance in science with advancing interdisciplinary approaches and novel methodologies. This interdisciplinary approach is important because, as discussed previously, the multiple sensorial aspects of dance (i.e. movement and music) are vital for the health and wellbeing benefits of dance.

Functional Changes: Mirroring and Empathy

The main body of the early research on dancers' functional brain changes predominantly investigated neuronal processes of passive action observation. This research was in particular stimulated by the finding of the 'mirror neurons' in the macaque monkey's frontal and parietal brain areas (Rizzolatti et al. 1996). The authors made the coincidental finding that neurons in the area relevant for motor execution (e.g. when the monkey grasped a piece of food) were also activated when the monkey passively observed an action (e.g. when it observed the experimenter grasping food), as if internally 'mirroring' or simulating the observed action and thus potentially building the basis for understanding others and experiencing empathy.

An interesting means of studying these mirror neurons is dance. Dance is a universal phenomenon, developed to a variety of cultural forms, with movements ranging from object-unrelated gestural to fully abstract actions. These characteristic properties allow studying action observation in refined forms. For example, comparing brain activity of spectators with different levels of physical and visual expertise in different styles of dance advanced our understanding of the role of context effects in abstract as well as gestural dance movements (Jola et al. 2012; Jola et al. 2013; Jola and Grosbras 2013). Largely, action observation studies with dancers showed that brain activity is dependent on physical familiarity with the observed movements. In other words, dancers who watched movements that closely matched the movements they master showed enhanced activity in areas considered part of the mirror neuron system (see Figure 1.3), also described as the action observation network (e.g. Calvo-Merino et al. 2005; Calvo-Merino et al. 2006; Cross et al. 2006).

Specific roles have been associated with the different parts of the mirror neuron system. The primary motor cortex is relevant for the motor action, the superior temporal sulcus—considered lacking motor execution functions (Rizzolatti and Craighero 2004; but see also Gazzola and Keysers 2009)—is relevant in the perception and recognition of a human body (see Noble et al. 2014) and thought to further process the visual properties of motor actions (Werner et al. 2012). While the parietal lobe has been described frequently as part of the mirror neuron system, its superior parts are more likely related with the preparation to imitate an action (Cattaneo and Rizzolatti 2009).

Finally, the role of the inferior frontal gyrus has just recently been associated with the processing of complex movement structures (e.g. Noble et al. 2014; Bachrach et al, 2016). Furthermore, the somatosensory cortex is the part of the brain that is involved in the sensation of motion, or in the case of passive action observation it signifies 'how the action would feel if executed' (Gazzola and Keysers 2009).[1]

It is interesting to note that one would expect dancers to engage particularly in the sensation of movements when watching dance. As Kandel (2012, p. 393) states: '. . . art is an inherently pleasurable and instructive attempt by the artist and the beholder to communicate . . . with each other.' He emphasizes the 'the sudden recognition' when we can, through art, see into another person's mind. In line with Kandel's quest into the perceptual, cognitive, and emotional response processes involved in looking at visual art, when looking at dance, the focus is on kinaesthetic processes of the spectator. Although dance spectators are immersed in a kinaesthetic, visual, and auditory stimulation (Glass 2005), audience interviews showed that the experience of pleasure when watching dance is predominantly rooted in the kinaesthetic sense (Reason and Reynolds 2010). Furthermore, dance has been described as a fundamentally kinaesthetic art form (Daly 2002). Therefore, one would predict that, particularly for professional dancers when they observe dance themselves, the exchange between the performer and the observer would happen through movement. However, even though dancers indulge in kinaesthetic pleasures of movements and potentially employ somatosensory information in lieu of visual information (e.g. Ehrenberg 2010; Jola, Davis, and Hoggard 2011), the somatosensory cortex activity was not consistently identified in studies designed to test the mirror neuron theory. Sensory experiences evoked through dance as well as the influence of context related elements (e.g. watching with or without music, as in Reason, Jola, Kay, Reynolds, Kauppi, Grosbras, Thoka, Pollick 2016) have been studied less. Hence, the seemingly obvious link between dancers' health and wellbeing (enjoyment) and activity in their neuronal action observation processes (enhanced somatosensory activity) may have been missed. In fact, since neuroscientific studies often neglected the rich variety of dynamic gestures in dance by defining dance along the lines of 'a kind of movement pattern' (see Christensen and Jola 2015: 230; for a critical review of dance in scientific studies see Jola et al. 2012), suggestions on how functional changes related to dancers' mirror neuron system activity can be linked to their health and wellbeing are hitherto limited. Yet there exists hope that future research in dance, art, and cognitive neuroscience will follow the ideas with dance not being a purely visual or cognitive art form, but embodied (e.g. Block and Kissell 2001; see Jola 2017).

An interesting aspect of functional brain imaging studies and dancers' health and wellbeing not yet discussed relates to dancing in synchrony with a partner or to a beat that potentially acts as a mood enhancer. For example, several studies found that prosocial behaviour is enhanced through moving in synchrony (Reddish et al. 2013; Hove and Risen 2009; Wiltermuth and Heath 2009; see also Keller et al. 2014). More specifically, Kokal et al. (2011) showed that drumming in synchrony enhances brain activity in areas that are active in reward contexts (that is, the caudate nucleus; see Figure 1.3) and facilitates future prosocial behaviour.

Since the seminal study by Hasson et al. (2004) on the synchronization of specta-tors' brain activity while watching parts of the feature film *The Good, the Bad and the Ugly*, methods to analyse neuronal synchronization across a group of spectators have advanced notably. For example, a group of novice spectators watching Indian dance in the scanner showed a wider network of brain areas synchronized when the music that accompanied the dance moves was audible (Jola et al. 2013). While the authors sug-gested that the increased synchronization is based on enhanced shared understanding of the movements by means of coherent multisensory stimulation (vision and audition), the exact source for increased synchronization when audio-visual stimulation in dance is combined could not be identified in this particular study. However, it encouraged a number of following publications that suggested activity in inferior frontal areas, also known for language production, to be enhanced through shared perceived boundaries of complex edited dance movement (e.g. Noble et al. 2014; Herbec et al. 2015).

Finally, spectators' resonance with a dance style was suggested to be affected by the narrative (Jola, Grosbas, and Pollick 2011), the live presence of the performers (Jola and Grosbras 2012), and their personality (Jola et al. 2014). Moreover, resources of cognition and emotion potentially compete when watching dance (Grosbras et al. 2012). Hence, dance may simply take your mind off other things and thus improve your health and wellbeing.

In conclusion, although we have learned considerably about modifiers of action observation processes over the last ten years (physical and visual experience, presence of the performer, complexity of dance structure), the links between functional brain pro-cesses and dancers' health and wellbeing are yet largely unexplored.

Structural Changes: Expertise, Specificity, and Efficiency

A close link between structural brain changes and health and wellbeing of an individual has been shown in both directions, positive (e.g. changes leading to enhanced health and wellbeing) and negative (e.g. changes leading to decreased health and wellbeing). Evident cause-and-effect relationships between structural brain changes and wellbe-ing are examples of brain lesions (i.e. damages to brain tissue) that significantly impact on an individual's health. For example, lesions by injury (e.g. stroke) or infections (e.g. multiples sclerosis, cerebral palsy) have significant effects on the individual's motor con-trol ability. Alzheimer and dementia are examples of disorders with detrimental effects on health and wellbeing that are accompanied by structural brain changes (i.e. pro-gressive loss of specific neuronal populations). Furthermore, ageing, with its evidently detrimental effects on health and wellbeing, was found to be related with reduced grey-matter thickness and white-matter signalling across sensory, somatosensory, and motor lobes, as well as in parts of the frontal lobe (Salat et al. 2009).

Although structural deterioration is linked directly to a decline in health and well-being, as already indicated, the causing effects are often unknown. Moreover, the cog-nitive, sensory, and motor functioning in the elderly are not necessarily impaired as a result of these structural brain changes. On the plus side, it is well known that acquiring new skills prompts positive structural and functional brain changes. Notably, physical activity in the form of sporting or musical expertise (Chang 2014) as well as physical intervention (Draganski et al. 2004) repeatedly showed increased grey matter volume in the areas of the trained activity, suggesting motor-training-induced neuroplasticity. While most research on neuroplasticity compared experts with novices in cross-sectional studies, longitudinal studies that measure the effect of training over time showed evidence that neuroplasticity is not only fast and efficient but that even low to moderate leisure activity can evoke structural improvement (e.g. Bezzola et al. 2012). Research on structural changes in dancers' brains is, however, unfortunately sparse and less conclusive (Chang 2014).

To our knowledge, only two studies have yet specifically investigated structural plasticity through dance training. Hänggi et al. (2010) compared white and grey matter volume and fractial anisotropy (FA) between professional ballet dancers and non-dancers. FA is a measure of diffusion (directionality of transfer of material, such as water molecules) from one spatial location to other locations over time, thought to vary with fibre density as well as myelination of axons, but is yet poorly understood. Contradicting a number of studies which showed a correlation between brain volume and physical expertise, the authors reported decreased GM and WM volume as well as decreased FA in dancers compared to non-dancers. While the interpretation of the latter is confined to speculations based on the lack of knowledge on the modifying mechanisms, the decreased GM and WM volume is surprising. Hänggi et al. (2010) provided a number of potential explanations, one of which is the model of expertise efficiency. The idea is that 'the higher the expertise, the more efficient the neuronal processing', which is based on the observation of decreased neuronal activity in experts' action execution and interpreted as a functional outcome of optimization of the underlying neuronal mechanisms (see Chang 2014). However, as acknowledged by Hänggi et al. (2010), the interpretation does not resonate with a number of findings. Notably, it is inconsistent with the assumptions of the mirror neuron theory and the increased activity measured during experts' action observation. Other suggestions given by the authors refer to the significant differences in dancers' weight and years of education. In fact, the latter relates to an earlier observation by Jola and Mast (2005). The authors noted that dancers compared to the control group had reduced levels of higher education (HE) and minimal computer experience, which potentially affected their mental rotation test scores. Hence, when comparing dancers as experts with a control group, rigorous control for potential confounding variables is crucial.

The second study which compared dancers' GM volume with that of non-dancers, controlled indeed for dancers' computer experience (Hüfner et al. 2011). In contrast to controls, the experts showed decreased GM volume of the anterior parts of the hippocampal formation (see Hippocampus in Figure 1.3); however, they also showed increased GM volume of the posterior parts of the hippocampal formation and in several other areas in the frontal, temporal, and occipital lobes and the cerebellum. Although explanations of the functional specificity for all of the areas with significant

volume differences between experts and novices can be given, the hippocampal formation was of particular interest for the authors due to its involvement in vestibulo-visual
stimulation, navigation, and memory. While this study was well-controlled for confounding factors as well as effects of expertise with a number of additional tests, it is not
clear which brain differences are specific for dance, as ice dancers and slackliners were
also included in this study.

More research is needed into how dancing experience leads to structural brain
changes in order to advance both direct and indirect neuronal exploratory mechanisms
on the dancing benefit for individuals' health and wellbeing. Further studies are needed
that control for different levels of intellectual abilities and different physical demands,
such as cardiovascular activity, across the range of dance styles. Finally, a major criticism of most studies on motor-induced neuroplasticity is that the special skills acquired
are often defined only on a descriptive qualitative basis. It is not unlikely that they are
expressed post hoc, following the identification of brain areas with significant changes
instead of a theoretically based approach.

Psychosocial Mechanisms

A variety of psychosocial factors that may justify the benefits of physical activity in wellbeing have been reported (Buckworth et al. 2013): increased perceived competence,
control of own body or physical appearance, increased perception of autonomy and
self-acceptance, affiliation, and belonging through improved social contact, are likely
to impact individuals' self-concept and self-esteem. In dance, these elements were often
identified as beneficial factors (Quiroga Murcia et al. 2010) but sometimes as detrimental (Aalten 2007). Therefore, we summarize the psychosocial mechanisms in body
image and self-perceptions, mastery and perceived competence, and social affiliation.

Body Image and Other Self-Perceptions

Body image is a psychological construct that represents the 'individual's perceptions,
feelings and thoughts about one's body and incorporates body size estimation, evaluation of body attractiveness, and emotions associated with body shape and size' (Burgess
et al. 2006: 57). Negative body image has been associated with low self-esteem, obesity,
depressive states, and other clinical conditions (e.g. eating disorders, social physique
anxiety) (Hausenblas and Fallon 2006). Burkhardt and Brennan's (2012) systematic
review showed limited effects on self-concept and body image of children and adolescents' participation in recreational dance. Connolly et al. (2011) observed significant
increases in self-esteem in adolescent girls in response to contemporary dance classes.
Notably, attitudes and intrinsic motivation were initially high, indicating that dance is
a promising avenue to promote active lifestyles, at least among females. However, the

lack of a control group undermines validity of the results. In a methodologically stronger study, Burgess et al. (2006) reported that involvement in biweekly aerobic dance sessions for six weeks significantly reduced body image dissatisfaction and enhanced physical self-worth in female adolescents, compared to swimming sessions in physical education classes. Specifically, self-perceptions of attractiveness, physical self-worth, feeling less fat and fit significantly improved after the aerobic dance class. The authors point out that aerobic dance may be particularly suited to promote psychological benefits in young girls, predominantly in those who have low levels of self-esteem (Biddle and Mutrie 2008). Other studies (e.g. Aşçi et al. 1998) failed to find significant differences in self-perceptions after an aerobic dance programme in college-aged women, which may indicate an age-moderating effect. However, Burkhardt and Brennan's (2012) meta-analysis provides limited evidence that dance may improve self-concept and body image in dancers aged 5 to 21 years old. In a systematic review on effects of dance intervention in cancer patients, Bradt et al. (2015) also failed to find positive improvements of body image. These controversial results may be due to developmental differences in the participants, as well as the level to which dance participants rely on dancing for self-definition (Quiroga Murcia et al. 2010; Padham and Aujla 2014).

Mastery Experiences and Perceptions of Competence

Another mechanism that can explain the effects of physical activity (and dance) on wellbeing is the mastery hypothesis. According to this hypothesis, the successful completion of a challenging and personally meaningful task brings about feelings of accomplishment and mastery (Biddle and Mutrie 2008). Considering the performing context of dance, particularly at the professional level, challenging tasks are required for dancers to achieve a degree of excellence. Therefore, it is not surprising that risk-taking is one of the sought features of contemporary dancers, as Dummont (2012) has illustrated.

Grounded on Bandura's (1997) self-efficacy theory, regardless of the level of the dancer, promoting mastery experiences will increase participants' self-efficacy which in turn influences participants' choice of task, perseverance in task completion, and positive affective states (Bartholomew and Miller 2002). Bartholomew and Miller (2002) demonstrated that participation in aerobic dance classes resulted in increased positive affect and vigour and in decreases in negative affect, tension, and tiredness. However, those who rated their performance as 'high' reported greater increase in positive affect five and twenty minutes after the class than did those who rated their performance as 'low', indicating that a mastery experience may have moderated the experience of positive affective states. Based on the knowledge that high challenges are an important aspect of dance for contemporary performers (Dummont 2012), the dynamic interplay of personal achievements and dance participants' health and wellbeing becomes apparent.

Haboush et al. (2006) found support for increase in self-efficacy and decrease in hopelessness as an outcome to a programme of ballroom dancing in depressed older adults compared to a group on a waiting list. It is thought that the ability to successfully master a particular task brings about positive emotional changes. Another dance intervention with middle-aged psychiatric patients resulted in reductions of depression compared to two control groups (music-only and exercise-only). Increases in vitality compared to the music-only group were further observed (Koch et al. 2007). In line with suggestions concerning general physical activity (e.g. Matos et al. 2009), dance/movement therapy—a psychological intervention that uses dance and movement as a way of exploring personal difficulties and relationships—can be an adjunct for the treatment of depression (Cruz and Sabers 1998; but see Meekums et al. 2012).

Social Affiliation

One important element of dance is the social bonding, based through touch and 'entrainment'—a spontaneous synchronization to the rhythm of others which is present in humans and animals (Phillips-Silver et al. 2010). It can be found in response to music and movement, while participating in dance (in the form of external, motor synchronization) or while watching dance (in the form of internal, sensory synchronization). Entrainment provides a strong sense of presence, liveness, and connectedness (Jola and Grosbras 2013), and thus potentially enhances psychosocial wellbeing through dance (Quiroga Murcia et al. 2010). Hence, entrainment may have a positive effect on wellbeing, as it may contribute to the fulfilment of individuals' basic psychological need of affiliation (amongst competence and autonomy) (Ryan and Deci 2000). Research is needed to explore this mechanism.

It has been argued that certain types of dance have the potential to improve participants' sense of connectedness (Burgess et al. 2006; Quested et al. 2011; Quiroga Murcia et al. 2010). In a participatory phenomenological study, Cook and Ledger (2004) reported that adult female participants in a 5 rhythms dance programme experienced a sense of social connection and belonging while experiencing a safe place where they could express themselves. However, these improvements were not sustained after termination of the programme. These results are consistent with literature in the physical activity domain (e.g. Biddle and Mutrie 2008), suggesting that long-term interventions are necessary.

The positive effects of dance on psychosocial health were also demonstrated in non-clinical and clinical populations in the elderly. For example, Mavrovouniotis et al. (2010) have demonstrated that 60–91-year-olds experienced reductions of anxiety and psychological distress after one session of Greek traditional dances, compared to a group who discussed and watched television for one hour. Kluge et al. (2012) further conveyed that women who were recently relocated to a care retirement community reported more social connectivity, realized they had found a new and improved self, and reported improved mobility. It appears that dance participation promoted personal growth and decreased stress associated with relocation.

Guzmán-García et al.'s (2013) meta-analysis has shown some evidence of increased social interaction and enjoyment among care-home residents with dementia, and care staff. Specifically, decreases in problematic behaviours, enhancing mood, cognition, communication, and socializing after the dancing session were observed. Recent Cochrane Reviews on dance movement therapy also suggest that there are some positive effects of this dance-based intervention for clients with dementia (Karkou and Meekums 2014) or schizophrenia (Ren and Xia 2013). Notably, this research is afflicted with methodological limitations, small sample sizes, and an overall small number of studies with randomized controlled trial design.

CONCLUSION

Dance has gained increased recognition as a form of physical activity with considerable benefits for health and wellbeing. However, research specifically conducted on psychosocial wellbeing in dance is limited compared to research on physical activity and exercise. Although it is reasonable to expect that some mechanisms are shared between dance and physical activity/exercise contexts, it is also reasonable to explore the uniqueness of dance as a creative and performance-related activity. Therefore, there is a need to engage with the different demands of different dance styles, separate recreational dance from elite or vocational dance contexts, and take a developmental approach by considering different elements according to age groups (Burkhardt and Brennan 2012) or other personal characteristics not discussed here (e.g. gender, social status, race). Unfortunately, research focusing on public and leisure settings is scarcer than research in clinical settings (Cook and Ledger 2004), which suggests the need to focus on the different communities within a broader health-promotion agenda. Such knowledge would improve the level of consultations on dance intervention programmes, allowing better identification of target groups and precision of optimal intervention designs, and provide a framework for predictable and testable intervention strategies.

For example, based on literature on music and movement, we found that dance with interactive, live music provides feedback that also increases levels of endorphins more than dance without live music. Moreover, we showed on the basis of recent research on functional brain activity that watching dance with music enhances spectators' brain synchronicity and has significant effects on the enjoyment of the spectators. We outlined that the current understanding of social cohesion further supports that entrainment (synchronization of movement and music) is a hugely relevant factor for successful intervention strategies—in particular, when working with groups and the elderly. Hence, explanatory mechanisms for the effect of dance with music are prevalent in all neuronal, psychological, and biochemical areas.

Furthermore, in order to better support dance intervention programmes it is essential to understand the level of cardiovascular intensity of different types of dance forms. As outlined, cardiovascular intensity is related to levels of endorphins and cortisol, which need to be known in order to activate the intended health and wellbeing changes related, for example, to unacknowledged nutritional needs (e.g. due to aesthetic demands and/

or appetite suppression) as well as increased risks of injury (e.g. continuous training despite injury or fatigue).

Researchers should also determine a dose-response relationship in relation to the proposed mechanisms and examine how the different mechanisms interact in the context of dance to promote wellbeing (Buckworth et al. 2013). For example, few authors have measured changes in the brain alongside physiological changes in the body. We believe that in the near future, interdisciplinary research will further advance and studies combining structural changes and functional brain activity with physiological and psychosocial measures will increase. Such approaches would allow us to more closely relate subjective health and wellbeing with objective brain measures.

To conclude, hopefully, we have clarified the importance of the interplay of the brain and the body when considering health and wellbeing effects in response to dance. Moreover, we believe that this is the first condensed review that presents dance-related processes on the outer cortical surface as well as the inner brain structures equal attention. We anticipate that the increasing presence of dance in science will further signify the value of dance as an embodied art form and evidence its benefits on recreational as well as professional level as a form physical practice that includes further psychosocial and artistic aspects worth practicing and researching (Giersdorf 2009).

NOTE

1. It must be noted, however, that Gazzola and Keysers (2009) contrasted brain activity within each individual participant during the execution of an action with the observation of the action. This is an appropriate approach to assess mirror neuron activity. Notably though, it is in contrast to most studies involving dancers, most of which only measured brain activity during passive action observation. (One exemption is the study by Brown et al. 2006, who measured tango dancers' brain activity during dancing steps using PET.)

REFERENCES

Aalten, A. (2007). 'Listening to the dancer's body', *Sociological Review*, 55(s1): 109–25.

Abizaid A. (2009). 'Ghrelin and dopamine: New insights on the peripheral regulation of appetite', *Journal of Neuroendocrinology*, 21(9): 787–93.

Angioi, M., Metsios, G., Koutedakis, Y., and Wyon, M. A. (2011). 'Fitness in contemporary dance: A systematic review', *International Journal of Sports Medicine*, 30: 475–84.

Aşçi, F. H., Kin, A., and Kosar, S. (1998). 'Effect of participation in an 8 week aerobic dance and step aerobics program on physical self-perception and body image satisfaction', *International Journal of Sport Psychology*, 29: 366–75.

Bachrach, A., Jola, C., and Pallier, C. (2016). 'Neuronal basis of structural coherence in contemporary dance observation', *NeuroImage*, 124(Pt A): 464–72.

Bandura, A. (1997). *Self-Efficacy: The Exercise of Control*. New York, NY: Freeman.

Bartholomew, J. B. and Miller, B. M. (2002). 'Affective responses to an aerobic dance class: The impact of perceived performance', *Research Quarterly for Exercise and Sport*, 73: 301–9.

Berndt, C., Strahler, J., Kirschbaum, C., and Rohleder, N. (2012). 'Lower stress system activity and higher peripheral inflammation in competitive ballroom dancers', *Biological Psychology*, 91(3): 357–64.

Bezzola, L., Mérillat, S., and Jäncke, L. (2012). 'Motor training-induced neuroplasticity', *Journal of Gerontopsychology and Geriatric Psychiatry*, 25(4): 189–97.

Biddle, S. J. and Mutrie, N. (2008). *Psychology of Physical Activity: Determinants, Well-being and Interventions*. 2nd edn. New York, NY: Routledge.

Blaesing, B., Calvo-Merino, B., Cross, E., Jola, C., Honisch, J., and Stevens, C. (2012). 'Neurocognitive control in dance perception and performance', *Acta Psychologica*, 139(2): 300–8.

Block, B. and Kissell, J. L. (2001). 'The dance: Essence of embodiment', *Theoretical Medicine and Bioethics*, 22(1): 5–15.

Boecker, H., Sprenger, T., Spilker, M. E., Henriksen, G., Koppenhoefer, M., Wagner, K. J., Valet, M., Berthele, A., and Tolle, T. R. (2008). 'The runner's high: Opioidergic mechanisms in the human brain', *Cerebral Cortex*, 18: 2523–31.

Bolandzadeh, N., Davis, J., Tam, R., Handy, T., and Liu-Ambrose, T. (2012). 'The association between cognitive function and white matter lesion location in older adults: A systematic review', *BMC Neurology*, 12(1): 126.

Bradt, J., Shim, M., and Goodill, S. W. (2015). 'Dance/movement therapy for improving psychological and physical outcomes in cancer patients', *Cochrane Database of Systematic Reviews*, 1: CD007103, doi: 10.1002/14651858.CD007103.pub3.

Brown, S., Martinez, M. J., and Parsons, L. M. (2006). 'The neural basis of human dance', *Cerebral Cortex*, 16(8): 1157–67.

Brown, D. and Wyon, M. (2014a). 'The effect of moderate glycemic energy bar consumption on blood glucose and mood in dancers', *Medical Problems of Performing Arts*, 29(1): 27–31.

Brown, D. and Wyon, M. (2014b). 'An international study on dietary supplementation use in dancers', *Medical Problems of Performing Arts*, 29(4): 229–34.

Buckworth, J., Dishman, R. K., O'Connor, P., and Tomporowski, P. (2013). *Exercise Psychology*. 2nd edn. Champaign, IL: Human Kinetics.

Burgess, G., Grogan, S., and Burwitz, L. (2006). 'Effects of a 6-week aerobic dance intervention on body image and physical self-perceptions in adolescent girls', *Body Image*, 3: 57–66.

Burkhardt, J. and Brennan, C. (2012). 'The effects of recreational dance interventions on the health and well-being of children and young people: A systematic review', *Arts and Health: An International Journal for Research, Policy and Practice*, doi: 10.1080/17533015.2012.665810.

Burkhardt, J. and Rhodes, J. (2012). 'Commissioning dance for health and well-being', *Guidance and Resources for Commissioners. Public Health England*. <http://www.noo.org.uk>

Burns, V. E. (2006). 'Psychological stress and immune function', in M. Gleeson (ed.), *Immune Function in Sport and Exercise*. London: Elsevier, pp. 221–45.

Calvo-Merino, B., Glaser, D. E., Grèzes, J., Passingham, R. E., and Haggard, P. (2005). 'Action observation and acquired motor skills: An fMRI study with expert dancers', *Cerebral Cortex*, 15: 1243–9.

Calvo-Merino, B., Glaser, D. E., and Haggard, P. (2006). 'Seeing or doing? Influence of visual and motor familiarity in action observation', *Current Biology*, 16: 1905–10.

Cattaneo, L. and Rizzolatti, G. (2009). 'The mirror neuron system', *Archives of Neurology*, 66(5): 557–60.

Chang, Y. (2014). 'Reorganization and plastic changes of the human brain associated with skill learning and expertise', *Frontiers in Human Neuroscience*, 8: 35.

Chaouloff, F. (1989). 'Physical exercise and brain monoamines: A review', *Acta Physiologica Scandinavica*, 137: 1–13.

Chaouloff, F. (1997). 'Effects of acute physical exercise on central serotonergic systems', *Medicine and Science in Sports and Exercise*, 29: 58–62.

Christensen, J. F. and Jola, C. (2015). 'Towards ecological validity in the research on cognitive and neural processes involved in dance appreciation', in M. Nadal, J. P. Huston, L. Agnati, F. Mora, and C. J. Cela-Conde (eds.), *Art, Aesthetics and the Brain*. Oxford: Oxford University Press.

Connolly, M. K., Quin, E., and Redding, E. (2011). 'Dance 4 your life: Exploring the health and well-being implications of a contemporary dance intervention for female adolescents', *Research in Dance Education*, 12(1): 53–66.

Connolly, M. K. and Redding, E. (2010). 'Dancing towards well-being in the Third Age: Literature review on the impact of dance on health and well-being among older people', *Report produced by Trinity Laban Conservatoire of Music and Dance and Commissioned by the London Thames Gateway Dance Partnership*. http://tiny.cc/DancinginOldAge (accessed 18 April 2014).

Cook, S. and Ledger, K. (2004). 'A service user-led study promoting mental well-being for the general public, using 5 rhythms dance', *International Journal of Mental Health Promotion*, 6: 41–51.

Crabtree, D. R., Chambers, E. S., Hardwick, R. M., and Blannin, A. K. (2014). 'The effects of high-intensity exercise on neural responses to images of food', *American Journal of Clinical Nutrition*, 99(2): 258–67.

Cross, E. S., Acquah, D., and Ramsey, R. (2014). 'A review and critical analysis of how cognitive neuroscientific investigations using dance can contribute to sport psychology', *International Review of Sport and Exercise Psychology*, 7(1): 42–71.

Cross, E. S., Hamilton, A. F., and Grafton, S. T. (2006). 'Building a motor simulation de novo: Observation of dance by dancers', *Neuroimage*, 31(3): 1257–67.

Cruz, R. F. and Sabers, D. L. (1998). 'Dance/movement therapy is more effective than previously reported', *The Arts in Psychotherapy*, 25: 101–4.

Daly, A. (2002). *Critical Gestures: Writings on Dance and Culture*. Middletown, CT: Wesleyan University Press.

Davies, C. and Few, J. (1973). 'Effects of exercise on adrenocortical function', *Journal of Applied Physiology*, 35(1): 887–891.

Davis, J. M. and Bailey, S. P. (1997). 'Possible mechanisms of central nervous system fatigue during exercise', *Medicine and Science in Sports and Exercise*, 29(1): 45–57.

Dishman, R. K. (1997). 'Brain monoamines, exercise, and behavioral stress: Animal models', *Medicine and Science in Sports and Exercise*, 29(1): 63–74.

Dishman, R. K., Dunn, A. L., Youngstedt, S. D., Davis, J. M., Burgess, M. L., Wilson, S. P., and Wilso, M. A. (1996). 'Increased open field locomotion and decreased striatal GABAA binding after activity wheel running', *Physiology and Behavior*, 60: 699–705.

Dishman, R. K., Renner, K. J., and Youngsted, S. D. (1993). 'Spontaneous physical activity moderates escape latency and monoamines after uncontrollable footshock' (abstract), *Medicine and Science in Sports and Exercise*, 25(Suppl.): S25.

Dishman, R. K., Renner, K. J., Youngstedt, S. D., Reigle, T. G., Bunnell, B. N., Burke, K. A., Yoo, H. S., Mougey, E. H., and Meyerhoff, J. L. (1997). 'Activity wheel running reduces escape latency and alters brain monoamine levels after footshock', *Brain Research Bulletin*, 42: 399–406.

Draganski, B., Gaser, C., Busch, V., Schuierer, G., Bogdahn, U., and May, A. (2004). 'Neuroplasticity: Changes in grey matter induced by training', *Nature*, 427(6972): 311–12.

Dunbar, R. I., Kaskatis, K., MacDonald, I., and Barra, V. (2012). 'Performance of music elevates pain threshold and positive affect: Implications for the evolutionary function of music', *Evolutionary Psychology*, 10(4): 688–702.

Dummont, A. (2012). 'Une perte de contrôle, une perte de confort: Louise Lecavalier. La question du risque dans un parcours d'interprète', *Repères-Cahier de Danse*, 29: 15–17.

Dunn, A. L. and Dishman, R. K. (1991). 'Exercise and the neurobiology of depression', *Exercise and Sport Sciences Review*, 19: 41–99.

Dunn, A. L., Reigle, T. G., Youngstedt, S. D., Armstrong, R. B., and Dishman, R. K. (1996). 'Brain norepinephrine and metabolites after treadmill training and wheel running in rats', *Medicine and Science in Sports and Exercise*, 28: 204–9.

Ehrenberg, S. (2010). 'Reflections on reflections: Mirror use in a university dance training environment', *Theatre, Dance and Performance Training*, 1(2): 172–84.

Ekkekakis, P. (2003). 'Pleasure and displeasure from the body: Perspectives from exercise', *Cognition and Emotion*, 17: 213–39.

Ericsson, K. A. (2008). 'Deliberate practice and acquisition of expert performance: A general overview', *Academic Emergency Medicine*, 15: 988–94.

Fernandez-Arguelles, E., Rodriguez-Mansilla, J., Antunez, L., Garrido-Ardila, E., and Munoz, R. (2015). 'Effects of dancing on the risk of falling related factors of healthy older adults: A systematic review', *Archives of Gerontology and Geriatrics*, 60: 1–8.

Fields, R. D. (2010). 'Change in the brain's white matter: The role of the brain's white matter in active learning and memory may be underestimated', *Science*, 330(6005): 768–9.

Foley, T. E. and Fleshner, M. (2008). 'Neuroplasticity of dopamine circuits after exercise: implications for central fatigue', *Neuromolecular Medicine*, 10(2), 67–80.

Fritz, T. H., Halfpaap, J., Grahl, S., Kirkland, A., and Villringer, A. (2013). 'Musical feedback during exercise machine workout enhances mood', *Frontiers in Psychology*, 4: 921.

Gardner, S., Komesaroff, P., and Fensham, R. (2008). 'Dancing beyond exercise: Young people's experiences in dance classes', *Journal of Youth Studies*, 11: 701–9.

Garfola, L. (2010). 'The travesty dancer in the nineteenth-century ballet', in A. Dils and A. Cooper Albright (eds.), *Moving History/Dancing Cultures*. Middletown, CT: Wesleyan University Press, pp. 210–17.

Gazzola, V. and Keysers, C. (2009). 'The observation and execution of actions share motor and somatosensory voxels in all tested subjects: Single-subject analyses of unsmoothed fMRI data', *Cerebral Cortex*, 19(6): 1239–55.

Giersdorf, J. R. (2009). 'Dance studies in the international academy: Genealogy of a disciplinary formation', *Dance Research Journal*, 41 (1), 23–44.

Glass, R. (2005). 'Observer response to contemporary dance', in R. Grove, K. Stevens, and S. McKechnie (eds.), *Thinking in Four Dimensions: Creativity and Cognition in Contemporary Dance*. Melbourne: Melbourne University Press, pp. 107–121.

Grosbras, M. H., Tan, H., and Pollick, F. (2012). 'Dance and emotion in posterior parietal cortex: A low-frequency rTMS study', *Brain Stimulation*, 5(2): 130–6.

Guzmán-García, A. H. J. C., Hughes, J. C., James, I. A., and Rochester, L. (2013). 'Dancing as a psychosocial intervention in care homes: A systematic review of the literature', *International Journal of Geriatric Psychiatry*, 28: 914–24.

Haboush, A., Floyd, M., Caron, J., LaSota, M., and Alvarez, K. (2006). 'Ballroom dance lessons for geriatric depression: An exploratory study', *The Arts in Psychotherapy*, 33(2): 89–97.

Hänggi, J., Koeneke, S., Bezzola, L., and Jäncke, L. (2010). 'Structural neuroplasticity in the senso-rimotor network of professional female ballet dancers', *Human Brain Mapping*, 31: 1196–206.

Haskell, W. L., Lee, I. M., Pate, R. R., Powell, K. E., Blair, S. N.,. Franklin, B. A., Macera, C. A., Heath, G. W., Thompson, P. D., and Bauman, A. (2007). 'Physical activity and public health: Updated recommendation for adults from the American College of Sports Medicine and the American Heart Association', *Circulation*, 116: 1081–93.

Hasson, U., Nir, Y., Levy, I., Fuhrmann, G., and Malach, R. (2004) 'Intersubject synchroniza-tion of cortical activity during natural vision', *Science*, 303(5664): 1634–40.

Hausenblas, H. A. and Fallon, E. A. (2006). 'Exercise and body image: A meta-analysis', *Psychology and Health*, 21: 33–47.

Herbec, A., Kauppi, J-P., Jola, C., Tohka, J., and Pollick, F.E. (2015). 'Differences in fMRI inter-subject correlation while viewing unedited and edited videos of dance performance,' *Cortex*, 71: 341–48.

Howe, S., Hand, T., and Manore, M. (2014). 'Exercise-trained men and women: Role of exercise and diet on appetite and energy intake', *Nutrients*, 6(11): 4935–60.

Hove, M. J. and Risen, J. L. (2009). 'Its all in the timing: Interpersonal synchrony increases affil-iation', *Social Cognition*, 27: 949–60.

Hüfner, K., Binetti, C., Hamilton, D. A., Stephan, T., Flanagin, V. L., Linn, J., Labudda, K., Markowitsch, H., Glasauer, S., Jahn, K., Strupp, M., and Brandt, T. (2011). 'Structural and functional plasticity of the hippocampal formation in professional dancers and slackliners', *Hippocampus*, 21(8): 855–65.

Hyde, A. L., Conroy, D. E., Pincus, A. L., and Ram, N. (2011). 'Unpacking the feel good effect of free-time physical activity: Between- and within-person associations with pleasant-acti-vated feeling states', *Journal of sport and Exercise Psychology*, 33(6): 884–902.

Jeong, Y. J., Hong, S. C., Lee, M. S., Park, M. C., Kim, Y. K., and Suh, C. M. (2005). 'Dance move-ment therapy improves emotional responses and modulates neurohormones in adolescents with mild depression', *International Journal of Neuroscience*, 115(12): 1711–20.

Jola, C. (2016). 'The magic connection: Empirical evidence of the dancer–audience interac-tion', in U. Eberlein (ed.), *Zwischenleiblichkeit und bewegtes Verstehen—Intercorporeity, Movement and Tacit Knowledge*. Transcript Verlag.

Jola, C. (2017). 'Choreographing science: Synopsis of dance and cognitive neuroscience', in B. Bläsing, M. Puttke, and T. Schack (eds.), *The Neurocognition of Dance: Mind, Movement and Motor Skills*. 2nd edn. Hove: Psychology Press, pp. 203–34.

Jola, C., Abedian-Amiri, A., Kuppuswamy, A., Pollick, F., and Grosbas, M.-H. (2012). 'Motor simulation without motor expertise: Enhanced corticospinal excitability in visually experi-enced dance spectators', *PLoS ONE*, 7(3): e33343.

Jola, C., Davis, A., and Haggard, P. (2011). 'Proprioceptive integration and body representa-tion: Insights into dancers' expertise', *Experimental Brain Research*, 213(2–3): 257–65.

Jola, C., Ehrenberg, S., and Reynolds, D. (2012). 'The experience of watching dance: Phenomenological-neuroscience duets', *Phenomenology and the Cognitive Sciences*, 11(1): 17–37.

Jola, C. and Grosbras, M.-H. (2013). 'In the here and now: Enhanced motor corticospinal excitability in novices when watching live compared to video recorded dance', *Cognitive Neuroscience*, doi:10.1080/17588928.2013.776035, 1–9.

Jola, C., Grosbras, M.-H., and Pollick, F. E. (2011). 'Arousal decrease in "Sleeping Beauty": Audiences' neurophysiological correlates to watching a narrative dance perfor-mance of 2.5 hrs', *Dance Research Electronic*, 29(2): 378–403.

Jola, C. and Mast, F. W. (2005). 'Mental object rotation and egocentric body transformation: Two dissociable processes?', *Spatial Cognition and Computation*, 5: 217–37.

Jola, C., McAleer, P., Grosbras, M.-H., Love, S.A., Morison, G., and Pollick, F. E. (2013). 'Uni- and multisensory brain areas are synchronised across spectators when watching unedited dance', *i-Perception*, 4: 265–84.

Jola, C., Pollick, F. E., and Calvo-Merino, B. (2014). '"Some like it hot": Spectators who score high on the personality trait openness enjoy the excitement of hearing dancers breathing without music', *Frontiers in Human Neuroscience*, 8: 718.

Kandel, E. R. (2012). *The Age of Insight: The Quest to Understand the Unconscious in Art, Mind, and Brain, from Vienna 1900 to the Present*. New York, NY: Random House.

Karkou, V. and Meekums, B. (2014). 'Dance movement therapy for dementia (Protocol)', *Cochrane Database of Systematic Reviews*, 3: CD011022.

Keller, P. E., Novembre, G., and Hove, M. J.. (2014). 'Rhythm in joint action: Psychological and neurophysiological mechanisms for real-time interpersonal coordination', *Philosophical Transactions of the Royal Society of London, Series B, Biological Sciences*, 19: 369(1658): 130394.

Keogh, J., Kilding, A., Pidgeon, P., Ashley, L., and Gillis, D. (2009). 'Physical benefits of dancing for healthy older adults: A review', *Journal of Aging and Physical Activity*, 17: 479–500.

Kluge, M. A., Tang, A., Glick, L., LeCompte, M., and Willis, B. (2012). 'Let's keep moving: A dance movement class for older women recently relocated to a continuing care retirement community (CCRC)', *Arts and Health*, 4: 4–15.

Koch, S. C., Morlinghaus, K., and Fuchs, T. (2007). 'The joy dance: Specific effects of a single dance intervention on psychiatric patients with depression', *The Arts in Psychotherapy*, 34: 340–9.

Kokal, I., Engel, A., Kirschner, S., and Keysers, C. (2011). 'Synchronized drumming enhances activity in the caudate and facilitates prosocial commitment—if the rhythm comes easily', *PLoS ONE*, 6(11): e27272.

Koutedakis, Y. and Jamurtas, A. (2004). 'The dancer as a performing athlete: Physiological considerations', *Sports Medicine*, 34(10): 651–61.

Koutedakis, Y. and Sharp, N. C. C. (1999). *The Fit And Healthy Dancer*. Chichester: Wiley.

Landers, D. M. and Arent, S. M. (2001). 'Physical activity and mental health', Handbook of *Sport Psychology*, 2: 740–65.

Lansley, J. and Early, F. (2011). *The Wise Body: Conversations with Experienced Dancers*. Bristol: Intellect.

Liiv, H., Jürimäe, T., Mäestu, J., Purge, P., Hannus, A., and Jürimäe, J. (2014). 'Physiological characteristics of elite dancers of different dance styles', *European Journal of Sport Science*, 14: S429–36.

Logothetis, N. K. (2008). 'What we can do and what we cannot do with fMRI', *Nature Reviews*, 453: 869–78.

Macleod, A. D. (1998). 'Sport psychiatry', *Australian and New Zealand Journal of Psychiatry*, 32(6): 860–6.

Marieb, E. (2012). *Essentials of Human Anatomy and Physiology*. San Francisco, CA: Pearson.

Matos, M. G., Calmeiro, L., and Da Fonseca, D. (2009). 'Effet de l'activité physique sur l'anxiété et la dépression', *La presse médicale*, 38: 734–9.

Mavrovouniotis, F. H., Argiriadou, E. A., and Papaioannou, C. S. (2010). 'Greek traditional dances and quality of old people's life', *Journal of Bodywork and Movement Therapies*, 14(3): 209–18.

McMurray, R. G., Hackney, A. C., Guion, W. K., and Katz, V. L. (1996). 'Metabolic and hormonal responses to low-impact aerobic dance during pregnancy', *Medicine and Science in Sports and Exercise*, 28(1): 41–6.

Meekums, B., Karkou, V., and Mala, A. (2012). 'Dance/Movement Therapy (D/MT) for depression: A scoping review', *Arts in Psychotherapy*, 39(4): 287–95.

Meeusen, R. and De Meirleir, K. (1995). 'Exercise and brain neurotransmission', *Sports Medicine*, 20: 160–88.

Mercer, T. (2014). 'Wakeful rest alleviates interference-based forgetting', *Memory*. ePrint ahead of publication, doi:10.1080/09658211.2013.872279.

Miller, G., Chen, E., and Cole, S. W. (2009). 'Health psychology: Developing biologically plausible models linking the social world and physical health', *Annual Review of Psychology*, 60: 501–24.

Noble, K., Glowinski, D., Murphy, H., Jola, C., McAleer, P., Darshane, N., Penfield K., Camurri, A., and Pollick, F. E. (2014). 'Event segmentation and biological motion perception in watching dance', *Art and Perception*, 2(1–2): 59–74.

Nordin-Bates, S. M., Walker, I. J., Baker, J., Garner, J., Hardy, C., Irvine, S., Jola, C., Laws, H., and Blevins, P. (2011). 'Injury, imagery, and self-esteem in dance healthy minds in injured bodies?', *Journal of Dance, Medicine, and Science*, 15(2): 76–85.

O'Neal, H. A., Dunn, A. L., and Martinsen, E. W. (2000). 'Depression and exercise', *International Journal of Sport Psychology*, 31: 110–35.

O'Neill, J., Pate, R., and Liese, A. (2011). 'Descriptive epidemiology of dance participation in adolescents', *Research Quarterly for Exercise and Sport*, 82: 373–80.

Padham, M. and Aujla, I. (2014). 'The relationship between passion and the psychological well-being of professional dancers', *Journal of Dance Medicine and Science*, 18(1): 37–44.

Pascual-Leone, A., Amedi, A., Fregni, F., and Merabet, L. B. (2005). 'The plastic human brain cortex', *Annual Review of Neuroscience*, 28: 377–401.

Penedo, F. J. and Dahn, J. R. (2005). 'Exercise and well-being: A review of mental and physical health benefits associated with physical activity', *Current Opinion in Psychiatry*, 18(2): 189–93.

Phillips-Silver, J., Aktipis, C. A., and Bryant, G. A. (2010). 'The ecology of entrainment: Foundations of coordinated rhythmic movement', *Music Perception*, 28(1): 3–14.

Pierce, E. F., Eastman, N. W., Tripathi, H. L., Olson, K. G., and Dewey, W. L. (1993). 'Beta-endorphin response to endurance exercise: relationship to exercise dependence', *Perceptual and Motor Skills*, 77(3, Pt. I): 767–70.

Quested, E., Bosch, J. A., Burns, V. E., and Cumming, J. (2011). 'Basic psychological need satisfaction, stress-related appraisals, and dancers' cortisol and anxiety responses', *Journal of Sport and Exercise Psychology*, 33(6): 828–46.

Quick, S., Simon, A., and Thornton, A. (2010). 'PE and sport survey 2009/10', *DFE RR032 (TNS-BMRB)*.

Quiroga Murcia, C., Bongard, S., and Kreutz, G. (2009). 'Emotional and neurohumoral responses to dancing Tango Argentino: The effects of music and partner', *Music and Medicine*, 1(1): 14–21.

Quiroga Murcia, C., Kreutz, G., Clift, S. and Bongard S. (2010). 'Shall we dance?: An exploration of the perceived benefits of dancing on well-being', *Arts and Health*, 2(2): 149–63.

Reason, M. and Reynolds, D. (2010). 'Kinesthesia, empathy, and related pleasures: An inquiry into audience experiences of watching dance', *Dance Research Journal*, 42: 49–75, doi:10.1017/S0149767700001030.

Reason, M., Jola, C., Kay, R., Reynolds, D., Kauppi, J. P., Grosbras, M. H., Tohka, J., and Pollick, F. (2016). Spectators' aesthetic experience of sound and movement in dance performance: a transdisciplinary investigation. Psychology of Aesthetics, Creativity, and the Arts, 10(1), 42–55.

Reddish, P. R., Fischer, R., and Bulbulia, J. (2013). 'Let's dance together: Synchrony, shared intentionality and cooperation', *PLoS ONE*, 8.

Remington, G. (2009). 'From mice to men: What can animal models tell us about the relationship between mental health and physical activity?', *Mental Health and Physical Activity*, 2: 10–15.

Ren, J. and Xia, J. (2013). 'Dance therapy for schizophrenia', *Cochrane Database of Systematic Reviews*, 10: CD006868.

Rieth, C. A., Cai, D. J., McDevitt, E. A., and Mednick, S. C. (2010). 'The role of sleep and practice in implicit and explicit motor learning', *Behavior Brain Research*, 214: 470–474.

Rizzolatti, G. and Craighero, L. (2004). 'The mirror-neuron system', *Annual Review Neuroscience*, 27: 169–92.

Rizzolatti, G., Fadiga, L., Matelli, M., Bettinardi, V., Paulesu, E., et al. (1996). 'Localization of grasp representations in humans by PET: 1. Observation versus execution', *Experimental Brain Research*, 111: 246–52.

Rohleder, N., Beulen, S. E., Chen, E., Wolf, J. M., and Kirschbaum, C. (2007). 'Stress on the dance floor: The cortisol stress response to social-evaluative threat in competitive ballroom dancers', *Personality and Social Psychology Bulletin*, 33(1): 69–84.

Russell, J. A. (2013). 'Preventing dance injuries: Current perspectives', *Open Access Journal of Sports Medicine*, 30(4): 199–210.

Ryan, R. M. and Deci, E. L. (2000). 'Self-determination theory and the facilitation of intrinsic motivation, social development, and well-being', *American Psychologist*, 55(1): 68.

Salat, D. H., Lee, S. Y., van der Kouwe, A. J., Greve, D. N., Fischl, B., and Rosas, H. D. (2009). 'Age-associated alterations in cortical gray and white matter signal intensity and gray to white matter contrast', *Neuroimage*, 48(1): 21–8.

Schwarz, L. and Kindermann, W. (1992). 'Changes in β-endorphin levels in response to aerobic and anaerobic exercise', *Sports Medicine*, 13(1): 25–36.

Sekulic, D., Peric, M., and Rodek, J. (2010). 'Research note: "Doping" and dancing substance use and misuse among professional ballet dancers', *Substance Use and Misuse*, 45: 1420–30.

Sevdalis, V. and Keller, P. E. (2011). 'Captured by motion: Dance, action understanding, and social cognition', *Brain and Cognition*, 77(2): 231–6.

Siddall, J. (2010). *Dance In and Beyond Schools*. London: Youth Dance England, p. 9.

Soares, J., Holmes, P. V., Renner, K. J., Edwards, G. L., Bunnell, B. N., and Dishman, R. K. (1999). 'Brain noradrenergic responses to footshock after chronic activity-wheel running', *Behavioral Neuroscience*, 113: 558–66.

Sothmann, M. and Kastello, G. K. (1997). 'Simulated weightlessness to induce chronic hypoactivity of brain norepinephrine for exercise and stress studies', *Medicine and Science in Sports and Exercise*, 29: 39–44.

Tarr, B., Launay, J., and Dunbar, R. (2014). 'Music and social bonding: "Self-other" merging and neurohormonal mechanisms', *Frontiers Psychology*, 5: 1096, doi: 10.3389/fpsyg.2014.01096.

Tremblay, M. S., Copeland, J. L., and Van Helder, W. (2005). 'Influence of exercise duration on post-exercise steroid hormone responses in trained males', *European Journal of Applied Physiology*, 94: 505–13.

Walker, T. (2010). 'BBC's Strictly Come Dancing obsession is not helping dance, claims ballet star Deborah Bull', *The Telegraph*, 22 October. <http://www.telegraph.co.uk/news/celebritynews/8078780/BBCs-Strictly-Come-Dancing-obsession-is-not-helping-dance-claims-ballet-star-Deborah-Bull.html>

Wang, G. J., Volkow, N. D., Fowler, J. S., Franceschi, D., Logan, J., Pappas, N. R., Wong, C. T., and Netusil, N. (2000). 'PET studies of the effects of aerobic exercise on human striatal dopamine release', *Journal of Nuclear Medicine*, 41: 1352–6.

Wanke, E. M., Mill, H., and Groneberg, D. A. (2012). 'Ballet as high-performance activity: Health risks exemplified by acute injuries in dance students' (in German), *Sportverletzung Sportschaden*, 26(3): 164–70.

Warburton, D. E., Nicol, C. W., and Bredin, S. S. (2006). 'Health benefits of physical activity: The evidence', *Canadian Medical Association Journal*, 174(6): 801–9.

Werner, J. M., Cermak, S. A., and Aziz-Zadeh, L. (2012). 'Neural correlates of developmental coordination disorder: The mirror neuron system hypothesis', *Journal of Behavioral and Brain Science*, 2: 258–68.

Wiltermuth, S. S. and Heath, C. (2009). 'Synchrony and cooperation', *Psychological Science*, 20(1): 1–5.

Winter, B., Breitenstein, C., Mooren, F. C., Voelker, K., Fobker, M., Lechtermann, A., et al. (2007). 'High impact running improves learning', *Neurobiology of Learning and Memory*, 87: 597–609.

Wyon, M. A. (2010). 'Preparing to perform: periodization and dance', *Journal of Dance Medicine and Science*, 14(2): 67–72.

Wyon, M. A., Twitchett, E., Angioi, M., Clarke, F., Metsios, G., and Koutedakis, Y. (2011). 'Time motion and video analysis of classical ballet and contemporary dance performance', *International Journal of Sports Medicine*, 32: 851–5.

CHAPTER 2

DANCE IN THE BODY, THE MIND, AND THE BRAIN

Neurocognitive Research Inspired by Dancers and their Audience

BETTINA BLÄSING

INTRODUCTION

ACCORDING to the author's personal experience, many people seem to share the perspective that dancing can make us feel happy and energetic, and that regular dance activities can contribute to our perceived quality of life on different levels. Experience gained from an increasing number of community dance projects with participants of all ages and social backgrounds has confirmed that dance can strengthen our social bonds and improve our self-esteem. How can dance have such far-reaching positive effects? Dancing allows us to be creative, to experience our body and its ways of moving in novel ways, and thereby to learn about ourselves. Dancing in sync with others or with a musical beat can elicit a feeling of joy, harmony, and alignment that can easily be shared. All of the above help us experience our bodies in a multiplicity of pleasurable ways, thus contributing to our sense of well-being. Furthermore, even if we do not dance ourselves, watching others dancing can be also enjoyable and energizing, and can thereby also have a positive effect on our well-being. Recently, dance has begun to attract scientists interested in how the brain links action with perception, how such processes are influenced by expertise, and how they evoke positive emotions. Various aspects of dance expertise have been addressed by neurocognitive research (see for reviews, Bläsing et al. 2012; Sevdalis and Keller 2011), and the dance community has begun to contribute to this development by providing their own questions and ideas (see Bläsing et al. 2010; May et al. 2011; Waterhouse et al. 2014). One of the most recent questions asked in this field is 'what makes dance pleasurable to watch?', and more specifically, 'which processes in the human brain underlie positive emotional responses to dance?' These questions have inspired studies in neuroesthetics (see Cross and Ticini 2012; Christensen and Calvo-Merino 2013), and recent research in this field has indicated how the function of one's central nervous system while watching dance relates to the generation of a sense of wellbeing, as a result of experiencing positive emotional responses. In the following, I will regard how the brain controls and processes movement in general, before I turn to dance as very special type of human motor action. I will then present neurocognitive studies with dancers and dance spectators, to propose a physiological perspective on how dancing and watching dance can contribute to wellbeing.

MOVEMENT AND THE BRAIN

We tend to think of our brain as a machine for reasoning and problem solving. However, if we look at the different tasks of our everyday life, it is clear how great an extent our brain is involved in generating and controlling motor actions, including locomotion, posture and balance control, facial expressions, and manual actions such as grasping, manipulation, and gestures. Remarkably, dance makes use of all these aspects of human motor action. Therefore, before we turn to more specific aspects of dance, let us briefly reflect on the various parts of the brain concerned with motor action.

The neocortex, the outermost and youngest part of the human brain, can be anatomically divided into four lobes (Figure 2.1A). The frontal lobe is most strongly involved in planning and executing movement. Adjacent to the central sulcus (which separates the frontal lobe from the parietal lobe) is the primary motor cortex (also called M1, see Figure 2.1B), which directly controls intentional movements. From here, large neurons project to the spinal cord via the pyramidal tract, where they connect to motor neurons that innervate the muscles in the body periphery. In front of the primary motor cortex is the premotor cortex (PMC), which contributes to motor control and motor planning, as well as integrating sensory and spatial information with the planned movements. Next when moving in the mediofrontal direction is the supplementary motor area (SMA), which is involved in posture control, alignment of movement sequences, and coordination of bimanual actions. The most frontal part of the brain, the prefrontal cortex (PFC), is concerned with action plans on a higher cognitive level, hierarchical organization of actions according to their goals and their context, and decision making.

The parietal lobe is involved in many different activities related to the perception and higher-level processing of perceived information that is crucial for motor action, including spatial integration and navigation. Its most frontal part, next to the primary motor cortex, is the primary somatosensory cortex (S1), in which all

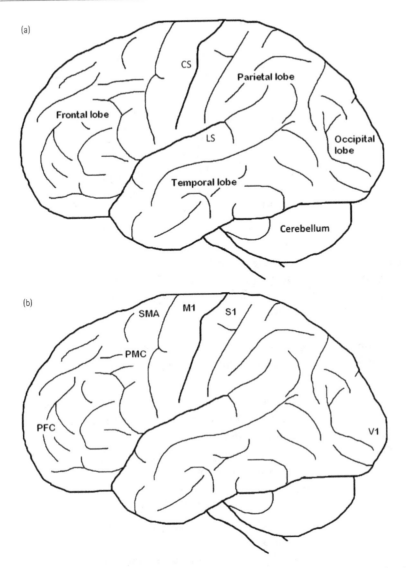

FIGURE 2.1. Human brain, from the lateral perspective. A: The neocortex can be subdivided into four lobes: the frontal lobe, the parietal lobe, the temporal lobe and the occipital lobe. The frontal lobe and the parietal lobe are separated by the central sulcus (CS), the temporal lobe is separated from the parietal lobe by the lateral sulcus (LS). The cerebellum, positioned below the hemispheres of the cerebral cortex, is strongly involved in motor control and motor learning. B: Areas of the cerebral cortex that are relevant for planning, performing, and perceiving movement: PFC Prefrontal cortex, PMC Premotor cortex; SMA Supplementary motor area; M1 Primary motor cortex; S1 Primary somatosensory cortex; V1 Primary visual cortex. (Credit: B. Bläsing.)

tactile, proprioceptive, and kinesthetic information is assimilated. In subsequent parts of the parietal lobe, this information is integrated with visual and other sensory information, contributing to multimodal representations of the body and the way it is embedded in its environment. The other two lobes of the neocortex also

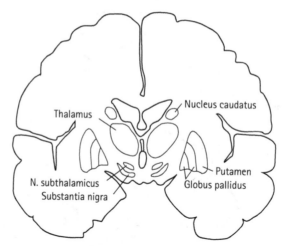

FIGURE 2.2. Subcortical areas of the human brain involved in movement production (coronal view). The basal ganglia include the Nucleus caudatus, Putamen, Globus pallidus, Nucleus subthalamicus, and Substantia nigra. The Thalamus acts as a relay between the basal ganglia and the cerebral cortex. (Credit: B. Bläsing.)

contain regions that process sensory information and contribute to multimodal perception, such as the visual cortex in the occipital lobe and the auditory cortex in the temporal lobe.

Below the neocortex, at the base of the forebrain, the basal ganglia (Figure 2.2) form a group of heavily interconnected nuclei with multiple functions, several of which are also crucial for motor control, motor learning, and the performance of voluntary actions. One main function of the basal ganglia is to generally inhibit motor systems and selectively allow access to motor output, thereby playing an important role in selecting actions. Several diseases with symptoms related to overshooting or the suppression of motor behaviors (e.g. Parkinson's disease, Huntington's disease, Tourette's syndrome) are linked to malfunction in the basal ganglia. Finally, the cerebellum (see Figure 2.1A), located below the occipital lobe of the neocortex, has most strongly been identified with motor control in the past, and its relevance for higher cognitive functions has only recently been investigated. The cerebellum is connected to the spinal cord and to most other parts of the brain, contributing extensively to the coordination, accuracy, and precision of movements, and carrying action plans to their relevant position in the body. The cerebellum also plays an important role in motor learning by monitoring the fit between executed and intended actions (in terms of an efference copy).

This brief overview of the brain gives an impression of the broad network of brain areas related to and necessary for performing motor actions. Dance, as a special type of complex human motor action, makes use of all these parts and their functions; however, dance is more than just movement, and it differs from everyday activities in several ways, as we will see in the following section.

WHAT IS SPECIAL ABOUT DANCE?

Dance can be seen as an art form intricately linked to the human body on different levels, from the most basic physical level to the higher-order conceptual level. Even though dancers performing on stage in classical, modern, or contemporary choreographies are movement experts comparable to athletes who perform with high skill in different sports disciplines, their expertise comprises additional features that makes dance an art form and the dancer an artist as well as an athlete. This can, of course, also apply to dancers engaging in other dance disciplines, such as traditional dance in many cultures, novel dance styles developed within urban subcultures such as hip hop or break dance, or competitive dancing that formally is a sports discipline. Additional to different movement vocabularies and expressive styles, all these types of dance have their own challenges, and, performed on an expertly level, can elicit amazement and admiration in the spectator. The content and character of what a type of dance can convey, however, is often inextricably linked to its cultural background and can hardly be determined with general validity.

Despite the differences and specialities, there are characteristics that seem to apply, on a broad level, to most types of dance. In addition to complex coordinated movement, dance typically involves entrainment on different levels to music or rhythm and between partners (Waterhouse et al. 2014), and interaction or communication among dancers and between dancers and their audience. Dance has been developed as part of almost every human culture, fulfilling various social functions. There is obviously something about dance that makes it useful and enjoyable for us humans, on a deeper level than can be explained by tradition or fashion. To find out more about how dance is embedded in our human nature, it is certainly worthwhile to take a closer look at the human brain. Neuropsychological studies have shown that the perception of others' bodies in motion is substantially influenced by reciprocal top-down and bottom-up processes between actors and observers (e.g. Blake and Shiffrar 2007). We perceive moving humans' (and also other animals') bodies differently from inanimate moving objects. Furthermore, specific parts of our brain have been shaped by evolution to preferentially attend to movements that are of the highest social relevance for us, those of our conspecifics, our partners and opponents. These specialized brain regions naturally respond to dance, indicating that, in certain contexts, dance can convey information about the dancer's emotional state (Dittrich et al. 1996; Sawada et al. 2003) and physical condition (Brown et al. 2005). Some dancers and choreographers deliberately make use of such effects by creating, modifying, and shaping the implicit and explicit messages that the movement of human bodies can convey, using metaphorical thinking as a cognitive and emotional mode of communication. Choreographies in contemporary dance often evolve in a creative process from the choreographer's ideas than can be based on concepts, feelings, words, images, or sounds, reflected and further developed by the dancers' thoughts and associations, and mediated through bodily action (see Stevens et al. 2003; Stevens and

McKechnie 2005; Zöllig 2010). Stevens and McKechnie point out that contemporary dance, as a heightened form of non-verbal communication rich in gesture, expression, and affect, can be viewed either as non-representational, non-symbolic, and formalist 'movement pure and simple', or as representational in some sense, a 'symbolic transformation of experience' (Stevens and McKechnie 2005). They suggest that different cognitive processes underlie these perspectives, including the direct perception of movement and force that does not depend on the observer's knowledge of performing the observed actions, and the neural mirroring of observed actions that involves the same repertoire of motor representations that is used for the production of these actions, and is therefore strongly influenced by motor expertise. As a third cognitive process, the authors add the implicit learning of the movement vocabulary and grammar that is specific for a dance style or the work of a choreographer. Even without being aware of this knowledge, an experienced spectator might therefore be more successful than an inexperienced one in predicting the trajectories and dynamics of movement in an unknown dance piece. Interestingly, the balance and tension between intrinsic reward following successful movement prediction and the surprise following a deviation from the prediction have been proposed as major sources of the pleasure experienced while watching dance (Hagendoorn 2004).

THE DANCING BRAIN IN THE SCANNER

After we have briefly reviewed how various parts of the human brain process movement, and subsequently focused on dance as a special type of human motor action, the question that naturally comes to mind is: What happens in the brain of a dancer while dancing? This question is not easy to answer, for mostly technical reasons; neuroimaging techniques such as functional magnetic resonance imaging (fMRI) or positron emission tomography (PET) require the participant to move as little as possible in order to minimize artifacts. But even though scanning a dancer's brain during active dancing is difficult, it has been mastered. In order to explore the neural correlates of specific tasks involved in dancing, PET was used to measure brain responses in ten amateur tango dancers (five women and five men) performing tango steps on an inclined board while they were lying in the scanner (Brown et al. 2006). The PET method makes use of a radioactive tracer to record three-dimensional images of metabolic processes in the brain. Molecules carrying a short-lived radioactive isotope are injected into the bloodstream and transported via the blood circulation to the area of interest. As the tracer decays, it emits positrons, anti-particles of electrons. When a positron meets an electron in the body tissue, both particles are annihilated and a pair of gamma photons is emitted. These gamma particles are recorded by a luminescent material in the PET scanner. As the blood flow is increased in brain areas with high activity levels, the gamma radiation measured from these areas will also be higher than the one from less active areas.

Brown and colleagues used PET to measure dancers' brain activity under six conditions: 1) while they were stepping to metric tango music (i.e., tango music with a regular rhythmical beat of equal time intervals); 2) while they were stepping to non-metric music; 3) while they were stepping without music; 4) while they were listening to metric music and contracting their leg muscles as if stepping, but without leg displacement; 5) while they were lying motionless listening to music; and 6) while they were lying motionless, resting without music. As expected, a large neuronal network of cortical, subcortical, and cerebellar regions was found to be active during dancing. Contrasting the different conditions revealed that certain brain areas are specifically involved in individual components of the dancing action. Movement to metric (in contrast to non-metric) music was found to correlate with activity in the right putamen, which is part of the basal ganglia, whereas movement to non-metric music correlated with activity in the ventral thalamus (see Figure 2.2). Entrainment to music was correlated with activity in the vermis, the medial part of the anterior cerebellum, and patterned stepping correlated with superior parietal activity. These findings support that dancing activates the brain regions commonly involved in complex motor action in general, and that individual regions respond selectively to dance-specific tasks, such as those related to music and rhythm.

IMAGERY AND CREATIVITY

The previous study has demonstrated that it is possible to dance even under very restricted conditions; however, experienced dancers are even able to dance without moving at all. Trained dancers are experts in movement imagery, and both motor and visual imagery are frequently used as tools in dance training to improve movement quality in terms of spatiotemporal adaptation and artistic expression, to exercise the memorization of long complex phrases, and even to create novel movements (e.g. May et al. 2011). Dance training has been found to increase the amount and efficiency of kinesthetic imagery, making kinesthetic sensations more complex and vivid (Golomer et al. 2008; Nordin and Cumming 2007). Alternative methods for dance training based on mental imagery have been recommended to decrease physical stress, especially during recovery from injury (e.g. Krasnow 1997). Theory states that motor imagery is based on simulation processes that recruit motor representations (Jeannerod 1995, 2004), and empirical findings have provided evidence that brain activity during motor imagery closely resembles brain activity during physical performance. During motor imagery, increased cortical activity of high frequencies has been observed in addition to increased cardiac and muscular activity, indicating states of high concentration and attention that are comparable to those seen during active movement (Blaser and Hökelmann 2004, 2009).

In a recent study, motor imagery was used to investigate brain processes underlying creativity in dance improvisation (Fink et al. 2009). Two groups of participants—fifteen trained dancers with a classical background who were also experienced in dance improvisation and seventeen dance novices who had only participated in a basic course in ballroom dancing—completed two motor imagery tasks while their brain activity was measured by electroencephalography (EEG). EEG records the activity of neurons mainly in the cerebral cortex using a set of electrodes placed on the scalp. Potentials of single neurons are summarized, and the resulting brain waves (characterized, for example, as alpha, beta, or gamma waves) can be used to monitor the activity of the cortex. In one condition of the study, the participants imagined dancing a waltz with a fixed simple stepping pattern, while in the other condition they imagined performing a dance phrase which they were spontaneously improvising, trying to make it as original and unique as possible. Additionally, all participants took part in a verbal test in which they were asked to quickly invent unusual applications for conventional objects. Dancers performed better than novices in the alternative uses test, and showed stronger alpha synchronization (known as an indicator of creative processes) during this task. Dancers also showed stronger right hemispheric alpha synchronization during the creative dance imagery task compared to novices, whereas brain activity did not differ between the groups during the waltz imagery. Studies like this one suggest that imagery and creativity are sensitive to training effects (as an alternative explanation, more genuinely creative minds might be found among dancers engaging in dance improvisation), and that such effects can be demonstrated on the neural level.

OBSERVING DANCE OBSERVERS' BRAINS

Evidence from studies investigating the activity in the human and non-human primate brain that is elicited by observing actions (see Rizzolatti and Craighero 2004; Rizzolatti and Sinigaglia 2010) suggests that when we observe actions performed by others, we simulate the observed actions without actually executing them, using similar brain regions as we would for executing the movements ourselves. A network of such brain regions has been found active during movement execution, imagery, and observation. This network, which mainly includes regions in the inferior parietal and premotor cortices (see Figure 2.3), has been described as the *human mirror system* (Grèzes and Decety 2001) or *action observation network* (see Calvo-Merino et al. 2005; Cross et al. 2009).

Scientists interested in studying action-perception links on the neural level have recently turned to working with dancers, using dance as a distinguished example of skilful human motor action. Several studies have applied this expertise-based approach for investigating how the brain is engaged in learning, executing, observing, and simulating complex coordinated full-body movements. One of the first studies in this line of research used functional magnetic resonance imaging (fMRI) to investigate the effects of movement expertise on movement observation (Calvo-Merino et al. 2005). fMRI is a method that measures brain activity on the basis of blood flow, or more specifically,

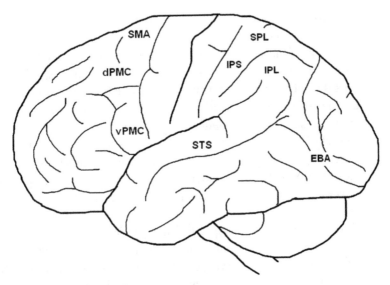

FIGURE 2.3. Areas of the neocortex that have found to be active during activities related to watching human movement such as dance (relevant studies are described in the text). SMA Supplementary motor area; dPMC Dorsal premotor cortex; vPMC Ventral premotor cortex; STS Superior temporal sulcus; SPL Superior parietal lobule; IPL Inferior parietal lobule; IPS Intraparietal sulcus; EBA Extrastriatal body area. (Credit: B. Bläsing.)

of the difference between levels of haemoglobin before oxygen release and after oxygen release. As active neurons need increased levels of oxygen, the blood flow is dynamically regulated to supply oxygenated haemoglobin to active brain areas. As oxygenated and deoxygenated haemoglobin differ characteristically in their magnetic susceptibility, activated brain areas show a different magnet resonance from less active brain areas. This effect—the blood oxygen level dependent (BOLD) response—is measured in fMRI.

In the study by Calvo-Merino and colleagues, short video clips of dance movements were presented to three groups of male participants: ten professional ballet dancers from the London Royal Ballet, nine professional capoeiristas, and ten non-dancers. The video clips showed typical movements from ballet or capoeira, matched for similarity of movement types. Brain activity was measured while the participants watched the clips, and the results revealed significant effects of the observers' own movement expertise. Brain areas belonging to the action observation network, including the PMC, the intraparietal sulcus (IPS), the right superior parietal lobule (SPL), and the left posterior superior temporal sulcus (STS) (see Figure 2.3), showed stronger activation in the experts than in the control group. Furthermore, responses were stronger when the experts watched movements from their own area of expertise (i.e., ballet dancers watching ballet movements and capoeiristas watching capoeira movements) compared to movements not belonging to their own repertoire, whereas the non-dancers showed no effect of movement type. The authors argued that the observers' movement expertise modified the responsiveness of the corresponding brain areas to the movements they were familiar with from their own training.

Notably, the findings of the latter study did not specify whether the observed effects were based on visual or motor familiarity of the presented movements, as ballet dancers and capoeiristas would be used to performing and watching only movements from their own discipline. An expedient situation to differentiate between visual and motor experience within the same expert population exists in classical dance, where a few movements are exclusively performed by male or female dancers, while the majority of movements are not gender-specific. As male and female dancers train and rehearse together, they are familiar with such gender-specific movements of the opposite gender, but have never performed these movements themselves. In an fMRI study, twelve male and twelve female ballet dancers from the London Royal Ballet watched short video clips of female-specific, male-specific, and gender-common classical dance movements (Calvo-Merino et al. 2006). The results revealed that within the action observation network, the left dorsal PMC, the IPS, and the cerebellum responded specifically to motor familiarity of observed movements from the dancers' own repertoire when compared to visual familiarity of movements performed exclusively by the opposite gender.

A study that aimed to further differentiate the responsiveness of the action observation network to observational versus physical learning made use of a dance video game (Cross et al. 2009). The sixteen student participants, all without dance experience, physically trained short sequences of steps presented partly by abstract cues (arrows) and partly by a human demonstrator, and watched comparable sets of stimuli without practicing them physically, over five consecutive days. Brain responses to watching the trained cues along with similar untrained cues were measured using fMRI before and after the training days, and participants reported that they spontaneously engaged in mental imagery while watching the rehearsed sequences. The fMRI results revealed:

- greater activity in the right premotor cortex and left inferior parietal lobule (IPL, see Figure 2.3) in response to trained compared to novel sequences, and
- greater activity in the right premotor cortex in response to physically trained sequences compared to sequences learned from observation.

These findings provide evidence that observational learning and physical practice engage several parts of the action observation network (specifically premotor and inferior parietal regions) in a similar way, and that part of these regions is specifically responsive to physical training compared to observational learning.

The presented studies suggest that brain regions belonging to the action observation network are responsive to watching dance, and that their activity is modulated by the observer's own visual and motor experience of the observed movements, with physical practice enhancing the brain's responsiveness even more strongly than repeated observation.

WATCHING DANCE AND LIKING IT

We stated previously that there is more to dance than just movement. In a similar way, we can argue that there is more to watching dance than just observing others performing more or less familiar actions—otherwise dance performances would not have an audience. There must be a reason why dance appeals to spectators, linking watching dance to wellbeing. Why and how an audience enjoys watching dance is not easy to pinpoint, given the various disciplines, styles, and artistic intentions. Dance can be beautiful, disturbing, touching, provocative, arduous, even terrifying; it can raise a multitude of emotions, making audience members feel happy, sad, angry, bored, contemplative, energetic, or exhausted. Interestingly, such emotional responses in the spectators can be evoked by the coordinated movement of human bodies. Neurocognitive research has developed a growing interest in the neural correlates of such positive emotional responses to watching dance, asking why spectators enjoy watching certain movements more than others, and how this is represented in their brains (see Christensen and Calvo-Merino 2013).

In an fMRI study that aimed at defining neural correlates of aesthetic evaluation of dance, scientists presented video clips of ballet and capoeira movements to six male participants who were naïve to both disciplines (Calvo-Merino et al. 2008). A year after the fMRI data were collected, the same participants were invited back for a questionnaire study. This time, they were presented the same dance clips and had to rate them in five aesthetic dimensions: how simple or complex, dull or interesting, tense or relaxed, weak or powerful they perceived each movement, and how much they liked or disliked it. From the participants' ratings, a general consensus was calculated for each movement and compared to the fMRI results. It turned out that high ratings for liking correlated with increased activity in the bilateral occipital (visual) cortices and in the right PMC, suggesting that these areas represent neural correlates of positive aesthetic experience of dance. Remarkably, no other aesthetic dimension from the questionnaire was significantly correlated to any brain response. The questionnaire also assessed movement characteristics related to aesthetic evaluation. It turned out that, according to the participants' consensus, full-body movements with strong horizontal or vertical displacement were liked best, whereas movements of single limbs without displacement of the body and without vertical variation were most disliked. This, however, represents only the preferences of the participants who took part in this study, and cannot be regarded as a general finding.

As shown by the previous study, the subjective assessment of liking can be used as a measure of aesthetic evaluation, and evidence for neural correlates of such personal preference has been found. A question that remains to be answered is what makes us like a dance movement or dance piece in general, beyond personal taste for certain movement characteristics. An fMRI study approached this question by linking the participants' aesthetic evaluation of dance movements to their estimation of their personal ability to perform the movements, thereby necessitating motor simulation (Cross et al. 2011). Twenty-two dance novices watched video clips of dance movements and had to indicate for each movement how much they liked it and how well they thought they could reproduce it. Results revealed that the two ratings were not independent of each other; participants liked those movements best that they rated as most difficult to perform. Ratings for liking movements and perceiving them as difficult were correlated to activation in the right IPL and in occipitotemporal brain areas, including those involved in the visual processing of motion patterns and human bodies. These findings suggest that spectators specifically enjoy watching dance movements they perceive as demanding, and that liking movements and judging them as physically difficult share neural correlates. Interpreting these findings remains a challenge: did the participants like certain movements best because they perceived them as the most difficult, or did they like certain movements and therefore made the strongest effort to simulate them, which made them perceive these movements as the most difficult?

Neuroimaging techniques such as fMRI or PET can reveal correlations between behavioral tasks and brain activity (measured via blood flow and oxygen metabolism). Transcranial magnetic stimulation (TMS), in contrast, influences neuronal activity in the brain and can thereby be used to investigate causal relationships by showing that certain tasks cannot be performed while the correlating brain areas are briefly 'knocked out' by strong magnetic pulses. Rapidly changing magnetic fields applied with high precision by an electric coil induce weak electric currents in the brain tissue. These electric currents interfere with the neuronal activity in the target areas, which can lead to measurable effects on task performance, such as increased reaction times, or even different response behaviour. In a recent study, TMS was shown to interfere with aesthetic judgements of dance stimuli (Calvo-Merino et al. 2010). In this study, sixteen dance novices rated images of dance postures and abstract patterns, indicating how much they liked them. Later, the same task was repeated while TMS was applied to the participants' ventral PMC or to their extrastriatal body area (EBA, see Figure 2.3), a small region in the occipital cortex that is associated with the visual processing of human bodies and body parts. The ratings obtained before and after TMS application were compared, showing that ratings differed significantly for stimuli depicting dance postures, but not for abstract patterns. Interestingly, the direction of the effect was different for the two brain regions to which TMS was applied: TMS over the EBA resulted in higher ratings, whereas TMS over the PMC resulted in lower ratings compared to the baseline. The authors produced a model for explaining these findings, according to which the PMC processes rather configural aspects of human bodies, whereas the EBA processes local aspects. Disconnecting the configural processing area in the PMC via TMS should result in heightened aesthetic sensitivity via the EBA (the local processing area), thereby decreasing liking ratings. Disconnecting the local processing area, the EBA, should result in blunted aesthetic sensitivity via the PMC (the configural processing area), thereby increasing liking ratings.

Findings from the presented studies emphasize the importance of sensorimotor mechanisms for the aesthetic experience of dance, suggesting the existence of a complementary network that includes visual and motor regions. Notably, these studies used a subjective approach for evaluating aesthetic quality (i.e., liking) that enabled them to examine which movements appealed most to their participants, rather than asking for objective movement characteristics. Information gained from such studies can be of interest for the dance community, as it reflects probable reactions of the audience, at least as far as a generally positive response is concerned. When choreographers aim at creating works which are aesthetically pleasant, they could use this information to anticipate which dance phrases would be perceived as such (Cross and Ticini 2012). The subjective nature of the aesthetic evaluation used in the presented studies also has potential relevance for exploring the aspect of wellbeing. These studies indicated that watching dance makes us feel good by engaging our brains more strongly in simulating the observed action, whether we are dancers or not.

CONCLUSIONS

When we dance, a broad neural network that includes regions in almost every part of our brain is activated. This network comprises regions commonly involved in controlling complex motor action and also additional regions related to tasks that are special to dance, such as entrainment to music or rhythm. When we watch others dancing, many of these regions are also active—our brain engages in the dance even if our body remains motionless, by simulating the observed movements. The degree to which our brain becomes active while observing dance depends on our own dance experience— the more we dance ourselves, the more strongly the motor areas in our brain respond to watching dance. Furthermore, the degree of our brain's activity while watching dance depends on how much we like what we see, and this seems to be linked to how challenging we judge the dance to be. As evidenced by empirical studies, the experience of being totally absorbed by watching a sophisticated dance piece, feeling almost as if we were dancing ourselves inside the dancer's body, does have neural grounding.

Dancing and watching dance are intricately linked, not only in the way that action and perception are interconnected in our brains, but also ecologically. Dance enables social interaction and communication on levels far more basic than language—there is hardly any other type of human motor action that is so closely related to watching others and being watched. Nevertheless, in terms of how dance in the body, mind, and brain can contribute to wellbeing, this is not the full story. Even though social interactions do not necessarily require movements to be complex, dance implies highly coordinated and orchestrated movements based on creativity and cooperation, challenging our neurocognitive apparatus to integrate sophisticated physical and social skills. We can argue that dancing has a highly beneficial effect on our whole system, as it has the potential to integrate our most basic and most advanced skills on different levels into one activity that has the intrinsic goal to be enjoyed by actors and observers. Due to the nature of our neurocognitive apparatus, simply watching dance shares many qualities with active dancing, but not all. Dancing, which always includes watching dance, can stimulate the best part of our abilities, including social, communicative, and creative skills. A high level of physical skill is less important for dance to have this beneficial effect; however, dancers who enjoy what they do will naturally be drawn toward acquiring more sophisticated and challenging movement skills.

Taken together, to make the most of dance for ourselves, we should first engage in some dancing activity that we personally enjoy, that involves creativity and social interaction, and that offers a way to reach a higher level of movement skill. Secondly, we should also at times engage in watching dance in an active way, simulating the dancers' movements and letting our mind dance while our body rests, and enjoy the way this perspective broadens our personal experience.

References

Blake, R. and Shiffrar, M. (2007). 'Perception of human motion', *Annual Review of Psychology*, 58: 47–73.

Blaser, P. and Hökelmann, A. (2004). 'Relationships between load and demand under the condition of the mental representation of a dance', *Journal of Human Kinetics*, 12: 15–30.

Blaser, P. and Hökelmann, A. (2009). 'Mental reproduction of a dance choreography and its effects on physiological fatigue in dancers', *Journal of Human Sport and Exercise*, 4(2): 129–41.

Bläsing, B., Calvo-Merino, B., Cross, E., Honisch, J., Jola, C., and Stevens, K. (2012). 'Neurocognitive control in dance perception and performance', *Acta Psychologica*, 139(2): 300–8.

Bläsing, B., Puttke, M., and Schack, T. (eds.) (2010). *The Neurocognition of Dance: Mind, Movement and Motor Skills*. London: Psychology Press.

Brown, W. M., Cronk, L., Grochow, K., et al. (2005). 'Dance reveals symmetry especially in young men', *Nature*, 438(7071): 1148–50.

Brown, S., Martinez, M. J., and Parsons, L. M. (2006). 'The neural basis of human dance', *Cerebral Cortex*, 16(8): 1157–67.

Calvo-Merino, B., Glaser, D. E., Grèzes, J., Passingham, R. E., and Haggard, P. (2005). 'Action observation and acquired motor skills: An fMRI study with expert dancers', *Cerebral Cortex*, 15(8): 1243–9.

Calvo-Merino, B., Grèzes, J., Glaser, D. E., Passingham, R. E., and Haggard, P. (2006). 'Seeing or doing? Influence of visual and motor familiarity in action observation', *Current Biology*, 16(19): 1905–10.

Calvo-Merino, B., Jola, C., Glaser, D. E., and Haggard, P. (2008). 'Towards a sensorimotor aesthetics of performing art', *Consciousness and Cognition*, 17(3): 911–22.

Calvo-Merino, B., Urgesi, C., Orgs, G., Aglioti, S. M., and Haggard, P. (2010). 'Extrastriate body area underlies aesthetic evaluation of body stimuli', *Experimental Brain Research*, 204(3): 447–56.

Christensen, J. F. and Calvo-Merino, B. (2013). 'Dance as a subject for empirical aesthetics', *Psychology of Aesthetics, Creativity, and the Arts*, 7(1): 76–88.

Cross, E. S., Kirsch, L., Ticini, L., and Schütz-Bosbach, S. (2011). 'The impact of aesthetic appreciation and physical ability on dance perception', *Frontiers in Human Neuroscience*, 5: 102.

Cross, E. S., Kraemer, D. J., Hamilton, A. F., Kelley, W.M., and Grafton, S. T. (2009). 'Sensitivity of the action observation network to physical and observational learning', *Cerebral Cortex*, 19(2): 315–26.

Cross, E. S. and Ticini, L. F. (2012). 'Neuroaesthetics and beyond: New horizons in applying the science of the brain to the art of dance', *Phenomenology and the Cognitive Sciences*, 11(1): 5–16.

Dittrich, W. H., Troscianko, T., Lea, S., and Morgan, D. (1996). 'Perception of emotion from dynamic point-light displays represented in dance', *Perception*, 25(6): 727–38.

Fink, A., Graif, B., and Neubauer, A. C. (2009). 'Brain correlates underlying creative thinking: EEG alpha activity in professional vs. novice dancers', *NeuroImage*, 46: 854–62.

Golomer, E., Bouillette, A., Mertz, C., and Keller, J. (2008). 'Effects of mental imagery styles on shoulder and hip rotations during preparation of pirouettes', *Journal of Motor Behavior*, 40(4): 281–90.

Grèzes, J. and Decety, J. (2001). 'Functional anatomy of execution, mental simulation, observation, and verb generation of actions: A meta-analysis,' *Human Brain Mapping*, 12(1): 1–19.

Hagendoorn, I. (2004). 'Some speculative hypotheses about the nature and perception of dance and choreography', *Journal of Consciousness Studies*, 11: 79–110.

Jeannerod, M. (1995). 'Mental imagery in the motor context', *Neuropsychologia*, 33(11): 1419–32.

Jeannerod, M. (2004). 'Actions from within', *International Journal of Sport and Exercise Psychology*, 2(4): 376–402.

Krasnow, D. (1997). 'C-I training: The merger of conditioning and imagery as an alternative training methodology for dance', *Medical Problems of Performing Artists*, 12: 3–8.

May, J., Calvo-Merino, B., deLahunta, S., McGregor, W., et al. (2011). 'Points in mental space: An interdisciplinary study of imagery in movement creation', *Dance Research* 29(2): 404–30.

Nordin, S. M. and Cumming, J. (2007). 'Where, when, and how: A quantitative account of dance imagery', *Research Quarterly for Exercise and Sport*, 78(4): 390–5.

Rizzolatti, G. and Craighero, L. (2004). 'The mirror neuron system', *Annual Review of Neuroscience*, 27: 169–92.

Rizzolatti, G. and Sinigaglia, C. (2010). 'The functional role of the parieto-frontal mirror circuit: Interpretations and misinterpretations', *Nature Reviews: Neuroscience*, 11(4): 264–74.

Sawada, M., Suda, K., and Ishii, M. (2003). 'Expression of emotions in dance: Relation between arm movement characteristics and emotion', *Perceptual and Motor Skills*, 97: 697–708.

Sevdalis V. and Keller, P. (2011) 'Captured by motion: Dance, action understanding, and social cognition', *Brain and Cognition*, 77: 231–6.

Stevens, C., Malloch, S., McKechnie, S., and Steven, N. (2003). 'Choreographic cognition: The time-course and phenomenology of creating a dance', *Pragmatics and Cognition*, 11(2): 297–326.

Stevens, C. and McKechnie, S. (2005). 'Thinking in action: Thought made visible in contemporary dance', *Cognitive Processing*, 6: 243–52.

Waterhouse, E., Watts, R., and Bläsing, B. (2014). 'Doing duo: A case study of entrainment in William Forsythe's choreography "Duo"', *Frontiers in Human Neuroscience*, 8: 812.

Zöllig, G. (2010). 'Searching for that "other land of dance": The phases in developing a choreography', in B. Bläsing, M. Puttke, and T. Schack (eds.), *The Neurocognition of Dance: Mind, Movement and Motor Skills*. London: Psychology Press, 115–122.

CHAPTER 3

SUBJECTIVE AND NEUROPHYSIOLOGICAL PERSPECTIVES ON EMOTION PERCEPTION FROM DANCE

MARIE-HELENE GROSBRAS, MATTHEW REASON,
HAODAN TAN, ROSIE KAY, AND FRANK POLLICK

INTRODUCTION

THE appreciation of art is a subjective process often linked to emotional/hedonic experiences. Emotional responses have been intensively studied in the measurement of the aesthetic evaluation of art (e.g. Belke et al. 2010; Daprati et al. 2009; Di Dio and Gallese 2007; Vartanian and Goel 2004). The responses to art that are measured (pleasure and preference) reflect the observer's emotional feelings towards those works of art. The emotions aroused from viewing art are defined as 'aesthetic emotions', and these are claimed to be closely related to artistic appreciation. Positive emotions have been studied most in aesthetic psychological studies; for example, pleasure (e.g. Fechner 1876) and liking (e.g. Belke et al. 2010; Daprati et al. 2009; Di Dio and Gallese 2009; Vartanian and Goel 2004). However, some other studies indicate that negative emotions may also be associated with art appreciation, such as anger, disgust (e.g. Silvia and Brown 2007) and hostile emotions (Silvia 2009). Silvia (2005a, 2005b) introduced an appraisal model of emotions into the psychology of aesthetics, which posits a linear relationship between emotion and aesthetic judgement. Other models take into account a more complex relationship that includes emotional, aesthetic, and cognitive appraisal. The 'hedonic fluency model' (Reber et al. 2004) claims that the appreciation of artwork is not limited to the perception of object properties, but is also influenced by pleasant feelings arising from the observation of artwork, and is closely related to successful cognitive processing. Leder et al. (2004) suggested that artistic experience may be based on the cognitive interpretation, with processing fluency leading to a feeling of aesthetic pleasure. They proposed an information-processing framework to explain why the appreciation of artwork is always accompanied by affective reactions. This multi-stage model involves different levels of processing: pre-classification, perceptual analyses, implicit memory integration, and explicit classification, as well as cognitive mastering and evaluation. Affective evaluation is continuously taking place, and impacts on the cognitive mastering process at each stage. In summary, according to this model, 'An aesthetic experience is a cognitive process accompanied by continuously upgrading affective states that *vice versa* are appraised, resulting in an aesthetic emotion' (Leder et al. 2004: 493).

These models are supported by studies in the Arts and Humanities, which have investigated appreciation and emotional responses. Considering the complexity of emotional reaction to art appreciation, qualitative research methods are often important approaches to understanding subjective feelings and audiences' individual experience involved in the appreciation process (Reason and Reynolds 2010). Neuroscience research has also started to shed light on the brain and body correlates of the arts appreciation and in particular the emotions evoked by arts, leading to the emergence of the field of neuroaesthetics (Di Dio and Gallese 2009). This research indicates that a network of brain structures involved in emotional processing is also associated with artistic appreciation (see Figure 3.1). These regions include the left anterior cingulate sulcus (see Devinsky et al. 1995 for a review), the insula and the amygdala (Phelps and

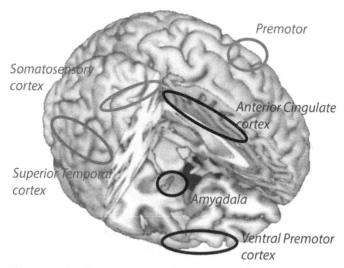

FIGURE 3.1. The network of brain structures involved in emotional processing and artistic appreciation. In black, regions commonly involved in emotion processing; in grey, regions commonly involved in person perception.

LeDoux 2005; Cupchik et al. 2009; also see Di Dio and Gallese 2009 as a review), the ventromedial frontal cortex (Calvo-Merino et al. 2005). Theses regions are activated in addition to regions involved in object or person perception in visual and premotor cortices (Calvo-Merino et al. 2006).

Empirical and theoretical work from all these fields of research (psychology, neuroscience, and qualitative audience research) support the idea that aesthetic experience is a complicated psychological state that involves multiple cognitive approaches, while emotional responses evoked from the experience are especially apparent and intermingled with different cognitive processes. In this context, the present study aims to provide a multidisciplinary account of the emotional response to dance. To this end we combine psychophysics, brain measures, and qualitative research to study the subjective emotions induced by watching dance. The originality of this approach offers a unique view of emotional engagement with dance, which could form the base for more applied research on dance as a mean of regulating emotions. Part of the data on which this paper is based has been published as a scientific report (Grosbras et al. 2012).

Dance is an art form that uses the dancer's body as a means to induce affective and aesthetic experience in the observers. It has been used in the field of qualitative audience research but also in psychology and cognitive neuroscience as a form of stimulus to study emotion perception (see also Blasing's chapter in this volume). Macfarlane, Kulka, and Pollick (2004) asked subjects to rate emotional valence after watching ten pieces of dance with different affects, and found that subjects were able to distinguish accurately the emotion portrayed by the dancers. This study, however, involved segments of dance, each 15 seconds long, with judgements of affective similarity made *after* the presentation of the videos. Yet emotional response to dance occurs in the immediacy and evolves as the dance performance unfolds (Jola et al. 2012). Thus in the present study we collected continuous ratings on a linear visual scale. Participants watched a 4-minute video constructed from the filming of a piece of contemporary dance choreographed for the purpose of the research project (Watching Dance n.d.), involving two dancers and three different music segments. They were asked to use a computer mouse to move a slider on a screen upwards when they felt positively aroused, and downwards when they felt a negative emotion. This provided us with a continuous rating of their subjective emotional response. We chose to focus only on valence and intensity rather than categorization of individual emotions (e.g. sadness, joy, fear, and so on) as those dimensions capture most of the experience of emotion and are less sensitive to interindividual differences in labelling feelings and emotions. Indeed, based on the circumplex model of affective experience—one of the most influential models in the field of emotion research (Russell 1980)—each emotion can be placed on a plan with the two bipolar dimensions representing valence (or pleasantness: positive or negative) and arousal (or activation, low or high). Importantly, both dimensions are independent and correspond well to the conscious experience or perception of emotion (Pollick et al. 2001). While previous studies have collected only self-reported positive emotion responses to dance, in reference to this model we felt that using a bipolar slider—measuring not only positive but also negative emotional changes—was pivotal. Similar ratings of the aesthetic response were also obtained in order to test the relationship between affective and aesthetic impressions during the continuous watching.

We used these ratings to investigate how the subjective judgement of the emotion induced by the dance modulates the brain response to the dance. To this end we used functional magnetic resonance imaging (fMRI)—a technique that provides us with an indirect measure of brain regional activity, exploiting the fact that brain regions that are active receive an increased afflux of oxygenated blood, which in turn changes the magnetic signal in a way that can be measured. We relied on a parametric approach (Buchel, Morris, and Dolan 1998) to map the impact of emotion on the regional neuronal activity.

This experiment was complemented by two lines of investigation. First, in order to draw causal links between the identified functional brain regions and emotional appraisal, we conducted a non-invasive brain interference study using Transcranial Magnetic Stimulation (TMS). Indeed, fMRI shows where in the brain the activity is *correlated* with the perception of dance while subjects are watching the video. It does not tell us anything about the causal nature of this relationship. TMS is a technique that allows us to transiently and non-invasively perturb local brain activity (reviewed in Walsh and Rushworth 1999). If as a result we observe a change in behaviour, then we can infer that the brain region targeted with TMS is causally involved in the behaviour under investigation, and not just incidentally activated. It works by applying a rapidly changing focal magnetic field near the scalp of the participants, which depolarizes the nearby neuronal populations and thereby interferes with their activity. If applied repeatedly during several minutes the effect of altered activity can outlast the stimulation by 10–15 minutes. In this study we used TMS to ask whether a small and transient manipulation of the regions identified in fMRI could modify the emotional appreciation of dance. We then conducted a qualitative investigation probing participants' subjective reflections on their reaction to the dance, in order to obtain further insight into the meaning of their responses during the experiments.

In summary, the aim of this project was to investigate the neural correlates of the subjective emotional reaction to dance, using functional brain imaging and non-invasive brain interference to investigate a causal link between regional brain activity and the subjective emotional response. This was complemented by structured interviews prompting the participants to reflect on their ratings. This chapter will present and discuss some of these findings with regards to their relevance for understanding the links between emotion and cognition. In doing so we will draw a link with wellbeing. For the purpose of this chapter, wellbeing will be seen as a state of health and positive functioning, and we will argue that it is strongly dependent upon the harmonious integration between cognitive and affective processing at the brain level. We will speculate about how considering dance perception in this framework could offer new research avenues for interventions promoting wellbeing.

METHODOLOGY

Subjects

Thirty-two subjects from Glasgow University participated in this study. Sixteen (eight females) took part in the first (FMRI) as well as in the third part (structured interview), and sixteen others in the second part (TMS). They were recruited from advertisements throughout the university, and were all naïve to the purpose of the study and had no experience in any dance-related activity in the previous year. They all had normal vision and had no past neurological or psychiatric history. The study was approved by the Ethics Committee of the College of Science and Engineering, University of Glasgow, and written informed consent was obtained from all subjects prior to inclusion in the study.

Experiment Stimuli

The stimulus material was an edited video of 3 minutes 38 seconds (at twenty-five frames per second) of a contemporary dance involving two dancers (one male, one female) with strong physical body movements (see Figure 3.2 and Video 3.1 on the Companion Website ▶). The dance was produced for the Watching Dance project (<http://www.watchingdance.org>) as part of a collaboration with the Rosie Kay Dance Company. The

FIGURE 3.2. Snapshots from the video showing moments described as synchronous (left) and asynchronous (right). Double Points: 3x, Rosie Kay Dance Company, dancers Rosie Kay and Morgan Cloud. (All consent is owned by Rosie Kay Dance Company. Credits: Double Points: K, with Rosie Kay and Morgan Cloud, by Rosie Kay Dance Company; photographer, Brian Slater.)

original dance was more than 20 minutes long and comprised the same 5-minute dance performed three times to different soundscapes (mechanical soundtrack with breathing sounds of the dancers, dance music, and a Bach concerto), as well as separate introductory and concluding segments. Cameras recorded the dance performance from different angles. The final video was the result of independent editing, and comprises a collection of excerpts from the original dance that included different camera angles and different soundscapes.

Functional Brain Imaging Methods

Procedure

Participants watched the dance video in the Magnetic Resonance Imaging (MRI) scanner, and gave their emotional and aesthetic ratings afterwards. At the time of scanning, subjects were not aware of the questions in the later behavioural tests and were instructed to passively view the dance performance. No task was used in order to avoid cognitive influences during scanning.

Post-Scanning Data

After the scanning session, subjects were taken to another room and the dance video was reshown to them twice. A slider was showed on the right side of screen while video was played. The sliders were bipolar. The ratings ranged from –230 to +230 pixels, but no number was shown on screen to indicate the scale; only the zero point was shown in the middle of the slider. Participants were instructed to move the mouse to indicate their emotional response to the dance performance continuously and as often as possible. Upper means more positive emotional feeling, while lower means more negative feelings. Subjects were instructed to make their ratings as close as possible, in accordance with their experience during scanning. The same procedure was repeated, asking participants their aesthetic judgement:

> This time you are going to be reporting the aesthetic experiences you have while watching the same movie. You will be reporting them using a mouse working as a slider. We define aesthetics as 'the extent to which the movie is appealing to you, or how intellectually engaging it is.' Move the mouse up if you feel that it is very appealing/intellectually engaging, or down if you do not think so.

Functional Brain Imaging (Scanning)

Brain activity was recorded on a 3 Teslas Tim Trio Siemens scanner (Erlangen, Germany). The video was projected on a translucent screen positioned at the back of the scanner, and which the subjects could see due to a tilted mirror. The sound was diffused via a pneumatic audio system with earplugs. Functional scans consisted of 117 full-brain volumes acquired one every 2 seconds at a resolution of 3 x 3 x 3 mm. At the end of the scanning session, high-resolution (1 x 1 x 1 mm) structural image was collected, which we used to localize the brain activity on brain anatomy.

Participants were instructed not to move the body and head during dance presentation.

Image Analysis

Analysis was carried out using the FSL suite (<http://fsl.fmrib.oxford.ac.uk>). First, standard preprocessing was applied, including correction for small head movements and drifts, and spatial smoothing. Then we estimated, at each voxel in the brain, the correlation between the fMRI time series and the slider data. To this end, the slider data were normalized and resampled to 2-second time-bins to match the fMRI time-series (for which one full-brain image was acquired in 2 seconds). This resulted, for each individual, in a correlation brain map, showing at each element of the brain image (each voxel) the correlation coefficient. These maps were transformed into a common standard space so that data from all participants could be compared and averaged. Group result maps indicate where in the brain the neuronal activity is related consistently to the *a posteriori* emotional judgements. To identify the regions with the most significant correlation between activity and judgement we applied a threshold to retain only clusters of activity with a significance of $P = 0.05$ (Worsley et al. 2005). We looked at both positive and negative correlations. In addition, we performed a second analysis to identify brain regions related to intensity judgement; that is, high or low emotional engagement, either positive or negative. To this end, we took the absolute values of the slider data and performed the brain-behaviour correlation analysis as described previously. The aesthetic judgement data were analysed in the same way.

TMS Method

The TMS experiment was carried out on a separate group of participants, targeting the brain region identified in the fMRI group analysis as showing the most significant and meaningful correlation between neural activity and emotion. This was done by transforming the coordinates of this region—identified in the group—into each individual brain space and using a dedicated system to place the TMS coil over this location (see Figure 3.3). We applied TMS for 15 minutes at 60% of maximum stimulator output, while continuously monitoring coil position and eventually adjusting it. Stimulation was delivered by a Magstim rapid-2 stimulator (Dyfed, Wales) through a 7-cm diameter figure-of-eight coil. Following the TMS session, participants took the subjective slider rating task as described in the *fMRI procedure*. In a separate session we stimulated the vertex as a control where no effect was expected. Both sessions were completed on the same day and were separated by at least 40 minutes. The order of the sessions was counterbalanced. Subjects wore commercial earplugs to attenuate the noise from TMS stimulator.

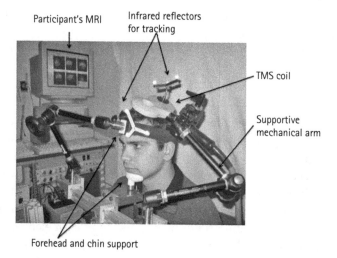

Participant's MRI   Infrared reflectors for tracking   TMS coil   Supportive mechanical arm   Forehead and chin support

FIGURE 3.3. A photograph of the set-up for the transcranial magnetic stimulation (TMS) experiment. Participants are seated on a comfortable chair, and the chin and forehead supports help them maintain their head still during the 15-minute stimulation. A camera system tracks infrared landmarks attached to the head and the TMS coil, allowing tracking of the position of the stimulation relative to the brain MRI of the participant.

We performed two analyses to compare the continuous ratings following active or control TMS. First, we analysed the entire duration of the slider data by computing the mean and standard deviations, and compared the control and the active TMS conditions. We then ran a separate analysis of variance for each of these measures to compare their values in the two TMS conditions (repeated factor). To take into account the effect of exposure we also added a between-subject factor to compare the TMS effect in the group of participants who received parietal TMS first, with those who had control TMS first.

Second, we carried out time-wise analysis to examine any TMS effect at specific moments of dance (Blair et al. 1993). We first resampled the data into 722 time points, used for smoothing data and limiting computation. Then, at each time point we performed a paired *t-test* across all the participants on each subject's parietal TMS condition and control condition.

To assess at which time points the t-value was significantly different from 0, we built a distribution of t-statistics by randomly permuting the sign of the t-values. (Under the null hypothesis, the values obtained for each subject are interchangeable and thus the sign of the difference is also changeable). For each permutation we extracted the maximal t-value (Tmax) across the time series, and built a distribution of Tmax for 10,000 permutations. To conduct two-tail tests while controlling for multiple comparisons, we determined the t-values that cut the Tmax distribution at 0.025 on each tail, and compared each of the 722 values of the original t-test to these values to determine significance at $p < 0.05$. In addition, we repeated the procedure to compare the groups of participants who had control TMS in the first or second session, and assessed whether the effects qualified as significant were higher than those due to multiple exposures.

Qualitative Methods

Semi-structured one-on-one interviews took place with twelve of the sixteen subjects who participated in the fMRI experiment a few weeks after the initial testing. The interviews began with participants watching the same 3 minute 38 second video that they had watched in the scanner. They were then invited to talk freely about the video recording before being shown their individual slider charts with the 'aesthetic' and 'emotional' responses that they had, indicating using the slider and in response to the instructions. The participants were invited to interpret their own slider charts, reflecting upon the significance of the highs and lows and on the relationship with the video performance (which included going back to the recording, sometimes several times, to try to match a moment on the slider to a moment in the dance). Participants were also asked to comment on how they had interpreted the instructions when using the slider.

The interest was in the participants' conscious reflection upon their own experience, and on using this to trace the relationships and divergences between emotional and aesthetic responses to watching the video performance. Located within the traditions of qualitative audience research, this approach was concerned with individual responses to the particular performance seen and in the ways in which individuals make sense of experiences for themselves, both in the moment of watching and after the event.

One of the primary objectives of all qualitative audience research is to elicit talk from participants, providing circumstances where they can respond to their experiences in their own words and in an open manner (see, for example, Barker 1998; Geraghty 1998). On this occasion this approach was adjusted to take into account the collaborative process with the neuroscience research, the nature of the stimulus being used (most audience research uses real-world stimulus, performances in theatres, very different from a short edited video recording), and in particular the use of slider measurements.

For these reasons the decision was made to focus the interviews around these aesthetic and emotional responses and, moreover, to do this through showing the participants their own slider chart results and inviting them to help us analyse the graphs. With the video recording on a laptop, the participants were able to watch and rewatch it, matching moment on the slider chart, and consciously reflecting on the responses and feeling that each moment elicited.

This approach was motivated by the ethos of participatory inquiry and action research—methodologies that seek to engage participants as active co-researchers in a process that acknowledges their own self-reflective expertise in their own perception and experiences. Creswell (2009, p. 9) describes the participatory worldview as one that sees meaning as 'constructed by human beings as they engage with the world they are interpreting'. Of course, within this perspective the nature of that 'expertise' is uncertain. For example, was the participants' operation of the sliders an instinctive and unreflective response to a stimulus, or a more or less conscious process of reflective meaning making? Equally, the relationship between the participants' understanding of how and why they responded in that moment, when asked a couple of weeks later, is unclear. Nonetheless, these very gaps and uncertainties are potentially valuable when considering what we mean by emotional and aesthetic responses to art. The slider charts produce moment-by-moment responses, produced in response to particular instances in the video and moreover influenced by what had just gone before. It is possible to argue that in contrast an aesthetic consideration requires some sense of overview and reflective distance. Responses to art, in other words, are produced both in the moment of watching but also through reflective consideration (Reason 2010). This perspective also draws on ideas of social phenomenology, of which Alfred Schutz writes:

> Meaning does not lie in the experience. Rather, those experiences are meaningful which are grasped reflectively. [. . .] It is, then, incorrect to say that my lived experiences are meaningful merely in virtue of their being experienced or lived through. [. . .] The reflective glance singles out an elapsed lived experience and constitutes it as meaningful. (Schutz 1967, pp. 67–71)

We might argue, rather, that meaning is produced through both affective and reflective processes (Sobchack 2004, p. 75). In the context of this research, the participants were therefore being asked to reflect upon their immediate responses and to consider what meanings could be constructed from them and through them.

RESULTS

Behavioural Results

Ratings of the two groups of participants (fMRI and TMS) are represented in Figure 3.4, showing no significant differences between groups. Despite some inter-individual variability, a general pattern emerged with globally the first half of the performance being linked to negative emotion and the second half to positive emotion, with higher ratings on the positive side of the scale. On the average and in most individual participants, clear transitions could be observed at the moments when the music changed.

The aesthetic judgements acquired in the group of subjects involved in the fMRI experiment showed less amplitude and more variability than the emotional judgements. On an individual level, significant correlations between the aesthetic ratings and emotion ratings were shown in fifteen of all the sixteen subjects ($p < .01$). At the group level, the rating of aesthetics (means ± SD) averaged from all subjects was 67.8 ± 27.193, and the rating of emotion was 47.16 ± 67.045 (see Figure 3.4). We also observed a significant correlation between aesthetics and emotion (Pearson $r = .661$, $p < .01$).

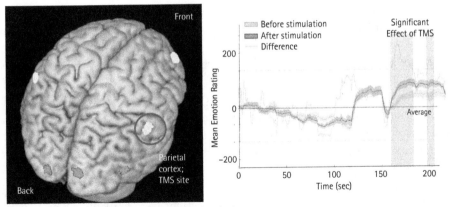

Positive correlation: Brain activity increases as emotion increases
Negative correlation: Brain activity decreases as emotion increases

FIGURE 3.4. *Left*: Averaged slider ratings over time on the 'emotion' (black) and 'aesthetic' (grey) scales. The shades underline the three sections of the video corresponding to the three different soundtracks. *Right*: Moment-by-moment correlation between the emotion and aesthetic ratings, computed in 10-second time bins.

Qualitative Results

The observations from the slider data were largely corroborated by the interview analyses, although talking to individual participants inevitably complicates the picture. Rather than engaging with averages, qualitative audience research reveals the details of individual responses—which are often heterogeneous and idiosyncratic and are strongly linked to participants' previous experiences and attitudes. Following Bourdieu (1984), qualitative audience research has explored the importance of previous experience and cultural capital in shaping an individual's taste and their engagement with art. The focus of the research in this instance was directed by the use of the emotional and aesthetic questions in the slider task.

In the interviews the majority of the participants used the music as the main reference point through which to talk about different sections of the video and to segment the performance. Equally, their comments suggested that, while watching, the music significantly shaped and directed their responses. Commentators have described how the lived experience of both music (Barthes 1986) and dance (Sheets-Johnstone 1979) are challenging, or even impossible, to put into language. In this instance, as our participants were inexperienced dance audiences, we may speculate that music represented a more familiar experience and therefore one where they were more able to articulate their experience. In their responses, and therefore also in this discussion, the video-edit was divided into three broad sections, as defined by the sound score. First, a 'mechanical' or 'industrial' music section, which was the least homogenous of the sections in terms of both the soundscape and the movements; second, a 'dance' or 'electro' music section; and third, a 'classical' music section. The last two sections were conceived as more homogenous and more similar, both internally and in relation to each other.

Between the second and third sections there was a short but clear and very widely per-ceived visual and sonic break that was noted by all the participants (140–154 on the time scale).

The first section was labelled by the participants as emotionally dark or negative (variously described as 'weird', 'sinister', 'scary', 'odd', 'aggressive', and 'uncomfortable'). Participants described this negative emotion as predominantly produced by the music, which during this section was mechanical, industrial, 'strange'. A secondary factor was choreographic movements, which were characterized by a lack of touching between the two dancers, oppositional facing-off across a dividing line, and more extreme or unu-sual body posture.

The second and third sections were, in contrast, perceived as an emotional high, particularly after this dark first section. These sections were marked by a more famil-iar style of music (respectively dance and classical) which brought in a higher tempo and a greater sense of sonic fluidity and flow. Choreographically the dancers also began moving more together, in synchrony, touching more and being closer. Both sections two and three were described as having more harmony between the music and movement, which was related to a positive emotional response (and, as will be discussed, also a pos-itive aesthetic response).

Between sections 2 and 3 was a short, darker moment, marked by a soundscape of high=pitched whistling and a particular choreographic and screen focus on the dancers' feet, tiptoeing round each other. This short section was often very visibly noticeable on the slider charts as a sharp and significant downward spike, and therefore when looking at these charts the participants were drawn to it and to the reflective task of identify-ing what had caused it. In this instance they found it easy and satisfying to match their reflective evaluation of their response to the slider data: they in a sense 'knew' what had been going on for them in that moment.

Overall, in terms of emotional responses there was a strong similarity between the respondents; nine of the twelve participants strongly matched the pattern described previously. This level of consistency would suggest that the participants were largely drawing their emotional interpretations from the recording (as opposed to what they brought to the experience), and that the music in particular was strongly coded in a cul-turally shared and broadly accessible manner.

It is valuable here to remember that the participants in this research were all inexperi-enced dance spectators, and to interpret their responses in the light of this. In particular, their responses match the description of Reber et al. (2004: 374), in which for novice spectators (and in contrast to expert or experienced spectators) positive aesthetic eval-uation is associated with more familiar stimuli that can be interpreted with greater processing fluency. Greater experience and exposure to the arts increases the ability to interpret complex stimuli with fluency and also to impose external judgements about taste, aesthetics, and value upon the performance (Bourdieu 1984).

The three exceptions to the typical interpretative pattern that were observed illustrate this in different ways, with, in each instance, participants overlaying their own individ-ual tastes onto the experience; in other words, the three exceptions are instances where participants' judgements of aesthetic value dictated their emotional responses (Reber et al. 2004). One participant, for example, shared the group emotional responses to parts 1 and 2 but had a negative emotional response to the third section. She reported that this was because it reminded her of ballet and that she did not like that kind of music or dance. Another participant fitted the group responses to parts 2 and 3 globally, but also had an idiosyncratic positive emotional response to some isolated sections of part 2. She reported this as being because she had liked identifying and enjoying the 'bird-like' movement in that section. The third exception was almost a reversal of the group response, which was directed by her liking the 'newness' of the first section over the known and 'boring' quality of the second two sections.

In different ways these three responses are directed by an aesthetic or interpretative position. The participants are activating personal taste or attitude, and in doing so are marking a more assertive individual ownership of their experience.

fMRI Results

In the 'valence' analysis—looking at where in the brain the activity was related to the positive or negative affective evaluation—we observed no significant positive correlation. We observed significant negative correlation in the bilateral occipito-temporal and fusiform cortex—regions known to be involved in high-level visual processing of objects, faces, and bodies. This means that there was more activity in these regions when the dance was perceived the least positive. In the 'intensity' analysis—using the absolute value of rating used as predictors—we observed positive correlation in the early visual cortex only. Negative correlation was observed in the occipito-temporal and fusiform cortex, as well as in the right parietalcortex. In contrast, the same correlation analysis run using aesthetic judgement results revealed brain activity in a small set of regions that are known to be involved in attention orienting, including the anterior cingulate cortex, the precuneus, and the basal ganglia.

The significant negative correlation between subjective affective ratings and activity in the posterior parietal cortex is reminiscent of reports of decreased activity in 'cognitive control' regions during emotional perception (Drevets and Raichle 1998; Greene et al. 2001). We thus characterized this region further by using meta-analytical tools. We searched the Brain Map database (a repository of brain imaging results from more than 3,000 experiments; see <http://brainmap.org/scribe/index.html>) and identified 259 brain-imaging experiments reporting brain activation in a 1,000 mm^3 region around the peak identified in our analysis. The majority of them (64%) belonged to the Cognition domain, 28% to Perception, 15% to Action, and 2% to Emotion. Thus this confirms that this region, which is more active when the subjects feel neutral emotionally than when they feel engaged positively or negatively, belongs to the 'cognitive' brain network (the circuit of brain regions engaged during cognitive tasks) and not the 'affective' brain network (the circuit of brain regions that are engaged when we experience a strong emotion; see Figure 3.1).

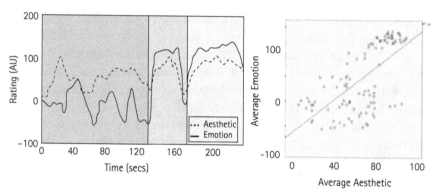

FIGURE 3.5. *Left*: Brain regions showing significant correlation between absolute values of emotional ratings and brain activity. Individual correlation maps were computed with individual ratings and not the average rating; the maps were then averaged across the sixteen participants. Dark grey spots: positive correlations; light grey spots: negative correlations. The circle indicates the site of TMS. *Right*: TMS results: averaged (n = 16) Z-scored ratings after parietal (black) or control (grey) rTMS ± standard errors and difference (paired t-statistic; pale grey) computed at each time point between the two time-series. Horizontal lines represent the threshold t-value (dotted line) or exact threshold t-value (plain line) for p < 0.05. The grey area represents regions of the curve showing statistical significance using non-corrected (light grey) or exact t-test (darker grey).

TMS Results

When we transiently interfered with the activity of this region in the parietal cortex, using low-frequency rTMS, we observed no effect on the global average or variance of raw data, nor a global average of absolute data (paired t-tests all p > 0.3). There was also no effect of order of either viewing, nor interaction between TMS condition and order. In the time-specific analysis, in contrast, we identified only one segment of the dance for which the emotional judgement significantly differed after parietal TMS compared to control TMS, independently of stimulation order. The positive judgement occurring in the last third of the dance video was rated as eliciting more positive emotion after parietal TMS. It is in this part of the dance video that the music changes to classical music. (See Figure 3.5.)

DISCUSSION

Our results from different methodological approaches converge in showing that emotional responses are an important part of the aesthetic experience and are linked to reduced activity in brain networks involved in cognitive control. The experience of emotion was largely shared between participants and was strongly influenced by the music score as well as the 'harmony' or fluidity of accord between movement and music. The video editing might have further enhanced this by juxtaposing excerpts from different visual angles.

Here the qualitative audience research suggested more similarities and shared responses in terms of the emotional responses, and more divergent responses in participants' aesthetic interpretations. This is probably because the emotional responses are affects produced in direct response to the stimulus, while the aesthetic responses are more interpretative and learned. In this particular instance the primary factor shaping emotional and interpretative responses to the recording was reported to be the music.

The findings of this study are partially consistent with underlying theories that the subjective assessment of the aesthetic value is influenced by affects evoked from the work of art, and that the aesthetic judgment has a linear relation with emotion in general. Moreover, the implications of our results are especially in accordance with the Reber et al.'s (2004) model suggesting an interplay between affective feeling and cognitive control. In this model, affective evaluation takes place continuously, influencing and being influenced by all stages of cognitive processing occurring during the aesthetic experience.

Our brain-imaging results are also in line with this model. They further indicate an antagonistic interaction between processes involved in cognitive reasoning and processes involved in affective reaction. Indeed, the higher the subjective emotional rating of the dance, the less activity was shown in regions important for reasoning and action control—in particular, in the region of the parietal lobe that we targeted with TMS. Beyond a simple correlation between an index of neuronal activity in this region, we also show that decreasing activity there can indeed cause an increase in subjective emotional judgement. This effect was dependent on context, occurring only for the part of the dance that was judged the more emotional, with increased fluidity and harmony. This is in accordance with the idea that resources engaged for emotion and executive control, respectively, can compete in some contexts. Indeed, while traditionally the affective and cognitive systems have been considered as separate, independent entities, at the conceptual as well as at the neurophysiological level of analysis, it is increasingly recognized that the interaction between the two systems is at the core of a large part of our behaviours (Pessoa, 2008). The expansion of cognitive neuroscience has contributed significantly to this paradigm shift across disciplines by allowing researchers to characterize the networks of brain areas involved in emotion and cognition, respectively, as well as their interactions. Such interactions are reflected by areas of overlap as well as antagonistic functioning. Brain-imaging studies have shown that regions involved in executive or cognitive control are less active when regions involved in emotion processing and perception are engaged, and *vice versa* (Mitchell et al. 2008; Greene et al. 2001; Drevets et al. 1998). Importantly, disruption of the harmonious integration between the control and affective system is associated with a manifold of mental disorders (Cole et al. 2014). Therefore, understanding this interaction, in different contexts, offers some leverage for researching novel intervention approaches that could restore normal integration between cognitive and affective processes. In this regard, our observation that a small manipulation of one node of the cognitive control network can change subjective emotional report opens interesting perspectives.

Another important result from both the qualitative and the quantitative measures is that positive emotional responses were more strongly held than negative emotional responses. Indeed, this is where the greatest consistency emerged. It is also the part of the judgement that could significantly be modulated by bringing down brain activity in brain networks involved in cognitive reasoning. This also has important implications in fostering research on the potential health benefit of watching dance. Indeed, mental health and wellbeing are deeply interconnected with the ability to experience positive emotions (Fredrickson and Joiner 2002). Identifying what specific aspects of music/ movements enhance the evoked positive feeling would be beneficial for therapies.

CONCLUSION

Our study suggests that the sense of harmony and fluidity are important for inducing positive affect. Moreover, our results show a direct relation between these evoked positive emotions and brain activity in specific networks. So far, emotional wellbeing has been related mainly to activity in prefrontal regions of the brain. Non-invasive brain stimulation targeting these prefrontal regions can influence emotional judgements of ambiguous stimuli (Donhauser et al. 2013) as well as response biases (Van Honk et al. 2002; Schutter et al. 2001). Moreover, rTMS is used clinically for treatment of depression or anxiety disorders (reviewed in George 2013). Our study adds to this research field by showing that activity in the parietal cortex could also modulate subjective positive feeling when watching dance. Importantly, lowering activity in this region led to enhanced judgements of the dance segments that were experienced positively. This highlights the contextual nature of the effects observed using these techniques. In terms of implications, it would be interesting to explore new therapeutic avenues for affective disorders. Indeed, TMS has been used successfully in combination with behavioural therapy for motor rehabilitation (Liew et al. 2014). Similar combined approaches could be envisaged for treatment of affective disorders, which would involve simultaneously inducing aesthetic emotions by the means of art and brain manipulation to facilitate those effects.

ACKNOWLEDGEMENTS

This research was funded by the Arts and Humanities Research Council (AHRC AH/F011229/ 1; project Watching Dance <http://www.watchingdance.org>). We would like to extend our sincere thanks to all the people who helped us with this study: the Rosie Kay Dance Company (<http://www.rosiekay.co.uk>), all the research participants who gave up their time, the Watching Dance project principal investigator Professor Dee Reynolds, and Ilka Schulz (independent film-maker) and Frances Blythe (photographer), for their invaluable help with filming and editing.

REFERENCES

Barker, M. (1998). *Knowing Audiences*. Luton: University of Luton Press.

Barthes, R. (1986). *The Grain of the Voice, the Responsibility of Forms*, transl. R. Howard. Oxford: Blackwell, pp. 267–77.

Belke, B., Leder, H., Strobach, T., and Carbon, C. (2010). 'Cognitive fluency: High-level processing dynamics in art appreciation', *Psychology of Aesthetics Creativity and the Arts*, 4(4): 214–22.

Blair, R. C. and Karniski W. (1993). 'An alternative method for significance testing of wave-form difference potentials', *Psychophysiology*, 30(5): 518–24.

Bourdieu, P. (1984). *Distinction: A Social Critique of the Judgement of Taste*, trans. R. Nice. London: Routledge.

Buchel, C., Morris, J., Dolan, R., et al. (1998) 'Brain systems mediating aversive conditioning: an event-related fMRI study', *Neuron*, 20: 947–57.

Calvo-Merino, B., Glaser, D. E., Grezes, J., Passingham, R. E., and Haggard, P. (2005). 'Action observation and acquired motor skills: An FMRI study with expert dancers', *Cerebral Cortex*, 15: 1243–9.

Calvo-Merino, B., Grezes, J., Glaser, D. E., Passingham, R. E., and Haggard, P. (2006). 'Seeing or doing? Influence of visual and motor familiarity in action observation', *Current Biology*, 16(19), 1905–10.

Cole, M. W., Repovs, G., and Anticevic, A. (2014). 'The frontoparietal control system: A central role in mental health'. *The Neuroscientist: A Review Journal Bringing Neurobiology, Neurology and Psychiatry*, 20(6): 652–64, doi:10.1177/1073858414525995.

Creswell, J. W. (2009). *Research Design: Qualitative, Quantitative and Mixed Methods Approaches*. Thousand Oaks, CA: Sage.

Cupchik, C. G., Vartanian, O., Crawley, A., and Mikulis, J. D. (2009). 'Viewing artworks: Contributions of cognitive control and perceptual facilitation to aesthetic experience', *Brain and Cognition*, 70: 84–91.

Daprati, E., Iosa, M., and Haggard, P. (2009). 'A dance to the music of time: Aesthetically-relevant changes in body posture in performing art', *PLoS ONE*, 4 (3): e5023.

Devinsky, O., Morrell, M. J., and Vogt, B. A. (1995). 'Contributions of anterior cingulate cortex to behaviour', *Brain* 118: 279–306.

Di Dio, C. and Gallese, V. (2009). 'Neuroesthetics: A review', *Current Opinion in Neurobiology*, 19: 682–7.

Donhauser, P. W., Belin, P., and Grosbras, M. H. (2013). 'Biasing the perception of ambiguous vocal affect: a TMS study on frontal asymmetry', *Social Cognitive Affective Neuroscience*, 9, 1046–51.

Drevets, W. C. and Raichle, M. E. (1998). 'Reciprocal suppression of regional cerebral blood during emotional versus higher cognitive implications for interactions between emotion and cognition', *Cognition and Emotion*, 12: 353–85.

Fechner, G. T. (1876). *Vorschule der Aesthetik [Preschool of Aesthetics]*. Leipzig: Breitkopf and Härtel.

Fredrickson, B. L. and Joiner, T. (2002). 'Positive emotions trigger upward spirals toward emotional well-being', *Psychological Science*, 13(2): 172–5.

George M. S., Taylor, J. J., and Short, E. B. (2013). 'The expanding evidence base for rTMS treatment of depression', *Current Opinion in Psychiatry*, 26(1): 13–18.

Geraghty, C. (1998). 'Audiences and "ethnography": Questions of practice', in C. Geraghty and D. Lusted (eds.), *The Television Studies Book*. London: Arnold, pp. 141–57.

Greene, J. D., Sommerville, R. B., Nystrom, L. E., Darley, J. M., and Cohen, J. D. (2001). 'An fMRI investigation of emotional engagement in moral judgment', *Science*, 293(5537): 2105e8.

Grosbras, M. H., Tan, H., and Pollick, F. (2012). 'TMS applied over the parietal cortex modulates appreciation of dance', *Brain Stimulation*, 5(2): 130–6.

Jola, C., Reason, M., Pollick, F., and Grosbras, M. H. (2012). 'Audiences' neurophysiological correlates to watching a narrative dance performance of 2.5 hrs', *Dance Research Electronic*, 29(2): 378–403.

Leder, H., Belke, B., Oeberst, A., and Augustin, D. (2004). 'A model of aesthetic appreciation and aesthetic judgments', *British Journal of Psychology*, 95(4): 489–508.

Liew, S. L., Santarnecchi, E, Buch, E. R., and Cohen, L. G. (2014). 'Non-invasive brain stimulation in neurorehabilitation: Local and distant effects for motor recovery', *Frontiers in Human Neuroscience*, 8: 378–82.

MacFarlane, L., Kulka, I., and Pollick, F. E. (2004). 'The representation of affect revealed by Butoh dance', *Psychologia*, 47(2): 96–103.

Pessoa, L. (2008). 'On the relationship between emotion and cognition', *Nature Review Neuroscience*, 9(2), 148–58.

Phelps, E. A. and LeDoux, J. E. (2005). 'Contributions of the amygdala to emotion processing: from animal models to human behavior', *Neuron*, 48(2), 175–87.

Pollick, F. E., Paterson, H. M., Bruderlin, A., and Sanford, A. J. (2001). 'Perceiving affect from arm movement', *Cognition*, 82(2): B51–61, doi:10.1016/S0010-0277(01)00147-0.

Reason, M. (2010). 'Asking the audience: Audience research and the experience of theatre', *About Performance*, 10: 15–34.

Reason, M. and Reynolds, D. (2010). 'Kinesthesia, empathy and related pleasures: An inquiry into audience experiences of watching dance', *Dance Research Journal*, 42(2): 49–75.

Reber, R., Schwarz, N., and Winkielman, P. (2004). 'Processing fluency and aesthetic pleasure: Is beauty in the perceiver's processing experience?', *Personality and Social Psychology Review*, 8(4): 364–82.

Russell, J. A. (1980). 'A circumplex model of affect', *Journal of Personality and Social Psychology*, 39: 1161–78.

Schutter, D. J., Van Honk, J., d'Alfonso, A. A., Postma, A., and De Haan, E. H. (2001). 'Effects of slow rTMS at the right dorsolateral prefrontal cortex on EEG asymmetry and mood', *Neuroreport*, 12(3): 445–7.

Schutz, A. (1967). *The Phenomenology of the Social World*. Evanston, IL: Northwestern University Press.

Sheets-Johnstone, M. (1979). *The Phenomenology of Dance*. London: Dance Books.

Silvia, P. J. (2005a). 'Emotional responses to art: From collation and arousal to cognition and emotion', *Review of General Psychology*, 9: 342–57.

Silvia, P. J. (2005b). 'What is interesting? Exploring the appraisal structure of interest', *Emotion*, 5: 89–102.

Silvia, P. J. (2009). Looking past pleasure: Anger, confusion, disgust, pride, surprise, and other unusual aesthetic emotions', *Psychology of Aesthetics Creativity and the Arts*, 3(1): 48–51.

Silvia, P. J. and Brown, E. M. (2007). 'Anger, disgust, and the negative aesthetic emotions: Expanding an appraisal model of aesthetic experience', *Psychology of Aesthetics, Creativity, and the Arts*, 1: 100–6.

Sobchack, V. (2004). *Carnal Thoughts: Embodiment and Moving Image Culture*. Berkeley, CA: University of California Press.

Van Honk, J., Hermans, E. J., D'Alfonso, A. A., Schutter, D. J., Van Doornen, L., and De Haan, E. H. (2002). 'A left-prefrontal lateralized, sympathetic mechanism directs attention towards social threat in humans: Evidence from repetitive transcranial magnetic stimulation', *Neuroscience Letters*, 319(2): 99–102.

Vartanian, O. and Goel, V. (2004). 'Neuroanatomical correlates of aesthetic preference for paintings', *NeuroReport*, 15(5): 893–7.

Walsh, V., and Rushworth, M. (1999). 'A primer of magnetic stimulation as a tool for neuropsychology', *Neuropsychologia*, 37(2): 125–35.

Watching Dance Project (n.d.). <http://www.watchingdance.org>

Worsley, K. J. (2005). 'An improved theoretical P value for SPMs based on discrete local maxima', *Neuroimage*, 28(4): 1056–62.

CHAPTER 4

EVIDENCE-BASED BIODANZA PROGRAMMES FOR CHILDREN (TANZPRO-BIODANZA) IN SCHOOLS AND KINDERGARTENS

Some Effects on Psychology, Physiology, Hormones, and the Immune System

MARCUS STUECK AND ALEJANDRA VILLEGAS

INTRODUCTION

IN order to increase wellbeing in children, it requires being with them in a systemic attentive, mindful, and loving way, which means to be fully present and to include parents, teachers, families, and the field, helping them to express their own identity, autonomously, initially in a non-verbal and later in a verbal way. Those working towards the wellbeing of children often need to understand that the body (e.g. senses and feelings) is the greatest thinking organ for children who feel the world through their bodies (Stueck 2010). Such physical experiences are often associated with play that can make a contribution to the child's sense of wellbeing, as argued by Krenz (2009), and with dance, that may enable a child to express instincts, needs, and feelings in connection with others (Stueck et al. 2010). Moreover, a sense of wellbeing in children can be enhanced through:

- The presence and the love of adults; for example, wellbeing can increase the development of self-awareness in children (Maturana and Verden-Zöller 2010; Stueck 2010).

- A relaxed, healthy environment; such an environment can increase empathic connections and self-efficacy (Stueck 2010).
- Empathic links to others and nature; for example, acquiring implicit and explicit knowledge can take place through such links (Stueck 2010; Stueck, Schoppe et al. 2013).

Within the Masterplan of Healthy Education developed by Stueck (2013a), the first three important steps that are recommended (Steps 1–3) are relational and affective. Step 1 involves raising awareness regarding the importance of being with children without any theoretical background, method, or aim, to focus intention. The next step, Step 2 (relaxation), is done by evidence-based programmes with elements of yoga for children (Stueck 1997, 2000, 2008). Further, verbal and non-verbal aspects of the work are integrated in Step 3 of the MasterPlan of Healthy Education, showing a systematic integrated approach as its overarching method. They are defined as essential steps towards establishing relationships, and are used among other methods (e.g. yoga, mindfulness) and dance practices (e.g. Biodanza for children, teachers, and parents) as a way of developing presence, relaxation, and empathy. Empathy is based on love, presence, and relaxation, and is the basis of wellbeing as a biological, affective, cognitive, and behavioural connection with oneself, between a child and their teacher or parents (Stueck 2015), and also towards nature. For empathy to take place there is a need for trust, autonomy, an interest in others, and the giving up of the desire to control or to compensate one's own discomfort states.

Steps 4–7 of the MasterPlan of Healthy Education involve more reflexive abilities concerning the content of educational performance of teachers, parents, and their institutions. They are rational–analytical steps, such as supervision, development of educational abilities, educational concepts, and addressing practical issues (e.g. number of teachers and children in the classroom, payment of teachers, teaching material).

Within this context, several evidence-based Biodanza programmes (Figure 4.1) have been developed and evaluated at the University of Leipzig (1998–2012), the University of Applied Sciences Saxony (DPFA), and the Institute of Biodanza Research Leipzig (IBR/BIOnet research network[1] since 2012), and used since 1998 in the practice (Stueck and

FIGURE 4.1. Examples of evidence-based Biodanza programmes (Logos). (Credit: M Stueck.)

Villegas 2008). They are called TANZPRO-Biodanza (TANZ, German for Dance; PRO, evidence-based programmes with Biodanza), mostly with ten sessions informed by evidence deriving from scientific studies. For each programme there is a logo, a handbook for 'train the trainer approach', and scientific publications (see <http://www.bionet. name>). TANZRPRO Biodanza is the synonym for a structured Biodanza programme, mostly with ten sessions informed by evidence deriving from scientific studies (OUT).

Until now there have been a number of different evidence-based Biodanza versions:[2] for adults (e.g. teachers, parents), for elderly people (evidence-based Biodanza program for seniors), in water (Biodanza programme for reparentalization: BIODANZA-Aquatica), and for children (TANZPRO-Biodanza for children) to increase empathy and wellbeing with themselves, with others, and with nature. Biodanza, as an integrative approach, was tested in German schools and kindergartens (Stueck 2003, 2004, 2011; Stueck, Villegas, et. al. 2007, 2008, 2009). In this chapter we will introduce the scientific basis of studies on Biodanza—a method of dance developed by Toro (2010). We will see dance as relating to the movement of life, and focus especially on work relating to children and adults.

Biodanza: Theory and Empirical Research

Dance is a deep movement arising from the most unfathomable depths of human beings; as the founder of the discipline Ronaldo Toro (2010) called it, this form of dance has to do with the movement of life. The name Biodanza makes these references: bios means 'life' and danza (Spanish) means 'dance', and his aim was for people to learn how to live well and happily together and how everyone can express its identity by dancing. Thus, Biodanza encourages movement that is full of meaning, because it expresses true feelings or emotions, its own identity, and is based on the development of nurturing relationships in the dances, while supporting personal integration. It works with four powerful factors: music, movement, emotion, and group. It is a technique that takes place in the here and now (Spanish: *Vivencia*) engaging with auto-regulation, self-organization, and affective integration. It means that everything that you dance or do should be connected with the feeling to yourself, with others, and with nature.

The theory of Biodanza is based on the concept of human integration on a personal, interpersonal, and transcendental or transpersonal level. The impact of Biodanza-*Vivencias* penetrates deeply on the central nervous system, immune system, and hormonal system. Toro (2010) has stated that 'Biodanza is not about peace of mind . . . it is about intensity of living', and he assumed that there was an association between people being optimistic, happy, and healthy, as various research approaches have shown (see, for example, the Positive Psychology approach of Seligman 2004). In order to achieve this he created Biodanza—a system of dances which consist of five Lines of Experience, as he called them. These were Vitality, Affectivity, Sexuality, Transcendence, and Creativity. In the 1990s, Marcus Stueck, Alejandra Villegas (coordinators and pioneers of the Biodanza research worldwide; see Institute of Biodanza Research Leipzig,

IBR integrated in the BIOnet research network of IBF/International Biocentric Foundation, <http://www.bionet.name>, <http://www.biodanza.org>) and colleagues[3] started to investigate Biodanza scientifically, together with Rolando Toro in Argentina (Univeridad Abierta Interamericana, Buenos Aires[4]) and at the University of Leipzig. In 2001, projects with the Institute of Clinical Immunology, University of Leipzig, started to investigate blood and saliva samples after Biodanza classes, to discover more about the effects on the immune and hormonal system (Stueck, Villegas, et al. 2002). Since 2012 the project continues at the University of Applied Sciences Saxony (DPFA) and the Institute of Biodanza Research Leipzig (IBR/BIOnet research network) in coopera-tion with the University of Leipzig (the latter since 1998). Stueck and Villegas published many results in journals, PhD work (Villegas 2006), and a professorial dissertation (Stueck 2007) on the effects of Biodanza on the wellbeing of students, teachers, elderly people, and patients (increasing feeling of relaxation, mood, and vitality), connected with hormonal, immunological, physiological, and psychological changes (Villegas et al. 2000; Stueck and Villegas 2008). In 2006 the investigation into Biodanza with children began. Historical and future accounts of research studies in Biodanza are also available and are integrated in an eight-point research plan for Biodanza[5] (Stueck and Villegas 2008). In the first journal of the research network BIOnet (Art/Biodanza Meets Science[6]), almost all doctoral theses on the subject are reported, these having been completed in different parts of the world: the first qualitative and quantitative empiri-cal PhD studies of Pereira (2005) with elderly people, Villegas (2006) at the University of Leipzig with 'normal neurotics', and participants with psychopathology, showed a clear effect of Biodanza classes on wellbeing and life satisfaction increasing optimism. Stueck's (2007) first professorial dissertation (for a second PhD at German universities, one criterion to gain full professorship, called 'Habilitation') highlighted the effects of Biodanza on teachers coping with negative frame conditions in schools. If the frame condition in institutions is poor, then teachers have a tendency to display the behav-iour pattern of 'withdrawing from work' (Schaarschmidt 2006) increasingly, which means withdrawing from interaction with children. This emphasizes the importance of looking further to dance intervention focusing on skills, supervision, concept, and improvement of conditions. The study of Stueck (2007) could demonstrate the benefits of Biodanza for teachers' non-verbal communication skills and stress reduction. Some research studies conclude that Biodanza appears to have an effect on the physiological (Stueck et al. 2007), psychological (Stueck 2007; Villegas 2008), and immunological sys-tems (Stueck et al. 2009). In light of these possibilities, Biodanza can have an impact on more than emotional expression. It has also been argued that it enhances integration between thinking, feeling, and acting, thus inducing harmony, unity, fluidity, pleasure, and plenitude. These can be shown by the changes in different psychological variables (higher optimism, relaxation, self-efficacy, the abilities to love, and feelings of empathy) (Villegas 2006; Stueck 2007; Villegas 2008; Stueck 2008; Stueck 2012). In these studies, it was found that Biodanza increased potential counterbalances to the excessive nega-tive impact on the system of stress, anxiety, depression, and the sublimation of instinct, and of turning self-expression into 'more culturally acceptable' behaviour. Studies have been carried out in Germany and Argentina with adults (teachers, psychiatric patients, employees, and elderlies; Fidora, Mader, and Stueck 2008) and children (Stueck, et al. 2008; Stueck and Villegas 2012). Also, a study about the efficacy of Biodanza for treating women with fibromyalgia (FM) shows improvements in pain, body composition, and FM impact in female patients (Carbonell-Baeza et al. 2010). The results of many studies (Stueck and Villegas 2008) argued for the cross-cultural effects of Biodanza on the reduction of psychosomatic symptoms, a more optimistic view of life and future, and a reduction of stress and hypersensitivity (Balzer and Stueck 2008). (For a list of all Biodanza research, see Stueck and Villegas 2016; <http://www.bionet.name>; <http://www.biodanza.org>.)

EVIDENCE-BASED BIODANZA PROGRAMMES AS LIFE-FOCUSED APPROACHES FOR CHILDREN

Evidence-based Biodanza programmes for children were developed within the theoretical model of the School of Empathy (SOE) (developed by Stueck 2013b), which consisted of both non-verbal and verbal aspects. It is understood that within the context of educational institutions, working with dance needs to be part of a 'larger' methodological and anthropological theoretical conceptualization, which needs to be evidence-based through scientific research while retaining a life-focused quality. As a life-focused approach, Biodanza for children involves the connection with oneself, with others, and with natural elements as central aspects (biocentric approach; Toro 2010). It has been adapted from Rolando Toro's system, which was used for adults by Cecilia Luzzi in Chile in the 1980s. For children, it is based on dances along four of the Lines of Experience: Vitality, Affectivity, Creativity, and Transcendence. The fifth Line of Experience (Sexuality) is excluded when Biodanza is used for children. In 2007, Stueck, Villegas, and others (Thinschmidt et al. 2012) undertook a four-year project for the German Ministry of Health and Education (Healthy Life Styles in Education, Technical University Dresden, Leipzig University, Department of Health for North Saxony). This was the first research worldwide on Biodanza with children. Stueck, Villegas and others adapted this method for work in institutions by developing evidence-based Biodanza programmes for kindergarten children and schoolchildren (Stueck and Villegas 2009; Stueck et al. 2010), based on the non-verbal aspects of the work as developed in the School of Empathy by Stueck (2013b). There is a verbal and non-verbal part. The Biodanza content as the non-verbal part of the School of Empathy uses TANZPRO-Biodanza for children and adults/parents (an evidence-based Biodanza programme based on the Biodanza model of Rolando Toro and the Biodanza-for-children work of Cecilia Luzzi). The verbal part of the School of Empathy is the evidence-based programme 'Respectful Communication' (Language of Life/way from the body to head) based on Marshall Rosenberg's nonviolent communication (Müller and Pörschmann 2009; Schoppe and Stueck 2012). This aspect was based on the verbal-reflexive activity of describing and expressing feelings and emotions in words (see Figure 4.2).

The programme Respectful Communication (Müller and Pörschmann 2009; Müller 2016) assumed that depending on the exact verbal expression of feeling words, it was highly probable that children could also express associated needs and communicate

School of Empathy (Stueck, 2013)

School of empathy (verbal)
Language of the north:
"From the body into the head"
= Verbal, reflexive aspects of Empathy
Theory: M. Rosenberg (USA)
Method: Nonviolent communication
"The Language of Empathy & Life"
4 steps to be empathic:
1) observation 2) verbal expression of feelings 3) verbal expression of needs
4) asking please instead of demand.Rosenberg describe this as the language of Giraffe vs. Wolf

School of empathy (nonverbal)
Language of the south
"From the head in the body"
= Nonverbal, experiencial, actional, biological, natural aspects of empathy.
Theory: R.Toro; H. Maturana
Method: Biodanza
"The Dance of Empathy & Life"
Empathy as a nonverbal behaviour in a biological based social autopoietic network with behavioural aspects: e.g., to act what I feel, to act in group networks rather than as individual egoistic. Stueck describes this as the language of Penguins vs. Polar Bears

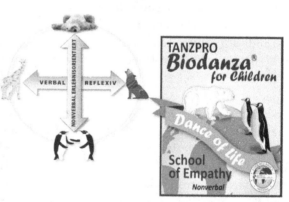

Evidence-based Program (Language–verbal)	Evidence-based Program (Dance–nonverbal)
RESPECTFUL COMMUNICATION® **(Marion and Norman Müller Pörschmann, Marcus Stueck, Sebastian Schoppe)**	**TANZPRO-Biodanza®** **Dance-oriented program with Biodanza for children (Marcus Stueck, Alejandra Villegas, Cecilia Luzzi, Rolando Toro)**

FIGURE 4.2. Overview of the School of Empathy. (Credit: M. Stueck.)

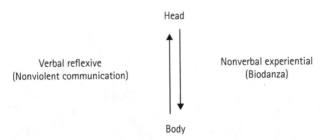

FIGURE 4.3. Two ways of intervention to gain empathy. (Credit: M Stueck.)

them to others as a basic ability for empathic behaviour. Stueck (2013b) called it the way '. . . from the body into the head'. The second way was to dance '. . . from the head into the body', which was necessary in order to experience physical arousal (feelings and emotions) and allow these to be expressed, without naming them. Thus, they were not immediately recognized by the rational structure of the spoken word.

An integrative model of empathy with verbal and non-verbal parts of the development of empathy in Biodanza and nonviolent communication are well integrated, because verbal and non-verbal expression of children's needs and feelings are possible (see Figure 4.3). Garcia described, in his book *Biodanza: Experience as a Therapy* (1997), the importance of the experience of dancing without words ('way from head to body') and the opportunity to experience a new feeling as a biochemical structure, without expressing it verbally or putting it into existing conceptual categories, which would destroy it. This head–body way is non-verbal, experiential, and practiced through Biodanza (see Figure 4.3). In this way, Biodanza has been taught in educational settings and institutions internationally, such as in Indonesia, Sri Lanka, Latvia, Austria, and Germany. The evaluation of the effects has been conducted in different cultural contexts and circumstances. It has also been used as a therapeutic method for children suffering trauma after natural disasters in Nepal, Sri Lanka, and Indonesia (Senerath 2010; Trimulyaningsih, Novitasari, and Qudsyi 2014). Because of the evidence-based character of TANZPRO-Biodanza for children, it is possible to train trainers who work in institutions[7] how to deliver it. This project (Healthy Lifestyles in Education) started with pilot studies in Latvia and Indonesia, by educating instructors in the method of School of Empathy (verbal: respectful communication; non-verbal: TANZPRO-Biodanza for children, adults, and parents).

Figure 4.4a shows the depth of the quality of contact with children dancing in Riga (Latvia) and Leipzig (Germany), conducted by psychologist and Biodanza teacher Vineta Greaves, who gave TANZPRO-Biodanza for children sessions (duration six months) in a Latvian school and found remarkable changes in children[8] (e.g. more openness and emotional differentiation, higher social competences, less internal behavioural problems, and less stress). Figure 4.4b shows the bioanalytic evaluation (saliva tubes for analysing cortisol, testosterone, and immunoglobulin A) which was carried out in Germany (Stueck and Villegas 2008) and, since 2014, also in Latvia (Greaves et al. 2016).

(a)
(b)

FIGURE 4.4. a) Celebrating life and joy of a group of 4–6-year-old children in kindergarten; b) scientific study (saliva and blood pressure). TANZPRO-Biodanza session with 8–9-year-old children in a school in Riga (Latvia) by TANZPRO-Biodanza instructor and psychologist Vineta Greaves from the Center of Educational Health Latvia (a), and bioanalytical evaluation at the University of Leipzig (b). (Credit: M. Stueck.)

Each session of the TANZRPO-Biodanza programme for children contains three parts. Firstly, there is a story about a journey in one country; for instance, reading aloud the story 'Travel to Egypt', which represents "joy". A Biodanza part follows which is accompanied by music and relatively energetic exercises, with faster music to promote not only the vitality but also the creativity of children. Then quieter exercises together with slower music are used to promote relaxation and interactive experiences through age-appropriate peer (partner) exercises. Finally, the session closes by encouraging the children to talk about their feelings, then to express them in paintings after the session. Further details of the content of a typical session can be found in Table 4.1, which introduces the exercises of the Biodanza part of the 'Egypt' session.

Table 4.2 shows the ten themes of the ten sessions of the basic version of TANZPRO-Biodanza. At the time of writing we are working on more sessions of TANZPRO-Biodanza for schoolchildren (sessions 11–20; 7–12 years of age) and on a version for adolescents. Every session is a 'journey' in a country and symbolizes a value or motive of life that is danced in the session: for example, in a Spanish session the value is 'love and care', and in an Egyptian session the value is 'joy'. In the kindergarten version the children produce little gifts which symbolize value and are put in their treasure box of life. In the end, the children receive a certificate, 'Master of Life'.

Effects of TANZPRO-Biodanza Among Children Aged 4–6 Years (Kindergarten Children)

The following effects in kindergarten children (ten sessions of TANZPRO-Biodanza, school version) can found in several studies (e.g. Stueck, Villegas et al. 2013; Stueck et al. 2015).

Table 4.1. Example of summary of TANZRO-Biodanza for children's session 'Travel to Egypt'.

No	Session	Description
1	Introduction	Loud reading the story 'Travel to Egypt'
2	Biodanza part	1) In circle 2) Round dancing: go to the music 3) Rhythmic variations: all children move after requested; Stop and Go 4) Go as a pair: walking in pairs 5) Play the mirror: children mirror the movement against other children 6) Silent dance / relax movement: smooth movement with arms; children stay in circle 7) Silent dance / relax movement: smooth movement with hips; children stay in circle 8) The snake: going in row; on the back start lying and wriggle around the room 9) Cradle in circle: relax dancing in circle; swaying movement 10) Progressive activation: increase of movement intensity
3	Closing part	Free painting after thoughts and music time

Table 4.2. Overview of sessions and related themes of basis version of TANZPRO-Biodanza.

Sequence	Theme	Notion (life focused value)
1	Travel to Spain	Love and care
2	Travel to Egypt	Joy
3	Travel to Tanzania	Leisure and courage
4	Travel to Chile	Wishes and risk
5	Travel to Brazil	Feeling of security and embrace
6	Travel to Mexico	Diversity and friendship
7	Travel to Ireland	Acceptance and integration
8	Travel to Russia	Humbleness and sportsmanship
9	Travel to China	Creativity and solidarity
10	Travel to Germany	Respectful communication

Note: Adapted from © ? 2011. Stueck, Villegas, and Toro (2010b)

Change in Cortisol Level in Kindergarten Children because of TANZPRO-Biodanza

This study showed the change in cortisol of kindergarten children after taking ten sessions of TANZPRO-Biodanza. Children initialized with high cortisol level seemed to be 'normalizing', whilst those with low cortisol level seem to be already 'normalized' (Stueck et al. 2015). Furthermore, the findings from this study suggested that there might be an autoregulatory effect of TANZRPO-Biodanza sessions in children of kindergarten age.

Effects on Emotional Recognition and Its Relation to Cortisol Reduction

The same study (ten children, aged 4–5; ten sessions of TANZPRO-Biodanza) confirmed that cognitive performance in children (e.g. emotion recognition, measured with the Emotion Recognition Test in the Vienna test system, whereby the children had to recognize different emotions from photographs) could be developed by dancing. The effects were on average greater when participants had higher initial cortisol levels in their saliva (before the TANZPRO-Biodanza sessions) than those with lower levels of cortisol (Stueck et al. 2015).

Heart Rate and the Improvement of Physiological Auto-regulation

In the same study, looking at the heart rate for each child before and after the TANZPRO-Biodanza course, there was a significant decrease in the average score, which was statistically significant ($p = 0.04^*$, $d' = 0.77$, $1-\beta = 0.68$). The low-level and high-level groups showed significant change of heart rate (average over ten session) between pre-session and post-session, towards the value of the medium heart-rate group (see Table 4.3).

Table 4.3. Post-session changes in average heart rate in groups with pre–session values low (100 beats/min), medium (120 beats/min), and high (170 beats/min).

Cluster time		Mean	SD	N	Significance (two-tailed)	Effect size d'	Power 1-β
Low heart rate	Pre	95.52	4.95	8	0.00**	1.66	0.53
	Post	114.75	10.97				
Medium heart rate	Pre	119.95	10.74	64	0.76	0.04	0.77
	Post	120.46	11.37				
High heart rate	Pre	175.75	26.04	14	0.00**	1.35	0.53
	Post	128.24	20.52				

(Credit: M. Stueck.)

Table 4.4. Post-session changes in average heart rate in groups with pre-session values low (100 beats/min), medium (120 beats/min) and high (170 beats/min).

Cluster time		Mean	SD	N	Significance (two-tailed)	Effect size d'	Power 1-β
Low pre-mood	Pre	3.13	0.96	16	0.036*	0.63	0.49
	Post	3.94	1.18				
High pre-mood	Pre	5.00	0.00	83	0.002**	0.34	0.85
	Post	4.81	0.59				

It seems that when children had a low and high heart rate they normalized significantly their vegetative working state (optimum of excitement; Stueck and Stueck 2011) and found a balance between sympathetic and parasympathetic activity. None of the samples was measured as hypersensitive. It means that none of the children were chronically stressed. The hypersensitivity itself was measured by observing the electrodermal activity (Balzer and Stueck 2013).

Psychological Findings

In the psychological evaluation, a significant improvement of self-rated mood (in a five-point rating scale) can be seen in the group which started from a low level. Children who already had a high score of positive mood regulated their mood even further (see Table 4.4).

Furthermore, additional findings were determined when course instructors observed the children, which included significant increases ($p \leq 0.05$) in empathy, interest, relaxation and motoric resting ability, and concentration. In the ability of social exchange, a significant tendency ($p \leq 0.10$) was found. Finally, parents observed a significant increase in social competences in the observation scale in their children ($p = 0.019$, $d = 0.84$, $1-\beta = 0.78$), in comparison to the teachers ($p = 0.47$, $d = 0.23$, $1-\beta = 0.17$).

Effects of TANZPRO-Biodanza Among Children Aged 7–12 Years (Schoolchildren)

The following effects for schoolchildren (TANZPRO-Biodanza school version; ten sessions; age 7–12 years) were found, concerning cortisol levels, immunoglobulin, testosterone, and hypersensitivity. In an extended study in a Latvian school, twenty-two TANZPRO-Biodanza sessions were carried out to measure psychological effects and the effects on cortisol.

Change in Cortisol because of TANZPRO-Biodanza for Children

In a study of twenty-three children of 7 and 8 years of age, who took part in ten TANZPRO-Biodanza sessions, their cortisol levels were tested. The results in Table 4.5 and the graph in Figure 4.5 show a significant stress reduction effect in cortisol (accepted at $p = 0.001$ level of significance). Averaging over all sessions, there was no significant decrease in testosterone in the whole group ($p = 0.195$, $d' = 0.14$, $1-\beta = 0.39$). Also, there could not be found a significant increase in immunoglobulin A (IgA) ($p = 0.145$, $d' = 0.16$, $1-\beta = 0.46$). Looking more closely, an immune-enhancing effect (increased IgA) was seen in the last sessions (Figure 4.5).

Table 4.5. Post-session changes in average IgA, cortisol, and testosterone (pre-/post-session).

Cluster time		Mean	SD	N	Significance (two-tailed)	Effect size d'	Power 1-β
IgA	Pre	150.06	76.45	95	0.195	0.14	.39
	Post	162.25	92.78				
Cortisol	Pre	0.093	0.046	95	0.001**	0.41	0.99
	Post	0.075	0.042				
Testosterone	Pre	84.38	38.26	95	0.145	0.16	.46
	Post	77.72	36.81				

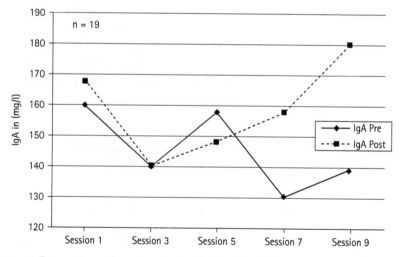

FIGURE 4.5. Pre-session and post-session IgA levels. After the later sessions (7 and 9) there was a visible IgA increase. (Credit: M. Stueck.)

Testosterone Levels in Boys and Girls after TANZPRO-Biodanza for Schoolchildren

Taking a closer look at testosterone levels, there was a difference between boys and girls. The hypothesis that the immune system could be regulated by TANZPRO-Biodanza was supported by the decrease in testosterone concentrations in the saliva of boys after the sessions (statistical tendency $p = .071$, $d' = 0.44$, $1-\beta = 0.68$) (see Table 4.6). The same level of reduction in testosterone levels was not observed amongst girls, but this would be due to the lower levels of testosterone in girls prior to the intervention.

Physiological Findings Concerning Hypersensitivity of the Skin (Chronic Stress State) and the Heart Rate

The concept was investigated among twenty-three children, in which four children (17.4%) in at least one out of the ten sessions were hypersensitive. In Table 4.7 the result

Table 4.6. Post–session changes in average testosterone in boy groups and girl groups.

Cluster time		Mean	SD	N	Significance (two-tailed)	Effect size d'	Power 1-β
Girl (aged 7)	Pre	81.56	37.33	70	0.54	0.11	0.13
	Post	78.28	38.48				
Boy (aged 7)	Pre	92.29	40.48	25	0.071	0.44	0.68
	Post	76.14	32.33				

Table 4.7. Cases of hypersensibility in each session.

Hypersensibility	Session 2		Session 4		Session 6		Session 8		Session 10	
	pre	post	pre	post	pre	post	pre	post	pre	post
S1	/ c	/	+ a	– b	+	–	+	–	–	–
S2	+	–	+	–	–	–	+	+	–	–
S3	–	–	+	–	–	–	/	/	/	/
S3	+	–	+	+	–	–	–	–	–	–

Note: a = hypersensible state; b = not in hypersensible state; c = not participated in this session. The amount of hypersensibility decreased because of TANZPRO-Biodanza in six cases (35.3%). In two cases (11.8%) there is no change (Chi/Pearson = 0.11). The results of the hypersensibility analysis are shown in a cross-tabulation in Table 4.8.

can be seen among four children before and after the session. The results of the hyper-sensitive analysis are shown in a cross-tabulation in Table 4.8.

In the same study we also looked at the heart rate for each child before and after the TANZPRO-Biodanza course (see Table 4.8). The low-level and high-level groups showed a significant change of heart rate (average over ten sessions) between pre-session and post-session, compared to the medium-level group (see Table 4.9), which means that the heart-rate values reached a balance between sympathetic and parasympathetic excitement.

Psychological Findings

A psychological evaluation of TANZPRO-Biodanza (school version 7–12) with twenty-two sessions (extension of the structurized programme) (Greaves et al. 2016), working with ten primary-school first-grade children aged 6–7 (experimental group) and nine children (control group) in a Latvian school, was carried out from the beginning of October 2014 until the end of May 2015. The parents' version of the Emotion

Table 4.8. Cross-tabulation of frequency change of hypersensitivity.

| Hypersensibility | | Post | | |
		No	Yes	Total
Pre	No	9	0	9
	Yes	6	2	8
Total		15	2	17

Table 4.9. Pre–Post Session Difference (average 10 sessions) between children with low and pre heart rate values.

Cluster time		Mean	SD	N	Significance (two-tailed)	Effect size d'	Power 1-β
Low heart rate	Pre	95.11	3.56	43	0.03*	1.44	0.96
	Post	113.18	14.49				
Medium heart rate	Pre	119.82	11.52	7	0.54	0.14	0.23
	Post	121.63	16.19				
High heart rate	Pre	171.28	19.53	10	0.00**	2.31	1.00
	Post	125.50	19.28				

Table 4.10. Internalized behaviour problems.

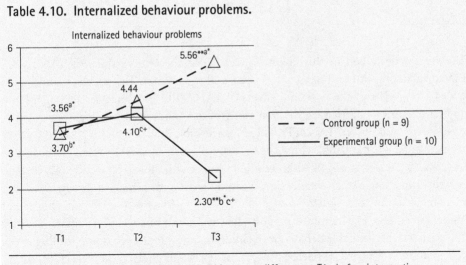

Note: $^+p < 0.1$; $^*p < 0.05$; $^{**}p < 0.01$. a, b, c – within-group differences. T1 – before intervention, T2 – after 10 sessions, T3 – after intervention.

Questionnaire (Rydell et al. 2003) was used to evaluate emotional competence: emotionality and emotion regulation. The parents' versions of the prosocial scale, internalizing and externalizing scale of the Strengths and Difficulties Questionnaire (SDQ; Goodman 1997) were used to measure social competence; that is, prosocial behaviour and nonexistence of behavioural problems. Testing was performed in three time points: before intervention, after ten sessions, and after intervention (twenty-two sessions). Pre-intervention and post-intervention results of social and emotional competence revealed different changes in experimental (n = 10) group and control (n = 9) group pupils. Experimental group pupils showed statistically significant improvement in emotion regulation results, prosocial and internalizing behaviour, but control group pupils showed decrease in emotion regulation results and an increase in internalizing behaviour results. Both between-group and within-group analyses indicated that internalizing behaviour results have most pronounced changes. Repeated measures with ANOVA and *post hoc* tests with Bonferroni adjustment revealed a statistically significant time effect for experimental group pupils ($F(2,18) = 4.81$, $p = 0.02$, $\eta^2 = 0.35$) and a tendency level with 90% probability for control group pupils ($F(2,16) = 3.40$, $p = 0.06$, $\eta^2 = 0.30$).

Internalizing behaviour problems includes emotional symptoms and peer relationship problems. Results suggest that the TANZPRO-Biodanza intervention programme of twenty-two sessions causes a decrease of emotional problems and improves peer relations, or at least prevents children from experiencing an increase in internalized problems, as was shown by the control group. Along with these psychological changes, a significant decrease of cortisol was also found (Greaves et al. 2016).

DISCUSSION

The studies described in this chapter investigated the two versions of TANZRPO-Biodanza among children of ages 3–6 years and 7–12 years). The selected studies produced a first view of the potential effects of TANZPRO-Biodanza for schoolchildren and kindergarten children. In the first study of ten children in kindergarten (ages 4–5 years), each taking ten TANZPRO-Biodanza sessions, those with high initial cortisol seemed to be 'normalizing', whilst those with low cortisol seemed to be already 'normalized' (Stueck et al. 2015). Although there were methodological limitations (e.g. no control group) and a small sample size, the findings from this small study suggested that there might be an autoregulatory effect of TANZRPO-Biodanza sessions in children of kindergarten age. The literature suggests that reduction of cortisol has many positive correlations with desirable behaviour in children; for example, relaxation leading to the deactivation of the cortisol release process. In a previous study, Ockenfels (1995) found that emotions, related to wellbeing, correlate well with lower cortisol levels. Kirschbaum (2008) also suggested that self-efficacy and anti-depressive optimistic–joyful reactions, and viewing a situation as challenging in conjunction with coping with problems, have been associated with low cortisol concentrations. The effects on emotional reduction and its relation to cortisol reduction were on average greater when children had higher initial cortisol levels in their saliva (before the TANZPRO-Biodanza sessions) than with lower levels of cortisol. Watamura, Coe, Laudenslager, and Robertson (2010) also found in a study of children aged 3–6 years that higher cortisol levels were associated with an increased risk of disease symptoms developing, especially in relation to the upper respiratory tract. The measured cortisol reduction suggested that TANZPRO-Biodanza (with its stress-reducing, prosocial nature) could potentially promote the development of emotion recognition abilities, thus enhancing the social skills of young children (Stueck and Villegas 2015). However, further studies are necessary regarding the effect of cortisol reduction among children. Another finding in this study showed the significant changing of heart rate for the low-level and high-level groups of children before and after TANZPRO-Biodanza. This indicates that low-pulse and high-pulse cases normalize significantly their vegetative working point in order to balance between sympathetic and parasympathetic activity. Similar results could also be shown in yoga among children through the use of the evidence-based programme 'relaxation training with elements of yoga for children/EMYK' (Stueck 1997, 2010; Stueck, Gloeckner, and Balzer 2002), whereby these physiological changes correspond to lower anxiety and stress scores (Stueck 2009).

The second study showed a significant stress reduction effect in cortisol among school-age children (7–8 years old). Cortisol is released when the hypothalamic–pituitary–adrenal axis has been activated and influences among others these immune regulatory processes (Ockenfels 1995). Accordingly, Ockenfels presented, with respect to the cortisol concentration in the saliva, a relationship to psychological variables whereby a negative affect correlates with higher cortisol levels, and positive emotions with lower cortisol levels. Lohaus et al. (2007) indicate in their discussion of mental stress effects a negative impact of stress on cognitive performance in children. Also, Jeong et al. (2005) found this modulation of neurohormones (increase of serotonin, decrease of cortisol level) in adolescents with mild depression after dancing (dance movement therapy). The decrease in testosterone concentrations in saliva among boys after the sessions was a significant finding that differentiated this group from the girls who participated in this study. A reduction in cortisol and testosterone most probably indicates an increased feeling of relaxation, which is connected with a higher sensibility and ability to enjoy contact (see studies by Spangler and Schieche 1994, cited in Stueck and Villegas 2010, about maternal sensitivity and cortisol reduction).

Taking a closer look at the low, middle, and high cortisol groups and the cortisol changes in the two studies, children with high pre-cortisol level benefit most from the dance-oriented programme after the interventions. With testosterone levels there was a difference between boys and girls. As Watamura (2010) has stated, the production of testosterone could be positively related to the amount of cortisol in saliva. In addition, there should be a closer examination of oxytocin, because this 'wellbeing hormone with others' which motivates tenderness and social interaction could influence cortisol and IgA. Immunoglobuline A showed in both studies no average effect, whereas in single sessions 7 and 9 there is an intended increase of IgA visible. The stable significant effects of the increase of IgA in adults after Biodanza in teachers (Stueck 2007) are obviously not found in children. It is assumed that the immune system still develops among children. Furthermore, the psychological effect relating to hypersensitivity has been investigated among school-age children. The hypersensitivity in the skin is a parameter which has been investigated in the context of chronic stress (Balzer and Stueck 2013). It can be defined as the pre-step before exhaustion and burnout, and was investigated by the authors in high-stress activities such as mountain climbing (Stueck, Balzer, Schroeder, and Rieck 2003), with teachers (Stueck 2007), and in Biodanza-interventions (Stueck and Villegas 2008). In general, it is reported that few studies exist regarding heart rate, blood pressure, cortisol, testosterone, IgA, and hypersensitivity in this age group.

Being an early study, the number of the sample sizes, deeper data exploration, and the lack of a control group were limitations. Thus, it is recommended that better-designed studies can take place on the same topics to determine whether the findings can be replicated. It could be helpful to make a comparison between experimental and control groups in TANZPRO-Biodanza and in interventions such as yoga for children (relaxation method), for example. Despite this fact, the results of these studies are worthy, because no studies of dance-oriented methods with children of this age range have been carried out until now. The cortisol in the two programmes decreased significantly, so that it could be argued that there was a stress reduction effect on the participating children, which may be connected with the particular intervention. It is possible that a particular intervention can help children concentrate and better recognize the emotions of other children. Because of this finding and the auto-regulative effect of decreased heart rates among children after the sessions, especially in the subgroups' low-pulse and high-pulse rates (in the programme for ages 3–6 years), it is possible that the intervention could be used in programmes relating to the prevention of violence or stress reduction in schools.

Conclusion

This chapter provides an overview of some studies on hormonal, physiological, and immunological effects of an evidence-based programme, using Biodanza for children. Research into the use of evidence-based Biodanza training for children (TANZPRO-Biodanza) was carried out in German schools and kindergartens. Because of its non-verbal focus on dancing, it can also be used in institutions in other countries, such as Latvia or Indonesia. There is no contradiction or expected conflict concerning religious attitude in this method, although a researcher should always bear in mind the possibility of these arising, in order to maintain the quality and to adjust the indication and contra-indication of the intervention.

To promote the wellbeing of children, it is necessary to support and maintain the interest of the adults and teachers in a systemic approach. This approach can give children the possibility to move freely to express feelings and needs autonomously. This could become the focus of further studies.

Other aims of TANZPRO-Biodanza for children are to reduce chronic stress, to enhance empathy, and to support the development of nonviolent behaviour in schools and kindergartens (Lahm et al. 2009).

Finally, TANZPRO-Biodanza for children has a role to play within a MasterPlan for Healthy Education (or a similar meta-plan), in which teachers, parents, and the conditions (such as class size, social differences, and financial status) are taken into consideration (Stueck 2009, 2013a). Further research in this area could explore ways in which this promising intervention can be incorporated within such policies.

Notes

1. <http://www.bionet.name >
2. See the videos of Marcus Stueck and others on the YouTube BIONET channel: 'Biodanza Aquatica/Evidencebased Biodanza', 'TANZPRO Biodanza for children', 'Biodanza and stress reduction', 'Biodanza en el espejo de la Ciencia'.
3. E.g. Villegas et al. (1999); Stueck et al. (2015).
4. See the video on the YouTube BIONET channel: 'Investigation about psychological and physiological effects of Biodanza' (Villegas and Stueck 2000).
5. In 2008, Rolando Toro, Marcus Stueck, and Alejandra Villegas compiled a list of past and future research challenges and created an overall research concept. This contains eight aspects, and seeks to integrate and coordinate global Biodanza research: (1) developing and updating the theoretical model of Biodanza; (2) experimental life sciences basic research on the effects of Biodanza (since1998); (3) quasi-experimental psychology studies with

weekly Biodanza classes (since 1998); (4) quasi-experimental research on Biodanza extensions (since 2006); (5) cross-cultural studies of Biodanza (since 2005); (6) studies on the quality of Biodanza teacher training (since 2003); (7) Biodanza with children (since 2008); (8) publications in scientific journals and high-quality scientific work (since 1998) (Stueck and Villegas 2012).

6. Since 2012 at the Educational University Riga, where Biodanza teachers listen to scientific presentations and scientists are dancing; see <http://www.bionet.name>.
7. Information at <http://www.bildungsgesundheit.de>.
8. With an extended TANZPRO-Biodanza programme (twenty-two sessions) (Greaves 2015; Greaves, Stueck, and Svence 2016).

REFERENCES

Balzer, H.-U. and Stueck, M. (2013). 'The psychological meaning of hypersensitivity', *Biopsychological Basics of Life: BIOnet*, 2: 23–35.

Carbonell-Baeza, A., Aparicio, V., Martins-Pereira, C., Gatto-Cardia, C., Ortega, F., Huertas, F., Tercedor, P., Ruiz, J., and Delgado-Fernandez, M. (2010). 'Efficacy of Biodanza for treating women with fibromyalgia', *Journal of Alternative and Complementary Medicine*, 16: 1191–200.

Fidora, N., Mader, G., and Stueck, M. (2008). *Befunde zu Biodanza mit älteren Menschen.* Leipzig and Granada: Verlag für Bildungsgesundheit. (In-depth research on Biodanza with older people.)

Goodman, R. (1997). 'The Strengths and difficulties questionnaire: A research note', *Journal of Child Psychology and Psychiatry*, 38: 581–6.

Greaves, V., Stueck, M., and Svence, G. (2016). 'Overview and psycho-biological effects of a long-term school project (22 weeks) in Latvia with an evidence-based Biodanza programme for children (TANZPRO Biodanza)', Web of Science (Thomson and Reuters).

Jeong, Y. J., Hong, S. C., Lee, M. S., Park, M. C., Kim, Y. K., and Suh, C. M. (2005). 'Dance movement therapy improves emotional responses and modulates neurohormones in adolescents with mild depression', *International Journal of Neuroscience*, 115(12): 1711–20.

Kirschbaum, C. (2008). *Biopsychologie von A bis Z.* Berlin and Heidelberg: Springer.

Krenz, A. (2009). 'Bildung' im Elementarbereich: Was ist los in deutschen Kindergärten?', *Die aktuelle Bildungspraxis im Fadenkreuz einer kritischen Betrachtung.* <http://www.win-future.de/downloads/bildungskritikeepaedagogik.pdf>

Lahm, B., Stueck, M., Mueller, M., Neumann, D., Poerschmann, N., and Mietzsch, B. (2009). *Fair sein: Ansätze zur Förderung von wechselseitiger Anerkennung und ewaltprävention in Kindertagestättenn.* Leipzig: Zentrum für Bildungsgesundheit, Messedruck.

Lohaus, A., Domsch, H., and Fridrici, M. (2007). *Stressbewältigung für Kinder und Jugendliche: Positiv mit Stress umgehen lernen, Konkrete Tipps und Übungen, Hilfen für Eltern und Lehrer.* Heidelberg: Springer Medizin Verlag.

Maturana, H. R. and Verden-Zöller, G. (2010). 'Biology of love', in G. Opp and F. Peterander (eds.), *Focus Heilpaedagogik.* Munich and Basel: Ernst Reinhardt.

Müller, M. (2016). *Respectful Communication in Schools: Handbook.* Leipzig: Gewaltfreies-leipzig.de.

Müller, M. and Pörschmann, N. (2009). 'Verbale Aspekte Wertschätzender Kommunikation im Kindergarten: Auf der Basis der Gewaltfreien Kommunikation nach Marshall Rosenberg (Empathieschule für Pädagogen)', in M. Stueck (ed.), *Beiträge zur Bildungsgesundheit*, vol. 7. Strasbourg: Schibri.

Ockenfels, M. (1995). *Der Einfluss von chronischem Stress auf die Cortisolkonzentration im Speichel*. Münster and New York, NY: Waxmann.

Pereira, B. (2005). *Biodance as a Process of Existential Renew for the Elderly*. PhD thesis. Fortaleza: Departament of Enfermagem, University Estadual do Ceará.

Rosenberg, M. (2009) *Gewaltfreie Kommunikation: Eine Sprache des Lebens*, 8th edn. Paderborn: Junfermann.

Rydell, A. M., Berlin L., and Bohlin G. (2003). 'Emotionality, emotion regulation, and adaptation among 5- to 8-year-old children', *Emotion*. 3(1): 30–47.

Schaarschmidt, U. & Fischer, A. W. (2006). Diagnostik des beruflichen Bewältigungsverhaltens. Teil 1: Sichere Arbeit 3, 32–35; Teil 2: Sichere Arbeit 4, 22–25.

Schoppe, S., and Stueck, M. (2012). 'Wertschätzende Kommunikation in Kindertagesstätten', *Prävention und Gesundheitsförderung*, 7: 229–36.

Seligman, M. (2004). *Authentic Happiness: Using the New Positive Psychology to Realize Your Potential for Lasting Fulfilment*. New York, NY: Adria.

Senerath, S. (2010). Adjustment and stress disorders in children and adolescents affected by the Tsunami in Sri Lanka and evaluation of a mediator-intervention method under use of the evidence based programme with Biodanza or children (Stueck, Villegas, Luzzi, Toro, 2010/ TANZPRO-BIODANZA). Dissertation. Faculty of Biosciences at the University of Leipzig.

Spangler, G. and Schieche, M. (1994). *The role of maternal sensitivity and the quality of infant mother attachment for infant biobehavioural organisation*. 9th International Conference on Infant studies, Paris, France.

Stueck, M. (1997). *Entwicklung und Evaluation eines Entspannungstrainings mit Yogaelementen für Mittelschüler als Bewältigungshilfe für Belastungen*. Dissertation. Fakultät für Biowissenschaften der Universität Leipzig.

Stueck, M. (2000). Handbuch zum Entspannungstraining mit Yogaelementen in der Schule. Donauwörth: Auer Verlag.

Stueck, M. (2003). 'Integrative Belastungsbewältigung in der Schule: Das IBiS-Konzept: Prävention', *Zeitschrift für Gesundheitsförderung*, 26(4): 115–18.

Stueck, M. (2004). 'Stress management in schools: An empirical investigation of a stress management system', *Social Work Practitioner-Researcher*, 16(2): 216–30.

Stueck, M. (2007). *Entwicklung und empirische Überprüfung eines Belastungsbewältigungskonzepts für den Lehrerberuf. Habilitation*. Leipzig: Fakultät für Biowissenschaften der Universität Leipzig.

Stueck, M. (2008). 'Neue Wege: Yoga und Biodanza in der Stressreduktion mit Lehrern', in M. Stueck (ed.), *Neue Wege in Pädagogik und Psychologie*, vol. 1. Strasbourg: Schibri.

Stueck, M. (2010). *Researchers, Artists and Constructors: Early Education Under Investigation*. Strasbourg: Schibri.

Stueck, M. (2011). 'The concept of system related stress reduction (SYSRED) in educational fields', *Problems of Education in the 21st Century*, 29: 119–34.

Stueck, M. (2013a). 'Masterplan healthy education', *Biopsychological Basics of Life: BIOnet*, 2: 23–35.

Stueck, M. (2013b). 'School of Empathy: Introduction and first results', in E. Witruk and A. Wilcke (eds.), *Beiträge zur Pädagogischen und Rehabilitationspsychologie: Historical and Cross-Cultural Aspects of Psychology*, vol. 4. Frankfurt am Main: Peter Lang, pp. 497–509.

Stueck, M. (2015). 'Biodanza: Inklusion geht nur mit geschlossenen Augen!', *Praxishandbuch Kinder unter 3*, Ausgabe 14.

Stueck, M. and Stueck, Th. (2011). 'Die wissenschaftlichen Grundlagen zum Kinder-Yoga', in M. Stueck (Hrsg.), *Neue Wege in Pädagogik und Psychologie*. Bd. 3. Strasburg: Schibri-Verlag.

Stueck, M., Schoppe, S., Lahn, F., and Toro, R. (2013). 'What is the use of empathy without doing? Development of an empathy scale based on a holistic empathy concept', *ErgoMed/Praktische Arbeitsmedizin*, 6(37): 38–46.

Stueck, M. and Villegas A. (2008) *Empirische Befunde zu Biodanza-Marathon*. Leipzig and Granada: Verlag für Bildungsgesundheit.

Stueck, M. and Villegas A. (2008) *Es ist wie eine Geburt: Empirische Befunde zu einjährigen Biodanza-Gruppen*. Leipzig and Granada: Verlag für Bildungsgesundheit. (A study of one-year courses and visible complex behavioural changes.)

Stueck, M. and Villegas, A. (2008). 'Zur Gesundheit tanzen? Empirische Forschungen zu Biodanza', in M. Stueck and A. Villegas (eds.), *Biodanza im Spiegel der Wissenschaften*, vol. 1. Strasbourg: Schibri. (In German, Italian, Spanish, and English.)

Stueck, M. and Villegas, A. (2009). *Dance Oriented Programme with Elements of Biodanza for Children (TANZPRO-Biodanza for Children)*. Leipzig: Healthy Education.

Stueck, M. and Villegas, A. (2010). 'TANZPRO Biodanza: the school of penguins', in M. Stueck, *School of Empathy*. Leipzig: Center of Educational Health Publishing.

Stueck, M. and Villegas, A. (2010). Handbook for Instructors: TANZPRO-children (Dance-oriented Programme with Biodanza for children). Print on demand. Leipzig: Pinguine-Polarbear.

Stueck, M. and Villegas, A. (2012). 'Overview on biodanza research: An 8-point masterplan', *Biopsychological Basics of Life: BIOnet*, 1: 7–15.

Stueck, M. and Villegas, A. (2012). 'Biodanza as a health-promoting intervention for teachers', *Biopsychological Basics of Life: BIOnet*, 1: 33–9.

Stueck, M. and Villegas, A. (2013). 'Effects of an evidence-based dance program (Tanzpro-Biodanza®) for kindergarten children aged four to six on immunoglobulin a, testosterone, and heart rate', *Problems of Education in the 21st Century*, 56: 128–43.

Stueck, M., Villegas, A., Bauer, K., Terren, V., Toro, R., and Sack, U. (2009). 'Psycho-immunological process evaluation of Biodanza', *Signum Temporis: Journal of Pedagogy and Psychology*, 2(1): 99–113.

Stueck, M., Villegas, A., Lahn, F., Bauer, K., Tofts, P., and Sack, U. (2015). 'Biodanza for Kindergarten children (TANZPROBiodanza): Reporting on changes of cortisol levels and emotion recognition', in *Body, Movement and Dance in Psychotherapy*, vol. 20. Routledge, Francis and Taylor.

Stueck, M., Villegas, A., Meyer, K., Bauer, K., and Sack, U. (2002). *Psycho-immunological process evaluation of a stress preventive intervention program for teachers*. 33. Jahrestagung der Gesellschaft für Immunologie. Immunobiology 206. 319.

Stueck, M., Villegas, A., Perche, F., and Balzer, H.-U. (2007). 'Neue Wege zum Stressabbau im Lehrerberuf: Biodanza und Yoga als körperorientierte Verfahren zur Reduktion psycho-vegetativer Spannungszustände', *Ergomed*, 3: 68–75.

Stueck, M., Villegas, A., Schoenichen, C., Bauer, K., Tofts, P., and Sack, U. (2013). 'Effects of an evidence-based dance program (Tanzpro-Biodanza®) for kindergarten children aged four to six on immuneglobuline a, testosterone, and heart rate', *Problems of Education in the 21st Century*, 56: 128–43.

Stueck, M., Villegas, A., Terren, R., Toro, V., Mazzarella, L., and Schroeder, H. (2008). 'Die Belastung tanzen? Biodanza als neue körperorientierte psychologische Interventionsmethode der Belastungsbewältigung für Lehrer', *Ergomed*, 2: 34–43.

Stueck, M., Villegas, A., and Toro, R. (2010). 'Nonverbale Aspekte Wertschätzender Kommunikation in Kindertagesstätten: Empathieschule für Pädagogen', in *Beiträge zur Bildungsgesundheit*, vol. 8. Strasbourg: Schibri.

Thinschmidt, M., Druschke D., Gruhne B., Kahle S., Stueck M., Mayer L., and Schoppe S. (2012). '"Starke Wurzeln": Aktionsbündnis gesunde Lebensstile und Lebenswelten im Setting Kita des Landkreises Nordsachsen', in L. Tillmann, K. Neitemeier, and K. Sterz (ed.), *Aktionsbündnisse für gesunde Lebensstile und Lebenswelten: Portraits der Aktionsbündnisse Ergebnisse der wissenschaftlichen Begleitung Tipps für die Praxis*. Berlin and Köln: Bundesministerium für Gesundheit and Lernende Region, S.50–4.

Toro, R. (2010). *Das System Biodanza*. Hannover: Tinto.

Trimulyaningsih, N., Novitasari, R., and Qudsyi, H. (2014). 'Nonviolent communication: An alternative approach for enhancing empathy among Indonesian children', *Biopsychological Basics of Life: BIOnet*: 34–46.

Villegas, A. (2006). *The Danced Way: Process and Effect Evaluation of Biodanza*. Strasbourg: Schibri. (PhD thesis.)

Villegas, A. (2008). *The Danced Way: Evaluation of Effects and Processes in Biodanza*. Strasbourg: Schibri. (PhD thesis.)

Villegas, A., Stueck, M., Terren, R., Toro, V., Schroeder, H., Balzer, H.-U., Hecht, K., and Mazzarella, L. (1999). 'Psychologische und Physiologische Wirkungen von Biodanza', in *Conexión Abierta UAI B. Aires*. pp. 15–18. (In Spanish.)

Villegas, A., Stueck, M., Terren, R., Toro, V., Schröder, H., Balzer, H.-U., Hecht, K., and Mazzarella, L. (2000). 'Untersuchungen zu psychologischen und physiologischen Effekten von Biodanza', *Biodanza/AEIB: Jährliche Zeitschrift*, 1: 37–42. (In German, English, Italian, and Spanish.)

Watamura, S. E., Coe, C. L., Laudenslager, M. L., and Robertson, S. S. (2010). 'Child care setting affects salivary cortisol and antibody secretion in young children', *Psychoneuroendocrinology*, 35(8): 1156–66.

CHAPTER 5

··

DANCING TO RESIST, REDUCE, AND ESCAPE STRESS

··

JUDITH LYNNE HANNA

INTRODUCTION

UNENDING horrific man-made and natural disasters as well as daily life lead almost all persons to complain of stress at some point in their lives. They call out for wellbeing—a feeling of satisfaction with one's physical and psychological health, social relations, and work situation. Adults, students in school and extracurricular activities, and family members at home may find an answer to coping with stress in dancing and watching dance. Like a diamond with radiant facets, dance attracts our attention, usually feels good to do, and has the potential to meet our needs for stress relief and good health.

In this chapter I address the concepts of dance, stress, and wellbeing. Then I offer evidence of coping with stress through dance: personal and cultural experiences, physical exercise research, and the language component that makes dance a unique form of physical exercise. I refer to studies of marginalized groups that cope with stress through dance. On the basis of involvement in the dance world for more than half a century, and numerous reports, I describe both the positive and negative stressors in dance education, professional dance, and amateur dance. I note research that documents dance therapy programmes for diverse populations and problems that help people deal with stress.

I intend to address what gives dance the potential power to help individuals and groups resist, reduce, or escape from harmful stressors. I draw upon field, historical, clinical, and laboratory work. Research studies in neuroscience provide evidence for the predominance of the brain in mind and body. We have learned about the plasticity of the brain, and thus a life-long ability for humans to make new synaptic connections (Ratey 2008), the basis of emotion and the links between body and feelings (Damasio 2010), and the role of mirror neurons in the brains of dancer and viewer linked to empathy (Bläsing et al. 2012; Calvo-Merino et al. 2010).

Human dancing emerges from an evolutionary process lasting millions of years. Across cultures, people do more than attend to motion as a tool for survival—to distinguish prey and predator, to select a mate, and to anticipate others' actions and respond accordingly for cooperation or fighting as other animals. Humans dance—a form of multi-sensory movement that also communicates as well as being a means of coping with stress. In addition, dance shapes and sharpens body and brain (Hanna 2015).

Dance, too, can be a stressor (especially for dancers, parents, choreographers, production staffers, dance critics, and others in the professional dance world). As is the case with all healing approaches, there may be counter-indications. What is a stressor for one person may not be for someone else. It all depends upon one's views about the body and dance as well as one's personality, culture, and social context. A person perceives and appraises an issue within a framework of beliefs, goals, personal resources, demands, constraints, and opportunities. Appraisal may be instantaneous or reflective (Lazarus 1966; McEwen 2002; Sapolsky 2004; Ratey 2008; Hoge 2010).

The Concept of Dance

Elaborated in *To Dance Is Human* (Hanna 1987), the word 'dance' refers to human behaviour composed of, from the dancer's perspective, purposeful, intentionally rhythmical, and culturally patterned sequences of nonverbal body movements other than ordinary motor activities in space with effort. The movement is frequently accompanied by music along with its particular health benefits (MacDonald et al. 2012). In addition, the movement may have an acting quality, such as pantomime and role-playing, and be performed alone or with others. Usually involving sight, sound, touch, smell, and kinaesthetic feeling, dance may provide the performer and spectator with a captivating multisensory experience.

The language of dance bears some similarities to verbal language (including sign language). Clegg (2004) points out that 'speech refers to the oral/auditory medium that we use to convey the sounds associated with human languages. Language, on the other hand, is the method of conveying complex concepts and ideas with or without resource to sound' (p. 8). Galaburda et al. (2002) argue that there are multiple possible 'languages of thought' that play different roles in the life of the mind but nonetheless work together (p. 1). 'Representations of information, representations of relations, and a set of rules for how the relations can be used to combine and manipulate representations' constitute a language (p. 200).

Both dance and verbal language have vocabulary (locomotion and gestures in dance) and grammar (rules in different verbal languages and dance traditions for putting the vocabulary together and, in each dance tradition, justifying how one movement can follow another). Both non-verbal dance and verbal language have semantics (meaning). Verbal language strings together sequences of words, and dance strings together sequences of movement. However, dance more often resembles poetry, with its multiple, symbolic, and elusive meanings, than it resembles prose. Dance can be mimetic or abstract. It is more difficult to communicate complex logical structures with dance than it is with verbal language. Although spoken language can simply be meaningless sounds, and movements can be mere motion, listeners and viewers tend to read meaning into what they hear and see.

Since everybody has some of the same features, and time, space, and energy are universals in human life, people may erroneously assume that these are experienced in a universal manner by everyone. Similarly, dance is assumed to be a universal form of communication. But culture, context, and knowledge of a dance genre affect one's understanding of it (Hanna 2002). Verbal languages, too, are usually not understood by people unfamiliar with them.

THE CONCEPT OF STRESS

Let me now turn to 'stress'. *Icy hands in a hot room; blushing, trembling extremities, shortness of breath, and furtive eyes; tears and other emotional outbursts; nervousness and increased perspiration; extra trips to the bathroom; a cry of pain due to injury; and a host of diseases.* These are the tell-tale signs of excessive stress.

At other times only the stressed person is aware of such symptoms as *a palpitating heart, muscular tension, faintness, back strain, depression, anxiety, difficulty in swallowing, headaches, loss of appetite, intestinal and eating disorders, insomnia, and emotions of frustration and resentment* (Yamaguchi et al. 2003; Wittstein et al. 2005; Wilson 1991).

Stress refers to the perception of threat of physical or psychological harm that pushes a person towards the limits of his or her adaptive capacity (McEwen 2002; Sapolsky 2004; Ratey 2008; Hoge 2010). Note that the fight-or-flight syndrome does not require an emergency. Even everyday worries and pressures or the anticipation of a threatening situation or extraordinary excitement may trigger the response.

The term 'stress' is relatively new. Stress was called 'shell shock' in World War I, 'combat fatigue' and 'concentration camp syndrome' in World War II, and 'post-traumatic stress disorder' following the Vietnam War (Brewin 2003). Today the term 'stress' is an umbrella for conflict, frustration, trauma, alienation, anxiety, and depression (Rand 2004). Many difficulties previously labelled in various ways from the time of our earliest records are now subsumed under the term 'stress' (Ben-Ezra 2002; Hanna 2006).

Chronic stress is ongoing and unresolved, whereas acute stress is brief and time-limited. *Eustress* refers to catalysing adaptive, productive, and creative efforts to solve problems and to motivate persons to high peaks of performance. *Distress* overworks and exhausts the body's defences against the harmful effects of stress.

Under stress, the brain's limbic system—responsible for emotions, memory, and learning—triggers an alarm reaction. The brain's amygdala orchestrates feelings with hormonal responses and mediates the influence of emotion (the awareness and appraisal of feeling) on cognition. The amygdala stimulates the hypothalamus (it controls heart rate, blood pressure, sleep/wakefulness, most of the information from the internal body system, the autonomic functions, and hormone regulation) to send a message to the adrenal glands that spill out stress hormones. These activate the fight-or-flight response, increasing the production of the inflammatory hormones adrenaline (epinephrine) and cortisol. They work together to speed heart rate, increase metabolism and blood pressure, shunt blood way from organs into muscles, lower pain sensitivity, and enhance attention—all beneficial for survival.

After the body has mobilized the alarm reaction and the stressful situation is coped with, the second phase of the stress response kicks in to produce from the adrenal cortex anti-inflammatory hormones that limit the extent of inflammation against stressors and return the body to normal.

However, constant stress prevents the body from returning to normal. High adrenaline and cortisol levels that persist may cause blood sugar imbalances, blood pressure problems, and a whittling away at muscle tissue, bone density, and immunity. Stressful experiences can change the physical structure and function of the brain, affecting wiring and thus cognitive performance, making a person feel unmotivated and mentally exhausted. Formation of new neural connections in the hippocampus—the part of the brain responsible for encoding new memories—becomes blocked, hindering memory and the mental flexibility needed to find alternative solutions. People under prolonged stress may suffer a changed sense of self that increases the probability of accidents and certain diseases. Long-term and short-term stress, even a mere few hours, can reduce cellular connections in the hippocampus.

Lazarus (1966) finds stress and emotion conjoined. Anger, anxiety (uncertainty), fright (a sudden and overwhelming concrete physical danger), guilt, and shame (not about a provocative act but the implication that we deserve to be disgraced or humiliated), sadness, envy, jealousy, and disgust may be a part of distress. 'Coping potential arises from the personal conviction that we can or cannot act successfully to ameliorate or eliminate a harm or threat, or bring to fruition a challenge or benefit' (p. 93). When we reappraise a threat, we may alter our emotions by creating new meaning of the stressful encounter. This may diffuse anger, fear, anxiety, and so on.

Dance has the potential to diminish threat and transform emotions. To prevent or cope with distress, some people talk with friends, drink, eat, become violent, seek solitude, or turn to religion (Snyder 2001; Tipton 2003). Yet others dance—do it or watch it. Of course, these activities are not mutually exclusive.

THE CONCEPT OF WELLBEING

Based on his summary of research and work as a therapist in positive psychology, Seligmann (2011) proposes components of a 'wellbeing theory' that coping with stress through dance has the potential to encompass. Wellbeing, he says, 'has several measurable elements, each a real thing, each contributing to well-being, *but none defining well-being*' (2011, p. 15). Wellbeing theory has five elements, and each of the five has three properties (pp. 16–20). The elements are

1) positive emotion (pleasurable, hedonic, altered state of consciousness, ecstasy, comfort);
2) engagement (absorption in activity);
3) meaning (belonging to and serving something beyond the self with subjective and objective logic);
4) accomplishment (achievement, winning, mastery); and
5) positive relationships (support, sympathy, sharing).

The properties of each element are contributing to wellbeing, pursuit for its own sake, and measurability independently of the rest of the elements. The following discussion suggests how dance may envelope these elements and properties.

EVIDENCE FOR COPING WITH STRESS THROUGH DANCE

Personal and Cultural Experiences

How do we know that dance can help us cope with stress? I can attest to personal experience in responding to family pressures and bad bosses. But more importantly, there is an amazing amount of historical, anecdotal, and scientific evidence (Hanna 2006). Humans turn to dance for self-protection and problem-solving—to resist, reduce, or escape stress related to birth, puberty, marriage, infertility, ecological harm, social disorder, death, and uncertainty. People meet their gods and demons with danced praise and appeal, possession, masking, and exorcism to prevent stress and to achieve healing (e.g. Kapferer 1983). The Italians performed the tarantella dance to expurgate the hairy wolf spider's agonizing venom and also to cope with such problems as a repressed sex drive (Schneider 1948; DeMartino 1966; Rouget 1985). Dance was thought to purify villages devastated by the Black Death that plagued medieval Europe over a period of many centuries (Hecker 1885; Benedictow 2004; Kelly 2005). Political conquest created stressors of lost land, group dignity, and self-identity (Mooney 1965; Mitchell 1956). Victims found relief through dance expressing catharsis (the recollection and release of past repressed distressful emotions such as anger and fear), identification with the aggressor, accommodation, or resistance. Bwiti and Beni Ngoma dances from Africa (Fernandez 1982) and the Ghost Dance (Mooney 1965), Coast Salish Spirit Dancing (Amoss 1978), Gourd Dance, powwow, and *danza de la conquista* from the Americas (Moedano 1972) are further examples.

Immigrants worldwide have carried their traditional healing arts to other countries. Some transformation occurs, but so does retention. In the same way that many people accept our grandparents' hand-me-down age-old remedies, such as chicken soup for a cold, many people also accept intuitive beliefs in the efficacy of dance to help them cope with stress and achieve wellbeing.

Physical Exercise

The most significant evidence that dance can help people reduce, resist, or escape stress comes from research findings on dance as physical exercise (Jackson et al. 2004; Brown and Lawton 1987; Penedo and Dahn 2005; Snyder 2001). Dance is exercise, and regular exercise is a critical component of ways that help us guard against the ravages of stress and be resilient to it. Nearly every set of recommendations for stress management includes exercise as therapy. When you neither fight nor flee from stress because physical action is not possible, biochemical elements of energy can remain in the body and cause harm. Exercise absorbs this energy. Moreover, exercise can provide distraction, reduce muscle tension, alter mood, improve mental health, and blunt the stress response. As an individual adapts to the increase in heart rate, pressure of the circulation of blood carrying oxygen to the muscles and the brain, as well as altering the level of certain brain chemicals and stress hormones, the body is strengthened and conditioned to react more calmly during stress. Depression, anxiety disorder, dementia, Alzheimer's disease, arthritis, coronary issues, and pain have been shown to be reduced with exercise (Fox 1999; Verghese et al. 2003; Stein 2005; Tipton 2003; Dunn et al. 2005; Moffet et al. 2002).

In addition, exercise promotes more than physical activity. Ratey (2008)—a psychiatrist at Harvard Medical School—presents research which found that exercise involves a plethora of cognitive brain functions. Throughout life, exercise stimulates neurogenesis, the formation of new brain cells that spark the key molecule of the learning process, glutamate, which stirs up a signalling cascade. One hundred billion neurons of various types communicate with each other through hundreds of different chemicals.

> Each brain cell might receive input from a hundred thousand others before firing off its own signal . . . Electrical charges reach synapses (spaces between neurons), a neurotransmitter carries the message across the synaptic gap in chemical form. The dendrite, or receiving branch . . . opens ion channels in the cell membrane to turn the signal back into electricity. (Ratey 2008, p. 36)

Exercise spurs new nerve cell growth from stem cells in the hippocampus and prepares and stimulates nerve cells to bind to each other—the cellular basis for acquiring new information. The brain circuits created through movement can be recruited by the prefrontal cortex for thinking and coping with stress.

As an activity in itself, exercise may lead to emotional changes or even altered states of consciousness. Exercise apparently releases a copious quantity of opiate beta-endorphins, which are magical, morphine-like brain chemicals that dull pain, distract one from problems, produce feelings of analgesia, euphoria, calm, satisfaction, and greater tolerance for pain. The Dogon of Mali describe their rapid *gona* dance movement as a relief, like vomiting (Griaule 1965; see Forman 1983; Insel et al. 2001; Heinrichs et al. 2003; Moffet et al. 2002).

Exercise Plus

So, why dance rather than engage in other forms of exercise to handle stress? 'The more complex the movements', Ratey (2008) says, 'the more complex the synaptic connections', (p. 56) and dance has various levels of complexity. *Dance is exercise PLUS.* Not only does dance release the potentially harmful energy in the body that cannot be used in a fight-or-flight stress response, but dance is also non-verbal language that is akin to cognitive therapy. Dance aesthetically expresses ideas and feelings. Dance is 'bodies sounding off'—a form of embodiment that gives concrete form to emotions and concepts. Moreover, dance can impact the brain's reward and pleasure system. Dopamine is a neurotransmitter that helps control this centre, which enables a person to take action to move toward rewards. Associated with pleasurable motivation, improved working memory, and taking action, dopamine is essential to learning (Floresco 2013). Partner dancing and group dancing with touching release oxytocin, the 'bonding' or 'feel good' hormone (Heinrich et al. 2003; Hanna 1988, 2012).

A dancer may simultaneously be a performer and also a spectator, imagining the dance as part of performance preparation, seeing oneself (and others in a group dance) in the studio mirror, or seeing others moving in a group dance on stage. A spectator may be an empathizing 'dancer' through mirror neuron action, more intensely felt by viewers with dance experience. When we watch someone performing an action, our brains may mirror, or simulate, performance of the action we observe.

Communication through dance can offer some of what reading, writing, and body-oriented psychotherapy offer—fantasy, story-telling, performer–audience connection, and spirituality. Mental representation plays a key role in dance. Mental representations are 'activated and produce images embedded in space and time, which can be translated introspectively, interpreted consciously, and described schematically' (Bläsing et al. 2009: 350).

Dance may reflect the status quo or suggest what might be. A person may escape stressors in a danced fantasy (Kandel 2012). The embodied practice of dance performance may spotlight themes such as the forbidden, sexuality, oppression, self-identity, ageing, death, and other possible stressors. In this way these themes may be scrutinized and imaginatively played with, distanced, and consequently made less threatening. Thus there are engagements with meaning, accomplishment, and positive emotion through dance—elements which Seligmann proposes contribute to wellbeing.

Because dance representations of ideas and feelings are pretend and symbolic and therefore without the impact of real life, the dance medium allows participants a safe opportunity to cope with threatening problems. Catharsis is common. The danced action is like a rehearsal. If you do not like a performance scenario, you can create or watch another, changing it in your mind or in a new choreography.

In giving testimony and retelling, dance making or viewing can help people to make sense of the incomprehensible (Nemetz 2004). By retelling a stressful situation, reliving one's harrowing experience over and over again, an individual gets used to telling and expressing the memory and realizing that it was in the past (Foa et al. 2013). Dance rehearsal offers a prolonged exposure.

In dance, military service men and women can confront traumatic experience toward modifying maladaptive beliefs about events, behaviour, and symptoms. They can thus begin to associate cues to bad memories with a sense of current safety. Dance is a venue in which to dream oneself anew (Gray 2001), even with abstract dances into which meaning can be read by dancer and spectator. Also, a focus on form may be a distraction from stress. When students dance their academic subjects, learning may be less stressful.

Bill T. Jones, a charismatic dancer/choreographer, lost his partner and lover, Arnie Zane, to AIDS. After the death, several of Jones's new dances confronted the pain; he even had one of his company's dancers, who also had AIDS, participate in a dance even though pain prevented him from standing on his own. Company members reported that the dances enabled them to better manage the pain and anguish of loss (Kisselgoff 1989; see also Wallach 1989; Wilson 1991; Gere 2004).

Although dance expression has the potential to move participants in a dance performance to gain distance and insight to evaluate problems, consider resolutions, and act in a constructive way outside the dance setting, less frequently the themes portrayed in dance may scrape against raw nerves and induce stress.

Cultural Dance

Marginalized groups—ethnic, racial, colonial, gender, sexual (DeFrantz 2004; Meyer 2003; Gold 2001), age, and occupational (Hanna 2012)—may be stressed by stigma, prejudice, and discrimination in a hostile social environment. There may be expectations of rejection, concealing, and internalized homophobia. Dance temporarily suspends an ecological setting. Alternatively, cultural dances 'speak' to a sense of belonging, bonding, and pride. Group inclusiveness is self-empowering. Dance with touch releases oxytocin (Heinrichs et al. 2003; Hanna 1988, 2012). Renowned African American dancer Pearl Primus (1968) described dance as 'the scream which eases for a while the terrible frustration common to all human beings who because of race, creed or color are "invisible". Dance is the fist,' she said, 'with which I will fight the scheming ignorance of prejudice. It is the veiled contempt I feel for those who patronize with false smiles, handouts, empty promises, insincere compliments' (p. 58).

More than letting off steam, or creating a safe haven, dance is a venue to reduce the stressful misuse of power and produce social change without violence. A political form of coercion in a shame-oriented society, unheeded dance communication led to the famous 1929 'women's war' in Eastern Nigeria. Women went on a rampage, prisoners were released, and people were killed. The repercussions were widespread both at local and intercontinental levels. Indeed, the mighty British were forced to alter their colonial administration (Van Allen 1972; Dorward 1982) and attend to messages conveyed in women's dancing.

Through the dance, young Ubakala Igbo girls in Nigeria try to cope with the stressors of maturing, marrying, living among strangers, being fertile, and giving birth. In the *Nkwa Edere* dance, shoulder shimmying and side-to-side pelvis swinging highlight breast development and other pubescent body changes. There are also dances for the death of an aged man or woman that remind participants of the coming of their own deaths and help them cope with the wrenched and dislocated part of the fabric of social relationships caused by a death (Hanna 1987).

Educational and Professional Dance

Individuals usually find strength against stress in the self-mastery required in learning a dance technique, from ballet to hip-hop. They may gain the support of others in cohesive group dancing that in itself is a kind of therapy (Heinrichs et al. 2003). Performers pay tribute to human fortitude as they express the sense of doing something and being in control. Of course, dance is art and entertainment that diverts performers and audiences alike from stressors.

In any setting, dance may have positive and/or negative stresses. Children's wellbeing is threatened when parents, teachers, or coaches ask them to accomplish more in dance than they are physically and emotionally ready for. A child younger than 8 years lacks bones that are sufficiently strong to withstand the prolonged physical discipline required to master techniques such as ballet. Age, development, and expectations affect readiness, although some youngsters are naturally precocious. Juggling academic requirements and dance classes, or being unable to go to friends' parties because of class or rehearsal commitments, may also be stressful.

Some parents impose stress on their offspring when they attempt to realize their own romantic theatrical ambitions through them, and the youngsters are unable or unwilling to do so (Conraths-Lange 2003). Youngsters may also impose unrealistic demands upon themselves. Students read about dance, the competitions, prizes, and scholarships—and some push themselves in ways that become stressful. Changes in puberty may lead to a pre-professional dancer's body becoming no longer appropriate for a ballet career (Buckroyd 2000).

Being the butt of bias, neglected, branded disloyal, or the victim of intrigue in someone's pursuit of self-advancement can stress any type of dancer. So too can competition, cooperation, and performance in class, for roles and on stage (Forsyth and Kolenda 1996). While students compete for the teacher's attention and approval, teachers compete for students. Students who want exposure to a variety of dance styles often face possessive teachers who 'want you under their wing'. Burnout—physical, mental, and emotional exhaustion from an inability to cope with the demands of dance and consequent loss of interest in dance—affect children and adults alike.

Pursuing a dance career is a passion that can reap great rewards. Motivation to dance professionally often includes the satisfaction of achieving what others want to do, try to do, but cannot do well, and the exhilaration of performance and audience approval. Professionals perform for others and in place of others. But as with most occupations, there are stressors, some specific to the dance profession (Abrams 1985–86; Bentley 1982, 1986; Helin 1989; Kirkland 1986; Hamilton et al. 1995). Financial rewards (except for a few superstars) are low, the economics of the dance process, production, and performance are difficult, and a performing career is brief. Watching one's weight and fitness are constant concerns. Perfectionists stress about whether their work measures up to high standards. Yet successful dancers have a burning sense of conviction that allows them to overcome these stressors as well as negative attitudes toward a dance career, physical demands, and hazards of injury, competition, and the occasional mistreatment by teachers, coaches, choreographers, and company managers.

Performance anxiety affects novice and pro alike (Aaron 1986). Paul Taylor (1999), the renowned choreographer, writes in his autobiography: 'Stage fright. Some clone, not me, is cowering offstage and covered with icy sweat, his palms and soles slippery, temples booming, tongue dry, seizured, sizzled. It's plain to see that the reason for greasepaint is to prevent your skin from betraying its cowardly color' (p. 39).

Choreographers may experience anxiety about being able to produce, especially under pressures of deadlines and limited resources. Although choreographers must innovate as Western aesthetics dictate, too much innovation can lose audiences unfamiliar with or unreceptive to the avant-garde. The creator as unique and marvellous has the negative counterpart as loner–outsider, troublemaker, and uncommitted.

Yet good stress often catapults dance participants toward recognition, and spurs the creation of innovative work and more effective dance education and arts management. Many in the dance world thrive because of its stressful challenges and risks.

Amateur Dance

Amateur dance is more relaxed and stress-free than professional dance. Individuals participate in social dance or dance classes for fun, exercise, self-expression, and socializing. Dance helps people to resist stress through developing physical fitness and building social support that extend beyond the dance setting. Stress reduction occurs through the dissipation of everyday tensions of work and family, as well as tensions that arise from crises. The fantasy and enchantment of a romantic dance genre offers escape from stress.

Of course, amateur dancers may feel stress because of the inability to master steps or embarrassment about partnering. Stressors also include inadequate dance-class support from teachers or classmates, ambiguous performance feedback, performance anxiety, and insufficient social dance invitations.

Sometimes dance triggers stress that enables you to deal with a greater stressor. Paradoxically, the pursuit of wellbeing through exercise may result in injury and impaired health. As critic George Jackson (2007) has said: 'Dance, that double-edged sword, ought to come with a warning label, "the spice of life or the kiss of death"' (p. 25). However, dance medicine directs us to ways of making dancing less risky and more effective in resisting and reducing stress (Solomon et al. 2005; Berardi 2005; Peterson 2011).

Treatment Programmes

More than a theatre art and a form of leisure, dance is also part of contemporary wellbeing and medical stress treatment programmes. Some dance studios advertise their classes as a way to 'dance away the blues'. Extracurricular activities offered to university students include dance as an antidote to stress. Similarly, self-help groups turn to dance as a stress reliever.

Dance/movement therapy (DMT), rooted in dance, psychology, and medicine, bears resemblances to the therapeutic stress-management dance practices found in non-Western cultures, past and present. DMT is included in psychiatric hospitals, community health centres, nursing homes, clinics, special educational settings, prisons, private practice offices, and the therapist's or client's home (Schmais 1985; Levy 2005; Chaiklin and Wengrower 2009; see Cruz and Berrol 2012). There are diverse populations and kinds of problems. For example, DMT is offered to people with anxiety (Lesté and Rust 1990) and depression (Rand 2004). DMT is provided to battered women (Chang and Leventhal 1995), sexually abused men (Frank 1997), torture victims (Gray 2001), sexually assaulted women (Bernstein 1995), American Indian college women (Skye et al. 1989), child soldiers for rehabilitation (Harris 2009), and refugees (Singer 2005). Stress from eating disorders, drug abuse, caregiving, and transitioning out of the military are other illustrative foci for DMT. This therapeutic approach provides a supportive environment in which clients usually warm up body parts, expand their range of movement, and create excitement with music and props. Improvisational exercises, mirroring the movements of another person, and holding movements are used to express troublesome issues and work through them.

Conclusion

In short, dance is a medium that humans have long held as a key weapon in their arsenal to cope with the stresses of life—birth, adolescence, sex, work, marriage, ecological harm, social disorder, uncertainty, crises, and death. On the basis of historical, ethnographic, scientific, and anecdotal evidence, it appears that dance has the power to help a person to resist, reduce, or escape stress.

Dance in relationship to stress certainly envelops components that Seligmann (2011) proposes contribute to wellbeing: dance can provide positive emotion, engagement, meaning, accomplishment, and positive relationships. Dance is a form of exercise plus the communication of thoughts and feelings, yielding more dividends than other forms of exercise. Because dance is physical, cognitive, and emotional, it is a vehicle for a person to cope with stress and become motivated and invigorated to achieve goals for wellbeing. Excessive stress and distress, on the other hand, can cause physical harm and impede accomplishments and even managing daily life. When one neither fights nor flees from stress because physical action is not possible, biochemical elements of energy can remain in the body and cause harm. However, dance is a medium through which to discharge the energy and, most significantly, to portray and scrutinize stressors in order to diminish their threat. Knowledge of the positive and negative aspects of stress and dance can lead one to appraise threat in order to alter one's emotion or interpret the threat in new ways.

References

Aaron, S. (1986). *Stage Fright: Its Role in Acting*. Chicago, IL: University of Chicago Press.
Abrams, G. L. (1985–86). 'Report on the dirst international conference on mind, body and the performing arts: Stress processes in the psychology and physiology of music, dance and drama, New York University, July 15–19, 1985', *Dance Research Journal*, 17(2) and 18.
Amoss, P. (1978). *Coast Salish Spirit Dancing: The Survival of an Ancestral Religion*. Seattle, WA: University of Washington Press.
Benedictow, O. J. (2004). *The Black Death 1346–1353: The Complete History*. Woodbridge: Boydell Press.
Ben-Ezra, M. (2002). 'Trauma 4,000 years ago?', *American Psychiatric Association*, 159: 1437.
Bentley, T. (1982). *Winter Season: A Dancer's Journal*. New York, NY: Random House.
Bentley, T. (1986). 'Reaching for perfection: The life and death of a dancer', *The New York Times*, 17 April, H1, 25.
Berardi, G. M. (2005). *Finding Balance: Fitness, Training, and Health for a Lifetime in Dance*, 2nd edn. New York, NY: Routledge.
Bernstein, P. (1995). 'Dancing beyond trauma: Women survivors of sexual abuse', in F. J. Levy with J. P. Fried and F. Leventhal (eds.), *Dance and Other Expressive Art Therapies: When Words are Not Enough*. New York: Routledge, pp. 41–58.
Bläsing, B., Calvo-Merino, B., Cross, E. S., Jola, C., Honsch, J., and Stevens, C. J. (2012). 'Neurocognitive control in dance perception and performance', *Acta Psychologica*, 139: 300–8.
Bläsing, B., Tenenbaum, G., and Schack, T. (2009). 'The cognitive structure of movements in classical dance', *Psychology of Sport and Exercise*, 10(3): 350–60.
Brewin, C. R. (2003). *Post-Traumatic Stress Disorder: Malady or Myth?* New Haven, CT: Yale University Press.
Brown, J. D. and Lawton, M. (1987). 'Stress and well-being in adolescence: The moderating role of physical exercise', *Journal of Human Stress*, 12(3): 125–31.

Buckroyd, J. (2000). *The Sstudent Dancer: Emotional Aspects of the Teaching and Learning of Dance*. London: Dance Books.

Calvo-Merino, B., Ehrenberg, S., Leung, D., and Haggard, P. (2010). 'Experts see it all: Configural effects in action observation', *Psychological Research*, 74: 400–6.

Chaiklin, S. and H. Wengrower (eds.). (2009). *The Art and Sscience of Dance/Movement Therapy: Life is Dance*. New York, NY: Routledge.

Chang, M., and Leventhal, F. (1995). 'Mobilizing battered women: A creative step forward', in F. J. Levy with J. P. Fried and F. Leventhal (eds.), *Dance and Other Expressive Art Therapies: When Words are Not Enough*. New York: Routledge, pp. 59–68.

Clegg, M. (2004). 'Evolution of language: Modern approaches to the evolution of speech and language', *General Anthropology*, 10(2): 1, 8–11.

Conraths-Lange, N. (2003). 'Pas de deux: Daughters, mothers, and dance talk', *Medical Problems of Performing Artists*, 18(2): 52–8.

Cruz, R. F. and Berrol, C. R. (eds.) (2012). *Dance/Movement Therapists in Action: A Working Guide to Research Options*, 2nd edn. Springfield, IL: Charles C. Thomas.

DeFrantz, T. (2004). *Dancing Revelations: Alvin Ailey's Embodiment of African American Culture*. New York, NY: Oxford University Press.

De Martino, E. (1966). *La terre du remords*, trans. C. Poncet. Paris: Gallimard.

Damasio, A. (2010). *Self Comes to Mind: Constructing the Conscious Brain*. New York, NY: Random House.

Dorward, D. C. (1982). *The Igbo 'Women's War' of 1929: Documents Relating to the Aba Riots in Eastern Nigeria*. New York, NY: Microform Ltd.

Dunn, A. L., Trivedi, M. H., Kampert, J. B., Clark, C. G., and Chambliss H. O. (2005). 'Exercise treatment for depression: Efficacy and dose response', *American Journal of Preventive Medicine* 28(1): 1–8.

Fernandez, J. (1982). *Bwiti: An Ethnography of the Religious Imagination in Africa*. Princeton, NJ: Princeton University Press.

Floresco, S. (2013). 'Prefrontal dopamine and behavioral flexibility: Shifting from an "inverted-U" toward a family of functions', *Frontiers in Neuroscience*, 7: 62.

Foa, E. B., McLean, C. P., Capaldi, S., and Rosenfield, D. (2013). 'Prolonged exposure vs supportive counseling for sexual abuse-related PTSD in adolescent girls: A randomized clinical trial', *JAMA*, 310(24): 2650–7.

Forman, J. S. (1983). *The Effects of an Aerobic Dance Program for Women Teachers on Symptoms of Burnout*. PhD thesis, University of Cincinnati.

Forsyth, S. and Kolenda, P. M. (1966). 'Competition, cooperation, and group cohesion in the ballet company', *Psychiatry* 29(2):123–45.

Fox, K. (1999). 'The influences of physical activity on mental well-being', *Public Health Nutrition*, 2(3a): 411–18.

Frank, Z. (1997). 'Dance and expressive movement therapy: An effective treatment for a sexually abused man', *American Journal of Dance Therapy*, 19(1): 45–62.

Galaburda, A. M., Kosslyn, S. M., and Christen, Y. (eds.) (2002). *The Languages of the Brain*. Cambridge, MA: Harvard University Press.

Gere, D. (2004). *How to Make Dances in an Epidemic: Tracking Choreography in the Age of AIDS*. Madison, WI: University of Wisconsin Press.

Gold, R. (2001). 'Confessions of a boy dancer: Running a gantlet of bullying and name-calling', *Dance Magazine*, 75(11): 52.

Gray, A. E. L. (2001). 'The body remembers: Dance/movement therapy with an adult survivor of torture', *American Journal of Dance Therapy*, 23(1): 29–43.

Griaule, M. (1965). *Conversations with Ogotemmeli: An Introduction to Dogon Religious Ideas.* London: Oxford University Press.

Hamilton, L., Hella, J. J., and Hamilton, W. G. (1995). 'Personality and occupational stress in elite performers', *Medical Problems of Performing Artists*, 10(3): 86–9.

Hanna, J. L. (1987). *To Dance is Human: A Theory of Nonverbal Ccommunication.* Chicago, IL: University of Chicago Press.

Hanna J. L. (1988). *Dance, Sex and gender: Signs of Identity, Dominance, Defiance and Desire.* Chicago, IL: University of Chicago Press.

Hanna, J. L. (2002). 'Reading a universal language?', *DCA News*, Spring, pp. 6, 15.

Hanna, J. L. (2006). *Dancing for Health: Conquering and Preventing Stress.* Lanham, MD: AltaMira.

Hanna, J. L. (2012). *Naked Truth: Strip Clubs, Democracy, and a Christian Right.* Austin, TX: University of Texas Press.

Hanna J. L. (2015). *Dancing to Learn: The Brain's Cognition, Emotion, and Movement.* Lanham, MD: Rowman Littlefield Education.

Harris, D. A. (2009). 'Dance and child soldiers', *Foreign Policy in Focus*, 15 June.

Hecker, J. F. C. (1885). *The Dancing Mania of the Middle Ages*, transl. B. G. Babington. New York, NY: J. Fitzgerald.

Heinrichs, M. T., Baumgartner, T., Kirschbaum, C., and Ehlert, U. (2003). 'Social support and oxytocin interact to suppress cortisol and subjective responses to psychosocial stress', *Biological Psychiatry*, 54(12): 1389–98.

Helin, P. (1989). 'Mental and psychophysiological tension at professional ballet dancers' performances and rehearsals', *Dance Research Journal*, 21(1): 7–14.

Hoge, C. (2010). *Once a Warrior, Always a Warrior: Navigating the Transition from Combat to Home, including Combat Stress, PTSD, and mTBI.* Guilford, CT: Lyons Press.

Insel, T. R., Gingrich, B. S., and Young, L. J. (2001). 'Oxytocin: Who needs it?', *Progress in Brain Research*, 133: 59–66.

Jackson, A. W., Morrow, J. R. D. Jr., Hill, W., and Dishman, R. K. (2004). *Physical Activity for Health and Fitness*, updated edn. Champaign, IL: Human Kinetics.

Jackson, G. (2007). 'Healthy dance, sick dance', *Ballettanz*.

Kandel, E. R. (2012). *The Age of Insight: The Quest to Understand the Unconscious in Art, Mind and Brain, from Vienna 1900 to the Present.* New York, NY: Random House.

Kapferer, B. A. (1983). *A Celebration of Demons: Exorcism and the Aesthetics of Healing in Sri Lanka.* Bloomington, IN: Indiana University Press.

Kelly, J. (2005). *The Great Mortality: An Intimate History of the Black Death, the Most Devastating Plague of All Time.* New York, NY: HarperCollins.

Kirkland, G. (1986). *Dancing on My Grave.* New York, NY: Doubleday.

Kisselgoff, A. (1989). 'Jones/Zane Company and loss', *The New York Times*, 20 March, C16.

Lazarus, R. S. (1999/2006). *Stress and Emotion: A New Synthesis*, 2nd edn. New York, NY: Springer.

Lesté, A. and Rust, J. (1990). 'Effects of dance on anxiety', *American Journal of Dance Therapy* 12(1): 19–25.

Levy, F. (2005). *Dance Movement Therapy: A Healing Art*, revised edn. Reston, VA: National.

MacDonald, R., Kreutz, G., and Mitchell L. (2012). *Music, Health, and Wellbeing.* New York, NY: Oxford University Press.

McEwen, B. (2002). *The End of Stress as we Know It.* Washington, DC: Joseph Henry Press.

McNally, R. J. (2003). *Remembering Trauma.* Cambridge, MA: Harvard University Press.

Meyer, I. H. (2003). 'Prejudice, social stress, and mental health in lesbian, gay, and bisexual populations: Conceptual issues and research evidence', *Psychological Bulletin*, 129(5): 674–97.

Mitchell, J. C. (1956). *The Kalela Dance*. Manchester: Manchester University Press for the Rhodes-Livingstone Institute.

Moedano, G. (1972). 'Los hermanos de la Santa Cuenta: Un culto de crisis de origen Chichimeca', in *Religion en Mesoamerica*. Mesa Redonda, Sociedad Mexicana de Antropologia 12, ed. J. L. King and N. C. Tejero. Mexico: La Sociedad.

Moffet, H., Noreau, L., Parent, É., and Drolet, M. (2002). 'Feasibility of an eight-week dance-based exercise program and its effects on locomotor ability of persons with functional class III rheumatoid arthritis', *Arthritis Care and Research*, 13(2): 100–11.

Mooney, J. (1965). *The Ghost-Dance Religion and the Sioux Outbreak of 1890*, ed. A. F. C. Wallace. Chicago, IL: University of Chicago Press. (Originally published in 1896.)

Nemetz, L. D. (2004). 'Being in the body: Finding reconnection after 9/11', *Dance Therapy Association of Australia Quarterly: Moving On*, 3(2): 2–11.

Penedo, F. J. and Dahn. J. R. (2005). 'Exercise and well-being: A review of mental and physical health benefits associated with physical activity', *Current Opinion in Psychiatry: Behavioural Medicine*, 18(2): 189–93.

Peterson, J. R. (2011). *Medicine Head to Toe: A Dancer's Guide to Health*. Hightstown, NJ: Princeton Book Company.

Primus, P. (1968). Quoted in *Dancemagazine*, 42(11): 56–60.

Rand, R. (2004). *Dancing Away an Anxious Mind: A Memoir about Overcoming Panic Disorder*. Madison, WI: University of Wisconsin Press.

Ratey, J., with Hagerman, E. (2008). *Spark: The Revolutionary New Science of Exercise and the Brain*. New York, NY: Little, Brown.

Rouget, G. (1985). *Music and Trance: A Theory of the Relations between Music and Possession*. Trans. and rev. B. Biebuyck. Chicago: University of Chicago Press.

Sapolsky, R. M. (2004). *Why Zebras Don't Get Ulcers: An Updated Guide to Stress, Stress Related Diseases, and Coping*, 3rd edn. New York, NY: Henry Holt.

Schmais, C. (1985). 'Healing processes in group dance therapy', *American Journal of Dance Therapy*, 8: 17–36.

Schneider, M. (1948). *La danza de espadas y la tarentela. Ensayo musicológico, etnografico y arqueológico sobre los ritos medicinales*. Barcelona: Instituto Espanol de Musicologia.

Seligman, M. (2011). *Flourish: A New Understanding of Happiness and Well-being*. New York, NY: Free Press.

Singer, A. J. (2005). '"Hidden treasures, hidden voices": An ethnographic study into the use of movement and creativity in developmental work with war affected refugee children (Serbia 2001–2)', paper presented at the Dance Ethnography Forum, Leicester, England.

Skye, F. D., Christensen, O. J., and England, J. T. (1989). 'A study of the effects of a culturally-based dance education model on identified stress factors in American Indian college women', *Journal of American Indian Education*, 29(1): 26–31.

Snyder, C. R. (ed.) (2001). *Coping with Stress: Effective People and Processes*. New York, NY: Oxford University Press.

Solomon, R., Solomon, J., and Minton, S. C. (eds.) (2005). *Preventing Dance Injuries*, 2nd edn. Champaign, IL: Human Kinetics.

Stein, M. B. (2005). 'Sweating away the blues: Can exercise treat depression?', *American Journal of Preventive Medicine*, 28 (1): 140–1.

Taylor, P. (1999). *Private Domain*. Pittsburgh, PA: University of Pittsburgh Press.

Tipton, C. I. (ed.) (2003). *Exercise Physiology: People and Ideas*. New York, NY: Oxford University Press.

Van Allen, J. (1972). ' "Sitting on a man": Colonialism and the lost political institutions of Igbo women', *Canadian Journal of African Studies*, 6(2): 165–81.

Verghese J., Lipton, R. B, Katz, M. J., Hall, C. B., Derby, C. A., Ambrose, A. F., Sliwinski, M., and Buschke. H. (2003). 'Leisure activities and the risk of dementia in the elderly', *New England Journal of Medicine*, 348(25): 2508–16.

Wallach, M. (1989). 'Bill T. Jones/Arnie Zane and Co. brave the waters', *New York City Tribune*, 15 March.

Wilson, A. A. (1991). *Rehearsals in the Anthropology of Performance and the Performance of Anthropology: Ritual, Reflexivity, and Healing in a Dance by Men Challenging AIDS*. MA thesis, University of Southern California.

Wittstein I. S., Thiemann, D. R., Lima, J. A. C., Baughman, K. L., Schulman, S. P, Gerstenblith, G., Wu K, C., Rade, J. J., Bivalacqua, T. J., and Champion. H. C. (2005). 'Neurohumoral features of myocardial stunning due to sudden emotional stress', *New England Journal of Medicine*, 352: 539–48.

Yamaguchi, K., Toda, K., and Hayashi, Y. (2003). 'Effects of stressful training on human brain threshold', *Stress and Health*, 19: 9–15.

CHAPTER 6

···

BODY MEMORY AND ITS RECUPERATION THROUGH MOVEMENT

···

HEIDRUN PANHOFER

INTRODUCTION

···

IF we acknowledge that dancers know something and that for the most part their knowing is nonverbal, it leads us to ask: *what* do they know, and even more importantly, *how* do they know? (Parviainen 2002: 13).

For most of us from the world of dance who dedicate many hours of our lives working with and through our bodies the idea of a body that feels, a body that knows and remembers, is nothing new. Nonetheless, our surrounding has been dominated, during the last centuries, by a Cartesian discourse that separated minds and bodies: on the one hand the mental, conceptual, rationale, cognitive, and theoretic, and on the other the imaginative, emotional, and practical. More so, the Cartesian split privileged the mind over the body (Meekums 2006), denigrating the body over the intellect. In dance, this attitude shows up when bodies are being used as objects for pure technical proficiency: instead of vehicles for critical understanding of the life world they are transformed into anonymous, preprogrammed body machines that do not sense or feel. Being able to explore and make use of a thinking and feeling body is an important task for all dancers, performers, teachers, dance movement therapists and researchers, in order to work with their bodies in a more integrated way.

This chapter is concerned with the epistemological questions of the body—in particular, the concept of body memory and its relevance for working with the body's knowledge and wisdom for wellbeing. The aim is to clarify the concept of 'body memory' as it has been defined by Fuchs (2003, 2012), and to highlight its implications for research, dance and Dance Movement Psychotherapy (DMP). Panhofer's (2009) study which explored ways of verbalizing the embodied experience serves as a base for further discussion and comparison of other contributions that have integrated the knowledge and memory of the body.

Moving on from the Cartesian Duality of Body and Mind

Important advances in neuroscience, philosophy, and cognitive linguistics during the last decades are seriously challenging this Cartesian duality of body and mind. In neuroscience, for example, Panksepp (2006b) shows up the importance of emotions for our way of functioning. Despite the difficulty to study those affective aspects of our minds he affirms that without our embodied, inherent, and neuronally activated capacity to feel good or bad in the world, we could not exist. Damasio (1994), on the other hand, connects emotions with what he calls 'somatic markers' (pp. 173–5) as the base for human conscience. For him, emotions are representatives of corporal states, and he thus considers the body as an important container for all past and present moments.

In cognitive linguistics, Lakoff and Johnson (1999a,b, 2003) show that all abstract significance in our language is formed upon our physical experience. About 70% of the expressions we use in our daily language are based on physical metaphors, such as 'feeling low', 'hollow words', or 'getting an idea across to somebody'. Kövecses (2003) illustrates how metaphors that are connected with emotions stem directly from the embodied experience (love is fire, happiness is up, sadness is dark, shame is a burden, and so on). Giving cross-cultural evidence he shows that human physiology is universal—for example, anger does indeed go together with objectively measurable bodily changes such as a rise in skin temperature, blood pressure, and pulse rate, and deeper respiration, in most cultures.

In philosophy, Merleau-Ponty had already developed the concept of 'intercorporeality' in 1964 as 'the capacity to understand another person's action through the body prior to, and as a condition for, cognition' (Atkins 2008, p. 48). Before the advances in developmental psychology of the 1980s he had postulated the importance of 'relationships between bodies' as a preverbal concept, thus underlining the early nonverbal relationships as a base and condition for all knowledge. The American dancer and philosopher Sheets-Johnstone (1999) argues that movement is the mother of all cognition, and that the tactile–kinaesthetic body is our epistemological gateway.

As Damasio (1994, p. 93) states: '. . . the mind is embodied, in the full sense of the term, not just embrained'. Accordingly, the contribution of embodiment to cognition is inescapable (Gallagher 2005), thus allowing for a psychocorporeal holism (Atkins 2008, p. 9). This vision influences how we work in the world of dance, as our bodies cannot be considered any longer as pure machines, referred to in German as *Körper*[1] or in Latin as *corpus*, which emphasises the structural aspects of the body, the biological body, the corpse. On the other hand, the *corps vivant*—called *Leib* in German—with its emotions, sensations, and perceptions, is considered, thus opening the dimension of the body as an individual, the animate form, as Sheets-Johnstone (1999) calls it.

This *Leib*, or sensing body, plays an important role in the somatic work whose goal is to take conscience of the sensations and emotions of the body, using perception, or 'somatic modalities of attention' (Csordas 1993: 193). It is a body that knows and remembers, as it is employed in DMP or Authentic Movement. A large number of dance educators and artists appreciate the knowledge of the body for their process of creating dances (e.g. Parviainen 2002; Anttila 2007; Hämäläinen 2007), as well as for investigation (e.g. Koltai 1994; Smith 2002; Ylönen 2003, 2004; Kaylo 2004; Riley 2004; Panhofer 2011).

Body Memory

The German psychiatrist and philosopher Fuchs (2001) connects body memory with the concepts of implicit and explicit memory. While declarative and explicit knowing contains information that can be described with a *knowing that* (Fuchs 2001: 324), implicit knowing refers to a *knowing how*. Polanyi (1983) illustrates that when we know a person's face we can recognize it among a million, yet we usually cannot tell how we recognize a face we know. He emphasizes that this tacit knowledge (Polanyi 1969, p. 144) therefore cannot be put into words: even though we can waltz, we would have difficulties in describing the activity itself. Despite our capacity to read the physiognomy of a person, we cannot tell exactly why somebody appears to have a specific mood, and without seeing we can find our way in the dark when arriving late in the cinema. We can see a tree and, despite of not having examined the tree from all sides or having been able to measure it, we produce for ourselves a clear idea about the shape of the tree (Polanyi 1967).

As Parvaiainen (2002) points out, there is a clear distinction and a connection between 'skill' and 'knowledge' in respect of the body's movement. Knowledge in dance involves more than bodily skills or knowing how to do movements: it is a bodily lived form of knowledge.

Fuchs (2003, p. 3) affirms that

> [. . .] bodily learning means to forget what we have learned or done explicitly and to let it sink into implicit, unconscious knowing.

Fuchs (2003) proposes five types of body memory that form part of our implicit memory: procedural memory, situational memory, intercorporeal memory, intercorporative memory, and traumatic memory, and (2012) he adds a sixth form of body memory: pain memory. Consequently, the six types will be explained briefly.

Procedural body memory contains habits such as playing an instrument or riding a bicycle that form part of repetition. They are stored in the body as well-practiced habits, skilful handling of instruments, or familiarity with patterns of perception, called 'kinetic melodies' by the Russian neuropsychologist Luria (1973, p. 32)—a chain of isolated motor impulses which, upon repetition, becomes stored in the body as kinetic melodies. Whoever knows how to drive a car changes the gears without conscious reflection, whoever can dance a waltz moves his feet to the music without counting or explaining the action, reading means capturing shapes and forms that a familiar to us without analysing every single one of them again. On the contrary, when we change the keyboard of our computers our hands have a hard time adapting to the new, external reality: they keep tapping onto where they 'think' the letters are, as if they had their own memory.

Situational memory is inseparable from physical, sensorial, and atmospheric perception. It helps us to become familiar with recurrent situations, to get our bearings in the space of our dwelling, in the neighbourhood or hometown. We recognize characteristics of specific situations without expressing them in words; for example, we can enter our flat and put the coat on the hanger without switching on the light, when running for the underground we will stretch out the correct hand to put the ticket through the slot (which in Barcelona, for example, would be on the right-hand side for trains but on the left-hand side for the underground), and we do all this without conscious reflection but out of experience.

Parviainen (2003: 163) and Sheets-Johnstone (2009, p. 1) refer to this as 'thinking in movement'. When for example, one is walking along a path and there is a big stone in the way, one automatically lifts the leg, and the walking proceeds in a very regular, unbroken fashion.

> There is no need to think——Oh, there is a stone in my path, I have to lift a leg, I have to extend it, I have to step over, make an effort. (Sheets-Johnstone 2007, p. 4)

To be familiar with recurrent situations is what we call 'experience', and situational memory shows that our experience is based upon the lived interaction of our bodies with the world.

Intercorporeal memory is connected with the concept of implicit relational knowing—a term coined by the Boston Change Study Group with the child psychiatrist Stern (Lyons-Ruth et al. 1998). It is a physical knowing of how to treat with others which is learned during early childhood, and is closely linked to Merleau-Ponty's (1964) previously mentioned idea of 'intercorporeality'.

> This early intercorporeality has far-reaching effects: Early interactions turn into implicit relational styles that form the personality. As a result of a learning processes which are in principle comparable to the acquiring of motor skills, people later shape and enact their relationships according to the patterns they have extracted from their primary experiences. (Fuchs 2003, p. 4)

Intercorporeal memory thus makes reference to a kind of knowledge between bodies, and places emphasis on the fact that all learning happens with and through other bodies and our environment. Parviainen's (2002) beautiful example of the act of how to learn to swim may allow us to extend this kind of memory 'between bodies' to 'body and environment': 'Ultimately, the water I place myself in and the body placed there teach me more than any set of words I read or hear' (19), adding an environmental focus on Fuchs' (2003) or Merleau-Ponty's (1964) original proposal to look on relationships and experiences between bodies.

Incorporative memory incorporates physical attitudes from others in our own movement vocabulary. This is not only connected with prereflective interactions, but also with incorporations of postures or gestures that are learned in school, dance class, television, and so on. The body acquires an external significance, transferring symbols and social roles, this being in posture or clothing. The body converts into the conveyor of habits (Bourdieu 1990), styles, and ways of acting that are usually assumed and are acquired through activities and daily life experience (Fuchs 2012, p. 16).

The fifth type of memory, *pain memory*, connects us with the proverb 'The burnt child dreads the fire'. The adult, too, becomes aware of this connection when entering the dentist's consultancy. Instinctively we tense up, draw back, or dodge when there is a danger of pain. Whoever has touched an electric fence once retreats immediately when it comes into sight—the painful contact remains in our memory. In the same way, experiences of pain and its surroundings are inscribed effectively in our bodies—a fact that has been used a long time in education, considering that only memories that are 'burnt into our memory' will remain.

Traumatic memory deals with repressed, forgotten, or neglected contents, as they are too painful to bear, such as physical or sexual abuse, torture, danger of death, and so on. Behnke (2012) uses the German term *enduring* and its double meaning:

> Enduring something means undergoing it in such a way that one is somehow able to bear what one is suffering (German *aushalten, ertragen*), while at the same time, this experience of withstanding what one is enduring is lasting rather than momentary (German *andauern, fortdauern*), demanding persistence and perseverance (German *anhalten, ausdauern*). (Behnke 2012, p. 83)

It means that we can support traumatic events when they occur, but they leave kinesthetic marks that can last a long time afterwards, even though the traumatic event has passed. The most indelible impressions of body memory are caused by trauma, according to Fuchs (2012).

Fuchs (2001) describes impressively how, for example, in schizophrenia the patient cannot use tacit knowing any more as a means of perceiving the world. He perceives a split between the body and the mind, and is no longer able to explain single details of movement and perception. What is appropriate and decent in everyday situations becomes lost—kinetic melodies, as they are described by Luria (1973), are interrupted or commenced outside of the context.

Practical comprehension in the life-world, according to Fuchs (2003), is therefore originally based on an implicit, intuitive conception mediated by the body.

> [. . .] implicit memory is not a mere reflex programme realised by the body machine. Merleau-Ponty was the first to conceive of body knowledge as a third dimension

between merely imagined movement and motor execution. The memory of the body is an impressive refutation of the dualism of consciousness and the physical body. (Fuchs 2003, p. 1)

For this reason, for example, when dementia deprives a person of all her explicit memories, she still retains the memory of her body: The history of her life remains present in familiar smells, the handling of objects, sights, and so on, and her body is the carrier of her personal continuity—a more felt than known recollection, the tacit but *enduring* memory of the body (Fuchs 2012: 20–1).

The Study

The implications of a body that feels, knows, and remembers are widely spread for education in dance and movement, but also direct how research is approached and how we can work psychotherapeutically. Subsequently, Panhofer's (2009) study and its results will be described briefly as an example of how to use the knowledge and the memory of the body in research. Stemming from DMP—a psychotherapeutic approach that integrates movement and dance as a means of growth and learning in therapy—it examined the extent to which the lived, embodied experience can be worded.

Methodology

One of the aims of Panhofer's (2009) research was to explore the extent to which the embodied experience can be communicated in words. Therefore, a mixed methodological strategy has been designed, drawing from qualitative approaches in the field of artistic research methodologies (Eisner 1981; McNiff 1986, 1992, 1993, 1998; Hervey-Wadsworth 2000; Hannula 2004) such as writing (Coffey and Atkinson 1996; Sparkes 2002, 2003) and movement and dance (Koltai 1994; Smith 2002; Riley 2004; Ylönen 2003, 2004).

A group of professional DMP therapists were invited to reflect upon significant moments that they had experienced with their clients. These moments of insight, of connection and change, formed the basis of a creative exploration through a process of writing–moving–writing.

Firstly, all coresearchers wrote an initial narrative of what they remembered from this significant moment. Then, they created a movement sequence: rather than applying a specific dance or movement technique or reproducing a scene through role play, 'somatic modes of attention' (Csordas 1993: 1), as described in Riley (2004), were used for these movement sequences. Comparable to Gendlin's (1996) 'focusing' technique, the researchers got in touch with the 'body-felt sense'. Attention was brought to exteroceptive sensations stemming from the environment, such as temperature, space, noises from the outside, and so forth. This helped to distinguish the inside and the outside, but also to become familiar with the surroundings and therefore feel more safety. Then, awareness was brought to proprioceptive sensations such as physical sensations of movement; for instance, the joints, muscles, and bones. Finally, interoceptive sensations were considered: awareness has been brought to the breath or heartbeat, slowly getting in touch with one's own body rhythms.

Similar to the process in Authentic Movement (Whitehouse 1978; Chodorow 1991; Payne 2006b), this inner focus allowed for free association in movement, based on the significant moment. Rather than pure expression, a dialogue between the conscious and unconscious that consists in attention, or listening, and response was proposed in order to '. . . tap into somatic images through all of our various sensory modalities' (Smith 2002: 133). A movement sequence emerged, offering a space of spontaneous, self-initiated, and self-directed activity, a reflection in movement, thus providing access to the aspects of the tacit dimension of nonverbal thought.

After this movement sequence the coresearchers created a final written narrative as a response to their movement narrative. Some of the procedures for the data analysis were Wolcott's three-step model, Labov's narrative analytical framework (Labov 1972; Toolan 2005), and Laban's movement analysis (LMA) (Bartenieff 1980; Laban 1987; Laban 1988; North 1990; Laban 1991), as well as a focus group (Stewart and Shamdasani 1990; Marczak and Sewell 2007), with the coresearchers that discussed the experience and the findings.

Findings

A clear outcome from the study was that the methodological procedures of writing–moving–writing enhanced the connection to the therapist's lived, embodied experience—a finding that was confirmed by the focus group and the final follow-up questionnaire responses from the coresearchers. The process of moving facilitated an engagement from the coresearchers' whole self, including their emotional attitude towards their clients. 'First [*making reference to the initial narrative, comment in italics from the author*] it became a description of another person, then it was rather an internal dialogue', one coresearcher stated.

Another coresearcher expressed surprise when comparing her two texts, supporting the finding that the method of moving and writing had brought her closer to her own personal thoughts and emotions, shifting from an aloof observer to an engaged participant. It seemed as though a simple consideration through reflective thought and verbalization could not bring them as close to their deep bodily knowledge than the act of moving itself. One coresearcher commented:

> The proposed experience of writing and moving has allowed me to reflect in a different way about the material and has provided me with new ways of how to focus in the therapeutic process. (Panhofer 2009, p. 212)

'It has enhanced the knowledge about me', another confirmed in her final feedback, underlining how the process of connecting personally through her body's movement brought her in touch with her tacit knowledge from 'behind the scene'.

> Because the earliest foundation of tacit knowledge is preverbal and disconnected from the verbal-thinking self ... changes in flawed tacit knowledge must take place through thought that is connected to preverbal, body-based, global experience of wholes rather than reflective reason' (Selar-Smith 2002, p. 62)

Selar-Smith speculates that it is not the thinking–observing self but rather the *I-who-feels* who is experiencing the feeling that provides access to the aspects of the tacit dimension of nonverbal thought. The procedures of writing and moving allowed the researchers to transfer from implicit to explicit ways of knowing through a practical, body-based, global experience. It is further suggested (Panhofer et al. 2011a, 2011b) that these procedures are used for clinical supervision to explore and deepen the intercorporeal perspective of the therapeutic relationship. An emphasis purely on verbalization, leaving aside the body, risks neglecting experiences which have been stored as body memories, or in other sensory modalities, and which are more easily accessible to DMP practitioners or other body-oriented psychotherapists.

DISCUSSION

In the field of research, many have asked for new methodological possibilities that move closer to the body's senses, feelings, and multisensorial communication (Winther 2008). Sparkes (2002) criticizes:

> Where bodies have been focused on, they have been heavily theorized bodies, detached, distant, and for the most part lacking intimate connection to lived experiences of the corporal beings that are the objects of analytical scrutiny. (p. 146)

Panhofer's (2009) investigation therefore sought to integrate the body as the *Leib*, the *corps vivant*, with its sensing and feeling capacities—a body that knows and remembers, such as described previously by Fuchs (2001, 2003, 2012).

It worked with the knowledge of the body, that

> [...] does not imply the exposition of bodily skills, though there is an intimate correlation of bodily knowledge and body's skills. The living body acquires knowledge by doing, moving itself, by not only aimless wandering, but also practicing socially and culturally shaped skills. (Parviainen 2002: 20)

Similarly, the dancers and researchers Hammergren, Lilja, and Román (2007) show how movement, perception, kinaesthetic consciousness, and the physical sense can be included in research as tools to generate and analyze data.

In dance the kind of knowledge that is not considered acceptable elsewhere becomes important. Our physical memories emerge as events of significance. Scents, tastes, movements, feelings, thoughts . . . The unexpressed . . . What is it that makes us believe that we know anything? Every day we tread the paths of memory and wander around in the tracks of what has been. I see this; I observe it. And then my work can take off and move forward. My body is my dwelling-place. I move within a context. My movement expresses my place, and it is through the body that I turn it into experience. (Lilja 2007)

The dance movement therapist Ylönen (2003, 2004) also bases her studies on the connection between physical existence and cognition, and uses dance as a method of investigation, creating a physical dialogue in dance between the participants of the investigation and the researcher herself. In the same way, she facilitates the contact with *prenoetic* factors (Gallagher 2005, p. 151), describing these aspects of our consciousness that normally do not enter into the phenomenal content of experience in an explicit way—aspects that are therefore often inaccessible to reflective consciousness.

An essential part of the creative process is the ongoing dialogue and exchange between unconscious and conscious practice, as described by Hartley:

The conscious mind penetrates the unconscious and unexpressed areas of the body, awakening awareness in the body and integrating body and mind into a coherent whole. (Hartley 2004, p. 55)

Chodorow (1994) points out how movement can activate both conscious and unconscious processes: on the one hand it may help to reinforce the ego-position by setting clear body boundaries and orientation in space, while on the other hand, movement can also open us to our inner worlds and the unconscious psyche. Through full devotion to the unconscious it may speak to us through our movement, and *move* us, allowing for very important information to emerge from unknown places. The movement analyst and dance movement therapist Kaylo (2004) confirms that 'bodily consciousness is our most primordial, underlying awareness of existence' (4).

CONCLUSIONS

This chapter has portrayed the important move from a Cartesian split between bodies and mind to a more holistic, integrated vision, as described by the embodiment approaches. It has shown how recent contributions from philosophy, neuroscience, and neurolinguistics have helped to gain a new view of the body, thus opening the dimension of a feeling, sensing, and thinking body. The different types of body memories that have been defined highlight the tacit dimension of the body and stress the inescapable contribution of embodiment to cognition. Aspects that are often inaccessible to reflective consciousness can be accessed through movement, as confirmed by Panhofer's (2009) study: movement finds a way to these prenoetic factors (Gallagher 2005) and thus lends us a valuable tool to reach out for this *knowledge behind the scene*.

It is hoped that this chapter will provide encouragement for educators, therapists, and researchers in dance and movement to step with confidence into the post-Cartesian area and use the knowledge base which is their bodies, to increase understanding of self in space and time, in their professional fields.

NOTE

1. The German language includes two words for 'body': *Körper* and *Leib*. Edmund Husserl, in his late phenomenology, stressed that the physical body (*Körper*) and the living/lived body (*Leib*) are essentially different (Husserl 1960, p. 97; Husserl 1970, p. 107).

REFERENCES

Anttila, E. (2007). 'Mind the body. Unearthing the affiliation between the conscious body and the reflective mind', in L. Rouhiainen (ed.), *Ways of Knowing in Dance and Art*. Yliopistopaino: Finnish Academy and the Arts Council of Finland.

Atkins, K. (2008). *Narrative Identity and Moral Identity: A Practical Perspective*. London: Routledge.

Bartenieff, I. (1980). *Body Movement: Coping with the Environment*. New York, NY: Gordon and Breach.

Behnke, E. A. (2012). 'Enduring: A phenomenological investigation', in S. Koch, T. Fuchs, M. Summa, and C. Müller (eds.), *Body Memory, Metaphor and Movement*. Amsterdam: John Benjamins.

Bourdieu, P. (1990). *The Logic of Practice*, transl. R. Nice. Stanford, CA: Stanford University Press.

Chodorow, J. (1991). *Dance Therapy and Depth Psychology: The Moving Imagination*. London: Routledge.

Coffey, A. and Atkinson P. (1996). *Making Sense of Qualitative Data: Complementary Research Strategies*. Thousand Oaks, CA: Sage Publications.

Csordas, T. (1993). 'Somatic modes of attention', *Cultural Anthropology*, 8(2): 135–56.

Damasio A. (1994). *Descartes' Error: Emotion, Reason and Human Brain*. London: Harper Collins.

Eisner, E. (1981). 'On the differences between scientific and artistic approaches to qualitative inquiry', *Teachers College Record*, 78(3): 345–58.

Fuchs, T. (2001). 'The tacit dimension', *Philosophy, Psychiatry, and Psychology*, 8(4): 323–6.

Fuchs, T. (2003). *The Memory of the Body*, unpublished manuscript, <http://www.klinikum. uniheidelberg.de/fileadmin/zpm/psychatrie/ppp2004/manuskript/fuchs.pdf> (accessed 8 December 2008)

Fuchs, T. (2012). 'The phenomenology of body memory', in S. Koch, T. Fuchs, M. Summa, and C. Müller (eds.). *Body Memory, Metaphor and Movement*. Amsterdam: John Benjamins.

Gallagher, S. (2005). *How the Body Shapes the Mind*. New York, NY: Oxford University Press.

Gallagher, S. (2008). 'Philosophical antecedents to situated cognition', in P. Robbins and M. Aydede (eds.), *The Cambridge Handbook of Situated Cognition*. Cambridge: Cambridge University Press.

Hämäläinen, S. (2007). 'The meaning of bodily knowledge in a creative dance-making process', in L. Rouhiainen (ed.), *Ways of Knowing in Dance and Art*. Yliopistopaino: Finnish Academy and the Arts Council of Finland.

Hannula, M. (2004). 'River low, mountain high: Contextualizing artistic research', in A. W. Balkema and H. Slager (eds.), *Artistic Research*. Amsterdam: Rodopi.

Hartley, L. (2004). *Somatic Psychology: Body, Mind and Meaning*. London: Whurr Publishers.

Hervey-Wadsworth, L. (2000). *Artistic Inquiry in Dance/Movement Therapy: Creative Alternatives for Research*. Springfield, IL: Charles C. Thomas.

Husserl, E. (1960). *Cartesian Meditation: An Introduction to Phenomenology*, transl. D. Cairns. The Hague: Martinus Nijoff.

Husserl, E. (1970). *The Crisis of European Sciences and Transcendental Phenomenology* [*Die Krisis der europäischen Wissenschaften und die transzendentale Phianomenologie: Eine Einleitung in die phanomenologische Philosophie*, 1954], transl. D. Carr. Evanston, IL: Northwestern University Press.

Kaylo, J. (2004). 'The body in phenomenology and movement observation', *E-motion*, XIV(7): 4–7.

Koltai, J. (1994). 'Authentic movement: The embodied experience of text', *Canadian Theatre Review*, 78: 21–5.

Kövecses, Z. (2003). *Metaphor and Emotion. Language, Culture, and Body in Human Feeling*. Cambridge: Cambridge University Press.

Laban, R. (1987). *El Dominio del Movimiento*. Madrid: Ed Fundamentos.

Laban, R. (1988). *Die Kunst der Bewegung*. Wilhelmshaven: Heinrichshofen Verlag.

Laban, R. (1991). *La Danza Educativa Moderna*. Mexico: Ed Paidós.

Labov, W. (1972). *Language in the Inner City*. Philadelphia, PA: University of Pennsylvania Press.

Lakoff, G. and Johnson, M. (1999a). *Philosophy in the Flesh: The Embodied Mind and its Challenge to Western Thought*. New York, NY: Basic Books.

Lakoff, G. and Johnson, M. (2003). *Metaphors We Live By*. London: University of Chicago Press.

Lilja, E. (2007). <http://www.doch.se/forskning/publikationer/bestall_material/movement_as_the_memory_of_the_body>, accessed 27 August 2012.

Luria, A. R. (1973). *The Working Brain: An Introduction to Neuropsychology*. Harmsworth: Penguin Books.

Lyons-Ruth, K., Harrison, A. M., Morgan, A. C., Nahum, J. P., Sander, L., Stern, D. N., and Tronick, E. Z. (1998). 'Implicit relational knowing: Its role in development and psychoanalytic treatment', *Infant Mental Health Journal*, 19(3): 282–9.

Marczak, M. and Sewell, M. (2007). 'Using focus groups for evaluation', <http://ag.arizona.edu/fcs/cyfernet/cyfar/focus.htm> (accessed 27 November 2007).

McNiff, S. (1986). 'Freedom of research and artistic inquiry', *The Arts in Psychotherapy*, 13(4): 279–84.

McNiff, S. (1992). *Art as Medicine*. Boston, MA: Shambhala Books.

McNiff, S. (1993). 'The authority of experience', *The Arts in Psychotherapy*, 20: 3–9.

McNiff, S. (1998). *Art-Based Research*. London: Jessica Kingsley.

Meekums, B. (2006). 'Embodiment in dance movement therapy training and practice', in H. Payne (ed.), *Dance Movement Therapy: Theory, Research and Practice*. Hove: Brunner-Routledge, pp.167–83.

Merleau-Ponty, M. (1962). *Phenomenology of Perception*. London: Routledge and Kegan Paul.

Merleau-Ponty, M. (1964). *The Primacy of Perception*, transl. C. Smith. London: Routledge.

North, M. (1990). *Personality Assessment through Movement*. Plymouth: Northcote House.

Panhofer, H. (2009). *New Approaches to Communicate the Embodied Experience in Dance Movement Psychotherapy*. Unpublished PhD thesis, submitted in partial fulfilment of the requirements of the University of Hertfordshire.

Panhofer, H. (2011). 'Languaged and non-languaged ways of knowing in counselling and psychotherapy', *British Journal of Guidance and Counselling*, 39(5): 455–70.

Panhofer, H., Payne, H., Meekums, B., and Parke, T. (2011a). 'The space between body and mind: Two models for group supervision', *10th ECARTE European Consortium for Arts Therapies Education. Ecarte e-publication*. <http://www.ecarte.info/> (accessed 14 January 2014).

Panhofer, H., Payne, H., Meekums, B., and Parke, T. (2011b). 'Dancing, moving and writing in clinical supervision? Employing embodied practices in psychotherapy supervision', *The Arts in Psychotherapy*, 38: 9–16.

Panhofer, H., Payne, H., Meekums, B., and Parke, T. (2012). 'The embodied word', in S. Koch, T. Fuchs, and C. Müller (eds.), *Body Memory, Metaphor and Movement*. Amsterdam: John Benjamins.

Panksepp, J. (2006b). 'Examples of application of the affective neuroscience strategy to clinical issues', in J. Corrigall, H. Payne, and H. Wilkinson (eds.), *About a Body: Working with the Embodied Mind in Psychotherapy*. London: Routledge.

Parviainen, J. (2002). 'Bodily knowledge: Epistemological reflections on dance', *Dance Research Journal*, 34(1): 1123.

Parviainen, J. (2003). 'Dance techne: Kinetic bodily logos and thinking in movement', *Nordisk Estetisk Tidskrift*, 27: 8.

Payne, H. (2006). 'The body as container and expresser. Authentic movement groups in the development of well being in our body mind spirit', in J. Corrigall, H. Payne, and H. Wilkinson (eds.), *About a Body: Working with the Embodied Mind in Psychotherapy*. London: Routledge.

Polanyi, M. (1967). *The Tacit Dimension*. Garden City, NY: Doubleday.

Polanyi, M. (1969). 'Sense-giving and sense-reading', in M. Grene (ed.), *Knowing and Being: Essays by Michael Polanyi*. Chicago, IL: University of Chicago Press.

Polanyi M. (1983). *The Tacit Dimension*. Gloucester, MA: Peter Smith.

Riley, S. R. (2004). 'Embodied perceptual practices: Towards an embrained and embodied model of mind for use in actor training and rehearsal', *Theatre Topics*, 14(2): 445–71.

Selar-Smith, S. (2002). 'Heuristic research: A review and critique of Moustakas's method', *Journal of Humanistic Psychology* 42: 53–88. doi: 10.1177/0022167802423004

Sheets-Johnstone, M. (1999). *The Primacy of Movement*. Amsterdam/Philadelphia: John Benjamins.

Sheets-Johnstone, M. (2007). Dance, movement, and bodies: Forays into the non-linguistic and the challenge of languaging experience: Evening II. Retrieved from http://www.youtube.com/watch?v_-pTxptDPQzI.

Sheets-Johnstone, M. (2009). *The Corporeal Turn: An Interdisciplinary Reader*. Exeter: Imprint Academic.

Smith, M. L. (2002). 'Moving self: The thread which bridges dance and theatre', *Research in Dance Education*, 3(2): 123–41.

Sparkes, A. C. (2002). *Telling Tales in Sport and Physical Activity. A Qualitative Journey*. Leeds: Human Kinetics.

Sparkes, A. (2003). 'Bodies, identities, selves: Autoethnografic fragments and reflections', in T. Denison and P. Markula (eds.), *Moving Writing: Crafting Movement in Sport and Research*. New York, NY: Peter Lang, pp. 51–76.

Stewart, D. W. and Shamdasani, P. N. (1990). *Focus Groups: Theory and Practice. Applied Social Research Methods Series*, vol. 20. Newbury Park, CA: Sage Publications.

Toolan, M. (2005). *Narrative: A Critical Linguistic Introduction*. 2nd edn. London: Routledge.

Whitehouse, M. (1978). 'Conversation with Mary Whitehouse and Frieda Sherman', *American Journal of Dance Therapy*, 2(2): 3–4.

Winther, H. (2008). 'Body contact and body language: Moments of personal development and social and cultural learning processes in movement teaching and education', *Forum Qualitative Sozialforschung/Forum: Qualitative Social Research*, 9(2): Art. 63, <http://nbn-resolving.de/urn:nbn:de:0114-fqs0802637> (accessed 7 January 2009).

Ylönen, M. (2003). 'Bodily flashes of dancing women: Dance as a method of inquiry', *Qualitative Inquiry*, 9(4): 554–68.

Ylönen, M. (2004). 'A dance by mother and daughter', *The Arts in Psychotherapy*, 3: 11–17.

....

CHAPTER 7

LISTENING TO THE MOVING BODY

Movement Approaches in Body Psychotherapy

....

LAURA HOPE STECKLER

Movement is our mother tongue.

Maxine Sheets-Johnstone (2011, p. xxv)

INTRODUCTION

....

IN a performance project entitled 'Hologram', I spent a number of weeks with a group of dancers attempting to sense each cell of our bodies as a hologram of the universe. I came upon the idea for this project after one of my Body Psychotherapy clients told me she felt as if she held the entire cosmos in her body. Figure 7.1, 'Touching galaxies' captures this notion for me.[1] We found this to be a nourishing and at times evocative process; I felt there were parallels with this process and Body Psychotherapy. There were also parallels with the work of other dance practitioners and body practitioners such as Deborah Hay's (2000) work in which she invites dancers to be aware of each cell of their bodies. For this to happen we often worked in a very slow and meditative manner, focusing more on our internal state than external form, similar to the way Butoh dancers work.

We discovered (or rediscovered) the wonderful capacity we have for sensation and awareness in all parts of our bodies, particularly when we slow down and allow ourselves to be still. As we do so, we can tap into the holographic nature of the body in which each aspect links into and holds every other aspect.

In this chapter I will discuss some of the therapeutic benefits that such attention, especially in conjunction with movement, can engender. The movement interventions described will elucidate the holographic concept as they reflect how emotions, memories, images, and psychological dynamics are held within the body.

FIGURE 7.1. 'Touching Galaxies, Video still from 'Hologram'. (Credit: Sabine Klaus-Carter, Creation Editor, and Laura Hope Steckler, Body/Theatre, 2011.)

I will describe how movement can be used in Body Psychotherapy and will provide examples from my clinical practice. There are a myriad of movement approaches available to the Body Psychotherapist, and this chapter is not meant to be exhaustive in its description of these, but to demonstrate some better-known approaches and those with which I am most familiar. I have done my best to credit techniques and approaches with their originators. Some approaches are widespread and longstanding, and it is difficult to determine their origins. I apologize for any such omissions. I draw on my training and experience as a Body Psychotherapist as well as my dance training.

I will consider 'movement' and 'dance' as interchangeable. Dance tends to be more deliberate in its execution than many of the movement approaches in Body Psychotherapy, and one might argue that the approaches that I present are not, in fact, dance. There is not the use of rhythm or music that one typically associates with dance. Nonetheless, they still focus on the moving body and thus are included in this chapter and in this book, because they can be seen as dance in a wider definition of the term that includes gestures, postures, pedestrian movement, and deeply felt bodily experiences.

WHAT IS BODY PSYCHOTHERAPY?

Body-oriented Psychotherapy—also referred to as Somatic Psychotherapy or Somatic Psychology—'takes into account the complexity of the intersections and interactions between body and mind' (European Association of Body Psychotherapy 2011, <http://www.eabp.org/about.php>). Body Psychotherapists believe that becoming aware of the body, and processing our somatic experiences, can help us better regulate our emotions and understand ourselves, leading to greater wellbeing.

There is a belief amongst Body Psychotherapists that when we make changes to how we move, our posture, and how we use our bodies, our emotional and psychological functioning may also change simultaneously. These processes often require deep attention and listening to the body, with stillness and emptiness.

We move continuously as long as we are alive. We breathe, our hearts beat, our cells divide and replenish. We are always buzzing and vibrating. Therefore, movement can be seen as a key aspect of life. While the body is the main area of attention for Body Psychotherapists, movement is the main focus and therapeutic agent in Dance Movement Psychotherapy. Body Psychotherapy and Dance Movement Psychotherapy are independent fields, having developed in different but parallel and potentially intertwining streams, as suggested by Steckler (2006) and by Payne et al. (2016). Some Body Psychotherapists integrate movement therapy methods in their work. Most, however, tend to use smaller, gestural movements or prescribe certain movement patterns to achieve particular therapeutic goals. A basic 'functional competency' of a Body Psychotherapist includes the utilization in therapy of 'channels of communication including touch, gaze, gesture, (and) movement' (Boening et al. 2012, p. 9). Thus Body Psychotherapists are aware of both gross and micromovement in their clients and how to use these psychotherapeutically.

Body Psychotherapy should be distinguished from body therapies such as massage and other forms of bodywork which may have positive psychological benefits but do not incorporate psychotherapeutic processes (Payne et al. 2016).

I am primarily a Body Psychotherapist, not a Dance Movement Psychotherapist. However, since I have had considerable dance training, movement has greatly influenced my work.

Theoretical and Methodological Influences

The Body Psychotherapy influences that are important for this chapter include the method that forms the foundation of my own work: the Rubenfeld Synergy® method (RSM). This method is a synthesis of the Alexander technique (a method of body awareness and education that facilitates more efficient use of the body in activity and stillness), the Feldenkrais® method (another movement education method that uses both hands-on bodywork and prescribed movement practices), and Gestalt Therapy, a humanistic approach to psychotherapy (Perls et al. 1951).

Rubenfeld Synergy® integrates subtle touch and movement with therapeutic verbal dialogue in a cohesive and integrated manner. Ilana Rubenfeld, the developer of the method, is widely considered to be a pioneer in the field of Body-oriented Psychotherapy.

Other significant influences on my work include:

- Bioenergetics (Lowen 1976), developed from the work of Wilhelm Reich.
- Somatic experiencing (Levine 1997).
- Authentic movement (Pallaro 1999; 2007).
- Marcher's bodynamic approach (Marcher and Fich 2010).
- Babette Rothschild (Rothschild 2000).
- Hakomi (Kurtz 2008; Weiss et al. 2015).
- Body-Mind Centering (Cohen 1993).
- 'Mindfulness-based' approaches to therapy (e.g. Segal et al. 2002).
- The disciplines of Butoh dance, dance improvisation, tai chi, chi gong, and yoga.

Psychodynamic and Object Relations theories are also included along with Jungian theory—all developments of Freud's Psychoanalytic theory (Freud and Bonaparte 2009) and Gestalt Therapy (a fundamental part of RSM) characterized by present-moment emotional awareness and expression. I include the emerging research into the psychobiology of trauma (e.g. Van der Kolk 2014) and the psychobiology of child development and human relationships (e.g. Schore 2003; Stern 1995).

Movement in Trauma-Focused Work

Many clients who come for Body-oriented Psychotherapy have been traumatized. They may have been abused or neglected as children. A lack of bonding, secure attachment, or dysregulated attunement by early caregivers can also be considered traumatic. Such experiences during the early developmental stages of life are often referred to as 'developmental trauma', and can have lasting effects on the body/mind (Cozolino 2002; Schore 2003; Van der Kolk 2014).

Body-based therapies, among others, have become important in supporting clients to recover from trauma, in what is known as 'bottom-up processing' (Van der Kolk et al. 1996). Traditional 'talking therapy' tends to be cognitive in nature, traditionally disregards somatic phenomena, and is thus considered as a 'top-down' approach. The growing understanding that the more primitive and less conscious parts of the brain are affected by trauma and need to be harnessed in treatment has led to the development of a number of somatically-based approaches that often include movement.

'Freeze' Response

Rothschild (2002)—a Body Psychotherapist specializing in trauma—asks people *not* to move for two minutes in her workshops. This is incredibly difficult. Our bodies are meant to move! Yet this is what happens in trauma. This is the result of what is known as the 'freeze' response in trauma. When confronted with danger, the instinctive and evolutionarily ancient aspects of our nervous systems gear up to either fight or flee. If we cannot do either, we freeze. This is akin to an animal 'playing dead'. However, the animal is not actually playing. She/he is overwhelmed with both arousing and subduing chemicals simultaneously, leading automatically to sudden and dramatic immobility (Rothschild 2000).

Many clients are stuck in such immobility long after a traumatic event has occurred, and one often observes a tendency towards excessive containment and rigidity in the bodies of such clients. Conversely, they may also be excessively floppy, without energy or tonus in their muscles. It seems natural, then, that the path to healing should include movement.

Ruth, a Frozen Child

Ruth was repeatedly raped by her father from a very young age.[2] If she tried to resist him he became more aggressive and punitive. The only thing she could do to survive was to keep still and quiet. She did what many victims of abuse do: she dissociated.

Dissociation is a very common response to unbearable and unmanageable stress (e.g. Van der Kolk 2014). It is a splitting of consciousness so that the unbearable experience is pushed to the side as if it were not happening. Ruth felt as if she were on the ceiling during the abuse. She developed a part of her personality that was split off from the rest of her awareness that believed it was dangerous to move. This part of her was very young and extraordinarily frightened. This phenomenon is known as 'dissociative identity disorder' (American Psychiatric Association 2013), and is also known as 'multiple personality disorder' (World Health Organization 1992), popularized in the media by the book *Sybil* (Schreiber 1973), which also became a television miniseries.

The frozen part of Ruth was stuck in the past experiences of abuse. She felt that if she moved she would be in danger and would be 'bad'. I felt that she needed to be gradually encouraged to move and to see that she was safe in doing so.

I spent one session with her blowing bubbles and asking her to watch them and sense that she could move her eyes. I later played a movement game with her in which I would tap out a rhythm with my hand and she would mirror me. Eventually she was able to initiate these rhythms herself and to move her entire body.

MOVEMENT IN IMAGINATION

Movement done in imagination (ideokinesis) has a measurable impact on the neuromuscular system (Sweigard 1974). Athletes and dancers often use imaginal movement to rehearse, train, or prepare for performance, without overtaxing their bodies. Recent developments in this area have allowed paralyzed patients to interface with computers so that they can use imagined movement to control equipment such as artificial limbs, a wheelchair, and other devices (e.g. Hochberg et al. 2006).

Marcher (Marcher and Fish 2010) and Levine (1997) both encourage clients to imagine themselves running to safety from early traumatic experiences. This may facilitate re-engagement of neuromuscular patterns and modulation of the fight/flight/freeze response (Picton 2004). Feldenkrais (1972) utilized ideokinesis to improve neuromuscular function. In RSM, ideokinesis is used to get in touch with and shift affective material.

Sharon's Dance

I once asked a client, Sharon, who was in a very dark period of her life, if she could find an image of herself in a better place. She was still for a long time while my hands were under her back, listening to the subtle movements taking place. Eventually an image emerged. She quietly said that she could see herself dancing. I encouraged her to stay with this image and sense what it felt like in her body in detail. She began to have pleasant sensations in her body for the first time in a long while. She felt tingling and warm wave-like sensations. This was a turning point in her therapy.

We could postulate that, as Sharon imagined herself dancing, she began to release neurochemicals such as beta-endorphins (our natural inborn opioids) and oxytocin (which promotes wellbeing and connectedness to others) into her bloodstream (Carter 2012). Perhaps this was a catalyst for something that was dormant within her, or perhaps, like William Arthur Ward (1970, p. 14) has stated: 'If you can imagine it, you can achieve it; if you can dream it, you can become it.'

MOVING OUR CLIENTS

In Rubenfeld Synergy® we sometimes use passive movement to facilitate freedom in the joints by moving a client's limbs in their sockets. Any blocks to freedom in these joints seem to have an emotional correlate.

When we move our clients in this way, this may connect them to very early emotional states. It may unconsciously remind the person of when they were totally helpless and had to have their diaper changed, or to be bathed and dressed by someone else. This can be a powerful intervention, especially for those who have had early experiences of abuse or neglect.

Sonya Allows Herself to be Moved

I was holding Sonya's right arm and moving it slowly and gently in its socket. This brought up feelings of guilt, as she felt she did not deserve this sort of nurturing and support, and that she should help me do it. She was concerned that her arm might be too heavy for me. I believed that this tied into her early parenting experiences. Her mother had had postnatal depression and had been inconsistent in attending to her daughter. Sonya was, at times, not fed when she was hungry, or changed when she was wet. Her crying was at times met with indifference or hostility. Sonya's mother often behaved as if her daughter was 'too much' for her.

This sort of early parenting may lead to what are known as 'attachment difficulties', the most severe of which is called a 'chaotic' or 'disorganized' attachment (Ainsworth et al. 1978; Main and Solomon 1986). Attachment theory suggests that the nature of our attachment to our original caregivers forms an indelible blueprint for later relationships (Bowlby 1988). Thus, people with such a history will find relationships challenging as adults, and their sense of self-worth and identity will be compromised. It may be difficult for them to modulate their emotions, to trust others, to feel authentic, and to have a sense of safety in the world.

I believe that revisiting these early experiences on a somatic level, and being met with consistency and unconditional positive regard (Rogers 1951), as well as accurate and sensitive attunement (Stern 1995), can help people develop a greater sense of internal safety.

If we have had the experience of being handled roughly and with disregard to our somatic experience as a child (that is, lack of attunement), then having someone listening deeply to our bodies can be healing. Body Psychotherapists pay attention to a client when she resists, when she lets go, when she has discomfort, and when her body has reached its limit of stretch or rotation. By honouring these boundaries and not pushing or criticizing the person, they are providing mirroring on a somatic level.

We know it is important for our development to receive verbal mirroring (see Bateman and Fonagy 2003). This means that our caregivers reflect back to us what we say and how we feel such that we feel validated and helps us have a sense of belonging. Our nonverbal behaviour can also be mirrored, and it is felt that this is also important for normal child development in being able to develop understanding and acceptance of ourselves and others (see Gergely and Watson 1996). This may be why we tend to instinctively mirror the movements and facial expressions of babies.

Traditional talking therapy can provide the verbal aspect of mirroring. Body-oriented Psychotherapy can add a somatic layer that talking therapy may not. Dance movement psychotherapists use the mirroring of movement therapeutically (see chapters 6 and 47 on Dance Movement Therapy in this handbook). Body Psychotherapists may also use similar techniques.

Children may blame themselves for their parents' lack of attunement, abuse, and neglect. Fairbairn has termed this the 'moral defence' (Fairbairn 1952). This is because a child will do almost anything to maintain the bond with their caregivers. To blame the caregiver might threaten the bond. It feels safer to blame oneself, leading to feelings of shame and low self-worth. Thus, Sonya did not believe she deserved support. She could not trust that any support or nurturing she did get was going to be safe and stable.

I suggested that Sonya experiment with (a) holding onto her arm and helping me, and then with (b) letting go of it and allowing me to support her. We explored the part of her that wanted to help me, as well as the part of her that yearned for, but was afraid of, being supported. We were able to work through these issues, and she eventually was able to let go of her arm. She could 'be moved', physically and metaphorically. Sonya later expressed amazement that she felt guilty 'just from movement'. She began to 'let go' of certain beliefs about her own worth and loveability, and her self-acceptance began to increase.

Movement as a Reflection of the Unconscious Mind

A goal of many forms of psychotherapy—particularly Psychodynamic Psychotherapy—is to help the client become more aware of unconscious material and integrate this into consciousness. In psychodynamic theory, emotional difficulties arise when clients have developed defence mechanisms to avoid being aware of this unconscious material, which they would otherwise find too threatening.

Body Psychotherapists often see subtle movements, gestures, and postural habits as 'leaking' unconscious material, as if the body is sending messages from the unconscious. One client's feet begin to contract without his noticing; another makes a fist; another places her hand on her cheek; another tightens her legs to cover her genitals. Whatever these gestures are, it is useful to bring these to the clients' awareness. It is as if the body sends messages from the unconscious mind; as if it holds what Jung (1965) calls the 'shadow' or the unconscious, unaccepted, and unprocessed emotions, thoughts, and feelings.

We can ask clients to repeat and exaggerate these movements or perform them in slow motion to promote awareness. This facilitates the message from the body to come to consciousness, where it can be processed. As clients become aware of the meaning of their unconscious movements, they can begin to understand and accept themselves. They can become more authentic and let go of the defences and masks—sometimes known as the 'false self' (Winnicott 1960).

Mitch Connects with Self-Soothing

Mitch kept rubbing his chest as he spoke of his relationship difficulties. His partner had been asking him to help with household chores. At times he resented doing these things, in spite of the fact that he wanted to help her. He then felt guilty about his resentment.

I asked Mitch to become aware of the movement his hands were making in rubbing his chest. He was able to attend to it with an attitude of curiosity. If we are to receive these messages from the body, we must let go of expectations about what we 'think they should mean', and really just listen to them in a mindful non-judgemental manner.

After a time, Mitch stated that this movement felt good to him. It was as if he were comforting and soothing himself. I invited him to carry on with the movement, but to slow it down so that his attention to it could become even more focused and subtle.

I knew that Mitch came from a family in which he felt he had to take care of his parents, rather than the other way around. I suspected that he did not really know how to nurture himself, either physically or emotionally.

As Mitch listened to this slow nurturing movement, he was able to get in touch with his deep longing for nurturing and support. He became tearful, and so began a process of grieving the loss of the nurturing that was his birthright but was never received.

In a later session, this same movement emerged again. This time I invited him to let this movement grow and expand. He began to stroke himself not only on his chest, but on his head, arms, and legs. He found this powerful as he became aware, at a deep level, of his ability to support and nurture himself. He began to report that he was feeling stronger in himself and was better able to cope with the challenges of life and relationships.

LISTENING TO STILLNESS

The longer I practise psychotherapy, the more I believe in the old adage that 'less is more'. This is a tenet of the Feldenkrais Method, in which micromovements are done in a slow and focused manner, leading to changes in the neuromuscular system such that movement becomes more fluid. Similarly, being with a client in stillness, without words, can be powerful. I believe that when we add touch to this stillness, we multiply the power exponentially.

My training with Rubenfeld involved learning, over several years, to develop sensitivity in my hands. We use a 'listening touch' (Rubenfeld 2000)—a similar technique used by cranial-sacral therapists (e.g. Kern 2005).

In practical terms we usually work with the client on a massage table, fully clothed. When I have my hands under a client's shoulder, for example, I can begin to perceive movement of various sorts. This movement seems to resonate with what the client is saying or thinking. I often begin a session by asking my client to find a message or image to send into their body, and can often determine whether they have done so by the movement I sense in my hands. Conversely, I can recognize when the message does not get through, through a sense of stagnancy.

Generally speaking, when a client is in touch with him/herself and the therapeutic process is moving well, the energy will feel circular and full, or wave-like. I often sense a 'flowering' of energy, as the person moves through a difficult issue. In a highly traumatized client, the energy often feels as if it is vibrating or oscillating very rapidly. This reduces over time in therapy. I see these phenomena as similar to what is described by cranial-sacral therapists as movement of the cerebrospinal fluid (e.g. Kern 2005). At times I will feel pain, as the client lets go of painful material. At other times I will feel a sharp pushing, which I generally interpret as the person's system wanting me to move away from them at that time, which I honour. The video still 'Immersion' (Figure 7.2) captures something of my experience of this.

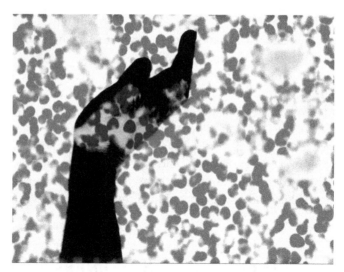

FIGURE 7.2. 'Immersion, Video still from 'Hologram'. (Credit: Sabine Klaus-Carter, Creation Editor, and Laura Hope Steckler, Body/Theatre, 2011.)

Sam Finds his Boundaries

When Sam was aged 12, his mother summoned him into her room, when she was undressed. This was a boundary violation, and inappropriate in most cultures. In addition, she would often complain about his father at these times, putting him in an untenable position given his loyalty to both parents. He was describing this to me, and my hands were under his left shoulder blade and upper back. I asked Sam how he felt during these occasions. He said: 'It was normal.' I immediately felt a constriction of energy and a tightening in his back. I asked him to become aware of sensations in his body. We stayed in stillness for some time. After a minute or two, he also became aware of this tightening. I said that I wondered if his body believed what he had just said. He then burst out with: 'No! It was not normal! It was incredibly weird!' He became upset, and I felt a release of energy in his back simultaneously. Months later, things began to shift for him in his capacity for intimacy in relationships.

At times I use listening touch in total silence and mirror back to the body the movement that I feel in my hands through subtle micromovement of my hands. This tends to lead to a sense of wellbeing in the client, and at times, an alleviation of pain or other symptoms.

MOVEMENT WITH AN INTERNAL FOCUS

In Japanese, 'Butoh' simply means 'dance step'. However, the word has taken on the meaning of a particular type of movement-based performance work that evolved post-World War II as a reaction to the establishment at the time. It has roots in Kabuki and Noh theatre, and has often reflected the horror of Japan's exposure to the atomic bomb (see, for example, Fraleigh 2010).

Butoh performers embody elements such as stone, wood, animals, or young children. They seem to slowly and effortlessly transform from one archetypal state to another. This may be the result of Butoh training, which involves the use of internally focused states, as opposed to external form. 'Suriashi'—which means 'walking'—is one such method, requiring deep concentration and awareness of the whole body, as well as the environment. It is often done very slowly with a low centre of gravity, but may also be done quickly.

In a therapeutic context, Suriashi can be used to promote 'affect regulation', or the ability to tolerate and manage strong emotions. In clients who feel overwhelmed by emotion, I have used Suriashi and the slow transformational practices of Butoh to help them acquire a sense of control and grounding of emotional states.

This has been particularly useful with clients with 'Emotionally Unstable Personalities'—also known as 'Borderline Personality Disorder' (American Psychiatric Association 2013)—most of whom have had multiple traumas throughout their lives, and find emotions so difficult to tolerate that they often resort to self-harm in order to cope.

Sometimes I simply walk slowly with my client, keeping ourselves connected by retaining the same speed and distance between us. This can give the client a sense that she or he does not have to rush or perform in the therapeutic process—that we can simply 'be together'. For clients who have never had a relaxed calm connection with another, this can be soothing.

Susan's Walk with Anger

Another use of Suriashi can be seen in my work with Susan, who had been horrifically sexually abused by her father. She had, for many years, repressed the rage that she felt towards him. She was terrified of experiencing this rage, but at the same time knew that it was bottled up inside her and needed some form of expression. She had at times been suicidal when in touch with her rage, and harmed herself brutally, burning or cutting herself.

In one session we used Suriashi to help with anger. Beginning in stillness, we began to walk side by side. We walked slowly, feeling each moment of contact with the floor, staying in contact with all parts of the body at once, as well as sensing our connection with each other. I then asked her to begin to allow her feelings of anger to develop in her body, noticing where she experienced them, what sensations they created, and how they affected her breathing, yet still walking slowly with awareness. I then asked her to let them grow slowly until we reached the far wall, at which point they would be at their strongest. We then turned around and invited the angry feelings to slowly diminish. This practice helped this vulnerable woman to accept and tolerate her deep and potentially violent rage in a contained and safe manner.

Movement Prescriptions

Many Body Psychotherapists prescribe particular movement patterns and exercises for their clients. Lowen and Lowen (1977) describe a number of Bioenergetics exercises which offer opportunities to 'break through' chronic muscular holding patterns, to create and discharge energy, and to promote energy flow, grounding, and emotional expression. They are inherently mindful in their nature, as they are performed with moment-to-moment awareness of how the body feels while doing the movements. The breath is integrated into the movement patterns. There are exercises to enhance sexuality and joy, to express anger, and to free the muscles of the face.

Lowen and Lowen (1977) are quick to offer the caveat that Bioenergetics exercises do not constitute therapy in and of themselves, and I concur. Any prescribed movement practices are adjunctive to, not the core basis of, Body-oriented Psychotherapy.

Claire Fights Back

I used a popular Bioenergetics exercise with a client, Claire, who had what Levine (1997) might consider as an 'incomplete defensive movement pattern'. Claire had been sexually assaulted as a teenager and had never received any support from her family, medical professionals, or school-teachers about this event. It still haunted her as a young adult. During a session, when we were processing this event, she remembered what it felt like to be pinned down and unable to move. She became panicky, even though she knew where she was and that she was safe.

I asked Claire to sense what movement her body felt like doing to escape. She became aware that her legs wanted to kick. I invited her to do so, and at the same time to shout 'No!' At first she felt unable to do so, but with encouragement she eventually 'came unstuck' and was able to complete the sound and movement practice. This facilitated her ability to move on from this terrible experience.

Ilana Rubenfeld's body–mind exercises evolved from Feldenkrais movement sequences. They are also mindful in nature and integrate the use of the breath with movement. As in Bioenergetics exercises, they can provide a deep sense of internal connection to, and flow in, the body. While Bioenergetics exercises can be highly vigorous, these movement sequences tend to be slow, subtle, and meditative. I learned many of these in my training with Rubenfeld.

In these exercises the body learns to find the easiest and most integrated pathway to movement. Movements are done repeatedly on one side of the body, with frequent mindful rests in between. As changes occur in the active side of the body, these are integrated into the nervous system during these rests. The information is passed on to the other side of the body via the corpus collosum in the brain, such that when the other side of the body becomes active, the movement is already easier. As movement becomes more integrated we seem to feel more whole in ourselves. This is important, as early emotional wounding tends to lead to a fragmented sense of self (Kohut and Wolf 1978). The development of a sense of wholeness and coherence in the body may support integration.

Here is an example of a Rubenfeld body–mind exercise. Ilana calls this exercise the 'bamboo', as she likes to use the image of a flexible bamboo plant while sensing the spine when doing the movements.

Beginning seated in a chair, move away from the back of the chair so that you can feel your sitting bones beneath you . . . Notice if you are leaning more heavily onto one or the other of your sitting bones . . . Notice how your spine is rising up from your pelvis and how your head is balanced at the top . . . Now slowly and mindfully allow your EYES to move to the RIGHT and allow your head neck and torso to go along for the ride . . . Rotate to the RIGHT as far as you can without straining. When you have reached a point where your body says 'stop', notice what you can see here and make a mental note of what it is.

Next pass your RIGHT hand over the top of your head to cover your LEFT ear . . . If you cannot keep your elbow over your head then just place your RIGHT hand on top of your head. Then, staying in this position with the window created by your arm and elbow staying open, allow your body to tilt gently to the RIGHT, imagining something soft and flexible in your spine as you do this, like a bamboo tree, soft cotton, or breath . . . Doing this a number of times, begin to integrate your breath with the movement, perhaps breathing out as you bend to the RIGHT and inhaling as you return to centre . . . You can try reversing this breathing pattern as well, i.e., breathing in on the bending. Notice as you do this movement any sensation in your ribs, your neck, your feet, or your pelvis . . . Where do you feel an opening, where a contraction? Find a way to make the movement as easy and comfortable as possible . . . After a number of times, take a rest, letting the arm release down to our sides and just noticing any sensations emerging from the practise . . . What is the difference between the RIGHT and LEFT side of the body?

Then repeat the entire exercise on the LEFT side, resting in awareness again when you have explored the movement sufficiently

Next, with the LEFT hand over the top of the head and covering the RIGHT ear, slowly rotate to the LEFT, again leading with the eyes, going only as far as the body wants to go . . . Next, coming back to centre, repeat the rotation but this time LEAVING THE EYES FACING FORWARD! This is confusing to the body/mind, so it is important to be gentle with yourself.

Now, finally, repeat the very first rotation with the arms resting at our sides, leading with the eyes . . . You will probably find that you rotate well beyond the place where you first made a mental note. The movement may also feel easier. Take another rest and notice how you feel internally. Has your posture changed? How is your mood? Take a brief walk around the room, sensing your contact with the ground, how your head balances on top of your spine, how easy or difficult your walking feels.
(From the author's Rubenfeld Synergy® Training 1993–97)

Many people have told me that this exercise has alleviated their headache, or pain in their shoulders. It can equally bring areas of holding and tension into relief so that we are more aware of them. Most people tell me that they feel more alive, calmer, and connected to themselves.

The confusion that arises when trying to move the head in opposition to the eyes can be disconcerting. However, this non-habitual movement seems to refresh the nervous system. When we practise the non-habitual, it seems to enhance our ability to deal creatively and flexibly with life's challenges.

Other movement prescriptions that are often used by Body Psychotherapists include hugging oneself in order to get a sense of containment and safety, or pressing into a wall or a therapists' hand, to acquire a sense of power and strength. I use the 'mountain pose' from hatha yoga, which is done standing and with a sense of grounding into the earth, while simultaneously lengthening the spine and feeling the head and neck rising towards the sky. I have also used chi gong exercises—particularly those from a set of exercises called 'stress relief chi gong' (Faulkner 2010).

Hartley (2004) explores 'developmental movement patterns' derived from the work of Cohen (1993). These are movements that we normally do at various stages of early development such as crawling. Some of these patterns are extant in utero. It can be helpful to suggest that clients engage with these movement patterns in response to a particular theme that may emerge in therapy. By doing so, we may shift the patterning of musculoskeletal as well as emotional functioning.

The Eyes Have It

Many Body Psychotherapists are interested in the movement of the eyes, (e.g. Kelley 1971). Tension in the ocular musculature can develop unconsciously, especially when we are anxious, as an automatic aspect of the fight/flight/freeze response. Porges (2009) tells us that the instinctive mammalian response to danger is to scan the horizon and visually seek connection with others. Some Body Psychotherapists thus utilize scanning eye movements to calm a stressed nervous system (see Ogden et al. 2006).

Feldenkrais and Rubenfeld use non-habitual ocular movement to help the eye muscles let go. The trauma-treatment technique eye movement desensitization and reprocessing (EMDR) (Shapiro 2001) also uses lateral eye movements to facilitate the nervous system's integration of traumatic experiences. A recent development of EMDR, called 'brainspotting' (Grand 2013), utilizes the eyes held in a stationary position while the client is emotionally aroused to process emotional material.

Mutual gaze with the primary caregiver—usually the mother—is important in infant development and the ability to form a secure emotional and relational attachment (Trevarthen 1979).

The infant is drawn to her/his mother's eyes, and if the mother is unable to meet the baby's need for visual attunement—if, for example, she looks away too often or conversely cannot tolerate the baby's looking away periodically—this disrupts the emotional equilibrium of the baby and can lead to difficulties in relationships as an adult. It is postulated that the lack of attuned gaze in early parenting can also lead to chronic ocular rigidity.

Body Psychotherapists can help to repair the lack of gaze attunement. By having clients explore eye contact, looking away and then coming back to our eyes, we are repatterning early attachment experiences.

CONCLUSIONS

Movement-based interventions in body-centred psychotherapy may not always be seen as what is popularly seen as 'dance', but yet are part of how movement can contribute to recovery from wounding experiences and promote psychological health.

Deep holding patterns in the body can be released, allowing freedom both physically and psychologically. People may feel more 'whole', more alive, and more connected to their bodies. We can decipher the symbolic unconscious messages from our bodies, developing a deeper sense and acceptance of self. We can explore therapeutic movement patterns that have the ability to make psychological and relational changes.

Conscious awareness of the moving body can engender all the benefits of mindfulness practices with regular use over time. Indeed, from the vast array of body-awareness practices used by body-oriented psychotherapists, many fall within the realm of 'mindfulness', and thus are likely to reap these benefits as well.

Daniel Siegel has written about the neurological benefits of mindfulness practice (Siegel 2010). He states that becoming aware of our thoughts, sensations, and feelings can build integrative fibres in the brain, particularly in the central prefrontal cortex. The benefits of this can include affect regulation, calming of fear, improved immune function, reduced impulsivity, improved insight, compassion, empathy, and morality. He posits that these are all features of psychological health.

Body Psychotherapists can expand on and deepen what clients can gain from mindfulness and somatic practices alone. Because many of our clients have been deeply wounded, as they practise these exercises, they may not be able to contain the affect, memories, and distress that can arise. We can support them to foster such containment, through our attuned presence and through other therapeutic practices.

It should be noted that the process of psychotherapy involves many more layers and types of intervention than just these movement interventions. These may be seen as companions to the process of therapy and do not constitute the entirety of the therapeutic process, which is complex and multidimensional.

There are many other systems that incorporate movement and bodywork into psychotherapy, e.g. Rosenwork (Rosen and Brenner 1992), Caldwell's Moving Cycle (Caldwell 2002), and others. There are certainly many approaches that regard psychological health as clearly interwoven with the body and movement. Marcher and Fich

FIGURE 7.3. 'Embracing the Universe', Video still from 'Hologram'. (Credit: Sabine Klaus-Carter, Creation Editor, and Laura Hope Steckler, Body/Theatre, 2011.)

(2010), for example, have detailed the psychological significance of the muscles and connective tissue. Cohen (1993) has described the 'mind' of developmental movement patterns (Hartley 2004), and Susan Aposhyan has developed Cohen's work into her own brand of psychotherapy that she calls body–mind psychotherapy (Aposhyan 2004). The curious reader may wish to explore further the rich and diverse literature in this field.

Regardless of how we delve into the wisdom and holographic nature of the moving body, and regardless of how much we understand about neuropsychology and the mind–body connection, there is still a bit of mystery as to why and how these holistic approaches lead us towards greater wholeness and wellbeing. Figure 7.3 depicts this wholeness and mystery for me. That bit of mystery can keep us humble and curious in our work.

ACKNOWLEDGEMENTS

I would like to thank Linda Hartley, Tina Stromsted, and Gill Westland for providing valuable feedback on earlier drafts of this chapter.

NOTES

1. The images in the chapter are from the 'Hologram' project, and each image reflects an aspect of my experience of working with the body in psychotherapy. All images are attritable to Sabine Klaus, Creation Editor, and Laura Hope Steckler, Body/Theatre, ©2011.
2. All names and personal details of my clients have been changed to safeguard confidentiality.

REFERENCES

Ainsworth, M. D. S., Blehar, M. C., Waters, E., and Wall, S. (1978). *Patterns of Attachment: A Psychological Study of the Strange Situation.* Hillsdale, NJ: Erlbaum.

American Psychiatric Association (2013). *Diagnostic and Statistical Manual of Mental Disorders,* 5th edn. Arlington VA: American Psychiatric Publishing.

Aposhyan, S. (2004). *Body–Mind Psychotherapy: Principles, Techniques, and Practical Applications.* New York, NY: Norton.

Batemanm, A. and Fonagy, P. (2003). 'The development of an attachment based treatment program for borderline personality disorder', *Bulletin of the Menniger Clinic,* 76: 187–211.

Boening, M., Westland, G., and Southwell, C. (2012). *Body Psychotherapy Competencies.* Amsterdam: European Association of Body Psychotherapy. <http://www.eabp.org/pdf/BodyPsychotherapyCompetencies.pdf>, p. 9.

Bowlby, J. (1988) *A Secure Base: Clinical Applications of Attachment Theory.* London: Routledge.

Caldwell, C. (2002). 'The moving cycle: A model for healing', in P. Lewis, *Integrative Health, Healing and Transformation: A Guide for Practitioners, Consultants and Administrators.* Springfield, IL: Charles C. Thomas.

Carter, S. (2012). *The Healing Power of Love: An Oxytocin Hypothesis.* Presentation at the 13th International EABP Congress of Body Psychotherapy, Cambridge.

Cohen, B. B. (1993) *Sensing, Feeling and Action: The Experiential Anatomy of Body–Mind Centering,* 3rd edn. Northampton MA: Contact Editions.

Cozolino, L. (2002). *The Neuroscience of Psychotherapy.* New York, NY: Norton.

European Association of Body Psychotherapy (2011). 'About Body Psychotherapy', <http://www.eabp.org/about.php> (accessed 26 February 2011).

Fairbairn, W. R. D. (1952). *Psychoanalytic Studies of the Personality.* London: Routledge and Kegan Paul. First published in 1981.

Faulkner, G. (2010). *Managing Stress with Qigong.* London: Singing Dragon.

Feldenkrais, M. (1972). *Awareness Through Movement.* New York, NY: Harper and Row.

Fraleigh, S. (2010). *Butoh: Metamorphic Dance and Global Alchemy.* Champaign, IL: University of Illinois Press.

Freud, S. and Bonaparte, M. (eds.) (2009). *The Origins of Psychoanalysis: Letters to Wilhelm Fliess: Drafts and Notes 1887–1902.* Whitefish, MT: Kessinger.

Gergely, G. and Watson, J. (1996). 'The social biofeedback theory of parental affect-mirroring: The development of emotional self-awareness and self-control in infancy', *The International Journal of Psychoanalysis,* 77: 1181–212.

Grand, D (2013). *Brainspotting: The Revolutionary New Therapy for Rapid and Effective Change.* Boulder, CO: Sounds True.

Hartley, L. (2004). *Somatic Psychology, Body, Mind and Meaning.* London: Whurr.

Hay, D. (2000). *My Body the Buddhist.* Hanover, NH: Wesleyan University Press.

Hochberg, R. L., Serruya, M. D., Friehs, M. G., Mukand, A. J., Saleh, M., Caplan, A.H., Branner, A., Chen, D., Penn, R. D., and Donoghue, J. P. (2006). 'Neuronal ensemble control of prosthetic devices by a human with tetraplegia', *Nature,* 442: 164–71.

Jung, C. G. (1965). *Memories, Dreams, Reflections,* transl. A. Jaffé. New York, NY: Random House.

Kelley, C. R. (1971). *New Techniques of Vision Improvement.* Stamford, CT: Interscience Research Institute. (Originally published as a series of articles in *Energy and Character,* 1971–72.)

Kern, M. (2005). *Wisdom in the Body: The Craniosacral Approach to Essential Health*. Berkeley, CA: North Atlantic Books

Kohut, H. and Wolf, E. (1978) 'The disorders of the self and their treatment: An outline', *International Journal of Psycho-Analysis*, 59: 413–25.

Kurtz, R. (2008). *Body-Centered Psychotherapy: The Hakomi Method*. Mendocino, CA: LifeRhythm.

Levine, P. (1997). *Waking the Tiger: Healing Trauma*. Berkeley, CA: North Atlantic Books.

Lowen, A. (1976). *Bioenergetics: The Revolutionary Therapy that uses the Language of the Body to Heal the Problems of the Mind*. New York, NY: Penguin.

Lowen, A. and Lowen, L. (1977). *The Way to Vibrant Health: A Manual of Bioenergetic Exercises*. Alachua, FL: Bioenergetics Press.

Main, M. and Solomon, J. (1986). 'Discovery of an insecure-disorganized/disoriented attachment pattern', in T. B. Brazelton and M. W. Yogman (eds.), *Affective Development in Infancy*. Westport, CT: Ablex Publishing, pp. 95–124.

Marcher, L. and Fich, S. (2010). *Body Encyclopedia: A Guide to the Psychological Functions of the Muscular System*. Berkeley CA: North Atlantic Books.

Ogden, P., Minton, K., and Pain, C. (2006) *Trauma and the Body: A Sensorimotor Approach to Psychotherapy*. New York, NY: Norton.

Pallaro, P. (ed.) (1999). *Authentic Movement: Essays by Mary Starks Whitehouse, Janet Adler and Joan Chodorow*. London: Jessica Kingsley.

Pallaro, P. (ed.) (2007). *Authentic Movement: Moving the Body, Moving the Self, Being Moved: A Collection of Essays, Volume Two*. London: Jessica Kingsley.

Payne, H., Westland, G., Karkou, V., and Warnecke, T. (2016) 'A comparative analysis of Body Psychotherapy and Dance Movement Psychotherapy', *Body, Movement and Dance in Psychotherapy*, doi: 10.1080/17432979.2016.1165291.

Perls, F., Hefferline, R., and Goodman, P. (1951). *Gestalt Therapy: Excitement and Growth in the Human Personality*. New York, NY: Julian

Picton, B. (2004). 'Using the bodynamic shock trauma model in the everyday practice of physiotherapy', in I. McNaughton (ed.), *Body, Breath and Consciousness: A Somatics Anthology*. Berkeley, CA: North Atlantic Books, pp. 287–306.

Porges, S. (2009). 'The polyvagal theory: New insights into the adaptive reactions of the autonomic nervous system', *Cleveland Clinic Journal of Medicine*, 76: 86–90.

Rogers, C. (1951). *Client-Centered Therapy*. Cambridge, MA: The Riverside Press.

Rosen, M. and Brenner, S. (1992) *The Rosen Method of Movement*. Berkeley, CA: North Atlantic Books.

Rothschild, B. (2000). *The Body Remembers: The Psychophysiology of Trauma and Trauma Treatment*. New York, NY: Norton.

Rubenfeld, I. (2000). *The Listening Hand*. London: Piatkus.

Schore, A. (2003) *Affect Regulation and the Repair of the Self*. New York, NY: Norton.

Schore, A. (2003). *Affect Regulation and Disorders of the Self*. New York, NY: Norton.

Schreiber, F. R. (1973). *Sybil*. Chicago, IL: Regnery.

Segal, Z. V., Williams, J. M. G., and Teasdale, J. D. (2002). *Mindfulness-based Cognitive Therapy for Depression: A New Approach to Preventing Relapse*. New York, NY: Guilford Press.

Shapiro, F. (2001). *Eye Movement Desensitization and Reprocessing: Basic Principles, Protocols, and Procedures*. New York, NY: Guildford Press.

Sheets-Johnstone, M. (2011). *The Primacy of Movement: Advances in Consciousness Research*. Amsterdam: John Benjamins, p. xxv.

Siegel, D. (2010). *Mindsight: The New Science of Personal Transformation*. New York, NY: Bantam Books.

Steckler, L. H. (2006). 'Somatic soulmates'. *Body, Movement and Dance in Psychotherapy*, 1(1): 29–42.

Stern, D. N. (1995). 'Affect attunement', in J. D. Call, E. Galenson, and R. L. Tyson (eds.), *Frontiers of Infant Psychiatry*, vol. 2. New York, NY: Basic Books, pp. 3–14.

Sweigard, L. (1974). *Human Movement Potential: Its Ideokinetic Facilitation*. New York, NY: Harper and Row.

Trevarthen, C. (1979). 'Communication and cooperation in early infancy: A description of primary intersubjectivity', in M. Bullowa (ed.), *Before Speech: The Beginning of Interpersonal Communication*. New York, NY: Cambridge University Press, pp. 321–47.

Van der Kolk, B. A. (2014). *The Body Keeps the Score: Brain, Mind and Body in the Healing of Trauma*. New York, NY: Penguin.

Van der Kolk, B. A., McFarlane, A. C., and Weisaeth, L. (eds.) (1996). *Traumatic Stress: The Effects of Overwhelming Experience on Mind, Body, and Society*. New York, NY: Guilford Press.

Ward, W. (1970). *Fountains of Faith: The Words of William Arthur Ward*. Anderson, SC: Droke House.

Weiss, H., Johanson, G., and Monda, L. (2015). *Hakomi Mindfulness-Centered Somatic Psychotherapy: A Comprehensive Guide to Theory and Practice*. New York, NY: Norton.

Winnicott, D. W. (1960). 'Ego distortion in terms of true and false self', in *The Maturational Process and the Facilitating Environment: Studies in the Theory of Emotional Development*. New York, NY: International Universities Press, pp. 140–52.

World Health Organization. (1992). *ICD-10: The ICD-10 Classification of Mental and Behavioural Disorders: Clinical Descriptions and Diagnostic Guidelines*. Geneva: World Health Organization.

CHAPTER 8

AUTHENTIC MOVEMENT AS A PRACTICE FOR WELLBEING

JANE BACON

Introduction

AUTHENTIC Movement (AM) is not a codified form of dance, and it relies on the individual having a particular attitude of openness toward working with the body. But what do we mean when we speak of being 'authentic'? How does the practice of AM facilitate being 'authentic' and, in turn, generate a sense of wellbeing? The process can be described as follows: one person moves, another watches/witnesses. They agree an amount of time for the process, and the witness is the timekeeper. The witness sits where the mover asks, then the mover closes his/her eyes and waits for an inner impulse to move. Whitehouse (1999a), the founder of AM, said: 'It is a moment when the ego gives up control, stops choosing, stops exerting demands, allowing the Self to take over moving the physical body as it will' (p. 82). During this time the witness does not move or in any other way intervene. When the time is finished, the two sit together with the mover speaking her experience followed by the witness offering her reflections on her own experience as witness in the presence of the mover. Both mover and witness speak about the anatomical, physical experience and the individual's internal or imaginary and emotional experiences. Both work to be aware of the experience of moving and an internal sense of being moved. In other words, *both* are concerned with 'an awareness of what I am doing and what is happening to me' (p. 82).

AM is a process of allowing an inner sensation or impulse to take physical form. Joan Chodorow (1995/99)—a prominent Jungian analyst—describes AM as 'active imagination in movement'. In AM we work to embody our internal world and allow it to take shape in our moving body.

> Following the inner sensation, allowing the impulse to take the form of physical action, is active imagination in movement, just as following the visual image is active

imagination in fantasy. It is here that the most dramatic psychophysical connections are made available to consciousness. (Whitehouse 1999b, p. 52)

Waiting in this way with eyes closed in the presence of a witness, the mover allows herself to give shape and form to whatever arises and is not checked or mediated by a conscious attitude relating to what one should look like or how one should behave. As Johnson (2004) describes:

> The practice involves teaching people how to wait for movement to arise and evolve as one gives oneself to it within an atmosphere of quiet attention, often with one person acting as a non-interpretative witness for the other. It is a sustained, tutored, disciplined waiting for movement to come from the self, instead of from habitual movements or moving as others would have us. (Johnson 2004).

The process provides a particular structure with uninterrupted time and space. The (limited) rules are clear: be open and attentive to the unconscious, be interested in how my body is moving, and learn to track and name my movement patterns; always speak from my own experience as both mover and witness; as witness, work toward an awareness of my projections that arise as interpretations of the mover's experience and restrain from offering these interpretations to the mover.

Writings about AM usually introduce the practice in much the same way as I have done here. But what happens when a mover finds herself in a dark and painful psychological state? Whilst this is regularly discussed in group and individual sessions, there is a paucity of writing on this subject. AM practitioners usually have excellent screening processes, and those interested in AM may be recommended to have a psychotherapeutic relationship, so material arising in the practice can be more deeply processed and integrated. Throughout this chapter I will draw on the writings and my personal experience of working with Janet Adler to explore how AM practice might transform traumatic memories and experiences which can then give rise to a greater sense of wellbeing.

WHAT IS WELLBEING?

Wellbeing is most usually discussed in contemporary cultures using quantitative measures. According to the UK National Account of Well-Being (2012),

> the science of subjective well-being suggests that . . . people need . . . a sense of . . . vitality . . . to undertake activities which are meaningful . . . and make them feel . . . autonomous (and) . . . a stock of inner resources to help them cope . . . Wellbeing is . . . the dynamic process that gives people a sense of how their lives are going.

Importantly, the Institute of Well-Being reminds us that wellbeing has been the concern of philosophers since the ancient Greeks, but now is more the domain of the scientists who are amassing evidence about what contributes to the quality of our lives. Perhaps AM is particularly named as a counter-balance to an attitude often evident in contemporary society that our body is simply a machine to be fixed, tuned-up, or souped-up, or have parts simply replaced when faulty. According to Body Psychotherapist Michael Soth (2006): 'The body is fast becoming a postmodern fashion accessory, treated like a car as a substitute for self, an advertisement for self' (p. 113). He continues, that this is an objectification of the body even though we might think of it as a more positive objectification than previous more callous and sexist images of the body. These images neglect, and invite us to neglect, the spontaneous life of the body in favour of an unattainable image. But Body Psychotherapists, Dance and Movement Psychotherapists, and artists all know that working with our bodies and creativity can be a deeply healing experience. We use our bodies, or bodies use skin and deeper fascia to record or sense all that goes on around and within it (Pinkola Estes 1992/96, p. 200). According to Jungian analyst Pinkola Estes, it might be helpful to imagine that it is the body that helps the soul adapt to mundane life, 'translates, gives the blank page, the ink, and the pen with which the soul can write upon our lives' (p. 206).

Philosopher Alva Nöe suggests that 'the locus of consciousness is the dynamic life of the whole, environmentally plugged-in person or animal' (2009, p. x). He goes on to say that 'the subject of experience is not a bit of your body. You are not your brain. The brain, rather, is part of what you are' (p. 7). In AM we work with all of who we are, all our experiences, not just our thinking minds. The work of Antonio Damasio (1996, 2000) also reminds us that the brain is part of the body and that emotional processing takes place in the environment of our body–mind. He calls these 'somatic markers'. Philosopher-turned-psychologist Eugene Gendlin refers to a very similar aspect using the term 'felt sense' (1978). For philosophers and psychologists such these, the body plays a central role and is more than the vehicle of the senses and the means by which we receive impressions of the world (Gold 2008, p. 3). And C. G. Jung (1961) spent an entire career with an implicit knowledge about the interdependence of body and mind as well as body, mind, and spirit. Jung described his discovery of psychiatry as his chosen career as a place where the two currents of his interest—the biological and the spiritual—'could flow together and in a united stream dig their own bed' (Jung 1961, p. 109). In his autobiography, *Memories, Dreams, Reflections* he writes:

> That was the primal stuff which compelled me to work upon it, and my works are a more or less successful endeavor to incorporate this incandescent matter into the contemporary picture of the world. (p. 199)

Perhaps Jung would have said that a sense of wellbeing is enhanced when one attends to and then replenishes processes of inner visualizing, the storehouse of symbolic material, in order that the meanings of life and the lives of others are not reduced to the cognitive processes of rationality that are often seen as the bedrock of twentieth-first-century living. I have had numerous psychotherapy clients and students say things such as 'I don't understand why I can't control my emotions more like a computer', or

'I don't know why I still feel like that, I have dealt with that issue', as though they have neatly put this or that feeling or traumatic experience tidily in a box and cannot face or do not know that all that we experience is part of a deeper field of experience beyond ego and the confines of the rational. A young female client told me she felt like she had a faulty wire in her brain and that if I could just fix that for her she would be fine. She could visualize both ends of the wire, and even knew that there was a particular experience that was connected to this. This was such a wonderful image of her experience, and yet she wanted a simple solution. She wanted a person from a medical or healing profession to literally (rather than symbolically) make the connection for her not understanding that to allow her inner river bed to run a new course—or as psychiatrist and neuroscientist Bessel van der Kolk (2013) explains, to develop new neural pathways to develop—is a process that requires new ways of working. She left therapy because these wires were not being connected quickly and efficiently in the way a technician might repair a faulty computer.

In Helen Payne's (2006) article 'The body as container and expresser', she claims that AM 'helps individuals and groups to engage with transpersonal experiences, develop an emotional literacy, interpersonal skills and processes, body awareness, somatic intelligence' (p. 162). She adds: 'Authentic Movement. . .can be used to promote emotional wellbeing and health, as it aims to increase connections between body, mind and spirit in the context of a group approach to health and wellbeing, embodiment and wellbeing through movement' (p. 162). This suggests that wellbeing is enhanced through a sense of wholeness that might emerge from connecting body, mind, and spirit.

AUTHENTIC MOVEMENT AS PHILOSOPHY: THE PHENOMENOLOGY OF EMBODIED UNFOLDING EXPERIENCE

Mary Starks Whitehouse, founder of AM, reminds us of the practical reasons for her use of the term 'authentic': 'When movement was simple and inevitable, not to be changed no matter how limited or partial, it became what I called "authentic"—it could be recognized as genuine, belonging to that person'(Whitehouse 1999a, p. 81). I would also suggest that the term was appropriate to the time in which it emerged. Johnson suggests that Adler, and others in the AM community, use the term 'authenticity' in a manner that may be practiced but also links to the philosophy of Heidegger—and more particularly, to Heidegger's use of the term 'authenticity' in *Being and Time*, which is taken from its Greek origin, *authentikos,* which means original and genuine, acting on one's own authority, and self-posited.

'My core being is mine to be in one way or another. That core being . . . is in each case mine . . . But only in so far as it is essentially something which can be authentic' (Heidegger, in Johnson 2006, p. 6).

I would like to suggest that Authentic Movement practitioners, although using the term 'authentic' for practical reasons (as Whitehouse did), are also using the term for philosophical reasons and most are working with the premise that those wanting to participate in Authentic Movement have a conscious or unconscious need for a process that will aid that person's 'individuation' process and/or connection to the unknown, unconscious or transpersonal. This might be typified in that person's interest in being honest with themselves or a search for deeper meaning in life. Heidegger says, 'we might, when a moment allows us, be honest with ourselves.' (Thompson 2003, p. 196)

Psychoanalyst Jon Mills, drawing on Heidegger's question of Being (*Sein*) offers the following reflection on the enigmatic question of authenticity as a means to becoming 'honest with ourselves':

> For Heidegger, authenticity is a uniquely temporal structure and a process of unfolding possibility. It is a state of being that is active, teleological, contemplative, and congruent—an agency with quiescent potentiality. As such, authenticity is the process of becoming one's possibilities and by nature it is idiosyncratic and uniquely subjective. (Mills 2003, p. 117)

This 'authenticity is a state of being 'active, teleological, contemplative, and congruent' (Mills 2003, p. 117). In this way, we choose to surrender to a process of 'becoming one's possibilities'. We can also call this process 'individuation', as Jung did: 'A person's becoming himself, whole, indivisible and distinct from other people or collective psychology (though also in relation to these)' (Samuels, Shorter, and Plaut 1986, p. 76). We begin to become whole, to grow into the person we were born to be. We unfold to ourselves rather than arriving at a fixed and stable point.

If Johnson is correct that Adler's use of 'authentic' is practical and philosophical in the sense that philosophy is a process of trying to understand something about the nature of our existence, then AM allows, facilitates, and even encourages such an exploration. These deeper moments of honesty with ourselves could be said to be 'core being' experiences in that we experience the unfolding of a process that was longing to come to consciousness (individuation). This is a reflexive self, which aids an individual's sense of agency. It is often also a feeling of wholeness or a uniting of all aspects of oneself, both known and unknown.

According to Mills, referring to Heidegger, this is ultimately about 'self-relatedness' and a responsibility toward self 'care' (Mills 2003, p. 134). For Heidegger, this process necessitates the 'call of conscience', the 'voice ... that summons us to respond to an authentic appeal and transcend the public everydayness of Being' (p. 134). In other words, we respond to an appeal to become who we were intended to be rather than who we have been taught or learned to be. Nietzsche said this was 'the person who is not afraid to stand up to the anxieties of living' (Thompson 2003, p. 196).

Contemporary 'anxieties of living' are of a different order to those of Nietzsche's time. This is not to romanticize past histories but to acknowledge the differences in daily life across times, places, cultures, and social systems. The speed and pace of contemporary life in many societies along with the easy access to information via the World Wide Web can generate anxieties of a particular nature. We do not have—and are often not taught—skills to access our internal world. We often do not have the time and space to develop a relationship to the unknown. We are taught to value rationality and progress, to seek out quick and easy answers to problems. We often have little or no knowledge of our spiritual or spirit world, whether that is inwardly perceived or externally manifest. Perhaps we have altered who we might become as we have strived toward integration with family and culture, or perhaps we are just weary of making constant decisions offered by the contemporary world of the Internet and consumer culture (Baumeister and Tierney 2012) and have lost any deeper sense of 'who I am'.[1]

A woman (who is a composite of many clients rather than a specific person) is lying on the floor in my studio. I will call her Bethan.[2] Her arms wrap around her torso and then rub her belly. She is in this place for what feels to me, her witness and psychotherapist, a very long time. Later she says:

> I don't have any legs, or I can't feel my legs. I am all torso. But as I say this, I feel myself wondering how I will walk, how I will stand my ground, or even how have I been grounding myself in my life.

We are to spend many months together as she slowly begins to find her own legs, to find her own way out of this place where she has lost her anchoring in a world that she imagines may once have felt secure to her ancestors. She is to discover and work with traumatic memories and dissociated parts of her self until they are integrated and she finds a new sense of 'who I am' in the here and now in relation to the there and then.

In working together within a psychotherapeutic frame which places the tenets of AM as a central organizing philosophy, she begins to discover what we might call her core being, her authentic self, and she also learns how to develop an inner witness or a consciousness that is embodied, rather than disembodied, and embedded. In the process she discovers she has an opportunity to experience radical acceptance, 'self-care' and 'authenticity'. For Heidegger this was characterized 'as a specific act or moment in any individual's life where the context in which a situation arises offers an opportunity to behave authentically' (Thompson 2003, p. 196). AM practice affords Bethan many opportunities to open to experience in this way which is, in and of itself, philosophical.

'The discipline of authentic movement' is Adler's (2015) articulation of her unique approach to AM which she describes as a 'potential model of embodied consciousness' (personal communication 2013). Terms such as 'direct experience', 'intuitive knowing', and 'witness consciousness' are all ways in which she hopes to convey the embodied nature of the mysterious processes of mind, body, and spirit. She is not concerned with philosophical concepts of 'authenticity'—which is not to say that these connections do not exist or might be fruitful. Adler (2007) does not use the word 'authenticity' but instead talks about 'direct experience', explaining that this 'evolves without a particular philosophy' (p. 264). But perhaps another way of saying the same thing is that 'direct experience' evolves as its own kind of philosophy, or that consciousness does not arise just in our brains but *from* and *with* the 'conscious body' (Adler 2002).

Johnson reminds us:

> Whitehouse, Adler, and their associates are exploring a much wider realm of different kinds of non-deliberate movements, opening up different realms of feeling, memory, and image . . . Adler extends this direction of movement into language and thought itself. This breadth of bodily exploration, seeking primal roots of movement and words in many new areas . . . Practice is in the foreground, constantly being the norm against which words and theory are being reshaped. (Johnson 2006, p. 6)

This is congruent with the writing of Alva Noë, who tells us that consciousness does not arise in our brains, but that the 'brain's activity gives rise to consciousness only when we appreciate that what matters for consciousness is not the neural activity as such but the neural activity as embedded in an animal's larger action and interaction with the world around it' (Noë 2009, p. 47). That is to say, as does Adler, our moving body is also our consciousness—what Adler (2002) refers to as 'body consciousness' or our 'inner witness' (Adler 2015). The brain's job is that of facilitating a dynamic pattern of interaction among brain, body, and world' (Noë 2009, p. 47). The facilitation of an unfolding experience of 'interaction of brain, body, and world' returns us to the notion of wellbeing as the connection of body, mind, and spirit. One such facilitation process is AM.

Authentic Movement and Trauma

In the previous section the focus was on articulating how AM can be considered an embodied philosophy. Now we turn to the way in which an embodied philosophical approach is a unique psychotherapeutic approach to working with trauma.

A woman in her early forties—another I will call Bethan—came to see me. She was interested in AM but was also afraid of what she might discover. She had experiences of past abuse and neglect. For Bethan it was important to work with the principles of AM practice, but within a therapeutic frame in an attempt to be alive to the danger of AM practice becoming retraumatizing. I was always her primary witness, she was always the mover, but I would often limit the time of moving to just one or perhaps two minutes. In this instance, learning to 'track' her inner and moving experience was vital to her, and allowed body and brain (Damasio 1996) or left and right hemisphere of the brain (McGilchrist 2009) to integrate and so process the past trauma. But this was difficult, and she could easily find herself in a place that felt like a familiar traumatic experience. When she closed her eyes it was usually to escape, because she experienced her inner world as a place of fear, shame, and darkness. So we would begin with tiny fragments of time where I invite her to explore her body—firstly to see and feel her physical anatomy, and then in order to name each experience. At the beginning I said to her: 'Let us just be together and you work on tracking your moving experience, and if either one of us feels you have somehow left the room or cannot remain present then we stop.' In this way I was fundamentally challenging her perception of the world as a hostile and unsupportive place, but she was also sufficiently aware of her own processes of protection. It seemed that her ego was strong enough to look at that which she could not bear. Often, those suffering from traumatic states such as dissociation and hyper- (or hypo-) arousal find it almost impossible to be reflexive (to look inward whilst also being aware of looking inward) because their inner world is such a hostile environment and can overwhelm; often, in such circumstances there is no differentiation between inner and outer experience. But Bethan had been in therapy for a long time, and she was able to try this exercise. She knew she dissociated when an experience was perceived to be overwhelming, and this knowing allowed us to work with the part of her that had a knowing. That would be the aspect of her personality that could track her experiences moment by moment. Adler would call this her 'inner witness' or 'witness consciousness'. Tracking requires us to stay fully present in a moment rather than allowing our ability to dissociate to take control. For Bethan, as for many of us, sometimes this was possible, while at other times it seemed impossible. At the beginning she was only able to stay fully present for a few seconds, just as we find it so difficult in meditation practice to stay present and alive to what is in each moment, rather than allowing our minds to wander off into thinking or getting stuck in this or that.

Adler suggests that 'tracking' is a way to develop our ability to work with direct experience, and this, I would suggest, is one of the ways that AM works with these states of dissociation. In relation to the question of retraumatizing, 'tracking', when done one to one rather than in a group, offers an opportunity for an individual to be seen just as they are and to be contained by the psychotherapist/AM practitioner in a way that gives time and careful attention to 'embodied detail, felt by the senses one by one' (Adler 2007, p. 263). By placing the practice of the moving body in the foreground, we work with 'direct experience' and then allow language to emerge. The focus on this embodied unfolding approach to the arrival of language is a philosophical approach also articulated by the philosophers cited in this chapter.

Adler is not of the opinion that language takes us away from our felt or direct experience but is an important part of becoming bodily conscious. She warns against referring to ourselves in the third person. Based on this, I offer the following example of gentle revisions for how we might speak about experience:

BETHAN: then the arm raises.
ME: you might try 'I raise my arm' and notice that. If you can tell me all that you
notice in this moment of 'I raise my arm'.

Adler suggests that 'the arm raises' is akin to asking a rhetorical question rather than owning our intention to say 'I think' or 'I want'. This third-person distancing fuels an inner dialogue with a self that is disconnected from parts of me. So, for Bethan to be able to say 'I raise my right arm' shifts her internal dialogue from a body that is objectified and often dissociated, to a human subject with body and mind who chooses to lift her arm and can then discover more about what happens when 'I lift my right arm'. She may discover:

SENSATIONS

I notice my arm feels heavy, it makes me think about how hard it always was to raise my hand in school.

FEELINGS

As my arm lifts I feel such a longing, I think I am longing to be seen, I can feel it in my heart.

IMAGES

As I raise my arm I see there are other people somewhere close to me, I do not know who or what they want, it is like I can see them in my mind's eye.

NARRATIVES

I was always the quiet child, the one who did not ask questions, who never put her hand up in class. I remember my mother saying 'don't be stupid, of course you know the answer'.

THE INEXPLICABLE/INVISIBLE/MYSTERIOUS

I sense a light is coming from within me, it seems clear somehow that the light is me and also not me.

All of these ways of being in relation to image and experience offer us the tracking of our moving process as we come closer to dark places within that often also contain our inner light, our inner intuitive knowing.

Adler reminds us that 'direct experience creates intuitive knowing' (Adler 2007, p. 262), and we attend to this experience through an awareness of embodied and felt detail. Perhaps what happens is that an individual can begin to experience having a body (of their own and the body of the witness) they can begin to trust; and in the moving, speaking, and being together the horror of past experiences transforms and can be integrated. It is not just that we have a body, but we also have our creative and intuitive sense of ourselves.

Noë (2009) reminds us that to perceive the world, to be shaped by it, is an embodied process, and that our brains are only one part of that process. We might say that this complex process engenders my 'authenticity'. In AM practice, Heidegger's 'call of conscience' demands that we pursue authenticity as 'self-relatedness', and this, in turn, allows the hurt or damaged inner child or adult to be heard and seen just as she is rather than as others expect. In this process we begin to allow the phenomenon of our traumatizing memories because we have a self-conscious, or self-reflexive, aspect that can help keep us safe on our journey. We begin to realize we are no longer the child or person who was hurt and damaged, but are a person who can choose our future. We allow our conscious body to take us on a journey. On that journey our markers for keeping to or finding the path are our 'felt sense' (Gendlin 1978) of the experience. We know in our bodies the feeling and sensation of our potential, our unfolding possibility, and we also know its lack.

As Heidegger says, authenticity can be 'in a moment', and we hope we might be honest with ourselves—we hope we might allow ourselves to see the truth as we experience it in that moment. To do that we will need to embrace the lightness and the dark and to know that there is a truth in what happened 'back then', which may not be congruent with our present reality. For Bethan, the dark places were like a possession by a persecutor/protector figure (Kalsched 1996, 2013).

Jungian analyst Donald Kalsched wrote in 1996 that for those with severe trauma, the demonic persecuting inner archetypal figures could not be transformed. But in his most recent book, *Trauma and the Soul: A Psycho-Spiritual Approach to Human Development and its Interruption* (2013), he revises his opinion, suggesting that bodywork such as AM offers a means to aid the deep healing of trauma. He says that psychoanalysts have begun to recognize that many individuals, seen from the outside, appear to live normal lives, but 'their bodies carry the sequelae of their early trauma in somatic symptoms that bear no obvious relationship to the early injuries' (p. 287). He suggests that for these people, a sense of 'aliveness' is not possible because the past trauma has become encoded in the physiological. He suggests that AM is one method to work with such states of traumatic dissociation, and also that if done along with psychoanalysis (particularly working with dreams) a much deeper transformation of these demonic or persecuting archetypal figures begins to take place. In this way the story of their lives begins to transform.

In AM we are practicing wellbeing, being well, in each moment when we allow our flesh to become a part of our being rather than subjecting ourselves to the confused and unhelpful notion of the body as concrete matter that can be altered to suit current media images of an objectified body. New methods of trauma treatment are quickly developing and building on insights from neuroscience (van der Kolk 2014), but most do not embrace the notion of embodied consciousness. Although beyond the scope of this chapter, a future area of research would be to compare the practice of AM to practices such as Peter Levine's (2015) somatic experiencing. This research would need to be conducted in a multidisciplinary environment in order to embrace both the philosophical underpinning of AM as well as the more physiological, cognitive, and neurological underpinnings of many trauma treatments.

AUTHENTIC MOVEMENT: FINDING AND ALLOWING OUR SOURCE OF WELLBEING

AM practice is inherently therapeutic, but is not therapy per se. It is practiced and facilitated by people with wider concerns beyond the therapeutic and the existential or transpersonal, such as dancers, actors, fine artists, educators, consultants, and so forth. As indicated in the section on wellbeing, practices that aid a connectedness between mind, body, and spirit may make our lives more meaningful. Working with AM invites a 'direct experience', a deep listening to the subtlety and power of that connectedness.

Jung—whose thinking informed the development of Whitehouse's 'movement in depth'—might have used the word 'psyche' to express the unity of mind, body, and spirit as it is internally and externally experienced. He was concerned to distance, or to reconfigure, dualist notions of mind and body imposed by Enlightenment thinkers such as Descartes and his infamous 'I think, therefore I am'. The (my) body is not merely a machine to be used by the (my) thinking mind. Jung believed that self and body are the same, saying that 'the difference we make between the psyche and the body is artificial . . . In reality there is nothing but a living body' (Jung and Jarrett 1989, p. 396). Furthermore, and paradoxically, he says that 'we must assume that the self really means us to live in the body, to live that experiment, live our lives' (p. 403). In other words, our living potentiality is spirit and body, and these two are essentially the same. For Jung, the 'symbols of the self arise in the depths of the body and they express its materiality every bit as much as the structure of the perceiving consciousness' (Jung 1940/80, par. 291).

Jung's symbols of Self can be compared to Adler's understanding of direct experience. For Adler, AM is a mystical practice (Stromsted 2007). It is different from a 'moving self and inner witness being merged or in a dialogic relationship' (Adler 2007, p. 262). These direct experiences, according to Adler, are synonymous with 'surrendering images of self, of an identity of self as one has known it', of a moving into and through 'the archetype of God, or the symbolic nature of God, into a clear silent awareness, an infinite emptiness' (p. 262).

The implication is that AM provides an opportunity or space and time for these experiences of 'clear, silent awareness' or a unity of mind, body, and spirit, and this, in turn, is a source of wellbeing. And in AM practice we have particular strategies for working with, and developing our conscious attitude to, our subjective experience. As previously explained, we work with language in the present tense. This subtle shift in language, to present and first person, keeps experience central and located as belonging to the speaker. I allow into consciousness more than the sensation of stretching up to reach for something, more than the personal memory of lifting my arm for permission to speak or to protect myself from being hurt. Now I lift my arm, and in lifting I learn about my place in the world and my connection to other people, places, and things in this moment of my experience and in relation to all other moments both known and unknown. Here is an example of such an experience, again as a composite vignette from many clients.

I feel a light appear in the far distance above me. Suddenly there is a stream of light from the source moving through the darkness until I feel it touches my chest. My heartbeat is clear and present, the light is touching my skin, penetrating my surfaces, connecting me to this source. I see clearly the line of light, the energy, connecting me to the source. I lay in stillness for sometime. Then it seems that my heart is emanating light, that the light in the distance is really coming from me. I marvel at this, it seems to be both my light and not my light.

In this vignette, the mover experiences the image as both separate and part of herself. I would describe this as a 'numinous' experience. Jung advised, 'in as much as you attain to the numinous experiences you are released from the curse of pathology' (1973, vol. 1, p. 377). He was not suggesting that the numinous, or spiritual, was the answer to our healing, but that these experiences needed to be thought of psychologically rather than in the frame of religion. Such experiences offer radical healing and, for Jung, come from the ego's recognition of our own (and world's) overpowering, numinous, unconscious structure. Jungian analyst Edinger (1972) suggests: 'If when the individual is thrown back on himself through the loss of a projected religious value, he is able to confront the ultimate questions of life that are posed for him . . . If he is able to work consciously and responsibly with the activation of the unconscious he may discover the lost value, the god-image, within the psyche' (p. 68). According to Capobianco, Jung insisted that therapy was a 'rebinding of consciousness with the unconscious process, a reconsideration by consciousness of the "overpowering", "numinous", unconscious process' (Capobianco 1993, p. 30). This is perhaps what Heidegger would call the truth of Being. Heidegger's version of the 'numinous' might be expressed as follows, in the words of Capobianco: 'Being as the Holy is the endless presencing process which is awesome, but also wholesome; and Dasein who dwells in nearness to the Holy is made whole, is healed' (p. 31). For Heidegger, the holy was not connected to religion nor anything else; it was chaos and inexpressible. But for AM practitioners,[3] such as Adler, it is the 'holy', the 'numinous', within each of us that compels and offers the potential for healing. This phenomena is what Jung was also concerned to discover. In *Psychology and Religion, West and East* (1975), he wrote: 'I restrict myself to the observations of phenomena' (par. 2). I suspect that this is what Adler (2002) means when she invites us to 'track our inner experience'. We find the answers we are searching for within ourselves rather than as projected on the outer world. And it is our capacity for consciousness—for knowing and speaking from and about these images and experiences—that aids that healing and supports our wellbeing.

AM is our *practice*, our phenomenological study, not of these psychological and philosophical theories, but of our 'Being as Holy'. Our radical healing comes through connection to the deep, numinous unconscious structure and our ability to allow spirit and matter (or mind and body, conscious and unconscious) to come into relation or even to become one. Most importantly then, the method and practice of AM is perhaps an embodied unfolding experience of self as a source of wellbeing. And this embodied theory, or praxis, is similar to Jung and other depth psychologists as well as many mystical scholars and philosophical phenomenologists. It is the practice, our lived and embodied experience, that allows us to connect to our deepest well of Being.

CONCLUSION

AM offers us a way of knowing that many other forms of experience may overlook and, as I have suggested, is a wellbeing practice. It draws our attention to perception and to experience that allows us to really notice who we are, where we are, and with whom we are as present unfolding moments of experience which contain vital fragments of our past, present, and future. Much of our daily experiences require us to work toward some sort of adaptation to others, either in the workplace, in our families, or in other settings. This external processing often means that we become lost to our inherent potential for an inner adaptation. Jung suggested that ego—our conscious attitude that navigates our daily living processes—needs to come into relation with the Self, or the internal God image, and then to offer what we find back to the world in which we live. As I have stated, that process he called individuation. To return to the words of the founder of AM, Whitehouse:

> What I began to understand during the beginning of my work in movement in depth was that in order to release a movement that is instinctive (i.e. not the 'idea' of the person doing that movement nor my idea of what I want them to do), I found that I had to go back toward not moving. In that way I found out where movement actually started. It was when I learned to see what was authentic about movement, and what was not, and when people were cheating, and when I interfered, and when they were starting to move from within themselves, and when they were compelled to move because they had an image in their heads of what they wanted to do; it was then that I learned to say 'Go ahead and do your image, never mind if you are thinking of it', and when to say 'Oh, wait longer. Wait until you feel it from within.' (Whitehouse in Frantz 1999, p. 23)

In my opinion, AM practice offers an opportunity to integrate past trauma when carefully handled, and is an excellent approach to wellbeing which does not foreground physical over psychic wellbeing or vice versa because of the inherent interrelatedness of the psychological and physical. In AM we are allowed to 'wait until you feel it from within', and we are seen in all that we are. And even if what you feel from within is painful and troubling, we learn to be present to our own suffering, and in so doing that very pain might begin to shift from its usual rigid, unmoveable, fixed attitude and defence. This can be life-changing. What was once unbearable and resulted in a trauma locating itself deeply in the depths of the body and unconscious, can now become more present with the caring support of an outer witness and the developing skill of the inner witness which brings about the individual's sense of agency and aliveness. AM is a process of integrating and processing these experiences so that they become meaningful aspects of our lives rather than splintered, fragmented aspects of personality that form the basis of pathology. If we are not recognized in this way then our psychic development, our sense of identity and worth, may be marred, thwarted, or more deeply damaged.

Without a deep recognition of 'who I am' I may find myself yearning to be seen, to be known by an Other, or I may find I lose my way in my life and yearn to find myself on the path or journey towards my Self once more. I want to allow for things beyond my conscious awareness, and believe that such experiences (so long as we have enough ego strength to contain and work with them—but who can know how much ego strength is 'enough') offer a sense of expansion, like the experience of the 'light' or 'numinous', 'authentic', experiences, that little else can. This is the search for Self, the Ultimate, God, or whatever name we feel truly reflects and encompasses our experience. These give us (to return to the definition of wellbeing) a sense of 'vitality' because we are engaged in 'meaningful' experiences that enhance our sense of agency, and these experiences, brought to consciousness, offer us a lifetime of 'inner resource'.

NOTES

1. Baumeister and Tierney (2012) suggest that contemporary living requires so much decision making that our ego's capacity for self-control and willpower is regularly depleted—what they refer to as 'ego depletion'. Glucose (offered by the food we eat) replenishes our ability to make decisions and to exercise self-control; and glucose is used much more quickly if we have a lot of decisions to make. It does not matter what type of decisions these are, and it is not that a lack of food shuts down the brain, but the decision making that then alters the way the we are able to think and behave.
2. The persons mentioned in this chapter are fictional but have been created from my personal experiences with those in analysis with myself or attending AM. All those who have helped to create these characters have read and given permission to what is written here, but I take sole responsibility for the creation of all vignettes.
3. Stromsted (2007) writes about AM as mystical practice.

REFERENCES

Adler, J. (2002). *Offering from the Conscious Body, The Discipline of Authentic Movement.* Rochester, VT: Inner Traditions.

Adler, J. (2007). 'From seeing to knowing', in P. Pallaro (ed.), *Authentic Movement: Moving the Body, Moving the Self, Being Moved: A Collection of Essays, Volume Two.* London: Jessica Kingsley, pp. 260–9.

Adler, J. (2015). 'The mandorla and the discipline of authentic movement', in J. Bacon (ed.), *Authentic Movement: A Field of Practices.* Special issue of *The Journal of Dance and Somatic Practices*, 7(2): 217–27.

Baumeister, R. F. and Tierney, J. (2012). *Willpower: Why Self-Control is the Secret to Success.* New York, NY: Penguin.

Capobianco, R. M. (1993). 'Heidegger and Jung: Dwelling near the source', *Review of Existential Psychology and Psychiatry*, 21(1–3): 50–9, <http://www.cgjungpage.org/index2.php?option=com_content&do_pdf=1&id=818> (accessed 13 August 2012).

Chodorow, J. (1995/99). 'Dance/movement and body experience in analysis', in P. Pallaro (ed.), *Authentic Movement, Essays by Mary Starks Whitehouse, Janet Adler and Joan Chodorow.* London: Jessica Kingsley, pp.253–66.

Damasio, A. (1996). *Descartes Error, Emotion, Reason and the Human Brain*. New York, NY: HarperCollins.

Damasio, A. (2000). *The Feeling of What Happens*. London: Vintage.

Edinger, E. (1972). *Ego and Archetype*. Shambala: London.

Frantz, G. (1999). 'An approach to the center: An interview with Mary Whitehouse', in P. Pallaro (ed.). *Authentic Movement: Essays by Mary Starks Whitehouse, Janet Adler and Joan Chodorow*. London: Jessica Kingsley, pp.17–28.

Gendlin, Eugene. (1978). *Focusing*, New York, NY: Bantam Books.

Gold, L. (2008). *Is Body Self or Other?* <http://www.somatics.com/pdf/Self_or_Other.pdf> (accessed March 2009).

Johnson, D. H. (2004). 'Body practices and human inquiry: Disciplined experiencing, fresh thinking, vigorous language', in V. Berdayes (ed.), *The Body in Human Inquiry: Interdisciplinary Explorations of Embodiment*. New York, NY: Hampton Press. <http://donhanlonjohnson.com/articles/bodypractice.html>

Johnson, D. H. (2006). 'The primacy of experiential practices in Body-Psychotherapy', in G. Marlock and H. Weiss (eds.), *Handbuch der Kšrperpsychotherapie* (*The Handbook of Body Psychotherapy*). Stuttgart: Schattauer GmbH. <http://donhanlonjohnson.com/articles/theprimacy.html>

Jung, C. G. (1940/80). 'The psychology of the child archetype', in *Archetypes of the Collective Unconscious: Collected Works*. London: Routledge, pp. 151–60.

Jung, C. G. (1961). *Memories, Dreams, Reflections*. New York, NY: Random House.

Jung, C. G. (1973). *C. G. Jung Letters: Selected and Edited by Gerhard Adler in Collaboration with Aniela Jaffé*, 2 vols. Princeton, NJ: Princeton University Press.

Jung, C. G. (1975). *Psychology and Religion, West and East: Collected Works*. Princeton, NJ: Princeton University Press.

Jung, C. G. and Jarrett, J. L. (1989). *Nietzsche's Zarathustra: Notes on a Seminar Given in 1934–1939, in Two Parts*. London: Routledge.

Kalsched, D. (1996). *The Inner World of Trauma: Archetypal Defenses of the Personal Spirit*. London: Routledge.

Kalsched, D. (2013). *Trauma and the Soul: A Psycho-Spiritual Approach to Human Development and its Interruption*. London: Routledge.

Levine, P. (2015). *Trauma and Memory, Brain and Body in a Search for the Living Past*. Berkeley, CA: North Atlantic Books.

McGilchrist, I. (2009). *The Master and His Emissary: The Divided Brain and the Making of the Western World*. New Haven, CT: Yale University Press.

Mills, J. (2003). 'A phenomenology of becoming: reflections on authenticity', in R. Frie (ed.), *Understanding Experience, Psychotherapy and Postmodernism*. London: Routledge, pp. 116–36.

Noë, A. (2009). *Out of Our Heads: Why You are Not Your Brain, and Other Lessons from the Biology of Consciousness*. New York, NY: Hill and Wang.

Payne, H. (2006). 'The body as container and expresser: Authentic Movement groups in the development of wellbeing in our bodymindspirit', in J. Corrigall, H. Payne, and H. Wilkinson (eds.), *About a Body: Working with the Embodied Mind in Psychotherapy*. Hove: Routledge, pp. 162–80.

Pinkola Estes, C. (1991/96). *Women who Run with the Wolves: Contacting the Power of the Wild Woman*. London: Rider.

Samuels, A., Shorter, B., and Plaut, F. (1986). *A Critical Dictionary of Jungian Analysis*. London: Routledge and Kegan Paul.

Soth, M. (2006). 'What therapeutic hope for a subjective mind in an objectified body?', in J. Corrigall, H. Payne, and H. Wilkinson (eds.), *About a Body: Working with the Embodied Mind in Psychotherapy*. Hove: Routledge, pp. 111–31.

Stromsted, T. (2007). 'The discipline of Authentic Movement as mystical practice: Evolving moments in Janet Adler's life and work', in P. Pallaro (ed.), *Authentic Movement: Moving the Body, Moving the Self, Being Moved: A Collection of Essays, Volume Two*. London: Jessica Kingsley, pp. 244–59.

Thompson, M. G. (2003). 'The primacy of experience in R. D. Laing's approach to psychoanalysis', in *Understanding Experience, Psychotherapy and Postmodernism*. London: Routledge, 180–203.

Thompson, M. G. (2005). 'Phenomenology of intersubjectivity: A historical overview of the concept and its clinical implications', in J. Mills (ed.), *Relational and Intersubjective Perspectives in Psychoanalysis*. New York, NY: Jason Aronson.

van der Kolk, B. (2014). *The Body Keeps the Score, Mind, Brain and Body in the Transformation of Trauma*. London: Allen Lane.

Whitehouse, M. S. (1999a). 'C. G. Jung and dance therapy: Two major principles', in P. Pallaro (ed.), *Authentic Movement: Essays by Mary Starks Whitehouse, Janet Adler and Joan Chodorow*. London: Jessica Kingsley, pp. 73–105.

Whitehouse, M. S. (1999b). 'Physical movement and personality', in P. Pallaro (ed.), *Authentic Movement: Essays by Mary Starks Whitehouse, Janet Adler and Joan Chodorow*. London: Jessica Kingsley, pp. 51–7. <http://www.nationalaccountsofwellbeing.org/learn/what-is-well-being.html> (accessed 17 July 2012).

....

CHAPTER 9

AUTHENTIC MOVEMENT AND THE RELATIONSHIP OF EMBODIED SPIRITUALITY TO HEALTH AND WELLBEING

....

ZOË AVSTREIH

INTRODUCTION

....

CURRENT research suggests a relationship between spiritual practices and healthier living, better social, emotional, and mental health, and increased self-esteem and perceived wellbeing (Plante and Thoresen 2007, p. x). Walsh (2000) distinguishes between religion and spirituality, defining *spirituality* as *direct experience* of the sacred (p. 3). He goes on to say that 'the ultimate aim of spiritual practices is awakening; that is, to know our true Self and our relationship to the sacred' (p. 4).

This chapter will discuss Authentic Movement as an embodied spiritual practice that fosters a connection to the true Self, promoting a sense of health and wellbeing that flows from an increase in empathy, compassion for self and other, and a deepening sense of the sacred quality of life itself.

HEALTH, WHOLE, HOLY, AND HALLOW

....

The English word 'health' is derived from the Indo-European root 'kailo', which is also the root of the words 'whole', 'wholesome', 'heal', 'holy', and 'hallow' (*American Heritage Dictionary* 1996, p. 2107). In its origins, the word 'health' is intimately connected to that which is whole, holy, and sacred, as is the practice of Authentic Movement. Authentic Movement serves the process of individuation—what Whitehouse refers to as the 'slow unfolding of a wholeness already there' (Whitehouse 1979, in Pallaro 1999, p. 78), and offers a portal to the sacred, a personal experience of the numinous—the term used by Rudolf Otto (1923) to describe the human encounter with the 'Holy'.

Whitehouse, influenced by both her personal experience in Jungian analysis and her studies of Jungian depth psychology, began to understand her movement work as a form of active imagination in movement, an embodied dialogue between the *self*, with a small 's' referring to the conscious ego/personality, and the *Self*, with a capital 'S' in Jungian thought referring to the totality of the psyche, both conscious and unconscious, as well as the archetype of wholeness that 'functions as an ordering and centring process of the psyche' (Chodorow 1991, p. 60). The core of the work for Whitehouse was: 'A centering, integrating, compelling obedience to something more than your personality ... The whole hinges on being, ready, willing and able to see the movement in the light of spiritual matter' (Wallock 1977, p. 71, as cited in Frieder 2007, p. 43). The words 'spiritual matter' embrace the body and mind as an integrated, unified whole, reflecting what Lowen (1990) calls the spirituality of the body, the capacity to feel 'a force within the self that is greater than the conscious self' (p. 44).

Authentic Movement supports the process of individuation—the unfolding of the individual towards their innate potential wholeness. Unlike individuality, which may lead to a sense of separation and self-preoccupation, the process of individuation serves to intimately connect one to the world.

> To individuate is to expand the boundaries of individual identity and personality to be rooted in our inner sense of totality. It is a growing sense of, in Jung's terms, the Self as the root of meaning and the archetype of wholeness within each of us. As we individuate we can experience our own deeper spiritual heart and then begin to express it in the world. This expression of individuation enables us to have a quality of inner authority, integrity, and knowledge of what is true for ourselves. It enables us to open to our unique responsibility in the task of our life for the welfare and good of all ... We stand upon a threshold where the individual meets the universal and yet retains a unique sense of self. (Preece 2006, p. 74)

To heal is to restore our sense of wholeness. In the practice of Authentic Movement, the spontaneous movements of the body become the pathway to remembering the innate wholeness of our being, the essence of our being that remains whole and unharmed as expressed by the words of this mover, a young woman who entered therapy to heal from the debilitating impact of childhood abuse:

> I enter the practice for the first time, fearful, fearful that I will meet once again the pain and fear that I have carried in my body for so long. Instead I am met with the pure joy of experiencing my body moving. I weep with joy, finding the part of me that remained untouched, unharmed by the years of abuse and trauma. I came home to my essence, to the truth of who I am. How grateful I am to find HER once again. Rooted in this centre, I have the support and the courage to allow my body to feel, to awaken once again and guide me in my healing process.

Through the direct experience of the body, Authentic Movement provides a way to heal the severance of mind and body. As 'we dance our sentient, embodied existence' (Fraleigh 1987, p. xvii), we come to know the true Self. The moving body becomes a sacred act of blessing the vital animating force within.

EMBODIED SPIRITUALITY: EMBRACING PARADOX

The derivative of the word 'spirituality' is the Latin word *spiritus*, which means 'breath'. It is related to the Greek work *pneuma*, which also means 'breath' and refers to a vital animating force. The physical act of breathing, each inhalation and exhalation, is an embodied declaration of our spiritual essence—each moment an opportunity to come home to our true nature.

The word 'spirituality' implies a sense of connection to an invisible essence that is larger than the personal self. Spirituality is connected to 'the feelings, thoughts, experiences, and behaviors that arise from a search for the sacred' (Boudreaux et al. 2002: 439, as cited in Young and Koopsen 2005, p. 8).

Embodied spirituality is used in this chapter to describe the body as a portal to the sacred, to the direct experience of the true Self. The term embraces the unification of body and spirit, the finite and infinite. It challenges the western Cartesian view that severed the intimate connection between the visible and invisible realms of existence, for the term 'embodied spirituality' embraces the incarnate mystery of human existence. As Jung (1933) has written:

> The body claims equal recognition; it exerts the same fascination as the psyche. If we are still caught in the old idea of an antithesis between mind and matter, this state of affairs must seem like an unbearable contradiction. But if we can reconcile ourselves to the mysterious truth that the spirit is the life of the body seen from within, and the body the outward manifestation of the life of the spirit—the two being really one—then we can understand why the striving to transcend the present level of consciousness through acceptance of the unconscious must give the body its due, and why recognition of the body cannot tolerate a philosophy that denies it in the name of the spirit. (p. 94)

Washburn (2003), in his book entitled *Embodied Spirituality in a Sacred World*, speaks of a 'deep psychic core (or deep psyche), which is inherited and, therefore, universal to the species' (p. 1). He calls this deep psyche the 'dynamic ground' (p. 2). For Washburn, the dynamic ground is a bridge between the psyche and the soma. The term resonates with what Jung called the *psychoid* level of the unconscious—the depth of the unconscious where the soma and psyche meet. It is here, at the meeting place of psyche and soma, that the true *Self* resides. In the practice of Authentic Movement, our embodied existence become the portal to the true Self, the archetype of wholeness within, the inherited and universal dynamic ground of our being.

Rooted in this understanding, the practice of Authentic Movement dances with the paradox that the body, which is finite and subject to illness, old age, and death, is in itself both the embodiment of the invisible ground of being and the gateway to the direct experience of the sacred, inexhaustible source of life itself (Avstreih 2007). This personal sense of connectedness to an ultimate source supports a profound sense of reverence for life, a sense of being connected to others, to community, to our shared existence on this planet and ultimately to the mystery of existence itself.

AUTHENTIC MOVEMENT

Originally rooted in the intersection of dance/movement therapy and Jungian depth analysis, Authentic Movement has evolved into a discipline with its own integrity informing psychotherapy, contemplative practice, prayer, ritual, creative process, embodied community, and the healing of body, mind, and soul. Authentic Movement is a profoundly simple form: a mover, a witness, and the relationship between them define its outer structure. For both the mover and the witness the work of Authentic Movement 'is centered on the development of an inner witness, which is one way of understanding the development of consciousness' (Adler 2002, p. xvi). Brown and Ryan (2003) define awareness and attention as components of consciousness:

> *Consciousness* encompasses both awareness and attention. *Awareness* is the background 'radar' of consciousness, continually monitoring the inner and outer environment. One may be aware of stimuli without them being at the center of attention. *Attention* is the process of focusing conscious awareness, providing heightened sensitivity to a limited range of experience. (822)

In the practice of Authentic Movement, one focuses *attention* inward, increasing receptivity and *awareness* of the vital animating force within as it becomes conscious through sensation, impulses, and energy patterns, allowing it to emerge into manifest form in movements visible or invisible to the external witness.

The core of the work of authentic movement is rooted in relationship: the relationship between the mover and the external witness, the relationship between the moving self and the internal witness, between the individual and the collective, and between the individual and the greater mysteries of life itself (Adler 1995, 2002, 2007; Avstreih 2002, 2005, 2007, 2008, 2014).

Fundamental to the practice is the experience of seeing and being seen reflecting the paradox that we are birthed into the fullness of our being through the attuned presence of another. The open, receptive, and non-judgmental attentive presence of the witness provides an environment of 'holding' (Winnicott 1965)—a metaphor for an affectively attuned relational field that provides a felt sense of safety and trust (Avstreih 2014). This relational field supports the mover to yield to the deepest levels of their kinesthetic reality, to know their truth in the presence of another, and to have it received free from projection.

In the practice, one comes to know the 'authentic' self as it emerges into consciousness and form through the spontaneous movements. Whitehouse used the word 'authentic' to describe the particular movements that she felt were genuine, true for the mover in the moment.

> When movement was simple and inevitable, not to be changed no matter how limited or partial, it became what I called 'authentic'—it could be recognized as genuine, belonging to that person. Authentic was the only term I could think of that meant truth—truth of a kind unlearned. (Whitehouse 1979, in Pallaro 1999, pp. 81-2)

At its core, Authentic Movement is about trust in the innate wisdom of the body to sense and express what may not be known on other levels of consciousness. The work offers an invitation to live a life that is rooted in direct contact with one's inner truth, and to come to 'treasure a way of life ruled by the dictates of (one's) 'alive center' (Wittine 1993, in Walsh and Vaughan 1993, p. 167). As the perennial philosophy and the ancient wisdom traditions teach, we become truly whole when 'we awaken to the wholeness of a deeper level of identity, the Self' (Wittine 1993, in Walsh and Vaughan 1993, p. 168).

THE PERSONAL TRUE SELF AND THE ARCHETYPAL TRUE *SELF*

The practice of Authentic Movement is rooted in the understanding that the personal self and transcendent Self are inseparable. The body is not only the vehicle for the direct experience of the sacred; it *is* the direct expression of the sacred. From this perspective, one's personal history and concerns for the experiences of everyday living is a pathway to a deeper connection with one's 'alive centre'.

In 1965 the late psychoanalyst and pediatrician D. W. Winnicott defined the *true self* as it emerged on the personal level as 'the inherited potential which is experiencing a continuity of being and acquiring in its own way and its own speed a personal psychic reality and a personal body scheme' (p. 46). Bollas (1989) states that 'this core self is the unique presence of being that each of us is' (p. 9), and depends on the facilitating presence of another to evolve. Our inherited potential is birthed in the presence of an attuned other 'who does not interfere or impinge on the representations of the true self as they emerge into manifest form' (Avstreih 2008, p. 215). Rooted in this understanding, the practice of Authentic Movement emphasizes the careful training of the external witness, the facilitating other, in order to create a 'facilitating environment' (Winnicott

1965) that supports the spontaneous gestures of the true self to emerge into movement as authentic declarations of one's core being.

Held in the attuned presence of another, the spontaneous gestures arise and are received free from projection, retaining their fundamental nature of authenticity. In her book *Finding Space: Winnicott, God, and Psychic Reality* (2001), Ulanov gives voice to Winnicott's understanding in this way:

> We arrive at what Winnicott calls a true self, which we experience as 'tissue aliveness' in our bodies and as imaginative aliveness in our psyches ... when true, our self at the core, feels real in the world. We can hold ourselves in being, inhabit our bodies and touch others. We can imaginatively elaborate our experiences and arrive at new perceptions. We can go on being, sustaining a sense of continuity through time and space, acquiring history, a narrative thread to our identity. Above all, we enjoy living creatively. A presence shines through ... This being of ours proves durable, even in the face of suffering ... a feeling that whatever happens, this living is worth it ... This is the soul we dare not lose, even if we were to gain the whole world. (pp. 46–7)

In the embodied form of Authentic Movement we come home and return again and again to the body, the dwelling place of the true self. We become alive, awake to the ongoing flow of life. We open to the direct experience of the vital animating centre of our being, the wellspring of vitality, creativity, and authenticity that nourishes every aspect of our life.

Although Winnicott did not speak directly of a spiritual core of being, his writings and his profound respect for his patients point to his deep appreciation of a sacred core of being that is the root of one's sense of aliveness and wellbeing. For Winnicott, this core of self-experience resists definition or labels. Ulanov (2001), reflecting on Winnicott's profound respect for the 'precious initiating self', uses these words:

> Out of this still, silent, singular primordial center of the personality all liveliness arises ... The excitement and inner gladness of being, the energy and freshness of instinct, the spontaneous gestures to communicate that arise from the core of our-selves in some tiny way reflect the unspeakable energy of God that only the word *love* captures. (p. 130)

The spontaneous gestures of the true self reflect the holy nature of our embodied exist-ence. The personal self is not separate from the true *Self*. The practice of Authentic Movement is a path to the direct experience of this simple yet profound realization.

THE SCHOOL OF THE BODY: A SACRED SPACE

In the practice of Authentic Movement, one enters the school of the body through the gateway of the senses. This is the paradox of embodied spirituality, for the senses that allow us to perceive the experiences of waking life are also the gateway into other realms of deeper awareness. A way of knowing reflected in the teachings of many ancient wisdom traditions is beautifully stated in these words of the great mystic poet Rumi: 'These gifts from the Friend, a robe of skin and veins, a teacher within, wear them and become a school' (Rumi 1995, p. 144). The learning here reflects the original sense of the Latin word 'educare', meaning to 'bring forth' what is already there.

In Authentic Movement, one receives life's lessons through the wisdom of the body. As the Buddha has said: 'Everything that arises in the mind starts with a flowing of sensation on the body' (cited in Johnson 2000, p. 22). Sensation becomes the guide or doorway to the wisdom of the inner teacher. As we develop the capacity to stay present with open, receptive attention, the body speaks, revealing the fixed patterns that restrict the fullness of our lived experience. The inner witness provides a safe container for these constricting patterns to emerge into awareness and release naturally and organically. Spontaneous movement arises, and our innate life-energy flows freely, bringing with it a sense of aliveness.

The ancient wisdom traditions say the truth lies within. Focusing attention inward with clear intention, one enters the school of the body and becomes a true student. Here we learn to live directly from the truth of our inner centre, which in itself is both restorative and healing (Wittine 1993). We become alive, awake to the ongoing flow of life—what Winnicott refers to as 'living the true self' (Ulanov 2001, p. 131).

The practice invites a yielding to both the personal and collective unconscious, while simultaneously offering the integrative potential of consciousness. It strengthens one's ability to attune to one's impulses, and helps develop respect and trust in the authenticity of one's movement. Learning to listen to one's inner cues, one emerges with a greater trust in the integrity of one's being and one's innate intelligence and self-regulating capacity for wellness.

Sacred Space: Honouring

The structure of Authentic Movement defined by the mover, the witness, and the relationship between them mirrors the structure of the therapeutic relationship, client, and therapist, and the relationship between the student/seeker and the teacher. In these structures, the witness, the therapist, or the teacher initially holds the larger responsibility of consciousness, thereby creating a safe container for the client, student, or mover to focus inward and make direct contact with the inner teacher, the inner knowing.

The structure and safety of the container is supported by the acknowledged trust in the integrity of the mover's direct embodied experience and the holding presence created by the open, receptive, non-judgmental attentiveness of the witness. The safety of the container allows that which is innately true to emerge and be seen. It is a process by which one repeatedly becomes emptied of preconceptions and preconditions and opens to the experience of the moment-to-moment unfolding dance of sensation, impulse, and energy in the present moment. Like play, which provides a space for the possibility of being, free from judgement and criticism, the form of Authentic Movement, the structure of mover, witness, and the relationship between them, provides a 'potential space' (Winnicott 1971) for spontaneity and authenticity.

In this space of vast alive potential, the true self is invited to come alive and express itself and embrace life enlivened with a sense of reality, embodied in an individual human form that exists at the juncture of the formless and its creative manifestations of form. This vast alive space of potential is sacred space—the space of 'primary creativity' which is an innate gift of our being. Winnicott believed in the innate presence of primary creativity—a space of absolute originality (Winnicott 1988). Creativity in this sense does not mean producing things. Ulanov (2001) articulates it this way:

> It means always perceiving freshly, feeling alive and real, in a self lodged in a body that we know as our own, out of which we live in shared existence with others but not from compliance, inhibition, or coercion. The mere act of breathing can partake of creative living. (p. 133)

The structure of the Authentic Movement container is an embodied commitment to honour the sacred nature of the spontaneous gestures that arises from the true self, the seat of primary creativity. In the practice, the role and training of the external witness are of utmost importance in order to protect the sacred expressions of the mover.

The external witness sits at the side of the movement space with eyes open, initially holding the larger responsibility for consciousness, with a commitment to protect and honour the spontaneous expressions of the mover. Through years of practice, the external witness has cultivated a strong inner witness, capable of tracking both the mover and tracking their own embodied experience including sensations, impulses, images, feelings, memories, and thoughts. 'The witness practices the art of seeing' (Adler 1996, p. 194), which entails not simply 'looking at' the mover, but rather allowing oneself to receive and attune to the mover while also attending to one's own experiences in response to the mover.

> Seeing clearly is not about what the mover needs or must do. The witness does not 'look at' the mover but, instead, as she internalizes the mover, she attends to her own experiences of judgment, interpretation, and projection in response to the mover as catalyst. As she acknowledges ownership of her experiences, the density of her personal history empties, enabling the witness at times to feel that she can see the mover clearly and, more importantly, that she can see herself clearly. (Adler 1996, pp. 194–5)

The witness practices the art of seeing to become a clear mirror for the mover, to embody a deep commitment to create a safe environment for the expressions of the true self to emerge and be received free from judgement, interpretation, and project.

In order to protect the integrity of the mover's experience from judgement, interpretation, and projection, Adler introduced the use of Percept Language (Weir 1975) into the practice (Adler 2002). Weir developed Percept Language—the use of the pronoun 'I' while speaking—to reinforce the concept of ownership and responsibility for one's perceptions. According to Weir (1975), the 'process of perception is selective . . . each of us is continually perceiving and organizing the world in a unique way' (p. 304). He further elaborates this idea as follows:

> You are there. So I experience you. But I can never experience an absolute or 'true' you, only the 'you-I-know-at-this moment', the 'you-I-perceive', the 'you-in-me'. I experience you in my own selective way, imposing my perceptual organization on the elements of you I am able and permit myself to experience. I form an internal image you, this 'you-in-me', and react to this perception as 'you' . . . In general, all my perceptions of others, my projections, my transferences, my blindnesses, and my illuminations take place within me. They are my doing and my responsibility. (pp. 305–6)

This care and precision in the use of language serves to protect the quality of sacred space, helping both mover and witness to cultivate a refined capacity to differentiate between clear perception and projection, thus honouring their commitment to neither usurp nor trample on the self-initiating offerings of the true self.

Creating Sacred Space: Individual Body and Collective Body

The school of the body houses the inner teacher for both the mover and the witness. The work ideally begins in dyads, with one mover and a trained witness, and may develop to include work in triads and groups. In the practice of Authentic Movement, the group—the collection of individuals—is referred to as the 'collective body'. Focusing attention inward with receptive openness, one crosses the threshold, entering the dwelling place of the inner teacher that resides in the school of both the 'individual body' and the 'collective body'.

Through years of facilitating the process I have come to understand ritual as the external expression of inner experience. Over the years, the following ritual has emerged as a way to both symbolically create a sacred space of practice and to prepare for the descent into the deeper levels of one's consciousness and knowing. The group gathers, standing in a circle, and begins the ritual of creating sacred space by communally walking counterclockwise. This circumambulation demarcates a centre space of emptiness. Circling around once, we return to the place where we started, face inward, acknowledging the empty space within the circle of our bodies, a central space of emptiness, symbolizing the sacred space of healing. At this moment, each member of the collective body renews their commitment to assume ownership and responsibility for their own experiences and thus keeps the space free from projection. Together, we create a sacred vessel for practice held by the integrity of our commitment and open to the inherent wisdom of the inner teacher.

> The body becomes the microcosm of the cosmos, the edge between the sacred and profane, and it, too, becomes a vessel within the larger communal vessel of the circle.

The sacred space is set and we enter into it as we choose to have faith in embodying the moment. (Burns 2008, p. 3)

Receiving: The Individual Body

Crossing the threshold, entering into the space of practice, opening to what is not yet known, we prepare to learn from 'the raw data of our own experience' (Shikpo 2007, p. 10). 'There is a word in Hebrew, *teshuvah,* that literally means "repentance" but more accurately refers to an inward *turning toward the truth* of the moment' (Bobrow 2010, p. 67). This is the essence of the practice of Authentic Movement. We 'start close in' (Whyte 2007, p. 362), and find our 'own way to begin the conversation' (p.362) between the conscious and the unconscious, between the manifest and the invisible, and between the finite and the infinite.

This simple yet profound truth is expressed by the experience of this young woman—a member of an ongoing group for young adults on their journey towards adulthood in the following way: 'I strive to restore transparency to my lived reality, to come to know more fully the ways I hide or obscure my authentic experience from myself and others.' She goes on to speak about the ongoing conflict she has with form and structure—a resistance which she feels stems from her life experiences of having had many expectations imposed on her from external sources. She enters practice one day with the intention to explore her resistance to form and structure as it relates to her relationship with a particular person in her early life. She uses these words to describe her movement experience:

> I come to ground, sit, and rest on my left hand. I feel stuck, stuck by form. I can't move. I'm trapped in stillness and I sense that energy wants to be liberated. My hands start brushing away, flapping against all that is caging me. I flap and brush off all the stuck energy around my body. I come into sitting upright, cross-legged. Yes, I am strong. A rope is in front of me; I climb it with my hands. It is [I am] pulling me into my dignity. My spine stretches upward and I become more confident. Still in a sitting posture, but climbing, one hand over the other, they finally meet as stacked fists over my solar-plexus/heart center. They feel solid there; this is a strength pose. This is my center of gravity. I am poised.

The teaching arrives through the wisdom of the body, releasing old entanglements and patterns, offering the embodied sense of a new way of being in the world, deeply rooted in her direct experience. This young woman is learning to access and trust the wisdom of her inner teacher, to begin the journey of becoming the author of her own life. She is restoring her capacity to live rooted in the truth of her inner experience, centred in a body that she experiences as strong and alive, and from this fundamental place of connectedness share herself with other, free from compliance, inhibition or coercion.

Receiving: The Collective Body

In the practice, the collective body of experienced movers and witnesses provides a powerful container for healing. As each member of the collective body surrenders to the wisdom of the inner teacher, they simultaneously open to receive the healing wisdom that emerges through the collective body. The following is a powerful example of such an experience. This mover, a young man in his late twenties, is a member of an ongoing Authentic Movement therapy group which has been meeting for over a year. There is a high degree of trust and trustworthiness in the group, which provides a safe container for the exploration and working through of early trauma. His experience in this movement time reflects the potency of a healing that arises as the wisdom of his inner teacher meets the emerging wisdom of the collective body. He describes his experience as follows:

> As I enter the movement space, I feel tense, somewhat triggered by events of the day. As I begin to move, I take a journey back into time and revisit a trauma from my childhood. I experience it this time, not as a helpless childhood, but with the embodied experience of the man that I now am. I see the events unfold as they had that day, but this time I, the adult, intervene to protect the small child that I was and that I still carry inside me. When I see my father advance to attack 'little me', I step in. I put my left hand on my heart and I move the little child behind me with my right hand so he could peek around my leg and still be protected. Now, I am in my fight stance and ready to fight if needed. Just as I was about to make a strong, powerful stabbing movement into the space, I cracked my eyes to make sure there was no one standing close to me that I could hurt. I found myself surrounded by movers. The forceful movement I had felt emerging was restricted, but to my surprise, this only facilitated what happened next.
>
> As my mind looked for a way out, energy flowed from my heart out through my arm and into my father's heart. There was no longer any need for violence, for when he felt the emotion in my heart it, it was more than he could bear. He found his tears in my rage, just as I had found mine in his. Then the rage that flowed from my heart turned into compassion, and I expressed what he could not. I cradled him in my arms and comforted him. By the time the movement session had ended, the compassionate adult that I embodied in that moment, merged with the old image of my father transforming him, and simultaneously allowing the wall of protection that I had built around me years ago to begin to dissolve.

This mover's experience reflects a central aspect of the practice of Authentic Movement. Entering practice with a commitment to not hurt oneself or another, each individual is free to choose moment-to-moment as they dance between will and surrender in response to the voice of the inner teacher what is the true movement or response now. 'In the midst of such concentration on owning one's own experience as mover or witness it matters that others are attempting the same practice, thus trusting some inherent order in the collective' (Adler 1996, p. 195). Often, in this field of integrity, spontaneous forms of synchrony arise in the group—an offering of the innate wisdom of the collective body that supports the healing process.

Conclusion: Embodied Spirituality, Health, and Wellbeing

Embodied spirituality is the direct experience of the body as a portal to the sacred. From its inception, Authentic Movement has been rooted in the direct experience of an invisible yet palpable existence of an inner animating source. As Whitehouse (1987) has stated: 'There is that in us which has moved from the very beginning; it is that which can liberate us' (p. 53).

In the practice of Authentic Movement, the body becomes the portal to the wisdom of the inner teacher, the Self. 'In each one of us is a living truth' (Aldridge 2000, p. 199). We dance with the paradox that the body, which is finite and subject to decay and disease, is a portal to the direct experience of what in the perennial wisdom or philosophy is known as the 'divine spark', the centre of transcendent awareness, pure consciousness, mind, spirit, or Self (Walsh 2000). In Authentic Movement practice, we consciously enter the school of the body; spontaneous gestures emerge into form as we encounter the living truth within. Here, the paradox of finite and infinite coexist. This encounter with our ever-present wholeness provides the ultimate foundation for healing and wellbeing. Each time we enter practice, we honour the gift of our embodied existence as a profound source of wisdom—a simple truth so eloquently expressed by the fourteenth-century poet Yunus Emre:

> We entered the house of realization,
> We witnessed the body . . .
> Truth is wherever you want it.
> We found it all within the body.

References

Adler, J. (1992). 'Body and soul', in P. Pallaro (ed.) (1999), *Authentic Movement: Essays by Mary Starks Whitehouse, Janet Adler and Joan Chodorow*. London and Philadelphia: Jessica Kingsley, pp. 160–89.

Adler, J. (1995). *Arching Backward*. Rochester, VT: Inner Traditions.

Adler, J. (1996). 'The collective body', in P. Pallaro (ed.) (1999). *Authentic Movement: Essays by Mary Starks Whitehouse, Janet Adler and Joan Chodorow*. London and Philadelphia: Jessica Kingsley, pp. 190–204.

Adler, J. (2002). *Offering from the Conscious Body: The Discipline of Authentic Movement*. Rochester, VT: Inner Traditions.

Adler, J. (2007). 'From autism to the discipline of authentic movement', in P. Pallaro (ed.) (1999), *Authentic Movement: Moving the Body, Moving the Self, Being Moved: A Collection of Essays, Volume Two*. London and Philadelphia: Jessica Kingsley, pp. 24–31.

Aldridge, D. (2000). *Spirituality, Healing and Medicine: Return to the Silence*. London and Philadelphia: Jessica Kingsley.

American Heritage Dictionary of the English Language (1996). 3rd edn. Boston and New York: Houghton Mifflin Company.

Avstreih, Z. (2002). 'Coming home', *A Moving Journal*, 9(2): 18–20.

Avstreih, Z. (2005). 'Authentic movement and Buddhism', *A Moving Journal*, 13(3): 8–10.

Avstreih, Z. (2007). 'Achieving body permanence: Authentic movement and the paradox of healing', in P. Pallaro (ed.) (1999), *Authentic Movement: Moving the Body, Moving the Self, Being Moved: A Collection of Essays, Volume Two*. London and Philadelphia: Jessica Kingsley, pp. 270–3.

Avstreih, Z. (2008). 'The body in psychotherapy: Dancing with the paradox', in F. Kaklauskas, S. Nimanheminda, L. Hoffman, and M. Jack (eds.), *Brilliant Sanity: Buddhist Approaches to Psychotherapy*. Colorado Springs, CO: University of the Rockies Press, pp. 213–21.

Avstreih, Z. (2014). 'Authentic movement and mindfulness: Embodied awareness and the healing nature of the expressive arts', in L. Rappaport (ed.), *Mindfulness and the Arts Therapies: Theory and Practice*. London and Philadelphia: Jessica Kingsley, pp. 182–192.

Bobrow, J. (2010). *Zen and Psychotherapy: Partners in Liberation*. New York and London: W. W. Norton.

Bollas, C. (1989). *Forces of Destiny: Psychoanalysis and Human Idiom*. Northvale, NJ, and London: Jason Aronson.

Boudreaux, E. D., O'Hea, E., and Chasuk, R. (2002). 'Spiritual role in healing: An alternative way of thinking', *Primary Care: Clinics in Office Practice*, 29(2): viii, 439–54.

Brown, K. W. and Ryan, R. M. (2003). 'The benefits of being present: Mindfulness and its role in psychological well-being', *Journal of Personality and Social Psychology*, 84: 822–48.

Burns, C. A. (2008). *Passages of Authentic Movement*. Unpublished manuscript.

Chodorow, J. (1991). *Dance Therapy and Depth Psychology: The Moving Imagination*. London and New York: Routledge.

Fraleigh, S. H. (1987). *Dance and the Lived Body: A Descriptive Aesthetics*. Pittsburg, PA: University of Pittsburg Press.

Frieder, S. (2007). 'Reflection on Mary Starks Whitehouse', in P. Pallaro (ed.), *Authentic Movement: Moving the Body, Moving the Self, Being Moved: A Collection of Essays, Volume Two*. London and Philadelphia: Jessica Kingsley, pp. 35–44.

Levy, F. J. (2005). *Dance Movement Therapy: A Healing Art*. Reston, VA: National Dance Association (American Alliance for Health, Psychical Education, Recreation, and Dance.

Lowen, A. (1990). *The Spirituality of the Body*. New York, NY: MacMillan.

Otto, R. (1923). *The Idea of the Holy: An Inquiry into the Non-Rational Factor in the Idea of the Divine and Its Relationship to the Rational*, transl. J. W. Harvey. London: Oxford University Press. First published in 1917.

Plante, T. and Thoresen, C. E. (eds.) (2007). *Spirit, Science and Health: How the Spiritual Mind Fuels Physical Wellness*. Westport, CT: Prager/Greenwood.

Preece, R. (2006). *The Wisdom of Imperfection: The Challenge of Individuation in Buddhist Life*. Ithaca, NY: Snow Lion Publications.

Rumi, J. (1995). 'The mouse and the camel', in C. Barks (transl.), *The Essential Rumi*. San Francisco, CA: HarperCollins, pp. 142–4.

Shikpo, R. (2007). *Never Turn Away: The Buddhist Path Beyond Hope and Fear*. Boston, MA: Wisdom Publications.

Ulanov, A. B. (2001). *Finding Space: Winnicott, God and Psychic Reality*. Louisville, KY: Westminster John Knox Press.

Wallock, S. (1977). *Dance/Movement Therapy: A Survey of Philosophy and Practice*. Unpublished manuscript.

Walsh, R. and Vaughan, R. (eds.) (1993). *Paths beyond Ego: The Transpersonal Vision*. Los Angeles, CA: Jeremy P. Tarcher/Perigee.

Walsh, R. (2000). *Essential Spirituality: The 7 Central Practices to Awaken Heart and Mind*. New York, NY: Wiley.

Washburn, M. (2003). *Embodied Spirituality in a Sacred World*. Albany: NY: State University of New York Press.

Weir, J. (1975). 'The personal growth laboratory', in K. D. Benne, L. P. Bradford, J. R. Gibb, and R. O. Lippett (eds.), *The Laboratory Method of Changing and Learning: Theory and Application*. Palo Alto, CA: Science Behavior Books, pp. 293–325.

Whitehouse, M. S. (1979). 'C. J. Jung and dance therapy: Two major principles', in P. Pallaro (ed.) (1999), *Authentic Movement: Essays by Mary Starks Whitehouse, Janet Adler and Joan Chodorow*. London and Philadelphia: Jessica Kingsley, pp. 73–101.

Whitehouse, M. S. (1987). 'Physical movement and personality', in P. Pallaro (ed.) (1999). *Authentic Movement: Essays by Mary Starks Whitehouse, Janet Adler and Joan Chodorow*. London and Philadelphia: Jessica Kingsley, pp. 51–7.

Whyte, D. (2007). 'Start close in', in *River Flow: New and Selected Poems*. Langley, WA: Many Rivers Press.

Winnicott, D. W. (1965). *The Maturational Process and the Facilitating Environment: Studies in the Theories of Emotional Development*. London: Hogarth Press.

Winnicott, D. W. (1971). *Playing and Reality*. London: Tavistock.

Winnicott, D. W. (1988). *Human Nature*. London: Free Association Books.

Wittine, B. (1993). 'Assumptions of transpersonal psychotherapy', in R. Walsh and F. Vaughan (eds.) *Paths beyond Ego: The Transpersonal Vision*. New York: Tarcher/Perigee, pp. 165–71.

Young, C. and Koopsen, C. (2005). *Spirituality, Health and Healing*. Sudsbury, MA: Jones and Bartlett Publishers.

CHAPTER 10

···

REIMAGINING OUR RELATIONSHIP TO THE DANCING BODY

···

ANDREA OLSEN

PRELUDE

···

RELATIONSHIP is a central theme in contemporary life, including relationship to self, other, and the natural world. Before beginning, let us draw a circle of appreciation around the colleagues whose work is included in this book and those who have brought this text to fruition: the scholars who have solicited and edited the writings, as well as the writers, editors, sales team, printers, and makers who collaborate to bring words to the page. And now you, the reader, are giving meaning to the written word through your own life experiences, collaborations, and companions. Models of relationship involve those closest to us.

Personal Narrative: Our Bodies Remember

I walk into a studio where I have danced for over twenty years, and close my eyes.[1] This is a practice called Authentic Movement, in which I invite movement impulses in the body to become more conscious (Adler 2015). Some of what emerges will find its way into dance performance; some is just for me. The process requires discernment, while recognizing the intrinsic intelligence of the body. Rather than seeking control over my movement, deep attending is involved. As my arm stretches upward, circling overhead, one hand grasps the other's wrist. A memory surfaces in my awareness of reaching to my father's hand, crossing a busy street as a young child, stretching up, up. My body remembers.

FIGURE 10.1. Skeleton and dancers. (Photo © Angela Jane Evancie.)

INTRODUCTION

Two themes are central to my work: First, body is earth: our bones, breath, and blood are the minerals, air, and water inside us. Body systems and earth systems are intricately interconnected (Olsen 2004). Arriving in this particular place—Northampton, Massachusetts, in the United States—three days ago to complete this chapter, the 70% of my body that is water is now from this watershed. The local eggs and greens, milk, and grains shaping my muscles and bones as I write are from this place. Humans are nature too, not separate but the same. There is no separation.

Second, dance—movement—is an essential way to experience this interconnectedness. Rather than being superficial, peripheral, or extraneous, dance is central, essential, the core to understanding what it means to be human (Olsen and McHose 2014). Sourced in over 3 billion years of evolutionary history, since the origins of the first cell, movement intelligence is inherent. Instead of seeking control over the body, we develop practices for deep attending.

Somatic Excursion: Orientation and Arriving

To explore these concepts at an experiential level, we practice arriving:[2]

You have to show up. Congratulations, you have already accomplished this task—finding this book, opening these pages, in a specific time, place, and state of mind. The next step is to become fully present in the moment. You may still be thinking about what is left undone from the day, a text message on your phone, or planning tomorrow. Three stages help us arrive together in depth, opening to more consciousness in any situation—bringing the body's intelligence 'on board' with the possibilities at hand.

First, you put your feet on the ground and feel the connection. (Can you locate them, spread their surfaces onto the floor?) Second, you free your spine, allowing all the holdings and longings of the day to release as you reach the crown of your head toward space. Third, you breathe—in, out, and through the whole body. If the oxygen from your plant relatives just stays in your lungs, you will die. Your bone cells breathe, muscle fibres breathe, and nerve cells engage cellular respiration with every breath.

Refreshing perception of these three relationships—ground and groundedness, space and spaciousness, and breath and responsiveness—supports creative thinking and imagination: the capacity to act with authenticity in the world. Perhaps we should have a cell phone 'app' whispering: 'Ground, space, breath. You are doing a very good job! Your oldest friend, gravity.'

This baseline of ease in the nervous system cultivates trust in our moving, dancing bodies, by optimizing the preset tone of the body. As an Aikido master might remind us, the fight is over before it begins. The pre-movement of the body–mind informs what will happen. Perception underlies coordination. Noticing sensations in the soles of your feet, palms of your hands, labyrinths of your inner ears, and engaging peripheral vision broadens awareness. This orienting system, called the 'tonic system', helps you engage with the immediacy of 'where', staying present to the experience at hand, rather than fixating on the past or future. Meaning-making or judgement—the 'why' or 'what' of the situation—comes later. The invitation is to stay in rapport with yourself in the context of other people and place (Frank 2004).

This attention to pre-movement is a theme discussed in relation to *tonic function* articulated by French anatomist Rolfer Hubert Godard. It is also described by McHose and Frank (2006), who offer protocols for inhabiting the body with more ease and awareness. The feet are essential. In conversation with others, McHose suggests that we remember that we are all standing on the same ground. As we engage in intercultural communication and face global challenges, understanding this foundational relationship helps us reimagine possibilities that are available to us through the body. (See Video 3.2 on the Companion Website ⊙.[3])

CHANGING LENSES

Teaching graduate students last spring at the Middlebury Institute of International Studies in Monterey, California, we developed specific tools for intercultural communication. In the two classes on Grassroots Leadership and Social Needs Assessment that I cotaught with Turkish scholar Nükhet Kardam, there were adult students from many countries— Afghanistan, Palestine, Guinea, Africa, Turkey, and the United States. These students, including former Peace Corps volunteers, United Nations affiliates, and World Bank employees, were action-oriented. They wanted useable skills to engage social change. Together we articulated a resource that we named 'Changing Lenses'. The goal was to bind subjective experience with a scientific foundation through embodied scholarship.

Somatic Excursion: Changing Lenses

Visualize that you are seated facing an ocean. It is a warm day with bright sunshine and a light sea breeze. People are strolling by, children and dogs are playing, and birds pass overhead. Enjoy the smells, sounds, and textures of this specific place gleaned from memory. Now imagine a pair of sunglasses (you will need five different pairs).

1. Begin putting on the glasses for a geological view. Focus on the ocean, ground, and sky of your place. This geological lens connects you to billions of years of earth's history as well as to the present landscape. If you were a geologist, surfer, or mountain climber, you might be drawn to the rocks, water, or weather patterns, reflecting the planet's origins some 4.6 billion years ago and changing through time. (Lower your arms, and 'glasses', to refresh.)

2. Try on a second pair of glasses for the biological view (lifting your hands to your face). Scan the horizon—what is happening in the unique life forms of plants and animals in this landscape. Often we recognize the truth of our emotional lives in the lives of animals. If you were a biologist, gardener, or dog-lover, your focus might be on the plants and animals of this place, connecting you back millions of years to the first boney fish and land plants some 400 million years ago. (Lower your arms, and 'glasses', to refresh.)

3. Put on the third pair of glasses for a cultural view. Consider the historical, political, religious, economic, and social heritage of this place, and how it is most visible in the present scene. Within the cultural view you can include the artists and writers who have preceded you in this place. This focus brings you to human history, which begins with the origin of Homo sapiens, around 200 thousand years ago. (Lower your arms, and 'glasses', to refresh.)

4. Try on the fourth pair of glasses for the familial view. Through connection to relatives and family, you can notice your perceptual preferences. Do you habitually look, listen, move, smell, or touch to perceive? You may have grandparents who walked here, parents whose ashes were spread at sea, picnics and boat trips on nearby islands, linking you back hundreds of years and continuing to the present day. (Lower your arms, and 'glasses', to refresh.)

5. And finally, experience the last pair of glasses—your personal view. This view, which underlies all perception, includes your education and training, beliefs and values, and the individual life experiences and memories that shape your attention to this place: a first kiss by the dock, performance on the beach, or a fight with a friend. Place is emotional, whether we are consciously aware of it or not. Now you are engaging decades of history, your life span. (Lower your arms, and 'glasses', and refresh.)

The problem with any lens (as with binoculars, for example) is that it can become stuck. When you are fixated on one view of the world, with no other possibilities, all the rest of the perspectives and ideologies are blurry or impossible to perceive. If, for example, you are working in a community with long-term distrust between families or tribes, including gender and economic inequalities (like my rural community in Maine, or my student's home community in Afghanistan), how do you move past fixed ideas and outcomes? How do you broaden the conversation? One possibility (from geography) is to look at a problem from a larger or smaller scale, a shift to a different perspective. It can be a relief to come together as a community to focus on water issues rather than staying stuck in family grievances or cultural inequities. And in dance, if there is pain in the knee, the cause might be misalignment at the ankle or hip; you look at the part above and below. Instead of focusing on the problem, you shift to lenses that support healing and change. All systems are inherently interconnected; starting with one will lead to the others. (See Video 10.6 on the Companion Website ▶.)

Understanding Perception

After forty years of teaching anatomy and kinesiology, it is always striking for me to remember that no two people perceive the same thing in the same moment. As you read this writing on perception, your nervous system connects to a vast array of associations, memories, and ideas that inform your view. Perception is a construct, impacted by the present state of your attention. You might be sleepy from lunch, elated after a run, or distracted by those irritating voices nearby. We each interpret the moment in our own way, based on past experience and the quality of our attention.

With this in mind, we can explore balancing the autonomic nervous system (ANS) to broaden perceptual possibilities. The ANS governs our vital actions and reactions. In dance and martial arts, the belly is considered the location for 'centred' energy, called the *hara* in Aikido and the *dan tien* in tai chi. ANS innervation engages automatic survival responses for fast, integrated movement, underlying a sense of body-level security and integrity so that we can be more present to the moment.

The ANS is part of the peripheral nervous system, outside the spinal vertebrae and skull. It is composed of nerves and ganglia located along the front of the spine, anterior to the bony vertebral bodies. Governing the vital organs and glands, the ANS affects heart rate, breath rate, and digestive and sexual functions. Messages go back and forth between body and brain, yet the ANS can function rapidly and continuously without conscious effort, regulating the visceral activities that maintain and support our dancing bodies.

The ANS is functionally divided into two parts: the sympathetic and parasympathetic nervous systems. The sympathetic division stimulates the body toward activity and engagement, the parasympathetic toward cycles of rest and digestion. The sympathetic and parasympathetic nerves work together, not antagonistically, to coordinate body functioning for optimal health.

During normal situations of alertness, the sympathetic nerves (thoraco-lumbar nerves) support clarity and directness of action (Cohen 2012). During what is perceived as a stressful situation, however, sympathetic nerves trigger the fight, flight, freeze, and friendly response. You can attack, run, disappear energetically, or try to smile, laugh, or talk your way out of what you perceive as a threatening situation (Porghes 2011). Physiological responses include dilation of pupils for increased vision, dilation of capillaries of the lungs for more oxygen, decrease in digestion and salivary gland secretions (dry mouth), increase in blood to skeletal muscles, and decrease of blood to the digestive organs, and increase in blood glucose concentration in preparation for activity, as well as release of bladder muscles to reduce energy expended. For example, before running a race, you generally are energized, clear your digestive tract by going to the bathroom, and lose your appetite.

For dancers, the edge of sympathetic activation brings dynamic range and 'larger than life' presence to performance. Overstimulation results in stress, falling off balance, and miscalculation of energy. When dancing, you can arouse your sympathetic nervous system by imagining that you are going to perform on a big stage, with dance critics in the audience, or whatever activates and heightens your stress levels. Notice that as your arousal level increases (skeletal muscles flush with blood, heart rate increases, pupils dilate, and glucose levels rise), it is exciting. The body often presses forward in the ribs and lumbar spine, ready to move!

The parasympathetic division (cranial-sacral nerves) is activated when the body is ready to relax and digest and there is time for integration, like a quiet afternoon after a big meal. In this situation the heart rate and breathing slow down, and the eyes relax and water. As the digestive system activates, increase in secretions and peristalsis sometimes cause familiar stomach grumbles. Reduction of blood and glucose levels in brain and skeletal muscles causes drowsiness. This restful digestive process allows recovery and integration for all the body systems. Parasympathetic activation also engages the vagal nerve complex, which can help regulate sympathetic over-activation (Porghes 2011).

In the creative process it is often during the parasympathetic state, including daydreams and doodling, that things start to 'make sense', and we have insights or images about seemingly disparate thoughts and experiences (Nachmanovitch 1991). When dancing, you can invite your parasympathetic nervous system to support your movement. Imagine you are in bed or on a wonderful, restful vacation. Allow digestion and integration. The body naturally relaxes in on itself, releasing front and back body tension. As you carry this quality into your dancing, you create the conditions for nuanced expressivity.

A cyclic balance between rest and activity is fundamental to the healthy functioning of internal organs, including the brain. We all know the situation, however, of eating a big meal and running off to a rehearsal or meeting. In this case, the nervous system sends contradictory messages: the parasympathetic nervous system stimulates the digestive system for integration, and the sympathetic nervous system is activated to deal with high-level functioning in the world. One physical result of these conflicting messages is indigestion. If this imbalance is a constant occurrence, the further result is nervous-system exhaustion. Wellbeing in dance involves listening to the internal balance, finding time for both activity and expression, and recovery and integration to build range and resiliency. Then we can amplify that which sustains, and diminish that which drains our energy and creativity day by day.

The enteric nervous system is the 'brain in the gut'. There are more nerves lining your digestive tract in this ancient part of the nervous system than in your spinal cord. And there are also more nerves to the brain than from the brain: it is surprisingly hard to override your gut experience by thinking (Gershon 1998). You may want to go to a party or compete in a dance audition, but if your gut says no, you will not walk in the door. Formed by more than 100 million neurons, the enteric nervous system involves two layers of tissue surrounding the esophagus, stomach, small intestines, and colon. Studies show that it can act independently, learn, remember, and feel.

Each of us can recall situations where we followed our instinct or gut feelings. We made a telephone call at the right moment, or met someone in an unexpected place. Functioning below rational thought, our visceral body picks up on information that may not register in our conscious minds. This 'instinctive' aspect engages another kind of intelligence and knowing, balancing our picture of ourselves as brainy and smart. Various models have been offered to explain the seemingly mysterious process of unconscious knowing. In our daily lives we notice that when we engage all the dimensions of our nervous system potential, we feel supported by, rather than in conflict with, our deepest motivations. When dancing, you can close your eyes and feel your way into moving. Keeping the front surface of your body open and receptive as you dance, you allow an integrative presence to inhabit your dancing.

Balancing these interconnected aspects of the nervous system (which govern life-sustaining processes such as breathing, digestion, heart rate, and reproduction) creates the conditions in which recovery and discovery can occur. A physical therapist or bodyworker will tell you that healing is not likely to take place when a patient/client is locked in the reactivity and defensiveness of the sympathetic nervous system (Juhan 1987). You need to access an integrative and digestive state to invite healing processes, as the parasympathetic nervous system and gut allow nourishment, release tension, and are open to change.

Somatic Excursion: Balancing the Autonomic Nervous System

Imagine it is morning, and you have recently risen from bed. You are still sleepy as you get in the car to drive to work. In the parasympathetic mode, you are probably thinking, 'I would really rather stay in bed and dream.' (Front and back spine are relaxed and easeful, staying with receptivity.) Then you realize you are late, and start to remember all you have planned for your day. Your sympathetic nervous system kicks in: 'Hurry up!' (Back spine pushes forward, moving into action.) Try these extremes experientially, imagining your hands holding the steering wheel: You are fully 'relaxed' and easeful—parasympathetic;

then 'hyper-alert' and pressing into action—sympathetic; and then balance. Notice the sensations and postural readiness of this embodied orientation.

Balance in the ANS is alertness. This is the ideal state for engaging relationship to yourself, others, and the world: you are not overly passive and are not already defensive—just open and inspirable. By supporting gut-level receptivity, you take in what you need, let go of what is unnecessary, and reconnect to the larger cycles of life systems. There is an inherent exchange with the sun, soil, air, water, and other animals on the planet through the digestive, integrative process.

The amygdala is considered the 'emotional sentinel' of the limbic brain (Levine 1997) (see Figure 10.2). Often studied in terms of fear and the processing of emotions, the amygdala registers anything new or unusual in the environment that might just be dangerous. Screening for emotional relevance at the level of survival, it determines the speed and complexity of processing, sometimes overriding higher thought processes. When healthy, the amygdala keeps you alert for safety; hyper-vigilance creates stress. Amygdala activation is based on your history. If you have seen lots of dances or snorkelled often with sharks, your 'newness' threshold for those experiences in the future is higher than that of a novice.

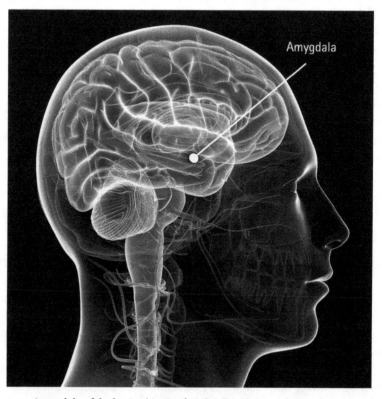

Amygdala

FIGURE 10.2. Amygdala of the brain. (Artwork © SciePro/Science Source.)

In dance making, the question becomes: how much newness do you need to stimulate alertness and stay awake to the moment, and how much makes you, your dancers, or your audience close down or leave the room? If the work is too safe, viewers settle back in their chairs and snooze; they have seen it before. When dancing, you can feed the amygdala with surprise. Try something that you have never experienced before. Find your unique edge between comfort and fear, and explore that terrain. Notice if the amygdala can become a little less reactive, more curious. Cultivating alertness rather than defensiveness, who knows what will happen? (See Video 10.7 on the Companion Website ⊙.)

Designing Space

As dancers, we design space with the body in mind. We shape the space inside the body (skinesphere), around the body (kinesphere), and throughout the environment where we are dancing (Koteen and Stark Smith 2008). Our body creates perceptual habits based on our history and experience. As babies, we measure the distance from hand to mouth, self to mother, chair to the open door leading outside. This 'measuring' through experiential learning underlies our capacity to abstract space, and the time it takes to move through space, informing choices (Cohen 2012). Place is space known through direct experience—you have been there, and mapped it with your body (Tuan 1977). When dancing, we rely on these perceptions to move quickly and intricately on stage or in the studio with other dancers, and also to calculate the design of body parts in relation to ourselves—between hand and face, foot and chest.

So important is our relationship to space and place that specific neurons in the brain map both internal and external landscapes. 'Place cells and grid cells are space-mapping neurons linked to memory forming regions in the hippocampus', state Blakeslee and Blakeslee (2007, p. 130). 'Place cells are context dependent; grid cells are context independent, combining the place you are right now, with an internal sense of body in space'. Place cells are mapping the environment where you are reading these words; grid cells monitor space 'independently from your environment. The space two feet in front of your nose is the space two feet in front of your nose' (Blakeslee and Blakeslee 2007, p. 130). Dancers often consider their body as home, yet dancing is impacted on multiple levels by the places we inhabit and spatial interactions.

Each of us needs a supportive home for the heart. Designing the interior space of the body also requires awareness—keeping inner spaciousness so that the heart and other vital organs are not compressed and compromised, even when using maximum muscular strength. Alignment and spatial orientation in all relationships to gravity (forward bends, back bends, twists and falls) increases ease and efficiency while retaining a responsive and spacious core. Bonnie Bainbridge Cohen, founder of the School for Body–Mind Centering, reminds us that 'The heart is not a pump, the heart is a history . . . it's a process of circulation and absorption' (Olsen 2014, p. 225). While dancing, we can support the heart rather than straining and compressing through excess tension. The lungs can cradle the heart, as well as providing massage through their expanding and condensing tissues; the rhythmic descent and release of the breathing diaphragm facilitates this movement if we do not think of our ribs as a cage (Farhi 1989).

Overcontraction of upper abdominal muscles can restrict movement of the breathing diaphragm (like old-fashioned corsets); tightness in the back muscles strains the posterior heart and kidneys. In forward bends and back bends, rather than compressing one surface while opening another, you can maintain spaciousness through head-to-tail orientation, ensuring the heart and other internal organs a spacious home. Then the lungs can cushion the heart instead of compressing the pulmonary arteries; blood flows freely away from the heart through the arteries, returning through the veins and lymph system. There is one continuum, pulsating the tides and rivers inside us. Unzipping back tension and feeling the upward wash of healthy flow through fluids and organs supports an experience of inner radiance; each cell is saturated and nourished. As the interconnected web of connective tissues remains responsive throughout, we encourage resilience and resourcefulness—fundamental qualities in dance training (Bernstein and Bernstein 2003). (See Video 10.4 on the Companion Website ▶.)

Creativity and Embodied Scholarship

Embodied scholarship is relational knowing. Multiple connections are involved: between self and other, movement and language, personal narrative and scientific fact. However much we pretend otherwise, knowledge has a perspective. There is no objective seeing. Readers want to know 'who' it is that is doing the writing/speaking, 'what' is the context in which these ideas were revealed and validated, and 'where' you imagine this investigation might lead. To integrate and communicate about the ephemeral knowledge of dancing, it sometimes helps to put words on the page—to move from sensory impression (taking in) to sensory expression (sending out)—making what is less conscious more available to the conscious mind. This includes moving unwanted memories out of the body and into a recognizable form where they are available for mature reflection in this period of your life. Some memories are put 'on hold' when you are young or in the midst of stressful situations, waiting until you have more resources for support. For example, the tension patterns stored from witnessing a death or injury to someone dear to you might now be understood and integrated more thoughtfully (Levine 2015). Places of holding require energy expenditure; release makes that energy available for living your present life.

Art making is one mode of investigation and assimilation. In my creative process I write to learn, I move to know. Dancing tells me if what I have said is true, from my body's perspective. Performance texts, combining words and movement, help to synthesize complex topics into communicable offerings. The additional challenge of speaking while dancing requires finding and claiming one's authentic voice or multiplicity of voices. The sustained need to create is linked to meaningful connection both to self and the world. If we are going to encourage our students and ourselves to care deeply about both body and earth, we need practiced forms for creative expression to avoid depression, aggression, and repression in relation to social and environmental challenges. And as reader or viewer, you never know what will touch you. It might be a word, an image, the quality of light in the room, or the person sitting next to you in a café or theatre. It is less about what you 'like' and more about what stays with you, motivating your dreams, memories, and investigations. (See Video 10.9 on the Companion Website ⊙.)

The aim throughout this chapter is to inspire you, the reader, through various modes of investigation, to invite your own stories and embodied experience. One memory links to another; we all have a rich movement life and deeply stirring stories. One of the challenges is to believe that our stories, our voices, have worth, and that we will not be overwhelmed in the process of attending. A student writes: 'I'm still a student. I can't have anything of use to share.' And yet authority—the right to speak with a certain kind of confidence—comes not just from reading and research but also from claiming the stories that shape your views.

Somatic Excursion: Pause

It could be useful to pause now, close your eyes, and let your body respond to what you are reading and viewing. This 'portal' or entranceway into embodied knowledge is present at every moment if you make time and open to the body's view.

Utilizing a variety of learning modalities allows one to cycle back to the physical building blocks of earth systems and to sensations within the body to affirm, confirm, or reject the words on the page. Research and literature review—particularly in the field of neuroscience—remind us that mind and body are one; scientific investigation partners dance training in affirming that the nervous system is whole body. As we have noted, more ancient autonomic aspects are capable of overriding conscious thought. From our understanding of neurotransmitters to current research on fascia as a semiconductor, it is important to recognize that facts are only facts until a new fact is discovered. Four decades ago, the earth's crust was thought to be solid; tectonic plates were unknown. Neurons could not regenerate, and neuroplasticity was scoffed at as a myth (Doidge 2007). Change and uncertainty are inherent in both experiential, movement-based learning and scientific investigation.

Cultivating the Imagination

At this point in my career I am most interested in the comments and investigations of those who are coming next—the younger voices. Let me share with you three statements from college students, just beginning their quest as adults, that invite further reflection. These voices are from my course called Body and Earth, taught with a creative-writing component within the dance and environmental studies programmes at Middlebury College in Vermont. Drawn from final papers, their words represent various ages, majors, and cultural perspectives, and are shared with permission.

Tawanda—a first-generation college student from Zimbabwe—states: 'The ability to see through the lens of the imagination, the power to create something that does not exist, and the capacity to dream are great gifts.' Sarah—a competitive athlete and environmental studies major from Connecticut—writes: 'As I have become familiar with the science behind earth's systems, I have become emotionally distant from nature itself. And as I focused on building strength and endurance as a competitive athlete and exerted my body to its limit, I ignored pain and fatigue symbols.' And Sophie—an anthropology major from England—writes: 'I inherited disengagement. The airplane indexes the arc of my journeys between boarding school in England and my parents' home in Switzerland.' These three capacious themes—the power to imagine and create, the challenge of partnering personal emotional response with intellectual and physical rigour, and the need to re-engage relationship with both body and place—provide clues for the work at hand in reimagining relationship to the dancing body.

What these students have in common within creative community is their willingness to risk. Author and writing colleague John Elder, in a discussion with our class (2013), stated: 'To teach creative writing, you have to celebrate the indeterminate aspects: the gaps. Those are the little spaces where something new can happen.' And he continued: 'If you want a vital creative life, which continues to be so, you have to find practices that relinquish and consolidate. We are required to grieve our way forward, relinquishing the past and opening to possibilities.' Grieving involves opening to the storied landscapes of body and earth.

We come here to the pages of this book, to dive into the gaps—cultivating the dynamic ecotone or edge-zone between knowing and not knowing. We can encourage each other in this process of inquiry and creative conversation at every stage of life. It is impossible to fixate one's passionate nature. Instead we practice resiliency and connection, returning again and again to resource. Within the dancing body we seek integrity within polarity—the capacity to stay centred, responsive, and resourceful, in the face of complex social and environmental challenges. Conscious embodiment practices help us avoid the depletion of exhaustive daily encounters that pull us off our essential natures, burying authentic impulses in the clutter of consumptive and addictive behaviours. Dance and movement are too easily reduced to stereotyped sexuality, competitive hierarchies (winners and losers), and consumer values, making the dancing body just one more thing to sell. A kind of vigilance is required.

Returning to what is fundamental, we find resources through reimagining the dancing body as interconnected to earth systems that refresh perception and enlarge our view. Dancing is for life; movement is our nature. This nature requires sustained intimacy. Cultivating the dynamic edge of dancing and dance making in the larger context of earth systems, we can open to fresh possibilities within the overlapping circles of dance practice and articulation—moving, dancing, performing, and writing—celebrating the intrinsic intelligence of the body. (See Video 10.8 on the Companion Website ▶.)

Personal Narrative: Storied Landscapes

I am driving southward along Route 7 in Vermont, a two-lane stretch of highway linking my home in Middlebury with my creative community in Northampton, Massachusetts. I have travelled this route for over thirty years, through loves, deaths, births, and multiple artistic collaborations. As I pass through Rutland, I think of an environmental studies student who was killed here in a car accident when returning to college; in Chester, Vermont, the lemon-chicken dinner with a friend, celebrating her new baby Caitlin; and at the juncture with Route 91, the first time I noticed a detailed geological cut through the highway, revealing ancient layers. The roadway is a textured map, not neutral but relational.

All stories are journeys. I am trying to evoke an ending: to this article, to my academic life, to driving this well-worn stretch of road with its implications for fossil fuels. Inner and outer dimensions merge. I have inhabited transitional terrain before, cultivating uncertainty while staying open. Reaching up, up for a hand, offering just enough support to cross a road safely. The memory of touch offers resource amid confusion: gentleness with a firm grip. The body remembers.

Conclusion

Reimagining our relationship to the dancing body refreshes perception. For easeful movement and effective communication, we can engage the web of connection between body systems and earth systems, remembering that humans are part of the natural world. As we build range and resiliency in our body–minds, we encourage the contagion of healthy organismal flow. Refreshing the primacy of sensation as the language of the body, we recover the easeful coordination in the nervous system that underlies creative thinking and healthful imagination—cultivating wellness in relationship to self, other, and the natural world. Reflecting on our journey, we can apply all these resources to embracing mystery, meeting the uncertainty and challenges of our days more consciously and with more spontaneous joy.

Somatic Excursion: Writing Dancing

Put pen to page or fingers to keyboard and write about your relationship to your dancing body. Keep going for five minutes, then find an end. Repeat your last sentence and write for another five minutes. Then stand up, close your eyes, and move—it does not matter where you are. (Open your eyes if you want to move fast or through space.) What does

FIGURE 10.3. Somatic excursion. (Photo © Angela Jane Evancie.)

your body think about what you have said in writing? Do not expect an answer, but notice what comes from entering into dialogue. There may be a feeling, emotion, thought, image, sensation, intuition, or full sentences or distinct movement phrases that emerge. Do not predetermine your findings. Write and move to explore. No worries! Your body remembers.

NOTES

1. The indented text throughout this chapter refers to the author's personal narratives.
2. All paragraphs in *italics* refer to invitations for the reader to engage in activities.
3. Videos 10.1–10.9 from the *Body and Earth: 7 Web-Based Somatic Excursions*, by Andrea Olsen, Caryn McHose, and Scotty Hardwig, © Andrea Olsen 2015, can be found on the Companion Website ⏵.

REFERENCES

Adler, J. (2015). *The Discipline of Authentic Movement.* <http://disciplineofauthenticmovement.com>

Bernstein, M. R. and Bernstein, R. R. (2003). *Martha Graham, Dance, and the Polymathics Imagination: A Case for Multiple Intelligences or Universal Thinking Tools?* Andover, NJ: J. Michael Ryan.

Blakeslee, S. and Blakeslee, M. (2007). *The Body has a Mind of Its Own: How Body Maps in Your Brain Help you Do (Almost) Everything Better.* New York: Random House.

Cohen, B. B. (2012). *Sensing, Feeling and Action: The Experiential Anatomy of Body–Mind Centering*, 3rd edn. Northampton, MA: Contact Editions.

Doidge, N. (2007). *The Brain that Changes Itself: Stories of Personal Triumph from the Frontiers of Brain Science*. New York, NY: Viking Press.

Elder, J. (2013). Body and Earth course discussion at Middlebury College, Middlebury, Vermont.

Farhi, D. (1989). *The Breathing Book: Good Health and Vitality through Essential Breath*. Markham, ON: Fitzhenry and Whiteside.

Frank, K. (2004). 'Tonic function: Gravity orientation as the basis for structural integration', *Hellerwork Newsletter*. <http://www.resourcesinmovement.com>

Gershon, M. (1998). *The Second Brain: The Scientific Basis of Gut Instinct and a Groundbreaking New Understanding of Nervous Disorders of the Stomach and Intestines*. New York, NY: HarperCollins.

Juhan, D. (1987). *Job's Body: A Handbook for Bodywork*. Barrytown, NY: Station Hill Press.

Koteen, D. and Smith, N. S. (2008). *Caught Falling: The Confluence of Contact Improvisation*. Northampton, MA: Contact Editions.

Levine, P. (1997). *Waking the Tiger*. Berkeley, CA: North Atlantic Books.

Levine, P. (2015). *Trauma and Memory: Brain and Body in a Search for the Living Past: A Practical Guide for Understanding and Working with Traumatic Memory*. Berkeley, CA: North Atlantic Books.

Linklater, K. (2006). *Freeing the Natural Voice*. New York, NY: Drama Book Specialists.

McHose, C. and Frank, K. (2006). *How Life Moves: Explorations in Meaning and Body Awareness*. Berkeley, CA: North Atlantic Books.

Nachmanovitch, S. (1991). *Free Play: Improvisation in Life and Art*. New York, NY: G. P. Putnam's Sons.

Olsen, A. (2004). *Body and Earth: An Experiential Guide*. Lebanon, NH: University Press of New England.

Olsen, A., and McHose, C. (2014). *The Place of Dance: A Somatic Guide to Dancing and Dance Making*. Middletown, CT: Wesleyan University Press.

Pallaro, P. (ed.) (2007). *Authentic Movement: Moving the Body, Moving the Self, Being Moved: A Collection of Essays, Volume Two*. London: Jessica Kingsley.

Pallaro, P. (ed.) (1999). *Authentic Movement: Essays by Mary Starks Whitehouse, Janet Adler and Joan Chodorow*. London: Jessica Kingsley.

Porghes, S. (2011). *The Polyvagal Theory: Neurophysiological Foundations of Emotions, Attachment, Communication, and Self-Regulation*. Norton Series on Interpersonal Neurobiology. New York, NY: W. W. Norton and Company. <www.stephenporges.com>

Tuan, Yi-Fu. (1977). *Space and Place: The Perspective of Experience*. Minneapolis, MN: University of Minneapolis Press.

PART II

....

DANCE WITHIN PERFORMATIVE CONTEXTS

....

INTRODUCTION TO PART II

VICKY KARKOU AND SOPHIA LYCOURIS

With a Contribution by Taira Restar on Her Work with Anna Halprin[1]

In this part the emphasis is on dance as an art form and its connections with thera-peutic or transformative performance, either in traditional contexts such as a stage or, often, in non-traditional contexts such as urban communities, derelict old build-ings, or selected locations in the countryside. The chapters included here often aim to challenge stigma around ageing, health, and mental health, and also to battle with the ultimate themes of life and death. The boundaries around disciplines are questioned and conventions are revisited and redefined, while the personal, often sensitive and vulnerable, becomes the inspiration for performative work.

We as editors, and the contributors included in this part, ask questions such as:

- How can dance as an art form contribute to and propose new approaches to wellbe-ing both semantically and experientially?
- How do audiences, performers, and choreographers/directors understand and experience aspects of wellbeing?
- What can they learn from each other and how can this inform interdisciplinary research on the conditions of wellbeing beyond the context of dance as an art form?

Although the questions asked are more than the answers found, this part certainly attempts to open up possibilities and encourage explorations of the crossover between dance as an art form and dance as therapy. Practice as research methodologies (Nelson 2013) are used (named or otherwise), next to phenomenology (Finlay 2009; Merleau-Ponty 1945; Heidegger 1927), the use of personal narratives, autobiography, and autoeth-nography (Lawler 2002).

Artistic explorations therefore remain at the heart of this part, which begins with an historical discussion of concepts of wellbeing from dance artists and educa-tors in Germany, the UK, and the USA at the beginning of the twentieth century. In Chapter 11, Michael Huxley and Ramsay Burt consider dance artists such as Hanya

Holm, Doris Humphrey, Diana Jordan, and Mary Wigman, and discuss the different ways in which dance began to be seen not only as a healthy exercise but also as a form of art that could deepen and expand people's experiences. In many ways, these early dance practitioners paved the way for a number of developments both in terms of dance as art as well as therapy.

Within the context of therapy, for example, Chapter 12, by Thania Acaron, offers an exploration of the therapeutic uses of choreography tools, dance technique, and performance. Thania—an active performer and a dance movement psychotherapist from Puerto Rico—discusses 'therapeutic performance' as a cathartic experience filled, however, with challenges around the need for a private, safe, and confidential space on the one hand and the value of sharing experiences publically on the other. Through a case study, she illustrates connections between such choreographic practices and wellbeing, while reminding the reader that this particular type of therapy has its origins within dance practice.

Similarly, the connection between therapy and dance is also explored in Chapter 13 by Marcia Plevin, an American dancer, therapist, and authentic movement practitioner working in Italy. She discusses how Authentic Movement—a practice extensively used within therapy, as we can see in other parts (for example, in Part I, Chapter 8 by Bacon and Chapter 9 by Avstreih)—became the central device for a choreographic project that involved ten women, not all of whom were dancers. Plevin argues that there was therapeutic value of this work for participants through what she calls the 'four portals of transformation'. Although the project did not intend to offer therapy, the deep personal exploration that Authentic Movement offered enabled participants to engage in what she describes as 'transformational choreography'. The edited video from the final performance that accompanies this chapter highlights the potential contribution of in-depth personal explorations not only to personal wellbeing but also to choreography and dance as performance.

From Italy, Paola Esposito and Toshiharu Kasai, take us, in Chapter 14, to Japan and butoh dance—a practice introduced in the 1950s by Tatsumi Hijikata. Butoh dance practitioners pay attention to small movement variations and wait 'to be moved', presenting striking similarities to practices and language used in Authentic Movement. However, rather than delving deep into one's psyche as Authentic Movement practitioners may do, butoh dancers focus on outer forces, such as gravity, and may engage with a set of exercises that can enhance their awareness. Examples of some of these exercises are included in this chapter (along with associated video material). Similar to claims made by Plevin, the authors argue that butoh dance has the potential to offer transformative experiences, and also suggest that it challenges ordinary notions of the body–mind, extending it beyond the physical limitations of the body.

Back to Europe and the UK in particular, Louise Douse explores, in Chapter 15, the concept of 'flow' as described by Mihaly Csikszentmihalyi, and shifts our attention back to performance and the dance-making process that precedes it. Douse—a dance artist herself—draws upon both positive psychology and phenomenology, connecting the concept of flow with dance, and dance improvisation in particular. She argues that 'flow enables the researcher/spectator to connect to, act into, and merge with the experience of the dancer, informing both their understanding of the dancer's wellbeing and their own wellbeing in the moment of observation'. As such, it becomes a concept that can enhance the spectator/dancer relationship and contribute to wellbeing.

In Chapter 16, Doran George—originally from the UK, but currently working as an academic, choreographer, and somatic practitioner in the USA—turns his attention to Rosemary Lee, a choreographer known for her large community-based somatically informed dance performances in the UK, referred to as 'choral dances'. Choral dances challenge prevailing distinctions between professional dance performed on stage and community dance with therapeutic or educational aims. Her work—diverse, intergenerational, and inclusive of both professional and non-professionals dancers—plays with integrating difference and supporting cohesion. Similar to Douse's chapter, George argues that in Rosemary Lee's work the flow of movement that emerges naturally from the dancers through somatic practice is made visible in her choreographic pieces, contributing not only to a sense of wellbeing for the individuals involved but also acting as a form of movement heritage for humanity.

Mixed groups of dancers and non-dancers are also involved in the choreographic work presented by Jan Bolwell in Chapter 17. In her New Zealand-based dance company Crows Feet Dance Collective, Bolwell argues that the older dancer, and the older female dancer in particular, finds her place, questioning stereotypes about both age and dance. Resilience, self-awareness, courage, at times recklessness, curiosity, joy, and creativity are some of the characteristics of the dancers with whom she works, and who, unlike what people often expect of them, engage in a forward-looking manner with the choreographic material, introducing a 'lived richness' to the work.

In Chapter 18, Mark Edward and Fiona Bannon continue with this topic by discussing not only the experience of the ageing dancer but also the effect that ageing can have on mental health. They also coin the term 'mesearch', denoting the study of one's own life in an autoethnographic/autobiographic manner. Through renarrating and relanguaging past experiences in the context of performative work, the authors explore concepts of self-identity and, paraphrasing Kaprow and Kelly (1992), argue that 'performance is not separated from the experience gained in making meaning of life'.

The exploration of the experience of the ageing performer continues in Chapter 19 by June Gersten-Roberts. A dance artist and video-maker from the USA practising in the UK, she approaches the concept of ageing sensitively and insightfully. She writes about her collaboration with Gerry Turvey in 'Body Stories'—a project which maps Gerry's dancing history, including interruptions through injuries and illnesses. Gerry's body becomes the map for this journey, which is filmed and projected in a series of performances/installations. With reference to three videos and a four-minute performance from this work, June discusses her own experiences as a collaborator, bringing together film-making literature with an interesting redefinition of the concept of wellbeing.

This part finishes with Chapter 20 by Beatrice Allegranti. The author, a choreographer, dancer, and dance movement psychotherapist, talks about loss as a physical ('corporeal') and performative experience. She draws upon feminist literature (Butler 2010; Barad 2007) in order to explore loss as a personal experience, within Dance Movement Psychotherapy practice and through a choreographic project. As with other chapters in this part, the borders between life and performance are once again challenged here. Furthermore, Allegranti argues that reclaiming loss through (im)possible performativity allows for the dead to find a place within us in a creative, ongoing, and thus transformative way. As such, it appears that performance crosses over not only to life, but also to *death*, to create artistically rich and potentially powerful therapeutic experiences.

Within a compilation of chapters that deal with dance and wellbeing, the work of Anna Halrpin cannot be omitted. Her interest in art as life and in topics such as death and dying, and her active encouragement of the performers to engage both with the development of the choreographic work and the experience of performing it, makes her work particularly relevant to this part. Her work 'Intensive Care: Reflections on Death and Dying', which premiered in the Cowell Theatre, San Francisco, in 2000, seems seminal. This piece grew out of Anna's own life experiences and the trauma of witnessing the physical suffering of her husband Lawrence Halprin, as a result of a routine operation which had unexpected complications. It was created following the Life/Art Process®—an approach developed by Halrpin in response to her own struggle with cancer. As a choreographic process it relies on one's own life experiences as inspiration for artwork, and includes five parts: identity, confrontation, release, change, and growth.[2]

Taira Restar—a dancer and close associate of Anna Halprin—has been invited to provide an account of how she experienced the development and presentation of the piece 'Intensive Care'. Her personal narrative included here evidences feelings of wellbeing as a dancer, maker, student, and person:

> In fall 2005, Anna Halprin invited me to perform in 'Intensive Care: Reflections on Death And Dying'—a twenty-five minute dance piece inspired by her experiences at the hospital bedside of her husband Lawrence Halprin, and developed through the use of her Five Part Life/Art Process. The four primary dancers were Anna Halprin, G. Hoffmann Soto, Brian Collentine, and myself. We performed at Kanbar Theater, Jewish Community Center of San Francisco, San Francisco, CA, in June 2006.
>
> The four performers each found their own entry point into the piece and into engaging with the theme of dying and death. Anna asked the dancers to work with their own personal realities during rehearsal and while performing. This created depth and authenticity. I was not dancing about death or dying as an abstract concept. I was exploring what death and dying meant to me at that time.
>
> Initially, my challenge was that I did not have much first-hand experience with death. At 47, I had not known many people who had died. Sometimes in rehearsal

I would remember my grandmother's death or imagine my mother's death. The creative process is mysterious, and somehow these were not the entry points that sparked me. Then, one day in rehearsal, Anna and I were exploring various ways in which we could cradle and hold one another. It was very tender. As I touched Anna, felt her delicate skin and thin arms, looked into her eyes, I saw her as any elderly woman, who will not live forever. I recognized how much she had inspired and influenced me as an artist and as an educator. I sensed the weight of her contributions to my life and the generosity of sharing herself for over twenty years. Emotions welled up. I started to cry. It was personal and intimate—not about her as a pioneer in the dance world, but about my own love and appreciation. As an artist, I was able to witness myself in my improvisational process. I encouraged myself to feel the poignancy of the moment—and of the theme of Anna's eventual death. I imagined how I will feel when Anna does die. This became the inspiration for accessing real emotions while performing. I am inspired by the fact that focusing on my own relationship with Anna emerged out of the physicality of the moment—out of touch and the senses.

In the shaping of the performance and in the Tamalpa Life/Art Process®, we work in 'real time'—that is, we attend to what is present in the moment, and this is what fuels the creative fire and is shaped into art. It is an enriching and fascinating way to work. For me, it is an active and artistic form of meditation.

As we utilized the Five Part Process map in the scoring and dancing of 'Intensive Care', I was simultaneously putting myself through the same process internally as an individual performer. First, I identified with the theme of death and dying. Second, I confronted this theme by exploring through movement, emotions, and imagination my own suffering, loss, and grief. This is a highly creative phase of improvisation—going deeply into the movements of physical pain. In order to access true discomfort, I would hold my own breath or contract my muscles. In these ways I was able to play with metaphors through movement. I then released. At last, a breaking point was reached. I let go of certain thoughts, body posture, or movements. Often, tears were shed or a loud breath or sound emerged from my body. There was then space within me for something new. I no longer felt sadness. I no longer struggled. I felt acceptance. My movements were lighter and more tender. I often felt love and appreciation. In these ways I truly experienced my self as changed in that moment. In the final stage, Growth, I walked towards my own death and faced the death of those I love. In many of the rehearsals and performances, in the final minutes, I actually experienced a longing to commune with God. I experienced my self as having grown and expanded beyond the individual self and into a state of communion.

The performance had a predesigned 'score', but within that the movements were improvisational. (Except for the final sequence, the dancers performed while seated. Each dancer sat on a wheeled chair, which was draped in white cloth). As an improvisor, I was committed to crafted spontaneity—responding to what is present, and focusing on what attracted me in the moment, developing and expressing that, dropping what was not working artistically. Like life, the performance was at times enlivening, at times uplifting, and at times extraordinarily scary. It required a lot of trust. Sometimes, to give myself a boost of confidence, I said to myself: 'If Anna has this much trust in me as a performer, than I can trust my own self.' It was such an honour to be able to dance side by side with her! Since 'Intensive Care', I have carried a renewed appreciation for Anna Halprin's approach to integrative dance. It is so fluid—allowing for each dancer to be uniquely his or her self, and allowing for each moment to be uniquely its self!

Improvisational performing is like riding a roller coaster. It is an electric blend of terror, anticipation, excitement, and climbing towards a drop-off into the unknown. And when the roller coaster includes dancing with Anna Halprin and being embodied in her methods, it is also a mindfulness practice. In the end, I am exhilarated, a bit shaken up, awake and alive, and wanting to go back for more.

The audience's experience is equally varied and powerful, as evidenced by several leaving the theatre during the piece. One witness told me after the performance: 'When I first saw you, I thought, "She looks too young to die. That's not realistic." But I found I could not take my ewyes off of you. I felt so sad . . . for the young adults and children that die each day.'

This diversity of audience response is not uncommon with performances based on this process, as Janice Ross (2009) writes in her book, *Anna Halprin: Experience as Dance*: 'With each performer drawing on her or his own storehouse of experiences, the result is a performance that hovers between rawness and realism, making viewing at times both uncomfortable and engrossing.' (See Video II.a on the Companion Website ⓐ.)

NOTES

1. We would like to acknowledge the inspiration Anna Halprin offered to the writing of Taira's text and her permission to use the abbreviated material from her performance available on the Companion Website ⓐ.
2. Later, Daria Halprin, Anna's daughter, developed this work for therapy, known as the Tamalpa Life/Art Process®.

REFERENCES

Butler, J. (2010). *Frames of War: When is Life Grievable?* London: Verso.

Barad, K. (2007). *Meeting the Universe Halfway: Quantum Physics and the Entanglement of Matter and Meaning.* Durham/London: Duke University Press.

Finlay, L. (2009). 'Exploring lived experience: Principles and practice of phenomenological research', *International Journal of Therapy and Rehabilitation*, 19(9): 474–81.

Heidegger, M. (1927). *Being and Time*, transl. J. Macquarrie and E. Robinson (1962). Oxford: Blackwell.

Kaprow, A. and Kelly, J. (ed.) (1992). *Essays on the Blurring of Art and Life.* Berkeley, CA: University of California Press.

Lawler, S. (2002). 'Narrative in social research', in T. May (ed.), *Qualitative Research in Action.* London: Sage, pp. 242–58.

Merleau-Ponty, M. (1945). *Phenomenology of Perception*, transl. C. Smith (2002), 2nd edn. London: Routledge.

Nelson R. (2013) *Practice as Research in the Arts: Principles, Protocols, Pedagogies, Resistances.* Basingstoke: Palgrave Macmillan.

Ross J. (2009) *Anna Halprin: Experience as Dance.* Berkeley and Los Angeles, CA: University of California Press.

CHAPTER 11

....

A GREATER FULLNESS
OF LIFE

Wellbeing in Early Modern Dance

....

MICHAEL HUXLEY AND RAMSAY BURT

INTRODUCTION

....

AT the start of the twentieth century, ideas of wellbeing were somewhat different from
twenty-first-century notions. However, dance can be identified as having contributed
significantly to the development of these ideas, as we will now discuss. A scene from the
German film *Wege zu Kraft und Schönheit* (*Ways to Health and Beauty*)[1] (1925) neatly
captures attitudes to health and wellbeing that were widely held in Europe and North
America in the early part of the twentieth century. A subtitle in the English-language
version[2] informs us that 'A body neglected from a child will grow older more quickly
than others'. We are shown a bespectacled businessman with slightly hunched shoulders
who, we are informed, is 50 years old and 'never went near a sports field in his life'. Either
because he is weighed down by the cares of the world, or because of his poor eye sight,
he steps off the kerb of an attractive, tree-lined suburban boulevard in front of a cyclist
who, another subtitle has informed us, is 62 years old and 'has been a sportsman since
a boy'. The bicyclist's whole manner is more upright and alert than that of the businessman. This sportsman deftly swerves in order to avoid running the younger, less
fit, man over, playfully rising up on his back wheel and looping round so as to stop and
greet him. The simplistic message of the sequence is that, in modern life, one should
not neglect physical activity. Ironically, though, the cyclist then asks the pedestrian for
a light for his cigarette, suggesting his affable congeniality and that fitness makes one
a better person. He and the film-makers were seemingly oblivious of the dangers of
smoking. This sequence is part of the first section of the film, which contrasts the ideals
of Ancient Greek culture with the generally poor state of health of modern man. People
of today, a subtitle tells us, are 'not always well built, not always good, but certain to be

always nervous. We must endeavour to emulate those ancient Greeks ourselves. Which is the road that leads us back to ancient strength and beauty? There are several'. The rest of the film surveys a wide range of sport, body culture, and recreational and professional dance activity, including some rare footage of some of the pioneers of modern dance. Dance, it argues, can lead us to strength and beauty.

A decade later, in the USA, a local newspaper reporter in Hartford, Connecticut, interviewed the German dance artist Hanya Holm, who was then running a dance school in New York. She observed that everybody could dance:

> Many who have no intention of entering the professional fields of dance are today discovering the joy of dancing as a remarkable exhilaration and a deeply satisfying emotional stimulation from the monotonous level of daily routine. Housewives, workers, school teachers, nurses, men, and women in all fields of activity have been able to find in this way a new stimulus, a new sense of well being. (Holm 1936)

Holm is arguing for the beneficial effects of dance on people's sense of wellbeing in the context of the monotony of twentieth-century working life. When one looks at what dancers and dance educationalists were writing about during the first few decades of the twentieth century, one finds that most of them believed that, because dance is an art form, it makes a positive and beneficial contribution to society. While they may not necessarily express this in terms of wellbeing, as Holm did in her 1936 interview, there is a strong desire to demonstrate that dance is art. Thus dancers such as Isadora Duncan and Martha Graham were keen to distance their dance performances from dancing as popular entertainment, as discussed by Daly (1995) and McDonagh (1973) respectively. Similarly, dance educationalists picked up on this idea of dance as art and used it as a means for arguing that they were teaching something more than physical education. Their argument, expressed simply, is that while dance performance can entertain and dance is of course a healthy form of exercise, it offers more. It offers 'a greater fullness of life'. This phrase, used in the title of this chapter, comes from a 1938 book by the pioneering British dance educationalist Diana Jordan, who borrowed it from the philosopher John Stuart Mill's *On Liberty*, published in 1859. Mill (1998) advocates personal development that, he argues, is not just good for the individual but for others as well. 'There is a greater fullness of life about his own existence, and when there is more life in the unit, there is more life in the mass which is composed of them' (Jordan 1938, p. 5).[3] This, Jordan argues, is why dance as art is important and valuable.

We are introducing these ideas alongside those of Holm (1936) and the makers of *Wege zu Kraft und Schönheit* (1925) because they usefully evoke a range of similar ideas around this time about dance, health, concerns about decadence and the lack of value in modern life compared with that of the Greeks, and the relation between amateur, professional, and educational dance. Dance writers of the period rarely spoke of wellbeing per se. To understand the significance of wellbeing in dance historically it is necessary to consider a number of ideas to make sense of the important contributions that dancers such as Holm and Jordan made to the development of what later came to be known as 'wellbeing'—by which we mean a positive sense of self involving the whole being.

This chapter is concerned primarily with professional dance practice, and focuses in particular on two dance works which exemplify key aspects of the discourse about the value of dance—and, by implication, its wellbeing contribution—during the period. Mary Wigman's short solo *Pastorale (Pastoral)*[4], from her cycle *Schwingende Landschaft (Swinging Landscape)* (1929), exemplifies a vivid and powerful sense of wellbeing—an ideal of expressive energy that is free of the contaminating influence of monotonous, modern working life. Doris Humphrey's work *New Dance*[5] (1935) creates, as we will show, a comparable sense of positive vitality in a group of dancers who are brought together in an integrated, harmonious sense of unity through choreographed patterns of movement variations. Whereas Wigman's piece celebrates qualities through which one might aspire to resist the harmful influence of modern life, Humphrey's piece is part of a trilogy that, taken together, grasps the problematic of modernity's effects and finds a way through them towards a greater sense of collective wellbeing.

This chapter surveys existing literature about modern dance during the period up to the outbreak of World War II. It considers writing from the period about the positive value of dance, looking first at the ideas of those who saw dance as a way of resisting modernity. This provides a context for a reading of Wigman's 1929 solo. We also look at other examples of writing that, while not explicitly challenging these ideas about dance's resistant potential, are more concerned with the way that dance can contribute to a sense of collective rather than individual wellbeing. The latter is discussed through an examination of Humphrey's 1935 choreography.

EARLY MODERN DANCE AND WELLBEING IN CONTEXT

There is currently no major recent publication dealing directly with dance and wellbeing in the early part of the twentieth century—the period we are considering. However, there is a growing body of dance scholarship that reconsiders the dance practices of the period in ways that help facilitate discussion about the broader perspective that dance and wellbeing invites. Twenty-first century dance discourses have opened up discussion about the role and purpose of dance. For instance, dance as performance is now considered in terms of human rights (Jackson 2004; Jackson and Shapiro-Phim 2008) as well as theatrical or educational practices. The early modern period has been the subject of much reinvigorated research recently, leading to some notable reinterpretations of what had been assumed to be a finite history. Morris (2006) has reconsidered post-war American modern dance in terms of the embodiment of community, with reference back to the 1930s. Manning (2004) discusses continuities and divergences between the development of white and African American concert dance in the 1930s and 1940s. Two major biographies, of Margaret H'Doubler and Anna Halprin, by Janice Ross (2000, 2007), have provided insights into American modern dance and the emergence of art practices that prioritized education and experience respectively. Susan Manning's (2006) major reassessment of one modern dancer, Mary Wigman, has done much to locate the dance of the period within the changing politics of the time. German dance performance has been reconsidered in Manning and Ruprecht's (2012) edited collection that places the work of artists such as Laban, Wigman, and Holm in a wider cultural and historical context. In this collection, Randall (2012), for instance, presents a new inflection to the established view of Holm's work in the USA by considering life reform and community as well as art as expression. The interactions of European, American, and Indian modern dance practices in the context of an overtly philanthropic and supportive community have been explored in Nicholas's *Dancing in Utopia* (2007). Reynolds (2007), in examining the place of rhythm as a driving force for the new modern dance, has directly compared the performance work of Mary Wigman and Martha Graham. The broader context within which dance can be placed during this period has been approached from a number of perspectives that are relevant to an exploration of wellbeing. Toepfer's (1997) *Empire of Ecstasy: Nudity and Movement in German Body Culture 1910–1935* has placed the art practices of Wigman, Laban, and many other modern dancers within the complex world of body culture and, in doing so, has helped highlight some of the aspects of these practices that distinguished dance from some of the 'healthy mind in a healthy body' practices of the time. Recently, Carter and Fensham (2011) have brought together, in an edited collection, a number of scholars to consider the idea of what was 'natural' in natural dancing: our chapter in that book (Huxley and Burt 2011) raises questions about the relationship of dance to modernity and the natural, while other chapters consider the approaches of individual artists, notably Humphrey (Main 2011).

MARY WIGMAN'S DANCE *PASTORALE*

Mary Wigman's 1929 solo dance cycle *Schwingende Landschaft*, which includes *Pastorale*, can be seen as the climax and culmination of her work in the 1920s. To understand how it brings together ideas about wellbeing from this decade, it is necessary to provide a brief survey of these, beginning with the ideas of her teacher, Rudolf Laban. In his book *Die Welt des Tänzers* (*The Dancer's World*) (1920), Laban argues that the practice of dancing offers the most complete expression of a reformed modern life. Echoing the philosopher Friedrich Nietzsche's idea of the *Übermensch* (the over man or new man), Laban (in McCaw 2011) defines the dancer as

> that new person, who does not draw his awareness one-sidedly from the brutalities of thinking, feeling, or will. He is that person who strives to interweave clear intellect, deep feeling, and strong will into a harmoniously balanced and flexible whole whose parts are interrelated (p. 45).[6]

What is clear from this quotation is that, rather than drawing from any one capacity in isolation, dancing involves the whole person by interweaving capacities into a harmonious, flexible whole. One of the things that Wigman helped Laban develop when she was his student during 1913–17 were his *Schwungskala* (*Swing Scales*, sometimes called 'movement scales'). Their purpose, Laban (McCaw 2011) wrote later, is to 'slowly educate the body in a more precise feeling of space' (p. 95). These are not intended merely as physical exercises and do not only express 'the ground rules of basic locomotion', but, along with other phenomena of movement, express 'the growth of the human being' as far as wellbeing is concerned. These scales were later used in Laban training and movement analysis. They help develop the new person referred to in *Die Welt des Tänzers* who is a harmoniously balanced and flexible whole. To express it another way, the approach to dance training that Laban is advocating is one that opens up a potential for experiencing a greater fullness of life.

What is important about Laban's approach, and distinguishes it from that of many of his contemporaries, is the fact that he did not prescribe exercises for developing physical fitness. The latter approach can be found in, for example, the writings of contemporaries such as the Austrian dancer and teacher of Rhythmic Gymnastics, Gertrud Bodenwieser, and of the English dancer and movement teacher, Margaret Morris. Bodenwieser's (1926) approach is unequivocally dualistic in the way she sees mind and body as separate spheres: 'The body having undergone training and exercise, is transformed into a sensitive and easily controlled instrument, and gradually comes to appreciate and to express itself in beauty of form' (p. 169). While she seems to believe that an almost mechanistic instrumentalization of 'the body' will lead to an appreciation of aesthetics, and by implication a greater sense of wellbeing, she provides no explanation as to how the one leads to the other. Morris (1925) also implies that dance exercise leads to a greater sense of wellbeing:

> There is no reason why average human beings should not develop strong, healthy bodies, and mental and physical control, as well as understanding and appreciation of form, colour, and sound, in nature and in art—and in many cases even the power of artistic creation. (p. 94)

In this way, she believes: '. . . health and happiness should be the basis for all art—it is reasonable that, to some extent at least, it should become a part of the life of all' (p. 94). The limitations in Morris's thinking here are not just the way that, like Bodenwieser, she separates the mental and the physical. They are also evident in the way she offers a long, all-embracing list of qualities and properties—of whose value no one would have any doubts—without any clear explanation about how these might arise from the practice of dancing. Wigman's *Pastorale*, as we shall show, is informed by a much more sophisticated understanding of the way dance expresses the needs of women of the period. She spoke of this in an article titled 'The dance and modern woman' (1927), preceding her first UK tour. Addressing an English readership, but speaking of her German experience, she says that youth has a considerable appetite for dance, and that women have many reasons for pursuing it. Whatever their reasons—emotional outlet, escape from the monotony of routine, artistic endeavour:

> The solution is in the dance, in the pure delight of movement which is the overflow of abundant vitality and is independent of all but physical expression.

Wigman's modern woman is a close relative of Laban's new man.

Reynolds, in her account of new approaches to energy and rhythm in the modern dance of Mary Wigman, Martha Graham, and Merce Cunningham, identifies the German approach to rhythm and space, deriving from Laban, as having particular import. She highlights the new idea of *Schwung*—one which 'designates a rhythmic, swinging movement in which tensions are discharged, and which integrates the whole body (2007, p. 68). Wigman's idea of rhythm is one that embodies *Schwung* in the dancer's use of space. She was renowned for evocative choreography in space, especially in her solo dances.

Mary Wigman's performances as a solo dancer ranged across the breadth of human experience, presenting both 'ecstasy and the demon', as Susan Manning (2006) would have it in her book with this title. Wigman's *Schwingende Landschaft* cycle[7] of 1929 evoked life in many aspects. A contemporary, Elizabeth Selden (1935), described it as follows:

> After she has shown us life solemn, life beautiful, life stark, dark, and perilous, she touches the chord of humour and does not even mind if her audiences think that they have had a good time . . . Hence the tremendously stimulating, vitalizing effect that one experiences from her programs. (p.73)

The idea of her dances being stimulating and vitalizing for her audience is one that, we would argue, is central to a notion of performance for wellbeing for all concerned. This cycle has been the focus of many writers on Wigman and the period, notably Manning (2006) and Reynolds (2007).

Taken together, the seven dances in the *Schwingende Landschaft*[8] cycle explore the dancer's range of emotions through the dynamic range of her dancing.[9] *Pastorale* occupies a focal place, as the central dance in the cycle, and exemplifies how Wigman attains a sense of wellbeing through her use of a swinging rhythm and space. *Pastorale* is a three-minute solo dance. Mary Wigman is dressed in a light, satin, full-length, flaring, panelled dress, which follows her movement and clings to her when the movement is arrested. The music is a simple repetitive flute melody with percussion accompaniment provided by two drums, a Chinese gong, and an Indian double bell. The dance begins with Wigman lying flat on her back. She gently raises her right hand, as if exploring the air above her. Her arms lead her languidly to a semi-recumbent position where she explores the world around her. She uses an arm to arch off the floor and then, finally, rises to her feet. Immediately she begins to circle—her arms continuing the rippling explorations of the first section. Her circular dancing

takes her into a state of evident pleasure, at which point she slows down and gradually returns to the floor. After a brief pause she returns to the semi-recumbent position and its accompanying arm movements. The dance concludes with her lying on
the floor again, as at the start, her legs apart with one knee akimbo. The last movements are echoes of the first, the right hand slowly and gently waving as she sinks into
stillness. The whole, brief, dance has a symmetrical structure around a vertical rising
and falling.

When the dance was seen live in performance it was interpreted as being about
spring, in contrast to the later *Summer Dance* of the cycle. For Selden she creates 'an
unforgettable idyll . . . in order to convey the atmosphere of spring' (1935, p. 71). The
reviews of her 1932 London performance also refer to spring, but as a season when the
dancer showed an inner state of 'rapture' which gave a 'vivid and powerful' impression,
rather than a 'pretty' one (Martin 1932).In an article published in 1931,[10] Wigman wrote
about how she came to make the dance. She describes how she went into the studio and
lay down with a 'feeling of complete relaxation'. She asked for someone to provide a reed
pipe playing a simple monotonous melody to evoke the feeling and provide a sense of
'lyrical tenderness' (Wigman 1931, cited in Sorell 1986, p. 143). Three decades later, recalling happier times in Germany during the 1920s, she reminisced about the years 1928 and
1929, and how *Pastorale* came to be made.[11] Her account differs from her contempor-
aneous one, but is still evocative of why the dance mattered for her.[12] Wigman's (1966)
description of *Pastorale* conflates its making, its performance, and her happy memories
of lying on the beach and doing nothing on holiday:

> The slightly raised arm swung to and fro in the air without resistance, the fingers
> moved playfully in the rhythm of wave and tide. Everything was so soft and warm, so
> pleasantly weightless, everything had the freshness of a dawning day about it (p. 63).

For Manning (2006), *Pastorale* has the capacity to expose the process 'whereby the
choreographer simultaneously recalls and abstracts her life experience' (p. 145). In
doing so, she makes that experience available for an audience. Reynolds (2007) makes
a similar point when she says that 'Wigman achieved the feat of visibly dancing as
a woman, evoking a femininity which was also perceived as "impersonal", thereby
resisting marginalization in terms of a specifically feminine "other"' (p. 83). That is
to say (and both writers make the point), she presented herself as a woman capable of
evoking the erotic without succumbing to masculine ideas of what that might mean.
Her sensual escapism is one that can be embraced by her audience, especially women.
Reynolds (2007) highlights particular qualities found in *Pastorale* as leading to a sense
of wellbeing:

> Each phrase melts imperceptibly into the next: there is no interruption to the flow,
> which is extremely free. Effort and shape-flow qualities combine to produce a sense
> of relaxation and wellbeing, particularly in the light, free-flowing qualities of the
> arms, which lead the body as they rise and stretch. (p. 84)

Wigman's *Pastorale* is a deeply personal statement. There is no doubt that the dance evokes an intense sense of self, and, in tune with the modern dance of the time, this is a sense of her as a whole vibrant human being. It is the free-flowing, swinging energy of this solo that does this, and in our view it is this that creates a sense of wellbeing. For Laban, the swing scales express the growth of the human being, the emergence of the modern man. Wigman performs as a modern woman who finds a security in her dancing that enables her to cope with the social and political vicissitudes of Germany in the closing years of the Weimar Republic.

DORIS HUMPHREY'S *NEW DANCE*

Modern dance in the USA changed significantly between 1934 and 1939, between the introduction of F. D. Roosevelt's New Deal and the outbreak of World War II. Much has been written about the flourishing of dance at this time. We approach this period—the context for Doris Humphrey's *New Dance*—by identifying a shifting discourse around the purpose of dance, where matters to do with politics, community, security, democracy, and the good life in America came to the fore. Hanya Holm, writing as a German in the USA in 1935, compared German and American approaches to dance. She found the former's dancers to be more subjective and expressive, and the latter's more objective, observational, and technical (Holm 1935). She was keen to stress that dance was not just about exercise, nor even just about art. Randall (2012) has recently written of how Holm established a sense of community that drew on the ideas of Laban and Wigman, but which were firmly located within an American social *and* (our emphasis) political context. In talking of Holm's idea of dance as life reform and the school as community, Randall (2012) says:

> The physical practice of 'release' created a responsive body, [Holm] explained, which was necessary for new, healthier movement patterns to emerge, 'The effortless flow of natural movement that can take place only in an unresistive, responsive body is the secret of that vividness and vitality that lifts dancing from the category of exercise to its true place as an expression of life.'
>
> Ultimately, this was always the goal—to lift dancing from mere exercise or fun to life consciously lived and vitally experienced. In lecture after lecture during her first few years in the United States, Holm asserted that modern dance was the 'doorway to a more intense and fuller life', not only an elite artistic technique. (p. 83)

Here there is concern with what we would wish to term wellbeing not just of the individual but also of the larger community, which had not appeared in previous writing during the period.

The dancers, who were later termed 'the four pioneers' of modern dance, developed their work through the 1930s and especially at the Bennington Summer Schools of Dance that opened up opportunities for the teaching, performance, and discussion of the new dance form.[13] It was at these summer schools that Martha Graham, Hanya Holm, Doris Humphrey, and Charles Weidman developed new ways of making group dance. It was these new approaches that were applauded and theorized by American dance critics, especially John Martin (1933, 1936) and Margaret Lloyd (1949), but they tended to focus their interest solely on the formal ideas of modern dance as an art form. There were some others writing in dance circles who were also considering the wider ramifications of dance for dancers, dance students, and the dance audience. For instance, Henry Gilfond (1936), a relatively conservative commentator, reported on the First New York Dance Congress of 1936 in *Dance Observer*. Echoing the demands of the time and the potential that dance had begun to tap into, he wrote how the Congress realized that 'dancers, no matter what the medium of their work ... have much in common—the common interest in a physical wellbeing, a security and a desire for a decent place in which to work' (Gilfond 1936: 1). Such pragmatic concerns resonated with the more philosophical treatise of Henry Beiswanger (1935/1981) in *Theatre Arts Monthly*. He suggests that the new modern dance had emerged in response to four contemporary wants: 'humanizing the machine', answering the question 'what is the good life?', 'the personal pattern', and 'modes of associate living' (pp. 280–2).

Modern dancers working in the USA began to make works in the mid-1930s that both challenged the politics of fascism in Germany, on the one hand, and sought to promote an American view of a better life, on the other. Their ideas were pioneered and performed at the Bennington Summer Schools. Ideas about social wellbeing and the new democratic community are most noticeable in Doris Humphrey's *New Dance* (1935), Hanya Holm's *Trend* (1937), and Martha Graham's *American Document* (1938). We will look at the first of these, as it embodies the ideas of the collective foundations of wellbeing, community, and democracy.

New Dance is the final part of Humphrey's *New Dance Trilogy*—the other two pieces being *Theatre Piece* and *With My Red Fires*. *New Dance* was actually made first, and given that each piece was at least forty minutes long, they were never intended to be performed in their entirety during one evening. Humphrey aimed to show through them that there is, as she wrote in an essay published only after her death, a 'modern brotherhood of mankind'. Of the three works, she preferred *New Dance*, which showed 'the world as it could be and should be where each person has a clear and harmonious relationship to his fellow beings' (cited in Cohen 1972, p. 238). *New Dance* was the most ambitious piece that Humphrey (or indeed any of the American modern dancers) had until then attempted. Margaret Lloyd (1949) called it a landmark because of its length—until then, modern dance works were generally much shorter. John Martin, reviewing it in *The New York Times* (11 August 1935) wrote:

> Certainly a more authoritative piece of creation in the dance has not been seen for many a long day. It is especially significant in this time when it has become habitual to question the validity of 'absolute' dance that here is a work which has the same power to stir the emotions, to kindle aesthetic excitement, as is to be found in symphonic music. (Cited in Kriegsman 1981, p. 130)

New Dance begins with a duet by a female leader (Humphrey) and a male leader (Weidman). They then lead the female and male dancers respectively in a series of dances which bring the group together into an integrated whole. These gradually develop material from the initial duet into a statement of group values, which are finally celebrated in the final part, the 'Variations and Conclusion'. This was recorded in Labanotation in 1938, and was often performed on its own. When *New Dance* was revived in 1972, apart from 'Variations and Conclusion', much of the piece had been largely forgotten. Humphrey (1972) has explained its significance in her scheme:

> Having unified the men's group and the women's group, one more section was neces-
> sary in order to express the individual in relation to the group. Too many people
> seem content to achieve a mass-movement and then stop. I wished to insist that there
> is an individual life within that group life. (p. 240)

Using a vocabulary of dynamic and exuberant movement—with sweeping, off-centre turns that use the body's momentum that had been developed earlier in the piece—Humphrey created complex centrifugal series of floor patterns for the group. While the group, including the two leaders, stand on raised cubes in the centre of the stage, each dancer takes his or her turn to perform their own solo while the rest watch and keep time behind. Each solo is singular, but there is a commonality between them all. It is as if the group's unity is mature enough to embrace a range of complementary differences. It is this high-energy finale that has left so many viewers with a feeling of radiance and optimism—a sense of wellbeing that is rooted in collective rather than individual experience.

Conclusion

The two dance works discussed here expressed a sense of wellbeing during the interwar years. The free-flowing, swinging movements in Wigman's *Pastorale* had a 'tremendously stimulating, vitalizing effect' (Selden 1935, p. 73). The more dynamic, sweeping off-centre turns and the symphonic sense of form in *New Dance* had a 'power to stir the emotions, to kindle aesthetic excitement' (Martin, cited in Kriegsman 1981, p. 130). Wigman showed what the modern woman in isolation was capable of becoming, while Humphrey aimed to show 'the world as it could be and should be where each person has a clear and harmonious relationship to his fellow beings' (cited in Cohen 1972, p. 238). While the German film *Wege zu Kraft und Schönheit* (1925), with which we began, suggested that healthy exercise, including dance, created a positive sense of wellbeing, we have shown that many writers and dancer artists during the period believed dance could do much more. Performances of *Pastorale* and *New Dance* showed their audiences a potential for a greater fullness of life, while Humphrey's piece demonstrated that the wellbeing of each individual could contribute to the greater wellbeing of society as a whole.

NOTES

1. Available in full on YouTube: see *Wege Zu Kraft und Schönheit* (2013), though the music used has been dubbed onto the original film.
2. Wilhelm Prager's *Wege zu Kraft und Schönheit* was published in Germany in 1925. It was subtitled *Ein Film über moderne Körperkultur*. The title translates as *Ways* (or *Paths*) *to Health and Beauty*, and the subtitle translates as *A Film on Modern Physical Culture*. A second, expanded edition was published in 1926. The English version was published *c.*1932, and was variously titled *Back to Nature* or *The Golden Road to Health and Beauty*, with a specially produced English introduction by Charlton Morton, and English subtitles, at the request of the British Association and the British Institute of Education. For further discussion see Franco (2012, pp. 67–73) and Toepfer (1997, pp. 373–4).
3. The original quote from John Stuart Mill is from section III, 'Of Individuality, as one of the elements of well-being', in his *On Liberty* (1859). It differs in three small ways from Jordan's usage: 'There is a great fullness of life about his own existence, and when there is more life in the units, there is more in the mass which is composed of them' (Mill 1998, p. 70).
4. Available on the DVD *When the Fire Dances Between Two Poles*; see A. F. Sneider (Director), (1991). A YouTube video (extant in 2013) has the original movie footage, but the music has been dubbed with a more recent reconstruction: *Pastorale* (2013).
5. Available in reconstruction on DVD; see *New Dance* (1978).
6. In the original Laban (1920) *Die Welt Des Tänzers*, 9.
7. Mary Wigman presented many of her solo dance works in thematic 'cycles' or 'suites'. In addition to the *Swinging Landscape* cycle of 1929, she choreographed *Sacrifice* (solo cycle) in 1931, *The Road* (group cycle) in 1932; *Women's Dances* (group cycle) in 1934, and *Autumnal Dances* (solo cycle) in 1937. This particular cycle is detailed in the next endnote.
8. *Schwingende Landschaft* translates literally as *Swinging Landscape*, but two different English titles are used in the literature. Reynolds (2007) uses *Swinging Landscape*, and Sorell (1975) and Manning (2006) refer to *Shifting Landscape*. The latter title does provide a good sense of the shifting perspective that Wigman evokes in the cycle. However, we prefer *Swinging Landscape* because of the sense of *Schwung* that it implies, and because translations of other similar works of the period, such as Laban's *Schwingende Tempel* of 1922, use *Swinging*.
9. The cycle comprises *Anruf, Seraphisches Lied, Gesicht der Nacht, Pastorale I, Festlicher Rhythmus, Sommerlicher Tanz*, and *Sturmlied* (*Invocation, Seraphic Song, Face of Night, Pastoral, Festive Rhythm, Dance of Summer,* and *Storm Song*). They were performed throughout Germany in 1929 and in the early 1930s, and during Wigman's 1932 London season and her 1930/31 and 1931/32 tours of the USA. There was a second dance called *Pastorale II*—a group dance, part of the group cycle *Der Weg*, premiered on 8 December 8th, which toured the USA and UK. A film was made of Wigman performing three dances from the cycle: *Seraphic Song, Pastoral, Dance of Summer*. The *Schwingende Landschaft* cycle premiered in Germany on 7 November 1929. The extant film, which is widely available, is held by the Danish Film Museum, which dates its copy to 1929 because of the film techniques: it is titled *Mary Wigman Danser*. Hedwig Müller refers to the film *Mary Wigman tanzt: Schwingende Landschaft und Hexentanz* as being from 1930. John Martin reported a showing of this film in New York in May 1931. This film record has become a main source for discussion of Wigman's work.

10. From Wigman, M. (1931), 'Composition in pure movement', *Modern Music*, 8(2): 20–2, cited (in German) in Sorell, W. (1986), *Mary Wigman: Ein Vermächtnis*. Wilhelmshaven: Florian Noetzel.

11. Wigman made the cycle at a difficult time—1929 being a low point for the world economy, and Germany in particular, with the clouds of European fascism gathered on the horizon. Financial pressures had forced Wigman to disband her group, and this was the first of a series of solo performances. It was part of the repertory that she took on the first of her American tours.

12. She describes a summer holiday to southern France in 1929, and the 'joy of life' for her at that time: 'Everything was constantly changing, but never restless, never hurried. Aloneness was as wonderful as being together was harmonious. I was very happy. Because it was the time of promise and blossoming—also of my blossoming' (1966, p. 48). The *Swinging Landscape* cycle was directly inspired by this holiday.

13. See especially Kriegsman (1981).

REFERENCES

Beiswanger, G. W. (1935/1981). 'The dance and today's needs', in S. A. Kriegsman (ed.), *Modern Dance in America: The Bennington Years*. Boston, MA: G. K. Hall, pp. 280–3. Originally published in 1935 in *Theatre Arts Monthly*, 19(6): 439–50.

Bodenwieser, G. (1926). 'Dancing as a factor in education', *The Dancing Times*, pp. 169, 171.

Carter, A. and Fensham, R. (eds.) (2011). *Dancing Naturally: Nature, Neo-Classicism and Modernity in Early Twentieth Century Dance*. Basingstoke: Palgrave.

Cohen, S. J. (ed.). (1972). *Doris Humphrey: An Artist First*. Middletown, CT: Wesleyan University Press.

Daly, A. (1995). *Done into Dance: Isadora Duncan in America*. Bloomington, IN: Indianapolis University Press.

Franco, S. (2012). 'Rudolf Laban's dance film projects', in S. Manning and L. Ruprecht (eds.), *New German Dance Studies*. Urbana, IL: University of Illinois Press, pp. 63–78.

Gilfond, H. (1936). 'Dance Congress and Festival', *Dance Observer*, III(6): 1.

Holm, H. (1935, 1970). 'The German dance in the American scene', in V. Stewart and M. Armitage (eds.), *The Modern Dance*. New York, NY: Dance Horizons, pp. 79–86.

Holm, H. (1936). 'Everybody can dance, Hanya Holm contends', *Hartford Connecticut Times*, 30 December.

Humphrey, D. (1935) *New Dance*, from *New Dance Trilogy*. Bennington College Theatre, 3 August.

Humphrey, D. (1972). 'New dance', in S. J. Cohen (ed.), *Doris Humphrey: An Artist First*. Middletown, CT: Wesleyan University Press, pp. 238–41.

Huxley, M. and Burt, R. (2011). 'Ideas of nature, the natural and the modern in early twentieth-century dance discourse', in A. Carter and R. Fensham (eds.), *Dancing Naturally: Nature, Neo-classicism and Modernity in Early Twentieth Century Dance*. Basingstoke: Palgrave, pp. 31–42.

Jackson, N. (ed.) (2004). *Right to Dance: Dancing for Rights*. Banff: Banff Centre Press.

Jackson, N. and Shapiro-Phim, T. (eds.) (2008). *Dance, Human Rights and Social Justice: Dignity in Motion*. Plymouth: Scarecrow Press.

Jordan, D. (1938). *The Dance as Education*. London: Oxford University Press.

Kriegsman, S. A. (ed.) (1981). *Modern Dance in America: The Bennington Years*. Boston, MA: G. K. Hall.

Laban, R. (1920). *Die Welt des Tänzers*. Stuttgart: Walter Seifert.

Lloyd, M. (1949). *The Borzoi Book of Modern Dance*. New York, NY: A. A. Knopf.

McDonagh, D. (1973). *Martha Graham: A Biography*. London: David and Charles.

Main, L. (2011). 'Nature moving naturally in succession: An exploration of Doris Humphrey's *Water Study*', in A. Carter and R. Fensham (eds.), *Dancing Naturally: Nature, Neo-classicism and Modernity in Early Twentieth Century Dance*. Basingstoke: Palgrave, pp. 98–109.

Manning, S. (2004). *Modern Dance, Negro Dance: Race in Motion*. Minneapolis, MN: University of Minnesota Press.

Manning, S. (2006). *Ecstasy and the Demon: The Dances of Mary Wigman*. Minneapolis, MN: University of Minnesota Press.

Manning, S. and Ruprecht, L. (eds.). (2012). *New German Dance Studies*. Urbana, IL: University of Illinois Press.

Martin, J. (1931). 'The dance, film versions: Motion picture of Mary Wigman reveals camera limitations and possibilities', *The New York Times*, 10 May.

Martin, J. (1932). 'The dance: Mary Wigman. The German artist's first London recital impresses England, but raises doubts', *The New York Times*, 12 June.

Martin, J. (1933). *The Modern Dance*. New York, NY: A. S. Barnes.

Martin, J. (1936). *America Dancing; The Background and Personalities of the Modern Dance*. New York, NY: Dodge.

McCaw, D. (ed.). (2011). *The Laban Sourcebook*. Abingdon: Routledge.

Mill, J. S. (1998). *John Stuart Mill on Liberty and Other Essays*. Oxford: Oxford University Press.

Morris, G. (2006). *A Game for Dancers: Performing Modernism in the Postwar Years, 1945–1960*. Middletown, CT: Wesleyan University Press.

Morris, M. (1925). *Margaret Morris Dancing*. London: Kegan Paul, Trench and Trubner.

New Dance (1978) (DVD). American Dance Festival, directed by Charles Reinhart and Martha Myers. Dance Horizons video. Hightstown, NJ: Princeton Book Company.

Nicholas, L. (2007). *Dancing in Utopia: Dartington Hall and its Dancers*. Alton: Dance Books.

Pastorale (2013) (Video file). <https://www.youtube.com/watch?v=37sEaUhFzpI> (accessed 22 March 2017).

Randall, T. (2012). 'Hanya Holm and an American *Tanzgemeinschaft*', in S. Manning and L. Ruprecht (eds.), *New German Dance Studies*. Urbana, IL: University of Illinois Press, pp. 79–98.

Reynolds, D. (2007). *Rhythmic Subjects: Uses of Energy in the Dances of Mary Wigman, Martha Graham and Merce Cunningham*. Alton: Dance Books.

Ross, J. (2000). *Moving Lessons: Margaret H'Doubler and the Beginning of Dance in American Education*. Madison, WI: University of Wisconsin.

Ross, J. (2007). *Anna Halprin: Experience as Dance*. Berkeley, CA: University of California Press.

Selden, E. (1935). *The Dancer's Quest*. Berkeley, CA: University of California Press.

Sneider, A. F. (Director) (1991) (DVD). *When the fire dances between two poles: Mary Wigman*. Hightstown, NJ: Dance Horizons.

Sorell, W. (ed.) (1975). *The Mary Wigman Book: Her Writings Edited and Translated*. Middletown, CT: Wesleyan University Press.

Sorell, W. (1986). *Mary Wigman: Ein Vermächtnis*. Wilhelmshaven: Florian Noetzel.

Toepfer, K. (1997). *Empire of Ecstasy: Nudity and Movement in German Body Culture, 1910–1935*. Berkeley, CA: University of California Press.

Wege zu Kraft und Schönheit (2013) (Video file). <http://www.youtube.com/watch?v= cHTk-KHZ3QjU> (accessed 26 January 2015).

Wigman, M. (1927). 'The dance and modern woman', *The Dancing Times*, November, pp. 162–3.

Wigman, M. (1929). *Pastorale (Pastoral)*, from *Schwingende Landschaft (Swinging Landscape)*, 7 November 1929.

Wigman, M. (1931). 'Composition in pure movement', *Modern Music*, 82(2): 20–2.

Wigman, M. (1966). *The Language of Dance*. Trans. W. Sorrell. London: Macdonald & Evans.

CHAPTER 12

....

THERAPEUTIC PERFORMANCE

When Private Moves into Public

....

THANIA ACARÓN

INTRODUCTION

....

DANCE Movement Psychotherapy (DMP)[1] developed from the alliance between dance practices and psychotherapeutic frameworks. The pioneers of DMP came from dance and performance backgrounds, and their work encouraged the development of an approach that connects body and mind and introduces the body as the focus of all experience and the principal agent in the healing process. Wellbeing encompasses the fulfilment of our own human potential while developing the resources to cope and transcend adversity (World Health Organization 2014). Movement within DMP acquires communicative, emotional, symbolic, and expressive qualities that take on an integrative role within the individual or group. Its pioneers viewed 'mastery or technique as functional and aesthetic platforms for expression' (Fraenkel and Mehr 2006, pp. 1–2). This included teaching dance technique to clients to create a basic non-verbal vocabulary. To many dance movement psychotherapists, however, the use of choreography or dance technique within a therapeutic framework may seem like a contradiction. Duggan (1995) states that some dance movement psychotherapists argue that conventional dance steps 'are inauthentic and keep individuals away from their feelings' (p. 229). Fraenkel and Mehr (2006) also state that the term 'dance technique' elicits a critical response which echoes the ambivalence of whether structuring a therapeutic process can thwart a patient/client's[2] own voice. Arnheim (1992) argues that aesthetics are an 'indispensable trait' of human behaviour, and can be useful, even at times necessary within therapeutic contexts. Choreography and performance, as major elements of dance, exhibit a controversial role within DMP, which will be unpacked in this chapter. I will focus on delineating the potential and limitations of the use of choreographic approaches, movement techniques, and performance opportunities within the DMP setting: how dance performance functions as a therapeutic tool. The therapeutic performance in DMP will be analysed as an intervention taking into consideration its benefits and risks to the therapeutic relationship and patient/client wellbeing. I will use examples from my practice to illustrate certain applications of choreography within DMP, and will refer to debates relating to ethical issues surrounding such applications.

As a dance movement psychotherapist, performer, and choreographer who is still creating work for the stage, my artistic background has offered many new perspectives that promote further communication between the ramifications of dance/movement as a discipline. However, I have felt the importance of also illustrating similarities and distinctions between artistic, educational, and therapeutic processes and their application. DMP holds many differences from dance education that have been a way to demarcate the DMP field from its inception and align it within psychotherapeutic contexts. Many authors, including Panhofer (2005), Schmais (1970), Duggan (1995), Fraenkel and Mehr (2006), Meekums (2002), and Hayes (2010) illustrate the fine and precarious line between dance technique, education, and DMP. In order to help my students and workshop participants understand these differences, I created a working diagram (see Figure 12.1) that encompasses the components of therapeutic processes in DMP. In summary, it is the focus on the therapeutic relationship between practitioner and client, and the structures and interventions based on the client's needs and from the client's movement and verbal contributions, that distinguishes DMP from other body-based or movement-based practices. Using this diagram, a movement-based practice can be distinguished from DMP. A delicate exception, however, would be Body Psychotherapy

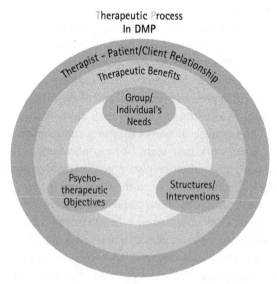

FIGURE 12.1. Diagram illustrating the therapeutic process interrelations that distinguishes DMP from other dance/movement-based practices. (Credit: Design by Claudia Peces.)

and Somatic Psychology, which would also use the body as the main focus of treatment, but may not use dance-based practices as a mode of intervention, and also may include touch. Considering differences between DMP on the one hand and Somatic Psychology and Body Psychotherapy on the other may require more of an in-depth theoretical and practical discussion which is outside the scope of this chapter, since their path and formation are indeed complementary to DMP.

DMP has traditionally been aligned with improvisational processes—the patient/client being in the moment in movement, the bringing forth of movement as a description of existence, of being. The objective is to develop awareness of and with the body (Csordas 1993, in Tantia 2012), letting it be a protagonist within the psychotherapeutic process, allowing expression to occur at a bodily level. The role of teacher or choreographer is abdicated, making a transition from teaching to therapy: judgement is suspended, aesthetics become secondary, and the patient/client's movement repertoire becomes the focus (Schmais 1970). This bidirectional process between therapist and patient initiation and movement dialogue shapes the therapeutic relationship and lays down the foundations for the therapeutic process, facilitating the delineation of therapeutic objectives in treatment.

The research focus on choreography, performance, and the use of dance technique in DMP sessions was originally introduced by DMP pioneers. However, apart from earlier writings from the pioneers, there is very little on choreography as a therapeutic tool (Victoria 2012). Duggan (1995) uses choreography as a flexible structure that both honours the clients'—in this case adolescents'—contributions (versus a therapist/choreographer-directed process) and provides a therapeutic framework. Her work was one of the first to mention choreographic dance structures as a therapeutic tool with adolescents. Swami and Harris (2012) and Hayes (2010) conducted their research on DMP with dancers, Hayes (2010) has described how DMP sessions influenced dancers' choreographic ability and technique, while Swami and Harris (2012) have focused on body image and body awareness. Jeppe (2006) suggests a model that incorporates music, poetry, and DMP with adults with mental illness, including several final performances that emerged from her work. Allegranti (2009) uses creative multidisciplinary approaches to DMP that culminated with a film generated by her clients' work. Bacon (2007) discusses the role of Jung's active imagination and Gendlin's focusing method within performance contexts in DMP, arguing in favour of the therapeutic processes involved in dance-making. Victoria (2012) proposes a 'choreo-therapeutic model using the psychodynamic concepts of externalization, transformation, and reinternalization in dance choreography to work through and heal inner states' (p. 168). She exposes a process where *choreo-clients*, as she terms them, are led through a creative process within sessions, using performance as a therapeutic tool. Her methodology, which is still in development, indicates why choreography has a wide potential to be used for therapeutic purposes. Victoria's (2012) model is perhaps a great starting point for continuing a discussion and developing practice-based models within DMP.

In terms of the use of specific dance forms, there has been a variety of applications to DMP. Capello (2007) reviews the American Dance Therapy Association International

Summary of Article by Patricia Capello (2007) Dance as Our Source in Dance/Movement Therapy Education and Practice in American Journal of Dance Therapy, 29(1), pp. 37-50.				
Panelist	Country of Origin	Dance Forms Mentioned	Populations worked for**	Therapeutic Objectives (if mentioned)
Jocelyne Vaysse	France	Ballet	Children with Autism	
		French Folik Dances	Paediatric Psychiatry	Collective memory Reminiscence* Sense of belonging Reinforcement of cultural identity
		Primitive Expression[2]		Corporal symbolisation of patent's personal history Expression through ritual*
Theodora Thatcher	Greece	Panygiriaw		Group Cohesion Attesting Cultural Values Confirming Local Identities* Sense of mastery
Susanna Bender[3]	Germany	Circle Dances Oriental/Belly Dance Social Dance Contact Improvisation Tango African Dance		
Lucie Bednarova	Czech Republic	Nursery rhymes	Adults with Psychosis	Identification with childhood through memory
		Social Dances (polka, waltz, samba)	Adolescents	Appropriate touch and space Social Interaction*
		Czech & Moravian folk dance)		Coping Skills Creative Problem Solving*
		Beseda (seven folk dances)		Distance/closeness Sense of belonging to a group Emotional expression
		Belly Dance African Dance Jewish Dance Samba		

FIGURE 12.2. Summary of Capello (2007): dance forms and therapeutic objectives. (Credit: Thania Acaron.)

		Noh/Shimai		Introductory form to dance
Shoichi Machida & Yukari Sakiyama	Japan	Nihonbuyoh		
		Bon Festival Dance	Mental health hospital settings	Sense of community Unity[1] group cohesion* Mutual cooperation
		Butoh		
Dr. Boon Soon Ryu	Korea			Community awareness Sense of belonging Emotional expression release Addressing inner conflicts arid desires
		Moon Dance		
Rita Parvia	Finland	Contemporary Dance		
Tsung Chin Lee	Taiwan	Chinese Dragon & Lion Dance		Emotional decompression in group
Maralia Reca	Argentina	Folk rhythms Zapateo	Adults with Psychosis Neurotic Adults	Grounding/Embodying sense of weight Impulse control Addressing compulsive tendencies Developing self-awareness
Sohini Chakaborty	India	Yoga/yogic elements		Internal awareness of rhythm* Mind/body integration Increased concentration Improved sense of control
		Kathakali Dance		Developing facial affect* Energy/tension release* Emotional discharge*
		Manipuri Dance		Increasing self-identity Realising Inner cairn
		Bharatnatyam		Body part isolation and integration*
		Folk Forms		Solidarity within group)* Relationship building Enhancing body language Communication Self-dignity and confidence Overcoming trauma and aggression

ADDITIONAL NOTES

* Paraphrased

** If left blank, panelist did not specify usage with a specific population

[1] Refers to French DMP pioneer Ruth Gaetner's use of ballet with children in psychiatric care and adults

[2] Developed initially by Herns Duplan and Katherine Dunham, and adapted to DMP by France Schott-Billmann

[3] Presented a general overview of influences in DMP in Germany

FIGURE 12.2 Continued

Panel's discussion during their 2007 annual conference. Several DMP delegates from all over the world focused on different elements of dance performance used both historically and contemporarily within the DMP profession. Capello's article encapsulates the integration of folkloric forms into DMP contexts as a way of using familiar and symbolic aspects of dance that are meaningful for the patient/clients' cultural realm in the service of therapy. Figure 12.2 shows a summary of the statements provided by the international panelists invited to this panel to speak on this context, and lists their mentions of the benefits of using their dance forms within DMP sessions. Some panellists offered examples of work with specific populations, while others selected specific dance forms and their applicability. This chapter presents some of these examples as possibilities for further research.

THERAPEUTIC PERFORMANCE

I define a dance performance as a set of movements, either choreographed and structured in advance, or improvised in the moment, intended to be seen by an audience. The creator(s) of the movement may develop a piece using material generated from their own internal states, their therapeutic process, various aesthetic vocabularies, inspiration from the environment (landscapes, buildings as in site-specific works), images, poems, other visual media, music, or any combination of these. As Bacon (2007) remarks: '... performance-makers working with therapeutic tools enter an imaginal world whenever they begin the creative process' (p. 20). There are endless relationships between the creation of material, the creator, and the audience. This is not to leave out the fact that even in the private sphere, a patient/client may 'perform' for the therapist—assuming roles that they think will please him or her—or may adopt and act out various roles as defences. In many ways this can be true in reverse, and the therapist may perform roles for the client. The private sphere within therapy contributes to a sense of mutual construction of reality. Within the arts therapies,[3] assuming different roles, acting out symbolically and embodying metaphor is instrinsic to the work (Ellis 2001). The concept of performativity, especially with regard to gender, has been much explored within the social sciences. Butler (1999) claims that every human being performs their own roles that are inscribed in the body (especially in terms of gender) within social contexts. One may even question: what is private and what is considered public? I highlight this aspect to argue that throughout our lives we manifest infinite types of private and public performances. However, for the purposes of this chapter the therapeutic performance is considered differently. As a client-led process of creation, the private self or private selves expressed via the therapeutic relationship make conscious decisions to create dance/movement material choreographed for an outside audience.

Some dance movement psychotherapists incorporate performance as part of their therapeutic interventions, while others use dance technique as a way to address the therapeutic objectives within sessions (some examples are summarized in Figure 12.2). Within this chapter I illustrate the key aspects of the therapeutic performance within DMP as follows:

1. Therapeutic performance is a part of a patient/client/group process of DMP.
2. The movement material is generated from patient/client/group work within the sessions.
3. The process of generation and selection of material is client-led.
4. Concepts from artistic dance-based processes are in dialogue with therapeutic connotations.

These aspects correlate to Figure 12.1, in that the therapeutic performance[4] (and embedded within it all the movement codes used to create it) remains within the structures/interventions, which are hence generated from the patient/clients and are tied into the therapeutic objectives of the session. Therapeutic performance is one of many interventions that emerge from the sessions, and serve as a vehicle to structure and clarify the material that the patient/clients bring.

Background

During my work as a dance movement psychotherapist in schools, I was often asked if I would do something for the annual Holiday Show. The students' gaze turned to me, expecting permission to bring the private into the public arena. My role was established as a dance movement psychotherapist, but the school demanded a show for the parents and community, and year after year, as I remained the only 'dance/movement person' within these settings, this performance expectation started to become a ritual. My initial compromise was to hold 'performance groups' separate from those therapeutic in nature. These performance groups had technique classes as part of their formation, and performed several times a year. I also held different types of session: individual therapy sessions, dyads and group therapy sessions, juggling a myriad of roles within this setting. The settings' expectations of a performance for the community felt at first an insult to my professional career—I felt I had to defend the privacy of DMP and the distinction from dance as a performing art and communicate this to the school—to administration directly, and then to the staff through professional development workshops. Additionally, I needed to explain this further to my young clients, since part of our therapeutic process was in defining how movement could benefit them, and how different our sessions were from a dance class or dance training. This blurring of boundaries in others enforced an internal boundary in myself: I needed to clarify these different roles within me in order to create safety and ethical lines within the setting. After transitioning to work community-based contexts with adults, and teaching DMP in higher education and in South America and Europe, I realized that therapeutic performances were quite common amongst practitioners, yet employing this tool needed careful unpacking and analysis.

THERAPEUTIC RATIONALE AND BENEFITS OF PERFORMANCE

Developmental psychologists and psychoanalysts, such as Winnicott (1971), argue that the existence of an Other shapes us from infancy and ultimately defines our sense of self. The Other is represented by multiple roles throughout our lives. In a formal performance situation, the Other becomes the audience and the situation is taken into a hyper-reality: All eyes descend on the performer. There is no escape from criticism or approval. There is no stopping or redoing. An external view of the performer is immediately injected into what was previously a dual or closed group process. In the practice of Authentic Movement, awareness of oneself is often developed through both being witnessed (by the therapist or fellow group therapy members) and witnessing our own experience (Musicant 1994, 2001; Adler 1996). Therapeutic performances to some extent can fulfil some of these experiences. The challenge, however, is that the audience-as-witness is not trained in DMP nor familiar with the therapeutic process involved. The audience member will not necessarily hold the patient/client, sustain and contain the emotional charge spent on what is presented, and might not be willing to manage the intricacies of the patient/client's world. In a public performance, both therapist and client take a risk plunging into the unknown hands of its audience members, and need to be prepared for all the configurations of reactions and feedback that are inherently involved. On the other hand, Jeppe (2006) reports a sense of confidence, and social affirmation as aftermath of the therapeutic performance, which links performance to patient/client wellbeing. The effects of witnessing a community's acceptance, and overcoming struggles and challenges to put up a specific product on stage, become instrumental for a patient/client's personal growth.

DECISION TO PERFORM

The process of deciding to get up on 'stage' (whether it is an open community room or a theatre) involves a unique process of preparation initiated by a self-reflective process and assessment of readiness and willingness. For many artists, even after decades of training, there is always the moment of anxiety before a performance. In the case of some patient/clients, where there is little to no performance background, the decision to place themselves on purpose in an anxiety-ridden situation may seem controversial and perhaps contraindicated. Pre- and post-performance assessments can ultimately determine its effects on the patient/client and therapeutic relationship.

Duggan suggests that the decision to perform depends upon the establishment of a performance contract versus a therapeutic contract (personal communication, 27 August 2012). She mentions that patient/clients (especially in school-based settings) have self-referred solely to participate in a DMP group for performance purposes. Their desire to perform fuelled their initial contact. She has hence formed specific performance groups with this output in mind. This is different from the cases in which the contract is initially a therapeutic one, in which there is a decision to perform that has emerged from the process. Both cases are included within my definition of therapeutic performance in DMP.

In my practice I constantly offered my patient/clients the option of not performing, and had to be sensitive to possible signs of their feeling overwhelmed, not ready, or assess potential psychological harm, as in the case of my child clients that had been previously traumatized. The work within the sessions needed to provide support, and as Winnicott (1971) terms it, a holding environment and a therapeutic relationship had to be well established before any decisions to perform were discussed. Many conversations and movement explorations constantly fed the possibility and intention behind performance, and the client's readiness was monitored until the moment before the performance.

THERAPEUTIC MATERIAL IN MOVEMENT

The body is able to express its inner workings through many pathways in DMP. Each therapist has her/his own style of working according to the needs of their client population. From my training in the United States, my approach has encompassed strong elements both from Authentic Movement and Marian Chace (Lewis 2004), and I have also been able to interweave my experience as a performer and dance educator. This section describes some of the choreographic tools I have employed in my sessions that have culminated in therapeutic performances.

Along with Victoria (2012), I too found extreme validity in DMP pioneer Trudi Schoop's claim that structuring unconscious material that had been brought to the conscious into movement phrases was a useful way of being able to organize thoughts and being able to ground perspectives. 'The process of formulating dance movement sequences served the function of slowing down the expressive process and in this way allowed more time for the exploration of inner conflicts. Through choreographing conflicts, Schoop believed the individual could gain some control, insight, and mastery over his or her problems.' (Levy 2005, p. 64). Hackney (2002) defines phrasing as 'perceivable units of movement which are in some sense meaningful' (p. 239). She speaks about 'practicing' new patterns as they are brought to awareness, in an effort to retrain the body to discover alternative ways of being. In my work, I use the making of phrases of movement as a tool in order to bring awareness to an individual's behavioural patterns. These themes of repetition, patterns, or 'stuckness' can be explored within the space, with specific movements which the patient/client generates. This tool is often used in dance education frameworks, yet within the concept of therapeutic performance in DMP it can be employed as a form of crystallization of internal into external states, to aid the identification of intrapsychic conflicts. It can help the client construct multiple perspectives with which to view a particular issue.

Other choreographic tools that involve explorations of space can be particularly useful. For example, in the case of one patient/client choreographing for the group, or in group choreography, the use of spatial formations, or the use of mapping of the space and allocating movement and meaning to specific locations, can be useful. This tool was particularly useful in my work with children in foster care, in which we explored transitions between the homes of biological parents to the foster homes. Pathways can be drawn on the map to symbolize a client's personal events or to indicate ways in which transitions between the events or places took place which the patient/clients can then enact through movement.

Incorporating dance technique into sessions can also be used to generate therapeutic movement material and expand the patient/client's movement repertoire. Maintaining clarity of intention, as Hackney (2002) suggests, helps structure our world. Through employing dance technique, however, the focus of sessions may become more 'educational', involving teaching specific steps or combinations which may then be applied to the choreography. This is not to say that teaching does not occur at times during therapy. With some clients, psychoeducational tasks may be incredibly beneficial. The challenge lies in the delicate balance between the patient/client's needs, their therapeutic process, and what elements within the dance technique may address them appropriately. However, the use of social dances and partner dances may enforce gender stereotypes and need careful consideration. Duggan (1995) argues that reinforcing traditional gender roles and dynamics may perpetuate oppressive societal norms. In these cases, the therapist can investigate creative ways in which these traditional dance forms and gender roles can be challenged, providing a safe place for differences in gender expression and sexual orientation.

The aesthetic value of dance technique is intrinsically linked to dance performance and the choreographic process. The choreographer employs a specific set of aesthetic values that shapes their vision of the work. This is a difficult challenge, as the integrity of the patient/client's material must not be sacrificed to put on something pleasing to the eye for a performance. It is, nevertheless, a rich discussion to have with patient/clients around what they consider aesthetically pleasing. Depending on their therapeutic framework, dance movement psychotherapists may become more directive in their interventions. Dance movement psychotherapists might also teach choreographic concepts and structures to form the material as well (i.e. canon, spatial formations, specific structures such as theme and variation, or ABA formats). They may also propose complementary movements that may support, contrast, or expand the patient/client's movement repertoire (Sandel et al. 1993). Some dance movement psychotherapists from more of a psychodynamic stance, however, would adopt a more therapist-as-witness role within session, not moving with clients, but holding their experience in their bodies and attuning to the client's movement.

Another device that can facilitate the generation of movement material is the video camera. Although videotaping might not be allowed in some settings—and patient/client consent is essential—it can become a useful tool for self-reflection and documentation of the process. Managing the anxiety of a 'technological eye' is not an easy process when working with a group or individual client, since enough time has to be allowed in sessions for patient/clients to feel comfortable with its presence. There is little mention in DMP literature about the use of video, with the exception of Allegranti (2009), who combines film-making as joint part with DMP with self-referred adults. Art therapist Henley (1991) describes the process and benefits of using videotaping with developmentally disabled clients within art therapy, adding an embodied way of both patient/client and therapist assessment during art-making. Henley (1991) states that 'video can increase awareness of self and others through body animation, facial expressivity, and interpersonal relating when taped sequences are played back as a prelude to drawing' (p. 443). Within my practice, videotaping clients and film-making have been an incredibly useful tool. An example of this was demonstrated by an adolescent client with selective mutism in my school-based therapy group. As part of a collective group film project, she was able to speak to the camera and manage her severe anxiety around adults, whilst providing a creative venue for social interaction and inclusion.

THERAPEUTIC RELATIONSHIP IN PERFORMANCE

Every element of the creation, development, performance, and evaluation of therapeutic performance material poses both a threat and an opportunity to the therapeutic relationship. Clarkson and Pokorny (2013) argue that one of the most effective types of therapeutic relationship is the working alliance relationship, in which client and therapist 'join forces' to engage in mutual cooperation (p. 32). The therapeutic relationship is hence negotiated throughout the performance, ebbing and flowing within a system of unknowns (i.e. audience reaction, client's perceived 'success' of the performance, effect on the relationships with the therapist). Duggan (1995) conveys the struggle to get her adolescents' choreography to the stage, and how performance impacted on the youngsters' lives within their school community. As with many of my patient/clients that chose to perform their therapeutic material, performance day becomes a synopsis about how the patient/client copes with stressful or difficult situations, which is one of the pillar elements of wellbeing. Some of my clients were incredibly determined to show their mastery. Some debated whether to perform almost seconds before going on. Some groups became fragmented due to the stress, or grew more cohesive. However, all knew that they had to make a clear choice to perform which could be rescinded at any point. As a therapist, these moments when a patient/client(s) were the most vulnerable became opportunities to offer support without judgement, and model ways of coping with stressful events.

Debriefing a performance with a client was one of the most fascinating and pivotal moments in our therapeutic process. They described, drew, or moved how they embodied exposure, criticism, anticipation, self-doubt, pride, anxiety, and/or mastery. The therapeutic performance does not end when the curtain falls or the audience stops clapping; it becomes embedded in the relationship and therapeutic development of the individual and marks an important point of growth, break, or transition in their life.

Ethics, Benefits, and Risks

Therapeutic performance in dance, as a process developed within the DMP context, carries several ethical issues. Confidentiality is *essential*. Within the therapeutic performance process in DMP, measures need to be taken to protect the confidentiality of the patient's specific history. In this way, since dance is inherently non-verbal and movement can be interpreted in an infinite number of ways, the advantage of using dance in this way becomes clear. The same can apply to the consideration of the performance space, which may include anywhere from the common treatment room with family and friends, to the school auditorium, or it may be a general area. The choice of space is important in preserving a client's confidentiality if he/she belongs to a mental-health setting. Videotaping also involves a heavy component of confidentiality and care as to who has access to the material.

Patient/client *safety* is also an important consideration—psychological, physical, and emotional safety. In terms of the physical dimension, for example, performance props should be chosen according to the capabilities of the patient/clients. Patient/clients with sensory integration problems should be considered, where the extreme noise or over-stimulation can be potentially detrimental to the client. This was often the case when I worked with children in the autistic spectrum. *If* they decided to perform, it was in small group settings or with family members. In other cases, collaboration with therapeutic assistants was crucial, since they could monitor specific individuals within a group and be able to leave the premises if needed in order for a child to have a break from the overstimulation. Additionally, measures of the patient/client's stamina, condition, and bodily abilities must always be monitored, since the adrenaline of performance can sometimes work against even the most trained bodies. Emotional and psychological safety should also be the priority when selecting therapeutic material. This is not to say that movement cannot betray even the most private of matters. The interpretation of what is seen by the audience cannot be controlled—but the way in which patient/clients choose their own material can be guided and discussed. The rationale behind the therapeutic performance is to provide a context of expression. The patient/client may feel too vulnerable about certain material, so it is important to consider the potential benefits and risks. Gender and sexuality need also to be considered among the dynamics of groups and to promote psychological safety amongst members regardless of their gender identity and sexual orientation within the group.

Snow et al. (2003) reiterated that the drama therapist should not foresake their clients' needs in order to prioritize their own artistic ambitions. This also applies to the distinct roles of choreographer and therapist. I must admit there were times in which I noticed during sessions, the choreographer role emerged in me. It was a moment of internal reflection, and I identified my own countertransferential feelings as an artist being called into question. At times I would find myself wanting the choreography to 'look good' or yearning to adjust or correct a client's steps, and needed to hold back. I understood it was my need; the aesthetics wanting to influence the process. Brown (2008) argues that dance movement psychotherapists must keep their own dance practice alive and consistent in order to address this. Brown (2008), Boris (2001), and Myers et al. (1978) recommend the maintenance of creative practices as a powerful burnout prevention and professional development tool for practising creative arts therapists. Brown (2008) states that 'creative arts therapists must continue to embody the creative spark that first birthed our respective disciplines and first drew individuals to this creative field' (201). I agree that nurturing our embodied practices and continuing to create artistic work or developing our movement skills can benefit ourselves as practitioners and our clients; the fulfilment of our own performance needs are realized and are kept separate from the patient/client process.

In the next section I will address a case from my practice in which therapeutic performance was implemented in order to paint a picture of its application in DMP.

CASE STUDY

I had been working at school-based setting as a dance movement psychotherapist where I had individual and group work for children aged 5–13. Sylvia—a client I had been seeing in individual sessions—asked me, much to my surprise, if she could be in the end-of-year performance at an after-school programme on which I had been working. Sylvia was 12 years old, very verbose, and extremely precocious, with incredible responsibilities for taking care of her younger siblings. She already thought of herself as a 'caretaker', and was able to rationalize and justify her situation in an adult-like manner. She had profound issues with her body image, and was very self-conscious about her body. She had a reputation among her peers as the 'tough one', and it made me extremely curious that by performing she was inviting others to see a vulnerable side of herself.

Sylvia had chosen as part of her sessions to use a Body Sox™ (see Figures 12.3 and 12.4), stating that she felt safe inside it. The Body Sox is a type of human-sized encasing made of lycra in which people can crawl inside and their body be covered completely, with an option to cover or reveal their face. It allowed Sylvia a way to cover her body while she moved. Sylvia often used the Body Sox with her head uncovered, finding comfortable ways of moving and exploring the space around her. The lycra provided

FIGURE 12.3. Body Sox™ (not actual client). (Photo credit: Ellen Ríos Padín (Puerto Rico); dancer: María de Lourdes Biaggi.)

FIGURE 12.4. Body Sox™ (not actual client). (Photo credit: Ellen Ríos Padín (Puerto Rico); dancer: María de Lourdes Biaggi.)

proprioceptive feedback, and she felt held by this flexible structure, providing her with the physical boundary she craved from the adult figures in her world, and the nurturance she lacked everywhere else.

I always had the option of a video camera available to clients, and Sylvia agreed that we videotape[5] her sessions in order to reflect on how she moved through the improvisations. The video footage was only to be seen by the two of us, and her parents consented that if needed, my clinical supervisor would have access to the material. Selecting the material for the performance was the most difficult process. Sylvia had a way of masking her emotions in movement in a similar fashion to how she used her language and adult-like behaviour to create alliances with the adult figures in the programme and alienate her peers. Some of her improvisations always included the theme of hiding, using external objects such as scarves. She had limited affective range in her facial expressions, and she used many props to cover her face. One of our therapeutic objectives was to be able to encourage a deeper involvement with the strong feelings she had about herself, her body, and the incredible burden of responsibility she carried.

Sylvia decided that she would perform her material with her head inside the Body Sox, and I remember her expressing that this way, she did not have to worry about her clothes nor accidentally revealing any skin or showing her face—a clear representation of the strong protective measures she had been applying, even throughout the sessions. She selected a very emotional song that had been played in our closing movement ritual that expressed the struggle between what was being demanded of her and what she should do, and, as expressed in the lyrics of the song, the 'need for a pause', to think for herself. The process of choreographing her piece involved certain shapes in conjunction to the music, and also included some structured improvisation.

Before the performance, Sylvia remained pretty calm, but at times was rather ambivalent about her impending performance. When the time came, she decided to perform—much to the surprise of her community. Her performance brought tears to everyone's eyes. Even though she was covered in the Body Sox, the emotionality and deep connection to her struggles were evident. The audience held her experience, and the energy felt in the room reaffirmed the power of her movement. When she had finished dancing she poked her face out of the Body Sox and smiled. Her performance marked the development of our work together—to be able to show vulnerability and emotion through movement. To her, in the confined boundary inside the Body Sox, she did not have to be a 'tough girl', nor the caretaker. She could just be Sylvia. Some staff members came to me afterwards and commented on how different Sylvia had portrayed herself versus her usual self within the school. They were surprised at her expressivity, and were glad that she had a place where she could explore this within DMP. As we debriefed the performance, she expressed she was pleased with what she did, and discussed the possibility of doing other dances without the Body Sox in the future. I took this as a gesture that her therapeutic performance had benefited her therapy in DMP; she was beginning to be ready to go deeper within herself, and without her 'mask'—a beginning of her journey towards wellbeing.

This case study presents the cathartic aspect of therapeutic performance in dance, and its possibilities for the development of the therapeutic relationship. The patient/client led the process, chose what she wanted to portray to her audience, what facets of herself she felt comfortable exposing. The Body Sox provided a protective barrier in her case, yet the shapes created were able to transmit much more than she probably anticipated. I interpreted the final detail of peeking out of the Body Sox to take a bow as a sign that she was willing to show a part of herself to the outside world. My role was not that of a choreographer, looking for the aesthetics of it, but more as a source of support and offering a contained environment where she could have the independence of her own voice. The process of selecting the material and shaping it involved asking questions both verbally and through inviting her to move certain emotions she wanted to portray, or offering other improvisations to develop her movement vocabulary as well, in conjunction with her theme. Sometimes we used the song she selected, and at other times we used different types of music to elicit other efforts and dynamics. The video provided us with the continuity and external eye, as she was able to further select movement sequences from her previous sessions to which she was drawn. The video footage also allowed her to view herself, and I guided the process of expressing feedback about seeing herself on camera, suggesting ways in which she could view herself without the overly critical eye she had about her body.

The case of Sylvia is only one out of the many powerful stories that came out of the use of therapeutic performance within my DMP sessions. At times, the experiences were not always positive, especially with particularly 'honest' audience members, whose feedback was not always censored and was at times quite destructive. However, even the difficult comments or feedback were useful tools within the context of our sessions. The performances were a hyper-reality of the outside world, with the exception that this was a world situation I could navigate and process with my patient/client while being there. I could embody with my client a live *mise en scene*, and I could incorporate the myriad of aspects within this experience into our therapy. The therapeutic performance is one of the few ways in which the dance movement psychotherapist and client both interact with an external audience.

CONCLUSION

Creativity is 'the doing that arises out of being' (Winnicott et al. 1986, p. 39). If the therapeutic relationship is prioritized, choreographic tools and dance forms/styles which are underpinned by movement techniques, with or without explicit aesthetic objectives, can be made available as therapeutic interventions. The practitioner, however, needs to be aware of how these interventions serve the patient/clients' therapeutic objectives and also be sufficiently familiar with choreographic principles and dance-based artistic concepts and structures. The dance movement psychotherapist's previous experience in choreography and performance can be extremely beneficial to the process, if the tools that are brought forth are used to clarify a patient/clients' artistic vision and are continually being checked for fulfilment of the patient/clients' needs. At all times, ethical guidelines must be upheld, and the balance between education and therapy needs to be maintained. Since a therapeutic performance can occur or be suggested at any time during the therapeutic process, the challenges and benefits to the client are intrinsically interwoven. To create something that links to a patient/client's life, to witness a client being seen by others, and to have a patient/ client witness themselves being seen by an outside community, can have a powerful effect, which can be incredibly constructive and/or possibly destructive to their process. Although the case study presented indicates that the therapeutic performance enhanced the client's wellbeing, this may not be the case for all therapeutic performances. However, at the times when it has been implemented in a safe way and through the considerations expressed in this chapter, the benefits to the patient/client have been immense. It is a delicate balance and risk, with an enormous amount of potential therapeutic opportunities which need to continue to be explored and researched.

NOTES

1. The term for the profession in the UK is 'Dance Movement Psychotherapy', though in the United States the term is 'dance/movement therapy'. The UK version of the term and British spelling is utilized in this chapter.
2. I use the words 'patient/client' with a separator in order to allow for the terminology to be applicable to a variety of settings. In the case of schools and my work with normal neurotic adults, I refer to them as clients, whereas in hospital settings they can be referred to as patients.
3. 'Arts therapies' is the British and European term that encompasses music therapy, art therapy, dramatherapy, and DMP. See the European Consortium for Arts Therapies in Education (<http://www.ecarte.info>) for more information. In the United States, this category is termed 'creative arts therapies', and includes psychodrama and poetry therapy. See the National Coalition for Creative Arts Therapies Association (>http://www.nccata.org>).
4. Therapeutic performance has also been utilized by psychodrama and dramatherapy, and within dramatherapy has been termed 'therapeutic theatre'.
5. Authorization for videotaping was obtained from parents and Sylvia, since it was an educational setting. Parents signed consent forms that authorized the use of videos in sessions, for therapeutic purposes, and for clinical supervision. At the end of the year, the children were given copies of all the sessions videotaped, for them to keep.

REFERENCES

Adler, J. (1996). 'The collective body', in P. Pallaro (ed.), *Authentic Movement: Moving the Body, Moving the Self, Being Moved: A Collection of Essays*. London and Philadelphia: Jessica Kingsley, pp. 190–208.

Allegranti, B. (2009). 'Embodied performances of sexuality and gender: A feminist approach to dance movement psychotherapy and performance practice;, *Body, Movement and Dance in Psychotherapy*, 4(1): 17–31.

Arnheim, R. (1992). 'Why aesthetics is needed', *The Arts in Psychotherapy*, 19(3): 149–51.

Bacon, J. (2007). 'Psyche moving: "Active imagination" and "focusing" in movement-based performance and psychotherapy', *Body, Movement and Dance in Psychotherapy: An International Journal for Theory, Research and Practice*, 2(1): 17–28.

Boris, R. (2001). 'The root of dance therapy: A consideration of movement, dancing, and verbalization vis-à-vis dance/movement therapy', *Psychoanalytic Inquiry*, 21(3): 356–67. doi:10.1080/07351692109348940

Brown, C. (2008). 'The importance of making art for the creative arts therapist: An artistic inquiry', *The Arts in Psychotherapy*, 35(3): 201–08. doi:10.1016/j.aip.2008.04.002

Butler, J. (1999). 'Bodily inscriptions, performative subversions', in J. Price and M. Shildrick (eds.), *Feminist Theory and the Body: A Reader*. Edinburgh: Edinburgh University Press, pp. 416–422.

Capello, P. (2007). 'Dance as our source in dance/movement therapy education and practice', *American Journal of Dance Therapy*, 29(1): 37–50. doi:10.1007/s10465-006-9025-0

Clarkson, P. and Pokorny, M. (2013). *The Handbook of Psychotherapy*. East Sussex and New York: Routledge.

Duggan, D. (1995). 'The "4s": A dance therapy program for learning-disabled adolescents', in F. J. Levy, J. Pines Fried, and F. Leventhal (eds.), *Dance and Other Expressive Art Therapies: When Words are Not Enough*. New York and London: Routledge, pp. 225–40.

European Consortium for Arts Therapies in Education (2013). <http://www.ecarte.info>

Ellis, R. (2001). 'Movement metaphor as mediator: a model for the dance/movement therapy process', *The Arts in Psychotherapy*, 28(3): 181–90.

Fraenkel, D. L. and Mehr, J. D. (2006). 'Valuing the dance teacher and dance technique in dance/movement therapy', in *41st Annual Conference American Dance Therapy Association: Choreographing Collaboration: A Joint Conference with NDEO*. American Dance Therapy Association.

Hackney, P. (2002). *Making Connections: Total Body Integration through Bartenieff Fundamentals*. New York, NY: Routledge.

Hayes, J. (2010). *Dancers in a Dance Movement Therapy Group: Links between Personal Process, Choreography and Performance*. Saarbrücken: LAP Lambert Academic Publishing.

Henley, D. R. (1991). 'Therapeutic and aesthetic application of video with the developmentally disabled', *The Arts in Psychotherapy*, 18(5): 441–7.

Jeppe, Z. (2006). 'Dance/movement and music in improvisational concert: A model for psychotherapy', *The Arts in Psychotherapy*, 33: 371–82.

Levy, F. J. (2005). *Dance/Movement Therapy. A Healing Art* (revised). AAHPERD Publications. <http://eric.ed.gov/?id=ED291746>

Lewis, P. (2004). 'The use of Marian Chace's technique combined with in the depth dance therapy derived from the Jungian model', *Musik-, Tanz Und Kunsttherapie*, 15(4): 197–203. doi:10.1026/0933-6885.15.4.197

Meekums, B. (2002). *Dance Movement Therapy: A Creative Psychotherapeutic Approach*. New York, NY: Sage.

Musicant, S. (1994). 'Authentic movement and dance therapy', *American Journal of Dance Therapy*, 16(2): 91–106. doi:10.1007/BF02358569

Musicant, S. (2001). 'Authentic Movement: Clinical considerations', *American Journal of Dance Therapy*, 23(1): 17–28. doi:10.1023/A:1010728322515

Myers, M., Kalish, B. I., Katz, S. S., Schmais, C., and Silberman, L. (1978). 'Panel discussion: "What's in a plié": The function and meaning of dance training for the dance therapist', *American Journal of Dance Therapy*, 2(2)L 32–3. doi:10.1007/BF02593065

National Coalition For Creative Arts Therapies Association (n.d.). <http://www.nccata.org> (accessed 3 December 2014).

Panhofer, H. (2005). *El cuerpo en psicoterapia: Teoría y práctica de la Danza Movimiento Terapia*. Barcelona: Gedisa.

Sandel, S., Chaiklin, S., and Lohn, A. (1993). Foundations of dance/movement therapy: The life and work of Marian Chace. *Columbia, MD: The Marian Chace Memorial Fund of the American Dance Therapy Association*.

Schmais, C. (1970). 'What dance therapy teaches us about teaching dance', *Journal of Research in Health, Physical Education*, 41(1): 34–5.

Snow, S., D'Amico, M., and Tanguay, D. (2003). 'Therapeutic theatre and well-being', *The Arts in Psychotherapy*, 30(2): 73–82.

Swami, V. and Harris, A. S. (2012). Dancing toward positive body image? Examining body-related constructs with ballet and contemporary dancers at different levels. *American Journal of Dance Therapy*, 34(1): 39–52.

Tantia, J. F. (2012). 'Mindfulness and dance/movement therapy for treating trauma', in L. Rappaport (ed.), *Mindfulness in the Creative Arts Therapies*. London: Jessica Kingsley, pp. 96–107.

Victoria, H. K. (2012). 'Creating dances to transform inner states: A choreographic model in dance/movement therapy', *Body, Movement and Dance in Psychotherapy*, 7(3): 167–83. doi:10.1080/17432979.2011.619577

Winnicott, D. W. (1971). *Playing and Reality*. New York, NY: Basic Books.

Winnicott, D. W., Winnicott, C., Shepherd, R., and Davis, M. (1986). *Home is Where we Start from: Essays by a Psychoanalyst*. New York, NY: Norton.

World Health Organisation. (2014). <http://www.who.int/features/factfiles/mental_health/en/> (Accessed 22 March 2017).

CHAPTER 13

....

PORTALS OF CONSCIOUS TRANSFORMATION

From Authentic Movement to Performance

....

MARCIA PLEVIN

INTRODUCTION

....

WITH an international following of practitioners, Authentic Movement has evolved from its roots in dance, dance movement therapy, and a base in the Jungian practice of active imagination (Whitehouse 1958, 1963, 1979) to a formalized movement practice that brings body, mind, and spirit together. For many, Authentic Movement offers a way to live in the body and to value all that it can bring to consciousness, including a healing of the body–mind separation which so many seek to move beyond. Mary Starks Whitehouse, the pioneer of this movement work, initially called it 'movement in depth' (1958, p. 41). It was further refined by two of her many students in two main directions. One direction was taken by dance movement therapist and Jungian analyst Joan Chodorow in the research and study of Authentic Movement principles in a clinical setting, while the other direction was taken by dance movement therapist Janet Adler, who developed it into a formalized practice and subsequently named it the 'discipline of AM',[1] addressing how the work develops inner witness consciousness. In early 2000, Adler (2002) shifted her practice even further to the study of mysticism and the influence of energetic phenomena, a state of higher consciousness, that arose during individual or collective practice of the discipline.

After evolving for approximately fifty-four years, the practice called Authentic Movement has become as varied as the people who have studied it and taught it. It is both practiced and taught in various ways, both in the formalized discipline as created by Adler and informally with practitioners using only specific elements of the practice. A few uses include as a creative source for visual artists, actors, dancers, choreographers, as meditation and mystical practice, and as training for dance movement therapists to experience and to understand somatic transference phenomena. I studied with Janet Adler through the 1990s, in the European group which helped her work out questions of the discipline. A former professional dancer, choreographer, and dance teacher before I became a dance movement therapist, my learning of Authentic Movement paralleled beginning Buddhist vipassana meditation practice, which resulted in my confronting experiences and questions in both approaches (Plevin 2005), which continues today. The impulse to bring Authentic Movement into performance germinated in me for quite a while, and when I finally began to let it grow I was not aware of all its ramifications. For me, a memory of an extraordinary moment on stage always hovered about, wanting to be understood. I remember dancing Shirah, a piece choreographed by Pearl Lang, who was a soloist in the Martha Graham Company and had her own company. It was a technically difficult piece. Standing on stage, with my head tilted back, eyes in the lights directly above me, my body moved down into a first position grand plié to the music's opening sounds. I remembered at that moment leaving my body. It was not I who was moving. I was being danced from another source. It was not until I met Authentic Movement that I could begin to comprehend what perhaps had happened. That moment on stage held a direct encounter with something other than my ordinary dancer self. My body became a portal—an entry or doorway to another level of consciousness. I had a direct embodied experience with transcendental phenomena. I was both very present to myself and my surroundings. and using what is known in Authentic Movement as 'inner witness consciousness'. I was in this world, but not of it. This experience catapulted me into what is defined in Adler's ground form as a unitive or higher consciousness which can lead to energetic phenomena.

Authentic Movement practice reveals its complexity and simplicity by three essential components: 1, a person who moves and is named 'the mover'; 2, a person who observes and gives testimony to the mover who is named a 'witness'; 3, the intrapsychic and interpsychic relationship that develops within and between the two people or two roles.

These three components together form the basis of what is known as the 'ground form' of the discipline, as defined by Adler (1987, 2002). The outer form of the work is simple. One person moves in the presence of another. The witness, especially at the beginning, carries a larger responsibility for consciousness, as she sits to the side of the movement space. She is not 'looking at' the person moving; she is witnessing, listening, bringing a specific quality of attention or presence to the experience of the mover. The mover works with her eyes closed in order to expand her experience of listening to the deeper levels of her kinaesthetic reality. Her task is to respond to a sensation, to an inner impulse, to energy coming from the personal unconscious, the collective unconscious, or what Wilber (1979) calls the 'superconscious'. After the mover moves, the mover and witness usually speak together about the material that has emerged during the movement time, thus bringing formerly unconscious processes into consciousness. (p. 142).

This is the dyad stage within the development of the Authentic Movement discipline—a portal through which a transformative experience becomes available to the one who moves and may also occur for the one who witnesses. Here the term 'portal' refers to the entryway mentioned previously. It is a passageway, facilitated by the presence of the outer witness, which changes self-awareness through what is known as 'inner witness consciousness'. This consciousness first develops by 'being seen' by a trusted and non-judgemental external witness. The safety and intimacy established by a relationship of trust allows for the mover to close his/her eyes, facilitating contact with unconscious or conscious thoughts, images, emotions, or memories that may arise in the self. The mover is encouraged to surrender and be moved by her inner impulses, or to use her will to practice how she wants or must move. It is a way of touching deeply the inner core of the self and its needs in the moment. She stays in a conscious relationship to how she moves or does not move, through the body's kinaesthetic sense—'a set of sensory signals that originate peripherally in the body, and inform the brain about positions and movements of parts of the body in space' (Jola 2010, p. 216). In a similar way, the external witness becomes conscious of what he/she experiences internally while observing the mover. A changing relationship to trust, intimacy, safety, and courage in oneself and in the presence of others is the cord which brought the participants in the project through the portals of transformation.

Authentic Movement to Performance

The project was structured in four phases, which became the four portals of conscious transformation. The template of the phases was: 1, the invitation to participate in the project, and the acceptance to do so—the first portal of 'being seen'; 2, the practice of Authentic Movement in the dyad stage—'seeing oneself being seen', the dance-making choreographic phase; 3, performing the dance in front of the collective who were the movers in the project, which opened awareness of transpersonal phenomena; 4, performing their dance in public. These phases seemed to broadly mirror a developmental path that Adler (1996) mapped out in the practice of Authentic Movement: acceptance of the invitation to practice Authentic Movement, affirming one's individual self within a relationship (in this context through our relationship and the making of a dance), performing this dance for the collective (being seen and acknowledged by the group of people involved in the project), while recognizing transpersonal phenomena within the collective and to bring it out into the world.

More than ten women of ages 35–60—or, as is called in Authentic Movement, 'movers'—responded. Two benefit performances were given in the Vascello Theatre in Rome to collect funds for UNICEF to aid Japanese children after the tsunami of March 2011. Another invitation was given to the movers after the performance to write about their experience about the project from any angle—how it began, its unfolding, or the ending. It was their decision. On average, I worked with each woman individually twelve times, for an hour and a half each time. The length of the dances ran from two and a half minutes to five minutes.

Remembering and repeating movements that emerge from Authentic Movement practice to create a dance or set them into choreography is not a part of the practice.

However, the nature of the movements that appear in the practice, the relationship of the mover and witness, and the formality of the discipline, can at times be related to both dance performance and to the art of theatre, which prompted me to begin this project. The choreography on which I focused is the result of a dance-making process by which the moments of moving in the dyad stage formed themselves into a repeatable dance through the Authentic Movement methodology of witnessing and the relationship created between us. This was achieved by the mover returning with eyes open to the instant of being moved. She bodily and emotionally recalled it into being, bringing those moments into conscious awareness and also with the possibility of giving form to the movement material. The context and meaning of the dance became clearer as movements were repeated, amplified, or discarded on their way to becoming form in the physical space. This process brought the women and myself through portals of transformation both in relationship to their inner witness and to my own internal witness as I witnessed them. The dances seemed to answer a need to integrate a small part of a mind–body split that they discovered within the dyad stage.

FOUNDATIONS FOR HEALING WITHIN THE DANCE MAKING: CHOREOGRAPHY

The reflections of this author and the movers' writings illustrate the complexity of the undertaking: how on a physical, emotional, and healing level, sourcing movement from Authentic Movement, creating their dances and performing them, became a transformational experience for the participants (see Video 13.1 on the Companion Website ▶[2]). Creating a dance was the conscious goal—the invitation for the project. Chodorow (1978) specifically addresses how Jung developed his methodology of active imagination in order to transcend the opposites of unconscious and conscious tension pulls in the psyche to realize original wholeness of being. He has named this healing function the 'transcendent function'. Within Authentic Movement practice the mover's inner witness consciousness may recognize and work with unconscious movement material at times to transcend the opposites. I believe this function can be traced throughout the process of this project. The healing that came out of the practice by going back into unconscious moments of movement and working them as one would with clay into a dance became choreography that heals. By healing, I mean the unifying nature of experiencing wholeness, as Jung addresses, rather than curing, which implies bringing an end to an ailment. Healing came through awareness of the changing relationship which the participant felt in relationship to her inner witness. At every portal there was another shift—an expanded consciousness in their relationship to themselves, to the dance, and to this author. The project seemed to develop and reinforce inner witness presence in the movers. Whitehouse, Adler, and Chodorow (in Pallaro 1999) have written extensively in their seminal essays about how the practice engenders healing, and have offered explanations about how the healing may be brought about and connected to inner presence which is a bare unadorned non-judgemental awareness of the self. Through evolution of the practice one can see these connections between healing and presence as well in dance performance (Olsen 1993), Somatic Psychotherapy (Stromsted 1998), meditation and spiritual practice (Avstreith 2007, Fields 2007, Plevin 2005), dance ritual (Lowell 2007), theatre performance (Koltai 2007), and in other contexts. Deeper self-acceptance as a consequence of integrating unconscious aspects of themselves became evident as the women and I moved through the four transformational portals: to be seen, to see oneself being seen, to be seen by the collective, and to be seen in a public performance.

From 'Being Moved' to Dance-Making to Choreography

There can be a locus, a common joining point of mental, physical and energetic phenomena in Authentic Movement, which reveals itself in the mover as a qualitative shift in the movement. This qualitative shift comes from what Whitehouse (1979) has identified as 'being moved':

> [. . .] I move' is the clear knowledge that I, personally am moving, I choose to move, I exert some demand (not effort) on my physical organism to produce movement. The opposite of this is the sudden astonishing movement when 'I am moved' [. . .] The moment when 'I am moved' happens is astonishing both to dancers and to people who have no intention of becoming dancers. (p. 82)

Something in the mover shifts, which may or may not be available to his/her consciousness. It does not matter how fast or slow, strong or light a mover is moving, nor the movement itself: it is a change of embodied presence, a change of relationship in the mover to the movement. I am in awe at what I feel and see. I feel a spaciousness open up in my body and mind; there is more 'room' for seeing and witnessing. I see a natural aesthetic and a 'rightness' to whatever the mover is doing or not doing that seems to light up the body from within. This is a subjective physical and mental perception which is hard to describe in words. I experience it as a metaphysical change of light and space which marks a shift in the mover's consciousness. This could be understood as a unifying light and sense of space connecting the unconscious and conscious parts of the self. The state of being in the mover's movement or stillness is transmitted to and embodied, as well by the witness. It is an experience that may or may not have words, may or may not be able to be talked about.

Adler (1992) writes about an internal state of being that is needed for transformation: 'To transform we must descend into the body' (p. 187). She follows this statement with a quote from contemporary mystic Satprem: 'The more we descend, the higher the consciousness we need, the stronger the light.' She calls upon the experience and statements of mystical spiritual leaders Sri Aurobindo, the Mother, and again Saprem, who, she says, writes about 'luminous vibrations'.

Adler's experience, my own, and others in the field talk about changing levels of consciousness, the aligning of energies; something takes place out of the ordinary, yet that could be part of an ordinary experience.

Segal (1990) speaks about an alignment of energies through attention, which I understand as a prerequisite to witness consciousness.

> Attention is the quintessential medium to reveal man's dormant energies to himself. Whenever one witnesses the state of the body, the interplay of thought and feeling there is an intimation, however slight, of another current of energy. Through the simple act of attending one initiates a new alignment. (p. 76)

There is no one way to perceive this alignment. Seeking to describe my inner experience as outer witness, I offer the following examples. I witness a mover's arm lift weightless from her side. Within me I do not sense or perceive a source of the movement. Its rising in space is both ethereal and other worldly. She moves from a source that seems not to be of her, but is her. In speaking about this experience, she says she was being taken by her arms from a force within her self, that she perceived as inevitable as her own inner witness observed the movement. In addition, I witness a mover pressing his back into the floor and sense a power and strength in me as this energy moves through him. He spoke about not finding strength in his body but of being 'strengthened' and sensing both the physical possibility and limits of his body. His mind was for him curiously quiet and calm, and brought with it a state of wholeness. Adler (2004) speaks to this direct embodied moment as a unitive state of being within the mover that is described by one of her own students as eternal, universal, beyond that which is ego or self. These instances embody a qualitative shift of presence in both mover and witness. These instances capture and hold my attention as something wanting to break through and establish a communication between the mover and witness. All stages of the Authentic Movement practice allow for a spontaneous transmission of embodied sensation within and between both the mover and witness. This transmission can be transformative to the consciousness of all movers and witnesses participating in that session, and carry on outside the practice into daily life. The movement I am witnessing may be as simple as walking, running, jumping, lying on the ground, moving hands and feet, or coming into contact with another mover.

A mover's movement, or the movers' collective work together generated by moving from the unconscious, referred to by Adler (2002) as a descent into matter into the material of the body, held me enraptured and in awe of a natural aesthetic that this state of being can reveal. With eyes closed, this descent can release powerfully emotional movement and gesture. As a witness, I asked myself whether this common, ordinary aesthetic found by the mover/movers could be given form through the mover/witness dyad relationship, molded into a dance and brought into performance. Could the original spark, that qualitative shift, be maintained in the light of consciousness and then public performance? What would be gained, or what would be lost?

Whitehouse (1979) acknowledges these moments of being moved in the following way:

> It is a moment of unpremeditated surrender that cannot be explained, repeated exactly, sought for or tried out. If it is used as raw material for a dance something is lost, but something has to be lost since that moment was an instant, a happening in and of itself—the structure needed for a lasting work of art is something else. (p. 82)

The question for the women, along with myself, was how to keep in a true relationship with these moments. What, if any, meaning was being articulated by them, and what kind of a dance, a piece of choreography, could come of it?

In hindsight, the project confronted dualities also found in the discipline of Authentic Movement: the polarity of will and surrender and the polarity of inside to outside, or internal to external body experience. Jung's transcendent function was constantly being solicited. Each woman's will to participate in the project brought her to experience moments of being moved by the unconscious. When brought to consciousness, movement was selected to be shaped into a choreographic form both by her will and in response to witnessing. Phrases of movement were developed to remember to repeat, and then finally she had to surrender to what would happen on the stage. Continually, there was the process of shifting between inner sourcing of movement, being present to what was felt intimately *in* oneself, and how it would change when it came *out* externally into a form. Could the spark of the original material remain intact? How would the performers reach a place of seeing the audience seeing themselves—how out can one take the intimate self? The journey of the participant's inner witness relationship from the invitation to participate (first portal), to the dyad sessions (second portal), to the collective viewing (third portal), to the public performance (fourth portal) offered a pathway through which it became possible to track how the healing dances came into being.

The First Portal: I Am Seen

As indicated previously, the first portal, the invitation, was based on simply being seen, being acknowledged. According to Authentic Movement language, the invitation was the result of a 'seeing'—a recognition of people who had studied with me in Authentic Movement practice, had trained in creative movement, or were dance movement therapy colleagues, only a few of whom had formally studied dance or were dancers. These individuals were 'seen' and acknowledged by myself as being able to participate in the project, as having solid enough ego boundaries to enter into and to come out safely of unconscious movement work which emerges in Authentic Movement practice. The proposal was to cocreate a solo dance together, opening the second portal, from movement emerging from Authentic Movement practice, and to perform the dance in front of the other participants of the collective, the third portal, and finally to bring it, the fourth portal, into public performance. The dance piece would be created in the dyad stage of the discipline, the second portal. In the spirit of being the witness which, in the Authentic Movement context, means to practice 'mindfulness', to be open to whatever arises in myself or the other, I would respond to the movement, and together we would find a way to shape and form it into a repeatable dance, a piece of choreography

Accepting the invitation became the participants' first inner-witness relationship, acknowledging that they had been seen. To accept the invitation was a statement from each of them to 'commit to an unknown'. Not all were like Costanza or Valentina (the women's real names, used with permission), who decided immediately that they would participate.

Upon receiving the invitation, Alessandra wrote about her experience of hearing her judgemental inner witness that told her she was fat, not a dancer, so she discarded the prospect immediately as preposterous. She returned a few moments later to write: 'Stop this, let go, throw yourself into it or you will feel remorse for the rest of your life. Life? How much time do I have left to live? Do it!'

Luisa felt fear that had no form or name that the project would fail, that it would be better if she was not involved. She recognized that something big was being asked of her and decided to head into it accompanied by the others.

Betta, in her mind's eye, witnessed herself playing. She imaged a wardrobe trunk from which she pulled out or let playfulness and enjoyment fall out. Her question was: could she come out to play?

Valeria immediately said 'yes' to the project, but after four months of dyad work and two nights before being seen by the collective of women (the third portal of transformation), fear paralyzed her. She could not be seen by others in such an intimate place. I accepted that this could be a possible outcome. What melted her fear was the warm non-judgemental response and acceptance of herself by the collective.

SECOND PORTAL: I SEE YOU SEEING ME AS I SEE MYSELF

After acceptance of the invitation we began the Authentic Movement practice in the dyad form. We would greet each other in the studio, speak for a few minutes, and then begin.

I witnessed one of the movers close her eyes, which allowed for a descent into what can metaphorically be considered a well—a dark unknown place where she waited for the impulse to move or began to move from her will. After moving for what could be ten or twenty minutes, she stopped moving naturally or I indicated by words or a sound that it was time to come out. We acknowledged together her movement work—particularly movement or gesture by which we both felt that an internal qualitative shift had taken place, a place of being moved. I allowed myself to speak about where I felt in my own body a movement wanted physical expansion, a rhythmic beat, perhaps with more force or stillness. There may have been a movement not spoken about that I spoke to in words, or demonstrated with my own body. These were instances where I intuitively sensed lay an unconscious truth, which I held in consciousness. All the women agreed that I could bring these movements out if they were not seen by their own inner witness. We were stimulated by what could be that lay in the shadow of consciousness that may want to be found. Was it ready to be seen? The mover could decide to work with what was found in that session.

The decision to choreograph and how to develop that which was revealed became the central axis of our mover/witness dyad relationship. We were both using the practice to find the material, yet seeking to stay with the quality of that astonishing moment, to work it like a sculptor stays with the clay, marble, or whatever material, to hone it and bring it into a form. The decision to stay or not stay with being seen in sensuality, anger, sadness, grief, or even happiness, or to hold the emptiness of form, to do nothing, became an opportunity for transformation, many times to accepting unacceptable parts of themselves. No longer only witnessing the mover, I became, at times, a mover in a shared process, playing and collaborating on the piece. It was not important to capture the instant of being moved, but to embody the qualitative shift which brought more attention and presence to their movement. The mover and I would both feel this place in our bodies, a shared knowing. From that felt sensation came movement phrases that began to shape and form themselves into choreography.

Two questions emerged in the initial period of this portal. How could the choreographer in me get out of the way in order to see the other clearly? How does a mover who may not be a trained dancer remember her movement decisions? The response to the first question was in firmly holding the witness position and field. Adler (2003) refers to her witnessing position in relationship to movers as being able to 'discover the gift of themselves, the gift of their own authenticity" (p. 27). Different from certain approaches to choreography in which dancers are expected to hold the movement vision of the choreographer's mind, I constantly asked myself: 'Where is the mover going in her piece?' I was not interested in a vision of where I wanted her to go. I was seeing the mover as she was, what she had chosen to work with: my role was one of midwife to her creative process. As the performance date drew closer, my choreographic intuition held a sense of timing. What does this woman need to find closure with her piece? Both similar to and in opposition to Authentic Movement practice, the witness does hold the timing for the mover, but in practice the mover is not finishing a piece. With these women, I pushed the boundaries in the practice by proposing choices of how to end through the mover's own movements. If we were in formal Authentic Movement practice, she could go back into the movement portion of the work, and by her will choose to work that piece of movement to see where she would want to go or be present when a movement incessantly appears time and time again, asking to be seen. Closure of the piece gave it a frame and aided adapting to the reality of the performance.

Being present to the kinaesthetic sense, the internal body position and place of the body in space, was the response to the second question of remembering movements. The fear of not being able to remember movements or movement sequences brought heightened internal attention to the kinaesthetic life of the mover's inner witness. In Authentic Movement practice, remembering is remaining in touch with movement and the emotion/sensation of that memory. It is a memory of a dance encoded within the kinaesthetic experience of the dance's movement (Sheets-Johnstone 2011). Once a quality of movement was found in the dyad relationship and woven into a phrase of repeated movements, it was the kinaesthetic memory and emotion of that spatial/muscle memory that recalled it.

Francesca

Francesca had completed a training in creative movement and was fairly new to Authentic Movement. She shared the following: 'My inner attitude towards Authentic Movement alternated between the fear of losing control, to find the unknown, and my wish to let myself flow into the unknown.' Her first memory in our dyad work was very strong: she recalled, as she was sitting on the ground, her hands and arms around her shoulders, an intimacy which opened, as she expressed it, 'a warm sensation in her heart.' Her body softened, and she cried softly. It was, as she wrote, 'out of the ordinary'. Little by little, the fear of this intimacy became apparent, together with symptoms of nausea, when she moved freely in space. If nausea came while she was moving from repeating movement phrases in setting her piece, this became a signal to heighten consciousness, to become aware of kinaesthetic sensations, and in particular, to plant her feet on the ground. Kinaesthetic sensations, the feedback loop of her body to her inner witness, and being seen by the external witness, all helped her find a more knowledgeable place, a lived-in relationship with her body, and aided in memorizing her dance.

Valeria

Valeria was aware after years of practicing Authentic Movement that repeatedly she began her movement with her back to her witness. This would be a place of healing if she could know it. Facing and moving towards me became a central part of our dyad work, and it found its way into her dance.

This is an excerpt of a poem which she offered about this challenge:

> [. . .] I am a snail rolled into myself,
> The gesture begins to dig from within
> an extreme gesture that is born from my cave,
> my body is a cave.

> I move forward
> overburdened
> inevitable
> out
> there is no space [...]

She continued:

> My dance needed to have space for my impetuous fury, my aggressiveness which comes out every time there is a cause. My witness encouraged me to go back into the practice to find this place in myself. No form came. A horrible fear to be seen in this rapacious place came instead. We found together that hiding my eyes, protecting myself made more sense. I walk forward with hands over my eyes.

Valentina

About to finish her training as a dance movement psychotherapist, she made the following revelation while improvising one section of the choreography:

> My witness guide suggested I try a brief sequence of movements to practice waiting until one movement came to a close in order to sense the emergence of the following movement. It seems simple to say but the more I tried to do this I realized that I could not do it. I broke into tears with the astounding consciousness that I did not have faith in my body. I do not have faith in my body?! But are we kidding?! [...] I, who always talked about how important it is to listen to the body [...] I discovered that in my deepest place exists distrust in what I feel are body sensations that make me anticipate successive movements, fearfully thinking that they could not emerge by themselves [...] I discovered something that gave me permission to risk more, to let myself go, to try to go beyond the fear, the risk to feel nothing. Risking not to feel, I could wait and feel the movements coming into being developing from my body instead of my head. I began to sense my body in a new way.

Valentina had awakened her body-and-mind connection.

Betta

Betta was concerned with the time she had to complete her dance:

> In the middle of the project I meet an inner mechanism that I know very well. I use my will to find forms that will tranquillize me. An old story. I arrive for my meeting with the witness and show her steps and phrases fixed to a piece of music.

After seeing it I asked her, 'Where is your dance?' It had disappeared, had become external with no deep contact with her essence. She found the courage to reopen her wardrobe trunk to, as she wrote, 'play, give myself caresses, shift my weight, scribble, squiggle, throw, push, be liberated by a dance which came.'

Alessandra

During Authentic Movement practice previous prior to this project, she became conscious of an inner witness that automatically 'commanded her like an owner'. She understood it as an authentic part of a past life that had grown stale. This project brought new emotions that were not encoded, halted, or sabotaged by these commands. She found what for her was unusual: stillness and small movements. Could she be still and not judge herself harshly, not look for approval? Silence and time, agents of Authentic Movement practice, had transforming effects. Alessandra experienced the absence of a judging audience or, more specifically, her own self as the harshest audience negating and obstructing any possibility to witness what was happening in her body clearly. As a former actress, she needed to distance herself from the actual but more difficult internal audience, to learn how to wait in silence and emptiness without fear. 'Walking', she said to me during a session, 'I need to just walk and see what happens.' Alessandra walked in the space until she found stillness. From holding stillness she experienced being moved.

THIRD PORTAL: I SEE MYSELF BEING SEEN
BY THE COLLECTIVE

We had completed four months of dyad work and were close to the public performance. The next phase—being seen by the collective—became a developmental passage which both rooted their individuality and transcended the process into something greater than themselves. Adler (1996) speaks about the 'unitive' state of the practice found within collective relationship. She admonishes:

> If you are me, you know how afraid I am, how hopeful, how doubting, how strong, how vulnerable I am. You know that I am doing the best I can and how deeply I need to be seen, embraced. If I am you, I know of your fear, your hope, your doubt, your strength and vulnerability. I know you are doing the very best you can and that you desire to be loved as you are. Remembering that 'I am because we are' can encourage a freedom of fear and doubt. Such freedom enables hope and strength. (p. 194)

As their primary witness, I held the knowledge that these women belonged together even though they had never seen each others' dances before this moment. On the evening of our collective showing I invoked the same non-judgemental atmosphere that

I tried to maintain in individual sessions. Each had been seen in my reflecting eyes and their own inner witness. It was now time to be seen in the larger circle. They were about to practice the art of silent witnessing for each other and to see themselves being witnessed by the collective.

Luisa wrote: '. . . there was this "other" that accompanied the voyage, this other that was close by but we never saw. This created expectation and the fear of being seen that revealed itself as a great treasure.' She added: 'I like to think it is because the breath of each one of us left in the studio was breathed in by the other who entered.' Francesca wrote: 'I felt we were always united even as the witness worked with each of us individually. My experience in seeing the dances of all my companions of this voyage were of synchrony, as if in seeing the birth of each dance, I gave birth to each one myself.'

Coming face-to-face with owning one's truth and performing and sharing it with the collective reinforced the ownership of their individual dances. It also put them into a transpersonal relationship with emotional themes with which they were all working, giving them a sense of belonging amongst themselves and not only to the project. Paradoxically, their own courage to face the unknown also proved to hold fear of being judged. Before the showing, Valeria wanted to pull out of the project. Her inner witness held paralyzing fear which was softened by the welcoming witnesses that pulled her back in. She held what, I believe, was the fear of being judged by all the women.

Fourth Portal: The Performance, I See Myself Being Seen by the Public

An Invitation to Shift from Audience to Witness

Before the performance I spoke to the audience briefly about the practice of Authentic Movement and the project. I told them that there would time to comment on the performance afterwards. I shared with them:

> In the beginning I was the witness for each of the women in the creation of their piece, they then became witnesses for each other and were seen in the larger collective. Tonight I want to orient you, the audience, to be witnesses as well, to give testimony, because that is what you are doing here tonight, giving testimony to a journey of deep personal work. I invite you to open a non-judgemental attention to what will be seen; a difficult task, as if bringing attention to something means to naturally judge it. Instead, I ask you to bring attention and consciousness to the lens out of which you see: that the dancer and the dance is her gift, a haiku poem to be read through her body. Although still in your chair you may experience 'moving' with each of the performers connecting the space that separates you. You are both observer and participant.

A Call to be Mover/Performer

The collective's support found in the third portal became the foundation from which the mover/performers could step onto the performing space and be seen by an unknown public. The final portal was at hand. The women were seated in the front row of the performing space with, as Alessandra wrote, eyes like 'burning embers'. Behind them was the audience. They were not in the circle of formal Authentic Movement practice, but sitting silently. Each one was ready to enter the performance space to be seen and to witness their companions.

Costanza wrote that it took courage to witness naked emotions, her own and others: 'To feel the thread that also connects our dances, the existence of one body dancing, to feel us together in front of all those eyes.' Betta, on the other hand, not only found playfulness but amused herself in the performance: 'In telling it I feel it is more true. I am present to every moment of my dance as I never have been before; I amused myself with myself.' Giovanna talked about her inner witness becoming an ally, helping her focus on each and every moment. While space held an emotion for Francesca—'I have found space for more love inside me'—Valentina witnessed and felt that the soul (anima) released by each mover raised the soul consciousness of the audience to an archetypal and universal dimension, the goal of theatre. Being seen in one's truth led to strengthening the self, and taking one's place in a collective, finding one's relationship to the whole, and transcending this to a collective place are all portals of transformation in the practice of Authentic Movement.

Conclusion

The initial goal of the project was to see if movement found in Authentic Movement practice could find a meaningful form for dancers and non-dancers and subsequently be brought out into the world. This is what we accomplished. The public responded by talking about the courage needed to reveal oneself, about seeing presence, how they witnessed and became emotionally involved and more present to themselves and to the movers/performers. The gifts of the entire project were different for all, but what was crucial and became apparent in the process was that these dances enabled healing. Authentic Movement practice, where the outward roles of mover and witness are accompanied by inner witness presence respectively, produces what is best called 'transformational choreography' which, brought to performance, has the power to heal. Every woman opened up to change, found it through the choreography, and owned it. Each found her piece of wholeness within her life at that moment. Years before, dancing Shirah—another choreographer's piece—I was moved to transcend my body, yet I held an inner witness presence. I was a witness to help birth their dances into existence. Transcendence and then wholeness were found through the base of Authentic Movement practice.

ACKNOWLEDGEMENTS

I would like to acknowledge the editing suggestions of the authors of this book, and, most warmly, the initial structuring of this chapter by my dear cousin Arlene Plevin, who rearranged words and thoughts dancing on the pages.

NOTES

1. Adler (2002) has named the formal discipline the 'ground form', which consists of a developmental sequence of practice with specific names—the dyad, triad, breathing, and long circle stages—whereas the exchange of what is known as 'mover' and 'witness' roles within each stage addresses the changing relationship and growth of 'inner witness consciousness'.
2. The video complements the article by illustrating segments of the theatre performance, the final portal of transformation (see 13.1 on the Companion Website ⊙). Envisioning the project, its process and theoretical constructs on which it was based are incorporated in this chapter. From imagining in word what the dances could be like, images of the dances can actually be seen. There is no audio for the images, since the movement and dance found through Authentic Movement practice emerged in silence. After the dance was created, music was found and integrated with the movement. The three basic components of Authentic Movement practice are: to be seen, to see, and the relationship between the two. By watching the video you become the observer/ participant in this process by becoming the one who sees. You will witness all the women in a brief segment in the beginning of the video in a group dance which the author composed of movements from each of the choreographies. Each woman's name appears with her movement piece. The entire performance, with the music chosen for each piece, is available on DVD. The running time is 57 minutes. Contact: marcia.plevin@alice.it.

REFERENCES

Adler, J. (1987). 'Who is the witness?', in P. Pallaro (ed.) (1999), *Authentic Movement: Essays by Mary Starks Whitehouse, Janet Adler and Joan Chodorow*. London: Jessica Kingsley.

Adler, J. (1992). 'Body and soul', in P. Pallaro (ed.) (1999) *Authentic Movement: Essays by Mary Starks Whitehouse, Janet Adler and Joan Chodorow*. London: Jessica Kingsley.

Adler, J. (1996). 'The collective body', in P. Pallaro (ed.) (1999) *Authentic Movement: Essays by Mary Starks Whitehouse, Janet Adler and Joan Chodorow*. London: Jessica Kingsley.

Adler, J. (2002). *Offering from the Conscious Body: The Discipline of Authentic Movement*. Rochester, VT: Inner Traditions.

Adler, J. (2003). 'From autism to the discipline of authentic movement', in P. Pallaro (ed.) (2007), *Authentic Movement: Moving the Body, Moving the Self, Being Moved: A Collection of Essays, Volume Two*. London: Jessica Kingsley.

Adler, J. (2004). 'From seeing to knowing', in P. Pallaro (ed.) (2007), *Authentic Movement: Moving the Body, Moving the Self, Being Moved: A Collection of Essays, Volume Two*. London: Jessica Kingsley.

Avstreith, Z. (2007). 'Achieving body permanence: Authentic Movement and the paradox of healing', in P. Pallaro (ed.), *Authentic Movement: Moving the Body, Moving the Self, Being Moved: A Collection of Essays, Volume Two*. London: Jessica Kingsley.

Chodorow, J. (1978). 'Dance therapy and the transcendent function', in P. Pallaro (ed.) (1999), *Authentic Movement: Essays by Mary Starks Whitehouse, Janet Adler and Joan Chodorow.* London: Jessica Kingsley.

Fields, C. (2007). 'Authentic movement: A theoretical framework based in Tibetan buddhist thought', in P. Palloro (ed.),*Authentic Movement: Moving the Body, Moving the Self, Being Moved: A Collection of Essays, Volume Two.* London: Jessica Kingsley.

Jola, C. (2010). 'Research and choreography: Merging dance and cognitive science', in B. Blasing, M. Puttke, and S. Thomas (ed.), *The Neuroscience of Dance.* New York, NY: Psychology Press.

Koltai, J. (2007). 'The pleasure of text: Embodying classical theatrical language through the practice of Authentic Movement', in P. Pallaro (ed.), *Authentic Movement: Moving the Body, Moving the Self, Being Moved: A Collection of Essays, Volume Two.* London: Jessica Kingsley.

Lowell, D. (2007). 'Authentic Movement', in P. Pallaro (ed.), *Authentic Movement: Moving the Body, Moving the Self, Being Moved: A Collection of Essays, Volume Two.* London: Jessica Kingsley.

Olsen, A. (1993). 'Being seen, being moved: authentic movement and performance', in P. Pallaro (ed.), *Authentic Movement: Moving the Body, Moving the Self, Being Moved: A Collection of Essays, Volume Two.* London: Jessica Kingsley.

Pallaro, P. (ed.) (1999). *Authentic Movement: Essays by Mary Starks Whitehouse, Janet Adler and Joan Chodorow,* 2nd edn. London: Jessica Kingsley.

Plevin, M. (2005). 'Breathing in the field: An inquiry into Authentic Movement and Buddhist vipassana meditation', in A. Geissinger, J. Webb, P. Sager (ed.), *A Moving Journal,* vol. 12. Rhode Island.

Segal, W. (1990). 'The force of attention', in Dooling D.M. (ed.), *Parabola: The Magazine of Myth and Tradition,* vol. XV, number 2. New York: Society for the Study of Myth and Tradition.

Sheets-Johnstone, M. (2011). 'From movement to dance', *Phenomenology and the Cognitive Sciences* 11 (1): 39–57. doi 10.1007/s11097-011-9200-8

Stromsted, T. (1998). 'The dancing body in psychotherapy: Reflections on somatic psychotherapy and Authentic Movement', in P. Pallaro (ed.), *Authentic Movement: Moving the Body, Moving the Self, Being Moved: A Collection of Essays, Volume Two.* London: Jessica Kingsley.

Whitehouse, M (1958). 'The tao of the body', in P. Pallaro (ed.), *Authentic Movment Essays by Mary Starks Whitehouse, Janet Adler and Joan Chodorow.* London: Jessica Kingsley.

Whitehouse M. (1969/1970). 'Reflections on a metamorphosis', in P. Pallaro (ed.) (1999), *Authentic Movement: Essays by Mary Starks Whitehouse, Janet Adler and Joan Chodorow.* London: Jessica Kingsley.

Whitehouse, M. (1979). 'C. G. Jung and dance therapy: Two major principles', in P. Pallaro (ed.) (1999), *Authentic Movement: Essays by Mary Starks Whitehouse, Janet Adler and Joan Chodorow.* London: Jessica Kingsley.

Wilber, K. (1979). *No Boundary: Eastern and Western Approaches to Personal Growth.* London: Shambhala.

....

CHAPTER 14

BUTOH DANCE, NOGUCHI TAISO, AND HEALING

....

PAOLA ESPOSITO AND TOSHIHARU KASAI

INTRODUCTION

....

BUTOH dance occupies an important place in the international contemporary dance scene of the twentieth century, since Japanese butoh dancers and groups introduced it in Europe and North America in the 1980s. The novelty and strangeness of this performance style, with its half-naked and white-painted dancers' bodies, surprised the Western audiences at first, yet butoh dance has been now widely accepted in countries other than Japan, incorporating some of their local characteristics. The most significant characteristics of butoh are its iconoclastic performance style and its approach to the bodymind. While the former contributed to its significant popularity amongst Western audiences, dancers, and choreographers, the latter has only recently started to be recognized (e.g. Nakamura 2007; Esposito 2013), as it is not an aspect of this dance that is visible on stage. It is an element that defines butoh dance training.

This paper focuses on butoh's underlying principles about the bodymind and training methods in order to discuss how butoh dance is concerned with body-oriented psychotherapeutic factors. In this context, relations between butoh and another Japan-based training method, Noguchi taiso, are highlighted. It is argued that both butoh and Noguchi taiso actualize notions of the bodymind as contiguous with the environment, fostering a sense of 'compatibility' with the world that it is potentially healing (Jackson 1989, p. 155). Throughout the discussion we adopt the compound word 'bodymind' in an attempt to challenge residual Cartesian assumptions of the 'mind' as separate from the 'body' (Farnell 1999). While opposing 'Western' dualistic conceptions, butoh also resists those interpretations that see the body–mind relationship as outright monistic in 'non-Western' epistemologies (e.g. Scheper-Hughes and Lock 1987). Transcending both perspectives, we contend that body–mind integration through butoh is not a given but a 'potential' (Ozawa De Silva and Ozawa De Silva 2011), as shown by butoh dancers' reliance on training in order to develop their creative practice. Also, given the nature of bodymind as an 'internal' and 'experiential' dimension, we argue that a 'first-person perspective' (Farnell 1999; Middleton and Chamberlain 2012, p. 96) is most appropriate to dealing with this subject.

The first part of this chapter outlines some key historical aspects concerning butoh. In the second part, a selection of exercises illustrates elements of psychotherapeutic efficacy of butoh-with-Noguchi taiso. Building on these illustrations, we will further contend that butoh training can be used as a healing method by virtue of the following characteristics: its potential to enhance the awareness of one's own bodymind; its suitability to people with or without mental or physical disabilities; its challenging of rigid or worn-out social boundaries.

Brief History of Butoh Dance

Tatsumi Hijikata started developing his provocative avant-garde dance form in Japan, in the aftermath of World War II. In 1959, he premiered what is generally regarded as his first butoh dance piece 'Kinjiki' (Forbidden Colours) in Tokyo, employing the same title as Yukio Mishima's novel. In this piece, Hijikata, who played the role of a Man, simulated same-sex eroticism with another dancer, Yoshito Ohno, who played the role of a Young Man. In one famously controversial scene, Yoshito Ohno crushed a live chicken between his legs, seemingly suffocating it. Yoshito later explained that the chicken was not killed, but lived a good life and even laid eggs (Yoshito Ohno, personal conversation with Kasai). Nonetheless, the extreme content of the piece shocked the audience and led to Hijikata's expulsion from the All Japan Art Dance Association. While the shock was certainly one of the main goals of Kinjiki, as 'largely achieved by breaking the social norm that prevented overt sexuality (and particularly same-sex eroticism) and violence from being presented on stage' (Baird 2012, p. 21), the complexity and depth of this piece should not be underestimated. In Baird's analysis, for instance, Kinjiki really is about unequal relationships, and the coercion of social forces acting upon the individual (pp. 28–30). Meanwhile, for Hornblow, Hijikata's work

> ... should not be seen as an overtly political statement, nor was the sexual content or the killing of an animal simply for shock value ... [Rather,] Hijikata's rebellion was one of seeking to reinhabit and reconstruct the body, a body denied and controlled by the rationalism and emerging consumerism of postwar Japan. (Hornblow 2006, p. 29)

Indeed, the critique of the social order through the investigation of the body is a recurring theme in Hijikata's work.

Members of the Japanese literary circles, including Mishima, who supported Hijikata substantially and later committed hara-kiri in 1970, praised the iconoclast, and called his dance 'ankoku butoh', literally meaning 'dark–black' dance, usually translated as 'dance of utter darkness' (e.g. Klein 1988). The performance 'Hijikata Tatsumi and Japanese People: Rebellion of the Body' (1968) was another important highlight in Hijikata's butoh career and a forceful example of his quest to expand the possibilities of the body, while reflecting on its limitations and constraints—physical ones, as well as those imposed by society and culture. In 'Rebellion', Hijikata challenged audience's expectations by bringing together disparate elements through the surrealistic method of juxtaposition, and drawing on a variety of sources, Western and Japanese alike (Baird 2012). The concern with the limitations of the body also characterizes his later performances, such as 'My Mother Tied Me on Her Back: a Story of Smallpox', in which he explores his own socialization in rural Japan (Baird 2012, p. 156). In his investigations to the limits of the body, he created an array of new movements, hitherto untapped in the dance world. His bodily vocabulary began featuring 'fragmentation, tension, instability, disequilibrium, and misdirection' (p. 145). In his attempt to recover the body that transcended social forces, he rediscovered traditional Japanese postures and 'techniques of the body' (Mauss 1979, p. 104), such as 'ganimata', the bandy-legged low posture. These were movements from the ordinary, peasant and urban world that had never appeared in dance before (Yoshioka 1987; Fraleigh and Nakamura 2006; Baird 2012).

Just as he was trying to expand the possibilities of the body, Hijikata also tried to expand the possibilities of language (Baird 2012, pp. 185–205). Beside his dance work, he produced a significant number of essays as well as posters and pamphlets accompanying butoh performances (Hijikata 1983, 1987). His writings challenge the reader or listener just as his dance production challenged his dancers and audiences. These two dimensions of expression, language, and dance, would overlap in the context of training and choreographing, drawing the dancers into unusual conditions for movement and perception. For instance, one of Hijikata's famous phrases, 'Butoh is a corpse standing straight up in a desperate bid for life' (Tanemura et al. 1993), besides being figurative or poetic, is meant to direct the dancer toward a particular bodymind condition that is seen as foundational to butoh. Kasai (2000) refers to such condition as butoh-*tai* (where *tai* means body/attitude). We can attempt an interpretation of what this condition is about, by drawing on Hijikata's pupil Kayo Mikami's explanation of an exercise called Ash Pillar Walk, which Hijikata identified with the walk of death row inmates.

Just like, in the Ash Pillar Walk, the walking ash figure 'has lost the power to control itself, and so moves in unpredictable ways' (Mikami, quoted in Baird 2012, p. 178), so 'the corpse standing desperately upright' suggests a state of annihilation of one's own will and intention, of being at the mercy of outer forces, of being simultaneously dead and alive. A related concern for unpredictability, open-endedness, and loss of control can be found in another of Hijikata's sentences: 'Even your own arms, deep inside your body, feel foreign, feel that they do not belong to you. Here lies an important secret. Butoh's radical essence is hidden here' (Tanemura et al. 1993). This sentence also points to a condition where the body is no longer perceived as one's own, but as if it were at the mercy of foreign forces, in this case as found within oneself (one's own arms). To the extent that butoh's *raison d'etre* is sought in Hijikata's vision of expanding the perceptual and imaginative possibilities of the human body, such imaginative instructions still constitute a point of reference for butoh practitioners. Thus butoh is often seen as going beyond performance into psychophysical explorations, and as defying conventional notions of dance.

After 1974, Hijikata did not perform and devoted himself to choreograph dances for his butoh disciples, who, however, became gradually independent and started their own butoh companies during the 1970s. These include Dairakudakan by Akaji Maro, Hakutobo by Yoko Ashikawa and Saga Kobayashi, Harupin-ha by Koichi Tamano, Hoppo Butoh-ha by Ippei Yamada, Sankaijuku by Ushio Amagatsu, and many others. These butoh artists gradually developed their own butoh styles and approaches. Sankaijuku—one of the most prestigious butoh dance companies in the world—started performing in the USA and Europe in the 1980s, and their work was received with much enthusiasm. A number of butoh dancers followed them, and influenced the Western dance world by introducing butoh's unique dance styles and philosophies in the 1990s. Hijikata passed away in 1986, and Hijikata's long-term collaborator, Kazuo Ohno, further developed their joint work and became internationally recognized for the ethereal and feminine style of his movements. Having performed around the world with his son, Yoshito (Ohno and Ohno 1992), Kazuo died at the age of 103 in 2010.

BUTOH DANCE WITH NOGUCHI TAISO

In the 1970s, young butoh dancers and students started including Noguchi taiso techniques in their butoh training. Noguchi taiso (the Japanese word *taiso* literally meaning 'physical exercise' or 'gymnastics') is a method of bodymind training that was invented by physical education teacher Michizo Noguchi (1914–1998). On the verge of suicide after World War II, Noguchi had come to the realization that, while being alive, his body had weight. This realization became central to his method, with the notion of body weight replacing that of the muscle–skeletal system when approaching human movement (Noguchi 1972, 1977, 1978). The following are central principles in Noguchi taiso: a) It is important to pay attention to passively induced movements; b) the muscles should be regarded as sensors rather than effectors when controlling the body; c) the heightened sensory awareness leads to movements performed with the minimum amount of energy. Noguchi taiso shares with butoh a concern for enhancing bodily sensitivity and responsiveness through a focus on gravity, inertia, the principle of an equal and opposite reaction for each action, and the use of imagery (Baird 2012, p. 172). While Baird contends that it is likely that Hijikata and Noguchi came in direct contact, and that Noguchi's method influenced butoh training (Baird 2012, pp. 171–3), the two approaches differ significantly. Noguchi advocates loosening and relaxing the body, as well as the efficient carrying of weight so as not to overwork the muscles, whereas Hijikata uses exaggerated tensions, contractions, and shifts of the centre of gravity away from the core, which require substantial muscular effort from the side of the dancer (Baird 2012, p. 172). We suggest that such differences are related to Noguchi and Hijikata's different aims, with the former focusing on efficient moving for the sake of wellbeing, while the latter privileging artistic exploration (and therefore not being concerned with efficiency). Aesthetic divergences aside, butoh and Noguchi taiso share a radical questioning of the principles that underlie movement.

After his death in 1998, Noguchi's ideas and exercises continued to be widely employed in Japan—not only in butoh, but also in other fields of dance, drama, and physical training. Butoh dancers around the world, including Sankaijuku leader Ushio Amagatsu, adopted Noguchi taiso exercises in their work. Yet Noguchi's name is seldom acknowledged. This is probably because, as outlined previously, Noguchi's aims were considerably different from those of butoh training and performance. This paper advocates Noguchi taiso to be explicitly included as an important part of butoh training, as performance as well as a healing method, because of its potential for enhancing body sensitivity and responsiveness, hence for 'transforming' one's bodymind. In particular, Noguchi taiso heightens the body's innate capacity to perceptually relate to and to respond to impulses from both inner and outer environments. Because of that, Noguchi taiso is suitable for exploring butoh's imagery, such as: 'Again and again we are reborn. It is not enough simply to be born of the mother's womb. Many births are necessary. Be reborn always and everywhere. Again and again' (Hijikata, quoted in Tanemura et al. 1993). This narrative suggests that butoh dancers should constantly aim to be (like a) newborn. What the narrative does not tell us, however, is *how* to do so.

In order to solve this riddle, one has first to try to see the world through a newborn's eyes, and then allow the mindset to change accordingly. This is exactly what psychologist Daniel Stern (1998) did, in his part-fictional, part-scientific account of the experiential world of an infant named 'Joey', through different stages of his life. At the earliest of these stages, when Joey is six-week old, his world is described as seamless. Objects and events are different, yet not so much in themselves as in the tone of *feeling* they evoke in him, as well as the 'opportunities for action they offer him' (p. 13). Stern draws an analogy between Joey's world at this age and the weather, whose 'unique mood and force derive[s] from its own combination of wind, light, and temperature' (p. 14). Joey experiences this 'weatherscape' not from an observer's perspective, but as though he is part of it, to the point that no clear distinction between his inner world and the world outside of him can be drawn. This implies a relation of deep reciprocity with the world, so that, for instance, 'the prevailing mood and force can come from inside you and shape or color everything you see outside' (p. 14). Stern tells us that we never lose completely this immersive sense of being the world. 'In adults, [however,] these partial breaches in the inside–outside barrier are short-lived. In infants, they are almost constant . . . Each moment has its own sequence of feelings-in-motion' (p. 14). In attempting to be 'reborn in each moment' through butoh, one attempts to extend the short-lived moments when the boundaries between inside and outside dissolve, and to return to a condition of oneness with the world.

Butoh Dance Enhances Sensibility

One of the essential ideas of Noguchi taiso is based on the awareness of body weight that one never loses while alive. Noguchi had realized that an 'anatomical' perspective on the body as a muscle–skeletal system often engenders a 'mechanical' understanding of how the body moves. As opposed to this notion, he introduced the image of the 'god of gravity', and proposed that the muscles of the human body should be regarded not as effectors but as sensors: 'Muscles do not exist for resisting and governing the gravity. Muscles are the ears for listening to the words of the god of gravity.' In other words, Noguchi substituted an image of the body as a 'muscle–skeletal system' evoking activity and rigidity, one of the body as subject to a somatically perceived entity—the god of gravity—evoking bodily passivity and yielding. His 'ne-nyoro' exercise presents us with an opportunity to relate physically to this idea.

Exercise 1: 'Ne-nyoro' lesson. (See Video 14.1 on the Companion Website ▶.)

1) Lie down on the floor on your back. Stretch your knees.
2) Your partner catches both your ankles and, holding them together, shakes your legs to the left and right briskly, making your entire body wave.
3) Check if the head is swaying to some extent as a result of this waving. Your partner changes the shaking speed and the amplitude so as to make an irregular movement in the body.

The Japanese name of this exercise, *ne-nyoro*, is composed of two words: *ne*, meaning 'lying', and *nyoro*, a mimetic word describing a 'snaky' movement. This name offers a cue as to the movement quality that this exercise is meant to produce. In this exercise, one can also imagine the human body as 'a flexible leather bag in which bones, muscles, viscera or brain are all floating'. Images of 'snake-likeness' and 'liquidity' should inform the movement, triggering a sense of the body as a jelly-like waving matter. When this condition is achieved in ne-nyoro, the body will be highly reactive to any movement variation that is applied by the (active) partner, including irregular or similarly unexpected movements.

An emphasis on what we could call 'passive' movements—that is, movements resulting from an (actual or imaginary) action applied onto a relaxed, receptive body—is what distinguishes butoh from other kinds of dance training. Western dances in particular tend to rely on a muscular–skeletal understanding of the body, hence privileging 'active' and 'intentional' movements, while neglecting 'passive' and 'unintentional' movements, such as those emerging from ne-nyoro practice in the form of passively induced, soft, flexible, and unexpected movements. Butoh dance training, as informed by Noguchi taiso, involves a combination of 'intentional' and 'unintentional', 'active' and 'passive' approaches to movement, hence actualizing notions of the body other than the muscle–skeletal one, and expanding notions of the moving body.

Having grasped the kinaesthetic reality of body weight and the basic principles of 'passive' movement through the practice of yielding to applied forces and to gravity, one can apply the same principles to explore the potential for passive movement in different parts of the body. The following set of exercises, while not Noguchi taiso exercises strictly speaking, are based on its principles. They can be included in butoh dance training in order to explore creatively the potential for passive and active movement alike.

Exercise 2: Simple arm rotation. (See Video 14.2 on the Companion Website ▶.)

1) Lift the right or left arm, release tension from the shoulder, and allow it to fall freely (while taking care not to hurt your elbow and shoulder joint).
2) Use the elbow to control slightly the arm's fall, and turn the arm's falling movement into a swinging movement.
3) By using the inertia of the arm's swinging movement, lift the arm again.
4) Keep swinging the arm by focusing on its weight and inertial movement, while avoiding muscle tension.

Exercise 2 is concerned with passively induced movement in arm rotation. The same logic of releasing muscle tension and of using body weight to fuel inertial movement can be applied to body parts other than the arms, though the resulting appearance of the movement may be different; for example, it may not be a falling but a flapping of the body part in question. In order to avoid muscle tension, it is important to try to breathe normally. Fast and strong muscle movements are governed by the fast muscle fibres, while slow movements are carried out by the slow muscle fibres. Although breathing tends to stop when there is a strong muscle contraction, by focusing on breathing normally one can maintain an awareness of the bodymind even in such conditions of fast movement.

Exercise 3: Arm-standing exercise. (See Video 14.3 on the Companion Website ▶.)

1) Lie down on the floor on your back. If you have back problems you may keep your knees bent. If you still find this position painful, then stop doing this exercise altogether.
2) Stretch your arms wide open, with your palms facing up.
3) Rest your arms on the floor.
4) Try to touch the floor with all your finger nails in order to stretch your arms farther.
5) Release tension from your entire body and take a rest for a while.
6) Slowly lift your forearms, keeping your elbows on the floor, until each arm forms a right angle.
7) Breathe normally. Try not to close your throat when you move your arms.
8) Slowly lift your entire arm. Do not rush. This is a precious moment to perceive your arm weight, and so encounter Noguchi's 'god of gravity'.
9) Continue lifting your arms, raising your shoulder blades off the floor.
10) Stretch your arms all the way upward. Keep this position for a while.
11) Release tension from your shoulders and allow your shoulder blades to rest on the floor while your arms are extended upward.
12) Feel your shoulder blades on the floor and try to locate the point on which the weight of the arm rests.

13) Try to suspend your arms up in the air with as little muscle tension as possible. Keep your arms in this position for a while.
14) When you feel tired, release tension from your shoulders and lower your elbows to the floor gradually. Feel how heavy your arms are while lowering them.
15) Rest your elbows on the floor. Then, release tension from your elbows, allowing your forearms to lower gradually.
16) Rest your arms on the floor. Feel that your body is more relaxed and tranquil.
17) Repeat the exercise a few times. Try to keep your arms up with as little muscle tension as possible.

Kasai composed Exercise 3 on the basis of Noguchi taiso principles of perception of body weight (Kasai 2005, 2009b). In this exercise, the focus is on the weight of the arms. Perception of the 'pull' of gravity is used to release the weight of the arms on the floor, hence facilitating the release of tension from the shoulders. The shoulder blades act as a basis for the straightened arms. If the person lying on the floor is not able to 'feel' his or her own shoulder blades, the instructor can hold the lying person's arm and delicately push it in the direction of his/her shoulder blade. This will help the lying person to perceive more clearly the point on which the weight of the arm rests.

The efficacy of both Exercise 2 and Exercise 3 relies on the practitioner's ability to increasingly recognize the difference between relaxation and tension and monitor it through small adjustments of the arm. In Exercise 3, the monitoring of the relationship between shoulder blade, floor, and gravity (as signalled by the weight of the arm) facilitates a mimetic integration between inner and outer physical forces that is key to both butoh and Noguchi taiso. That is, the shift from active muscular effort to an attitude of 'listening' and 'yielding' to physical forces external to the body brings the tacit mutual relationship between person and environment to a level of explicit or conscious awareness (Esposito 2013, p. 134–8). The expanding of awareness through subtle body movement feeds back into one's experiential notion of the bodymind, as indissolubly 'enmeshed' (Ingold 2013) in the force fields that make up the world. We suggest that this sense of enmeshment is 'unifying' and 'integrating', and is therefore healing (Jackson 1989).

We are now in a better position to understand the meaning of Hijikata's exhortation: 'Again and again we are reborn. It is not enough simply to be born of the mother's womb. Many births are necessary. Be reborn always and everywhere. Again and again' (Hijikata, quoted in Tanemura et al. 1993). Butoh and Noguchi taiso entail a healing potential through their use of dynamic convergence of imagination and sensoriality. Not only do the imageries of Noguchi taiso and butoh training emphasize the body's innate capability to perceptually relate, by directing perceptual attention to energies, dynamics, and qualities in movement; they also emphasize the body's in intimate relation with the world. This leads to a softening of the experiential boundaries between 'inside' and 'outside', 'self' and 'non-self.' Thus, both the butoh dancer and the Noguchi taiso practitioner attempt to approximate the worldview of a newborn, who is perceptually caught up in the 'weatherscape' (Stern 1998, p. 4) of forces, dynamic and intensities that make the world, and unable to tell inside from outside.

Butoh can be Used with Anybody, With or Without Disabilities

In most dance styles, dancers are expected to reproduce a movement based on its 'form' or exterior appearance. Dance routines and choreographies can be seen as detailed scores for the production and reproduction of movement phrases and dynamics. The predominance of a 'view from the outside' tends to 'objectify' the movement, often turning the dancer into a mere executor of established forms which are meant to please the eye of a viewer. The basis of this relationship is the dancer's perceptual engagement with the movement as an outwardly projected form. In contrast, in butoh, dancers are not expected to reproduce a movement as form, but to experientially engage with the process that makes a particular movement possible. They are not concerned so much with the final result as with the 'origin' or 'cause' of a movement, which can be physical, imaginative, or both. Also, movement in butoh unfolds internally, within or very close to the dancer's body. Thus, a butoh dance is often projected inwardly or close to the body, rather than outwardly into an optically constructed space. The visible form of a movement in butoh is incidental to this primarily internal or close-up engagement. The resulting form of a dance is 'emergent' (Ingold 2013) in the unfolding of perception and action in interplay with actual or imaginary forces. As a consequence of such logic of emergence, a butoh dancer's movements can remind one of the processes of becoming and growth, which 'give rise to the forms of the living world that we see all around us— in plants and animals, in waves of water, snow, and sand, in rocks and clouds' (Ingold 2013, p. 21). In this respect, it is not surprising that butoh dancers draw inspiration from movements from nature and the everyday. Their dances reflect the multidimensional and seemingly chaotic and idiosyncratic side of life itself. Hijikata's work, for instance, drew inspiration from the movements of aged, disabled, or working people, and so eluded conventional parameters of beauty. His 'butoh-fu', or butoh notation, is filled with ideas and images from the human and nonhuman world around him, as well as from his imagination.

Akiko Motofuji—Hijikata's wife and cofounder of butoh dance—wrote that she had trouble in mending a pair of his trousers because one of his legs was a few centimetres shorter than the other, due to an injury in his high-school days (Motofuji 1990). Since Hijikata's body shape did not fulfil the parameters of Western dances such as ballet and modern dance, this might have been an intrinsic motivation to his resorting to a completely new and rebellious philosophy of dance (Kurihara 1996, pp. 17–18). Hijikata's own writing and speeches (e.g. Hijikata 2000) suggest that he was a keen observer of the reality surrounding him, and that his dance might have been affected by the floods, famines, and poverty in rural Tohoku, where he grew up. His understanding of the harshness of life as lived by common people, and of its intertwining with death, may explain Hijikata's distancing himself from Western attitudes toward dance (pp. 78–9).

Hijikata insisted that butoh should begin with discovering one's lost legs. We can try to guess what he meant by this, by going back to one of his speeches, Wind Daruma (*Kazedaruma*), which he presented at the Tokyo Butoh Festival in 1985. In Wind Daruma, Hijikata (2000) sketches episodes from his childhood in rural Japan that he believes had an impact on the consequent development of butoh. He tells, for instance, of farmers who went to work in rice fields and brought small children along tied in straw baskets called *izume*. They would leave four or five of these baskets, with the children inside, in the middle of the field, while they went off to work. Hijikata describes such a situation as very distressing for the children:

> Of course, the children sit down to defecate and urinate and their bottoms get all itchy. But the children are tied in the baskets, which are stuffed with all kinds of things so that they are unable to move, and they bawl [. . .] The children bawl endlessly. In the damp open sky a gluttonous wind swallows those children's screams', while the adults are not able, or willing to, hear them. (Hijikata 2000, pp. 77–8)

When, at the end of a long working day, the parents went back and pulled their children out of the *izume*, they would find that their legs were 'all folded up, [and that the children] can neither stand nor stretch their legs' (p. 78). Those legs would be numbed, or 'lost' (Tanemura et al. 1993). The children would have to relearn what it means to move their legs.

We can interpret Hijikata's anecdote of the children's 'lost legs' as a metaphor of the process of socialization; that is, the conforming to the mode of life of a particular social group. Like one of the children stuck in the *izume*, one may lose awareness, forget or suppress dimensions of their own very bodies because of socialization, or because of traumatic events beyond the person's control (Hanna 1988, p. xiii). Rediscovering one's own body that has been forlorn is the ideal aim for butoh. In fact, one could say that butoh corresponds to a questioning of one's known body in order to explore its hidden or forgotten potentialities. Butoh's driving force, even today, is the questioning of the taken-for-granted body. Yet such process of rediscovery is not immediate or straightforward. 'Tuning in' one's 'lost' body requires a particular kind of concentration and heightened movement sensitivity that can be achieved, as in other forms of physical training, through practice.

Enhanced kinaesthetic perception implies an increased sensitivity to movement quality and detail (Esposito 2013). It is generally accepted that, in butoh, one's kinaesthetic perception should be attuned to movement changes as minute as one millimetre (Kasai, personal conversation). Kasai experienced this notion first-hand when he attended a butoh workshop led by Semimaru in Japan in 1988. As part of the practice, participants engaged in trying to place a raw egg in upright position (personal conversation). Kasai argues that Michizo Noguchi also used the 'egg-standing' exercise with his students, and that the 'arm-standing exercise' (Exercise 3), devised by Kasai, is a development of the same exercise, as applied to one's arm (personal conversation). Another butoh exercise that is meant to develop perception of minute movement variations consists in opening one's fist very gradually (Esposito 2013, p. 7–8). In the version reported in what follows, by Takeuchi (2011), one is asked to open one's hand and fingers for the time-length of three minutes. Even with such a short time-frame to execute the exercise, one is forced to reduce the scale of one's movement drastically, hence training one's kinaesthetic awareness.

Exercise 4: Three-minute palm opening and the finger dance (Takeuchi 2011). (See Video 14.4 on the Companion Website ▶.)

1) Make a fist and spend at least three minutes to open your hand.
2) The palm opening movement should be continuous, though you might experience awkward reactions or 'squeaky' movements in the finger joints. Keep breathing normally.
3) After this exercise, try a 'dance of fingers.' Explore the movement of fingers such as stretching, bending, and twisting (with and without wrist movements).
4) If you are lying, you can try this exercise after the arm-standing lesson (Exercise 3) and create a whole arm-dance, engaging finger, elbow, and shoulder movements.

Awareness of 'hair-splitting' variation means that butoh movements tend to be scaled down and minute when compared to other dances. In fact, while most dances tend to gratify the audience's gaze through the enacting of ample movements that can be seen from a distance, butoh's use of minute movement encourages a 'close-up' modality of visual awareness, as blurring with the sense of touch—'haptic vision'—which tends to be most effective in small performance settings (Esposito 2013, pp. 112–19, 285–7, 305). Butoh dancers' dismissal of 'optical' or distanced notions of visual engagement, and emphasis on kinaesthetic attention, is evidenced by their habit of covering the mirrors in the rooms or halls where the train. This is in order to avoid watching themselves in the mirrors and, as a result, producing visually (and, specifically, optically) constructed movements. In fact, when looking at one's moving body in a mirror, one is giving priority to such a kind of visual perception at the expense of a more directly kinaesthetic engagement with self-movement (Williams 2011, pp. 73–7). As a result, one is neglecting a whole array of movements which occur inside oneself, such as the movement of one's emotions. Dance anthropologist Drid Williams (2011) pointed out that 'visual images nearly always originate from a source *outside* the students' bodies, unlike kinaesthetic imagery, which originates from *within* the students' bodies' (p. 76; emphasis in the original). The mirror image of the body is one such kind of visual images, diverting one's attention from the bodymind as a source of movement. In contrast, kinaesthetic imagery allows one to link dance movements directly with their kinaesthetic source in the bodymind.

Another byproduct of butoh dancers' enhanced kinaesthetic focus is that butoh performances are sometimes criticized for being 'painfully slow'. Yet such criticism overlooks that the very experience of time is altered in butoh performances, due to a converging of the performers' and the audience's focus on the kinaesthetic dimension (Esposito 2013, pp. 273–9). Butoh dancing does not usually follow any particular rhythm, and dancers do not count the beats. In most cases, music is used only to create an atmosphere. Thus, traditional relationships between music and dance are transcended in butoh. Moreover, dancers often use stillness as part of their dance. Such stillness has nothing 'static' in it, as it is grounded in perceptual attention to involuntary self-movement. As such, stillness is charged with the experiential intensity of being alive. Philosopher Sheets-Johnstone (2010) has captured the intrinsic 'musicality' of this dynamic aliveness:

> [Such feeling of aliveness] depends upon one's attention to the actual experience of self-movement, which is to say to the kinaesthetic dynamics of movement and in forms as simple as breathing, sneezing, yawning, and blinking. Each of these simple pan-human movement forms has a unique dynamic, yet one that, like a theme with variations, has multiple possible dynamics. A sneeze can erupt in a staccato manner, or be singularly abrupt or singularly attenuated, and so on . . . Attention to the kinaesthetic dynamics of such involuntary movement can awaken feelings of aliveness. Something is not just happening to you but *moving* you. You do not have to do anything. You just have to sit back, so to speak, and listen to its dynamics. (Sheets-Johnstone 2010, p. 3; emphasis in the original)

When attempting to stay still, one realizes that there is no such a thing as complete immobility, because of the many forms of involuntary movement that keep us alive, such as breathing, the beating of the heart, or the micromovements involved in adjusting one's balance. Inspired by the butoh's approach to dance, Kasai (2009a) has developed dance therapy programmes at mental health clinics, in which patients are let to dance freely, without having to follow a rhythm or in a rigidly choreographed way. He also introduced elements of butoh dancing such as small-scale, minute, and slow movement. This has allowed patients, with and without disabilities, to enjoy themselves and find ways to relax through movement.

Bodily 'vibrations', resulting from release of tension or from an 'impasse' in the direction of an action, provide yet another source of movement material for butoh dancing. In psychology it is said that antagonistic movements and opposite mental factors—two notions which refer to an internally felt and physically experienced conflict with relation to a course of action—can create involuntary 'vibrations' in the body (Kasai 2009b). For instance, when a person wants to hit someone out of anger, he may experience physically and mentally suppressing reactions against the impulse to perform the hitting movement. A conflict arises between the impulse to perform the hitting movement and the socially imposed need to control such impulse.

While these are usually involuntary movements, techniques have been devised to generate bodily vibrations for therapeutic aims. Autogenic training is one such method, which originated in Germany during the years 1984–1903, through research on sleep and hypnosis conducted by neuropathologist Oskar Vogt and his assistant Korbinian Brodmann, and later developed by psychiatrist and neurologist Schultz (Schultz and Luthe 1969, pp. 4–5). Autogenic training consists of a series of physiologically oriented and meditative exercises—including verbal formulae, training postures, breathing and visualizations—allowing relaxation and release of stress (pp. 1–6). The term 'autogenic' means 'self-generating', and refers to the fact that autogenic exercises are meant to support the organism's self-regulatory mechanisms which participate in 'homeostatic, recuperative, and self-normalizing processes' (p. 1). It also refers to the fact that patients are responsible for carrying out their own treatment by performing the exercises regularly, without having to rely on the therapist. 'Autogenic discharges' may occur as a result of engagement in autogenic training (p. 20) in the form of convulsion, spasm, and jerky movements. These discharges are considered to be normal compensating reactions of self-recovery of the bodymind equilibrium, and a sign that the therapy is effective (p. 20). However, it is important that patients maintain 'a passive, spectator-like attitude when such autogenic discharges occur' (p. 20). That is, patients need to suspend the socially conditioned notion that these temporary losses of control are disagreeable or negative. The following exercise, based on the notion of autogenic discharge, can be used in butoh practice for its stress-releasing as well as aesthetic effects.

Exercise 5: Convulsion, spasm, and jerky movement. (See Video 14.5 on the Companion Website ▶.)

1) Allow a part of your body to start jerky movements, or start convulsions or spasms by using the antagonistic muscle contraction.

Kasai (1999) has suggested that body distortion may be a result of encountering the suppressed dimensions (dark side) of our mindbody through butoh movement. While body distortions in butoh performances can look awkward and disturbing, and can even shock an unprepared audience, they should not be seen as gratuitous, as distortions usually reflect a dancer's self-probing movements into the deep layers of his or her bodymind. Distortions may be accompanied by pain, which signals the encountering of one's own physical and mental limits when exploring and challenging habitual movements and ways of being. As Stein (1986) put it, this is 'a key to butoh: working beyond self-imposed boundaries, passing through the gates of limitation into undiscovered territory' (p. 116).

Exercise 6: Distortions. (See Video 14.6 on the Companion Website ▶.)

1) Twist a part of the body, and allow other body parts to distort as in a chain reaction.

To summarize, butoh dance expands conventional notions of dance by introducing the following elements:

- There are no rules with regard to how to move or dance.
- It is irrelevant whether a movement corresponds to a pre-established form.
- There is no obligation to dance following a rhythm.
- Stillness is also considered as dance.
- The amount and scale of the movements are irrelevant—though butoh movements tend to be small and subtle.
- Convulsions, spasms, or distortions can also be considered dance movements.

- Everybody with or without disabilities can engage in the exercises described in this chapter to develop his or her own dance, for performance or healing aims alike.

It is fundamental that instructors are aware of the particular needs of participants in butoh training, and that they create a safe, non-judgmental environment in which students can experiment with movement. Each context of training is different and may require special precautions, so instructors need to prepare in advance.

Butoh Dance Liberates from Rigid Social Boundaries

The legacy of Hijikata's butoh is that dance can stem from the deep layers of oneself, from one's own motivations, intentions, memories, or emotions. Also, that dance can become a medium to access and expand one's imagination through the body, releasing it from social norms or conventions, and so actualize 'otherness' in oneself (Esposito 2013). In her study of the perceptual actualization of the butoh body, Esposito (2013) argued that butoh dancing is a perceptual as much as it is an imaginative endeavour. A butoh 'choreography' usually alerts the dancer to the experiential and sensuous dimensions within a movement or gesture, rather than its form. When, for instance, we extend an arm toward the sky in butoh, it is not in order to show the physical gesture of extending an arm as merely a 'beautiful' shape, but rather, to let our and the audience's attention converge onto the imagining that *something* is going on. For instance, in extending the arm we may be encountering something or someone just above us, or reaching out for something lost or out of reach. (See Video 14.7 on the Companion Website ▶.) Or, when taking a step forward, this might not be just in order to move to the next position, but to gradually discover one's 'lost leg'. Whichever 'meaning' a dancer imbues into a movement, it is not important that the audience reads the same meaning into it. What is important is that the movement triggers the audience's imagination, in the form of memory, sensory engagement, or free association. As dancer Nakajima explains, 'the gestures [in butoh] do not tell a story but evoke associations—to explain a movement is to undermine its meaning' (Nakajima, quoted in Klein 1988, p. 21). Not only is the dancer's imagination set free in butoh, but the audience's imagination as well.

Imagination and perception, body and mind, playfully converge in butoh, in ways that do not usually occur in everyday life. Through the adoption of kinaesthetic imagery alongside rigorous physical practice, butoh allows one to make the body into something other than it is normally conceived of, and to join in the world's processes of becoming. This approach brings about feelings of intimacy, connectedness, and even identity with the world. Following a definition of healing as the capacity to unify and to make whole (Jackson 1989), we argue that butoh is healing in its encouraging integration of the person with the nonhuman as well as with the human world. By allowing individual and group imagination to overlap, butoh dance has the potential to bridge the gap that some of us experience with relation to the social world in times of increasing complexity, fragmentation, and insecurity (Jackson 1989, p. 155).

The notion of 'communitas', introduced by anthropologist Victor Turner (1969), can help us clarify this aspect of the healing potential of butoh training. In communitas, the 'structural', differentiating paradigms that are at work in society, such as class, or roles inherent to one's age or position, are suspended, and people are able to confront each other as bare 'human identities' (Turner 1969, p. 132). In other words, in communitas, people meet each other 'directly', without the mediation of their social statuses or roles (pp. 131–2). In butoh, the suspension of value judgement of 'good' or 'bad', or of the distinction between 'dance' and 'ordinary' movement, or between voluntary and involuntary movements, allows participants to free themselves from the 'structuring' devices of the social order. By allowing involuntary and 'dysfunctional' movements such as trembling, convulsing, stiffening, or abrupt or 'painfully slow' movements, butoh introduces an aesthetic of disorder and grotesqueness that, in turn, releases participants from the normalizing demands of conventional social life. Participants in a butoh dance training setting transcend the social order through their bodies by allowing repressed emotions and images to inform their movements, and by letting corporeal imagination unfold, observing and accepting themselves and others in the process. Indeed, the collective dimension of butoh training is crucial to its effectiveness as a therapeutic process, provided that the framework of training offers a safe and secure container for all participants. The session instructor must be able to judge whether butoh dance exercises are safe enough for people with mental or physical disabilities.

As anthropologist Rappaport (1999) has pointed out, communitas is not only an alternative state of society, but also of 'mind' (p. 219). In contrast with the consciousness that dominates mundane time, in communitas the boundaries that we place between ourselves and the world dissolve, reconnecting us with others and with the environment, and revealing something primal and sacred: a larger sense of self. Similarly, butoh training has the potential of transforming the daily state of consciousness by putting aside the social world which is taken for granted (Schutz 1967)—a change that Kasai and Parson (2003) describe as a transition from social time to body time. Kasai (1991) also refers to the 'ethnomethodological challenge' (Garfinkel 1967) of undoing the socially conditioned body as a process of body 'desocialization'. Although 'desocialization' through body 'deconditioning' is a very difficult if not impossible aim to fulfil (Kasai 1994, 1996; Kasai and Zaluchyonova 1996), the perception of renewal and release that can be experienced through group training is very real (Baird 2012, pp. 215–16). In accordance with our theoretical premises of conceiving bodymind integration as 'potential' (Ozawa De Silva and Ozawa De Silva 2011, p. 96), the notion of body 'desocialization' in butoh stands as an ideal aim. It is an imaginative framework which supports the need and effort to be 'whole'.

CONCLUSION: BUTOH DANCE FOR SPIRITUAL HEALING

This chapter purposes to clarify the uniqueness of butoh dance and why Japanese butoh dancers sometimes think that butoh dance is not merely a performing art (Nakamura 2007; Esposito 2013). Butoh goes beyond the notion of performance as entertainment or as display of aesthetic values or technical skill, and it can make us feel uneasy. Eroticism, grotesqueness, and nonsense, often found in butoh performance alongside other aesthetic dimensions, are not meant to simply unsettle or shock an audience for entertainment purposes. Rather, these qualities may be connected to existential themes, such as hunger for love, loss of vibrant life, and meaningless of life.

While butoh dance started as a 'dance of darkness', even the faintest positive emotions should be conversely lit up in today's butoh, as if we could see the weakest stars in the darkest night. Butoh dance in the twenty-first century asks us to explore its approach to the bodymind for spiritual healing. This is possible through butoh's dialogue with other healing techniques based on similar principles, such as Noguchi taiso. Both butoh and Noguchi taiso ask not so much to 'learn' or 'create' as to 'observe' what is already there, and let it have its say. These approaches actualize movement 'via negativa', through a perceptual attention to forces other than one's own and through a 'passive' rather than 'active' attitude to the moving body. The attitudes of listening and paying attention can lead one to question prefabricated notions, as attached to one's body and to oneself as a consequence of socialization, culture, or habit.

Hijikata's investigations have transformed the world of modern and contemporary dance, changing the parameters of movement aesthetics, connecting 'Western' and 'Eastern' sensibilities and conceptions of the body. The next step is to allow such innovations to seep into our everyday consciousness of the bodymind. While bodymind unification is an ideal aim in butoh as in other physical and spiritual disciplines, butoh practice can contribute to changing the perception of the body that has been shaped and constrained by habit or custom, hence offering opportunities of healing. 'Desocialization of the body' through butoh training can support bodymind integration by enhancing the perception of the corporeal body, while freeing our imagination of what or who we are, thus promoting an enhanced state of wellbeing.

REFERENCES

Baird, B. (2012). *Hijikata Tatsumi and Ankoku Butoh: Dancing in a Pool of Gray Grits*. New York, NY: Palgrave MacMillan.

Esposito, P. (2013). *Butoh Dance in the UK: An Ethnographic Performance Investigation.* PhD. thesis, Oxford Brookes University.

Farnell, B. (1999). 'Moving bodies, acting selves', *Annual Review of Anthropology*, 28: 341–73.

Fraleigh, S. and Tamah N. (2006). *Hijikata and Ohno*. New York and London: Routledge.

Garfinkel, H. (1967). *Studies in Ethnomethodology*. Englewood Cliffs, NJ: Prentice-Hall.

Hanna, T. (1988). *Somatics: Reawakening the Mind's Control of Movement, Flexibility, and Health*. Cambridge, MA: Perseus Books.

Hijikata, T. (1983). *Yameru Maihime (Sick Dancing Princess)*. Tokyo: Hakusuisha.

Hijikata, T. (1987). *Bibou no Aozora (The Blue Sky of Beauty)*. Tokyo: Chikuma Shobo.

Hijikata, T. (2000). 'Wind daruma', *The Drama Review*, 44(1): 71–81.

Hornblow, M. (2006). 'Bursting bodies of thought: Artaud and Hijikata', *Performance Paradigm*, 2: 26–44.

Ingold, T. (2013). *Making: Anthropology, Archeology, Art and Architecture*. London and New York: Routledge.

Jackson, M. (1989). *Paths Toward a Clearing: Radical Empiricism and Ethnographic Inquiry*. Bloomington, IN: Indiana University Press.

Kasai, T. (1991). 'Body de-socialization and Butoh dancing', *Memoirs of Hokkaido Institute of Technology* 19: 1–8. In Japanese, with English abstract.

Kasai, T. (1994). 'The psychological strategies in the arm relaxation', *The Japanese Journal of Humanistic Psychology*, 12(2): 212–19.

Kasai, T. (1996). 'The reconfirmed difficulty of the arm relaxation task', *Japanese Journal of Hypnosis*, 41(1–2): 34–40. In Japanese, with English abstract.

Kasai, T. (1999). 'A Butoh dance method for psychosomatic exploration', *Memoirs of the Hokkaido Institute of Technology*, 27: 309–16. In Japanese, with English abstract.

Kasai, T. (2000). 'A note on Butoh body', *Memoirs of Hokkaido Institute of Technology*, 28: 353–60. In Japanese, with English abstract.

Kasai, T. (2005). 'Arm-standing exercise for psychosomatic training', *Sapporo Gakuin University Bulletin of the Faculty of Humanities*, 77: 77–8.

Kasai, T. (2009a). 'Sense of safety and security for creative works nurtured by meditative Butoh dance movements', *European Consortium for Arts Therapies Education in London*. 16–19 September, Presentation abstract. <http://relak.net/toshi-kasai/> (Accessed 21 March 2017).

Kasai, T. (2009b). 'New understandings of Butoh creation and creative autopoietic Butoh: From subconscious hidden observer to perturbation of body–mind system', *Sapporo Gakuin University Bulletin of Faculty of Humanities*, 90: 85–141.

Kasai, T. and Parsons, K. (2003). 'Perception in Butoh dance', *Memoirs of Hokkaido Institute of Technology*, 31: 257–264.

Kasai, T. and. Zaluchyonova, E. (1996). 'An experimental study of the difficulty in the arm relaxation task', *The Japanese Journal of Humanistic Psychology*, 14(2): 195–202. In Japanese paper, with English abstract.

Klein, S. B. (1988). *Ankoku Butō: the Premodern and Postmodern Influences on the Dance of Utter Darkness*. Ithaca, NY: Cornell East Asia Series 49.

Kurihara, N. (1996). *The Most Remote Thing in the Universe: Critical Analysis of Hijikata Tatsumi's Butoh Dance*. PhD thesis, Ann Arbor UMI, New York University.

Mauss, M. (1979). *Sociology and Psychology: Essays*, transl. B. Brewster. London: Routledge and Kegan Paul.

Middleton, D. and Chamberlain, F. (2012). 'Entering the heart of experience: First person accounts in performance and spirituality', *Performance and Spirituality*, 3(1): 95–112.

Motofuji, A. (1990). *Hijikata Tatsumi to tomoni (Together with Hijikata Tatsumi)*. Tokyo: Chikuma Shobo.

Nakamura, T. (2007). *Beyond Performance in Japanese Butoh Dance: Embodying Re-creating of Self and Social Identities.* PhD thesis, Felding Graduate University.

Noguchi, M. (1972). *Gensho Seimeitai toshiteno Ningen (Man as a Primordial Form of Life).* Tokyo: Mikasa Shobou.

Noguchi, M. (1977). *Karada ni kiku (Obey the Body).* Tokyo: Hakujusha.

Noguchi, M. (1978). *Omosa ni kiku (Obey the weight).* Tokyo: Hakujusha.

Ohno, K. and Ohno, Y. (1992). *Ontono Sora wo Tobu: Butoh no Kotoba (The Palace Soars through the Sky: Kazuo Ohno on Butoh).* Tokyo: Shichosha.

Ozawa De Silva, C. and Ozawa De Silva, R. B. (2011). 'Mind/body theory and practice in Tibetan medicine and Buddhism', *Body and Society,* 17: 95–119.

Rappaport, R. A. (1999). *Ritual and Religion in the Making of Humanity.* Cambridge: Cambridge University Press.

Scheper-Hughes, N. and Lock, M. (1987). 'The mindful body: A prolegomenon to future work in medical anthropology', *Medical Anthropology Quarterly,* New Series 1(1): 6–41.

Schutz, A. (1967). *The Phenomenology of the Social World.* Evanston, IL: Northwestern University Press.

Schultz, J. H. and Luthe, W. (1969). *Autogenic Therapy.* New York, NY: Grune and Stratton.

Sheets-Johnstone, M. (2010). 'Why is movement therapeutic?', *American Journal of Dance Therapy,* 32: 2–15.

Stein, B. S. (1986). 'Twenty years ago we were crazy, dirty, and mad', *The Drama Review,* 30(2): 107–26.

Stern, D. (1998). *Diary of a Baby: What your Child Sees, Feels, and Experiences.* New York, NY: Basic Books.

Takeuchi, M. (2011). *Three-minute Palm Opening and the Finger Dance* (DVD). ADTA. *18th International Panel 'A Panorama of New Directions for Dance/Movement Therapy',* cited by panelist Yukari Sakiyama, Minneapolis, 2011.

Tanemura, S., Motofuji, A., and Tsuruoka, Y. (eds.) (1993). *Butoh Taikan (All about Butoh).* Tokyo: Yuuchisha.

Turner, V. (1969). *The Ritual Process: Structure and Anti-Structure.* London: Routledge and Kegan Paul.

Williams, D. (2011). *Teaching Dancing with Ideokinetic Principles.* Urbana, Chicago, and Springfield, IL: University of Illinois Press.

Yoshioka, M. (1987). *Hijikata Tatsumi Sho (The praise of Hijikata by Tatsumi).* Tokyo: Chikuma Shobo.

CHAPTER 15

FLOW IN THE DANCING BODY

An Intersubjective Experience

LOUISE DOUSE

INTRODUCTION

'FLOW' is an area of research that explores optimal experience from a psychological perspective. Mihalyi Csikszentmihalyi, a positive psychologist, is considered to be the founder of flow in the context of positive psychology. His research addresses the state of mind an individual enters when totally immersed in an activity. Csikszentmihalyi's interest in flow began with decades of research on the positive aspects of human experience. According to Csikszentmihalyi the term 'flow' itself 'is what anthropologists call a native category—a word frequently used by the informants themselves to describe their experience.' (Csikszentmihalyi 1975, p. 36). Within his research, Csikszentmihalyi (1975) initially interviewed participants who typically experienced such flow phenomena, including chess players, rock climbers, musicians, social dancers, and basketball players, to name a few. Flow defined by Csikszentmihalyi (1975) is as follows:

> Action follows upon action according to an internal logic that seems to need no conscious intervention by the actor. He experiences it as a unified flowing from one moment to the next, in which he is in control of his actions, and in which there is little distinction between self and environment, between stimulus and response, or between past, present, and future. (Csikszentmihalyi 1975, p. 36)

Flow research falls largely within empirical literature on intrinsic motivation in studies of wellbeing (Deci and Ryan 1985; Csikszentmihalyi and Rathunde 1993; Waterman 1993; Waterman et al. 2008). However, within research on wellbeing, and central to recent discussions of flow, there is an increasing distinction being made between hedonic wellbeing and eudaimonic wellbeing (Deci and Ryan 2008; Henderson and Knight 2012; Huta and Waterman 2014; Ryan et al. 2008; Ryan and Deci 2001; Waterman

1993, 2007; Waterman et al. 2008). Hedonic wellbeing is typically considered to equate with pleasure and happiness, and most research drawing on the hedonic definition of wellbeing has used assessment of subjective wellbeing (SWB). This consists of measures of life-satisfaction, the presence of a positive mood, and the absence of a negative mood (Miao et al. 2013; Pavot and Diener 2013). Eudaimonic wellbeing on the other hand 'is concerned with living well or actualizing one's human's potentials' (Deci and Ryan 2008: 2). The relationship between hedonia and eudaimonia is a complicated one; eudaimonia is considered a subset of hedonia insomuch as all eudaimonic activities must include hedonic enjoyment, but not all examples of hedonia will include eudaimonic enjoyment (Waterman et al. 2008). While some characteristics of eudaimonia are debated among scholars, core elements of eudaimonia, as distinct from hedonia, typically include self-realization, personal expressiveness, excellence, and relatedness (Huta and Waterman 2014).

Within this chapter, flow is considered an example of eudaimonic wellbeing. This is somewhat debated in the literature (Henderson and Knight 2012), with some scholars suggesting it make up a third category of wellbeing in relation to engagement (Schueller and Seligman 2010). The aim of this chapter is to elucidate the eudaimonic nature of flow experiences in improvisation, and further suggest that flow enables for an intersubjective experience of wellbeing, drawing on the writing of phenomenologists Maurice Merleau-Ponty (1945, 1964) and Martin Heidegger (1927, 1954).

The chapter draws on case-study research conducted by the author as part of a practice-led PhD at the University of Bedfordshire (Douse 2014). The PhD explored flow in improvisation using technologically innovative ways to capture the experience. Central to the research presented in this chapter is the perspective of improvisation as the generative stage of creation (Cerny Minton 2007). It must be emphasised that the context of this study is Western contemporary theory and practice, and notions of flow in improvisation are therefore both contextually and culturally specific. This chapter addresses the dialogic processes involved in capturing the flow experiences of dancers from a dance spectator or choreographers' perspective, and begins with a discussion of the characteristics of flow, drawing on the interview transcripts and journal entries of the two dance practitioners within the study.

For the purposes of confidentiality, these participants are labelled as Dancer 1 and Dancer 2. Both participants were female and were recruited through acquaintance with the researcher. Dancer 1 had been a colleague of the researcher for one year, and Dancer 2 for three years. Within the research, drawing on a hermeneutic phenomenological approach, 'the biases and assumptions of the research are not bracketed or set aside, but rather embedded and essential to interpretive process' (Laverty 2003: 28). Thus, the relationship between the participants and the researcher informs and supports the research.

Dancer 1, aged 25, is a Lecturer in Dance at a UK university and studied at a UK university, attaining a BA and MA, and is currently undertaking a PhD. She is currently situated in the Midlands, and has worked as a freelance dance artist undertaking teaching, performance and choreographic roles. Dancer 1 studied improvisation at university, and has used it as a tool when working with choreographers on various projects. Dancer 1 has described herself as comfortable with improvisation, but no expert. Her knowledge of flow research is only through this research project.

Dancer 2, aged 34, is a Senior Lecturer in Dance at a UK university and has a background in dance spanning sixteen years, including eight years of post-18 (UG and PG) dance education and training and ten years dance teaching experience. She is situated in south-east England, and has performed and choreographed as part of her own company for five years and has experience of working in a range of community settings. Dancer 2's experience of improvisation spans her career; embedded in her training, choreography, teaching, and performance work. Her previous knowledge of flow research is a result of the work of two other colleagues around this area and the support of those two colleagues in developing a collaborative project in 2010 that had flow as part of the research focus, though she concedes that flow was not an area which she had considered particularly within her own practice.

Both participants were provided with an introduction to the theory of flow, and as part of the case-study research they were asked to improvise to a set of six three-minute tasks which drew on a number of different image-based exercises. After choosing one of these tasks as the most enjoyable, participants were then asked to improvise freely for an unlimited amount of time. After each of the tasks the participants were asked to complete a stream-of-consciousness writing task as reflection of the task and on their experience of flow, and were then interviewed after the event in a semistructured interview format.

Philosophical Approaches to Flow

Csikszentmihalyi (1990) is credited with identifying around eight characteristics of flow, through his observations and interviews with respondents. These include clear goals and feedback, the merging of action and awareness, the transformation of time, a balance between the skill and challenge within the task, the possibility of control, concentration on the task at hand, a loss of self-consciousness, and the autotelic experience. Csikszentmihalyi (2000) cites phenomenology as the source of his method. He describes a 'systematic phenomenology', drawing on a description of the stream of consciousness that had influenced him when reading the key texts of the early phenomenologists. Csikszentmihalyi does not, however, provide a complete phenomenological analysis of flow, and thus it is the purpose of this chapter to explore the ways in which a phenomenological analysis of flow can enhance an understanding of that experience, drawing on responses from the participants of the case-study research to further support this understanding.

This section in particular will address Merleau-Ponty's conceptualization of the body as a site for knowing the world. Drawing on his theory of the habit body, the section will explore an understanding of self through the inextricable link of mind and body. The key tenets of Merleau-Ponty's *Phenomenology of Perception* (1945) will be drawn upon, including his intimate relation of body and world, and the nature of time. Merleau-Ponty's understanding of the body as a spatiotemporal 'anchor' in the world will be addressed in order to further Csikszentmihalyi's definition of flow and its particular relation to the eudaimonic characteristic of wellbeing regarding personal expressiveness (Huta and Waterman 2014).

Heidegger can also be linked to flow with regards to the eudaimonic characteristics of self-realization and excellence (Huta and Waterman 2014) through his understanding of authenticity, mind, and being. The section will draw on Heidegger's (1927) understanding of temporality and address his theories on freedom and choice as a positive experience. 'Along with the sober anxiety which brings us face to face with our individualized potentiality-for-Being, there goes an unshakeable joy in this possibility' (Heidegger 1927, p. 358). It is this potential for joy which is the most profound similarity between Heidegger and positive psychology (Crow 2009). In particular, it can be argued that the similarity lies with the eudaimonic concept of wellbeing in relation to self-realization: 'developing one's unique individual potentials and furthering one's purposes in living' (Waterman et al. 2008: 42).

The chapter then progresses by discussing the work of Dr Linda Finlay, and her method of 'reflexive embodied empathy' in understanding the role of the researcher/observer in the interpretation of meaning as a method for accessing the flow experiences of the dancers.

> [Reflexive embodied empathy is] a reciprocal process where one seeks to find ways to allow the Other to present him- or herself to and through one. It involves an intersubjective process of imaginal self-transposition and mutual identification where self-understanding and Other-understanding is intertwined. (Finlay 2005: 289–90)

The process of reciprocal understanding is furthered through reference to the later writings of Merleau-Ponty (1964) in regards to the reciprocity of touch and connects with the eudaimonic characteristic of relatedness (Huta and Waterman 2014). The use of language, both physical and linguistic, as a tool for expressing an individual's thought is drawn upon, as well as the use of interpretation in understanding the Other. The study was conducted through both observation and interview, and addresses an embodied approach to understanding the dancer. The body is thus engaged by the researcher as a way of understanding '"physical" exchanges that occur in a reciprocal manner between the researcher and the participant' (Burns 2003: 230). The manner of observation/interview conducted therefore neglects neither the verbal or physical exchanges between researcher and participant. In the discussion, reflection is employed by the researcher, in order to acknowledge and critique their own embodied relation to the participant.

Personal Expressiveness

Within research on the eudaimonic concept of wellbeing, personal expressiveness 'refer[s] to perceptions that an activity advances the development of personal potentials and the attainment of personally salient goals' (Waterman et al. 2008: 48). It is related to terms such as 'authenticity', 'identity', 'autonomy', 'constitutive goals' and 'integrity' (Huta and Waterman 2014: 1435). Within flow theory these concepts can be teased out in relation to Merleau-Ponty's theory of the body and in particular to his theory of habit as both challenge to and construction of self. Improvisation as a generative tool within choreography requires the individual to produce an instant flow of movement, where it is considered that they must avoid habitual movement patterns in order to invent original material. This brings into focus questions of autonomy, authenticity, and the constitution of self through goal-orientated activity.

Clear Goals and Feedback

In many instances of flow, Csikszentmihalyi cites the characteristic of clear goals and feedback, such as in mountain climbing. The goal is obvious, to reach the top, and the feedback simple, 'I am not falling'. However, often it is more complex than this, particularly in creative pursuits; for example, within dance improvisation there is often not a clear goal or feedback, or at least not one that is articulated. In this sense, 'the rules governing an activity are invented, or negotiated on the spot . . . The goal of such sessions emerges by trial and error, and is rarely made explicit; often it remains below the participants' level of awareness' (Csikszentmihalyi 1990, p. 56). There is, however, a fundamental type of feedback within dance improvisation, as it 'demands a reflexive awareness of when the known is becoming a stereotype' (Foster 2003, p. 7). The dancer must have a clear idea of what constitutes improvised movement in order to avoid habitual movement patterns.

> I was setting myself the task of trying to work in & move in all 3 planes clearly & I liked trying to do this faster & faster . . . I am aware I get stuck in my arms when I do this kind of task—my right arm particularly often leads the material & is the catalyst for whole body action which irritates me when I reflect on it—as it is habitual & I should be trying to challenge those habits when I dance. (Dancer 2 2013a)

One of the dancers was able to find flow in this particular task, though she was very conscious that her familiarity with the task engendered a habitual movement pattern in which she tended to lead the movement with her right arm. Merleau-Ponty's theory of body schema and understanding of embodied knowledge can be linked to this clear understanding of feedback in the body.

For Merleau-Ponty (1945) the body is immediately present, in that an individual knows where their limbs are without having to look for them: they possess a body schema. This 'body schema' provides an individual with a prereflective knowledge of the location of their limbs, but only insofar as an individual's awareness of his body is inseparable from the world of that individual's perception:

> A movement is learned when the body has understood it, that is, when it has incorporated it into its 'world', and to move one's body is to aim at things through it. (Merleau-Ponty 1945, pp. 160–1)

Within Merleau-Ponty's own examples, to learn to type or play a musical instrument 'is to be transplanted into them, or conversely, to incorporate them into a bulk of one's own body' (Merleau-Ponty 1945, p. 66). Within the example of the dancer, the dancer often does not 'know' how the individual movements become habitual in a reflective sense; the form of knowledge an individual has is a practical, embodied knowledge. There is a dependence on the individual's knowledgeable body for its practical meaning. The body schema is thus an implicit procedural knowledge encoded in the body, and flow is tacitly anchored in bodily modes of action and reflection.

Merging of Action and Awareness

Merleau-Ponty's (1945) theory of body schema informs his work on habit and the habitual body. The habit to which Merleau-Ponty (1945) refers is far from being a mechanistic or behaviourist tendency to respond to fixed stimuli in a fixed way, implying passivity, but rather it permits new ways of acting and understanding, thus relating to the notion of personal expressiveness in eudaimonic wellbeing (Waterman et al. 2008). Merleau-Ponty (1945) uses the example of the musician who is at once familiar with a new musical instrument. It becomes a question of the bodily comprehension of a motor significance, which enables musicians to lend themselves completely to expressing the music without having to think about the position of their fingers:

> Between the musical essence of the piece as it is shown in the score and the notes which actually sound round the organ, so direct a relation is established that the organist's body and his instrument are merely the medium of this relationship . . . in giving himself entirely to the music, the organist reaches for precisely those stops and pedals which are to bring it into being. (Merleau-Ponty 1945, pp. 168–9)

This draws a parallel to the characteristic of action and awareness merging within Csikszentmihalyi's theory of flow. This characteristic addresses the moment when an individual is no longer aware of the actions required to complete the task; it is the period when those actions become automatic and spontaneous. It is not the case that the individual is no longer engaged in the challenge of the task, but the application of skill is automatic, innate; it does not require any conscious reflection, only immediate and reflexive action. Within the third task Dancer 1 noted this sensation when drawing on habitual movement patterns:

> Lots of the kind of aesthetic of dance that I've done, work I've done with choreographers, has been quite detailed in the hands and quite articulate in the body, and that was the kind of movement I was doing, and so then I guess it felt, um, more habitual to me to move in that way. So it wasn't that I was kind of going oh I'll do a bit of dance from that piece or something, but it was those kind of movements that felt better for me, or I kind of like doing or that I would create myself. So I naturally did that and it felt much easier, like that was the most time that I kind of felt I had flow. (Dancer 1 2013b)

In this sense, habit is not prescriptive but 'endow[s] the instantaneous expressions of spontaneity with "a little renewable action and independent existence"' (Merleau-Ponty 1945, p. 169). For Csikszentmihalyi (1990), while in flow consciousness works smoothly and action follows seamlessly, an individual is aware of his actions but not of the awareness itself. Within Dancer 1's journal entry for this task, she notes an absence of awareness but heightened physical sensation: 'Feeling dizzy. Like smoke weaving in and out of itself. In a sense you have dissapeared [*sic*] but in another sense you are everywhere' (Dancer 1 2013a). Whilst Csikszentmihalyi (1990) addresses the body and the role of action in flow, the mind is still elevated in his conception of flow. His chapter 'The body in flow' (1990) largely addresses the types of activity which produce flow experiences rather than elucidating the role of the body within such experiences. Merleau-Ponty's writing thus helps to identify embodiment as a condition of flow experience.

The Transformation of Time

> ... the thing about time is interesting because certainly yesterday you don't realise how long you're moving for and it goes so quickly ... (Dancer 1 2013b)

Flow experiences tend to focus the mind temporally, to the present moment, but there is often an altered sense of that moment. Time can appear to move really quickly, or alternatively a few seconds can feel like a few minutes. In this sense an individual's sense of time bears little relation to the conventional clock but to an internal time consciousness:

> Although it seems likely that losing track of the clock is not one of the major elements of enjoyment, freedom from the tyranny of the time does add to the exhilaration we feel during a state of complete involvement. (Csikszentmihalyi 1990, p. 67)

The habit body as well as being spatial and embodied has a temporal structure which is not of the order of objective time or 'clock time'. Here, it is important to address

Heidegger's notion of temporality in relation to Dasein, in his *Being and Time* (1927). Heidegger based his theory of temporality on what he called the 'care structure'—that Dasein's Being is orientated toward the future, while acknowledging itself as past with an openness to the present:

> Temporalizing does not signify that ecstases come in a 'succession'. The future is *not later* than having been, and having been is *not earlier* than the Present. Temporality temporalizes itself as a future which makes present in the process of having been. (Heidegger 1927, p. 401)

This ecstatic quality shows the human capacity to be at once ahead, behind, and alongside the individual; it is a self-generating, self-defining process.

Where Heidegger insisted upon the unity of the three ecstasies, it is Merleau-Ponty who clarifies their relation to temporality as experienced by the individual. Merleau-Ponty's conception of temporality has its roots in both Heidegger's *Being and Time* (1927) and Husserl's *Cartesian Meditations: An Introduction to Phenomenology* (1931). According to Merleau-Ponty there are three levels of temporality. The first level or world is where transcendental time is public and measured time which is located in the world. The second level or internal, immanent time is private; it is the sequences of experience that occur before, after, or concurrent with another, yet is not measurable in the same way that a clock measures time. Finally, the third level addresses the consciousness of internal time which accounts for the experience on the second level. Internal time consciousness is more immanent than the individual's subjective temporal processes, and underlies both the subjective flow of internal time and the objective flow of world time.

Internal time consciousness retains its own preceding living presents and builds up its own continuous identity. The living present is the full and immediate experience of temporality that an individual has at any instant, and as Merleau-Ponty suggests, 'my present, which is my point of view on time, becomes one moment of time among all the others, my duration a reflection or abstract aspect of universal time' (Merleau-Ponty 1945, pp. 81–2). This notion then of 'being in the moment' is when one's perception of time becomes transformed or altered as in flow experiences; it is the conscious experience of the fleeting living present.

Challenge/Skill Balance and the Paradox of Control

For Merleau-Ponty, temporality is a constituting structure for an embodied agent.

> Every present grasps, by stages, through its horizon of immediate past and near future, the totality of possible time; thus does it overcome the dispersal of instants, and manage to endow our past itself with its definitive meaning, reintegrating into personal existence even that past which the stereotypes patterns of our organic

behaviour seem to suggest as being at the origin of our volitional being. (Merleau-Ponty 1945, pp. 97–8)

Thus, while arising from the spatiotemporal history of an individual's actions in particular situations, habits develop which enable them to act on the world. Habits are therefore the basis of an individual's agency and in the context of eudaimonic wellbeing—a basis for their own autonomy and personal expressiveness (Huta and Waterman 2014). While Merleau-Ponty did not use the term's agency or autonomy, he did utilize a Sartrean vocabulary for discussing 'freedom' and 'choice' (Merleau-Ponty 1945, pp. 504–30). Merleau-Ponty's (1945) conception of choice is that it cannot be absolute; habits root an individual in the world that makes choice possible. Agents have knowledge about their situation, and their knowledge is integral to the successful accomplishment or 'doing' of that situation which links to the control component of flow in which Csikszentmihalyi describes the '*possibility*, rather than the *actuality*, of control' (2000, p. 60).

Csikszentmihalyi (2000) describes the control component as the confidence an individual has in their abilities. However, it is not necessarily about exerting control but is more concerned with the possibility of control, and links to the element of challenge within the flow activity which requires a particular set of skills. He noted that this challenge does not need to be physical, as, for example, in appreciating art a skilled art critic takes enjoyment from analysing a conceptually challenging artwork. However, the skill needs to match the challenge in a delicate interplay, where the activity is never too difficult to accomplish, nor too easy that the individual loses interest.

> So, first of all I thought I would choose the planes one, because that was the one that I experienced most flow in, and it's the one I felt most comfortable in and then I thought is that a bit of a cop out by choosing something that maybe I've done a lot of, so I kind of felt more comfortable with, and I thought I would try something that was a bit more, that would challenge me. And I had, when I was doing the shorter task, I did experience flow. (Dancer 2 2013b)

Dancer 2 acknowledges that when choosing the final task to improvise to she wanted more of a challenge, thus balancing her level of skill to the challenge of the task in order to find flow.

The presence of a high level of challenge balanced with a high level of skill is seen as a key component of eudaimonic wellbeing (Waterman 1993; Waterman et al. 2008). In a study conducted by Waterman (1993) the skill/challenge balance component of flow activities was strongly correlated with that of personal expressiveness and self-realization.

> From a eudaimonist perspective, in which feelings of personal expressiveness are experienced in connection with the furtherance of one's skills and talents, it is expected that such feelings will arise because of the process of self-realization occurring when the level of challenges afforded by an activity is high and the level of skills brought to it is commensurate. (Waterman 1993: 681)

In improvisation, the challenge of the task and of avoiding habitual movement patterns results in the furthering of one's skill, but only through a process of self-realization.

Self-Realization and Excellence

Eudaimonic wellbeing can be considered as 'the striving for perfection that represents the realization of one's true potential' (Ryff 1995: 100). There is a progressive element to self-realization which is associated to the development of one's skills in flow activities. The level of excellence one develops in an activity will depend on the continual refinement of the flow activity. As one becomes more proficient, presumably, the less challenging the task will be, and therefore the less likely one is to experience flow. Individuals must therefore engage in a process of self-reflection and desire to reach a high standard in order to maintain the flow experience: '... in this manner, potentials for personal excellence can be progressively actualized' (Waterman 1993: 681).

Within flow, the challenge of the action is enjoyable to the agent, as with the prospect of control. However, as Csikszentmihalyi (1975) states, this is only in retrospect:

> He has no active awareness of control but is simply not worried by the possibility of lack of control. Later, in thinking back on the experience, he will usually conclude that, for the duration of the flow episode, his skills were adequate for meeting environmental demands; and this reflection might become an important component of a positive self-concept. (Csikszentmihalyi 1975, p. 44)

In order for the challenge/skill balance to promote the development of one's potentials, there needs to be a complete focus on the task. This is often described as a lack of unwanted disturbances such as personal issues, doubts, and insecurities.

Concentration on Task and Loss of Self-Consciousness

For Csikszentmihalyi, the characteristic of concentration within flow can also create a loss of an individual's own self-consciousness. 'One item that disappears from awareness deserves special mention, because in normal life we spend so much time thinking about it: our own self' (Csikszentmihalyi 1990, p. 62). Yet this loss of self-consciousness is not a loss of self or a loss of consciousness, as particularly in dance, an awareness of an individual's body, breathing and the feel of the dance is very important. However, it seems that the loss of self-consciousness in the flow experience often builds a stronger sense of self for the person afterwards.

> I was very aware of the notion of sensation today—I wonder if it is the suit. Because you can feel it against your body & skin & it restricts—not fully—not like you can't do

a movement—but because it is not loose & you are aware of it. So I think this made me aware of other sensations—the floor the fabric etc. & so there seemed to be a lot to investigate as well as to challenge and push me out of my comfort zone. (Dancer 2 2013a)

In this task, it could be argued that Dancer 2 experienced a new sense of self by being pushed out of her 'comfort zone'. For Csikszentmihalyi (1990) then, self refers in some respects to an individual's own objectified representation of their being. A loss of self-consciousness refers to the focusing of an individual toward the subjective experience of the activity, thus enabling an individual to develop new ways of being in the world.

The Autotelic Experience

This links with Heidegger's notion of Dasein (1927). Heidegger played a key role in examining the question of 'being-in-the-world'. Dasein (being there) is an existence which understands that it exists, and what is more, the being of Dasein is, in part, shaped by that understanding. Heidegger described three particular characteristics of Dasein; firstly, that it relates itself to its own Being, that 'Dasein is in each case essentially its own possibility, it can, in its very Being, 'choose' itself' (Heidegger 1927, p. 68). Secondly, that it has an implicit understanding of this relationship: '. . . in determining itself as an entity, Dasein always does so in the light of a possibility which it is itself and which, in its very Being, it somehow understands' (Heidegger 1927, p. 69). Finally, Heidegger explicates a third priority 'as providing the ontico-ontological condition for the possibility of any ontologies' (Heidegger 1927, p. 34), thus defining the capacity for understanding the Being of all entities.

The idea that Being is an issue for itself is inherent within the characteristic loss of self-consciousness within the flow experience for which a conscious acknowledgement of the human relation to Being emerges stronger afterward.

> The self emerges when consciousness comes into existence and becomes aware of itself as information about the body, subjective states, past memories, and the personal future. Mead . . . distinguishes between two aspects of the self, the knower (the 'I') and the known (the 'me'). In our terms, these two aspects of the self reflect (a) the sum of one's conscious processes and (b) the information about oneself that enters awareness when one becomes the object of one's own attention. The self becomes organized around goals. (Nakamura and Csikszentmihalyi, cited in Snyder and Lopez 2002, p. 91)

Heidegger (1927) then distinguishes between two modes of existence: '[a]s modes of Being, *authenticity* and *inauthenticity* (these expressions have been chosen terminologically in a strict sense) are both grounded in the fact that any Dasein whatsoever is characterized by mineness' (Heidegger 1927, p. 68). The inauthentic reflects the every-dayness of Being—a mode in which an individual exist most of the time and refers to the way in which the individual is not always caught up in things, when they are no different than others. Authenticity, on the other hand, is when Being is revealed in a first person way, when the individual is most 'at home' with their self, and is characterized by a 'moment of vision' in which we have the 'authentic potentiality-for-Being-a-whole' (Heidegger 1927, p. 277).

> [R]esoluteness is our name for authentic existence, the existence of the Dasein in which the Dasein is itself in and from its own most peculiar possibility, a possibility that has been seized on and chosen by the Dasein. (Heidegger 1954, p. 287)

Since Being is an issue for Dasein, only a life in which a conscious acknowledgement of the human relation to Being, such as in authentic experiences, can be understood as a 'good' life in the eudaimonic tradition. Thus a shared characteristic of Heidegger's *Dasein* and Csikszentmihalyi's *Flow* can be seen in their quest for moments of 'authenticity' and references the final characteristic of flow, that of the Autotelic experience, as an intrinsically rewarding experience:

> LOVE IT—the planes are an interesting form to work within & I enjoyed trying to cognate where the body was actually going. (Dancer 2 2013a)

Flow experiences are fundamentally intrinsically rewarding; that is, they provide pleasure and enjoyment in and of themselves. The term 'autotelic' can be broken into '*auto* meaning self, and *telos* meaning goal' (Csikszentmihalyi 1990, p. 67). In autotelic activities the reward is a subjective one, through the completion of a personal goal. This is unlike activities which have an external reward, such as dancing for money, or recognition for an award. In this instance, an external reward would be second to the feeling of dancing for the dancer. For Csikszentmihalyi this is evident in the way in which flow enriches an individual's life:

> The autotelic experience, or flow, lifts the course of life to a different level. Alienation gives way to involvement, enjoyment replaces boredom, helplessness turns into a feeling of control, and psychic energy works to reinforce the sense of self, instead of being lost in the service of external goals. When experience is intrinsically rewarding life is justified in the present, instead of being hostage to hypothetical future gain. (Csikszentmihalyi 1990, p. 69)

Intrinsic motivation is a key component of eudaimonic wellbeing, and flow in the context of improvisation enables an individual to experience a 'potential-to-be-whole' through those moments when an individual's embodied being is brought into question and revealed through action.

RELATEDNESS

Another of the key characteristics of eudaimonia is relatedness—a term developed within self-determination theory (Deci and Ryan 2000, 2008; Huta and Waterman 2014; Ryan and Deci 2000, 2001). Relatedness is 'the need to feel belongingness and connectedness with others' (Ryan and Deci 2000: 73) Relatedness, however, does not refer to all human relations, but specifically to those aspects of relationships which engender wellbeing. In this section, the notion of flow as an intersubjective state will be discussed as an example of relatedness through the application of Merleau-Ponty's theories of reciprocity.

In Part Two of *Phenomenology of Perception* (1945), titled 'The world as perceived', Merleau-Ponty's opening chapter title explains: 'The theory of the body is already a theory of perception' (p. 235). His aim is to show that consciousness and the world are mutually dependent. He writes: '. . . the world is inseparable from the subject, but from a subject which is nothing but a project of the world, and the subject is inseparable from the world, but from a world which the subject itself projects' (Merleau-Ponty 1945, pp. 499–500). There must therefore be both a subject and world, which interact through perception. However, there is a further dimension to an individual's existence in the world; each individual inhabits a world that is shared with other people. Merleau-Ponty developed his thinking on intersubjectivity at the end of Part Two in 'Other selves and the human world'; however, it was not explicitly formulated until his final writings, particularly in the unfinished work, *The Visible and the Invisible*, published after his death in 1964.

This section details the initial interpretations of the two dancers by drawing on the author's perceptions during these tasks as detailed in the author's journal. It aims to clarify the subjective experience of the researcher in identifying the experiences of flow in both participants. In doing this it draws on the subjective experiences of the participants and develops an interrogation of the intersubjective nature of the research and the use of 'reflexive embodied empathy' as defined by Linda Finlay.

Finlay is a psychotherapist based in the UK who addresses a qualitative research method for addressing lived experience. Her numerous articles (2005, 2006, 2009a, 2009b) address a phenomenological approach to lived experience, in which she attempts to articulate a practical methodology based on hermeneutic phenomenological descriptive practices. She suggests a particular way of engaging with others which addresses the intimate role of the researcher in engaging with, and understanding, the participant. 'Reflexive embodied empathy' addresses the researchers 'need to learn to read and interrogate their body's response to, and relationship with, the body of the research participant (the Other)' (Finlay 2005: 272).

Finlay's distinct method of 'reflexive embodied empathy' 'advocate[s] a research process that involves engaging, reflexively, with the participant's lived body, the researcher's own body, and the researcher's embodied intersubjective relationship with the participant' (272). As a method, it involves a process of hermeneutic reflection which 'can be understood as a process of continually reflecting on one's experience as a researcher, alongside the phenomenon being studied, so as to move beyond the partiality and investments of one's previous understandings' (279). Through a discussion of Finlay's method of reflexive embodied empathy, this section provides a method for understanding the experience of the participants while enabling an examination of the researcher's intimate role in the construction of that interpretation.

Within this section there is a shift in tone. The use of the reflective journals and semi-structured interviews, mentioned previously, was utilized in the collection of verbal dialogic data. The experiential data collected is important in identifying the subjective experiences of both the author and participants. In traditional academic terms, dance is considered to give primacy to subjective experience; as a work of art it is 'an expressive form created for our perception through sense or imagination, and what it expresses is human feeling' (Langer 1947, p. 15). The evaluation of such data thus requires different analysis to that of quantitative empirical data, and language is considered closest to the subjective and experiential. Thus not only are entries from both the researcher's and the participants' journals referred to directly, but the use of first-person pronouns is also employed in order to indicate the researcher's intimate role in the construction of the data.

During the tasks set for the dancers, and, articulated within the stream-of-consciousness reflective writing conducted after each task, it was clear that my perception of the dancers in improvisation indicated when the dancers had achieved flow. This was in both a generalized sense, with regard to the overall sense of flow within a particular task, and in a more specific sense, during particular phrases or movements of the dancers. This perception came from an embodied connection that I experienced to particular phrases of movements, in which I describe being 'drawn' to them. I grappled in the journal with the idea that I was either 'sharing' or empathising with their experience of flow, or else achieving flow myself, through watching them dance.

> I was wondering if the moments of dancing [which] I connect with, actually reflect my own flow movement qualities? Or whether I am sharing in her flow experience? Or neither? (Douse 2013)

This reflects the multiple layers in which Finlay (2005) describes our ability to empathize with the 'Other', including connecting of the Other's embodiment to our own, and acting into and merging with the Other's bodily experience.

Connecting of the Other's Embodiment to Our Own

The first layer Finlay (2005) denotes as 'connecting of', in which one connects with the Other through using one's own embodied reactions; for example:

I felt my presence was a disturbance to begin with, but I think that was also true of the space, the suit, the whole research environment ... I think [Dancer 1] did get into it more, though I am not sure she achieved flow. I noticed she closed her eyes—I imagine to get into it and not feel those external pressures. (Douse 2013)

In this instance, my understanding of Dancer 1's experience of flow is mediated by our shared experience of the research environment and my own identification with the action of closing one's eyes.

In Merleau-Ponty's understanding of the Other, the mediating term between self and Other is not bodily similarity, but the external world. For Merleau-Ponty, the concern is not that of the gesture but that the gesture is directed toward a shared object in the world: 'The gesture which I witness outlines an intentional object. This object is genuinely present and fully comprehended when the powers of my body adjust themselves to it and overlap it' (Merleau-Ponty 1945, p. 215). This also relates to mirror-neuron research, which suggests that empathy is only activated in goal-specific action (Rizzolatti and Craighero 2005). This resonates with the first characteristic of flow: that of clear goals and feedback. In this instance the feedback is my own embodied recognition of the Other's embodied goals.

Acting into the Other's Bodily Experience

The second layer Finlay calls 'acting into', in which 'understanding, therefore, comes from somehow taking up, identifying with, and then enacting the Other's experience' (2005: 281). When observing Dancer 2 I noted that 'there [were] some really interesting moments. And I was completely involved in it and developed (?) some kinaesthetic empathy towards it' (Douse 2013). It is important to note that kinaesthetic empathy fundamentally involves the observance of physical bodily action. However, it is not the case that I am passively observing the Other, but that I am actively embodying the experience of the Other. Merleau-Ponty's understanding of the reversibility of experience between self and Other is important to consider here:

We must habituate ourselves to think that every visible is cut out from the tangible, every tactile being in some manner promised to visibility, and that there is encroachment, infringement, not only between the touched and the touching, but also between the tangible and the visible, which is encrusted in it, as, conversely, the tangible itself is not a nothingness of visibility, is not without visual existence ... every vision takes place somewhere in the tactile space. There is double and crossed situating of the visible in the tangible and of the tangible in the visible; the two maps are complete, and yet they do not merge into one. The two parts are total parts and yet are not superposable. (Merleau-Ponty 1964, p. 134)

The kinaesthetic empathy I experience is thus an active embodied experience in which I mirror the dancer's bodily experience. The bracketed question mark in my observation above also indicates my ambivalence to the term 'developed' as I wrote my response, perhaps indicating the embodied nature of the experience and the difficulty in precisely portraying that experience through words. This links with the characteristic in flow of action and awareness merging. Rather than in the first layer of 'connecting of' where I am aware of my conscious reflection of the Other's experience, in this layer I more directly experience that which the Other experiences whilst still acknowledging it as of the Other.

Merging with the Other's Bodily Experience

The final layer is that of 'merging with', in which Finlay describes an experience where she, 'as researcher, became so thoroughly immersed in [her] participant's experience that [she] (momentarily) lost sight of [her] own' (2005: 284). In Dancer 2's sixth task I describe 'moments when I felt connected and in flow myself' (Douse 2013). In these moments I acknowledge feeling in flow as a spectator; I am engaged with the dancer's embodied experience and am able to capture this experience through my own sensations of being in flow. Flow for me was a physical response to watching them dance, but further, in those moments, I feel I am resonating with the experience of the dancer, and experiencing their own enjoyment and flow in the task.

Merleau-Ponty acknowledges this experience in his discussion of intersubjectivity as involving an individual experiencing his self as something that others can experience in the same way that they experience them. He states that, as collaborators, 'my thought and his are interwoven into a single fabric . . . they are inserted into a shared operation of which neither of us is the creator' (1945, p. 413). He goes on to discuss the 'consummate reciprocity' (1945, p. 413) an individual experiences when both participants are actively engaged in the event of consciousness. In this experience, a connection with the flow characteristic of concentration and loss of self-consciousness is apparent, in which for both the dancer and myself, a more positive sense of self emerges.

Challenges

What is interesting about these observations, however, is that my experience and perception of flow relates largely to Dancer 2 and not Dancer 1. This also reflects the dancers' own perceived experiences of flow. In the final task, for example, Dancer 2 notes six moments of flow, while Dancer 1 notes only two. This is also acknowledged by Dancer 1 in the interview, in which she states: 'I've kind of found it hard to imagine where [flow] is when you're dancing' (Dancer 1 2013b), and indeed, when asked if she had ever experienced flow in anything else, she replied: 'No I, I guess not'. This therefore calls in to question the importance of the skill/challenge balance characteristic of flow in relation to intersubjectivity. For example, in one of my journal entries I note:

[The task] didn't really seem to go anywhere, I felt quite outside from it . . . I didn't feel compelled to watch or drawn into the movement, I wonder if it reflects a lack of flow for [Dancer 1], but certainly for me. I was partly distracted, thinking about things, I can't remember what now. (Douse 2013)

This distraction and lack of flow from the perspective of the spectator also indicates an imbalance of skill to challenge. It could be argued that my previous entry indicates a mirroring and 'acting into' the identity of the Other. Dancer 1, in the same task, notes:

Sometimes I thought about connection between 2 points like a puppet but that always broke off because it limited what I could do with my body. (Dancer 1 2013a)

Perhaps the increased challenge and broken flow of Dancer 1 was mirrored in my distracted experience of the task. It could therefore be suggested that flow is itself an example of relatedness, which 'is a necessary condition for a person's growth, integrity, and well-being' (Ryan et al. 2008: 153). It is important, therefore, to distinguish between the terms 'relatedness', 'reflexive embodied empathy', and 'intersubjectivity'. Reflexive embodied empathy can be considered a methodology for engaging in intersubjective relations, and while relatedness can be considered an example of intersubjectivity, not all intersubjective interactions are positive. Thus, reflexive embodied empathy can facilitate a 'merging with' the positive flow experience of the Other (enabling a sense of relatedness), but also enable the 'acting into' and identification with the distracted experience of the Other.

CONCLUSION

This chapter provides a transdisciplinary definition of flow which draws on both the psychological and physical component of this experience. It extends Csikszentmihalyi's definition of flow within positive psychology by drawing on the work of phenomenologists Merleau-Ponty and Heidegger in order to align flow with current research on eudaimonic wellbeing. In particular, it makes reference to the eudaimonic principles of personal expressiveness, self-realization, excellence, and relatedness. Merleau-Ponty's theory of body schema and bodily habit informs Csikszentmihalyi's characteristics for flow in regard to the dancers' experience of feedback in the body in improvisation, and their ability to both recognize habitual movement patterns and to move beyond these patterns. This enables the dancer to develop a sense of personal expressiveness through the balance of challenge and skill. It also recognizes Heidegger's theory of Dasein as a constituting structure for self-realization, thus allowing one to develop an 'authentic' experience of self through pursuit of excellence—an intrinsically rewarding experience.

Finally, through the process of hermeneutic embodied reflection, this chapter argues for flow as an intersubjective experience. Observers of dance are able to empathize with this experience of flow in the dancers they observe, developing a sense of relatedness. Drawing on Finlay's theory of reflexive embodied empathy, the chapter addresses the role of the researcher/observer in the interpretation of meaning, engaging with both the observer's own body and the body of the dancer. This 'reciprocity' of experience with the Other enables the observer to connect to, act into, and merge with the experience of the Other, informing both their understanding of the Other's wellbeing and their own wellbeing, in the moment of observation.

REFERENCES

Burns, M. (2003). 'Interviewing: Embodied communication', *Feminism Psychology*, 13(2): 229–36.

Cerny Minton, S. (2007). *Choreography: A Basic Approach using Improvisation*, 3rd edn. Leeds: Human Kinetics.

Crow, S. (2009). *Phenomenally Happy: An Examination of the Ways Heidegger can Critique and Support Positive Psychology*. Master's thesis, University of Notre Dame Australia.

Csikszentmihalyi, M. (1975). *Beyond Boredom and Anxiety: The Experience of Play in Work and Games*. San Francisco, CA: Jossey-Bass.

Csikszentmihalyi, M. (1990). *Flow: The Psychology of Optimal Experience*. New York, NY: Harper & Row.

Csikszentmihalyi, M. (2000). *Beyond Boredom and Anxiety: Experiencing Flow in Work and Play*, 25th anniversary edn. San Francisco, CA: Jossey-Bass.

Csikszentmihalyi, M., and Rathunde, K. (1993). 'The measurement of flow in everyday life: Towards a theory of emergent motivation', in J. E. Jacobs (ed.) *Nebraska Symposium on Motivation, Vol. 40: Developmental Perspectives on Motivation*. Lincoln, NE: University of Nebraska Press, pp. 57–98.

Dancer 1 (2013a). Personal journal, 13 June.

Dancer 1 (2013b). Skype conversation with Louise Douse, 14 June.

Dancer 2 (2013a). Personal journal, 13 June.

Dancer 2 (2013b). Skype conversation with Louise Douse, 14 June.

Deci, E. L. and Ryan, R. M. (1985). 'The general causality orientations scale: Self-determination in personality', *Journal of Research in Personality*, 19(2): 109–34.

Deci, E. L. and Ryan, R. M. (2000). 'The "what" and "why" of goal pursuits: Human needs and the self-determination of behaviour', *Psychological Enquiry*, 11(4): 227–68.

Deci, E. L. and Ryan, R. M. (2008). 'Hedonia, eudaimonia, and well-being: An introduction', *Journal of Happiness Studies*, 9(1): 1–11.

Douse, L. (2013). Personal journal, 13 June.

Douse, L. (2014). *Moving Experience: An Investigation of Embodied Knowledge and Technology for Reading Flow in Improvisation*. PhD thesis, University of Bedfordshire.

Finlay, L. (2005). ' "Reflexive embodied empathy": A phenomenology of participant-researcher intersubjectivity', *The Humanistic Psychologist*, 33(4): 271–92.

Finlay, L. (2006). 'Dancing between embodied empathy and phenomenological reflection', *The Indo-Pacific Journal of Phenomenology*, 6 (Special Edition).

Finlay, L. (2009a). 'Exploring lived experience: Principles and practice of phenomenological research', *International Journal of Therapy and Rehabilitation*, 19(9): 47–481.

Finlay, L. (2009b). 'Debating phenomenological research methods', *Phenomenology and Practice*, 3(1): 6–25.

Foster, S. (2003). 'Taken by surprise: Improvisation in dance and mind', in Cooper Albright, A. and Gere, D. (eds.), *Taken by Surprise: A Dance Improvisation Reader*. Middletown, CT: Wesleyan University Press, pp. 3–10.

Heidegger, M. (1927). *Being and Time*, transl. J. Macquarrie and E. Robinson (1962). Oxford: Blackwell.

Heidegger, M. (1954). *The Basic Problems of Phenomenology*, transl. A. Hofstadter (1988). Indianapolis, IN: Indiana University Press.

Henderson, L. W. and Knight, T. (2012). 'Integrating the hedonic and eudaimonic perspectives to more comprehensively understand wellbeing and pathways to wellbeing', *International Journal of Wellbeing*, 2 (3): 196–221.

Husserl, E. (1931). *Cartesian Meditations: An Introduction to Phenomenology*, transl. by D. Cairns (1991). London: Kluwer Academic Publishers.

Huta, V. and Waterman, A. S. (2014). 'Eudaimonia and its distinction from hedonia: Developing a classification and terminology for understanding conceptual and operational definitions. *Journal of Happiness Studies* 15(6): 1425–56.

Langer, S. (1947). *Problems of Art*. New York, NY: Charles Scribner's Sons.

Laverty, S. M. (2003). 'Hermeneutic phenomenology and phenomenology: A comparison of historical and methodological considerations', *International Journal of Qualitative Methods*, 2(3): 21–35.

Merleau-Ponty, M. (1945). *Phenomenology of Perception*, transl. C. Smith (2002) (2nd edn). London: Routledge.

Merleau-Ponty, M. (1964). *The Visible and the Invisible*, ed. C. Lefort, transl. A. Lingis (1968). Evanston, IL: Northwestern University Press.

Miao, F. F., Koo, M., and Oishi, S. (2013). 'Subjective well-being', in I. Boniwell, S. A. David, and A. Conley Ayers (eds.), *The Oxford Handbook of Happiness*. Oxford: Oxford University Press, doi: 10.1093/oxfordhb/9780199557257.013.0013.

Pavot, W. and Diener, E. (2013). 'Happiness experienced: The science of subjective well-being', in I. Boniwell, S. A. David, and A. Conley Ayers (eds.), *The Oxford Handbook of Happiness*. Oxford: Oxford University Press, doi: 10.1093/oxfordhb/9780199557257.013.0010.

Rizzolatti, G., and Craighero, L. (2005). 'Mirror neuron: A neurological approach to empathy', in J. P. Changeux, A. R. Damasio, W. Singer, and Y. Christen (eds.), *Neurobiology of Human Values*. Berlin: Springer, pp. 107–23.

Ryan, R. M. and Deci, E. L. (2000). 'Self-determination theory and the facilitation of intrinsic motivation, social development, and well-being', *American Psychologist*, 55(1): 68–78.

Ryan, R. M. and Deci, E. L. (2001). 'On happiness and human potentials: A review of research on hedonic and eudaimonic well-being', *Annual Review of Psychology*, 52: 141–66.

Ryan, R. M., Huta, V., and Deci, E. L. (2008). 'Living well: A self-determination theory perspective on eudaimonia', *Journal of Happiness Studies*, 9(1): 139–70.

Ryff, C. D. (1995). 'Psychological well-being in adult life', *Current Directions in Psychological Science*, 4(4): 99–104.

Schueller, S. M. and Seligman, M. E. P. (2010). 'Pursuit of pleasure, engagement, and meaning: Relationships to subjective and objective measures of well-being', *The Journal of Positive Psychology*, 5(4): 253–63.

Snyder, C. and Lopez, S. (eds.). (2002). *Handbook of Positive Psychology*. New York: Oxford University Press.

Waterman, A. S. (1993). 'The conceptions of happiness: Contrasts of personal expressiveness (eudaimonia) and hedonic enjoyment', *Journal of Personality and Social Psychology*, 64(4): 678–91.

Waterman, A. S. (2007). 'On the importance of distinguishing hedonia and eudaimonia when contemplating the hedonic treadmill', *American Psychologist*, 62(6): 612–13.

Waterman, A. S., Schwartz, S. J., and Conti, R. (2008). 'The implications of two conceptions of happiness (hedonic enjoyment and eudaimonia) for the understanding of intrinsic motivation', *Journal of Happiness Studies*, 9(1): 41–79.

CHAPTER 16

COMMON EMBRACE

Wellbeing in Rosemary Lee's Choreography
of Inclusive Dancing Communities

DORAN GEORGE

ESSAY

SINCE the mid-1980s, British choreographer Rosemary Lee has produced large choral dances with performers that have diverse levels of training, and range in age from older than eighty to as young as six. She thus challenges contemporary dance's conventions about what bodies can perform, while querying distinctions between professional (or concert) dance and community practice. Community dance has tended to envision itself as a means to enhance its participants' social or personal health (Foundation for Community Dance 2014), while on the concert stage, professional dancers have historically understood their role as fulfilling a choreographer's vision (Martin 1985: 54). This distinction lines up with one set out by Thompson and Schechner (2004), who differentiate 'social' and 'aesthetic' theatre, which they argue privilege community improvement and aesthetics respectively. However, while casting non-professionals with whose welfare she concerns herself, Lee clearly hones her dances for viewership. Choreographing uncompromising theatrical visions of social cohesion using methodology that promotes the dancers' 'wellbeing', Lee eludes easy categorization. (See Figure 16.1.)

Art historians have recently theorized how broad participation and the notion of 'community' can be intertwined with the aesthetics and representation of a work (Bishop 2006; Bourriaud 2002; Kester 2004). Yet applied to 'participatory dance' like Lee's, their terms overshadow the historical development of choreographic strategy that configures the performers' wellbeing as central to a concert's expressive aims. Furthermore, the genealogy of the ideas in Lee's choral dances challenges a tendency to read the work through romantic, essentialist notions of the human condition that erase cultural specificity and the labour entailed in the choreographic process. For example,

FIGURE 16.1. Some of the intergenerational cast in Lee's *Common Dance* (2009). (Photo credit: Simon Weir. with permission from Rosemary Lee.)

Dove (2014) insists that when companies include amateurs as opposed to being made up of only professionals, universal truths are revealed. In opposition to 'work that is primarily an exercise in skill display', he proposes that Lee's choral, intergenerational *Square Dances* (2011) are 'not a distracting "show" of skills, but rather a deeply engaging celebration of what it is to be human' (Dove 2014). He thus suggests that jettisoning concern with the performers' appearance enables a rejuvenating recovery of humanity. But Lee critiques 'virtuosity' by teaching skills that have been under development for at least fifty years.

With the absence of a critical language for Lee's methodology, in the reception of her work, the term 'community dance' has signified her use of inclusivity and the dancers' welfare to contest professional concert dance conventions. In reviews of *Egg Dances* (1988/1990), scholars Valerie Briginshaw and Christy Adair reference Lee's history of community practice to explain how she choreographs her performers' wellbeing (Adair 1990; Briginshaw 1989)—a textual strategy that Catherine Hale recapitulates in her writing about *Passage* (2001) (Hale 2001). For example, Adair verifies Lee's ability to choreograph non-professionals by mentioning her work with 'communities' not represented in the concert (Adair 1990). This is notable, because reviews rarely mention an artist's teaching endeavours to explain their choreographic practice. Briginshaw (1989) and Hale (2001) similarly reference community dance to bolster their claims that, through mutual care, intimacy, and belonging among the cast, Lee stages an idealized sociality, which, along with Adair (1990), they characterize with affectionate nostalgia.

Although Lee and her casts hold wellbeing as a shared value, central to creating and performing the work, Lee demands that the dancers fulfil her artistic vision of community, and she points to key differences between her work and that of community practitioners, as I touch on below. Critical appreciation of her aesthetic of wellbeing has thus been sacrificed by framing her work as either revealing intrinsic human welfare by rejecting display, as Dove suggests (2014), or restoring a lost sense of community, as Briginshaw (1989), Adair (1990), and Hale (2001) imply. By contrast, I suggest that Lee choreographs a 'movement culture' by creating social bonds amongst her cast, based on a specific performer identity that she synthesizes through dance practice. As a result, the dancers both experience and represent wellbeing. To articulate Lee's movement culture, this essay first maps historical precedents from which Lee draws ideas about the dancers' wellbeing and broad participation. Then, to discern how she combines the ideas in her methodology, I analyze Lee's rehearsal procedures and choreographic modality.

Redefining Contemporary Concert Dance

An American avant-garde tradition deeply influences how Lee blurs distinctions between professional and community dance. Although this aesthetic legacy is familiar for students of modern dance history, scholars have rarely addressed how it underpins the valuing of the performers' wellbeing in participatory dance. When American modern dance first achieved institutionalization in the 1950s through state funding for the arts (Morris 2006; Prevots 1998), artists such as Merce Cunningham and Anna Halprin challenged aesthetic limitations that arose through canonization (Gilbert 2014, pp. 72–82). Building on their innovations, dancers in New York's Greenwich Village in the 1960s resisted what they saw as the exclusivity of modern dance authoritarianism. As evidence that any-and-everybody could participate, performances across various artistic disciplines included colleagues not trained in the given discipline, in order to reject what was thought to be the artificiality and constraint of institutionalized aesthetics (Banes 1993). Artists such as Simone Forti, Steve Paxton, and Trisha Brown rejected idealized body types and virtuosity. For example, writing about Paxton's 1967 *Satsifyin' Lover* in which dancers simply walk across the stage, critic Jill Johnston revels in the 'incredible assortment of bodies' (Banes 1993, p. 60). Meanwhile, in Forti's 1960 dance *Huddle*, one dancer at a time separates from, clambers over, and rejoins a tightly formed standing group (Banes 1980, p. 27). Rejecting the refinement of vocabulary that distinguished those with and without professional dance training, artists used everyday movement that appeared more 'natural' (Gilbert 2014, pp. 88–91).

Against what became know as a 'pedestrian aesthetic of everyday action and the awkward quirkiness of untrained diverse bodies' (Foster 2002, p. 64), modern dance virtuosity came to represent institutionalized training as opposes to universal human ordinariness (Gilbert 2014, p. 86). The idea that dance achieved universal significance through broader participation, as identified previously in Dove's (2014) reading of Lee's work, thus accompanied the push against canonization. Yet it also recapitulated modern dance's abiding claim to embody something essential about humanity. With their anti-virtuoso bodies, Forti, Paxton, Brown, and others seemed to fulfil the aim, set down by previous modern dance generations, of staging universal human truths (Manning 2004, p. 118).

Ideas now broadly understood as somatic training fuelled and benefited from the challenge to modern dance (Gilbert 2014). With the belief that they were reconnecting with inherent bodily capacity, evident in anatomy's design to negotiate gravity and other terrestrial forces, dancers displaced or modulated existing training. Often focusing on skeletal–muscular structure and function, somatics contributed to pedestrian aesthetics by claiming to relieve dancers of kinetic artificiality imposed by modern and classical training. The technique of Anatomical Releasing, for example, purports to restore natural facility obscured by other techniques, while contact improvisation (CI), which enjoys a mutually influencing historical relationship with Anatomical Releasing (Gilbert 2014, p. 11), focuses on mechanical properties in the motion of two dancers sharing weight (Gilbert 2014, p. 282). Many practitioners believe that they access primal kinetic patterns through these and other techniques that exhibit somatic ideas. This provides a convincing logic for the belief in dance's universality and inclusivity, even though somatics and CI now produce virtuosos (Novack 1990, p. 188), and have a history of being dominated by white dancers (Novack 1990, p. 10). When Dove (2014) reads Lee's work as restoring innate human qualities by rejecting virtuoso skills, he thus recapitulates a fifty-year-old discourse.

Schooled in British contemporary dance that was initiated in the late 1960s with the significant involvement of Americans (Preston-Dunlop and España 2005), Lee exhibits the influence of New Dance—an artistic movement that consolidated in the 1970s, echoing many of the critiques of classicism and modernism staged in New York (Jordan 1992; Mackrell 1992). Like the experimentation across the pond, New Dance artists pushed against the limited subjects, aesthetics, and methods which they perceived in ballet and Britain's recently established Graham-based modern dance. Lee developed a concern about elitism and what she perceived as an insider conversation, committing to make high-quality inclusive work. Like many of her generation she travelled to New York in the early 1980s, where she saw intergenerational concerts and was drawn to choreography that included untrained dancers and 'unconventional' dance vocabulary (Lee 2012).[1]

Determined to be an artist of utility based on her interest in inclusion, Lee also benefited from New Dance's effort to take art practice beyond the concert stage. The influence of German modern dance on American approaches taking root in Britain, was key to this move. As an academic requirement, students at Dartington College worked in non-arts settings following the philosophy of modern dance pioneer Rudolph Laban, who, as an exile from Nazi Germany, had based himself at the arts institution in south-west England (De Wit 2000; Preston-Dunlop and España 2005). When the American educator Mary Fulkerson instituted New York experimental practices at Dartington, she used the educational mission of working beyond arts contexts to extend the turn toward inclusion developed in Greenwich Village. Fulkerson developed her version of Anatomical Releasing, which, along with CI that Paxton taught at the college, was designed for dancers and non-dancers to train together (De Wit 2000, p. 108–34; Novack 1990, p. 68).

Lee attended the last of Dartington's dance festivals, and interfaced with Laban's philosophy at London's Laban Centre in the early 1980s, where, training to be a dancer, she
also studied a Dartington student project in working-class Rotherhithe, in north-east
London. In addition, New Dance felt Dartington's philosophical impact more generally
when Fulkerson's first graduates, some of whom Lee worked with, participated in the
emerging scene for which the collective X6, started at London's Butler's Wharf in 1976,
formed an epicentre (Gilbert 2014, p. 225).[2]

The British stage was also set for Lee's vision when New Dance choreographed the
progressive political zeal of the 1970s. In the first half of the decade, the pioneering
experimental company Strider moved beyond the proscenium arch, aiming to divest
theatre dance of its elitism (Jordan 1992, p. 39). Other artists furthered this mission by
vehemently rejecting the presumption of the necessity for virtuosity in concert dance,
central to a classical stronghold in the establishment. X6 pursued a feminist agenda, evident in their publication *New Dance Magazine* (Lansley 1977), and, as well as working
in non-arts contexts, dancers turned to folk culture. Folk festivals and fairs engendered
a subversive grass roots milieu that was not officially governed, and emphasized participation rather than consumption and its association with spectacle. For a generation
seeking independence from corporate commercialism and state control, folk culture,
through its association with the natural environment in rural contexts, embodied local-
ity and microeconomies (McKay 1996, p. 35). Avant-garde dancers invested in the ideology, evidenced in, for example, an X6 New Dance seminar at which attendants agreed
with Kate Flatt's assertion about folk dance's value, arguing that it was a means by which
their art form could make an ideological intervention (Early 1977). Flatt—whose work
for extemporary dance had a big influence on Lee[3]—spearheaded the use of folk culture
to foreground broad involvement against elitism based on the refining of skills (Early
1977). This ethic echoed some of the central aims of a CI network rapidly growing in the
United States (Novack 1990).

Lee's Methodology of Wellbeing through Broad Participation

Lee's concept of wellbeing, in various aspects of her methodology, evidences these
influences in a way that builds upon a somatic aim of nurturing postural health. In
their redefinition of contemporary dance, practitioners not only changed their training procedures, but found connections between a new theory of the moving body, and
how to reorganize classes, company structure, and the modality of presenting choreography. In contrast with ballet and the Graham technique, which a new generation
saw as overworking superficial muscles, somatics offered to connect practitioners with
deep muscles beyond voluntary control, developing good posture and creating space,
or 'openness', in the joints, purportedly promoting more natural, effortless, movement,
less focused on appearance. Using ideas from key texts by Mabel Ellsworth Todd (1937)
and F. M. Alexander (1932), dancers argued that injury results from working against the

body's natural logic by compressing the joints, which accelerates ageing (Gilbert 2014). They expanded the concept of cooperating with nature to an ethic of cooperation in dance classes, rehearsals, and the choreographic process, arguing that the modern and classical models promote competition as dancers aim to fulfil an idealized outward appearance, neglecting their bodily nature. With its culture of personal and mutual care, somatics ushered in dramatic change in the organization and execution of dance. In training and the creative process, artists rejected authoritarianism that was thought to disconnect dancers from their inner knowledge (Gilbert 2014). In the way that she pro-cures, rehearses, and choreographs her casts, as well as how she conceives of her dances, Lee institutes an ethic of personal and mutual care that extends from a somatic theory of the body, and she thereby integrates inclusivity and wellbeing.

Lee intervenes in dance-making culture in its broadest terms by conceiving of her casting approach to take into account the broader impact of her projects. To procure dancers for *New Springs from Old Winters* (1987), local newspapers in Oxford, which is where the project was based, carried an open call, while Jointwork—the company that commissioned the project—drew performers from schools and community groups. With sections choreographed to cater for different skill-levels and availability, Lee opened up the ways in which people could participate. Approximately 150 performers joined the core cast of fifty-seven dancers for a procession through Oxford that pre-ceded the concert (Lee 2012), offering multiple ways of being engaged in, and feeling ownership over, the dance[4] (see Figure 16.2). Yet Lee pursued her social or 'community'

FIGURE 16.2. Children of Oxford participate in the procession for *New Springs from Old Winters* (1987). (Photo credit: unknown, with permission from Rosemary Lee.)

concerns as part of her artistic vision rather than to its detriment. While forging connections between existing groups and individuals, and thereby strengthening a local dance network through collaboration, Lee insisted upon the ability of non-professionals to perform high-quality dance. She also depended on the cross-section of aged and trained bodies to represent mortality and regeneration as transcultural themes. Basing her dance on annual rituals (including Christian, Jewish, Pagan, and Buddhist) associated with coming from darkness to light, winter to spring,[5] the casts' diversity conveyed, and constituted, a community in celebration.

Like *New Springs,* in order to claim the universality of their themes, many of Lee's large dances depend upon what is conveyed by a diversity of bodies. Lee thus recapitulates how earlier generations had replaced virtuosity with 'pedestrian' bodies and movement to claim the essential nature of human ordinariness. Novack (1990) proposes that CI's anti-elitism accompanied a loss of 'faith in communicating solutions to large problems and expressing the human condition on a grand scale'—ideas in which modern dance had invested (p. 136). Lee's work diverges from Novack's analysis in that to solve what she sees as the problem of contemporary dance's elitism, it represents inclusivity through the diverse embodiment of 'grand scale human truths'. In Lee's *Common Dance* (2009), an elderly man and a young girl exemplify this strategy by evoking different relationships to mortality. Gradually moving their centres of gravity forward to precipitate a controlled stumble, they seem to fall into the 'unknown', where they embrace the space into which they step with their arms, before retreating and performing the gathering of air back into themselves. The simultaneous but distinct execution of the action, along with the rest of the cast, evokes pondering the future, grasping at that which cannot be held, while the precarious falling steps communicate expectation, uncertainty, and hope, configuring humans as universally fragile in our mortality. Yet disparity in the old man and the young girl's ages suggests different amounts of time they might expect to be on the planet, and different experiences they might have. In line with Paxton's *Satisfyin Lover* noted previously, Lee multiplies what dance can say by breaking limits upon what bodies populate the stage; yet she does so by expressing grand-scale human truths such as mortality or seasonal change. She thus recycles how, in its progressive era previrtuosity beginnings, American modern dance dismissed cultural differences, being used against New York's Jewish immigrants for example, by staging seasonal rituals as the shared experiences of ordinary people (Tomko 1999, pp. 93–5).

It is with folk-dance modalities, which carry the association of timeless customs kept alive by generations of ordinary people, that Lee establishes broad participation as a means of communicating universal human truths. In his study of British countercultures since the 1960s, such as the folk-culture Barsham Fairs in which Lee participated, George McKay argues that seasonal rituals, such as the pagan summer solstice, played a central role for folk revivalists (McKay 1996). Lee benefits from folk dance's symbolic significance as communally celebrating seasonal and life changes, such as in *New Springs* and *Common Dance.* The dancers evidence the inclusive, shared nature of the themes by performing mutual participation in a collective project, rather than the spectacular presentation of skills or an idea. As they face each other rather than the audience, the dancers share a fairly simple vocabulary that underpins their choral movement patterns and flouts concert dance's demand for precise unison. With inclusion that conveys toleration of difference in everyday movement, rather than the elite display of physical superiority, Lee uses folk dance to intervene in contemporary dance, like New Dance artists had suggested was possible.

Yet to establish the accessibility associated with folk dance, Lee cultivates skills in her dancers that promote inclusivity in the studio and communicate it in performance. For this she builds upon the New Dance initiative of taking dance into non-arts settings. To learn to dance confidently as individuals and a group with varying levels of training and capacity, the cast must relinquish expectations about what constitutes accomplished movement. While teaching in 'community' (rather than professional) contexts, Lee found that because professional training strives for perfection, it stratifies dancers based on previous experience, which works against her aim of social cohesion. Students not accustomed to dancing on count, for example, lost what she calls their 'physicality' when learning phrases set to music, because, caught up in the cerebral demand of fulfilling steps, they lost their comfort with moving. To avoid a pecking order of competence, Lee replaces modelling dance phrases with cultivating mutual appreciation using, for example, the metaphor of 'embracing different ways of seeing the world'. Partners develop empathy by taking turns imagining that they are looking at the world through each other's eyes, following in silence, attempting to see what they imagine their colleague sees. They also learn to be attentive to each other by following and leading each other's movement. Furthermore, to demonstrate to potential participants in *Common Dance* the openness she requires, Lee employed a young girl with whom she showed the exercises in an introductory workshop. Together they modelled a middle-aged woman and child partnering each other. Lee thus aims to supplant any tendency toward judgement between cast members with mutual appreciation, and thus engenders equanimity as an experience.[6] She builds collective bonds by integrating individual difference into a horizontal social modality. The expressive aims (aesthetic theatre) depend on the cast's wellbeing (social theatre), which is achieved through the mutual inclusion that governs Lee's vision of competent performance.

Much like amongst her cast, Lee carefully nurtures relations between herself and the dancers by representing herself as anti-authoritarian, exhibiting the ethos of 1960s and 1970s experimentation. In rehearsals for *Common Dance*, for example, she communicates misgivings about her authority even while pushing for her artistic vision (Lee 2013). As with all her large choral works, prior to working with the cast, Lee carefully plans the rehearsal process based on previously envisioned sections, and directs her dancers to convey a contemplative and quotidian, as oppose to presentational and spectacular performance style. But when giving feedback, Lee expresses shock at her own forthrightness, candidly using self-deprecating humour in her communication with the cast (Lee 2013). By presenting her leadership as approachable, fallible, and playful, rather than as demanding obedience, she creates a milieu of shared responsibility, engendering the feeling of a community of individuals invested in a collective project.

Choreographing an Inclusive Performer Identity

Lee connects the various aspects of her methodology by constructing a performer identity, based on somatic ideas about natural facility, to which the integration of wellbeing and participation in the group is central. In the metaphor 'presence', a state her dancers aim to achieve, Lee theorizes inclusivity as inevitable, because for her cast to connect with 'nature' and reveal their 'humanity', they must do so as a 'community'. She insists that, rather than fulfil an externally imposed idea of performing, her dancers are most powerful as their authentic selves on stage, and cultivates skills to achieve this sense of 'presence' with exercises that emphasize the role of the group. For example, by brushing down each other's bodies in turn, and letting go of tension, the cast aims to sense downward flow in their bodies, which Lee proposes helps them to connect to the ground. She frames this as allowing the usual masks of everyday life to fall away, stripping the dancers down to their real selves. Those who brush, stand away momentarily to look at the effect of their work, which for Lee reveals everybody as gorgeous in a way that transcends conventional ideals of beauty evident in much concert dance. Her belief in each person's intrinsic beauty lines up with how the commentators on her work, whom I have referenced, suggest that her dancers recover an innately human sense of healthiness.

By insisting that they contribute value to the dance simply by being who they are, manifested in the sensory and image-based metaphors of a performance practice, Lee instils confidence in her diverse performers. In this way, she builds on the universal ordinariness of pedestrianism that replaced modern dance virtuosity. The cast learns to 'be themselves', with the idea that they are recovering a birthright through connecting with natural physical laws. In the brushing exercise, gravity functions as a sensory metaphor for a universal force through which the beauty of the true self can be revealed. Lee thus sustains the argument, inaugurated in the 1960s, that aesthetic value inherent in the body has been obscured by culture. In the contexts that Lee works, the veracity of Newtonian physics is almost certainly unquestioned. So, when dancers accept gravity as a means to self-revelation, they feel that, through connecting with the shared reality of a body negotiating terrestrial forces, they relinquish social masks, discovering an essential connection to each other, and theoretically to all humanity. Potentially new sensations reveal what seems like a familiar and self-evident scientific truth as the dancers come to know an individual experience of gravity as unique and profound, while also universal and mundane. The communal nature of the brushing exercise also frames the achievement of the sensation of gravity as dependent upon cooperative exchange. Lee therefore conjoins individuality and community in a way that seems logical and obvious yet outstanding and magical. Along with the exercise itself, she engenders group coherence ideologically by configuring each cast member as a spectacular part of the ordinary truth of the natural, universally shared reality of being human.

Using exercises designed to engender sensory awareness, Lee further promotes group coherence by averting her dancers' concern from the appearance of movement. In this sense, 'presence' underpins a cooperative rather than competitive culture using the focus in somatics and CI on the tactile sense (Cohen-Bull 1997; Gilbert 2014). For example, in rehearsals for *Common Dance*, to help the dancers strengthen their kinaesthetic awareness and experience of their own and their colleague's bodily motion,[7] cast members place a flat hand—one that 'listens'—softly on the back-centre of the pelvic girdle of a partner. The person receiving touch aims to sense their sacrum—the bone that joins the two halves of the pelvis—and connect it to their own moving arms through to the fingertips. Lee informs her dancers that a prevailing perception of the arms beginning at the shoulder inhibits the 'fuller' movement achieved with an awareness of the connection between the sacrum and arms. A teenage girl watches Lee demonstrate with a tinge of cynicism, unconvinced, perhaps, by the choreographer's flowing dance (Lee 2013). Yet with the focus on sensation of the partner being touched, and on following motion for those offering tactile feedback, the procedure displaces embarrassment or judgement aroused by concerns about the appearance of movement. As they exchange roles, the dancers also develop empathy for each other's experience, learning to attend to sensation. By sensing and facilitating movement, which is understood as based on a common physicality, they learn what Lee calls 'openness' to the diverse bodies, training backgrounds, and ages in the cast.

Both the brushing exercise and connecting the sacrum to the arms are modulated somatic sensory exercises, which often include tactile feedback, such as one partner lifting another partner's relaxed limb to help each of them sense the weight, location, and

FIGURE 16.3. In rehearsal for *Common Dance* (2009), some of the cast practice listening to each other's bodies. (Photo credit: Lucy Cash, with permission from Rosemary Lee.)

shape of the boney structure. Lee insists that diverse cast members develop movement competence through these processes because there is a focus on how a practitioner feels rather than how high they can lift their leg or execute other skills that demand years of training, such as movement memory and dancing on count.

As well as cultivating shared responsibility in rehearsals, Lee rechoreographs such somatic exercises to convey mutual care in her choreography in a way that promotes the experience and the appearance of community wellbeing. For example, a motif of dancers listening to places on each other's bodies recurs in her large group works. Building on the attentiveness developed in the rehearsals, dancers place an ear against a partner's knee, shoulder, or belly, recalling the hand placed on a sacrum (see Figure 16.3). Listening to a partner's body with the head or hand evinces contemplative mutual caring, because, figuratively and literally, dancers attend to the 'nature' of each other. The cast thus learns to perform the act of caring and being cared for as an experience, an authentic act, rather than the presentation of an idea. By performing caring for a colleague, they compound Lee's idea of presence. Even while the cast learns such skills over the rehearsal period, because the dances appear to strip away theatrical artificiality, they seem to reveal intrinsic humanity, just as Dove (2014) suggests. The resulting compositional modality asserts individual difference as integral to group movement by representing a community that embraces the natural uniqueness of each performer in a shared culture of wellbeing.

Nurturing Nature in Choral Flow

Based on the individual-group performer identity that Lee cultivates, she conveys wellbeing through her composition of choral movement. With reference to her work *Common Dance*, this section focuses on her choreographing of mellifluous flow, which, among other patterns, stages the dancers' unique embodiment of a common trajectory, evoking inclusivity by asserting the natural status of group belonging to which individual difference is integral. In sections of many of Lee's choral works, the dancers execute a common language of what seems like ordinary movement travelling in the same direction. Rather than exhibit either uniformity or transgression in their common motion, the dancers perform fluidity through the harmonious integration of kinetic inconsistency. Lee's compositional lyricism thus appears to embody natural phenomena, suggesting that mellifluous flow is a foundational terrestrial pattern, innate to humanity and recovered in inclusive community. For example, in a section of *Common Dance* the performers surge backwards and forwards in four directions like the swell of a tide (Lee 2013). Discrepancies in their individual execution of moving in the same direction evokes the unpredictable cosmic logic we associate with natural forces such as the effect of the wind and the pull of the moon on the ocean. Furthermore, seeing mellifluous flow on human bodies that seems to reference marine motion, procures a physical feeling of familiarity. The dancing thus lulls its audience into a sensation of witnessing human community that integrates individual difference as part of a natural and harmonious universal logic.

The choreographed surging demonstrates the ineluctability in many of Lee's large choral works of the cast's diversity and the compositional references to natural phenomena. Bodies of differing ages and levels of dance training create latitude in the compositional lyricism, thereby emulating, for example, oceanic motion. Lee choreographs inconsistent but common vocabulary using broadly accessible image-based prompts. In the surging section the dancers internalize the idea of feeling a force emerging deep inside that wells up and reaches out to grab something in the space that they take back within. Meanwhile, in the section referred to previously that communicates different experiences of mortality in an elderly man and a young girl, all the dancers work with an image of contemplating wide-open possibility with the whole front of their bodies. Lee wants her performers to be 'possessed' by rather than illustrate such images, betraying the influence of ideokinesis and the Skinner Releasing Technique. In these techniques, dancers use sensory awareness to physically experience and be propelled into movement by images, rather than represent them with established forms of dance (Gilbert 2014). Embodying the prompts with their diversity in age and motile capacity, Lee's cast provides individual unpredictability, which the choreographer maintains is more difficult to procure from professional dancers. With years of training to fulfil a standardized ideal, she holds that professional dancers are sometimes trapped by their carefully honed skills, struggling to abandon concern with how they appear (Lee 2012). It is clear, then, how, in trained dancers, the prompts might fail to produce the appearance of ordinary motile difference, which is crucial for evoking natural unpredictability.

To congregate her cast's diverse embodiment of the images into choral flow, Lee uses their skills in sensory awareness to nurture a collective experience of a particular dynamic quality. Having jettisoned counting, the timing is unmetered, so in an orchestral fashion the dancers learn, as a group, to change the power and direction of their action by following Lee's conductor-like gestures. By gaining clarity in their group flow under Lee's direction, the dancers integrate their individual embodiment of the prompts into ensemble choreography. They thus continue to execute different kinetic versions, sustaining their sense of 'presence' within shared movement while moving in a group trajectory. Through repetition, the performers cultivate attentiveness to their embodiment of an image while developing codependence within the group. They do this by listening to each other for cues as to when the movement should happen, ultimately establishing the cast's independence from Lee's gesturing arms. Forging a group flow that is irrevocable from individual sensation, each dancer executes with certainty action that binds them to the flow of the whole cast, and thus manifest unpredictable and inconsistent movement relative to their colleagues as part of a recognizable kinetic flow.

Lee choreographs the cohesion of difference with the logic that the performers are empowered through an actual connection to nature achieved by virtue of the dance practice. For her, somatics restores an essential sense of belonging to the natural world, likening the heightened sensory awareness with the experience of being in a 'natural' landscape. Arguing that in contemporary society there are few opportunities for sensing the relationship between the body and its natural environment, she feels that the experiences cultivated in somatics enable transcendence from contemporary alienation, such as her belief that the brushing exercise reveals each dancer's intrinsic beauty. The logic goes that to the degree that the body, like all material, is subject to gravity, so too is corporeality part of nature, and bringing this connection to consciousness restores an intrinsic sense of belonging. Again, by embodying images of waves, the dancers achieve an elevated sense of self through their connection to the natural world, affording them group belonging with their dancing colleagues, expressed in the choral dimension of the image, and ultimately a universal connection to humanity and the cosmos. Lee therefore choreographs a concept of nature that supports individual 'presence', while functioning as a binding logic of sociality in the group, and potentially with all humanity.

Culturally Specific Nature

Given that Lee's work seems to recover a natural sense of inclusive community, it is not surprising that Dove (2014) reads *Square Dances* as clearing away the demonstration of skill to reveal human truths, and that Briginshaw (1989), Adair (1990), and Hale (2001) find in her work a lost sense of community. Lee herself makes a distinction between what I am characterizing as compositional references to natural phenomena, and somatic ideas about the body's nature. She proposes that

> ... we share physical experiences or sensations of being alive like breathing, our heart beating, that's what we have in common hence the title [*Common Dance*] ... I believe we share common natural processes, I'm trying to find a shared experience through sensation that's not the same as claiming that nature provides a universal experience ... I'm talking about a shared sensation of a natural force. The work comes from the shared experience of those images and tasks.[8]

However, I maintain that individual and social wellbeing achieve a sense of inevitability in Lee's vision of inclusive community, because her dancers and audiences are familiar with the natural phenomena that her choral movement evokes. Somatic theories of the body, along with the aesthetic history of 'pedestrian' vocabulary, provide Lee's cast, and her audiences, with a convincing link between the body's 'mundane nature' and the natural phenomena.

The problem with the idea that nature provides an essential foundation for human connection, even when the aim is to cut through cultural difference and overcome exclusion, is that it risks concealing the specific cultural perspective through which the idea is forged. Since at least the 1980s, cultural studies scholars researching race, sexuality, gender, and other social identity categories, have revealed problems with recourse to a universal 'nature' to understand human social relations (Ahmed 2006; Butler 1990; Foucault 1978). Only representations that dominant ideology endorses accrue universal status, so minority positions are excluded by default. For example, right-wing Dutch politicians corralled Western rhetoric about individual freedom being a universal right, to demonize the Islamic faith. They argued that observance of Islam necessarily entails subjugation to a tyrannical authority (Puar 2007). The politicians were able to place Islam 'beyond reason' because the conceptualization of freedom as manifest in individuality accrues self-evident status in the West, even amongst progressives (Mahmood 2012). Lee opposes prejudices such as Islamaphobia with her agenda of inclusion; yet by staging individuality through seemingly self-evident metaphors of natural bodily processes and forces, she risks concealing cultural specificity in her idea of wellbeing, and glossing over conflicts in the notion of community by claiming her perspective's naturalness.

Of course, by integrating individual difference Lee holds out for a community that moves beyond conflict, the hopeful nature of which we see in Briginshaw (1989), Adair (1990), and Hale's (2001) nostalgia for the sense of community which Lee represents. By imagining that a lost social cohesion becomes recuperated, these writers validate Lee's project, which struggles to find a place within contemporary dance's idiomatic history, as the labour I have detailed demonstrates. However, by drawing attention to the historical and cultural contingency of Lee's concept of wellbeing, I wish to challenge, while also affirm the efficacy of, investing in ideas about precultural human nature. For example, when viewed against early twentieth-century mass spectacles, Lee's lyrical vision of heterogeneous community exposes its dependence on the historically specific idea that nature is integral to wellbeing. The 1930s saw a radically different idea of human welfare staged in mechanically equivalent chorally moving bodies. Such dances represented technology's promise of a better society—an idea invested in by a spectrum of political ideologies. Yet as the century progressed, streamlined efficiency became associated with war and authoritarian fascist and Stalinist systems, as well as intense state interference, exemplified by McCarthyism. Taking on a sinister quality, mechanization signified destruction, the foreclosure of freedom, and the extinguishing of diversity (Burt 1998). When early 1960s artists included untrained performers in their work, they contributed to a new corporeal logic in which natural diversity represented liberation from institutional authority—a move that Lee extended. She recalibrated Greenwich Village's untrained bodies by harmonizing awkward quirkiness into oceanic motion. Like the seemingly irrefutable truth manifest in the 'pedestrian' movement of 'ordinary bodies', references to wave-like motion are so widespread that it would seem odd if someone in Lee's native London was unfamiliar with the idea. As a metaphor, marine movement thus functions like a natural self-evident truth which, when used to represent the resolve of individual difference within a communal social movement, establishes inclusive community as irrefutable. It is probable, then, that Lee's audience feels they know the social model's truth as a precultural physical experience, even while that sense of knowing depends upon specific historical and cultural circumstances. The feeling of inclusive community's natural inevitability is precisely what makes the hope for harmonious social resolve convincing in Lee's work.

Lee is not unaware of the cultural specificity of her vision. She insists that the choral works are concert dance, contrasting them with work undertaken by practitioners who, through ongoing regular groups, work with people who normally would not have the opportunity to participate in dance classes, or artists who specialize in dance with specific constituencies such as the disabled or disenfranchised young people. Generally limited to rehearsing over a few months to create a professional work, Lee concedes that her participants are often middle-class people, and are usually already interested in contemporary dance, even if they are not professionals.[9] In her large choral works, rather than embracing an existing community's dynamic social complexity, as some artists do, Lee asks people to join her in a process through which they represent an idealized vision of community inclusion. The limits that Lee identifies upon participation in her work, and the historical and cultural specificity of her vision of wellbeing, reveal the problem with Dove's (2014) assertion that Lee choreographs 'what it means to be human', as well as Briginshaw (1989), Adair (1990), and Hale's (2001) nostalgic reading of her representation of community. While Lee stages a convincing vision of inclusive community supported by widespread beliefs in universal forces that govern bodies, if her ideas are taken as self-evident, different concepts of sociality risk appearing to be artificial by comparison, and thus vulnerable to the kind of disenfranchising that Dutch politicians enacted upon Islam.

Nevertheless, through her concept of wellbeing, Lee has spearheaded in contemporary dance the staging of diverse casts, particularly in terms of age and experience. Dove's (2014) claims, while misleading, gesture toward the significance of her achievement. By employing terms related to science and nature, as well as individual and community wellbeing, which are self-evident in her cultural context, Lee has, for more than thirty years, contested what for most artists are unquestioned conventions in contemporary dance that are based upon the exclusion of a whole range of bodies. Furthermore, with a conspicuous absence of the nuclear family in the danced relationships, Lee stages a communal rather than heterosexual imperative as the basis for human connection. She therefore constructs a vision of human nature alternative to the widespread naturalization of the heterosexual nuclear family (Roughgarden 2004), insisting upon a diversity of ways in which humans achieve kinship and a sense of belonging and wellbeing.

Notes

1. Lee lists Doris Humphrey, in whose work, as a student, she first saw a child perform alongside adults, and the likes of Meredith Monk and Kei Takei, who worked with lots of differing bodies and ages, though not children. Lee herself also worked with the New York company Spoke to Hub, which carried out big projects involving untrained and trained people of all ages.
2. Sue MacLennan, for whom Lee danced in a touring company for several years, as well as Kirstie Simpson, Laurie Booth, and Julyen Hamilton, were among Dartington College graduates who participated in New Dance.
3. E-mail from Lee to the author, 20 July 2015.
4. The numbers that participated in *New Springs From Old Winters* is Lee's estimate. E-mail from Lee to the author, 23 July 2015.
5. E-mail from Lee to the author, 19 February 2015.

6. I am building on Cynthia Novack's proposition that CI generates and sustains shared rather than individual responsibility within the 1970s community that practiced the dance. She proposes that social arrangements were embedded in, and extended from, the dance form (Novack 1990).

7. E-mail from Rosemary Lee to the author, 19 Feburary 2015.

8. E-mail to the author, 19 February 2015.

9. Lee pointed out that it is especially in London that her casts are predominantly middle class, and that in the more recent projects *Without* (2014) and *Under the Vaulted Sky* (2014), that the casts have been more mixed than is usual. E-mail to the author, 19 February 2015.

REFERENCES

Adair, C. (1990). 'Review of Rosemary Lee's work at the Place Theatre', *Dice Magazine: The Magazine for Community Dance*, 11.

Ahmed, S. (2006). *Queer Phenomenology: Orientations, Objects, Others*. Durham, NC: Duke University Press.

Alexander, F. M. (1932). *The Use of the Self, its Conscious Direction in Relation to Diagnosis, Functioning and the Control of Reaction*. New York, NY: E. P. Dutton.

Banes, S. (1980). *Terpsichore in Sneakers: Post-Modern Dance*. Boston, MA: Houghton Mifflin.

Banes, S. (1993). *Greenwich Village 1963: Avant-Garde Performance and the Effervescent Body*. Durham, NC: Duke University Press.

Bishop, C. (2006). *Participation*. London and Cambridge, MA: Whitechapel and MIT Press.

Bourriaud, N. (2002). *Relational Aesthetics*. Dijon: Les Presses du réel.

Briginshaw, V. (1989). 'Egg dances' at the Place, *Laban News*, 7 December.

Burt, R. (1998). *Alien Bodies: Representations of Modernity, 'Race', and Nation in Early Modern Dance*. London and New York: Routledge.

Butler, J. (1990). *Gender Trouble: Feminism and the Subversion of Identity*. New York, NY: Routledge.

Cohen-Bull, C. J. (1997). 'Sense meaning and perception in three dance cultures', in J. Desmond (ed.), *Meaning in Motion: New Cultural Studies of Dance*. Durham, NC, and London: Duke University Press, 269–85.

De Wit, M. (2000). *New Dance Development at Dartington College of Arts, UK, 1971–1987*. Ph D, Middlesex University.

Dove, S. (2014). 'Who gets to perform? The ethics and aesthetics of social practice. *B.A.M. Blog*. <http://bam150years.blogspot.com/2014/12/who-gets-to-perform-ethics-and.html> (accessed 28 December 2014).

Early, F. (1977). 'Report on new dance seminar', *New Dance Magazine*, 3 (summer).

Foster, S. L. (2002). *Dances that Describe Themselves: The Improvised Choreography of Richard Bull*. Middletown, CT: Wesleyan University Press.

Foucault, M. (1978). *The History of Sexuality*. New York: Pantheon Books.

Foundation for Community Dance (2014). Professional Code of Conduct. <http://www.communitydance.org.uk/member-services/professional-code-of-conduct.html> (accessed 27 November 2014).

Gilbert, D. (2014). *A Conceit of the Natural Body: The Universal Individual in Somatic Dance Training*. PhD thesis, University of California at Los Angeles.

Hale, C. (2001). 'In rehearsal with Rosemary Lee', *Dance Theatre Journal*, 12(2): 14–17.

Jordan, S. (1992). *Striding Out: Aspects of Contemporary and New Dance in Britain*. London: Dance Books.

Kester, G. H. (2004). *Conversation Pieces: Community and Communication in Modern Art*. Berkeley, CA: University of California Press.

Lansley, J. (1977). 'Writing', *New Dance Magazine*, 1.

Lee, R. (2012). Discussion with the author.

Lee, R. (2013). 'On taking care'. UK: Arts Admin. Video recording.

Mackrell, J. (1992). *Out of Line: The Story of British New Dance*. London: Dance Books.

Mahmood, S. (2012). *Politics of Piety: The Islamic Revival and the Feminist Subject*. Princeton, NJ: Princeton University Press.

Manning, S. (2004). *Modern dance, Negro Dance: Race in Motion*. Minneapolis, MN: University of Minnesota Press.

Martin, R. (1985). 'Dance as a social movement', *Social Text*, 12: 54–70.

McKay, G. (1996). *Senseless Acts of Beauty: Culture of Resistance since the Sixties*. London and New York: Verso.

Morris, G. (2006). *A Game for Dancers: Performing Modernism in the Postwar years, 1945–1960*. Middletown, CT: Wesleyan University Press.

Novack, C. J. (1990). *Sharing the Dance: Contact Improvisation and American Culture*. Madison, WI: University of Wisconsin Press.

Preston-Dunlop, V. and España, L. M. (2005). 'The American invasion, 1962–1972'. Friends of the Laban Center. Video recording.

Prevots, N. (1998). *Dance for Export: Cultural Diplomacy and the Cold War*. Middletown, CT, and Hanover, NH: Wesleyan University Press and University Press of New England.

Puar, J. K. (2007). *Terrorist Assemblages: Homonationalism in Queer Times*. Durham, NC: Duke University Press.

Roughgarden, J. (2004). *Evolution's Rainbow: Diversity, Gender, and Sexuality in Nature and People*. Berkeley, CA: University of California Press.

Thompson, J. and Schechner, R. (2004). 'Why social theatre?', *The Drama Review—A Journal of Performance Studies*, 48(3): 11–16.

Todd, M. E. (1937). *The Thinking Body; A Study of the Balancing Forces of Dynamic Man*. New York and London: P.B. Hoeber.

Tomko, L. J. (1999). *Dancing Class: Gender, Ethnicity, and Social Divides in American Dance, 1890–1920*. Bloomington, IN: Indiana University Press.

CHAPTER 17

WELLBEING AND THE AGEING DANCER

JAN BOLWELL

... the ageing body leaves ability behind, but experience, which cannot be gained in any other way than by ageing, fills this absence with a lived richness.

Edward and Newall (2011, p. 7)

INTRODUCTION

THE connections between dance and wellbeing are currently being revisioned in the context of a twenty-first-century lifestyle, but they are not new. As far back as the 1920s, British dance pioneer Margaret Morris worked both as a dance artist and as a trained physiotherapist devising remedial dance programmes for diverse sectors of society. She understood that an aesthetic and creative approach to dance technique, improvisation, and choreography could be just as easily applied to the aged and those with special needs as it could to professional dancers. Her emphasis on posture, breathing, spinal mobility, flexibility, strength, rhythm, alignment, and coordination provided the solid core of MMM (Margaret Morris Movement) and remained the bedrock of any dance education. Exemplifying her philosophy of creativity, exercise, and a healthy diet, Morris died at the age of eighty-nine having lived a full and active dancing life.

As with Morris, the fusion of dance aesthetics with principles of exercise has become a preoccupation in my work with mature women. After decades of working in primary and secondary school dance programmes and educating teachers, I have focused my teaching and choreography on this older age group—an area of dance that brings me intense challenge, joy, and satisfaction. In this chapter I chart my experiences of teaching two different cohorts of middle-aged women, one of them a twice-weekly dance exercise programme, and the other, Crows Feet Dance Collective—a performance-based group I began over a decade ago. One cannot work in this area without reflecting on the ageing body and ageist attitudes; therefore, the larger framework of discussion in this chapter is how ageism manifests itself in the worlds of community and professional dance, and how dancers in both contexts deal with these artistic and societal challenges.

A Dance Exercise Class
for Mature Women

On Monday and Thursday mornings a group of middle-aged women bounce into the dance studio full of chat and laughter. They wear brightly coloured loose T-shirts, tights, and trainers, and are happily seen after class in the same clothes at the local shopping mall. In New Zealand we are accustomed to dressing casually most of the time, but even so, when I look at myself in the studio mirror in my sixty-fifth year and at the women in front of me, I am struck by the huge contrast, in only fifty years, between women of our age today and what my grandmother looked like at a similar age. Born in 1896, she was a large, tall woman with a pouter pigeon chest, trussed up in a full body corset beneath matronly dresses of muted shades with stockings and low-heeled court shoes. This was the fashion of her middle and old age, and she was never seen in a pair of trousers, or 'slacks', as she would have called them. She had a lurching 'trendelenburg' gait typical of people with an osteoarthritic hip that eventually was attended to when she was in her eighties. I, on the other hand, am tall, but not as tall as my grandmother. I wear casual, brightly coloured clothes—mostly trousers or jeans—and a corset has never touched my body. I am toned and reasonably muscular after a lifetime's adherence to dance and other forms of physical exercise. I too have osteoarthritis in my hip, but with an active lifestyle of dancing, acting, and teaching dance and yoga, waiting until the age of eighty to have a hip replacement was never an option. I had the operation when I was fifty-eight, which enabled me to continue as normal all my physical activities. Such a life-style would have been utterly unimaginable to my grandmother in her sixties. Within two generations the notion of ageing has altered dramatically, but with all such apparent freedoms, society has yet to embrace the idea that there has been a distinct change in the way we carry ourselves into our middle and later years. Still, we are on the cusp of an ageing revolution as the baby boomers, my generation, redefine what it means to be an older person in a society. How I live out the next two decades of my life will be far removed from my grandmother's experience of old age.

The women in my dance exercise class are not dancers, but I teach them as if they will all acquire a dancer's posture. Heads erect, shoulders down, scapula muscles work-ing, pelvis correctly held. I tell them that the slow careful stretches and core strength exercises we do at the beginning of class should be done for the rest of their lives. My responsibility as a teacher is to ensure that the programme is fun and well balanced, and does not induce injuries. That means a mix of high-impact and low-impact dance move-ments where there is an element of choice; for example, 'you can walk, jog, or run this pattern'. Safe dance practice is essential, for women in this age group come with a range of physical issues that need to be worked around. Music is a powerful motivator in the classes. Margaret Morris maintains that it is 'the aesthetic value of the movement and the music that makes the exercises so satisfying to do, and sustains interest over long periods'. In my experience this is an accurate observation. Music is enabling and I choose it with great care, across a range of genres and styles, as it impacts so significantly on the expressive quality of movement. Apart from the clear physical benefits, psychosocial factors are equally important. In interviewing the women they cite the 'feel-good' factor that dancing brings them, the release of stress, the challenge and sense of mastery, being taken into another realm, doing something just for themselves, making friends, and entering a welcoming and non-threatening environment. This twice-weekly dance class enhances their lives, and attendance is consequently extremely high.

While it is undoubtedly true that young people are successful teachers of older people, there are certain advantages in being of the same age as the class participants. You serve as a role model for them while acknowledging that you face the same issues of the ageing body as they do—a slowing metabolism that can lead to weight gain, knee and hip problems, and cardiovascular disease. In my country those aged 65–74 suffer the highest rates of obesity, with almost two in five adults in that age group obese. Those aged 55–64 are not far behind. University of Otago health researcher Jim Mann finds obese elders suffer diabetes and cardiovascular disease associated with high body weight and sedentary lifestyles with significant costs to the public health system. In New Zealand, even though government social policy (2001) promotes 'active ageing' and 'positive ageing', no public-health dollars target healthy lifestyle initiatives for older people, and such discrimination is not confined just to health.

A Silver Tsunami

Societal prejudice and discriminatory behaviour against older people led to the concept of 'ageism'—a term first coined in 1968 by gerontologist Robert N. Butler (2008). As I write this chapter forty or so years later, ageism has increased in significance because the world is facing a 'silver tsunami'. Population figures released by Statistics New Zealand (2012) reveal that those aged over eighty are the fastest-growing age group, now with one out of every seven New Zealanders over sixty-five. It is not only these figures, mirrored in other developed countries, that give pause for thought, but also that we are ageing differently than ever before. Longevity has become a contemporary social, medical, political, and cultural issue. While lives may be increasingly different for older people, societal attitudes are slower to change. Angus and Reeve (2006) contend that despite empirical studies and public-health initiatives, ageism has not diminished in the early twenty-first century:

> The ageing of society has not significantly changed our perceptions of ageing and the elderly. Ageism—the discrimination against individuals based on their age—is widespread, generally accepted, and largely ignored. Stereotypes that underlay the

pervasiveness of ageism have become so embedded in our perceptions of human life that they are taken for granted and have become unexamined tacit assumptions. (p. 138)

As a baby boomer I am accustomed to reading publicity about how our generation is going to challenge social planners with the cost (read 'burden') of our increasing dependence on society. In contrast to this scenario, recent statistics (Chaston 2012) reveal that one worker in twenty is now aged sixty-five or older—more than 5% of the total workforce in the Western world. In New Zealand more than 18% of everyone over sixty-five is in the workforce—double the number of a decade ago. (Similar trends are seen in the United States.) One of the challenges of the longevity revolution is that we baby boomers may not have the financial resources to sustain a lengthy retirement and will have to work to supplement our incomes. Remaining healthy enough to work may become a major goal of our generation. I remain healthy by using dance as my primary form of physical recreation, teaching my dance exercise class for mature women and running a contemporary dance group, Crows Feet Dance Collective. The former is perfectly acceptable for older women, but theatre dance is more problematic, as one confronts societal barriers and stereotypical ideas of who should dance outside the studio and in the public arena. However, in the past decade, particularly in the United Kingdom, the picture has begun to change. Sadlers Wells has a well-established Company of Elders, and Green Candle Dance Company has created a new diploma course in Leading Dance for Older People. From Here to Maturity is an artist-led company founded in 2000 by former Rambert dancer Ann Dickie, to provide opportunities for mature performers. Scotland's Barrowland Ballet (of 2005) leads the way in intergenerational work, and its recent *Dancing Voices* featured two hundred participants, all of whom were over sixty. Luminate!, Scotland's creative ageing festival, is intent on providing an increased number of older people with high-quality arts activities, whether as participants or as consumers. Even in a country as small as New Zealand we have four dance companies whose focus is older people. While such initiatives give cause for optimism, even celebration, it is also true that ageism is still deeply embedded in Western theatre dance. In the next section I attempt to tease out this phenomenon and profile some individual artists who have made the successful transition from highly athletic young dancers into consummate senior artists.

AGEISM IN WESTERN THEATRE DANCE

Ageism in dance is not new. Decades ago, Marcia Siegel (1976) addressed the topic in a poignantly titled article, 'Growing old in the land of the young'. With regard to ballet, she writes:

The dancer's goal is not only to become a more than perfect being but to remain there, one having achieved the identification. The first place in the ballet company goes to the ballerina, the princess, and not to the friend, the older sister or the wise confidante. Seniority in a ballet company does you some good only if you conceal it. This means that a dancer's experience and maturity have no value in the coin of his/her profession. Older dancers make good teachers, coaches, choreographers, but they cannot use their years on the stage, except in lesser roles. (250)

In comparison with other art forms in which artists often reach their peak in their forties and fifties, the cessation of a career by experienced dancers in their late twenties and mid- to late thirties, common in both ballet and contemporary dance, represent a vast waste of talent. The greater athleticism and technical virtuosity required of today's dancers—higher, faster, further, which mirrors extreme sports—the less the likelihood that senior dancers will find a lasting career in a company. The question remains: how does the mature dance artist leap over the ageist hurdle to sustain a long-term performing career? The answer is that they cannot do this alone. It requires a changed vision and attitude by arts funding bodies, producers, and choreographers to realize the untapped potential of senior dancers.

Cultural norms can change only by active intervention. As Angus and Reeve (2006) state, despite its entrenched nature 'ageism—being socially constructed—can be overturned' (150). Disregard and devaluing of older dancers on stage needs to be confronted and challenged. We need to look afresh at Western dance stereotypes of who can and should, and what, can be performed in the public arena. If more choreographers were to present combined-age dance works, then audiences would gain a richer perspective and deeper appreciation of the scope of Western theatre dance. For dance companies to embrace senior dancers in an age-appropriate manner, the terms of engagement may also need to alter with the implementation of workplace flexibility. Schwaiger (2006) points out, in her doctoral study on the sustainability of dance careers amongst older dancers, that the responsibility of children, houses, and mortgages are not an easy fit with the rigours of dance company touring schedules.

Schwaiger (2006) interviewed thirty dancers who were mostly over forty and ranged in age from twenty-six to sixty-eight. According to some of the older interviewees there is a distinct mismatch between emotional and physical maturity. While a dancer may peak physically in her twenties, full maturity as a performer can happen much later, at around forty:

> Retirement from performing before this point is reached occludes any possibilities of reaching one's performing maturity. (p .3)

Like Siegel before her, Schwaiger concludes that it is Western cultural attitudes in valuing youth, strength, and beauty above all else that result in ageism in the dance world. One hopes—with the culture of rejuvenation evident now amongst the older generation as they challenge perceptions about being 'old'—that dance will be pulled into a re-examination of its prevailing norms.

To date, a minority of Western dance artists have sustained their careers well into middle age, and in some cases old age. What personal characteristics and/or circumstances have enabled them to remain as dancers? Mikhail Baryshnikov, most notably, has, I believe, successfully transitioned from one of the world's outstanding and famous ballet dancers to a contemporary dancer and some-time actor. Baryshnikov and his compatriot, Rudolph Nureyev, both toured New Zealand on different occasions in their mature years, and the contrast between the two artists could not have been greater. Whereas Nureyev drew attention to his waning powers by donning white tights and attempting to dance Balanchine's 'Agon' with a cast of much younger performers, Baryshnikov, dressed in black shirt, trousers, and street shoes, performed a sparse, distilled contemporary dance work which emphasized his mastery of timing and movement, regardless of the genre. But Baryshnikov is not free from constant scrutiny from the media about his age and imminent retirement from dancing. In a visit to Israel where he was acting in a new play 'In Paris', he, exasperatedly, had this to say to reporter Elad Samorzik (2012):

> Listen, I am 63 years old. It depends what you're dancing . . . The piece we did with Ana Laguna [Mats Ek's 57-year-old wife dancing with Baryshnikov in Israel in 2011] we played ourselves, our age. We are not dancing 'Romeo and Juliet'. You know, pas de deux . . . I'm dancing in street shoes and in jeans sometimes. It's called dance too. There are all kinds of movement—look at artists in tango or flamenco or butoh or hula. People dance at any age.

To make wise choices as a senior artist means working with choreographers and directors who understand the limitations placed upon the ageing body, and yet are able to draw upon the strengths that an older dancer brings to the stage in their bodily wisdom and expressiveness.

Lloyd Newson, director of DV8 Physical Theatre, is a prominent artist who has consciously challenged ageism in dance. His work invariably focuses on difference—whether that is age, size, sexual orientation, or physical handicap—in a deliberate attempt to subvert the stereotype of the young, beautiful, and athletically gifted dancer. Newson admits to a low boredom threshold when it comes to an undiluted diet of beautiful dancers making beautiful movement.

Sixty-four-year-old Diana Payne-Meyers appeared in his 1992 work 'Strange Fish'. In an interview in 1992, Newson explained why he chose to work with an older woman:

> I use her because—even now, with the company in their mid-thirties I still find them very young. It is a very young company for me, although for most companies it is probably very old. I am very eager, as I get older, to work with my peers . . . I am very eager to take movement, maybe not pure movement, but I want to be able to look at how older people's lives are revealed through movement . . . I find it a bit arrogant when I go to performances and see eighteen- and nineteen-year-olds trying to tell me about life—and most of the audience is double their age!

At age eighty-four, Meyers is still going strong, performing in a range of different dance theatre works.

The presence of older dancers on stage with younger performers invites the audience to draw comparisons. I recall a memorable performance by the Merce Cunningham Dance Company at the 1979 Edinburgh Festival. The audience was perched on tiered scaffolded seating down one end of a hot, airless gymnasium, while John Cage and his musicians, situated underneath the scaffolding, ensured our full attention by banging loudly on the metal bars that sent constant vibrations up through our seats. In the midst of this cacophony of sound, Merce Cunningham limped on stage in his leotards and tights, turned away from the audience, and performed a constrained solo, occasionally interacting with a single or small group of dancers. Then he limped off stage again. At first I was astounded and discomforted to see this sixty-year-old man on stage, moving amongst svelte athletic dancers. But his presence on stage was riveting and command-ing, and it was impossible not to be deeply moved by his dancing. At the end of the per-formance, half the audience rose to their feet and cheered, while the other half sat in the seats and booed. Were they cheering and booing the man, the work, the company, or all three? It was hard to determine.

Cunningham died at the age of ninety. In his obituary notice in *The New York Times*, Alistair Macaulay (2009) tells us that until the age of seventy Cunningham danced in every single performance given by his company. At eighty he danced a duet with Baryshnikov, albeit holding onto a barre, and was choreographing up until his death. Siegel (1976) reflects on the role Cunningham has played with his company, and in so doing raises the issues/dilemmas that age presents in theatre dance in a way that is never considered problematic in theatre or music:

> The old dancer is past his technical power but wise as a performer. The young dancer's technique gets used in great displays of brilliance but his qualities as an individual are submerged. The old dancer has learned who he is and how he dances, but the dance is passing him by. And both of them are poised where the audience can't quite put itself, doesn't quite want to be, in a state between mystic intelligence and sweat. (254)

In New Zealand, Sir Jon Trimmer is our 'Merce Cunningham'—an artist who has had a fifty-year career with the Royal New Zealand Ballet.

SIR JON TRIMMER

Sir Jon Trimmer's career flies in the face of the trend towards untimely early retirement amongst ballet dancers. Seventy-three-year-old Trimmer is employed as a Senior Artist with the company. Five years ago, aged sixty-nine, he played the lead role in ex-director Gary Harris's new version of *Don Quixote*, during which he was on stage, dancing, and miming virtually the whole time (see Figure 17.1). In an interview with Sir Jon he

FIGURE 17.1. Sir Jon Trimmer in the lead role in the Royal New Zealand Ballet's 2007 production of *Don Quixote*. Reproduced with the kind permission of the Royal New Zealand Ballet. (Photo credit: Maarten Holl.)

attributed his longevity to robust health, eating well throughout his career, and having a natural dancer's body. It is clear that he has managed transitions due to age very skilfully. He believes you can modify classical technique and still have artistry, and it is artistry rather than technique that carries him on. At fifty-five he stopped doing ballet class; 'It wasn't doing anything for me any more. I didn't feel satisfaction with it either mentally or physically.' Even as a young dancer he always practiced yoga—'yoga breathing is the most wonderful thing in the world'—and now yoga and Pilates are his forms of movement training and conditioning. The motivation to keep dancing is because it is still intrinsically and internally part of his life, and he enjoys doing it. 'Your inside is all full of rhythm, you're moving inside and it's wonderful to be able release that through the body.' While he says he sometimes feels on the 'outer edge' as a grandfather figure and craves 'adult company', he still feels needed, and is respected by the much younger dancers who ask his advice, which gives him a role feeding back to the profession. However, he admits that being a member of the company is not enough for him these days, so he teaches mime to drama and dance students, is involved in theatre work, and is an enthusiastic and prolific painter.

The artists profiled here have not attempted to sustain or recreate their younger dancing selves. Working within their physical limitations they have metamorphosed into new and different performers, drawing upon physical skills learned decades earlier and honing them into a rich amalgam that is the mature dancer.

The Habit of Creation

What motivates a dancer to keep performing for years beyond what is customarily thought of as their technical peak? UK choreographers Jacky Lansley and Fergus Early (2011) interviewed twelve distinguished older dancers from a variety of different dance genres. In a radical reappraisal of the cultural norms of who dances and for how long, these artists provided a rich insight into a sustained performance career. The most striking commonality is that they are all choreographers and are vitally interested in the creation and exploration of new movement ideas in different social and cultural contexts. Also, their longevity informs the way they work in rich and complex ways that is part and parcel of their lifestyle. They work in farm buildings, garages, houses, factories, or outside. They have created spaces to work in that reside outside the constraints of institutions and their prevailing movement ideologies. While all have made names for themselves as younger artists, this does not mean that working as older artists is without its challenges. As Lansley and Early (2011) point out, many have struggled economically, and some have also struggled to find a place for themselves in the world of professional dance:

> Despite these realities it is important to understand that this vibrant independent sector has not resulted from artists 'dropping out' of some actual or notional mainstream dance world; on the contrary they have chosen to create and be part of an alternative professional context that has within its practices the resources to be part of much broader cultural fields, encompassing a wide variety of people, disciplines, and social issues. (p.187)

A deep, abiding interest in the art form and intrinsic motivation to continue intellectual, spiritual, and physical exploration of movement must surely be present when it comes to longevity in dance. Delbanco (2011) uses the term 'lastingness' to describe the characteristics of artists who continue to create and produce significant work as they age, while others do not. In his study of Hardy, Haydn, Matisse, Moore, Neel, Sand, Williams,

Casals, O'Keefe, Yeats, and Liszt, among others, he found that while age changed and slowed their output, it did not alter their compulsion to be alive to sensory input and to act upon it:

> What they have in common also is unabated energy—at least in terms of imagination and insofar as physically plausible. They kept on keeping on. Our artists, male and female, do share this attribute of karacter as energeia, both potential and kinetic: an unyielding fealty to the yield of work. (p. 240)

Delbanco's study embraces visual art, literature, and music, but his findings could equally apply to dance artists. Merce Cunningham, on his deathbed, was still creating dances in his head, Martha Graham continued creating despite her increasing infirmity, and Margot Fonteyn danced on (cleverly) into her sixties. Although one can select certain outstanding and idiosyncratic individuals, it still remains true that the societal norm is for dancers not to continue their performing and/or choreographic careers into old age, because, unlike other arts, dance is so closely associated with one's physicality. Western theatre dance, regardless of genre, has a code of physical expectations reliant upon youth and physical virtuosity that instantly makes the older dancer some sort of anomaly.

So far, this discussion has looked almost exclusively at Western dance traditions in terms of ageist attitudes and the constraints placed upon dancers to continue in their careers. I now want to look at specific examples from non-Western cultures from where emerges a very different value system.

Dancing into Old Age in Asia and the Pacific

In 1993 I attended the Japan Asian Dance Event (JADE '93) in Tokyo. The final concert presented as part of this international conference was entitled 'Hogi no Mai', 'Dances for Blessing the Elderly', performed by dancers in their seventies, eighties, and nineties. Kichikoma Wakayagi, then aged ninety-six, danced a classical Japanese dance (nihon buyo) with exquisite skill and sensitivity, and the great Butoh artist Kazuo Ohno, then aged eighty-six, gave a riveting thirty-minute performance that enthralled the packed concert hall. He was still performing at the age of 100, and died at the age of 103 in 2010. His son, Yoshito Ohno, has continued his father's tradition, dancing into his seventies (Lansley and Early 2011). Addressing the conference, Professor Gunji, an eighty-year-old dance artist and scholar, whose own mother was 103, spoke of the power of old age and explained that in Japanese classical dance it is three-tenths technique and seven-tenths spirit. You are criticized if the technique is too much in evidence, for it is the spirit infusing the technique that is important. 'I am a better performer at eighty than

I was at forty because now I am not constrained by technique, and I feel totally free as a dancer.'

In my part of the world—the South Pacific—it is customary for Maori and Pasifika artists to have extended performance careers, but the motivations are very different from those of Western artists. Ageist attitudes are less evident amongst these communities, because older dancers are regarded as repositories of cultural knowledge and not simply as practitioners with fading powers. Cultural preservation is equally as important as pushing creative boundaries. There are cultural leaders throughout Maoridom who see that their role is to create the new and at the same time preserve the old. One such leader is Kuini Moehau Reedy of the Ngati Porou iwi, or tribe from the East Coast of the North Island. Learning traditional Maori performing arts since childhood, this seventy year-old woman is now their guardian:

> Being a keeper of those treasures is important to me because this is the language of the soul; it is not just the spoken language but the body language and it is really important for me to express this through dance and songs and chants. That's how it was kept—by just doing it. This is who I am—communicating with the environment and the environment communicating with me. I feel connected and as one with the universe. (Horsley 2007: 14)

Kuini Moehau Reedy is intensely involved as a performer, creator, and adjudicator in Te Matatini, the national kapa haka (traditional Maori song and dance) competitions, in which the best kapa haka teams from throughout New Zealand compete fiercely for top honours. She is clear in her distinction of what is a dance and music heritage to be preserved, and what can be used as a leaping-off point into the future (Waka Huia 2011) Many older dancers graduate from Te Matatini into a new performing arena that has been set up specifically for kaumatua (elders). The Trust is called He Kura Te Tangata ('The human being is precious'), and provides an opportunity for senior Maori performing artists to share their experience, knowledge, and love of kapa haka (see Figure 17.2).

Kapa haka is a group activity, and although individual performers may feature it is only ever in the context of the group. Most of the performers are over sixty years of age, and they sing waiata (songs) and perform haka (dances) in an authentic manner. Many of these kaumatua have Maori as their first language, so their performances are a means of preserving a language that is under threat, as well as showcasing a subtle style of performance that educates younger performers.

Kapa haka is increasingly seen as a means of contributing to health and wellbeing. A Maori medical professional (Paenga 2008) has described the health-related benefits of kapa haka in a recent study:

> The major findings were that kapa haka is an important vehicle for; the learning and teaching of Maori knowledge, construction of a secure Maori identity which was part of wellbeing, whanaunatanga (making familial connections), and learning skills that could transfer into other areas of life. (pp. vii–viii)

FIGURE 17.2. Kaumatua kapa haka group 'Te Roopu Pakeke o Whakaohoake'. The performers are Raakauoteora Te Maipi, Lovey Kajavala, and Nani Oriwa Law. (Photo Credit: Dick van den Oever.)

In Hawaii, as in New Zealand, a cultural renaissance amongst the indigenous peoples has been under way since the 1970s. One manifestation of this is the Merrie Monarch Hula Competition—the largest Hula Festival in the world. It is a community event, not designed for tourists, and embraces all age groups, from keiki (children) to kupuna (elders). There is also the Kupuna Hula Festival—a special competitive festival held annually for those over fifty-five years of age. Song and dance is the embodiment of Hawaiian culture, and as such, these dancing elders reconnect with their language, mythology, history, and genealogy. But that is not all. Increasingly it is being recognised that there are also positive health outcomes from participation in traditional Polynesian dance for elders. Heart disease disproportionately affects Native Hawaiians and other peoples of the Pacific. A recent study (Look et al. 2012) examined the role that traditional hula dance can play in a cardiac rehabilitation programme. Culturally congruent programmes of exercise can have more appeal and be more motivating for participants than the conventional gym apparatus routine. Results from this study suggested that a hula-based cardiac rehabilitation programme was both appropriate and effective, warranting further development.

A similar initiative for Tongan and Samoan elders has begun in New Zealand (Taoma 2010). The dance exercise programme is called Langi Mai, which means 'sing me a song'. As part of an injury prevention programme run by New Zealand's Accident Compensation Corporation, the elders were participating in tai chi classes, though some were reluctant. They questioned why they could not do their own songs and dances, and so Langi Mai was born, with a steadily increasing number of Pacific-island elders now participating in the programme in the Auckland area. The motivating factors are the fact that the songs are known and understood and that it is natural to dance to them:

> Langi Mai is thus a total experience. It incorporates dance and music but is also about the connection between the participants (and the instructor). It isn't quite zumba but it's just as much fun, easy to do, and being low-impact and gentle on the body is perfect for the elderly. (10)

I have drawn upon examples from Asia-Pasifika cultures to illustrate the different cultural norms towards the ageing dancer. As Schwaiger (2012) points out, the function of dance in non-Western cultures is fundamentally different, with regard to spectacle and physical virtuosity, and therefore the way in which older dancers are viewed is through a very different lens. The narrowness of the Western dance aesthetic and the concomitant waste of talent has been challenged in the past—by Pina Bausch, Liz Lerman, and Ann Dickie, to name but three—and with a swathe of baby boomers redefining what it means to grow older we can expect more and more variants on the model of the Western professional and non-professional dancer. Following this so far wide-ranging discussion about ageism and dance amongst different cultures and types of dance experience, I now to focus on one specific dance group with which I have been intimately involved over the past thirteen years in Wellington, New Zealand.

Crows Feet Dance Collective

Crows Feet Dance Collective, founded in 1999, came about through a series of events. In 1998, at the age of forty-eight, I was twice diagnosed with breast cancer and had a double mastectomy. The illness changed my life. I resigned from my position as head of performing arts at a tertiary education institution, and in order to come to terms with my mutilated body I began dancing again. I wrote my cancer story (Clark 2000). I devised a dance called 'Off My Chest' that featured in a documentary about breast cancer called *Titless Wonders*. With the encouragement of a dance colleague I set up a community dance company for mature performers, and I also became a playwright and creative non-fiction writer. Creative endeavours that were once fitted around the edges of a busy life in education now took centre stage, and have remained there. (See Figure 17.3.)

What began with four dancers in their thirties and forties has expanded into a collective of thirty-five dancers, spread across four different distinct groups whose average age is now fifty-five, with the eldest seventy-two. They are middle-class professional women—heterosexual, lesbian, mothers, grandmothers, artists, arts administrators, counsellors, designers, librarians, writers, teachers, and physical therapists.

There are no auditions for entry into Crows Feet Dance Collective, but to join you must be over thirty-five. Beginners are welcome, but the majority of Crows have some type of dance training (ballet, jazz, contemporary, folk, and/or ballroom dancing),

FIGURE 17.3. Jo Thorpe and Tania Kopytko rehearsing *The Armed Man*, Crows Feet Dance Collective's 2014 World War I dance theatre work. (Photo credit: Penny Evans Inspire Photography.)

which usually did not last beyond childhood or adolescence. Prior learning in, and a strong love of, dance seems to be the prominent motivating factor in joining Crows Feet, and a perception that the Collective was tailor-made to fit their needs. Some of the women found their way to Crows Feet after unsatisfactory experiences in the fitness industry environment doing inappropriate routines to loud music led by young, unsympathetic gym instructors (Liechty and Yarnak 2010).

Lynne—a former professional skier—joined Crows because 'it sounded like the most exciting form of exercise I could do. It seemed to suggest challenge, as I had not danced for years because of lack of opportunity for older women.'

The only barriers or reservations the women identified to joining Crows Feet Dance Collective were the juggling of work/family commitments and the anxiety that they would be not be good enough or would not keep up with the rest. Such fears were usually assuaged because of the inclusive nature of the group, the lack of any competitive attitudes, and a lot of peer tutoring that happens quietly on the side. The initial concept of the Collective was that it would be a performance group; we are always working on new choreography leading to a performance. The repercussions of this decision are that there is a specific focus to the work, the dancers are disciplined in their class attendance and practice conscientiously to be the best they can be, and technical and other performance skills increase, and the Collective has developed a considerable public profile. Documenting their own progress, the Crows Feet dancers have identified the following aspects:

- Increased coordination and flexibility.
- Increased confidence as a performer.
- Able to learn material more quickly.
- Developing a movement memory.
- Learning to move freely and intuitively, anticipating better.
- Daring to improvise and be creative.
- Using our brains.

Liz, a long-term Crows Feet member, has concluded:

> I have always found my ability to remember complex movement sequences as embodied knowledge really challenging, and in the early years of performing with Crows Feet this caused me great anxiety and the feeling of not being good enough. I now realize that although it takes me a long time, I usually get there in the end and stressing is counter-productive.

For Ann, it was the rediscovery of her dancing body: 'I can feel my body returning to that toned state; a reminder of how great it is to be in control of your body.'

One could predict the sort of physical transformations that occur as a result of training and performance, but the emphasis on the cognitive aspect of dancing mentioned by many of the Crows was equally significant and gives support to research, (Verghese, Lipton, Katz et al. 2003) showing the cognitive benefits of dancing for older people.

When asked what was most important about being in the Crows Feet Collective, the women overwhelmingly identified the social aspects. They mentioned the supportive atmosphere, the establishment of real friendships, and the fun and challenge of dancing with a like-minded group of women. The physical challenges of the dance class are met positively because of the empathetic atmosphere in which humour abounds and less experienced or skilful dancers are assisted and feel supported.

Sally, one of the oldest dancers has said: 'Being in Crows Feet I keep fit, physically, emotionally, and spiritually because of my passion which is dance.'

For Tania, the support and assistance given to the less experienced dancers is an important part of the group dynamics: 'The women are amazing and everyone gets along. I like being in a team which generally works well as a unit; we all want the same thing.'

For Crows Feet Collective the psychosocial factors predominate. Studies (Thomas and Cooper 2002; Paulson 2005) reinforce the fact that while the physicality of dance is important for older people, the social context is crucial to their enjoyment. In a comparative study of 'fitness exercise' and 'dance exercise' groups for older people, Paulson found that the fitness group focused on their individual health in physiological terms, whereas the dance group 'focused on moving gracefully in relation to each other as they discipline their minds to control their bodies during the sessions.' As with Crows Feet, they met each other outside class, socializing and arranging extra rehearsals. Camaraderie and the striving for group rather than individual success, where competition is a driving factor, replace the solipsistic nature of the young dancer's world.

Given the prevailing strong association of Western theatre dance with young, beautiful, highly skilled, and athletic bodies, it could be regarded as a subversive act to create a dance performance group of older trained and untrained dancers. As director of Crows Feet I was all too aware of placing the women is a situation in which they could be exposed to ridicule or on the receiving end of scathing comments from critics. In fact, quite the opposite has happened. Crows Feet instantly acquired a loyal and enthusiastic following, largely from women in our age group, and critical commentary has been overwhelmingly positive, placing the Collective's work in an appropriate context and showing a deep appreciation of the women's commitment and artistry. Crows Feet has developed a repertoire of more than twenty works ranging from the serious to the comedic. As a choreographer I feel free and fearless, knowing the Crows will go with me on any journey because we have nothing to lose and no reputations to be upheld—just a love of creating and working together. As dancers, we have a sense of liberation.

A number of the women admit that performing on stage is their greatest fear and their greatest challenge. While many find it stressful, it is 'good stress' because it keeps the group goal driven, raises the skill level, leads to great camaraderie, and leaves everyone with a great sense of joy and achievement. Crows Feet Dance Collective offers a very public challenge to ageist attitudes that are prevalent in our society. Here are older women that are fit, disciplined, creative, and capable of moving an audience to tears or laughter through their artistry. They are not ashamed of ageing bodies; they exude a positive self-image, and present a type of theatre dance that is rare in New Zealand. Asked to respond to the statement that 'the ageing performer is both a potent narrative and a harsh reality' (Edward and Newall 2011) seventy-two-year-old Rachel, the oldest Crow, retorted: 'For whom? The audience? Potency is indeed there in the wisdom, or knowingness, gleaming through the eyes of the ageing dancer. We are not innocently cavorting under the illusion that we are young and gorgeous. We may be self-parodying or reflecting or just having fun, but we have seen it all. We defy you to humiliate us with your condescension. Yes, we are a harsh reality, in that we are your future. What will you be doing from 40 to 90—sitting in the shadows watching the world go by? We are the alternative: embrace it!'

Asked recently by a Crows Feet dancer whether I thought we would still be dancing in twenty years time, my thoughts turned immediately to the memory of ninety-six year old Kichikoma Wakayagi performing her nihon buyo in front of a rapt audience in Tokyo. This was my epiphany on the ageing dancer. This is the reason I could confidently reply: 'Given good health and a continuing love of dance, I cannot see why we will not be dancing into our eighties and beyond.'

CONCLUSION

Whilst dance in the Western world has succumbed largely to the stereotypical view of ageing, it also has the potential to transform that view. Dance can be a potent vehicle for personal growth, freedom, and development as the older person transitions to a new stage in his or her life. The ageing dancer discovers newly found freedoms, and displays self-knowledge and a depth of understanding and interpretation in performance. The ageing dancer is resilient in the face of unpredictable physical and social changes, and is capable of skilful adaptation. The ageing dancer can express and acknowledge personal loss physically and emotionally, but at the same time can look forward rather than back to new joys, new discoveries, and a new level of creativity in a body that encapsulates a 'lived richness'.

REFERENCES

Angus, J. and Reeve, N. (2006) 'Ageism: A threat to "aging well" in the 21st century', *Journal of Applied Gerontology*, 25: 137

Butler, R. N. (2008). *The Longevity Revolution: The Benefits and Challenges of Living a Long Life.* New York, NY: Public Affairs

Clark, M. (ed.). (2000). *Beating Our Breasts*. Auckland, NZ: Cape Catley Ltd.

Delbanco, N. (2011). *Lastingness: The Art of Old Age*. New York, NY: Grand Central Publishing.

Edward, M. and Newall, H. (2011). *Temporality of the Dancing Body: Tears, Fears and Ageing Dears*. IDP Publishers, ebook.

Horsley, F. (2007). 'Guardian of the Dance', *DANZ Quarterly New Zealand Dance*, 8: 14.

Lansley, J. and Early, F. (2011). *The Wise Body: Conversations with Experienced Dancers*. Bristol: Intellect.

Liechty, T. and Yarnal, C. (2010). 'Older women's body image: A lifecourse perspective', *Ageing and Society*, 30: 1197–1218.

Look, M. A., Kaholokula, J. K., Carvhalo, A., Seto T., and de Silva, M. (2012). 'Developing a culturally based cardiac rehabilitation program', *Progress in Community Health Partnerships: Research, Education and Action*, 6 (1).

Macaulay, A. (2009). 'Merce Cunningham dies', *The New York Times*, 27 July.

Paenga, M. D. Te Ahu (2008). *Te Maoritanga Wellbeing and Identity: Kapa Haka as a Vehicle for Maori Health Promotion*. MHSc thesis, AUT University, Auckland.

Paulson, S. (2005). 'How various "cultures of fitness" shape subjective experiences of growing older', *Ageing and Society*, 25: 229–44.

Powers, R. (2010). *Use It or Lose It: Dancing Makes You Smarter*. <http://socialdance.stanford.edu/syllabi/smarter.htm>

Samorzik, E. (2012). 'Mikhail Baryshnikov dances his way to Tel Aviv', *Haaretz*, 29 May.

Schwaiger, L. (2006). *Ageing, Gender and Dancers' Bodies: An Interdisciplinary Perspective*. PhD thesis, Victoria University of Technology, Melbourne.

Schwaiger, E. (2012) *Ageing, Gender, Embodiment and Dance*. London: Palgrave Macmillan.

Siegel, M. (1976). 'Growing old in the land of the young', *The Hudson Review* 29(2).

Statistics New Zealand. (2012). *New Zealand in Profile. Ministry of Foreign Affairs and Trade*. <http://www.stats.govt.nz/browse_for_stats/snapshots-of-nz/nz-in-profile-2012.aspx> (accessed 21 March 2017).

Thomas, H. and Cooper, L. (2002). 'Dancing into the third age: Social dance as cultural Text. research in progress', *Dance Research: The Journal of the Society for Dance Research*, 20(1): 54–80.

Verghese, J., Lipton, R., Katz, M., Hall, C., Derby, C., Kuslansky, G., et al. (2003). 'Leisure activities and the risk of dementia in the elderly', *The New England Journal of Medicine*, 348:2508–16. <http://www.nejm.org/doi/full/10.1056/NEJMoa022252#t=article>.

Waka Huia. (2011). A documentary profiling Kuini Moehau Reedy, prolific composer, kapa haka exponent, writer, and Maori language expert. Television New Zealand, 18 December.

CHAPTER 18

BEING IN PIECES

Integrating Dance, Identity, and Mental Health

MARK EDWARD AND FIONA BANNON

INTRODUCTION

IN writing this chapter our aim is to share a series of remembered life episodes in relation to dance, identity, and mental health. What has become evident in this process is the uncertainty of the present. 'Now' does not exist within its own right; it is a mongrel with a past that still resonates and a future impatient to become present. In composing the journey of a life narrative, we have to leap backwards and forwards, drawing on lived experiences via memory in the moment of writing. What we seek to reveal are pieces of a life, and the cumulative impact of these life episodes from various narratives within which identity is constructed. It is through our individual will to grasp an identity that we seek to discover self-knowledge and to realize wisdom.

In acknowledging that we are each a multiplicity of selves, this chapter centres on a discussion of ageing and mental illness as narrative components of the concept of identity. The reflective narration of one of the authors (Mark Edward) explores ways in which his career in dance has been challenged through mental illness. Equally, a further challenge was to cope with the emotional impact of the foreshortened careers for a dancer. Customarily, dancers have been presented as young, energetic, and graceful, thus requiring ageing dancers to journey towards becoming choreographers or teachers, or to retire. Yet this need not be the case, as Mark witnessed when he was invited to present a keynote speech at the Art of Age (2014) conference, as part of the Elixir Festival at Sadler's Wells, London. Here, mature movers performed powerful dance works that drew the gaze of admiration from critics, audiences, and colleagues. These mature dancers demonstrated that dance can be performed across age ranges without prejudices about their age that seems to be so widespread in professional Western dance contexts. These ageing yet dynamic bodies, including Dominique Mercy (one of the original members of the Pina Bausch Company) and Mats Ek, with his long-time dance companion Ana Laguna, performed contemporary dance works with a rich embodied subjectivity, informed by a wealth of their performance experience. It was mesmerizing to watch. These are dynamic ageing dance bodies that show new possibilities for dance in the future and contribute to ongoing research on ageing in professional dance contexts. Their dancing presence was loud and clear. Dancers can keep dancing beyond 'expectation'.

Both mental illness and ageing affect the body in time, presenting challenges to the body that require negotiation. After experiencing mental illness, and the impact of the onset of ageing, it takes courage and strength to emerge resolute with a determination to live life well and to keep dancing. In choosing to write about these experiences our aim is to situate the performer as self; and as both the researcher and subject of the research. Through our writing process, transitions in identity are formulated through reflexive narrations, traced through embodied memory, dancing nostalgia, loss, reluctance, vulnerability, and mental illness. For, as sociologist Steph Lawler suggests: 'identities are produced through the autobiographical work in which all of us engage every day' (2014, p. 26). In addition, we visit and revisit performances of the past that, whilst created during the ongoing life journey, demonstrate fruitfulness in ways by which we might each embrace change.

ME, MYSELF, AND I(DENTITY)

Bauman states that identity is a theme that has garnered much interest within our time—'identity is the loudest talk in town' (Bauman 2004, p. 7). Identity has panned all academic disciplines within the arts and social sciences, as researchers and authors have begun to turn subjectively to the self. Lawler suggests that in the formation of an individual identity, the use of narrative serves to construct identity; we literally tell our own stories, writing ourselves into being. She discusses how episodic narratives contribute to identity formation and self-understanding:

> In narrating a story, social actors organise events into 'episodes' which make up the plot. In doing so, of course, they draw on memories. But, not only do they interpret those memories, the memories themselves are interpretations. It is not simply that memory is unreliable (although it is): the point is that memories are themselves social products. (Lawler 2014, p. 30)

The stories we tell about our lives and about others, and that others tell about us, all serve to construct an identity. This identity is never concrete, and could more usefully be recognized as something fluid; a mosaic built on narratives. Lawler's work on identity (2014), from a sociological perspective, has a significant contribution to make to discussions of dance and wellbeing. Identity is not a rigid, preordained state of being; rather, it is fluid and changeable. It is this understanding of the nature of identity which corresponds well to discussions of wellbeing. According to Lawler, realizing that identity is never set means that our wellbeing can be more usefully appreciated as a fluid state of interconnecting possibilities. As Catherine Bateson suggests in work where she writes of the ways in which we might be seen to compose our lives,

> . . . we need ways to tell stories that are interwoven and recursive, that escape from the linearity of print to incite new metaphors. I believe that the choices we face today are so complex that they must be rehearsed and woven together in narrative. (Bateson 2000, p. 247)

From this subjective starting point, our first concern in exploring narrative is its current status as a research area. Exploring life stories as a sociological enterprise provides a rich platform from which research paradigms can emerge in dance and somatic practice. That said, life-story investigation can often be discarded as self-indulgent and self-serving. What we argue here is that such endeavour ultimately enables individuals to come to value others, because during this process one learns to retain self-awareness within a context of a duty of care for self, and others. As such, research that is self-serving is absolutely essential to integrating an art form, a life, and one's wellbeing. This is nothing new. In the 1950s, Mooney wrote: '. . . research is a personal venture which, quite aside from its social benefits, is worth doing for its direct contribution to one's own self-realization' (1957, p. 155). In a desire to move away from the assumed power of rationality in terms of knowledge and the gradual move towards engagement with qualitative research as a valid methodology, putting oneself in the place of a non-neutral research subject adds new weaponry to the battle of the worth of knowledge. In striving for rigour, objectivity, and scientific sanitization within research, the self has often been closeted or, at worst, buried.

Our second concern is one in which we acknowledge that the research area is murky, simply because there is no objective journey to the past. Indeed, the past is negotiated and renegotiated in order to provide a comprehensible sense of the subject's identity. Ricoeur (1991b) calls this 'narrative identity'. Lawler (2002) shares this concern when she argues that 'neither researcher nor researched can fully access or inhabit a past which is inevitably gone' (p. 248). Yet what is significant is the present negotiation and renegotiation of the past. It is the present interpretation of the past that helps us to make sense of our lives and ourselves. Being both the storyteller and the interpreter of one's own life is a position which allows us to reflect on our own identity and wellbeing. Ricoeur agrees when he argues that '. . . narrative mediation underlines this remarkable characteristic of self-knowledge—that it is self-interpretation' (1991a, p. 198).

DANCE AND WELLBEING

In framing what they call a 'lifespan model', Myers et al. (1998) define wellness as 'a way of life oriented toward optimal health and well-being in which the body, mind, and spirit are integrated [. . .] to live more fully'. These sentiments are evidently based on the longstanding pledge shown in the preamble to the Constitution of the World Health Organization (1946) that health is 'a state of complete physical, mental, and social well-being, and not merely the absence of disease or infirmity'. With this as our shared foundation it is evident that physical, psychological, and social factors contribute direct vitality to our life experience—something distinctly different to what some see as only utopian ideals.

Writing in 1934, pragmatist aesthetician John Dewey highlighted the importance of maintaining interactions between our sensory experiences, the environments in which we live, and work coupled with our critical abilities. His arguments remain relevant today, for if we cannot give attention to the complex patterns of our interactions then we might expect only a narrowing of experience and aspiration. In what we have started to frame for Mark as an everyday aesthetic life-world, the desire to draw together evaluations that are stimulated and realized through bodily sense remains clear. To come to rely during the formative parts of one's life on a self-identity characterized as a moving thinking being can present issues later. These issues occur when one's life-world remains framed as a nostalgic view of a past that is reinforced by a societal habit that capitalizes on youth culture.

There is an art to living well, to attending and taking care of oneself, and this follows the lead of Foucault when he speaks of 'epimeleia heauton'—a care of the self (Foucault 1988). In what is primarily an ethical drive to examine who we are, who we might come to be, and what we ultimately find ourselves capable of doing, there is a style of life in which acknowledging the pieces that contribute to the whole, that shape our presence and embodiment, is vital. In facing human life directly, Foucault argues, we face the possibilities of suffering, injury, dreams, and difference that we each need to work to integrate into 'a coherent whole' (Lotringer 1989, p. 319) and so in time take possession of ourselves differently and facing what Foucault refers to as 'producing ourselves'.

It was Husserl (1936) who introduced the metaphor 'life-world', though according to Eckartsberg (1998) what is perhaps most important to retain from the concept is that it attempts to account for the fullness of experience; a purposeful attending to 'lived' experiences. The prize is to remember, recognize, and revalue the potential richness and flourishing that experiences offer throughout a life journey. To live well is to be aware of the many facets of your own being, and this exists in continuous negotiation with the fluid nature of experiences. Segal (1999) captures these sentiments effectively when she argues that we need to think in terms of determined self-study rather than evade it:

> ... our own most cherished conceits, stubborn evasions, or persistent illusions are all fashioned by a growing stock of cultural narratives, as we try to make sense of the past and its connections to our lives in the present. (Segal 1999, p 118)

In exploring such an integration within a dance setting, we engage with a realization of selves, where the performance of the artist is not separated from the experience of making meaning of life (Kaprow and Kelly 1992). Our interest is to embrace living life more fully through enhanced personal knowledge, where 'being-embodied' acknowledges the multiple narratives which produce one's identity, including the stories we tell about ourselves and the stories other people tell about us. Thus, the phenomenon of wellness of self relies on our identity being intact—a position that is both singular and multiple. This tasks each of us with the curious phenomenon of self-interpretation in seeking to know oneself.

To consider the affective resonance of such self-recognition, we have chosen examples in which Mark has situated himself within the practice, as actor, dancer, drag queen, and imitator of iconic dance images. These projects include *Falling Apart at the Seams* (2008), *Council House Movie Star* (2012) and *Dying Swans and Dragged Up Dames* (2013). The three research projects provide access to Mark's collaborative work as he narrates the negotiations of ageing and ability, valuing his new embodiment and journey towards mental wellbeing. For Mark, mental wellbeing is always a journey, not a destination. *Falling Apart at the Seams*, *Council House Movie Star*, and *Dying Swans and Dragged Up Dames* are works that deliberately make visible the changing nature of bodies and our embodied selves, investigating the variability and potentiality of self-identity.

PERFORMANCE, AGEING, AND MENTAL HEALTH

Studies that consider how mature artists negotiate age are relatively recent, while studies that consider how artists negotiate mental health remain rare. Recent scholarship in the field of ageing studies among mature movers includes the research of Helen Thomas (2013). She notes how the study of the body in traditional sociology was seldom explored, and that its focus was on the social in dialogue with natural sciences, during modernity. Thomas claims that 'the radical cleavage between the natural sciences (*Naturwissenschaft*) and the cultural sciences (*Geisteswissenschaften*) in German sociology in particular reinforced this separation of the social over the natural' (2013, p. 9). She goes on to explain 'that it was not only the body that was neglected in classical sociology; other topics such as touch, emotions, and sexuality, which are also associated in some way with the body, were also marginalized' (p. 10). Thomas's work is highly significant in that it provides a bridge to address the lacuna in debates about age and performance. In other work—for example, that of Coupland (2003)—consideration is given to a persistent duality between the ageing body with the 'self' as mind, proposing that the mind does not experience the same vulnerability to time:

> Our bodies are old, we are not. Old age is thus understood as a state in which the body is in opposition to the self. We are alienated from our bodies. (Coupland 2003, p. 5)

Similarly, Featherstone and Hepworth (1991) discuss a 'mask of ageing', which reflects the dualism of ageing, as the mind and body have contrasting and conflicting experiences.

In their study, ageing is considered a 'mask' in which an individual may suppress their subjective sense of age in contrast to the appearance of the body. Thomas agrees with the perspective, arguing that 'there is a gap between the recognition of the outward physical appearance of the ageing body' (2013, p. 110). Whereas the mind will contain the narrative and memory of the body, the body itself comes under scrutiny for critique. Simply expressed, the mind does not age, and the older body places restrictions on this youthful mind with memories of the athleticism and a particular type of beauty the body used to be able to produce. This emerges as an imperfect juxtaposition where the mind and body remember the past, which could be experienced as a form of grieving for the past. Gullette (1999) states:

> It would appear that an increased visibility of ageing flesh in dance concerns the dismantling and the disrupting of the stereotype and visually challenges the legitimatization of what body should or should not dance. It involves a cultural critique of ageing and for the older dancer to 'reconnect with one's distinctive life story and unique subjectivity. (p. 55)

As Gullette states, it is important to note how the cultural and social contexts denote a negativity towards ageing, as witnessed through consumerist culture. Featherstone and Hepworth's research in the 1980s and 1990s brought to light how ageing is affected by images of the aged and a policing of the skin through the media and advertising. Their studies explored the frameworks for an extended lifespan and sought to extend the middle-aged period for a much longer duration.

Aside from age, it is important to consider other dialogues on the relationship between the mind/spirit and the body. An example of this is the work of sociologist Erving Goffman. Within his contribution to Shilling's volume *The Body and Social Theory* (1993), Goffman cites three key concepts addressing the self and external policing of the body and the self-expression, social, and self-identity of the body:

1 The body is the material property of individuals, which individuals control and monitor in order to interact.
2 Individuals present and manage their bodies in accordance with shared vocabularies of body idiom that are not individually controlled but are hierarchically set and symbolically charged.
3 The body mediates the relationship between self-identity and social identity; consequently, the social meanings attached to bodily display and expression are an extremely important factor in an individual's sense of self, and his or her feelings of inner worth. (Goffman, in Shilling 1993, pp. 82–3)

Thus the regulation of bodies by mainstream traditional Western dance culture is one which seeks to remove personal expressions, and places an emphasis on lean bodies. The result is the promotion of an eradication of visual signs of physical ageing, such as wrinkles and fat. This can be experienced as a form of controlling, monitoring, and

policing the matured body. Thomas discusses the visual manifestation of ageing, following Featherstone and Hepworth, who argue:

> The perceived signs of ageing are not individual, but are part and parcel of a restrict-
> ive discourse of ageing which, as Featherstone and Hepworth (1991) argue, impedes
> the possibilities for a different mode of self-expression. (Thomas 2013, p. 112)

Within the arena of professional dance, the persistence in terms of demand for bodies, which are strong, muscular, and physically vibrant, perpetuates age discrimination.
Intense training to achieve and maintain such ideals begins at a very young age, and this
forces dancers to have relatively short career-spans. In mainstream conservative dance
there appear to be specific criteria regarding an ideal leg extension or idealized/idolized
body, ultimately drawing us towards an approach to the body as commodity. Society
prefers bodily aesthetics that please the gaze in a very particular way: a gym culture worthy of sweat, pain, and 'muscularization', a 'techno body' (Cooper-Albright 1997, p. 28),
or a body sculpturing worthy of the gaze.

Dance as an industry, career, and discipline needs to increase the visibility of older dancing bodies in order to dislodge age discrimination. We need to encourage the visibility
of the ageing form in order for it to become 'normalized' within performance contexts.
The increasingly frequent participation of ageing dancers within performance would
challenge the assumption that performers should be always youthful, and would normalize the presence of ageing dancers on stage. The unpacking of ageing, vulnerability,
and normative bodies through performance visibility, theories, and practice of deconstruction need to be developed further if we are to move the art form on from its fixation
with youth. The value of including ageing bodies within dance performance cannot be
negated. Aside from the living archive which is embodied in skeletal and muscular form,
there is also a sense of 'loss' which is embodied, as the dancer has had to negotiate his or
her own capabilities. We should seek to eradicate notions of the older dancing body being
less valuable or unable, as there should be 'a practice in which societies negotiate around
bodily value and bodily order' (Shepherd 2006, p. 20) and 'where the limits of the body
are negotiated [. . .] imagined somehow else' (Shepherd 2006, p. 20). We hope to expand
the cultural and social significance of the ageing performer through developing a deeper
understanding of performing one's own age and a body reflexive practice.

Moving from this extensive discussion of ageing, our attention now turns to mental health. Mental illness is traumatic. That does not mean that mental illness needs to
have been linked and traced back to a traumatic event. People who suffer from mental illness experience similar symptoms and traits with survivors of trauma. This is further compounded to some degree by the external and internalized negativity or lack of
understanding towards mental illness in which we live, grow, and come to know ourselves. Those who experience mental illness understand the ordinariness of trauma all
too well. It is a never-ceasing trauma. The movement from modernity to postmodernity is also one of significance in terms of mental wellbeing. Gilbert (2011) states that 'in
terms of mental health, then, a move from modern to postmodern forms of identity has

both advantages and disadvantages' (p. 159). As Foucault reminds us, modernity was not driven by any straightforward liberation of people to be their own being. Instead, it hailed the introduction to the notion that each of us faces a continuing task of producing ourselves, inasmuch as we have to learn to negotiate our ever-changing context. Life, with all its wandering, differences, and lines of flight, positions us as a being constructed of many pieces (Rabinow 1997).

In what appears to be a growing cultural acceptance of the use of synthetic chemical controls as a method of treatment, it seems that the profits of global pharmaceutical industry have priority over the treatment of individuals suffering from a mental illness. The relative ease with which repeat prescriptions can be written and reissued decreases an individual's access to the sense of 'flourishing' that we aim to promote here. Given time to be in dialogue with our ideas and ourselves, in moving and in conversation with others, we might come to understand the connectivity of life experiences, and of the very ways in which we can come to make sense together. If our time is lost in a haze of only drug-induced suppression, then our ability to live with the nuances of change around and within us is deflated too.

What Mark continues to explore is the creation of new performances drawn from the very life narratives that are the pieces of his complex life, where emotion, memories, and personal associations coalesce as ways to form thought. In this practice of living well resides the ethical drive to examine the multiple pieces of his life, coming to know who he is, what he can do, and in the ever changing advances of time, what he is capable of coming to be. This involves engaging in uncertainty, and learning to be comfortable in this uncertainty. This allows us to come to know ourselves differently.

In the next section, Mark narrates his own trauma rooted in the experiences of his long-term mental illness. Coupled with the realization of the impact of ageing on his dancing form and technique, Mark's narrative depicts how identity was renegotiated and then rerepresented within three performance works: *Falling Apart at the Seams* (2000, 2006, 2008), *Council House Movie Star* (2012), and *Dying Swans and Dragged Up Dames* (2013, 2014).

VULNERABLE VISIBILITY? 'COMING OUT' AND MENTAL HEALTH

Regarding academic housekeeping in the production of this chapter, first-person pronouns (I/my) are used to relate to Mark's experiences. What also becomes evident in this chapter is the journey that the co-authors Fiona and Mark share, where there are echoes of many of the conversations that they have together—across late-night e-mails about theorists, performances, conferences, and life. The chapter explores the journey they have undertaken together, including some of the themes, which highlight their ongoing relationship and scholarship.

In making the decision to share my narrative about dance, wellbeing, and mental health from a personal perspective I enter into a dialogic negotiation with my own process of ageing, reflecting on, and coming to value my maturing performing form. This is something that not only necessitates a degree of self-exposure but an inevitable accompanying vulnerability. Through my performance investigations I explore a personal paradigm for the expression of myself, sustaining the possibilities of performance beyond the discriminating cultural backdrop of dancing youthful elitism. Dancer, composer, and somatics practitioner Scott Smith (2008) highlights the importance of experience as beneficial to the mature mover, as he or she moves away from the more codified and rigid dance technique forms. I am in agreement with his advocacy of an appreciation of one's individual selfhood, which should be prioritized over rigid technique forms:

> There is something about the accumulation of experience that emerges in performing that has very little to do with technique . . . As time goes on, dance becomes less about technique and more about somatics, about the uniqueness of the individual body, rather than having to conform to a set of practices and ideas. (2008, p. 10)

My practice in *Falling Apart at the Seams*, *Council House Movie Star*, and *Dying Swans and Dragged Up Dames* interrogates the process of those bodies that have moved beyond the physical inscriptions of a stylized language in dance performance, relating to age, bodily aesthetics, and (cap)ability to maintain a technical athleticism.

It is the summer of 2014 and I am writing this part of the chapter whilst sitting on my friend's balcony high up in the hills of La Siesta in Ibiza. I have taken a holiday, as I needed some time to reflect and allow myself some healthy headspace before continuing with this collaborative chapter. As I type, my mind reflects on my past and the impact that mental illness and ageing angst has had and still has on me. I hear in the background on the Spanish news station that the Hollywood actor Robin Williams has committed suicide through the effects of depression. This has thrown some of my thoughts into those dark moments when I had to resist those strong desires and urges to overdose on my hoard of pills or jump into the canal water that is near to my hometown. Maybe the former would have been painstakingly long. Maybe the latter would have impacted upon an innocent passer-by. Two of my aunties, who I adored as a child, killed themselves: one was found dead in the bath after overdosing on pills, and the other through jumping into the canal at Wigan Pier. On reflection, maybe I resisted the urge to die as I did not want to be another family suicide statistic, or I just did not have the courage it takes to end a life. Whichever it may be, I am still here to share my story, and they are not.

Regarding my own mental health I have what I term 'transient mental illness', which put simply means I have good and bad days. For those who work professionally within the arts and academia and, like myself, suffer from the challenge of maintaining one's mental wellness, my narrative may help pave the way for further awareness for those who suffer. Of course, there are those who suffer from the challenges of mental ill health without any reference to this part of their identity; they achieve their aim in passing as mentally well. I have been very accomplished at pretending the latter, but it is fruitless. Like all identity politics, which involve a process of 'coming out', I am fully aware this can be a liberating experience. But this process of 'coming out' should not be misunderstood as a recovery process. Nor do I see my reflections here as a form of narrative therapy. My aim is to share my experiences in order to pit myself among those who feel they are imprisoned by their own illness. The act of sharing these experiences allows the silence on mental illness to be broken, and it becomes possible to articulate the suffering and impact this has on some people's lives.

I have never had to 'come out' to my family as gay. They did not flinch when I swapped my hairdressing scissors for ballet pumps and attempt to shock my Dad by gaining my first employment as a drag queen. Nor have I had to 'come out' to my family as mentally unwell. I think there is a mutual understanding between my sisters and myself and my parents and myself, and a discussion of medication, paranoia, and the problems with psychiatry are just as commonplace in my family home as my 42-year-old self trying on stilettos and charity-shop chic gowns to dress for my latest performance. Let me just adhere to the 'coming out' analogy before I move on. My only 'coming out' has been in relation to my own mental health. I think it is important for those who cannot 'read' mental illness that I am able to tell them I am not feeling too good on a particular day; that in itself is an achievement. Here there is a sense of learning to recognize my signs, after having spent time knowing what I need and appreciating that context, relation-ships, and mutual respect make a difference. Day-to-day existence has required con-tinuous renegotiation in order to create the capacity to adapt as a survival mechanism, but also to acknowledge when time-out calls and I need to step away. This relies on a continuing improvization that often exhibits itself as a form of collaborative caring with significant others in my life.

As an ageing performance artist and self-identifying gay man with long-term men-tal illness, I seek to challenge areas of performing sexuality, gender, ageing, and ability through the works I choreograph, perform, and exhibit. Within the range of work I have created, both practical and written, I explore intersections between my own ageing in dance, my onset of arthritis, and constant fluctuations in body weight. For those who do not know my work, the themes I investigate do not take mental illness as the major focus. Instead, the recurring threads in my work are of playful absurdity in a distilla-tion of what I experience as reality. Examples include six-foot dancing rabbits in *Falling Apart at the Seams* (2000, 2006, 2008). *Dying Swans and Dragged Up Dames* (2013) performs re-enactments of me/I as dance legends Martha Graham, Moira Shearer, and Anna Pavlova. In *Council House Movie Star* (2012) I resurrected a council house within a derelict building to reignite the warbles of my past through an ageing drag queen per-sona; after all, art imitates life.

The starting point when creating *Falling Apart at the Seams* was my own interest as a dancer to explore the ageing process for dancers who spend their careers working in an arena where an elite level of physicality and athleticism are typical expectations in the professional field. *Falling Apart at the Seams* began as a debate between notions of repertory versus the individual performer, and explores the theme of the ageing practitioners, their egos, insecurity, denial, and destruction. The work was originally developed in a rehearsal laboratory over a number of weeks in 1999, and was presented as a twenty-minute dance theatre duet in 2000. The dance theatre piece focuses on two performers who appear on stage as gladiators of the long-gone past, yet both are in severe denial. Dark humour, cracking hip bones, dodgy lip synching, substandard phrase work, and a constant urge to take centre spotlight is the undercurrent of the piece.

The work highlights that dance is an arena where contract leads to competition. Similarly to sportspersons, the traditional career trajectory of a dancer is restrained through bodily facility or injury. There are added pressures in terms of the availability of work and the high levels of competition for both men and women in securing a contract. Dancers in their early thirties are considered ripe for retirement. In 2007, *Falling Apart at the Seams* was revisited, culminating in a seventy-minute dance theatre performance for two contemporary dancers and a former British variety octogenarian. At the time, as a thirty-something dancer, I had the physical capability to execute the piece: I aged myself through parodying the technique I could still perform quite easily. In 2008 I suffered from an acute bout of mental illness, immediately following the re-production of the work. The real irony of the piece came post-performance. The Mark who I aged up in order to perform the piece was ageing beyond control as I sought to survive each day and escape the battlefield of the mind. People around me who gave support and protected me during that time sought to investigate what the trigger to this episode was. (See Figures 18.1 and 18.2.) Had I taken too much on in creating a full-length performance piece in addition to working full time in a leadership position within the university? Was it fluctuations in my personal life? Was it God? The questions were numerous, but there was just one simple conclusion: being mentally unwell was a part of me. I thought I had escaped it, but it came back to remind me of its hold. The hold is no longer there. I know where I have been, and I know I have the strength and capacity to survive. And the patience.

In the future I may consider revisiting the original twenty-minute dance theatre performance of *Falling Apart at the Seams*, working through bodily memory, accompanying visual documentation, and written reflective diaries. The objective would be to revisit, re-examine, and reconcile physical disruptions between my performance re-enactment and my own facility in dancing a work hosted by a much younger and slimmer me. This process of re-presenting this work challenges me critically and reflectively in terms of a dance theatre project spanning ten years of touring. Mentally I know I can recreate the performance in my sleep, but the physical capacity required to do so may need some further investigation.

Dying Swans and Dragged Up Dames is a collaboration with my colleague Professor Helen Newall. It explores and interrogates iconic cultural images of the agile and able performer. The photographs represent iconic images of dance artists, from modern dance and traditional ballet, which are reinterpreted and 'queered'. The images include re-enactments of dancers such as Moira Shearer, Martha Graham, Rudolf Nureyev, and

FIGURE 18.1. Mark Edward in Falling Apart at the Seams. (Photo credit: Stuart Rayner.)

Vaslav Nijinski. The work presents a living archive of my body, revisiting of past dance repertoire, and bringing back to life iconic dance imagery. Although I am not an historian, I am delving into my own biography where the study of a distant dancing self and the somatic archaeology of my past(s) are being retrieved. This self-body archaeology is further developed by Davis et al. (2011), who value 'the cultural position from which we revisit the past being as potent as the contexts of the past we seek to investigate' (p. 96). The piece explores the myths of the dance world that these images become iconic and stationary, but my experience of dance is one of an ever-changing self. The piece required me to reassign my embodied feelings and sensibility to performing another. In sourcing the costume for the piece, there was a playful parody in visualizing dance in a way that traditional dance has avoided. I experience a perverse pleasure in knocking the modernist dance giants from their pedestals. These were the dance giants whose

FIGURE 18.2. Mark Edward in Falling Apart at the Seams. (Photo credit: Stuart Rayner.)

techniques and body languages got under my skin, gradually penetrating my bones, muscles, and identity. Now my bones were experiencing the early onset of arthritis, and the muscle memory was stronger than the muscle capacity.

Within *Dying Swans and Dragged Up Dames*, I offer myself for scrutiny as I put a visual image of my body in different forms up for public spectatorship. As I re-enacted previous dance pieces from iconic past performers, my body revisited techniques I may not have used for decades. (See Figures 18.3–18.5.)

Council House Movie Star began from a passing comment; even insult turned on its head. On exiting a fun pub in the late 1980s, someone commented on my recent success in performances and labelled me a '*Council House Movie Star*'. Embracing the subjectivity of such a statement, combined with an appreciation of my working-class roots, I began to explore the resurrection of my first performance experiences as a drag

FIGURE 18.3. Mark Edward as 'Moira's Angst' in *Dying Swans and Dragged up Dames*. (Photo credit: Helen Newall.)

FIGURE 18.4. Mark Edward as 'Arthur Graham' in *Dying Swans and Dragged up Dames*. (Photo credit: Helen Newall.)

FIGURE 18.5. Mark Edward as 'Angina Pavlova' in *Dying Swans and Dragged up Dames*. (Photo credit: Helen Newall.)

queen, long before modernist dance invaded my frame. Indeed, this exploration of performance that did not rely on traditional technique or acknowledgement of traditional dance history was a feeling of liberation.

The personal saturated the creation of the performance, as production materials sourced were original, personal possessions I had kept over time. The characters in the piece, including my 83-year-old mother (Sylvia), matriarchal drag queen Chris D' Bray, and the local council estate youths, were all personal friends and previous collaborators of mine. (See Figures 18.6–18.9) Maddison argues that 'drag's status as performance keeps it safely at a distance' (2002, p. 158), yet my performance arena included public settings such as shops, and a former industrial warehouse in the north-west of England where the piece was shown. Such dislocation removed the 'safe space', yet being surrounded with familiar friends and collaborators enabled such a risk-taking performance piece to offer some personal security.

CONCLUSION

This chapter moved from the theoretical to the practical appreciation of the wellbeing of an individual performer. We must remember that performers are entwined in

FIGURE 18.6.   Gale Force and Chris D' Bray in *Council House Movie Star*. (Photo credit: Victoria Tetley, *Liverpool Echo*.)

stories that not only include the piece they are interpreting, but also the stories that are significant parts of their lives, whether hidden or open to view. With dance remaining saturated in a gaze of bodily aestheticism privileging young age, it continues to be demanding of strength of mind as well as physical stamina. What is needed is for the practice to be equally as demanding in terms of embracing the individual performer with an holistic, person-centred method. Mark's retelling of performances punctuated with the personal life-stories signposts the path for a subjective turn to self within the arts, through which research does not seek to dull the emergence of the inherent 'mesearch'. For it is in the stories that we experience and share that we come to construct our identities and experience the world.

We acknowledge the individual as more than being a tool for technical achievement, and that dance is maturing, as is information about many different aspects of the art

FIGURE 18.7. Mark Edward in the process of becoming Gale Force in *Council House Movie Star*. (Photo credit: Stuart Rayner.)

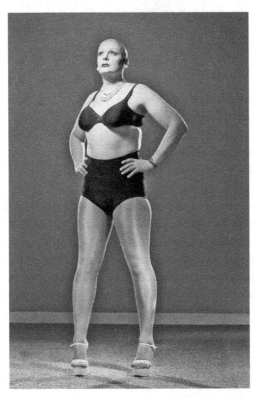

FIGURE 18.8. Mark Edward in the process of becoming Gale Force in *Council House Movie Star*. (Photo credit: Stuart Rayner.)

FIGURE 18.9. Mark Edward (as Gale Force) and his 83-year-old-mother in *Council House Movie Star*. (Photo credit: Chris D' Bray.)

forms. Dance has come to mean different things to Mark. His investigating how this art form can continue to make significant difference to his life and living well without the aid of psychological sciences is evident in his body of works. There is something about the captivating experience of creating and performing that helps Mark understand himself as a moving thinking dancer and a person living well.

Despite the focus on ageing and wellbeing as core themes in this chapter, we wish to conclude with a final yet significant observation. Wellbeing is not the privilege of the experienced and ageing performer. Arts-based practitioners and educational settings need to support and embed mental wellbeing practices as integral to their core mission statement for all ages—from youth to mature settings. The potential correlation between arts-based creative industries and mental illness should not be underestimated. Some argue that the arts can enable positive mental wellbeing to flourish, through building confidence, positive self-esteem, and exploring the relationships we have with ourselves, whether through dance, theatre, music, storytelling, or visual art. Within such context, and in addition to performing well, we must ensure that we live well. For as Joan Tronto suggests in calling for a route to sustained enrichment, what we need is to adopt a species view that interweaves ways that we might 'maintain, continue, and repair our world' (Tronto 1993, p. 103).

References

Bateson. C. (2000). *Full Circle Overlapping Lives*. New York, NY: Ballantine Books.

Bauman, Z. (2004). *Identity Conversations with Benedetto Vecchi*. Cambridge: Polity Press.

Cooper-Albright, A. (1997). *Choreographing Difference: The Body and Identity in Contemporary Dance*. Hannover, NH: University Press of New England.

Coupland, J. and Gwyn, R. (2003). *Discourse, the Body and Identity*. London: Palgrave.

Davis, J., Normington, K., Bush-Bailey, J., and Bratton, J. (2011) 'Researching theatre history and historiography', in B. Kershaw and H. Nicholson (eds.), *Research Methods in Theatre and Performance*. Edinburgh: University of Edinburgh Press.

Dewey, J. (1934/1980). *Art as Experience*. New York: Perigee Books.

Featherstone, M. and Hepworth, M. (1991). 'The midlife style of "George and Lynne": Notes on a popular strip', in M. Featherstone, M. Hepworth, and B. S. Turner (eds.), *The Body: Social Process and Cultural Theory*. London: Sage.

Foucault, M. (1988). *Technologies of the Self: A Seminar with Michel Foucault*, ed. L. H. Martin, H. Gutman, and P. H. Hutton. Amherst, MA: University of Massachusetts Press.

Fraser, M. and Greco, M. (2005). *The Body: A Reader*. London: Routledge.

Gilbert, P. (2011). 'Mental health, spirituality and religion', in J. Atherton, E. Graham, and I. Steedman (eds.), *The Practices of Happiness: Political Economy, Politics and Wellbeing*. Abingdon: Routledge.

Gullette, M. M. (1999). 'The other end of the fashion cycle', in K. Woodward (ed.), *Figuring Age: Women, Bodies, Generations*. Bloomington, IN: Indiana University Press, pp. 34–55.

Husserl, E. (1936). *The Crisis of European Sciences and Transcendental Phenomenology*, trans. David Carr (1970). Evanston, IL: Northern Illinois University Press, p. 139.

Kaprow, A. and Kelly, J. (eds.) (1992). *Essays on the Blurring of Art and Life*. Berkeley, CA: University of California Press.

Lawler, S. (2002). 'Narrative in social research', in T. May (ed.), *Qualitative Research in Action*. London: Sage, pp. 242–58.

Lawler, S. (2014). *Identity*. Cambridge: Polity Press.

Lotringer, S. (ed.) (1989). *Foucault Live: Interviews, 1966–84*. New York: semiotext(e).

Maddison, S. (2002). 'Small towns, boys and ivory towers' in J. Campbell and J. Harbord (eds.), *Temporalities, Autobiography and Everyday Life*. Manchester: Manchester University Press.

Mooney, R. L. (1957). 'The researcher himself', in *Research for Curriculum Improvement: Association for Supervision and Curriculum Development, 1957 Yearbook*. Washington, DC: Association for Supervision and Curriculum Development, pp. 154–86.

Myers, J. E., Sweeney, T. J., and Witmer, M. (1998). *Wellness Evaluation of Lifestyle*, <http://www.mindgarden.com> (accessed 10 May 2011).

Rabinow, P. (ed.) (1997). *Michel Foucault: Ethics, Subjectivity, and Truth*. New York: The New Press.

Ricoeur, P. (1991a). 'Narrative identity', transl. D. Wood, in D. Wood (ed.), *On Paul Ricoeur: Narrative and Interpretation*. London: Routledge.

Ricoeur, P. (1991b). 'Life in quest of narrative', transl. D. Wood, in D. Wood (ed.), *On Paul Ricoeur: Narrative and Interpretation*. London: Routledge.

Segal, L. (1999). *Why Feminism? Gender, Psychology, Politics*. Cambridge: Polity Press.

Shepherd, S. (2006). *Theatre, Body, Pleasure*. London: Routledge.

Shilling, C. (1993). *The Body and Social Theory*. London: Sage.

Smith, S. (2008, Winter). Cited in Diane Parker, 'What's Age Got to do With It?', *Dance UK* 67, pp. 10–11.

Thomas, H. (2013). *The Body and Everyday Life*. New York, NY: Routledge.

Tronto, J. (1993). *Moral Boundaries: A Political Argument for an Ethics of Care*. New York, NY: Routledge.

World Health Organization (1946). Preamble to the Constitution of the World Health Organization as adopted by the International Health Conference, New York, 19–22 June 1946; signed on 22 July 1946 by the representatives of 61 States (Official Records of the World Health Organization, no. 2, p. 100) and entered into force on 7 April 1948.

CHAPTER 19

WRITING BODY STORIES

JUNE GERSTEN ROBERTS

INTRODUCTION

IN 2013, dance artist Gerry Turvey marked her sixtieth birthday with performances of *Body Stories*—a solo dance, visual art, and digital video installation mapping the life journeys of her dancing body through the scars and memories of injury and surgery.

Body Stories offers a suggested autobiography, alluding to the ten operations that Turvey[1] describes as 'pauses' in her thirty-year career as a dance artist. The stories of these surgeries, on her knees, breast, and appendix, are implied through fragmentary traces of memory—some shared with the audience, on small handwritten luggage tags, hanging within the installation (see Figure 19.1), and others highlighted through their resultant scars, inscribed on Turvey's body and revealed through installation videos. Most of the stories are left untold, allowing Turvey's performance to create its own narrative continuity through the powerful presence of her dancing body.

The performative and filmic language of *Body Stories* resolves in a descriptive physicality, emerging from the processes of framing, marking, and body mapping. Turvey repeatedly draws attention to her abdomen, legs, and chest, sequentially noting each site of trauma with an uninflected functionality (see Figure 19.2). In one of the four videos screened in the dance installation, she delicately scrolls a line of red thread to locate her damaged knee, repeating the action on her exposed belly and then on her bare breast.

In performance, barely visible behind a tracing-paper banner, Turvey coolly lifts her dress to reveal where she is scarred, while in another video, projected above her head, she is seen in extreme close-up, drawing on her knee with a spiked wheel-marker (see Figure 19.3), the decorative lines suggesting hennaed chains of flowers and then inferring the marking-up before invasive surgery, as she pulls the marker across the sites of appendectomy and biopsy, digging deep into her flesh. This descriptive physicality

FIGURE 19.1. Video still from a live performance of *Body Stories*, Huddersfield Art Gallery, November 2013. (Credit: Video still June Gersten Roberts, Dancer Gerry Turvey.)

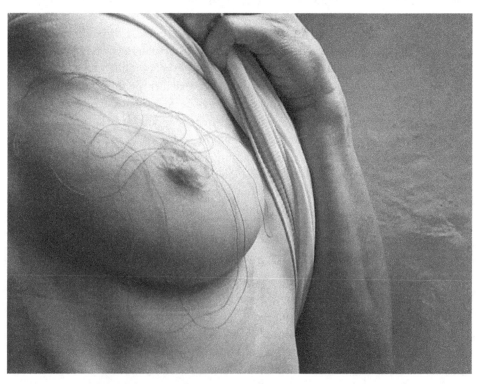

FIGURE 19.2. Video still from *Installation Video Body Stories 4*. (Credit: Video still June Gersten Roberts, Dancer Gerry Turvey.)

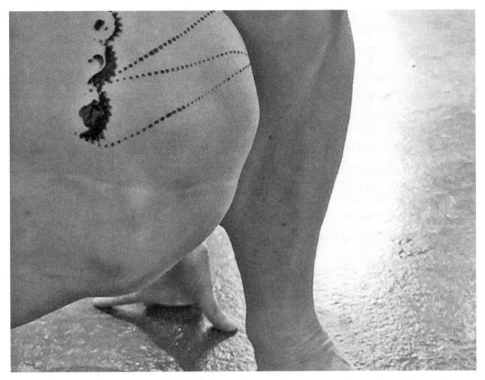

FIGURE 19.3. Video still from *Installation Video Body Stories 3*. (Credit: Video still June Gersten Roberts, Dancer Gerry Turvey.)

powers the work with the immediacy of stories told and recognized through, of, and by the body.

The *Body Stories* project was co-created through 2012 and 2013 in residencies in museums and art galleries in Leeds, Halifax, and Huddersfield.[2] The work was developed as a collaboration, with Gerry Turvey as solo performer and artistic director, working alongside visual artist Roger Bygott, movement director Vanessa Grasse, sound artist Daniel Weaver, and myself as video maker.[3]

Writing experientially, from my perspective as a participatory artist and with particular focus on the four videos[4] screened within the *Body Stories* installation, I aim to locate potential sites for exploring wellbeing within the filmic images and the creative processes of making videos that offer absorbing, visceral framings of Turvey's injuries and close-focus intimations of both her vulnerability and her physical power.

I suggest that the filming and screening approaches, of close-up and ambiguity, along with the choreographic devices of mapping, framing, and marking, bring the viewer into haptic visual contact with the image of the dancer's body, allowing a fleshly connectivity with the material presence of skin, scars, and Turvey's physical strength, offering the potential for enhancing and questioning the experience of wellbeing, through sensuous encounters with the body and through witnessing injury as a physical knowledge, which Turvey (2013)[5] describes as having 'informed me as a dancer'.

WELLBEING REDEFINED

The preamble to the World Health Organisation's constitution (2006) defines health as a 'state of complete physical, mental, and social wellbeing and not merely the absence of disease or infirmity', suggesting an understanding of wellbeing as in excess of and differently constituted from the binary constructs of wellness and illness. The UK Department of Health report (2014) refers to two interconnected strands of wellbeing, the objective and subjective—the first focusing on the fulfilment of basic needs, and the latter referring to an individual sense of life-satisfaction, positive emotion, and purpose. This definition of subjective wellbeing (SWB), in common with much current literature on the subject (Alea and Bluck 2013; Dodge et al. 2012; Hone et al. 2014; Hefferon 2013), refers to Diener's research, with its emphasis on subjective self-evaluation and understanding that 'wellbeing necessarily includes positive elements that transcend economic prosperity' (Diener et al. 1999: 276) encompassing, though not necessarily always including, satisfaction with life, high levels of positive affect, and low levels of negative affect.

Writing in 1999, Diener identified SWB with happiness, which he considered to be at least partially determined by factors of heredity and personality, as well as intrinsic goal fulfilment, adaptability, social relationships, and environmental conditions. This led him to conclude:

> The happy person is blessed with a positive temperament, tends to look on the bright side of things, does not ruminate excessively about bad events and is living in an economically developed society, has social confidents and potential adequate resources for making progress toward valued goals. (Diener et al. 1999: 295)

This emphasis on the 'blessings' of an extrovert personality, positive temperament, and conditions of privilege suggests a concept of SWB that is inherently dualistic, exclusive, and potentially beyond individual agency. According to Hefferon (2013): 'This overemphasis on the benefits of happiness, positivity, etc. was, and is, short sighted, especially as research has continually shown the potential for enlightenment and growth through adversity' (p. 7).

More recent movements in positive psychology engage with functional models for enhancing wellbeing through personal and social responsibly. Csikszentmihalyi (2002) projects that 'happiness is a condition that must be prepared for, cultivated, and defended privately by each person' (p. 2)—a process which, he suggests, we make happen through engaging in the challenges of meeting personal goals and 'a sense of participation in determining the content of life' (p. 4). Seligman's (2011) wellbeing theory (WBT) shifts the terminology from happiness to flourishing, the new term suggesting a broader concept of wellbeing opening to and growing through self-motivated action. Seligman (2011) identifies five components contributing to wellbeing, together referred to by the acronym PERMA: positive emotions, engagement, relationships, meaning, and accomplishment. His theory suggests these are constructive pillars for wellbeing and, like Csikszentmihalyi (2002), shifts the emphasis from personal disposition to supportive life choices.

The New Economic Foundation (2009) think-tank report suggests socially active strategies for enhancing wellbeing, emerging from its global and environmental perspectives. It places emphasis on responsible interaction, advocating 'connect, be active, take notice, keep learning, and give'. Dodge et al. (2012) move the foundations of Seligman's stable conceptualizations of WBT to offer a see-saw model and a definition of wellbeing based on dynamic equilibrium, shifting the static concepts of quality of life to consider wellbeing as active balancing between being challenged and finding the psychological, social, and physical resources to meet these challenges. In a Radio 4 interview in 2012, New Economic Foundation's Nick Marks also offered a dynamic metaphor for wellbeing as a 'sort of dynamic dance and there's movement in that all the time and actually its the functionality of that movement which actually is true levels of wellbeing' (Marks, 2012).

The concept of an SWB invites personal reflection, and mine comes from the dissident stance of an introvert with a sceptical and Pythonesque view of looking on the bright side of life. The sunnier brands of dispositional wellbeing may be beyond the scope of my more pessimistic perspectives. The functional PERMA constructs and New Economic Foundation directives provide viable guidelines for life choices and social interactions, which could (and do) provide a spring from which personal and social engagement may flow. Nonetheless, I might experience these outpourings as vexing difficulties. Dodge's wellbeing see-saw model and Nick Marks' dancing metaphor both offer evocative imagery for understanding the dynamics of my own shifting and ephemeral experiences of wellbeing, and yet offer little connection with how or where I might feel, locate, recognize, or embody that experience.

As a dance film-maker, my most personal experiences of wellbeing are located within, and flow into and from, those sensuous sites where I find connections between body, place, and image. I freely admit to this producing a solipsistic understanding of wellbeing, which may shift the colours of SWB but still responds to hedonic models. I sense wellbeing as located within my body—a voluptuous, internalised fizz of awareness and presence that may bubble up as felt satisfaction but also resonates at other frequencies, within melancholy, vulnerably, humility, or even in the energies of anger. I experience wellbeing as internalized, but also vibrant in connectivity, perhaps in communion with other people, but not exclusively. I also find wellbeing in sensuous empathy with places, memories, and music, through diving into the experience of colour and dwelling within the visual nuances and auric presence of particular objects. The focused acts of filming open my connective rapport with the moment found; film editing offers me a depth of engagement within the interfaces of memory and experience, movement and materials.

My experiences with Buddhist teachings[6] and meditation enliven my understanding of wellbeing as the outcome of an active subject view, rather than of given circumstance. Informed by Buddhism, I tend to recognize wellbeing as fleeting and incidental; welcome, but not specifically identified as an aim. Dzonsar Jamyand Khyentse (2012)—a contemporary Tibetan Buddhist teacher with a penetrating view of current Buddhist practitioners—suggests that 'if you are only concerned about feeling good, you are far better off having a full body massage' (p. 4) and advises that 'Buddhism is not therapy' (p. 8). Referring to the words of Kongol Rinpoche, Kythentse teaches: 'we pray to the . . .

Buddhas . . . so I may give birth to the heart of sadness' (p. 6), thus opening to an emotional pallet that allows all experience to become the path—an approach summarized poetically in the thirteenth-century *Vairo Drabag*:

> Without needing to be forsaken, the emotions are the five great wisdoms. Without needing to be removed, the three poisons are the perfection of Body Voice and Mind.
>   Without needing to be eliminated, samsara is the path that leads to the bliss of Bodhi.
>   Thus has the state of knowledge of the Buddhas of the three times arisen in me.
> (Anon., cited in Norbu and Clemente 1999, p. 37)

My sense of personal fulfilment tends to be located within the Buddhist practice of mindfulness, an act of non-judgemental, inclusive, and attentive awareness of the flow of experience, emotion, sensation, and thought that I may experience as a felt mental presence, an opening of the skin, an internal reverberation, a recognition of feeling and sensing as a site of embodied knowing and of knowing as a place of feeling. It is the colours of attentive experience that most open me to mindful awareness and where I find my most valued and personal sensations of wellbeing.

LOCATING SITES FOR WELLBEING WITHIN THE *BODY STORIES* PROJECT: TOWARDS A SENSUOUS METHODOLOGY

It is this embodied mindfulness, this focused attentiveness on a non-judgemental, sensuous empathy, that I aim to elicit when sharing the *Body Stories* videos, asking the viewer for an active sensory engagement through close attention to the emerging moment, embracing a shared experience of felt being. This responds to the work of film critics Marks (2000, 2002), Barker (2009), and Hezekiah (2010), whose writings on haptic visuality and tactile cinema inspire my approaches to video making and nourish my approach to writing.

Marks (2002) discusses haptic perception as 'the way we experience touch both on the surface of and inside our bodies' (p. 2), and links this to her discussion of haptic visuality, as an experience of the eyes 'function[ing] as organs of touch'. In her earlier text, *The Skin of the Film* (2000), Marks suggests that 'haptic looking tends to move over the surface of its object rather than plunging into illusionistic depth not to distinguish form so much as to discern texture' (2000, p. 162), and that haptic images 'invite the viewer to respond to the image in an intimate embodied way' (p. 2). The *Body Stories* videos attempt to dwell with the body through the material surfaces of the image and elicit a sensuous connectivity, through haptic visuality, inviting an enhanced embodied mindfulness. It is from my experiences of working with this connection that I suggest the films may generate a sense of SWB, inviting attentive focus on being in and being with a spectrum of felt and remembered bodily experiences and engaging in an enlivening visceral connection with the felt presence of the image.

It should be noted that *Body Stories* is not an arts-for-wellbeing project, and has no intended agenda to generate, promote, or research wellbeing. Unlike projects specifically designed to support wellbeing, with an emphasis on experiential effectiveness (Stuckey and Nobel 2010), the *Body Stories* project is firmly grounded in the artistic production. There are some overlaps of processes. The body mapping and autobiographic strategies used in *Body Stories* are also used in wellbeing and therapeutic practices (Solomon 2008; Bluck and Gluck 2004). These processes are employed for a different purpose in *Body Stories*, where they are utilized as artistic tools for exploring and generating visual and movement material (Turvey, personal communication, 30 May 2014). Any wellbeing benefits from these would be incidental to the project's aims and intentions.

Nonetheless, my experiences of working on the *Body Stories* project have offered personal moments of wellbeing through creative engagement in collaborative art making and the positive reception of the performances. During the months of project development, I was part of a responsive and supportive community of collaborative artists, working towards a collective purpose. These circumstances offered me the buzz of belonging and social acceptance and of having a place in the world. Through our public performances I felt the confidence of having made a positive social contribution, while our collective accomplishments offered me a sense of shared mastery. These are welcomed wellbeing benefits, which could also be the outcomes of any successful collaborative performance project.

Of more relevance to this specific project, although incidental to its aims, are my experiences of wellbeing emanating from particular processes. *Body Stories* works with autobiographic memory, specifically drawing on Turvey's histories of injury. The project also incorporates the shared body stories of our audiences and of the participants in Turvey's workshops,[7] who, like Turvey, hand-wrote their personal memories of physical trauma on luggage tags, which were embedded, with Tuvey's stories, in the installation. As the project developed and this collection of shared stories grew, I was increasingly opened to a sense of awe and wonder at the depth of so much human resilience and generosity.

AUTOBIOGRAPHICAL RESPONSES TO *BODY STORIES*

This growing collection of stories also elicited my own memories. I repeatedly found myself adding my tags to the collections. Through the process of making stories of my past injuries and illness, I found an increasingly sympathetic connection to my past and a loosening of fear of the future. Alea and Bluck's study (2013) contextualizes this experience. Their cross-generational study of autobiographical meaning-making among adults in Trinidad and North America suggests that while this is not consistent across both cultures, for older adults from North America experiencing autobiographical memories engenders SWB in the present and positive views of the future. Referring to studies by Freeman (2010) and Newby-Clark and Ross (2004), Alea and Bluck (2013) note that 'individuals search for meaning in the context of constructing and reconstituting their life story; a story in which they evaluate and make sense of the past but that also helps them to map out or envision a positive future' (58). They conclude that while their study does not suggest a causal relationship, the 'general tendency to use autobiographical memory for meaning making appears to be positively (and not negatively) related to SWB'. Within the *Body Stories* project, reviving my histories into shared stories generated a sense of self-acceptance. Adding my stories to the project collection enabled the construction of a new autobiography—a story in which my history gains new meaning though its connection with the stories of so many others.

This process of reconstructing my personal stories also emerged through the film-making process. Reflectively observing Turvey's body, through filming and editing, allowed me to relocate my perception of my own body and find a site for renegotiating my fears of vulnerability and aging (Turvey and I are the same age). Focusing on scars and maturing skin, finding these touching film subjects and gorgeous resultant images, offered me a less judgemental view of my body. Working with the palpable evidence of Turvey's strength has offered me an unsolicited and unexpected emotional fund for living well, within my body and with my body stories.

The gentle resilience of these experiences also permeates as redemptive narratives that seep into the poignant imagery of both the *Body Stories* performances and the videos. Referring again to Alea and Bluck (2013): 'redemption occurs when a difficult past is narrated as one that has turned into a positive generative future' (57).

Body Stories alludes to deep vulnerabilities, suggesting Turvey's histories of pain and surgery, yet her performance also elicits a redemptive presence of strength, risk-taking, and commanding dance skills. In live performance (see Video 19.1 on Companion Website ⊙). Turvey manipulates, drags, swings, and holds aloft the bulky window frames that are the constructive materials of the installation, reshaping the installation environment. She slides along the floor, folds and unwinds, cramps herself into minuscule spaces, and emerges with seeming ease. Her presence controls the audience, who follow her through the installation and fan out from her pathways, allowing her reigning power within the performance space. In the final scene of the live performance (not visible in the available performance video), Turvey, half naked, tightly binds herself in the skeins of red wool that have linked the spaces and scenes throughout the performance. Accelerating into a spin, she frees herself of her bindings and out of the room, leaving behind the trails of wool and the frames that she has been dragging throughout the performance (see Figure 19.4).

Similar themes of vulnerability and liberation emerge through the installation videos. In *Body Stories 1* (see Video 19.2 on Companion Website ⊙), Turvey's image appears as fragile and insecure—a ghostly reflection of a dancer trapped within the glass panes of pitted and flaking window frames, propped against a dirty wall (see Figure 19.5). The dancer's reflection fragments in the glass panes as her image half rises from a deep crouch. As she exhales, her reflection creases into low drops, cupping knees, enfolding her centre, protecting the sites of her historic pain and injuries. The camera moves closer, revealing a lithe muscularity, the dancer's flexibility and movement control. Cut to a new image: a fast-paced series

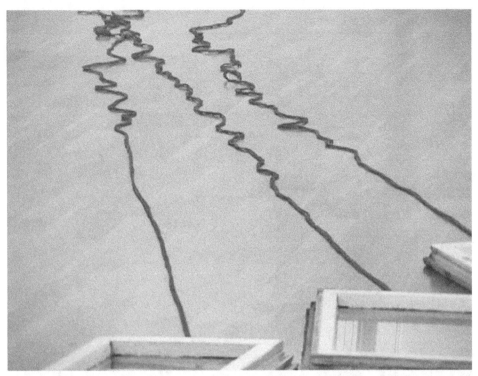

FIGURE 19.4. Video still from a live performance of *Body Stories*, Huddersfield Art Gallery, November 2013. (Credit: Video still June Gersten Roberts.)

FIGURE 19.5. Reflections in frames and image fragmenting. Video still from *Installation Video Body Stories 1*. (Credit: Video still June Gersten Roberts, Dancer Gerry Turvey.)

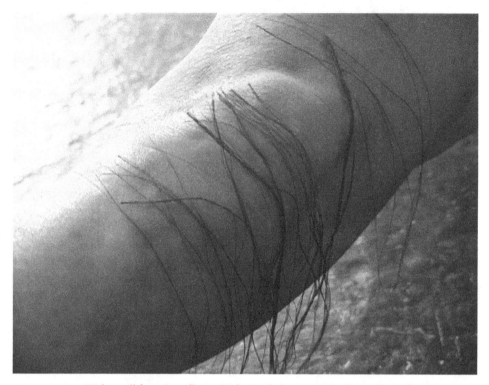

FIGURE 19.6. Video still from *Installation Video Body Stories 4*. (Credit: Video still June Gersten Roberts, Dancer Gerry Turvey.)

of extreme close-ups locates bare knees playfully changing directions as the dancer swings the window frames in which her reflection was previously captured (see Videos 19.2 and 19.3 on Companion Website ▶).

In *Body Stories 4*, (see Video 19.4 on Companion Website ▶) a slow, extreme close-up follows the line of a deep crack along a rough stone floor, coming to rest on a scarred knee. A red thread drops lightly onto the knee, delicately encircling the scar. A cross-fade reopens into the same scene and the red thread now rapidly winds around the scarred knee, pulling into the flesh, binding, the treads cutting, the camera tightly gripped to the image of the skin, trussed and puckering. Cut to slow fade-in to the same view; in a series of broken clips a small scissor snips through the bindings. The knee tilts towards the camera, exposing the residual bind marks as they fade from the skin. The threads slowly drop off and slip away (see Figure 19.6) (see Video 19.4 on Companion Website ▶).

TOWARDS A HAPTIC VISUALITY
IN *BODY STORIES*

Phelan (2004) contends that 'representation follows two laws: it always conveys more than it intends; and it is never totalizing. The "excess" meaning conveyed by representation creates a supplement that makes multiple and resistant readings possible' (p. 2). The redemption narratives that may be read into the *Body Stories* videos are also excessive interpretations of videos that are emphatically non-narrative, resistant to narrative readings. Rather than presenting causal narratives, to be read through time and seen from a distance, the *Body Stories* videos offer opportunities for haptic readings, allowing the viewer to 'contemplate the image itself instead of being pulled into narrative' and 'pulling the viewer in close' (Marks 2000, p. 163) through myopic filmic mappings of Turvey's scars and close-focus visual descriptions of the anatomical sites of her injuries. Short clips and tightly edited repetitions suspend any narrative temporality. Background and contextual information are absent from the videos (though offered in the performance and installation). Sporadic camera movements fixate on the surfaces of the skin, or shift in response to Turvey's movements. All available information is locked into condensed images of self-contained body parts, animated through close focus on small movements and the dancer's actions of marking and framing. As such, the stories are embodied in the dancer's body and action, relocated as single moments in the act of filming and the choices of editing.

These close-up images and the repetitive edit sequences offer a caught-in-the-moment, enclosed, and attentive hyper-focus, which offers me, and I suggest may offer the viewer, a sense of wellbeing within a heightened mindful attention to the sensory experiences of being in the body. If, as MacDougall (2006) suggests, we film-makers are 'putting ourselves in a sensory state that is one of vacancy and of heightened awareness . . . preparing ourselves for a different kind of knowledge' (p. 7), the *Body Stories* videos attempt to vacate the search for narrative causality in favour of intensifying awareness of bodily presence and offer what MacDougall refers to as a mindful visual 'embrace [of] the knowledge of being' (p. 6). Drawing on Merleau-Ponty's concepts of phenomenological seeing, film theorist Hezekiah (2010) further suggests that 'the body is inherently sensible because it is sensual . . . The essence of things . . . is attained through heightened awareness of sensory perception' (p. 9). This experience resonates with Lawless and Allen's (2003) descriptions of the Buddhist practices of *rigpa*, a being-in attentiveness integrating mindfulness with bodily awareness in a sense of heightened wakeful presence (pp. 50–2). This attentive state of dwelling with the human body, according to Hezekiah, 'reaches out to the world' through embodied consciousness (2010, p. 9).

The *Body Stories* videos use haptic images to reach out to the viewer, to touch and in turn invite touch to offer a heightened sense of connectivity through intimate close-up attentiveness to the creasing give of the skin, to flinches, and to clumsy jutters and the sudden jolts of resistance. As the dancer marks her body, the close-up camera traces the touch onto the body of the viewer (see Figure 19.7). The video editing sustains the touch into a deepening press, arresting the skimming of time with repeated sequences that impel the viewer into the images. And the images hold, enclosing the viewer within the recycling embrace of the dancer framed and framing (see Figure 19.8) (see Videos 19.2 and 19.3 on Companion Website ⓟ).

The videos also touch through uncertainty and discomfort, unsettling the visceral attachment of the viewer, traumatizing the experience, and heightening the sensory perception of vulnerability and insecurity. In *Body Stories 2*, (see Video 19.3 on Companion Website ⓟ) heavily glazed window frames weigh on the thighs, abdomen, and chest

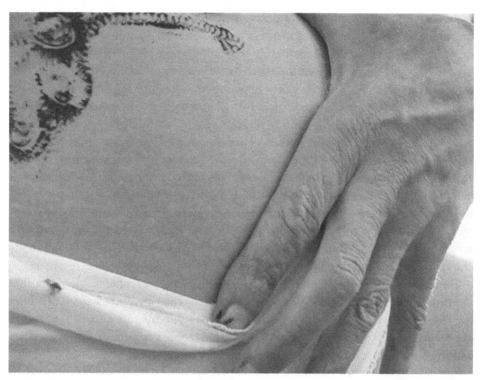

FIGURE 19.7. Video still from Installation Video *Body Stories 3*. (Credit: Video still June Gersten Roberts, Dancer Gerry Turvey.)

of the prone and naked dancer (Turvey). As she manoeuvres under the weight of the windows, the camera fixates on the surface textures of the pocked glass and the peeling paintwork. The raw edges of the frames slice the viewing surface and cut across the pictorial image, their pitted glass forming a corrupted second skin as the dancer drags them across her naked breasts and stomach, obscuring and revealing the flesh beneath. Ambiguously aggressive reflections collide on the panes, marking the dancer's body and intruding on the viewer's vision, and through the bridge of haptic viewing making vulnerable the viewer's body, exposing the viewer to a sense of vulnerability.

This exposure to vulnerability offers an embodied site in which to relocate the experience of wellbeing. In her TEDx Houston address, Brown (2010) notes the social tendency to numb the experience of vulnerability, and in this numbing to also numb our capacity for 'gratitude and happiness'. Identifying the experience of 'vulnerability as the birthplace of joy, of creativity, of belonging and love' (2010) in the same web broadcast, Brown refers to vulnerability as making possible the experience of living wholeheartedly. I would also suggest that vulnerability allows openheartedness—a receptivity and heartfelt connectivity. Understandings of openhearted or wholehearted vulnerability indicate experiences of vulnerability that differ significantly from those attending to the threat or risk of abuse or danger, and are quite separate from concepts of vulnerability

FIGURE 19.8. Video still from Installation Video *Body Stories 2*. (Credit: Video still June Gersten Roberts, Dancer Gerry Turvey.)

as a condition of being victimised. Openhearted vulnerability resonates with sensations of permeability, exposure, and revelation, while wholeheartedness invites emotional inclusivity. Both offer an understanding of vulnerably as a potentially transformative wellbeing experience, which, Brown (2010) contends, opens us to be deeply seen, allowing authenticity and connectivity. The *Body Stories* videos aim to elicit this sense of connective opening through extreme close-up imagery, exposing the viewer to, by, and with the body of the dancer.

Ethnographic film-maker MacDougall (2006) suggests that filmic close-ups offer 'a proximity to . . . bodies of others that we experience much less commonly in daily life. The conventions of social distance normally restrict proximity except in moments of intimacy' (p. 21). Dwelling in continuous close-up, the *Body Stories* videos allow an unusual depth of physical encounter, offering 'a secondary sense in the film viewer of being personally exposed by witnessing the others exposure' (p. 21).

The videos further heighten the experience of exposure and haptic connectivity by almost wholly eliminating opportunities for seeing the dancer's face. In those few moments when Turvey's face becomes visible, fleetingly, the sensory connection seems to momentarily rupture, returning the visual experience to seeing the dancer as a filmed character, creating a separation that vacates the body of the viewer. By contrast, when facial contact is eliminated and the filmic images dwell in close-up intimacy with the body, the videos invite the viewer to inhabit the film image, locating the experience viscerally in the body of the viewer, and offering a visual and sensory ownership. While MacDougall suggests that the 'face in films ... becomes ... a receptacle for many of our feelings about the body as a whole' (2006, p. 22), the *Body Stories* videos instead enface the body with distinct, expressive, and mobile close-ups engaging the power of the touching image to move with the viewer into and with the body of the dancer, offering visceral ownership of being in the body.

Towards a Haptic Ambiguity

As I locate these haptic and embodied experiences of vulnerable connectivity, emotional inclusivity, and sensory ownership, speaking to and from and also, as Hezekiah (2010) suggests, writing 'into the videos', my sources are the four recordings as they stand today—extant visual documents remaining on my computer files, a year or more after production and now isolated from their intended site, within the *Body Stories* performance and installation.

The stand-alone videos available with this publication (see *Body Stories 1, 2,* and *4*) are the videos as they were created in edit: intensified and enclosed miniature image worlds of frames within frames and sensorial worlds of naked skin, close-up objects, and marked body. As stand-alone visual artefacts, viewed within the confines of a digital screen, the videos offer images that are distinct and stable, if often ambiguous and sometimes out of focus. The videos have fixed beginnings, middles, and ends, albeit repeating beginnings, and middles recycled into endings that finish without conclusions. These are very different viewing experiences from the videos as they are screened within the installation environment and performance. It is worth illuminating the contexts for which they were developed.

The *Body Stories* videos were created without sound, to be viewed within the soundscapes of the installations. For the Huddersfield performances, Daniel Weaver composed a gentle undulating multitracked environment of gravelly textures, industrial sounds, and melodic interludes. Tracks from Weaver's score have been added to the videos. These offer continuity and create a sustained timeline through what could be seen as fragmentary visual sequences of short clips, jump cuts, and accumulating repeated images.

Within the *Body Stories* installations, the videos are played on continuous loops and are revealed, or concealed, at selected moments in the performance. Once revealed, the audience may enter or leave the world of the video at any point in the sequence. In performance, the videos are among several viewing events. The audiences' attention and viewpoint are continuously reorientating as the performance moves through the installation site. Focus on the videos may be transitory and fleeting, while readings of sequence are necessarily condensed into moments—moments caught in movements repeated.

The screening scenarios create visual ambiguities, which further disrupt sequential readings through time. The first video encountered in the installation is projected onto four long banners of tracing paper hanging from the ceiling and spilling onto the floor, shimmering in the projected light of the barely perceptible image. Greenish grey tones shift between and across the banners, escaping onto the surrounding walls. Movements appearing on one paper banner leap onto another, changing size as they re-emerge. Between the banners, shards of the video splinter onto the adjacent walls. Flesh tones and recognizable fragments of a body guide the imagination to resolve filmic images: a bare shoulder multiplies, rises in the corner of one banner, falls into another, and disappears. Edges of window frames break across the paper surface, bare knees appear, change direction, flaking frames glide across and off the banners.

Videos are projected so large that the image dissolves into available light, and then momentarily rendered hyper-distinct as Turvey moves the projector close. Video images collide as she manipulates one projector into the viewing path of another, splicing the two image worlds (see Figure 19.9). The images are rendered unstable, mysterious, and fleeting. Linear time is suspended as the images repeat, dissolve, and reappear as the audience moves through the site to reconstruct the fragmentary images.

The ambiguous screening scenography and repetitive editing strategies in the *Body Stories* installation disrupt sequential readings, preclude cause and effect, and interrupt opportunities to construct meanings through time. In fact, they extend and make vividly visible the ephemerality of dance with fleeting moments of attention continually lost. MacDougall (2006) proposes that 'a filmmaker's knowledge is often believed to lie in the film's conclusion' (p. 5). These screenings elude conclusions. As such, the videos are screened and edited to eschew direct engagement with causal narratives in preference for engaging the viewer in the immediacy of physicalized experiences through structures that accumulate imagery in short repeating clips, designed to be assimilated through glimpses and experienced as moving moments.

The attention to surface detail along with the repetition-based edit structures, visual ambiguity and elimination of causal linear development, all collude to enfold the viewer in a sensory experience that attunes with Marks' (2002), descriptions of haptic visuality as 'a way of seeing in which the eye lingers over innumerable surface effects' (p. 6) and through which 'the viewer is called on to fill in the gaps in the image, engage with the traces the image leaves' (p. 13). The haptic experience offers the viewer an empowering ownership of caught-in-the-moment sensory presence, vulnerable with structural ambiguity, open to sensual connectivity and choice.

These approaches to ambiguity, experiential ownership, and sensory presence are rooted in the practices of surrealism, minimalism, and early postmodern dance, resonating through the twentieth century into the visual poetics of the current European cinema of the body, which Walton (2013) describes as 'eschewing dialogue, character psychology and linear narrative . . . in favour of crafting elliptical and yet exquisitely vivid sensory worlds'. Within the sensory worlds offered in the *Body Stories* videos, these approaches invite an experience of wellbeing located within the aware, mindful, and knowing body connected through haptic imagery to a sensuous embodied empathy with memories and experiences of vulnerability.

FIGURE 19.9. Video still from a live performance of *Body Stories*, Huddersfield Art Gallery, November 2013. (Credit: Video still June Gersten Roberts, Videos: June Gersten Roberts.)

CONCLUSION: *BODY STORIES* WELLBEING IN THE MAKING

I have suggested that although *Body Stories* has no intended agenda to promote or research wellbeing, the project nonetheless offers potential for enhancing and questioning where and how SWB may be located in artwork that stems from experiences of physical trauma. Working with Turvey's histories of injuries and invasive surgeries, the *Body Stories* performance and installation offers shared memories and implied stories. Turvey's stories mingle with experiences shared by the *Body Stories* audiences and workshop participants, who wrote their autobiographies of injury on luggage tags, incorporated into the installation. Alea and Bluck's (2013) studies suggest that these acts of autobiographic making can enhance wellbeing and offer opportunities for redirecting past experience into more optimistic views of the future. These redemptive potentialities are further woven into *Body Stories* through the implied narratives of recovery, which thread illusively among the possible readings of the performance and filmic materials.

Drawing on theories of haptic visuality and imagery, I suggest that the project may also offer another, less evidenced, site for sensing wellbeing through enhanced connectivity and attentive being-in and being with the body. As Turvey maps the sites of her scars, the choreographic strategies of marking and framing, evident throughout both the performance and videos, invite a heightened focus on the body. The close- focus filming approaches further enhance sensory attentiveness and invite an embodied reciprocal connectivity between the image body and the viewer body. The visual hyper-focus of the close-up video imagery offers a site for being in and being with the body, and through haptic connectivity with the close-focus body of dancer, offers potential for deeper connection with one's own.

The visual and temporal ambiguities of the video images, the repetitive edit structures and the broken screening strategies further enhance a participatory engagement and ownership. As Marks (2002) contends, it is through the surface plays of unresolved images that the haptic experience can be located. I suggest that it is through the haptic experiences of sensory engagement that the *Body Stories* project may offer a heightened sense of embodied awareness—an experience that I might personally identify as a wellbeing resonating with the Buddhist understanding of mindfulness, a being-within experience of non-judgemental embodied attentiveness that encourages inclusion and openhearted connectivity.

From the perspective of my experience as a participatory artist and video maker, the *Body Stories* project offered experiences of inclusion in a wider artistic community, offering a socially active sense of wellbeing that the New Economic Foundation (2009) suggests may be found through connecting and giving, and that Seligman's (2011) WBT suggests can be found through relationships and accomplishment. The project was challenging and demanding artistically, technically, and physically. Yet, as Csikszentmihalyi (2002) and Dodge et al. (2012) suggest, wellbeing may be found in the experience of flowing engagement with challenges that lead to achievement. Working on *Body Stories* may have been challenging, but working with these challenges utterly absorbed me, offering a heightened sense of purpose and fulfilment.

While my bluesy temperament may not have allowed me to wash these experiences with the brighter shades of positive emotion, the process of filming and editing *Body Stories* offered a deepening engagement with the more subdued colours of my own emotional pallet. The grey-toned sensory worlds of the *Body Stories* video images seeped into my body, my sensory responses dissolving into the imagery. Through working within the embrace of haptic visuality, feeling the visceral imagery of the close-up footage of Turvey's body, I enter into an experience of sensorial intimacy with my own. Her vulnerability and her strength opened me to mine. I find myself embodying a version, my version, of her strength, and through her exposure, also exposing the soft centre of my own vulnerably.

Is this wellbeing? I would suggest that it is. Vulnerability encourages or, as Brown (2010) suggests, enhearts, a connective openness. In my experience, it is through that vulnerable exposure that the mindful heart opens, allowing the sensuous, attentive, embodied, empathetic, and owned awareness in which I find wellbeing can be felt.

Further explorations of vulnerability as a potential site for experiencing wellbeing could allow for understandings of SWB beyond binary exclusivity and causal conditions. Hefferon (2013) notes that wellbeing can be generated through trauma and that 'suffering and grief can co-exist with enlightenment and growth' (p. 94). While clarifying that she does not deny the negative side of trauma, Hefferon offers the possibility that distress, illness, and disruption can also offer conditions through which we can become aware of, and re-engage with, the body to allow post-traumatic growth or positive changes through awareness of self, the body, and mortality.

Hefferon suggests a redemptive approach with an emphasis on recovery, and her tests for evidence of post-traumatic growth (p. 107) focus on attaining identifiable states of positive wellbeing with implications of increased stability and reduced vulnerability. Buddhist teachings destabilize this concept of positive redemption, holding vulnerability, impermanence, and mortality as conditions of sentience and living. It is awareness of this impermanence, with its ensuing vulnerability, that pervades the Buddhist body of mindfulness and opens our capacity for compassion.

Butler (2006) offers insightful dissections of vulnerability in her discussions of grief and global politics. She presents an understanding of vulnerability that bypasses attempts to solve or dissolve its presence and allows for its necessity in our social, collective, and connective humanity, suggesting that 'loss has made a tenuous "we" of us all' (p. 20). She offers the prospect of vulnerability as powerfully transformative but as open-ended, uncertain, and collective, 'something fundamental about the social condition of our very formation' (p. 23), and as embodied: 'The body implies mortality, vulnerability' (p. 26). Butler presents vulnerability as a primary condition that we deny at the risk of violating our connectivity and global responsibility that we need to sustain, be mindful of, attentive to, and 'tarrying with' (p. 30) as a resource for recognizing our interdependency.

The *Body Stories* project locates itself within, touches with, and touches on our acceptance and recognition of vulnerably. If it holds a site for understanding wellbeing, it is perhaps best felt through its call to open to being-in wellness as being-with and being within our vulnerability—an area, perhaps, for further study in the understanding of wellbeing.

Notes

1. Interview with Ruth Gamble for Huddersfield Art Gallery in 2013. Obtained with permission from Gerry Turvey; not retrievable.
2. *Body Stories* residencies and performances were hosted by Armley Mills Industrial Museum, Leeds (2012); IOU Gallery, Dean Clough, Halifax (2013); and Huddersfield Art Gallery (2013). The *Body Stories* project was funded by Arts Council England (2013) and the IOU *Time, Space, and Advice* programme.
3. Special thanks and credit are also offered to Hannah Leighton Boyce (visual artist) and Daliah Le Toure (choreographer), both of whom collaborated in the early stages of the *Body Stories*

project and contributed to the filming of *Body Stories 3* and *4*. Thanks are also due to Nicola Forshaw, who provided the musical accompaniment for performances in Leeds in 2012.

4. This chapter is accompanied by three of the four videos screened in the *Body Stories* installation, and also a four-minute video documentation of the *Body Stories* performance at Huddersfield. The performance video is referred to as '*Body Stories*, Huddersfield', (see Video 19.1 on Companion Website ▶) and the installation videos are referred to as '*Body Stories 1, 2, 3 and 4*', (see Videos 19.2–19.4 on Companion Website ▶) indicating the order in which they are revealed in the installation. The videos were filmed on a DV camera and edited digitally, and are available in digital formats. The images, however, are sometime referred to as 'filmic', as there is no equivalently evocative word for a digital image. The camerawork is also referred to as 'filming' or 'videoing', deliberately avoiding the aggressive language of shoot and capture.

5. Turvey, Arts Council Application, 2013. Optioned with permission from Gerry Turvey; not retrievable.

6. My contact with Buddhism is primarily through the Mahayana Tibetan traditions. I offer thanks to the many teachers and sangha who have given teachings through the years, with particular thanks to my first teachers, Geshe Techog, Geshe Kelsang, and Lama Yeshe; also to Lopon P. Ogyan Tanzin for his generous retreat in Bentham, North Yorkshire, and to Chogyal Namkhai Norbu, whose regular webcasts on Dzogchen have reignited my practice.

7. Audiences and workshop participants were invited to write their body stories on luggage tags and place these within the installations. Museum guests who visited our open rehearsals also offered their stories. As an integral part of the *Body Stories* project, Gerry Turvey offered a series of workshops in Leeds, Halifax, and Huddersfield, exploring the performance processes of framing and body mapping. Turvey's workshop for women aged over fifty produced a collection of evocative photographs, which were screened alongside *Body Stories* performances at Armley Mills Industrial Museum, Leeds, in 2012.

References

Alea, N. and Bluck, S. (2013). 'When does meaning making predict subjective well-being? Examining young and older adults in two cultures', *Memory*, 21(1): 44–63.

Barker, J. (2009). *The Tactile Eye Touch and the Cinematic Experience*. Berkeley, CA: University of California Press

Bluck, S. and Gluck, J. (2004). 'Making things better and learning a lesson', *Journal of Personality*, 72(3): 543–71.

Brown, B. (2010). *Brune Brown: The Power of Vulnerability*, Ted Talk TEDx Houston, <https://www.ted.com/talks/brene_brown_on_vulnerability#t-289920> (accessed 23 November 2014).

Butler, J. (2006). *Precarious Lives*. London: Verso

Csikszentmihalyi, M. (2002). *Flow*. London: Rider

Diener, E., Suh, E., Lucus, R. E., and Smith, H. (1999). 'Subjective well-being: Three decades of progress', *Psychology Bulletin*, 125(2): 276–302.

Dodge, R., Daly, A., Huyton, J., and Sanders, L. (2012). 'The challenge of defining wellbeing', *International Journal of Wellbeing*, 2(3): 222–35. <http://www.internationaljournalofwellbe­ing.org/index.php/ijow/article/viewFile/89/238> (accessed 17 June 2014).

Freeman, M. (2010). *Hindsight: The Promise and Peril of Looking Backward*. New York: Oxford University Press

Hefferon, K. (2013). *Positive Psychology and the Body: The Somatapsychic Side to Flourishing*. Maidenhead: Open University Press

Hezekiah, G. (2010). *Phenomenology's Material Presence: Video, Vision and Experience*. Bristol: Intellect.

Hone, L. C., Jarden, A., Schofield G. M., and Duncan, S. (2014). 'Measuring flourishing: The impact of operational definitions on the prevalence of high levels of wellbeing', *International Journal of Wellbeing*, 4(1): 62–90. <http://www.internationaljournalofwellbeing.org/index.php/ijow/article/view/2 86/395> (accessed 10 June 2014).

Khyentse, D. J. (2012). *Not for Happiness: A Guide to the So Called Preliminary Practices*. Boston: Shambala.

Lawless, J. and Allan, J. (2003) *Beyond Words, Dzogchen Made Simple*. London: Element.

MacDougall, D. (2006). *The Corporeal Image, Film Ethnography and the Senses*. Princeton, NJ: Princeton University Press

Marks, L. (2000). *The Skin of the Film, Intercultural Cinema, Embodiment and the Senses*. Durham, NC: Duke University Press

Marks, L. (2002). *Touch, Sensuous Theory and Multisensory Media*. Minneapolis, MN: University of Minnesota Press.

Marks, N. (2012). *Reasons to be Cheerful*. BBC Radio 4 (7 January 2012).

Newby-Clark, I. R. and Ross, M. (2004). 'Conceiving the past and future', *Personality and Social Psychology Bulletin*, 29, 807818.

New Economic Foundation (2009). *National Accounts of Well-Being*, <http://www.nationalaccountsofwellbeing.org> (accessed 10 June 2014).

Norbu, C. N. and Clemente, A. (1999). *The Supreme Source: The Fundamental Tantra of the Dzog Chen Semde Kunjed Gyalpo*. Ithaca, NY: Snow Lion.

Phelan, P. (2004). *Unmarked: The Politics of Performance*. New York: Routledge

Seligman, M. (2011). *Flourish*. New York, NY: Free Press.

Solomon, J. (2008). *Living with X: A Body Mapping Journey in the time of HIV*. Johannesburg: Regional Psychosocial Support Initiative.

Stuckey, J. H. L. and Nobel, J. (2010). 'The connection between art, healing and public health: A review of the literature', *American Journal of Public Health*, 100(2): 254–63. doi10.2105/AJPH.2008.156497

UK Department of Health (2014). Well Being Why it matters to health policy. <https://www.gov.uk/government/uploads/system/uploads/attachment_data/file/277566/Narrative__January_2014_.pdf> (accessed 22 March 2017).

Walton, S (2013). 'Enfolding surfaces, spaces and materials: Claire Denis' neo-Baroque textures of sensation', *Screening the Past*. <http://www.screeningthepast.com/2013/10/enfolding-surfaces-spaces-and-materials-claire-denis'-neo-baroque-textures-of-sensation/> (accessed 17 May 2014).

World Health Organisation (2006). *Constitution of the World Heath Organisation*. <Retrieved from <http://www.who.int/governance/eb/who_constitution_en.pdf> (accessed 6 June 2014).

CHAPTER 20

(IM)POSSIBLE PERFORMATIVES

A Feminist Corporeal Account of Loss

BEATRICE ALLEGRANTI

INTRODUCTION

Loss and grief are paradoxical: in the 'peaceful' West there is an uneasy (human) relationship with mortality—loss is publicly hidden if not privately ubiquitous (Mellor and Shilling, 1993). Clinical discourses of grief are often pathologized (Davies 2013, 2012) and, by contrast, we are routinely exposed to still and moving media images of conflict, war, and torture, potentially anaesthetizing our capacity to witness with embodied empathy or even acknowledge our collective responsibility for the physical lives of one another (Butler 2006). All this prompts me to call forth Judith Butler's political question: What makes for a grievable life? (Allegranti 2014; Butler 2006).

In acknowledging the paradox of grievability, little is said of the taboo of loss and grief in the public performance of everyday life, of telling the story of loss by way of disrupting dominant narratives and iterating the value of private suffering (Davies 2012). Even less is said about the process of loss and grieving as both corporeal (Allegranti 2005; Allegranti and Wyatt 2014; Allegranti 2014) and as a performative process (Butler 1993; Barad 2007). Hence, this chapter builds on previous research that establishes the interwoveness between psychotherapeutic and performance processes (Allegranti 2011), within the context of loss (Allegranti and Wyatt 2014; Allegranti 2014). Here my intent is to explore the complexity of loss and grief as a corporeal process—one that involves our attention to, in Karen Barad's (2007) terms, the 'entangled' material (biological, kinaesthetic, non-human) and discursive (psychological, sociopolitical) construction of bodies in motion (Allegranti 2011, 2013; Allegranti and Wyatt 2014). In so doing, I aim to convey the relationship between loss and wellbeing not as a stable state, but as a tension between a precarious equilibrium and its constant re-establishment within a biopsychosocial system.

MOVING VOICES

Emerging from personal experiences of the death of a loved one, the *Moving Voices* project was a collaboration between Jonathan Wyatt—counsellor, autoethnographic researcher, writer, and myself—dance movement psychotherapist, choreographer, filmmaker. It was an UnLtd-funded[1] practice-based research project about loss and grief, focusing in particular on the experience of the death of a loved one. The project was borne out of our own personal experiences of working creatively following the death of a parent (Allegranti 2005; Wyatt 2005). To this end, *Moving Voices* comprised three interrelated and material-discursive aspects: (i) workshops combining dance movement psychotherapy and writing;[2] (ii) a 15-minute screendance, *Your Story Calls Me*, comprising ten autobiographical stories of loss; and (iii) ten qualitative interviews[3]. The project culminated with the *Embodying Loss* symposium that explored the impact of our work for arts and health professionals.[4]

The aim of the research project was to work with loss and subsequent grief by developing an embodied story of the ongoing and changing relationship with the person who has died. The emphasis was on working creatively with a blend of Dance Movement Psychotherapy and writing by way of affirmation, but also as a possibility of 'moving through' the sometimes conflicting and overwhelming feelings that arise after the death of a significant person in one's life. To this end, the *Moving Voices* project provided a facilitating environment for participants to create multilayered 'embodied performances' that encapsulated autobiographical, relational, and political aspects (Allegranti 2011), of their own losses and those of others.

PERFORMANCE AND PERFORMATIVITY

As a choreographer I regard the notion of performance as an art form. Although my background and professional training was in contemporary dance and choreography, I have evolved my own working definition of performance to include a broad range of multidisciplinary activities which may be understood under the banner of 'performance' to the extent that the notion may be viewed as a 'constellation of practices' (Huxley and Witts 2003, p. 2). What characterizes all these practices is the established relationship of a performer and a spectator, whether this is live performance as for dance/theatre, or through new media such as film. Moreover, the locus of my own performance practice is an unequivocal engagement with the psychophysical body. Also, as a result of my own idiosyncratically positioned body, in both performance practice and dance movement psychotherapy, I recognize that there exists a further layered hybridity as well as an uneasy and unarticulated relationship between the two (Allegranti 2011).

I also align myself with sociolinguists Thornborrow and Coates (2005), who use the term 'performance' in two different ways: the first is in relation to the performance of identity and the social self, and the second is the telling of a story as performance (this story can of course be a dance, a film, a psychotherapeutic conversation, or in written form).

A further (political) layer which intersects with and expands the notion of performance is Judith Butler's (1994) consideration of performativity 'as *that aspect of discourse that has the capacity to produce what it names* . . . this production actually always happens through a certain kind of repetition and recitation' (33) (author's emphasis), suggesting that identity is something that is 'done' and that it is 'done' over and over again. Building on Butler's notion of performativity in the context of Dance Movement Psychotherapy and performance practice, previous research shows how the iteration and reconstitution of identities—specifically sexuality and gender—is possible through movement improvisation (Allegranti 2011).

An extension of the performative premise is developed by Barad, (2003, 2007) who builds on Butler's notion of performativity, suggesting it as a process of 'intra-activity': 'All bodies, not merely "human" bodies, come to matter through the world's iterative intra-activity—its performativity' (Barad 2003, p. 823). In this way, Barad argues for a relational ontology or 'agential realism'. This suggests a shift from representationalism (reflecting on the world from outside) to a way of understanding the world from within and as part of it. To this end, the *Moving Voices* research shows how embodied selves 'doing' loss leak beyond the confines of discursive labels, diagnosis, and narrow views of human suffering to an understanding of loss and grief as a performative, mutually entangled process between self, other and the person 'lost' (Allegranti and Wyatt 2014).

PSYCHOTHERAPY–PERFORMANCE
INTRA-ACTIONS

In this writing I am interested in aspects that emerged for research participants in the '*intra*-actions' (Barad 2007) between the *Moving Voices* psychotherapeutic (private) workshops and the subsequent choreographic and performance process for the (public) screendance: *Your Story Calls Me* (Allegranti 2012). Reflections on these experiences were captured during individual interviews with all those who participated in both the workshops and the film. For the purposes of this chapter I also chose to conduct an interview with my collaborator, Jonathan Wyatt, in order to better understand his engagement with both cofacilitation of the workshops and performing in the screendance, and to enfold his corporeal presence into my writing.

A significant aspect of the *Moving Voices* research was to build on Barad's work in seeing 'ourselves'—human, non-human, and more-than-human—as always co-implicated, as always 'intra-acting':

> The neologism 'intra-action' *signifies the mutual constitution of entangled agencies.* That is, in contrast to the usual 'interaction', which assumes that there are separate individual agencies that precede their interaction, the notion of intra-action recognizes that distinct agencies do not precede, but rather emerge through, their intra-action. It is important to note that the 'distinct' agencies are only distinct in a relational, not an absolute, sense; that is, *agencies are only distinct in relation to their mutual entanglement; they don't exist as individual elements.* (Barad 2007, p. 33, italics in original)

Hence, the 'mutual entanglement' of Jonathan and myself, our losses, our participants and their losses, the spaces in which we worked (the workshop studio, the rehearsal studio, the outdoor film locations, and so on), non-human performative agents such as the camera (as 'seer'), props and costume, the choice of the Balanescu Quartet's 'Life and Death'[5] as the musical backdrop to some of the workshops, and the material-discursive practices of transitioning between psychotherapeutic and performative; between writing and moving (as if 'writing' is not always 'moving' and 'moving' not always 'writing'), and between writing, moving and performing (Allegranti and Wyatt 2014). By engaging in this relation between material and discursive phenomena I attempt to privilege neither bodies nor language in oppositional hierarchy.

One key aspect for our collaboration was a material-discursive engagement with the interview data: 'data' for us are 'what we think with when we think about a topic' (St Pierre 2011, p. 621); in other words, they are *all* of this. The film is 'data': it shows aspects of how loss matters, the ways in which loss is 'evidenced'; the interviews that followed the making of the film are data. During the interviews with participants, both Jonathan and myself iterated the importance of 'reflecting together' on the process of the workshop and making the film in a way that did not play the 'god trick' (Haraway 2006); instead, we took part in a process of 'knowing-in-being' or 'onto-epistemology' (Barad 2007), in which we performed an analysis from a position of being with and co-implicated in the event of analysing the data. Hence the process of 'gathering' the data was always already *intra*-corporeal: it was within and outside us, and we are within and outside others (Allegranti and Wyatt 2014).

This 'mattering' of the research process (Allegranti 2013: 397) led me to inquire into two entangled aspects that locate subjectivity and consciousness in the body: (i) how *intra*-corporeal shifts emerged (in)between the psychotherapeutic process of the workshops and the choreographic process for the film; and (ii) how these aspects demonstrate corporeal traces—that is, a co-implication between the performer, the person 'lost', and the (non-human) performative environment.

INTRA-CORPOREAL SHIFTS

We are outside in the blazing summer sun—the expanse of green grass vividly con-trasting a cloudless blue sky. Yards of red silk billow in the warm wind alongside pil-lars of a mock Greek temple.[6] A buzz of people—the film crew and photographer[7] with their technical apparatus—move around the participants who are ready to perform on this first day of filming. We have journeyed—the research participants, Jonathan, myself—from the intimate therapeutic studio space with its large windows and grey linoleum floor, into the bigger and less personal rehearsal studio with ceiling to floor mirrors. And now, we are outside, in the world. As I stand next to Garry—one of the camera operators—I recognize that I am holding a different kind of relationship: a newly formed sense of time, space, and witnessing. Holding my own loss and the losses of all the performers. The task ahead is to strike a balance between my already embod-ied experience of loss during the workshops, and the demands of capturing necessary and formed material for film. Of honouring each individual's idiosyncratic, intimate yet entangled experience. What will this constellation of compositions tell me about my own relationship with my mother?

In and Out of Relationship

During the act of filming her movement phrase, one of the participants, Cecilia, reflects on the process of becoming 'undone' by grief (Butler 2004):

> I think when you said 'do you mind if we wrap you in the material?'
> I remember becoming . . . feeling really overwhelmed.
>   I didn't really know what that was about and I was quite upset.
> But then, not upset with you for asking me, just the sort of emotions of just every-thing, kind of those memories because we had to,
>   when she was in . . . I had to actually help her put her sari on
> in the coffin . . .
>   when she was laid in with other people in the family so . . .
> it was all those memories and I wasn't sure if I could manage that but actually,
>   during the filming, it was almost that sort of . . .
> theatrical distance . . .
>   that allowed it to become something that was really powerful and . . .
> I don't know, it was quite healing I suppose, in some ways, yeah.[8]

The red silk was a feature throughout the film. I invited Cecilia to improvise with it in relation to her movement phrase and to wrap the silk around her body. Speaking of this, Cecilia highlights the unexpected experience of being *in* the overwhelming

FIGURE 20.1. Photo of Cecilia Bissesur performing her story during the filming of *I Can't Find Myself.* (Photo credit: Jackie King.)

experience of grief: remembering the preparations for her mother-in-law's body in her coffin. This has echoes of being 'transported' (Leahy et al. 2012), being moved elsewhere in the process of her grief. Notably, this transport emerges as a result of a tactile–kinaesthetic process of wrapping the silk around her body—a non-human boundary. For Cecilia, this transport became an *intra*-corporeal experience— between her performing body and the tactile kinaesthetic memory of her dressing her mother-in-law's body in a Sari and, as Butler (2010) observes: 'The boundary of who I am is the boundary of the body, but the boundary of the body never fully belongs to me' (p. 54). What is afforded to us, I wonder, if we begin to understand in our intersubjective engagements that we do not inhabit ourselves by ourselves? (Allegranti 2013).

Later in her interview, Cecilia talks of the usefulness of 'theatrical distance' as a way of mitigating the initial and possibly traumatic intensity of grief:

> I think when we were doing the filming, I distanced myself in the way that, sort of, theatre, because it was filming, it was theatre.
> But I allowed myself to come closer to some of those, more,
> I don't know,
>   difficult feelings while we were doing the workshop and
> Yeah . . .
> I think having time to sort of think about it and process it in between . . .

Cecilia's voice seems to speak of her experience of the paradox of distance—a distance that brought her closer to the 'difficult feelings' in relation to her experience of grief. I propose that the 'theatrical distance' Cecilia speaks of is both material and discursive: it acts in Barad's (2007) sense as an 'agential cut' between her own experience and what an external witness might perceive. Agential cuts are the non-binary critical constitutive 'actors' in the relation that allow for shifting subjectivities. In the filming of *Your Story Calls Me*, the agential cuts were experienced in different ways for each participant: the change of environment, from the seclusion and privacy of the workshop space into an outside filming location; the use of the camera apparatus as 'intersubjective seer'

FIGURE 20.2. Photo of Jonathan Wyatt performing his story during the filming of *I Can't Find Myself*. (Photo credit: Jackie King.)

(Allegranti 2011); the materiality of each person's dance phrase requiring a different set of kinetic dynamics, conditions, costume and props. As such, all these components are akin to Barad's description of 'apparatuses', which are

> not mere static arrangements *in* the world, but rather *apparatuses are dynamic (re) configurings of the world, specific agential practices/intra-actions/performances through which specific exclusionary boundaries are enacted* . . . Apparatuses are open-ended practices. (Barad 2003, p. 816, author's emphasis)

For the participants there was a corporeal adjustment—between workshop and filming and between past and present—thus allowing for a range of different affective understandings, or ontological 'knowings' of how to 'do' loss. Such an experience highlights different possibilities for performing our everyday relationship with loss, and also highlights how the aesthetics of these performances are evident in both everyday life as well as in the artistic process.

Also reflecting on the process of shifting between workshop and filming, Jonathan echoes the paradox of distance and intimacy in his relationship with his father:

> I remember saying to you at the time and at various points that . . .
> I kind of moved in and out of relationship with my dad.
>   There were times when this was about him and me.
> And some times I felt that I was very distant from that.

Our bodies are layered with the developmental experience of being with another, and loss is invariably part of this intersubjective reality. Many of the participants in the project, including Jonathan and myself, had experienced the death of a parent, thus bringing into sharp relief how grieving potentially enacts our autobiographical developmental processes as part of the complex web of loving and making sense of losing (Allegranti 2014).

Jonathan's words seem to highlight the dynamic nature of his ontogenetic body—how he 'moved' in and out of relationship with this father, a realization prompted perhaps by, as Barad (2007) would say, the 'dynamic reconfigurings' between the workshops into preparing for and during filming. Each of these reconfigurings was layered with the kinaesthetic intimacy of each individual's personal movement phrase which was re-formed for the camera, as well as the intermodal and performative shifts between speaking, writing, and movement.

In My Body

The workshop's cycles of writing and moving were intended to offer a temporal shift or oscillation even, from being alone with loss to being with others and their losses. However, in preparation for, and during, filming, a different spatiotemporal experience emerged. In her interview, Maura speaks of this qualitatively different experience:

FIGURE 20.3. Photo of Maura O'Connell performing her story during the filming of *I Can't Find Myself*. (Photo credit: Jackie King.)

> I . . . when in the process work,
> [in] music terms, I would say it's *allungato* . . .
> > it's sustained, it's suspended in time, it's indulging in time.
> Whereas the film process is very much staccato, [clicks to indicate haste] and fighting against and resisting time,
> > and get this done and move this, and get there and go there, and do it.
> You know, it's very much a different experience . . .
> > > . . . and it's a different experience in my body . . .

The therapeutic process necessarily involves immersion in a relational experience over extended time. Time stretches between past autobiographical experiences and present perceptions, feelings, and the living of everyday life. By contrast, the choreographic process necessitates a refining of raw material that may have unfolded over extended time but that necessitates a new shape—a compositional form. Thus the 'agential cut' (Barad 2007) involves establishing a compositional boundary—a containment of (personal) process: if we had continued to allow time and space to reflect in the rehearsal and filming process then further material would have been elicited.

I am struck by Maura's explanation of 'a different experience in my body', and crucially, for her, the transition seems to be articulated in musical terms that capture *time*—'Allungato . . . Staccato'—and *space*:—'. . . move this, get there, and go there . . .' This changing rhythm has echoes of infant meaning-making in the developmental process

(Gallagher 2013), and seems to provide Maura with a direct felt sense (Gendlin 1996) of perceiving the dynamics of her movement located with/in time and space. Thus, Maura is aware of the 'out-thereness' of her experience in relation to the surrounding environment—appreciating her own spatiotemporal dynamics in her performance of loss, but also incorporating an understanding of the complexity of her creative process within the overall project. It is, therefore, the kinaesthetic rhythm of her experience that seems to allow Maura to reconstitute her experience and make an 'agential cut' (Barad 2007) between therapeutic and performative.

In his interview, Jonathan elaborates on the difference of his embodied experience in the transition between therapeutic and performative:

> . . . for me it's not such a binary it's a different way of . . . of . . .
> so when we're in the workshop and we're creating text and movement in the room
> that is also a performance and . . . and
>   it's therapeutic and when we move into the making of the film,
> that's also a performance and it's therapeutic.
> So those are the kinds of. . .
>   there was a shift in my . . . in what I did with my body . . .
> in making the film and how I was . . .
>   I was working with a different shape and . . . and . . .
> my role of whatever I was doing was . . .
>   . . . with a kind of . . .[intake of breath]
> was looking through a different lens or a different angle but it still felt like it was part
> of the same process.

Jonathan articulates the intermodal shifts between visual and lived proprioceptive experience: 'Shift in what I did with my body . . . different shape . . . different lens . . . different angle'. As Gallagher (2013) attests, this somatocentric capacity emerges from infancy, where vision directs the child outward toward the world of others, and proprioception is concerned with the sense of self. That Jonathan experienced the shift as 'not such a binary' seems to highlight how he was 'apprentice' of his corporeal-kinetic body (Sheets-Johnstone 2000), learning his body and learning himself into performing loss across the entangled processes of moving, writing, and performing—alone and with others. I am left wondering: what kind of (adult) developmental stage is mourning?

Corporeal Vulnerability

Shifting between workshop and performance presented participants with a series of dynamic vulnerabilities in relation to their own experiences of loss and how these personal experiences *intra*-act with formation of movement and text for the camera, and the shared environment of the filming process. During her interview, Theresa reflected on the conflicting feelings that emerged for her during this process:

FIGURE 20.4. Photo of Theresa Messenger performing her story during the filming of *I Can't Find Myself.* (Photo credit: Jackie King.)

I found myself feeling completely different, very vulnerable, and very like, oh, right, ok, you know, I've come out of this safe therapeutic space into a performance space now, and I don't know if I can do it.
I felt very vulnerable.
                              That shift was something I haven't experienced before.
I haven't come out of a creative into a performance specifically in that way before and actually seeing both of you and having you two both in a different light as well, you know, now you're kind of directing, and you were actually guiding me as to how you'd like my movement to be, and that was kind of like, you know . . .
                      oh right, so I'm not going to sort of have the whole movement.
My sort of sense of it being . . . having the whole movement,
and no, that's not going to happen now, it's going to be pieces of my movement.
So, there was a breaking down of that kind of [movement] phrase, which was, yeah,
I found that quite difficult actually.
                      I'm like, 'What's happened to my phrase', you know?
And I think I wrote something about that, yeah, something about sort of feeling, somehow sort of . . . something in that process of feeling marginalized
                              of feeling kind of side-lined somehow
Which I think this was a sort of, was a kind of link into other areas of my life, that that triggered something,
you know . . .
that triggered something and I went sort of away and thought, well, you know, I thought of it then in pragmatic terms, well, this is what happens when you go into

producing. We're now into producing a film, and it's not like I've let go of what I did in this creative space.

I've brought it in, and it's now been sort of produced in a different way, but it's all still there, you know.

It's all still there.

But it was a curious sort of process to go through.

I never expected to feel like that at all.

Extending Butler's (2006) notion of corporeal vulnerability, Theresa's words seem to highlight several complex political and ethical aspects which may mirror the grieving process: producing a different bodily sense of self or identity; engaging in a different kind of witnessing of one's own material and forming, and editing personal material for public performance (of self). It is impossible to locate corporeal vulnerability and mourning without entering the sphere of politics, and, as Butler (2006) clarifies: 'Loss and vulnerability seem to follow from our being socially constituted bodies, attached to others, at risk of losing those attachments, exposed to others, at risk of violence by virtue of that exposure' (p. 20). In the context of Theresa's words, I am curious about what kind of body becomes 'produced' after loss? Perhaps Theresa hints at this when she asks: 'What's happened to my phrase . . .?'

In preparation for filming, the breaking down of each person's movement phrase—gesture by gesture—was an essential component in maintaining a safe holding environment, much like the intersubjective bodily resonance between mother and infant (Winnicott 1971; Beebe et al. 2005). Each movement phrase was edited and formed by participants and choreographically reshaped for camera by me. The aesthetic (re)composition allowed for a process of metabolisation, for personal material to be seen or 'exposed' and worked through. It allowed the work to shift from unformed therapeutic disclosure to autobiographical aesthetic intervention, as captured in Theresa's words, 'it's been produced in a different way'.

However, as a result of kinaesthetic engagement with reshaping and re-forming her movement phrase, Theresa seems to have experienced a presence–absence in terms of embodied 'I's, which is evident in her comment on how choreographic editing produced 'a process of feeling marginalized . . . [and] sidelined' and that this was a 'familiar' everyday life trigger. The paradoxical sense of dispossession in the grieving process seems to be evoked here—and Butler (2006) is aware of this incorporation too: 'I think I have lost "you" only to discover that "I" have gone missing as well' (p. 22). Butler goes on to explain that

perhaps what I have lost 'in' you, that for which I have no ready vocabulary, is a relationality that is composed neither exclusively of myself nor you, but is to be conceived as *the tie* by which those terms are differentiated and related. (p. 22)

Loss evokes this disruption of ipseity—the feeling of identity, corporeality, existential orientation, and being the perspectival origin of one's own experience: all these are basic components of the experienced differentiation of self from non-self (Gallagher 2013; Parnas and Handest 2003). And yet Theresa comments in her interview that 'It's all still there', perhaps suggesting that she has created a new kinaesthetic memory within the process of losing.

Often, in choreographic and clinical arenas as well as therapy training contexts, I have noticed that people unfold a movement phrase and then need to go back to it to understand its constituent parts in order to appreciate and make meaning from what they have produced. This seems to highlight how our bodies anticipate conscious experience (Gallagher 2013), which is also evident in Theresa's realization that 'I never expected to feel like that at all'. The materiality of movement in Theresa's dance seemed to have allowed her to experience an 'I' that never stands still; that is unknowing (though not epistemologically so). This oscillation between emotions and cognitive adaptation highlights an evolutionary corporeality where bodily self-perception is formed on the basis of past information— which is always out of date with our current physical body (Fausto-Sterling 2000).

Later, Theresa identifies how this paradoxical process was made possible through a 'holding trust':

> I think what was useful in that process was having those feelings,
> but actually trusting, trusting that what was happening was ok.
> > I didn't feel as if anything was going to be lost.
> I still felt kind of accompanied in my process.
> So . . .
> > there was a powerful kind of holding trust there.
> So that's what came out of that really.

A powerful holding trust is significant here as a fundamental aspect of developing the ontogenetic body as well as the therapeutic alliance. A safe holding environment (Winnicott 1971) is a basic premise and is crucial for facilitating an unfolding of intense emotional material in an ethical manner. Speaking to this aspect of safety, Theresa's words describe how she felt 'accompanied' during the rehearsal and filming process. This accompaniment became an *intra*-corporeal process comprising my kinaesthetic engagement with each individual and their movement phrase and a co-creation of each phrase as choreography for the camera, thus allowing a collaborative approach of individuals' contribution to the overall aesthetic.

In her interview, Silja elaborated on the collaborative nature of choreographic development for the camera. Like Theresa, she identified the issue of safety:

> And I think it was really nice to have lots of choreographic help and spacing, and in terms of everything, it was nice to know that I was looked after,
> > so it wasn't I was just left alone to do a dance, and let's film it,
> and, it was nice to know it was very set, and I think it gave it,
> > yeah, some sort of frame,
> and I felt safe to do it.

Silja's words seem to highlight the need for developmental holding: 'It was nice to know that I was looked after'. Again, I draw attention to the developmental process precisely because body-based processes of meaning-making and intersubjective relating develop in infants in a way that is carried forward into our adult experience (Johnson 2007; Beebe et al. 2005). As Johnson (2007) somewhat provocatively proposes, we are 'Big Babies'—the point here being to remind us how we learn to understand not from conceptual knowledge but though intersubjective bodily interactions and feelings. Hence, during this particular choreographic holding I was acutely aware of a different kind of intersubjective engagement; there was a range of vulnerabilities present and, as I witnessed Silja repeatedly falling to the ground and getting back up on her feet, I recognised her embodied performance of loss because I knew the meaning and feeling of *my own* bodily gestures and movements of loss.

Since choreographers increasingly work more transparently with dancers' autobiographical and collective movement motifs, developing the ability to facilitate movement unfolding and compositional aspects with a 'holding trust', is a crucial consideration for the evolution, composition, and flourishing of any personal movement material into the public choreographic domain. Moreover, for dance movement psychotherapists this compositional holding is also an essential aspect of assisting clients to integrate raw material into the performance of their everyday lives.

CORPOREAL TRACES

Although it is midsummer the rain drives ceaselessly all day. The camera crew try as best as possible to protect the equipment with large umbrellas. On this third day of filming we prepare for the next performances. Framed against the backdrop of an outside chapel white wall, Alison's movement is visceral: lifting, pulling, rippling, and twisting the long, now soaking wet yards of silk as it flies through the air. As I witness Alison, in front of the camera, I am reminded of fragments of her narrative, developed in the workshops and now providing the soundscore for her performance in the film: 'Red blanket, red blanket, red, blanket, a sign, a signal, a symbol [. . .] fear and love [. . .] red blanket, never spoken of, release it to the wind and air . . .' Now, I wonder what the silk becomes for her, and who she becomes in this embodied performance with the silk.

Transformation

It feels lovely. It was actually lovely being in the rain.
Well, I think something of the liberation of . . . of the blanket made me . . .
                                    It was just great, and . . .

I, I can see, I can kind of feel the real blanket. It was that sort of honeycomb, you know, the standard sort of issue which . . .

and I can see the colour and everything, and seeing the beautiful sort of silk, obviously *completely* different to the, to the blanket,

but it felt . . .

something really felt appropriate,
and I think I might have said on that day, about transformation,

from this thick blanket that's been so stuck in my mind, in my mind's eye, on the bed, and somehow about the sort of, that movement, so sort of freeing and flying and, and the and the, I think the transformation from the, this woolly blanket into that beautiful silk, and from being in the hospice bed to being,

you know, in the ground. And actually the rain was . . . felt rather lovely.

But the material changed a bit as it got wet, and . . . no, I really, really enjoyed that.

And I thought that was really, it felt for me like a massive part of the process of . . . of transformation.

And I suppose that's what was happening over the weekend for me really, of something transforming inside . . .

I'm really moving . . .

FIGURE 20.5. Photo of Alison Kelly performing her story during the filming of *I Can't Find Myself.* (Photo credit: Jackie King.)

Alison's words seem to evoke how the materiality of the performative process mirrors the materiality of loss, and yet something different was iterated in Alison's performance of loss in her experience of 'freeing and flying' with the red silk. My choreographic intervention was for Alison to have a kinaesthetic experience of moving with the red silk—I wanted to honour her experience of the 'red blanket' of which she speaks in her narrative for the film—which in turn allowed for a positive experience: a 'liberation ... [and] ... transformation'. This has echoes of the transformative power of mourning, as Butler (2006) explains:

> ... one mourns when one accepts that by the loss one undergoes one will be changed, possibly forever. Perhaps mourning has to do with agreeing to undergo a transformation (perhaps one should say *submitting* to a transformation) the full result of which one cannot know in advance. (p. 20)

The kinaesthetic shift into a public performative allowed for possible restorying (Willis 2009) of participants' relationship with loss, with the grieving process, and with the loved one who has died; for Alison, this experience became 'something transforming inside'. However, this transformation is paradoxical, both in the shift from therapeutic to performance space as well as *within* the process of grieving, since, as Derrida (2001) and Butler (2004) remind us, the person lost is inescapably 'in us'.

In her interview, Silja speaks of the materiality of engaging with nature during her performance, and I am struck by the entangled relationship between artistic process, nature, and loss.

> I think it was really, I was really glad my piece was filmed outside, you know,
>   on a green grass.
> Because to me it was almost like ... I don't know if a closure is probably not the right word, because it's not closed, the whole process, of course not ... but to the workshops, in terms of the workshops, it was a nice closure, of bringing it back to the nature. Because to me it's very important,
>   because that's, that's where my step-dad is,
>   and that's where we come form, that's where go,
>   and doing it in an open space, in fresh air, it's,
>   it's, I think it was really important.
>   Rather than doing it in some closed theatre space.

The workshops and the choreographic and film-making process allowed for participants to recognize, in Derrida's (2001) words, interiorization—the incorporation of the person lost into one's sense of self as ongoing; and Silja recognises this: '... it's not closed, the whole process, of course not'. And yet, interiorizing the other and recognizing that this is an ongoing (incomplete) process seems to be paradoxical, since the

FIGURE 20.6. Photo of Silja Ilmonen performing her story during the filming of *I Can't Find Myself*. (Photo credit: Jackie King.)

bodies of those we have lost are with within us, for us to see, yet 'intersubjective seeing' (Allegranti 2009, 2011) is not reciprocal.

In the *Moving Voices* project, the transition from workshops to filming worked actively with the process of witnessing self and other(s), which enabled a witnessing of the person lost (Allegranti and Wyatt 2013). Bearing embodied witness to the singularity of a relationship with the person who has died—and more than this, to the precarious-ness of bodies and our corporeal vulnerability—was strongly evoked in Silja's repeated crashing to the ground and in her recognition of the importance of '. . . bringing it back to the nature'.

OUR STORY CONNECTED WITH OTHER STORIES

We carry our ancestral, genetic line, other bodies, other stories, in our body. Later in her interview, when reflecting on her participation in the film, Cecilia speaks of the materiality and importance of this co-implication:

> I enjoyed doing it. I'd never been part of a film before so that was a really new experience for me and yeah,
> I did enjoy doing that, putting on the costume, seeing other people doing their bits, being outside and the colours, the heat of that day, yeah,
> just overall I think just being heard,
> being witnessed,
> being seen
> and also being able to respond to other people's stories in a kind of,
>
> yeah,
>
> where there's that kind of shared,
>
> shared experience, it's just really powerful,
> and that just reminded me how important it is to provide those opportunities to other people as well I think.

Young (2005) writes that '... stories must be told and retold to each new generation to keep a living, meaningful history' (p. 143). These stories are embodied in our memories, emotions, and psychophysical selves, and as each individual performed, my witnessing provided felt-sense and multisensory kinaesthetic responses that shift beyond an emphasis on visual representation into an *intra*-corporeal engagement (Allegranti and Wyatt 2013). Our kinaesthetic *intra*-actions produced a series of 'I's, resulting in embodied performances that are multilayered: autobiographical, relational, and political (Allegranti 2011). In so doing, we began to find a sense of community for the conditions of vulnerability (Butler 2006)—the 'shared' and 'powerful' experience to which Cecilia refers. Butler, too, understands how 'loss has made a tenuous "we" of us all' (Butler 2006, p. 20). And so, how can we use the deaths of others and lessons learned from them to understand the deaths of those dear to us and to engage with our own mortality? How do we become other than who we are after loss (White 2000)?

Echoing Cecilia's words, Jonathan also reflects on how the experience of making the film is now incorporated into this experience of his father:

> I ... I ... I think of the film and his name on the credits
>   and I think of the reading of him by me
> and the filming of that scene is now part of how I think about my dad.
> It's part of the whole ... um ... picture that I have when I think about my dad.
> It's not always there but still it's in there amongst a lot of other image that I have.
> And the way in which his story,

our story connected with other stories.
So that was alongside a number of other people's performances and ... performances of their losses,

um ... is also part of how I ... now ...
that's kind of added something to how I experience my father.

Jonathan's corporeal experience of seeing and being in the film is 'now part of how
I think about my dad', chiming with Gallagher's (2013) observation that 'body schemas,
working systematically with proprioceptive awareness, constitute a proprioceptive
self that is *always already* coupled with the other' (p. 81). This corporeal ontology calls
individualism—that great master discourse of 'I'—into question. We are 'processual'
beings, unbound, in a way that draws attention to Butler's sense that 'the body does not
belong to itself' (2010, p. 52–3).

AFTERLIFE

It is our ethical responsibility to 'reimagine the possibility of community on the basis
of vulnerability and loss' (Butler 2006, p. 20). The workshops, the film, the interviews,
shifting between moving, writing, and performing, and the transitions (in)between—all
of these have allowed for unthought-of possibilities to emerge. In her interview, Kate
spoke of the experience of writing in preparation for *Your Story Calls Me*:

I think that because you'd edited what I'd written,
I actually really liked the way it was edited and it did seem to me to encapsulate
something.
So, to come and do that, I actually felt quite excited about it, and I guess it also spoke
to a part of me that was a performer, so there was that sense of using my voice and
being ...

... and feeling that I had the right,
when we did the second read through of it,
to take my time, and, you know,
to mark those images in my head and to see them, which is very much how I act as
well as visualize, you know.
So, I really, really enjoyed that. And I really feel like there's something ... a sort of
tribute to Daniel that I can ... that will be in the film, you know ...

... that I feel very proud of.

Kate's words evoke the process of narrating herself, her story, and her brother into existence, perhaps acting as a ritual of mourning and a tribute for her brother. Similarly,
evoking Derrida's ghost, Butler (2006) speaks of the afterlife of words:

We inherit traces of the dead even when we are not the intended recipients, but in the
moment that we give away our own words, we participate in a certain wild future of
inheritance, one for which no framework for kinship exists. (p. 32)

In the *Moving Voices* project, what became apparent were the corporeal traces—the afterlife of embodiment. There is an afterlife that is kinaesthetically mediated by the experiences of moving, writing, filming, and witnessing the film for those who took part and for public audiences. Thus, by remembering the person lost, it was possible to engage in a material-discursive (dancing-writing) ritual of mourning in which we were 'giving an account' or 'reckoning with the dead' (Derrida 2001). The extent of this 'reckoning' is, of course, contingent upon the historicity of each embodied performance. However, there may be a possible corporeal reclaiming after loss: the dead can be in us, the living, and this (im)possible performative can give rise to our stories and their stories and provide a creative ongoing relationship with the person who has died.

Notes

1. UK UnLtd Social Enterprise Grant received by Allegranti and Wyatt in 2010.
2. There were two cycles of stand-alone workshops, each two days in duration. Sixteen women attended in total, and four attended both cycles. Since we were supported by the grant, the workshops were offered free of charge as part of a psychosocial support service.
3. Following the workshops, participants were invited to contribute to the screendance and subsequent interviews. In addition to Jonathan and myself, eight participants decided to take part. All participants gave formal consent to 'visibility' in the film and interviews. Ethical decision making unfolded at various stages where, as researchers, Jonathan and myself held a private screening of the film for participants prior to its public screening. This allowed for further discussion and reflection on the process and on the experience of loss.
4. National symposium *Embodying Loss*, at the Siobhan Davies Dance Studios, London, 2012. <http://embodyingloss.blogspot.co.uk>.
5. Balanescu Quartet and Balanescu, 2005.
6. Ponsonby Temple, Froebel College, University of Roehampton. In 200, stones from a neo-classical temple were discovered. These stones had been safely stored by the Jesuit Priests who had dismantled the temple in the early part of the twentieth century.
7. All photographs were taken by Jackie King on location.
8. I follow Etherington (2004) and others in presenting participants' words in stanza form, which 'allows for the disjointed natural breaks and hesitations, more normal in speech, to be maintained' (p. 56).

References

Allegranti, B. (2005). *In My Body* (film). Director, B. Allegranti, Media Arts Productions, Video Channel Cologne.

Allegranti, B. (2011). *Embodied Performances: Sexuality, Gender, Bodies*, London: Palgrave Macmillan.

Allegranti, B. (2012). *Your Story Calls Me* (film). Director, B. Allegranti, Assistant Director, J. Wyatt, UnLtd Catalyst, N Creative, Nest Films.

Allegranti, B. (2013). 'The politics of becoming bodies: Sex, gender and intersubjectivity in motion', *The Arts in Psychotherapy, Special Issue on Gender, Health and the Arts Therapies*, 40: 394–403.

Allegranti, B. (2014). 'Corporeal kinship: Dancing the entanglements of love and loss', in J. Wyatt and T. Adams, *On (Writing) Families: Autoethnographies of Presence and Absence, Love and Loss*. Rotterdam: Sense Publishers.

Allegranti, B. and Wyatt, J. (2014). 'Witnessing loss: A feminist material-discursive account', *Qualitative Inquiry*, 20(4): 533–43.

Barad, K. (2003). 'Posthumanist performativity: Toward an understanding of how matter comes to matter', *Signs: Journal of Women in Culture and Society*, 28(3): 801–31.

Barad, K. (2007). *Meeting the Universe Halfway: Quantum Physics and the Entanglement of Matter and Meaning*. Durham, NC: Duke University Press.

Beebe, B., Knoblauch, S., Rustin, S., Sorter, D., (2005). *Forms of Intersubjectivity in Infant Research and Adult Treatment*. New York, NY: Other Press.

Butler, J. (1993). *Bodies That Matter: On the Discursive Limits of Sex*. New York, NY: Routledge.

Butler, J. (1994). 'Gender as performance: An interview with Judith Butler', in 'Interview by Peter Osborne and Lynne Segal', *Radical Philosophy*, 67.

Butler, J. (2004). *Undoing Gender*. Oxfordshire: Routledge.

Butler, J. (2006). *Precarious Life: The Powers of Mourning and Violence*. London: Verso.

Butler, J. (2010). *Frames of War: When is Life Grievable?* London: Verso.

Davies, J. (2012). *The Importance of Suffering: The Value and Meaning of Emotional Discontent*. London: Routledge.

Davies, J. (2013). *Cracked: Why Psychiatry is Doing More Harm Than Good*. London: Icon Books.

Derrida, J. (2001). *The Work of Mourning*, ed. A. P. Brault and M. Naas. Chicago, IL: University of Chicago Press.

Etherington, K. (2004). *Becoming a Reflexive Researcher*. London: Jessica Kingsley.

Fausto-Sterling, A. (2000). *Sexing the Body: Gender Politics and The Construction of Sexuality*. New York, NY: Basic Books.

Gallagher, S. (2005). *How the Body Shapes the Mind*. Oxford, UK: Oxford University Press.

Gallagher, S. (2007). 'The natural philosophy of agency', *Philosophy Compass* 2(2): 347–57.

Gallagher, S. (2013). *How the Body Shapes the Mind*. Oxford: Oxford University Press.

Gendlin, E. T. (1996). *Focusing-Oriented psychotherapy: A Manual of the Experiential Method*. New York, NY: Guilford Press.

Haraway, D. (2006). 'Encounters with companion species: Entangling dogs, baboons, philosophers, and biologist', *Configurations*, 14(1–2): 97–114.

Huxley, M., and Witts, N., (2003). *The Twentieth Century Performance Reader*, 2nd edn. London: Routledge.

Johnson, M. (2007). *The Meaning of the Body: Aesthetics of Human Understanding*. Chicago, IL: University of Chicago Press.

Leahy, M. M., O'Dwyer, M., and Ryan, F. (2012). 'Witnessing stories: Definitional ceremonies in narrative therapy with adults who stutter', *Journal of Fluency Disorders*, 37: 234–41.

Mellor, P. A. and Shilling, C. (1993). 'Modernity, self-Identity and the sequestration of death', *Sociology*, 27: 411–32.

Parnas, J. and Handest, P. (2003). 'Phenomenology of anomalous self-experience in early schizophrenia', *Comprehensive Psychiatry*, 44(2): 121–34.

Sheets-Johnstone, M. (2000). 'Kinetic–tactile–kinesthetic bodies: Ontogenetical foundations of apprenticeship learning', *Human Studies*, 23: 343–70.

St Pierre, E. A. (2011). 'Post qualitative research: The critique and the coming after', in N. Denzin and Y. Lincoln (eds.), *Handbook of Qualitative Research*, 4th edn. London: Sage, pp. 611–25.

Thornborrow, J. and Coates, J. (eds.) (2005). *The Sociolinguistics of Narrative: Identity, Performance, Culture*. Amsterdam: John Benjamins.

White. M. (2000). *Reflections on Narrative Practice: Essays and Interviews*. Adelaide: Dulwich Centre Publications.

Willis, A. (2009). 'Restorying the self, restoring place: Healing through grief in everyday places', *Emotion, Space and Society*, 2(2): 86–91.

Winnicott, D. (1971). *Playing and Reality*. New York, NY: Routledge.

Wyatt, J. (2005). 'A gentle going? An autoethnographic short story', *Qualitative Inquiry*, 11(5): 724–32.

Young, I. (2005). *On Female Body Experience: 'Throwing Like a Girl' and Other Essays*. Oxford: Oxford University Press.

PART III

....

DANCE
IN EDUCATION

....

INTRODUCTION TO PART III

VICKY KARKOU AND SUE OLIVER

With Contributions by Julie Joseph, Jo Bungay-Orr, and Foteini Athanasiadou

THIS part presents views of dance across a broad spectrum of educational settings, from mainstream schooling to higher education, from working with children with learning difficulties to working with dance and movement educators and therapists. These diverse perspectives stem from various locations across the globe, with the concept of wellbeing as a catalyst for successful learning being the common thread binding them.

Writing from a Canadian perspective, in Chapter 21 Ann Kipling Brown notes that educators acknowledge the benefit of arts in general in school curricula to encourage creative minds in children, but questions how well prepared their teachers might be, particularly for teaching dance, due to shortfalls in teacher training. Such gaps in pedagogical teaching manifest themselves in patchy implementation of dance across the geographical area, which, she argues, has a direct impact on students' wellbeing. She tells of her own experience of teaching in a tertiary education setting, insisting that dance offers possibilities for self-expression, connecting the personal with the historical and as such contributing to individuals' sense of wellbeing.

In the UK, and in England in particular, Jayne Stevens continues the pedagogical theme in Chapter 22, endorsing the belief in the place of dance in education, but raising awareness of the lack of research into the pedagogies underlying the modes of delivery. Focusing on youth education settings, she outlines the development of dance teaching pedagogy and highlights the disparity in training and backgrounds of those who deliver it. She also argues that integrated practices that bring together professional educational and community dance practices can be of value, especially with regards to developing subjective wellbeing.

In Chapter 23, a European 'snapshot' is taken by Sue Oliver, Monika Konold, and Christina Larek, who pool their knowledge of educational dance to compare creative dance in schools in areas of Germany and Scotland. Underpinning the decision to pursue this topic has been the view that, while both countries have been part of the European Union, there could be some degree of conformity in educational provision. However, as education has been a devolved issue in Europe, their findings inevitably reveal significant differences in provision at present. Focus on pupils' wellbeing through creativity and dance is an area of ongoing development in the curricula of these countries.

Remaining in Germany, in Chapter 24 Claire Schaub-Moore, a British psychodynamic psychotherapist and dance movement psychotherapist, describes a programme of a whole-school psychotherapeutic intervention in a German secondary school, which offered a choice of creative outlets to pupils who had been branded 'difficult'. This was a multistranded project that incorporated not only dance/movement but also art, music, filming, singing, and graffiti. It involved not only direct work with the young people participating (pupils with a very diverse cultural background, all of whom were struggling emotionally and educationally), but also teaching staff (through supervision) and families (through weekly visits), as well as social-work students. The project aimed to help these pupils find a way to connect back into the school system to complete their studies rather than drop out.

Similarly multi-stranded is the work presented in Chapter 25 by Nancy Beardall in the USA. Three projects are described: one on dance, another on dance/movement therapy, and a third on the use of creative/expressive arts in secondary schools. In all cases these projects attempted to handle potentially challenging behaviour before it became a problem, aiming to support self-esteem, relationship building, empowerment, and the prevention of bullying, in addition to the promotion of respect for differences and the creation of a supportive community. By linking it with dance and other creative arts, schools were able to offer a more holistic approach to education, addressing the physical, cognitive, social, emotional, and relational needs of these adolescent pupils. Beardall lets the reader know about the outcomes of the evaluations of these programmes while making useful links with theory.

In Chapter 26, Abdulazeem Atolaibi, Vicky Karkou, Marieta van der Linden, and Lindesay Irvine offer a unique insight into the use of movement therapy with children who have special educational needs in Saudi Arabia. The setting presents particular challenges to the implementation of this therapeutic programme (for one, movement therapy, the preferred term for this culture, has only recently been introduced in Saudi Arabian schools). A very well attended and evaluated programme, however, gives us some exciting statistical evidence that supports assumptions of the link between motion and emotion and beliefs that movement therapy can support the integration of these two areas.

Sue Mullane and Kim Dunphy continue the theme of dance movement therapy in Chapter 27—this time in special education in Melbourne, Australia. They focus on how educational policies set the context for the curriculum, within which dance movement therapy can contribute to students' wellbeing, hence encouraging successful learning. They also explore the many facets of wellbeing and evaluate this therapeutic approach as a mechanism for promoting deep engagement in the learning process. A case study of a particular programme in a special school is presented, illustrating some of the points argued for in the chapter. The brief video material accompanying this work also brings an understanding of some of the key points.

The wellbeing of dance movement therapy students in higher education is the subject of Chapter 28, by Hilda Wengrower. This international study draws upon a survey of the perspectives of trainers and teachers, and compares the wellbeing of the students in dance movement therapy programmes with that of students studying medicine and social science. Wengrower considers the impact of dance on students' stress levels, as well as the impact the characteristics of the trainers and teachers have on the teaching and learning process.

Exploring and cultivating the feeling of wellbeing further is the topic of Chapter 29, by Anna Fiona Keogh and Joan Davis. The context of their enquiry is a somatically-based training programme delivered in the Irish Republic, developed by Davis, and on which Keogh, a qualified dance movement psychotherapist, was a student at the time of writing. It is called 'Origins', and is approved by International Somatic Movement Education and Therapy Association (ISMETA). The authors consider the 'felt sense' of wellbeing as experienced by students on the course, and discuss the benefits of cultivating an awareness of wellbeing for students and educators. They pose intriguing questions when they ask: 'How do we know we are feeling well?', and 'How can we teach our students or clients to have an awareness of their own experience of wellbeing?'

As editors, we also ask further questions, which we invite readers to consider:

- Within the context of education, is wellbeing an essential consideration?
- What are some effective ways in which wellbeing can be supported?
- What is the contribution of different types of dance within this work?
- How can cross-disciplinary work operate in ways in which education becomes a conducive and welcoming environment for the emotional/social health of learners?
- Within the context of global recession and financial cuts, is specialist provision within a school context essential or a mere luxury?

Looking at the last of these questions a little closer, it is worth considering the potential contribution of Dance Movement Psychotherapy in this debate. As indicated in other publications, and as explored in this part, school environments are traditionally a common area of work for dance movement psychotherapists in the UK (Karkou 2010; Karkou and Sanderson 2001a, 2001b). This can be seen as the result of the early development of the profession from teachers with a strong creative and/or dance educational background. Although Dance Movement Psychotherapy practitioners are currently working in diverse contexts, original links with education seem to persist. Currently however, unlike its origins, the discipline is not just a sensitive form of dance teaching.

As a form of psychotherapy it has clear psychotherapeutic aims to offer support to the overall wellbeing of children who are struggling with their learning. We can see this point made strongly in this part by Schaub-Moore, for example.

We can also see this even more clearly in three brief examples presented here, two of which come from mainstream education (primary and secondary), and one from a special school. All three projects illustrate (i) the development of an in-depth understanding of children's issues, (ii) movement-based and creative means with which some of these issues can be explored, and (iii) useful ways in which the work can complement and support the work of teaching staff.

All three examples also have in common the use of artistic inquiry as their methodology. This research methodology integrates thinking and creativity, and is linked with postmodern qualitative enquiry that allows for multiple meaning and encourages critical awareness (Leavy 2009). Wadsworth Hervey (2000) defines it as a research methodology that follows the creative process, incorporates aesthetic/artistic criteria, and uses artistic methods for all its stages (collection, analysis, and presentation of findings). As a result, in the accompanied video material (see the online version of the book), creative, movement-based findings are presented as answers to the research questions asked. The aim is not to share knowledge as such, but to share affective aspects of the topic of investigation (Finley 2005; Leavy 2009). The viewers are therefore invited to approach this video material as emotional references to the clinical work and the research questions of each of these projects.

In the first of these three projects, moments of chaos and order in Dance Movement Psychotherapy with children in a mainstream primary school are explored. Jo Burgay-Orr, an English dance movement psychotherapist, influenced by attachment theory (Bowlby 1988) on her final project from her Masters training, writes:

> This project refers to a small-scale study on moments of chaos and order within weekly Dance Movement Psychotherapy sessions within the primary school. Relevant literature suggests that children first need to be chaotic in order to reorganize themselves into something they can understand and manage. Similarly, others argued that children need to make a mess but also have a longing to contain it.
>
> However, in the work I did with four girls aged nine to eleven, I felt overwhelmed by the amount of chaos that these children, struggling with neglect, were presenting. In the process of the study I found that three moments offered particular insights in the therapeutic process and became turning points for both myself and the children attending: (i) 'Acceptance' was the first—a moment that was important for both myself and one of the children with whom I had more difficulties connecting. (ii) 'Safe holding', involving the sensation of being held and supported. (iii) 'Finding a space for chaos', referring to the need to create a safe space and 'getting it all out'. (See Video III.a on the Companion Website ▶.)

Similar themes are present in the second study, which was completed by Julie Joseph (Joseph and Karkou 2013, 2017a, 2017b) in a secondary school in Scotland. The accompanying video refers to the final creative reflection of the researcher/student-therapist on three moments of holding. She writes:

> As part of my final clinical project I asked the question: 'How did a twelve-session Dance Movement Psychotherapy group facilitate moments of holding with adolescents in a mainstream school?' 'Holding' was defined in Winnicottian terms (1965) as not only the physical holding of the infant 'but also [to] the total environmental provision' (pp. 43–4), including the particular space and time where it may take place.
>
> The study was based on postmodern philosophical principles that valued multiple perspectives. In accordance to artistic enquiry principles, it used artistic methods to gather, analyse, and present data. The methods included (i) art-making by six adolescents (15–16 years old) at the end of each session, (ii) video recording of the therapist's movement responses to the group after each session, and (iii) reflective notes of the therapist after each session. The analysis included an ongoing 'dialoguing' with data and a final creative synthesis.
>
> Findings revealed that holding took place through (a) the use of objects that connected participants with their breath and thus their own 'body' selves (session 5); (b) the relationship with another—a mirroring exercise between one participant and the therapist, enabling this young person to 'be seen' (session 7) and subsequently to open up; and (c) the relationship with the group. During the final session (session 12), the group 'held' certain members while they revealed losses and issues around self-worth (see Video III.b on the Companion Website ⦿).

Finally, Athanasiadou (Athanasiadou and Karkou 2017), a Greek dance movement psychotherapist, refers to her study in special education with children with autism, influenced by interactive ideas (Stern 2000; Trevarthen et al. 1998). Her findings are brought together in a creative synthesis (see Companion Website, ⦿). She summarizes this project as follows:

> It is generally believed that children with ASD struggle with forming relationships. However, there is growing literature that stresses the significance of non-verbal interactions, such as gestures and facial expressions within a non-threatening, warm therapeutic environment for the formation and establishment of relationships with this client group.
>
> This project explored the use of Dance Movement Psychotherapy with children with autistic spectrum disorders as a support in forming relationships. Dance movement psychotherapy was seen as a form of arts therapies that uses movement as a means for communication, and as such as an intervention that may support the development of relationships. Data was generated through methods such as (i) video recordings of sessions, (ii) embodied tools such as drawings of a body figure and video recording of the researcher/therapist's somatic responses, and (iii) written reflection on observations, feelings, and ideas relating to the study question recorded in a journal.
>
> Challenging general perceptions around autism, two types of relationships were identified: one-to-one and group relationships. Physical awareness through sensorimotor activities, the use of rhythm in mirroring (otherwise known as attunement),

purposeful misattunement, and role playing seemed to be important factors supporting the development of such relationships (see Video III.c on Companion Website ⏵).

References

Athanasiadou, F. and Karkou, V. (2017). 'Establishing relationships with children with autism spectrum disorders through dance movement psychotherapy: A case study using artistic enquiry', in S. Daniel and C. Trevarthen (eds.), *Rhythms of Relating in Children's Therapies*. London: Jessica Kingsley, pp. 272–292.

Bowlby, J. (1988). *A Secure Base Clinical Applications of Attachment Theory*. London: Routledge.

Finley, S. (2005). 'Arts-based inquiry', in N. K. Denzin and Y. S. Lincoln (eds),. *The Sage Handbook of Qualitative Research*, 3rd edn. London: Sage, pp. 681–94.

Joseph, J. and Karkou, V. (2013). 'Research into dance movement psychotherapy with adolescents: A rationale', in E. Krevica and K. Martinsone (eds.), *Arts Therapies for Different Client/Patient Groups*. Riga: Janis Zeimanis, pp. 102–7.

Joseph, J. and Karkou, V. (2017a). 'The moving and movement identities of adolescents: Lessons from dance movement psychotherapy in schools', in R. MacDonald, D. Heardgreaves, and D. Miell (eds.), *Handbook of Musical Identities*. New York: Oxford University Press, pp. 232–245.

Joseph, J. and Karkou, V. (2017b). Holding and adolescent angst: Significant moments within a dance movement psychotherapy group in a mainstream secondary school, in H. Payne (ed), Essentials of Dance Movement Psychotherapy: International Perspectives on Theory, Research and Practice. London and New York: Routledge, pp. 201–222.

Karkou, V. (ed). (2010). *Arts Therapies in Schools: Research and Practice*. London: Jessica Kingsley.

Karkou, V. and Sanderson, P. (2001a). 'Dance movement therapy in the UK: Current orientations of a field emerging from dance education', *European P.E. Review*, 7(2): 137–55.

Karkou, V. and Sanderson, P. (2001b). 'Report: Theories and assessment procedures used by dance/movement therapists in the UK', *The Arts in Psychotherapy*, 28: 197–204.

Leavy, P. (2009) *Methods Meets Art: Arts-Based Research Practice*. New York: Guilford Press.

Stern, D. N. (2000). *The Interpersonal World of the Infant: A View from Psychoanalysis and Developmental Psychology*. New York, NY: Basic Books.

Trevarthen, C., Aitken, K., Papoudi, D., and Robarts, J. (1998). *Children with Autism: Diagnosis and Interventions to Meet their Needs*, 2nd edn. London: Jessica Kingsley.

Wadsworh Hervey, L. (2000). *Artistic Inquiry in Dance Movement Therapy: Creative Alternatives for Research*. Springfield, Illinois: Charles C. Thomas.

Winnicott, D. W. (1965). *The Maturation Process and the Facilitating Environment*. London: Karnac Books.

CHAPTER 21

PROVOKING CHANGE

Dance Pedagogy and Curriculum Design

ANN KIPLING BROWN

INTRODUCTION

IN this chapter I address how arts education is being supported and sustained through UNESCO initiatives, undertakings by dance and arts education scholars, and the specific programming that exists in Saskatchewan, Canada. These initiatives are discussed in reference to curriculum development and in-service teacher education in the arts. With reference to dance I speak to the importance of high-quality curriculum design and pedagogical practice in the training of pre-service teacher education. The premise is that through arts/dance education students develop perceptual, imaginative, and sensual abilities, come to understand others, and find their voices to express ideas, thoughts, and feelings about their world.

Research has suggested that many people are not aware of the benefits of the arts in relation to health and wellbeing and the impact of an arts-rich school environment on student engagement or how arts may be used as a pedagogical tool to help students learn (McCarthy, Ondaatje, Zakaras, and Brooks 2005, p. 22). They identify that significant experiences in the arts, whether throughout the curriculum and/or through a range of extracurricular activities in the arts, can lead to improved attitudes toward arts and school, improve social behaviour, and encourage self-confidence and self-efficacy (p. 24). In the Forum Summary report of the Canadian Forum on Arts and Health (2006), recurring themes from the forum's discussions in relation to the arts and health were identified: 'arts and creativity promote a sense of control and empowerment in people'; 'the arts facilitate human relations and connections'; 'creativity is a need'; 'new understandings of the nature and the experience of illness are revealed through art'; 'the arts help patients become active partners in their own care'; and 'the arts are transformative and facilitate change' (p. 1). Quiroga Murcia et al. (2010) undertook a study that asked 475 non-professional adult dancers to complete a survey, which revealed that ' . . .

dancing has potential positive benefits on wellbeing in several aspects. In particular, beneficial effects were found related to the emotional dimension, as well as physical, social, and spiritual dimensions' (p. 149).

MY PERSONAL JOURNEY

I embarked upon a career in dance education because I found something in dance that encouraged, shaped, and empowered me. Like any other teacher I struggled with the politics of the school context, the design of curriculum, the lack of respect for dance and the arts, and the ever-changing demands made on the school by administrators, teachers, parents, and students. My values and beliefs often clashed with others and left me feeling unsure and confused. I believed there was a way to teach dance other than in the traditionalist method, and there could be a way in which dance could be used to express oneself and the world around us. I persevered with my ideas, learned from my mistakes, and listened to my colleagues, and I think that I am now able to reflect on that journey and describe where I am today. What were those influences? How do I feel about what is happening in arts education today? Have there been changes?

THE IMPORTANCE OF ARTS EDUCATION

It is not an easy task being a teacher, and certainly not when you are working in the arts. Many scholars have talked about the importance of the arts in education. Maxine Greene (1991) states that 'one of the functions of the arts is to subvert our thoughtlessness and complacencies, our certainties about art itself' (33). Eisner (1994) clearly states that 'the arts' position in the school curriculum symbolizes to the young what adults believe is important' (88). Goldberg (1999) adds to the argument for the place of arts in education. She firmly believed that we could expand our knowledge and understanding of the world through study in the arts. Specifically, she outlines three aspects through which the arts can be used to understand the world. Firstly, she says, 'A student may learn *with* the arts; that is, explore subject matter with the aid of an artwork'; secondly, a student may learn '*through* the arts by creating works of art that express his or her reflections concerning specific subject matter; and thirdly, a student may learn '*about* the arts as a subject in and of itself' (p. 17). Richards (2005) makes the critical connection between artistic activity and human nature, asking:

> Why does the human being long to work artistically? Why are the art programs in public schools and communities so popular? Because there is the natural enthusiasm for creative activity built into their bodies. The arts are the ground of our intuitive understanding of ourselves and the world around us. (p. 94)

Naidus (2005) confirms the power of the arts when she says:

> I remain optimistic that more of us will use the arts to provoke dialogue, empower
> the invisible and alienated, raise questions about things we take for granted, educate
> the uniformed, heal rifts in polarized communities and within individuals wounded
> by society's ills, and provide a vision for the future where people can live in greater
> harmony with each other and the natural world. (p. 182)

Johnson and Lew (2005) comment on the role of the arts in their work as elementary
and early childhood professionals: 'The groundedness of the artist, the work of art, and
ourselves as perceivers reflect the significance of social and historical contexts for the
construction of meaning' (p. 82). Dance educators Cone and Cone (2011) justify dance
education as

> a crucial component of a comprehensive education for all students. It is a movement
> art form that promotes learning to communicate and express ideas, feelings, per-
> spectives, and concepts through kinesthetic modes of learning . . . Dance is for all
> students of all abilities; everyone can participate, create, learn, and experience the joy
> of dancing with others. (p. 29)

In 'Rationale for Dance Education', Manitoba Education (2011) states that 'dance has the
potential to promote responsibility and leadership and to prepare and inspire future citizens of the world to understand and address the most critical challenges of their times.'
Anderson (2004) includes in his list of educationally important aspects about dance that
it 'can contribute to a person's overall health and well-being—mental, emotional, spiritual, social, and physical (p. 85). There is no doubt in the eyes of the artist and arts educator that the arts are empowering and are important in the lives of our students.

THE ROLE OF ARTS EDUCATION IN CANADA

In Canada, in the early 1990s, there was a call to prepare students for the twenty-first century. Tomkins and Case (2012) identified that educational reform was needed. There was
much criticism that students in Canada compared 'unfavourably to other industrialized
countries' and that the 'perceptions of excessively high student drop-out rates' required
attention. Concern that the curriculum did not take into consideration the diversity of
the nation's classrooms resulted in curricular developments on two fronts: 'establishing
sets of common or essential elements that formed the 'basics for all', and 'the new "core"
of the curriculum [that] reduced focus on academic study, emphasizing vocational and
career-related development, particularly in the areas of technology, mathematics, and
science, problem solving, critical thinking, literacy and communication.' Although the
arts were not mentioned directly, many provinces, including Saskatchewan, retained
the arts as core, identifying them as part of literacy. These reforms had great effect on

how teachers were expected to deliver the curriculum; namely, allocating fifty minutes per week for each art form in an already crowded week of curriculum expectations, and being proficient in teaching each of the four art forms (dance, drama, music, and visual arts).

Information pertinent to the status of arts education comes to us through the report, *Learning to Live, Living to Learn: Perspectives on Arts Education in Canada* (UNESCO 2005). Dr Max Wyman, OC., President of the Canadian Commission for UNESCO, explains in his introductory message in the report that it provides

> ... a concise snapshot of the thinking that currently surrounds the issue of the programming in arts education that is currently available, and of the potential for development and growth in this area. In particular, it highlights the significance and importance of arts education in Canada, providing both philosophical argument and a practical description of programs, organizations, and teacher education, as well as identifying some of the major players and challenges they face. (para. 4).

In late 2004 and early 2005, the Commission undertook consultations across Canada to identify the current state of arts education in Canada, supporting the work of the Canadian project *Arts and Learning: A Call to Action*. The consultations were also in preparation for two major events: the Europe Regional Conference on Arts Education in Vilnius, Lithuania, in 2005, and the World Conference for Arts Education in Portugal in 2006. The report of the First World Conference on Arts Education (2006) highlighted that many agencies, such as 'ministries of education, universities, school boards, private schools, cultural organizations, government and non-governmental agencies, community centres, and arts production companies' (p. 10), are involved in arts education and provide a range of courses, programmes, and activities. Following these initiatives, UNESCO's Second World Conference on Arts Education was held in May 2010 in Seoul, Republic of Korea, with a further report: *The Seoul Agenda: Goals for the Development of Arts Education* (UNESCO 2010). The goals affirm the importance of arts education, encouraging a focus on infrastructures, policy development, research, and practice that will provide 'lifelong and intergenerational learning in, about, and through arts education' (pp. 1–10). One of the major goals that apply particularly to this writing emphasizes the importance of 'ensuring that sustainable training in arts education is available to educators, artists, and communities' (p. 6). It is mentioned specifically that 'sustainable professional learning mechanisms' should be provided for teachers and artists, that 'artistic principles and practices' should be integrated within pre-service teacher education, and that such in-service and pre-service activities should be carefully monitored through 'supervision and mentoring' (p. 6).

In Canada, while in-service activities are offered by various agencies cited in the report *Learning to Live, Living to Learn: Perspectives on Arts Education in Canada* (Canadian Commission for UNESCO 2005), the pre-service education of teachers is the responsibility of designated universities in each province and territory. This report briefly identifies what is important in pre-service education, and outlines the range of offerings:

> Future teachers need to know what the arts can do and how individuals learn in and through the arts. Not enough time is given to pre-service arts education programs to teachers and there are great discrepancies and inconsistencies in the programs that are offered. Program courses can range from as little as 12 hours in length to 5 years in certain provinces. In most, teachers' arts education takes place over an 8 to 12-month period. (p. 11)

It appears that the concerns stated in these reports have not lead to much change in pre-service or in-service training in Canada. This inaction prompted the formation of the National Roundtable for Teacher Education in the Arts (NRTEA), led by Michael Wilson and Madeleine Aubrey, both avid advocates for arts education and co-chairs of the Roundtable. Its has met on two occasions—May 2011 and June 2012—and its vision is 'to engage, empower, and inspire arts educators in both public and private sectors through new insights into pre-service and in-service training and learning in the Arts to enhance delivery of arts education across Canada' (2011, p. 1). As a participant in the two Roundtable discussions that involved professors, teachers, artists, pre-service and graduate students, arts administrators, government officials, and school board consultants and superintendents, it was interesting to learn of the paucity of training offered across the country and the limited access of sound programmes to all learners. Through the discussions we examined the various programmes available for pre-service and in-service teacher education in the arts, and concluded that guidelines were needed for an appropriate and supportive programmes in teacher education in the arts. In 2012 the participants investigated four areas, the outcomes of which I summarize here: the need for a strong philosophical base; a balanced inclusiveness of all artistic expressions, focusing on learning in, through, and about the art forms; meaningful aesthetic experiences and practical training in the arts for all in-service and pre-service candidates; and programmes that include strategies dealing with certification, structure, and models of delivery.

ARTS EDUCATION IN SASKATCHEWAN

In the province of Saskatchewan, arts education has long been provided through programmes offered by professional artists and community programmes. Additionally, arts courses in the Faculty of Fine Arts and Education at the University of Regina provided access to certain art forms. In 1982 the implementation of the Arts Education programme in the Faculty of Education influenced and supported the need for a comprehensive arts education programme for schools and specialist and generalist teachers who would be trained to teach arts in schools. Since its inception the Arts Education programme has established a five-year BEd degree and an after degree in Arts Education. The Arts Education programme requires that the students follow five arts areas (dance, drama, literature, music, and visual arts) for the first two years of the programme, and then select a major and minor from those areas. During the five years the students follow courses in the selected major and minor areas together with courses in educational psychology, professional studies, aesthetic education, technology, and selected areas in arts, such as sociology, philosophy, and anthropology. These studies lead to a comprehensive education in the teaching of arts, full teacher certification, and a combined BA in each of the arts areas. In addition, we offer a Certificate in Dance Teacher Education for those who wish to teach in private studio and community settings.

In 1990 the implementation of the arts education curriculum for all K-12 students began. The 1990 Saskatchewan Arts Education Curriculum documents identified the aim of arts education as 'to enable students to understand and value arts expressions throughout life' (Saskatchewan Education 1991, p. 3). The broad areas of learning of the curriculum include the following about arts education:

> In arts education, students learn how the arts can provide a voice and means to make a difference in their personal lives and in peer, family, and community interactions. The arts give students multiple ways to express their views and to reflect on the perspectives and experiences of others. Students learn how to design, compose, problem solve, inspire change, and contribute innovative ideas that can improve the quality of their own lives and the lives of others. Students in the arts seek to discover who they are, envision who they might become, imagine possibilities and alternatives for their communities, and provide new ideas and solutions for building a sustainable future. Students also gain an understanding of the immense contributions that artists and the arts offer to the world. (p. 4)

In the academic year 1996–97 an evaluation of the implementation of the Arts Education curriculum was undertaken, and in 1998 the Arts Education Grades 1–9 Curriculum Evaluation Report was presented. The evaluation was undertaken in order to evaluate the extent of implementation in the province, to collect information about practices and student experiences, to identify supports and barriers to implementation, and to provide information for future implementation and maintenance. Interviews, focus groups, and telephone surveys were employed to access information from administrators, teachers, students, parents, and local arts communities. In addition, case studies of classrooms of six schools were conducted. The universities also provided information about teacher education programmes. The following summary reveals the situation in 1996–97.

> Most administrators, teachers, students, parents and members of the communities in Saskatchewan believe in the aim, goals and objectives of the Arts Education Curriculum. The curriculum evaluation project has revealed that some elements of the curriculum are being implemented as intended in some locations around the province, and in some cases very successfully. However, implementation is not

progressing at a desired pace, and will require measures to enhance the process. (Saskatchewan Education 1998, p. v)

It appeared that dance was the least taught of the four strands (dance, drama, music and visual arts), with teachers saying that it was difficult to teach if they did not have any experience in the area. There was confusion as to whether dance would be covered by the Arts Education or Physical Education teachers, and observations that there was little time or space for a dance programme in the schools. It was recommended in the evaluation report that a clarification of the differences between dance in Arts Education and Physical Education should be made, and that there should be more professional development for the dance strand.

At the time of writing it appears that the same problems exist. Even though professional development has been offered, the presence of dance in schools is very low. Where graduates of the programme, working in a generalist or specialist role, are in the schools, there is success—but we hear the same arguments of space, time, and lack of confident teachers.

Dance Education

> The role of dance in the education system or in the lives of children is unknown, though dance forms part of the curriculum in several provinces, and dance has a role in learning and in therapy.
>
> T. J. Cheney Research Inc. (2004, section 7)

This statement, as well as the summary of the 1998 Arts Education Grades 1–9 Curriculum Evaluation Report mentioned previously, is supported by a review of dance in the province by the Saskatchewan Arts Board in collaboration with Dance Saskatchewan Inc. (2009). The final report (2009), *A Review of Dance in Saskatchewan*, described that through community consultations 'the goals of the review were: to find what currently exists in dance in Saskatchewan; to ignite people's imagination of what could be; and to generate new information that may expand, build, or replace' (p. 3). The report revealed that there were inadequate facilities for dance, a challenge geographically for access, a lack of awareness of what dance is and could be, inadequate training for dancers and dance educators in both public and private settings, and above all, a 'dissatisfaction with the implementation of the elementary and high school dance curricula' (p. 8).

As a dance educator within the Arts Education programme that I have described, I am interested in the role of the arts in the education of all students. However, I am particularly focused on how dance shapes future arts educators and what kind of dance educators we should be striving to nurture and prepare for teaching in our community. Many of our students are graduates of the public schools in our province, and they, like many of their students, have limited backgrounds and experience in the arts. Even though the arts are core curriculum in this province, not all students have access to a meaningful arts education. Many will have had some form of visual arts, a few may have had access to a music programme, and a very few will have had experiences in dance and drama. Those who have experience in dance come from the dance studios and community programmes in which performance is the focus of the curriculum. It is not surprising, therefore, that many of our undergraduate pre-service teachers have little understanding of the role of the arts in young people's growth and development. Some may have the view that the arts may help other subjects or are for recreational purposes. Few understand the symbolic function of the arts and do not grasp how the arts may provide means for young people to express their thoughts, feelings, and ideas.

Who decides what dance curriculum will be in our schools? What is it that makes for a good dance curriculum? Whose and what dance is in the curriculum? How is dance being taught? How is the dance curriculum meeting the needs of the diversity of our classrooms?

Education theorists such as Larry Cuban (1995) and Eliot Eisner (1994) describe the curriculum as that which is officially or explicitly designed to be taught, and that which is learned implicitly because of the way the school is organized and teachers and administrators behave. We know that what teachers leave out of the curriculum is no less important than that which they include. So if there is no time for arts, the message is that arts are not important! As Eisner (1994) states: 'These messages are often numerous, subtle, and consistent' (p. 88). Thus our arts education students as part of their studies examine in detail the official curriculum that reflects the content prescribed by the Ministry of Education. They become aware of the taught curriculum, that which the teacher chooses to teach, and in the recollections of their own schooling they realize that these two do not often match. They are confused, and at the same time feel they learned some things that they both wish to and do not wish to carry with them into their own teaching. I am interested in how we help our pre-service teachers to understand curriculum and pedagogy and, of course, to go beyond the teaching of steps in dance. So, what is it that we strive for in our dance education programme?

DANCE PEDAGOGY

In the August 2006 edition of *Dance Magazine* (Perron 2006), 'eighteen dancers, choreographers, coaches, and teachers talk about the teachers who made a difference' (p. 30). Many describe earlier teachers as role models—as giving them direction in their life and supporting them. Melissa Morissey, formerly with the Dance Theatre of Harlem, talks of a teacher with whom she began her dancing and has returned to as someone with 'a lot of energy and gives lots of corrections'. Anna Laghezza, a dancer with the Metropolitan Opera Ballet says of the same teacher: 'She creates an environment where everybody is working super hard. It's a good space to try to do new things and not be afraid to fall over. She encourages dancers of all types' (p. 31). Elizabeth Walker, a dancer in the corps of the New York City Ballet, describes two additional qualities of the same teacher: 'She's very clear in demonstrating and she'll stop and ask it it's too fast or too slow' (p. 31). There are descriptions of teachers who 'would scream and yell', who were 'sarcastic', and who intimidated the students. More positively, Derek Grant—tap dancer, choreographer, and director—summarizes what is so important for students: 'She [the teacher] makes a bridge for you to connect who you are as a person with who you are as an artist (p. 34).

Certainly, those experiences we have had with teachers and administrators in any learning context, whether negatively or positively, have an impact on how we learn and subsequently how we teach. In the Arts Education programme we believe it is important to critically reflect upon our experiences and assumptions. We ask students to examine their ideas and assumptions about schools, students, teaching, and learning. Hinchey's (2006) research supports this belief. When talking of American schools (and this can certainly apply to Canadian schools) she says that 'we can no longer afford schools peopled by educators who act without being conscious of their assumptions, their choices, and the likely consequences' (p. 4). She extends the notion when she articulates that 'teacher education courses focus most often not on the *whys* but on the *hows* of schooling' (p. 5).

Embracing critical feminist dance pedagogy as outlined by Shapiro (1998), I endeavour to challenge the traditional dance class where the teacher is the authority and the student is the silent follower. I hope that students understand that the learner is at the centre of the curriculum and that personal ideas and social issues become the core of the dance content. Shue and Beck (2009) confirm this when they say we want dance students who 'think critically and creatively about their work, develop an emotional link to their work, and appreciate the value of collaboration in the learning process' (p. 125). Finke (2000) suggests that when we want to empower students we

> seek to give 'voice' to those who have been silenced and alienated by traditional pedagogical practices that privilege hierarchy, authority, 'rigour', and exclusivity, and that value abstract and objective knowledge over subjective and experiential knowledge. (p. 529)

I want students to have effective behaviours in the classroom, and thus discussion of how something is being taught is as important as what is being taught. It is important to review those implicit messages in what and how we choose to teach. Addressing traditional and damaging notions of dance practice can lead dance educators to teach students to understand that 'dance aesthetics are culturally constructed', 'to value and trust their own bodies as a legitimate source of knowledge', and to 'demonstrate to students they themselves can be agents who change harmful aspects of dance discourse' (Shue and Beck 2006, p. 140). Ann Dils (2007) conjectures that 'to move the expressive body in from the margins of schooling? How might it enrich how we teach traditional subjects, help us rethink difference in schooling, and provide more integrative experiences for students? How might this help us create schools that recognize the richness of human intelligence and prepare children to meet the demands of a rapidly changing world' (p. 3).

In most teaching contexts, Western dance education predominates, and the dance heritages of 'other' cultures are ignored or are relegated to a cursory mention. As we learned from Kealiinohomoku's famous essay on ballet as ethnic dance (1970), all dance is a cultural form of expression. Ashley (2008) encourages educators to embrace a 'pedagogy that would treat culturally diverse dance traditions equitably', and reminds us that this requires 'inclusion of conservation conversations in the classroom' (p. 1). Risner and Stinson (2010) challenge us to think about ourselves as 'cultural leaders and critics in our own classrooms', and that if we do so, 'then we might also gain significant energy by seeing our roles as collaborators with our students, teaching and learning from them and the diverse cultural capital they bring to school' (14). In this way we may be able to work towards social justice through dance, 'guiding students in critical self-reflection of their socialization into this matrix of unequal relationships and its implications, analysis of the mechanisms of oppression, and the ability to challenge these hierarchies (Cochran-Smith 2004).

Exploring Curriculum Possibilities and Pedagogical Concepts

Striving towards a transformative and democratic dance education, I attempt to create experiences that challenge students to think about their assumptions about dance and teaching and to make the dances we learn and create culturally relevant. The framework for movement exploration and analysis is based on creative/modern work influenced by the work of Rudolf Laban (1879–1958), and the bridging between the traditional dance education practice and critical dance education is supported by the midway model outlined by Jackie Smith-Autard (2002). From short dance expressions that explore 'who am I?' to choreography inspired by a current issue to research writing about the role of dance in education, the teacher and the learner shape course content and assignments, generating the inclusive dance pedagogy that Risner (2007) suggests. In describing the following project I want to contextulize possibilities that have shaped critical discourse about dance education, allowing students and myself to unravel the mysteries of teaching and learning.

In 2006, inspired by and based on a project by Sema Brainin and Salla Saarikangas at the Lincoln Centre Institute in 1998, I wanted to look at how we talk about and lead our students in recognizing pedagogical concepts and teaching strategies (2005, p. 114). Together with Shapiro's (1998) 'embodied knowing' in which 'the body is a vehicle for understanding oppression, resistance, and liberation' (p. 15), and following the idea of using movement and dance to promote and understand pedagogical craft, I approached a teacher of Kathak dance in the community and together we designed dance sessions to explore the craft of teaching through story and the vocabulary of Kathak dance. We discussed specific teacher qualities and skills and, in particular, the concept of 'with-it-ness'. Brainin and Saarikangas (2005) quote Kounin (1977) as defining ' "with-it-ness" as the most important teacher characteristic that distinguished good classroom managers from poor ones' (p. 118). Further, they state that 'with-it-ness' 'encompasses a kind of internal hyperawareness and reflective ability regarding the needs of each learner, the proverbial " 'eyes-in-the-back-of-the-head" teacher. It implies the capacity to overlap attention, to "switch gears" as needed, and overtly, to approach the teaching challenge in a lively and responsive manner' (p. 118).

The project—accepted by the University of Regina Research Ethics Board—was designed to take place over three sessions of a professional studies course that is offered in the fourth year of the five-year Arts Education programme. The focus of this course is the professional development of each student as future educators through consideration of professional qualities and practices, the Saskatchewan curricula, planning and instructional strategies, and assessment and evaluation procedures. As part of this course, students are placed in an elementary classroom for one day each week in the autumn semester, and in a high school for one day each week in the winter semester. In each teaching context, a cooperating teacher and a faculty adviser support them.

The twenty-nine students participating in the project were all fourth-year students. All of them has taken three dance courses in their first and second years, some had previous dance experience in dance studio settings, all were pursuing major and minor studies in the arts, approximately a quarter of the group were dance majors, and only one of them had experience in Kathak dance. Three seventy-five minute sessions took place over a three-week period. The sessions included a brief overview of the dance form, the teaching of specific Kathak vocabulary and dances, the story 'Churning of the Milk Ocean' plus other stories to be used for dance-making, videotaped performance of the marriage of Rama and Seeta, and, in the final session, an assignment to arrange a section of a story that they could tell through movement. After each session we would return to the classroom and briefly review the session, at which time the students would talk generally about what they had learned and how they had coped in the session. We asked them to write critically about their experience, addressing the following questions: What strategies were used to teach the dance? What did you learn about yourself as a student and as teacher? What challenges did you face as a performer that you might encounter as a teacher?

The responses, coded S.1–S.21, from the first session revealed that they found the experience daunting. They said that the teacher moved far 'too fast' (S.6), and that there was 'a lot to take in all at once' (S.3), making the experience 'overwhelming' (S.3). In general, they had a 'hard and tough time following the movement of the dance' (S.9), and commented that 'as the movements were so unfamiliar it was especially hard'(S.10). One student commented: 'It was hard to stay focused because of the turns, different arm and hand positions as well as feet positions' (S.21). Some felt 'extremely rushed, uncertain, and baffled not only with the moves but because the new language that went along with them' (S.19). One thing that did help was the 'story aspect of the dance' that assisted 'visually because a lot of the actions were familiar to my body and to my memory (such as gathering flowers, the seashell, the snake, and so on). I could relate these movements to past experiences and to real life' (S.16). Several commented on a circle activity that they had experienced in their dance and drama classes, finding the activity a familiar and reassuring moment in the class. One student identified the power of the moment, saying:

> I loved when we formed the circle and had to make up a movement and then mimicked that movement all the way round the circle. The concentration in the room was incredible. Everyone was so focused on the movement. Being a dance minor I loved this! The silence and communication through the various movements moved me. (S.20)

We were pleased with the participation and focus of the class in this first session. We recognized the students' struggles and felt that this would reveal some interesting insights into their personal journey in learning a new dance form as well as their thinking about learning and teaching in general.

All wrote after the second session that it was 'more enjoyable' (S.6) and that it was 'much easier to learn the movements because the movements were no longer as foreign' (S.10). The use of story once again helped some: 'I think it was easier today because there was a "story" involved and more room for exploration and repetition of certain movements' (S.11). Additionally, '. . . watching the video showed a whole new perspective of the "story" element present in Kathak dance' (S.22). We observed this change in comfort level, and were encouraged that the students would be able to reflect deeper on the experience. The final task, which required the students to work in groups and create their own dances based on the previous sessions, created general excitement in the room—partly, I believe, because they would be working in groups.

It was evident in the third session that the groups had come together during the week and worked on their dances. Our observations were that the students had used suitable stories and were using movements appropriately from the Kathak vocabulary as well as their own. Each group used props, three groups found music, and one group used percussion instruments and made their own vocal sounds. They felt great commitment to their pieces, and considered that this third session was very rewarding 'because we got to see the results of everyone's ideas and work' (S.14). They were excited about the particular story that each group had selected, and applauded the performances, one student saying: 'Everyone performed with commitment' (S.13). Many commented on the 'talent' and 'creativity' of their classmates. One student summarized the thoughts of the group when she said: 'Everyone enjoyed what they were doing, and everyone was equally impressed about the dances performed by others' (S24).

In considering their role as students they commented on the need for commitment, challenge, and safety in the learning environment. One student commented: 'As a class we jump in with both feet. This meant for me that I had to go somewhere beyond my personal comfort level' (S.11). Another said that 'the teacher was very patient and created a safe learning environment, so I bit the bullet and let go my inhibitions' (S.9). They found learning a new dance form both a challenge and enjoyable, necessitating 'a lot of concentration but also the ability to let go and be loose' (S.19).

Each found the experience not only meaningful as a student but also as a teacher: 'As we were asked to think of this experience from the perspective of teacher, I realized things about pedagogy, content and motivation' (S.4). Another student talked about the importance of artists in the classroom, saying that it 'gave me the opportunity to see the value in doing so' (S.5). One student, addressing the importance of cultural studies, stated that 'this can be so easily done through the arts' (S.6). Several commented on the integration of the art forms, identifying that 'Kathak dance is an excellent form because of the way it incorporates the five arts areas' (S.19).

In addition to the comments about their learning as student and teacher they commented in more depth about pedagogical craft. They said that the dance teacher was 'an amazing teacher', that she was always 'patient and caring', and that she kept the 'environment very personable and fun at all times'. One student commented astutely that 'it reminded me that like teaching a dance that involves many parts of the body working together, teaching in general requires the teacher to be doing many things at the same time' (S.21). They identified that the teacher needs to be 'aware of different learning styles' (S.21), to 'slow down' at times, and to be 'sensitive to the feelings of students and check out how they are coping and understanding' (S.5). Several talked about encouraging students to have a sense of ownership over their work, one student commenting: 'This ownership was created for us when we were asked to create our own dance' (S.13). Some expressed how frustrating learning can be: 'I am interested in the "getting right" factor. I wonder if it is important to others as it is for me. I have witnessed children get so frustrated if they do not understand something, and seen them completely shut down' (S.7). The student agreed that it is important to 'give students time to become comfortable with what they are learning', and that the teacher 'needs to be supportive in little achievements' (S.6).

Several talked about the experience requiring them to take risks, and one student articulated that it is hard as a student to 'take a risk in learning something new and quite challenging! As a teacher, the risk would be to put myself in a very vulnerable position in attempting to learn a challenging dance form. It would demonstrate great leadership as a teacher as it would encourage the students to take the risk with you' (S.12). They were unanimous that a teacher needs to 'know what is going on at all times', and that 'teachers need to have good classroom management skills. I have realized this from this class that you have to be completely clear when giving directions' (S.10). 'It is true', said one student 'you need to have eyes in the back of your head. You must be aware/know your students well enough to know if they are struggling or falling behind in the steps' (S. 5). 'I think it would help', said another student 'if I can develop this "with-it-ness" so that I know what is happening with everyone in class, not just if they are misbehaving but if they are having success or difficulties' (S.4). One poignant comment about this experience was that 'this experience created a sense of community' (S.16)—a factor that stayed true for this group as they embarked upon their teaching and further class experiences. We felt that this project was extremely rewarding and valuable in many respects. When I reflect on the first session and the nervousness of the majority of the students, I recognize how quickly they became comfortable as the dance instructor provided tasks that were attainable. Many students found comfort in familiar activities, and were much more at ease in the second and third sessions. It was important that they felt good about their experiences and grow in confidence and belief in their ability to complete tasks and reach goals of the sessions.

There was awareness of the different learning styles and, as Gardner (1999) points out, individuals use many forms of intelligence in the learning process, and these capacities are much broader than the linguistic and logical/mathematical modes of learning emphasized in most school programmes (pp. 181–2). It helped us to understand that through an arts experience there is much to be learned about the art and craft of teaching, and that being immersed in an arts experience provides a sense of wellbeing for both students and teacher.

Conclusion

It seems that we have the best intentions to implement arts education experiences for all children, and to provide pre-service and in-service professional development for those who will be responsible for teaching. Reports clearly indicate the benefits of an arts-rich education as one that acknowledges the value of arts activities and recognizes student participation and achievement. We also recognize the intrinsic benefits of an arts education for all students that provides students with a sense of place, contributes to health and wellbeing, and helps to develop positive attitudes and gain confidence. Teachers are examining and changing their practice, and scholars write articulately in support of arts education. And yet we do not see sufficient activity. There are still many children who are not receiving arts in their schooling, and we do not see equal access for students at the tertiary level to study in the arts. On the other hand, projects such as the one on educational craft, which I developed in collaboration with the Kathak dance teacher, provide evidence that the appropriate type of arts/dance education can initiate change.

References

Anderson, A. (2004). 'Moving in a circle', in D. Booth and M. Hachiya (eds.), *The Arts Go to School: Classroom-based Activities that Focus on Music, Drama, Movement, Media and More*. Markham, ON: Pembroke Publishers.

Ashley, L. (2008). '?' Metamorphosis in Dance Education, in C. F. Stock (ed.), *Dance Dialogues: Conversations Across Cultures, Artforms and Practices*. Canberra: Australian Dance Council and Queensland University of Technology.

Brainin, S. and Saarikangas, S. (2005). 'Bharata Natyam as a metaphor for the concept of 'with-it-ness': Teaching pedagogic craft through story and dance', in M. Fuchs Holzer and S. Noppe-Brandon (eds.), *Community in the Making*. New York, NY: Teachers College Press.

Canadian Commission for UNESCO (2005). *Learning to Live, Living to Learn: Perspectives on Arts Education in Canada*. Preliminary Report on Consultations. Ottawa.

Canadian Forum on Arts and Health (2006). 'Forum summary report', *Arts Research Monitor*, 4(9). <http://www.hillstrategies.com/content/canadian-forum-arts-and-health-%E2%80%93-forum-summary-report>

Cochran-Smith, M. (2004). 'Developing social justice literacy: An open letter to our faculty colleagues', *Phi Delta Kappan*, 90(5): 345–52.

Cone, S. and Cone, T. (2011). 'Assessing dance in physical education', *Strategies: A Journal for Physical and Sport Educators*, 24(6): 28–32.

Cuban, L. (1995). 'The hidden variable: How organizations influence teacher responses in secondary science curriculum reform', *Theory and Practice*, 34(1): 4–11.

Dils, A. (2007). 'Why dance literacy?', *Journal of the Canadian Association for Curriculum Studies* 5(2): 95–113.

Eisner, E. (1994). *The Educational Imagination: On the Design and Evaluation of School Programs*. 3rd edn. New York, NY: Macmillan College Publishing.

Finke, L. (2000). 'Knowledge as bait: Feminism, voice and the pedagogical unconscious', in J. Glazer-Raymo, B. K. Townsend, and B. Ropers-Huilman (eds.), *Women in Higher Education: A Feminist Perspective*. Boston: Pearson Custom Publishing, pp. 526–39.

First World Conference on Arts Education. (2006). *Building Creative Capacities for the 21st Century*. Lisbon: UNESCO.

Gardner, H. (1999). *The Disciplined Mind: Beyond Facts and Standardized Tests, The K-12 Education that Every Child Deserves*, New York, NY: Simon and Schuster.

Goldberg, M. (1999). *Arts and Learning: An Integrated Approach to Teaching in Multicultural and Multilingual Settings*. New York, NY: Longman.

Greene, M. (1991). 'Texts and margins', *Harvard Educational Review*, 61: 1.

Hinchey, P. H. (2006). *Becoming a Critical Educator: Defining a Classroom Identity, Designing a Critical Pedagogy*. New York, NY: Peter Lang.

Kealiinohomoku, J. (1970). 'An anthropologist looks at ballet as a form of ethnic dance', in M. Van Tuyl (ed.), *Impulse*. San Francisco: Impulse Publications, pp. 24–33).

Johnson, H. L. and Lew, J. (2005). 'Learning to talk: Reflections on the first-year faculty seminar', in M. Fuchs Holzer and S. Noppe-Brandon (eds), *Community in the Making: Lincoln Center Institute, the Arts, and Teacher Education*. New York, NY: Teachers College Press, p. 82.

Kounin, J. S. (1977). *Discipline and Group Management in Classrooms*. Huntington, NY: R. E. Krieger.

Manitoba Education (2011). 'Dance: Rationale for dance education. <http://www.edu.gov.mb.ca/k12/cur/arts/dance/rationale.html>

McCarthy, K., Ondaatje, E., Zakaras, L., and Brooks, A. (2005). 'Gifts of the muse: Reframing the debate about the benefits of the arts', *Research in the Arts*, The RAND Corporation. <www.rand.org/content/dam/rand/pubs/monographs/2005/RAND_MG218.pdf>

Naidus, B. (2005). 'Teaching art as a subversive activity', in M. C. Powell and V. M. Speiser (eds.), *The Arts, Education, and Social Change: Little Signs of Hope*. New York, NY: Peter Lang, pp. 169–84.

Perron, W. (ed.) (2006). 'My favourite teacher'. *Dance Magazine*, August.

Quiroga Murcis, C., Kreutz, G., Clift, S., and Bongard, S. (2010). 'Shall we dance?: An exploration of the perceived benefits of dancing on well-being', in *Arts and Health: An International Journal for Research, Policy and Practice*, 2(2): 149–63.

Richards, M. C. (1980). *Toward Wholeness*. Middletown, CT: Wesleyan University Press.

Risner, D. (2007). 'Dance education in social and cultural perspective', in L. Overby and B. Lepczyk (eds.), *Dance: Current Selected Research*, vol. 6. Brooklyn, NY: AMS Press, pp. 153–89.

Risner, D. and Stinson, S. W. (2010). 'Moving social justice: Challenges, fears and possibilities in dance education', *International Journal of Education and the Arts*, 11(6). <http://www.ijea.org/v11n6/>

Saskatchewan Arts Board and Dance Saskatchewan Inc. (2009). *A Review of Dance in Saskatchewan*. A final report.

Saskatchewan Education (1991). *Arts Education: A Curriculum Guide for Grade 5*. Regina: Saskatchewan Education.

Saskatchewan Education. (1998). *Arts Education: Grades 1–9 Curriculum Evaluation Report*.

Shapiro, S. B. (ed.) (1998). *Dance, Power, and Difference: Critical Feminist Perspective on Dance Education*. Champaign, IL: Human Kinetics.

Shue, L. L. and Beck, C. S. (2009). 'Stepping out of bounds: Performing feminist pedagogy within a dance education community', *Journal of Communication Education*, 50(2): 125–143.

Smith-Autard, J. (2002). *The Art of Dance in Education*, 2nd edn. London: A. & C. Black.

T. J. Cheney Research Inc. (2004). *The Growth of Dance in Canada over Three Decades*. Prepared for the Canada Council for the Arts, Section 7. <http://canadacouncil.ca/research/research-library/2004/04/facts-on-dance>

Tomkins, G. S. and Case, R. (2012). 'Curriculum development', in *The Canadian Encyclopedia* (including *The Encyclopedia of Music in Canada*). Canada: Historica Foundation. <http://www.thecanadianencyclopedia.com>

UNESCO (2010). Seoul Agenda: Goals for the Development of Arts Education. The Second World Conference on Arts Education. Seoul, Korea.

Wilson, M. and Aubrey, M. (2011). *Summary of Participant Comments in Small Group Discussion*. The National Roundtable for Teacher Education in the Arts. <http://www.nrtea.ca/p/background.html>

Wilson, M. and Aubrey, M. (2012). Draft Report of the National Roundtable for Teacher Education in the Arts.

CHAPTER 22

PEDAGOGIES OF DANCE TEACHING AND DANCE LEADING

JAYNE STEVENS

INTRODUCTION

THERE is considerable evidence of a prodigious growth in the number of children and young people engaging in dance in the UK in recent years (Bond 2011; Burns 2008; Hall 2007). The expansion of opportunities for children and young people to dance in both formal and informal education sectors has arisen as a result of, for example, investment in the dance development sector,[1] a growing number of specialist arts and sports colleges, initiatives to expand creative and cultural education, and to respond to central government's health and inclusion agendas. The latter, in particular, has led to increased interest in how dance can impact positively on the wellbeing of children and young people.

This expansion of opportunities has created a demand for dance leaders who can engage and inspire young people. There has been a concomitant demand from employers and parents for assurances that young people will be safe and well taught (Burns 2008, p. 6). This is unsurprising given that dance teaching in the UK is largely unregulated. Those teaching dance in state- maintained schools must hold Qualified Teacher Status.[2] Some are specialist dance teachers, though most are physical education teachers with, frequently, limited dance experience. In the private sector, teachers are likely, but are not required, to hold a qualification from one of the dance-teaching associations[3] in order to practice. In addition, there are considerable numbers of dance artists for whom teaching dance to children and young people is a part of their portfolio of freelance, self-employed work. The dance-teaching workforce is, therefore, very diverse. The increased demand for dance has led many schools, along with youth, arts, sports, and community services to employ dance practitioners, who are not necessarily trained teachers, to teach and lead dance activities for young people. Audits[4] have revealed the professional development and support needs of such practitioners (Bond 2011, p. 47) and prompted initiatives[5] to provide and accredit opportunities for dance artists to develop pedagogical knowledge and practice.

This chapter explores current dance pedagogy in the light of such initiatives. It is especially concerned with the pedagogies of dance artists and practitioners in the informal education and youth sectors. In recent years such pedagogy has acknowledged its impact on young people's wellbeing. This chapter proceeds by considering aspects of relationships between wellbeing, young people, and dance. Despite evidence of the impact of dance on young people's wellbeing, the pedagogy that delivers it is relatively under-researched. The chapter then traces pedagogical developments that have integrated aspects of professional, educational, and community dance practices. It then suggests aspects of this pedagogy that are key to the promotion of wellbeing.

DANCE, WELLBEING, AND YOUNG PEOPLE

It has become commonplace to promote the benefits of dance for young people's educational attainment, health, and wellbeing. Fleming suggests that justification for arts education reflects concerns of the times in which it is made (2012, p. 13). It is not surprising, then, that claims for the positive impact of dance on wellbeing follows a growing concern, noticeable since the late 1990s, to understand, monitor, and improve the wellbeing of children and young people.[6]

Despite frequent use of the term 'wellbeing', there are differences in meaning and ideas as to how it may be identified, measured, and achieved (Cronin de Chavez et al. 2005, p. 70). The Department of Health defined wellbeing as 'A positive state of mind and body, feeling safe and able to cope, with a sense of connection with people, communities, and the wider environment' (2009, p. 18). This embraces some key elements, about which consensus may be possible. Firstly, it encompasses physical, social, and psychological perspectives, and secondly it emphasizes, in common with many definitions, feeling and functioning (McLellan et al. 2012, p. 13). In fact, the New Economics Foundation defines wellbeing simply as 'how people feel and how they function, both on a personal and a social level, and how they evaluate their lives as a whole' (Michaelson et al. 2012, p. 6). These two aspects are reflected in measures of wellbeing, which include both subjective and objective indicators.[7]

It is generally acknowledged that different groups of people have differing priorities regarding wellbeing, and that care should be taken to understand what matters to participants themselves, not just to the professionals delivering services. Recent research into the subjective wellbeing of children and young people aged between eight and sixteen across the UK identified six priorities that the young people themselves saw as significant in promoting their wellbeing. These are:

1. The right conditions in which to learn and develop.
2. A positive view of themselves and a respect for their identity.
3. Enough of the items and experiences that matter to them.
4. Positive relationships with their family and friends.
5. A safe and suitable home environment and local area.
6. Opportunities to take part in positive activities that help them thrive. (Children's Society 2012, p. 14)

These reflect a shift in recent years beyond negative indicators (what people lack, for example, in terms of basic material needs, care, and health) to more positive indicators—what aspects of life give pleasure, purpose, and a sense of achievement and autonomy.[8] In this view of wellbeing, the arts, it has been suggested, have a significant contribution to make (Arts Council England 2007; Scottish Arts Council 2006). Increasing numbers of research studies and project evaluations have revealed the contribution to wellbeing made specifically by dance, which, it is argued, combines physical activity, social interaction, and creative expression into experiences attractive to young people (Burkhardt and Rhodes 2012, p. 8).

Since 2005 a number of studies have employed dance science and educational research methodologies to evidence the impact of dance on the physical health, psychological wellbeing, and social inclusion of young people.[9] A review of fourteen studies of recreational dance activity involving 5–21-year-olds (Burkhardt and Brennan 2012) found consistent evidence that dance could improve aspects of physical health (such as cardiovascular fitness and bone health), and also found more limited evidence of improvements in psychological wellbeing (such as self-concept, body image, and reduction in anxiety). Harland et al.'s (2005) study of the impact of arts interventions on young people found that a distinctive feature of dance was its ability to generate teamwork—a major contributor to social development and wellbeing—and physical wellbeing outcomes.

Some studies have emphasized dance as a non-competitive, physical activity offering an alternative to sport or exercise, especially for young women. Others have emphasized dance as a creative art form. The forms most frequently featured in projects for young people were contemporary, street, and creative dance.[10] Sessions were generally led by dance artists, and occasionally included professional development, for example, in 'how to use dance to promote health' (Nordin and Hardy 2009, p. 13). Some studies provided brief information on the structure and content of sessions—most commonly, a combination of technical skill development and creative exploration (see, for example, Connolly et al. 2011, 56–7). Since many studies, however, are implicitly looking to support investment in dance (Quin et al. 2007b, 31), their focus is on the 'why' of dance rather than the 'how'. Very few explore the nature or effectiveness of the pedagogies involved. This is despite the close relationship deemed to exist between the quality of dance teaching and outcomes for participants (Buckroyd 2000; Harland et al. 2005; Hall 2007). This begs the question: 'What kinds of pedagogical practice in dance best enhance the wellbeing of children and young people?' To begin to explore the complexities involved it is useful to understand how elements of the pedagogic traditions of professional, educational, and community dance have come together in the UK over the last thirty years, and how they inform current practice.

THE DEVELOPMENT OF ARTIST-LED PEDAGOGY

There is a tradition of dance artists working in formal and informal education in the UK to teach and lead dance activities for young people. In the mid-1970s and early 1980s, many such artists came from professional training backgrounds (in contemporary dance and ballet) that consisted primarily of 'technique training delivered through a didactic, teacher-driven, student-response method' (Price 2009, p. 80). Such training did not include a preparation to teach. It was frequently assumed that professional dancers were 'inherently good teachers solely by virtue of being top performers' (Brinson and Dick 1996, p. 112). Some, therefore, taught as they themselves had been taught, thereby uncritically, and perhaps unwittingly, perpetuating aspects of pedagogical practice that did not prioritize the wellbeing of learners.[11] Frequently, teaching was through established repertoire and 'inherited practice', with priority given to the acquisition of technical and performance skills.

The dance that children and young people were most likely to experience within the formal English educational system, or indeed any other part of the UK, at this time bore little relationship to the world of professional dance (Sanderson 1996, p. 5).[12] Often this was 'creative movement' or 'modern educational dance', and was in large part derived from the theory and movement analysis of Rudolf Laban. Although 'wellbeing' was not a term much used at this time, the emphasis on 'the process of dancing and its affective/experiential contribution to the participant's overall development as a moving/feeling being' (Smith-Autard 2002, p. 4) meant that concepts now recognizable as central to wellbeing were key. This was indicative of arts education generally, which was, up to the 1980s, shaped by progressivism and modernism (Abbs 1987, in Fleming 2012, p. 14). Progressivism and child-centred ideas in education meant that priority was given to free self-expression and creativity rather than appreciating the art of others or acquiring technical skills (Fleming 2012, pp. 15–16). Fleming warns against overgeneralization and suggests that many arts educators took a developmental approach to place more emphasis on the appreciation of professional art, form, and tradition as pupils grew older (p. 15).

Nevertheless, there existed a pedagogical divide—sometimes sharply felt—between those who emphasized developing high-level skills towards 'theatrically defined dance products for presentation to audiences' (Smith-Autard 2002, p. 4) and those who were more concerned with 'investigation, social interaction, and the value of transferable skills engendered in arts practices' (Jeffery 2005, p. 90). There were, however, a number of factors driving a resolution of such differences. Modern educational dance was proving less attractive to older pupils as new forms of dance, such as contemporary and jazz, gained popularity. As Smith-Autard (2002) writes: '. . . adolescents and young adults were ready and had a need for the development of technical skills' (p. 7). Moreover, dance provision in secondary schools was limited (Calouste Gulbenkian Foundation 1980, p. 54). Both factors may help explain why more and more young people in the 1980s were participating in youth dance activities outside of school. Such provision was part of a new understanding of 'the importance of the arts as part of social policy outside school, especially for young people' (Robinson 1989, p. xvii). Here they learned dance technique, engaged in performance, and often came into contact with a new kind of dance practitioner: the dance animateur.

Dance animateurs played a key role in expanding out-of-school, youth dance provision in the 1980s (Brinson 1986). Some had teacher training as well as dance training (Jasper 1995, p. 183), which meant they could teach within, as well as outside, the formal curriculum. More importantly, perhaps, they had knowledge and experience to bridge the worlds of professional and educational dance. Animateurs often worked within or alongside community arts organizations, adopting and adapting methods of inclusion and participant empowerment that characterized community arts practice. Despite an emphasis on process in community dance at the time, dance animateurs appreciated the value of performance in motivating young people and in making their achievements visible. In the mid-1980s and throughout the 1990s there emerged a community of practice that developed and shared ways of teaching, leading, and creating dance for young people in informal educational settings (see Stevens 2013). This pedagogy, by synthesizing traditions of educational dance, theatrical dance, and community arts, began to dissolve distinctions between teaching for product, technique, and performance and teaching for process, expression, and individual development. (It is worth noting that some of those who pioneered such pedagogy as animateurs are now key to current initiatives to provide and accredit pedagogical development for dance practitioners.)[13]

Such developments in the informal sector coincided with a major reconception of dance within formal education gaining momentum throughout the 1980s.[14] Central to this was a new emphasis on dance as performance (Haynes 1987, p. 141; Smith-Autard 2002, pp. 5–6). A 'midway' model of dance education, promoted by Smith-Autard, was now being widely adopted. As Table 22.1 (Smith-Autard 2002, p. 27) indicates, this also amalgamated elements of educational and professional practice. This repositioning of dance in education helped create an environment with greater potential for interaction and exchange between school teachers and dance artists.

Such developments established a pedagogical framework capable of supporting the expansion of dance for children and young people that occurred throughout the 1990s and 2000s. Concerns for the physical wellbeing of young people, their social and educational inclusion, and the enrichment of their creative and cultural lives, especially around the turn of the millennium, led to a series of initiatives that saw 'government, the dance sector, and the education sector coming together at different levels both within school and beyond to enhance the take-up of dance by children and young people' (Hall 2007, p. 11). One such initiative—Creative Partnerships (funded between 2002 and

Table 22.1. From The Art of Dance in Education (Smith–Autard 2002, p. 27).

Table demonstrating features of the art of dance in education model

EDUCATIONAL	*MIDWAY*	*PROFESSIONAL*
Process	Process + Product	Product
Creativity Imagination Individuality	Creativity + Knowledge of Imagination public artistic Individuality conventions	Knowledge of theatre dance repertoire
Feelings Subjectivity	Feelings + Skill Subjectivity + Objectivity	Skill acquired Objectivity
Principles	Principles + Techniques	Techniques
Open methods	Open + Closed	Closed methods
Creating	THREE STRANDS Composition Performance Appreciation OF DANCES Leading to ARTISTIC EDUCATION AESTHETIC EDUCATION CULTURAL EDUCATION	Performing

2011)—promoted partnerships between teachers and creative practitioners to foster creativity and encourage creative learning. It also supported research into, for example, the
impact of projects on wellbeing (McLellan et al. 2012) and the nature of artist-led pedagogies (Pringle 2008).

A recently published framework suggests that policy makers and service providers
seeking to promote positive wellbeing for children and young people should consider
providing opportunities to play and be active, to achieve, to enjoy positive relationships, and to exercise choice and autonomy (Children's Society 2012). How, then, do the
pedagogies developed and employed by dance artists promote positive wellbeing for the
children and young people with whom they work?

Artist-Led Pedagogy and Wellbeing

As mentioned previously, there is a growing body of evidence to show that dance can
have a measureable impact on young people's physical wellbeing. It is clear that young
people enjoy the challenge of learning new movement and executing 'cool moves'

(Nordin and Hardy 2009, p. 44). Dynamic and structured dance classes delivered through demonstration and direct instruction can motivate, build strength and endurance, and extend and refine movement vocabulary. In a 'command style' of teaching, used extensively in dance technique and exercise classes, the teacher makes decisions and frequently provides the movement material. The learner's role is to perform, follow, and obey (Mosston and Ashworth 1986, p. 12). This style of teaching and learning often produces synchronized, precise performance and can engender the sense of belonging that can come with moving as part of a group (McNeill 1995). Kuppers also suggests that this style of teaching and leading can help participants feel reassured and safe and can provide a group with a shared sense of purpose (2007, p. 96) Dance artists, however, must be sensitive to participants' ability to respond appropriately and be alert to any abuse of the power relationships that this style of teaching and learning can engender. Even in projects whose prime aim is to improve physical wellbeing, a balance of teaching methods and activities for young people which include, for example, creative tasks, peer critique, and encouragement are used (Connolly et al. 2011; Castle et al. 2002; Urmston 2012).

There is general agreement that a learning environment that enables learners to demonstrate competence and achievement can raise self-esteem and self-efficacy, thereby enhancing psychological wellbeing (Miulli and Nordin-Bates 2011). There have been many examples of how performance—both informal to peers and invitees and more formal, public performance—can have a transformative effect on how young people view and value themselves and how others see them.[15] It is often the case that dance artists are employed to create performance with and for young people. Butterworth (2004) presents a continuum model of processes employed by dance artists in making dances. The model resembles Mosston and Ashworth's (1986) spectrum of teaching styles referred to previously. It identifies five approaches and details teaching methods and learning opportunities characteristic of each. These range from directed—teaching by showing, or a 'didactic' approach—to a shared, collaborative, 'democratic' approach (Butterworth 2004).

A dance artist may employ any or all such approaches in the process of making a dance, and some may prefer certain approaches depending on the nature of the performance or dance style. So, for example, a didactic approach in which the learner is required to observe, imitate, reproduce, and replicate dance material and style precisely was used extensively in Ballet Hoo's production of the ballet Romeo and Juliet, performed by young people with no previous experience in ballet (Ballet Changed My Life: Ballet Hoo! 2006).

It is, however, more usual for dance artists to actively engage young people in contributing ideas and materials by setting tasks or problems for them to explore. The artist may act as facilitator, enabling young dancers to not only contribute movement content but also to decide on purpose, style, and structure. In her studies of artists as educators, Pringle (2002, 2008) found that most artists preferred to adopt a facilitative rather than an authoritative role, engaging learners in processes of enquiry and evaluation that mirrored the artist's own practice. A later study noted that in some instances artists recognized the need to instruct rather than explore, especially when new knowledge or skills needed to be introduced and that this was particularly the case in dance (Galton 2008, p. 34). Styles of teaching, whether employed in dance classes or dance making, that are, to use Mosston and Ashworth's (1966, 1986) taxonomy, more inclusive, discovery-based and divergent afford young people degrees of choice over what they do, and provide opportunities for self-direction and self-determination. Being able to exercise choice and experience autonomy has been shown to enhance wellbeing (Layard and Dunn 2009).

Understanding and using a range of teaching styles is an important aspect of pedagogical knowledge and practice, and is often emphasized in the provision of professional development for artists. At one time, studies of pedagogy focused almost exclusively on the activity of the teacher and the teaching styles, characterized as authoritarian or democratic (Watkins and Mortimore 1999, p. 3). A broader view of pedagogy, however, recognizes that what is learned relates not only to how it is taught but also to the situation, especially the social situation, in which it is learned. At the core of the learning environment (and indeed of any teaching style) are relationships—between teacher/artist and learners, and between learners. This chapter goes on to argue that it is the *quality* of these relationships that is especially significant for wellbeing and is that which dance pedagogy should seek to optimize. It also suggests that establishing effective relationships is as much about who the artist is as it is about what the artist does.

Pedagogical Relationships

The Good Childhood Inquiry found that the quality of children's and young people's relationships was key to their subjective wellbeing (Children's Society 2012, p. 8). Most significant were relationships within families, but relationships with teachers and peers were also important. The survey reports that one in ten children was unhappy about his or her relationships with teachers, and that one in six was unhappy about the amount they felt listened to in school (Children's Society 2012, p. 6).

Studies of creative practitioners working with children and young people have consistently noted that they tend towards dialogic, open, and informal working practices and adopt roles more akin to coworker than to teacher (Galton 2008; Pringle 2008; Chappell et al. 2011; McLellan et al. 2012). One study of artists' pedagogies found that on meeting a new group artists tended to tell them about themselves:

> "I'm Alex and I'm a dance artist and I live in Portsmouth. I've worked with lots of junior groups and parents and tots. I've been a dance artist on Creative Partnerships for two years and it's made me realise this is the work I like doing; it's the kind of work I enjoy doing most", whereas teachers begin along the lines of 'I'm Mr Smith and I'll be taking you for history'. (Galton 2008, p. 28)

Galton suggests that whereas the latter introduction seems designed to establish the respective roles of the participants and, to a certain extent, reinforce the power relationship between teacher and taught, the former appears to take the form of opening a conversation and invites an equal relationship (2008, pp. 28–9). Lynch and Allan found that secondary-school pupils responded positively to artists because 'they talk to you like an ordinary person' (2006, p. 27). The interest pupils took related more to the artists' personality than to any skill. Pringle found that artists resisted describing themselves as 'teachers', instead positioning themselves as co-learners in an open-ended, co-constructed process (2008, p. 46). Katy Mckeown—formerly a dance artist working for Y-Dance in Scotland—for example, often attempts moves that she is unsure about to reveal her own vulnerability and encourage a sense of learning together (Lynch and Allan 2006, p. 95).

This may help explain why young people often see artists as role models. As such, artists may provide positive views of identity (Chappell 2008, p. 6), challenge young people in ways not usual in school settings (Chappell et al. 2011, p. 137) raise aspirations (Fensham and Garner 2005, p. 17), and influence behavior through example. As a dance artist working on the *Go Dance* project explained:

> When we started the project it was a struggle to get [participants] to class on time, they straggled in. But after three or four weeks, they are now early, lining up at the door, no nagging about clothing, etc. required. Just ready and focused and eager to go. I've just kept at it, behaved in a way in which I want them to behave and expected them to rise to that too. I've been aware of myself as the role model here, and from what I see in their behavior, they too are expecting more, demanding more of themselves, and appear motivated to work together. Very interesting to witness. (Quoted in Urmston 2012, p. 9)

There is a danger that artists—especially those working closely with schools—may be cast as the charismatic, creative 'other', and teachers as 'didact or classroom police' (Pringle 2008, p. 47). Chappell et al. (2011), and Jeffery (2005), however, have demonstrated that such dichotomy can be avoided and co-participative partnerships of interactive, rather than simply complementary, roles developed.

Relationships with adults based on respect for a young person's identity and capabilities contribute positively to social wellbeing. Equally important are relationships with peers. Social isolation has been linked directly to low levels of wellbeing, and as children reach adolescence their relationships with peers become more significant in their social and emotional growth (Children's Society 2012, p. 7). Social and educational inclusion through participation and community connectedness has been a key aim of some dance projects for young people. Although learning and making dance is an inherently social activity peer interaction, an essential aspect of the psychosocial development of adolescents (Buckroyd 2000, p. 108) needs to be fostered and managed. Miulli and Nordin-Bates (2011) suggest that motivational climates (the psychological environment in which dancers learn) have a significant impact on wellbeing. Their research suggests

that learning based on setting and completing tasks is more likely to encourage dancers to interact and learn together. A further way in which dance artists working with
young people have developed significant levels of interaction characterized by trust and
cooperation has been through the use of touch, physical support, and contact work. In
2003, for example, Dance United ran a project for young male offenders (aged between
15 and 17). The resulting performance, *Third Symphony: Men at War*, used contact work
and lifts extensively to develop trust and reciprocity between participants. Participants
felt that they worked together as a team and the institution's staff noted improved relationships with and between participants (Bramley and Jermyn 2006). Where cooperative and collaborative working are established, dance can create communities that offer
young people support, a sense of belonging, and identity (Fensham and Garner 2005).
There is considerable evidence that young people enjoy and value the social interaction
generated by dance participation.

Conclusions

In conclusion, a growing body of evidence demonstrates the positive impact that participation in dance can have on young people's physical, psychological, and social wellbeing, but the specific pedagogy involved is relatively under-researched. This chapter has
surveyed some recent developments to suggest that relationships within the learning
situation are key to enhancing subjective wellbeing. The recent expansion in children's
and young people's participation in dance activity and performance in the UK has led
to greater involvement of dance artists in teaching and leading dance. Their ability to
establish and manage effective relationships is central to pedagogy for wellbeing. It is
this that enables a wide range of teaching and choreographic methods to be employed in
ways that enhance the subjective wellbeing of the young people involved.

Notes

1. YDance in Scotland (2002>) and Youth Dance England in England (2004–2016) have led
   developments in youth dance over recent years. Part of their remit has been to enhance
   the quality of leadership, teaching, and facilitation of participatory dance and support the
   development of a qualified and skilled workforce.
2. This frequently involves postgraduate teacher training.
3. Such associations include, but are not limited, to the Imperial Society of Teachers of
   Dancing, the British Ballet Organisation, the British Dance Teachers Association, and the
   Royal Academy of Dancing.
4. See, for example, Hall (2007). Youth Dance England suggested that there was a national
   shortage of suitably qualified dance teachers (Siddall 2010, p. 46), as did a recent review of
   the dance sector in Scotland (Clark 2012).
5. These include the work of the National College for Community Dance (2009>); the Dance
   Training and Accreditation Partnership (2006>), including development of a Diploma in

Dance Teaching and Learning (Children and Young People); and *Dance Links* (2005>), providing training for out-of-school dance providers. Arts Council England publications, including *Providing the Best* (2005) and *Keeping the Arts Safe* (2005), encouraged and helped artists working with children and young people to assess the quality and safety of their arts provision. Creative Partnerships has (2002–11) nurtured creative practitioners to work with educators.

6. The British government's ambition to improve children's health, wellbeing, and achievement was set out in two Green Papers: *Every Child Matters* (2003) and *Youth Matters* (2005). Arts Council England's responses (2005, 2006) championed the potential of the arts to contribute to the achievement of the five outcomes specified: being healthy, staying safe, enjoying and achieving, making a positive contribution, and achieving economic wellbeing. The Social and Emotional Aspects of Learning (SEAL) programme was introduced in 2005. Also in 2005, the Children's Society launched its wellbeing research programme to investigate young people's own views on wellbeing, most recently publishing its findings in *The Good Childhood Report* in 2012.

7. Subjective measures might include how satisfied people feel about their relationships, experiences, and prospects. Objective measures include indicators such as educational achievement and life expectancy. A degree of caution has been expressed about the use of subjective measures.

8. In 2010 the British National Office for Statistics launched a national wellbeing programme that was committed to using measures of wellbeing that focused on 'quality of life' as well as economic growth.

9. For example, Quin et al. (2007a, 2007b), Nordin and Hardy (2009), North Kent Local Authorities Arts Partnership and Laban (2009), and Urmston (2012).

10. Creative dance sometimes refers to a dance form and sometimes to the creative processes involved in composing dances in other dance forms such as contemporary, street, and ballet.

11. Lakes (2005), Ross (2004), and Smith (1998) have described the authoritarian approach that characterized some teaching in the 'classic modern dance and ballet worlds', especially in the USA in the past.

12. Although there was separate curricular documentation for Wales, Scotland, and Northern Ireland at the time, the children's experience in each country was very similar.

13. For example, Linda Jasper (Director of Youth Dance England), Marie McClusky (Director of Swindon Dance), and Chris Thomson (Director of Creative Teaching and Learning at The Place).

14. This was also a time when dance movement therapy (DMT) was being developed in the UK. Karkou and Sanderson (2000) suggest that although DMT was to become a separate discipline it originated from principles that also underpinned modern educational dance, and that prior to the 1980s, educational dance could be said to be more 'therapeutic' than artistic (69).

15. See, for example, Harrison (2007) and Miles (2008).

References

Arts Council England (2007). *The Arts, Health and Wellbeing: A National Framework*. London: Arts Council England.

Ballet Changed My Life: Ballet Hoo! (2006). Directed by Michael Waldman, Diverse TV, Bristol. First broadcast September 2006. London: Channel 4.

Bond, A. (2011). *Youth Dance England National Development Programme 2008-2011. Final Evaluation Report.* London: Youth Dance England.

Bramley, I. and Jermyn, H. (2006). *Dance Included: Towards Good Practice in Dance and Social Inclusion.* London: Arts Council England.

Brinson, P. (1986). *The Development of Youth Dance and Mime.* Laban Research. Unpublished.

Brinson, P. and Dick, F. (1996). *Fit to Dance? The Report of the National Inquiry into Dancers' Health and Injury.* London: Calouste Gulbenkian Foundation.

Buckroyd, J. (2000). *The Student Dancer: Emotional Aspects of the Teaching and Learning of Dance.* London: Dance Books.

Burkhardt, J. and Brennan, C. (2012). 'The effects of recreational dance interventions on the health and well-being of children and young people: A systematic review', *Arts and Health: An International Journal for Research, Policy and Practice,* 4(2): 148–61.

Burkhardt, J. and Rhodes, J. (2012). *Danceactive: Commissioning Dance from Health and Wellbeing: Guidance and Resources for Commissioners.* Department of Health, West Midlands.

Burns, S. (2008). *Dance Training and Accreditation Project: Research Phase Report.* London: Dance Training and Accreditation Project.

Butterworth, J. (2004). 'Teaching choreography in higher education: A process continuum model', *Research in Dance Education,* 5(1): 45–67.

Calouste Gulbenkian Foundation (1980). *Dance Education and Training in Britain.* London: Calouste Gulbenkian Foundation.

Castle, K., Ashworth, M., and Lord, P. (2002). *Aims in Motion: Dance Companies and their Education Programmes.* Slough: NFER.

Chappell, K. (2008). *Pick up the Pace 2004–2007: Final Report.* London: Laban, Paul Hamlyn Foundation.

Chappell, K., Rolfe, L., Craft, A., and Jobbins, V. (eds.) (2011). *Close Encounters: Dance Partners for Creativity.* Stoke on Trent: Trentham Books.

Children's Society (2012). *Promoting Positive Well-being for Children.* London: The Children's Society.

Clark, A. (2012). *Review of Dance in Scotland.* Edinburgh: Creative Scotland.

Connolly, M. K., Quin, E., and Redding, E. (2011). 'Dance 4 your life: Exploring the health and well-being implications of a contemporary dance intervention for female adolescents', *Research in Dance Education,* 12(1): 53–66.

Cronin de Chavez, A., Backett-Milburn, K., Parry, O., and Platt, S. (2005). 'Understanding and researching wellbeing: Its usage in different disciplines and potential for health research and health promotion', *Health Education Journal,* 64(1): 70–87.

Department of Health (2009). *New Horizons: A Shared Vision for Mental Health.* <http://webarchive.nationalarchives.gov.uk/+/www.dh.gov.uk/en/consultations/liveconsultations/dh_103144> (accessed 22 March 2017).

Fensham, R. and Garner, S. (2005). 'Dance classes, youth cultures and public health', *Youth Studies Australia,* 24(4): 14–20.

Fleming, M. (2012). *The Arts in Education: An Introduction to Aesthetics, Theory and Pedagogy.* Abingdon: Routledge.

Galton, M. (2008). *Creative Practitioners in Schools and Classrooms, Final Report of the Project: The Pedagogy of Creative Practitioners in Schools.* Cambridge: University of Cambridge.

Hall, T. (2007). *The Dance Review: A Report to Government on Dance Education and Youth Dance in England*. London: Department for Children, Schools and Families.

Harland, J., Lord, P., Stott, A., Kinder, K., Lamont, E., and Ashworth, M. (2005). *The Arts–Education Interface: A Mutual Learning Triangle?* Slough: National Foundation for Educational Research.

Harrison, S. (2007). *From Leaps and Bounds to Ballet Hoo: Summary Report*. Youth at Risk.

Haynes, A. (1987). 'The dynamic image: Changing perspectives in dance education', in P. Abbs (ed.), *Living Powers: The Arts in Education*. London: Falmer, pp. 141–62.

Jasper, L. (1995). 'Tensions in the definition of community dance', in J. Adshead (ed.), *Border Tensions: Dance and Discourse*. Guildford: University of Surrey, pp.181–90.

Jeffery, G. (2005). 'Professional identities: Artist and activist teachers?', in G. Jeffery (ed.), *The Creative College: Building a Successful Learning Culture in the Arts*. Stoke on Trent: Trenthan Books, pp.79–101.

Karkou, V. and Sanderson, P. (2000). 'Dance movement therapy in UK education', *Research in Dance Education*, 1(1): 69–86.

Kuppers, P. (2007). *Community Performance: An Introduction*. Abingdon: Routledge

Lakes, R. (2005). 'The messages behind the methods: The authoritarian pedagogical legacy in Western concert dance technique training and rehearsals', *Arts Education Policy Review*, 106(5): 3–16.

Layard, P. R. G. and Dunn, J. (2009). *A Good Childhood: Searching for Values in a Competitive Age*. London: Penguin.

Lynch, H. and Allan, J. (2006). *Social Inclusion and the Arts: Final Report to the Scottish Arts Council*. Stirling: University of Stirling.

McLellan, R., Galton, M., Steward, S., and Page, C. (2012). *The Impact of Creative Partnerships on the Wellbeing of Children and Young People*. Cambridge: University of Cambridge, Creative Partnerships.

McNeill, W. H. (1995). *Keeping Together in Time: Dance and Drill in Human History*. Cambridge, MA: Harvard University Press.

Michaelson, J., Mahony, S., and Schifferes, J. (2012). *Measuring Well-being: A Guide for Practitioners*. London: New Economics Foundation.

Miles, A. (2008). *The Academy: A Report on Outcomes for Participants*. Manchester: ESRC Centre for Research on Sociocultural Change.

Miulli, M. and Nordin-Bates, S. (2011). 'Motivational climates: What they are and why they matter', *IADMS Bulletin for Teachers*, 3(2): 5–7.

Mosston, M. and Ashworth, S. (1986). *Teaching Physical Education*. 3rd edn. London: Merrill.

Nordin, S. M. and Hardy, C. (2009). *Dance4Health: A Research-Based Evaluation of the Impact of Seven Community Dance Projects on Physical Health, Psychological Wellbeing and Aspects of Social Inclusion*. Warwickshire County Council County Arts Service.

North Kent Local Authorities Arts Partnership & Laban (2009). *Dance 4 Your Life. A Dance and Health Project*. London: NKLA Arts Partnership.

Price, H. (2009). 'Pedagogy in ballet studies at the undergraduate level in the United Kingdom', in T. Randall (ed.), *Global Perspectives on Dance Pedagogy: Research and Practice*. De Montfort University, Leicester, 25–27 June 2009, Congress on Research in Dance, pp. 80–5.

Pringle, E. (2002). *'We Did Stir Things Up': The Role of Artists in Sites for Learning*. London: Arts Council of England.

Pringle, E. (2008). 'Artists' perspectives on art practice and pedagogy', in J. Sefton-Green (ed.), *Creative Learning*. London: Creative Partnerships and Arts Council England, pp. 41–50.

Quin, E., Redding, E., and Frazer, L. (2007a). *The Effects of an Eight-Week Creative Dance Programme on the Physiological and Psychological Status of 11–14-year-old Adolescents: An experimental Study*. London: Hampshire Dance and Laban Centre.

Quin, E., Redding, E., and Frazer, L. (2007b). 'The health benefits of creative dance: Improving children's physical and psychological wellbeing', *Education and Health*, 25(2): 31–3.

Robinson, K. (1989). *The Arts in Schools: Principles, Practice and Provision*, 2nd edn. London: Calouste Gulbenkian Foundation.

Ross, J. (2004). 'The instructable body: Student bodies from classrooms to prisons', in L. Bresler (ed.), *Knowing Bodies, Moving Minds: Towards Embodied Teaching and Learning*. Amsterdam: Kluwer Academic Publishers, pp.169–81.

Sanderson, P. (1996). 'Dance within the national curriculum for physical education of England and Wales', *European Physical Education Review*, 2(1): 54–63.

Scottish Arts Council (2006). *ArtFull: Arts, Mental Health and Well-being Strategy 2006–08*. Edinburgh: Scottish Arts Council.

Siddall, J. (2010). *Dance in and Beyond Schools: An Essential Guide to Dance Teaching and Learning*. London: Youth Dance England.

Smith, C. (1998). 'On authoritarianism in the dance classroom', in S. B. Shapiro (ed.), *Dance, Power and Difference: Critical and Feminist Perspectives on Dance Education*. Champaign: Human Kinetics, pp. 123–46.

Smith-Autard, J. (2002). *The Art of Dance in Education*, 2nd edn. London: A. & C. Black.

Stevens, J. (2013). 'The National Association of Dance and Mime Animateurs (1986–9): A community of practice', *Dance Research*, 31(2): 157–73.

Urmston, E. (2012). *Go Dance: Inspiring Children to Dance to 2012 and Beyond*. Ipswich: East Youth Dance.

Watkins, C. and Mortimore, P. (1999). 'Pedagogy: What do we know?', in P. Mortimore (ed.), *Understanding Pedagogy and its Impact on Learning*. London: Paul Chapman, pp. 1–19.

CHAPTER 23

....

CREATIVE DANCE IN SCHOOLS

A Snapshot of Two European Contexts

....

SUE OLIVER, MONIKA KONOLD,
AND CHRISTINA LAREK

INTRODUCTION

....

WHILE acknowledging the many manifestations of dance in curricular contexts—social
or ethnic, for example—this chapter focuses on the art of creative dance in education,
as found (or not, as the case may be) in schools in some Scottish and German education
authority areas, and how it is perceived and valued by those who teach and learn it as
a means of enhancing wellbeing. That statement itself raises huge philosophical questions. What is the purpose of dance as art? Can creativity be taught? Can it be assessed?
We, the authors, do not attempt to address these questions here, but only to acknowledge them. The questions of *how* creative dance is experienced and valued, and how
it can enhance pupils' sense of wellbeing, are more pertinent to this study. We begin
with a glimpse of the issues regarding definition; we progress to descriptions of how
creative dance is presented in the selected Scottish and German education systems and
explore pupils' and teachers' perceptions of the process at curriculum level. We then
look through the European lens to see how the two systems match up to the ideals of
unity while honouring national identity and differences, which broadly sums up the
position of the overarching European Union authority. The ensuing discussion raises
more questions than the chapter attempts to answer.

Tempting though it might be to sneak a look at dance in education from a more
global perspective, we resist the temptation and leave that to such authors as Gilbert
(2005), who discusses dance in education in various countries and raises questions

concerning what should be taught and who should teach it, and Bellinger (2013), whose focus is on teaching West African dance in an American university, to mention two in a vast field.

LITERATURE FRAMEWORK: DANCE, CREATIVITY, AND WELLBEING

Advocating creativity in education, worldwide education adviser and Professor Emeritus Sir Ken Robinson states that

> (e)ducation should develop the whole child and not just their academic abilities. It should include processes that engage their feelings, physical development, moral education, and creativity. (p. 160)

In similar vein, Gardner's (2006) theory of Multiple Intelligences promotes the concept of arts being central to the learning experience, as in his Project Zero[1] experiment. When words are deemed inadequate due to their dependence on common usage, an art form can transcend the limitations of spoken language in articulating a feeling (Best 1985; Royce 2001). The success of this must be limited by the knowledge and understanding of the percipient—Langer's (1953) term—which goes some way to justifying the inclusion of arts in children's education (Eisner 2002; Gardner 2006). By extending their artistic experience they have a greater basis for communication. We have adopted Langer's term 'percipient' as opposed to 'perceiver', because we believe it reflects the intuitive nature of the understanding—not a passive process, but one which requires active engagement between subject and object. It suggests something of the cognitive process which takes place in the assimilation of knowledge.

Smith-Autard (2002) links the word 'aesthetic' with 'enjoyment', endorsing the idea that sensory satisfaction lies at the root of its meaning and that it can be nurtured and developed to enable the individual to make better sense of her/his world. It becomes a form of knowledge, and as, in our view, aesthetics cannot be divorced from art, it follows that art education promotes knowledge and understanding about life experience—one's own, and, vicariously, that of other people. It is a window on the world. Therefore, we adopt the position that the main tenets of arts education include a) to learn something about oneself, b) to learn about other people and cultures, and c) to learn how people from other cultural backgrounds view us: in the words of Scottish poet Robert Burns, 'to see oursels [sic] as others see us' (Fraser and Fraser 1983). We suggest that, through creative dance, children can gain a clearer and deeper understanding of 'being-in-the-world' (Heidegger, 1996), and so enjoy a greater feeling of both physical and social wellbeing. For the purpose of this study, 'wellbeing' is defined as a person's level of social and emotional comfort and enjoyment of opportunities to express her/his individuality (Nussbaum 2000; Harris and Hastings 2006; Oliver 2010). Factors affecting this might include physical health, where that aids or hampers social inclusion, and self-image, home, family, and cultural life. Wellbeing is therefore a holistic concept embracing personal, sociocultural, and environmental factors.

We draw from a vast body of knowledge to arrive at an understanding of creativity, including the ability to create, as well as solve, problems (Robinson 2001), the ability to produce original ideas in any discipline (Esquivel and Hodes 2003), and to employ various different personal attributes in a creative task, from styles of thinking, to personality, and reaction to one's environment (Sternberg 2006). Robinson (2001) and Gardner (1999, 2006) route creativity firmly in a cultural framework, which is acquired by individuals through their personal experience. 'Nothing is created in a cultural vacuum' (Oliver 2010, p. 33). Hence it is a subjective process with implications for wellbeing.

RATIONALE

Claims for many types of dance in the curriculum include promoting cultural awareness, social skills, and personal identity (Brinson 1993; Robinson 2001). These attributes can justify the conclusion that dance can enhance people's lives in the same way as other arts. The combination of the physical, emotional, and cognitive elements in creative dance are widely reported and acclaimed (e.g. Hanna 1999; Holtz 2006; Smith-Autard 2002). However, in accepting the claims, the allocation of overstretched public funds to support cultural activities may be tantamount to making a leap of faith in some policy makers' eyes—mainly, we suspect, because the effects of dance education are not directly quantifiable. Whether the product is as important a, or less important than, the process is a moot point, on which Oliver (2010) differs from Craft (2005) and Chappell (2007). The latter two deem the journey of accruing self-knowledge to be more important than the destination. Oliver (2010) agrees that the journey is crucial, but that the discipline of crafting the work into a finished entity is a useful educational discipline and a source of satisfaction for the dancer(s): a positive experience which enables them to say 'I achieved that!', and feel proud of the outcome. We believe that time spent on group and personal reflection at the end of a project is valuable to everyone involved.

Beecher (2005) believes that the Western lifestyle can put the concept of an holistic state of wellbeing under strain, and that in schools, creative dance can be a useful tool in restoring balance:

> Creative dance movement may bridge the gap between mind, body, and spirit by engaging and combining the imagination and thinking body with the physicality of doing. (Beecher 2005: 43–4)

Karkou (2010) makes the point that arts therapy, including Dance Movement Psychotherapy (DMP), in mainstream education can support pupils' learning through cognition and skills development: by addressing social and emotional needs, the foundation is set (or repaired), upon which the educational outcomes can be built. In particular, pupils in secondary schools can benefit from DMP (Karkou et al. 2010) to help them cope with emotional and physical changes. These authors included teachers in their project on the basis that in order to support mental health promotion, it would be useful to offer training to teaching staff about mental health issues and about the role of DMP in addressing them. BenZion (2010) explains how kinaesthetic stimuli can help to overcome the barriers of dyslexia and dysgraphia in school-based learning. Removed from the psychotherapeutic application of dance in schools, Kenrick, Lappin, and Oliver (Chapter 30 in this volume) found that dance as a performance art conducted outside school met many of the needs of teenage girls who had become disenfranchized within the school system in parts of Scotland for reasons concerning physical and socioemotional development. That project was delivered by YDance, the government-funded Scottish Youth Dance company. Perhaps if it could have been accommodated more widely within school curricula, these girls would not have become alienated from school in the first place.

METHODS

This was not a full-scale research project but rather an observation on how areas of two European nations regard creative dance in schools, and the samples from each country were small (Scotland: pupils, $n = 13$; teachers and dance providers, $n = 4$; Germany: pupils, $n = 18$; teachers, $n = 4$). It was never intended to draw far-reaching conclusions, but to tease out feelings and stimulate further thought. Pupils and dance educators volunteered their views on creative dance in semistructured interviews (Robson 2011). Questions included:

- *For teachers.* Why and how do you include it in the school curriculum? How do you think the pupils benefit from it? How rewarding or otherwise has your experience of teaching it been?
- *For pupils.* Did you have a choice in whether you dance at school or not? If so, why did you choose it? What do you feel you derive from it? How do you feel when you are dancing?

There was a clear gender bias (all the respondents were female), which we have not addressed, as it was outwith the remit of this chapter. Standard ethical procedures were followed: interviewees (and their parents, in the case of pupils) gave written consent, pupils were interviewed in groups, and transcripts were member-checked. Names were changed to ensure confidentiality. The data were then analysed thematically (Robson 2011; Creswell 2012), with an emphasis on themes such as feelings about self and others, enjoyment of the creative process, and self-empowerment.

Dance as Art in the Scottish Education System: Practical Application of Policy

Education is a crucial factor in maximising the creative potential of a community or a nation (Brinson 1993; Harris and Hastings 2006; Scottish Executive 2006), and is underpinned by cultural values instilled into pupils, strengthening their bonds with their own community while, ideally, giving them insight into other cultures. If people feel comfortable with their cultural heritage they can work together creatively, generating social and cultural capital which, in turn, will enrich their community (Bourdieu 2005; Grauer et al. 2001). This feeling comes with knowledge and understanding of the cultural milieu in which one lives, and the current Scottish educational policy, Curriculum for Excellence (CfE) (Scottish Executive 2006, 2009) seeks to promote it.

CfE aims to combine creative arts in the core curriculum with the philosophy of child-centred education. It is not a rigid system, but allows flexibility for schools and individual teachers to accommodate the prevailing needs and circumstances of pupils while aiming to encourage:

- Successful learners.
- Confident individuals.
- Responsible citizens.
- Effective contributors to society. (Scottish Executive 2006)

Within that framework, two subject areas are relevant to this chapter: Expressive Arts and Health and Wellbeing. Dance has a unique status in straddling both: although clearly an expressive art, its contribution to health and wellbeing is also acknowledged. It is assessed in terms of attainment targets rather than rigid grades except at certificate level for senior pupils, when more rigorous assessment is required.

Dance as an expressive art is viewed in CfE as a vehicle for 'expressing feelings, ideas, thoughts, and solutions' (Scottish Executive 2006), implying a degree of metacognition in children's response to stimuli, and a direct link between what a child feels and how that feeling is manifested. Creative dance is valued as a vehicle for self-expression, for skills acquisition (specific to the dance and transferable to other situations), and for fostering understanding of aesthetic and cultural values. Children learn to communicate emotional content to other people in performance and personal response through observation and evaluation. These skills can contribute to the building of relationships and respect for others across social and cultural spectra. As a vehicle for promoting health and wellbeing, the same principles apply, with the addition of the adage that 'a healthy mind grows in a healthy body'. The Scottish Executive (2006) states that a 'healthy lifestyle supports physical, social, and emotional wellbeing, and underpins successful learning' (p. 13).

Against this background of philosophy, policy, and politics, creative dance in primary schools is potentially provided by:

- Class teachers.
- Specialist physical education (PE) teachers.
- Dance artists employed by the local council.
- Freelance dance artists by invitation.
- Performing companies who have educational programmes linked to their productions and who are performing locally.

There are strengths and weaknesses in all these methods of provision.

Class teachers in primary schools (pupils aged 5–11 years approximately) do not always feel comfortable teaching creative dance, especially to the older children who are more judgemental about their teacher's abilities. Despite the fact that dance as an Expressive Art is integral to CfE, many teachers have had very little training to deliver it (National Dance Teachers' Association 2004)—especially those who are older, perhaps nearing retirement age, and have received little guidance in, or since, their initial teacher training. A primary-school teacher who also teaches dance in the community comments:

> It used to be part of PE[2] . . . and now it's part of Expressive Arts . . . I suppose there's a bigger emphasis on it in general. However, I think that dance is one of those things that people are scared of teaching because they don't feel confident in it a lot of the time. They get their SCD[3] as part of gym (PE) usually around Christmas time; maybe at Burns[4] time they'll get SCD but I think that class teachers tend to be a little bit more sort of—'what else can we teach as dance?' PE teachers obviously have a bit more training in that aspect but—I love teaching it [laughs]—it's great fun! I think there's reluctance to teach it, probably because of a lack of training . . . I have lots of experience in dance and I've (recently) had a theme to work with, which was great. (Emma)

Upper primary school pupils report that they feel more motivated if the teacher is also motivated: they can tell whether the teacher is doing it because (s)he has to or because (s)he wants to. Both genders enjoyed 'making up' dances because it lets out emotions and really fun plus helps you keep fit' (Primary school pupil aged 11, 2012).

Reports from older pupils also suggest that creative dance provision in primary schools is at best patchy, as revealed in interview (interviewer's questions in italics):

> *And, thinking back to when you were in primary school, did you do much dance there?*
> Not an awful lot . . .
> I did some tap dancing outside school . . .

But did you ever do any creative dance? Were you given an idea and allowed to explore the movement round it yourselves?
Not really, not in primary school. We had competitions and we made up
    dances . . . and you could do what you wanted in that, like sing or dance.
Were you guided by a teacher, or was it just a group of you together at some point?
We just made it up ourselves.
As part of the curriculum?
No, we didn't get that sort of dance at school.
(*Interviewer* and secondary school (S.4) pupils)

There is evidence suggesting that dance—especially creative dance—is not well provided for in PE training in Scotland. A day of dance delivered at a Scottish teacher-training facility by one of the authors revealed that postgraduate PE students in the second year of their two-year diploma course had had no dance input whatsoever other than on that day, yet they would soon be expected to deliver it themselves in schools. Similar pictures emerge from establishments which train primary-school teachers and drama teachers in Scotland (Blanche 2007). If the teachers do not feel comfortable teaching it, how is that going to impact on the learning experience and therefore on the wellbeing of pupils?

Most Local Education Authorities (LEAs) have Dance Artists in Residence or Dance Development Officers, who assume much of the responsibility for implanting dance in schools, especially in secondary education, where pupils can gain certification through National Progression Awards (NPAs)[5] in the Scottish education system. The onus is therefore removed from PE staff.

> It really does depend on the local authority area and what support they (the teachers) have in each local authority area. I tend to find that it's normally led by one or two people and if you don't have those proactive people in the area, then there's very little dance in primary and secondary schools. (Alice, Dance Development Officer)

In another LEA, the Dance Artist in Residence nurtures a group of senior high-school girls through their NPA Level 2 award. In two years, she reports that the girls' attitude has turned around:

> . . . two years ago I had a group of twelve kids started [the course] and I think seven of them started because they just wanted a bit of a skive . . . and by the end of the year, I wouldn't have even recognised them! I'm not saying it's all because of the dance, but a large part of it—one girl used not to come into any other classes, but she used to come in to dance . . . [At first] they were kind of coming in, completely not equipped—hair down—then they'd come with their hair pinned back, a big change in itself! They came in wearing thick leggings and T-shirts, and jogging bottoms and—yes their attitude completely changed. Actually, even towards me—they had no respect at first—not that I was out to command respect, but they didn't listen to me. You know you can tell that general chit-chat when you're talking, that kind of laughing; if you say something, it's like, giggling, and they completely

turned round—they were so lovely by the end of the year. (Rebecca, Dance Artist in Residence)

The dancers themselves expressed delight in what they had achieved, as demonstrated in the following interview:

> You're yourself; you don't have to think about everything else. Also it clears your mind if you've got problems going on, and it's exercise so it . . . makes you feel good about yourself, because when you exercise there's a hormone that gets released that helps you relax and feel better—endorphins.
> *There are so many facets to this sort of dancing—dance as art—the social, expressive . . . what is it that appeals to you?*
> The fact that it takes you out of yourself, like in some of the normal classes we have, we don't really get to talk to that many people, but since this is a small class we get to talk and if we're stuck on something, the teachers can help. So we get a chance to explore different techniques. And because in most classes you're sitting down and working, it's something that you're actually up and doing, and for people that don't like PE or something, it's not like you have to change what you're doing all the time—and it's quite easy, and if you enjoy it, then why not just keep doing it, basically. I think it's socially good as well, because you gain confidence, like at the beginning of the year, I didn't really (know the others), but now we're a really close group.
> *In what way has it improved your confidence?*
> You get the chance of expressing yourself and just letting go. With us being such a small group being really close to each other, we've helped each other and within the group it feels better.
> *Do you feel less shy now than you did with each other at the beginning?*
> Yes [collective answer]. And doing the dance show helped us gain a bit of confidence being in front of people, and not just being around each other. Because it's different when you're dancing in front of people who you know rather than people who are strangers. Dancing in front of strangers helps you just get to know why you get to express yourself, more than being [shy]) about people you don't know.
> (*Interviewer* and senior pupils, NVQ certificate candidates)

As their course involved them in composition and choreography, they were also faced with the novel situation of having to teach their dances to the rest of the group. This posed its own challenges:

> It was quite scary because you didn't know if they would pick it up or if you were teaching them right or . . .
> Because you actually then have to be the teacher and we had to do duets—choreography and . . .
> We did solos themselves, but then we had to teach the duets and because you had to be two people, teaching (and learning).

So, you were in control of that process. What was it like having control?

Quite weird at the beginning because you're used to listening to what the teacher says, but it gives you the chance of expressing yourself and making it your own, and showing what you can do to other members of the group.

I thought it would be quite hard because you have to get the idea you had in your head across to them but in the end you did get it right.

But what an achievement! Were you pleased with it?

Yes [general agreement] . . . We did a dance show with other schools . . . It was nerve-racking because of having to do it in front of so many people and we did some mistakes but judging by the reviews, nobody noticed because we just kept on going . . . We kept on smiling!

(*Interviewer* and senior pupils, NVQ certificate candidates)

The evidence here suggests that the pupils were learning to be agents in shaping their own identity, taking control of the process, pushing beyond the restrictions of 'habitus', (Bourdieu 2005) and embracing a wider set of norms and values, choosing what they wanted and who they wanted to be (Oliver 2010).

In Scottish state schools, freelance artists often work alongside class teachers to give pupils a quality experience underpinned by educational principles. By investing in cultural capital in this way, the authorities are judged to be promoting creative indus-tries for the future benefit of the country (Garnham 2001). Even the most cynical educationalist in Western society has to admit that by fostering a symbiotic relation-ship between creative industries and education, the system is at the very least boost-ing future audiences and spectators, hence generating cultural, or 'symbolic', profit (Bourdieu, 2005, p. 118). This can translate into commercial success and consequent societal wellbeing. A more enlightened view might be that even such passive partici-pation in dance as art will go a long way to nurture fulfilment in adulthood by encour-aging positive attitudes through cognitive and social engagement which will foster feelings of personal wellbeing (Seligman et al. 2005). An interest in dance might start in the formal school system, but can transcend it to influence adult life in the same way as any curricular subject.

Dance as Art in the Education systems of Germany: Practical Application of Policy

In Germany, the national government only dictates aspects of general education pro-vision, and Culture and Sports responsibility rests with the appropriate ministry. The responsibility for curriculum content lies with the different states (Holtz 2006). In Bavaria, a nominal amount of dance is compulsory, and the system is flexible enough so that teachers who are not confident about teaching it, would, theoretically, not be expected to do so. Dance obligations can also be fulfilled as after-school activities as well as within the curriculum (M. Konold, personal communication, 15 October 2012). The same approach to dance provision can be found in Lower Saxony:

> In the curriculum, they say you might have to do dance for four hours in half a year but if you don't do, well, nobody is blaming you. And most of the teachers don't do it because they don't feel really comfortable with it . . . It's all sorts of dance (not just creative). And well, you can choose what you like to do because nobody was teaching you really in university. And most of the teachers don't have any other experience with dance. (Krista, middle-school teacher, Hannover, 2011)

As is the case in Bavarian schools, Krista observed that dance needs are often met as after-school classes.

On the German websites there is plenty about dance *and* school but just a few articles about dance *in* school. Various projects are offered to schools which are interested in dance education, led by independent dancing schools or even special Government organizations.

Another problem is the competition between dance and popular sports such as soccer and hockey, which are compulsory in all German schools, with formal assessment. Because of perceived difficulties in teaching creative dance, teachers tend to resort to filling the sector with male-dominant topics (Kleindienst-Cachay et al. 2008: 100). Kleindienst-Cachay et al. warn that the culture of sports and movement in school turns slowly in the direction of male stereotype, and the promotion of wellbeing is not an overt aim.

The German school timetable contains only one to three hours of PE per week. Dance is an option, sometimes occurring at the end of a school year. Many German teachers do not have time to teach dance, even if they had the competence and confidence to teach it.

Nevertheless, in all PE curricula there is a section on 'Gymnastic, Rhythm, and Dancing Presentation/Exercise' (Niedersächsisches Kultusministerium 2006, p. 15). It is one of six fields of learning in primary school (children are aged 6–10 years). These might differ from region to region, but the general target is to achieve basically coordinated skills—skills to develop a feeling of rhythm, to use the body to express different feelings.

The curriculum in the region of Hesse adds the experience of dancing with instrumental accompaniment and vocal and visual inputs (Hessisches Kultusministerium 2010, p. 18). Interdisciplinary learning enables teachers to connect dance with music education, especially in primary schools. At the end of primary school, pupils should be able to 'think of and develop different dances, and show improvement in movements and steps' (Ministerium für Schule und Weiterbildung des Landes Nordrhein-Westfalen 2008, p. 94). Yet if teachers are not adequately trained to deliver dance, how can this be fulfilled? What will this do for *their* sense of wellbeing?

The basic curricular requirements are stipulated by the German Government and contain areas with compulsory and optional topics, such as athletics, apparatus gymnastics, gymnastic/dance, and judo/wrestling (Ministerium für Bildung, Wissenschaft und Kultur Mecklenburg-Vorpommern 2002, p. 17). Sometimes in high schools, topics are chosen by teachers in collaboration with pupils. It is interesting that dance is specified for girls, and judo/wrestling for boys, reinforcing Western cultural stereotypes. It is not clear from the document whether dance can be also taught to boys. That is another decision of the staff.

Social skills are promoted through the affective curriculum, especially for teenagers. Through the physical aspects of the curriculum (whether PE or dance), they become sensitized to issues of health, their changing bodies, and the mental states of themselves and others. They can also learn about different cultures, and this can sometimes be interpreted through dance (Ministerium für Bildung, Wissenschaft und Kultur Mecklenburg-Vorpommern 2002, p. 30).

In some German universities, students of PE get the opportunity to attend courses on dance. Because of the disparity among participants regarding their knowledge of dance, respondents reported that only basic movement technique is taught rather than the chance to explore creativity. Methods or ideas for teaching creative dance to children in school are not given. As in Scotland, at the end of their training young teachers often lack the confidence to teach dance in school. Respondents reported that perhaps two PE classes per year would be devoted to 'dance', but that included gymnastic dance and was not necessarily creative. Krista, from a middle school near Hannover, stated that in her experience the aesthetic aspect of dance was not touched upon in her university course. When she teaches dance in her PE lessons it tends to be contemporary, whereby she teaches a dance routine to her pupils. Consequently, the emphasis was on the 'doing', not the 'feeling' or the appreciation or evaluation of the task, which, she believes, is the status quo in most of Germany. If student teachers are not given the chance to develop an understanding of creative dance as a discipline in its own right, it will not find its way into school curricula, except by virtue of individual teachers' preference.

By contrast, Gaby, a PE teacher in Bavaria, reported that she did have several hours of creative dance input in her teacher training course—not just practical, but theory as well. It was compulsory for females, but male students had the choice. The course provided insight into

> the effect of dance on the body and the body expression with dance [which] plays a particular role. The effect of dance on group experience and social behaviour [of)] kids belongs mainly to the lectures in theory. Development of different dance styles (hip-hop, jazz) [encourages] social unity. (Gaby, transl. M. Konold, data collection, 21 May 2012)

Armed with that knowledge, PE teachers then have some autonomy in how to implement it in the curriculum. From the fifth to the twelfth class, pupils in her school learn dance—in the earlier years, the emphasis is on technique whereby the pupils are taught a dance, on which they can build their own variations. Later, the pupils have increasingly more opportunity to use their dance skills to create their own original work. Gaby, who teaches girls only, believes that issues of wellbeing are implicit in the pupils' dance experience, and may be discussed with the older pupils: they, not the teachers, are the best judges of how it affects their feelings and self-confidence. The younger pupils might feel it; the older ones are better able to articulate it. The teacher cannot readily perceive how the pupils are feeling about the work they are doing; (s)he can only observe their reactions and deduce what they might be feeling.

Waldorf schools (following the principles of Rudolph Steiner) offer Continuing Professional Development (CPD) for PE teachers, which include dance as well as other aspects of PE (Trittner 2012). Some privately run Waldorf schools offer Eurhythmie as a form of expressive dance, but the overall impression among teachers is that it is not a free form of expression; it is strictly technique-based. When asked about what stops it from being creative dance, one teacher replied:

> It's because of the rules you don't find in normal dance. For example, if you hear an 'A' you have to dance a special form. (Claudia, Waldorf teacher)

A former Waldorf pupil, Nadia, explained how Eurhythmie was not about self-expression but of body and movement in a defined space—a disciplined dance form, leading to a performance. In her view, the product was at least as important as the process. This resonates with the practice of assessing dance in state schools, which, Gaby believes, motivates pupils to raise their standards. By contrast, opinions are divided in Scotland about assessment in the arts, particularly in primary schools, where some teachers feel that it could be demotivating for less able pupils.

Pedagogically, then, the Waldorf approach to dance teaching seems to be very rigid. If this is where teachers are receiving CPD, this rigidity must influence what is taught in schools. Conversely, Holtz (2006) supports the inclusion of creative dance in the curriculum as a vehicle for children's exploration of self, feelings, and movement potential: while there is an underlying acceptance of the cognitive, physical, and spiritual components sharing importance in dance provision, she notes that individual schools have freedom to choose how they integrate dance into the curriculum; for example, as a subject in its own right, or as an add-on to cultural programmes.

Pupils in Bavarian high schools and one primary school reported that in most cases the classes were exclusively female. When creative dance was part of PE it was taught only to girls, while in the primary class it was part of music, so boys were included. Paula, aged 10, had enjoyed creative dance in her primary school, partly because she felt that the teacher also enjoyed it, and was able to convey her confidence and enthusiasm. Juliette, aged 16, had had very little experience of dance of any sort in school. The closest thing to creative dance which she had encountered was a dance with a skipping rope, outside one winter. Part of the dance was set by the teacher, while the rest was choreographed by the pupils. Susie, aged 14, composed a dance with another pupil. She found that experience rewarding and would have liked to do more, but curriculum constraints prevented it. Susie surmised that although the teacher had been willing to accommodate it, she was perhaps not personally confident about dancing.

In response to the question as to how their dance experiences had impinged on their sense of wellbeing, the pupils' opinions varied. Juliette had a clear idea of what she thought wellbeing should be:

> It's important to have a good class community and not so much stress. And even if we have stress, it's important we still have our fun. (Juliette, transl. Konold)

She did not, however, derive much fun from dance, and sought a sense of wellbeing from other activities with her friends. It was the fact of being together that made her feel good, rather than the nature of the activity.

Susie noted:

> It reduces stress. I can go to my limits and afterwards I feel much better. [My body perception] has improved definitely... [Wellbeing means that] related to dance, I shouldn't feel uncomfortable with what we are doing. Generally it means, that I'm well; that I have friends and family. (Susie, transl. Konold)

For Patsi, like Juliette, fun was a key element in wellbeing:

> [There] should be someone around me I know. I like to run and cycle, and music also shouldn't be missed. I like to do what is fun for me. (Patsi, transl. Konold)

Holtz (2003), writing from a German perspective, acknowledges that dance in general has much to offer the development of self-worth and feelings of wellbeing, as much through the physical demands as the psychosocial, but supports the comments of the respondents inasmuch as these benefits are best experienced in a stable community environment: that includes family, friends, school, and any other contact which helps to shape one's life experience. Bourdieu (2005) describes this as 'habitus': the network of social forces which protect as well as contain us. For most people, the main influence in the socialization process comes from the immediate family. A child adopts the mores and behavioural code of the family, which ensure a safety net of social and behavioural guidelines before (s)he is exposed to wider social influences—pre-school, school, community, and so on. The child is then likely to start negotiating and possibly rebelling against perceived confines of an imposed habitus, as (s)he assumes agency for creating her/his own self-image (Oliver 2010). The process has implications for her/his feelings of wellbeing.

Tanzplan Deutschland is a system devised by the dance community in Germany, commissioned by the Federal Cultural Foundation, which aims at widespread adoption throughout the country's education establishments in an effort to bring consistency of experience to school pupils and vocational students alike. The Tanzplan vision is to target all areas of education, from school to tertiary and higher education with contemporary dance, to engage pupils and students in the breadth of its application, from broad dance *education* to specific dance *training*. It aims to address changing social, cultural, and political trends, and echo these in its educational programmes.

DISCUSSION

A European Perspective

Whether united under the administrative umbrella of the European Union or not, one might hope that Scotland and Germany are close enough geographically and culturally to make connections through education policies, while maintaining cultural diversity. Indeed, the European Commission for Public Health (2009) has acknowledged the similarities in children's educational needs irrespective of political boundaries:

> Children and young people spend a large proportion of their days in educational settings, making them one of the key environments for mental health promotion . . . aligning the climate and practices in educational settings with children's mental health needs has been shown to improve academic achievement and social behaviour. (European Commission 2009)

It seems, then, that programmes like Tanzplan could garner funding from the EU to reach more pupils, as could Scottish dance artists, to implement creative dance projects in Scottish schools. Might government or EU funding even allow them to have cultural exchanges and deliver their programmes in each other's country?

Hardman (2007) reports that education policies in many European countries are in a state of flux, trying to adapt to changing societal pressures. The disparity of the member countries makes it virtually impossible, not to mention undesirable, to apply a rigid model across the EU. Moreover, the arrival in Europe of immigrants in large numbers from the Middle East and beyond will have brought their various cultures, which are potentially a subject for the celebration of diversity, even if challenging to integrate. One of the difficulties in justifying investment must be the problem of measuring the benefits of art. How can one measure the effectiveness of an arts education programme against the cost of provision? How can educators be sure that they are attaching equal value to attainment standards and to the personal and social benefits of pupils? Scottish LEAs are accountable for the allocation of public funds, as are German state governments. Training artists to a high standard requires a narrow, linear approach to funding, while enabling pupils to have wider access to arts education requires a broader application of funds—the dilemma of 'raising' and 'spreading' (Garnham 2001; Bourdieu 2005)—yet authorities cannot ignore the terms of the United Nations Convention on the Rights of the Child: Article 31 (1990), which gives the right of every child to participate fully in the arts and all aspects of cultural life.

Policy makers must look beyond the figures, embrace the position that education should be holistic, and treat it as an investment in a country's most precious resource: its children. That is nothing new: in Scotland, the holistic approach has been enshrined in law for decades (Scottish Education Department 1965; Scottish Office Education Department 1992). However, one wonders about the efficacy of a system which shows such disparity of children's and teachers' experience. Gardner (2006) also points out the importance of teachers having a deep knowledge of the art they are teaching: to afford children the chance to learn how to engage critically with it:

> If the area is music, the teacher must be able to think musically—and not merely introduce music via language or logic. (p. 154)

The same must surely apply to dance and other arts.

CONCLUSION

The picture emerging from this study is of a somewhat haphazard approach to dance provision in at least some Scottish and German schools. In both countries, the current, largely pragmatic, approach to dance—especially creative dance—leaves too much to teachers' personal choice as to whether it is provided and so an opportunity for promoting wellbeing could be missed. Yet personal feelings of wellbeing were important to the pupils who were interviewed, and that had as much to do with the social context and delivery as with the content. Can teachers' CPD address that need? And do these experiences resonate with those of pupils elsewhere in the EU?

Perhaps the German Tanzplan approach has more in its favour. If it is implemented across Germany, it could ensure parity and consistency of experience for pupils. The fact that it is the brainchild of dance artists as well as educationalists outside any state system will hopefully allow it to remain fresh and vital, in touch, and evolving with current trends. Through the European link, perhaps it could extend beyond Germany's borders. Perhaps we need a European forum for dance to share best practice so that we can learn from each other.

Acknowledgements

The authors wish to express thanks to the respondents, in both Germany and Scotland, for giving freely of their time to share their views on creative dance and wellbeing.

Notes

1. Project Zero is maintained by Harvard University Graduate School of Education, to study the learning processes of children.
2. Physical education.
3. Scottish Country Dancing.
4. The anniversary of the birth of Scottish poet Robert Burns (25 January 1759).
5. These are part of the National Vocational Qualifications (NVQ) in Scotland.

References

Beecher, O. (2005). *The Dance Experience and the Sense of Being: Therapeutic Application of Modern Dance*. PhD thesis, University of Limerick.

Bellinger, I. (2013). 'Dancing through time and space: African dance and the Géwël tradition of Senegal at Suffolk University', *Journal of Pan African Studies*, 6(5): 1–23.

BenZion, G. (2010). 'Overcoming the dyslexia barrier: the role of kinesthetic stimuli in the teaching of spelling', in B. Bläsing, M. Puttke, and T. Schack (eds.), *The Neurocognition of Dance: Mind Movement and Motor skills*. Hove and New York, Psychology Press, pp. 123–50.

Best, D. (1985). *Feeling and Reason in the Arts*. London: Allen and Unwin.

Blanche, R. (2007). *Delivering Dance in the Curriculum for Excellence: Research and Consultancy Commissioned by the Federation of Scottish Theatres*. Edinburgh: Blanche Policy Solutions.

Bourdieu, P. (2005). *The Rules of Art*. Cambridge: Polity Press. First published in 1996.

Brinson, P. (1993). *Dance as Education: Towards a National Dance Culture*. London: Falmar.

Burns, R. C. (1983). 'To a louse', in E. Fraser and A. Fraser, *My Heart's in the Highlands . . . An Anthology of Verse by Robert Burns*. Norwich: Jarrold and Sons. Poem originally published *c.*1784.

Chappell, K. (2007). 'Creativity in primary level dance education: Moving beyond assumption', *Research in Dance Education*, 8(1): 27–52.

Craft, A. (2005). *Creativity in Schools*. London: Routledge.

Creswell, J. (2012). *Qualitative Inquiry and Research Design: Choosing among Five Traditions*. London: Sage.

Eisner, E. (2002). *Arts and the Creation of the Mind*. Newhaven, CT: Yale University Press.

Esquivel, G. B. and Hodes, T. G. (2003). 'Creativity, development and personality', in J. Houltz (ed.), *The Educational Psychology of Creativity*. Cresskill, NJ: Hampton Press, pp. 135–65.

European Commission on Public Health. (2009). *Promotion of Mental Health and Wellbeing of Children and Young People: Making it Happen*. Conference proceedings, Stockholm. <http://ec.europa.eu/health/mental_health/events/ev_20090929_en.htm>

Fraser, E. and Fraser, A. (1983). *My Heart's in the Highlands . . . An Anthology of Verse by Robert Burns*. Norwich: Jarrold and Sons.

Gardner, H. (2006). *Multiple Intelligences: New Horizons*. New York: Basic Books.

Garnham, N. (2001). 'Afterword: The cultural commodity and cultural policy', in S. Selwood (ed.), *The UK Cultural Sector*. London: Policy Studies Institute, pp. 445–58.

Gilbert, A. G. (2005). 'Dance education in the 21st century: A global perspective. Dance education around the world faces common challenges: Who should teach, Who should teach the teachers, and what should they teach?' *JOPERD: The Journal of Physical Education, Recreation and Dance*, May–June: 26–35. <https://www.questia.com/read/1G1-132848059/dance-education-in-the-21st-century-a-global-perspective> (accessed 7 July 2014).

Grauer, K., Krug, D., Loucheur, Y., Mackinnon, E. (2001). 'Culture, education and skills for living', in F. Matarasso (ed.), *Recognising Culture*. Comedia, the Department of Canadian Heritage, and UNESCO, pp. 61–7.

Hanna, J. L. (1999). *Dance and Education: Intelligent Moves for Changing Times*. Champaign, IL: Human Kinetics.

Harris, A. and Hastings, N. (2006). *Working the System: Creating a State of Wellbeing*. Edinburgh: Scottish Council Foundation.

Heidegger, M. (1996). *Being and Time: A Translation of Sein und Zeit*, transl. J. Stambaugh. New York: State University of New York Press.

Hessisches Kultusministerium.(2010). *Bildungsstandards und Inhaltsfelder: Das neue Kerncurriculum für Hessen*. Wiesbaden: Primarstufe Sport.

Houltz, J. (ed). (2003). *The Educational Psychology of Creativity*. Cresskill, NJ: Hampton Press.

Karkou, V. (ed.) (2010). *Arts Therapies in Schools Research and Practice*. London: Jessica Kingsley.

Karkou, V., Fullerton, A., and Scarth, S. (2010). 'Finding a way out of the labyrinth through dance movement psychotherapy: Collaborative work in a mental health promotion programme in secondary schools', in Karkou, V. (ed.), *Arts Therapies in Schools Research and Practice*. London: Jessica Kingsley, pp. 59–84.

Kleindienst-Cachay, C., Kastrup, V. and Cachay, K. (2008). 'Koedukation im Sportunterricht: Ernüchternde Realität einer löblichen Idee', *Sportunterricht*, 57(4): 100–2.

Langer, S. (1953). *Feeling and Form: A Theory of Art*. London and New York: Routledge and Kegan Paul.

Ministerium für Bildung, Wissenschaft und Kultur Mecklenburg-Vorpommern (2002). Rahmenplan. Regionale Schule, Hauptschule, Realschule, Gymnasium, Integrierte Gesamtschule. Jahrgangsstufe 7–10; adiant Druck Roggentin.

Ministerium für Schule und Weiterbildung des Landes Nordrhein-Westfalen (2008). Grundschule: Richtlinien und Lehrpläne. Musik. Ritterbach Verlag, p. 94.

National Dance Teachers' Association (2004). *Maximising Opportunity: Policy Paper*. Burntwood, Staffordshire: National Dance Teachers' Association.

Niedersächsisches Kultusministerium (2006). Kerncurriculum für die Grundschule. Sportjahrgänge 1–4. Sport; Unidruck Hannover.

Nussbaum, M. (2000). *Women and Human Development*. Cambridge: Cambridge University Press.

Oliver, S. (2010). *Creative Dance for Adolescents, and their Social Wellbeing: A Community-Based Study Set in Scotland*. Saarbrücken: VDM Verlag Dr Müller.

Robson, C. (2011). *Real World Research: A Resource for Users of Social Research Methods in Applied Settings*. Chichester: John Wiley and Sons.

Robinson, K. (2001). *Out of Our Minds: Learning to be Creative*. Chichester: Capstone.

Royce, A. P. (2001). *The Anthropology of Dance*, 2nd edn. Bloomington and London, Indiana University Press.

Scottish Education Department (1965). *Primary Education in Scotland.* Edinburgh: Her Majesty's Stationery Office.

Scottish Executive (2006). *A Curriculum for Excellence: Building the Curriculum 1.* Edinburgh: Scottish Government.

Scottish Executive (2009). *A Curriculum for Excellence: Building the Curriculum 4.* Edinburgh: Scottish Government.

Scottish Office Education Department (1992). *Expressive Arts 5–14: National Guidelines.* Edinburgh: Her Majesty's Stationery Office.

Seligman, M., Parks, A., and Steen, T. (2005). 'A balanced psychology and a full life', in F. Huppert, N. Baylis, and B. Keverne (eds.), *The Science of Well-being.* New York, NY: Oxford University Press, pp. 275–84.

Smith-Autard, J. (2002). *The Art of Dance in Education*, 2nd edn. London: A&C Black.

Sternberg, R. (2006). 'Creating a vision of creativity: the first 25 years'. *Psychology of Aesthetics, Creativity and the Arts*, 5(1): 2–12.

Tanzplan Deutschland (n.d.). <http://www.tanzplan-deutschland.de/ausbildungsprojekte.php?id_language=2> (accessed 27 August 2012).

Trittner, G. (2012). 'Bewegung Stützt seelische Entwicklung: Waldorfschule richtet derzeit international Tagung für Turnlehrer aus', *Heidenheimer Neuen Presse*, 29 May.

CHAPTER 24

....

MOVING SYSTEMS

*A Multidisciplinary Approach to Enhance Learning
and Avoid Dropping Out*

....

CLAIRE SCHAUB-MOORE

INTRODUCTION

....

TWENTY-SIX pupils of an eighth grade at a lower secondary school (*Hauptschule*[1]) in Germany were selected to participate in a school project that aimed at preventing pupils dropping out and leaving school without achieving a qualification. The prognosis made by the teachers was bleak: they expected only 75% of the class to pass all examinations and receive the lowest possible school qualification (*Hauptschulabschluss*). The figures reflect years of experience at that school: according to the headmaster, their average dropout rate was 25% (Düpree 2009)—higher than the average number of early school-leavers in Germany at the time (15%) (Eurostat and European Commission 2014).

These so-called 'dropouts' or 'early school-leavers' constitute a group that is heavily at risk (Rumberger 2004; Psacharopoulos 2007). According to De Witte and Cabus (2013) they have a relatively high risk of '(1) entering a vicious circle in which in turn their children obtain lower education levels . . . (2) having long-term unemployment . . . (3) suffering from health problems . . . or (4) feeling a low social cohesion' (155). The reasons for young people to drop out and leave school without a qualification are manifold. Research and literature reviews point to factors such as socioeconomic status (SES) (Heckman and Krueger 2005; Orfield 2004), poor academic achievement (Christenson and Thurlow 2004; Lehr et al. 2004), academic self-efficacy (Caprara et al. 2008), student motivation (Rumberger 2004), and problem behaviours (Hickman et al. 2008). Furthermore, as Alivernini and Lucidi (2011) point out, the theory of self-determination (SDT)—in particular, how a pupil perceives his or her competence and autonomy (Deci and Ryan 2002)—seems to play an important role in understanding the intrinsic motives for 'leaving'.

A social constructionist view on the relationship between school and pupil was offered by Australian researchers whose findings emphasize the importance of pupils feeling a sense of belonging to their school. When pupils experience a supportive environment in school, such as having friends or teachers who support their academic goals, they are more likely to experience positive outcomes (Newman et al. 2000). These findings suggest that a sense of belonging within school is important in facilitating intellectual and social wellbeing. Pupils who do not feel that they 'belong' at school often attempt to satisfy this need through membership of antisocial groups, or they drop out from school altogether (Lee and Breen 2007). In his seminal meta-analysis of the influences on achievement in school-aged students, Hattie (2013) develops a model of learning and understanding based on a co-constructed teacher–pupil relationship. Positive learning outcomes will occur, he claims:

> . . . when learning is the explicit goal, when it is appropriately challenging, when the teacher and the student both (in their various ways) seek to ascertain whether and to what degree the challenging goal is attained, when there is deliberate practice aimed at attaining mastery of the goal, when there is feedback given and sought, and when there are active, passionate, and engaging people (teacher, student, peers, and so on) participating in the act of learning. It is teachers seeing learning through the eyes of students, and students seeing teaching as the key to their ongoing learning. (p. 22)

This view sums up the importance of 'relationships' for the physical–psychological–social development of a person. In the intersubjective field of a relationship, each partner is able to explore, communicate, and act upon past and present experiences, questions, and wishes. Yalom and Leszcz (2005) describe these processes in the context of group therapy. By allowing relationships to form, an in-depth understanding of self and other can develop, thus fostering the client's self-acceptance, self-efficacy, self-confidence, and wellbeing.

In the Finnish need-adapted approach for patients with schizophrenic symptoms (Alanen 1997; Alanen et al. 1991), relationships are pivotal. From this, the open dialogue (OD) approach was developed for treating patients with psychosis in their homes (Seikkula et al. 2006). Seven main principles are key to this approach (pp. 215–16):

1. *The provision of immediate help.* The aim is to integrate interventions as soon as possible with the patient's everyday life.
2. *A social network perspective.* The patients, their families, and other key members of the patient's social network are always invited to the first meetings to mobilize support for the patient and the family.
3. *Flexibility and mobility.* These are guaranteed by adapting the therapeutic response to the specific needs of each case, using the therapeutic methods that best suit each case. The meetings are often organized at the patient's home, with the consent of the family.

4. *Responsibility.* Whoever among the staff is first contacted becomes responsible for organizing the first multiprofessional family meeting, in which decisions about continuation and site of treatment are made.

5. *Psychological continuity.* The role of the team is not only to take care of the treatment as such but also to guarantee both the creation of new psychological meanings for symptoms and shared experience of this process. Members of the patient's social network are invited to participate in the meetings throughout the treatment process.

6. *Tolerance of uncertainty.* Building a relationship in which all parties can feel safe enough in the joint process strengthens this.

7. *Dialogism.* The focus is primarily on promoting dialogue and secondarily on promoting change in the patient or in the family. In dialogue, patients and families increase their sense of agency in their own lives by discussing the patient's difficulties and problems.

The strength of this approach lies in the realization that progress can only be promoted if the many experts (patient, family, helpers, social network) form equal relationships, and jointly and openly communicate, interact, reflect, and make decisions. Essential to this approach is an understanding that all members of the Open Dialogue Team bring their own physical–psychological–social life histories and meanings into a relationship. These need to be heard, seen, felt, sensed, and understood in order for new meanings to develop. Thus, learning can be viewed as a lifelong process of integrating past and present experiences on the physical, psychological, and social levels. This process is both conscious, preconscious, and unconscious.

According to memory research, two knowledge systems mirror this process. From the beginning of life, the body is able to store all sensory, emotional, and behavioural (automatic, such as skills) aspects of experience. This *procedural or implicit knowledge* is non-verbal and cannot be retrieved consciously (van der Kolk et al. 2005; van der Kolk 1994). Facts and language are stored in *declarative or explicit memory*. This system can be accessed consciously. The earliest retrievable memory is usually from the age of 2. In situations of (extreme) stress, the body reacts in a very healthy way: The declarative system 'shuts off', breaks incoming information apart, and memorizes facts in fragments. The procedural system, however, continues to store all sensory information, thus causing the body to react physiologically but not cognitively. Seen from a trauma-centred perspective, the body 'keeps the score' (van der Kolk 1994), which means that traumatic events are memorized on a somatosensory level and not forgotten (Reif-Huelser 2015; Ogden et al. 2012; Lieberman 2011; Moore 2009, 2006). Even though a person may not have explicit, conscious (declarative) memory of a traumatic event, the body will memorize all sensory, emotional, and behavioural (implicit) aspects before, during, and after the event. According to van der Kolk (2003), trauma does not affect primarily cognitive functions, but the entire organism: '. . . trauma-related hyperarousal and numbing is experienced on a body level' (p. 310).

Perry (2001) asserts that our different brain structures develop sequentially and in a 'use-dependent' manner. The lower structures including the brain stem and mid-brain develop before limbic and cortical regions. The over- or under-development of these regions depends upon their activation, and this in turn determines how both internal and external experience are organized and interpreted. The more often a neural network is activated, the more a particular internal representation of experience is established. Prolonged exposure to traumatic experiences in childhood, such as domestic violence or flight, may result in abnormal patterns of neuronal activation. In persistent states of extreme fear, the child's response is driven from the lower structures of the brain. The ability to think, which requires higher brain functioning, is diminished. Over time, the higher brain systems that would normally modulate a child's responses to fear and danger may be compromised whilst lower brain systems responsible for states of arousal may over-develop (Baldwin 2013). Although these adaptations serve to protect the child in violent surroundings they are debilitating in other environments, such as at school. Furthermore, information is internalized, stored, and retrieved in a 'state-dependent' fashion (Perry 2001). A child exposed to subjectively perceived persistent violence is likely to process incoming information through the subcortical and limbic regions of the brain rather than the neocortex. The child focuses upon non-verbal cues that may indicate a potential threat, but may be unable to process verbal information, leading to difficulties with learning and social interaction. When children subjectively experience ongoing, threatening events, the 'use-dependent' development of the brain and the 'state-dependent' processing and retrieval of information lead to significant difficulties in social, emotional, and cognitive functioning (Perry 2001). These children might develop difficulties with self-regulation, including the lack of a continuous, predictable sense of self, disturbances of body image, a poor sense of separateness, distrust, or an inability to concentrate (Moore 2006).

The Project in Practice

The two-year project[2] (four terms) described in this chapter applied a multidisciplinary and multidimensional understanding to the aspect of 'individual learning'—in particular on how current and past life experiences affect a young person's capacity to learn, understand, communicate, and relate. The *hypotheses* were that achievement or failure at school are essentially dependent on

- past and present experiences in the family and in school;
- interactions with important others (such as family, school, peers) and the co-creation of relationships; and
- future chances for development.

Participants

Two Pupils: I

Deniz,[3] 18 years old, was the oldest in his class. After having fled with his family from Kurdistan to Germany five years ago, he was put into a school that allowed him to settle in gradually and to learn German. He was very polite and friendly, and his peers liked him even though they called him 'dumbhead' because of his bad marks and his difficulties in expressing his thoughts.

Lisa, 14 years old, was considered to have a low IQ—at least, this is what her teachers believed. She regularly forgot her homework, could not concentrate, and frequently fell asleep in class. When reprimanded, she lowered her eyes, shrugged her shoulders, and retreated inwardly.

Most of the twenty-six pupils in this project class had been together since grade 5; that is, for three years. The teachers and headmaster had chosen this particular class as they considered it to have the most 'difficult' pupils. Eight different languages (German, Platt,[4] Polish, Russian, Turkish, Kurdish, Arabic, and Sinti) were spoken in the homes of the pupils. The ages of the sixteen boys and ten girls ranged from 13 to 18 years. Three of the adolescents had been born in their home countries (Poland, Turkey, Kazakhstan) and had moved to Germany in their late childhood. One adolescent lived in a residential service, ten in single-parent or patchwork families, and fifteen with both parents. All had at least one sibling at home. Eight parents, respectively caregivers, were out of work or in low-paid work jobs, and lived on social welfare.

The school employed thirty-two teachers: one social worker, one headmaster, and his deputy. Five teachers (four men and one woman) taught in this class, and, together with the headmaster, were part of the project. The social worker decided not to participate, as she did not believe in the value of time-limited projects.

The project group consisted of two leaders (the author, and a male psychiatrist and psychoanalyst), a female art therapist and social worker, and sixteen social work students (eleven females and five males) who were in the final year of their Bachelor degree course.

Methods

Based on the theoretical background mentioned previously, the project aimed at applying a need-adapted approach and to encourage an open dialogue with all participants (Seikkula et al. 2006).

Twenty-six 'difficult' pupils of an eighth grade at a German *Hauptschule*, their teachers, and their families were offered the chance to participate in one, several, or all of the following research modules:

- The class—that is, the pupils—participate in *'creative movement'* work (dance, art, music, filming, singing, graffiti) on a weekly basis for ninety minutes in order to improve the pupils' self-awareness, their affect regulation, their linguistic competencies, and their abilities to form relationships.

- The teachers of this class and the headmaster participate in a *supervision (Balint) group*[5] (Schaub 2014, 2008; Schaub and Schwall 1992, 1995) every three weeks, led by the two project leaders. In this group they are able to reflect on their work and working relationships with the pupils, with the aim of improving their work.
- The *families* of the pupils are contacted and visited twice by the project leaders, with the aim of improving their cooperation with school.
- Sixteen social-work *students* accompany and support the pupils once a week by joining the creative movement groups, offering out-of-school activities and helping them with their school work.

Furthermore, all participants were invited to bimonthly meetings at which the development of the project was discussed and further interventions were co-created. For example, to foster group cohesion and a sense of 'belonging' (Lee and Breen 2007), terms 1–3 ended with an out-of-school activity (1, ice-skating; 2, bowling; 3, a day outing to one of the adjacent North Sea islands), to which the project group invited the pupils and their teachers. The final term ended with a public performance at which all pupils presented the work they had done in the creative movement groups.

All research modules were analysed and assessed throughout the entire project phase (Moore and Schaub 2013) by using semistructured interviews, movement observation, (Kestenberg Amighi et al. 1999), protocols, and questionnaires. In addition, the students reflected on their work with the pupils in a weekly supervision group offered by the two project leaders.

What happened?

'Creative Movement' Work

At the beginning of the project phase the pupils were informed about the goals of the project, told that the project team had two school hours each week for working directly and creatively with them, and told that they could determine how the time might be filled. The mood was clearly negative. Most pupils considered school to be 'a waste of time', teachers 'stupid', and only a third of them knew what they wanted to do after two years, when this stage of schooling was over. They formed at least four subgroups, each sceptical and mistrustful of one another. After a lively and long discussion, the pupils jointly agreed to work on 'their' topic: 'Life in the street'.

The topic progressed in six workgroups of their choice, each accompanied by at least two students:

- *Band*: Four boys wanted to write their own music and learn to play drums, keyboard, and percussion, and sing.

- *Dance*: Six girls developed their own choreography.
- *Drama*: Three boys and one girl decided to write and perform a play about young people in the street.
- *Art*: Three girls and one boy created the stage decoration for the drama.
- *Graffiti*: Four boys sprayed writing and drawings on canvas walls.
- *Film*: Four boys recorded the developments in the workgroups, edited the scenes, and made a film of the pupils' processes.

In the first year the workgroups steadily, and with increasing confidence, developed their individual stories of the topic. Every week, they presented the results of their processes in front of the whole class and discussed the need to embed and interweave each other's work in a 'whole picture'. Thus, they developed from six initially separate to six interactive workgroups. The second year began with a crisis, Due to changes in the educational system, the headmaster was asked to retire earlier than planned. His deputy took over, and exchanged the class teacher for one whom the pupils feared and disliked. The 'creative movement' workgroups stopped functioning, regressed to their initial 'I hate school' attitude, and used the time to debate and discuss their 'plan to rebel'. This time was important for the class teacher and for the pupils, as it was used to reconcile differences and to change attitudes on both sides. After a month, the themes in the groups gradually changed, and the pupils picked up their creativity once more and began talking about their own lives, fears, wishes, hopes, and dreams. The two hours in the project became a creative mix of verbal and non-verbal expressions of personal stories, and the original topic—'Life in the street'—moved into the background. In their last term, the pupils decided to work at their original topic only once a month, and to use the other weeks to learn together for the final examinations.

Two Pupils: II

Deniz opted for the band. His father, he remembered, had played many instruments, but since their arrival in Germany, life was very quiet at home. Deniz tried out various instruments until he dared to say that he wanted to rap a text he had written about the tragic killing of a mother in his neighbourhood. When he presented his rap song to the class, there was silence, followed by tears and endless applause.

Lisa surprised all. Known as 'quiet and sleepy', she actively showed the girls in her group how to move and dance, and drew choreography scripts in which she integrated the ideas from other workgroups.

Families

The project leaders were able to visit twenty-five families in the first half year of the project and for a second time in the second half year. One mother did not want immediate contact with the school or their associates, but gave permission for her son to participate in the project. The high interest of the families in the project was surprising for the teachers, as the show-up rate of parents at school (at conferences or school activities, for example) was usually 25%, which was interpreted as 'disinterest'. Most families particularly appreciated the fact that they were visited and not expected to 'show up' at school; they felt 'seen and respected'. The hospitality and the willingness (and desire) to speak about their family stories were overwhelming.

Supervision (Balint) Group

The model of a psychoanalytically oriented, person-related group (Balint) supervision, as used in medical and psychosocial settings (Schaub 2008), was offered to the five teachers and the headmaster of the project class (Schaub 2014). Here they were able to bring in a case story or vignette of one of their pupils, and use the space to share their thoughts, ideas, questions, and feelings about the individual's behaviour in class. Initially, the teachers found it very challenging to reflect on the teacher–pupil relationships, as their role model was that of a 'distant and neutral observer' whose task was to pass on knowledge without the interference of a 'personal' relationship. The more they knew and understood about the personal backgrounds and histories of their pupils, the harder they found it to remain 'neutral'. They all reported feelings of surprise, sadness, fear, anger, and confusion about the often surprising, saddening, fearful, and confusing stories of their pupils, but also empathy, feelings of attachment, and a deeper sense of understanding for the difficulties their pupils presented.

Two Pupils: III

The teachers often talked about Deniz, raising their concerns that he was 'too old and slow' to be successful. They could not understand why, after five years in Germany, he was apparently not able to speak properly and suggested that he might be better off at a school for learning difficulties. After the project leaders had visited Deniz's family, a deeper understanding developed. His father had been persecuted and tortured for his religious beliefs (Yezidi), he, his wife, and their three children flew to Germany, and, after two years of uncertainty, were given right of residence. Five years later, Deniz's parents obtained a work permit. They lived in a council flat with hardly any furniture. Traumatized by the experiences, the parents were frozen in their past. They barely left their home, and Deniz, their oldest son, acted as their translator. The feelings of insecurity, fear, grief, loss, and speechlessness had become a transgenerational issue.

Even though Lisa was lively in the workgroups, she regularly 'disappeared' in the lessons, often unable to stay awake after 11.00 a.m. The teachers felt annoyed at her apparent disinterest, talked about possible 'punishments', such as giving her extra homework 'to catch up'. After the family visit, the teachers understood more: Lisa was the oldest of four children, and her father worked as a lorry driver, which meant long absences from home. Her mother was a chronic psychiatric patient, and when she was in hospital social services sent a family help in to look after the children. She also suffered from severe panic attacks at night, and could be calmed down only if Lisa talked to her. Lisa had never spoken to anyone about her domestic situation, she felt a need to protect her family, and was afraid that the children might be put into foster homes. In the supervision group, the teachers developed a support scheme to enable Lisa to keep up with the curriculum.

Conclusions

The school project aimed at preventing pupils from dropping out and leaving school before having achieved a qualification. All pupils passed their examinations, ten moved on to grammar school (*Gymnasium*), and sixteen started professional training.

It can be assumed from the outcomes of these pupils' stories that the multi-layered, movement-oriented approach had an impact on both the pupils', teachers', and families' wellbeing as well as on their capacity to 'learn'. *Movement* was offered in various ways:

1. The open dialogue approach (Seikkula et al. 2006) fostered a flexible and continuous response to the specific and changing needs of the pupils, families and teachers, as well as of the project team.
2. 'Creative movement' work allowed the pupils (and teachers) to step out of the school curricula for two hours. The merging of two levels—body sensations/implicit knowledge and cognitions/explicit knowledge—evidenced the uniqueness and creativity of each pupil and gave them a 'language' to express their inner and outer worlds (Moore 2009, 2006). By creatively working through a topic they had chosen, they developed a sense of self-efficacy, self-confidence, and trust in themselves as well as in others.
3. The supervision (Balint) group enabled the teachers to move to and integrate a new understanding of their pedagogical work, from 'neutral, distant observers' to 'feeling, empathic professionals' (Schaub 2014).
4. By moving towards the families and showing interest in their unique life stories, each individual felt seen, heard, and respected. The meaning of 'school' changed in a positive way, both for the families as well as for the pupils, and evoked a sense of 'belonging'. (Lee and Breen 2007)

The positive, moving effects of (therapeutic) group work, as described by Yalom and Leszcz (2005), were evident in all research modules of this project. The recognition of shared experiences and feelings among group members helped to remove an individual's sense of isolation, to raise self-awareness and self-esteem (*universality, interpersonal learning*). The interpersonal context of the group served each member to feel a sense of belonging, acceptance, and validation (*cohesiveness*).

All systems moved. The pupils were able to move from isolated subgroups to interactive individuals that supported, encouraged, and inspired each other, thus lifting self-esteem and improving coping and learning styles and interpersonal skills. They were increasingly able to share their individual themes with others, and to develop positive life visions. The teachers and pupils (and families) moved from negative projections onto the outer environment to an inner understanding, and respect for the others, their life stories, and the impact these stories had on individuals. The project team was moved by the demanding and sometimes challenging processes of the pupils, teachers, families, and themselves. Movement, creativity, and relationships were key to the success of this project: all pupils were determined to pass their examinations and move on.

Notes

1. Until 2010, the German secondary school system had a three-tier system: *Hauptschule* for slow learners, *Realschule* for medium fast learners, and *Gymnasium* for quick learners.
2. The local ethical committees (town and school councils) gave permission for the project, and every family and pupil gave written informed consent to participate.
3. The names of the project participants have been changed.
4. A regional language in its own rights.
5. The Balint group is named after the psychoanalyst Michael Balint (1896--1970). The approach was developed for medical doctors to explore interpersonal aspects of their work with patients, to encourage them to see their patients as human beings outside of the consulting room and to gradually develop a deeper understanding of their patients' feelings and their own.

References

Alanen, Y. (1997). *Schizophrenia: Its Origins and Need-Adapted Treatment*. London: Karnac Books.

Alanen, Y., Lehtinen, K., Räkköläinen, V., and Aaltonen, J. (1991). 'Need-adapted treatment of new schizophrenic patients: Experiences and results of the Turku Project', *Acta Psychiatrica Scandinavica*, 83: 363–72.

Alivernini, F. and Lucidi, F. (2011). 'Relationship between social context, self-efficacy, motivation, academic achievement, and intention to drop out of high school: A longitudinal study', *The Journal of Educational Research*, 104: 241–52.

Baldwin, D. (2013). 'Primitive mechanisms of trauma response: An evolutionary perspective on trauma-related disorders', *Neuroscience and Biobehavioral Reviews*, 37(8): 1549–66.

Caprara, G., Fida, R., Vecchione, M., Del Bove, G., Vecchio, G., Barbaranelli, C., and Bandura, A. (2008). 'Longitudinal analysis of the role of perceived self-efficacy for self-regulated learning in academic continuance and achievement', *Journal of Educational Psychology*, 100: 525–34.

Christenson, S. and Thurlow, M. (2004). 'School dropouts: Prevention, considerations, interventions, and challenges', *Current Directions in Psychological Science*, 13: 36–9.

Deci, E. and Ryan, R. (2002). *Handbook of Self-Determination Research*. Rochester, NY: University of Rochester Press.

De Witte, K. and Cabus, S. (2013). 'Dropout prevention measures in The Netherlands: An explorative evaluation', *Educational Review* 65(2): 155–76.

Düpree, H. (2009). Interview, 10 July 2009. Unpublished manuscript.

Eurostat and European Commission (2014). *Eurostat Regional Yearbook 2014: Education.* Luxembourg: Office for Official Publications of the European Communities.

Hattie, J. (2013). *Visible Learning for Teachers: Maximizing Impact on Learning.* London: Routledge.

Heckman, J. and Krueger, A. (2005). *Inequality in America: What Role for Human Capital Policies?* Cambridge, MA: MIT Press.

Hickman, G., Bartholomew, M., Mathwig, J., and Heinrich, R. (2008). 'Differential developmental pathways of high school dropouts and graduates', *The Journal of Educational Research*, 102: 3–14.

Kestenberg Amighi, J., Loman, S., Lewis, P., and Sossin, M. (1999). *The Meaning of Movement. Developmental and Clinical Perspectives of the Kestenberg Movement Profile.* Amsterdam: OPA/Gordon and Breach Publishers.

Lee, T. and Breen, L. (2007). 'Young people's perceptions and experiences of leaving high school early: An exploration', *Journal of Community and Applied Social Psychology*, 17: 329–46.

Lehr, C., Sinclair, M., and Christenson, S. (2004). 'Addressing student engagement and truancy prevention during the elementary school years: A replication study of the check and connect model', *Journal of Education for Students Placed at Risk*, 9: 279–301.

Lieberman, A. (2011). 'Infants remember: War exposure, trauma and attachment in young children and their mothers', *Journal of the American Academy of Child and Adolescent Psychiatry*, 50(7): 640–1.

Moore, C. (2009). 'Bewegungsbeobachtung in der traumazentrierten Fallsupervision', in C. Moore and U. Stammermann (eds.), *Bewegung aus dem Trauma. Traumazentrierte Tanz- und Bewegungspsychotherapie.* Stuttgart: Schattauer, pp. 237–55.

Moore, C. (2006). 'Dance movement therapy in the light of trauma: Research findings of a multidisciplinary project', in S. Koch and I. Bräuninger (eds.), *Advances in Dance/Movement Therapy: Theoretical Perspectives and Empirical Findings.* Berlin: Logos Verlag, pp. 104–15.

Moore, C. and Schaub, H.-A. (2013). 'Aspekte der Handlungsforschung; Am Beispiel eines Projektes an der Hauptschule', in B. Birgmeier and E. Mührel (eds.), *Handlung in Theorie und Wissenschaft Sozialer Arbeit.* Wiesbaden: Springer Verlag, pp. 249–63.

Newman, B., Lohman, B., Newman, P., Myers, M., and Smith, V. (2000). 'Experiences of urban youth navigating the transition to ninth grade', *Youth and Society*, 31: 387–416.

Ogden, P., Pain, C., Minton, K., and Fisher, J. (2012). 'Einbeziehung des Körpers in die Hauptrichtungen der Psychotherapie mit traumatisierten Klienten. Zeitschrift für Psychotraumatologie Psychotherapiewissenschaft', *Psychologische Medizin*, 10(2): 7–17.

Orfield, G. (2004). *Dropouts in America: Confronting the Graduation Rate Crisis.* Cambridge, MA: Harvard Education Press.

Perry, B. (2001). 'The neurodevelopmental impact of violence in childhood', in D. Schetky and E. Benedek (eds.), *Textbook of Child and Adolescent Forensic Psychiatry.* Washington, DC: American Psychiatric Press, pp. 221–38.

Psacharopoulos, G. (2007). *The Cost of School Failure: A Feasibility Study.* European Expert Network on Economics of Education.

Reif-Huelser, M. (2015). 'Kindersoldaten und ihr Weg zurück ins Leben', *Zeitschrift für Psychotraumatologie und ihre Anwendungen*, 13(1): 62–70.

Rumberger, R. (2004). 'Why students drop out of school', in G. Orfied (ed.), *Dropouts in America: Confronting the Graduation Rate Crisis.* Cambridge, MA: Harvard Education Press, pp. 131–55.

Schaub, H.-A. (2014). 'Die pädagogische Beziehung zwischen Lehrern und Schülern', in R. Plassmann (ed.). *Die Kunst, seelisches Wachstum zu fördern. Transformationsprozesse in der Psychotherapie.* Gießen: Psychosozial-Verlag, pp. 109–27.

Schaub, H.-A. (2008). *Klinische Sozialarbeit: Konzepte, Methoden und Forschung.* Göttingen: Vandenhoeck and Ruprecht unipress Verlag.

Schaub, H.-A. and Schwall, H. (1995). 'Fallsupervision und Teamberatung in medizinischen und psychosozialen Institutionen', *Gruppenpsychotherapie und Gruppendynamik*, 31: 331–45.

Schaub, H.-A. and Schwall, H. (1992). 'Auf dem Wege zu einem Supervisionskonzept', *Gruppenpsychotherapie und Gruppendynamik*, 28: 158–68.

Seikkula, J., Aaltonen, J., Alakare, B., Haarakangas, K., Keränen, J., and Lehtinen, K. (2006). 'Five-year experience of first-episode nonaffective psychosis in open-dialogue approach: Treatment principles, follow-up outcomes, and two case studies.' *Psychotherapy Research*, 16(2): 214–28.

van der Kolk, B. (1994). 'The body keeps the score: Memory and the emerging psychobiology of post traumatic stress', *Harvard Review of Psychiatry*, 1: 253–65.

van der Kolk, B. (2003). 'The neurobiology of childhood trauma and abuse', *Child and Adolescent Psychiatric Clinics*, 12: 293–317.

van der Kolk, B., Roth, S., Pelcovitz, D., Mandel, F., and Spinazzola, J. (2005). 'Disorders of extreme stress: The empirical foundation of a complex adaptation to trauma'. *Journal of Traumatic Stress*, 18: 389–99.

Yalom, I. and Leszcz, M. (2005). *The Theory and Practice of Group Psychotherapy.* New York, NY: Basis Books.

....

CHAPTER 25

DANCE/MOVEMENT AND EMBODIED KNOWING WITH ADOLESCENTS

....

NANCY BEARDALL

INTRODUCTION

....

Dance/Movement Therapy and Embodied Knowing

Dance and movement were incorporated into my social studies class in the first year I worked as a teacher. I believed that to understand history, students might enact and experience the event to fully understand what was unfolding and occurring at a particular time. I also organized and taught an afterschool dance class that was open to anyone who wanted to participate. During this time I observed that as the students danced they related to each other positively, became more inclusive, worked collaboratively, and were more expressive and empowered.

At the end of the year, a parent of one of my students who was in the social studies and after school class mentioned that dance had made a significant difference for her daughter in how she felt about herself. She indicated that her daughter had been depressed and selfdestructive, but the dance experience had helped transform her. The parent affirmed my observations and intuitive discovery of the importance and power of dance for her daughter to experience and embody a more integrated sense of self. This early experience influenced my decision to pursue a graduate degree in dance/movement therapy.

Embodied knowing is a term that captures a concept described by others, including Merleau-Ponty (1962), Gendlin (1978), and Hervey (2007). The expression relates to body-centred experiential activities that contribute to an emerging sense of self—one that is felt and experienced. It is an inner knowing or body sense that you know more than you can tell. One does not have to think about it; one feels it. Through dance and movement, students can become more connected with their body and mind. This allows a more integrated understanding of self that can support health and wellbeing.

Historically, dance/movement therapy principles or core beliefs have evolved from an understanding of dance/movement and body/mind experiences, as well as through observations of dancers and interactions between the early dance/movement therapy pioneers and their students. These dancers later became the initiators of the emerging dance/movement therapy field. Pioneers in the field such as Marian Chace, recognized as the founder of dance/movement therapy, as well as Trudi Schoop and Mary Whitehouse, were early leaders who contributed to the basic theoretical principles of the dance/movement therapy work. Examples of these principles consisted of Chace's notions about *therapeutic movement relationship, body action, mirroring or attuning, symbolic movement,* and *group rhythmic expression,* all of which created the foundation for the *Chace technique* (Fischer and Chaiklin 1993, p. 138). Schoop's technique included integrating movement improvisation, leading to the creation of repeatable sequences of dance and drama to help bring unconscious patterns forth (Levy 2005, p. 71). Whitehouse's contributions were *active imagination, witnessing, and authentic movement process* creating an empathic presence (Levy 2005, p. 55). These concepts have become thoroughly integrated into the commonly understood dance/movement therapy theory and practice that I have incorporated into my work with students. These early pioneers worked with psychologists and psychiatrists and were part of a team approach working with varying populations.

In addition to dance therapy theory, dance therapists are trained in developmental psychology, psychotherapeutic theories, and movement observation and assessment. In addition, they have much to offer educators in the physical, cognitive, social, emotional, and relational psychoeducational development of children and adolescents.

Somatic processes help support students in listening and becoming more mindful, assisting them in integrating and transferring their embodied knowledge into embodied action, whether it be in connecting to other people or to themselves. According to Studd and Cox (2013), 'Our bodies provide the means to take in (perceive), connect, and interact with the world. Knowing is based in experience and experience is embodied (p. 15).

Gendlin (1978) believed that listening to the body was key to the healing process, and demonstrates this through his work with *Focusing.* Perl (2004) invokes Gendlin's (1978) process of experiential knowing when she writes: 'Ultimately, a theory of embodied knowing begins with felt sense and draws from it a theory of experiencing ... one that says: All knowing is embodied in persons; no knowing happens outside of that; without the body, we know nothing' (p. 60).

In addressing the physical, cognitive, social, and emotional developmental challenges that adolescents face, dance/movement and the expressive arts can provide a creative, expressive outlet—both individually and collectively—bringing awareness to their own challenges and to those of others. It is my experience that the use of the creative process, mindfulness, and dance/movement therapy experiences lead to a more conscious and integrated *body sense* whereby students become more aware, empathic, and able to support themselves and each other. As a dance/movement therapist and educator, I have used a psychoeducational approach with adolescents in the schools. This model draws upon the work of Guerney et al.'s (1971) psychoeducational definition that promotes 'teaching of personal and interpersonal skills which the individual applies to solve present and future psychological problems to enhance his satisfaction in life' (p. 277).

Dance/movement therapists have become important team members in many schools for students ages 3 through 18. It has been my experience that they provide individual therapy programmes and interventions one-on-one, as well as in small groups to students who are on Individualized Educational Plans (IEPs). However, this chapter focuses on three programmes using a psychoeducational approach applied to the general population of students in grades 6–12. The three secondary school programmes highlighted include Creative Dance, Creating a Peaceable School, and Mentors in Violence Prevention. These programmes draw upon commonly understood dance/movement therapy concepts and are applied to specific experiences that students encounter, such as diversity issues and bullying, sexual harassment, increasing self-esteem, and building individual and collective connections.

Additional Theoretical Foundations

Relational Cultural Theory (RCT)

According to relational theory as developed through the Stone Center at Wellesley College (Jordan et al. 1991), human beings of all ages desire and thrive in connected relationships. As stated in this theory, participation in authentic, responsive, and mutual connections is central to healthy psychological growth and development. RCT (Miller and Stiver 1997) emphasizes the basic human yearning for connection and the growth potential inherent in building authentic and responsive connections. A concept central to an understanding of healthy growth is relational development; that is, the nature of a person's psychological health can be observed and experienced through the movement of connection/disconnection that he or she creates with others. The health of the community can also be observed through this lens.

At the heart of this model is the concept of the *We*. In addition to self and other, I and you, the *We*, is the third element in human experience which involves *the relationship*, or the *connection* (Beardall et al. 2007). Adolescence is a stage of life where students are finding their own voice while navigating relationships and connections with others. The dance of connection, disconnection, and reconnection can be observed in middle-school and high-school hallways, classrooms, and activities. In the corridor and in the classroom, one can observe how students approach and avoid connection with each other. It is evident in both verbal and non-verbal interactions. 'In a classroom that values authentic connection, and develops a class *We* and a school *We*— more marginalized voices have greater opportunity to speak and be heard. They are brought into the mainstream not by being part of the dominant culture, but through the dialogue of different voices' (Beardall et al. 2007, p. 22).

The Laban/Bartenieff Work

The Laban work provides a conscious movement vocabulary and experience in educating adolescents as well as increasing awareness of their body through the fundamental work of Irmgard Bartenieff. Bartenieff spoke of achieving a balance between the therapeutic, the recreational or arts, and the learning experience of school. (Bartenieff and Lewis 1980, p. 6). This balance is what I incorporated into the three programmes addressed in this chapter.

Rudolf Laban (1966, 1971) spoke about *movement thinking* in the *The Language of Movement* and the *The Mastery of Movement* and wrote about its three aspects— physical experience, observation—and a more abstract analysis of meaning which helps the student transfer this embodied thinking into action. He believed that the connection between *movement thinking* and word thinking must be found. As far as *movement thinking* is concerned, he claimed that: 'This thinking does not, as thinking in words does, serve orientation in the external world, but rather it perfects man's orientation in his inner world' (Laban 1971, p. 17). Laban believed that outward actions reflect inner attitudes or feelings (p. 3). In addition, he believed that practicing *humane effort* enabled people to become aware of negative habits and to develop qualities and inclinations creditable to man (p. 15). Incorporating the work of Laban and Bartenieff into the programmes mentioned in this chapter provides a conscious movement vocabulary and somatic basis from which to work. The *dance theatre*—or as Laban refers to it, *tanztheater*—is present in the role-play scenario work in the Creating a Peaceable School curriculum and in the Mentors in Violence Prevention programme. Laban's theory forms a clear foundation for using dance/movement and the expressive therapies in the development of adolescent problem solving by providing an expansive movement vocabulary and flexibility in the development of resiliency skills. Since movement is the common denominator of all the arts, Laban's language of movement and Bartenieff's (1980) body fundamentals speak to how movement patterns influence the ways we relate to each other and solve problems. They also become movement metaphors for how we are and how we live in the world.

Neuroscience: Dance of the Mind/Body Social Circuitry

Neurophysiologist Rizzolatti and colleagues discovered the existence of what they termed *mirror neurons* through their research with monkeys. Goleman (2006), citing Rizzolatti (2006), writes that neurons are part of a system that 'allow us to grasp the minds of others not through conceptual reasoning but through direct simulation: by feeling, not by thinking' (p. 43). The research of Rizzolatti (2006) supports what they call an *empathic resonance* (Goleman 2006, p. 43). Stern (2004) 'concludes that our nervous systems are constructed to be captured by the nervous systems of others, so that we can experience others as if from within their skin' (Goleman 2006, p. 43). Dance/movement therapist Cynthia Berrol (2006) speaks of 'Stern's transfer of meaning to another (that is, ascribing to that person feelings, sensations, emotions, and thought) a form of "empathic projection"—a concept significant to D/MT clinicians' (p. 8). Berrol (1992) also stated that 'movement can serve as the mediator, intervening to organize and reorganize the neurologic underpinnings of cognitive, physical, and emotional function to facilitate behavior change and wellbeing"' (p. 28).

Teachers have a role in a student's development. 'The relationships that teachers have with their students and the experiences they provide for them directly shape the neural circuitry of the next generation. Teachers in this way can be seen as the neurosculptors of our future' (Siegel 2008, p. 1). I believe Siegel's statement also applies to DMT's role in the schools.

Social and Emotional Intelligence

Discussing society's belief about education, Goleman (1995) states in *Working with Emotional Intelligence*, 'our entire system is geared to cognitive skills. But when it comes to learning emotional competencies, our system is sorely lacking. Capacities like empathy or flexibility differ crucially from cognitive abilities; they draw from different areas of the brain' (p. 244). In Goleman's (2006) book *Social Intelligence* he speaks of the biological basis of the 'social brain referring to the particular set of circuitry that is orchestrated as people relate to each other' (p. 80).

Adolescence is a challenging time when students are experiencing and navigating their own physical and psychological growth. 'Adolescence requires a coordinated set of expectations about oneself and others and well integrated social and emotional skills for handling complex life situations, especially when under emotional pressure" (Elias et al. 1997, p. 40). Due to the neurological wiring of the adolescent brain, Goleman (1999) claims that emotional intelligence continues to develop throughout adolescence and into adulthood. The scientific data he cites to support this hypothesis generates the rationale for delivering programmes that help adolescents develop their social and emotional intelligence. These programmes are significant because they equip students in developing relationships, self-awareness, empathy, and the capacity for decision making that can be seen as important to successful maturation.

The Spiral Integrated Learning Process

The Spiral Integrated Learning Process is a term I coined to denote the weaving of theoretical concepts with experiential threads into a multidimensional learning

FIGURE 25.1. The Spiral Integrated Learning Process. (Credit: N. Beardall.)

approach leading to embodied knowing and embodied response in adolescents. This process was informed by my dance/movement therapy training and by my role as counsellor and educator. The process contributes to students' physical, cognitive, social, emotional, and relational growth inherent in the programmes described in this chapter. The Spiral Integrated Learning Process provides experiences for the students to move, sense, create, witness, and dialogue as they become more mindful and empathic, assisting them to embody and transfer their knowledge into action. As can be seen in Figure 25.1, the spiral process rotates clockwise and counterclockwise and is overlapping. Students are encouraged through this multidimensional learning process to support their own wellbeing as well as that of others, thus leading to a more connected community.

Programme Examples

Creative Dance Elective

The Creative Dance class—a school arts elective offered to sixth, seventh, and eighth graders—included an eclectic mix of dance styles. It also allowed students to experience a movement vocabulary based on Laban/Bartenieff theory. The students who chose to enrol in the elective met twice weekly for an entire year. They created their own dances as well as joining together in creating a collective piece. This creative group process taught students to listen, compromise, solve problems, and express themselves. It is my belief that adolescents need to define who they are and to feel good about themselves as well as be able to relate to the group. According to Chace (1975): 'There is therapeutic dance, dance therapy, or just dance, depending upon the needs of the participants, the particular setting, the goals of the leaders, and the leader's comprehension of what she is trying to accomplish, how, and why' (p. 144). It was my intention to support students at this vulnerable developmental time in their life and use dance as a tool for adolescents to consciously connect with and accept their bodies and express themselves. This is an example of the psychoeducational approach I used in the schools.

Dance the Dream

Dance the Dream (Beardall 2005) was the name students gave to a dance they choreographed in response to a racial incident that had caused disconnections in the school and community. The process took place during an eighth-grade creative dance class where the dialogue model (Shem and Surrey 1998) and RCT were used with a diverse group including African-American and European-American English language learners and students who were deaf. Students were introduced to a model where verbal and non-verbal dialogues were experienced. The class was designed to guide the group to connect and dance together on themes about race, ability, and ethnic and cultural differences as a way to better understand and support one another.

The initial step was to organize the class into affinity groups working together with an adult facilitator. The goal was for students to communicate within their group about their experiences and eventually come together with greater awareness and understanding to create a community dance piece. Students discussed several questions in the affinity groups:

How do you feel when you are asked questions about differences?
How might you like to be understood or treated?
What would you like others to know about you?

As a group we had danced together since the beginning of the school year, but in this project we focused on learning about ourselves in the affinity groups and then about our differences and similarities in the larger group. From there, we created a dance to share with all of the students at their school, along with teachers and parents. Movement connected us to each other through the dance, though it was the reflective dialogue that helped to make the process more conscious. This aided each dancer to become more culturally aware and embody a sense of self and other, leading to a better understanding of differences and connection. Each group came to understand their affinity group's contribution to the entire class. The dance evolved and flowed. Frustrating moments provided opportunities to talk about disagreements and how to express ideas through the choreography. Dialogue allowed us to reflect and expand as a community with greater connection and understanding and a feeling of the group *We*. Working on the choreography encouraged problem solving, sharing, and collaborative efforts.

The students decided they would read aloud, or through an American Sign Language translator, the comments that had been generated through the dialogue process before beginning the dance. A few of the statements were:

> You don't know what it's like until you've been there.
> Treat me with respect.
> People treat me as if I am not there.
> It feels good when people ask me about my differences because then, POW, it's out there.
> When you know, you act and *dance the dream.*

As the last student uttered those words, the dance began, with each person moving first in solo and then dancing with their own affinity group, and ultimately with all the groups moving together. In the end, the students were very proud of the dance and enjoyed performing for their peers and parents. The students had danced and embodied the process leading to increased empathy, attunement, and a greater sense of community through dance.

The following year I contacted the students who were then in high school to ask what they remembered from our community dance. The following thoughts were shared:

> I learned that I loved expressing myself through the art of dance.

> When we had group discussions, our feelings just poured out, and even now, it affects us, because we still say hi to each other and make a point of smiling when we see each other, because we had bonded during that experience.

> I found that diversity and individuality very welcoming. I didn't have to act a certain way anymore. I could be myself.

> Everyone stayed helpful. We would help each other out.

> All people want the same things. I learned we all want to be supported.

> Well for me, I was always afraid to even speak to a person who is deaf because I thought they would think I was ignorant. That has changed—I talk and listen to each person.

The students had connected to themselves, to each other, and to the community.

Dance the Dream was part of the community's healing journey, affirming the transformative power of dance.

Four years later, when the students were in twelfth grade, my dance therapy intern and I had a reunion with the dancers. The students had gone their different ways but were very conscious about how the dance experience in eighth grade had bonded them throughout their high-school years. They mentioned going to each other's sports games and performances, and supporting each other in various activities. Their embodied dance experience and connection lasted through high school.

Surrey's (2005) work in RCT deals with the concept of *relational mindfulness* and is relevant to this creative dance experience. She speaks about the notion of *I, You,* and *We,* and how they are expanded by means of their interactions through the creative process of the RCT model. The dynamic quality of relationships, the group *We,* and a supportive community are also important to RCT's creative process. This theoretical model provides a developmental and psychological framework for students' learning and for their understanding of and navigating through relationships. The use of Laban/Bartenieff themes, group process, affinity groups, choreographing, dialoguing, and witnessing all contributed to a healing experience—one that the students integrated and embodied as they proceeded through high school. According to Eddy (1998), 'performance affords an opportunity to contribute to the wider community, increasing the sphere of relationship (and hence, hopefully extending the range of behavioral accountability) and supporting the development of confidence and pride' (p. 335).

In Our Words: Dancing for Development and Discovery

In Our Words: Dancing for Development and Discovery is an example of a school-based research study that was conducted in an eighth-grade Creative Dance class. The study was conducted to document the effects of dance on self-esteem at the junior-high-school level, with the ultimate goal of sharing the results with a wider community.

The study documented the girls' process in finding their own creative voice and learning how to express themselves through dance, which in turn empowered them at a period of their development that Gilligan and Brown (1992) refer to as 'a lost time'—a time when adolescent girls silence their voice.

The study included:

- Administering the Piers-Harris Self-Concept Questionnaire to twenty-eight eighth-grade dance students in September and again in May. The questionnaire cites six domains: Behaviour, Intelligence, Physical Appearance, Anxiety, Popularity, and Happiness
- Audio taping an interview with each student in the autumn and in the spring.
- Videotaping several students' individual progress as well as videotaping the dance class throughout the year.
- Administering questionnaires that were completed by former eighth-grade dance students at their high school in grades nine, ten, eleven, and twelve at the time of the study.
- Sending questionnaires to former eighth-grade students who participated in making a documentary film entitled *Day Dances* ten years before this study.

Seventy-four students of ages 13–23 years participated in the study. There were twenty-eight eighth-grade students, forty high-school students in grades nine through twelve who were interviewed and/or answered questionnaires regarding their experience in the eighth-grade Creative Dance class, and six students who previously had made the documentary film entitled *Day Dances*. The high-school students who had taken the class in eighth grade and the students who had participated in making the documentary provided a retrospective view of the programme.

The following results affirmed the therapeutic value of dance at this age and also shed light on a number of developmental challenges affecting students.

- The twenty-eight eighth-grade students who took the Piers-Harris Self-Concept Questionnaire scored on average 11 points higher on their combined self-concept total score (TOT) in the spring than they did in the autumn. This was a notable increase. When students feel good about themselves, they are more likely to do better academically and be more relationally connected.
- The high-school students responses to the questionnaire described feeling empathy for the eighth-grade students, recalling their own emotional struggles at that age. They repeatedly spoke of how dance helped them become more aware, resilient, and empowered during this time.
- An additional unexpected finding of the study was a passionate outpouring from the eighth-grade students about many issues they were either observing or experiencing—eating disorders, media stereotypes and body-image distortion, substance abuse, peer pressure, harassment, and sexual harassment within the schools. The students' descriptions of these struggles highlighted the pressing need for a wellness and prevention programme. It is also noteworthy that this study occurred before the tragic shootings of Columbine, when social and emotional support and bullying prevention programmes were not a primary focus in educational communities.
- Shortly after the results of the study were shared with administration and community, focus groups of teachers, students, and parents came together to target the issues that needed to be addressed.

Dancing together, expanding their movement vocabulary in the areas of body, effort, space, and shape through the Laban/Bartenieff work, and creating and dancing their individual and collective choreography, led to a relationally connected group—one in which the students acknowledged that they felt seen, accepted, and empowered.

By listening to the students and their experiences, this study led to the creation of a new health education programme in the secondary schools entitled *Health, Wellness, and Prevention*. Dance therapist Norma Canner (1992), mentions: 'The time is ripe for us to begin to focus our efforts away from the medical model in the field of mental health. Prevention is what interests me. Dance therapists need to work in the schools—both public and private—from pre-school through high school and in Head Start programs" (p. 129). This innovative *Health, Wellness, and Prevention* programmme was a beginning.

Creating a Peaceable School: Confronting Intolerance and Bullying

An example of one of the successful programmes in the *Wellness and Prevention* curriculum was *Creating a Peaceable School: Confronting Intolerance and Bullying* (Beardall 2005). This was a sixth-grade course organized to promote respect for differences. Every student in the school took the class, which met twice weekly for ten weeks.

Course goals were to promote respect for cultural differences, present guidelines around anti-bullying behaviour, and to illustrate the role of the witness and active bystander. This was accomplished by offering interactive experiences, including dance/movement and the expressive arts, which were designed to help students navigate relationships and build community. The core components of the curriculum provided a school-wide vocabulary around bullying prevention for students, school staff, and parents, and adhered to the Guiding Principles and Learning Standards of the state where this took place.

Two sample exercises from this curriculum follow.

Non-Verbal Communication Warm Up

- Work with a partner.
- Demonstrate different meanings of movements by acting out the following: tone of voice, facial expressions, gestures, posture, eye contact, and nodding.
- Discuss how the different movements convey different messages with the partner, then with the entire class

(4) *Bullying Cast of Characters*:

- Break up into groups of five.
- Create a 'silent film' scenario of the cast of typical characters in a bullying episode: instigator, bully, target, witness, follower, and activist.
- Present role plays to the class as pantomime (as if it were a silent film).
- Identify the qualities of each character in a follow-up discussion.

The movement sequences—such as depicting the cast of characters in bullying scenarios, along with witnessing and dialoguing about these situations—provided students with an embodied awareness and conscious understanding about how these situations can occur. The exercises above are just two examples; the curriculum included many other mindful exercises and cooperative movement activities that contributed to the students' understanding of the qualities of healthy relationships. By embodying and moving through connection, disconnection, and reconnection, students integrate a physical and emotional understanding of their experience and are able to identify the qualities of these varying relationships. This experience reflects the dance of connection and disconnection (Beardall et al. 2007).

School-based evaluations, funded through Safe Schools Grants, were conducted on the *Creating a Peaceable School* curriculum. The survey was conducted at baseline to inform administrators, parents, and teachers with the first group of students using the curriculum, and then again four years later to determine whether or not the programme supported change. Dan Olweus (1993), an international leader in bullying prevention, allowed us to adapt his questionnaires based on his core principles and ongoing research in Norway to evaluate our programme.

Over the four-year period during which the curriculum was being used there was a significant decrease in bullying episodes, and students were more frequently able to identify specific ways to interrupt bullying (Cummins 2004). Also over this time span, data from the Vice Principal's office showed a reduction in the number of students disciplined for bullying and fewer suspensions, further documenting the impact of the programme on the school community.

Martha Eddy (1998), a somatic-based therapist, educator, and Laban trained analyst, in her dissertation 'The Role of Physical Activity in Educational Violence Prevention Programs for Youth', observed and studied the *Creating a Peaceable School* programme and others that used movement and kinaesthetic activities in violence prevention. She summarized tactics that 'establish trust and peaceable behavior" (p. 11) that are inherent in successful prevention programmes. They are shown in Table 25.1.

According to Eddy's research, the *Creating a Peaceable School* curriculum incorporated all of these key teaching tactics. Goleman (2006) reports that

> the best social and emotional programs are designed to fit seamlessly into the standard school curriculum for children at every age, [and] include skills like self-awareness and managing distressing emotions, empathy, and navigating relationships smoothly. A definitive meta-analysis of more than one hundred studies of these programs showed that students not only mastered abilities like calming down and getting along better, but, more to the point here, learned more effectively. (p. 283–4)

Another example of a DMT intervention in a UK secondary school is seen in the labyrinth project (Karkou et al. 2010), in which overall improvement in social and emotional health such as dealing with stress, depression, and connecting to peers was demonstrated after ten DMT sessions. DMT therapists Rena Kornblum and Lynn Koshland conducted studies on their individual DMT programmes in elementary schools in the US. Kornblum and Hervey's (2006) study showed that students demonstrated 'more effective self-regulation and increased non-verbal attunement and empathy" (p. 127). Koshland and Whittaker's study indicated positive outcomes in reducing aggressive behaviours and providing self-control skills (p. 72) with their students.

Table 25.1. Key teaching tactics for violence prevention programmes.

ENGAGES STUDENTS

Works to get students actively involved with activities

Uses peer leadership

Solicits opinions

Invites questions and feelings

SHARES FEELINGS

Is honest and sincere

Shares own feelings, is vulnerable

PROVIDES CHOICES

Provides options in classes: allows students to make decisions/set goals

Shares new ideas and opportunities

Exposes students to varied community experiences

IS SENSITIVE TO INCLUSION

Affirms all students self worth

Avoids discrimination, notices own biases

Is systematic about setting up groups

Incorporates and affirms all students' ideas

ACKNOWLEDGES COMPLEXITY

Validates the difficulty of many decisions

Is comfortable dealing with complex issues

Is interested in establishing a real learning environment

USES HOLISTIC APPROACHES

Refers to the wisdom of the body

Refers to the potential of the mind in affecting physical behavior

Uses the voice non-verbally; incorporates attention to breathing

Thinks about all the various needs of individuals and the group

PRACTICE CONFLICT RESOLUTION

Uses clear consequences

(continued)

Table 25.1. Continued

Provides opportunities for students to practice conflict

Does not make authoritative decisions

Uses clear consequences

Provides opportunities for students to practice conflict resolution

MODELS GOALS

Is consistent with values and behaviour; builds equity/fairness

No put-downs

Does team teaching: collaborates on the learning environment

PROVIDES SYNTHESIS

Reviews learning outcomes and student discoveries

Makes integrative statements

Provides opportunities for meaning-making

BUILDS ON-GOING RELATIONSHIPS

One on one attention

After-school attention

Listens to personal concerns

Provides tutoring and other resources

COUNTERS THE MEDIA, PROVIDES ALTERNATIVE IMAGES

(Eddy 1998, pp. 393–4, cited with permission.)

Mentors in Violence Prevention (MVP) Programme

MVP was a leadership programme that trained high-school students to be mentors to their peers as well as mentors to eighth-grade students. The programme focused on training student mentors to promote a respect for differences, to become aware of stereotypes in the media, and to recognize qualities of healthy and unhealthy relationships. It also encouraged them to be active bystanders in preventing harassment, sexual harassment, and teenage dating abuse.

MVP originated with author, educator, and activist Jackson Katz, who began the programme at Northeastern University, originally designed for male college athletes to mentor high-school athletes about men's violence against women. Katz and MVP trainers from Northeastern University worked with me to launch a pilot programme I adapted for high-school students (Katz et al. 1994).

High-school students interested in being MVP mentors (who grew in number to more than two hundred) applied to the programme and completed fifteen hours of training. There were two components to the programme: one based in the middle school and one based at the high school. The middle-school part consisted of high-school students travelling to mentor the nearly 1,000 eighth-grade students across the four middle schools in the city, three times a year. The MVP mentors used role-play scenarios to teach about media literacy and the prevention of bullying, *cyberbullying*, and sexual harassment. The mentors helped eighth-graders develop action plans to make positive changes in their schools. The second component was to create annual *MVP Days* in the two high schools, which were attended by high-school students. These events consisted of many activities, including guest speakers, media presentations, visual art, songs, and 'speak-outs'. Special projects, such as the students' version of the *Clothesline Project* that lists quotes and statistics about sexual harassment and relationship violence on T-shirts, also brought awareness. Movement, and what Laban termed 'dance theatre', played a key role in the day, particularly in role-play scenarios which illustrated challenging situations such as relationship abuse, sexual harassment, and discrimination of LGBTQ (lesbian/gay/bisexual/transgender/queer) students. The role-play format which used the audience as the 'witness' (Adler) allowed for a group experience. The group became more present, empathic, and mindful about what they were sensing and feeling.

MVP training activities and protocol included many aspects of an evolving movement process including cooperative movement activities, relaxation, body awareness exercises, visualizations, 'focusing' questions and listening to the body's wisdom (Gendlin 1978) regarding their experiences. These experiences were then visually depicted, moved to, and written about which led the students to create authentic scenarios. Students were guided through an experiential learning process including body sensing, mindful exercises, moving, creating scenarios, expressing, witnessing, dialoguing, and reflecting, both individually and collectively. The process assisted students to embody their experience and integrate the messages derived from the scenarios, ultimately leading to actions that support their health and wellbeing. The high school's MVP programme provided an educational process that combined the creative/expressive therapies (drama, dance/movement, art), violence prevention strategies, and a theoretical framework of social, emotional, and relational development.

Through student-directed lessons and experiences presented to middle-school students and by sponsoring *MVP Days*, the improved climate of all secondary schools in the city helped students feel safe, more supported, and increasingly empowered. The MVP training encouraged mentors to become more mindful, empathic, active bystanders and allies, and facilitated more respectful environments in their own school and the broader community.

Laury Rappaport (2009), an author and art therapist, applies Gendlin's ideas to the arts as follows: 'Focusing provides mindful access to inner resources of the bodily felt senses where art therapy carries its rich source of imagery and wisdom into an outward visual artistic expression' (p. 88). It is my belief that artistic expression can be manifested as a dance or role-play scenario as well.

One focus of the programme is the effect the interactive/creative role play process (including moving, focusing, drawing, writing the scenario, performing, witnessing, and reflecting) has on peer behaviour. There is a further assumption that the students who witness the role-plays become more aware of their sense of relational mindfulness, which 'is the mindfulness of self-in-relation, mindfulness of other-in-relation, and mindfulness of the qualities and movement of [a] relationship' (Surrey 2005, p. 94). A goal of the mentoring programme was to encourage the active bystander—a person who assists someone else in an emotional, physical, or manipulative *power over* situation by taking an active role. Aiding the targeted person, speaking to the harasser, getting the help of a teacher or counsellor, or contacting professional resources for further assistance, are ways in which the active role can be manifested. Because this work can trigger students' past memories and experiences, counselling support and school and community resources must be made available.

Through the process of witnessing and dialoguing about the role-play scenarios as a community, it is believed an individual can embody the experience through his or her kinaesthetic sense, or what was previously mentioned as a body sense. Body sense is an embodied experience that can be sensed, felt, or acted upon (Cohen 1993) through a person's mindful awareness of what he or she is feeling and experiencing. Dance/ movement therapist Adler (2002) and her idea of 'conscious embodiment' speaks to the mind/body integration that takes place when the observer witnesses the mover. A different but similar relationship can be applied, in this case, to the actor, with the audience as witness. A collective *felt sense* (Gendlin 1978) can occur when a group becomes more mindful about what they are sensing and feeling. I suggest that a collective *felt shift* (Gendlin 1978) can happen when some members of the group understand, feel empathy, and are moved by what they are seeing and feeling. This can be accompanied by a physical release that can be kinaesthetically felt as well as observed. An example of this was demonstrated at the end of the performed MVP scenario in the theatre in the round where the focus was on identifying red flags leading to relationship violence. A 16-year-old male student stood up at the end and said 'this happened to my friend, and even after time she still suffers from this experience.' His was a spontaneous, heartfelt comment, and the audience responded with an audible, collective intake of breath that seemed to encircle the room.

The dramatic scenarios created and acted out by the students in the mentors programme exemplify what Laban believed in—that movement and theatre are capable of enacting *humane effort*. This experience can contribute to the self-development of each student and allows for embodied integration. As Laban pointed out, 'theatre gives an insight into the workshop in which man's power of reflection and actions is generated' (Laban 1971, p. 6). 'We need an authentic symbol of the inner vision to effect contact with the audience, and this contact can be achieved only if we have learned to think in terms of movement' (Laban 1971, p. 20). The role-play scenarios created, acted out, witnessed, dialogued, and reflected upon by audience and actors assist in what Siegel (2007) calls the 'integrative process'. This leads to health and wellbeing, and reinforces Laban's idea of an integrated sense of 'movement thinking' applied to *humane effort* and authentically acted out in life.

An evaluation on the MVP programme was administered at one high school in order to assess its effectiveness. One aspect of the study included a questionnaire administered to all high-school students who attended *MVP Day*. The common themes that emerged from the post-test questionnaire was an increased awareness of harassment and dating abuse and a willingness to interact and to intervene as an active bystander in harassment, sexual harassment, and teenage dating abuse situations (Beardall 2011).

Another aspect of the evaluation study consisted of interviewing MVP alumni to obtain their retrospective view of the programme. They were passionate as they spoke of continuing to embody MVP's values to the present day. They spoke of life skills that they developed, such as increased empathy, leadership, and the ability to make healthy choices that influenced their behaviour and actions. The students were articulate and spoke from their past experiences and involvement in the programme. One student mentioned: 'We've seen a legacy that has developed around MVP and its messages.' Their responses reflect the positive long-term results of the Spiral Integrated Learning Process described (Figure 25.1). One alumni student commented: 'I have taken MVP's message of anti-violence to my college campus. I am part of a men's group looking at issues of sexual abuse and how we as men can bring about a positive change.'

It is important to note here that the MVP mentors who completed the feedback questionnaires after participating in *MVP Day* reported higher awareness, interaction, and perceived intervention than the high-school students not trained in the mentoring programme.

CONCLUSION

These programmes affirm that the Spiral Integrated Leaning Process, inspired by dance/movement therapy principles, has a role in the schools and can guide DMTs and dance educators to support their students' embodied knowing in their physical, social/emotional, relational, cognitive development.

Dance/movement therapy practice can be viewed on a continuum (Imus 2012) in how DMTs work with different populations in varying settings while maintaining clear intention and ethical standards. Individuals develop and learn through their bodies, our early memories are stored in our bodies and we attune and connect through our bodies. The three programmes mentioned in this chapter assisted in building awareness of the body's wisdom, increased expressive repertoire, involvement in the creative process, and mindfulness of self. This developmental psychoeducational approach using dance, movement, dance/movement therapy core principles, and the creative/expressive arts helped to facilitate growth and change through the challenging transitional time of adolescence. Students were guided to experience their own potential, to listen to their bodies' wisdom and embodied knowing, to develop empathy and respect for others, and to support their own wellbeing. Their integrated, embodied response often led to social action initiatives within the school and larger community.

The school-based programme evaluation studies demonstrate promising results for all three programmes. The findings provide both a baseline to work from and offer best practices for increasing the success of these initiatives. Educating teachers, administrators, and expressive therapists about this work, as well as conducting more rigorous research, is our next frontier in advancing the development of dance, dance/movement therapy, embodied knowing, and the psychoeducational experience in schools.

References

Adler, J. (2002). *Offering from the Conscious Body*. Vermont: Inner Traditions.

Bartenieff, I. and Lewis, D. (1980). *Body Movement: Coping with the Environment*. Toronto: Gordon and Breach.

Beardall, N. (2005a). *Creating a Peaceable School: Confronting Intolerance and Bullying*. Newton, MA: Newton Public Schools.

Beardall, N. (2005b). 'Dance the dream', in M. C. Powell and V. Marcow Speiser (eds.), *Little Signs of Hope! The Arts, Education and Social Change*. New York: Peter Lang, pp. 7–17.

Beardall, N. (2011). 'Spirals dancing and the Spiral Integrated Learning Process: Promoting an embodied knowing', *Journal of Applied Arts and Health* 2(1): 2–23.

Beardall, N., Bergman, S., and Surrey, J. (2007). *Making Connections: Building Community and Gender Dialogue in Secondary Schools*. Cambridge, MA: Educators for Social Responsibility.

Berrol. C. (1992). 'The neurophysiologic basis of the mind–body connection in dance/movement therapy', *American Journal of Dance Therapy*, 14(1): 19–29.

Berrol, C. (2006). 'Neuroscience meets dance/movement therapy: Mirror neurons, the therapeutic process and empathy', *The Arts in Psychotherapy*, 33(4): 302–15.

Canner, N. (1992). 'At home on earth', *American Journal of Dance Therapy*, 14(2): 125–31.

Chaiklin, H. (ed.) (1975). *Marian Chace: Her Papers*. Columbia, MD: American Dance Therapy Association.

Cohen, B. B. (1993). *Sensing, Feeling and Action: Experiential Anatomy of Body–Mind Centering*. Northampton, MA: Contact Editions.

Cummins. M. (2004). *Bullying Survey: Selected Results.* Burlington, MA: Social Science Research and Evaluation.

Eddy, M. (1998). *The Role of Physical Activity in Educational Violence Prevention Programs for youth.* Unpublished PhD thesis, Columbia University, New York.

Elias, M. et al. (1997). *Promoting Social and Emotional Learning.* Alexandria, VA: Association for Supervision and Curriculum Development.

Fischer, J. and Chaiklin, S. (1993). 'Meeting in movement: The work of the therapist and client', in S. Sandel, S. Chaiklin, and A. Larkin (eds.), *Foundations of Dance/Movement Therapy; The Life and Work of Marian Chace.* Columbia, MD: The Marian Chace Fund of the American Dance Therapy Association, pp. 136–53.

Gendlin, E. T. (1978). *Focusing.* New York: Bantam Books.

Gilligan, C. and Brown, L.M. (1992). *Meeting at the Crossroads: Women's Psychology and Girl's Development.* Cambridge, MA: Harvard University Press.

Goleman, D. (1995). *Emotional Intelligence.* New York, NY: Bantam Books.

Goleman, D. (2006). *Social Intelligence.* New York, NY: Bantam Books.

Guerney, B., Stollak, G., and Guerney, L. (1971). 'The practicing psychologist as educator: An alternative to the medical practitioner model', *Professional Psychology,* 2: 276–82.

Hervey, L. (2007). 'Embodied ethical decision making', *American Dance Therapy Association,* 29(2): 91–108.

Imus, S. (2012). *Dance/Movement Therapy's Scope of Practice in Healthcare: Soaring to New Heights.* Conference Presentation, American Dance Therapy Association 47th Annual Conference. Albuquerque, NM.

Jordan, J., Kaplan, A., Miller, J., Stiver I., and Surrey, J. (1991). *Women's Growth in Connection: Writings from the Stone Center.* New York: Guilford Press.

Karkou, V., Fullarton, A. and Scarth, S. (2010). 'Finding a way out of the labyrinth through dance movement psychotherapy', in V. Karkou (ed.), *Arts Therapies in Schools.* London and Philadelphia: Jessica Kingsley, pp. 59–84.

Kornblum, R. and Hervey, L. (2006). 'An evaluation of Kornblum's body-based violence prevention curriculum for children', *The Arts in Psychotherapy,* 33: 113–29.

Koshland, L. and Wittaker, J. (2004). 'PEACE through dance/movement: Evaluating violence prevention program', *American Journal of Dance Therapy,* 26(2): 69–90.

Katz, J., O'Brien, J. and Hurt, B. (1994). *The MVP Playbook.* Boston, MA: Northeastern University Press.

Laban, R. (1966). *The Language of Movement: A Guidebook to Choreutics.* London: McDonald and Evans.

Laban, R. (1971). *The Mastery of Movement.* London: McDonald and Evans.

Levy, F. J. (2005). *Dance/Movement Therapy: A Healing Art.* Reston, VA: AAHPERD.

Merleau-Ponty, M. (1962). *The Primacy of Perception.* New York, NY: Humanities Press.

Miller, J. B. and Stiver, I. (1997). *The Healing Connection.* Boston, MA: Beacon Press.

Olweus, D. (1993). *Bullying at School: What We Know and What We Can Do.* Malden MA: Blackwell.

Perl, S. (2004). *Felt Sense: Writing with the Body.* Portsmouth, NH: Heinemann.

Piers, E. V. and Harris, D. B. (1986). *Piers Harris Self Concept Scale,* 2nd edn. Los Angeles CA: Western Psychological Services.

Rappaport, L. (2009). *Focusing-Oriented Art Therapy.* London: Jessica Kingsley.

Rizzolatti, G. (2006). 'Cells that read minds', *The New York Times,* 10 January, p. C3.

Shem. S. and Surrey, J. (1998). *We Have to Talk: Healing Dialogues between Men and Women*. New York, NY: Basic Books.

Siegel, D. (2007). *The Mindful Brain*. New York, NY: Guilford Press.

Siegel, D. (2008). 'The fourth "R" of education', *Garrison Institute Newsletter*, 6, summer, 1–3.

Stern, D. (2004). *The Present Moment in Psychotherapy and Everyday Life*. New York, NY: W. W. Norton.

Studd, K. and Cox, L. (2013). *Everybody is a Body*. Indianapolis, IN: Dog Ear Publishing.

Surrey, J. (2005). 'Relational therapy, relational mindfulness', in C. Germer, P. Fulton, and R. Siegal (eds.), *Mindfulness and Psychotherapy*. New York: Guilford Press, pp. 91–110.

CHAPTER 26

MOVEMENT THERAPY PROGRAMME WITH CHILDREN WITH MILD LEARNING DIFFICULTIES IN PRIMARY SCHOOLS IN SAUDI ARABIA

Links between Motion and Emotion

ABDULAZEEM ALOTAIBI, VICKY KARKOU,
MARIETTA L. VAN DER LINDEN, AND
LINDESAY M. C. IRVINE

INTRODUCTION

MOVEMENT therapy[1] is a form of psychotherapy that is based on the principle that there are links between motion and emotion and between body and mind (Karkou and Sanderson 2006). As a result, bringing together emotional, cognitive, and social aspects of oneself through physical engagement is a key therapeutic aim for movement psychotherapists. For example, in the official definition used by the Association for Dance Movement Psychotherapy UK (2017) the discipline is described as 'a relational process in which client/s and therapist engage creatively using body movement and dance to assist integration of emotional, cognitive, physical, social and spiritual aspects of self' (p. 1). One could argue that this integration leads to therapeutic change, healing, and enhanced wellbeing.

However, and despite growing research evidence in the field, the degree to which integration is indeed achieved still remains insufficiently investigated. Instead, existing evidence suggests that movement therapy can be beneficial for individuals with difficulties relating to emotional problems and distress, personal communication skills, self-exploration, or self-understanding, as well as people who cannot easily communicate through words in general (Koch et al. 2014; Strassel et al. 2011; Karkou and Sanderson 2006; Payne 2006; Meekums 2002; Cruz and Sabers 1998; Ritter and Low 1996; Meekums et al. 2015).

The most recent meta-analysis, for example, looked at the effectiveness of movement therapy and dance from twenty-three primary trials ($N = 1078$), including studies with children and adolescents. Results suggest that these interventions can increase quality of life and decrease clinical symptoms such as depression and anxiety. Positive effects were also found on the increase of subjective wellbeing, positive mood, affect, and body image. Changes on interpersonal competence were encouraging, but due to the heterogenity of the data this effect remained inconclusive.

An older meta-analysis on the effectiveness of movement therapy, using sixteen studies, with varied populations undertaken by Ritter and Low (1996) and recalculated by Cruz and Sabers (1998), identified that movement therapy demonstrated a 30% positive treatment effect—a rate that is comparable to other psychosocial therapies in terms of improvement of motor skills, balance, and spatial awareness among children. As a form of psychotherapy that uses movement as its main media, movement therapy seems to show some usefulness as an intervention for varied client groups in diverse settings.

Several studies on movement therapy for children and adolescents (Karkou et al. 2010; Eke and Gent 2010; Jeong et al. 2005) hint about the relationship between motion and emotion that movement therapy draws upon. The quantitative study by Jeong et al. (2005) is of unique significance here, as it suggests that there is a link between physiological and psychological changes attributed to movement therapy. Jeong et al.'s study follows a twelve-week movement therapy course among forty middle-school senior girls with mild depression. The average age of the participants was 16, and equal numbers (twenty each) of participants were allocated into the movement therapy group and the control group. The results of the study indicated that all subscale scores of psychological distress and depression of the movement therapy group were found to be significantly lowered after the twelve-week period. Of even more interest is that within the movement therapy group the hormonal levels of plasma serotonin were found to be higher and the hormonal levels of dopamine lower than that of the control group, leading the authors to suggest that it appeared that movement therapy could have a very positive effect on stabilizing the sympathetic nervous system. Jeong et al. (2005) concluded that movement therapy could prove beneficial in modulating the concentrations of serotonin and dopamine in the bloodstream and therefore be used to successfully improve psychological distress. However, this is a fairly limited study with a small group of people ($N = 40$), while no attempt was made to examine the relationship between the neurohormone modulation and the emotional responses measured. It is clear, therefore, that further work needs to be undertaken to substantiate this effect. Furthermore, research that explores whether movement therapy enables psychological and physical changes in children with learning difficulties remains limited.

In England, the Department of Health (2012) describes learning disability as a 'significantly reduced ability to understand new or complex information, to learn new skills, along with a reduced ability to cope independently'(p. 1) that usually starts from childhood and is often expressed as poor academic performance. People with learning disabilities appear to face more challenges than just the limitation in intellectual capacity.

Evidence suggests a significant difference in motor and cognitive capacities between children with mild disabilities and typically developing students as seen in the study by Munkholm and Fisher (2008). According to Forness and Kavale (1996), it is estimated that as many as 40% of individuals with learning disabilities experience social, emotional, and behavioural problems. People with learning disability also seem to have increased health risks stemming from loneliness, difficulties with social engagement, and reduced physical activity (Margalit 1998; Messent et al. 1998; Deb et al. 2001).

The existence of these concomitant occurrences in children with learning disabilities highlight the need for interventions to consider the impact of medical, motor, and psychological problems that may follow learning disabilities (Margalit 1998; Alexander et al. 2002; Arthur 2003). This is because the understanding of all these factors is necessary for delivering treatment programmes that meet the diverse needs of people with learning disabilities.

The few available studies investigating the usefulness of movement therapy with people with disabilities provide evidence that it can improve motor function, mental state, functional capacity, physical performance, and health-related quality of life in various studies (Couper 1981; Berrol 1984; Ritter and Low 1996; Strassel et al. 2011). Couper's (1981) intervention study with ten children of ages 7–10 years reported increased gains on motor performance for the movement therapy group, even though the study had very small sample size and did not provide results that were statistically significant.

Similarly, Berrol's (1984) study in California with sixty-eight pupils ($N = 68$), which examined the efficacy of two remedial movement interventions (movement therapy and sensory motor activity) and their effect on the academic achievements, physical performance, and sociobehavioural adjustments of first-grade children with learning and perceptual-motor problems, noted some positive results for the movement therapy group. Although the results of the study were inconclusive, the author found that the effects of movement therapy were important enough to suggest that movement therapy may be effective in ameliorating some hyperactive behaviours in children with learning difficulties.

Notable as Couper's (1981) and Berrol's (1984) studies among others may seem, they remain fairly small-scale and with a high risk of bias. Furthermore, there is no analysis of the changes in correlation in the motor parameters and the emotional indices that may illuminate the observed impact of movement therapy on the integration of psychosocial and perceptual-motor functions of children with learning disabilities. More so, these studies are quite dated, and not much has been done recently leading to a continuing gap in knowledge base. As a result, the current study aims to contribute to the existing body of knowledge by investigating the correlation between emotional wellbeing and perceptual-motor ability fostered by movement therapy. In this chapter in particular, changes in the correlation between emotional wellbeing and perceptual-motor ability parameters of children with learning difficulties that have participated in a group movement therapy programme will be discussed. The study tests the hypothesis that movement therapy will contribute towards the integration of emotional/social skills and perceptual-motor ability of children in the study group.

METHODOLOGY

This study is an open-labelled Randomized Controlled Trial (RCT), with the allocation of participants into two groups: movement therapy intervention group and a control group. Since it was registered as a doctoral study in a UK university, it received research ethical permission from the research ethics committee of this university before it gained approval from the Saudi Arabian ethics department, where the fieldwork took place. Informed assent (verbal) and consent (written) was received from all the participants, including their teachers and parents after providing adequate and satisfactory information about the study. Quantitative data for the study were gathered through standardized testing with Purdue Perceptual-Motor Survey and Goodman's Strength and Difficulties Questionnaire (SDQ) in two schools for boys in Saudi Arabia. The official school records of the pupils in the two schools served as the source of background information, since it covered areas such as the number of pupils who had learning difficulties, age of pupils, cognitive skills, and health status. To recruit the study participants, a meeting with all the parents of the children was organized with the help of the school authorities. During this meeting, participants and their parents were given relevant information about the study, provided with the information sheet, and given adequate opportunity to ask questions which were duly addressed.

Inclusion and Exclusion Criteria

The criteria set out by the British Institute of Learning Disability (BILD) for diagnosis of learning disabilities (see Holland 2011; Department of Health 2013) were used in determining and selecting candidates who qualified for the study: boys aged 6–9 years with IQ scores between 50 and 70, indicating mild learning disability. Those with identifiable problems, a low intelligence quotient (IQ) (below 50), or a higher IQ (above 70), were excluded, since the programme was not designed to adequately cater for their needs. Children with deafness, blindness, those who would not speak, or those with severe anatomical and/or physiological impairment were also excluded, since the programme did not make provision for individualized special needs. As it was necessary for the study for participants to be actively engaged and interact with one another during the programme, the selection process ensured that all the boys who participated in the study had vocal capacity and that all could walk without support.

A random selection procedure produced thirty participants for each of school A and B from a total of forty-one and forty-four boys respectively who fitted the inclusion criteria and who agreed to participate in the study. The process entailed the children blindly picking from a box that had thirty tabs marked 'Yes' and the remaining (eleven and fourteen for schools A and B respectively) marked 'No'. Those who chose tabs marked 'Yes' were recruited into the study.

Selected participants in each of the two schools were then made to dip a hand into a blind bag with thirty tabs with equal numbers of tabs marked '1' or '2', after which a coin was flipped by the first author to decide allocation of these numbers to either the intervention or the control group.

Outcome Measures

The study followed a pre-test/post-test sequence. Perceptual-motor ability and emotional wellbeing were measured through Purdue Perceptual-Motor Survey and Goodman's SDQ respectively. According to Alrobe (1995), the Purdue Perceptual-Motor Survey serves as a comprehensive measure for perceptual-motor skills in children. The availability of the Arabic version of the Purdue Perceptual-Motor Survey and its high validity and reliability (Hasan 2007) made this a choice instrument for this study. The Goodman's SDQ screens children for psychiatric disorder(s), exploring their emotional and behavioural difficulties (Goodman et al. 2000). In this study, the Goodman's SDQ was considered suitable for measuring emotional wellbeing, since it is known for being fairly robust in measuring attitudes and eliciting emotional impact from research participants and also demonstrating moderately high measurement reliability (Goodman et al. 2000).

The scores for the five perceptual-motor ability parameters in Purdue Perceptual-Motor Survey range from 1 to 4 except for the Balance and Posture scale, which ranges from 1 to 12, as this includes three subscales. Lower scores indicate more problems/symptoms and the total perceptual-motor ability score (range 1–28) is derived by summing scores from all of the scales. The Purdue Perceptual-Motor Survey was performed by the first author. Scores for the five SDQ scales range from 0 to 10, with higher scores indicating more problems/symptoms except for the prosocial behaviour scale where the reverse is true. The total difficulties score (range 0–40) is derived by summing scores from all of the scales except the prosocial behaviour scale, which is treated independently and has a score range of 0–10. The SDQ has both parents and teachers versions, both of which were used in this study, though only the teachers' scores are presented in this paper.

Procedure

In each of the two study centres (two schools for boys), fifteen boys were randomized into the intervention group and the same number into the control group. The boys in the intervention group were further divided into two subgroups (of seven and eight boys) for effective observation and intragroup participants' interaction required in the movement

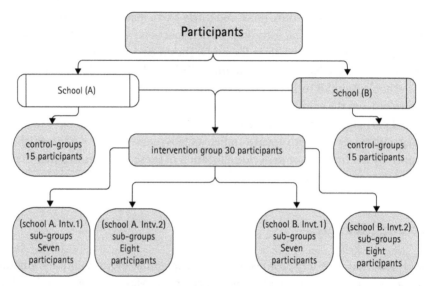

FIGURE 26.1. Participants in groups and subgroups in the two schools. (Credit: Abdulzeem Alotaibi.)

therapy programme. Each study centre, therefore, had thirty study participants—two main groups (intervention and control group) of fifteen pupils each—and the intervention group was further divided into two subgroups (see Figure 26.1).

The intervention programme consisted of three sessions of movement therapy activities per week for eight weeks, and was provided by the first author, who has experience in movement therapy as part of his doctoral research. Each session lasted for forty-five minutes, producing a total of 135 minutes of therapy per week. The control groups had a similar number of sessions, which represents the number of classes in a regular physical education programme of the schools. The works of Marian Chace, as elaborated in Karkou and Sanderson (2006), and Sherborne (2001) formed the foundation of the theoretical frame and principles guiding the movement therapy programme implemented in this study. The programme sessions were articulated to impact on the motor and emotional wellbeing of children with mild learning difficulties. Although flexibility was allowed in the implementation of the programme, each session's structure comprised a warm-up, theme development, and closure.

- Warm-up. These activities aimed to prepare the body and mind for the programme, brought the group together, and helped to prevent injuries. This section also encouraged participants to explore body action in space, build trust and develop relationships, and engage in a simple but common group rhythm.
- Theme development. This was built around the developmental themes of 'caring', 'sharing', and 'against' relationships (Sherborne 2001). Chace's (1975) ideas relating to the development of dyadic and group therapeutic relationship as presented by

Karkou and Sanderson (2006) acted as methodological guidelines. For example, the therapist was picking up on non-verbal clues: broadening, extending, and clarifying actions; using particular activities that supported caring, sharing, or against relationships; and encouraging other activities such as role playing and symbolic action.

- Closure. Here a drawing activity took place. This section of the sessional allowed for the expression of individual and/or communal movement/gestures, sharing of feelings, and a closing discussion.

Analysis

Descriptive and inferential statistics were used to analyse the quantitative data obtained from the outcome measures (Purdue test and SDQ). Data were screened for normality using the Kolmogorov–Smirnov test (Greasley and Hill 2008), necessitating the use of nonparametric tests, since the data were found not to be normally distributed. Since one of the hypotheses of the study (and the one reported here) asserted that there would be a change in the relationships between SDQ scores and Purdue Perceptual-Motor Survey scores of children with learning disability after participating in an eight-week movement therapy study, the Spearman's correlation coefficient was used to explore the relationships between the SDQ factors and the perceptual-motor ability scores before and after the movement therapy intervention.

SPSS version 19 was used to perform data analysis, and the level of statistical significance was set at $p = 0.05$.

Results

The thirty pupils—fifteen from each school—who took part in the movement therapy programme attended all three sessions of the programme per week for the eight-week period of the study, as did the control group in the regular physical education sessions. Therefore, all study participants attended all twenty-four sessions delivered during the study period. Furthermore, all study participants, as well as their teachers, completed the pre- and post-intervention tests and questionnaires, hence there were no missing data. Both groups had comparable age and IQ score profiles. The average age and average IQ score of the intervention group was 8.1 years (SD 0.86, range 6–9) and 59.8 (SD 4.67, range 50–66) respectively, while the same data for the control group were 7.8 (1.19, range 6–9) years and 58.5 (SD 5.62, range 51–69) respectively.

Table 26.1 shows the statistically significant difference ($p < 0.001$) between the average of the pre- and post-test measurements for the intervention group in factors of teacher SDQ scores and perceptual-motor ability parameters.

Table 26.1. Median and Interquartile (IQ) scores before and after movement therapy of the teachers SDQ scores and Perceptual–Motor ability and results of Wilcoxon test.

	Factor	Median (IQ)			
		Pre	Post	Z-value	p-value
Teachers SDQ scores	The emotional symptoms	5(0)	0(0.25)	4.94	<0.001
	The conduct problems	5.(1)	1(1)	4.75	<0.001
	The hyperactivity/inattention	7(0)	2(1)	4.88	<0.001
	The peer problems	6(0)	3(1)	4.42	<0.001
	The prosocial	0.75(2.25)	5(0.25)	4.57	<0.001
	Total difficulties	23(1)	7(3)	4.73	<0.001
Perceptual motor ability	Balance and posture	4(1)	11(1)	4.83	<0.001
	Jumping	1(0)	3(1)	4.97	<0.001
	Identification of body parts	1(0)	4(0)	5.07	<0.001
	Imitation of movement	1(1)	4(0)	4.90	<0.001
	Obstacle course	1(0)	3(1)	5.04	<0.001
	Perceptual motor ability	8(2)	26(2)	4.80	<0.001

The statistically significant changes seen between the post-test and pre-test of the SDQ scores and aerceptual-motor ability measures indicate a positive improvement for the children who engaged in the movement therapy programme.

Table 26.2 results show the baseline correlation coefficients between factors of Teachers SDQ and perceptual-motor ability scores for all sixty study participants. The results indicate that there were very few statistically significant correlations between the factors of perceptual-motor ability and Teachers SDQ scores: of the thirty-six points of reference there were only seven relationships which were of statistical significance. The strength of correlation ranged from mostly weak to fairly moderate correlation, with the strongest correlation ($\rho = -0.379$) between the prosocial component of the SDQ and the perceptual-motor ability scores. As the same trends were observed between the perceptual-motor ability factors and Parents SDQ scores these were not included in this chapter.

Table 26.3 shows the correlation coefficients between the post-test scores of the factors of Teachers SDQ and perceptual-motor ability for the thirty boys in the control group. Again, these results show few statistically significant correlations—nine of the thirty-six points of reference—with the strength of correlation also ranging from weak to fairly moderate, as seen in the pre-test. This indicates little or no change in the integration of emotional and motor skills in the participants of the control group. More

Table 26.2. Spearman's Correlation between each factor of the Teachers SDQ scores with factors of the Perceptual–Motor ability pre intervention (n= 60).

| | | Factor of Perceptual Motor ability | | | | | |
		Balance and posture	Jumping	Identification of body parts	Imitation of movement	Obstacle course	Perceptual Motor ability (total)
Factor of teachers SDQ scores	Emotional symptoms	0.077	0.120	−0.075	−0.036	−0.050	−0.030
	Conduct problems	−0.280*	−0.075	0.072	−0.100	−0.038	−0.210
	Hyperactivity/ inattention	0.088	0.033	0.034	0.141	0.073	0.112
	Peer problems	0.158	0.127	−0.110	0.336**	0.214	0.238*
	Prosocial	−0.180	0.246*	0.414**	0.248*	−0.073	−0.379**
	Total difficulties	−0.138	0.015	0.029	0.059	0.090	−0.054

** Correlation is significant at the 0.01 level (2-tailed).

Table 26.3. Spearman's Correlation between each factor of the teachers SDQ scores with factors of the Perceptual Motor ability after 8 weeks of regular Physical Education sessions for the control group (n=30).

| | | Factor of Perceptual Motor ability | | | | | |
		Balance and posture	Jumping	Identification of body parts	Imitation of movement	Obstacle course	Perceptual Motor ability
Factor of teachers SDQ scores	Emotional symptoms	0.066	0.063	0.046	− 0.198	− 0.182	− 0.041
	Conduct problems	0.295*	0.243	0.068	0.251	0.079	0.213
	Hyperactivity/ inattention	0.233*	0.102	−0.283*	0.185	0.0619	0.221
	Peer problems	0.150	0.130	−0.094	0.320**	0.211	0.232*
	Prosocial	−0.185	0.242*	−0.334**	0.243**	−0.247	−0.375**
	Total difficulties	−0.224	−0.091	−0.105	−0.043	0.025	−0.181

** Correlation is significant at the 0.01 level (2-tailed).

Table 26.4. Spearman's Correlation between each factor of the Teachers SDQ scores with factors of the Perceptual Motor ability in the posttest for the Intervention group.

		Factor of Perceptual Berrol's Motor ability					
		Balance and posture	Jumping	Identification of body parts	Imitation of movement	Obstacle course	Perceptual Motor ability
Factor of Teachers SDQ scores	Emotional symptoms	−0.774**	−0.807**	−0.832**	−0.828**	−0.877**	−0.803**
	Conduct problems	−0.678**	−0.761**	−0.767**	−0.749**	−0.794**	−0.696**
	Hyperactivity/ Inattention	−0.740**	−0.820**	−0.838**	−0.837**	−0.861**	−0.797**
	Peer problems	−0.621**	−0.687**	−0.729**	−0.673**	−0.713**	−0.651**
	Prosocial	0.703**	0.780**	0.790**	0.718**	0.765**	0.726**
	Total difficulties	−0.693**	−0.760**	−0.761**	−0.768**	−0.794**	−0.713**

** Correlation is significant at the 0.01 level (2-tailed).

so, the observation that most of the SDQ scores correlation with the perceptual-motor ability factors was seen with the 'prosocial' factor—a pattern that mirrors the pre-test correlation—may be reflective of the impact of group activity/exercise in which the control group engaged. A similar pattern of few correlations was seen between Parents SDQ factors and perceptual-motor ability scores for this group.

Table 26.4 shows the Spearman correlation coefficients between the factors of the Teachers SDQ scores and factors of the perceptual-motor ability after the movement therapy intervention (N = 30). A statistically significant inverse relationship (negative) was found between all factors of perceptual-motor ability and total difficulty scores and the following teacher SDQ scores: emotional symptoms, conduct problems, hyperactivity/inattention, peer problems ($-0.877 \leq \rho \leq -0.621$, p <0.01). In contrast, a highly statistically significant positive correlation existed between all the factors of perceptual-motor ability and the prosocial factor within the teachers SDQ scores ($0.718 \leq \rho \leq 0.790$, p, p < 0.01). The same trends were observed for parents' scores.

DISCUSSION

One of the hypotheses for this study was to test the widely help assumption that movement therapy will contribute towards integration of physical and emotional skills. This was done through the examination of changes in relationships, before and after the intervention, of SDQ scores and Purdue Perceptual-Motor Survey scores of children with learning disability participating in an eight-week movement therapy study.

The study showed considerably higher and stastistically significant correlations between the children's emotional wellbeing and the perceptual-motor ability after the eight-week movement therapy programme which was not seen in the control group. The strong inverse relationship post-intervention between all factors of perceptual-motor ability and SDQ scores (teacher) on emotional symptoms, conduct problems, hyperactivity/inattention, peer problems, and the positive correlation between all factors of perceptual-motor ability and the prosocial factor suggest an integration relationship of emotional/social skills and motor skills fostered by movement therapy intervention. This observed strong relationship between psychosocial indices and motor skills after movement therapy can be analysed and/or interpreted in two ways:

1. Movement therapy fosters proportional (and perhaps predictable) improvement in the psychosocial wellbeing and perceptual-motor ability of children with learning disabilities through the integration of physical and emotional skills;
2. There exist a biological relationship between psychosocial state and motor skills such that a change in one generates a proportional change in the other.

While each of these two positions can independently give rise to the observed relationship between the SDQ scores and the Perceptual-Motor indices, it must be borne in mind that the positions are not mutually exclusive as both may have influenced the results. For instance, Berrol's (2006) paper on the link between movement therapy and neuroscience appears to support this idea by hinting on the association of motoric and psychological processes through 'mirror neurons' which may underpin movement therapy effects. The association between motoric events and psychological processes is rightfully reflected in the description of movement therapy as a 'body and mind' intervention through which motion movements impact on the emotions of the participants.

Furthermore, the results showed that a statistically significant positive improvement was noted in the SDQ scores and Purdue Perceptual-Motor Survey scores of the movement therapy group after the intervention. In contrast to the movement therapy group, the pre-test/post-test comparison of the outcome measures for the control group—prepared for publication in another paper—did not show significant statistical changes. The improvement in the wellbeing of the movement therapy group as reflected in the reduction of post-test SDQ scores for emotional symptoms, conduct problems, hyperactivity/inattention, peer problems, and the increment in prosocial scores demonstrates the positive impact of the intervention on the social life of the children. Similarly, the significant increase in the post-test scores of the movement therapy group on Perceptual-Motor scores on 'balance and posture', 'jumping', 'identification of body parts', 'imitation of movement', and 'obstacle course' seem to substantiate earlier claims that movement therapy may improve motor skills.

These findings of the study agree with earlier studies (Couper 1981; Berrol 1984; Ritter and Low 1996; Strassel et al. 2011) that claim that movement therapy has a beneficial effect on psychosocial wellbeing and/or motor function.

A major limitation of this study is that there is no follow-up evaluation of this observed effect of movement therapy with children with learning disabilities to determine whether the relationship between SDQ scores and perceptual-motor ability indices are sustained over time. More so, the small sample size of the study and the lack of girls participating in the study heightens the need to replicate this study with a larger sample size and involving girls, perhaps in diverse cultural contexts. In addition to the previous, the study design was not blinded.

Conclusion

The positive impact of movement therapy on emotional wellbeing and perceptual-motor ability, and the observed strong positive relationship seen in the outcome measures of these two parameters after movement therapy, can be seen to have several implications. One of such is that it reinforces the need for further exploration of the impacts of movement therapy with various clients, as has been advocated by earlier studies. And, if this positive observation can be substantiated, many children with learning disabilities may be availed of the opportunity of having movement therapy as an alternative choice of therapy other than the regular programmes they may have in mainstream schools. More so, these findings seem to heighten the need to conduct further blinded randomized controlled trials on movement therapy to also explore the relationship between the psychosocial changes and motor skills with larger sample sizes and diverse clients, including girls. This will further illuminate the 'body and mind' connection pathway which seems to be the foundation of several body-based, movement, and arts therapies (Karkou and Sanderson 2006). Other therapists, especially psychologists, whose practice draws upon this assumption, may also need to critically evaluate the 'body/motoric' effects of their interventions in a quantitative manner as a way to further explore the depths and dimensions of this crucial relationship.

NOTE

1. Movement therapy is also known as dance movement therapy, dance movement psychotherapy, dance therapy, and movement psychotherapy. The term 'movement therapy' is

used throughout this chapter, since it appears to be the one with the best cultural fit in Saudi Arabia, where the notion of dance can be received with scepticism.

References

Abdul-Hameed Hasan (2007). 'Validity and reliability indices for the Arabic version of the Purdue Perceptual-Motor Survey in Sultanate Oman', *Jordan Journal of Educational Sciences*, 3(4): 331–49.

Alexander, R., Piachaud, J., Odebiyi, L., and Gangadharan, S. (2002). 'Referrals to a forensic service in the psychiatry of learning disability', *The British Journal of Forensic Practice*, 4(2): 29–33.

Alrobe, A. (1995). *Perceptual Motor Ability for Children*. Egypt: Dar Al Fikre Publishing.

Association of Dance Movement Psychotherapy UK (ADMP UK). (2017). What is Dance Movement Psychotherapy? http://admp.org.uk/dance-movement-psychotherapy/what-is-dance-movement-psychotherapy/ (Retrieved 20 March 2017).

Arthur A. (2003). 'The emotional lives of people with learning disability', *British Journal of Learning Disabilities*, 31: 25–30.

Berrol, C. (1984). 'The effects of two movement therapy approaches on selected academic, physical and socio-behavioral measures of first grade children with learning and perceptual-motor problems', *American Journal of Dance Therapy*, 7(1): 32–48.

Berrol, C. F. (2006). Neuroscience meets dance/movement therapy: Mirror neurons, the therapeutic process and empathy. *The Arts in Psychotherapy*, 33(4), 302–15.

Chace, M. (1975). *Marian Chace, Her Papers*. Columbia, MD: American Dance Therapy Association, p. 261.

Cook, B. G. (2001). 'A comparison of teachers' attitudes toward their included students with mild and severe disabilities', *The Journal of Special Education*. 34(4): 203–213.

Couper, J. L. (1981). 'Dance therapy: Effects of motor performance of children with learning disabilities', *American Physical Therapy Association*. 61(1: 23–6.

Cruz, R. F. and Sabers, D. L. (1998). 'Dance/movement therapy is more effective than previously reported', *The Arts in Psychotherapy*, 25(2): 101–4.

Deb, S., Thomas, M., and Bright, C. (2001). 'Mental disorder in adults with intellectual disability. 1: Prevalence of functional psychiatric illness among a community-based population aged between 16 and 64 years', *Journal of Intellectual Disability Research*, 45(6): 495–505.

Department of Health (2012). *Public Health England*. <http://healthandcare.dh.gov.uk/category/public-health/phe/> (accessed 12 March 2012).

Eke L. and Gent, A. (2010). 'Working with withdrawn adolescents as a moving experience: A community resourced project exploring the usefulness of group dance movement psychotherapy within a school setting', *Body, Movement and Dance in Psychotherapy*, 5(1): 45–57.

Forness, S. R. and Kavale K. A. (1996). 'Treating social skill deficits in children with learning disabilities: A meta-analysis of the research', *Learning Disability Quarterly*, 19(1): 2–13.

Goodman, R., Ford, T., Simmons, H., Gatward, R., Goodman, R., Ord, T. F., and Simmons, H. (2000). 'Using the Strengths and Difficulties Questionnaire (SDQ) to screen for child psychiatric disorders in a community sample', *The British Journal of Psychiatry*, 177: 534–9.

Greasley, P. and Hill, M (2008). *Quantitative Data Analysis Using SPSS: An Introduction for Health and Social Sciences*. Buckingham: Open University Press.

Holland, K. (2011). 'Factsheet: Learning disabilities', *British Institute of Learning Disabilities, Campion House*, 10(1): 1–7.

Jeong, Y., Hong, S., Lee, M., Park, C., and Suh, C. (2005). 'Dance movement therapy improves emotional responses and modulates neurohormones in adolescents with mild depression', *The International Journal of Neuroscience*, 115(12): 1711–20.

Karkou, V. and Sanderson, P (2006). *Arts Therapies: A Research Based Map of the Field.* Edinburgh: Elsevier.

Karkou, V., Fullarton, A., and Scarth, S. (2010). 'Finding a way out of the labyrinth through dance movement psychotherapy: Collaborative work in mental health promotion programmes for secondary schools', in V. Karkou (ed.), *Arts Therapies in Schools: Research and Practice.* London: Jessica Kingsley, 59–84.

Koch, S., Kunz, T., Lykou, S., and Cruz, R. (2014). 'Effects of dance movement therapy and dance on health-related psychological outcomes: A meta-analysis', *The Arts in Psychotherapy*, 41: 46–64.

Low, K. G. and Ritter, M. (1998). 'Response to Cruz and Sabers', *The Arts in Psychotherapy*, 25(2): 105–7.

Margalit, M. (1998). 'Loneliness and coherence among preschool children with learning disabilities', *Journal of Learning Disabilities*, 31(2): 173–80.

Meekums B. (2002). *Dance Movement Psychotherapy: A Creative Psychotherapeutic Approach.* London: Sage.

Meekums, B., Karkou, V., and Nelson, E. A. (2015). 'Dance movement therapy for depression', *Cochrane Database of Systematic Reviews*, Issue 2, Art. No. CD009895. doi: 10.1002/14651858. CD009895.pub2. <http://onlinelibrary.wiley.com/doi/10.1002/14651858.CD009895.pub2/abstract>

Messent, P. R., Cooke, C. B., and Long, J. (1998). 'Physical activity, exercise and health of adults with mild and moderate learning disabilities', *British Journal of Learning Disabilities*, 26(1): 17–22.

Munkholm, M. and Fisher, A. (2008). 'Differences in schoolwork performance between typically developing students and students with mild disabilities', *OTJR: Occupation, Participation and Health*, 28(3): 121–32.

Payne, H. (1993). *Handbook of Inquiry in the Arts Therapies: One River, Many Currents.* London: Jessica Kingsley.

Payne, H. (1994). 'A pilot study into DMT with women with eating disorders'. University of Hertfordshire: study funded by the Eating Disorders Association.

Payne, H. (2006). *Dance Movement Psychotherapy: Theory, Research and Practice.* London: Routledge.

Ritter, M. and Low, K. G. (1996). 'Effects of dance/movement therapy: A meta-analysis, *The Arts in Psychotherapy*, 23: 249–60.

Sherborne, V. (2001). *Developmental Movement for Children*, 2nd edn. London: Worth Publishing Limited.

Strassel, J. K., Cherkin, D. C., Steuten, L., Sherman, K. J., and Vrijhoef, H. J. (2011). 'A systematic review of the evidence for the effectiveness of dance therapy', *Alternative Therapies in Health and Medicine*, 17(3): 50–9.

CHAPTER 27

DANCE MOVEMENT THERAPY, STUDENT LEARNING, AND WELLBEING IN SPECIAL EDUCATION

SUE MULLANE AND KIM DUNPHY

I have come to believe that improvised dance involves literally giving shape to oneself by deciding how to move in relation to an unsteady landscape. To engage oneself in this manner, with a sense of confidence and possibility, is a powerful way to inhabit one's body and to interact with the world.

Danielle Goldman (2010)

INTRODUCTION

DANCE movement therapy[1] (DMT) is posited as an effective approach to learning through the arts for students who have greater learning challenges. However, while DMT is applied in special education contexts in Australia and other countries, it is not implemented comprehensively or as a well-recognized dimension of effective pedagogical approaches. At the same time, the inclusion of dance in the educational experience of Australian students is becoming more prevalent, as the new national curriculum includes dance, along with drama, media arts, music, and visual arts as mandatory arts-focused learning areas central to the first eight years of students' education (ACARA 2013a). The Australian curriculum is designed to be inclusive of a diverse range of students, provided 'necessary adjustments are made to the way in which they are taught and to the means through which they demonstrate their learning' (ACARA 2013b, p. 20). A specific curriculum for arts-based learning for students with a disability has now been

FIGURE 27.1.   (Credit: © Sunshine Special Developmental School.)

developed. This skills-based approach is potentially beneficial for students, but it does not enable the broader possibilities for learning offered by dance movement therapy.

This chapter addresses this challenge, examining the potential for DMT programmes to contribute in special education as depicted in Figure 27.1. Theoretical and practice-based knowledge about how DMT can advance student wellbeing and learning is presented. The international literature and Australian perspectives on wellbeing in education are surveyed for a definition and conceptions of wellbeing. The strong confluence between outcomes of creative educational dance and DMT, and elements of wellbeing is explicated. Principles of existential phenomenology are discussed in their provision of a philosophical framework for therapeutic practice with this student population. Influential ideas from education on relational learning and constructivist pedagogies are also explored because of their potential to inform learning through DMT.

The chapter is illustrated by a detailed example of a DMT programme in a special developmental school in Melbourne, Australia, that draws on principles of creative educational dance and existential phenomenology to promote wellbeing for students. The programme's goals are outlined, complemented by a discussion of classroom activities and principles that inform their selection and development. (See also Video 27.1 on the Companion Website ⓟ.)

WELLBEING IN THE CONTEXT OF SCHOOLS AND SCHOOLING

Promotion of the wellbeing of young people is acknowledged as a vital role for Australian schools (MCEECDYA 2008, p. 4), and there is a well-agreed accord for the need to 'consider, monitor and respond to student well-being' (Fraillon 2005, p. 1). However, despite this agreement in principle there is not yet an agreed definition of wellbeing, nor a uniform model of wellbeing applied within the Australian educational sector (Masters 2004; Fraillon 2005; NSW Department of Education and Communities 2011). Whilst a singular approach would provide consistency to programmes, the sector is hesitant to adopt one given the recognition that the local school community, as the setting in which student wellbeing is nurtured, is the most appropriate body to determine how this process should occur (DECS 2007; Fraillon 2005).

Although there is not yet an agreed definition of wellbeing in relation to education, there is a range of conceptualizations as to its nature. Wellbeing for school students has been described as a subjective state that reflects a range of personality aspects unique to each person (Awartani et al. 2008; DECS 2007; Kickbusch et al. 2012; Sarvimaki 2006). It is considered to be multidimensional, with interdependent dimensions seen as relevant to the unique whole-person learning potential of a student. Typically, Australian school policies reference wellbeing in relation to learning that is clustered into cognitive, emotional, physical, social, and moral/ spiritual dimensions (MEECDYA 2008). The Universal Education Foundation (UEF)— a group that advocates for the educational wellbeing of children—posits a similar broad set of wellbeing relevant learning domains that are informed by the international literature.

These domains comprise physical wellbeing (bodily pleasure, sensations, and vitality), physical and emotional safety, emotional wellbeing, satisfying relationships, confidence in capabilities, pleasure and joy in learning, inner strength and spirit, a sense of interconnection with all of life, and overall satisfaction with life (Ostroff et al. 2007). These domains encompass signposts of wellbeing identified by the Department of Education and Children's Services which include confidence and self-esteem, a sense of self-identity and vitality, enjoyment and a sense of humour, self-direction, openness, optimism pleasure in exploring, social initiative, participation and cooperation, coping flexibility, robustness and persistence, and the ability to rest and relax (Goldspink 2009, cited in DECS 2010).

As understandings of wellbeing develop, so too do conceptualizations of how it can be measured. The international literature is concordant with the perspective in Australian schools that learner wellbeing reflects a dynamic, integrated, subjective state, best framed in the light of positive, strengths-based indicators and competencies (DECS 2007; Kickbusch et al. 2012). A full measure of wellbeing is considered to require subjective data from student voice such as self-reports, reports from teachers and parents, and objective data such as national statistics (Awartani et al. 2008; DECS 2007; Kickbusch et al. 2012; Rodgers and Raider-Roth 2006; NSW Department of Education and Communities 2011).

THE SIGNIFICANCE OF WELLBEING
TO STUDENT ENGAGEMENT WITH LEARNING

As wellbeing is better understood, the vital relationship between student wellbeing and learning is increasingly evident. Students who experience a strong sense of wellbeing in the classroom tend to be more motivated towards, and involved with, their learning, which in turn promotes 'deep engagement' with learning (DECS 2007, 2010; Kickbusch et al. 2012). Hallmarks of deep engagement include a positive receptivity to learning, focused energy for the task at hand, and engrossment in learning activities with a reluctance to cease involvement (Goldspink 2009, cited in DECS 2010). Deep engagement in learning is positively influenced by a number of factors, including the quality of the learning environment, and experiences provided by the teacher for student learning. To promote deep engagement, teachers must facilitate immersion in learning that stimulates and challenges, but does not overwhelm, students (Csikszentmihalyi 1990; DECS 2010).

Deep engagement is also influenced by the quality of teacher–student relationships (DECS 2010; Kickbusch et al. 2012), which is acknowledged in the model of relational pedagogy. This approach recognizes the importance of the teacher's connection: with themselves as facilitator, with the students and their learning, and with the subject matter and relevant pedagogical knowledge, in the creation of a safe, secure, and productive learning environment (Bigger 2011; Fraser et al. 2007; Rodgers and Raider-Roth 2006; Sidorkin 2000).

Optimal relational learning occurs in an environment which is interactive and where knowledge is built dynamically on what is already known by students (Willis 2009). In this constructivist paradigm, adapted from the theory of Lev Vygotsky (1896–1934), the process of learning is made more of a focus than outcomes (Shepard 2000; Willis 2009). Students are encouraged to make active choices about their learning and so reflect their individual experiences, interests, needs, and differences (DECS 2007). By taking this approach to learning for wellbeing, teachers are best able to cater for individual student requirements, including those of students with disabilities (DECS 2007). These students usually require additional support and programme adjustments to optimize their well-being potential (Commonwealth of Australia 2006). Such specialized strategies are seen to be most effective when built on wellbeing strategies implemented for all students within the particular school context (DECS 2007).

ARTS LEARNING AND WELLBEING

The unique potential for arts-based learning to contribute to wellbeing is recognized, for example, by Fraser et al. (2007). Within arts-based learning, student wellbeing is cultivated in the student's relationship with self, as they learn to express themselves verbally and non-verbally, and through collaborative self-expression with other students. Wellbeing is also understood to be cultivated in the relationship that develops between the student and the actual art form. Students develop trust by exploring possibilities for safe personal, physical, and emotional self-expression within the art medium (Fraser et al. 2007, pp. 43, 45). These connections are enhanced by the teacher's careful observation of, and subsequent response to, the quality of all interactions in the classroom (Burrows 2010). The arts teacher or therapist must ensure that the conditions within the learning environment are conducive to students feeling accepted and safe to explore, experiment, and take risks with the materials of art-making (Blom and Chaplin 1988, p. 54). Within a supportive, safe, and secure arts-based learning environment, students can be encouraged to become aesthetically attentive. With an emphasis on intuitive and emotional as well as intellectual ways of knowing, students can explore their inner and outer worlds and make connections between them with greater candour and clarity (Vasko 2007: 12).

THE IMPERATIVE FOR WELLBEING LEARNING FOR STUDENTS WITH DISABILITY

The changing nature of childhood disability, particularly as it presents in schools, and its subsequent implications for wellbeing learning is documented in recent literature. Halfon et al. (2012) identify the pervasiveness of biopsychosocial forms of disability in comparison with physical disabilities in current childhood health (13). Comparing trends from US-based data with that from other countries, they contend that these biopsychosocial disabilities range across developmental, emotional, behavioural, and neurological impairments. Caused in part by changes to children's physical, social, psychological, and cultural environments, these disabilities include Attention-Deficit

Hyperactivity Disorder (ADHD), autism spectrum disorder, learning disabilities, developmental delay, and speech and language disorders. When compared to the more obvious physical or sensory-based disabilities, these forms of childhood disability are less identifiable and may well have not emerged prior to the child reaching school age (Aron and Loprest 2012). Moreover, they impact greatly on many of the wellbeing learning domains discussed earlier.

The 'Students with Diversity and the Australia Curriculum 2013' advice recognizes many of Ostroff et al.'s (2007) wellbeing domains as essential aspects of personal and social learning for students with disabilities (ACARA 2013b). Using a Personal and Social Capability continuum, students with diversity, including disabilities, are supported to

> recognize, understand, and label their own emotions, values, strengths, and capacities; manage and regulate their own emotions and behaviour; persist in completing tasks and overcoming personal obstacles; perceive and understand other people's emotions and viewpoints; show understanding and empathy for others; and form strong and healthy relationships. Without personal and social capability, students with disability will struggle to 'relate to others; develop resilience and a sense of self-worth; resolve conflict; engage in teamwork and feel positive about themselves and the world around them' (ACARA 2013b, p. 17).

These findings about students with a disability inform understandings of the potential of DMT to contribute to students' wellbeing and overall learning, as discussed in the next section.

THE RELATIONSHIP OF WELLBEING TO APPROACHES IN EDUCATION: CREATIVE EDUCATIONAL DANCE AND DANCE MOVEMENT THERAPY

While a focus on student wellbeing is relatively new in educational pedagogy, creative dance educators and dance movement therapists have long applied principles similar to those currently recognized as important for wellbeing.

In the mid-twentieth century, influential dance educator and theorist Rudolf Laban devised a developmental movement approach that informed much of the antecedent dance education (Hanna 2008). Like contemporary relational approaches to learning discussed previously, which emphasize the student–teacher relationship and value process above outcomes, Laban prioritized the process of participation in dance and the way this can provide creative expression appropriate to the person's skill, ability, and stage of development. Laban was much less concerned with outcomes of dance learning

FIGURE 27.2. (Credit: © Sunshine Special Developmental School.)

in terms of artistic product, such as technical skill and performance making. In Laban's 'modern dance', participants were encouraged to exercise, and so preserve, their innate capacity for spontaneous expression in order to experience the flow inherent in all human movement possibilities. As long ago as 1948, Laban understood the importance of a whole-person approach that is now being recognized for its significance for wellbeing. He believed that the creative dance process was particularly valuable in schools as it integrated the intellect with creative capacity, ultimately leading to the overall development of the child as a whole person (Laban 1988) as seen in Figure 27.2.

Subsequent dance educators also espoused the benefits of their programmes with respect to the development of student whole being (Exiner and Lloyd 1987; Joyce 1980; Stinson 1990). H'Doubler, who was first writing in 1940, perceived a range of qualities of 'personality' that would resonate with contemporary wellbeing experts in that the 'expressive total' of a person included 'physical, intellectual, emotional, and spiritual energies' (1998, p. 64). Dance was seen to foster individualized student development because it merged action with awareness. Recognized outcomes of creative dance such as body mastery and control, self-awareness and self-identity, stimulation of the imagination and intellect, confidence in one's own capabilities, and communication with and sensitivity toward others (Exiner and Lloyd 1987; Joyce 1980; Stinson 1990) align closely with current ideas about the physical, cognitive, emotional, personal, and social domains of wellbeing discussed previously. And like contemporary educational approaches that value inclusive practice (MEECDYA 2008), creative educational dance was considered equally relevant for mainstream and special needs students (see for example, Cust 1976; Exiner and Lloyd 1987; Guthrie and Roydhouse 1988; Slater 1987; Sherborne 1990; Stinson 1990).

The significance of deep engagement, while only relatively recently understood in its relationship to wellbeing and learning, has also long been recognized by dance educators. For example, 'engagement' was identified as the moment when students' 'concentration and awareness are fixed on the act of moving' (Joyce 1980, p. 5). Exiner and Lloyd (1987, p. 23) referred to this as the process of 'commitment', when a student applies their 'whole self' to the full possibilities of exploration in a motion, gesture, or shape.

These ideas about the potential for wellbeing, whole-person development, and deep engagement through participation in creative educational dance are also apparent in conceptions of DMT, which as an embodied art form is based on the fundamental principle of the importance of whole-person experience.

DMT considers the mind and body as inseparable, seeing what is experienced in the mind as also experienced in the body, and vice versa (Schmais 1986; Exiner and Kelynack 1994; Bond 1994, 1999). DMT is used to assist participants to integrate mind and body, and in so doing, to find heightened awareness of and sensitivities to their own particular state of wellbeing, and their interaction with others and their environment. The focus is on connection of an individual with the self, given that humans are understood to live their world through their body in relation to others (Fraleigh 1996). DMT encourages the expression of the participant's existing physical and emotional states, and seeks to provide expressive non-verbal experiences to clarify and develop these states (Schmais 1980). As a process-oriented approach, DMT shares with creative educational dance and constructivist pedagogy a valuing of process over product.

The pioneers of DMT were dance performers and educators familiar with natural self-expression as it had been evolving in the modern dance movement in the US during the 1940s (Levy 1988). They developed a range of therapeutic intervention styles, which, like creative educational dance, valued 'individual movement preferences' and 'personal expression through uninterrupted improvisation' (Levy 1988, p. 39). Early European dance movement therapists were strongly influenced by the non-codified movement approach of Laban (Karkou and Sanderson 2006; Levy 1988; Meekums 2002; Payne 1992). Bernstein (1975) considered that DMT was about working from 'what could be seen' (p. 11), which required the therapist to assist the client to enlarge or diminish their *existing* movement pattern, rather than imposing specific movement patterns or gestures.

Australian dance movement therapists Exiner and Kelynack (1994) were similarly influenced by Laban—in particular, by his notion that spontaneous improvised dance could be expressed from the participant's 'centre' or 'from within' (p. 14). Exiner and Kelynack valued this centred movement as reflecting depth and real connection in the mover. This conception is similar to contemporary pedagogical ideas about deep engagement in learning, in which students benefit by being connected fully within themselves to the learning process.

Like creative dance, DMT is an inclusive practice, and is suited to people at different life stages and with a range of abilities and needs (Levy 2005; Schmais 1980). It is well established as a useful modality for children with special needs and in special education (Dunphy and Scott 2003; Guthrie and Roydhouse 1988).

Levy (2005) documents DMT programmes for children and adolescents with disabilities, including those with learning and developmental disabilities. More recent investigations report the use of DMT with students whose special needs are related to autism spectrum disorder (Baudino 2010), Attention-Deficit Hyperactivity Disorder (ADHD) (Gronlund et al. 2005), and multiple sclerosis (Salgado 2010). Many dance movement therapists work in school settings around the world, including in Australia (Dunphy et al. 2009) and the UK (Karkou 2010). The wide acceptance of creative educational dance programmes for early years and primary-school students throughout the mid-1990s is considered to be the antecedent of the establishment of DMT practice in UK schools (Karkou 2010).

While DMT-based learning in schools can be seen as challenging, given that it disrupts some of the established dualisms in learning such as mind/body, thought/action, individual/group and theory/practice (Hager 2005), DM therapists view this disruption as a positive, intentional contribution to realizing alternative ways of learning that can be beneficial for students.

Thus to summarize this section, student wellbeing is strongly associated with learning which takes place in an environment that supports the student to explore what is meaningful to them. These characteristics resonate with principles of creative educational dance and DMT, in which the person is placed in the centre of their movement experience. A further concept that relates enhancement of wellbeing with ideas about the whole person is that of existential phenomenology. This is discussed in the next section.

FIGURE 27.3.   (Credit: © Sunshine Special Developmental School.)

PRINCIPLES OF EXISTENTIAL PHENOMENOLOGY IN RELATION TO WELLBEING AND DANCE LEARNING

Developed originally in the philosophy of phenomenology by Edmund Husserl (1859–1938) and expanded in the writings of Martin Heidegger (1889–1976), among others, existential phenomenology is largely concerned with notions of existence. This philosophy posits the concept of 'being-in-the-world'; that is, ideas about an individual's being and relationship to the world and to others (Spinelli 1995, p. 26). It suggests that humans are unique in the ability to be aware of our own existence, which cannot be shared, but which also reveals 'an inseparable relationship between existence and the world' (Spinelli 1995, p. 108). In this paradigm, all conscious experience of our world is understood as coming from an interrelational standpoint, so our awareness is therefore intersubjective seen in Figure 27.3. Intersubjectivity is concerned with examination of the interaction between individuals' subjective experiences and concomitant personal understandings (Buirski and Haglund 2001). This philosophy resonates with the notion of personal wellbeing, as it values 'being at home in the world' and 'knowing one's way around' as daily lives are lived out for ourselves and in relationship with others (Sarvimaki 2006, p. 6).

Existential phenomenology can provide a philosophical framework for therapeutic practice. It is particularly useful for dance movement therapists, as it aligns well with concepts from creative educational dance and DMT—particularly the recognized relationship between body and mind, and the impact of this on wellbeing. The term 'lived body' used in existential phenomenology was coined by the French philosopher and phenomenologist Maurice Merleau-Ponty in 1945, in his seminal work, *Phenomenology of Perception*. He used this term to indicate 'bodily intentionality' (Carman 1999, p. 206), or the weaving together of the physical elements and experiences of body with consciousness or intention to form two aspects of a unified whole (Carman 1999; Polkinghorne 1994). Carman (1999) views this as an awareness of *being* a body and not just *having* a body (208).

Dance academic and performer Sondra Fraleigh (1991, 1996) affirms the work of Merleau-Ponty specifically in relation to dance. Upholding the 'lived body' concept as supportive of a subjective, experiential-based, non-dualistic understanding of the human body and its interactions in the world, Fraleigh asserts that dancing requires 'a concentration of the whole person as a minded body' (1996, p. 9), and, because the body 'is continuous with the mind' (p. 17), the person is able to experience all of themselves in their body through dance expression. Fraleigh suggests that this attribute of dance as a vital expression of the lived body is 'life engendering' (1996, p. 56). In existential phenomenology, life experience is not considered in terms of separate physical, emotional, social, or personal states, but rather (as described by Goldman in the opening quote), via a whole-person response to the unfolding of ordinary life on a daily basis (Sarvimaki 2006).

The principles of existentialist phenomenology can inform the specific way in which therapeutic engagement takes place as part of the relationship between the therapist and client. Using the lens of existential phenomenology, the role of the therapist can be viewed as that of a co-clarifier who attempts 'an adequate entry' (Spinelli 1996) into the lived world of the client. *With* the therapist, the client can bring into explicit awareness beliefs and assumptions about their world that previously may have remained unexamined and implicit. This therapeutic process supports the client to gain more mastery and control over their lives so that they may experience more fully their own being-in-the-world.

Issues brought to examination need not necessarily be changed, but rather accepted, in the belief that acceptance is often change enough (Spinelli 1996). The therapeutic goal is to assist the person to establish *what matters to them*, so that they can become more in tune with themselves, and therefore, more real and alive (van Deurzen-Smith 1988). Three key elements from Husserl's (1970) phenomenological method—'bracketing', 'description', and 'equal valuing' (Husserl 1970)—can usefully inform DMT practice.

'Bracketing' is likened to a 'knowing nothing' about a client and their way of being. This can be practiced by the therapist in order to discover the lived-reality of the client. The concept involves a withholding of assumptions, especially to do with predicting and/or expecting certain behaviour. 'Bracketing' requires that the therapist uses 'fresh eyes', or the capacity to be open to the way the client is presenting in that moment. It also requires the therapist to have a genuine curiosity or a 'needing to know' about the client. This attitude is acknowledged as impossible to hold, but should nonetheless be the therapist's intention (Spinelli 1995).

The concept of 'description' requires that the therapist maintain an expressive awareness of what is being presented by the client and staying just with that, rather than going beyond it. The therapist examines what the client presents *from what is there* rather than from what may lie underneath or behind it. This negates the need to determine *why* a client is moving in the manner they have chosen. This is also considered impossible to do but is nevertheless desired. 'Description' values explanation rather than interpretation, and respects that 'meaning-making' is ultimately the client's prerogative (Spinelli 1995).

Lastly, 'equal valuing' is the attitude the therapist holds that treats each client statement, gesture' or action equally, rather than forming a hierarchical value judgement as to what is meaningful or most important to the client in what they say and/or do. 'Equal-valuing' supports the descriptive process, and draws the therapist's attention to the transitory as well as the more involved movement motifs, and to the subtle, quiet moments in a client's dance as well as the more obvious expressive moments. By adopting this mindset, the therapist ensures that it is the client who determines what is significant and insignificant in the process (Spinelli 1995; Van Deurzen-Smith 1988).

Typically, these three strategies (bracketing, description, and equal valuing) are most useful to the therapist at the start of the therapeutic relationship, as they facilitate coming to know the client. In the ensuing developing relationship, the therapist also pays attention to any ambiguity or incongruence in the client's verbal and non-verbal behaviour. As the aim of the therapeutic process is to support the client to find greater connection to and cohesion within their life, as they understand it, the therapist's role shifts so as to sensitively invite the client to interact with their consistencies and inconsistencies to shed light on new possibilities for ways of being (Todres 2007).

Having introduced three fields of theory and practice that connect enhancement of wellbeing and learning with dance participation—creative educational dance, DMT, and existential phenomenology—this chapter next outlines a DMT programme that is informed by all of these ideas.

Dance Movement Therapy Programme in a Special Developmental School

In 2009 a DMT programme was introduced in a large special developmental school by special education teacher and dance movement therapist Sue Mullane. Like other such schools in Australia, this school caters for students assessed as having intelligence quotients below 50. The DMT programme, which students attend once a week with their class group, forms part of the school's range of specialist programmes. The dance movement therapist is supported in the programme by classroom assistants who work full time with particular class groups throughout their school day.

The programme draws on Mullane's extensive experience as a dance educator and therapist with a wide range of children and adults with special needs and disabilities. Whilst it is informed by creative educational dance as an accessible means by which students with disability can find self-expression, the programme is distinct from dance education in its therapeutic intention. The focus is on students' experience of dance as an expression of social and emotional aspects of being, rather than on artistic development (Karkou and Glasman 2004; Karkou 2010). Student progress in this programme is considered across all aspects of development and change, and is underpinned by the principle that 'artistic change gives information about associated psychological change' (Karkou 2010, p. 11).

The programme is also supported by concepts from existential phenomenology, as discussed previously, that ascribe value to the student's active and integrated whole-person relationship with their world as they are experiencing it. This practice makes use of the tools of 'bracketing', 'description', and 'equal valuing' from Husserl's (1970) phenomenological method, as discussed in the previous section.

A learning focus or goal is chosen for each class of students at the beginning of the year by the dance movement therapist in consultation with their classroom teacher. These goals are included in students' Individual Learning Plans (ILPs) for the year. The learning focus is selected from a range of outcomes related to student wellbeing and learning that are pertinent to students with an intellectual disability and have the potential to be developed through DMT. These outcomes have been explicated in a *Framework for Dance-Movement Assessment* developed by the current authors (Dunphy and Mullane 2015).

The selected learning focus articulates the primary purpose of the DMT sessions for that group, and is sufficiently broad to cater for individualized student needs within each class group. Learning foci emphasize student development with respect to physical mastery of the body in creative expression, fitness and coordination, the capacity to relax, connection and communication with others (other students in the group and/ or the attending adult), emotional expression and regulation, initiative, decision making, and leadership skills; connection with the here and now; connection between thought, imagination, and the body; and a sense of fun and enjoyment.

These are congruent with Hanna's (2008) universal descriptors of dance-based learning that include physical, cognitive, emotional, interpersonal and expressive/aesthetic domains, and the schema of wellbeing domains offered by Ostroff et al. (2007) discussed previously.

PHASES OF THE SESSION

Each DMT session has a defined structure of four main phases: 'accompanied solo', group movement, cushion rest, and session closure, although the structure is sometimes varied in response to students' dispositions at the time of the session.

Phase 1: The 'Accompanied Solo'

This phase aims to settle students into the dance space and orient awareness to the self via the body. Students remove socks and shoes, then sit with the class assistant and await their turn to be invited individually by the dance movement therapist into the space for an 'accompanied solo'.

The 'accompanied solo'—a practice coined by Mullane—is danced in turn by each child in the company of the therapist, and serves to focus the shared movement on choices determined by the child pictured in Figure 27.4. The accompanied solo utilizes improvised movement—a fundamental practice of both creative educational dance and

FIGURE 27.4. (Credit: © Sunshine Special Developmental School.)

DMT—because of the opportunity it provides for unfettered personal movement expression. Also informed by principles of existential phenomenology in relation to personal experiencing as it exists in the 'here and now', this solo encourages the open, embodied expression of student self 'in relation to self', as it is spontaneously experienced in that moment and presumably in a manner that is enjoyable to the student. The therapist invites the student to engage in movement comprised of self-initiated motion, gesture, and/or action. During the 'accompanied solo', the therapist's role is to encourage the student's curiosity in their physical engagement as it is occurring, without coercion or prompts.

The therapist inwardly engages with the child using the phenomenological concept of 'bracketing', described previously, which permits him/her to pay attention to the child's movement choices afresh and with inquisitiveness as to what the child is expressing. The therapist also remains mindful of Husserl's concept of 'equal valuing', also described previously, so as to notice and accept the full movement repertoire being explored by the child in their solo.

The therapist also supports the student in the solo by paying close attention to their chosen movement expression, 'to simultaneously reflect and respond to the movement' (Schmais 1980). This practice is informed by 'mirroring'—the concept introduced to DMT by Marian Chace in the 1940s, which requires the therapist to imitate the physical and emotional expression of a client as a way to non-verbally validate and empathize with the client's whole-person expression (Berrol 2006; McGarry and Russo 2011). Tortora (2011) determines that close observation and reflection of client non-verbal action and gesture as an expression of communication allow the therapist to 'come to know and engage in dialogue' with the client (14). Further, it is through this process that 'a sense of trust and relationship develops, strengthening the therapeutic milieu' (8). As suggested by Burrows (2010) with respect to teacher practice in relational pedagogy, the therapist *mindfully* supports the students to direct their focus towards the choices they are making and to encourage sustained movement expression.

As the moving relationship between therapist and student is initiated and develops within the accompanied solo, so the therapist sensitively offers bodily responses to the student which reflect the quality of their shared, developing relationship (as described earlier by Todres). In these solos, the therapist may move as one with the student, such as mirroring them side by side or face to face; moving with, toward, or away from the student in a complementary or contrasting manner, or maintaining in-place movement or stillness to offer support by intention. This delicate bodily reflection back to the student of what he/she is seen to be experiencing is usually very pleasurable for students.

As many students with intellectual disabilities do not have strong verbal communication, this non-verbal style of engagement can be much more accessible than talking. DMT practices such as the therapist's use of body posture and gesture, eye contact, facial expression, and proximity with the student are applied throughout the activities to engage and support them. Solos are undertaken without musical accompaniment to encourage students to move from an inner awareness or impulse (as recommended by Laban) rather than external rhythm and/or song lyrics.

Students may be offered physical support for their solo, in the joint holding of a length of fabric with the therapist. The fabric acts to physically connect the student to the therapist, and supports shared engagement in the movement. Long lengths of fabric enable the student and therapist to explore proximity in the dance, with concepts such as 'close to' and 'far apart', without losing the connection between each other. By jointly holding fabric, the student and the therapist can also find strength in movement with pulling and tugging, and resistance to being pulled and tugged. Wrapping up body parts or the whole body with the fabric offers the student experiences of body boundaries and containment. Different types of fabric can add an aesthetic dimension to the student–therapist connection and enhance student movement. For example, a small arm gesture made by the student can result in a much larger and more encompassing 'response' in the fabric that is being held by the student. This use of the fabric is also supportive of students who are shy or timid in making initial movement patterns or who are touch-sensitive to physical contact with others.

Phase 2: Group Movement

Phase 2 is social, directing student awareness towards self in relation to others and the environment. This aspect of the programme also incorporates improvised movement,

FIGURE 27.5. (Credit: © Sunshine Special Developmental School.)

but as part of a group rather than solo. Group improvisation is undertaken because it can stimulate confidence and clarity of self in the mover as they explore ways to interact and engage with others. In this exploration, students can be inspired into new movement experiences (Blom and Chaplin 1988). Initial movement stimulus is usually offered by the therapist. This serves to invite spontaneous, collaborative, and connected engagement whilst still allowing for individual student responses. This group movement activity emphasizes playfulness and the enjoyment of moving together and in unpredictable ways. Play is used here because of its centrality in child development, contributing significantly to the cognitive, physical, social, and emotional wellbeing of children and youth. Play allows children to use their creativity while developing their imagination, dexterity, and physical, cognitive, and emotional strength (Ginsberg 2007: 183). Play is also understood as an essential part of the creative process, and in therapy has the potential to generate new self-recognition and understanding (McNiff 1981). Play creates a transitional space from which new concepts of the self can be explored safely and symbolically, and in which clients may 'try on' different ways of knowing and expressing themselves, which includes relating to others (Winnicott 1971) as seen in Figure 27.5 below.

As with the accompanied solo, during the group movement phase the therapist employs the tools of 'bracketing' and 'equal valuing' to sensitively facilitate the degree of inclusion and engagement of the students as the group movement unfolds. The phenomenon of 'group' can be experienced by some students *directly*, through active,

FIGURE 27.6. (Credit: © Sunshine Special Developmental School.)

involved participation, and by others more *indirectly*, via noticing, feeling, and/or sensing others near to and around them.

Music is usually used in this phase to stimulate interaction and increase engagement with and between others. Music with strong rhythmic, vibrant qualities is often selected. Large fabric pieces are sometimes incorporated into the movement activities for the whole group to hold on to and shake, stretch, pull, or hide under, as a tangible means of connecting self to the others in the group. Through this physical connection, students are afforded opportunities to respond independently and collectively to those around them.

Phase 3: Cushion Rest

This phase provides an opportunity for students to recuperate from the active movement section and sense the qualitative difference between the body in motion and the body in stillness see Figure 27.6 below. Students are invited to sit or lie individually or in a group on cushions covered with blankets or fabric usually chosen by them. Therapeutically, this phase is intended to offer a moment for private reflection on what was experienced during the session, while also addressing the wellbeing signpost noted by Goldspink (2009, cited in DECS 2010), of the ability to rest and relax. The therapist and/or the classroom assistant (as directed) may rub and pat individual students to assist their repose. Soothing music is usually played to support the restful mood. Soft toys are sometimes incorporated into this phase as comfort objects, especially for younger students.

Phase 4: Closure

Closure follows directly after cushion rest and incorporates a brief movement ritual led by the therapist. This usually includes stretching and shaking of hands and feet, then arms and legs, followed by a whole-body wriggle and stretch. This serves to physically re-enliven students' bodies from their state of rest and to indicate that the dance session has finished. Students are thanked for their participation and directed to put on socks and shoes.

THE EMBODIED RELATIONSHIP

In some sessions, students are asked by the therapist to identify what it was they liked about their solo once they have finished. This feedback process is integral to DMT, as it encourages participants to make the transition between their non-verbal, bodily expression of thought and feeling to the higher cognitive process and more abstract verbalizing of thought and feeling in order to integrate their experience and give it meaning. Students' verbalizing of their experiences informs the therapist more directly about what was meaningful for the student in their movement choices, and also how the student understands their experience of dance. Similarly, the other students, as observers, are also invited to comment on what they liked most about their peers' movement.

These feedback moments afford the therapist the opportunities to practice the phenomenological technique of 'description', whereby they describe to a student what they noticed or enjoyed in the students' dance without requiring the student to explain *why* they moved in the manner that they did, or whether the movement could be rated 'good' or 'bad'. The student may then respond further by agreeing with or clarifying with the therapist what they particularly noticed and/or enjoyed. This inclusion of student voice and subjective and peer evaluation is concordant with concepts of constructivist pedagogy, as discussed previously.

Conclusion

Strong parallels can be identified between contemporary perspectives of wellbeing in relation to education and learning, and outcomes of creative dance and DMT, that have been posited by theorists and practitioners for decades. These fields share the goal of students achieving wellbeing across domains of learning that cover cognitive, emotional, physical, social, and moral/spiritual dimensions. This interesting confluence is documented in detail in this chapter, specifically in relation to students with learning disabilities, whose needs are often not well met by traditional teaching practices.

The relational pedagogy of contemporary education, which acknowledges the quality of the teacher–student relationship as central to effective learning, is explored in depth in relation to learning through dance and DMT, as is the constructivist paradigm for learning, with its priority on interactive learning practices, the building of knowledge on what is already known by students, and the process of learning above outcomes.

These ideas are illustrated in the example of a DMT programme led by dance movement therapist and teacher Mullane in an Australian special developmental school. This programme's informing methodologies of creative educational dance and DMT are explained along with ideas from existential phenomenology, including intersubjectivity and whole-person responding to life experiences, that inform the programme's activities.

While this chapter offers comprehensive articulation of theory about this DMT programme's contribution to student wellbeing, illustrated by a detailed programme example, it does not provide unequivocal substantiation. Research that properly evaluates outcomes of such a DMT programme (that is supported by relational pedagogy and constructivist paradigm of learning, as presented here) would be a useful development. The issue of how student progress within the DMT programme can be assessed has not been tackled here either. Challenges for this vital aspect of educational practice include the difficulties of measuring wellbeing outcomes of a DMT programme in a way that is useful in the therapeutic process, while also being meaningful for school leadership, teaching staff, and parents/carers. Further research to explore assessment and evaluation of such programmes would be useful in the context of a special developmental school as discussed in this example, and also other settings outside of education, and/or for children without disability.

NOTE

1. The term 'dance movement therapy' is used in Australia for the practice known as 'dance movement therapy' or 'dance movement psychotherapy' in the UK and 'dance/movement therapy' in the USA.

REFERENCES

Aron, L. and Loprest, P. (2012). 'Disability and the education system', *The Future of Children*, 22(1): 97–122.

Australian Curriculum (ACARA), Assessment and Reporting Authority (2013a). *The Shape of the Australian Curriculum v.4.0*. Sydney, NSW. <http://www.acara.edu.au/verve/_resources/The_Shape_of_the_Australian_Curriculum_v4.pdf>

Australian Curriculum (ACARA), Assessment and Reporting Authority (2013b). *Student Diversity and the Australian Curriculum: Advice for Principals, Schools and Teachers*. Sydney, NSW. <http://www.australiancurriculum.edu.au/StudentDiversity/Pdf/StudentDiversity>

Awartani, M., Whitman, C. V., and Gordon, J. (2008). 'Developing instruments to capture young people's perceptions of how school as a learning environment affects their well-being', *European Journal of Education*, 43(1): 51–70.

Baudino, L. (2010). 'Autism spectrum disorder: A case of misdiagnosis', *American Journal of Dance Therapy*, 32: 113–29.

Bernstein, P. L. (1975). *Theory and Methods in Dance-Movement Therapy*, 3rd edn. Iowa: Kendall-Hunt.

Berrol, C. (2006). 'Neuroscience meets dance/movement therapy: Mirror neurons, the therapeutic process and empathy', *The Arts in Psychotherapy*, 33: 302–15.

Bigger, S. (2011). *Self and Others: Relational Pedagogy for Critical Pupil Engagement*. Swindon Philosophical Society, 14 January 2011. Unpublished. <http://eprints.worc.ac.uk/1304/2/Self%2C_Others_and_Pedagogy.pdf> (accessed 13 October 2013).

Blom, L. A. and Chaplin, L. T. (1988). *The Moment of Movement*. Pennsylvania, PA: University of Pittsburgh Press.

Bond, K. (1994). 'Personal style a mediator of engagement in dance: Watching Terpsichore rise', *Dance Research Journal*, 26(1): 215–25.

Bond, K. (1999). 'Perspectives on dance therapy', in J. Guthrie, E. Loughlin, and D. Albiston (eds.), *Dance Therapy Collections II*. Melbourne: Dance Therapy Association of Australia, pp. 2–5.

Buirski, P. and Haglund, P. (2001). *Making Sense Together: The Intersubjective Approach to Psychotherapy*. London: Jason Aronson.

Burrows, L. (2011). 'Relational Mindfulness in Education', *Encounter: Education for Meaning and Social Justice*, 24(4): 24–29.

Carman, T. (1999). 'The body in Husserl and Merleau-Ponty', *Philosophical Topics*, 27(2): 205–26. <http://ist-socrates.berkeley.edu/~hdreyfus/188_s05/pdf/Carman_Body.pdf>

Commonwealth of Australia (2006). *Disability Standards for Education 2005*. <http://docs.education.gov.au/system/files/doc/other/disability_standards_for_education_2005_plus_guidance_notes.pdf>

Cust, J. (1976). *Creative Dance as an Integrated Subject in the Primary School Curriculum*. Sydney: Physical Education Publications Cooperative.

Csikszentmihalyi, M. (1990). *Flow: The Psychology of Optimal Experience*. New York, NY: Harper Collins.

Department of Education and Children's Services (DECS) (2007). *Towards a Learner Wellbeing Framework for Birth to Year 12*. Adelaide: South Australia Department of Education and Children's Services.

Department of Education and Children's Services (DECS) (2010). *Understanding Student engagement–rationale*. Adelaide: South Australia Department of Education and Children's Services.

Dunphy, K., Hearnes, T., and Toumbourou, J. (2009). 'Dance movement therapy in Australia: A survey of practitioners and practice', in K. Dunphy, J. Guthrie, and E. Loughlin (eds.), *Dance Therapy Collections 3*. Melbourne: DTAA

Dunphy, K. and Mullane, S. (2015). *Framework for Dance-Movement Assessment*. <http://www.makingdancematter.com.au>

Dunphy, K. and Scott, J. (2003). *Freedom to Move: Movement and Dance for People with Intellectual Disabilities*. NSW: Elsevier.

Exiner, J. and Kelynack, D. (1994). *Dance Therapy Redefined*. Springfield, IL: Charles C. Thomas.

Exiner, J. and Lloyd, P. (1987). *Learning Through Dance: A Guide for Teachers*. Melbourne: Oxford University Press.

Fraillon, J. (2005). *Measuring Student Well-Being in the Context of Australian Schooling: Discussion Paper*. Adelaide: South Australian Department of Education and Children's Services.

Fraleigh, S. (1991). 'A vulnerable glance: Seeing dance through phenomenology', *Dance Faculty Publications*, Paper 4. <http://digitalcommons.brockport.edu/dns_facpub/4>

Fraleigh, S. (1996). *Dance and the Lived Body*, 2nd edn. Pittsburgh, PA: University of Pittsburgh Press.

Fraser, D., Price, G., Aitken, V., Gilbert, G., Klemick, A., Rose, L., and Tyson, S. (2007). *Relational Pedagogy and the Arts*. <http://www.educationscotland.gov.uk/images/Relational%20pedagogy%20and%20the%20Arts_tcm4-529562.pdf>

Ginsberg, K. (2007). 'The importance of play in promoting healthy child development and maintaining strong parent–child bonds', *Paediatrics*, 119: 182–91.

Goldman, D. (2010). *I Want to be Ready: Improvised Dance as a Practice of Freedom*. Ann Arbor, MI: University of Michigan Press.

Gronlund, E., Renk, B., and Weibull, J. (2005). 'Dance movement therapy as an alternative treatment for young boys diagnosed with ADHA: A pilot study', *American Journal of Dance Therapy*, 27(2): 63–85.

Guthrie, J. and Roydhouse, J. (1988). *Come and Join the Dance: A Creative Approach to Movement for Children with Special Needs*. Melbourne: Hyland House.

H'Doubler, M. N. (1998). *Dance: A Creative Art Experience*, 3rd edn. Madison, WI: University of Wisconsin Press.

Hager, P. (2005). 'Philosophical accounts of learning', *Educational Philosophy and Theory*, 37(5): 649–66.

Halfon, N., Houtrow, A., Larson, K., and Newacheck, P. W. (2012). 'The changing landscape of disability in childhood', *The Future of Children*, 22(1): 13–42.

Hanna, J. L. (2008). 'A nonverbal language for imagining and learning: Dance education in K-1 curriculum', *Educational Researcher*, 37(8): 491–506.

Husserl, E. (1970). *The Crisis of European Sciences and Transcendental Phenomenology: An Introduction to Phenomenological Philosophy*. Evanston, IL: Northwestern University Press.

Joyce, M. (1980). *First Steps in Teaching Creative Dance to Children*, 2nd edn. Mountain View, CA: Mayfield.

Karkou, V. (ed.) (2010). *Arts Therapies in Schools: Research and Practice*. London: Jessica Kingsley.

Karkou, V. and Glasman, J. (2004). 'Arts, education and society: The role of the arts in promoting the emotional wellbeing and social inclusion of young people', *Support for Learning*, 19(2): 57–65.

Karkou, V. and Sanderson, P. (2006). *Arts Therapies: A Research-Based Map of the Field*. Edinburgh: Elsevier.

Kickbusch, I., Gordon, J., and O'Toole, L. (2012). *Learning for Well-being: A Policy Priority for Children and Youth in Europe. A Process for Change*. Learning for Well-being Consortium of Foundations in Europe, Universal Education Foundation.

Laban, R. (1988). *Modern Educational Dance*, 3rd edn. Plymouth: Northcote House.

Levy, F. (1988). 'The evolution of modern dance therapy', *Journal of Physical Education, Recreation and Dance*, 59: 34–41.

Levy, F. (2005). *Dance Movement Therapy: A Healing Art*, 2nd edn. Virginia: NDA.

McNiff, S. (1981). *The Arts and Psychotherapy*. Springfield, IL: Charles C. Thomas.

Masters, G. N. (2004). *Conceptualising and Researching Student Wellbeing*. <http://research.acer.edu.au/research_conference_2004/1> (accessed 9 October 2013).

McGarry, L. and Russo, F. (2011). 'Mirroring in dance/movement therapy: Potential mechanisms behind empathy enhancement', *The Arts in Psychotherapy*, 38(3): 178–84.

Meekums, B. (2002). *Dance Movement Therapy: A Creative Psychotherapeutic Approach*. London: Sage.

Ministerial Council on Education, Early Childhood Development and Youth Affairs (MCEECDYA) (2008). *Melbourne Declaration on Educational Goals for Young Australians*. Canberra: MCEECDYA. <http://www.curriculum.edu.au/verve/_resources/National_Declaration_on_the_Educational_Goals_for_Young_Australians.pdf>

NSW Department of Education and Communities (DEC). (2011). *The Psychological and Emotional Wellbeing Needs of Children and Young People: Models of Effective Practice in Educational Settings*. Sydney: NSW Department of Education and Communities (DEC).

Ostroff, S., O'Toole, L., and Kropf, D. (2007). *Reflections for Well-being in Education*, Universal Education Foundation. <http://www.uef-eba.org>

Payne, H. (ed). (1992). *Dance Movement Therapy: Theory and Practice*. London: Routledge.

Polkinghorne, D. (1994). 'A path of understanding for psychology', *Journal of Theoretical and Philosophical Psychology*, 14(2): 128–45.

Rodgers, C. R. and Raider-Roth, M. (2006). 'Presence in teaching', *Teachers and Teaching: Theory and Practice*, 12(3): 265–87.

Salgado, R. (2010). 'The use of dance in the rehabilitation of a patient with multiple sclerosis', *American Journal of Dance Therapy*, 32: 53–63.

Sarvimaki, A. (2006). 'Wellbeing as being well: A Heideggerian look at wellbeing', *International Journal of Qualitative Studies on Health and Well-being*, 1: 4–10.

Schmais, C. (1980). 'Dance therapy in perspective', in K. C. Mason (ed.), *Dance Therapy: Focus on Dance VII*. Reston, VA: American Alliance for Health, Physical Education and Recreation, pp. 7–12.

Schmais, C. (1986). 'Introduction to dance therapy', *American Journal of Dance Therapy*, 9: 23–30.

Shepard, L. (2000). 'The role of classroom assessment in a learning culture', *Educational Researcher*, 29(7): 1–14.

Sherborne, V. (1990). *Developmental Movement for Children: Mainstream, Special Needs and Pre-School*. Cambridge: Cambridge University Press.

Sidorkin, A. M. (2000). 'Toward a pedagogy of relation', *Faculty Publications* , Paper 17. <http://digitalcommons.ric.edu/facultypublications/17>

Slater, W. (1987). *Teaching Modern Educational Dance*. Plymouth: Northcote House.

Spinelli, E. (1995). *The Interpreted World: An Introduction to Phenomenological Psychology*. London: Sage.

Spinelli, E. (1996). *Workshop Notes, Changing Self-Changing World, Master Class*. Melbourne: Psychotherapy Australia.

Stinson, S. (1990). *Dance for Young Children: Finding the Magic in Movement*. Virginia: American Alliance for Health, Physical Education, Recreation and Dance.

Todres, L. (2007). *Embodied Enquiry: Phenomenological Touchstones for Research, Psychotherapy and Spirituality*. London: Palgrave Macmillan.

Tortora, S. (2011). '2010 Marian Chace Lecture. The need to be seen: From Winnicott to the mirror neuron system, dance/ movement therapy comes of age', *American Journal of Dance Therapy*, 33: 4–17.

Van Deurzen-Smith, E. (1988). *Existential Counselling in Practice*. London: Sage.

Vasko, Z. (2007). 'The arts and the authentic learner', *SFU Educational Review*, 1: 11–16.

Willis, J. (2009). *Assessment for Learning: A Sociocultural Approach: Proceedings of Changing Climates*. Education for Sustainable Futures Conference, Queensland, Australia, 2008. <http://eprints.qut.edu.au/29323/1/29323.pdf>

Winnicott, D. (1971/2005). *Playing and Reality*. New York, NY: Routledge.

....

CHAPTER 28

THE WELLBEING OF STUDENTS IN DANCE MOVEMENT THERAPY MASTERS PROGRAMMES

....

HILDA WENGROWER

INTRODUCTION

....

THIS inquiry deals with the link between dance/movement and wellbeing in postgraduate students in Dance Movement Therapy (DMT),[1] as perceived by lecturers and training programme directors. My interest in this subject came from many years of teaching, training, and supervising in DMT as well as my own experiences as a trainee. I realized, for example, that movement and dance may have very positive intrapersonal and interpersonal effects, at the same time as potentially presenting emotional challenges. This is especially so in an academic setting that combines scholastic demands with experiential/embodied learning.

In all DMT training programmes, experiential/embodied learning is intertwined with theoretical and clinical components to varying degrees. By experiential/embodied learning, I refer to the dance/movement experiences students go through in order to learn about development, therapeutic concepts, therapeutic modes of intervention, and so on, particularly through movement. These dance/movement experiences are unique to DMT. Other training programmes in clinical professions may include experiential teaching, but they do not include bodily or movement/dance experiences. In other helping professions there is also more differentiation between courses: theoretical, clinical, and personal–professional groups (Binks et al. 2013).

There are reports about stress in postgraduate students of the helping professions (Binks et al. 2013; Dyrbye et al. 2006; Dziegielewski et al. 2004; Feiner 1998). It is stated that these specialities—such as psychology, nursing, and social work—that bring together classroom work and research with a clinical training component, might induce more stress than other programmes.

Another point is brought forth by Brodbeck's research. He focused on anxiety from the psychoanalytic candidates' point of view in their training, which takes place in psychoanalytic institutes, outside the orbit of universities (Brodbeck 2008). Although psychoanalytic training is carried on in private institutions, Brodbeck (2008) brings up some points that are relevant to the training of dance/movement therapists. In both practices, as well as in many health professions, the personal aptitude of the professional plays a key role in the effectiveness of the treatment, 'therefore, the person, as a whole, is trained and evaluated' (329). This, he says, is an unavoidable source of anxiety. In this aspect, the training in DMT has commonalities with training in psychotherapy and counselling. However, the particular bodily involvement marks an important difference between them.

Wellbeing

Keyes et al. (2002) consider wellbeing as a composite construct that combines subjective wellbeing (SWB) and psychological wellbeing (PWB). These concepts stem from two traditions: one associated with happiness (hedonic wellbeing) and the other with human potential (eudaimonic wellbeing). 'Subjective wellbeing is evaluation of life in terms of satisfaction and balance between positive and negative affect; psychological wellbeing entails perception of engagement with existential challenges of life' (1,007). SWB comprises overall appraisals of affect and life quality, and is related to feelings of happiness and cognitive evaluations of life satisfaction. PWB relates to perceived self-fulfilment and development when confronting life's challenges (such as learning a profession, growing and developing as a person, or pursuing significant goals). Although empirically different, these concepts are related; combined, they are associated with sociodemographic features and personality. I will return to these concepts in the 'Discussion' section.

Stress and Wellbeing in Students

The most-used definition of stress states that it is 'a relationship between the person and the environment that is appraised by the person as taxing or exceeding his or her resources and endangering his or her wellbeing' (Lazarus and Folkman 1984, p. 19). Furthermore, there is ample research discussing and establishing the impact of anxiety and stress on SWB and PWB in the general population. (For some examples, see Casey 2012; Cohen and Wills 1985; Harrell 2000; Norris et al. 1992; Nyklíček and Kuijpers 2008.)

Postgraduate students, and in our case, those enrolled studying a helping profession, confront stress in high percentages. In a survey of 438 psychology graduate students, more than 70% of them reported a stressor that hindered their sensation of wellbeing (El-Ghoroury et al. 2012; Pakenham and Stafford-Brown 2012). Payne (2001, 2004) published a survey on personal development groups run in postgraduate training of counsellors and arts therapists, and several articles on the issues raised by the members of a particular group in a British Masters programme (Payne 2001, 2004). Payne's study focused on personal development groups. It did not relate to curriculum courses characterized by different kinds of learning—experiential and theoretical—and did not include academic evaluation such as it is manifested in marks and their possible influence on students' experience of wellbeing.

Experiential/Embodied Learning

The term 'experiential learning' refers to mainly movement experiences aimed to grasp body–mind reciprocal interactions, concepts, theories, and dance/movement therapeutic processes. Hobbs (1992) underlines that 'the experiential learning process has to be a collaborative venture between teacher and learner. It involves all participants . . . in a process of mutual vulnerability and risk taking, of personal challenge and learning' (Hobbs 1992, p. xiv). I propose that this personal challenge may have some impact on the SWB and/or the PWB of the students. Nevertheless, I agree with Hobbs (1992) when he criticizes the solely theoretical presentation of information in an intellectual way, since it does not involve the person in an examination of her reaction to the subject matter. In his opinion, this could result in an unsuitable use of knowledge. In this experiential learning process, the whole learner is involved and invited to engage in an attitudinal and behavioural change. This emotional involvement is true for training in any helping profession, and as Hobbs states, implicates the tutor as well (Binks et al. 2013; Dudley et al. 1998; Meekums et al. 2010).

Since DMT emphasizes the influence of the non-verbal in many aspects of healthy and pathological aspects of life, experiential embodied learning is necessary for thorough training, although not exempt of risks, as stated previously. I hypothesized that since universities still centre a large part of their instruction on classical academic teaching, experiential learning in university settings might add a factor of stress that could impinge on the students' wellbeing due to conflicts between the university as institution and the DMT programme.

Questions of the Research

1. Do directors, conveners, and lecturers observe their students feel high emotional demands that stem from the experiential/embodied learning?

2. Do they perceive any risk to the wellbeing of the students connected to this issue?
3. How do DMT programmes deal with the conflicts between evaluation and facilitating self-disclosure in the experiential aspects of training?

METHODOLOGY

The research paradigm adopted is hermeneutical phenomenology. A questionnaire with open-ended questions was designed in order to respond to the three questions. The first step was to reach directors, conveners, and core lecturers teaching at the postgraduate DMT programmes run in universities in Asia, Europe, the Middle East, North America, and South America. The intention was to obtain a wide array of answers encompassing different cultures in order to reveal whether there are cultural particularities that affect the questions that motivate this research. E-mails were sent to thirty-three addressees aiming to cover all the master programmes in university settings. The topic was presented to them, and they were asked if they would collaborate by filling in the questionnaire. Three persons refused to participate, indicating that they needed more time than they had in order to speak about the institution where they worked. Eighteen colleagues from fifteen institutions answered, and I am grateful to all of them (see Acknowledgements).

The topics in the questionnaire were related to institutional aspects, the students' profile, if they were required to prove previous personal therapy, and their earlier studies. Class atmosphere and sources of stress for the students according to the respondents' perspective were also asked. The data collected were analyzed according to thematic analysis procedures (Braun and Clarke 2006). Excerpts from the answers received are presented in italics in the next section. Clarifications by the author are included in brackets in non-italics.

FINDINGS

Institutional Aspects

The questionnaire addressed organizational issues such as the character of the university as expressed in its values or mission stated, their harmony/discord with the DMT programme, and administrations' attitude towards the programme. One of the conclusions of Pascarella and Terenzini (2005) after twenty years of research is that the context, mission, and environment of the university exert an important influence on the students' personal development and learning. Every institution creates its own demands on the faculty, but it is with the students where this authority is more clearly perceived. The authors focused on undergraduate students. The answers of the respondents to my survey did not find any substantial connection to the research questions, although a participant wrote:

What I hear from friends on the faculty is usually about struggles to really understand what our work aims for and needs.

A professional working in a very similar establishment experienced collaboration and dialogue for many years, and a reciprocal movement of mutual understanding. As an example, she mentions the subdivision of the students into small groups, which is not always convenient in financial terms. So this aspect requires further examination. Closely related to this topic are some of the following categories covered in the questionnaire used in this survey.

Students' Backgrounds

The hypothesis for asking about previous studies or professions of the students is that different backgrounds may affect two aspects: students' adroitness to handle the emotional demands of experiential/embodied learning, and their ability to move with an inner, intrapersonal focus, as is needed in DMT practice. This ability sets students in a positive frame of mind to meet an important challenge in their studies.

According to the respondents, trainees come from a wide assortment of fields: health sciences, education, dance, and even business management. Dance and movement experience is asked of candidates. Interestingly, the major reference to obstacles stemming from the undergraduate education concerned those with a strong dance background. Participants in the survey reported that those students were specifically challenged for two reasons. They had to change their approach to dance/movement from a performing art to a mode of introspection and interpersonal communication, and secondly, to connect to their personal movement unhampered by style and technique. One participant observed:

In my experience, students with a dance background have had a harder time letting go of their training and aesthetic values of movement, and have had to delve deeper into an exploration of who they are apart from their training—finding their own movement-based discovery of their personality, and developing it as a future therapist. This often comes up in discussions within movement observation, where they need to develop awareness of their own movements' preferences, and how these can affect the patient/ client—therapist relationship.

However, one respondent mentioned that dancers chose to study DMT with a clear motivation:

... dancers ... find the most satisfying part of their dance activity is the creative process and working with others.

The director of a programme found it challenging helping students at the beginning of the course to relax and allow their expression and creativity to flow freely. This may also be an issue for trainees from different backgrounds that stems from the anxiety of being subjected to new situations. This last finding takes us to the following point.

Requirements of Any Kind of Personal Psychotherapy

When dealing with stress and its impact on wellbeing, the assistance of personal therapy can become relevant. Nowadays, no programme demands personal psychotherapy from their candidates prior to admission. One course adopting the norms of the national association of psychotherapy in its country accepted the student's personal psychotherapy before entering the training. Any form of psychotherapy with a licensed psychotherapist was accepted in this case in order to obtain the MA qualification. Students might have done this before entering the programme, or might undergo psychotherapy during the programme.

Regarding personal therapy during the studies, there was a clear difference between European universities and those situated on other continents, with one exception in the latter group. The former demanded some kind of personal therapy during the studies. Most but not all of the respondents of non-European countries reported that they did not officially require this; instead, personal therapy was recommended. In some countries it was illegal to make such a demand on students in universities. Nonetheless, personal therapy, be it individual or a group setting, was seen as important for personal and professional development. As in other helping professions, personal development was considered inextricable from the professional. In many programmes it was recommended as a support for the emotional issues emerging in the students from experiential/embodied learning. The emotional impact of this learning and its impact on wellbeing was recognized; therefore, personal therapy was considered as a means to buttress the students' learning, enhance their capability to stay in the apprentice role, and to profit adequately from their studies.

One programme that had primarily an academic character and viewed professional education of secondary importance did not require therapy. In this country, as in others, the profession was not officially recognized, and registration as a professional was based on one's undergraduate studies. This was the explanation given for not asking for personal therapy. However, they reported that during staff meetings they were beginning to ponder about the value of personal therapy. Staff felt that although the programme had an academic focus, the use of experiential learning was, at times, raising stressful experiences in the students.

One respondent from a university in the United States, which did not require therapy (though it recommended it), commented that their students used the university counselling service. This was available on

> a no-fee basis, and we've been told that our students are very heavy 'consumers' of this service. Students who have the financial means sometimes enter dance/movement therapy with therapists in the community. Legally this cannot be a requirement.

If this programme would have been allowed to include dance/movement therapy in this counselling service, this would have meant more recognition of DMT and an opportunity for students to have easier access to it.

In another North American institution, it was found that the trainers' recommendation was *reinforced by second-year students when they met with incoming students in orientation. They spoke from their own experience of the value of personal therapy had been* [*sic*] *to their training and ability to manage the first year.* The 'ability to manage' refers to the aptitude to cope with stressing situations that may affect wellbeing.

A lecturer in a European university states that personal therapy supports students to *maintain the professional boundaries of their ... training and professional working relationships with their tutors, peers, and processing of client material.* In addition, *many of them are international, and finding their feet in a new country and culture can be difficult.*

Other colleagues mention directly one of the main interests of this research: the emotional demands the experiential/embodied learning exerts upon the trainees:

> *The rationale for personal therapy is to provide particular support throughout the intensive immersion within DMT as the opening up of the body usually uncovers personal issues that cannot be addressed within an academic setting. When students have difficulties throughout the programme, they are referred to bring their issues to their own therapy.*
>
> *During our experiential classes that take part on a regular basis, many of these personal issues may be touched upon—students may become aware of important aspects that have to do with their private lives. We believe that these contents cannot be contained or covered in the training itself but need personal attention outside ... From our experience it has been very useful for our students to have such a personal space and, wherever students have not been in therapy* (for whatever reason), *this has been very obvious to us through their process and development within the course.*

Personal therapy during the studies is also seen as contributing to students´ identity as future professionals: *I think personal therapy is necessary in the process of becoming a psychotherapist. Still I leave it to personal autonomy because it is difficult to be managed within a school education system.*

In another training programme, although there is no official requirement for personal therapy, *it was a strong message transmitted to the pupils, and there was no case that somebody finished her studies without being committed in a therapy.* This was a question that was raised in the individual tutorials, not as a command but as an advice, relating it to learning to be a therapist: *to understand the therapeutic encounter, personal growth, awareness of one's own reactions, countertransference.*[2]

Emotional Class Atmosphere, Advantages, and Risks

Some questions in the survey aimed to distinguish between the atmosphere in theoretical and experiential courses, and asked whether unspoken wishes for personal therapy had been detected and how the trainer–trainee relationship was kept without sliding into a psychotherapeutic one. Unexpressed wishes for therapy with a lecturer might generate frustration in the student and probably discomfort in the trainer. This situation could be considered a hindrance to maintaining the academic setting and affect the experience of wellbeing in this specific situation.

A lecturer, who included theory in her teaching, affirmed that the atmosphere in class was different from therapy, and she strived to create a favourable relational ambiance. She did not perceive 'therapeutic fantasies', *since the frame of reference is very clear, differences are stated clearly from the beginning: artistic creation/learning/therapy.* This respondent considered that the elucidated differentiation between the different areas concerned with dance/movement was enough to preserve a safe learning environment in class.

The convener in a programme with emphasis on professional training reported that the class atmosphere was very special and there was meaningful feedback from the students. Regarding the management of the emotional processes in class, she added:

> (We say) *there will be* (emotions and processes) *that won't be closed* (worked through) *in class, the experience is in service of learning. We listen to the experience* (what the student tells about it) *without entering into personal histories and we link it with the learning content. We try to contain the frustration and turn them to personal therapy. Although sometimes stories are opened . . . we found a balance, I did not receive complaints.*

She clearly referred to the frustration of experiencing some strong emotion or some personal issue that could not be dealt with immediately in a learning context:

> *It happens quite often. If that occurs it is taken into consideration. But it shouldn't prevent from fulfilling educational tasks. Then the task of the teacher is to use it as an example to explore dynamics of the therapy ... The teaching process is directed by learning goals. In other words we can say that everything in class is submitted to the learning goals. But when all the students are in therapy, usually enough awareness is developed about what to bring to the study situation and what not.*

This idea is also mentioned by a colleague teaching in another continent.

> *If it is difficult for some students to carry on learning tasks and personal process starts prevailing. Sometimes a student can have a meeting with the director to talk about what is difficult in the studies, and if a person is going through a crisis (a difficult life situation), an individual plan can be thought for the person (studies can be taken for a longer period of time than usual).*

One colleague admits that: *Certain experiential courses for example aim to be as close as possible to a conceivable clinical setting, so criteria such as punctuality, participation, reflection, and so on, are essential.*

This means that experiential learning does not imply loss of boundaries or less important learning. On the contrary, in order to deal with delicate issues, the framework has to stay stable, clear, and consistent through time—particularly because, one respondent reported, there is the probability of *a general belief* (between students) *that the tutor is always available and that there is a telepathic relationship between staff.* This colleague maintains the boundaries of student–teacher by employing concepts from educational psychotherapy that addresses learning difficulties on an emotional basis.

We may consider the illusion of a telepathic linkage as a manifestation of the feelings of dependency from some students towards staff members that may arise in many learning situations and that are increased due to the emotional arousal rooted in experiential learning.

An interesting comment came from a European colleague: the atmosphere from experiential learning may radiate into different settings in the studies in a positive way.

> ... the teachers of theoretical subjects are very satisfied with the classes of arts therapies students because they are very curious, cooperative, creative, interested in interactive teaching-learning process. I suppose that students' involvement in a special class dynamics in the experiential teaching settings influences on [sic] the theoretical settings.

Does the related clinical DMT experience create some negative effect in class? This question aimed to engender further detail and give participants another opportunity to reflect on their experience and to share it. All the respondents very firmly backed experiential/embodied learning, some of them could not see any negative aspect:

> I don't really see the negative impact ... Most often I see students learning and growing from these experiences.

Nonetheless, some qualified their statement as follows:

> I have seen this rare, in instances of a student who did not have the maturity or self-reflective capacity necessary for self-regulation.

A colleague added another issue:

> No, I do not see any negative effect. But, what is difficult is how to help the students get relaxed and to stimulate and open their creativity and expressiveness at the beginning, which is the key to digest their experiential courses.

The following statements were provided by two younger respondents who had fresh memories from their time as students.

First colleague:

> The journey of self-discovery through experiential work can be extremely painful and overwhelming for students. It ruffles feathers in bringing unconscious processes to the surface and making them conscious ... I feel from my own personal experience of undertaking a training programme, it felt enough of a struggle attending the course on a part-time basis.

Second colleague:

> I think, stemming from my own experience when I was a DMT student, that the self-knowledge and body-based information that derives from the experiential work in class can be very intense. I often equate it with opening the floodgates, where the body is finally given a voice within your personal process. I believe that for some students, this opening of a floodgate can be overwhelming—there is a lot of self-growth that occurs within DMT training—and coming to terms with one's movement background.

Stress

Different aspects were indicated as stressors for graduate students: personal sources for stress encompass economic, work, and family factors, or breaking an intimate relationship. Stressors properly related to studies were those connected with academic demands, test anxiety, evaluation of professional competence, and fitness. Specifically in our case, self-disclosure in movement experiential learning was a factor to be considered. Nichol (1997), for example, carried on a research study on emotional pain in learning when applying group analysis, and found that the prospect of self-disclosure brought anxiety. Binks et al. (2013) interviewed group facilitators of clinical psychology students about their perceptions of students' experience in the reflective practice groups, which are different from classes in DMT. These facilitators reported anxiety and emotional pain in the students. Some of the professionals leading these groups expressed their preoccupation for students' wellbeing.

Most of the respondents to our survey considered that studying DMT can be very demanding and included similar concerns as those found by Binks et al. (2013). In this survey, the challenge of internships was particularly noted by many colleagues: anxiety about meeting patients, questioning what they knew and how they would perform, understanding what therapy was, handling uncertainty, and balancing all of these with academic demands.

Some of the training programmes participating in the survey admitted foreign students: Argentina's programmes were a pole of attraction for persons from other Latin American countries, while some USA and European Masters programmes admitted foreign students from all over the world. For these trainees the processes of sojourn augment the stressing issues they had to deal with, thus their subjective perception of wellbeing might be impaired. Fulfilling the diverse academic demands with personal life might be very thorny for some students.

In the category of personal stressors, a colleague included the lack of body-dance training; she observed a limitation in the interpretation of one's own body manifestations. I can also report that, based on my own personal experience as a trainer, student constraints around improvisation or attending to the body signs were additional factors of stress in DMT training. Finally, students often compared themselves with others or felt they could not live up to the desired standards.

Self-disclosure

There might be a cultural aspect in self-disclosure as a source of stress. However, answers indicated that they did not consider self-disclosure a stressor for students who came from countries so diverse as Argentina, Slovenia, and UK.

> *Through this embodied training students go through deep personal transformation. Sometimes it is not possible to foresee the depth and the pain the individual can encounter during this process. In all cases everyone becomes more oneself and in touch with real needs and quests. Sometimes the individual can realize that DMT is not the profession but the way for personal growth and healing; some can meet unresolved issues and changes in life which can ask for a pause in DMT studies to solve them.*

We could say that the movement experiences 'move a person from her known place'.

Another factor may be the different impacts this strain causes upon the trainers themselves. At least one colleague answered relating to her experience of stress and not to the students' experience. Binks et al. (2013) also received testimonies of the facilitators' stress when leading the personal–professional groups. Hobbs (1992), too, realized that experiential learning comprises uncertainty and anxiety for facilitators as well as for trainees. The responses included the following remarks:

> *Students are satisfied to have such an opportunity* (for self-disclosure).
> *Yes, it takes and needs care from the group members and teaching staff to develop and support respect and trust. It can become an issue for a number of students. From my perspective, those students who have enough inner security for self-disclosure— can get more from the studies and from their therapy and have more resources to deal with difficulties in study situation. And it's easier for a teacher to consider, negotiate, and contain and to share responsibility for carrying out learning tasks. In this case the exchange, communication, and awareness are easier for both sides.*
> *Self-disclosure can also be a distraction when it opens something the class doesn't serve or a new experience for the student who has trouble with the openness exercised.*

The next comment incorporates the consideration that students may have regarding their image in their peers' eyes for their future career, while the second quotation points to the students being aware of the delicate boundaries between training and therapy, their capability to contain themselves and be contained:

> *It causes high stress for some students. Self-disclosure is stressful for the students because they should continue to study and work within the same community.*
> *Many students question how much can I disclose that is safe? Safe within the context of the group they are sharing and disclosing to, and also how much they can cope with unpacking difficult and emotional material.*

Payne (2001) and Binks et al., (2013) met the concern for safety in self-development groups in some British training programmes. Payne (2001) researched a group in DMT training, Binks et al. (2013) students of clinical psychology. Although there are differences in the setting between the self-development group and an academic programme, in all the cases there is a common concern about how much to express, what to express, and how this disclosure will influence the student's image in her present role and in her future career development. This is an important consideration for trainers.

Another colleague adds the interpersonal disclosure:

> ... allowing themselves to be seen and known by others as they get to know themselves in a deeper way.

Participants in the survey were asked whether they witnessed some difficult or negative effects in class and how they interpret this. For some colleagues, the beneficial contribution of dance/movement is so significant that they could not understand the question. Almost all the answers stated the helpful influence on students' personal development and learning.

> Most often, I see students learning and growing from these experiences.

Problems were observed in those students without previous experience in reflective work through movement, or in those that have to overcome the image/identity of the professional dancer. Another source for difficulties was seen in the lack of personal therapeutic experience; some of those students had to learn to regulate how much to open themselves in the learning setting. In the words of one of the respondents:

> I have seen this rarely and in instances of students who did not have the maturity or self-reflective capacity necessary for self-regulation ... programme exerts more of a demand, since it is based on the body, and embodied practice, which can be stressful, but in the longer run is more beneficial for our students.

Another one added: *I observe that the creative process and the relations in the group of students help to overcome the negative aspects.*

A colleague wrote a statement that complements the above:

> No, I do not see any negative effect. But, what is difficult is how to help the students get relaxed and to stimulate and open their creativity and expressiveness, especially at the beginning, which is the key to digest their experiential courses.

DISCUSSION

For many years, many training programmes for different health professions have been leaning on experiential learning of some kind (Truax and Carkhuff 1964; Feiner 1998). There is research that informs about high levels of stress, anxiety, and emotional pain.

It seems that some threat to wellbeing in experiential learning or any other apprenticeship of a helping profession is unavoidable or intrinsic to the learning process and
is also valued as preparing for future work and professional identity. This stems from
research addressing trainees (Brodbeck 2008; Nichol 1997) as well as trainers (Binks
et al. 2013). There is no research on the training of dance/movement therapists on
this issue.

All of the sources reported previously arrive at similar conclusions: facilitators have
to present clear objectives and the course plan at the beginning. Interweaving of theory, research and practice with the experiential teaching is necessary in order to avoid
psychological harm and prepare students for professional demands (Dudley et al. 1998;
Feiner 1998). When trainees are exposed to relevant information, the level of anxiety
decreases; they can see how their experiences were already described and lived by others. This is very similar to what Yalom (Yalom and Leazcz 2005) denominated universality as a therapeutic factor in groups: group participants can discover that their challenges
are also the troubles of others. Knowledge may be generalized to other situations as well
(Dudley et al. 1998). Pakenham and Stafford-Brown (2012) propose the introduction of
stress management techniques based on mindfulness for clinical psychology trainees.

All the colleagues responding to the present survey resort to at least some of the
didactic steps mentioned in the previous paragraph. They reported establishing boundaries through the creation of links between embodied experiences with learning outcomes. From the very beginning of the course they explained the difference between
experiencing in class and in personal therapy. Other measures employed included personal interviews—referral to a personal therapy.

Most of the respondents did not find the experiential learning through dance and
movement counterproductive to students' wellbeing; rather, they saw it as inherent
to DMT. It was integrated with other pedagogical measures and was used to evaluate
positively the personal process of growth in their students. They considered dance/
movement as a tool/process to learn about oneself, others, and a profession. This was
not threatening the students' wellbeing, provided that trainees were assisted by personal therapy, use of the tutorial time, transmuted their stereotypes about dance, and
abandoned the emphasis on technical ability to give way to self-reflection and basic
movement. However, two younger colleagues, newer to the role of trainers, conveyed
very clearly their perceptions of the challenge that the experiential/embodied learning
imposed on the students. As presented previously, their testimonies were more emotionally charged or more empathic to the students' process, probably because they were
closer to them in time in this experience.

Respondents did not perceive universities' institutional characteristics as impinging
on their work, though some of them acknowledged conflicts and confirmed that solutions had to be found.

Another measure taken to help students to confront the emotions that might affect
their wellbeing was to include personal therapy for the trainee as either as requisite
or as a recommendation, depending on the country's regulations and their experience. Students were referred to the counselling services of the university when those
were available and were considered to be 'heavy consumers' of these services, as one

respondent expressed it. It would be very helpful if DMT were one of the available choices.

There was a clear difference between programmes in North America, South America, Asia, and Europe. The European Association DMT (EADMT, 2017) establishes personal therapy as a requirement. Associations in other continents recommend it. States' legal regulations for higher education as well as the lack of official recognition were adduced as causes for this. Nevertheless, the profession was not officially recognized in some European countries either, and still the requirement for therapy was kept.

Further consideration is needed with regards to viewing students' challenges of experiential/embodied learning through the constructs of PWB and of SWB, introduced at the beginning of this chapter. PWB involves the perception one has of oneself as confronting life's challenges, enabling the containment of negative emotions or difficult situations lived throughout the learning process. According to Keyes et al. (2002), there is a direct relation between optimal wellbeing (high SWB and PWB) and age, education, extraversion, and conscientiousness, and an inverse relationship to neuroticism. In their research, adults scoring higher in PWB than SWB were younger, had more education, and showed more openness to experience. Goodman and Holroyd (1993) found that DMT students scored higher than a control group of social welfare and psychology students in openness to experience or receptivity. More than this, the DMT trainees entered the programme with higher levels of these features than their counterparts in the comparison group formed by other mental-health trainees. This 'suggests either that individuals attracted to this area of study have a propensity for the experiential set, and/or that selection processes have implicitly chosen those with a talent for this way of functioning' (Goodman and Holroyd 1993: 43). These characteristics are appropriate for experiential/embodied learning, imply a yielding of control and a degree of relaxation that may enable one to go through the demands it sets in an easier way. We can add that probably the trainers share these characteristics, therefore they themselves are less impacted by the students' difficulties than are their counterparts, the clinical psychology facilitators interviewed by Binks et al. (2013). Since Goodman and Holroyd's (1993) research studied a small number of students, this finding needs to be further investigated.

According to Keyes et al., PWB is related with perceptions of self-fulfilment and personal development, which probably are felt by students and help them to endure the challenges they meet during their studies, even though if sometimes their SWB decreases.

The positive effects of dance on affect, relaxation, and mood might influence the SWB of the students as defined by Keyes et al. (2002) and moderate the strain elicited by the aspects already mentioned.

Another contributing factor to the trainers' perspective may lie in dance's and DMT's effect as decreasing stress, facilitating stress management, improving perception of wellbeing, and positive affects (Bräuninger 2014; Jeong et al. 2005; Koch et al. 2014; Quiroga Murcia et al. 2010; West et al. 2004).

The unique use of movement/dance in the training of DMT students is seen as a positive characteristic in spite of, or perhaps because of, the challenge it poses to students in an academic setting.

CONCLUSION

Throughout this chapter I have brought together many references that mention the emotional challenges that experiential learning poses on the trainees. Research has been based on students' reports, measures, or interviews, as well as on trainers' perspectives.

Experiential teaching in DMT is distinctive in that it is based on movement/dance. The colleagues participating in this survey admitted being aware of the difficulties it poses to the students: the anxiety related to self-discovery, self-disclosure, changing their approach to dance, and moving 'from within' instead of emphasizing external appearance. Nonetheless, they evaluate the benefits as being higher, and acknowledge that the students overcome the momentary impact on their wellbeing. The positive effects of dance and movement on stress management, positive affects, and wellbeing are probably an intervening factor.

We still lack research on what goes on with this learning in terms of its influence on students' wellbeing, but this chapter is an initial contribution to this subject, and the next step addresses the learners' voice as the focus of interest. The testimonies of the younger colleagues participating in this research brought the strongest emotional tone of all the answers received. The metaphorical expressions that were used may provide a hint of the emotional pain Nichol (1997) discussed, and which seems to be more present in these respondents. To close, I offer two excerpts—one from one of these young colleagues, and the other from an expert:

> I think, stemming from my own experience when I was a DMT student, that the self-knowledge and body-based information that derives from the experiential work in class can be very intense. I often equate it with opening the floodgates ...
> ... (the) programme exerts more of a demand, since it is based on the body, and embodied practice, which can be stressful, but in the longer run is more beneficial for our students.

ACKNOWLEDGEMENTS

I express my gratitude to the following colleagues who gave their time and thought to make this research possible: Thania Acaron, Queen Margaret University, Edinburgh, Scotland; Zoe Avstreih, Naropa University, Colorado; Irina Biryukova, Director of Dance/Movement Psychotherapy, Department of the Institute of Practical Psychology and Psychoanalysis, Moscow; Marcela Bottinelli, Instituto Universitario de las Artes, Buenos Aires; Jill Bounce, University of Derby, England; Gitit Burstyn, Academic College of Society and the Arts, Netanya, Israel; Aurelia Chillemi, Instituto Universitario de las Artes, Buenos Aires; Karin Fleischer, Instituto Universitario de las Artes, Buenos Aires; Birgitta Härkönen Smidhammar, Dans-och cirkushögskolan, Stockholm; Breda Krofilc, Faculty of Education, University of Ljubljana, Slovenia; Julie Leavitt, Lesley College, Boston, Massachussetts; Susan Loman, Antioch University New England, New Hampshire; Carly Marchant, Queen Margaret University, Edinburgh, Scotland; Julie Miller, Pratts, New York; Heidrun Panhofer, Universitat Autónoma de Barcelona, Spain; Maralia Reca, CAECE, Buenos Aires; Bon Soon Ryu, Graduate School of Healthcare Science, Soonchunhyang University, Seoul; Ellen Schelly Hill, Drexel University, Philadelphia.

Notes

1. The abbreviation DMT is used in this text for naming the profession Dance Movement Therapy or Dance Movement Psychotherapy.
2. Countertransference: briefly, the emotions, thoughts, and sensations a therapist feels related to a patient.

References

Binks, C., Jones, F. W., and Knight, K. (2013). 'Facilitating reflective practice groups in clinical psychology training: A phenomenological study', *Reflective Practice*, (ahead-of-print), 1–14.

Braun, V., and Clarke, V. (2006). 'Using thematic analysis in psychology', *Qualitative Research in Psychology*, 3(2): 77–101.

Bräuninger, I. (2014). 'Specific dance movement therapy interventions—which are success-ful?: An intervention and correlation study', *The Arts in Psychotherapy*, 41(5): 445–57.

Brodbeck, H. (2008). 'Anxiety in psychoanalytic training from the candidate's point-of-view', *Psychoanalytic Inquiry*, 28(3): 329–44.

Casey, L. (2012). 'Stress and wellbeing in Australia in 2012: A state-of-the-nation survey'. <http://www.psychology.org.au/Assets/Files/Stress%20and%20wellbeing%20in%20 Australia%202011%20Report%20(2)[1].pdf> (accessed 8 September 2013).

Cohen, S. and Wills, T. A. (1985). 'Stress, social support, and the buffering hypothesis', *Psychological Bulletin*, 98: 310–57.

Dyrbye, L. N., Thomas, M. R., and Shanafelt, T. D. (2006). 'Systematic review of depression, anxiety and other indicators of psychological distress among US and Canadian medical stu-dents', *Academic Medicine*, 81(4): 354–73.

Dudley, J., Gilroy, A., and Skaife, S. (1998). 'Learning from experience in introductory art ther-apy groups', in S. Skaife and V. Huet (eds.), *Art Psychotherapy Groups: Between Pictures and Words*. Florence, KY: Taylor and Frances/Routledge, pp. 181–203.

Dziegielewski, S. F., Roest-Marti, S., and Turnage, B. (2004). 'Addressing stress with social work students: a controlled evaluation', *Journal of Social Work Education*, 40(1): 105–19.

El-Ghoroury, N. H., Galper, D. I., Sawaqdeh, A., and Bufka, L. F. (2012). 'Stress, coping, and barriers to wellness among psychology graduate students,' *Training and Education in Professional Psychology*, 6(2): 122–34.

European Association Dance Movement Therapy (EADMT). http://www.eadmt.com/? action=article&id=39 (accessed 23 March 2017)

Feiner, S. E. (1998). 'Course design: An integration of didactic and experiential approaches to graduate training of group therapy', *International Journal of Group Psychotherapy*, 48(4): 439–60.

Goodman, L. and Holroyd, J. (1993). 'Are dance/movement therapy trainees a distinctive group?', *American Journal of Dance Therapy*, 15(1): 35–45.

Harrell, S. P. (2000). 'A multidimensional conceptualization of racism-related stress: Implications for the well-being of people of color', *American Journal of Orthopsychiatry*, 70(1): 42–57.

Hobbs, T. (ed.) (1992). *Experiential Training, Practical Guidelines*. London: Tavistock/ Routledge.

Jeong, Y. J., Hong, S. C., Lee, M. S., Park, M. C., Kim, Y. K., and Suh, C. M. (2005). 'Dance movement therapy improves emotional responses and modulates neurohormones in adolescents with mild depression', *International Journal of Neuroscience*, 115(12): 1711–20.

Keyes, C. L., Shmotkin, D., and Ryff, C. D. (2002). 'Optimizing well-being: The empirical encounter of two traditions', *Journal of Personality and Social Psychology*, 82(6): 1007–22.

Koch, S., Kunz, T., Lykou, S., and Cruz, R. (2014). 'Effects of dance movement therapy and dance on health-related psychological outcomes: A meta-analysis', *The Arts in Psychotherapy*, 41(1): 46–64.

Lazarus, R. S. and Folkman, S. (1984). *Stress, Appraisal, and Coping*. New York, NY: Springer.

Meekums, B., Allegranti, B., and Bunce, J. (2010). 'Developing Constructive tutor-student communication by becoming more aware of "thinking through the body"'. Obtained privately from the first author.

Nichol, B. (1997). 'Emotional pain in learning: Applying group analytic experience in non-clinical fields', *Group Analysis* 30: 93–105.

Norris, R., Carroll, D., and Cochrane, R. (1992). 'The effects of physical activity and exercise training on psychological stress and well-being in an adolescent population', *Journal of Psychosomatic Research*, 36(1): 55–65.

Nyklíček, I. and Kuijpers, K. F. (2008). 'Effects of mindfulness-based stress reduction intervention on psychological well-being and quality of life: Is increased mindfulness indeed the mechanism?', *Annals of Behavioral Medicine*, 35(3): 331–40.

Pakenham, K. I. and Stafford-Brown, J. (2012). 'Stress in clinical psychology trainees: Current research status and future directions', *Australian Psychologist*, 47(3), 147–55.

Pascarella, E. and Terenzini, P. (2005). *How College Affects Students: Findings and Insights from Twenty Years of Research: Vol. 2. A Third Decade of Research*. California: Jossey-Bass.

Payne, H. (2001). 'Students' experiences of a dance movement therapy group: The question of safety', *The European Journal of Psychotherapy, Counselling and Health*, 4(2): 167–292.

Payne, H. (2004). 'Becoming a client, becoming a practitioner: Student narratives from a dance movement therapy group', *British Journal of Guidance and Counselling*, 32(4): 512–32.

Quiroga Murcia, C., Kreutz, G., Clift, S., and Bongard, S. (2010). 'Shall we dance? An exploration of the perceived benefits of dancing on well-being', *Arts and Health*, 2(2): 149–63.

Truax, C. and Carkhuff, R. (1964). 'Toward an integration and didactic approaches to training in counseling and psychotherapy', *Journal of Counseling Psychology*, 11(3): 240–7.

West, J., Otte, C., Geher, K., Johnson, J., and Mohr, D. C. (2004). 'Effects of Hatha yoga and African dance on perceived stress, affect, and salivary cortisol', *Annals of Behavioral Medicine*, 28(2): 114–18.

Yalom, I. and Leazcz, M. (2005). *Theory and Practice of Group Psychotherapy*. New York, NY: Basic Books.

CHAPTER 29

CULTIVATING THE FELT SENSE OF WELLBEING

How We Know We Are Well

ANNA FIONA KEOGH AND JOAN DAVIS

INTRODUCTION

> As you are reading this, how well do you feel? How do you know that you
> are feeling well at this moment? What is your 'felt sense' of wellbeing?

We are interested in how we learn to recognize this bodily experience; how we learn to cultivate it; how we can then find a way to give it form through language or imagery; and finally, how it can be communicated and expressed. We argue that it is important for somatic, dance, and movement educators and practitioners to be able to develop in ourselves and our students and clients a capacity for attuning to the felt sense so that they may be able to recognize and modulate how they can be well.

We will discuss felt sense and how learning to read sensation is central to developing a capacity for felt sense—particularly for those working with the body. We will consider our understanding of wellbeing and then discuss the benefits of cultivating a capacity for attuning to our felt sense for our wellbeing. Finally, as we are interested in how we can guide others in developing this skill, we will guide the reader through the stages of developing this skill based on our experience.

Our enquiry is situated within, and is informed by the experiences and process of discovering the felt sense of wellbeing of students and facilitators of ORIGINS—a somatic and movement therapy training which is based on an in-depth exploration of our embryological and post-natal early development from pre-conception to standing. The three-year training programme has been developed by Joan Davis, who is a certified Body–Mind Centering (BMC®) practitioner, Authentic Movement practitioner, and a Hakomi Sensorimotor Trauma Psychotherapist based in Wicklow, Ireland.

The uniqueness of ORIGINS is that it aims to weave together new and existing strands of movement and somatic-based practices, including BMC, Authentic Movement, bio-dynamic craniosacral therapy, and Hellinger's Family Constellation work. The training is primarily experiential in nature, in which students are invited to engage with guided movement exploration, somaticization and embodiment practices, and hands-on body work. The training covers aspects of embryology, experiential anatomy, and physiology; developmental psychology and movement patterns; movement observation and repat-terning; object relations and attachment; attunement, resonance, and mindfulness; and group process and Authentic Movement as embodied spiritual practice.

On completion of the training, students who have fulfilled the course require-ments will become accredited as ORIGINS practitioners and may register as profes-sional members with the International Somatic Movement Education and Therapy Association (ISMETA).

Davis (2012) describes the ORIGINS approach as 'wholistic':

> Through the experience of ORIGINS, it is hoped that students will cultivate an enhanced quality of life and an enriched participation with the world, and as a natu-ral consequence of this, an increased sense of wellbeing. In ORIGINS, we are learn-ing about early development by exploring how through cultivating felt sense we can re-member our own early development. Through movement explorations which allow re-membering, our felt sense begins to take shape.

The first author of this article is a participant on the training programme and is involved in documenting the development of the programme. Throughout this chapter we invite you to read it—not just with your cognitive and thinking self, but with your embod-ied self. We invite you, as you read, to not only track your mental processes as you fol-low the discussion, but also to try to track your inner processes—bodily sensations and emotion.

WHAT IS FELT SENSE?

In considering the question 'What does wellbeing feel like?' we have found the concept of felt sense helpful. Felt sense is a concept that was originally coined and developed by Eugene Gendlin (1981) as part of his psychotherapeutic process called 'focusing'. Although originally developed within a psychotherapeutic framework, it has come to be widely used within somatic and movement-related fields; for example, Somatic Experiencing® and trauma healing (Levine and Frederick 1997; Levine 2008), Authentic Movement (Bacon 2007, 2012), ecosomatic therapy and ecopsychology (Beauvais 2012; Burns 2012), and craniosacral biodynamics (Sills 2009).

In essence, felt sense is the ability to be able to notice and attend to the happenings of the body. We experience these happenings as sensation. Gendlin (2003) describes it as the body-sense of a situation—the unclear, preverbal sense of 'something there'. This 'something' is always experienced in the body. It is always unclear and hazy. It is always more than a 'something' that can be put into words.

Gendlin argues that we must simply receive and welcome the felt sense:

> We try to receive whatever comes from a felt sense. We let it be, at least for a while. We try not to edit it, change it, or immediately push it further. Neither do we agree with what first comes from a felt sense . . . We develop an attitude of welcoming whatever comes, even if it seems negative or unrealistic. (Gendlin 1984, section 1)

This approach to welcoming is similar to the attitude of 'acceptance without judgement' encouraged within mindfulness (Kabat Zinn 1990), in which we aim to simply sit with the experience. Within the 'focusing' framework, however, the felt sense can help to bring about a resolution to an inner conflict. By attending to these 'happenings', we become observers of our inner processes. Our awareness of hitherto unconscious processes increases, and as our self-awareness increases we are able to find resolutions to inner conflicts. When a felt sense comes, one concentrates on its quality and tries to find a handle-word for that quality. When this word comes, there is an 'aha!' moment (Gendlin 1981, 1984, 2003). In this 'aha', I have the sense that 'now I can find a resolution to whatever it is that is bothering me. I will be able to get to the bottom of it.' This is not just a mental process, but is experienced as a *felt shift*—we feel differently after this moment (Sills 2008, p. 98)

Levine and Frederick (1997) explain how the felt sense is so central to our experience of being human that we take it for granted until we purposely attend to it. 'Through the felt sense we are able to move, to acquire new information, to interrelate with one another and, ultimately, to know who we are" (p. 70).

In all cases, we are talking about the experiencing body. When the body is experienced from within, the body and mind are not separated but are experienced as a whole (Bainbridge Cohen 2003, p. 1). To perceive felt sense is to realize that 'self is an embodied experience' (Sills 2008, p. 98). It is a feeling realm that holds meaning and can be accessed via a natural movement of awareness. For the purposes of ORIGINS, we find Sills' explanation and summary of the felt sense most helpful (Sills 2008, p. 99). The felt sense is:

- the global, whole-body sense of something;
- organized around and holds felt meaning;
- not just physical, but underlies more formed sensations, emotional tones, feelings, senses, and even images;
- accessed within the body space;
- an expression of how one embodies and gives meaning to our experience; and
- initially nebulous, undefined, hard to grasp or name.

Although the felt sense is described as a global experience, we argue that learning to be with sensation, to experience the 'totality of sensation' (Levine and Frederick 1997,

p. 67), is core to cultivating felt sense, particularly for those who work directly with the body.

Sensation, as Davis (2012) explains, is the operation or function of the senses. It is the physical feeling resulting from stimulation of a sense organ or from internal bodily change such as cold or pain. Sensation is a direct experience that arises from our senses. It is what is being 'impressed' in this moment. We do not enter the world with our senses fully formed. Senses begin to develop in utero as potential and develop and sharpen in response to experience in utero, after birth and throughout life. The vestibular nerve is the first of the cranial nerves to develop, and it is concerned with the sensations of movement and touch, which develop in synchrony with each other. Therefore, these are our first introduction into the world of sensation and they are experienced in utero in a fluid environment. The amniotic fluid moves, and we feel the touch of that movement and fluid contact on our developing skin. Our mother moves and breathes, and we feel the movement of that reflected in our fluid environment.

In our understanding, emotions too are always sensation-based. For example, the feeling of joy is excitement, and the sensation of excitement is a rising of energy in my body, perhaps a tightening of my musculature, depending on whether the excitement is leaning towards joy or tinged with fear or possibly both. Thoughts are also sensation-based; for example, if I think about a sunny day I may feel my body relax, whereas if I think of a cold day I may feel a headache starting. From our experience, everything can be traced back to the body's sensations or built up from the body's sensations and linked back into emotions, thought, concept, or belief.

Reading sensation is central to wellbeing. Consider what life would be like without the ability to read sensation. For example, if I cannot read the sensation of heat in my fingers, I will not know that I am burning myself when I touch the fire. On the other hand, I may be oversensitive to sensation, and the slightest feeling of warmth can make me shrivel up and pull away from its source. Thus, being able to read our felt sense of any stimulus is an essential part of being able to navigate our environment with an ease and grace that in its turn can promote the felt sense of wellbeing.

By giving time and significance to exploring sensations, the organizing mind is allowed to serve the knowing body. Our body re-members, and our attention to felt sense allows the re-membering to surface and become conscious, and the implicit realm to become explicit.

Whereas Levine and Frederick (1997, p. 66) talk about how the felt sense can be used in transforming trauma—'The felt sense encompasses the clarity, instinctual power, and fluidity necessary to transform trauma'—we are interested in how we can use the felt sense to remain in a state of wellbeing.

So reader, would you like to continue reading this article? Take a moment now to explore your felt sense in response to this question. Notice any sensations you are having right now as you prepare to read further. Are you interested, irritated, curious, bored, well? What tells you that you are experiencing any or all of these?

What do we Mean by Wellbeing?

Having reviewed our understanding of felt sense, let us now consider what we mean by wellbeing. Our considerations thus far have led us to understand wellbeing to be a dynamic state. As human beings, body, spirit, emotion, and thought all evolve in relationship to each other and in relationship to others and the environment. When we are well, we have a sense of vibrancy and aliveness rooted in our tissues. D. H. Lawrence found words to describe it:

> My belief is in the blood and flesh as being wiser than the intellect. The body unconscious is where life bubbles up in us. It is how we know that we are alive, alive to the depths of our souls and in touch somewhere with the vivid reaches of the cosmos. (Cited in Levine and Frederick 1997, p. 65)

Physiologically, we see basic wellbeing as being cellular—the quality of the tone that is the readiness to relate. The cytoplasm (the fluid inside the cell) and the cell membrane, and indeed all the sub-cellular structures that make the cell work efficiently, are essential to the quality of vibrancy and aliveness within each cell. Within this sense of aliveness and integration that is central to wellbeing, is also a capacity for responding to, relating to and modulating our experience of sensation, energy, and information flow.

Wellbeing is not necessarily about being without pain, discomfort, or distress. If I am giving birth, I experience many intense sensations, both pleasurable and displeasing, some of which I may describe as painful. However, I also know that I am well in this experience. I experience a felt sense of wellbeing whilst giving birth.

Wellbeing is about being resourced so that we can respond to the forces and stimuli with which we come into contact, and so we can be present in the here and now. For example, consider the sensation of a headache. It is very tempting to make a judgement on this felt sense in the moment and give it a story. 'I have an ache in my head . . . again . . . oh no, I'm stressed. I must reduce my stress . . . but how can I when I have so much to do . . .' However, when acknowledged without judgement, it can lead me to identify my needs and see my options: 'I have an ache in my head. It is located behind my nose and my eyes. It feels like a tightness and a pressing. I want to press it with my hands. I press with my hands. I consider what I can do to release the sense of tightness.'

In our article, we can focus on how dance and movement students can use felt sense to recognize when they are well. Having discussed what we mean by wellbeing, consider the following narrative in which Davis (2012) attunes to her sense of wellbeing. You may be interested to try to attune to your felt sense and see what your experience is like as you read the narrative. What happens for you as you try this? Take as much time as you need in a relatively quiet environment where you will not be disturbed.

> When I touch on a felt sense of alignment, there is a strongly felt experience of wellbeing which is very much in the present moment and I imagine could be different for

each person. I orient my attention towards the midline of my body from my head to my tail and deep in the centre of my body, not to the front or back but down the centre. In that experience of midline orientation the rest of my body has a sensation of 'coalescing' or knitting together as it were, orienting to this midline. There is warmth coupled with relaxation and alertness and I can say with congruence . . . 'I am here'. (Davis 2012)

In the previous narrative the author's sense of wellbeing encompassed a sense of focus: attunement to her internal world and her environment. She experienced a sense of wholeness, that 'all of her' was tuned in. This sensation is perhaps akin to what Siegel (2010, p. xxii) describes as 'neural integration', the underlying mechanism of wellbeing and overall mental health.

The Benefits of Cultivating a Capacity for the Felt Sense

Many authors have discussed the benefits of developing a capacity for felt sense (Bacon 2007; Gendlin 2003; Levine and Frederick 1997; Sills 2008). Levine and Frederick (1997, p. 82) describe it as a tool that allows us to come to know ourselves as 'complex, biological, and spiritual organisms'.

> [The felt sense] heightens our enjoyment of sensual experiences. It can be a doorway to spiritual states . . . The felt sense helps people feel more natural, more grounded, more at home in their bodies. It can enhance our sense of balance and coordination. It improves memory and provides us deeper access to the subtle instinctual impulses that guide the healing of trauma. It increases creativity. It is from the felt sense that we experience wellbeing, peace, and connectedness. It is how we experience the 'self'". (p. 71)

We would like to offer some of the benefits of cultivating the capacity for felt sense based on our experience on ORIGINS. Within this programme it is assumed that a cultivated felt sense will (i) encourage a sense of wellbeing, (ii) foster a sense of grounding and body presence, (iii) enhance communication and expressive skill, (iv) increase communication and respect for one's own learning needs, (v) increase ability to teach and guide others in movement. More specifically, an increased felt sense will contribute towards these skills and abilities as described here.

Encourage a Sense of Wellbeing

On a most basic level, developing the skill of tracking felt sense can greatly enhance potential for wellbeing because it may help me to learn to recognize what it feels like to experience wellbeing. Through cultivating felt sense, I can learn to understand what it is I need to attain a sense of wellbeing in this moment. I can learn to recognize, acknowledge, and accept without self-judgement or criticism when I am feeling unwell, be it on a physical, mental, emotional, social, or spiritual level. Staying attuned to, and being able to track, my own physical, mental, and emotional state, allows me to make decisions which support my wellbeing. For example, I will learn to recognize when I need a rest or something to eat or when a muscle is vulnerable.

Furthermore, being able to track felt sense over time can help to raise awareness of habits, patterns, and continuing needs. For example, not only do I become skilled at preventing hurt or injury, I also become skilled at recognizing wellness and what helps me feel well and healthy. I learn to recognize when I feel a sense of wellbeing during training and performances. This can lead to increased self-esteem, accomplishment, satisfaction, and joy.

Foster a Sense of Grounding and Body Presence

When attention can be focused on what is being sensed and when body sensations can be tuned into and acknowledged, it may help us to realize that we have a body. For example, when I realize I have a body I have substance, weight, form, and shape. I experience a sense of being real and really present. This may help contribute to a sense of being grounded and present in the body. Being present in the body can contribute to a sense of safety from which I can then find expression through my body, movement, and dance.

Enhance Communication and Expressive Skill

The capacity to stay with felt sense, to stay in tune with oneself, is central to being able to communicate and express. Being able to communicate our own sense of wellbeing—of vibrancy, alertness, coalescing—is an aspect of our art. Martha Graham, the renowned choreographer, described it beautifully to her biographer, Agnes deMille: 'There is a vitality, a life force, an energy, a quickening that is translated through you into action, and because there is only one of you in all of time, this expression is unique' (DeMille 1991, p. 264).

As an example of this, consider the following narrative in which Davis describes how she accessed a felt sense of wellbeing during a performance.

> I did a solo piece about 25 years ago. In it I told a story about two giraffes trying to get into a Mini Minor car as I danced around the stage. The piece took a good deal of skill in timing, of when to speak and dance or when to only dance or only speak. It also took enormous breath control and I had to attain a high level of physical fitness to execute it. These were satisfying tasks to accomplish and offered me a strong felt sense of wellbeing, which came in the form of satisfaction of accomplishment

and self-agency on the one hand; and on the other, was the felt sense of wholeness, that is, all the parts of me working in harmony with each other, and this was
even more heightened when I could hear the delighted response from the audience
and to know that some of them at least had a felt sense of wellbeing too in their
watching of the performance. I guess there are varying degrees of wellbeing from
the euphoric to the ordinary. To this day, people come up to me and remind me of
this solo! (Davis 2012)

Increase Awareness and Respect for One's Own Learning Needs

A cultivated felt sense can be very helpful for dance, movement, and somatic practitioners to understand and respect their own movement patterns and learning needs; their
movement gaps and competencies. Consider this example given by the first author:

> Through coming to respect my felt sense of anxiety and frustration when learning
> a dance sequence, I have come to recognize and accept that I need a lot of time to
> learn a sequence. Firstly, I need to get a sense of the whole piece and a sense of what
> it intends to communicate. The technical details and precise movements come after-
> wards. In order to learn it, I need time out of a pressurized environment.
>   I recall the relief when I first encountered a dance teacher who, having taught
> us a sequence, allowed us time to play around with it, alone or with others. What
> a relief! And what fun! When I encounter a teacher who does not work in this way,
> I have come to know that it is not that I'm stupid, but that I need time. (Keogh 2012,
> personal notes)

Increased Ability to Teach and Guide Others in Movement

As somatic and movement educators and therapists, we have found that developing a
cultivated felt sense has helped us give clearer guidance and feedback to our students
and clients based on our own experienced felt sense. As we cultivate our felt sense, we
find our own personal sensation vocabulary and become fluent in our own felt sense
language, thereby giving us means to communicate our felt experience if we wish.

HOW CAN WE CULTIVATE FELT SENSE?

Others have developed guidelines or ways to cultivate the capacity for felt sense (see for
example, Gendlin 2003). Here we offer guidelines based on our experience.

First Stage: Tuning In

The first stage of cultivating felt sense is about tuning in: How do we tune in? How do we learn to recognize this bodily experience?

a) Become aware of where your attention is.

Perhaps it is on the reading of this article, or a task you have to do, or the people or sounds around you. Notice what is capturing your attention.

b) Bring your attention inwards—into your body.

Take a few moments to do this. Try not to force it. It is almost like waiting for a pool of water to become still after it has been disturbed. What is capturing your attention now? You might find that you are noticing a sensation related to an emotion, such as the feeling of butterflies in your belly that can come with anxiety, or the feeling of heaviness that can come with boredom.

c) Bring your focus and concentrate your attention now on sensations that are presenting themselves.

Perhaps you notice an itch or tightness somewhere. When you become aware of such a sensation, take note of exactly where it is; for example: 'I feel an itch on the skin on the top of my left hand, near to the wrist, below my thumb.' Can you simply welcome the sensation experience with warm-hearted curiosity in its nakedness without trying to change it or label it? Can you allow the sensation to be there in its fullness? Can you allow yourself to not do anything at all with this sensation? Can you breathe 'behind' it as it were? You might like to explore this process with your breath. We invite you now to simply notice your breath. As you do this, you might realize that you are beginning to change your breathing—making it deeper or slower. If you become aware that you are doing this, see if you can step back from the desire to make an assessment of your breath, change it or think about it, and return to simply being with your breath. Step back, welcome, observe, and allow.

d) Eventually, with practice, we can learn to go deeper into our bodies—through the layers, skin, tissue, muscle, fascia, organs, cells . . .

Seek to acknowledge and accept all the sensations that present themselves, without picking and choosing. And cultivate an attitude of warm-hearted curiosity about them all. Another way of phrasing this is to suggest you 'accept what comes'. Our attitude to sensations we experience is significant, as it is our attitude which will promote a sense of wellbeing or non-wellbeing.

We invite you to let go of thinking about this chapter for a moment and explore for yourself what tuning in feels like for you.

Second Stage: Giving Form to the Sensation

The second stage of cultivating felt sense is about finding a way to give the sensation form.

> We learn to read sensation without interpretation; to experience sensation without putting a story or interpretation onto it. We simply rest with the sensation itself and explore the felt sense of that in a particular body part. As you rest with the sensation you are experiencing, let your attention spread out. You might begin to get a sense of all of it together, the whole-body sense. This will initially be hard to grasp or name. Do you find an image forming of this whole-body sense? Perhaps it is taking on a shape, a colour, or a texture. Perhaps it has a tone or a sound. This is personal. It only needs to make sense to you and not necessarily others. The difficult thing here is to stay with the sensation and not let the intellect take over. It is very easy at this stage to get into a dialogue with yourself: 'Oh, yes, I feel a tightness because I . . .' Try to let go of the 'because'.

Third Stage: Communicating the Felt Sense

The third stage of cultivating felt sense is about finding a way to communicate it to others.

> a) As you explore the various forms this whole-body sense, you will eventually find that a single word or even a few words might echo or resonate with this feeling . . . hot, cold, tingling, shaky, tight, buzzy?
>
> b) As you hit upon a word, see if you can fill it out with a metaphor . . . like a . . . or give it colour and sound? Let your curiosity guide you. Is this tightness a feeling of being pressed in or of bursting out, is it soft or hard, is it pleasurable or unpleasant? What sound comes out when I give this sensation attention? What is my felt sense of this? Over time, you will build up a list of your own sensation words, phrases, and metaphors.
>
> c) If you have found a metaphor such as 'I feel like I'm bursting', you might think to yourself, 'Well, I could have told you that in an instant. I didn't need to go through this whole process to know this is what I feel!' However, it is precisely the process of exploring the sensations behind the felt sense which is what is empowering and enabling. Indeed, primary metaphors are developed out of our embodied day-to-day experience, and structure our reasoning, our experience, and our everyday language (Lakoff and Johnson 1999). In cultivating felt sense, we return to the re-membering of where these metaphors originated. These additions should not come instead of the felt sense or we are in danger of skirting around the sensation experience.

As we conclude, we would like to offer some additional guidelines on cultivating felt sense.

Explore It

The cultivation of felt sense can be an enjoyable experience. Simple experientials working with the senses provide fertile grounds for exploration: squeezing and patting; rubbing and stroking; exploring a variety of movement qualities and dynamics; listening to loud and soft sounds; exploring smells and tastes; noticing our felt sense response to art and nature.

Practice It

An important thing to remember is that it takes practice until it becomes a practice. Initially exploring felt sense can be an intense and sometimes uncomfortable experience. Mindfulness practices (see for example, Kabat Zinn 1990, 1995; Siegel 2010; Williams and Penman 2011) can be very helpful in assisting us to learn to focus on small body areas and cultivate a capacity to tolerate small amounts of the less pleasant sensations, thus learning to modulate our experience of sensation—learning to move back and forth between what is pleasant and not so pleasant. We can develop a sense of agency which also cultivates the felt sense of wellbeing. This is particularly the case when there has been any trauma. This is an essential skill, otherwise we may end up living a life shut down from our sensations and therefore our felt sense.

Go gently

To bring up the experience of sensation in those people who have closed down their senses to the world and become desensitized/depressed, or who have simply closed down to the rough and tumble of the interactive world, or who have become lost in a cognitive world only, it is necessary to work slowly with bringing up this awareness to sensation again. It can be both enlivening and frightening. Movement, touch, and a well developed capacity for attuning to the sensorial needs of the student or client are ideal methods for this work.

Conclusion

In this chapter we have argued that in order to experience wellbeing, we must know what it *feels* like—what is the 'felt sense of wellbeing for me'. We have discussed some of the ways by which it is beneficial for somatic, dance, and movement educators and practitioners to develop this awareness in ourselves and in our students and clients.

Developing our sensitivity to our felt sense can be practised and learned. By regularly attending to our felt sense, we can learn to track it and how to receive information from it, from which we can make choices which will contribute to our wellbeing. Not only can it help us to prevent physical, mental, emotional, or social discomfort, disease, and injury, but it can help to us maintain a general state of wellbeing and improved quality of life.

We will become familiar with what our felt sense of wellbeing is. As the body and the mind create themselves through movement and touch, we can sense our way to wellbeing and health.

References

Bacon, J. (2012). 'Her body finds a voice: Authentic Movement in an imaginal world', *Body, Movement and Dance in Psychotherapy*, 7(2): 115–27

Bacon, J. (2007). 'Psyche moving: "Active Imagination" and "Focusing" in movement-based performance and psychotherapy', *Body, Movement and Dance in Psychotherapy*, 2(1): 17–28

Bainbridge Cohen, B. (2003). *Sensing, Feeling, and Action: The Experiential Anatomy of Body-Mind Centering*. Northampton, MA: Contact Editions,

Beauvais, J. (2012). 'Focusing on the natural world: An ecosomatic approach to attunement with an ecological facilitating environment', *Body, Movement and Dance in Psychotherapy*, 7(4): 277–91.

Burns, C. A. (2012). 'Embodiment and embedment: Integrating dance/movement therapy, body psychotherapy and ecopsychology', *Body, Movement and Dance in Psychotherapy*, 7(1): 39–54.

Davis, J. (2012). Personal correspondence.

DeMille, A. (1991). *Martha: The Life and Work of Martha Graham: A Biography*. New York, NY: Random House.

Gendlin, E. T. (2003). *Focusing*. 25th anniversary edn. London: Rider.

Gendlin, E. T. (1984). 'The client's client: The edge of awareness', in R. L. Levant and J. M. Shlien (eds.), *Client-Centered Therapy and the Person-Centered Approach: New Directions in Theory Research and Practice*. New York, NY: Praeger. <http://www.focusing.org/client_one_a.htm>

Gendlin, E. T. (1981). *Focusing*, New York: Bantam Books.

Kabat Zinn, J. (1990). *Full Catastrophe Living: Using the Wisdom of Your Body and Mind to Face Stress, Pain, and Illness*. New York, NY: Delta Trade Paperbacks.

Kabat Zinn, J. (1995). *Wherever You Go, There You Are*. New York, NY: Hyperion Books.

Lakoff, G. and Johnson, M. (1999). *Philosophy in the Flesh: The Embodied Mind and its Challenge to Western Thought*. New York, NY: Basic Books

Levine, P. and Frederick, A. (1997). *Waking the Tiger. Healing Trauma: The Innate Capacity to Transform Overwhelming Experiences*. Berkeley, CA: North Atlantic Books.

Levine, P. (2008). *Healing Trauma: A Pioneering Program for Restoring the Wisdom of Your Body*. Boulder, CO: Sounds True.

Siegel, D. (2010). *The Mindful Therapist: A Clinician's Guide to Mindsight and Neural Integration*. Norton Series on Interpersonal Neurobiology. New York, NY: W. W. Norton.

Sills, F. (2009). *Craniosacral Biodynamics Volume Two: The Primal Midline and the Organization of the Body*. Berkeley, CA: North Atlantic Books.

Sills, F. (2008). *Being and Becoming: Psychodynamics, Buddhism, and the Origins of Selfhood*. Berkeley, CA: North Atlantic Books.

Williams, M. and Penman, D. (2011). *Mindfulness: An Eight-Week Plan for Finding Peace in a Frantic World*. Emmaus, PA: Rodale Books.

PART IV

....

DANCE IN THE COMMUNITY

....

INTRODUCTION TO PART IV

VICKY KARKOU AND SUE OLIVER

With Contributions by Carolyn Fresquez and Barbara Erber

AT the time of writing, community-based dance has surely reached its zenith in popularity. Globally, it seems that people are recognizing its potential to improve their feelings of positive health and wellbeing. Both private initiatives and publicly funded ventures are providing opportunities for people of all ages to try various forms of dance outwith the formal health contexts or educational system. This part takes the reader on a cultural journey, exploring how dance can be used as a positive influence among widely disparate groups of dancers. Whether the contexts relate to therapy groups or more open community dance settings, the effect of participation is viewed in terms of the perceived wellbeing which the dancers experience.

In Chapter 30, Anna Kenrick, Carolyn Lappin, and Sue Oliver report on a Scottish project targeting teenage girls who had opted out of physical education at school, offering them the chance to learn how to create dances and, in some cases, to become certificated dance leaders. This opportunity motivated the girls to become active and stay active through dance, contributing to their sense of wellbeing by changing their lifestyle.

Kestenberg Movement Profile is the vehicle used by Susan Loman (Chapter 31) in her therapy work in the USA with children and their families in various stages of development, promoting healthy development using rhythm and dance. Particular attention is paid to the ages 3–6 years—a time when it is assumed that gender development takes place. Her aim is to demonstrate how particular developmental needs can be met through the use of developmentally appropriate movement responses, to encourage parents to understand these needs, and to form better relationships with their children. Loman is located within a university establishment (Antioch) but offers this service to local families.

Similar links are available for Cynthia Pratt (Chapter 32). Based at Butler University in Indiana, Pratt takes her inspiration from Rudolph von Laban's concept of 'movement choirs' in which large numbers of amateur dancers danced together by way of celebrating community spirit. She applies the model to twenty-first-century American community settings by creating large-scale dances in outdoor venues with the aim of promoting social connectedness and wellbeing in individuals and communities.

Outdoor spaces also feature in Petra Kuppers' Chapter 33, but her (ongoing) Tiresias Project is focused on disabled artists using their bodies and the spaces they occupy to create their dance. Contributions come from the participants in this project: Lisa Steichmann, Jonny Gray, Melanie Yergeau, Aimee Meredith Cox, Nora Simonhjell, Neil Marcus, Elizabeth Currans, Amber DiPietra, and Stephanie Heit, who, through creative writing methodologies, share their explorations of eroticism as defined by Audre Lorde (1984), challenging societal notions that deny sexual and loving pleasure to people with disabilities. This is clearly the work of theoretical, practical, and artistic activism, delivered sensitively by a group of people committed to make their voices heard and their bodies acknowledged.

In Chapter 36 the concept of aesthetic activism is also explored by Sherry Shapiro, through the lenses of social, educational, and political pedagogies. 'Community' is central to Shapiro's work, for expressing solidarity and the experience of interconnectedness to bring about change. Drawing on her work with a group of community dancers in South Africa, she describes the process of empowerment through dance to transcend the stereotypes of physical appearance.

Continuing the South African context in Chapter 37, Athina Copteros, Vicky Karkou, and Tally Palmer write about the first author's experiences in qualifying as a dance movement psychotherapist in the UK, in order to work with South African women struggling with cultural inequality in that country. Cultural translations are the main focus of this work, explored through both journals and word-written and body-based experiences remembered. The video that accompanies this chapter speaks of the main themes discovered: the need to connect with the environment, becoming aware of power and difference, sharing leadership, and the need for therapeutic adaptability.

In Chapter 38, Andre Reis and Sue Oliver do not speak about therapy. Still, they argue that capoeira (see the associated video) can influence intragroup relationships and the social wellbeing of dancers in this dance-fight game, and how these can be extrapolated to a wider context. Set in Brazil, the participants reflect on their experiences as individuals and as group members, and the authors postulate that these group dynamics are a microcosm of the wider community.

The system of dance known as 5Rhythms developed by Gabrielle Roth is the subject of Chapter 39 by Mati Vargas-Gibson, Sarena Wolfaard, and Emma Roberts. Their enquiry into the practice drew on responses from practitioners in Australia, Europe, and the USA, as well as their own practice, and through these they describe how five fundamental movement dynamics known as 'the wave' enable individuals to heighten their awareness of how their bodies move, which can lead to increased wellbeing. A beautifully created video accompanies this chapter, reminding us of reasons of why many of us have retained an active engagement with community dance—an engagement that does not ask for skill and technical expertise, while often offering deeply personal and meaningfully social experiences.

Back to the idea of dance as therapy, this part includes a number of references to dealing with trauma caused by conflict. For example, Allison Singer (Chapter 34) uses dance ethnography and dance movement psychotherapy in her work with internally displaced families in war-damaged Serbia. She explains how the building of new social and cultural relationships is the keystone to coping with trauma and rediscovering a sense of wellbeing by creating new opportunities for individuals and families in the process of resettlement.

In Chapter 35, Maralia Reca discusses the use of dance/movement therapy with victims of torture in Argentina. She argues that through dance/movement therapy the natural body rhythms are restored and connected to the brain via the nervous system, to aid the restoration of emotional and cognitive functioning, hence re-establishing a sense of wellbeing.

Trauma—an area that appears to receive a lot of attention recently—is also the topic of investigation in the following two projects, both of which involved dance movement psychotherapy with women. The first comes from Barbara Erber, a dance movement psychotherapist from Austria. Barbara looked, heuristically, at 'resonance' within the therapeutic relationship with a client living in the community who had experienced domestic abuse. Given the nature of trauma and the particular experiences of clients, within the therapeutic process, Barbara attempted to establish trust, support emotional regulation, and encourage a secure sense of self. Attunement (Devereaux 2008) was used extensively next to structures from Authentic Movement (Pallaro 1999, 2007) within a wider context of person-centred and Jungian psychodynamic thinking.

The term 'resonance' was used to describe both embodied empathy and somatic countertransference. With this definition in mind she aimed to distinguish between the material she shared with her client through embodied empathy and material she experienced on behalf of her client as somatic countertransference.

As a heuristic study it focused on her own inner process and sought to describe experiences, rather than identify causal effects (Moustakas 1990). Processes recommended in heuristic inquiry were followed, such as self-dialogue, tacit knowing, intuition, indwelling, focusing, and the internal frame of reference. The process was often ongoing and emergent, but came to a relative closure through a final piece referred to by Moustakas as 'creative synthesis' and is included on the book's Companion Website (see Video IV.a ▶). Barbara describes the methodological process that she followed very clearly:

> I noted my physical state before each session. After each session I wrote reflective notes and video recorded my own movement in the form of Authentic Movement in response to the session and the client. I then wrote down what I witnessed whilst watching the video. Once the therapeutic work and weekly data collection had been completed, the material I witnessed was divided into three columns, which separated

three categories of resonance: my personal material, shared material, and the client's material.

For the findings of the study and the creative synthesis that brought all the findings together, my personal material was dismissed as it was not relevant for this study. I interpreted the category of shared material as embodied empathy, and my client's material as somatic countertransference.

On findings, she tells us:

My findings depict five central themes in resonance, all felt very clearly and deeply in my body: fear, maternal, waiting, bliss, and connection. I generally perceived embodied empathy and somatic countertransference as complementing each other over the duration of the eleven sessions; fear in the beginning of my work with the client was certainly a feeling that bridged the two concepts. Still, as the work progressed, bliss and connection appeared to refer to an empathetic response to the therapeutic relationship, while maternal feelings and waiting were thought of as the effect of somatic countertransference.

The creative synthesis in the form of video material makes references to these key themes. It also incorporates my sense of my findings as a linear process that resembles re-enactment of traumatic experiences, regression to an embryological stage of development, followed by an emergence into a more integrated, resilient way of being.

Carolyn Fresquez, a dance movement psychotherapist from the USA offers the second clinical example on trauma. In the final placement on her Masters training, she worked with women who had committed crime. She writes:

As a dance movement psychotherapy trainee, I was on clinical placement working in a community-based setting for women who had committed crime. Part of a larger programme of intervention that sought to address clients' behaviour, health, mental wellbeing, and social and community integration, I ran a dance movement psychotherapy group once a week for eight weeks. There were four group members, ranging in age from early 20s to late 40s.

Given the serial marginalization of my clients, I adopted a social constructionist therapeutic perspective, shaped by a not-knowing approach that assumes the client is her own expert and focuses on the here and now (Anderson and Goolishian 1992; McNamee 2006). This provided scaffolding for my understanding of what the women brought to our group—especially when it felt to me that the group stayed 'on the surface', with only brief moments of depth poising a counterweight. Following the parameters of an artistic inquiry (Wadsworth-Hervey 2000), I decided to explore the themes of surface and depth further, identifying ways in which they manifested within dance movement psychotherapy sessions (see Video IV.b on the Companion Website ▶).

A discussion of the results of artistic data analysis shows 'surface' corresponded with a need for boundaries, in combination with relationship patterns that did not seek strong connection. 'Depth' appeared as interruptions to habitual patterns, incorporating the establishment of boundaries and connections. On the whole, the themes revealed client needs around boundaries, safety, and relationship building. Exploring the topic allowed me to acknowledge and understand the difficulties I felt engaging with the 'surface'. It also allowed me to fully appreciate the power my clients rightfully took regarding their own processes engaging with a service they were in legal and social ways obliged to attend. Additionally, it helped me understand why certain moments that stood out were in fact important. These brief moments, formed through collaborative, expressive action, had an integrated, multisensory quality of 'depth' that clarified intra- and interpersonal relationships.

References

Anderson, H. and Goolishian, H. (1992). 'The client is the expert: A not-knowing approach to therapy', in S. McNamee and K. J. Gergen (eds.), *Therapy as Social Construction*. London: Sage.

Devereaux, C. (2008). 'Untying the knots: Dance/movement therapy with a family exposed to domestic violence', *American Dance Therapy Journal*, 30: 58–70.

Lorde, A. (1984). 'Uses of the erotic: The erotic as power', in *Sister Outsider: Essays and Speeches*. Freedom, CA: Crossing Press, pp. 53–9.

McNamee, S. (2006). 'Therapy as social construction: An interview with Sheila Mcnamee, interviewed by C. Guanaes and E. F. Rasera', *Interamerican Journal of Psychology*, 40(1): 127–36.

Moustakas, C. (1990). *Heuristic Research: Design, Methodology and Applications*. California: Sage Publications.

Pallaro, P. (ed.) (1999). *Authentic Movement: Essays by Mary Starks Whitehouse, Janet Adler and Joan Chodorow*. London: Jessica Kingsley.

Pallaro, P. (ed.) (2007). *Authentic Movement: Moving the body, Moving the Self, Being Moved*. London: Jessica Kingsley.

Wadsworth-Hervey, L. W. (2000). *Artistic Inquiry in Dance/Movement Therapy: Creative Alternatives for Research*. Springfield, IL: Charles C. Thomas.

CHAPTER 30

FREE TO DANCE

Community Dance with Adolescent Girls in Scotland

ANNA KENRICK, CAROLYN LAPPIN,
AND SUE OLIVER

INTRODUCTION

LITERATURE reveals that feelings of negativity about the self bear influence on levels of achievement in social and educational experience (Thomas 2003; Bracey 2004). The benefits of physical exercise are lauded in the media in an effort to improve health on a wide scale. However, all too often young people opt out for various reasons, to the detriment of their physical health and general wellbeing (Biscomb et al. 2000; Wilkinson and Bretzing 2011). Numerous physical activity projects—some inspired by dance role models seen on television—are available to Scottish children and adolescents in community venues (Tweedie 2011), and claim positive results in terms of confidence and enjoyment, while combating the effects of a sedentary lifestyle. Often, however, these are short-term, and end before a lasting influence is established.

Free To Dance was a community dance project which ran for three years, and was delivered by Scottish Youth Dance (YDance)—the national dance agency for children and young people in Scotland. The project ran in rural, urban, and island communities in Scotland, and aimed at motivating teenage girls who had become alienated from regular physical activity at school or elsewhere. This public-funded project offered them the chance to get fit and feel good about themselves through dance, without having to pay. Research by Youth Scotland (2006) shows that by the age of 18, 40% of girls have dropped out of sport and physical recreation. Free To Dance offered girls from a range of backgrounds the chance to access and participate in a positive dance experience which was fun and appropriately challenging.

The project was viewed through a multifaceted lens—by participants, dance leaders, and funding partners—and was rigorously evaluated to gain a clear picture of both how and whether the dancers' feelings of wellbeing are enhanced from the dance experience.

RATIONALE

During adolescence, numerous factors impinge upon a young person's state of being:

a) They are changing physically and are aware of the change.
b) The locus of control over their lives is shifting from family to self.
c) External influences—peers or media-related, for example—can distract them from previous interests.

Somehow they have to make sense of the changes they perceive in their bodies, emotions, and environment, to enable them to forge their personal identity. These sources of emotional turbulence interplay to form a complex web of conditions experienced in adolescence—no less so for the adolescent dancer. We examine the factors more closely:

a) Hormonal changes linked to puberty and related growth are likely sources of concern to teenage girls, causing a change in self-perception, both physically and emotionally. An early-teen growth spurt can result in bones lengthening at a different rate from muscles (Kimmerle and Cote-Laurence 2003). As a result, girls in physical education or dance classes are likely to find themselves less able to perform certain moves rather than more able, because the muscles are being put under strain, and, combined with a redistribution of fatty deposits in their bodies, their self-confidence can be threatened. Consequent weight gain or loss has implications for self-image, performance, and feelings of wellbeing for dancers and non-dancers alike.

The contrast between young people pursuing a dance career and those engaged in dance for recreation could not be sharper. For instance, girls who want to be ballet dancers begin training at an early age and will start dancing *en pointe* usually between the ages of 10 and 12, depending on their physical maturity (Oliver 2007). This way, their still malleable bodies are manipulated into the requisite shape and they develop the necessary strength to withstand the demands of the discipline. At the other end of the spectrum we find girls in British schools who have no desire to embrace a dance discipline and, in fact, who have become disenfranchised from physical education and recreation in upper primary or early secondary school because of their changing bodies and consequent self-image. This can spark a downward spiral by imbuing their attitudes with negativity, which in turn inhibits confidence, creativity, social bonding, and even school achievement (Craig 2007). Free To Dance was seen as the ideal project to invest funding for the provision of dance classes in communities, and break the cycle for these girls.

b) Bourdieu (2005) presents the concept of 'habitus' as being a layer in the early socialization process of individuals, whereby they learn to adopt the norms and values of family and close community. Habitus has the effect of restricting the individual's social experience, while, by contrast, providing protection from the wider social field.

Bourdieu's model of 'habitus' is not a static position. It is the result of constant interplay between the individual and those who set the parameters of social behaviour—in the first instance, probably the family. This is a step removed from the social constructionist position of the early Foucault (1980), for whom the 'docile body' (p. 198) was acted upon by social forces in a one-way relationship. Placed in a modern framework, Thomas (2003) describes it as the result of external pressure to conform to the expectations of others in a position of authority or influence, to mould the social body. This is a restrictive aspect of the habitus.

The other view of the habitus is of a caring, nurturing network of socially determined norms in which the individual is protected from conflicting influences from the wider social 'field' (Bourdieu 2005)—a comforting 'nest' to grow up in. Nestlings, however, become fledglings, and as the child explores the wider realms of his/her environment, making new friends and having new experiences, such as going to school, he/she assimilates new norms and values (Smith 2002; Adkins 2004). Now the individual has some bargaining chips to help to negotiate her/his habitus, so that the once rigid 'nest' becomes a pliable protective 'membrane', shaped by the individual inside as well as the social forces outside.

c) Having gained a modicum of control of their lives, young people seek to establish new networks of peers with whom to identify. In seeking to determine a new or altered identity, they look to their peers (Moshman 1999) to find models they like. During these formative years, adolescents are gaining cognitive powers (Byrnes 2003; Gardner 2006) and communication skills (Vygotsky 1986). This accommodates social interaction, which in turn brings about a reappraisal of self-identity. They might look for new peer groups to befriend, adopting symbols of identity, such as jewellery or tattoos (Riley and Cahill 2005), with which they may or may not feel comfortable, but at least it gives them a feeling of belonging. That, in turn, can lead to a more positive feeling of self-esteem and, consequently, confidence.

In addition to visible signs of group membership, other aims which contribute to positive feelings about oneself in a group include:

- Adopting an appropriate behaviour style within the peer group.
- Constantly modifying the 'labile' or flexible self, finding one's unique place in the group, and being an individual within the parameters of the group. (Moshman 1999, p. 78)

But what sort of indicators give an adolescent the feeling of being valued? A survey of Glasgow teenagers was conducted by Gordon and Grant (1997), in which positive indicators included:

- Helping others.
- Being helped and trusted by others.
- Sharing interests with others.
- The feeling of belonging to the group.
- Experiencing success.
- Having freedom to make one's own choices.
- Having a supportive family.

If the latter could be achieved—if their families supported what they were doing while they could enjoy group membership—the teenagers' morale was boosted. However, they would feel negatively about themselves if they felt rejected by the group and had no-one either to give support to, or receive support from. Such social isolation contributes to negative self-image. Tweedie (2011) reports that parental support is a powerful factor in encouraging young people to adopt healthy activities in their community.

Negative body image is often associated with dance, especially in Western society, and more often in ballet and contemporary forms of dance which are given wide exposure in the media (Thomas 2003; Green 2004; Hämäläinen 2004). In sport and in fashion magazines, the perception of the ideal body being slim or even thin is portrayed by athletes and models (Biscomb et al. 2000), which can be a challenge for the impressionable teenage girl to reach for the unattainable, causing her either to fail and become depressed, or to develop eating disorders and become ill. The body has become socially constructed, constituting what Bourdieu (2005) refers to as 'physical capital', which can be extremely elusive for a teenage girl. Peer pressure at this point can be either destructive or constructive. Girls might feel threatened if they cannot conform to the accepted norm; conversely, they might feel supported by their peers if they all strive for a common aim (Biscomb et al. 2000).

On the basis of that uncertainty, it could appear that a project such as Free To Dance was extremely ambitious and even a large gamble. It was pitched at groups of adolescent girls who had opted out of physical activity. Teenage girls' disengagement with physical education is well-documented (Enright and O'Sullivan, 2010; Ryan and Poirier 2012), and one reason offered for this is that providers do not listen to them. At an age when they are developing their own voice, they want to have some say in what is relevant to them; that is, in taking control of their 'habitus'. Curriculum planning criteria which were appropriate when they were aged 12 are not always appropriate when they are aged 15. Ryan and Poirier (2012) note:

We know that girls steer clear of participation in elective secondary physical education for several reasons . . . self-confidence; lack of motivation; low perceived value of physical education; lack of opportunity for physical activity; marking scheme; competition; co-ed classes; teaching approach; and peers. (p. 178)

To fill the void successfully, one option is to involve the girls in planning an alternative (Peclova et al. 2008), and allowing flexibility to hold the alternative outwith the school environment, to escape any feelings of negativity which the girls might be harbouring. A community class can be just as disciplined and demanding of the participants, so that they do not consider it to be a soft option. In that environment, the girls can experience social as well as artistic challenges. They learn to be part of a group, as when learning a piece of choreography, and they learn to be team leaders when they are choreographing their own composition for a group. They become agents in shaping their own identity (Kroger 2004; Oliver 2010) instead of being Foucauldian 'docile bodies' (1980, p. 198), constructed by people with power over them.

THE PROJECT

The Free To Dance project, funded by NHS Health Scotland, ran in North, South and East Ayrshire (each being a separated Local Authority), Orkney, and Glasgow from September 2008 to August 2011. Ayrshire is a local authority area in south-west Scotland which is mainly rural, but with larger conurbations nearer its northerly limits. The Orkney Islands lie off the north coast of Scotland, with Orkney itself being the biggest of the group. Glasgow is Scotland's largest city. The Health Improvement Strategy Division of the Scottish Government specified that delivery be tailored to the differing needs of island, rural and urban areas to enable future use of the project structure as a template for activity. Free To Dance was designed to provide links between dance provision offered within curriculum time, outside of the school day and within community settings, building on existing partnerships and establishing new collaborations.

The vision of the programme aimed to enable teenage girls (ages 13–19) to become more physically active and to realize their potential as individuals through a positive dance experience. YDance had completed delivery of a three-year Dance in Schools Initiative (DISI)[1] (Muldoon and Inchley 2008), working across Scotland in primary and secondary schools, funded by the Scottish Government Health Improvement Strategy Division, and in 2008 the Government's Physical Activity Strategy prompted a more targeted approach, focused on teenage girls.

The pilot three-year Free To Dance programme began in 2008, as part of a national programme funded by the Scottish Government and managed by NHS Health Scotland, and was extended for an extra year. The national programme aimed to give girls and young women opportunities and choices to achieve the social, psychological, and physical health benefits possible through physical activity. It formed part of the national strategy to increase the nation's levels of physical activity by getting people more active more often. A key concern in Scotland was that numbers of those meeting the recommended levels of physical activity reduced dramatically with age, and girls are less active than boys—a gap which widens during adolescence. The 2003 Scottish Health Survey (Scottish Executive 2005) showed that by the age of 14, 65% of girls did not reach the levels of physical activity recommended to benefit their health (sixty minutes or more, seven days per week). Later, the 2008 survey showed that whilst 79% of 8–10-year-old girls met recommendations, only 41% in the 13–15 age group also met them, compared to 70% of boys.

The emphasis of Government strategy was to increase the activity levels of girls who do not meet recommendations, rather than getting girls already physically active to do more. The programme was therefore designed to give girls choices and opportunities, encouraging and supporting them to become more physically active and more likely to stay active throughout adulthood (see Figure 30.1).

One factor contributing to the decline in female activity levels is a difference in the types of physical activities preferred by boys and by girls. Walking for exercise, running, and jogging are popular activities for both genders, whereas dance appears to be a popular activity for girls. When compared to other physical activities there is a lesser rate of decline, as 60% of girls took part in dance at least once a week in P7, declining to 53% by S4. According to sportscotland (2006), increased competitiveness in sport in later years influenced many girls to drop out—especially those who did not consider themselves to be good at sport. Those who view sport in school as too competitive tend only to participate because it is compulsory to take part rather than optional. Only one in four girls believe 'it's cool' to be sporty, and find team sports especially

FIGURE 30.1. Encouraging girls to be more physically active. (Credit: Paul Watt/YDance.)

male-dominated. Girls associate with the social benefits more than the competitive aspects of physical activity.

The principal aims of the programme were:

- To use dance to promote physical activity in secondary age girls who are not participating in other physical education and sport activities.
- To use dance to promote a sense of physical and emotional wellbeing.
- To develop the individual through dance.
- To use dance to attain and develop core skills such as communication and teamwork.
- To focus on working within the recommendations made by the Report of the Review Group on Physical Education (Scotland 2004), the Physical Activity Strategy 'Let's Make Scotland More Active' (2003) and Sport 21: The National Strategy for Sport documents.
- To encourage secondary pupils and school leavers to take certificated courses or community leader courses in dance.

Target Groups

Primarily, the programme targeted 13–19-year-old girls who were physically inactive and/or hard to reach. For example, young teenage mothers may be at risk from becoming inactive, and therefore were targeted throughout the programme. The target groups were categorized as primary and secondary target groups.

Primary Target Group: Physically Inactive Girls

These were not reaching the weekly recommended physical activity (RPA) levels of five hours or more per week.

Secondary Target Group: Hard-to-Reach Girls

Hard-to-reach girls were identified as those who experience particular barriers against taking part in dance or physical activities for reasons such as:

- Inaccessibility (for example, geographical, affordability, and personal physical limitations).
- Language (such as not using English as a first language)
- Cultural perceptions and traditions (such as ethnicity, faith, country of origin, and so on)

For example, the programme specifically targeted minority ethnic/faith communities, young asylum seekers/refugees, young carers, young mothers, girls with learning difficulties or physical disabilities, and those from disadvantaged communities (such as those facing social, economic, and health inequalities, or rural/island disadvantage).

Programme Delivery (Outputs)

The programme was delivered by YDance, which, as the national youth dance organization, works across three strategic areas—participation, education, and talent development—maintaining core company values of excellence and quality in the provision of participatory and performance-based activities. YDance's work impacts on health inequalities and issues, development of increased wellbeing and confidence, learning skills, and inclusion issues.

Free To Dance involved three main types of programme delivery:

- Schools programme: introductory sessions marketed in schools to encourage girls to participate in after-school sessions, community-based sessions, or a rolling programme in Special Educational Needs schools.
- Community programme: working in partnership with a wide range of community-based organizations from the statutory and voluntary sector to offer a range of introductory sessions and tailored follow-up programmes according to needs and demands.
- Training and additional activities: a series of leadership courses, performances, events, and mentoring opportunities to build the skills and experience of participants, support workers/teachers and YDance staff, and reflect on and improve practice.

Over the course of the project delivery, 926 groups met for weekly dance sessions, with 5,670 sessions being delivered (excluding the introductory taster sessions designed to attract participants and leadership training sessions for young women and adult volunteers). A total of 2,995 girls registered for the programme, with, on average, 45% being in the primary target group (range 42–55%) and 57% falling within the secondary 'hard to reach' target group (range 49–75%). Seventy-four girls completed the Award in Dance Leadership (ADL), and forty of those newly trained leaders went on to receive further mentoring support in exchange for leading dance sessions in their school or community (see Figure 30.2). In addition, ninety-four adults from partner organizations were trained on the benefits of supporting dance sessions and activities with girls.

Free To Dance was independently evaluated by Catch the Light—a youth and community development consultancy. The evaluation approach adopted followed the assumptions of LEAP for Health (NHS Health Scotland 2003):

- Evaluation should be an integral part of promoting community health and wellbeing.
- Both the providers and the users of a community health programme should take part in its planning and implementation.
- The main aim should be for continual improvement in the effectiveness and efficiency.
- Future work should be informed by lessons learned.

FIGURE 30.2. Training dance leaders. (Credit: Paul Watt/YDance.)

Three main categories of stakeholder were identified: girls participating in the pro-gramme, partner organizations/support workers, and the Free To Dance team of Dance Workers/YDance. Specific outcomes were tailored to each stakeholder group.

Data Collection and Evaluation Methods

The Free To Dance evaluation started at the same time as the programme, in September 2008, and continued until the end of the programme, which was extended to March 2012. It is outcome-based, assessing the extent of any changes or improvements which the programme set out to achieve.

Data collection methods comprised:

- Registration form completed by all participants including, the Warwick-Edinburgh Mental Well-Being 14-point Scale 7 (Scottish Government Indicator) and an adaptation of the PAQ-C short questionnaire (as recommended by the Scottish Physical Activity Research Collaboration, SPARcoll)—monitoring levels of uptake from target groups engaged with the project, levels of participation in physical activity and sport at the start of the project, and emotional wellbeing.
- Attendance records monitoring attendance weekly.
- End-of-quarter review completed by a sample group monitoring key progress made by young people and dance workers.
- Training evaluation form monitoring benefits of dance leadership training.
- Partners' evaluation form monitoring benefits of working through Free To Dance.
- Case studies to provide a more in-depth exploration of the project's impact on individuals—monitoring changes since joining the project, achievements, and progression routes, and the roles of the dance worker and support worker.
- Focus-group evaluation using video to record a dance session and engage young people in dialogue on their experience of Free To Dance at the beginning, middle, and end of programme
- YDance records monitoring attendance and dance workers' feedback.

These provided the basis for project evaluation and subsequent feedback to the funding body.

Outcomes by Stakeholder Groups

For Girls

More Girls Achieve and Maintain the Recommended Physical Activity (RPA) Levels

By the end of March 2011 more than two thirds (68.2%) of the sample group were meeting RPA levels—an increase of 13% on the baseline figure of 55% of participants meeting RPA levels when they joined Free To Dance.

More Commitment and Desire to Continue with Dance or Other Physical Activities Beyond the Programme

Free To Dance has increased the number of participants sustaining their involvement for one year or more from less than 5% at the end of the first year to 60% by the end of the third year.

Evidence of Physical, Social, and Mental Health Benefits that may be Sustained in Future Life

More than three quarters (76%) noted a big improvement in their ability to perform (see Figure 30.3). More than two-thirds (70%) observed a big improvement in their ability to

FIGURE 30.3. Improving confidence to perform. (Credit: Paul Watt/YDance. Paul Watt ceded all rights to YDance.)

enjoy physical activity more. Slightly fewer (68%) believe they made a big improvement in learning new dance skills and being better at working in a team (64%). A big improvement in confidence was noted by more than half (58%) of sample group respondents in March 2011. Since Free To Dance began there is an overall positive improvement in the WEMWBS[2] from 51.05 to 53.28 (with some fluctuations over time and across areas).

Participants can Demonstrate Skills being Transferred to Other Contexts such as Learning or Employment Opportunities

Examples emerged where being involved in Free To Dance led to connections with wider opportunities and experiences in the home, work, education, and the community. As a specialist youth dance provider, YDance offers opportunities to join additional activities that are not part of the Free To Dance programme. Examples include more advanced and intensive training sessions ('the Elements') and Project Y summer dance programmes and exchange trips. Similarly, there was a number of employment or voluntary work opportunities filled by participants in partner organizations, in YDance, or in other NHS Health Scotland funded programmes.

Participants Start to Set Up/Lead Dance or Physical Activities in their Communities

Free To Dance offered participants aged 16 and over the opportunity to complete an Award in Dance Leadership, in partnership with 'Girls on the Move' (Youth Scotland 2006)—a nationally recognized award for those interested in leading dance sessions, allowing successful candidates to lead small groups in dance activities while they are under the supervision of a tutor. Since Free To Dance began, seventy-four girls completed the award and many went on to share their skills with other young girls taking part in the Free To Dance project. Forty participants entered the mentoring support scheme, available as a continuum of support for young people as they develop their new skills in dance leadership.

The girls who successfully completed the Award in Dance Leadership programme then had the chance to use and develop these skills through the mentoring programme. Under the watchful eye of the Free To Dance teaching team, they led sessions and developed choreography for a number of new Free To Dance groups. Three mentees won an Active Award[3] because of their work assisting with a young mothers' group, a community session, and a primary 'after school' club. The girls also helped to run the teacher training programme in dance in Ayrshire, which was a real achievement for them. Bearing these developments in mind, one can appreciate that the supervisory role of the tutors was crucial. They would have responsibility for the girls' wellbeing, as well as encouraging the girls to take responsibility for themselves. Under supervision, the girls could learn to be proactive in making a difference in their own lives, as well as helping others to achieve similar benefits. They had chosen a physical activity in which they felt happy; it was not competitive, but they could challenge themselves. They did not need a lot of equipment or space; they could practise at home on their own if they desired, or they could practise with their friends.

For Partner Organizations

Barriers are Removed so that More Organizations use Dance to Address Health Inequalities and Work with Target Groups

Almost half (47%) of the partners responding to the questionnaire believed that their expectations were exceeded regarding improvements in their own or their organization's ability to be fully aware of the benefits of dance and physical activity. The majority (78.8%) felt that they better understood the role and purpose of Free To Dance.

Partners Continue to Support Girls to Remain Active by Providing a Range of Suitable Activities

Teachers and support workers responding to the questionnaire (48 of 74) valued the opportunity to learn how to support dance in their own schools or organizations. More than three quarters (76%) rated the standard of training provided as excellent. More than two thirds (69.6%) also rated the dance skills learnt during the training as excellent.

For YDance

Free To Dance Becomes a Flagship Model of Dance Activity and Partnership Working that is Rolled out Scotland-Wide

Dance workers perceived that the greatest improvement they made over the duration of the Free To Dance programme was in their ability to contribute to making Free To Dance a flagship model of dance activity. At the end of the final year of the programme, responsibility for physical activity within the Scottish Government moved from the Health Department to the Sports Policy Division, with a subsequent change in emphasis away from the focus on inactive and hard-to-reach young people. Whilst YDance is now working on a new programme developing dance leadership skills for girls and adult volunteers throughout Scotland, the company intends to promote the model established by the Free To Dance programme to local health boards and local authorities as a method of increasing physical activity amongst teenage girls. A successful six-month project based on this model ran in Edinburgh in 2011/12, supported by the Edinburgh Physical Activity Alliance.

Dance Gains a Higher Profile and Recognition for Its Role in Addressing National Health Policies and Campaigns

Dance workers improved their capacity to overcome the challenges of working with the target group and tailor dance programmes to meet their needs. This learning has been used to support national policies and campaigns in which YDance continues to have a leading role, including the development of Get Scotland Dancing—a Scottish Government policy initiative aimed at increasing dance participation in the lead up to the 2014 Commonwealth Games in Glasgow and more recently, YDance Active (YDance 2015). This latter scheme, funded by the Government body *sportscotland*, takes forward the experience and knowledge acquired over the course of the Free To Dance programme, by encouraging girls to engage in physical exercise and by supporting those who have gained their nationally recognized Dance Leadership Award. It will continue to input into future debate and policy development in the fields of physical activity, youth arts provision, and increase in the profile of dance in Scotland.

Improved Reputation and Track Record in Providing a Range of Specialized Dance Programmes

Dance workers perceived that they increased girls' physical activity levels and highlighted the increasing levels of mentoring support which they provided to newly trained dance leaders, as more people took up this offer. Similarly, dance workers gave participants a wide range of positive experiences. YDance's specialist focus on youth dance and its ability to offer specialized training and support gave added advantages which drove forward the success of Free To Dance. YDance used its own resources and expertise to good effect, and worked well with partners to diversify the opportunities and benefits gained. The Free To Dance team provided strong evidence that the programme contributed to the achievement of national health targets. Equally, YDance has increased its capacity to deliver similar programmes with this highly challenging target group in future.

CONCLUSION

Research has shown that the drop in physical activity in adolescence is not a purely female trait, nor a purely British one, but spans Western culture widely (Pelclová et al. 2008; Hall 2011). To address this, it is recognized that appropriate activities have to be offered in schools, to keep teenagers motivated (Peclova et al. 2008; Wilkinson and Bretzing 2011). Free To Dance, while focusing only on female adolescents, went a step further by offering the opportunity to dance in the community, so that it broke the association with school, which had been a source of negative physical experience for the girls. Hall (2011) observes that the social skills and social capital thus gained are not just an asset for the dancers, but also a community asset:

> Dance classes are thus environments in which social skills can be learned and social capital developed, providing benefits that exceed economic considerations and so representing unique community capacity building opportunities. In terms of capacity building, Hall and Banno (2001) also found that public performance of activities such as dance (for young females) and exhibition games of rugby sevens (for young males) were effective both in developing a sense of belonging to community and in contributing to its vibrant life.

Free To Dance, then, not only gave the girls the chance to achieve a high standard in their chosen physical activity, but also gave them life-enhancing tools to help them in their social integration. Perhaps if schools were to provide more choice of physical activities, it might prevent girls becoming alienated from physical education in the first place. Wilkinson and Bretzing (2011) suggest that

> yoga, kickboxing, and spinning (to name but a few) ... could help generate interest in fitness activities, not just while students are in school but outside of school, and such activities could ultimately become a lifetime activity.

Questions arising from the project include:

- Would the girls' new fitness level be sustained after their series of classes had finished?
- Would the project have a lasting effect on their social network?

- Would it continue to influence their self-esteem and therefore their confidence in their everyday lives?
- Would the girls continue dancing as their chosen form of physical expression and exercise?
- Would the adoption of role models from the world of dance be conducive to keeping the girls focused?

YDance Active is well positioned to answer these questions and stimulate further debate. Burkhardt and Brennan (2012) conducted mixed methods research and agree that there is 'some evidence to suggest that involvement in dance may have some positive outcomes on physical and psychosocial well-being' (p. 148), but that there is scope for much more in-depth research on the subject. In terms of the Free To Dance participants' personal perceptions of their wellbeing, it would be interesting to conduct a hermeneutic study, as they progressed along the journey of exploration through creative dance, learning about themselves through the kinaesthetic and social experiences, and taking control of their own development as individuals. A study of that nature (Oliver 2010) explored the experiences of teenage dancers who were selected for a community dance group, and who were already active and predisposed to dance. The findings of that study addressed the dancers' experiences as they became agents in shaping their own identity. A similar study of the Free To dance participants and subsequent YDance Active participants could provide insight into their own feelings of wellbeing, as opposed to the Dance Workers' perceptions of these. Clearly, the purpose of the Free To Dance project was to deliver quantitative findings as much as—or more than—qualitative. Without more funding, a deeper and more introspective exploration remains tantalizingly just out of reach.

NOTES

1. The Dance-in-Schools Initiative ran from 2005 to 2008. It was funded by the Scottish Government Health Department, created and delivered by YDance, and linked to Curriculum for Excellence (the Education curriculum document for Scotland). YDance Active continues to promote dance among girls who have become alienated from other forms of physical exercise.
2. Warwick-Edinburgh Mental Well-Being Scale (2006).
3. Active Awards are small, UK Lottery-funded grants, primarily for sport but extended to other physical activities such as dance.

REFERENCES

Adkins, L. (2004). 'Reflexivity: Freedom or habit of gender?', in L. Adkins and B. Skeggs (eds.), *Feminism after Bourdieu*. Oxford: Blackwell, pp. 191–210.

Biscomb, K., Matheson, H., Beckerman, N., Tungatt, M., and Jarrett, H. (2000). 'Staying active while still being you', *Women in Sport and Physical Activity Journal*, 9(2): 79–97.

Bourdieu, P. (2005). *The Rules of Art*. Cambridge: Polity Press.

Bracey, L. (2004). 'Voicing connections: An interpretive study of university dancers' experiences', *Research in Dance Education*, 5(1): 7–24.

Burkhardt, J. and Brennan, C. (2012). 'The effects of recreational dance interventions on the health and well-being of children and young people: A systematic review', *Arts and Health*, 4(2): 148–61.

Byrnes, J. (2003). 'Cognitive development during adolescence', in G. R. Adams and M. D. Berzonsky (eds.), *Blackwell Handbook of Adolescence*. Oxford: Blackwell, pp. 227–46.

Catch The Light. (2011). *Free To Dance 2008–2011: End of Programme Review*. Prepared on behalf of YDance (Scottish Youth Dance). Unpublished.

Craig, D. (2007). 'An exploratory study of the concept of meaningfulness in music', *Nordic Journal of Music Therapy*, 16(1): 3–13.

Enright, E. and O'Sullivan, M. (2010). 'Can I do it in my pyjamas? Negotiating a physical education curriculum with teenage girls', *European Physical Education Review*, 16(3): 203–222.

Foucault, M. (1980). *Power/Knowledge: Selected Interviews and Other Writings 1972–77*, ed. C. Gordon. London: Harvester Press.

Gardner, H. (2006). *Multiple Intelligences*. 2nd edn. New York: Basic Books.

Gordon, J. and Grant, G. (1997). *How We Feel: An Insight into the Emotional World of Teenagers*. London: Jessica Kingsley.

Green, J. (2004). 'The politics and ethics of health in dance education', in L. Rouhiainen, E. Antilla, S. Hämäläinen, and T. Löytönen (eds.), *The Same Difference? Ethical and Political Perspectives on Dance*. Helsinki: Theatre Academy, pp. 65–78.

Hall, N. (2011) '"Give it everything you got": Resilience for young males through sport', *International Journal of Men's Health*, 10(1): 65–81.

Hämäläinen, S. (2004). 'Ethical issues of evaluation and feedback in a dance class', in L. Rouhiainen, E. Anttila, S. Hämäläinen, and T. Löytönen (eds.), *The Same Difference? Ethical and Political Perspectives on Dance*. Miktor, Helsinki: Theatre Academy, pp. 79–108.

Kimmerle, M. and Cote-Laurence, P. (2003). *Learning Dance Skills: A Motor Learning and Development Perspective*. Andover, NJ: Michael J. Ryan.

Kroger, J. (2004). *Identity in Adolescence: The Balance Between Self and Other*. 3rd edn. Hove: Routledge.

Moshman, D. (1999). *Adolescent Psychological Behaviour*. London: Laurence Erlbaum Associates.

Muldoon, J. and Inchley, J. (2008). *The YDance 'Dance in Schools' Initiative: Final Evaluation Report*. Edinburgh University: Child and Adolescent Health Research Unit. <http://cahru.org/content/04-publications/04-reports/disi_final_report.pdf> (accessed 8 April 2015).

Oliver, S. (2007). *Little Girls en pointe, Dance Expression*. Epsom: A. E. Morgan Publications.

Oliver, S. (2010). *Creative Dance for Adolescents and their Social Wellbeing: A Community-Based Study Set in Scotland*. PhD thesis. Saarbrücken: VDM, Verlag Dr Müller; Edinburgh, Queen Margaret University.

Pelclová, J., Frömel, K., Skalik, K., and Stratton, G. (2008). 'Dance and aerobic dance in physical education lessons: The influence of the student's role in physical activity for girls', *Acta. University Palacki. Olomouc., Gymn.*, 38(2): 85–92.

Riley, S. and Cahill, S. (2005). 'Managing meaning and belonging: young women's negotiation of authenticity in body art', *Journal of Youth Studies*, 8(3): 261–79.

Ryan, T. and Poirier, Y. (2012). 'Secondary physical education avoidance and gender: Problems and antidotes', *International Journal of Instruction*, 5(2): 173–93.

Scottish Executive (2005). The Scottish Health Survey 2003. <http://www.scotland.gov.uk/Publications/2005/12/02160336/03367> (accessed 2 February 2012).

Smith, M. (2002). 'Moving self', in *Research in Dance Education*. London: Taylor and Francis, pp. 123–41.

sportscotland (2006). 'School playing fields design'. <http://www.sportscotland.com> (accessed May 2012).

Thomas, H. (2003). *The Body, Dance and Cultural Theory*. Basingstoke: Palgrave Macmillan.

Tweedie, K. (2011). 'Jump to it: Kids love healthy options on offer from great projects', Glasgow, *Daily Record*, 11 March.

Vygotsky, L. (1986). *Thought and Language*, ed. A. Kozulin. Cambridge, MA: MIT Press. First published in 1934.

Wilkinson, C. and Bretzing, R. (2011). 'High school girls' perceptions of selected fitness activities', *Physical Educator*, 68(2): npn.

YDance (2015). 'Y it's good to dance', *Particpate*, (2), pp.2–3. <http://communitydance.org.uk>

Youth Scotland (2006). *Girls on the move*. YWCA, Scotland. <http://www.youthscotland.org.uk/projects/girls-on-the-move.htm> (accessed 17 August 2012).

....

CHAPTER 31

METHODS OF PROMOTING GENDER DEVELOPMENT IN YOUNG CHILDREN THROUGH DEVELOPMENTAL DANCE RHYTHMS

A Kestenberg Movement Profile (KMP) Dance/ Movement Therapy Approach

....

SUSAN LOMAN

INTRODUCTION

....

YOUNG children express themselves through their bodies' language. During the first 6 years of life, the way children communicate their needs and feelings is often shown through non-verbal behaviour. Not all of the young child's movements are random. Child and adult psychoanalyst Judith Kestenberg (1975) discovered that during the first 6 years of life, ten predictable rhythmic patterns of muscle tension (tension flow rhythms) could be observed and actually recorded. Although these rhythms function to help children satisfy biological needs and drives, such as sucking to obtain nourishment, they may also serve to elicit attachment and connection with others. Each of the ten rhythms has a period of prevalence in the child's life, such as a patting/biting rhythm during teething, but all the rhythms are available at birth and continue throughout the lifespan. Adults continue to move with these rhythms and show their own proclivities towards specific ones. Recent studies indicate that in adults, rhythm also influences attitudes (Koch 2014). Both children and adults can combine rhythms to reveal their own movement and personality signatures. Dance/movement therapists with a

Kestenberg Movement Profile (KMP) lens have an opportunity to reach young children through attuning to them by matching their tension flow rhythms. When dance/movement therapists attune to children's rhythms through dancing with their preferred and phase-specific tension flow rhythm patterns, children feel responded to and understood (Loman 1998). Attunement leads to a sharing of feelings or empathy. This concept of attunement is exceedingly simple, but is not often followed. Very often, young children express their frustrations and needs and are met by a discordant movement pattern.

The original context for this dance/movement therapy (DMT) work with young children and their parents was in a primary prevention setting directed by Judith Kestenberg called The Center for Children and Parents. The focus at the Center was to help parents and their children to communicate more effectively together through non-verbal methods such as attunement, mutual holding patterns, breath support, and dance and creative arts, within a community setting. One of the Center's missions was to address issues of isolation for new parents, and a benefit of attending the Center was to have a sense of belonging to a group whose goals were to promote community spirit during the challenging process of parenting. The Center was open to local children from birth to 4 years of age accompanied by a parent, relative, or caregiver. It provided parents and caregivers with a chance to play with, as well as understand, the children's development. An additional benefit for parents was to begin to understand the various stages in movement development that their children were experiencing. They began to be able to predict the challenges that their children were undergoing, rather than be taken by surprise each time the child entered a new stage of development.

The goals of The Center for Parents and Children were to prevent emotional disorders in young children, to optimize development, and to facilitate harmonious relationships between family members utilizing non-verbal, as well as verbal when possible, methods of communication. Part of the prevention philosophy was based on the concept of providing an optimal environment for growth in each developmental phase. Pleasurable creative art activities were offered which enhanced and supported the child's mastery of the developmental tasks.

As the dance/movement therapist at The Center for Parents and Children, I observed the movement dialogue between parent and child—looking for times of matching rhythms and affective sharing, to find ways to build on these emerging skills. Noticing when clashing or discordant rhythms occurred in the relationship was also vital in order to find ways to bring awareness of the differences and to work on mutually satisfying patterns (LeMessurier and Loman 2008). The Center's work was based on the assumption that a dance/movement therapist who understands the predictable phases associated with children's development is able to provide clearer intervention strategies when working with both typically developing children and children with disorders, in order to promote wellbeing. In this context, a philosophy of primary prevention of emotional disorders was highlighted that involved supporting the families' journeys through developmental challenges, vulnerable periods, transitions, and stress. There was an assumption in the work taking place in the Center that even typically developing children could be faced with difficulties such as weaning, separation, sleep disturbances, or illness, to name a few, all of which could be manifested through movement expression. Helping families negotiate the rough times as well as the smooth ones was facilitated in a community environment. Ultimately, the wellbeing of children was seen as relating to self-confidence, being able to make wide choices for self-expression, and being able to self-regulate. Movement, dance, and creative arts were the fundamental strategies for supporting mastery of developmental tasks and channelling frustration into creative expression. Dance was a major activity for enhancing family and community harmony (Loman 1994).

This chapter presents KMP approaches to wellbeing that support the child's developmental progression and emotional regulation through interactive dance connected to specific movement phases of development. After an introduction to Kestenberg's ten developmental rhythms and background information on gender development in particular, the chapter presents clinical vignettes of my DMT work with children from 3 to 6 years old addressing the topic of wellbeing with an emphasis on gender issues.

The following summary of KMP phases (which parallels Anna Freud's Metapsychological Profile; Freud 1965) places gender development within the framework of normal developmental stages (see Figure 31.1). Martin and Ruble (2004) point out that children begin to know if they are a boy or girl by the age of 3, and form concepts of gender by the age of 2. Particular attention is placed on interventions for children aged 3 to 6, as developmental themes during these ages may be less clear to both dance/movement therapists and caregivers.

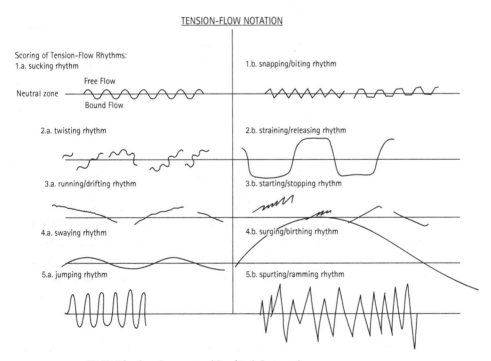

FIGURE 31.1. KMP Rhythm Sequence. (Credit: S. Loman.)

KMP Rhythms Sequence

First Year of Life Rhythms

Oral Sucking

During the first half year of life, an infant seeks union with primary caregivers through smooth, repetitive, rocking movements. These 'sucking rhythms' originate in the mouth and serve the needs of sucking for nourishment as well as self-soothing. The rhythms spread throughout the body and serve the task of attachment. The primary plane in which movement takes place is the horizontal. Children in this phase enjoy putting objects in their mouths and sucking on them: pacifiers, fingers, toys, and blankets all serve as pleasurable objects for this purpose. Music that is soothing and repetitive, such as reggae, can be used as a backdrop for a 'rocking the baby' dance. Adults can hold the baby in a rocking chair or dance in a waltz style to capture the essence of a 'sucking rhythm' dance.

Oral Snapping/Biting

With the advent of teething in the second half of the first year, an infant begins to bite to alleviate oral discomfort. 'Snapping/biting rhythms' are characterized by sharp transitions from contracted to released muscle tension. They serve the practical function of cutting through solid food, as well as the developmental functions of separation, differentiation, and boundary formation. The child enjoys patting and tapping, shaking rattles, clapping games, and banging on any convenient surface. Repetitive tapping music, such as Makeba's 'Pata pata' can be used to support a patting dance such as pat-a-cake. Instruments such as shakers and bells are enjoyable props for eliciting the 'biting rhythm' dance.

Second Year of Life Rhythms

Anal Twisting

Beginning at the end of the first year and continuing into the beginning of the second year, the child becomes flexible at the waist and pelvis in the service of crawling and adjusting to spatial demands. 'Anal twisting' rhythms appear in spinal motions that originate in the anal sphincter and spread throughout the body. The child is playful, teasing, and coy, and begins to practice locomotor skills. At times, the child enjoys smearing food and such creative messiness as finger painting. Music such as belly dance or Middle Eastern music supports the child's meandering exploration and playful moves to create the 'twisting rhythm' dance.

Anal Strain/Release

Typical of an 18-month-old child, tasks in this phase are the beginnings of bowel control, climbing skills, autonomy, stability, organization, confrontation, verticality, intentionality, presentation of self, and contending with the force of gravity. In this phase the child makes the transition into the vertical plane, becoming upright to face the world. Children enjoy squeezing and pressing clay, throwing objects into containers, and asserting themselves by saying 'no' with great intensity. This is also the age when temper tantrums begin in earnest. Powerful music that has a long hold and then a release, such as 'The stroll', can support energetic pushing and tug-of-war dances using the 'strain/release rhythm'.

Third Year of Life Rhythms

Urethral Running/Drifting

This developmental stage begins in the 2-year-old child. Tasks are to master walking, carry out operations, and learn to run without yet being able to stop. It is a phase of free-flowing mobility and wandering with no specific aim. It marks the transition from being stable in the vertical plane to becoming fluid in the sagittal plane (moving back and forth). The rhythm originates in the urethral sphincter muscle initiating the flow of urine. Typical activities in this phase include play with water and sand, as well as chasing and catching games. Flowing music such as 'New Age' music, that simulates the flow of water, may be played for a follow-the-leader sequence with scarves for the 'running/drifting rhythm' dance.

Urethral Starting/Stopping

At around the age of 2½ years, children learn to initiate and stop the flow of urine as well as to stop their bodies, without falling, while running. Movement qualities develop an abrupt sharpness that has an urgent or impatient sense of time. Favorite activities include squirting water and stop–start games such as freeze and move, musical chairs, and red-light–green-light. The use of up-tempo music that can be paused and restarted elicits the 'starting/stopping rhythm' dance.

Fourth Year of Life Rhythms

Inner-Genital Swaying

The inner-genital phase is the developmental stage beginning around 3 years old, and the task is to integrate past and present needs. Children feel internal wavy sensations that stem from their reproductive organs that come and go intermittently. They may complain of 'tummy aches'. Boys and girls are interested in babies and playing with dolls in a nurturing fashion. Typically, they alternate between mature behaviour and regressing to earlier and more disorganized patterns. Both girls and boys begin nagging, and are unclear about what they require to satisfy their needs. Music such as a lullaby or waltz-type beat suggests wave-like circular movement to create the 'swaying rhythm' dance (see 'inner-genital swaying' Video 31.1 of a child dancing with a hula hoop on the Companion Website ▶).

Inner-Genital Surging/Birthing

In the second part of the phase, around 3½ years old, 'surging/birthing' rhythms of grad-ually rising and falling waves of high-intensity muscle tension manifest themselves. Children squeeze through tunnels and small spaces (see the 'inner-genital surging/birthing' Video 31.2 of a child trying to squeeze through a folded mat on the Companion Website ⓟ), love to play inside forts and houses, and then burst out. This phase allows children who may not have had vaginal deliveries to 'rebirth themselves' through head-initiated movements and tactile pressure. Whale and dolphin melodies create the slow deepening rhythm needed for this 'surging/birthing rhythm' dance.

Fifth–Sixth Year of Life Rhythms

Outer-Genital Jumping

The 4-year-old child begins to use outward directed 'jumping' rhythms, typified by an increase in gross motor activity, showing off, accidentally crashing into people, and playing superheroes. At this age, movements are intense, percussive, and abrupt, and jumping and leaping are favourite activities. Children develop a strong sense of relation-ships and friendships. Rock music and drumming circle music support the exuberant jumping-bean bouncing of the 'jumping rhythm' dance (see the 'outer-genital jumping' Videos 31.3 and 31.4 of the young girl's jumping dance, ⓟ and the boy's gathering of scarves and throwing them in the air with high intensity and abruptness ⓟ).

Outer-Genital Spurting/Ramming

The 5-year-old enters the spurting/ramming phase, leaping abruptly and using a sharper and more directed high-intensity rhythm. These movements are seen in karate-type movements that may be ballistic and combative. The 5–6-year-old child wants to crash into objects and people (see the 'outer-genital spurting/ramming' video clip of a boy crashing into soft mats; Video 31.4 ⓟ). Children of this age enjoy role-playing super-heroes and precise games of kicking and punching. Zumba-type music helps children express 'spurting/ramming rhythm' dances.

Because in this chapter we are most interested in the establishment of healthy gender development, we will concentrate in more detail on the two phases that emphasize gen-der development: the inner and outer genital phases of 3–6-year-old children.

Inner-Genital Phase Development

Although some adults have difficulty believing that children experience any sexual feel-ings at all, it is also farfetched to assume that sexuality emerges for the very first time in adolescence. Judith Kestenberg has outlined periods in a child's growth when gen-der development becomes prominent (Kestenberg Amighi et al. 1999). As Kestenberg (1975) argues, in typical growth and development, children experience increases in male and female hormone levels, promoting internal sensations and jumping and intrusive behaviours, and they exhibit curiosity about gender differences. Biological approaches of gender development in early childhood emphasize the role of genes, hormones, and the brain in physical and psychological sexual differentiation (Ruble et al. 2006). The types of sexual feelings in the young child are clearly not the same as those of adults; rather, they are precursors of adolescent and adult expressions of sexuality.

Kestenberg (1980) based her developmental discoveries on the following sources: cross-sectional and longitudinal observation of infants, children and adolescents, and adults (when they became parents); memories and reconstructions from the analyses of adults, adolescents, and latency children; the analysis of pre-school children from the ages of under 2 to 6 years old; developmental assessments on children from birth to 6 years using the KMP as well as verbal behaviour; clinical findings at The Center for Parents and Children in Long Island, New York; and studies on hormonal changes in children and adolescents.

The sequence of motor development that Judith Kestenberg (Kestenberg Amighi et al. 1999) has outlined parallels psychodynamic theory, but adds a stage observed in the 3–4-year-old that she discovered during her clinical observations of young children. This additional phase, called the 'inner-genital phase', offers valuable information about gender and sexual development in both boys and girls. In a longitudinal study of ethnic-minority children and gender-typed behaviours in early childhood, researchers Halim et al. (2013) discovered that the transition from ages 3–4 years is an especially important time in children's gender development for the active consolidation of gender information.

Judith Kestenberg (1980) and colleagues observed 3-year-old children at The Center for Parents and Children in the 1970s, and discovered that they were undergoing developmental transitions not described elsewhere. They identified a new developmental phase that they named the 'inner-genital phase', when toddlers are in a time of transition—leaving behind babyhood, but not yet a big boy or girl. Children begin to have maturing interests in creativity and integration, but also feel sporadic interference from earlier phases. While 3-year-old children are drawn to their past babyhoods, they are also pulled to the future, resulting in confusion. Three-year-old regression to earlier phases may become exacerbated when the older child gets a sibling. Anthropologist Janet Kestenberg Amighi (2004), who conducted research in Bali observed:

> Especially upon birth of a new sibling, the 3-year-old Balinese child typically experiences a dramatic shift in mother–child contact, with weaning from the breast, weaning from the hip (being carried), and removal from the next-to-mother sleeping position. This weaning process is usually accompanied by temper tantrums, whining, or aggressiveness toward the mother. (p. 37)

Parents may become disappointed because their do not understand the minute-to-minute changes children are going through at this age. They expect that because their children can now act more grown up, they will always act maturely. When children do regress to earlier phases, it may serve as an opportunity to work out unresolved issues from their past. Regressions to earlier phases through play about unresolved issues are actually potential signs of health and wellness, and can lead to resolution (Loman et al. 2009). The KMP approach offers ways to rechoreograph these regressions and unresolved developmental issues, and work with families to help them understand and meet these challenges. Through rechoreographing regressions, children have the opportunity to progress. Potential issues which the child may be dealing with are unresolved separations (biting-phase issues), power struggles and temper tantrums (strain/release issues), or bedwetting (starting/stopping phase issues).

According to Kestenberg (1975) the 3-year-old child's task is the integration of past and present needs. The child's behaviour wavers between mature and immature actions, and regressions are typical. At times the child behaves like a big boy or girl, and at other times wants to act like a baby. A confusing, nagging feeling begins at this stage, and children are unclear about what they want or need to help them feel satisfied. This vagueness stems from a nagging sensation emanating from the pelvis and internal organs that comes and goes intermittently. Children become interested in their bellies and put soft objects underneath their shirts as if they were pregnant. Children are very interested in playing with dolls (Halim et al. 2013), and they are very interested in babies and nurturing activities. The rhythm in this phase is called 'swaying', and is of low intensity, gradual, and undulating. Children become very creative, dancing and drawing faces and circles inside circles. They like to hide in enclosed spaces, keep secrets, tell long stories, and feel inside sensations all in keeping with an internal focus. Children often ask never-ending 'why' questions and complain about feeling bored, but also have surges of creativity and receptivity.

Kestenberg (1975) has described the following:

> Children of both sexes solve the problem posed by the vagueness of inside sensations by externalizing them to the outside. The girl seems to experience periodically recurring vaginal tensions as something unfocused, 'nagging' her from the inside. She tends to nag others, especially her mother, and, in identification with her mother, her baby doll. The unclear tensions inside give rise to fantasies that she has a baby there, but she transfers her inner-genital impulses to dolls and toys. The boy at that time equates his testicles with male babies; but the testicles can be palpated, moved, and even visually observed through the thin scrotal sac. Consequently, the girl's need for fondling on the outside that which cannot be reached inside is much more imperative than that of the boy. The boy is much bolder in experimenting with the inside of objects and chooses a greater variety of models of his inside. He becomes interested in everything that moves and he tries to find out how it works. He is trying to solve on objects the intricate mechanics of erections and testicular movements, which he interprets as imposed on him from the inside of the body. (pp. 320–1)

Under optimal conditions, parents are proud of their children's creativity, drawing, singing, story telling, and the other imaginative aspects of their children's play. However, many caregiving adults tire of perennial play, regressive fantasies, nagging, and untiring questions, whose answers never satisfy the children. Caregivers need to be prepared for the challenges they face when raising children in this phase. It is helpful to be accepting when boys in this phase play with dolls, talk about wanting to be a mummy, and identify with their mothers.

Outer-Genital Phase Development

At the end of the inner-genital phase, children end their close identification with their mothers and turn to identifying with their fathers and males (Kestenberg and Kestenberg Amighi 1993). The outer-genital child is outward oriented and is in love with movement and spatial exploration. Hughes (2003) observed that pre-school boys are likely to choose adventure or action-oriented roles such as superheroes in their dramatic play. Behaviours derive from an interest in the external aspects of the body and the overflowing of those interests into the outside world. Children may become preoccupied with their external genitals. The external genital excitement sharply rises and falls. Children become infatuated with their own bodies and their new abilities of jumping. Their bodies are held as a united whole that they thrust into things or people. They throw their entire bodies fearlessly into activities. Their emotions range from loving to hate, active to passive. They need a framework to help contain their energy and be encouraged to vent their excitement into creative channels.

Kestenberg (1975) describes the 4-year-old child's overflowing activity as an expression of body and mind becoming increasingly sexualized. Children's exhibitionism may become excessive; they brag, clown, exaggerate, and show off. They know no bounds. They jump for jumping's sake until exhausted, and leap and ram against people. Global motor urges are undefined and do not allow for subtle approaches. When people shrink away from intrusive advances, the 5-year-old child is especially vulnerable to rejections. Exuberant joy can turn into inconsolable crying when feelings are hurt or knees skinned. Four-year-old children frequently hurt themselves and others primarily because they seem to want to master things with their total body, urgently seeking out objects and outlets for their global drives.

In the later part of the phase, around 5 years old, children become more focused. They can control their drives and aggression by channelling their energy into precise motor skills. They enjoy roughhousing. The 5-year old sees things black or white, right or wrong, good guys and bad guys. They invent excuses for misbehaviour. They project bad behaviour onto others, such as 'he made me do it'. Children may not always recognize right and wrong, because they believe their excuses.

Kestenberg (1975) portrayed the spurting/ramming phase in both boys and girls as a time to differentiate between various forms of extremes: real and unreal, true and untrue, good or bad, male or female. An overzeal in differentiation is apparent in all activities. The 5-year-old tends to be concrete and realistic.

It is helpful for dance/movement therapists and adult caregivers to become active with children of this age and provide opportunities for free play, rhythmic dance with percussive beats, and gross motor outlets. Children enjoy having mattresses or trampolines to jump on and daily opportunities to physically express themselves.

Examples of Promoting Wellbeing Through Dance/Movement Therapy (DMT)

My current work with this population draws from my experiences at Judith Kestenberg's Center for Children and Parents. The Center was a model for the Creative Movement Group for Infants, Toddlers, and Caregivers that I run as a practicum class for DMT students at Antioch University New England. The group comprises approximately ten families, including individual children or siblings and their parents or caregivers. Both group interaction and one-to-one work are encouraged, as needed, within the group. My work incorporates the key concept of attunement to recognize and understand childrens' needs and temperaments and their level of development (Loman 1998). The technique of attunement, or reflecting muscle tension, rhythm, or body shape, can be quite effective for developing non-verbal empathy. Judith Kestenberg's developmental rhythms serve as the foundation for understanding the underlying motor qualities in children's growth.

Some of the highlights of this approach to working with young children are meeting the child's developmental needs through pleasurable creative art modalities, channelling aggressive impulses into appropriate and interesting motor avenues, creating and maintaining a consistent 'holding environment' (Winnicott 1965) that establishes a basic trusting relationship, and strengthening the child's movement resources so that the child is better able to cope with challenges in the environment.

Props such as scarves, parachutes, soft balls, hoops, and stretch materials are made available to young children and serve as 'neutral' objects (Loman 1994). The children can use these materials in their own individual way to help them express their moods and feelings. For example, if a child comes to the group in an angry mood, a scarf can be waved vigorously up and down or thrown, which helps the child creatively express these feelings. If, on a different day, the child was sad, the scarf could be waved slowly and delicately. In the community setting, caregivers are encouraged to reflect these expressive movements with their own scarves, and themes that promote mutual understanding are developed. Sharing movement communicates support, recognition, and builds a sense of self-confidence in children (Tortora, 2006).

At other times, a scarf may become a bridge between people. Caregivers and children may move together as they hold different ends of the scarf. When the child or caregiver ends the interaction, the child can carry the image of this interaction in the realm of the imagination.

Parachutes are used to encourage group community activity even when individual group members move in different ways. For example, as several 3½-year-old girls jump in the middle of a large parachute, the dance/movement therapist and caregivers holding onto the edge of the parachute attune to the girls' rhythmic jumping by making jumping-type bounces and vocalizations in time with the girls. This example of group rhythmic action intends to promote the feeling of community spirit and belonging. Children of different age groups can tune into each other and cooperate by sharing similar rhythms.

In this particular approach to DMT, acknowledgement of the full range of feelings is encouraged through the creative arts. We often need to deal with a variety of forms of aggression and provide safe ways for our clients to express themselves (Kornblum 2002).

Dance/movement therapists encourage our clients to move with more variety of movement patterns and more flexibility. This aids in the availability of choices through creative expression. For example, when a 3-year-old child was angry and would not participate in the activity, singing the song 'When you're angry and you know it' prompted her to show us three or four dances about feeling angry.

Understanding that children have their own movement styles and preferences educates us in how to approach children individually. One child, who was pretending to hide, liked to be cajoled into interactions. When I exclaimed 'Where is Katie? Where could she have gone? I don't see her anywhere, do you?', the child began to smile and then appeared. Other children may like to be approached with hesitation, coyness, or directness.

Dance/movement therapists may use dance and movement to connect with clients, help them explore social and emotional dynamics, express feelings, build self-regulation, and integrate the whole self. Using an approach that combines relational and developmental perspectives, dance/movement therapists use the body and movement to help caregivers and children work through challenging behavioural issues. Movement is used for assessment, to build therapeutic relationships, and as a way to support clients in healing.

Through a DMT perspective, children use movement to tell us how they feel and what they need. Relationships and emotions are demonstrated through the body: muscle tension, facial expressions, body shaping, eye contact, breath, gestures, and full body movement. Dance/movement therapists observe the movement qualities in children and caregivers very carefully, and use their own bodies to try on the client's movement and to attune with the person on a body-felt level. Children are very responsive to this; most very young children seem to engage quickly in relationship when they see others connecting with them non-verbally.

An ongoing goal in the KMP approach to DMT is to support progression through developmental phases and healthy growth (Loman 1998). An environment is created to help a child explore movement dynamics that encourage joyful play and growth. A key concept is to provide creative outlets for expression of developmental and emotional release (Loman 1994).

Building self-regulation is an important task of early development that grows out of a caregiving relationship (Bowlby 1969; Sossin 1999, 2007; Stern 1985). Similar to a parent or caregiver, the dance/movement therapist matches the movement quality of a child and then either enhances or lessens the quality to teach self-regulation. By helping to modify negative states and amplify positive states through non-verbal interactions, children learn to regulate themselves and experience good feelings.

Validating emotions, increasing feeling recognition, and learning to identify feelings are goals to support young children's social and emotional development. Understanding feelings and being able to read non-verbal expression are important for successful social interactions (Kornblum 2002).

It has been argued (Goodill 2005) that discharging negative emotional content physically helps us think clearly and prevent physical illness. Children spontaneously find physical outlets for the expression of their feelings. The following vignettes illustrate examples of DMT groups in community settings and individual DMT with children from 3 to 6 years old.

Working with Issues in Three to Four Years Olds

To illustrate DMT with a child coping with challenges stemming from the birth of a sister, I will describe family DMT with Polly, a 3-year-old girl. Polly, her mother, and new baby, Sharon, were participants in the group for caregivers and their young children. Polly and her mother were participants in the group for the months preceding Sharon's birth. Now that the baby was born, Polly demonstrated both nurturing toward the baby as well as periods of rolling on the floor, kicking out, and clinging to her mother, in keeping with Kestenberg's (1975) description of the nurturing vs. nagging tensions typical of the inner genital phase. Mother reported that at home, father was becoming increasingly frustrated with Polly, and often restricted her to a 'time-out' separating her from the family. The parents did not know how to handle their daughter, and I spoke with the mother, suggesting that Polly's behaviours were part of a typical developmental phase of the 3-year-old. I described how Polly now wanted to pretend that she was a baby at times, and that it was acceptable to cuddle her and treat her as if she were a baby. Polly wanted to get into Sharon's baby carrier, and her mother began to tell her not to do that. I told her mother that this would be acceptable, and Polly happily rocked herself in the carrier as if she were a baby, using the swaying rhythm of gradual low-intensity wavy movements. Later, Polly was creating a 'house' for herself out of mats and scarves, simulating the internal aspect of this phase, putting herself inside an enclosed space. The mat tumbled down, and Polly became distraught and threw herself on the floor, whining, revealing the regressive aspect of the inner genital phase of not being satisfied. With mother observing, I spent much time with Polly, asking if the mat should go this way or that way, and demonstrating many varieties of how the mat could be placed—all the time Polly answering with 'no!' Her mother was able to notice how I remained patient with Polly and stayed with the process even when Polly was frustrated and seemed angry. At one point, when the mat was shaped like a tent, I placed myself low on the ground, peeked through the opening, and looked sideways at Polly with a smile. I was at her level on the floor and created a peek-a-boo dance with her. This was the breakthrough moment, and Polly sat up and began playing happily again. Mother and I discussed later how much patience it takes to work through the 'dissatisfaction dance' typical of this phase. In subsequent groups, Polly enjoyed dancing in circles with hoops, using the swaying rhythm and sharing her mother's lap with baby Sharon. Mother learned to make room for both children and feel less frustrated with Polly's 'nagginess'. Mother and father became more accepting, and understood Polly's inconsistent behaviour and vacillation between organized creative play and nurturing in contrast to unexpected bouts of nagginess, dissatisfaction, and provocations. Being able to categorize this confusing behaviour within a typical developmental phase was comforting to the parents.

DISCUSSION

Knowing that 3-year-old children enjoy themes of being babies as well as nurturing babies, being contained and going inside enclosed spaces, as well as dancing in circles and spinning, helps guide the dance/movement therapist. The fact that the 3-year-old may regress, nag, and work through earlier unresolved stages or issues, makes this 'second chance' stage especially supportive in achieving integration and contributing towards a healing process. Therapists can ensure that they are prepared when age-inspired issues arise, and can ensure that the holding environment offers intriguing possibilities. For example, a popular theme for 3-year-olds is the creation of big and small ocean waves by waving a parachute or a large scarf up and down gently or vigorously. The children can create themes of water environments and swim in the ocean on top of the waves or go underneath it and swim underwater. Children may dance as mermaids underwater, pretend they are sharks trying to bite others, or swim away from other biting sharks. Images of fish swimming, finding their fish houses, finding food for themselves and their babies, and avoiding fish monsters are all story-lines that I have encountered. Children remember themes from earlier weeks, and begin to make requests for creative play activities based on previous groups.

The development of age-appropriate movement themes, such as becoming popcorn for 4-year-olds who love to jump, supports children in expressing their own creativity and their need to jump for promoting the development of the outer-genital phase. Children can determine how small they will be as kernels of popcorn, and how big they will be when they are ready to jump up and down as popping popcorn. Finally, they decide when the popcorn is ready and if they will have a popcorn party.

A 5-year old child who wants to ram his body into people around him can be creatively encouraged to ram into props such as large pillows or mats suited for this purpose. Large therapy balls, exercise mats, large pillows, or stretch bands can all be adapted for children to safely charge into. To prevent injuries, soft surfaces such as mattresses can also be made available for children's exuberant jumping. Games such as building and knocking down tall towers can provide the safe containing structure that is needed to allow the 5-year-old child an opportunity to release the pent-up feelings associated with intense motor urges. Other ways to channel jumping and ramming impulses are through dancing to lively music such as African drum music or disco-type music with a strong regular beat and 'call and response' interactions between drummers and dancers.

Children love to have their energetic jumps validated through resonating percussion sounds.

Since the central theme of this KMP approach is to follow the child's movement lead, particularly their movement rhythms, working with 3-year-old inner-genital swaying rhythms involves harmonizing with the gradual and low-intensity wavy rhythms and being prepared for shifts into regressive derailment. Through this attunement in rhythmic shifts, caregivers and dance/movement therapists can support young children's fragile sense of self and promote mutual understanding and integration, including necessary regressions.

The KMP approach assumes that in typical development, children at a specific developmental level will naturally be drawn to themes representing their own phase. When children have experienced challenges such as abuse, neglect, or trauma, their developmental progression and their needs may be delayed or prematurely accelerated. It may be difficult for therapists to determine where the child is functioning developmentally. The KMP can be used as a clinical, observational assessment tool to help identify the child's predominant movement rhythms. Children reveal what issues are most challenging for them through displaying prevalent movement patterns over and over, and by repetitive behaviours that represent a recurring theme. The dance/movement therapist meets the child on its own movement level, and co-creates spontaneous movement scenarios with the child that lead towards resolution. The child may wish to repeat these scenarios over and over until they have worked through the issue to their satisfaction. In order to gain the child's trust, the dance/movement therapist provides consistency, regularity, and predictability through movement empathy and support.

Conclusion

Essential elements of the KMP DMT approach are creating and maintaining a consistent 'holding environment' that establishes a basic trusting relationship, channelling children's overly energetic and socially inappropriate impulses into creative and expressive dance/movement avenues, and strengthening the child's movement resources so that the child is better able to cope with challenges in the environment (Loman 2010).

Judith Kestenberg's developmental rhythms provide the foundation for understanding the underlying motor qualities in children's growth, including gender development. Movement behaviours that seem confusing can be viewed from a developmental framework and understood as part of the typical developmental progression. Through the understanding of this predictable developmental sequence, both dance/movement therapists and caregivers can empathize with children and build healthy communication patterns. They can follow the child's lead and redirect those potentially sexualized and interpersonally inappropriate behaviours into satisfying and creative dance outlets. Children are continuously evolving and growing, and having knowledge of Judith Kestenberg's developmental progression is a helpful guidepost to predict where the child is developmentally, leading to wellness and fulfilment. The opportunity to work with young children and caregivers in a community setting enhances social development and provides outlets for creative self-expression and pathways toward wellbeing.

References

Bowlby, J. (1969). *Attachment and Loss.* London: Hogarth Press.

Freud, A. (1965). *Normality and Pathology in Childhood: Assessments of Development.* Madison, WI: International Universities Press.

Goodill, S. (2005). *An Introduction to Medical Dance/Movement Therapy: Health Care in Motion.* Philadelphia, PA: Jessica Kingsley.

Halim, M., Ruble, D., Tamis-LeMonda, C., and Shrout, P. (2013). 'Rigidity in gender-typed behaviors in early childhood: A longitudinal study of ethnic minority children', *Child Development,* 84(4): 1269–84.

Hughes, F. (2003). 'Sensitivity to the social and cultural context of the play of young children', in J. Isenberg and M. Jalongo (eds.), *Major Trends and Issues in Early Childhood Education.* New York, NY: Teachers College Press, pp. 126–33.

Kestenberg, J. S. (1975). *Children and Parents.* New York, NY: Jason Aronson.

Kestenberg, J. S. (1980). 'The inner-genital phase: Prephallic and preoedipal', in D. Mendel (ed.), *Early Feminine Development: Contemporary Psychoanalytic Views.* New York, NY: Spectrum Publications.

Kestenberg, J. S. and Kestenberg Amighi, J. (1993). *Kinder Zeigen, was sie brauchen: Wie eltern kindliche signale richtig deuten. (Early Child Development: Theories and Techniques for the Intellectual and Emotional Joys of Child Rearing).* Salzburg: Verlag Anton Pustet.

Kestenberg Amighi, J. (2004). 'Contact and connection: A cross-cultural look at parenting styles in Bali and the United States', *ZERO TO THREE: Bulletin of National Center for Infants, Toddlers, and Families,* 24(5): 32–9.

Kestenberg Amighi, J., Loman, S., Lewis, P., and Sossin, K. M. (1999). *The Meaning of Movement: Developmental and Clinical Perspectives of the Kestenberg Movement Profile.* New York, NY: Brunner-Routledge.

Koch, S. (2014). 'Rhythm is it: Effects of dynamic body feedback on affect and attitudes', *Frontiers in Psychology* 5: 1–11. doi:10.3389/fpsyg.2014.00537

Kornblum, R. (2002). *Disarming the Playground: Violence Prevention through Movement and Pro-Social Skills.* Oklahoma City, OK: Wood and Barnes.

LeMessurier, C. and Loman, S. (2008). 'Speaking with the body: Using dance/movement therapy to enhance communication and healing with young children', in D. McCarthy (ed.), *Speaking About the Unspeakable: Non-verbal Methods and Experiences in Therapy with Children.* London: Jessica Kingsley, pp. 45–59.

Loman, S. (1994). 'Attuning to the fetus and the young child: Approaches from dance/movement therapy', *ZERO TO THREE: Bulletin of National Center for Clinical Infant Programs,* 15(1): 20–6.

Loman, S. (1998). 'Employing a developmental model of movement patterns in dance/movement therapy with young children and their families', *American Journal of Dance Therapy,* 20(2): 101–15.

Loman, S. (2010). 'Interaction with children with aggression', in S. Bender (ed.), *Movement Analysis of Interaction.* Berlin: Logos Verlag.

Loman, S., Cellini, N., Johnson, M., and Hallett, E. (2009). 'Magical moments in move-ment: Antioch University New England dance/movement therapy and counseling students quest in the real world', *American Journal of Dance Therapy*, 31(2): 159–69.

Martin, C. and Ruble, D. (2004). 'Children's search for gender cues: Cognitive perspectives on gender development', *Current Directions in Psychological Science*, 13(2): 67–70.

Ruble, D., Martin, C., and Berenbaum, S. (2006). 'Gender development', in W. Damon (ed.), *Handbook of Child Psychology*, vol. 3, 6th edn. Hoboken, NJ: Wiley, pp. 858–932.

Sossin, M. (1999). 'The KMP and infant–parent psychotherapy', in J. Kestenberg Amighi, S. Loman, M. Sossin, and P. Lewis (eds.), *The Meaning of movement*. New York, NY: Brunner-Routledge, pp. 191–209.

Sossin, M. (2007). 'History and future of the Kestenberg Movement Profile', in S. Koch and S. Bender (eds.), *Movement Analysis: The Legacy of Laban, Bartenieff, Lamb and Kestenberg*. Berlin: Logos Verlag, pp. 103–18.

Stern, D. (1985). *The Interpersonal World of the Infant*. New York, NY: Basic Books.

Tortora, S. (2006). *The Dancing Dialogue: Using the Communicative Power of Movement with Young Children*. Baltimore, MD: Brooks Publishing.

Winnicott, D. W. (1965). *The Maturational Process and the Facilitating Environment*. New York, NY: International Universities Press.

CHAPTER 32

TOGETHER WE MOVE

Creating a Laban-Style Movement Choir

CYNTHIA PRATT

Behind external events the dancer perceives another, entirely different, world. There is an energy behind all occurrences and material things for which it is almost impossible to find a name. A hidden, forgotten land-scape lies there, the land of silence, the realm of the soul . . .

Rudolph Laban (1975, p. 89)

INTRODUCTION

ON a mild September evening in 2009, approximately 500 individuals came together to take part in a choreographed, mass-movement event. Spilling over a hill at the edge of an outdoor football field, the participants moved slowly to their places, taking moments in their crossing to create living statues by freezing in a position of their choice. The participants represented a wide range of ages and walks of life, and most had no previous movement experience. The football field was an ideal location for the event, providing ample space for the dancers as well as being flanked on three sides by hills that offered perfect viewing opportunities for onlookers (see Figure 32.1). As the entrance was completed, the dancers gathered at the back of the field, then, as a unit, moved 'downstage' to begin their dance.

This event was, to date, my most ambitious attempt to stage a large-scale dance. My goal in instigating this event was to provide a vehicle for community-level artistic expression, and was inspired by the movement choirs created by Rudolph Laban in early-twentieth-century Germany. From my ongoing investigation into Laban's life and work, I had recognized many parallels between societal concerns a century ago and our increasingly isolating world today—specifically, a sense of personal disenfranchisement and a loss of community. The isolation enforced by our escalating engagement with modern media and the proliferation of personal digital devices—from text-messaging

FIGURE 32.1. Participants during a rehearsal prepare to begin choreographed movements. (Photo credit: Peter Alexander.)

and Twitter feeds to web-surfing among Facebook pages, YouTube videos, and more—is part of this phenomenon. We have so many ways to be connected to the world through our computers that we need not be aware of the world that is right in our room. Technological advances thus have the effect of maximizing individual control over sensory input. Being with others, whether moving with them through open spaces or sharing conversation in intimate settings, is a noisy affair that requires deliberate attention and intentional awareness of one's surroundings. When we can replace the external world with an internal one, we grow intolerant of the messy ways in which others make demands of us.

Writers such as Robert Putnam in his book *Bowling Alone* (2000) have pointed out the social and civic cost of Americans' disengagement from group participation and discourse. This trend is why I wanted to experiment with Laban's idea of large-scale group dance as a means of fulfilling what he termed *Festwille*—'the natural drive to joyfully participate in a symbolic group activity' (Preston-Dunlop 1998, p. 72). Community dance has traditionally been the means to satisfy this urge, but in a modern, urban world, dance for the purpose of solidarity has declined greatly (McNeill, 1995). Following Laban's philosophy, I could see a connection between this disintegration and the overarching anxiety and pessimism present in many individuals today. I felt that instigating the practice of a large group moving together would be an ideal way to revitalize my community and break down barriers between people in a positive, life-affirming way.

The virtues of dance for individuals are well known and much discussed. Dance can be a powerful contributor to the wellbeing of an individual because it relieves stress and anxiety and offers an escape from the pressures of daily life. The sheer physicality of dance can be a powerful means of release, leaving one feeling awake, alive, and fully present in the moment. Anyone who has given themselves over to the full experience of rhythmic movement can attest to the feelings of hyperawareness that accompany dance and the sense of euphoria that carries over even after the dance has stopped. Dance also provides a means of personal expression, since everyone has a distinct style of movement. Through the use of imagery and movement metaphor, it can be used to convey feelings that might not be verbally accessible (Meekums 2002).

What is less discussed is the impact of dance on social groups. Community dance channels the positive feelings of individuals into radically shared emotions, while universal feelings of elation generate a sense of community spirit and camaraderie for the participants. The lines between individuals are blurred, and people find a common ground through a shared experience. Group dance gives participants a sense of belonging to something bigger than themselves, and imbues a community with purpose and meaning. Historian William McNeill has termed the transformational experience of community movement 'muscular bonding', and describes the feelings of euphoria that come from participating in rhythmic group activity: 'A sense of pervasive wellbeing is what I recall; more specifically a strange sense of personal enlargement; a sort of swelling out, becoming bigger than life, thanks to participation in collective ritual' (McNeill 1995, p. 3).

Traditionally, community dance has held a special place in the human experience and has had myriad uses: as a means of cultural identity and social bonding; to express collective feelings such as celebration or grief; for courtship; to prepare for warfare; and for worship, to name but a few (Hanna 1988). Group dance has been present in virtually every civilization and has been a critical vehicle for both community bonding and individual wellbeing (Hanna 1988). However, dance as a structured, intentional group activity seems to be dwindling in popularity, making me ask myself the following questions. If *Festwille* is a fundamental human experience used in order to stimulate social attachment and positive emotions, what outlet do we have for such experience in today's world? What opportunities do we have to come together physically and blur the boundaries between us in a collective celebration of simply being alive? If dance is marginalized in our society as a trivial pastime rather than an important community event, how does that affect the way we view and interact with one another? And finally, if I staged a large-scale movement choir with firmly committed participants, would it result in the sense of collective unity and wellbeing that Laban's movement choirs did? It was this line of inquiry that led me to try to create an experience that would help to answer these questions.

Martin Seligman (2011), the founder of the field of positive psychology, outlines in his book, *Flourish*, five elements of wellbeing: positive emotion, engagement, meaning, accomplishment, and positive relationships. These elements were precisely at the core of my hopes for my movement choir and, I believe, the desired outcome of Laban's movement choirs as well. As we will see in my brief outline of Laban's life, the impetus behind his work was, ultimately, to use movement to bring a sense of purpose and fulfilment to people. In his movement choirs he was able to engage a group in a meaningful artistic process that gave them a sense of connection as well as individual achievement. In his writings, he described the intense positive feelings that were associated with these experiences as well as the commitment of the participants. I wished to do this as well. By emulating Laban's work with large groups, I wanted to see if a modern community dance could provide a way for people to unite and create an artistic product that celebrated the individual while establishing both a viscerally and spiritually shared experience. Ideally, individuals would feel a sense of accomplishment that would result in positive, life-affirming emotions—critical feelings to have in order to overcome the ever more present sensations of isolation and loss of community in today's society (Seligman 2011).

Dance Artist and Innovator: A Short Biography of Rudolf von Laban

Few dance artists have had as broad a vision as Rudolf Laban (1879–1958). The son of a high-ranking officer in the Austro-Hungarian military, Laban travelled widely at an early age—specifically, to the Balkan region, where his father was stationed. The area lagged behind Western Europe in terms of urbanization and sustained the rural cultures and traditions that were prevalent in Western Europe before the Industrial Revolution (Tilly 1967). Laban's biographer, Valerie Preston-Dunlop (1998) discusses two important early influences that laid the groundwork for his perspective on dance. As a leading member of a folk-dance troupe, he had first-hand knowledge of the critical role dance played in solidly bonding a community and providing an outlet for marking important events. Secondly, Laban encountered the rituals of Sufi dancers in the form of whirling dervishes, who would spin themselves into trance states (Preston-Dunlop 1998). When he inquired about the purpose of this practice, he was told that the dervishes did this for 'immunity to cuts and thrusts' (Laban 1975, p. 52). In other words, the act of dancing projected an individual into an almost superhuman state that would enable him or her to perform incredible feats of strength and endurance. One can only imagine the impression that this must have made on a young man, and Laban's later work certainly reflected his regard for the spiritual and transformational power of dance.

As Laban grew older he became part of a group of young artists who gathered in a utopian community on a mountainside outside Ascona, Switzerland. Monte Verita—the 'Mountain of Truth'—was part artist colony, part nature cure retreat, whose inhabitants were seeking an alternative lifestyle and new ways of artistic expression (Green 1986). Visitors to Monte Verita included many of the greatest minds of the twentieth century, such as Carl Jung and Herman Hesse, whose ideas on spirituality and self-awareness reflected values of the community (Green 1986). The Dada movement flourished here as well as the ideas of Vassily Kandinsky—particularly the importance of spiritual connection in the artistic process (Preston-Dunlop 1998). Laban taught dance at Monte Verita and was able to experiment with his ideas of movement, including dance as a natural, integral part of life. While at Monte Verita, Laban staged the first of what, perhaps, were the seeds of his subsequent movement choirs: a group dance titled Song of the Sun. In his book, *Mountain of Truth*, sociologist Martin Green (1986) describes this open-air event as part of an anti-war protest organized by the head of an irregular freemasonry order established at Ascona. Song of the Sun was an elaborate dance drama staged in three sections performed at sundown, midnight, and dawn, and reflected Laban's values of the ritual elements in dance and his fascination with mysticism and the occult (Green 1986, p. 105).

The idea of balance, or 'harmony', was a fundamental component of Laban's perspective on dance throughout his life (Preston-Dunlop 1998, p. 11). Laban's theory of space harmony—or choreutics, as he termed it—is an intricate and detailed system for describing and observing movement. However, its underlying premise is simply that 'movement has a harmonic structure analogous to that of music' (Moore 2009, p. 5). While the term 'harmony' refers to formal elements in movement such as balance and symmetry, it also metaphorically alludes to the balance of the inner and outer aspects of the individual. A consistent theme in Laban's investigation of harmony was the relationship between one's inner impulses and their subsequent outward manifestations in movement and behaviour. As Laban historian Carol Lynne Moore states: 'Harmony is the broad conceptual framework that Laban developed to address how the inner and outer domain are integrated in the seamless unfolding of voluntary human movement' (Moore 2009, p. 188).

From this perspective, Laban developed a movement vocabulary based on spatial tensions and movement dynamics. This basic vocabulary was accessible to experienced movers as well as beginners, underscoring Laban's core belief that dance was for everyone, not just for a trained elite. A recurring idea in Laban's work was the idea of movement as a vehicle to mind–body unity and the power of movement to express one's inner life (McCaw 2011). These two fundamental concepts led to the integration of one's emotional, physical, and mental processes, and contributed to a sense of wholeness for the individual. This viewpoint was in keeping with a trend in popular culture during the early twentieth century that acknowledged and explored the significance of the psyche on one's perception of the world and spilled into many areas, including psychology, literature, and fine arts (Preston-Dunlop 1998). Laban's fascination with the 'magical' powers of dance and dancers, however, could well be what has continually undermined the credibility of his theory of space harmony. Moore (2009), for example, argues that while Laban's idea of space having a harmonic structure similar to music is certainly sound, his writings are infused with fantastical references to the magical and metaphysical properties of dance. Contemporary dance researchers, particularly in the field of dance movement therapy (DMT), now have reliable measures to validate the mind–body connection with dance and to determine the transformative effects of dance on human behaviour (Meekums 2002, loc. 143). In Laban's time there were no such standards, and observations were coloured by his personal experiences with the occult.

Laban had formal training in music, art, and architecture, but not in dance. This is, perhaps, one reason why his ideas on dance were such a radical departure from the performance genre of the day, which was primarily ballet. His initial exposure to dance was not by an external means—that is, by trying to master a vocabulary of steps toward an elaborately structured and stylized ideal—but rather by allowing the form of movement to evolve from an inner motivation (Preston-Dunlop 1998). The resulting form that is generated from this internal impulse is distinct to each person, since everyone has a unique set of genetics, culture, memories, and experiences that inform their inner life. Laban loathed the artifice and superficiality in theatrical dance and felt that dance should be more than a shallow form of entertainment (Preston-Dunlop 1998). Laban's viewpoint on the relationship between music and dance was also somewhat unorthodox. He briefly explored Dalcroze eurhythmics (Preston-Dunlop 1998)—an approach that uses movement and rhythm to enhance musical expression—but his attitude toward the relationship between music and dance seemed almost the antithesis of the Dalcroze method. He maintained that dance should not be dependent on music—music should contribute to the atmosphere and expressivity of the dance without confining it rhythmically. He viewed music as a sort of theatrical prop to the movement, something to enhance the message of the dance rather than dictate it.

Laban settled in Munich in 1910, eventually becoming a German national. There, he continued his teaching, writing, and investigation of movement. The Germany to which Laban immigrated was undergoing a major cultural paradigm shift (Tilly 1967). Prior to the Industrial Revolution, Germany, along with the rest of Europe, had been primarily an agrarian society that included all the conventions and customs associated with a rural culture, including folk dances. With the migration of people into city life, however, there was a tremendous lack of meaningful communal activity, including group dance, which contributed to the stress of an urban existence. As Freud wrote in *Civilization and Its Discontents*: '. . . it is impossible to overlook the extent to which civilization is built upon a renunciation of instinct (Freud 2005, p. 84). The urban style of life simply did not provide for the basic human urge to come together and move collectively with the sole purpose of fostering a sense of kinship with one's fellow man (Preston-Dunlop 1998). With this new urban lifestyle came an epidemic of emotional tension, anxiety, and feelings of general malaise, and, as with today, there was a great deal of concern about this problem and how to resolve it (Green 1986).

Laban recognized that there was a longing for establishing and affirming community feeling. In essence, when society has a focus that is self-referential rather than community-oriented, life is a lonely endeavour. Urban inhabitants needed a replacement for the festivals and celebrations that no longer existed. Universally, people seek out collective experiences; as Laban put it, 'the will to live is bound up with the will to live together' (Preston-Dunlop 1998, p. 72). However, he felt that it was not simply social gatherings that were needed, but rather meaningful symbolic community activities that could reaffirm and define an individual and engender a spiritual tie to fellow participants. Laban saw group dance as a means to a healthy, happy, integrated life, and wanted to create a new German dance—one that included theatrical dance as a professional component, but which would also provide experiences in which everyone could participate regardless of the level of their dance experience. With this objective, Laban continued teaching and choreographing for serious dancers, but he also held workshops for individuals who wanted to delve into the physicality of dance without any professional aspirations (McCaw 2011).

In these public-oriented workshops, Laban used simple movement sequences that could be interpreted according to individual skill level, making the tasks accessible to everyone. These tasks translated into large group dances containing both improvisation and structured, choreographed passages that came alive when performed together by the ensemble. Laban described the charged atmosphere of these workshops as follows: 'The sensitivity and spontaneity of expression of the participants were greatly heightened and clarified through moving together in common rhythm' (Laban 1975, p. 155). He went on to describe cultural conditions that led to the evolution of the movement choir: 'It was a time when the world was filled with vague unrest on the one hand and a forced desire for unlimited amusement on the other. In both these mental attitudes there was a lack of dignity and innocent enjoyment, of healthy delight in physical ability and of natural poise which is implicit in the human form and its simplest movements' (Laban 1975, p. 155). It is easy to imagine the excitement in a group of individuals who have collectively experienced the force of artistic creation and the impression it must have made on their lives. Indeed, in one of these workshops the participants were so invested in their activities that they were reluctant to disband when their time was finished. The activities in the workshops were initially closed to audiences other than the occasional visitor, because the focus was not on presentation to an audience, but rather on the experience of the mover (Laban 1975). As the popularity of these workshops increased, Laban's group opened them to the public. At this juncture, the question arose as to what to name the events, since they had a radically different purpose than professional dance theatre. Laban stated: 'Then from somewhere a voice said: "Really, we are a movement choir'"' (Laban 1975, p. 156), and a new dance form was born.

Laban's movement choirs were not the only mass group expressions in pre-World War II Germany. There were also singing choirs (*Singchor*) and speaking choirs (*Sprechchor*) that involved large numbers of assembled participants. All of these were part of the nationalistic fervour that took hold in Germany before World War II. While German regions were looking to merge into a single state, individuals were seeking ways to define a fresh, unified country. This led to a scramble by various dance artists, including Laban, for the 'new German Dance', which would represent the values of the new state (Preston-Dunlop 1998). Laban's ideal for German dance was in keeping with popular cultural aspirations for a healthy, vigorous body, but he also valued an artistic expression based on the inner life of the individual. Therefore, his movement choirs contained spiritual and theatrical elements. Contrary to the group gymnastics that were also popular during this era—seemingly mile after mile of pretty, fit young women executing specific, unified, athletic movements—Laban's movement choirs contained an aesthetic and expressive component that made them art rather than sport. This contrast in values was evinced when Laban was commissioned by Hitler to choreograph the opening ceremony for the 1936 summer Olympic Games in Berlin. Laban's elaborate production aimed for the large effect and included movement choirs from all over Germany that had been rehearsed by his assistants. The production was abruptly halted after Hitler watched the dress rehearsal and commented: 'This has nothing whatever to do with us' (Preston-Dunlop 1998, p. 196). Indeed, Laban's vision of an individual listening to his or her inner voice and celebrating one's identity in the larger picture of the human race was virtually the antithesis of the Nazi ideal of honouring a segregated, superior race. Through his early interest in the metaphysical properties of ritual, it would seem that Laban identified with a world that was beyond the ego, a place that dance has accessed since the beginning of mankind.

An Example of a Movement Choir

It was with a fascination for Laban's ideology that I began experimenting with mass group movement. My position as a professor in a sizeable university dance department had given me ample opportunities to choreograph for large numbers of people. I would frequently find myself working on sizable dances with upwards of forty or fifty people simply to accommodate all our dance department students in performances. Although I was aware that dancers usually bond when working on a project, I found this to be intensified when I used particular choreographic elements. When choreographing for large numbers I would rarely use music to establish a common rhythm; rather, I would allow the rhythm to evolve from the groups of individuals moving together. I noticed that when given this freedom, the dancers were much more aware of one another and worked more cooperatively than when they were confined to a specific movement on a specific count. Indeed, when the dancers were given specific counts, it often resulted in disagreements and a divisive atmosphere in rehearsals. I also found that when I gave assignments that allowed for individual interpretation, an uplifting, supportive atmosphere prevailed in a community that was otherwise highly self-critical and at times oppressive in its striving for technical perfection.

The department where I teach has a strong ballet focus; therefore the curriculum is highly technical and rooted in tradition. The daily training reflects this, with an eye toward providing students with the rigorous physical and mental discipline of multiple technique classes. In this atmosphere it is sometimes difficult for an individual to experience dance as having any purpose other than physical proficiency. As a teacher of Laban's theories, my job is to make student performers feel dance on a deeper, less self-conscious level. I try to assign tasks that will either introduce or reconnect students with dance as a means to move beyond their rational mind, to access the place that Laban called 'the land of silence' (Laban, 1975, p. 89) This inner journey is critical to any individual who is devoted to a life in the arts because it gives access to a rich resource of infinite possibilities. It also tends to make the artist value the universal importance of creative expression rather than the applause at the end of a performance. Although it is often said that a ballet dancer has a short career due to the excessive physical demands on the body, I would also say that at a certain time of life, the extreme attention to the external ideal simply becomes boring. There is a finite limit to physical virtuosity in every person, but there is no limit to the imagination. When a dancer is accustomed to using dance as a means of obfuscating their inner life rather than expressing it, entering the realm of the imagination can be vastly empowering. Through his statement that the movement choir 'is to a great extent an inner experience and, above all, a strengthening of the desire for communion', Laban (1975, p. 157) asserted that it was this sense of empowerment that developed from individual sensation to collective feeling in community dance.

I had noticed that certain assignments on the creative process had the effect of intensifying the atmosphere in the studio and allowing students to experience this inner journey. The most effective tasks involved groups creating and executing movement together. Particularly successful were groups that utilized simple yet inventive movements that had an inner intention or characterization motivating them, as opposed to pre-existing steps. I also became aware of the enthusiastic support of the groups for one another's work, and the feeling of camaraderie that ensued at the end of the class. For many students this was a new and profound experience with dance. Other assignments—including creating dances from inspirational sources other than music, particularly from poetry—also seemed to evoke strong, supportive feelings in the students as they explored dance as a vehicle for individual expression rather than technical skill.

These discoveries in class inspired me to think about the ideals Laban expressed when creating his movement choirs, and I wanted to take those experiences that we had shared to a larger population. I was interested in following Laban's example of working with individuals with little to no dance experience to see if the same sort of positive ambience would result. For this reason, when the class with dance students had completed a short assignment choreographing movement inspired by a haiku, I asked them to each bring in three non-dancer friends in order to teach them our movement sequences. Approximately twenty people were enrolled in the class, so our visitors would swell the population to around eighty—a perfect number for a movement choir. At the outset there was a lot of nervous energy and self-consciousness on the part of the visitors, but this was soon quelled as they focused on executing the challenging but manageable movement tasks. Since the studies were based on imagery, each participant could shape the basic idea into a movement that was appropriate to their physical capabilities and still share in the group experience.

After the movement phrases were mastered by all participants, I gave instructions to the group that manipulated basic choreographic elements such as timing and spatial patterns to produce an overall 'harmonious' visual effect. Cooperation and group problem solving was required to complete the assigned tasks, and it was clear from the enthusiasm of the participants that they were invested in the process of creating a dance. The overall impression I sensed in the studio was extremely positive, for even the most reticent of the group were fully engaged in the work. It was, however, when I added two more elements that I felt the atmosphere evolve to something that was more spiritual and communal. The addition of music that was in keeping with this evolution was extremely helpful in leading the dancers away from their self-consciousness. This gave a calming unity to the entire group. Although the dancers were not assigned specific movements to specific phrases, the groups instinctively found their own rhythms that fit perfectly to the music. It was the next element, however, that seemed to offer a transformative experience to the group. As an introduction to our dance I had everyone hold hands and walk in a large circle for several minutes before releasing hands and moving to their places. According to Sachs (1963), the circle pattern is one of the oldest and most ubiquitous forms of ritual dance. Moving in a circle defines the space within the circle as sacred, thereby sanctifying events within the circle. Even though we were in a completely bare-bones dance studio, when the dance was done there was a sense of the unnameable bond that happens among people who intentionally move together (see Figures 32.2 and 32.3).

Watching this event was very moving. The participants also spoke enthusiastically about the experience: some spoke of having strong feelings of connection to each other while doing the dance, and many were interested in the possibility of participating again. I had the most positive feedback from the participants who had never danced before, particularly from some of the young men in the group. One of these young men, who has consistently participated in movement choirs I have structured

FIGURE 32.2. Dancers define the space by moving together in circles. (Photo credit: Peter Alexander.)

FIGURE 32.3. A section of the movement choir. Most of the choreography was inspired by imagery from haikus. (Photo credit: Peter Alexander.)

more recently, described strong optimistic feelings that came from the 'physical cooperation' required in the movement tasks. 'I felt as though I wanted to do my best so the dance would be the best. It was meditative and supportive at the same time. It felt really good; when I left, I rode that high all day.' This type of feedback made me ask questions. What if I could create a really big movement choir with people who would never have even imagined dancing in this way? Would that same communal feeling be generated? Would it have a positive influence on the individuals involved? I set for myself the goal of recruiting 1,000 people to participate in an enormous movement choir with these questions in mind. I targeted a date that was about eight months away and began laying plans.

Putting together a dance of this size is an enormous undertaking. While I had a fair number of resources in terms of space, both for rehearsals and for the event itself, my biggest obstacle was convincing people to commit to participating. Many times I heard the phrase 'I can't dance' or 'it sounds like a great idea; I'd like to watch it'. I found that non-movers were extremely uncomfortable with the idea of dancing, particularly when they knew they would be watched. It was difficult for many to view dance as an expressive, natural form of communication for which every human has an affinity. Many people with whom I spoke had never danced, and communicated a general lack of understanding and discomfort with moving their body. There seemed to be many negative connotations that were associated with dance and an overriding opinion that it was a somewhat marginal activity.

Within the field of higher education, my experience has been that while all expressionistic and abstract arts that lie beyond the purview of 'the academy' are considered fringe, dance has always been the most suspect. Laban speaks of the 'damned equivocal smile' (Preston-Dunlop 1998, p. 64) that he would invariably encounter when he spoke of his vocation in dance, and today's dance artist frequently encounters the same antipathy, whether passive or overt. The instinct to dance has been oppressed by the fragmenting of mind, body, and spirit in our society, which increasingly values specialization and compartmentalization rather than holism, integration, and universality—aspects of a community that dance is intended to foster. Furthermore, the visceral nature of dance, which requires that one encounter her or his body in an intimate and uninhibited way, is often associated with exhibitionism and sexuality (Buonaventura 2004). In America, Wagner (1997) argues, a Puritan heritage has caused people to traditionally frown upon dance in any form. Many people are extremely uncomfortable and self-conscious in moving their body in an intentional or meaningful way, and therefore the practice of utilizing movement to express oneself is a foreign concept to most individuals. While these inhibitions were, perhaps, not as much of a concern in a more physically open society such as 1920s Germany, the fact that Laban was able to mobilize thousands of people to move together in a massive dance speaks to his combination of charisma, organizational skills, and tremendous commitment to the ideal of mass movement contributing to a greater good.

While my own charisma and organizational skills fall far short of Laban's, I still had a great commitment to making this project happen. I wanted to ensure that I had a cross-section of populations represented in this event, particularly in terms of gender. Buonaventura (2004) argues that dance has been viewed as being primarily a female activity, and one historically linked with prostitution. On the subject of post-Romantic era ballet in late-nineteenth-century Europe, she states: 'The opera house was a shop window for women looking to sell themselves to the highest bidder and ballerinas were mistress, rather than wife, material' (Buonaventura 2004, p. 10) A carry-over of this perception could be another reason why dance, in many cultures, is marginalized as an art form and certainly a deterring factor in enlisting men for the movement choir in Indiana. To involve more men in the project, I visited several fraternities on campus and persuaded them to use this activity as a component of their requisite community service. It is notable that in rehearsals and performances it was these young men, initially the most reluctant, who engaged in the dance most enthusiastically and with the most commitment. I also contacted high schools, civic groups, and businesses to recruit participants. I was striving for diversity in my population, and did achieve that to a certain extent. In the end, most of the individuals involved were residential college students who had easy access to the event location. Although my goal was to have a total of 1,000 people, in the end I had about 500 individuals who committed to the performance.

I had a team of three assistants who led the movement sequences in rehearsals. The movement score itself was actually choreographed by different students in our dance department, but I chose the sequence and design of the dance. Although I admired Laban's standard of dancers receiving rigorous training before a movement choir

(Laban1975), it was impossible for me to demand that much commitment from such a large group. Each participant was asked to attend two rehearsals before the performance, one being the final rehearsal involving the entire group. I taught the movement to groups of between thirty and fifty individuals in rehearsals lasting between one and two hours. The movement was set to haiku poems, so it was comparatively easy for the less experienced movers to have a point of reference related to the imagery with which they were working. At the last rehearsal, our entire department of 125 dancers was also present in full force, and the dancers salted themselves throughout the crowd in order to guide the less experienced participants. I had structured a section in the movement choir to be danced solely by the university dance students (see Figure 32.4), in keeping with Laban's idea of integrating professional and amateur dancers, with the experienced movers leading the novices.

The performance itself went smoothly. The bowl of the football field provided a perfect viewpoint for the audience: there were hills surrounding the field on three sides, with stadium seating on one of the rises. The participants began on the far side of one of the hills, and as they came into view they set the tone of the dance by holding shapes that referred to images in the poems being read over a loudspeaker. While one person posed, others would pass them—a pattern that was repeated over and over and created a wave-like effect as the dancers moved into their places. When they had all assembled, the leader of the dance began a movement sequence that all the participants knew and followed—an opening to call everyone together. Music was playing

FIGURE 32.4. Butler University dance students in a smaller group section of the movement choir. (Photo credit: Peter Alexander.)

over the loudspeakers, and the poetry that inspired the sequences continued to be read. There was an air of excitement and anticipation, combined with a complete willingness on the part of the performers to enter into the spirit of the dance. At the last minute I chose to join in the choir rather than observe. When I came into the crowd there was an overwhelming welcoming feeling that I can only describe as joyful. During the event I experienced the same satisfying sensation of belonging that Laban described almost a hundred years ago and, judging from the overwhelmingly positive feedback I received from other participants after the event, I believe this feeling was shared.

Discussion

Recently there has been a return of organized dances in the form of 'flash mobs'—large groups of people who come together in unexpected places to perform an impromptu dance. In 2009 some 14,000 people in Mexico City participated in a flash mob that attempted to set a Guinness World Record (YouTube, Mexico City 2009). Another 2009 event, in an Antwerp railway station, organized as a commercial for the Flemish Television Company, has been viewed more than 14 million times online (YouTube, Antwerp 2009). At first I was reluctant to see these activities as being comparable to a movement choir because they seemed so sensationalized and presentational—the antithesis of the Laban ideal. After choreographing several of these events myself (YouTube, Indianapolis 2010), I have since come to rethink that opinion. While the final form and intention of the dance does not have the same ritualistic feeling as a movement choir, the impulse that motivates a flash mob can be seen as another manifestation of *Festwille*. In experiences I have had with large group movement, including flash mobs, the result is the same: a strong sense of camaraderie among participants, a commitment to create something of worth that inspires the individual to rise above oneself, and a post-event feeling of satisfaction and contentment. Does dancing together require an aura of solemnity and reverence to qualify as a movement choir? Not necessarily. The opening ceremonies of the Olympic Games in London (2012) were the perfect example of a modern-day movement choir, covering numerous subjects from celebrating Great Britain's National Health Service to chronicling British rock and roll (YouTube, London 2012). The spectacular group movement sections lasting almost two hours continued in the Laban tradition of employing simple yet meaningful steps and gestures that under-scored the cultural identity of a group of people.

The field of DMT has also incorporated and codified many of the same ideals Laban valued in its practices, synthesizing the esoteric nature of the mind–body connection with practical, measurable methodology. In her treatise on DMT, Bonnie Meekums (2002) mentions her use of ritualistic practices including a circle dance to mark space and time. She discusses using Gabrielle Roth's five rhythms as inspiration for improv-isational dance. These five rhythms (flowing, staccato, chaos, lyrical, stillness) were created as a form of shamanism to heal and empower an individual through dance

(5Rhythms)—perhaps the same phenomenon Laban alludes to when he refers to dance as 'magic'. Meekums (2002) also describes using a circle dance to mark space and time as distinct, and cites its ubiquitous usage throughout history as having healing properties. While I was aware of the field of DMT, I was not fully informed of these practices when constructing my movement choir. I only followed an instinct based on observations in my years as a dancer and choreographer—the feelings of connectivity and fulfilment in dancing, but also the engagement and sense of accomplishment in building an artistic product together. In virtually every creative process I have had, I have felt a sense of community. It was interesting to note that these feelings led me to some similar forms and values that are incorporated in DMT.

Many sociologists, educators, and psychologists point to the fact that social connectedness is critical to our wellbeing, and note that the decline in community-based activities directly corresponds with a rise in societal problems. Robert Putnam (2000) states: 'Though all the evidence is not in, it is hard to believe that the generational decline in social connectedness and the concomitant generational increase in suicide, depression, and malaise are unrelated' (loc. 4739). Martin Seligman (1991) backs this up: 'In a society in which individualism is becoming rampant, people more and more believe that they are the center of the world. Such a belief system makes individual failure almost inconsolable' (loc. 92). Regardless of what time they live in or how virtually connected they might be, people need meaningful community bonds to thrive. It was, and still is, my goal as an artist to continue to provide vehicles for this to happen.

Conclusions

Today's world is simultaneously exciting and overwhelming. As in Laban's time, we have a cultural paradigm shift as interaction between people becomes increasingly depersonalized (Putnam 2000). At a recent rehearsal I saw, first-hand, an example of this. Dancers who were waiting to be called upon to learn choreography each had a mobile device in hand and were deeply involved in individualized activities. Only a few years ago they would have been talking to each other. I recognize this trend in myself as well—when I am engrossed in an activity on my computer, particularly when it is entertainment rather than work, I am much less receptive to a visit from a student or even my own children. Rather than welcoming the companionship of another individual, my feelings are much more in keeping with Jean-Paul Sartre's (1944/1989) play *No Exit*, in which a character states: 'Hell is other people' (p. 45). While these two examples represent only a tiny segment of the overall population, they are reflective of a distinct trend in our society. It is easy to disregard people in one's immediate surroundings in favour of an electronic community where one can create relationships without having to actually deal with the compromise and responsibility that comes from face-to-face interaction.

People are also choosing lifestyles that are increasingly solitary; more individuals are choosing to live alone, particularly in urban settings. Our choices of how to structure our lives are greater than ever, but the basic urge to live in a community still exists and needs to be expressed. While remote communication is wider-ranging in our time than in the past, opportunities for individuals to come together viscerally and bond through a shared, artistic, celebratory activity such as group dance are few and far between. Meaningful group activities reinforce the value of community and remind us of our commonalities while honouring the contribution of the individual. While I do not think that group dance alone can solve all the world's problems, I do maintain that any opportunity to share the collective experience of artistic expression reminds us of our universal connection. In turn, this can only continue to inform us of the empathy needed to contribute positively in our community.

References

5Rhythms. 5Rhythms Global. <http://www.5rhythms.com> (accessed 13 December 2013).

Buonaventura, W. (2004). *Something in the Way She Moves.* Cambridge, MA: DaCapo Press.

Freud, S. (2005). *Civilization and Its Discontents,* ed. L. Menand. New York, NY: W.W. Norton.

Green, M. (1986). *Mountain of Truth: The Counterculture Begins: Ascona, 1900–1920.* Lebanon, NH: Tufts University Press (University Press of New England).

Hanna, J. (1988). *To Dance is Human: A Theory of Nonverbal Communication.* Chicago, IL: University of Chicago Press.

Laban, R. (1975). *A Life for Dance: The Autobiography of Rudolf Laban.* Princeton, NJ: Princeton Book Company.

McCaw, R. (2011). *The Laban Sourcebook.* New York, NY: Routledge.

McNeill, W. (1995). *Keeping Together in Time.* Cambridge, MA: Harvard University Press.

Meekums, B. (2002). *Dance Movement Therapy: A Creative Psychotherapeutic Approach.* London: SAGE Publications Ltd. Kindle edition.

Moore, C. L. (2009). *The Harmonic Structure of Movement, Music, and Dance According to Rudolf Laban.* Lewiston, NY: Edwin Mellon Press.

Preston-Dunlop, V. (1998). *Rudolph Laban: An Extraordinary Life.* Binsted: Dance Books.

Putnam, R. D. (2000). *Bowling Alone: The Collapse and Revival of American Community.* New York, NY: Simon & Schuster. Kindle edition.

Sachs, C. (1963). *World History of the Dance.* New York, NY: W. W. Norton.

Sartre, J.-P. (1944/1989). *No Exit and Three Other Plays.* New York, NY: Vintage International.

Seligman, M. E. P. (1991). *Learned Optimism: How to Change Your Mind and Your Life.* New York, NY: Knopf. Kindle edition.

Seligman, M. E. P. (2011). *Flourish: A Visionary New Understanding of Happiness and Well-being.* New York, NY: Free Press. Kindle edition.

Tilly, R. (1967). 'Germany: 1815–1870', in R. Cameron (ed.), *Banking in the Early Stages of Industrialization: A Study in Comparative Economic History.* New York, NY: Oxford University Press, pp. 151–82.

YouTube, Antwerp, 2009. <http://www.youtube.com/watch?v=bQLCZOG2o2k> (accessed 17 December 2013).

YouTube, Indianapolis, 9 September 2010, Butler University Dance Department. <http://www.youtube.com/watch?v=duRlwHhGzKg> (accessed 17 December 2013).

YouTube, London, 27 July 2012. Opening Ceremony, London 2012 Olympic Games. <http://www.youtube.com/watch?v=4Aso e4de-rI> (accessed 17 December 2013).

YouTube, Mexico City, 2009. <http://www.youtube.com/watch?v=f7z8ZiRcQ9Q> (accessed 17 December 2013).

Wagner, A. (1997). *Adversaries of Dance*. Urbana, IL: University of Illinois Press.

CHAPTER 33

TOUCHING DISABILITY CULTURE

Dancing Tiresias

PETRA KUPPERS

With contributions by Lisa Steichmann, Jonny Gray, Melanie Yergeau, Aimee Meredith Cox, Nora Simonhjell, Neil Marcus, Elizabeth Currans, Amber DiPietra, and Stephanie Heit

> Once we begin to feel deeply all the aspects of our lives, we begin to demand from ourselves and from our life-pursuits that they feel in accordance with that joy which we know ourselves to be capable of. Our erotic knowledge empowers us, becomes a lens through which we scrutinize all aspects of our existence, forcing us to evaluate those aspects honestly in terms of their relative meaning within our lives.
>
> Audre Lorde (1984)

BRAIDING MOVEMENT AND WELLBEING: THREE STRANDS

THIS chapter explores the Tiresias Project (2007–ongoing, multiple sites, mainly in the USA) by the Olimpias Disability Culture collective. The project invites disabled artists and their allies to play with the portrait camera, to expose themselves and explore erotic spaces. Many of the *Tiresias* workshops happen in outdoor spaces, where disabled nudity is odd and challenging. Some happen in dance studios, where we can lean back more luxuriously. We focus on Audre Lorde's use of eroticism, and apply it to disability culture work: an analysis in connection with joy, a bodily lens that allows us to see ourselves holistically, as bodymindspirits, and as people whose bodies and minds have often been denied sexual and loving pleasure by a culture who sees our bodies and minds as abnormal.

With these erotic lenses we develop, articulate, and share examples of spaces within which disabled people and their allies can flower. I propose a political position towards wellbeing—one which can only be accessed once the cultural character of current medical knowledge is revealed and shifted, thus allowing certain groups who are not usually welcome to 'take up space' to do so.

The art project discussed here uses a holistic view of art/life practice too: based on the moving, breathing self, but expressed through multiple modalities—dance, performance, visual art, writing. All these practices aim at taking up space sensuously, to become expansive, to uncoil, often (but not always) nude. The nudity here is completely optional, often just in a one-on-one in the encounter with the camera. It is an experience of air on skin, of airing out, of light on skin, of sensuous showing. The nudity offers itself as a small dance: feeling the movement of wind and sun on skin that very rarely is exposed outdoors, moving hairs and muscles and blood in response. Nudity here is erotic, not an invitation to sexual activity, but we acknowledge the deliciousness of the edge space.

This chapter uses a creative writing approach to develop its themes. Community participants created these writings as forms of witnessing performance. The writings offer insights into how many different people link concepts of wellbeing, beauty, human complexity, and connectivity, focused through Tiresias, the blind seer, gender transitioner, and oracular Greek figure familiar from much Western dramatic work.

Holistic humanity, movement, wellbeing, resilience, location, self-acceptance, self-worth, communal humour, laughter, respect, and grace. These are words that define for me the connections between disability culture, dance, and wellbeing. With these concepts I already make a significant incursion into the conceptual space of disability. I cite it in a non-medical connection, and I value disability's physical, cognitive, and emotional differences as sources of beauty, even in pain and depression, as sites of complex humanity—with medical knowledge and intervention as a support mechanism, as a resource.

Cultural survivance is a term explored by Anishinaabe/Ojibwe philosopher and writer Gerald Vizenor, who writes: 'Survival is a response. Survivance is a standpoint, a worldview, a presence' (Vizenor and Lee 1999, p. 93). It is 'an active repudiation of dominance, tragedy and victimry' (Vizenor 1998, p. 15). Disability approaches can learn much from concepts of survivance. Disability is not a cultural formation with narratives of homelands, spiritual connections, and genealogies. But disability is an historical process—one associated with the parsing and categorization of human knowledge in modernity. It is a complex of associations and ideas that merge together different people and makes them an 'other'. Disability and race share a history of devaluation based on a mixture of biological and cultural narratives: certain ways of being in the world are valued more than others, while others are seen as 'less developed', 'unfit for modern life', or 'savage'.

Given that we understand 'disability' to be a cultural concept, it is hard for us to insert 'disability' into categories of health and wellbeing that are not culturally focused. I am presenting here, briefly, three areas in which our particular art project leans into cultural concepts of wellbeing.

1. Marking timespace as potentially otherwise is a core value of much oppositional cultural writing that needs to reclaim colonized or, in the context of disability culture, stigmatized ground. My allies here are Audre Lorde's (1984) writing on the erotic with which I opened this chapter, and healers such as Nadia Ferrara (2004), who works on ritualized space and Cree people in art therapy (2004). She speaks about the cultural value of silence, and of creating images (and I extend that to movement) *before* speaking and writing.

Other allies include Metis writer Fyre Jean Graveline (2004), whose autobiographic work in *Healing Wounded Hearts* uses unusual Englishes (for there is more than one way to speak/write English), full of strange orthographies and marks to undo the authority of the colonial voice:

Dis Journey.

Travel with me. like Mahe'kun tracking Wapoos (Rabbit). iStorm.

sometimes Trail will be hard to See. maybe lose Tracks. of where we are goin' (11)

In this chapter we are tracking ourselves, deliciously losing track of the thread from time to time, too—pooling energies into sensations and experiences, into touch and the swing of an arm or the loving contact of a tree with our naked skin.

2. Another reason to take inspiration from non-Western scholars and healers is a focus on honouring what is, and taking things from there—something I find at work in the *Pedagogy of Aloha* by Ku Kahakalau (2002, 2013), where inclusive education means that every child is seen to have 'special needs', a term usually much despised by people affected by this labelling who have come to equate it with normalizing and patronizing practices. In Hawaiian charter schools, the emphasis on everybody's special needs and gifts means that every school child has an Individualized Learning Plan, destigmatizing cultural and bodymind difference, and allowing all of us to flower. (Kahakalau 2002, 2013)

A focus on individual expression is thus also a feature of this collaborative chapter: listening to different voices in their differences. As the choreographer of writing and images, I am not trying to smooth a coherent narrative. I set this introduction as a place from which all these themes shoot out, stories and image complexes that are taken up in different ways in the collage which follows. This space to flower is a marker of wellbeing itself—a place to be, in a world that tells many disabled people that they are not welcome to take up space, or that they are only allowed access if they tell stories of overcoming. There are many different emotions and moments in the writings collected here, and we invite our readers to find their own balance in response to our collective.

3. The third inspiration focuses on the interdependency of life, and of art, and of art and life. In many cultures, dance, ritual, visual art, play, poetry, and recitation are not parsed apart and named as separate forms. It is this much more encompassing sense of creative activity, in touch with the land and the bodymindspirits that inhabit it, that animates Olimpias projects like the one we are sharing here.

With these three strands to braid through this chapter, showing praxis, theory in action, my aim as a writer is not to claim (any one) indigenous knowledge. I write as a white colonizer settler, as a disabled woman, as a ritualist and performance maker who delights in being in touch with many different somatic and creative healing and expression modalities. But by foregrounding rather than appropriating diverse cultural knowledges and theories in this exploration of disability culture practice, we shift what is understood to be the centre, we rattle the certainties of what constitutes knowing, feeling, sensing and healing. In this way, respectfully, we can hopefully create a more capacious space for us all.

CHOREOGRAPHIES OF TOUCH: TIRESIAS

This chapter enacts effects of movement and image improvisation at the site of disability, performance, erotics, and play. We met in different sites, for a day or a weekend. One weekend took place during the *Sedimentations: Art Nature Culture* conference in Rhode Island in 2007, and two weekends happened in the Duderstadt Video Performance Studio at the University of Michigan in 2007. We had more single-session *Tiresias* shoots during the *Disability/Culture: Arts-Based Research Symposia* of 2012 and 2015, both also at the University of Michigan, and two longer shoots at Olimpias Disability Culture summer retreats in Berkeley, California—one in 2009, and one in 2012. All these explorations were part of *Tiresias*, an Olimpias Performance Project. The Olimpias is a disability-focused artists' collective, and I have been the Olimpias artistic director since the project's inception in the mid-1990s in Wales.

In *Tiresias* we reinvented the blind seer who lived both as a man and a woman, the old man who moves with his staff, who speaks hir[1] oracular words and watches the world go by.[2] Tiresias is never the protagonist in the old Greek dramas, but is always in the background: in *Oedipus Rex, Antigone, The Bacchae*.

We take on this ambiguous gender bender, call her out of the shadows, and take on his mantle. In our project, we played with movement and video, wrote poetry, and photographed our bodies, often in movement, or surrounded by traces of our moving, breathing selves.

FIGURE 33.1. Adam (the late Paul Cotton), Neil Marcus, and Kristina Yates reading poetry and preparing for a Tiresias photo shoot in Berkeley, California. (Photo credit: Lisa Steichmann.)

We revealed ourselves, and shrouded ourselves, and remained mobile in front of cameras. All photography was process work: photographs were not released without an extensive process of permission and reflection, and many of the *Tiresias* photographs will remain part of our unseen archive, never to be shared in public.

NEIL MARCUS: POET AND PERFORMANCE ARTIST

my tiresian journey

maybe they would have called me a spastic mute in ancient times
I am spastic
Meaning
I dance
My muscles dance
. . . all the time and act as if weightlifting

... all the time (except when I sleep or swim or laf or cry)
mute, I kind of like mute
its like muse
A muse.
What does he who rarely speaks and yet who seems to have so many 'voices'
Who chooses his word so carefully and economically
What does HE think??
What is HIS View of the world
I feel like an oracle
Looking so closely, watching the world
Thinking about it
Loving it sooo much
Loving my perspective
What I can offer
And I do look different, dancing all the time
What's that like ?
Curious
We all want to know what THIS life has to offer
hmmmmmmmmmmmmmmmmmmmmmmmmmmm

LOCATION: RHODE ISLAND,
THE HOTEL ROOM

Petra

I had a very intimate experience, a quietness: humour, but also a tenderness. We were in a hotel room. Lisa called it a space that is both anonymous and human. We laughed as we tried to hide the faded flowers on old bedspreads, kept fake wood headboard out of view, let an extension cable dangle into our images, spice up and subvert it all into magic play. We played a lot with red cloths, draping them over us, using them as structural, architectural elements of restriction and binding, as well as a flowing, open energy. The cloths changed from one mode to the other with the flick of a hand, glided over skin, supported poses, and captured our limbs. There was lots of laughter in this shoot: we posed as Tiresias in a robe, lay in each other's arms like sisters, like lovers. We revealed tattoos, felt different kinds of softnesses as breasts touched and pressed, and laid different skins against one another.

Our perspectives were different: Alison, whose work often focuses on the fetishist community, people who are obsessed with amputees, spoke about making sure that the images do not land on some of those websites. I improvised with hiding and revealing my own body, played with my insecurities, social judgement, size, the invisibility of pain.

Our antidote to oppression is called beauty. The oos and aas as we complimented each other on our movements and our poses were fun, but also serious play, performative wishes, transformative mantras.

Jonny and Alison are part of the queer presences in this project. They make me think about desire lines, about how sexual differences are read against other kinds of intimacies, other forms of non-sexual sensual support. How can we make visible the different support systems available to us in disability culture? How can we show the kind of physical closeness that often characterize crip meetings, where many physical scripts that are taboo in mainstream society are broken through and rearranged in improvisatory play? And how can we reveal/unveil/veil and keep private the fears and tears and pains of living in bodies that continue to be marginalized, made objects of ridicule, unwanted desire, or disgust? All these questions. We watch Jonny and Alison and myself arrange ourselves, carefully, tuck cloth into place as we present ourselves to be seen. Lisa's camera care translates itself in many different ways in this shoot. Although we all improvise together, she composes her shots carefully, asking us to freeze in positions, and she steps amongst us, close to us, as she frames our bodies.

This is the wildness I sense in *Tiresias*; here we are getting right into it. I step around ferns that are barely coming up and unfolding, the light is soft through the overcast sky,

FIGURE 33.2. Jonny Gray at Touposett Pond, Rhode Island. (Photo credit: Lisa Steichmann.)

a softness of forms against the damp, broken ground, the rocks with all the moss. I keep thinking about the thorns that snatch at us, snagging and clawing and poking. The beautiful tension between the skin and the organic decay all around us, fully away from the human-shaped environments we have been working in. Everything emerging, uncurling, coming up from the earth: a birth all around us. It feels as if there are twenty different languages spoken at once: the bird songs around us, so close.

Touposett Pond and Nearby Beaches

Petra

Tiresias Shoot Rhode Island. We are working at the Wildlife Refuge Center. Over lunch, a Narranganset Indian woman spoke to us of the traditional wisdom embedded in the area, and she spoke of cup and saucer stones: huge boulders that lie on top of stone tablets. When put in motion, they rock back and forth, create vibrations in the earth that

FIGURE 33.3. Petra Kuppers on Charlestown Beach, near Ninigret National Wildlife Refuge, Rhode Island. (Photo credit: Lisa Steichmann.)

FIGURE 33.4. Autumn Dann, Berkeley photo shoot. (Photo credit: Lisa Steichmann.)

communicate to the next set, miles and miles away. A deep, sonorous boom sounds when these boulders, erratics placed in the landscape by retreating glaciers, become mobile. Erratics in the landscape: unusual shapes, yet natural, belonging to, belonging of, belonging with.

> I find the erotic such a kernel within myself. When released from its intense and con-strained pellet, it flows through and colors my life with a kind of energy that height-ens and sensitizes and strengthens all my experience. (Lorde 1984, p. 58)

JONNY GRAY: PERFORMANCE ARTIST AND PERFORMANCE STUDIES SCHOLAR

Tiresias is notoriously oblique in the way he answers questions. He predicts the future, but rarely to the benefit of those who seek (?) his advice. Only afterwards—usually tragically—do his predictions prove useful.

So too, Petra—though minus the tragic consequences. I meet her and Alison and Lisa for dinner, at an Indian restaurant in East Greenwich, Rhode Island. I am late because my capacity to follow directions is confounded by my frequent inability to ask for them. These three women are welcoming when I finally arrive, but clearly laughing together over inside jokes about red satin and photo shoots. A late email might have provided clues, but we are collectively uncertain about what it contained. I certainly am clueless and trying to catch up over samosas and poppadums. Petra diverts my inquiries in her sly way—all will become clear, she tells me. Oh, and am I comfortable with nude photography? How do I say 'yes'—because I am—and yet still mark my startlement at the request? What *is* going on?

On the other side of the (first) photo shoot, I am still not entirely certain I know the answers to any of my questions. For me, though, uncertainty is a central part of *Tiresias*. Why must I know? It will happen. Art goes on. And so, I follow suit (pun intended) and strip, drape myself in red cloth, move and embrace and follow directions. As Petra and Alison join me or do their own posing, I try to be observant but not prurient—a fully present audience with active feedback, but not a vocal voyeur. And yes, I do connect. In part, I draw on my limited queer experience of the 'hook-up'—those anonymous, brief sexual encounters with men just met. Dominant culture tries to tell me that such encounters are shameful. Yet I have always experienced such encounters as sex-positive articulations of brotherhood, of community. My photo shoot with Petra and Lisa and Alison is not sexual in the way of those hook-ups, but it does similarly involve overcoming societal norms of appropriate contact, skin on skin. It is beautiful to me in a similar way.

So there I am in a hotel room with women I have more or less just met, each of us being brave with each other, being present to each other, being intimate with each other, making connections in the name of art and community and process.

True to her Tiresian augury, there *was* red cloth involved, there *was* nudity, there *was* photography. The predictions, in other words, came true. I have had encounters, embraced difference (literally, even), and challenged myself to know myself through such encounters. We move bravely from strangers to new friends to community with an interesting, immediate history. And if uncertainty remains, was it not always there in the first place? Will it not always be there to some significant degree? And is not that part of Tiresias's lesson?

Now, at the end of our weekend, we have taken pictures together in a hotel room, we have taken pictures together in the woods, we have taken pictures together on the beach. We have shared meals and shared art together, the life-sustaining forces of each sharing curdling into a hybrid and indeterminate form of vital sustenance. And I, for one, feel healthier for it.

LOCATION NO. 2: DUDERSTADT VIDEO PERFORMANCE STUDIO, UNIVERSITY OF MICHIGAN

FIGURE 33.5. Nora Simonhjell, Duderstadt Video Studio, University of Michigan. (Photo credit: Lisa Steichmann.)

NORA SIMONHJELL: CRITICAL THEORIST AND POET, NORWAY

This weekend I have read a strange but also interesting book by a woman called Erin Manning, *The Politics of Touch* (2007). She set all form of linear thinking aside and is arguing for an ethics of touch—as an encounter between people, movements, and politics.

I am not sure if I understand what she is arguing (using Deleuze/Guattari and Heidegger), but she is also using the Argentinean tango and the role of the leader and follower as a framing image of what is going on when different bodies meet and make contact—her reading of Wong Kar-wai's 'happy together' is almost as sensual and hurting as the film itself—and while I was reading her book all these Tiresian emails came crawling into my reading of Manning's philosophy . . . and there I sat still . . . with the book and my computer on my lap . . . and 'they' started to talk to each other . . . in a so abstract and meta-something language that I could not follow the movements in the words discussing the time–space dimensions . . . but . . . after I had read Jonny's email I thought:

> a touch is both a movement and a moment
> a touch has as least six dimensions: physical, emotional, temporal,
> spatial, cultural and an 'X'-dimension (the encounter)
> a touch is more than skin meeting skin, person meeting person
> a touch does not have to be physical
> a thought can be a touch
> if one is to touch another person the other must be willing to be touched
> and then I started to write about the movement of shadows—and the touch of shadows

MELANIE YERGEAU: AUTISTIC SELF-ADVOCATE AND RHETORIC SCHOLAR

I am what my mother calls an apologetic personality. I have often felt that this prevents me from being a poet. What is the opposite of *sorry*? I am sure someone can, and has, answered this, probably in a poem that I do not know. But I prefer not to know. I am sorry for this.

My head is attached to a body. I am sorry for my body. I am sorry for my pronouns. I'm sorry for *the* pronouns. But my head is attached to *a* body, and teachers have long felt sorry for this body. Its movements lack purpose, and what is poetry without purpose?

I do not dance. There is literal tension within literal me. My movements, stiff. My gaze, stiff. My speech, stiff. My touch—I do not touch.

All things make me nervous. But a performance-based symposium—*attending* a performance-based symposium—summoned some really bad (figurative) (occasionally literal, depending on anxiety level) shit. People milling, people touching. Late, I arrived to a small group of people milling and touching, milling and touching. As with most millers and touchers I know, they seemed to be movement poets. As though there were some invisible dotted line to which they wheeled, walked, limped, rolled, fell. They understood the spaces between bodies and objects. They understood pronouns. This was crip space, but a crip space of performers and understoodness and the sort of eroti-cization that signals touching and milling and where are the sorry people?

Part of being *a* sorry personality is being *the* sorry personality. When using sorry pronouns, it is hard to make room. Years removed from playground bullies and physical abuse and pitying teachers, I am still awash in my sorryself. I describe myself, I *know* myself, through apology. I am sorry for being asexual. I am sorry for cutting myself. I am sorry for fingers that cannot clasp buttons that cannot cut food that cannot type home row that cannot cannot cannot cannot cannot be your dexterous hot and bothered dream. Muscle memory, alas, I apologize as I forget. I am sorry for eyes that divert. I am sorry that I am asexual and queer, sorry that I put both of those in the same sentence (the oxymoronic ulnar nerve). I am sorry that I write this diatribe about being sorry. I may well be the DSM embodied. So sorry.

Where is the (in)(direct) object? The onus is on me and for.

Sorryself basks in cripspace as bodyminds ebb and invisible lines guide. There is this photo. Sorryself wants to say that this photographed autself stims *beyond* sorryself. But sorryself worries that saying so will make some ironic, overcoming commentary on depression that sorryself does not intend. Sorryself apologizes for third-person disclaimers.

FIGURE 33.6. Melanie Yergeau, Duderstadt Video Studio, University of Michigan. (Photo credit: Lisa Steichmann.)

The onus is on me and for. Autistext. Am I to analyze this photo with Donna Williams precision? Am I to list the ways in which photographed psychoself and unphotographed sorryself are divergent personalities under the taloned umbrella grasp of autistic psychopathy? Am I to analyze this photo *á la* Bettelheim? Am I to bellow *I am rigid*, bellow *I am rigid*, bellow *I am rigid*—repetitive commentary on a repetitive autistextsorryqueerwhat?

In this photo, I am sorry for being sorry. My irony stims. There is trope in my rigid mouth. Knees locked, sixth grade dance hell, I am a robot, there is a doctor, *I am sorry for telling this fucked up, internalized narrative.*

I am sorry that Autistic people are not poets.

AIMEE MEREDITH COX: CULTURAL ANTHROPOLOGIST

Today was so much fun. I walked into the room—I breathe out, get ready. But nothing to prepare for. Cannot get ready for this type of thing, just have to be. My first thought

FIGURE 33.7. Aimee Meredith Cox, Duderstadt Video Studio, University of Michigan. (Photo credit: Lisa Steichmann.)

was how good everyone smelled. I like sun on skin, remnants of incense, traces of soap and oils.

Today, for me, the floor beneath me felt almost as good as the smooth and hairy, taut and soft skins I touched. All the creaks and pains in my body gave way to liquid movement and caresses.

Today, for me, there was less fear and more blind trust. The stage was set and we all came to play in our own unique ways. People flowed in and out of touch, snapshots, frames and movement respecting and gently challenging their own and each others' boundaries.

Oh, and then in the audio room. Like in a church confessional, secrets were shared knowing that they would be kept and respected.

LOCATION NO. 3: OLIMPIAS DISABILITY CULTURE RETREAT, UNIVERSITY OF CALIFORNIA FACULTY GLADE AND PEOPLE'S PARK, BERKELEY

FIGURE 33.8. Neil Marcus, Olimpias Disability Culture Retreat, 2012. (Photo credit: Lisa Steichmann.)

FIGURE 33.9. Movement sequence from Olimpias Disability Culture Retreat, 2012. (Photo credit: Lisa Steichmann.)

ELIZABETH CURRANS: SCHOLAR OF GENDER, PERFORMANCE, AND PUBLIC SPACE

I participated in a series of helping dances during the National Women's Studies Association national conference in 2012. Positioning ourselves outside the conference hotel in Oakland, five of us came together to support each other. Alternating between being members of the circle and the centre, we each named what we needed and then accepted that help. The publicness was challenging at first. There we were just outside an academic conference doing something that does not fit within rational explanations of experiences of social hierarchies or usual methods for resisting oppression. Then I let myself be in that space, opened up to touching and being touched as a way to address my needs and the needs of others. I am not sure if we were watched or how closely. We became our own audience.

These dances do not have much movement. They remain in a small space and focus more on subtle shifts than sweeping movements. They are embodied and move, but focus on participants rather than external audiences. Care requires give and take. The cared for must seek care and consent to the way it is given in order for it to truly count as care rather than patronizing attending to. The suspended movement of the bodies in the image communicates that give and take, the back and forth required to give and receive support. People reach for each other. No one is retreating. The dance they did and the ones I participated in communicate consent, comovement, improvisational support.

STEPHANIE HEIT: DANCER AND POET

Abandonment of clothes creates a new climate in the Duderstadt studio with its black marley floors and high-tech light schematics. Skin glows with momentum. There is speed to the process of this lunch-hour kinaesthetic feast in the midst of day three of the Disability Culture Symposium. Quick shots and movement from individual photos and preferences to group engagement. Present tense and improvisation without staging or time to think. Corporeal buzz of skin unwrapped from layers of Michigan requisite winter garb. Outburst of laughter as five of us gather closer and I turn to the man next to me extending a hand: 'We haven't met. Hi, I'm Stephanie.' Delight in naked greetings. A vibrancy in exposure that does not hurt like too much sun or cold. Warmth of witnessing and being witnessed through sight, touch, camera lens. Lisa and her camera create a container where I feel held in the relief of split-second choices. I enter the rest of the day with a lightness in my chest and renewed energy that comes from being seen. Later I think about how just a couple months before I would not have allowed myself to be photographed clothed or naked. During the prior five years of intense illness with bipolar disorder, I did not want to capture my body or mood or fifty-pound psych drug weight gain in any indelible way. Photographs became markers of forgetting/loss as I looked at past images from moments shocked out of my brain by electroconvulsive therapy. The comfort of photographs holding memories was stripped away. Yet here I am now in this cluster of naked bodies laughing and alive and grateful for this enlivened moment.

PETRA KUPPERS

Tiresian play of alternative eros, of exploring new gendered behaviours and public intimacies, keeps its edge, even as what I feel, in this moment, is the lean of warm-blooded skin and cushioned bones against my own, and the rhythm of our breath stirring the circle of our momentary connection.

Pema Chodron is an American Buddhist teacher whose words often come up in art/life projects like ours. She writes:

> Someone once gave me a poem with a line in it that offers a good definition of peace: 'Softening what is rigid in our hearts.' We can talk about ending war and we can march for ending war, we can do everything in our power, but war is never going to end as long as our hearts are hardened against each other. (Chodron 2007, p. 17)

As a disabled woman of size, I am well familiar with disability hate in public. I have been spat on in public buses, people point me out and call me 'disgusting'. My form of embodiment triggers many people, and the fact that disabled people are perceived to be powerless means that sentiments that might remain hidden in other contexts are uttered and acted upon, as people like me are not supposed to constitute a threat. I am a white person who can safely be looked down upon, and I can become a valve for expressions of frustration.

Awareness of these mechanisms of frustration, expression, and danger constitute a basis for Olimpias actions: 'freedom' requires an acknowledgement of interdependence, as 'freedom' as independence is not available to anybody. So how can we revalue the rigid lines that keep people from one another, that make us devalue each other, and set up rigid boundaries around who can be considered co-human and valuable? Olimpias actions as melting pots: this seems a rich metaphor to me, a melting of flesh into flesh in the presence of a flame, of danger. In public, we are not safe, and I cannot, as choreographer and producer, guarantee anybody's safety. But we can create seductive spectacles of the loss of control, of vulnerability as a warmth that acts upon hate.

FIGURE 33.10. Mark Romoser, shimmering next to a tree, near Lake Anza, California, during the Olimpias Disability Culture Retreat, 2012. (Photo credit: Lisa Steichmann.)

Privilege subtends our projects in many ways: many of our group are white and have learned to understand space to be open to us. My size and disability status does not erase my privilege, and how I have learned to read and act in space. One of the Olimpias members, Mark, an autistic self-advocate, is very clear on the relationship between race privilege and his embodiment, and succinctly articulates the situation in this way: he has tantrums, and if he, as a large male, were black, he would most likely be in prison.

My own whiteness means that our taking up space in public, making ourselves comfortable, is much less fraught with dangers of arrest and citation as it might be. We smile at security guards, and confuse them. Eventually, we do tend to get shut down—but usually, only after we have done what we came to do, exhibited ourselves in new forms of public intimacy, in train stations, on pavements, in public pools. Opening up windows of space and time, and kneading rigidity.

Amber DiPietra: Poet and Body Worker

I have worked right under the (University of California at Berkeley's) 'faculty glade's radar', as Neil Marcus puts it. What has the work been? To learn to use my body to generate currency, but also to labour, with exquisite and balanced reciprocation, in the tiny

FIGURE 33.11. Amber DiPietra and Neil Marcus, Berkeley, California. (Photo credit: Gary Ivanek.)

FIGURE 33.12. Alisha Maria Vasquez, Olimpias Disability Culture Retreat, 2012. (Photo credit: Lisa Steichmann.)

intimate spaces of my little apartment, as an erotic artist. To provide 'healing' erotic encounters, as three of my recent clients, all of their own accord, have named it. It starts with holding a body, or being the body that lets go and lets itself be held, and rocking. Sometimes naked and sometimes not. Or just the tiniest little finger, making patterns on the back of a neck. I am new to this work of sensual encounters. I am new to knowing how to use my body in 'work'. Our dances, in which we all moved like an anemone pod, in grubby old, loud, chaotic People's Park (Berkeley)—where the man with the football helmet threw an imaginary ball for his dog, and some other bodies, on our periphery, were jouncing for a fix. Movements, social practice dance of this type have been central in teaching me how to use my body as the art form it is. And also, to manifest what is needed to live: food, rent—as in literal, enclosed space—and such. Not the only work I could have chosen, but the work that is most entwined with my body, that harnesses the intimacy I regularly want to extend to people. My sexual, my disabled, my artistic body as part of the labour of the world that can give and sustain. Illicit, on the margins, in public, holding and swaying.

CONCLUSION: LEARNING ABOUT COMMUNAL INTIMACIES

Tiresias is timeless and ongoing. Years into the Tiresias Project, I continue to learn new ways of finding experimental intimacy. I shiver as people merge skins, as their bare skin glides over the fine hairs of my arms, and my nerve endings tingle. I learn how to move respectfully with autistic self-advocates, begin to understand how I can rethink the erotic beyond eye contact and touching skins. I begin to work out that amputees can find particular challenges with the set-up of *Tiresias*, given the large devotee scene out there which greedily sells and circulates nude photographs as fetishes. I learn that some of my trans friends value the opportunity to expose their shape-shifting bodies to the camera, but hold the results very close: intimate markers of movement not only between bodies, but within them, and within the categories that curious gazes wish to fix upon them.

FIGURE 33.13. Petra Kuppers, Olimpias Disability Culture Retreat, 2012. (Photo credit: Lisa Steichmann.)

FIGURE 33.14. Writing and sharing poetry at Tiresias shoot in Berkeley, California: Kristina Yates, Autumn Dann, Neil Marcus, Adam (the late Paul Cotton), and Petra Kuppers, 2008. (Photo credit: Lisa Steichmann.)

FIGURE 33.15. Tiresias Photo Shoot, Duderstadt Video Studio, Michigan: Bronwyn Preece, Antonio Lyons, Beth Currans, Stephanie Heit, and Petra Kuppers, 2015. (Photo credit: Lisa Steichmann.)

Queer, weird, crip, autistic, spastic, fat: we reclaim some of the space to breathe into, but I know well that many of us, as we exhale, think of shame and hurt. Melanie and I dance together with the help of a scarf wrapped around our hands. Mark finds ways of being present with us, even though economics and the denial of a driving license means that he has to come from afar, and has to stay overnight with some of us, to get his movement fix. I myself learn to rock my body, which is becoming heavier as the project proceeds, and which feels to me so much more immobile now, five years after the start of the project. I rock myself gently, and lean into trees, and into my beloved community.

NOTES

1. 'Hir' is part of a range of linguistic practices to denote non-binary gender positions, and it might be a preferred pronoun for some genderqueer or trans people. In my writing here, about a mythological figure, I mix he, she, ze, his, she, and hir when referring to Tiresias. In real life, it is best to ask people for their preferred pronoun.
2. 'Crip' is a form of reference that has emerged out of disability culture, a form of reclaiming and renaming. There are intriguing and emerging politics attached to the use of the word, and of associated ones, such as 'neuroqueer' (which has currency in particular in neurodiverse communities) and 'queercrip'. See, for instance, McRuer (2006) and Kafer (2013).

REFERENCES

Chodron, P. (2007). *Practicing Peace in Times of War*. Boston, MA: Shambala.

Ferrara, N. (2004). *Healing through Art: Ritualized Space and Cree Identity*. Montreal, QC: McGill-Queen's University Press.

Graveline, F. J. (2004). *Healing Wounded Hearts*. Halifax, NS: Fernwood Publishing.

Kahakalau, Ku Hinahinakuikahakai (2002). *Kanu o ka'Aina: Natives of the Land from Generations Back. A Pedagogy of Hawaiian Liberation*. PhD thesis, Union Institute and University.

Kahakalau, Ku Hinahinakuikahakai (2013). *Pedagogy of Aloha: Trumping Dominant Models with Indigenous Practices*. Pacific Rim International Conference on Disability and Diversity, Honolulu.

Kafer, A. (2013). *Feminist, Queer, Crip*. Bloomington, IN: Indiana University Press.

Lorde, A. (1984). 'Uses of the erotic: The erotic as power', in *Sister Outsider: Essays and Speeches*. Freedom, CA: Crossing Press, pp. 53–9.

Manning, E. (2007). *Politics of Touch: Sense, Movement, Sovereignty*. Minneapolis, MN: University of Minnesota Press.

McRuer, R. (2006). *Crip Theory: Cultural Signs of Queerness and Disability*. New York, NY: New York University Press.

Vizenor, G. (1998). *Fugitive Poses: Native American Scenes of Absence and Presence*. Lincoln, NE: University of Nebraska Press.

Vizenor, G. and Lee, A. R. (1999). *Postindian Conversations*. Lincoln, NE: University of Nebraska Press.

....

CHAPTER 34

BUILDING RELATIONS

A Methodological Consideration of Dance and
Wellbeing in Psychosocial Work with War-Affected
Refugee Children and Their Families

....

ALLISON SINGER

INTRODUCTION

....

IN this chapter, the integration of dance ethnography and Dance Movement Psychotherapy (DMP) is considered as a methodology to explore the relationship between dance and wellbeing within psychosocial work with war-affected refugee and internally displaced (IDP) children and their families. It is based on one year's ethnographic research undertaken in Serbia between September 2001 and September 2002, shortly after the end of the war in former Yugoslavia. The research was primarily focused on a Serbian non-governmental organization (NGO) called Zdravo Da Ste, also known as Hi Neighbour.

The United Nations High Commissioner for Refugees (UNHCR) defines 'psychosocial' as 'the intimate relationship between psychological and social factors' (UNHCR 1998, p. 13). They consider psychosocial work with children to have two main features: a preventive measure 'enhancing all those factors which promote the wellbeing of children', and special remedial assistance 'to ensure that children who have been harmed or have special needs are provided assistance to ensure a full recovery' (p. 13).

The term 'refugee' as used in this chapter is based on the definition given in the United Nations Convention Relating to the Status of Refugees:

> ... any person who owing to a well-founded fear of being persecuted for reasons of race, religion, nationality, membership of a particular social group or political opinion, is outside the country of his nationality and is unable or, owing to such fear, is unwilling to avail himself of the protection of that country; or who, now having a nationality and being outside the country of his former habitual residence as a result

of such events, is unable or, owing to such fear, is unwilling to return to it. (United Nations 1951, pp. 1–2, Article 1A(2))

Zdravo Da Ste was founded by a group of Serbian psychologists and academics in response to the influx of refugee people at the beginning of the war in former Yugoslavia. Their central concern was for the welfare of the refugee children. Zdravo Da Ste stated that its main aims were 'protecting and promoting development during war and post-war crisis . . . [and] provid[ing] . . . support in building social communities' (Zdravo Da Ste 2006). In 2006 it had up to 25,000 beneficiaries a year whose ages ranged from babies to elderly people (Zdravo Da Ste 2006). The activities in which the organization was involved were described as psychosocial support, cultural and social integration, professional training and skills development, income-generating programmes, summer and winter camps for children, exhibitions, humanitarian assistance, etno[1] programmes, and intercultural exchange.

Underlying my research was the premise that there is a relationship between notions of creativity,[2] culture, and human development that can be harnessed within psychosocial work with war-affected refugee and IDP children and adults in order to facilitate processes of integration and resettlement. Central to these processes are the building of new social and cultural relationships and the creation of opportunities for individuals and groups to discover, or rediscover, and develop innate potentials within that can be used as resources in the context of forced displacement. Vesna, one of the co-founders of Zdravo Da Ste, stated: 'Human beings have an endless capacity for change and development' (Singer 2007, pp. 55–6). The key to this development lies in the interactions themselves and the ability to be receptive to new people and new ideas. Members of Zdravo Da Ste referred to this work as 'building relations', which extended beyond relations between people to include the development of relationships with culture and its creation. These ideas are the foundations for my definition of wellbeing in this chapter.

METHODOLOGY

The basis of my research methodology was dance ethnography, though I also integrated methodology from DMP. Through this integration I felt I could bring an important cultural perspective to clinical study whilst at the same time facilitating the examination of the interaction between social and psychological processes in the context of an ethnographic study of war-affected refugee people.

Different historical and philosophical approaches to the study of the dances of 'others' have emerged that can be roughly categorized as anthropological, folkloric,[3] and ethnochoreological[4] or ethnological. Dance anthropologists are concerned with understanding a particular group of people through comprehension of the dance systems they use. From the perspective of dance anthropology, dance can be perceived as 'structured movement systems . . . [socially constructed] systems of knowledge' (Kaeppler 1999, p. 16), which provide insight into the values and structures within a particular society. A contemporary approach towards dance anthropology views dance as a form of human action (Hughes-Freeland 1999; Williams 1991). Dance anthropology utilizes ethnography as the primary method, where ethnography is both the process of gathering data, using participant observation,[5] and the final written document that constitutes the analysis of these data. Using ethnographic methods, the dance researcher aims to understand the perspectives of the people in the field with respect to the meanings they give to movement and the context within which it is surrounded (Cowan 1990; Ness 1992; Sklar 2001). This is a classical approach to ethnography based on the ideas of anthropologist Bronislaw Malinowski (1992 [1922]), who described the aim of ethnography:

> . . . to grasp the native's point of view, his relation to life, to realize his vision of his world. We have to study man, and we must study what concerns him most intimately, that is, the hold which life has on him. (p. 25)

The 'native' in relation to this piece of research was Zdravo Da Ste as an organization, its members, and the participants in the workshops that Zdravo Da Ste facilitated. Although the field constructed for this research centred around Zdravo Da Ste and its work with refugee and IDP children and their families, it also extended to the family with whom I lived, post-war Belgrade and Serbia, and the other organizations with whom I occasionally participated. Within the field, meanings were negotiated between members of Zdravo Da Ste and myself. The negotiations extended to the planning and evaluation of the workshops, the use of fieldnotes, video, and photographic documentation, and access to the field. The field thus becomes a space that contains multiple truths, and the researcher becomes one of numerous 'storytellers . . . [and] truth keepers' (Buckland 1999c, p. 205) whose authority is derived from their academic status.

I chose to work with Zdravo Da Ste because I wanted to understand what the local people who had experienced the war considered important in their work with the arriving refugee people, rather than working with the interpretations of the international community. Although I initially wanted to understand whether and how dance and movement could be used in psychosocial work with war-affected refugee children, my research became a study of the ways in which Zdravo Da Ste used different artistic media, including dance, movement, story, and etno, in their work with war-affected refugee children and adults and IDPs. This change in focus is in line with ethnographic method, which seeks to reveal perspectives, values, and activities of the people under study. I chose to focus on Zdravo da Ste's workshops with children as the cornerstone of my research because I wanted to understand the effect of war on the development of children and the relation of work with arts media to this development. My research thus aimed to understand Zdravo Da Ste's aims and objectives within its work with war-affected refugee children and adults and IDPs, and the application of arts media within this.

In terms of applying methodology from DMP, I approached Zdravo Da Ste's workshops as a clinical practitioner and concentrated on the process of the work rather than being concerned with products. I tried to interact with the children through the arts media which Zdravo Da Ste used, slowly developing relationships with the children through these media, and observing changes in their relationships to one another and to the media themselves. The primary medium of communication between the children and myself involved the activities themselves and the arts media used within the activities. I also undertook intensive Serbian language training to allow me to communicate verbally. I became a member of Zdravo Da Ste's children's team and Belgrade team, and in this capacity contributed to the preparation and evaluation of the workshops in which I participated. In my fieldnotes I considered how the children had responded to the different media and how the workshops could be developed in response to the children's engagement with the artistic media and activities. Much of my work in the field was about developing relationships, with members of Zdravo Da Ste, with their methods and approaches, with the children and their families, with the family with whom I lived, and with Belgrade itself and the Serbian language. As my work in the field developed, I realized that this focus on relationships mirrored Zdravo Da Ste's approach.

DMP presupposes that the mind and body mutually affect one another and are interlinked so that a change in movement results in a change in the whole person (Payne 1992a, 1993a; Bernstein 1979a; Schoop 1974, p. 44; Meekums 2002). The Association for Dance Movement Psychotherapy (ADMP) states that DMP

> ... is a relational process in which client/s and therapist engage creatively using body movement and dance to assist integration of emotional, cognitive, physical, social, and spiritual aspects of self. (ADMP 2014)

Through movement improvisation an individual can explore 'new ways of being' (Meekums 2002, p. 8). Dance and movement are considered to be media of communication and expression, and are assumed to have a symbolic function, which allows them to be representative of unconscious processes (Meekums 2002; Chaiklin and Schmais 1979; Payne 1992b; Stanton-Jones 1992). Within DMP the individual is considered as having 'an innate capacity for continuous growth' (Bernstein 1979b, pp. 111–130) facilitated through the therapeutic relationship and process and mediated through movement, words, and imagery.

The next section describes an example of a children's workshop led by Zdravo Da Ste during the course of a ten-day summer camp for four hundred refugee and IDP children from Serbia and Republika Srpska held in Montenegro in 2002. The workshop was held at Zjanica—a popular beach area on the Lustica peninsula of Boka Kotorska, located where the bay opens to the sea. The example illustrates the integration of a variety of creative and performing arts media within Zdravo Da Ste's approach, including dance and movement, sound, visual images, and the natural environment. It also elucidates how Zdravo Da Ste's approach contributed to a sense of wellbeing—based on the definition outlined in the introduction to this chapter—for the children with whom they worked, and how my methodology provided me with insight into these processes.

Zjanica

The workshop at Zjanica was an ecological workshop that occurred four times to allow all the children at the summer camp to have an opportunity to attend. It began and ended with a journey by boat from Bijela, where the children were staying, to Zjanica. The summer camp was based at a large hotel that bordered the sea to the left of the picture. Workshops happened both in and around the hotel and at local places of historical, cultural, or geographical interest.

Two small tour boats arrived at Bijela after breakfast, and each boat quickly filled with a group of waiting children. As the boats travelled down Boka Kotorska towards Zjanica, the children waved to each other, looked out at the sea, moved to prerecorded popular music, and listened to the fragmented commentary of places of historical and cultural interest given by one of the drivers of the boat. The boats passed medieval villages and towns, modern glass-fronted hotels, and entrances to caves used by the navy for submarines. The teachers on the boat on which I travelled were unhappy with the commentary, finding it superficial and insensitive to the fact that the children on the boat were refugees. To the best of my knowledge, the children did not respond to the commentary. When the boats arrived at Zjanica the children were led past a small cluster of restaurants and cafés to an open space surrounded by trees and close to the sea. Each of the summer camp groups of about twenty children with two teachers—one from Serbia and one from Republika Srpska—chose a space for themselves under the trees and took some time to swim, explore the new environment, and have their lunch.

After lunch, all the groups came together in a large standing circle to begin the workshop. Everybody was asked to say their names simultaneously, repeating them as loudly as possible and then as quietly as possible. They then raised their arms above their heads to wave to one another. Smaller summer groups were formed, and many returned to their chosen place for the teachers to explain what they would be doing.

Branka, a member of the children's team, handed out small envelopes and showed the children how to operate the dictaphones. She and the teacher from Republika Srpska led the group into the woodland area behind the clearing. The group weaved its way under and over branches and past large spiders' webs. The sun was hot, and the brittle undergrowth scratched everyone's legs as they passed. The children and young people collected plants, pieces of bark, flowers, and seeds, and recorded selected sounds from the environment. They also shared their findings and observations with one another as they journeyed and learnt about the plants from Branka's colleague. They travelled in a large circle, eventually returning to their chosen place, where they put everything they had collected in a pile. The whole group then crossed the clearing to collect more objects and sounds from the rolling sea.

Led by Branka and her colleague, the children used their bodies to create different sounds with the water, lying on their stomachs and kicking the water with their legs, splashing water with their hands, hitting the water in rhythmical patterns, and blowing into the water to make bubble sounds. They struck large and small pebbles together, creating short random rhythmic phrases, and threw pebbles and rocks into the water. Branka and her colleague followed and supported the activities that the children initiated, recording the sounds they created. When the group finished collecting, they played in the sea before returning to their base to add the objects they had collected to the pile. At their base, Branka laid a large white cloth on to the ground for everyone to put the objects they had collected. The children selected materials with which to work, and gathered around the cloth to arrange the objects to create a collage. The children in Branka's group worked without intervention from the two teachers, though the teachers made their own contributions to the collage.

While the collages were being made, I travelled around the different groups in order to capture on video the emerging creations. Each group's collage had its own identity. Some appeared to be three-dimensional representations of Zjanica, while others were more narrative and included painted images of dolphins, faces, hearts, the sun, waves, and palm trees. A few images were abstract, displaying collections of different painted colours and designs made from plaited wool. Participants had also made objects from the collected materials, which they attached to the collages, such as a bouquet of flowers, a spider's web made of wool, and painted pebbles. Figures 34.1–34.4 show examples of the collages made at Zjanica. The photographs were taken after the collages had been brought to the hotel in Bijela. In the first example the children have added their own names to the objects, pictures, and colours of the collage. The second example takes on a three-dimensional form. The third example is more abstract. The final image appears to be a narrative representation of the children's experience within which the group have painted the group's name, Prijatelji Mora (Sea Friends) in the centre.

As each collage was completed, the children and teachers carried them to the central area in the clearing where the workshop had begun, and laid the collages on the ground alongside one another. All the participants gave a rousing round of applause as each collage was placed on the ground. The participants made a large circle around the collages when all the groups had arrived; simultaneously, each group played back the sounds they had collected. This created a cacophony of sound, movement, and images as the participants took it in turn to walk within and around the circle, listening to the individual and blended sounds while looking at the pictures. The large group then reformed into a circle, and the teachers asked the children to find a name for the workshop. The facilitators acknowledged all the suggestions. Every group then collected its collage and belongings and created a long informal procession to the waiting boats for the return trip to Bijela, carrying their collages canopy-like above their heads. After the children's return to Bijela, the collages were placed in the landings and corridors next to their bedrooms at the hotel. At the daily evening workshop, when all four hundred children gathered together, each group used movement and sound to present their experiences of the day. Each group worked with the two teachers who

FIGURE 34.1. Example of a collage from Zjanica (example 1). (Photo credit: Dr Allison Singer.)

FIGURE 34.2. Example of a collage from Zjanica (example 2). (Photo credit: Dr Allison Singer.)

FIGURE 34.3. Example of a collage from Zjanica (example 3). (Photo credit: Dr Allison Singer.)

FIGURE 34.4. Example of a collage from Zjanica (example 4). (Photo credit: Dr Allison Singer.)

were responsible for that group of children and reflected on their experience of the day and then, through discussion and action, created still or moving images through their bodies to represent these experiences. Sometimes the groups presented individually, and sometimes alongside the other groups. The day was closed with celebratory dancing to popular music.

The integration of different media was a feature of Zdravo Da Ste's workshops with children. The workshop at Zjanica included work in the natural environment, dance and movement, visual images, sound, journeys, procession, and performance (in the evening presentations). Branislava—a member of Zdravo Da Ste's children's team—said that children 'express themselves mainly through movement' (informal communication, Belgrade, 2001). Through observation of the children's movements, she felt that it was possible to see the 'inner state of soul' of a child, how the child was and who they were, and by working with movement to create changes through the discovery of new ways of perceiving. To emphasize this idea, Branislava told me: '[I] heard one grown-up man who said once "I am a handicapped person because I am not taught to express myself through movement"'. Within Zdravo Da Ste's workshops, meanings appeared to be negotiated through the interaction of individual and group responses to the activities. The group itself became a receptacle and transformer of meaning.

Dance anthropologist Anya Peterson Royce (2002) stresses the mulitvocalic nature of dance and movement. She describes dance as being 'polysemous as well as multivocalic' (p. xxiv), capable of stimulating all of the senses simultaneously. In this way, dance and movement can be powerful as media of communication and expression because they can convey ideas and emotions through different levels and senses at the same time. Royce, however, stresses that this multichannel expression is also open to misunderstanding, implying that it is only the moving person who really knows what they are communicating, and to whom. Ethnochoreologist Anca Giurchescu (2001) suggests that the polysemic nature of dance facilitates its potential as a medium for symbolic transformation. The notion of the potential for dance and movement to facilitate symbolic transformation underlies DMP.

Choreographer and dance theorist Rudolph Laban (1971 [1950]), who was an important influence on the development of DMP in the UK and the USA, stated:

> ... the world too deep for speech, the silent world of symbolic action, most clearly revealed in ballet, is the answer to the inner need of man. (p. 91)

Laban suggested that symbolic action, as expressed and revealed through the media of dance and movement, has the power to communicate aspects of the inner world of a person, or the unconscious or subconscious world, that may be hidden or remain silent in other forms of expression, representation, and communication. Symbolic actions are considered as more than representations of daily life. They are also able to convey 'inner responses' (Laban 1971 [1950], p. 92) to the external world and the internal world of a person, where the internal world is the world of dreams, images, ideas, emotions, memories, and associations. Laban believed that movement could communicate these aspects more clearly than words, and communication and expression through symbolic action is an important part of the process of becoming, of the individual fulfilling and expressing the potential that is within him or her. This potential to facilitate symbolic transformation allows therapeutic work with dance and movement to help an individual realize their potential.

In DMP there is considered to be a direct relationship of 'motion and emotion' (Payne 1992b, p. 4). Meaning is discovered through the therapeutic process and the relationship between the therapist and client. Dance movement psychotherapist Bonnie Meekums

(2002) suggests that the movement metaphor is the basis of DMP (pp. 22–5). It mediates between unconscious and conscious material, and both the therapist and the client bring meaning to the metaphor. From a Jungian perspective, the unconscious undergoes or creates change; it is a process in which 'the psyche is transformed or developed by the relationship of the ego to the contents of the unconscious' (Jung 1995 [1961], p. 235).[6] The changes in the psyche do not occur simply at an individual level, however, but also at a collective level.

The link between individual and collective or social development was an important idea within Zdravo Da Ste's approach. They often talked of the importance of 'building relations', though they were not only trying to build relations between people, but also to build relations 'with the culture, with the social society, not only with a group of people but with different things which are culturally important' (extract from interview, Belgrade, March 2002). Branka—a founding member of Zdravo Da Ste—said that these relationships were important for all children, but especially pre-school children because they have 'a lot of needs, social needs . . . [they are] especially sensitive'. Zdravo Da Ste's work was influenced by the ideas of the Russian developmental and social psychologist Lev Vygotsky (Vygotsky 1986 [1934]; Rieber 1998; Luria and Vygotsky 1992 [1930]), who suggested that social interactions are the foundation from which a person develops. Furthermore, a child assimilates and transforms social interactions as a source of mental development.[7] Within Zdravo Da Ste's work an informant once told me how she had seen a piece of artwork in a teenagers' bedroom that the teenager had created in a Zdravo Da Ste workshop when they had been a pre-schooler. The informant suggested to me that the meanings generated through the group activities in the workshops remained with the children for many years, and was part of an ongoing process of development for that child.

Some members of Zdravo Da Ste considered movement to be just one of a number of 'human potentials for expression'—tools that could be 'discovered and actualised' (extract from interview with Vesna, Belgrade, November 2001). These tools could be used alongside one another to find and develop the hidden potential within each person and the 'voices of the future'—the potential for the future development of the society. Vesna considered these potentials to be fundamental to human nature and indestructible, echoing Jung's idea that 'each of us carries his own life-form within him—an irrational form which no other can outbid (1995 [1961], p. 211).

Within the Zjanica workshop, movement was used alongside other tools, including visual images and the natural environment. For example, the collages created by the children at Zjanica and shown in Figures 34.1–34.4 became part of a procession to the waiting boats for their return journey to the hotel. Once at the hotel, the children placed the collages in the landings and corridors outside their bedrooms, where they became part of an informal gallery of images made over the ten days of the summer camp. In this way, the children were surrounded by their own and others' experiences and representations of the summer camp through the objects they had made, and could interact with these whenever they chose.

Psychologists Beverly Roskos-Ewoldson, Margaret Inton-Peterson, and Rita Anderson (1993b) suggest: 'Images are often produced with intention for some purpose. As such, images tend to be inherently meaningful" (p. 317). From this perspective the image can be seen as an expression and representation of one or a number of emotions and relationships. The image as product has the potential to produce an emotional response both in the creator and in the person witnessing the image, and is also a form of communication. Interpretation of the image and the motivations behind this interpretation determine what is considered good or bad, and in this way determines the individual and cultural value given to the image. Furthermore, the importance assigned to the image by both the person creating it and the person receiving it determines the extent to which it is maintained in the memory (p. 317). Images are representational both in what they show and in what they hide, and are conceived and generated in different ways. Images can range from 'conceptual images (such as intentional thought) to spatial images to mental pictures (such as experiential sensation)' (p. 317). In the Zjanica workshop, images were created through movement, pictures, words, and sounds. The workshop thus appeared to create the opportunity for the children to engage conceptually, spatially, mentally, and kinaesthetically, and, through this process, attempt to activate the whole person.

Jung suggests that the images that emerge in dreams and art-making processes are not necessarily initially understood but are those that ' "want" to become conscious' (Jung 2002 [1959], p. 49). The individual has an unconscious need to allow these images to move from the unconscious to consciousness in order to facilitate the process of individuation,[8] the process of becoming whole (Jung 2002 [1959]). In relating to the experience of war, these unconscious aspects can be thought of as experience that has been suppressed. The group interactions in Zdravo Da Ste's workshops allowed participants to both witness and experience the transformation of these images and experiences and thus help to develop a sense of self and other.

Many of the images created in the workshop appeared to be representations of the landscape and natural environment of Zjanica. In contemporary writings from archaeology and anthropology (Ucko and Layton 1999b; Cooney 1999; Darvill 1999; Mulik and Bayliss-Smith 1999; McGlade 1999) landscape refers

> ... both to an environment, generally shaped by human interaction and to a representation (particularly a painting) which signifies the meanings attributed to such a setting. (Ucko and Layton 1999b, p. 1)

With reference to this definition of landscape, it would appear that the workshop at Zjanica both created environments through the activities of the workshop and the contributions to the informal galleries the children created in the hotel, and created a representation of Zjanica. Folklorist Mihaly Hoppal (2002) suggests that space, like spoken language, 'mediates a value system', and the use of space follows 'culturally defined patterns' which contribute to 'marking out value norms for the individual' (p. 9). This workshop could thus be perceived as giving the children an opportunity to define their individual and collective value systems through the interaction with the materials, the creation of the collages, and the relationship and re-creation of the environments. The children at Zjanica had an opportunity to find their own symbols and images to represent an environment that was part of their new home country.

Displacement is a central feature of the refugee experience within which familiar social, physical, cultural, and geographical environments are replaced by unfamiliar and often hostile and confusing new environments. Realizing the potential to build new relationships with unfamiliar or known environments and cultural structures facilitates the potential to change the relationship with the past (McGlade 1999, p. 459), creating new possibilities in the present and for the future, and thus begins to develop a sense of wellbeing. By working with physical environments it could be suggested that Zdravo Da Ste was giving people back a choice of how to create and respond to an environment and how to work together to create in a new environment in order to generate meanings and a sense of belonging and ownership.

Conclusion

Art therapists Debra Kalmanowitz and Bobby Lloyd (2005a, p. 24) found in their work with survivors of political violence in the UK and in Bosnia that many of the people with whom they worked spent a great deal of time looking for meaning. This meaning was manifested within social, religious, and psychological contexts through various media. By integrating different arts media within their aims and objectives, I suggest that Zdravo Da Ste facilitated the development of meaning for the children and their families through verbal, non-verbal, embodied, and tangible representations of experiences. Through the activities in the workshops, participants had the opportunity to begin to understand and redefine themselves and their relationship to other people, and the social and physical environments by which they were surrounded, and to make choices.

The ability to make choices is important within the context of displacement. This is because one of the aspects of forced displacement is the loss of choice within basic life decisions. Many informants from both within and outside Zdravo Da Ste suggested to me that children stand a better chance of building a new life after war than do adults. They felt that this was because children are still able to adapt relatively easily, whereas adults can feel powerless, as Vesna suggested:

> I really think that children have a chance they will keep this experience [of war], but they can overcome this through development, through education, through meeting people. No one has the right to say 'It's ended'. We have to do our best, as we did in 1992, that's to keep this process [the workshops and the possibilities for social and cultural interactions] going on. (Extract from interview, Belgrade, November 2001)

Children who know that they can make choices and change their situation create the potential for new possibilities both for themselves and within their communities. The activities within Zdravo Da Ste's workshops created opportunities for the children to make choices and to have those choices acknowledged. They were springboards towards further development of the individual child, the community of children, and by implication the wider community, and in this way contributed to a sense of wellbeing for the refugee and IDP children and their families.

The methodology I adopted for this research allowed me to come to some understanding of Zdravo Da Ste's approach and witness and experience some of the different aspects and processes of their work. In terms of the integration of dance ethnography and DMP, the dance ethnographer, like the DMP clinician, tries to organize and shape multiple levels of communication in order to understand their significance; unlike the DMP clinician, the dance ethnographer is not trying to effect change. The dance ethnographer uses this information to document and explain the field and danced movement action within the context of the field. These two different intentions identify a potential conflict when one researcher adopts both methodologies within a research project. The use of DMP within dance ethnography in the context of refugee studies, however, is an intellectual and kinaesthetic language and method through which the ethnographer can engage in the study of processes of psychological transformation that accompany forced displacement and resettlement. In addition, the integration of dance ethnography and DMP within the context of psychosocial work with war-affected refugee children and adults gives an academic validity to the place of the arts within this work. The responsibility of the researcher is not stable, because the field is in a process of continual change and the researcher's interpretation is open to challenge from both members of the field and other academics. As dance anthropologist Georgina Gore (1999) points out, the completed ethnography is not the end of the ethnographic process, but 'one privileged moment in the ethnographic enterprise' (p. 208). The ethnography is thus a negotiated construction created and situated in a specific time and place with a particular group of people. Its truth lies within this negotiation.

NOTES

1. 'Etno' is Serbian for 'Ethno'—a prefix derived from the Greek language that means 'people'. Members of Zdravo Da Ste used the term 'etno' to describe regional dance, music, and craft forms, including embroidery and carpentry, considered as arts of the people of former Yugoslavia, or Yugoslav folk arts. The term was also used to designate folk arts from other countries and regions. Etno represents specific regions of former Yugoslavia, recognized through particular visual motifs, rhythms, costumes, or dance forms. Members of Zdravo Da Ste explained, for example, how the complex rhythms in Macedonian music gave it its beauty, and praised the dancing skills of the Roma women, purportedly the best dancers in former Yugoslavia.

2. For the purposes of the research I defined creativity as a generative process through which an individual has the opportunity to express, communicate, exchange, and develop their unique vision and resources within a specific context, and create something that has not existed previously.

3. In the twentieth-century approach, folklorists were concerned with documenting specific dance forms in order to preserve them and understand their form and structure.

4. Ethnochoreologists are concerned with the 'symbolic function' (Giurchescu 1999, p. 41) of dance systems and the implication of this in terms of notions of individual, social, and cultural identity. Like folklorists, the ethnochoreologist collects and examines dances and dance repertoire in different social contexts and through processes of change. The ethno-choreologist may already be part of the society in which the research takes place, entering and leaving the specific field at various points, possibly over several years or even decades, in order to monitor change (Giurchescu 1999; Felfoldi 1999).

5. Participant observation can be considered more of a 'research strategy than a unitary research method' (Aull Davies 1999, p. 67). This is because it intrinsically employs many methods, including formal and informal interviews, fieldnotes and journals, visual documentation, and life histories. In participant observation, the researcher participates in the lives of the people being studied over an extended period of time, traditionally at least one year, in order to attempt to understand their perspectives of their lives and activities. This is called 'fieldwork'. The researcher attempts to gain both an insider's and an outsider's, or emic and etic, perspective within the context of the field.

6. Jung's notion of the ego is of a driving force with which the unconscious strives to engage, while the psyche can be equated with the idea of the soul of a person, their essence.

7. Vygotsky's approach was known as the sociocultural approach.

8. Jung's notion of individuation is as a process of development by which a person becomes whole and there is integration of the conscious and unconscious. Individuation is considered an important process for the attainment of adulthood (Jung 2002 [1959]).

References

Association for Dance Movement Psychotherapy (2014). *Home.* <http://www.admt.org.uk> (accessed 1 May 2014).

Aull Davies, C. (1999). *Reflexive Ethnography: A Guide to Researching Selves and Others.* London and New York: Routledge.

Bernstein, P. L. (ed.) (1979a). *Eight Theoretical Approaches in Dance-Movement Therapy.* Iowa: Kendall/Hunt.

Bernstein, P. L. (1979b). 'The use of symbolism within a gestalt movement therapy approach', in P. L. Bernstein (ed.), *Eight Theoretical Approaches in Dance-Movement Therapy.* Iowa: Kendall/Hunt, pp. 111–30.

Buckland, T. J. (1999c). '[Re] Constructing Meanings: The dance ethnographer as keeper of the truth', in T. J. Buckland (ed.), *Dance in the Field: Theory, Methods and Issues in Dance Ethnography.* Houndmills and London: Macmillan Press, pp. 196–207.

Chaiklin, S. and Schmais, C. (1979). 'The Chace approach to dance therapy', in P. L. Bernstein (ed.), *Eight Theoretical Approaches in Dance-Movement Therapy.* Iowa: Kendall/Hunt, pp. 15–30.

Cooney, G. (1999). 'Social landscapes in Irish prehistory', in P. J. Ucko and R. Layton (eds.), *The Archaeology and Anthropology of Landscape: Shaping your Landscape.* London: Routledge, pp. 46–64.

Cowan, J. K. (1990). *Dance and the Body Politic in Northern Greece.* Princeton, NJ: Princeton University Press.

Darvill, T. (1999). 'The historic environment, historic landscapes, and space-time-action models in landscape', in P. J. Ucko and R. Layton (eds.). *The Archaeology and Anthropology of Landscape: Shaping your Landscape.* London: Routledge, pp. 104–18.

Felfoldi, L. (1999). 'Folk dance research in Hungary: Relations among theory, fieldwork and the archive', in T. J. Buckland (ed.), *Dance in the Field: Theory, Methods and Issues in Dance Ethnography*. Houndmills and London: Macmillan, pp. 55–70.

Giurchescu, A. (1999). 'Past and present in field research: A critical history of personal experience', in T. J. Buckland (ed.), *Dance in the Field: Theory, Methods and Issues in Dance Ethnography*. Houndmills and London: Macmillan, pp. 41–54.

Giurchescu, A. (2001). 'The power of dance and its social and political uses', in *2001 Yearbook for Traditional Music*, pp. 109–121.

Gore, G. (1999). 'Textual fields: Representation in dance ethnography', in T. J. Buckland (ed.), *Dance in the Field: Theory, Methods and Issues in Dance Ethnography*. Houndmills and London: Macmillan, pp. 208–20.

Hoppal, M. (2002). 'Tradition, value systems and identity: Notes on local cultures', in L. Felfoldi and T. J. Buckland (eds.), *Authenticity: Whose Tradition?* Budapest: European Folklore Institute, pp. 1–18.

Hughes-Freeland, F. (1999). 'Dance on film: Strategy and serendipity', in T. J. Buckland (ed.), *Dance in the Field: Theory, Methods and Issues in Dance Ethnography*. Houndmills and London: Macmillan Press, pp. 111–22.

Jung, C. G. (1995) [1961]. *Memories, Dreams, Reflections*. London: Fontana Press.

Jung, C. G. (2002) [1959]. *The Collected Works of C. G. Jung 9* (1): *The Archetypes and the Collective Unconscious*. 2nd edn. London: Routledge.

Kaeppler, A. (1999). The mystique of fieldwork', in T. J. Buckland (ed.), *Dance in the Field: Theory, Methods and Issues in Dance Ethnography*. Houndmills and London: Macmillan Press, pp. 13–25.

Kalmanowitz, D. and Lloyd, B. (2005a). 'Art therapy and political violence', in D. Kalmanowitz and B. Lloyd (eds.), *Art Therapy and Political Violence: With Art, Without Illusion*. Hove: Routledge, pp. 14–34.

Laban, R. (1971) [1950]. *The Mastery of Movement*. 3rd edn. London: MacDonald Evans.

Luria, A. R. and Vygotsky, L. S. (1992) [1930]. *Ape Primitive Man, and Child: Essays in the History of Behavior*, New York and London: Harvester Wheatsheaf.

Malinowski, B. (1992) [1922]. *Argonauts of the Western Pacific: An Account of Native Enterprises and Adventure in the Archipelagos of Melanesian New Guinea*. London: Routledge and Kegan Paul.

McGlade, J. (1999). 'Archaeology and the evolution of cultural landscapes: Towards an inter-disciplinary research agenda', in P. J. Ucko and R. Layton (eds.), *The Archaeology and Anthropology of Landscape: Shaping your Landscape*. London: Routledge, pp.459–82.

Meekums, B. (2002). *Dance Movement Therapy*. London, Thousand Oaks, New Delhi: Sage.

Mulik, I.-M., and Bayliss-Smith, T. (1999). 'The representation of Sami cultural identity in the cultural landscapes of northern Sweden: The use and misuse of archaeological knowledge', in P. J. Ucko and R. Layton (eds.), *The Archaeology and Anthropology of Landscape: Shaping your Landscape*. London: Routledge, pp. 358–93.

Ness, S. A. (1992). *Body, Movement, and Culture: Kinaesthetic and Visual Symbolisms in a Philippine Community*. Pennsylvania, PA: University of Pennsylvania Press.

Payne, H. (ed.) (1992a). *Dance, Movement Therapy: Theory and Practice*. London and New York: Routledge.

Payne, H. (1992b). 'Introduction', in H. Payne (ed.), *Dance, Movement Therapy: Theory and Practice*. London and New York: Routledge, pp.1–17.

Payne, H. (ed.) (1993a). *One River, Many Currents: Handbook of Inquiry in the Arts Therapies*. London and Bristol, PA: Jessica Kingsley.

Rieber, R. W. (ed.) (1998). *The Collected Works of L. S. Vygotsky, Volume 5: Child Psychology.* London: Kluwer Academic/Plenum Publishers.

Roskos-Ewoldsen, B., Intons-Peterson, M. J., and Anderson, R. E. (eds.) (1993). *Imagery, Creativity, and Discovery: A Cognitive Perspective.* Amsterdam: Elsevier Science Publishers.

Royce, A. P. (2002) [1977]. *The Anthropology of Dance.* Alton: Dance Books.

Schoop, T. (1974). *Won't You Join the Dance: A Dancer's Essay into the Treatment of Psychosis.* Palo Alto: National Press.

Singer, A. J. (2007). *Hidden Treasures, Hidden Voices: An Ethnographic Study of Movement and Dance in Psychosocial Work with War-Affected Refugee Children and Adults (Serbia 2001–2002).* Unpublished PhD thesis, De Montfort University, Leicester.

Sklar, D. (2001). *Dancing with the Virgin: Body and Faith in the Fiesta of Tortugas, New Mexico.* Berkeley, Los Angeles, and London: University of California Press.

Stanton-Jones, K. (1992). *An Introduction to Dance Movement Therapy in Psychiatry.* London: Routledge.

Ucko, P. J. and Layton, R. (eds.) (1999b). 'Introduction: Gazing on the landscape and encountering the environment', in P. J. Ucko and R. Layton (eds.), *The Archaeology and Anthropology of Landscape: Shaping your Landscape.* London: Routledge, pp. 1–20.

United Nations (1951). *The 1951 Convention Relating to the Status of Refugees (28 July 1951).* <www.unhcr.org/protect/PROTECTION/3b66c2aa10.pdf> (accessed March–July 2001).

United Nations High Commission for Refugees (UNHCR) (1998). *Refugee Children: Guidelines on Protection and Care.* Geneva: United Nations High Commissioner for Refugees.

Vygotsky, L. (1986) [1934]. *Thought and Language.* Cambridge, MA: MIT Press.

Williams, D. (1991). *Ten Lectures on Theories of the Dance.* Metuchen, NJ, and London: The Scarecrow Press.

Zdravo Da Ste (2006). *Zdravo Da Ste/Hi Neighbour.* <http://users.teol.net/~svjetion/www/zds/> (accessed 24 February 2006).

CHAPTER 35

RECONSTRUCTING THE WORLD OF SURVIVORS OF TORTURE FOR POLITICAL REASONS THROUGH DANCE/ MOVEMENT THERAPY

MARALIA RECA

INTRODUCTION

THIS chapter discusses how dance/movement therapy promotes recovery from severe relational trauma, as will be seen in two case studies of people who have survived the military dictatorship period in Argentina.[1] Torturers around the globe undermine the integrity of the individual; the uniqueness of body and mind. Harris (2002) states that this is happening ostensibly for profit in a specific historical and sociopolitical moment. Since 1997, Amnesty International (2000) has documented the existence of torture in more than 150 countries, and the Center for Victims of Torture (2000) in the United States has produced an estimate of 400,000 torture survivors. In Argentina during 1976–82, 30,000 people disappeared; according to Conadep National Advice Commission (1985), they were tortured and thrown into the sea.

Typically, the abuse of the body and the application of absolute and intolerable pain are meant to afford the perpetrator access to the victim's mind, or to obliterate all capacity to function. Torture may involve, all at once, an attack on the flesh, the psyche, and the symbols that give life its meaning.

Dance/movement therapy´s basic concern is 'to mobilize the body/brain relationship through movement' (Dulicai 2006, p. 1). When working with torture survivors, the goal of this intervention is often to reconstruct their life and to integrate the individual´s physical, emotional, cognitive, and social world. It attends to the implicated disarray of the nervous system, seeking to overcome the interactional and devastating crisis that has destroyed the totality of the human system's organization. The theory supporting the particular work to which I will refer to is Goodill's (2005). According to this author, development encompasses individual, biological, family, social, and group processes as interactive webs.

The inescapable stress resulting from torture is the acquisition of specific behaviours and the alteration of multiple brain systems. Van der Kolk (1994) states that strong emotional experiences have an impact on body functioning and work on the trauma, focalizing the patient's gestures. Damasio (1999) admits that pain is associated with punishment and is expressed through paralysis. Chaiklin, Lohn, and Sandel (1993) use kinaesthetic empathy, and Anzieu (1987, p. 25) believes that 'the skin is a set of different organs', all destroyed by torture.

The clinical material to which this chapter refers emerged during 1977–78, with persons who have suffered torture and organized violence by the Argentinean government, which was in power from 1976 to 1983. Clients attended the therapist's private practice, and the work focused on political and social violence that had taken place prior to their attending therapy within this particular sociopolitical context.

SOCIOPOLITICAL CONTEXT

Oszlak and O'Donnell (1981, p. 121) define context as 'the set of factors extrinsic to the more specific subject of a research, which is indispensable in order to understand, describe, and explain the subject and the effects over the variables.' The extrinsic factors to the more specific subject of this research are related to a system supported by the military authoritarian rule that resulted in the disappearance of many persons and a new population: survivors of torture for political reasons. According to Conadep (1985), the values and norms in that period produced disputes, and the authorities addressed this problem by establishing a coup d'état to restore public order. A series of circumstances influenced Argentinean social behaviour. Memories, goals, realizations, and organizations created a special social context of threats that changed the ideological system, standards, and values in that society. The military used the National Security Doctrine (NSD) for South America to provoke fear and to impose a new economic and sociopolitical form. Under NSD, the military became the force ultimately responsible for Latin American security and development. This information is crucial in understanding, describing, and explaining the specific object of this study: torture survivors who, for security reasons, lacked family or community support, were victims of a systematic plan of anxiety and disappearance. The concept of the body as the central target of the torturer's attack belonged to a society living under its own violence. For this reason, Reca (2010) argues that such trauma goes beyond post-traumatic stress disorder (PTSD), due to the fact that although it is suffered in isolation, it originates from a sociopolitical context. Bettelheim (1981) locates the trauma's political causality, alluding to the event's historical dimension: a traumatic experience which can emerge and be explained within a sociopolitical context. This author infers this as an event which exceeds the PTSD denomination. Martin-Baró (1990) was the first to devise with the term 'psychosocial trauma', and Madariaga (2002) contemplates the inadequacy of addressing the torture trauma as post-traumatic stress, since it fails to recognize the psychosocial problem. Sociopsychological trauma has a profound impact on the functional organization of individuals, since their systems do not allow connections with reality, and they become disorganized, resulting in loss of balance, personal limitations, and problematic boundaries.

DANCE/MOVEMENT THERAPY

The National Institute of Health (NIH) in the United States, cited by Goodill (2005), has categorized DMT as a form of intervention in the body–mind field, stating that the body–mind concept is used to refer to the mutual, bidirectional relationship in which the body affects the mind and vice versa. It is a process which cannot be divided into its components, since it does not constitute a separable phenomenon but two aspects of the same information system. In addition, as Rossi (1986, p. 67) has stated: '. . . biology is a process of information transduction. Mind and body are both aspects of one information system. Life is an information system. Mind and body are two facets or two ways of conceptualizing this single information system.' From the standpoint of a biopsychosocial model, the theory of the information system represents a solid theoretical ground for DMT on the basis of 'the solidarity of simultaneous, overlapping systems, one constructed on top of, with, and against the others', as explained by Morin (1988, p. 4). Wainstein (2002, p. 89) defined it as a system which 'includes a structure, while adding the properties resulting from the interactions occurring between its parts, and from its exchanges which affects it or which it is itself capable of affecting.' In this model, both the patient and the disorder are included, as well as the participation of social, psychological, and biological factors. At the same time, it is fundamentally connected to the concept of kinaesthetic empathy and its use in the population described previously. To use kinaesthetic empathy in DMT means to empathize with the other person's, including feelings that give way to bodily sensations and expressions. This modality primarily points to emotions that rest on the limbic system—the brain's system, which is evolutionally older than the cortex development—and then points to the rational–emotional link existing and produced each time behaviour is generated. In the use of kinaesthetic empathy in Chaiklin, Lohn, and Sandel (1993), reaching to understand the patient in their body means that the therapist becomes a mirror or a witness reflecting the other person's non-verbal expression. In so doing, the therapist allows the brain to re-establish its function of interpreting the experience coming from the senses and from the outside world. As an overall aim, it is proposed that DMT could be considered a specific and positive path in the reconstruction of the world's victims of torture, while it attends to the physical, emotional, cognitive, and social aspects of individuals, organizing and restoring their basic movement, which causes a permanent flow of sequential actions and experiences in the human organism. The core of this therapeutic process lies in the fact that what cannot be processed through words is processed through movement in a deeper and more effective way.

The literature review's origins derive from the material that includes theories, case studies, and group analysis carried out in Europe by Callaghan (1993, 1995) and Scarry (1985), in the United States by Epstein (2003), Gray (2001a, 2001b, 2002), and Harris (2002, 2007), and in Argentina by Reca (1997, 1999, 2005, 2010). Also included in the data is a panel discussion that took place at the 2002 ADTA Conference in Denver, and at least one available audiovisual resource filmed fifteen years after therapeutic processes were over: the ADTA Video Project on Violence (ADTA 2001), curated by Dianne Dulicai, which includes footage from Buenos Aires of the movement therapy work of panelist Maralia Reca, who is also author of a Spanish-language book on DMT that incorporates a case study of her work with the family of a person who 'disappeared' under Argentina's military dictatorship. The video material is to be screened during the workshop, allowing for spontaneous commentary by both Reca and other members of the panel.

Finally, in order to clarify this approach, a thematic analysis by Braun and Clarke (2006) has been used as a method for identifying, analyzing, and reporting patterns derived from data, and also Duverger (1986), who divided data into qualified unities and predefined categories through which the analysis addresses relationships and results.

PRESENTATION OF TWO CASE STUDIES

The aim that dance/movement therapists pursue, according to Reca (2000, p. 26), is 'to seek, feel, and perceive the individual's unique and particular body in order to touch it later with words and movements.' What is intended is the reparation of suffering, considering developmental issues, placing emphasis on relationships, the reconstruction of confidence, resocialization of object relations, intrapersonal and interpersonal relations, and those related to identity issues (Schmais and Felber 1977; Kestenberg 1974). It is acknowledged that this population suffers the rupture of their relational world with regard to themselves and others, due to an extreme experience which has annihilated the ordinary parameters of survival and coexistence. Scarry (1985) suggests, in her insightful meditation on torture and responses to it, that as a strategy for unmaking the personal and collective through brutality and force, torture may involve the body as the object as well as the subject of torture, embodying at the same time the society which is under attack.

Since, according to Bernstein (1979), the body defines separateness and mortality, and is the primary focus of freedom or the lack of it, DMT aims at making individuals feel secure in their own bodies, and helping torture survivors to be empowered (Harris

2002), which means taking control and responsibility for their own physical, psychological, and social body.

In torture survivors the major insult to their psychological system is the deep feeling of being isolated from the rest of the world for having been tortured. Torture implies that the connections taken for granted, the mere confidence necessary to keep living on a daily basis, are shattered, and one is left totally alone, without anyone's help and without anything to be done about it.

The International Rehabilitation for Torture Victims (2000) establishes the following consequences of torture: hyperarousal, restlessness, alertness, startle reaction, sleeping and breathing problems, recurrent intrusive memories, avoidance behaviour, powerlessness and helplessness, loss of values, vulnerability, and space–time confusion. The same source suggests that the two most common affects showing up in torture survivors correspond to two survival strategies: dissociation and hyperarousal. The former is a complex mental process during which a change appears in the person's consciousness, interrupting the normal connections of functions such as identity, memory, thoughts, feelings, and experiences. The latter is a multidimensional process involving physical and mental changes in terms of extreme vigilance and poor tolerance. Therefore, it is believed that DMT permits an on-site reconstruction precisely where the breaking of the boundaries has occurred, in and from the same place of torment and paralysis, providing a form of movement dialogue which can mobilize that part which was physically, emotionally, cognitively, and socially paralyzed. Basically, in the reconstruction of the world of this population, the problem posed is that of reconnecting the body with emotions. Van der Kolk (1994) states that strong emotional experiences have an impact on body functioning, and he works on the trauma by focusing on the patient's gestures.

DMT's approach to working with these trauma cases consists of bringing the smallest, least obvious movement qualities into focus; likewise the possible movement phrases, the relationship of the different body parts with each other, and its succession into gesture expression, to which the therapist will respond. Bercelli (2004) recommends working essentially on the possibility of relaxing the iliopsoas muscles, which contract during the traumatic event due to electric discharges, immobility by being tied to a bed, the inability to perform any defensive movement or escape which connotes the four basic threat-related reactions: fight, flee, face, faint, and the inability to respond to violence. None of these can be an alternative in the particular situation of torture, and therefore the organism's natural defences are annihilated. This chapter deals with two of the four major adaptive responses cited here: hyper-arousal (or fight), and dissociation (or faint). Damasio (1999) states that pain is associated with punishment and is expressed through paralysis withdrawal behaviour. On the other hand, pleasure is associated with reward is and expressed through searching and advancing behaviour. Punishment makes the organism close up on itself, freeze, and separate from its environment, and this is what DMT seeks to modify.

The following clinical cases illustrate and unravel the path that runs from the pain, anger, rage, and hatred to the deep mourning of needs that were destroyed by the actions of another.

The sequence that the therapist uses for the treatments include these concepts: empathy, mirroring, movement reflection, active dialogue, and active witnessing. The main technique is free movement improvisation.

- During mirroring, the visual and kinaesthetic aspects are differentiated as dance. The therapist invites the person to dance, and thus relates with his/her movement or the absence of it.
- Through dancing, the mirroring took shape as a process of dialogue rather than mimicking the movement.
- Through the mirrored dialogue, the patients achieved greater openness to their own language of movement.
- The spoken dialogue added new meanings to the movement language.
- Kinaesthetic empathy is a key factor because it makes possible for some parts of the body, those that move, to help the immobile ones to be rebuilt in their meaning, and from there consolidate a transient unit and the sequential flow of movement. Reuniting and relocating the natural flow of movement generates feelings of being cared for: the connection between the body and the emotional pain. Just reuniting small space distances such as going to and returning from the site of origin permits spatial relocation which enhances and generates certain independence for Lola, one of the survivors. The following is her case.

Case Study 1: Lola

Lola had obtained the therapist's telephone number through some friends who watched over her, despite the danger at that moment, after being imprisoned in a jail in the north of the country. During her captivity she drew and painted all day when she was not being tortured. Lola said she often had to literally eat her paintings, but at other times one of her torturers appreciated what she did and was able to give away her creations. Lola believes that this act saved her life. This was the first experience of destruction in the relation between body–space–time that she shared with the therapist.

The first encounter with the therapist was held only through visual contact and in absolute silence. Lola arrived, and she sat on the floor and started to tremble. The therapist quietly and slowly held her until the trembling stopped. She said she could not tolerate the feelings that returned to her again and again because they were stored within her.

In her first sessions she walked along the perimeter, close to the walls of the room, without ever stepping near to the centre of the place, even though she tried to conceal from the therapist what she was doing. During all the sessions she wore gloves and said that as she was a plastic artist she did not want to touch and stain the walls.

The spatial relocation generated by the therapist's movement approaches dialoging with Lola, opened Lola´s feelings of being in a protected space, and from them on continued their work. By the fifth session Lola said:

When I first came I felt like I was a puzzle, the pieces were located but not pieced together, this gave me the feeling that at any time or in any adverse situation I was going to fall apart and the pieces would lose their place. The encounter with you and DMT allowed my pieces to join definitely; this gave me a sense of unity that I lacked before because I was not this or that piece, I was a whole.

Lola slowly and gradually began to use up more space, even though she still leaned against the wall without touching it:

. . . something has changed in my relationship with others. I do not feel that I can disintegrate or fall apart and lose my pieces anymore. I can accept myself better than I had before and I'm slowly starting to trust myself again. This improved my relationship not only with other people, but also with me. I can not only rely on others but also trust myself. I learned to trust and take risks. When I first arrived here I felt I had had enough.

Lola continued to wear her gloves while moving. On one occasion she told her therapist:

. . . you always respected my dignity. You knew that I did not want to be referred to as 'the poor little thing'. You helped me sort my world and my needs. Helped me understand my words, my unique way of understanding, touching and feeling the world and what had happened to me.

At another time, after an exercise, Lola said:

I just went through an experience that allowed me to realize that through this work, I was able to reset my body, I can now understand better what has happened and I think I understand the key of my devastation . . . I remember one night, that I had not slept in my apartment, someone came to search it; I was not there, so they just turned the place upside down. Sometime after, I thought that if I had been there and once again taken, my parents would not have looked for me. At that time I had not understood the risks, even the suicide attempts I have lived alone and with guilt. I did not understand what I felt. I could not see me or feel me as a whole. I only saw parts of myself, and some parts horrified me. I did not know how to love myself, but there was love somewhere and you rescued it and showed it to me because you treated me as a person. Now I know Maralia (therapist) and DMT helped me cope with the horrible abuse that I went through.

What had happened to her, with her body? From the first session her body was the main character:

When I returned back home after being taken, everything hurt but in a strange way, the skin was more sensitive. I felt the pain penetrate me from the outside in. I have receptivity now; it's broader and it makes me less vulnerable. I'm a stronger person now.

Lola did not stop wearing her gloves during the therapeutic process—and twenty years later her therapist found her by chance in the street, wearing gloves. She did not mention the torture, but one day a wonderful painting with her signature was delivered to the therapist's office.

Movement takes place in time. It is part of a continuum that can differentiate from long to short sequences or parts of the movement which determines its speed. In Lola's case, her flow of movement was not a mechanical sequence. It played from emotional circumstances. This allowed her to perform and master certain actions sometimes, but she was paralyzed against the wall at other times. For instance, the structuring of various sequences of body movements was achieved by working on her body rhythmicity, to suddenly stop and go. This allowed her to work with those expressions of instantaneous stiffness, which ultimately led her to the ability of temporal organization that is understood as rhythm. This factor, because of its regulating and organizing character, enabled Lola to open and share her feelings. Later, this work led to an important dialogue of movements with the therapist, whom she had started to trust in terms of stability and continuity.

In one session, in the middle of Lola working with patterns of movements that were fairly simple and some of them joyful, she asked for several blankets and soft music.

She piled the quilts on top of each other until the structure was reliable, and then began to slide between them, entering through one side and, with a swimming-like movement, appearing on the other side, repeating the action again and again until she said that she had set up the dance of her martyrdom.

It is possible that Lola's ritual dance was a metaphor of the underworld through which she had travelled during her captivity.

Discussion of Case 1

The classification of these disorganized patterns is important because it refers to disorganized patterns in relation to the elements of space, time, and body weight (Laban 1960), which have all been found, in one way or another, to be compromised in the majority of survivors of torture for political reasons.

In Lola's case, fragmentation in the relationship of body parts was detected, as well as an evident decrease in their amount of energy: hands that can barely move or hold themselves look flaccid and soft. Exaggeration of defensiveness, such as walking in a fixed and invariant manner while sustaining an active control for the possible emotion, as well as a reduced mobility and lack of vital dynamics, were also detected. Inability to explore the horizontal direction, only to be attentive to front and back, is also another sign of rejection. In relation to space there was a lack of multifocal attention, replaced by the narrow vision which looked like tunnel vision that referred only to confinement and threat.

Considering these latter unique elements that are repeated in this population, the purpose of describing them was to analyze the experience of the tortured body in relation to the use of space, time, and weight expressed in the body messages of survivors of torture (Reca 2010). It is known that movement unfolds in space and that the spatial dimension is felt, perceived, and explored through kinaesthetic sensations and movement of the body itself. This space is therefore experienced in oneself and in relation to the environment and others. It is possible to distinguish between outer space and inner space. The skin is the binding limit and the connection between inside and outside, but also between separation and differentiation.

Body movement is experienced in relation to gravity and the possibility of keeping the weight in a continuum that requires energy and the regulation of it. Thus, the ability to remain standing relies on the voltage between the upper and lower body. In circumstances in which this vertical balance—up–down—is affected, it tends to a misbalance, and therefore to collapse, because of the unevenly distributed tension. The weight factor is a very important variable in terms of the quality of movement required to perform an action and to interact with objects and with others. This element depends on the emotional state as well as the individual's will, intention, and strength applied to its goal.

Space, time, and weight are dramatically affected in the body of the survivors of torture. It was observed that difficulties arose in the natural flow of body parts in the three dimensions of space, and also in the organization and utilization of them. Significant deterioration was found overall in the horizontal dimension, even though difficulties were found in all three. The significant lack of use in the horizontal dimension implied difficulties in emotional relationships and in the relations with the surrounding world objects, which appeared clearly diminished.

Case Study 2: Manuel

Manuel is another fictitious name for a survivor. Manuel's case reflects the elements mentioned previously. He was taken prisoner with ten other people in a restaurant at night. All of them were hooded, thrown into cars, and taken to an unknown location. Manuel was put in the trunk of one of the cars in which there was a small light, which helped him not to despair.

Manuel later revealed in his treatment that he had been tortured all that night. He had been bound to a grill and then poked with an electric pick, while at other times his head was submerged in a tub of ice-cold water, which only ceased when he passed out. His wrists and ankles ached because of the hyperextension to which he had been subjected. His head also hurt. He understood this to be due to being questioned incessantly, and also because he was forced to touch corpses and was told that he would look like them if he did not cooperate.

During therapy, Manuel said that the morning after he was tortured he was taken naked into the street. His captors told him to run, without turning back, otherwise he would be shot immediately. All of his belongings, including his ID, his house keys, and his clothes, had been taken from him. He took refuge at his brother's house, and that same morning he came to the therapist's office, where he showed him multiple cigarette burns and traces of the electric shock applications.

A major difficulty was revealed in the way that Manuel expressed what had happened to him. Torture had happened in and to his body, and as the damage was located there, he needed relief for the body which did not respond to him. The emphasis of the therapeutic encounters was placed on the paralysis and dissociation of his movements, and his feelings. During the sessions he was encouraged to feel and admit that his body was part of him, and that therefore the experience was his. In order to restore his body, he had to hear and pay attention to it that so he could develop a new relationship with it and himself. He had to start relating to his emotional pain: the impact on his feelings, the depression and the anxiety.

Manuel recovered his upward mobility in a short period of time, slowly achieving some regularity in its sagittal plane, and mobility, which usually tended to retreat or fall behind.

Horizontal mobility remained fixed and invariant, as the effective change regarding lateral focalization, which would modify his attention and allow the passage to and from, appeared inhibited. The joint use of his hands and the extension of his arms were not possible either. In Manuel's case, the treatment was followed by developments (Espenak 1981), since they proved effective with regard to hip mobilization and also allowed the possibility of relaxing the iliopsoas muscles, which, as mentioned previously, tend to stiffen during a traumatic event (Bercelli 2004). This experience revealed that the iliopsoas muscles had shrunk due to the repeated electric shocks, immobility while being strapped to a gurney, the impossibility of making any defensive moves or attempts to escape, to being paralyzed from the lying position, and of the electric pick to his legs and testicles. Gradually, he made movements that involved increasing amounts of physical courage. The therapist invited him to work in a multifocal space, in order to help him gain some resistance and to tolerate his anxiety and frustration. The control of anxiety and fear were the most important issues, since they inhibited the expression of his feelings and movements. During one session, Manuel and the therapist worked on the floor, thereby achieving safety for the body. The challenge was the freedom of his mind, because physical courage and fear have to do with the ability to control a situation.

Manuel's loss of spatial orientation was a consequence of the injuries he had received, which made the hypothalamus unable to relay its patterns of information to the cortical motor system. This makes some survivors of torture extremely vulnerable to experiencing a variety of negative emotions. Manuel's therapy focused on reinforcing his self-image from incursions on the ability to be and appear. Gradually, he came to stand briefly on his tiptoes and to remain standing for a short while. Later, he could walk on his tiptoes through the place, with his arms opened wide. Some time afterwards he was instructed to imagine a safe place: it could be real or fictitious, but it had to be a very safe place that he could evoke every time he needed to return to safety. During Manuel's therapy, the therapist sought to see and understand these signals, respecting the silence compressed below the level of speech, the magnitude of the trauma.

Impairments were not only seen in Manuel's mobility in general, but also at the dermal system level, due to cigarette burns and subjection to the ice-cold water, and to the electric picks and the head submersions. Manuel felt that his skin was pierced in many places. Thus, it was important to explore and address this system, since the skin and nervous system are linked, the two tissues having the same embryonic origin and appearing in the embryo prior to the other sensory organs. All information, change of temperature, pressure or aggression to the skin is transmitted to the brain through nerve fibres. The brain responds by ordering the release of neurotransmitters that allow the skin to act against these attacks. Recent research studies from Germany, carried out by Joachim, Kuhlmei, Dinh, et al. (2007), indicate that the perception of stress in the nervous system is transferred to peripheral tissues like the skin—not only in the classical hormonal sense, but through neuropeptides and neurotrophines. Although the existence of such a brain–skin connection is supported by steadily increasing experimental evidence, it remains unclear as to what extent perceived stress affects the sensory hardwiring between the skin and its afferent neurons.

Discussion of Case 2

In general, during the experiences of therapeutic process with torture survivors, it was found that the strongest feeling that permeated the self was that of being skinned or in raw flesh, even after having regained freedom for a long time. Therefore, therapy revolved around restoring safety limits to the nerve endings and their reactive connections, and also in pursuit of restoring the skin's protective function of the body: its being a wrap, a film, a membrane, a shell. Anzieu (1987, p. 25) says that 'the skin is a set of different organs. It's anatomical, physiological, and cultural complexity anticipates at the body level, the complexity of the self in the psychic realm.' He also argues that of all the sensory organs, the skin is the most vital sense because it precedes the other proximal systems: smell and taste, the vestibular and distal systems, and auditory and visual. The skin is thus a system of various sensory organs: touch, pressure, pain, heat. In close connection with other external sensory organs (hearing, sight, smell and taste) and along with kinaesthetic sensitivity, it is an essential balance in the therapeutic work in DMT.

Manuel drastically changed his life after the torture experience and his therapeutic work. He entered a religious community, in which he still lives, being a useful and emotionally rich person, different from whom he had been before.

CONCLUSION

The evaluations of patterns and sequences indicate that an extremely disruptive experience impacts the body in its full physical, emotional, cognitive, and social development. Dance therapy was therefore used to care for the emotional body, while avoiding overwhelming feelings. Working with minimal movements and use of space distances, the therapist's work focused on trying to reconstruct the biological body—one of the routes of entry of the traumatic experience.

The problem of emotional control and the splitting of suppressed feelings, as consequences of the experience, was met by inhibiting the reprocessing of what had been felt, smelled, touched, and lived, which, because of its unexpected and brutal characteristics, remained within sensations and perceptions of oneself.

Therapy worked in depth with the physiological patterns involved in torture and with the feelings and emotional reactions. Therapy sought to reinstate a new experience, more adapted to the present time, through the immediacy of movement and the safety that this involved, because although circumstantial, the threat of the experience happening all over again was always present.

Lola and Manuel show results of attuning to the rhythm and body organization at the same site at which torment and immobilization were inflicted. DMT techniques help to restore the nervous system's disarray and its basic movements, responsible for generating a sequential flow of experiences and actions. It is also possible to unblock what was paralyzed, and its main sequels: hyperarousal and dissociation. Kinaesthetic empathy enables an early approach, which by itself opened up the possibility of producing a change, preventing becoming emotionally overwhelmed or flooded. It is often the case that kinaesthetic empathy is the only pathway for the therapist to access a survivor of torture when there is no availability of either internal or external resources.

Both survivors could access a new organization with them and with the community, since torture and the permanent threat disrupted the entire structure and the system's balance. The strategy held draws the attention to the irreversible fact that whatever had happened, had happened to a part of the person and not to the whole, and that there is another part that can ask for help and try to overcome the disruptive experience. Understanding oneself in terms of parts helps also to accept the therapist's role.

According to the criterion that movement has a mobilizing power on the psyche, it is assumed that body–mind is a system which must function in harmony, each component mirroring each other mutually, since any dysfunction in the sequential flow of movement and in the unity can indicate the presence of stress and psychological or physical conflict. The case presented here explains how organizational systems are interconnected, and how they are all affected by torture. There is not one system that does not suffer or is not damaged by the aftermath and consequence of the ferocity experienced.

As DMT operates on the same principles as the organizational systems, self-sustaining constant activity and self-transformation, it is considered that the problems and solutions are bidirectional and are therefore interactional. Thus, systems theory helps to make possible the search for the meaning of social behaviors by analyzing the social group and the constructive ways that sustain behaviour.

NOTE

1. This chapter is based on the PhD thesis of the same title presented at Palermo University, Argentina, in 2009, for a doctorate in clinical psychology, directed by Dr Dianne Dulicai and Dr Graciela Tonon.

REFERENCES

Anzieu, D. (1987). *El Yo Piel* (2°. Ed.). Madrid: Biblioteca Nueva.

American Dance Therapy Association (ADTA) (2001). ADTA Video Project on Violence, United States: ADTA. Videotape shown at the International Panel of the 36th Annual Conference of the ADTA, Raleigh, NC.

Amnesty International. (2000). <www.amnesty.org> (accessed 20 November 2000).

Bercelli, D. (2004). *Bio-Mechanics and Mind/Body Techniques of Stress Release*. Orleans: Yoga Site.

Bettelheim, B. (1981). *Sobrevivir El Holocausto una generación después*. Barcelona: Grijalbo.

Braun, V. and Clarke, V. (2006). 'Using thematic analysis in psychology', *Qualitative Research in Psychology*, 3(2): 77–101.

Callaghan, K. (1993). 'Movement psychotherapy with adults survivors of political torture and organized violence', *The Arts in Psychotherapy*, 20: 411–21.

Callaghan, K. (1995). *The Body in Conflict: Arts Approaches to Conflict*. London: Jessica Kingsley, pp. 151–62.

Chaiklin, S., Lohn, A., and Sandel, S. (1993). *Foundation of Dance/movement Therapy: The life and work of Marian Chace*. Columbia: The Marian Chace Memorial Fund of the American Dance Therapy Association, pp. 25–29.

Conadep (1985). Informe Nunca Más, Bs. As: Eudeba.

Damasio, A. (1999). *The Feeling of What Happens: Body, Emotion and the Making of Consciousness*. San Diego: Harcourt Brace.

Dulicai, D. (2006). *Evidence-Based Outcomes: Humanistic and Arts Therapies. 1*. Long Beach, CA: American Psychological Association.

Duverger, M. (1986). *Método de las Ciencias Sociales*. México: Ariel.

Epstein, J. (2003). *Healing the Unnameable*. Unpublished Master's thesis. Naropa University.

Espenak, L. (1981). *Dance Therapy: Theory and Applications*. Springfield, IL: Charles C. Thomas.

Gray, A. (2001a). Dance/movement therapy with a child survivor: a case study. *Dialogus*, 6(1), 8–12.

Gray, A. (2001b). 'The body remembers: Dance movement therapy with an adult survivor of torture', *American Journal of Dance Therapy*, 23(1): 29.

Gray, A. (2002). 'The body as voice: Somatic psychology and dance/movement therapy with survivors of war and torture', *Connections*, 3(2): 2–4.

Goodill, S. (2005). *An Introduction to Medical Dance/Movement Therapy*. London: Jessica Kingsley.

Harris, D. (2002). *Mobilizing to Empower and Restore: Dance/Movement Therapy with Children Affected by War and Organized Violence*. Ann Arbor, MI: UMI Dissertation Services. Video.

Harris, D. (2007). 'Pathways to embody empathy and reconciliation after atrocity: Former boy soldiers in a dance/movement therapy group in Sierra Leona.' Unpublished paper.

Joachim, R. A., Kuhlmei, A., Dinh, Q. T., Handjiski, B., Fisher, T., Peters, E. M., Klapp, B. F., Paus, R., and Arck, P. C. (2007). 'Neuronal plasticity of the brain Connections', *International Journal of Research*, 85(12): 1347–49.

Kestenberg, J. (1974). The role of movement pattern in development. *This Quarterly*, XXXIV.

Laban, R. (1960). *The Mastery of Movement*. London: Macdonald and Evans, pp. 5–30, 70–90.

Madariaga, C. (2002). *Trauma psicosocial, trastorno de estrés postraumático y tortura*. Chile: Cintra, pp. 74–80.

Martin-Baró, I. (1990). *Psicología social de la guerra: trauma y terapia*. San Salvador: UCA.

Morin, E. (1988). *El conocimiento del conocimiento. El método, 1, II*. Madrid: Cátedra.

National Institute of Health (NIH) (2004), 'What is CAM?', in Goodill (2005).

Oszlak, O. and O'Donnell, G. (1981). *Estado y políticas públicas en América Latina: una estrategia de investigación*. CLACSO, 4. Bs.As: CEDES.

Reca, M. (1997). 'Coping with disappearance in Argentina: The impact on the body of the family', *Proceedings of American Dance Therapy Association*: 34–6. Copyright Beckett Papers.

Reca, M. (1999). 'The manifestation and treatment of violence', JADTA News, 40-7-11.

Reca, M. (2005). 'Qué es Danza/movimiento terapia: el cuerpo en danza.' Bs. As: Lumen.

Reca, M. (2010). *Tortura y Trauna: Danza/movimiento terapia en la reconstrucción del Mundo del sobre viviente de tortura por causas políticas*. Buenos Aires: Biblos.

Rossi, E. (1986). *The Psychobiology of Mind-Body Healing*. New York: Norton.

Scarry, E. (1985). *The Body in Pain: The Making and Unmaking of the World*. New York: Oxford University Press, pp. 124–40.

Schmais, C. and Felber, J. D. (1977). 'Dance therapy process analysis: A method for Observing and analyzing a dance therapy group', *American Journal of Dance Therapy*, 1(2): 18–26.

Van der Kolk, B. (1994). 'The body keeps the stored memory and the evolving psychotherapy of post-traumatic stress', *Harvard Review of Psychiatry*, 1 (5): 253–65.

Wainstein, M. (2002). *Comunicación: un paradigma de la mente*. Buenos Aires: Eudeba.

CHAPTER 36

HAUNTED BY MEANING

Dance as Aesthetic Activism

SHERRY B. SHAPIRO

INTRODUCTION

IN this chapter I want to explore the meaning of wellbeing in ways that differentiate it from the more familiar perspectives of physical, emotional, and spiritual health, and connect wellbeing to the context of political and social efficacy. My concern is the way that human beings are able to represent and express their resistance to, and transformation of, oppressive and unjust social conditions. In this context I define aesthetic activism as forms of practices that empower those living under dehumanizing conditions and seek to heal the human brokenness that is the result of these conditions; and further, to reimagine lives that might flourish with radical social change.

I begin with some personal experiences. In the summer of 2011, while riding in a taxi in Tel Aviv we turned onto Rothschild Boulevard, one of Tel Aviv's oldest leafy and affluent streets, when we came upon tents erected in the grassy median. Indeed, a very unusual site. Above the tents were banners with the phrase 'Aesthetic Activism'. I asked the driver why the tents were there. He mumbled something about people not being happy about the housing situation. With little research, I learned that the tents were a chosen aesthetic act—an act that sought to bring attention to the dissonance between existing inequalities around access to affordable housing to Israelis. This kind of intertwining of the aesthetic and political has become central in struggles from New York to Cairo to Moscow. In this epoch of globalization, as Tiina Rosenberg (2009) describes:

> Current issues such as militarization, poverty, trafficking, global warming, the AIDS crisis, violence, homelessness, homophobia, sexism, racism, and disrespect for human rights demand proactive measures if philosophers not only wish to interpret the world in various ways, but also to change it, as Karl Marx and Friedrich Engels once so famously put it. (1)

In places around the world, activists have found ways to go beyond critical interpretation developing a praxis-oriented approach to social and economic injustices through creative forms of expression. In so doing, they have created 'communities of solidarity and resistance' (Welch 1985). And—an important point made by Chandra Talpade Mohanty (2003)—this reflexive practice of solidarity foregrounds communities of people who have chosen to work and fight together. This idea of reflexive solidarity is useful, as it allows us a way of thinking about collectivity based on shared interests without colonizing or dominating others. Attention is given to the importance of collective interest that has brought the group together, and this in itself is a component of social wellbeing. Wellbeing, as noted in Keyes' (1998) study, includes the social dimensions: 'In short, this study suggests that life includes numerous social challenges; therefore wellbeing includes social dimensions such as coherence, integration, actualization, contribution, and acceptance' (p. 133).

In this chapter I examine the nature of aesthetic processes within existing communities connected to social change. Central to my work is the concern for the way the body, or embodiment, becomes the vehicle for challenging, interrogating, and resisting forms of social oppression. While I am aware of the dangers in essentializing the body, I believe it is a rich source for understanding the concrete experiences of the cultural/political/social forces that shape our lives. Feminist theorists (Hartsock 1997) have argued that these concrete experiences, at a particular time and place located within a particular set of social relations, provide a position for action. It is from this position, or standpoint, from which any emancipatory action can be undertaken. Here, the wellbeing of human beings is, in the first place, connected to their understanding of how they are positioned in the society. It is out of this understanding that they become capable of living in ways that empower them to be fully agentic individuals within a supportive and compassionate community. I draw on the work of social theories including those introduced by Terry Eagleton, Maxine Greene, and Herbert Marcuse, as well as contemporary feminist theory such as introduced by Patricia Collins, Judith Butler, and bell hooks, all of which can provide useful frameworks for a better understanding of activists' art making. The central concern of this discussion focuses on how aesthetic processes are joined to feminist and critical pedagogies creating spaces in the classroom, studio, or community for a better understanding and conscious engagement with one's life. In her book *The Dialectic of Freedom* (1988), Maxine Greene refers to Virginia Woolf's reference to the 'breaking of the disinterest of twentieth-century artists' and their absence of care towards the social/political world. Woolf wrote (p. 2) that 'to break with the "cotton wool" of habit, or mere routine, of automatism, is to seek alternative ways of being, to look for openings. To find such openings is to discover new possibilities—often new ways of achieving freedom in the world.' Here we imagine that it is possible to revisit lived experience as a means of challenging fixed meanings, and by so doing, seeing oneself or one's world in a new perspective. This questioning and renewed sense-making helps to shed some light on how we approach the world through common sense, which is usually shaped by several unexamined assumptions, and often the idea that our own perspective is the only valid one. Part of the work discussed in this chapter is about how to transcend our particular viewpoint and recognize that there are always multiple perspectives and multiple vantage points, and therefore no accounting can ever be complete or finished. Yet, from these anti-essentialist and multiperspective communities, democratic objectives can be formulated. As Greene (1988) reminds us: 'There is always more. There is always possibility. And this is where the space opens for the pursuit of freedom' (p. 128).

I will illustrate my understanding of aesthetic activism in dance pedagogy through my recent experience within a community in the Western Cape, in South Africa. Here, activist art, as described by Nina Felshin (in Rosenberg 2009), 'represents a confluence of the aesthetic, sociopolitical, and technological impulses of the past twenty-five years or more . . . This cultural form is the culmination of a democratic urge to give voice and visibility to the disenfranchised, and connect art to a wider audience' (p. 1).

Taking the body, and in particular hair as the thematic focus, I will describe the way in which the 'familiar can become strange, and the strange familiar' (Greene 1988). This process of questioning assumptions grounded in our everyday world can become a catalyst for a transformed understanding of identity, race, and gender. Cultural assumptions about boundaries for girls and young women's bodies and the narrow definitions of femininity are the central theme. Laid bare are some of the struggles to change the historical normative standards for femininity, power, and distinctions of identity, while a given society is moving towards a new political awareness. In this context, dance becomes a process of aesthetic activism in which the body provides a tool for both troubling essentialist assumptions and offering alternative possibilities shaped by the histories of its struggle. My intention is to make clear that aesthetic activism can be a catalyst for creating a more meaningful and empathic community. My concern is to illuminate the meaning and possibilities of aesthetic activism as they further the moral agenda of social justice and human rights. Here, there is an inextricable connection between the personal and the social; the development of more humane and interdependent context must produce a greater sense of wellbeing, efficacy, and fulfilment.

GROUNDING AESTHETIC ACTIVISM IN COMMUNITY

My discussion on aesthetics and activism is grounded in a wider debate on issues of community. Community is based upon a concept that we do not exist alone in the world, but alongside others. Archbishop Desmond Tutu (1999) explains that one cannot exist as a human being isolated from others. Of course, Tutu's vision makes it clear that the quest for community is inseparable from a deep understanding of human connection, of interdependence. For him this is expressed by the African term *Ubuntu*.

> *Ubuntu* is our way of making sense of the work. The word literally means 'humanity'. It is a philosophy and belief that a person is only a person through other people. In other words, we are human only in relation to other humans. Out humanity is

bound up in one another, and any tear in the fabric of connection between us must be repaired for us all to be made whole. This interconnectedness is the very root of who we are. (Tutu 2014, p. 8)

Who we are is always situated and positioned within a social, historical, political, and cultural context. We are all involved in 'life politics', as Zygmunt Bauman (in Collins 2006) tells us. The personal is connected to the social and therefore the political, as feminist scholars have made clear. Yet too often our concept of life is one that has been greatly based on principles of individualism and understood as a series of private choices; this approach specifically avoids the political. Obviously we do not live our lives fully in the private area nor in the public area, but rather in the meeting point between the two, and it is here where democracy becomes the place of dialogue between the two (Bauman, p. 201).

But let us return to the idea of individualism that is so well embedded in many aspects of contemporary life in various parts of the world. 'Contemporary culture teaches us to think of ourselves as individuals, separated from one another' (Shapiro 2010, p. 182). Most of what we define as successes or failures is thought about in individual terms. Indeed, our successes are often understood within the context of others' failures. The emphasis, Shapiro tells us, is constantly on 'me' and 'my', and what is mine and belongs to me. This ideology of individualism not only separates us from other human beings, but is a constant reinforcement of divisive imagery in which 'my group' (whether race, ethnicity, faith, nationality, team, and so on) is pitted against another. We might find ourselves seeing 'other human beings' as an obstacle to our safety, our success, our health, or our economic wealth. It becomes a problem of the stranger, and each society produces its own kind of stranger (Bauman 2001). Our worldviews become defined in terms of fear and suspicion, and our efforts are directed towards 'keeping things in order, in place'; that is to say, removing those who are different and appear to disturb our world. All of this leads to isolation, separation, and alienation—all antithetical to a sense of social integration, acceptance, or valued contributions. Whether the empowered or disempowered, Rabbi Michael Lerner (2006) concludes that 'most people feel underrecognized, underappreciated, and underrespected' (p. 251). The cynical realist worldview, states Lerner (2006), 'sees humans as independent little monads seeking to maximize self-interest and thus unlikely to sacrifice for some higher purpose' (p. 313). One cannot imagine here, in this highly separate, competitive, and individualized worldview, a perspective where participation, dialogue, empathy, and respect for others may become embodied, creating a space for a civil society to breathe and for true dialogue to emerge, and where empathy can prepare the ground for compassionate living—where, indeed, wellbeing is experienced.

Transcending Limitations and Boundaries

Today we live in a global society in which cultural globalization, the transnational migration of people, the impact of information circulation, and the centrality of consumer culture, are all prevalent. Coming to recognize the imaginary nature of our boundaries—the narratives of country, race or ethnicity, gender or sexuality—has spurred us to deconstruct what was thought of as 'real' or 'traditional'. Although simple deconstruction is not enough, rationality is not enough. Responding to this shift in theory, artist actions and activities have found ways of exposing, challenging, and presenting new awarenesses. Terry Eagleton (1990) posits that an aesthetics 'born of the recognition that the world of perception and experience cannot simply be derived from abstract universal laws, but demands its own appropriate discourse and displays its own inner, if inferior, logic' (p. 16). Or, put more succinctly by Eagleton: 'The aesthetic, then, is simply the name given to that hybrid form of cognition which can clarify the raw stuff of perception and historical practice, disclosing the inner structure of the concrete.' Eagleton's argument is one that reminds us that the aesthetic, grounded by our bodies, emerges from experience and perception. A discourse, as Eagleton suggests, that emerges from experience and perception speaks to a kind of rationality distinct from one that is only intellectually rooted. It speaks to the specificity of individual experiences and testifies against any simple abstraction of any category or label. This movement from an abstract discourse to one grounded in experience and perception has been a strong focus in feminist theory and pedagogy (Weiler 1988). Studying the past, confronting the present, and envisioning a new future have been central to women's liberation movements across the globe (Burn 2005). Weiler (1988) defines the space in which teachers are engaged in feminist pedagogy:

> They are describing the classroom as a place where consciousness is interrogated, where meanings are questioned, and means of analysis and criticism of the social world as well as of a text or assignment are encouraged. For these teachers, the goal of teaching is grounded in a respect for human value and cultural worlds of their students, and what it encourages is the development of both criticism and self-criticism . . . Feminist teachers share a commitment to a more just society for everyone, but they have a particular sense of themselves as women teachers and are conscious of their actions as role models for students. (pp. 114–15)

The emphasis in feminist pedagogy has ensured that the personal or subjective life-stories are central in understanding how culture and public policies shape lives. In this we can view how the social worlds in which we form our identity affect our bodies directly, at a visceral level; they become part of our bones and musculature. Our views of ourselves, of others, our ethics, values, manners of being, and understandings are instilled in our bodies—a place in which our thoughts and actions are instantiated. The 'body/subject' is the ultimate destination of cultural forming, both local and global. This point of cultural ingestion is where both projections and formations mingle in creating a double-edged process. The body of the postmodern subject, as Eagleton (1996) states, 'is integral to its identity" (p. 69). For modernity, the body was where there is something to be done, a place for betterment; in postmodernity it becomes a place where something—gazing, imprinting, regulating—is done to you. The global body imprinted by the concentrated power of the Western media is intensified, and a sense of a local self becomes less important. Human suffering extends through and beyond the boundaries of nationality, race, ethnicity, gender, social class, and sexual or religious preference—all ways of marking ourselves off from others. Here, in our shared physical suffering, in the commonality of the body, is a place of deeper and mutual understanding, and thus of transcendent possibility. The possibility for social wellbeing increases when empathic responses can be nurtured.

In order to increase our empathetic response towards others' sufferings requires an aesthetic process that directs us towards critical understanding, empathy, and imagination. Barber (2001) writes: 'Imagination is the link to civil society that art and democracy share . . . It is the faculty by which we stretch ourselves to include others, expand the compass of our interests, and overcome the limits of our parochial selves. Only then do we become fit subjects to live in democratic communities' (pp. 111–12). To address the issue of our immersion in a culture of privatism, fragmentation, inequality, and separation we must cultivate our imagination in order to transcend the 'what is' of our realities.

Historically, the arts have always played a critical role in helping to see 'what is and what might be'. Dance, particularly, has provided us with ways of understanding culture, history, and human desires, seeing both who we are and who we might become. Notwithstanding how the arts have played other kinds of roles in our cultures, such as a form of entertainment, as an avenue for escape, or as a form of exercise, here my focus is on dance as a form of intervention in our social realities—as an action for the purpose of effecting self and social change and promoting social justice. This kind of aesthetic action has been cultivated throughout history in different cultures as an avenue of jolting us out of our everydayness, as a process of opening spaces for us to examine what have been designated as socially acceptable ways of being, as a catalyst for challenging labels and restrictions, and as an experience that sensually educates us to think beyond and imagine what is not yet. It is at times called 'activist art', offering a counter-discourse to the official one.

The Discourse of Activist Art

Activist art means community or public participation as means of effecting social change and promoting social justice.

(Rosenberg 2009)

William Marotti (2006) provides us with a description of how artistic activism has been energized in Japan:

And what were the practices that attracted repression, and energized artistic activism? Interestingly, they anticipate the key strategies associated with the explosive activism marking the second half of the 1960s in Japan: the analysis of the everyday world through its signs and fragments for the operations of hidden forms of domination; the focus on local practice, the here and now, as a space implicated in larger structures and events, and the locus either for their replication, or transformation; strategies of radical defamiliarization and disidentification against unconscious forms of routine; the unearthing of hidden connections to politics and history in the simplest object of daily life; and above all, the identification of the world of the everyday itself as the central space for investigation and transformation. (614)

It is no accident that we see the connections Marotti makes between unearthing and laying bare policies that have in some way tried to silence the dominated and disempowered with artistic activism. This kind of action, Bernice Reagon (1990) reminds us, does not happen accidentally; it is a choice. She states: 'Socially conscious artists are not born. We are culturally oriented and trained . . . You have to choose and keep on choosing . . . It is our work (as artists) to show you what we see and to nurture, cradle, and change these images' (pp. 8–9).

As we have seen in more recent examples, activist movements have chosen aesthetics as a way of making statements, such as 'Arab Spring' (*The New York Times* 2011), 'Occupy Movement' (*The Guardian* 2012), 'Women in Black' (womeninblack.org) 'Argentina Mothers of Plaza de Mayo' (Women's News Network 2012), 'Aids Quilt' (Aids Memorial Quilt 2012), and the 'Clothesline Project'. The Clothesline Project, for example, creates a discourse of domestic abuse that recognizes the range of emotion experienced by abused bodies, and offers a community of hope to survivors (Jones 2009). In each of these we see forms of aesthetic activism. They are the emphasis in all of these struggles that the aesthetic is, to quote Picasso, 'a deceit that tells the truth'. In other words, the aesthetic allows us to exaggerate, condense, and highlight social realities in order to focus our attention and mobilize our energies against injustice and other forms of dehumanization. Rosenberg (2009) tells us:

> Activist art, in both its forms and methods, is process- rather than object- or product-oriented. Activist art takes place in public sites rather than within the context in art-world venues. As practice it often takes the form of temporal interventions, such as performance or performance-based activities, media events, exhibitions, and installations. (5)

Artistic expression becomes inseparable from a politics that seeks to notice what is, and, equally important, to imagine what is not yet. In this sense, the aesthetic becomes the critical component of how human beings can see their world in ways that are more critical and create meanings that transcend present forms of suffering. For example, the 'Occupy Movement' (*The Guardian* 2012) imaginatively reappropriates public space formerly possessed by the rich and the powerful; or democratic resisters in Cairo's Tahrir Square construct new images of a democratic and socially responsive civic order; or in the documentary '5 Broken Cameras' (Burnat and Davidi 2012), images record what it means to be living as a Palestinian under occupation. In the United States, women peace activists within the community of 'Code Pink' demonstrate in their physical appearance an assertive opposition to the war economy by subverting traditional gender notions associated with the colour pink. In places across the globe, 'flash mobs' refuse the

narrowly defined and traditional dance and performance spaces. In fact, it is my con-
tention that wherever there is a politics of resistance to injustice and inequality one will
find creative reimaginings of human possibility. This is true across the performing arts,
whether in poetry, theatre, music, or dance.

Human refusal of the present world is always paralleled by new visions of meaning
and discourse. Lucy Lippard (1995)—activist, artist, and scholar—saw art and politics
as linked, for, she believed, they both held 'the power to envision, move, and change'
(Collins, 2006, p. 10). Lippard saw a developed feminist consciousness as leading to a
new kind of art, a new way to experience art, and a new role for it—one with crucial
links to feminist activism. She explained:

> A developed feminist consciousness brings with it an altered concept of reality and
> morality that is crucial to the art being made and to the lives lived with that art. We
> take for granted that making art is not simply 'expressing oneself' but is a far broader
> and more important task—expressing oneself as a member of a larger unity, or
> comm/unity, so that in speaking for oneself one is also speaking for those who can-
> not speak. (1980, p. 363)

Surely, as mentioned previously that interpreting the world is not enough, we can better understand this today as meaning that the mobilization of people does not happen
through the process of dry, abstract reasoning, but requires a felt, full-bodied emotional
engagement with the life-world. Of course, it is necessary to add that such aesthetic
activism is not restricted to those seeking human progress, but is also found in less salu-
tary and reactionary movements. One only has to think about the Nuremberg Nazi ral-
lies as a prime example, or today the 'Tea Party' right-wing politics in the United States.

It is worth noting that while the Internet and social media have vastly expanded our
ability to communicate with others, nothing replaces the powerful immediacy of co-
present bodies, the shared physical experience, intimacy, and warmth that comes from
embodied proximity. What gives the aesthetic so much power is that it transforms critical reason into a process that works through emotion, feelings, and the sensibilities of
bodies. I heard this action described recently by George Takei (who played Mr Sulu in
Star Trek), discussing his new musical about the internment camps for American citizens of Japanese descent, as something that goes straight to the heart and then to the
mind. Dance can offer an especially rich vehicle for this process in the way it can draw
directly from the embodied and sensual experience of individual lives. Choreographers
have often chosen such life-stories or historical memories to create dance. Gottschild
explains (2008):

> Dancemakers have responded to social ills throughout the history of modern dance.
> Racism captured the imagination of mid-twentieth-century Americans: Charles
> Weidman's *Lynchtown* (1936), Pearl Primus' *Strange Fruit* and *Jim Crow Train*
> (both 1943) and *Slave Market* (1944), and Katherine Dunham's *Southland* (1951)
> all dealt with this issue. In Germany, Kurt Jooss created *The Green Table* (1932), a
> 'dance of death' about the horrors of war. A new crop of socially engaged works has

contemporary artists following in the footsteps of their aesthetic ancestors, particularly since the wake-up call of the 9/11 terrorist attacks. (pp. 62–3)

These artists have brought to consciousness, by raising awareness, some of the horrific chapters of human history. Many other examples can be found throughout the contemporary dance world of today, challenging issues of gender, sexuality, social class, race—most any issue of human concern. What I want to draw attention to, however, is not so much the aesthetic product but the aesthetic process. I contend that too often in dance the product is judged not by criteria developed from a framework of activist art, and the dancer is too often treated simply as a body, as an object or image fuelling the creation of a dance.

TANGLED THEORIES

My own struggle to connect dance pedagogy to aesthetic activism has led me through tangled histories, from the political theories of Marx to the life-world of Imelda Marcos.[1] I have explored relationships between economic systems and the kind of shoes women choose to wear. More succinctly, I introduced my concept of 'critical pedagogy of the body' in dance while teaching at a small, southern, private liberal-arts college for women in the United States. Subverting the traditional pedagogic formulas for dance, I was able to reflesh the dancer to an embodied existence through a choreographic process that makes connections to both feminist and liberatory pedagogies aiming to deliver activist intentions. With my students, we critically examined how we feel about, live in, with and through our own bodies. My intention in all of this is to connect women with a pedagogy which emphasizes their life experience and values their voices—one that has as its purpose the empowerment of women by means of gaining critical understanding of the self in relationship to society, and by understanding their bodies, not as objects of hostility, but as something that is to be valued, indeed cherished. It is in this act that wellbeing is rooted; it begins with the body. The body carries a living record, an autobiography or life story, as Estes (1992) writes:

> Life given, life taken, life hoped for, and life healed. It is valued for its articulate ability to register immediate reaction, to feel profoundly, to sense ahead . . . It speaks through the leaping of the heart, the falling of the spirit, the pit at the center, and rising hope . . . Like a sponge filled with water, anywhere the flesh is pressed, wrung, even touched lightly, a memory may flow out in a stream. (p. 200)

The body refuses to be understood as an abstract object. It is real. It is the presence of all that we know, albeit housed in narratives of meaning (Shapiro 2008). To understand the knowledge of the body, in this sense, is antagonistic to the dominant traditions in dance situated in a society that attempts to circumscribe women's ways of knowing by objectifying the body, carving it up and starving it out, and creating fractures and fissures that in turn fragment possibilities of empowerment (Shapiro 1998).

The Process

Pedagogically we begin with the body—the body understood as the concrete material inscribed by cultural values, local and global, and the vehicle for transcending our limited social identities. Pedagogic practices that draw upon the body, and aesthetic processes which provide ways of understanding the world and ourselves intellectually, sensually, mentally, and emotionally are all but non-existent in traditional educational texts, teacher education programmes, classroom practices, or dance studios. This absence is troubling at a time when the body has become so central to theory and cultural practice. Some of the reasons for the dismal construction of pedagogic practices that exclude embodied knowledge and aesthetic processes include the lack of prior educational experiences of teachers, the lack of understanding of how body knowledge can contribute to a broader social critique, the inability to turn it into a standardized test, or perhaps the need to be able to order and control knowledge which is defined by a curriculum in which students genuinely seek their own meaning.

In the next section I want to share an example of how one might draw upon embodied knowledge and connect it to social and ethical critique. This act of educating for a kind of activist aesthetics cuts across cultures and unites the arts/dance in the struggle for connection, healing (that is, overcoming fragmentation and making whole), and compassion. *Each of these speaks to the need for us to see ourselves, and experience ourselves, as part of a larger community in which the quality of our lives is inextricably connected to the wellbeing of others.* Although I will be describing a process I have created for dance, it is by no means only for dance, or only for the arts.

Such a pedagogy engaged in ideological critique inevitably raises moral concerns. It exposes questions of social injustice, inequality, asymmetrical power, and the lack of human rights or dignity. This educational discourse is meant to provide a theory and a process for critiquing all that privileges some rather than all, separating us into categories of those who deserve to live well and those who do not. Critical inquiry here means to learn to question what we take for granted about who we are, and how the world functions. What is central to critical pedagogy is a kind of understanding where students come to 'make sense' of their lives as they come to an awareness of the dialectical relationship between their subjectivity and the dominant values that shape them. These values may be ones fixed locally in early life, though in contemporary culture they are more likely to be part the result of the influence of a global ideology. It is helping students to learn to examine, reflect, ask questions, look for relationships, and seek understanding of themselves and their world.

In my position as a dance educator/choreographer I have had the opportunity to evolve in my own thinking about dance education. From the most primitive ways of teaching, of having students to reproduce the steps they have been given, progressing to creative movement where students learn to create from a movement vocabulary, and finally to a philosophy for education/arts/dance which has as its focus the development of a critical global aesthetic process which takes students through questions of identity and otherness, and, I hope, towards compassionate and ethically responsible behaviour. I have worked on choreographic projects that examined women's relationship to food, exposing the often ill results of young girls and women in a dance titled 'Dying to Be Thin'. Images of girls and women in the media were a rich ground for exploring ways female identities are being shaped by the media and advertising ('Body Parts'). The biblical story of Sarah and Hagar's relationship took us through a critical process, examining ways in which we choose to include and exclude others ('. . . and, Sarah Laughed'). And there were other themes, all chosen because they offered the students an opportunity to better understand how they thought about, felt, and lived out the cultural inscriptions.

Here, I will share in more detail one example of my choreographic work as an example of my pedagogic philosophy; it is this philosophy through which all the courses I teach are filtered. This particular project began with a Fulbright grant in South Africa in 2009 Knowing that dance education was now part of the schools of the Western Cape, and having contact with the government administrator of the programme as well as a contact in the dance programme at the University of Cape Town (UCT), I knew this would be fertile ground to research if and how dance in the schools could be helping to meet the post-apartheid curriculum goals directed toward social justice and equality in the support of a new democratic state. Part of my research was structured to gather information about dance programmes offered in three different high schools. One programme was in a township and had only black students, another programme served mixed-race middle-class students, and the third programme was offered in an affluent and mostly white area. Another focus area of my research was in the choreographic process which I have described. It was structured towards working directly with female dancers from different social/economic and racial backgrounds in a choreographic project. This is what became a dance called 'Hair South Africa'.[2] It was performed for their home communities in May 2009. In developing this project I kept in mind what bell hooks (2000, p. 133) taught me: 'Talking together is one way to make community'.

How Do You Begin

The body is the surface of the inscription of events.

(Foucault 1977, p. 25)

Working within a community that is ten years out of an apartheid government and is still struggling to make concrete the hopes and dreams they have for a country that is to be grounded in social justice and democratic values, but still too often wears the clothes of the old oppressive regime, I was walking on tender ground.

All stories begin in context. This is no different. My project began by mapping out a community dance project for young women in South Africa that would engage them in exploring personal experience and body memories. The research focused on how dance can contribute to the formation of a national identity oriented towards democratic values. The curriculum consisted of the dancers' own autobiographies. Through the choreographic process, utilizing both feminist and critical pedagogical theories, the dancers were to examine the shaping of their identities and consciousness as young women in the new South Africa. Searching for questions I might ask as a cultural outsider, and one that could speak to being female and to racial issues, I chose hair. Hair became the medium for examining questions of race, equality, economic determination, and feminism (hair on the head, opposed to other parts of the body). Discussion, dialogue, and movement that drew upon readings of written personal reflections on body memories provided material for the dancers in creating movements that reflected their life stories. Throughout the four months of working together, a community between a diverse groups of young women was established.

Before I proceed with the description of the project, I want to step back and discuss the idea of community dance and working within communities as an act of aesthetic activism. Creating community dance as defined by Kuppers (2006) is helpful, as she defines community dance as work that facilitates creative expression for aims of self-expression *and* political change. The dances created are done so communally and are not authored individually. This points back to the earlier arguments in this chapter about the need for social integration as part of the foundation for social wellbeing. The end product or outcome, if one is developed, is not predetermined by the choreographer or facilitator but instead is open, though it may be within a thematic field structured by the facilitator. This process and perspective towards the product challenges conventional approaches of community dance making and aesthetics. Kuppers states:

> With this approach, community dances challenge conventional performance aesthetics. Equally important, in my definition, is that community dance's power rests in process rather than product; in the act of working and moving together, allowing different voices, bodies, and experiences to emerge. A new way of understanding 'art making' can emerge from this: an aesthetic of access that redefines who can dance, what dance is, the nature of beauty and pleasure, and appropriate ways of appreciating dance. (p. 3)

What Kuppers makes clear is that the purpose of creating community dance takes seriously the process of creating the dance through the participants. She goes further to clarify how working in community dance is not only an aesthetic process but can also be a political one:

> As a second category, I would add politics. Many community dance practitioners (and again, not all) move towards changing wider issues in the world through participatory dance making. Various expressive art therapies, including dance therapy,

usually aim to enable change within an individual, so that this individual can function better within the already given social world. Community dance, on the other
hand, often aims to enable change both within individuals and within wider social
structures. In some form or other, many community dance practitioners understand
their work to be a form of political labour: facilitating creative expression as a means
to newly analyse and understand life situations, and empowering people to value
themselves and shape a more egalitarian and diverse future. (pp. 4–5)

In emphasizing knowledge for empowerment and moving beyond individual change
for social change, Kuppers is connecting community dance to aspects of critical pedagogy. This view of community dance takes seriously the belief that wellbeing cannot be
created within private worlds alone; it is also dependent upon a sense of social integration and acceptance. Being valued for the contributions one can make, having a sense
of empowerment and hope for positive change is central to the purpose of my work and
my belief about the nature of wellbeing.

After identifying the group, bringing clarity to my own motivations, and coordinat-
ing the place and time, I began to further develop methods that I believed could, in a
sensitive manner, bring forth a discussion about identity around issues of race, class,
and gender through body/hair memories. As in any feminist pedagogy, this process valued subjective knowledge, the voice of the knower, and what was known as the 'taken for
granted' assumptions. Feminist pedagogy is also keenly aware that the body/subject is
where social ideals and cultural standards are often deeply inscribed and lived out.

Throughout the community dance making process we explored the dynamics
between the power of cultural inscriptions and social institutions, and the consciousness of the dancer/participants. As Paulo Freire points out in his theory for education,
this recognition is the starting point to destroy oppressive ideas, thoughts, or feeling.
But what also must not be overlooked is the view of the teacher, choreographer; whoever
that is who provides the leadership and sets out the methodology of the project.

THE CHOREOGRAPHER/EDUCATOR

As the community dance choreographer/educator, I am not an impartial observer.
I come with my own knowledge, experiences, and ideologies, and with a particular ethical view of humanity. In other writings I have developed a framework for a universal
aesthetic, and argue for the need to illuminate not only the differences but also our commonalities (Shapiro 2008):

There is a compelling need to see the commonalities of human life—the shared and
universal quality of human life (indeed of *all* life)—as central to our quest for purpose
and meaning. More than anything, I believe, the body, *our bodies*, is what grounds
our commonalities. To address the importance of a common humanity grounded

in universality is to understand that the struggle for human rights and human liberation is necessary even while recognizing the danger of the term *human* as a vehicle
for imposing a particular concept of who we are. It is hard to see how one can make
the case for greater freedom, for greater justice, for the end to violence, for greater
human rights, without an appeal to the notion of a common humanity. (p. 260)

I elaborate on this idea of a universal aesthetics and how this connects to ethical practices (p. 261):

> The universal is not some abstract idea or ideal; rather, it is to acknowledge
> someone as a subject granting them the same status as oneself, to recognize their
> sacred otherness. Ethical practices occur in specific situations. Practices in and
> of themselves may or may not be ethical; rather, the 'rightness' of the action, as
> it affects the lives and experiences of those it is directed towards, determines
> ethical behaviour. The 'rightness' of an action is not reducible to a response
> to the other. It includes responsiveness to their values, beliefs, and principles,
> aesthetic and religious sensibilities—the values and meanings of their worlds.
> (Farley 1985)

Working within this specific situation—clear about my purpose and sensitive to ethical
issues—I began this work. My own journey which I travelled with the dancers was transformative for me as well, as I was privileged to have heard their stories, to be respected
and trusted to lead them through this process of reflection, and to have developed a
lasting feeling of creative transformation. I can only use the words here that I think Tutu
might use to describe this event as having been blessed. As we understand that history is
best learned through its struggles.

The Dancers

I made it clear to the dancers that this dance would be a story of their own lives developed through this critical/choreographic process where their body memories would
provide the impetus for creating movement. Each movement came from their stories,
their lives. Their ages ranged from 14 to 22, though most were between 16 and 20. One
group of dancers came from a community-based dance project established in 2002 in
the Western Cape called The Jikeleza Dance Project (in Xhosa, 'Jikeleza' means 'turn
around'). They define their mission as follows:

> To add value and uplift the Areas in which we serve, and to nurture and improve
> the quality of life of children and youth from impoverished target areas and then
> take the Jikeleza successful Model and implement in areas that are riddled with
> Poverty and Crime through the medium of creative dance and music. (Jizelka Dance
> Project 2002)

This programme serves the informal settlements of Imizamo Yethu and Hangberg Harbour of Hout Bay—two of the most disadvantaged, impoverished, and excluded communities in the Western Cape. I asked the director to select young women dancers who would, and could, participate in this project over a period of four months. We made an agreement to meet every Saturday morning at one of the UCT dance studios to work together to create a dance for a community performance. This was all the information they had. Eight dancers signed on.

The other groups of dancers came from the UCT dance programme. I was able to meet with the UCT dance majors and tell them about the project, and along with faculty recommendations, six students signed up to work with me on this project. Later, one dropped out due to an old injury that was bothering her. The different groups of students did not know each other, so the initial sessions were directed towards sessions that made the dancers comfortable and feel a sense of safety, where the possibility of social wellbeing might be felt.

Threads Through the Process

Movement instructions in the first classes were kept to abstract improvisations that eventually led to the dancers acknowledging each other's presence in the space. I provided them with a journal and colourful markers with which they could write down thoughts, feelings, and responses to questions that I used to direct them towards thinking about who they are, and later more specifically about their hair. Reflective questions are a powerful pedagogical tool in this process. I teach out of this recognition, as Elie Wiesel (1960) shared: 'Every question possesses a power that does not lie in the answer.' I asked the dancers to write about their hair—how they think about it, and how they felt about it. From their written work they chose three words or phrases to create a short movement phrase. After creating their phrases they shared them with each other and spoke about how they felt and thought about their hair. They shared their hair stories. I selected a section to read from a talk Alice Walker (1987) had given at Spelman College in Atlanta, Georgia, titled 'Oppressed Hair Puts a Ceiling on the Brain'. I asked them to talk about 'perfect' hair and where pressures 'to get hair', 'to be' something other than its natural state, comes from. The dancers with blond hair spoke of the stereotype of dumb blondes, and the dancer with dreadlocks shared experiences of not being accepted for jobs because of her hair, which was considered to be part of a way of being (in the dance she uses the phrase smoking ganja weed). She connected her hair to economic disempowerment. We looked at magazines and talked about the ideal image of beauty and where this beauty aesthetic comes from, and how Western ideas of beauty often dominate. I asked them what hair symbolized. The young women from the township shared stories of spending hours getting their hair straightened and suffering through the smelly and timely process as they tried to look like the preferred social image of women. I read to them a section from Susan Brownmiller's book *Femininity*. I showed them an assortment of pictures of women of colour—what their culture refers to as white, black, or coloured. I asked them what they 'saw' when they looked at these pictures, and how it made them feel. I asked them to talk about what the pictures were saying to us. Here I draw on John Berger's work, as he conveys the life world of the subjects in a photograph to tell us something about the culture (Another Way of Telling). During all of this the dancers were writing reflections, creating movement, sharing, learning each other's movements, and talking about their thoughts and discoveries. What was becoming clear was that a tension was developing about who is considered to be South African. As they learned to move the stories of each other's lives, they became more connected. They listened and they heard. They laughed, and they began making bodily contact through dancing. I purposefully added a class with some contact improvisation, as they had been shy about moving beyond the cultural boundaries of touching each other. They touched each other's hair, often for the first time having felt the differences between the silken lengths that lie flat to the kinky textures that curl every which way. Hair, our hair, is something that labels us, can give us pleasure and strife, and is something that as being female we struggle with most every day. And it often determines how we feel about ourselves. 'Bad hair days' has, across cultures, become a commonly understood expression for denoting our mood, sense of agency, and attractiveness. The dancers felt, they listened, they spoke, and they danced. Together, over this period, they created a dance that told their stories of resistance, struggle, hope, and reality.

THE PERFORMANCE

Moving the dance from the closed and protected space of the studio to the stage demands thoughtful preparation. The dancers mould the dance to one that is in the process of becoming to one that is. As the choreographer, I selected movements created by the dancers, organized them into sequences and patterns, and put them into an order, hoping to create an honest representation of what was created during our time together. I selected the music and costuming, as well as the programme notes.

The Dance

Section One: Early Memories

Remembering our hair when we were young—cut, plucked, dyed, straightened, braided, greased, bleached, tinted, dyed, and decorated. We learn early that hair is the medium that signifies conformity or rebellion, youth or old age, restraint or freedom.

Section Two: Voices in the Head

Powerful messages become internalized; who decides how I should look or what is considered attractive? Cultural forces determine beauty, aesthetic values, the construction of gender, and sometimes, even our economic futures.

Section Three: Making Waves

Moments of awareness are also times of possibility. As we come to understand ourselves in the context of culture, so we create spaces in which to affirm our identity and choose our future.

Section Four: Hair on My Mind

Identity is who we are in relationship. So, how do others see me? Do I impress or am I invisible? Am I a threat or am I 'safely' feminine? These programme notes were offered to the community audience.

ENDINGS

The performance presented for the larger community began with a talk by myself, helping to situate the audience into our larger discussion. I shared with them that in South Africa, just as in the United States and in so many other countries, girls and women are often valued by their physical appearance, as an object. And, in the field of dance, bodies are often 'used' simply as an instrument of the choreographer. So here, in this process, the dancer is valued not simply as a 'body', but instead her experiences are valued, which makes it possible for us to reposition ourselves in terms of power. When we begin to understand how we are shaped by culture, our position to power changes—where we are no longer simply acted upon—but can take actions ourselves. We discussed the many different historical laws that had prevented women from owning property, having a bank account, voting, serving on juries, gaining access to higher education—and many other rights given to men both culturally and legally. Even though today in many parts of the world these barriers have been crossed, in some countries women still cannot attend higher education, vote, own property, nor even drive a car, and face honour killings or prison for acts that men take upon them. So, I tell the audience, part of my work has been to educate women about women's history, but even more about their lives: what shapes how they think, feel, and act. I try to help them experience their own bodies as subjects of their world—not mere objects to be seen and used. I value their voice. I embody their knowledge. I tell them I hope that from this experience the dancers have learned how to use their own critical lens to educate themselves about who they are, and how they came to be that person and to become responsible for either accepting how things are or act for change. I shared this quote from the author and political teacher Marianne Williamson: 'In every community, there is work to be done. In every nation, there are wounds to heal. In every heart, there is the power to do it.' I tell them that it has been my work as an artist to mirror the world we experience, and at times, imagine something different.

We ended the performance with the dancers coming onto stage to have a conversation with the audience. Audience members shared their own hair stories. We listened about

678   SHERRY B. SHAPIRO

the choice of women to shave their heads. We struggled through a discussion about young white women who wanted to claim their South African identity alongside the South African blacks. And we laughed. They asked the dancers specific questions about their individual parts in the dance. Together we honoured the work of the dancers who shared some of their world as they told some of their life stories through movement.

After the performance, I met with the dancers, completing my research work with a final interview asking them to talk about how this community dance project was similar to or different from other dance performances in which they had been involved.[3] I asked them to talk about what they had learned about themselves, others, and their culture. They told me of their transformations, their strength, and how they had developed new understandings and new friends.

CONCLUSION

Aesthetic activism, yes. Maybe the form or the product would not be recognized as such, but the content and the process melds together threads of consciousness and the body to surpass what is hoped for. As Reagon (1990) reminds us:

> We artists have no special answers unavailable to other people. What we have is work that is intricately entangled in our people's dreams, hopes, and self-images. Like it or not, we are part of society's process of dreaming, thinking, and speaking to itself, reflecting on our past, and finding new ways forward. (p. 24)

My belief is that there is no real ending to such a process. I expect that as the dancers return to their everyday lives, subject to all the conventional cultural messages, some of the immediate impact of the dance process will be lost. Yet I remain convinced that once questions are posed, ideas deconstructed, beliefs challenged, and connections made, there remains embedded within them an embodied knowing that has transformative power. I am reminded here of the work of the great English critical scholar Raymond Williams, who talked of a 'long revolution'. By this he meant the slow chipping away at ideas and beliefs that are buried deep within us, and the continuing possibility of reimagining our lives and our world. Notwithstanding the ups and downs of hope and change in our world, I remain committed to the concept of a pedagogy that may enable our students to not only critique their world but to seek new meanings to their lives. In this, my work continues to represent a path towards wellbeing—one in which human fulfilment and efficacy are always grounded in the inextricable relationship between the personal and the political, the individual and the social, the spiritual and the material. I believe that the wellbeing of each of us depends on the degree to which our social relationships are those that nurture and ground us in compassionate, loving, and just communities.

NOTES

1. Imelda Marcos, widow of President Ferdinand Marcos, is remembered for her collection of more than 1,000 pairs of shoes. The acquisition of shoes was connected to the corruption of government funds during her husband's term of office.
2. See YouTube, Sherry Shapiro, Dance Research, < https://youtu.be/v4bJqT_dkS4>
3. See YouTube, Sherry Shapiro, Dance Research Hair, <https://www.youtube.com/watch?v=hnwaEZHaaRU>

REFERENCES

Aids Memorial Quilt. (2012). 'Women in Black', 4 November, <http://www.aidsquilt.org>, <http:::://www.womeninblack.org>, <http://www.artwomen.org/wib/wibmain.htm>.
Barber, B. and Watson, P. (2001). *The Struggle for Democracy*. Key Porter Books.
Bauman, Z. (2001). *The Individualized Society*. Oxford: Blackwell.
Burn, S. (2005). *Women Across Cultures: A Global Perspective*. New York, NY: McGraw Hill.
Burnat, E. and Davidi, G. (2012). *5 Broken Cameras*, <http://www.kinolorber.com/5broken-cameras/>
Collins, L. (2006). 'Activists who yearn for art that transforms: Parallels in the black arts and feminist art movements in the United States', in *New Feminist Theories of Visual Culture*. Chicago, IL: University of Chicago Press, pp. 717–52.
Eagleton, T. (1990). *The Ideology of the Aesthetic*. Cambridge: Basil Blackwell.
Eagleton, T. (1996). *The Illusions of Postmodernism*. Cambridge: Basil Blackwell.
Estes, C. (1992). *Women Who Run with the Wolves*. New York: Ballantine Books
Farley, W. (1985). *Eros for Others; Retaining Truth in a Pluralistic World*. University Park, PA: Pennsylvania State University Press.
Foucault, M. (1977). *Discipline and Punishment*. New York, NY: Random House.
Freire, P. (1998). *Pedagogy of Freedom; Ethics, Democracy, and Civic Courage*. Oxford: Rowman & Littlefield.
Gottschild, B. (2008). 'The movement is the message: Five dance makers who dare to mix activism with art', *Dance Magazine*, January.
Greene, M. (1988). *The Dialectic of Freedom*. New York, NY: Teachers College Press.
hooks, b. (2000). *All About Love: New Visions*. New York, NY: William Morrow and Co.
Jikeleza Dance Project (2002). <http://www.jikelezaprojects.co.za>
Jones, R. (2009). 'The aesthetics of protest: Using image to change discourse', *Enculturation*, 6(2). <http://enculturation.gmu.edu/6.2/jones>
Keyes, C. (1998). 'Social well-being', *Social Psychology Quarterly*, 61(2): 121–40. The American Sociological Association.
Kuppers, P. (2006) *Community Dance: A Resource File*. New Zealand: DANZ.
Lippard, L. (1995). *The Pink Glass Swan: Selected Feminist Essays on Art*. New York, NY: New Press.
Lerner, M. (2006). *The Left Hand of God*. San Francisco, CA: Harper Collins.
Marotti, W. (2006). 'Political aesthetics: Activism, everyday life, and art's object in 1960s Japan', *Inter-Asia Cultural Studies*, 7(4): 606–17.
Marx, K. and Engels, F. (1845). *The German Ideology*. New York, NY: Prometheus Books.

Hartsock, N. (1997). 'The feminist standpoint: Developing the ground for a specifically feminist historical materialism', in D. T. Meyers (ed.), *Feminist Social Thought: A Reader*. New York and London: Routledge, pp. 461–83.

Mohanty, C. (2003). *Feminism Without Borders: Decolonizing Theory, Practicing Solidarity*. Durham, NC: Duke University Press.

New York Times (2011). 'Arab Spring', 18 March. <http://www.nytimes.com/2011/03/18/world/middleeast/18youth.html>

Reagon, B. (1990). 'Foreward', in M. O'Brien, and C. Little (eds.). *Reimagining America: The Arts of Social Change*. Philadelphia, PA: New Society Publishers, pp. 8–9, 24.

Rosenberg, T. (2009). 'On feminists activist aesthetics', *Journal of Aesthetics and Culture*, 1. doi: 10.3402/jac.v1i0.4619

Shapiro, H. S. (2010). *Educating Youth for a World Beyond Violence*. New York, NY: Palgrave Macmillan.

Shapiro, S. (1998). *Towards A Pedagogy of the Body; A Critical Praxis*. New York, NY: Taylor and Francis.

Shapiro, S. (2008). 'Dance in a world of change: A vision for global aesthetics and universal ethics', in S. Shapiro (ed.), *Dance in a World of Change: Reflections on Globalization and Cultural Difference*. Champaign, IL: Human Kinetics, pp. 253–74.

The Guardian (2012). 26 July. < http://www.guardian.co.uk/world/occupy-movement>

Tutu, D. (1999). *No Future Without Forgiveness*. New York, NY: Doubleday.

Tutu, D. (2014). *The Book of Forgiving; The Fourfold Path for Healing Ourselves and Our World*. New York, NY: Harper Collins.

Walker, A. (1987). *Oppressed Hair Puts a Ceiling on the Brain*. Speech Presented at Spelman College, Atlanta, Georgia.

Weiler, K. (1988). *Women Teaching for Change*. South Hadley, MA: Bergin and Garvey.

Wiesel, E. (1960). *Night*. New York, NY: Bantam Books.

Welch, S. (1985). *Communities of Solidarity and Resistance*. New York, NY: Doubleday.

Women's News Network (2012). 31 July. <http://womennewsnetwork.net/?p=3763>

CHAPTER 37

CULTURAL ADAPTATIONS OF DANCE MOVEMENT PSYCHOTHERAPY EXPERIENCES

From a UK Higher Education Context to a Transdisciplinary Water Resource Management Research Practice

ATHINÁ COPTEROS, VICKY KARKOU, AND TALLY PALMER

INTRODUCTION

AT the time of writing this chapter, the first author (Athiná) was engaged in research to explore the ways in which dance movement psychotherapy (DMP), a body-based creative form of psychotherapy, could be applied within transdisciplinary research practice that aims to address the challenges between human wellbeing and ecological sustainability. For this DMP-led research to be realized in South Africa, a qualification in DMP and registration with the Health Professions Council of South Africa was essential. DMP is a relatively new form of psychotherapy worldwide, and in South Africa there is currently no formally registered DMP training available. Practitioners have to obtain an internationally accredited Master's degree, after which they can apply to register (HPCSA 2015; SANATO 2016).

Gaining qualifications in DMP took place at a university in the United Kingdom (UK) that offered a DMP Masters programme. In this chapter an exploration will be presented of how the experiences of the training in the UK were translated into a culturally relevant practice in South Africa.

THEORETICAL FRAME

In contemporary Darwinian ecological thinking, mankind is seen as neither separate from nor master of nature, but is embodied within it (Buchdahl and Raper 1998). This embodiment has unfortunately been severely challenged by peoples' alienation from their environment, which has led to violence against the environment itself (Abram 1997). McCallum (2008) writes about the human-nature split and the consequences of people putting themselves at the apex of creation. Due to this splitting, the destructive, self-deceptive trend in humans has grown to untold proportions and challenges life on the planet. As a result, Schmuck and Schultz (2002) claim, the sustainability of the earth's natural resources to sustain all life on the planet is eroding. Postel (2008) argues that what is missing from efforts to conserve water is modern society's fundamental disconnection from nature's web of life and the role of water as the foundation of that life. Healing and transforming the human-nature split requires a profound change in attitude to oneself and to the world we live in (McCallum 2008).

This split, and ways of addressing it, is also the area of exploration for ecopsychology. Even the pioneers of psychology acknowledged that the deepest levels of the psyche merge with the biological body and the physical make-up of the world (Hillman 1995). According to Dodds (2011), the pressing issue of climate change and its relationship to psychological wellbeing has contributed to the growth of an ecopsychological perspective that challenges the power relations between the human and non-human elements of the wider ecology. It offers a radical framework within which to view the therapeutic encounter as the self becomes defined within an ecological matrix as a dynamic and mutually dependent organism, rather than a separate self-sufficient entity. For ecopsychologists, to heal the wounds of the past and present the land and the people need to be reoriented to a connection to each other and thus to themselves and the people from whom they originally came (Naess 1995).

Dance has been used for centuries as a means of healing and effecting change, both at an individual and community level (Karkou and Sanderson 2006; Hanna 2004). According to Primus (1998), who studied and choreographed African dance, dance in Africa is about community, education, magic, and spirit. It is not a separate art, but part of the whole experience of living. Zulu culture has an ecological approach to health, in that health is not only about a healthy body but about the relationship of self to the Universe and everything existing within it (Makanya 2014).

Movement and dance are used in DMP as the medium of connectedness and communication to promote the health of individuals, groups, and communities (Koch and Fischman 2011). Central to this are the relations between mind and body, and interpersonal relations. If one adopts an ecopsychological therapeutic frame, the relatedness of the person to the environment also becomes important. Working creatively with body and movement can access aspects of people not easily spoken about, as part of creating opportunities for change (Stanton-Jones 1992). This way of working becomes particularly relevant in a post-apartheid South Africa.

Many authors recognize the indicators of social and community disruption, loss, and trauma in South Africa's dynamic but troubled young democracy (Meyer 2014). The peaceful transition from apartheid to democracy, however, prevented its recognition as a post-conflict country (Mogapi 2003). Furthermore, within a context of reconstruction and development, mental health issues are often viewed as secondary matters that individuals and groups can deal with on their own (Mbona 2011). Researchers such as Gear (2002), however, argue that psychosocial support is essential in order to offer opportunities for healing from psychological stress that continues to influence present conditions and contribute to the high levels of violence. According to Henley (2010), psychosocial support, and its associated concept of wellbeing, can be achieved through engaging both psychological, internal, and social, external factors. It is possible that such engagement can take place through theoretical principles and methodological ideas stemming from DMP. For a practice, however, which has developed largely in the West, it is important that the specific challenges of post-apartheid South African society are considered and adaptations are made to accommodate this context.

THE STUDY

The overall empirical context is defined by the practical challenges of ensuring that sustainable, equitable, and secure water is provided in South Africa (Department of Water Affairs 2013) using the principles and practices of integrated water resource management and water governance. In 1998 the National Water Act (No. 36 of 1998) was passed, aiming to achieve water equity and sustainability by reorienting people to water as a scarce resource in South Africa and developing a community-based approach of reconciliation, participation, and change (Asmal and Hadland 2011). Despite legislation that received world acclaim for water allocation being grounded in the principles of equity and ecological health (Postel 2011), the ecological condition of South Africa's river systems continue to deteriorate (Du Toit et al. 2013).

Technical information and skills are not enough to change people's behaviour where negative social circumstances such as poverty, gender, and other power inequalities limit people's control over their behaviour (Campbell and Cornish 2012). Participation in water quality debates and actions is influenced by the fact that many people do not have the skills and information needed to participate effectively in water resource management and actively exercise their agency (Lotz-sisitka and Burt 2006).

Natural resources such as water are essentially embedded in social systems (Roux et al. 2010). Social–ecological systems are inherently complex, multidimensional, and not confined by the boundaries of one disciplinary framework (Roux et al. 2010;

Wickson et al. 2006). Transdisciplinarity involves the concurrent building of knowledge between and among disciplines, practitioners, and participants as various ways of knowing are brought to bear on a grounded problem (Palmer 2007). This supports investigations that acknowledge life on this planet as complex bio-physical–social systems (Cilliers 2000; Pollard and Du Toit 2011).

Transdisciplinarity and complexity studies that address the challenges of the complex relationship between human wellbeing and ecological sustainability provide the opportunity to create new ways of engaging. Within a complex social–ecological system, the acknowledgement of trauma associated with the loss of land and identity, due to the history of colonialism and apartheid, adds a further dimension to considering appropriate psychotherapeutic support that encourages creative engagement of all stakeholders. Finding ways in which a UK-based DMP training could be translated from one culture to another formed the focus for this first stage of the overall research study on the use of DMP within a transdisciplinary complex social–ecological systems research context.

Research Objectives

The following objective constituted the first exploration into the wider topic of the relevance of a DMP-based approach:

- To develop culturally relevant themes from professional DMP training in the UK for application in a South African water resource management context.

Other objectives aimed to explore these themes further and apply relevant DMP principles within a transdisciplinary complex social–ecological systems researcher group.

Methodology

According to Merleau-Ponty, the living body is the true subject of experience (Varela et al. 1991). The sensuous and sentient life of the body is at the heart of lived experience (Abram 1997). Being a dance movement therapist who engages the body as the agent for change (Koch and Fischman 2011; Meekums 2006), and answering research questions about human experience and the meaning of lived experience in particular, has led this study to engage methodologically with the principles of phenomenology (Langdridge 2007). In phenomenology, people's relationships with the world are seen as intersubjective; there is a shared, overlapping, and relational nature to engagement with the world (Larkin et al. 2011).

According to Heidegger (cited in Hoeller 1993), the task of phenomenology is hermeneutic—meaning interpretive, and concerned with the meaning of being. In hermeneutic phenomenology the epistemological focus is on experience or narrative, and thus requires ways of capturing this that are subjective and involved (Langdridge

2007). According to Ashworth (2008), we live in an interpreted world and are ourselves interpreters of our lived experience. This perspective in phenomenology encourages the researcher to engage in enriched awareness of his/her own consciousness as part of the process of research and the dedication to transformation of researcher and participants (Rehorick and Bentz 2009; Lather 1991).

The study was qualitative in essence. Qualitative research takes into account different viewpoints and experiences, and acknowledges the depth and richness of data (Somers 1996) with an interest in personal views and circumstance (Denzin and Lincoln 2011). According to a constructionist perspective of qualitative methods, the research activity is regarded as an interpretation by the researcher who is not considered as separate from the research (Ashworth 2003). People are both constructions and constructors of their reality, which is influenced by the coexistence and interaction with others (Ashworth 2003).

Data Collection

Data were obtained from journal entries and e-mail communication during the MSc training in DMP that took place in the UK. Data were collected within different time frames (see Table 37.1), and each was considered a separate 'transcript' for the interpretative process of analysis.

Each time frame was divided into individual weeks of training, and all the activities of each week were listed. Within the breakdown of each week of the course, experiences and feelings were recorded as journal entries.

Data Analysis

Interpretative phenomenological analysis (IPA) is often used as a way of analysing data collected through a hermeneutic phenomenology perspective (Boden and Eatough 2014). IPA studies focus on what a particular experience means to people, and that the production of this knowledge will genuinely contribute to real and useful social change (Langdridge 2007). Concrete portrayals of lived experiences are offered, followed by insightful reflections on the meaning of the experiences for participants as well as the researcher (van Manen 2002). The researcher is encouraged to reflect on these experiences again and again, engaging in what is often referred to in hermeneutic phenomenology as the 'hermeneutic circle' (Smith et al. 2009). The relationship between the part and the whole is acknowledged as dynamic, and thus in IPA the process of analysis

Table 37.1. Time frames of data collection.

TIME FRAME	Beginning of course and getting to the UK	October 2012 to December 2012	January 2013 to August 2013	September 2013 to December 2013	January 2014 to May 2014

(Credit: A. Copteros.)

is iterative and non-linear. The meaning of text can be made at a number of different levels all of which relate and create different perspectives. As part of working at different levels, artistic enquiry (Wadsworth-Hervey 2000) was used to creatively reflect on the themes that emerged through IPA. This is a method for analysing and presenting data that uses and acknowledges a creative process as an inherent part of research in creative arts therapies.

In IPA work, semistructured interviews are the exemplary data collection method, but other data collection methods include diaries, personal accounts, and focus groups (Smith 2004; Larkin et al. 2006). IPA is an approach committed to the detailed exploration of personal experience. In this study, this was done through the use of journal entries and e-mail communications. Smith (2004) argues that there is a double hermeneutic in IPA, in that the participants are trying to make sense of their personal and social world, and at the same time the researcher is trying to make sense of participants making sense of their personal and social world.

In this study, the complexity was compounded by Athiná being both participant and researcher. In this process it was necessary to develop awareness of role/s, perception/s and experience/s. Athiná was reflectively making sense of the training and her personal social world through recorded perceptions of the phenomenon of the training while it was taking place, in the context of having returned to South Africa. The recorded perceptions during training form the data set for the study, which were then analysed while in South Africa. The geographical and time distance allowed Athiná to create a relative distance from the material learned and the experiences recorded in the journal. It allowed her to treat these entries as data that could be analysed with less emotional entanglement. In terms of the hermeneutic circle, the entrance into the meaning of the text shifted and brought in different perspectives.

Within the epistemological focus of IPA there is room to manoeuvre in terms of the analytical strategies used (Larkin and Thompson 2012). The analyst is encouraged to explore and innovate when it comes to organizing the analysis (Smith et al. 2009). The researcher thus engaged in an interpretive relationship with the transcript of each recorded experience that was taken through the following process of analysis:

1. Free contextual analysis during which the transcripts were read several times and comments noted.
2. The contextual analysis as well as the transcripts were uploaded onto ATLAS.ti (qualitative data analysis and research software) in which emergent themes began to be identified and coded. The entire transcript of each time frame was treated as data, and no attempt was made to select or omit passages for special attention (Smith and Osborne 2008).
3. The codes or themes were then clustered according to "Family Units" in ATLAS.ti as part of thematic development (Larkin and Thompson 2012).
4. The clustering of themes went through a further process of reflection and analysis as patterns of meaning emerged.

5. This led to the development of the final structure of superordinate themes (Smith et al. 2009) upon which initial narratives and arguments were based.

6. They also provided the basis for a creative response (Wadsworth-Hervey 2000) to the themes that emerged by embodying them in the lived context of South Africa and a town within it (see Video 37.1 on Companion Website ⓟ). This experience informed analysis and discussion.

Findings and Discussion

The following is a discussion based on the superordinate themes found:

- Awareness of Power and Difference.
- Therapeutic Adaptability.
- Sharing Leadership.
- Connecting with the Environment.

Athina's voice (the first author's voice) is now heard.

Awareness of Power and Difference

Video Creative Response 37.1 ⓟ: This theme was embodied and expressed outside the Magistrate's Court. This is a space that holds a lot of history in terms of power, exclusion, and at the same time justice and reparation.

The experience of the training began while still in South Africa. There was a lot of stress involved in making the opportunity to study overseas possible as a South African entering the UK:

P 1: Contextual Analysis-Beg of course and getting to Scotland.docx—1:1 [I am missing this! I hope I wo..] (84:84)

I am missing this! I hope I won't be too late. I hope I can go!

P 1: Contextual Analysis-Beg of course and getting to Scotland.docx—1:7 [I am carrying on regardless. W..] (70:70)

I am carrying on regardless. Will our passports come through and the application for entry for my family?

It was particularly stressful because I was a mature student with a partner and two young children whom I could not leave behind. The course began in mid-September, and by the time the funding, the passports, and the entry permits came through I could only begin my training in mid-October (week six of the course). Obtaining sufficient funding was difficult, as I needed a number of sources to cover the fees. The student fee for international students was three times higher than for local students. The increasingly unfavourable currency exchange rates created further difficulty in paying fees and meeting living costs. The pressure was extreme:

> P 3: Contextual Analysis- Jan 2013 to Aug 2013.docx—3:1 [I am petrified about finding t..] (142:142)

> I am petrified about finding the second half of the funding we need to complete the second year of the course. I don't have money to cover the fees!

As a South African wanting to practise DMP in South Africa, I had no option but to study overseas. Yet it appeared that costs reduced access to the training of those few people who either had the financial means or the skills and support needed to obtain the funding required. Even while I found myself struggling with finances throughout the process of my training, as a 'white' educated South African woman I was more empowered to access the support I needed. Caldwell (2013) writes about limiting the variables of power, privilege, and difference in DMP. My awareness of the privilege involved in training as a dance movement psychotherapist in the UK was heightened during my training and certainly after I returned to South Africa.

De Yong (2002) argues that on the whole, within Africa, Asia, and parts of Latin America there are relatively few mental-health professionals; this certainly includes dance movement psychotherapists. DMP literature makes reference to the fact that dance as healing has been part of indigenous cultures (Karkou and Sanderson 2006). Dance is an integral part of an African cultural heritage that continues the struggle for human dignity and cultural certitude (Nettleford 1998). DMP literature makes reference to diverse cultures (Levy 2005), yet the 'voice' of these cultures from the perspective of people from these cultures is mostly absent. Makanya (2014) echoes the view that the African has been Westernised and that the colonial frame of writing and thinking about arts therapy practice denies her a way of expressing herself that comes from the history, culture, and language of her people.

Acknowledging difference and allowing for alternative perspectives was an important personal challenge during my training. As a South African having grown up under apartheid, social transformation and justice were fundamentally important to me. This position became even clearer when, in one of my first days of my placement in a mental-health charity I attended as part of my training, I came across the following:

> P 4: Contextual Analysis-Sept 2013 to Dec 2013.docx—4:3 [A case was presented of a woma..] (475:475)

> A case was presented of a woman who has to be deported to India after her final application was rejected. She is apparently okay with it but may be facing an honour killing back in her home village. I felt really sick in my stomach. I suggested some inquiry be done into possible support she can receive in India so that she either doesn't have to go back to her village or some other support is offered her. It felt crazy

to me that the group wasn't thinking that far. That there is a sense there is nothing more they can do now that she has to be deported!

It became very clear to me that as a developing therapist I needed to negotiate my belief in social justice and activism on the one hand, and reflect on the traditional limits of the role of the therapist on the other. Back to the South African context, Meyer (2014) warns that arts therapists need to be aware of what it means to engage with the social, political, and cultural spheres, both in the ways they practise and also how they reflect about their practice. Recent creative arts therapy literature questions how Western-based therapeutic practices may shift to a more social justice agenda in order to understand the impact of the social, economic, and political contexts on the therapeutic relationship (Sajnani and Kaplan 2012).

Arts therapists carry a responsibility to confront their own positions of power, race, and privilege (Hadley 2013; Sajnani and Kaplan 2012) in order not to reproduce privilege and limit social transformation and justice (Meyer 2014). Within the theoretical components of my training, ideas from postmodern thinking stemming, for example, from social constructionism (McNamee 2004) and narrative therapy (White and Epston 1990), were all opening up the discussion of culture, power, and justice. They also offered me some first directions of how to navigate psychotherapeutic roles and boundaries in a manner that valued differences and allowed for co-construction of meaning within the psychotherapeutic relationship. In a South African water resource management context, for DMP to have an impact on the need for agency, the knowledge of people created within their own contexts is at the forefront if there is to be any possibility for beneficial change (Burt et al. 2015; Visvanathan 2005). Adaptations by the therapist are essential when engaging with a personal as well as a social justice agenda.

Therapeutic Adaptability

Video Creative Response 37.2 ▶: As part of exploring adaptability, I engaged in an embodied response at a polluted stream in the town in which I live. It is one thing to write or think about social injustice, but when I was confronted personally by having to put my feet into polluted water and be with the dirt and litter in the space that represents a lot of what most South Africans live with and in on a daily basis, it brought up a lot of discomfort and at the same time, amazingly, hope.

My placement at Irini (pseudonym) for two years working with black minority ethnic (BME) women provided me with insights into the value of offering a culturally recognizable and tolerant space for people who were displaced. Irini followed the tenets of research which showed that BME women did not feel comfortable in accessing services in which their own language was not spoken, they could not identify with the staff, they had fears of racism, and they experienced a lack of tolerance of their culture (Ota and Digpal 2012).

At Irini I worked with a diversity of clients from cultural and religious traditions different from my own.

> *P 4: Contextual Analysis-Sept 2013 to Dec 2013.docx—4:4 [At Irini I will be working wit..] (391:391)*
>
> At Irini I will be working with two women who do not speak English much. This is going to be an interesting challenge. Of course the cultural dynamics come up here for me and the significance of literally just being with the body and self-expression, because words will not be easy to share. I must look up readings around this area. I also need to find out more about the Muslim culture and religion and the different interpretations of it depending on where a person is coming from.

Due to my own life experiences and the diversity of clients at Irini, I learnt that it is important not to assume a particular cultural stereotype and to maintain a lively curiosity (Boas 2006). Culture does not maintain a coherent static and unchanging set of values (Hanna 2004). Acknowledging my own prejudice was critical, as well as the fact that I come from a particular cultural background and historical reference (Hadley 2013). I had to be aware, and work with the fact that non-verbal cues can vary greatly across cultures (Bradt 1997). Harris (2007) speaks about his awareness of 'sociocentric' cultures where the 'group' identity is important. In his experience, DMP and creative expression goes beyond words, and that offering the group a safe environment with culturally recognizable props was enough for them to access their indigenous body memory of the significance of dance to heal and move forward. A flexible therapy frame extends the way by which the therapeutic relationship is often defined in Western terms.

An example of this in my experience can be found in a client I call MB here. She was a single mother with a two-year-old daughter, her husband had left for their 'home country', and they were divorcing. Her passport was with Home Affairs for months while she waited to find out about her immigration status. She had no way of returning home, and no family to support her. She arrived for the session with her two-year-old daughter, who was taken to the crèche so that her mother could have space in the session for herself. The little girl was terrified and insisted on being with her mother:

> *P 4: Contextual Analysis-Sept 2013 to Dec 2013.docx—4:5 [I encouraged MB to try with th..] (263:263)*
>
> I encouraged MB to try with the little girl in the space with us. I brought toys and put out paper and crayons but she was completely distrustful of it all and cried desperately. She only wanted to be with her mom by herself. MB decided to leave and I walked with her to the bus to help with the pram. We chatted a bit more on the way and then I had to leave them.

I was aware that this woman had tried really hard to get the help she needed. I adapted as much as is possible to her needs for support, but she was not able to continue with the therapy. The reality of her circumstances made the help inaccessible, since not only was it difficult for her to leave her child to someone else for an hour, but she also had to travel for two hours to get to the free service offered at the centre. Knowing that she would not be able to come back, walking her to the bus felt like something I could offer her in terms of acknowledging her need for support. Maintaining the boundary of the therapeutic relationship within the predefined time and space at that time would have denied the opportunity to show this woman some warmth and kindness that she needed both as a mother and as a foreigner with no family to support her.

Gray (2001) argues that for DMP to work effectively with trauma there needs to be a strong supportive system in place that is culturally recognizable and offers help to manage external resources. Through building a trusting and safe relationship, the therapist can then work with the internal resources. In South Africa, opportunities for healing and change have to acknowledge the consequences of disempowerment and poverty (Aliber 2003), and that additional support may be needed. Offering a therapeutic space is invaluable, and offering it within an organization where there is additional practical support makes it even more accessible and valuable. This context also offers support to the therapist. By working as part of a team, it is easier to confront uncomfortable and unjust life circumstances.

Sharing Leadership

Video Creative Response 37.3 ▶: This theme was embodied and expressed at a traffics circle that links different parts of town, from the wealthy private school to the government clinic and the 'township', the centre of town and the largely 'white' suburb.

As a South African I responded well to the DMP group work of Marian Chace.

P 4: Contextual Analysis-Sept 2013 to Dec 2013.docx—4:7 [There is something very approp..] (341:341)

There is something very appropriate about Chace's approach of DMP to South Africa. It promotes equality, sharing, bonding, understanding, and growth of the whole group. These are critical parts of healing in South Africa. The circle formation—the primary structure from which other forms of relating can develop has strong links with traditional dance and indigenous culture.

Chace viewed distortions in the body shape and function as a result of disconnection in response to conflict and pain (Chaiklin and Schmais 1986). Dance actions, particularly in a circle (Levy 2005), expand patient's motility and in so doing develop emotional responsiveness. The sense that people can heal and that their 'conditions' are due to a response to conflict and pain, gives less emphasis to 'naming' the condition and more to creating opportunities for healing within a group process. This echoes Harris's (2007) work and his awareness of group identity in 'sociocentric' cultures. African notions of community emphasize the relationship of the individual with the community, including deceased family members (Makanya 2014). The health of the individual is dependent on the health of the community, and vice versa.

In my journal entries I find similar thoughts recorded:

> *P 4: Contextual Analysis-Sept 2013 to Dec 2013.docx—4:8 [Chace was aware that answering..] (341:341)*
>
> Chace was aware that answering movement through movement dissipates the feeling of apartness, whereas a battle of words increases that feeling. Apartness/apartheid—I think this is key in terms of South Africa and the feelings of apartness amongst and between all people.

In Chace's work there is acknowledgement of psychodynamic concepts in terms of references to unconscious material and inner conflicts, but it can be closely associated with the broad umbrella of humanistic thinking (Karkou and Sanderson 2006). The humanistic trend influences a variety of approaches used within psychotherapy, and includes work with individuals and groups (Yalom 1995; Ratigan and Aveline 1988). A key feature of the humanistic perspective is focusing the work on the here and now, highlighting empathy, and considering client and therapist as equal partners on the therapeutic journey (Karkou and Sanderson 2006).

South African history is replete with the wielding and consequences of wielding unequal power. In South Africa today, water service provision is still based on affordability and thus continues to be based on demographic inequalities (Burt et al. 2015; Swatuk 2002). Thus the emphasis on equality and the sharing of leadership are critical. In Chace's sessions, clients are given leadership at different points within sessions. Leadership is passed back and forth from members of the group to the dance movement psychotherapist (Chodorow 1991). Passing leadership involves a natural usurpation of power as different participants take the lead.

In a country with so much wielding of power that created division, pain, and trauma, the symbolic sharing of leadership is critical. Extending the healing to the wider community to fulfil notions of community in indigenous healing that moves beyond the group (Makanya 2014) is something that can be explored further in terms of Chace's approach in a South African water resource management context. The National Water Act made strong provision for civil society to participate in natural resources management. There is great scope for engaging with a community-based practice that acknowledges indigenous knowledge systems as a valid form of knowledge that has a role to play in empowerment and emancipation so that often marginalized 'voices' are heard. DMP could provide a space for a re-engagement with this knowledge. The following theme offers the opportunity for taking up this challenge.

Connecting with the Environment

Video Creative Response 37.4 ▶: *This embodied expression took place on the hill over-looking Grahamstown from which amaXhosa warriors attacked the British in 1819 in an attempt to reclaim their land and rights. From this history of division now comes the need for a united response and return to an ecological identity.* (Burns 2012).

The impact of the environment on our embodied experience was important for me throughout my training. I also felt it intensely from the moment we arrived in the UK.

P 1: Contextual Analysis-Beg of course and getting to Scotland.docx—1:9 (19:19)

We don't know where we are, where the University is, and the cold makes it hard to be outside with the kids. Inside it is exhausting living in a tiny space. Our bodies need to adapt to living in a cold place. I took the kids for a swim at an indoor pool and walking back they both developed bronchitis!

Within the training I was taken by an experience with a dance movement psychotherapist from Latvia who collected shells from the beach and shared them as part of a DMP workshop I attended:

P 2: Contextual Analysis-Oct to Dec 2012.docx—2:20 (174:174)

I really enjoyed the Mindfulness movement. It is very much where I am coming from. The facilitator collected shells to share from the beach—I loved that nature came into it and a sense of connection to ourselves, each other, and nature through the sharing of sea shells.

Our history in South Africa is one of deep divides, but, as Frizell (2011) argues, we currently face the collective trauma of experiencing environmental conditions that are increasingly unstable and unpredictable, and cross-cultural divides. A spirit of inclusive community is now called for as an inherent part of our healing and this includes the more-than-human world. Burns (2012) writes that DMP can be a means of connecting to sensory experience, the environment, and an embodied sense of belonging within the personal, cultural, and/or collective unconscious in order to bring about healing and greater connectivity. Reeves (2011)—a dance movement psychotherapist with an ecopsychology perspective—claims that corporeal, embodied change can take place by engaging with an ecological, psychophysical movement practice. At a body level, Olsen (2002) describes how to work with the body in relation to the circulation of the earth. She draws deep parallels between inhabiting earth and inhabiting our bodies.

In terms of DMP as part of water resource management that seeks to align human with environmental needs and deal with social injustice, the body becomes critical as the site for healing this split. Some of the first peoples of South Africa—the Khoisan and Khoikhoi—had an intimate relationship with, and shared in, the bounty of the country, being aware of the reciprocal relationship between nature and people (Funke et al. 2007). Mbona (2011) undertook research on the effectiveness of ecotherapy as a therapeutic model in post-conflict healing with individuals involved in armed struggle during apartheid. It contributed to a more positive outlook on life, and an increased sense of worth and personal development in relation to themselves and their communities. Nature endures and renews itself, despite the enormity of the trauma and loss, and there is hope that by re-establishing our relationship we can save it and ourselves.

Conclusion

DMP is a new profession in South Africa, and practitioners face a unique challenge. New ways of understanding and working as mental-health professionals are critical if social transformation and healing are to be achieved. Preparing therapists for such a context is challenging. Political and social histories influence how different countries and cultures perceive mental health and the role of a body-based creative form of psychotherapy. The UK has a very particular and relatively long history and context within which DMP has emerged. Training in the UK as a South African was a privilege which not many other South Africans could gain.

In South Africa there is no option but to strive for social transformation. It is hoped that the non-verbal, relational, and egalitarian nature of certain approaches to DMP may be well suited to the South African context, allowing for truly engaged and non-hierarchical collaboration between practitioners and the people and communities they serve. This is of particular relevance to water resource management and effective community engagement. Looking at DMP through contemporary therapeutic perspectives that challenge power differentials in the therapeutic relationship (such as social constructionism and narrative therapy), while creating active links with the environment (through perspectives from ecopsychology, for example), are approaches with potential value within a South African context. The body as the site for healing through dance and movement carries particular relevance to this context. The use of dance and music as a traditional mode of healing is particularly effective in people strongly connected to traditional culture (Dunphy et al. 2014). Further exploration of spiritual components, not sufficiently addressed within most UK trainings, is also worth considering, and its links to indigenous knowing and healing. These cultural adaptations would facilitate the ongoing development of DMP as a therapeutic practice that works with both internal, external (and even transcendental) factors, and ultimately make a useful contribution to the wellbeing of individuals, groups, and the environment in different parts of the world.

References

Abram, D. (1997). *The Spell of the Sensuous: Perception and Language in a More-than-Human world*. New York, NY: Vintage Books.

Aliber, M. (2003). 'Chronic poverty in South Africa: Incidence, causes and policies', *Chronic Poverty and Development Policy*, 31(3): 473–90.

Ashworth, P. (2003). 'The origins of qualitative psychology', in J. A. Smith (ed.), *Qualitative Psychology: A Practical Guide to Research Methods*. London: Sage, pp. 4–24.

Ashworth, P. (2008). 'Conceptual foundations of qualitative psychology', in J. A. Smith (ed.), *Qualitative Psychology: A Practical Guide to Research Methods*, vol. 2. Wiltshire: The Cromwell Press, pp. 4–25.

Asmal, K. and Hadland, A. (2011). *Kader Asmal: Politics in My Blood: A Memoir*. Auckland Park, SA: Jacana Media.

Boas, S. (2006). 'The body of culture: Transcultural competence in dance movement therapy', in H. Payne (ed.), *Dance Movement Therapy: Theory, Research and Practice*, vol. 2. London: Routledge, pp. 112–31.

Boden, Z. and Eatough, V. (2014). 'Understanding more fully: A multimodal hermeneutic-phenomenological approach', *Qualitative Research in Psychology*, 11(2): 160–77.

Bradt, J. (1997). 'Ethical issues in multicultural counseling: Implications for the field of music therapy', *Multiculturalism in the Arts in Psychotherapy*, 24(2): 137–43.

Buchdahl, J. M., and Raper, D. (1998). 'Environmental ethics and sustainable development', *Sustainable Development*, 6: 92–8.

Burns, C. A. (2012). 'Embodiment and embedment: integrating dance/movement therapy, body psychotherapy, and ecopsychology', *Body, Movement and Dance in Psychotherapy*, 7(1): 39–54.

Burt, J., Wilson, J., and Changing Practice Participants (2015). *The River Speaks*: Series of papers for the ALARA conference. *Changing Practice*: A course to support water activists in South Africa.

Caldwell, C. (2013). 'Diversity issues in movement observation and assessment', *American Journal of Dance Therapy*, 35: 183–200.

Campbell, C., and Cornish, F. (2012). 'How can community health programmes build enabling environments for transformative communication? Experiences from India and South Africa', *AIDS and Behavior*, 16(4): 847–57.

Chaiklin, S. and Schmais, C. (1986). 'The Chace approach to dance therapy', in P. L. Bernstein (ed.), *Theoretical Approaches in Dance Movement Therapy*. Dubuque, IA: Kendall/Hunt Publishing Company, pp. 17–36.

Chodorow, J. (1991). 'The nature of my work', in J. Chodorow (ed.), *Dance Therapy and Depth Psychology: The Moving Imagination*. London: Routledge, pp. 111–16.

Cilliers, P. (2000). 'What can we learn from a theory of complexity?', *Emergence*, 2: 23–33.

Copteros A (2017) Drawing on Principles of Dance Movement Therapy practice in a South African Water Research Context. Unpublished PhD Thesis, Rhodes University, February 2017.

Copters A, Karkou V and Palmer T (in preparation) The use of dance movement therapy principles in a water resource management research context in South Africa.

de Yong, J. T. V. M. (2002). 'Public mental health traumatic stress and human rights violations in low-income countries', in J. T. V. M. de Jong (ed.), *Trauma, War, and Violence: Public Mental Health in Socio-cultural Context*. New York, NY: Kluwer Academic, pp. 1–98. Electronic resource.

Denzin, N. K. and Lincoln, Y. S. (2011). *The Sage Handbook of Qualitative Research*, vol. 4. Thousand Oaks, CA: Sage.

Department of Water Affairs (2013). *National Water Resource Strategy: Water for an Equitable and Sustainable Future.*

Dodds, J. (2011). *Psychoanalysis and Ecology at the Edge of Chaos: Complexity Theory, Deleuze Guattari and Psychoanalysis for a Climate in Crisis.* New York, NY: Routledge.

Du Toit, D., Pollard, S., Burt, J., and Von Balkom, M. (2013). *The Shared River Initiative, Phase II Part 1: Collective Action for Improved Water Resources Management.* Gezina, SA.

Dunphy, K., Elton, M., and Jordan, A. (2014). 'Exploring dance/movement therapy in post-conflict Timor-Leste', *American Journal of Dance Therapy*, 36(2): 189–208.

Frizell, C. (2011). 'Association of dance movement psychotherapy conference, 10th September 2011', *E-Motion Association for Dance Movement Psychotherapy (ADMP) UK Quarterly*, XXI(4): 6–17.

Funke, N., Nortje, K., Findlater, K., Burns, M., Turton, A., Weaver, A., and Hattingh, H. (2007). 'Redressing inequality: South Africa's new water policy', *Environment: Science and Policy for Sustainable Development*, 49(3): 12–23.

Gear, S. (2002). *Wishing Us Away: Challenges Facing Ex-Combatants in the "new" South Africa.* Pretoria, SA: Centre for the Study of Violence and Reconciliation. Pretoria.

Gray, A. E. L. (2001). 'The body remembers: Dance/movement therapy with an adult survivor of torture', *American Journal of Dance Therapy*, 23(1): 29–43.

Hadley, S. (2013). 'Dominant narratives: Complicity and the need for vigilance in the creative arts therapies', *Gender and the Creative Arts Therapies*, 40(4): 373–81.

Hanna, J. L. (2004). 'Applying anthropological methods in dance/movement therapy research', in R. F. Cruz and C. F. Berrol (eds.), *Dance/Movement Therapists in Action*. Springfield, IL: Charles C. Thomas, pp. 144–67.

Harris, D. A. (2007). 'Dance/movement therapy approaches to fostering resilience and recovery among African adolescent torture survivors', *Torture: Quarterly Journal on Rehabilitation of Torture Victims and Prevention of Torture*, 17(2): 134–55.

Henley, R. (2010). 'Resilience enhancing psychosocial programmes for youth in different cultural contexts: Evaluation and research', *Progress in Development Studies*, 10(4): 295–307.

Hillman, J. (1995). 'A psyche the size of the Earth', in T. Roszak, M. E. Gomes, and A. D. Kanner (eds.), *Ecopsychology: Restoring the Earth, Healing the Mind*. San Fransisco, CA: Sierra Club Books.

Hoeller, K. (1993). 'Introduction', in K. Hoeller (ed.), *Merleau-Ponty and Psychology*. Atlantic Highlands, NJ: Humanities Press International, pp. 3–22.

HPCSA. (2015). Health Professions Council of South Africa: Occupational Therapy, Medical Orthotics, Prosthetics and Arts Therapy Registration. <http://www.hpcsa.co.za/PBOccupational/Registration>

Karkou, V. and Sanderson, P. (2006). *Arts Therapies: A Research-Based Map of the Field.* Edinburgh: Elsevier/Churchill Livingstone.

Koch, S. and Fischman, D. (2011). 'Embodied enactive dance/movement therapy', *American Journal of Dance Therapy*, 33(1): 57–72.

Langdridge, D. (2007). *Phenemenological Psychology: Theory, Research and Method.* Essex: Pearson Education.

Larkin, M., Eatough, V., and Osborn, M. (2011). 'Interpretative phenomenological analysis and embodied, active, situated cognition', *Theory and Psychology*, 21(3): 318–37.

Larkin, M. and Thompson, A. R. (2012). 'Interpretative phenomenological analysis in mental health and psychotherapy research', in D. Harper and A. R. Thompson (eds.), *Qualitative*

Research Methods in Mental Health and Psychotherapy. West Sussex: John Wiley and Sons, pp. 101–16.

Larkin, M., Watts, S., and Clifton, E. (2006). 'Giving voice and making sense in interpretative phenomenological analysis', *Qualitative Research in Psychology*, 3(2): 102–20.

Lather, P. (1991). *Getting Smart: Feminist Research and Pedagogy with/in the Postmodern*. New York, NY: Routledge.

Levy, F. J. (2005). *Dance Movement Therapy: A Healing Art*, vol. 2. Reston, VA: American Alliance for Health, Physical Education, Recreation and Dance.

Lotz-Sisitka, H. and Burt, J. (2006). *A Critical Review of Participatory Practice in Integrated Water Resource Management Water Research Commission Report No. 1434/1/06. Research Gate*. Pretoria, SA: Water Research Commission.

Makanya, S. (2014). 'The missing links: A South African perspective on the theories of health in in drama therapy', *The Arts in Psychotherapy*, 41(3): 302–6.

Mbona, S. (2011). *Ecotherapy in Post-Conflict Healing: A Study of the Experiences of Ex-Combatants in the Eastern Cape Township of Mdantsane*. Alice, SA: University of Fort Hare.

McCallum, I. (2008). *Ecological Intelligence: Rediscovering Ourselves in Nature*, vol. 2. Golden, CO: Fulcrum Publishing.

McNamee, S. (2004). 'Draft therapy as social construction: Back to basics and forward toward challenging issues', in T. Strong and D. Pare (eds.), *Furthering Talk: Advances in the Discursive Therapies*. New York, NY: Kluwer Academic/Plenum Press, pp. 1–28.

Meekums, B. (2006). 'Embodiment in dance movement therapy training and practice', in H. Payne (ed.), *Dance Movement Therapy: Theory, Research and Practice*. London: Routledge, pp. 167–83.

Meyer, K. (2014). 'Making fires: Rethinking the possibilities of creative arts therapy practice in South Africa', *Journal of Applied Arts and Health*, 5(3): 303–18.

Mogapi, N. (2003). 'Reintegration Process: The missing piece', in *XIth International Symposium on Victimology, Stellenbosch*, vol. 6. Stellenbosch, SA: Stellenbosch University.

Naess, A. (1995). 'Self-realization: An ecological approach to being in the world', in G. Sessions (ed.), *Deep Ecology for the Twenty-First Century*. Boston, MA: Shambala Publications, pp. 225–39.

Nettleford, R. (1998). 'Forward', in K. Welsh-Asante (ed.), *African Dance: An Artistic, Historical and Philosophical Inquiry*. Asmara: Africa World Press, pp. xiii–xviii.

Olsen, A. (2002). *Body and Earth: An Experiential Guide*. Lebanon, NH: University Press of New England.

Ota, K. and Digpal, S. (2012). 'Making the mental health service accessible for black and minority ethnic (BME) women: Training presentation'. Edinburgh: Irini (pseudonym).

Palmer, C. G. (2007). 'Finding integration pathways: Developing a transdisciplinary (TD) approach to the Upper Nepean Catchment', in *5th Australian Stream Management Conference*, Albury, NSW.

Pollard, P. and Du Toit, D. (2011). 'Towards adaptive integrated water resources management in southern Africa: The role of self-organisation and multi-scale feedbacks for learning and responsiveness in the Letaba and Crocodile catchments', *Water Resources Management*, 25: 4019–35.

Postel, S. (2008). 'The missing piece: A water ethic. <http://prospect.org/article/missing-piece-water-ethic> (accessed 10 July 2015).

Postel, S. (2011). 'The water legacy of Kader Asmal flows far beyond South Africa', *National Geographic* (blog). <http://voices.nationalgeographic.com/2011/06/29/postel-asmal/> (accessed 8 July 2015).

Primus, P. (1998). 'African dance', in K. Welsh-Asante (ed.), *African Dance: An Artistic, Historical and Philosophical Inquiry*. Asmara: Africa World Press, pp. 3–12.

Ratigan, B. and Aveline, M. (1988). *Group Therapy in Britain*. Milton Keynes: Open University Press.

Reeves, S. (2011). 'Moving towards an ecological body with Sandra Reeves', *E-Motion Association for Dance Movement Psychotherapy (ADMP) UK Quarterly*, XXI(4): 18–21.

Rehorick, D. A. and Bentz, V. M. (2009). 'Transformative phenomenology: A scholarly scaffold for practitioners', in D. A. Rehorick and V. M. Bentz (eds.), *Transformative Phenomenology: Changing Ourselves, Lifeworlds and Professional Practice*. Plymouth: Lexington Books, pp. 3–32.

Roux, D. J., Stirzaker, R. J., Breen, C. M., Lefroy, E. C., and Cresswell, H. P. (2010). 'Framework for participative reflection on the accomplishment of transdisciplinary research programs', *Environmental Science and Policy*, 13(8): 733–41.

Sajnani, N. and Kaplan, F. F. (2012). 'The creative arts therapies and social justice: A conversation between the editors of this special issue', *The Arts in Psychotherapy*, 39(3): 165–7.

SANATO (South African Network for Arts Therapies Organisation) (2016). <http://sanato.co.za/> (accessed 14 January 2016).

Schmuck, P. and Schultz, P. W. (2002). *Psychology of Sustainable Development*. Amsterdam: Kluwer Academic Publishers.

Smith, J. A. (2004). 'Reflecting on the development of interpretative phenomenological analysis and its contribution to qualitative research in psychology', *Qualitative Research in Psychology*, 1(1): 39–54.

Smith, J. A., Flowers, P., and Larkin, M. (2009). *Interpretative Phenomenological Analysis: Theory, Method, Research*. London: Sage.

Smith, J. A. and Osborne, M. (2008). Interpretive phenomenological analysis', in J. A. Smith (ed.), *Qualitative Psychology: A Practical Guide to Research Methods*, vol. 2. Wiltshire: The Cromwell Press, pp. 53–80.

Somers, J. (1996). 'Approaches to drama research', *Research in Drama Education*, 1(2): 165–73.

Stanton-Jones, K. (1992). *An Introduction to Dance Movement Therapy in Psychiatry*. London: Tavistock/Routledge.

Swatuk, L. A. (2002). 'The new water architecture in Southern Africa: Reflections on current trends in the light of "Rio + 10"'. *International Affairs*, 78(3): 507–30.

van Manen, M. (2002). *Writing in the Dark: Phenomenological Studies in Interpretive Inquiry*. London, ON: Althouse Press.

Varela, F. J., Thompson, E., and Rosch, E. (1991). *The Embodied Mind: Cognitive Science and Human Experience: The Embodied Mind: Cognitive Science and Human Experience*. Cambridge, MA: MIT Press.

Visvanathan, S. (2005). 'Knowledge, justice and democracy', in *Science and Citizens: Globalization and the Challenge of Engagement*. Chicago, IL: University of Chicago Press, pp. 83–94.

Wadsworth-Hervey, L. (2000). *Artistic Inquiry in Dance/ Movement Therapy: Creative Research Alternatives*. Springfield, IL: Charles C. Thomas.

White, M. and Epston, D. (1990). *Narrative Means to Therapeutic Ends*. Adelaide: Dulwich Centre.

Wickson, F., Carew, A., and Russell, A. W. (2006). 'Transdisciplinary research: Characteristics, quandaries and quality', *Futures*, 38(9): 1046–59.

Yalom, I. D. (1995). *The Theory and Practice of Group Psychotherapy*, vol. 4. New York, NY: Basic Books.

CHAPTER 38

CAPOEIRA IN THE COMMUNITY

The Social Arena for the Development of Wellbeing

ANDRÉ LUIZ TEIXEIRA REIS AND SUE OLIVER

INTRODUCTION

CAPOEIRA has been described as a 'dance-fight-game' (Capoeira 2012, p. 38), and is thought to have originated in the early days of the West African slave trade in Brazil, when slaves were forbidden to dance their cultural dances or practice martial arts (Capoeira 2012). Their solution was to develop this 'game', which incorporated elements of both prohibited practices and was performed to music. It is recognized as a dance form (Capoeira 2012; Calvo-Merino 2012) in its own right, given its emphasis on the aesthetic qualities of the movement and rhythm, the corporeal demands, and the neural stimulation, all bound together by the music.

Professionals of dance activities, health, and social sciences have welcomed the challenge of promoting health and wellbeing in communities. 'Enjoying groups' such as tai chi, yoga, kung fu, salsa, and capoeira are of particular interest for such promoters. Kovac (1995), for example, argues that they may act as unofficial 'social workers'.

Capoeira, this exotic dance-fight-game from Brazil, has the capacity, in Reis's experience, to motivate 'hard-to-reach' groups because it seems fun and enjoyable, helping to fulfil personal needs for engagement in somatic exertion and expression, and consequently promoting social, as well as physical, wellbeing. Moreover, it is an inclusive activity, open to those of all abilities: those who are unable to participate physically can sing or play instruments (Silva and Heine n.d.).

As a 'product' of Brazilian culture, capoeira synthesizes elements of dance, fight, acrobatics, and play (see Video 38.1 on the Companion Website ⊚). In it, the dancers imitate movements and attitudes of certain animals by performing specific movements with their bodies, especially with feet and legs (Almeida 1986). The game is played inside a circle formed by musicians and players, who arrange themselves in a certain order. This is not always obvious to the spectator. Two players squat under the *Berimbau* (one of the musical instruments), exchange greetings, and move to the centre of the circle. Then they start the game with its harmonized, flowing movements, acrobatics, feints, and kicks. To the spectator it appears like an improvised choreography, prompting the players to follow a sequence of attack and escape from one another. This is called *jogo de capoeira*. During the game, the *capoeiristas*[1] explore their strengths and weaknesses, confronting any lack of knowledge, fears, and fatigue that they feel in an enjoyable, challenging, and constant process of self-improvement.

Musical instruments and rhythms determine the speed and attitude of the game. The group playing musical instruments and singing add fluidity and energy to this social activity and lend unique colour to the capoeira sound. Singing traditional, folkloric, and improvised songs with clapping enhances the energetic atmosphere and enjoyment of the game. The music is important for the development of a good fighting rhythm, timing, body dialogue with partners, and concentration.

Capoeira, Reis (2005) found, is an interesting 'toy' for delivering an opportunity to experience wellbeing, and in this chapter we explore the possibility of extrapolating the findings to the wider community.

LITERATURE REVIEW

The Sense of Wellbeing in Community Groups

We start from the premise that capoeira, as a dance activity played in groups, promotes personal development, at least partly, through social interaction (Reis 2005). We see wellbeing as a multidimensional concept (World Health Organization 1999) in which the group setting constitutes the social arena for discovering, discussing, reflecting, and absorbing social behaviour and life experiences. It facilitates the continuous process of knowledge development, personal interactions, and collective experiences. We therefore argue that capoeira can potentially enhance this sense of social life and influence social wellbeing; however, it is a subjective experience because it is unique for each participant (Reis 2005).

How is dance linked to the development of social wellbeing? Cooper (1992) states that since the earliest studies of subjective wellbeing, social interaction has been considered a potential determinant of happiness. Palys and Little (1983) demonstrate that the presence of a supportive social network is more critical to a person's life satisfaction than the raw number of people with whom they interact. Consequently, social wellbeing is concerned with how relationships contribute to a person's positive or negative emotions and his/her social identity. Ellemers (1999) argues that the motivation to establish a positive social identity can modify one's overt behaviour, as people strive to manipulate their own identity. Gecas (2000) states that identities anchored in value systems are important elements of self-concept, since values give meaning, purpose, and direction to our lives. A sense of belonging can reinforce the underlying human need for self-concept and self-esteem (Greene 1999; Oliver, 2009).

Social wellbeing can include numerous states: somatic, psychological functioning, family values, aspects of environment, personal development, choice and autonomy, community integration, and social interaction (Kovac 1995, Oliver 2009). These states are neither simple nor static (Diener 1999), as they comprise global judgements, momentary mood changes, physiology, memory, and emotional expression. Adding to the complexity, the subjective experience of wellbeing can also be measured by physiological characteristics, behavioural reactions, and memories which are linked to ideas of time, space, body, and human relations (Van Manen 1990). These latter are some *objective* elements through which the human experience of life may be observed, described, and explained.

As well as benefiting physical health, exercising in company has been found to improve life satisfaction and emotional wellbeing by reducing loneliness and promoting the sense of one's self as a social being (Steptoe 1996, Herzog 1998, McAuley 2000, Ross 2000). It seems that this social element is one of the most important aspects of exercise for promoting social wellbeing. Dance—and in this case capoeira—is both a physical activity and a group activity. It can therefore be linked to the human desire to belong to a group, and has the potential to contribute to a sense of social wellbeing.

Humans as Social Beings

Starting from the premise that capoeira is a group activity, we need to understand the social functions inside the group. Building on Forsyth's (1996) 'big five traditions of groups,'[2] one can define the core concepts of social wellbeing as (i) friendship, (ii) peer relationship, (iii) leadership, and (iv) group identity (Reis 2005).

(i)   Friendship can be one of the most important elements that motivate people to participate in a group. Hartup (1995) argues that clear distinctions need to be drawn between the construct of having friends, the identity of one's friends, and the quality of friendship in childhood and adolescence. The need for social contact and shared interests are important components in friendship, as are the dynamics of relationships within groups (Zeggelink 1995).

(ii) Peer relationship studies include fluidity and reliability of relationships, group cohesion, and trust between members as key features for positive social experiences (Cairns 1995; Koerner 1999; Rittner and Smyth 1999; Tsuji 1999). These aspects have been found to increase self-esteem, reduce negative thinking, enhance coping abilities, delimit substance abuse, and encourage the ability to seek and enjoy pleasurable activities with peers (Rittner and Smyth 1999). Relationships might change in different stages of life according to the personal development of individuals, causing changes in social order (Shulman 1995; Tsuji, 1999) and affecting trust and cooperation between members. They might not develop into friendship per se, but they present an optimized way of living in society, affecting behaviours and fostering a sense of meaning in people's lives (Baum 1999).

(iii) Leadership is important in order to keep a group united (Boinsk 2000). It can exist among peers on several levels (Reis 2005) and, even between two people, it can switch from person to person according to the situation. In general, leaders maintain the cohesiveness of the group and uphold special rules for commitment and belonging, establish rituals, and induct new members.

(iv) Groups use rituals to create and preserve collective identities and values (Hermanowicz and Harriet 1999). These rituals are linked to group codes of conduct, which include clothes, body language, and spoken language. They are culturally constructed. Goodenough (1999) argues that cultural traditions (including languages) are transmitted across generations through learning by individuals in their social groups. Conflicts of interest in culture and tradition can arise from political and economic issues. Wade (1999) discusses this theme in relation to the efforts of young blacks—members of Ashanti—in the city of Cali, Colombia, who use rap music to make their cultural identity a way of life. Uniforms or special clothes can be significant for establishing identity and belonging, and Chou (1999) investigates whether participating in uniformed groups is likely to be beneficial for adolescents' psychosocial competence. This, of course, is also relevant to capoeiristas. Results indicate that participation in uniformed groups is associated with higher levels of social skills, encouraging initiative and leadership, and can, under certain circumstances, promote democracy and community (Gurin et al. 1999).

These core concepts of social wellbeing– friendship, peer relationship, leadership, group identity, and a sense of belonging—represent the social experience in capoeira.

Experiencing the partner's body in the act of dancing-playing capoeira denotes trust and fellowship. Dancing in a group requires interacting with others. This physical reality of play opposes the societal trend of spending more time alone (Glover 1998).

An intrinsic body-connection through partners in dancing-fighting movements is characterized by fluidity. People play differently because their bodies have different backgrounds and upbringings: bodies that might cross on the street might not otherwise interact. At the moment of playing, the body languages show different ways of living. As a result, a process of understanding each other as human beings and their differences is being experienced. There is a personal process of accepting or rejecting someone who is different. According to the findings it does not indicate prejudice, but a slow process of unfolding themselves to each other. Personal temperament influences moods, and that can affect tolerance. From this, the dark side of relationships—anger or depression—might be manifested as conflict (Baum 1999).

Bodies in dialogue in capoeira can experience a difficult process of learning (Reis 2005). The game requires continuous contact between players, reacting and paying attention to each other's body. In this sense, changing partners during the training seems uncomfortable because it may require adapting to different partners' bodies all the time and in the same lesson: it would be less stressful to keep with the same partner. Despite this, it allows the positive process of adapting to the others' bodies. It is a reciprocal process.

Conflicts arising from movement interaction happen between bodies in capoeira. There are movements of bodies that are fast, better-skilled bodies, and 'disliked' others. However, these different bodies need each other in order to learn in capoeira. Reaching the level of not envying other players' skills and tolerating individual differences is an aim which might promote psychosocial intimacy and integrated involvement—social provision fostering social skills (European Federation of Sport Psychology 1996). Consequently, despite the differences, bodies play 'with' bodies. Prejudices and humiliation of one's body's differences can occur during the process of teaching and learning from each other. Conversely, capoeira is seen as a process of teaching people how to deal with strong personalities, competition, distress, aggression, cognitive limitation, emotion, and self-control. This process can promote the understanding of judgement or non-judgement and a caring attitude (European Federation of Sport Psychology 1996), including thinking about not harming or injuring the weaker person (Howard 1994).

In this sense, the dance-fight-game is an honourable way of showing the weaknesses of different players' bodies when playing the game. This means that human rights, fairness, and respect for each other's physical integrity are more important than the element of the fight itself; there is no intention of knock-out. Failure to respect this makes some feel entitled to be violent. Consequently, in addition to the kinaesthetic element of the movement, experiencing capoeira in a group is viewed as a school of life encouraging bodies to remove inhibitions, meet others, make friends, understand rivalry, and avoid enmity. Thus capoeira can promote the ethics of social attitudes and sportsmanship—social behaviour, affecting personal traits, interpersonal interactions, and consensual agreement (European Federation of Sport Psychology 1996; Vallerand 1996).

Accordingly, this chapter attempts to show how capoeira can help wellbeing development in community settings.

METHODOLOGY

This research leans towards hermeneutic phenomenology and traditional methods developed for ethnographic studies. The experience of the dance activity engages subjective elements of the mind, such as thoughts, reflections, beliefs, and values, guiding the research process toward methods that are designed to explore subjective attitudes natural to human consciousness and comprising intention and *intentionality* as they are directed onto objects, people, events, and situations (Yedgich, 2000). The acceptance of subjectivity lays down the criteria for establishing what can be considered as 'true' or 'relationally true': what is objectively true does not change from day-to-day, but the subjective belief about what is true constantly shifts (Hendel 2001). Reis's (2005) research is based on human actions that are assumed to link with subjective meaning, intentions, and beliefs. We accept that human autonomy and choices are fundamental factors that are under conscious control but, given that subjectivity is neither measurable nor accountable, Reis's study acknowledges that there is internal, relative, and subjective 'truth'.

This study of capoeira for promoting wellbeing in a community is an exploratory one, based on the post-positivist paradigm, through which researchers study human behaviour and search for understanding through action (Reese, 2011).

There are concerns about how participants' consciousness and intentionality affect their perception and description of an experience (Van Der Zalm and Bergum 2000), so hermeneutic phenomenology (Heidegger 1962) was an appropriate discipline for the research, to illuminate the range of human experiences, being concerned with facts, feelings, concepts, dream images, sensations, fantasies, thoughts, and referential objects related to the topic and the experience (Maggs-Rapport 2001). To separate a person from the world is impossible; to be a person is to be in the world (Becker 1992). Social sciences recognize that human life is conscious and intentional and that free-willed individuals are actively involved with their dynamic, temporal, and cultural worlds (Giorgi 1970; Guba and Lincoln 1994; Heidegger 1962; Taylor and Armor 1985). This approach accepts that individuals are co-authors of their existence and not mere objects of the environment (Merleau-Ponty 1962).

Recognizing that enquiry is always value-laden influenced the shape and focus of Reis's research, in which three techniques were used for data collection: semistructured interviews, observation, and Reis's own reflexive journal.

The interviews provided an opportunity to explore, illuminate, and gently probe participants' descriptions (Kvale 1996), to cover the depth of the social wellbeing experience within capoeira.

Observation was used to gain insight into the participants' *life world* (Heidegger 1962) and involved not only the spoken words but also the capoeira dance. This included physiological, psychological, social, and temporal aspects of the participants' experience of the dance (Mischler 1979), and facilitated the recall, description, and understanding of the social setting, the people involved, and the action.

Practical fieldwork enabled Reis to play and talk with the capoeira participants, the movement being a common bond between them. This gave him a closer appreciation of the participants' lives and the lives around them. The reflexive journal, as a natural follow-up to participant observation (Gray and Malins 2004), involved Reis in describing day-by-day experiences. He used it to gauge the depth of his involvement, helping him to remain grounded in the action as a dancer and a capoeira instructor (Reis 2005), rather than detached and objective. The data collected were transcribed and interpreted to reach an understanding of the participants' experience of capoeira dancing and its implications for their social wellbeing.

FINDINGS AND DISCUSSION

The vast reservoir of data collected needed careful organizing, interpreting, and understanding of 'meanings' through the narratives, observations, and personal reflections, for which Reis used reflexive 'bracketing' (Robertson-Malt 1999). A range of significant statements were then extracted from all the transcripts (Creswell 1997) to become the main themes as identified in the literature review: a) friendship, b) peer relationships, c) leadership, and d) group identity.

a) Friendship

A significant number of bracketed narratives helped to uncover the experiences of the capoeira dancers. For example:

> I've noticed that when I am playing capoeira, somehow I know who I can really trust ... (Roberto).
>
> We [spend] a lot of time together, [so] we become good friends (Fred). People get closer slowly. Capoeira connects different people (Roberto, Cleber). Another good thing: there's no division—boys and girls play together ... (Luiz). Surely there is a social aspect in capoeira. Whenever [we are] at play, we show how different it is [from] the way we live (Edson), and, through this, I understand myself and others: the way we play is a way for us to get to know the other person as a human being (Fatima, Ernane). I think that any common hobby is a great possibility for people to make friends (Magda). It does not matter [if] it is capoeira, football or any other activity. They connect people (José).
>
> Capoeira is body language: [I can see when you are] nervous, helping, showing off (Flavia). But I just try to have fun with the other player, not to fight or compete.
>
> [Considering personal feelings,] there are some conflicts: [the dancers are] not always in a good mood (Henrique). I have been getting used to regular psychological breakdowns and paranoid attacks of bad moods, which are supposed to be tolerated by my poor colleagues and partners (Melissa).

There is no aggression—in the negative sense (Ester). Nobody humiliates others because they are not so good at capoeira (Maria). Skills can arouse conflicts because there are discriminations against each other: good or bad performers, being jealous or laughing at others (Flavio), but the black sheep of our group is someone that humiliates people (Rogerio).

I've never beaten anyone and I am proud of this, but it is possible that one day I might—it is part of the game (Isabela). [Once] one guy was happy because he kicked someone and I showed him that it was not right (Edson).

People meet spontaneously and naturally, becoming closer to those whom they instinctively like, fostering friendships. From that, subgroups appear as members and become attuned to each other through the exchange of information in teaching and learning. A cooperative state based in trust is achieved as the key element among the members of the group (Tsuji 1999), helping and being helped, respecting others and their common rights. In general, an atmosphere of cooperation and friendship was reported during the lessons.

b) Peer Relationships

The following bracketed narratives, from participants with varying amounts of capoeira experience, are useful for exploring how this dance-fight can foster improvement of personal wellbeing through peer relationships:

I am getting to understand people with whom I play (Flavia). I [try] to know [a dancer] before I judge him or her (João). It's a good way for breaking walls between people (Geraldo). I had some strong argument with someone, but we played together and afterwards we shook hands (Geraldo). [Consequently,] I am feeling less aggressive. I have started to respect people and care about them (Daniel).

My physical condition is getting better and I'm learning how to work in a group. Playing capoeira you meet people, learn to trust your partner and to be responsible for your acts (Claudio).

c) Leadership

There are conflicting views on how to lead the capoeira group. Leadership is defined, on one hand, by being charismatic and persuading people to act, and on the other hand, by keeping a professional distance and punishing undisciplined participants. These conflicts may be routed in prejudices that come from physical activities in schools. Such discriminations originate from long-time consideration of physical activities as unstimulating and physically punishing (Reis 2005).

Comments from the students reveal their constructs of good leadership:
Leaders [have] to be sensitive towards every act of aggression or unfairness (Geraldo). I think that the leader must discipline the group, make people respect him

(Luiz). I would not like to have a trainer who shouts all the time, like in the army (Flavia).

Our leader cares about people and I like it. He is very nice, an open person (Jose, Flavio). [He has] the ability to connect people, indicating a common goal (Isabela), great sense of humour, leaving us free, and people respect him somehow (Flavio). He is not aggressive toward us. He solves the problems in a very calm way, helping people to discover that [they sometimes] act against themselves. It works. He will shake hands with everyone and shows friendship. The atmosphere at trainings is great (Isabela). Maybe he is too gentle. He should be a little bit harder in particular situations (Pedro).

Extracts from the researcher's personal reflective journal demonstrate the effectiveness of good leadership:

Two days before, the instructor asked them to form up with partners in three queues. Yesterday, they did it by themselves.

One girl arrived late to the lesson. She was warned, and the instructor showed the watch—she [apologized].

Leadership can be problematic in groups. In this study it became evident that there was a juxtaposition between discipline and respect in leadership, possibly due to differences in the interpretation of the leader's role by students and the leader himself.

The group's behaviour is likely to reflect the leader's attitude. Importantly, this accentuates the need for facilitators to take their skills a step further by becoming aware and capable of managing social interaction (Danish et al. 1996).

d) Group Identity

The process of getting to know each other in a group comprising disparate characters can expose differences in people's character and skills. It is a reciprocal process: an individual initiates an exchange (verbal or physical) with someone, but in the expectation that he/she will receive this same attitude back in the future (Bullen and Onyx, cited by Bayly and Bull 2001). Acknowledgement of this may help to modify a person's behaviour, in turn affecting friendship and other relationships. In capoeira, the dance-fight can be a way of exposing differences while respecting the other's opinions. It can be both unifying and divisive, as the data show.

In this research, physical conditions and social life were both found to be influenced by capoeira. Socially, a network base of this nature could facilitate general communication and interaction (Forsyth 1996), so it could affect the participants' sense of wellbeing. Aspects of the capoeira network mirrored the support structure and the tensions of the wider community, as the following narratives show:

I come here to meet people (José), to spend my time well and it does not matter about the skills (Fred). I think that capoeira is a good place for meeting people (Davi). [As an example] I've met some of my neighbours here. We did not talk with each other before [enrolment in capoeira lessons] (Rogerio).

The joy of capoeira unites people and it seems that we [have known] each other for ages (Flavia). It's a wonderful group with 80–100 committed people [despite] some problems and arguments (Geraldo). Of course, there are some conflicts, because it is unavoidable in big groups of people (Maria, Rosana). There are lots of people and the whole group cannot be so [well] integrated (Monica). People can be divided [but] others are connected (Rogerio). There are smaller groups of people who keep together (Jose, Simone).

The roda . . . is the most important idea in capoeira (Flavia). In it, people motivate each other. [There is] a bit of competition, but in a positive way (Marcia).

It is very nice to belong to a group and to have something to do in your spare time. Meeting people . . . we have common interest (Laura). It's a special group—based on trusting others, caring about a partner—that's what our instructor teaches us (Paulo).

Capoeira does not exist without people and you play with someone, never alone (Geraldo). [Some] people should give more from themselves to make training better (Pedro). What irritates me? Five or six advanced students who play only among themselves (Pedro) . . . to start a conversation with somebody from the advanced group is very difficult. Even playing with us, they are not able (maybe don't even try) to come into a dialogue with us beginners. How annoying! (Lilian).

Hence the roda can be seen as a microcosm of the wider community. However, despite this latter negative comment, extracts from Reis's personal reflective journal supported the notion of capoeira building community spirit and uniting dancers with different levels of skill:

[It promotes] motivation and creates a good atmosphere for the lesson: stretching; warming up (basic movements and sequence in pairs); new sequences or movements; roda.

[For playing in the roda,] first step: beginners playing among them; second: beginners playing with advanced; later: [mixed playing] with anyone.

Implications of Capoeira as a Catalyst in the Community

Capoeira lessons consist of a space for meeting people where physical skills are not the only focus. The space doubles up as a location for people to meet neighbours and fellow citizens. In this way, capoeira can help to decrease the number of people spending more time alone in communities (Australian Bureau of Statistics 1999). Friendship is a natural process: some people make friends easily, others are neutral, some others do not think strongly about it. It depends on the individual need for social contact (Diener, cited by Cooper 1992), the presence of similar others as friends (Zeggelink 1995), how critical the supportive network is to a person's life (Palys and Little 1983), and the difference between social and emotional loneliness (Weiss 1986). In any case, the attainment of common goals keeps people together.

Common hobbies can make space for social connectedness, but the codes of behaviour in organized physical activities can either facilitate or prevent friendships. Belonging to a group can put pressure on members to adopt the shared values and beliefs which are seen as mandatory for membership and relate exclusively to others like themselves Riley and Cahill, 2005). This may promote isolation and lead to polarization when the individual participates in different groups. He found that it can generate a hatred of participants in other groups because they are not 'us', and so it can increase negative action against others.

The capoeira roda permits an exchange of skills without fierce rivalry; the attitude that 'for me to win, you must lose' (Howard 1994) does not apply here. The space allows the use of personal skills, accommodating the different levels of every individual, and develops an environment that creates opportunities for a variety of interactions (Baum 1999). The structure can help to increase self-esteem, reduce negative thinking, enhance coping abilities, and the ability to seek and enjoy pleasurable activities with peers (Rittner and Smyth 1999). Capoeira creates an environment that encourages intimacy between the inhabitants of that space. It can reveal problems and arguments, which are normal in big groups, but will not necessarily solve core problems. According to Forsyth (1996) there is a positive process of adaptability, allowing opportunities for refinement of ideas, self-improvement, understanding of self and others, and honing interpersonal relations. The capoeira space plays a role in maintaining and enhancing participants' sense of connectedness and inclusion (Australian Bureau of Statistics 1999), enabling their positive social 'growth' (European Federation of Sport Psychology 1996), despite the capoeiristas having different skills levels which define the social hierarchy in the roda.

Some of the narratives revealed the level of insight the capoeiristas could gain into their own selves and their social functioning in the group:

> [There are] different people around here, if I saw them for the first time in their usual clothes, I would never make contact with them . . . so it's breaking stereotypes (Davi). Some guys do not accept people as they are and capoeira makes contact with other people, whoever they are (Edson). [From this, I suppose] some guys started to become more conscious about some values for their social lives (Edson). Some people accept me, others don't. I am who I am. I don't pretend (Paulo). Capoeira fosters a feeling of familiarity. It is about respecting the other person (Edson). In this group, I try to help other people and sometimes I receive help from them. So, it is a kind of exchange (Pedro). If you do not respect other people, you will not respect common rights (Edson). First, I need to know people well before I trust them. Now I can say this group is like my second family (Fred).
>
> We learn here a kind of responsibility [for] our partner. We can play hard or soft. It's a feature that we can use in everyday life. So the ethics from here we take outside. That is what our teacher tries to teach us (Fred). Unsolved problems appear much later . . . I believe that this energy which exists here will survive and help to keep us together (Geraldo). Maybe capoeira can teach cooperation, being together in a group and to help other people.

In the social setting of capoeira, the leaders keep the common aim of understanding, arbitrating, and, in spite of differences, making and keeping people connected. However, there are still uncertainties about the best method of leading: calmness or hardness, freedom or punishment, democracy or fascism, sharing responsibility for discipline or being strict.

As part of the human relationship dimension of capoeira, there is a range of different people and characters, and the breaking of prejudices about clothes and appearance occurs as people become aware of each other's social values. Despite this, friendship and acceptance of different people can still be a problem because it varies according to personal needs and temperament. Hence this dance-fight-game should not ignore its social duty, which has been responsible for determining its unique character (Brinkhoff 1996).

The game reflects some conflicts because there are aggressive ways of playing as well as more friendly, deferential ways, depending on the players–dancers. Intrinsic elements of capoeira discourage the display of negative attitudes because it is a social dance too; however, negativity can be tolerated if it is part of the process of dealing with emotional experiences (Davis 1996). Playing 'hard' or 'soft' is an ethical consideration that people can take outside the capoeira setting, into their everyday lives. Such social dilemmas encountered in the group can influence the relationship between two or more persons (Tsuji 1999). Others include dealing with conflict, hostilities, and differences within the group (Baum 1999), which can reflect on feelings experienced outside it (Davis 1996). In this way, capoeira as a shared activity contributes to peers' overall relational closeness (Floyd and Parks, 1995).

CONCLUSION

This exploratory study follows people experiencing capoeira as a community dance-fight for wellbeing, and offers a tool for understanding how it can affect people's social lives. The literature provided the lenses through which the narratives of the capoeira students' own experiences could be viewed and linked with the researcher's field notes. This comparison portrayed the effects of capoeira for social wellbeing.

The opportunity for community work with capoeira in this project was a natural process that explored participants' need of social contact. The concept of relationships presented two sides. The negatives were sometimes a lack of respect for a participant's action and opinion regarding capoeira, and in these cases the students lacked commitment to their participation in this dance-fight-game activity. The positives were the support from friends and family and sustained personal investment by the participants in the group. Additionally, there was an understanding that common goals keep people connected. Ultimately, individual differences account for disparities in the capoeira experience, and this can be extrapolated to a wider social setting. The physical activity alone could not make changes in people's attitudes: it is the fusion of the social and physical aspects which make the difference to the social setting—the intersubjectivity of the all people interacting. In agreement with existing literature, the research findings accept that individuals are also co-authors within a context and not mere objects of the environment.

The research shows that leaders are important in maintaining the connectedness of the players–dancers and also their focus on attainment. Recognizable conflicts occurred between participants about the balance between fight-dance, fun, and hardness or softness of attitude. In these situations the leader was the mediator of the conflicts. Being together in a group develops a sense of community, but external social factors can influence internal relationships.

The research also indicates that human relationships have an effect on people's goals within and outside the capoeira practice: personal and collective improvement made in the lessons can be transferred to other community settings. Actually, it might highlight one of the most important elements of social wellbeing: living harmoniously within the society. Considering that extraneous factors are constantly affecting friendships and relationships, we suggest that therapists, programme planners, service providers, and policy makers might consider the relevant theories and the results of research on friendship when developing intervention strategies and analysing their consequences for social wellbeing.

NOTES

1. Dancers/players of capoeira.
2. Forsyth's (1996) 'big five traditions' are: (1) belonging that provides the opportunity for contacts and relationships with others in an organized social network; (2) intimacy that provides opportunities for supportive relationships with others; (3) generativity for productivity, achievement, success, and task-orientation; (4) stability that increases or decreases anxiety, tension, self-esteem, hardness, self-satisfaction, and others; and (5) adaptability which provides the opportunity for creativity, refinement of ideas, self-improvement, improvement of interpersonal relations, and others.

REFERENCES

Almeida B. (1986). *Capoeira: A Brazilian Art Form*. Berkeley, CA: North Atlantic Books.
Australian Bureau of Statistics (1999). *Australian Social Trends*. Canberra: Australian Bureau of Statistics.
Baum, F. (1999). 'Building healthy communities: Health development and social capital project, western suburbs of Adelaide', *SA Community Health Research Unit and Department of Public Health*. Adelaide: Flinders University.
Bayly, L. and Bull, F. (2001). *How to Build Social Capital: A Case Study of an Enduring Community Walking Group*. Eastern Perth Public and Community Health Unity and Department of Public Health, University of Western Australia.
Becker, C. (1992). *Living and Relating: An Introduction to Phenomenology*. London: Sage.
Boinsk, S. (2000) *On the Move: How and Why Animals Travel in Groups*. Chicago, IL: University of Chicago Press.

Cairns, B. (1995). 'Friendships and social networks in childhood and adolescence: Fluidity, reliability, and interrelations', *Journal of Child Development*, 66(5): 1330–45.

Calvo-Merino, B. (2012). 'Neural mechanisms for seeing dance', in B. Bläsing, M. Puttke, and T. Schack (eds.), *The Neurocognition of Dance: Mind, Movement and Motor Skills*. New York: Psychology Press, pp. 153–76.

Capoeira, N. (2012). *Capoeira: Roots of the Dance-Fight-Game*. Berkeley, CA: North Atlantic Books.

Chou, K. (1999). 'Influences on adolescents in an ecosystem: uniformed groups', *Journal of Genetic Psychology*, 160(3): 270–9.

Cooper, H. (1992). 'Social activity and subjective well-being', *Personality and Individual Differences*, 13(5): 573–83.

Creswell, J. W. (1997). 'Qualitative inquiry and research design choosing among five traditions', in R. Vaile and M. King (eds.), *Phenomenological Alternatives for Psychology*. London: Sage.

Danish, S., Stevens, J., Nellen, V. C., and Owens, S. S. (1996). 'Community-based life skills programs: Using sports to teach life skills to adolescents', in J. Van Raalte and B. Brewer (eds.), *Exploring Sport and Exercise Psychology*. Washington DC: American Psychological Association, pp. xxix, 205–25.

Davis, K. (1996). 'Defining questions, charting possibilities', *The Counseling Psychologist*, 4: 144–60.

Diener, E. (1999). 'Subjective well-being is essential to well-being', *Psychological Inquiry*, 9: 33–7.

Ellemers, N. (1999). *Commitment and Strategic Responses to Social Context*. Oxford: Blackwell Science.

European Federation of Sport Psychology (1996). 'Position statement of the European Federation of Sport Psychology (FEPSAC): II. Children in sport', *Sport Psychologist*, 10(3): 224–6.

Floyd, K. and Parks, M. (1995). 'Manifesting closeness in the interactions of peers: a look at siblings and friends', *Communication Reports*, 8(2): 69–76.

Forsyth, D. (1996). 'Why so social an animal? The functions of groups.' <http://www.has.vcu.edu/psy/faculty/fors/functions.html>

Gecas, V. (2000). 'Value identities, self-motives, and social movements', in S. Stryker, T. J. Owens, and R. W. White (eds.), *Self, Identity, and Social Movements*. Minneapolis, MN: University of Minnesota Press, pp. 93–109.

Gray, C. and Malins, J. (2004). *Visualising Research: A Guide to the Research Process in Art and Design*. Aldershot: Ashgate.

Giorgi, A. (1970). *Psychology as a Human Science*. New York, NY: Harper and Row.

Glover, S. (1998). 'Social environment and the emotional well-being of young people', *Family Matters*, 49: 11–17.

Goodenough, W. (1999). 'Outline of a framework for a theory of cultural evolution', *Journal of Comparative Social Science*, 33(1): 84–107.

Greene, J. (1999). 'Can support group heal?', *The New England Journal of Medicine*, 14(2): 34–45.

Guba, E. and Lincoln, Y. (1994). 'Competing paradigms in qualitative research', in N. K. Denzin and Y. S. Lincoln (eds.), *Handbook of Qualitative Research*. Thousand Oaks, CA: Sage, pp. 115–17.

Gurin, P., Peng, T., Lopez, G., and Nagda, B. R. (1999). 'Context, identity, and intergroup relations', in D. Prentice and D. Miller (eds.), *Cultural Divides: The Social Psychology of Intergroup Contact*, New York: Russell Sage Foundation.

Hartup, W. (1995). 'The three faces of friendship', *Journal of Social and Personal Relationships*, 12(4): 569–74.

Heidegger, M. (1962). *Being and Time*, transl. J. Macquarrie and E. Robinson. New York, NY: Harper and Row.

Hendel, C. (2001). 'The nature of knowledge: Pitfalls of science as religion.' <http://www.doctorcarl.org/knowledge.html>

Hermanowicz, J., and Harriet, M. (1999). 'Ritualizing the routine: collective identity affirmation', *Sociological Forum*, 14(2): 197–214.

Herzog, A. (1998). 'Activities and well-being in older age: Effects of self-concept and educational attainment', *Psychology and Aging*, 13(2): 179–85.

Howard, P. (1994). *The Death of Common Sense*. New York. NY: Random House.

Koerner, A. (1999). 'Relational schemas: The universal grammar of relationships', Dissertation Abstracts International. *The Sciences and Engineering*, 59(9-B): 5168.

Kovac, D. (1995). 'Man's quality of life: A cliché or a scientific category? Bratislava, Slovak Republic', *Journal of Studia-Psychological*, 37(1): 47–55.

Kvale, S. (1996). *InterViews: An Introduction to Qualitative Research*. Thousand Oaks, CA: Sage.

Maggs-Rapport, F. (2001). '"Best research practice": In pursuit of methodological rigour', *Journal of Advanced Nursing*, 35(3): 373–83.

Merleau-Ponty, M. (1962). *Phenomenology of Perception*, transl. C. Smith. London: Routledge and Kegan Paul.

McAuley, E. (2000). 'Social relations, physical activity, and well-being in older adults', *Preventive Medicine*, 3: 1608–17.

Mischler, E. (1979). 'Meaning in context. Is there any other kind?', *Harvard Educational Review*, 49: 1–19.

Palys, T. and Little, B. (1983). 'Perceived life satisfaction and the organization of personal project systems', *Journal of Personality and Social Psychology*, 44: 1221–30.

Reese, H. (2011). 'The learning-by-doing principle', *Behavioral Development Bulletin*, 11: 1–19.

Reis, A. (2005). *Capoeira: Health and Social Wellbeing*. PhD thesis, University of Bristol.

Riley, S. and Cahill, S. (2005). 'Managing meaning and belonging: young women's negotiation of authenticity in body art', *Journal of Youth Studies*, 8(3): 261–79.

Rittner, B. and Smyth, N. (1999). 'Time-limited cognitive–behavioral group interventions with suicidal adolescents', *Journal of Social Work with Groups*, 22(2–3): 55–75.

Robertson-Malt, S. (1999). 'Listening to them and reading me: a hermeneutic approach to understanding the experience of illness', *Journal of Advanced Nursing*, 29(2): 290–7.

Ross, A. (2000). 'The psychosocial and physical impact of exercise rehabilitation following coronary artery bypass surgery', *Coronary Health Care*, 4(2): 63–70.

Oliver, S. (2009). *Community-based Creative Dance for Adolescents and Their Feelings of Social Wellbeing*. PhD thesis, Queen Margaret University, Edinburgh. <http://etheses.qmu.ac.uk/139/1/139.pdf>

Shulman, S. (1995). *Close Relationships and Socioemotional Development: Human Development*. New York, NY: Ablex Publishing Corporation.

Silva, G. de O. and Heine, V. (n.d.). 'Capoeira and social inclusion', in *Texts from Brazil No. 14: Capoeira*. Brazil: Ministry of External Relations.

Steptoe, A. (1996). 'Stress, social support and health-related behavior: A study of smoking, alcohol consumption and physical exercise', *Journal of Psychosomatic Research*, 41(2): 171–80.

Taylor, S. and Armor D. (1985). 'Positive illusions and coping with adversity', *Journal of Personality*, 64: 873–98.

Tsuji, R. (1999). 'Trusting behavior in prisoner's dilemma: the effects of social networks', *Dissertation Abstracts International Section A: Humanities and Social Sciences*, 60(5-A), 1774.

Vallerand, R. (1996). 'Toward a multidimensional definition of sportsmanship', *Journal of Applied Sport Psychology*, 8(1): 89–101.

Van der Zalm, J. E. and Bergum, V. (2000). 'Hermeneutic phenomenology: Providing living knowledge for nursing practice', *Journal of Advanced Nursing* 31(1): 211–18.

Van Manen, M. (1990). *Researching Lived Experience*. Ontario: State University of New York Press.

Wade, P. (1999) Working culture: Making cultural identities in Cali, Columbia', *Journal of Current Anthropology*, 40(4): 449–71.

Weiss, M. (1986). ' "That's what friends are for": Children's and teenagers' perception of peer relationships in the sport domain', *Journal of Sport and Exercise and Movement Science*, 18(4): 347–79.

World Health Organization (1999). *Balancing Mental Health Promotion and Mental Health Care: A Joint WHO/EC Meeting*. Belgium: WHO MNH/NAM/99.2, 22–4.

Yedgich, T. (2000). 'In the name of Husserl: Nursing in pursuit of the things-in-themselves', *Nursing Inquiry*, 7: 29–40.

Zeggelink, E (1995). 'Evolving friendship networks: An individual-oriented approach implementing similarity', *Journal of Social Networks*, 17(2): 83–110.

CHAPTER 39

THE 5RHYTHMS® MOVEMENT PRACTICE

Journey to Wellbeing, Empowerment, and Transformation

MATI VARGAS-GIBSON, SARENA WOLFAARD,
AND EMMA ROBERTS

INTRODUCTION

GABRIELLE Roth's 5Rhythms® is an exploration of five different energetic states of being which invite each individual to discover their own unique way of moving. It is a flexible practice where self-awareness, freedom in the body, and creativity develop through regular dancing and traversing several specific maps, or levels. Each map explores emotions, relationships, and psychological patterns.

In this chapter we provide a general overview of the 5Rhythms® practice, with the Wave as the basis of its cosmology and its relationship and relevance to wellbeing. Experiences from participants in the 5Rhythms® community were collected through open-ended questionnaires, and the data was approached through a hermeneutic phenomenology perspective that "unveil(s) the world as experienced by the subject through their life world stories". (Kafle, 2011) We also write about the practice from our own experience as 5Rhythms® teachers. (Oliver, 2009, quoting Heidegger, 1996).

GABRIELLE ROTH

Gabrielle Roth (1941–2012) was a movement innovator, theatre director, community leader, and musician with a special interest in shamanism. She was a workshop teacher and a bestselling author of three books: *Sweat Your Prayers: Movement as a Spiritual Practice, Maps to Ecstasy: Teachings of an Urban Shaman,* and *Connections: The Five Threads of Intuitive Wisdom.* With her band The Mirrors she created more than twenty albums of trance dance music, and she directed or has been the subject of several videos and theatre performances.

She began teaching at 16 years of age and trained in traditional dance methods. It is interesting to note that according to Roth (1989) herself, she suffered from anorexia during her teenage years. Whilst a young adult, Roth paid for college education by teaching movement in rehabilitation centres. In her 20s she sustained a knee injury and, after surgery, she was told she would never dance again. Following a period of depression she retreated to the Esalen Institute in Big Sur. Here she healed her body through dancing, and, with encouragement from Fritz Perls, she began facilitating dance (Roth 1989). Martha Peabody (2014) says the practice of 5Rhythms® began to evolve intuitively and organically through observation and experimentation. In the 1970s the Esalen Institute was a hub for the human-potential movement, and the body was one primary site for investigation. Processes such as gestalt practice, holotropic breathwork, and other disciplines explored the edges of perception and altered states of consciousness (Esalen Institute n.d.) Roth was part of this laboratory, and her work continued to be influenced by the great diversity of teachers and artists she encountered: Arica's Oscar Ichazo, the Nigeran drummer Babatunde Olatunji, and Dick Price. She did not work with professional dancers (Roth 1989). It appears that 5Rhythms® and its primary form, the Wave, arose, essentially and almost shamanically, from an intuitive dialogue between dancing that followed the drum, and drummers who followed the dancers. Roth's work was born from her own experience of healing. She described her own initiation into freedom of movement as blissful, and was compelled to map the way there and back so that she might escort others to that ecstatic place. She travelled inside to the essence, to the core of it all, to create this map.

> It came out of, and I consider it to be, the essential Feminine Spiritual path which comes from the body. I was the captive audience, I named and articulated them, but the rhythms were there. It is a path designed to give you the tools and maps to resurrect yourself, reinvent yourself, to heal, to bring oneself back into wholeness and therefore holiness or sacred self. (Grey 2012, p. 1)

Roth spent the next fifty years taking inspiration from theatre, music, spiritual practice, and always the dance itself to continually evolve the maps of this work, train teachers, and seduce thousands of people into moving and reconnecting with their authentic and creative selves.

WHAT ARE THE FIVE RHYTHMS?

5Rhythms® is a flexible practice in which self-awareness, freedom in the body, and creativity develop through regular dancing and traversing several specific maps, or levels. Each map explores emotions, relationships, and psychological patterns. 'It is a map to everywhere you want to go, on all planes of consciousness—inner and outer, forward and back, physical, emotional, and intellectual' (Roth 1999, p. 194).

Through 5Rhythms® practice, dancers become attuned to sensation, emotion, mind states, and connection to space and the environment. They also obtain direct information and discernment about pain, suffering, joy, emotional states, and relationship dynamics. By cultivating present moment awareness, centredness, and groundedness, 5Rhythms® dancers develop a greater capacity to see new possibilities, individually and collectively. Wellbeing is a possibility on all levels with this practice: physical, mental, relational, social, and spiritual.

The physiological responses to moving—breath, sweat, endorphins, presence, and collective connection—could contribute to an overall sense of wellness. In this chapter we show that the practice acts as a catalyst for healing, change, and wholeness. Mindfulness is also encouraged in this practice by engaging a focused attention while moving all body parts, moving with others, and exploring the dynamics of relationship. Many studies have shown that meditation and mindfulness may also contribute to wellbeing and happiness in a direct way (Brown and Ryan 2003).

Over many years, at the Esalen Institute and other venues, Roth studied dancers in her movement classes and saw the same patterns emerging. She categorized her observations into five specific sequential rhythms that follow a pattern similar to a wave. She then found a language of patterns—a language which is universal and is supported by quantum physics theory (Juhan 2003, p. 53): 'Energy moves in waves. Waves move in patterns. Patterns move in rhythms. A human being is just that, energy waves, patterns, rhythms. Nothing more. Nothing less. A dance' (Roth 1999, p. 194).

From her observations she named five rhythms—qualities that can be explored through movement: flowing, staccato, chaos, lyrical, and stillness. Each suggests a vibration, a state of mind or consciousness, and a state of being (Juhan 2003, p. 85), whilst all together constitute the Wave. There are no choreographed steps or 'right' ways of dancing the Wave and each of the rhythms. However, one of the main principles of this practice is the cultivation of awareness of and attention to the body. The dancer grounds their awareness in their feet, and then brings attention to a specific body part. Attention becomes a point of consciousness moving around in this field of awareness (Roth 1999, p. 29), each dancer following their own internal impulse into the energetic field of each rhythm. The Wave, as Roth called it, is 'a flexible practice, meant to reflect the level of your energy rather than force you to conform to it as a rigid discipline. The only discipline it requires is for you to show up and be true to the part of yourself that is committed to moving' (1999, p. 15). (See Video 39.1 on the Companion Website ▶.)

Flowing

> Let whatever you are feeling unravel. Don't force it. Surrender to your feet.
>
> Gabrielle Roth (1999, p. 55)

Flowing is fluid, round, and continuous, being relaxed and flexible in our bodies. In Flowing 'there are no separations or distinctions between things, only continuous change' (Roth 1999, p. 51). We become aware of our inhalation and how we take things in. Flowing teaches us to follow the natural momentum of the moment, to stay fluid in a changing environment. Two main qualities we meet in Flowing are grounding and feeling our connection to self, which allows us to restore our relationship with our instincts. We then reconnect to our environment and our bodies' relationship to the world by surrendering to our weight and trusting the pull of gravity. We regain our connection to the earth and rest in harmony with the rhythms of nature, her cycles and moods (Roth 1999, p. 51).

Flowing gives us access to our inner rhythm and shows us the feminine, receptive nature within. Roth describes this rhythm as 'an energy field in which the feminine aspect of the soul is revealed in all its awesome beauty, fierce power, and animal magnetism. Deep within each of us is a mother longing to nurture, a mistress impatient to flirt, and a *madonna* serene in her wisdom' (Roth 1999, p. 54).

Staccato

> Define yourself. Move as if your body were a huge heart, pumping, beating.
>
> Gabrielle Roth (1999, p. 86)

Staccato is punctuated, linear, percussive, defined, and angular, and its movement is edgy and clearly articulate. This rhythm connects us to our expressive energy, the beat of our heart and passions, and the masculine fire within us. If Flowing is receptive, Staccato is responsive and active. Energy moves out from our centre into the world, and we practice shaping our dance in clear, defined forms. We also practice expressing feelings, giving them delineation and clarity. If Flowing shows us how we feel, Staccato teaches us how to move and to express and project those feelings. Roth describes it as dancing with your bones, creating all kinds of angles and edges like geometry in motion (Roth 1999, p. 83).

In Staccato we get to know our limits and boundaries. It is the part of us that makes plans, thinks about the future, knows what we want and go after it. Staccato also has the call of the wild (Roth 1999)—the rebel who 'acts his passion, and lives his dreams'. As Roth so eloquently says: 'To be truly wild and free you have to follow your heart, not your head', 'go for the anger and find out what it has to teach you' (pp. 98–9). Staccato is emotionally expressive; it is where we reach out to connect and communicate our truth. In Staccato we also start practicing the dance of dyad relationship, how to express what is happening to us in relationship to other dancers in the room.

Chaos

> Don't impose a pattern on your dance. Let them emerge.
>
> Gabrielle Roth (1999, p. 131)

Chaos is often described as release, unconfined, random, spontaneous, undirected, and letting go. Physically it is the dance of rooting our feet into a pattern and releasing the different parts of the body into spontaneous seizures of abandonment (Roth 1999, p. 115). Our feet are locked in the beat, our arms moving freely, our spine undulating, our head loose. We are vibrating and shaking out, softening, releasing, and falling off and onto the beat. The movement has an unpredictable, ever-changing, spontaneous form; spine, head, and limbs soft and loose like a rag doll. We practice letting go of tension and conditioned holding patterns. 'In Chaos we learn how to dive below the surface, logical mind into the intuitive mind; how to get in touch with our whims and impulses, our spontaneous, poetic intelligence, and free them to move through our bodies and hearts' (Roth 1999, p. 118). Chaos, says Roth, teaches us 'how to move in the unknown, how to die and be reborn' (p. 119). It is as if we become plugged into something bigger than ourselves; we are connected to the universe and our bodies become vibrantly alive (Roth 1998, p. 33). Juhan (2003, p. 86) describes Chaos as an internal dissolving of all known structures and the complete surrender to what is.

Lyrical

> Lighten up. Stay on the beat, free and wild and rooted but lighter. Drop the effort. Enjoy the ride.
>
> Gabrielle Roth (1999, p. 161)

In Lyrical we physically lighten up and feel our weightlessness. We remain rooted in the body, but lighter, with eyes often focused on finger tips. If there was any effort it is gone now, and we even let go of letting go. Roth (1999) describes this rhythm as 'when the body, heart, and mind are working as a unit, we're not spaced out, we're perfectly tuned in' (pp. 161–2). It is the most elusive of the five rhythms. If we have not experienced the rhythms of Flow, Staccato, and Chaos fully, we cannot fake the aftermath—an aftermath where we realize we are works in progress, nothing is fixed, particularly our identities. Lyrical is when we finally find the ease and natural quality of our own movements; where the dancer finds her/his own personal patterns, style, and interpretation. When witnessing a room in the lyrical phase of the Wave, one sees dancers making connections and improvisations with little effort.

Lyrical holds the energy of shape-shifting; we dance the freedom of possibilities, of shifting energies, of not getting stuck in any one place. 'When we finally divest ourselves of everything that weighs us down, we lighten up. Lyrical is the process of delightment' (Roth 1999, p. 157). Asking any 5Rhythms® dancer to describe Lyrical as a rhythm, you will receive as many answers as people. It is where we find our individuality in its most expressed form. As seen in the description of Juhan (2003), 'the energetic result of Chaos, a light emptiness, a freedom, a sense of ease or mindful effortlessness, an expanded, timeless, completely awake trance (p. 86).

Stillness

> Sink into the emptiness. Disappear in the dance. Embrace the mystery
> that is you.
>
> Gabrielle Roth (1999, pp. 180–1)

'Stillness is the pool at the end of the energetic descent' (Juhan 2003, p. 86). Physically, the body becomes a vibrant quiet place, resting, feeling, waiting for the impulses, playing in the spaciousness of a body, mind, heart, soul, and spirit completely united. Juhan acknowledges the individual experience of Stillness in that it can be simultaneously full of personal meaning and also of universal or archetypal significance. It is where the dance can turn into a blessing or a prayer, where we meet a sense of fullness and emptiness at once, as well as oneness and connection.

Physically, we wind down and move in slow motion while gathering energy inward. We might stop and feel our shape, watch our breath, and we focus our attention on the flow of our breath, the beat of our heart, the pulsing of our cells (Roth 1999). It is in the rhythm of stillness where we can place the 5Rhythms® as a spiritual and transformational practice. It takes a lot of movement to empty out and find a thorough sense of peace and contentment, a deeper connection to the spirit moving in and through us. It is here where we start becoming an empty field and are able to fully cruise the emptiness (Roth 2009).

5Rhythms® as a Movement Practice

In this section we elaborate and demonstrate how dancing 5Rhythms® is experienced by participants as a practice supporting wellbeing. According to Oliver (2009), 'wellbeing comprises a number of factors, including physical health, recognition of personal identity, and the level and quality of interaction with one's social network' (p. 88). While on the surface 5Rhythms® may seem to be about dance, movement is merely the vehicle for a powerful, healing process of meditation-in-motion, aimed at unifying the body, heart, mind, soul, and spirit into our original wholeness, and addressing our collective cultural disease of fragmentation, or what Roth has called 'trizo-phrenia': thinking one thing, feeling another, and doing a third (Sobel 2009). Oliver (2009, p. 89) also quotes Beecher (2005) as saying: 'Creative dance movement may bridge the gap between mind, body, and spirit by engaging and combining the imagination and thinking body with the physicality of doing' (p. 44).

As mentioned in the introduction, we follow a hermeneutic phenomenological approach with open-ended questionnaires and our own experiences as teachers. Andrea Juhan (faculty member of 5Rhythms®, 1994–2013), following a combined phenomenological and hermeneutic research model in her thesis, writes: '. . . it seems that in the last decade researchers have moved more towards the use of phenomenological-based research methodologies to mine and articulate the experiences, effects, and techniques of dance/movement therapy.' She also says, 'as many of the researchers themselves are dancers or movers engaged in the disciplines they seek to study, the heuristic components of phenomenological research bring an invaluable structure in which to include the intersubjective nature of movement and the creative and psycho-spiritual processes involved in dance/movement group experiences. (2003, p. 74).

In this chapter we have followed a hermeneutic phenomenology in which the experience is the source of knowledge. We devised a questionnaire for participants to respond to questions on different areas of wellbeing in 5Rhythms®. We e-mailed these early in 2014 to our students in the UK, and to teachers in Europe, Australia, and the United States to forward to interested participants in their groups. Participants could choose if they wanted to take part. We did not define age, ethnicity, physical fitness, gender, range of mental health, or regularity of dancing the 5Rhythms®. Neither did we interview or survey those who have been diagnosed with a mental health illness, nor asked participants if they have a mental illness. Our group was mostly from a middle-class, financially capable group, and mostly white. We did not follow up on responses to clarify meaning; for example, where a participant said they lose inhibitions, we assumed this to be positive. Others mentioned being self-conscious at first, which could mean that mostly those who were already confident would more easily take part. We were aware that mostly those who like 5Rhythms® took part in the survey, and that we did not collect information from those who had a negative experience. We received twenty-six responses. In this chapter we quote participants' responses in italics to differentiate them from the authors' experiences and comments.

We based our approach on Roth's view that, as teachers, we get who we need in front of us in a class. This is not a practice for everyone, but has the potential to allow transformation for those who feel drawn to it. The rationale of the brief study was to glean information from current participants with regard to their experience of wellbeing from engaging in 5Rhythms®. Roth (1999) defined the 5Rhythms® as a practice, never as a therapeutic modality. Yet we cannot exclude the therapeutic effects that dancers experience. Juhan (2003) states that 'the use of dance and movement tends to have the opposite effect (from expressive art therapy), as the movement of one's body often creates a direct and intimate experience of internal processes and emotions, dropping below or moving right into the experience of one's defenses' (p. 41). It is often challenging to describe in words what is usually a wordless experience. In our research, dancers contributed their inspired voices to reflect on the physical, emotional, mental, creative, and spiritual aspects of their practice. They are presented in the following groupings, and we allow for anonymity by not using names in the chapter when we quote feedback given in italics.

5Rhythms® and Physical Wellbeing

5Rhythms® dancers describe the physical effects of the practice in a variety of ways, from general fitness, to feeling grounded, to releasing tension. For the purpose of our (for teachers and students alike) practice, wellbeing is indicated by a heightened and distinct awareness of the body and increased pleasurable sensation. Typically dancers make comments such as '*I feel totally in my body and relaxed, it makes me feel more fit, strong and supple. I am more aware of the physicality of the body—of the body as movement and expression.*' To describe their experience, they use words such as '*sensuousness*', '*vibrate more*', '*warmth in my belly returning*'; '*it is the only form that comes close to playing; a good workout, no strain or overstretching*', '*complete freedom throughout each and every part of my physical body*', '*improves flexibility*', and '*always feel good physically after it*'. They feel calm afterwards, as well as energized, or simply: '*Physically I feel better.*'

As teachers we know that the practice increases awareness and creates mindfulness and self-acceptance. In the dancers' words:

> It brings awareness to me of my full body, the areas that do not move and those that do. I become aware of the movement qualities of my body and the distinct vocabulary of these movements. Most importantly, I own the movements, I am not copying or trying to 'do it right' because the only 'right' is how I choose in the moment, and end up energized, sweating, and glowing inside and out.

True to Roth's (1999) maxim 'if you don't do your dance, who will?', 5Rhythms® sessions allow dancers to be with their state of being, exactly as it is, and realize they have full permission to own their experience:

> 5Rhythms® allows me to meet myself physically where I am. I can move with the dynamic that best suits my physical body. I can play with the movement; luxuriate and sink into my lethargy or exhaustion, or I can expand it and speed it up, see what happens as my energy shifts to various parts of my anatomy. 5Rhythms® creates acceptance for how my body is right in this moment . . . to move the way the body wants to.

Mindful presence is reflected as:

> 5Rhythms® is one of the primary ways to know how I am doing in present time and what is trying to shift in my body/mind. The practice helps me both to discover and then facilitate what is ready to shift. Unlike in the majority of other movement practices, my body is grateful that I allow it to move the way it feels like moving.

In comparison to other physical practices, our 5Rhythms® dancers claim to enjoy it so much, and benefit from it in so many ways, that it is easy to keep it up regularly and, in their words:

Unlike other physical activities that I have undertaken in the past purely for the sake of fitness, which have tended to fall by the wayside eventually. Also, 'although I do other types of training (cycling/gym), 5Rhythms® allows my entire body to develop, align and connect. My muscles are stronger and my coordination has improved. I dance with a lot of energy and 5Rhythms® is as good a physical workout as any other. [I] love the sweat!

Moreover, as teachers we know that release in the body creates a direct felt sense of physical patterns of tension that can start to unfreeze and shift, creating an increased state of wellness. One dancer says that *'my body can feel tight, particularly when I feel busy and preoccupied with work, and I feel tension in my neck and shoulders. When I dance I am able to release that tension'.* Another says that *'the dance also helps facilitate the resolution of old unhelpful patterns/traumas which have been held as energetic blocks in the body and have given rise to painful/ troublesome physical symptoms, my experience of the body has been increasingly blissful and pleasurable, especially whilst I am dancing.'*

5Rhythms® and Emotions

Feedback from dancers showed a maturity in describing the emotional effect of 5Rhythms®, how the practice allowed a non-judgemental environment to explore and experience emotions. Wellbeing is indicated by the concept of acceptance and having freedom to experience and express. In the dancers' own words:

As I express myself emotionally through the dance, I feel release and also a sense of cleansing; but also the strengthening and expansion of positive emotions. I feel 'lit up' and 'lifted up' [. . . also] growing up, it was vital for me to repress my emotions and focus on the emotional needs of others. I never knew what I was feeling and rarely expressed my authentic self. When I started to move, I found I could freely express myself in a safe and non-judgemental environment.

The emotional experience in the dance encourages and facilitates a range of feelings not often available in other settings. Some dancers have found themselves uplifted, slightly overexcited. At other times there is a sense of balance; recognition of tension and such feelings *'in myself more quickly than I may have previously'.* Being able to dance emotions as and when they present themselves is perceived as a way of healing. In the dancers words: *'On a couple of occasions it revealed feelings of anger and loneliness that were much stronger than I had acknowledged, which helped to recognize and deal with them'.* Another dancer says *'I dance for pleasure and I dance when I am in pain or feeling sad'*, and yet another says *'I ALWAYS find the dancing gives me what I need to heal my emotional pain at that particular time'* and *'there is magical healing and it is a fantastic way of dancing through the emotions from anger through to blissful peace!'* We note here that Heartbeat,[1] or the emotional exploration of the rhythms, requires experience of practicing and embodying the Wave. As the body releases tension and opens to sensation, feelings and emotions have room to arise, and some dancers will experience discomfort as they experience energy that has been locked or unacknowledged. It is here that the practice provides much wellbeing as dancers redefine how they relate to their emotional selves. 5Rhythms® becomes a wellbeing tool in the way it gives permission to move diversely in experiencing emotions.

Dancers describe the following:

> I find that it is impossible to engage wholeheartedly with 5Rhythms® practice and not become acutely aware of the subtleties of my emotional life. Dance almost invariably alters my emotional state, and each session is very much experienced as an emotional journey. Although I can begin a session in all sorts of emotional states, once I start dancing the emotional experience is one of bliss, gratitude, love, joy, and a sense of freedom. Immediately following a class there is very often a lot of painful emotional content arising without any 'story' attached, which I experience as release.

The sense of catharsis often affects life in general, as both old painful emotions and current emotional pain are met and released, so that the body and emotional system are not so clogged up. This means that reactivity is reduced and there is less projection in relationships with others in daily life than there would otherwise be, less energy bound up in keeping painful emotions repressed. For example:

> I have the possibility to explore the feelings and the option to drop in or out of them by changing posture. I have uncovered volcanic rage and 5Rhythms® gave me a tool for safe expression of anger. As a female, I was missing a socially acceptable method of expressing anger and aggression. Regular 5Rhythms® gives my emotions a way of expressing themselves, regardless of which emotions want to come through.

5RHYTHMS® AND THE MENTAL STATE

Roth insisted in her workshops that we put our mind in our feet to get out of the constant chatter in our heads. By giving mindful attention to what is moving, instead of what we are thinking, 5Rhythms® allows for mental relaxation, especially for those who find sitting meditation difficult. Dancers describe wellbeing with regard to the mental state as related to an open attitude, less rumination and overthinking, breaking a pattern, and liberation from the often dominant possession of the soul by thought. In their own words:

> It's helping me to become more connected to my body and get out of the trap of constantly being stuck in my head. Positively it enables equanimity; acceptance for how my mental state is right in this moment; allowing myself to leave my mind and surrender to the music and my body is an incredibly liberating experience for me; it supports my mental wellbeing, releasing unresolved issues and reminding my mind that there is

more to me than the chatter of my ego; a holiday from the constant mental chatter; and the practice gives rise to mental clarity and a sense of profound spaciousness devoid of conceptual thought.

There is also the wellbeing of being fluid mentally, as '*it seems to unblock certain cognitive processes, and I often find that I have a sudden insight into an area that I've been thinking about; it feeds my intellectual enquiry too, as I am interested in learning through the body*'. Dancers also mention that they find wellness through new intuitive insight. They begin to perceive and act on new possibilities of ways of being and seeing. A new sense of trust and openness arises. For example:

> *I think it has made me more confident, more able to take risks in my teaching and in the ways in which I present my intellectual work in public. As a result of stepping out of the conceptualizing mind and dropping deep into the body, there is access to a deep intuitive clarity, knowing, and wisdom. Different types of insight frequently arise out of this.*

When caught in the throes of the dance, the mind cannot keep up sufficiently to judge, criticize, or evaluate the experience. Dancers report that this '*leads to a state of mental clarity and the freedom to perceive things as they really are, with less projection.*' As we release and shake out the body in Chaos, we also release many of the preconceived notions and ruminations that cause so much disease and discomfort. In the dancers' words:

> *There's no time for the critical mind to take the stage when I am in the frenzy of 5Rhythms®. It helps clear out the unnecessary baggage of nagging, depressing mind talk and switch gear into positive growing healthy mind-awareness. The dance allows for noticing where one is stuck and where change can occur: mental states give an overall shape to the body and 5Rhythms® can help me move with [them]; something which I do entirely for my own joy and wellbeing, and completely without shame. It makes me feel free and gives me the opportunity to dance with others without inhibition.*

CONNECTION, CREATIVITY, AND RELATIONSHIP

Since we are often given steps and rules to follow, first-time dancers are often surprised, and at times uncomfortable, when they meet their own self-consciousness on the dance floor. It was Roth's belief that 5Rhythms® taps into the DNA of the creative process, and our task in the dance is to find the discipline to become a free spirit; that is, to keep showing up past fixed notions of ourselves and let movement inform us as a vehicle to turn our life into a work of art. With practice and the willingness to dive into the unknown parts of ourselves, creativity and freedom begin to feed back as sources of inspiration and catalysts for change. Not having steps and not having any rules in the movement is regarded by one dancer as a source of wellbeing, and '*allows me to journey through a loose framework in a way that I choose because there are no steps, no rules; a container that allows me to express different aspects of how I feel; especially when I can do so freely, in the way that I choose.*' Others describe it as

> *being liberated from my obsessive need to be right. Opening to my indivisibility with the universe I can be rejected or accepted by other people, or like or dislike the music or a dozen other things and (potentially!) learn from all of them. I have been searching for this kind of dance for a long time, one that allows me to be me and fully lose myself in the dance in a beautiful and expressive way. It is really simple, the dance is purely a reflection of me, of what I express. Nothing to follow, no confining structure . . . As long as there is physical space in the room, my dance is limitless, my movements unbridled, my energy limitless.*

What is different about 5Rhythms® from other movement practices is that, although it provides a structure and 'pointers', the bottom line is that it is about listening deeply to, and being true to, one's own process—about integrity and authenticity, rather than imposing anything universally from outside oneself. As well as being an extremely effective orientation, it also deepens the trust in the 'inner guide'. A non-judgemental environment fosters free expression; a discovery of the body's own language as powerful and articulate as the mind, but free from any self-judging filters. In a dancer's words: '*Connection with the real self, a vehicle for learning who I really am, and a sanctuary from the mental busy-ness I created in response to the rest of my life.*'

One of the most distinct processes in 5Rhythms® is the exploration of different levels of relationship: dancing with oneself; dancing with another; dancing in connection to the whole group (dancing alone, in partnership and in tribal form). Much healing happens here as dancers meet their openness or resistance in relating to themselves and to others in ways that are different from, but reflective of, life off the dance floor.

COUNTER-INDICATIONS

This chapter would not be complete if we did not take into account that there are many who have tried the practice and did not experience 5Rhythms® as a practice of wellbeing. Among a myriad of other possibilities there are those who might have a history of trauma and could have a lower sensory tolerance that requires further expert support. As teachers we are aware of these dynamics in our classes and can help these dancers seek additional healing options. Each container of the practice will have its own unique structure and circumstances. Some classes and workshops may be as large as a hundred people, and it is understandable that all the needs in the group will not be met. Also, each teacher brings her or his own style and interpretation. It might be that an individual has a negative experience with one teacher, but then has a positive one with another.

CONCLUSIONS

Individually and collectively, practice of 5Rhythms® is an ever evolving process. Each time we step onto the dance floor, we step into a mystery, as we do not know exactly what will arise from our dance, what will be felt, what will need to be moved through, what insight is to be experienced. When we put ourselves in motion and start to seek space within our bodies, we can relax, find new and original energy available to us, and connect with our deep, instinctual truth. We can listen to ourselves and know what we really need, what we need to do, what we have to let go, what we can look forward to, and how to just be alive in the moment. The longer people engage in the practice, the deeper layers of being will surface. The layers may not always lead to states of bliss, peace, or happiness. As trust and willingness strengthen, perhaps we touch on old personal and ancestral traumas and are able to be with more of the difficult states of being human. As the body opens to more sensing and feeling, resilience and sensitivity grow, and the individual and collective are able to visit what often remains in the shadows. Wellbeing from this perspective is a greater understanding of what we each hold, placing it within the bigger picture. This can become personal and collective healing. How many layers one will peel away depends on the time which the individual practices and their readiness to change, let go and move towards new ways of being. All of this is in constant flux and change.

This chapter is by no means the complete vision of 5Rhythms®. It presents a theoretical flavour of the practice and how it has therapeutic effects towards some areas of wellbeing. The words on the page can never stand for the actual experience of moving through the rhythms. ▶

NOTE

1. In the 5Rhythms® cosmology laid out by Gabrielle Roth in her first book (1989), the work evolves in several levels, or maps, Waves being the physical embodiment of the practice, Heartbeat the territory of the emotions, Cycles an exploration of our life story, Mirrors working with the ego, God, Sex, and the Body to move with feminine and masculine archetypes, and the Silver Desert, where the task is to explore the power of healing.

REFERENCES

Beecher, O. (2005). *The Dance Experience and Sense of Being – Therapeutic Application of Modern Dance*, PhD thesis, University of Limerick.

Brown, K. W. and Ryan, R. M. (2003). 'The benefits of being present: Mindfulness and its role in psychological well-being', *Journal of Personality and Social Psychology*, 84(4): 822–48.

Esalen Institute (n.d.). <http://en.wikipedia.org/wiki/Esalen_Institute> (accessed 19 September 2014).

Gestalt at Esalen (2014). <http://www.esalen.org/page/gestalt-esalen> (accessed 19 September 2014).

Grey, A. (2012). 'In memory of Gabrielle Roth'. <http://alexgrey.com/gabrielle-roth/> (accessed 5 November 2012).

Juhan, A. (2003). *Open Floor: Dance, Therapy, and Transformation through the 5Rhythms®*. PhD thesis, Union Institute and University Graduate School of Interdisciplinary Arts and Science.

Kafle, N. P. (2011). 'Hermeneutic phenomenological research method simplified', *Bodhi: An Interdisciplinary Research Journal*, 5: 181–200.

Oliver, S. (2009). *Community-Based Creative Dance for Adolescents and Their Feelings of Social Wellbeing*, PhD thesis, Queen Margaret University.

Peabody, M. (2014). Interview with Mati Vargas-Gibson, 18 September.

Roth, G. (1989). *Maps to Ecstasy: Teachings of an Urban Shaman*. San Rafael, CA: New World Library.

Roth, G. (1998). *Maps to Ecstasy: The Healing Journey for the Untamed Spirit*. California, Natawraj Publishing.

Roth, G. (1999). *Sweat Your Prayers: Movement as Spiritual Practice*. Dublin: Newleaf.

Roth, G. (2009). Breath of Life Conference, video lecture, London.

Sobel, E (2009). 'The tribal embrace: On grief and vulnerability in the presence of others', *Psychology Today*, <http://www.psychologytoday.com/blog/the-99th-monkey/200909/the-tribal-embrace>

PART V

DANCE IN HEALTHCARE CONTEXTS

INTRODUCTION TO PART V

VICKY KARKOU AND SUE OLIVER

With Contributions by Chan Nga Shan and Ania Zubala

THIS last part deals with the use of dance within health care contexts including work taking place in primary care, hospitals, or, broadly speaking, work that is somehow linked with medical thinking. Perspectives challenging medical thinking are also included. References are made to dance as a form of therapy as well as an art form. In all cases, the aim remains to alleviate ill health and to strengthen wellness.

The discussion around whether or not dance can have an active contribution within a hospital context, how this may be the case, and what type of evidence is needed to demonstrate change, remains a very alive discussion in this part. In Chapter 40, Brauninger and Bacigalupe offer an interesting overview of dance movement therapy practice in European hospitals. They ask the question:

- Is dance movement therapy a viable treatment modality in health care?

We certainly join them to ask even more questions:

- What are the 'active ingredients' of the intervention?
- What are the best ways to establish effectiveness?
- Are there areas in common practice that need to be revisited, revised, and improved?
- How can health services take advantage of best practice?

In the case of Brauninger and Bacigalupe, they explore the role of dance movement psychotherapy in oncology, neurology, and geriatrics, while proposing that this intervention has a contribution to make not only to the treatment of ill health but also to prevention, in rehabilitation and in health promotion. Clinical vignettes illustrate these arguments, introducing the reader to wide clinical applications, diverse client populations, and a useful discussion about the potential input of this practice in assessment, treatment documentation, and evaluation.

Chapter 41, by Diane Amans, offers an overview of the work of dance artists in hospitals. Unlike the previous chapter, the emphasis here is on dance practice rather than therapy. Although overlaps with dance movement therapy are discussed, this chapter presents a clear argument that even within a hospital context, dance artists pursue work that remains ultimately an artistic event. The challenges of offering such work within a hospital context are presented and discussed.

In Chapter 42, Helen Payne presents her recent work on The BodyMind Approach™—a unique approach that has been developed specifically to address medically unexplained symptoms and associated issues relating to insecure attachment and alexithymia. Influenced by the practice of Authentic Movement (see online video material), The BodyMind Approach™ can be delivered by people who are specifically trained in this work. Payne argues that because it is designed for the non-psychologically minded who have a physical explanatory model for their bodily symptoms, it can be appealing to a diverse audience around the world. The chapter also discusses the role of this work within the national health system in the UK, and offers arguments for its value for people with medically unexplained symptoms. Interestingly, although Helen Payne is regarded as one of pioneers of dance movement psychotherapy in the UK, she explains that The BodyMind Approach™ is not a psychotherapeutic approach. Primitive Expression—the topic of Chapter 43, by Alexia Margariti and a team from the Psychiatric Department of the University of Athens— often occupies this territory between therapy and dance. In several European countries, Primitive Expression—a practice that began in the USA, drawing largely upon Afro-Caribbean traditions and rhythms—is often referred to as a form of therapeutic dance, and not as a form of dance therapy. In Greece, however, Primitive Expression is seen and practised as a form of psychotherapy. Furthermore, the application of this practice with psychiatric patients with psychotic and depressive disorders forms the topic of Margariti's doctoral research study. The use of data from electroencephalograms next to standardized questionnaires makes this a cutting-edge study a major contribution to the discussion around evidence. The video that accompanies this work is also worth seeing, as it is both informative as well as of high aesthetic quality.

Client populations that are regarded as readily falling under mental health, such as mothers and children, older people with dementia, and adults with depression and schizophrenia, are some of the areas of work explored by Loughlin and Hill in Australia, Punkanen et al. in Finland and Koch et al. in Germany.

Elizabeth Loughlin, for example, focuses on the liveness of the intercommunication between mother and infant, which is especially relevant when mothers are faced with postnatal depression, anxiety, or postpartum psychosis. Within an outpatient clinic and inpatient ward hospital, Loughlin describes, in Chapter 44, the aesthetic processes of dance, and claims that they contribute towards new ways of relating and improved responsiveness in the mother–child dyad. Still within the same country, but with a different client population, another dance movement therapist, Heather Hill introduces resilience and flow as two non-dementia-specific concepts with potential value towards the wellbeing of people with dementia. In Chapter 45, her exploration, which is largely phenomenological, questions not only the biomedical framework often associated with dementia, but also the concept of wellbeing itself, arguing that 'flourishing' might be an interesting and a potentially useful alternative concept.

In Chapter 46, Punkanen et al., of the University of Jyväskylä, Finland, address the topic of depression using motion capture technologies that accurately record the movement of a group of patients with depression and a group of people without depression. The findings revisit well-known assumptions about the connections between motion and emotion (see Chapter 26), and offer an evidence-based description of some movement characteristics of patients with depression. These exciting findings are made even clearer through video clips from motion-captured movement. Associated studies are also presented that look quantitatively at the effectiveness of dance movement therapy for this population, while following the journey of one participant qualitatively—both hard evidence and depth are demonstrated by this team.

Similarly, at the University of Heidelberg, the research team called German National Project Body Language of Movement and Dance, focus some of their work on mirroring. They explored mirroring philosophically, and through a phenomenological perspective in particular, but also engaged in exploring the experience and interaction skills of patients with schizophrenia in a psychiatric hospital setting and the impact of this work on body awareness, empathy, social skills, and an overall sense of wellbeing.

Furthermore, medical dance movement therapy is introduced—a term coined by Goodill (2005) in the USA to refer to both a particular approach to dance movement therapy as well as the use of this discipline within hospitals to address client populations such as cancer and cardiac rehabilitation. Two chapters in this part address exactly this, working with women recovering from breast cancer—Chapter 48 by Serlin et al.—and cardiac heart disease—Chapter 49 by Mchitarian et al. Serlin et al. attempt to define medical dance/movement therapy within the context of working with women with breast cancer as 'an intervention that, through a safe and supportive environment that encourages creativity, can help develop psycho, social, and spiritual dimensions of women's lives at a time when their life-trajectory has been interrupted.' The extensive literature review on the topic, accompanied by a video from work completed on this topic in the past, are two of the strengths of this contribution.

The part finishes with Chapter 49 by Mchitarian et al., with two studies in cardiac rehabilitation: one in Cyprus and the other in the UK, and one in a tertiary hospital and the other in a rehabilitation centre. The team—nurses, doctors and dance movement psychotherapists—argue that findings from these two pilot studies are promising, and although they acknowledge the methodological limitations and small scale of the research, they argue that dance movement psychotherapy has a lot to offer to this relatively new area of work.

In most of the chapters in this part, wellbeing is perceived holistically, especially as a counterbalance to the pure and physical perceptions adopted in medical contexts. Even in medical dance movement psycho/therapy presented in Chapter 48 by Serlin et al. and Chapter 49 by Mchitarian et al., holistic perceptions of wellbeing are adopted and highly valued. Interestingly, phenomenology (Hill; Koch et al.), existentialism (Mchitarian et al.), and spirituality (Serlin et al.) become important additions to the prevailing medical thinking for which health contexts are known. Such alternative approaches to health become particularly relevant to patients who have been threatened or are faced with the end of their life. It is possible that dance-based therapeutic interventions that offer opportunities for transcendental experiences allow one's journey towards the end to become bearable and meaningful, and, some argue, if appropriately used, may contribute to a sense of spiritual healing.

In this part we also see that although dance-based work offers alternative options to traditional approaches to health, most authors engage with definitions of evidence as understood through a medical/health perspective and the hierarchy of evidence in particular (NICE 2004). Research designs adopted here involve randomized controlled trials, controlled trials, or pre- and post-testing. New technologies are used, such as motion capture and EEG. Within these, quantitative evidence of improved mental health and quality of life are discussed, while patients' views of the process and outcomes from a qualitative perspective are highlighted.

The use of video material in a number of the chapters in this part is also interesting. Payne, Margariti et al., Punkanen et al., and Serlin et al. all submit videos that offer snapshots of the work involved in training and in clinical practice. All manage to address ethical risk by focusing either on the work of trainers, hiring actors/actresses to role play, or using technology to eliminate facial recognition, and ensuring that in all cases full consent is given.

A further addition to the literature may also come from the use of dance as art within such health/medical contexts. The work completed by Shan Nga Chan and Ania Zubala is worthy of our attention as an interesting 'other' perspective. Chan, during her studies as a dance movement psychotherapist in a UK higher-education institution, where she was supervised by Zubala, looked at her work with clients with schizophrenia within a hospital context. Through a heuristic process (Moustakas 1990), by which she focused on her own somatic responses to the work, she engaged in understanding both the clients and the work they did together. The outcome of this process took the shape of a video piece that is available with the online version of this book (see Video V.a on the Companion Website ⊙). They write about this work:

> Interconnection of the body and the mind and a belief in the healing qualities of dance lie at the very basis of dance movement psychotherapy—a form of therapy in which engagement in movement and formation of a therapeutic relationship have a potential to enhance the wellbeing of clients, regardless of their underlying condition. The study involves a personal account of a researcher and a dance movement psychotherapist, whose heuristic exploration led her to intentionally embody symbolic movement from her work with patients. People with symptoms of schizophrenia are likely to experience hallucinations or delusional thoughts. These thoughts, often warned by the medical profession to not indulge in, find their way into movement expressions through symbols and metaphors, and may act as an important conduit of emotional material.
>
> In this heuristic study, the therapist/researcher committed to exploring symbols and metaphors and the impact these had on her own body, acknowledging rather than negating them as important information shared by the patients. Data collected in the form of somatic responses to symbolic movement material within sessions were processed through ongoing reflection, as suggested by the heuristic methodology adopted. Meaning was attached to these personal body-based responses, followed by self-reflection on the process as a whole. The findings were brought together into a final choreographic video piece. During the creation of the work, the residue from symbolic information shared by patients within the confidential space of therapy became reactivated and rediscovered by the therapist/researcher. The experiences of patients became her experience, at times unsettling and disjointed. And her body, the body of the therapist and researcher, became the body of the dance artist who carried and shared affective information about the therapeutic process. All non-verbally.

We think this piece is powerful.

REFERENCES

Goodill, S. W. (2005). *An Introduction to Medical Dance/Movement Therapy*. Philadelphia, PA: Jessica Kingsley.

Moustakas, C. (1990). *Heuristic Research: Design, Methodology and Applications*. Thousand Oaks, CA: Sage.

NICE (2004). *Guideline Development Methods: Information for National Collaborating Centres and Guideline Developers*. London: National Institute for Clinical Excellence.

....

CHAPTER 40

DANCE MOVEMENT THERAPY IN HEALTHCARE

Should We Dance Across the Floor of the Ward?

....

IRIS BRÄUNINGER AND GONZALO BACIGALUPE

INTRODUCTION

DANCE is a universal ritual with a long history as a healing form. In healthcare, beginning in the 1940s, dance movement therapy (DMT) took hold in psychiatry, and began entering into fields such as geriatrics, neurology, oncology, pain and palliative care, and psychosomatics. In this chapter we explore the role of DMT (or dance therapy as otherwise known) and its current healthcare assessment and intervention applications in the preventive, curative, rehabilitative, and promotional modalities. We highlight the state of the art in empirical research and its application, with illustrations drawn from case examples, to a wide range of populations.

Should we dance across the ward floor? Commonly, people who dance do experience feelings of joy and satisfaction during and after moving. Research shows that quality of life and stress management improves on the short term and long term after participating in DMT (Bräuninger 2006, 2012a, 2012b), and dancing together disrupts isolation (Hill 2009), connects people (Hamill et al. 2011; Harris 2007), and fosters spirituality (Bräuninger 2012b). Moreover, DMT addresses the person in a holistic way in a healthcare environment that remains rooted within a deficit-oriented philosophy. Dance therapists are in a privileged position to work holistically (addressing mind, body, and spirit), and are able to work both in primary and secondary healthcare. Primary healthcare provides essential care universally accessible to all people in the community, instilling full empowerment, autonomy, and self-determination at low cost. Its ultimate goal is better health for all (WHO 2012). Secondary-level facilities concentrate on more complex services provided by medical and allied health professional specialists (WHO 2007).

'Health is a state of complete physical, mental, and social wellbeing and not merely the absence of disease or infirmity' (WHO 1946). Huber et al. (2011) have recently challenged the WHO's focus on complete wellbeing. As chronic diseases become mainstream worldwide, we need to reformulate the definition of health to emphasize the 'ability to adapt and self manage in the face of social, physical, and emotional challenges' (Huber et al. 2011: 1).

DMT can promote both; it can support adaptation and encourage self-management to a changing environment:

> The therapist encourages development and integration of new adaptive movement patterns through acknowledging and evaluating clients' movements, while supporting the emotional states that might arise with such changes. (European Association Dance Movement Therapy 2012)

Our analysis of the role of DMT in healthcare—preventive, curative, rehabilitative, and promotional—includes a review of its key characteristics, research findings, applications, and case vignettes drawn from the first author's practice. Evidence-based practices are also discussed. Finally, we evaluate DMT's potential in healthcare services.

Dance Movement Therapy in Healthcare

DMT in healthcare aims to improve clients' wellbeing and strengthen their capacity to adapt and self-manage. Dance therapists assume that mind, body, emotions, and relationships are integrated and body language and movement reflect internal processes and provide the means of assessment and the mode of intervention (European Association Dance Movement Therapy 2012). With a growing number of therapists worldwide, it has the potential to become mainstream in healthcare (Goodill 2010; Quiroga Murcia and Kreutz 2012). The increasing interest in DMT is also reflected in evidence provided by research: The meta-analysis by Koch et al. (2014) examined the effectiveness of DMT and dance on health-related psychological problems. The analysis included twenty-three primary intervention studies ($N = 1,078$) that had at least a control group design with pre- and post-test. Variables on quality of life, body image, and wellbeing, and on depression, anxiety, and interpersonal competence were analysed. Results suggest that DMT and dance have a positive impact on quality of life, subjective well-being, mood, affect, and body image, and on the reduction of depression and anxiety.

A Cochrane protocol aims to assess the effects of DMT for depression compared with no treatment (waiting list), standard care in both child and adult populations, other psychological interventions, pharmacological interventions, other physical interventions, and different forms of DMT (Meekums et al. 2012). A scoping review on the effectiveness of DMT, dance, and arts therapies on depression included studies that fulfilled at least one inclusion criterion (published or non-published study, (quasi-)experimental design) (Mala et al. 2012). Out of nine studies, six followed a randomized controlled trial design, and three a non-randomized design. The authors concluded that DMT and related interventions were effective in the treatment of depression, and recommended a systematic review of DMT on depression.

One randomized control trial confirmed its effectiveness on modulating concentrations of serotonin and dopamine, and in improving psychological distress in middle-school seniors with mild depression (Jeong et al. 2005). Another randomized control trial showed that DMT decreased the depression level in university students (Akandere and Demir 2011). An exploratory randomized controlled trial of Body Psychotherapy for twenty-one patients with chronic depression showed that the depressive symptom scores reduced significantly in the Body Psychotherapy group after twenty sessions over a ten-week period compared to the control group (Röhricht et al. 2013). Heimbeck and Hölter's (2011) comparison of unspecific versus disorder-orientated movement therapy demonstrated that both interventions increased body awareness and decreased depression in the short and long term, with the assumption that unspecific interventions are slightly more successful. Another study of psychiatric patients with depression revealed that the DMT group intervention showed significantly more vitality and less depression after the intervention compared to the music and ergometer control group intervention (Koch et al. 2007).

Ren and Xia (2013) updated an earlier review by Xia and Grant (2009) on dance therapy in schizophrenia in their systematic Cochrane review and again included the randomized controlled trial by Röhricht and Priebe (2006) in the analysis of systematic reviews, since no recent studies had been published in the meantime on the effectiveness of DMT in schizophrenia. The RCT by Röhricht and Priebe (2006) compared the effectiveness of body-oriented psychotherapy and related approaches to the negative symptoms of schizophrenia with standard care or other psychosocial interventions. Patients attending body-oriented psychotherapy for twenty sessions over ten weeks showed significantly lower negative symptom scores after treatment and during the four-month follow-up compared to the control group (supportive counselling). Treatment satisfaction and ratings of the therapeutic relationship were similar in both groups. Ren and Xia (2013) concluded that due to the small number of cases there was no evidence for or against the effectiveness of dance therapy in schizophrenia, and recommended further research on dance therapeutic efficacy in schizophrenia, especially in patients with negative symptoms.

Two randomized control trials demonstrated significant improvement in the DMT groups in the quality of life for breast cancer survivors (Sandel et al. 2005), in body symptoms such as vigour, fatigue, and somatization, and a minimal improvement in mood, distress, body image, and self-esteem (Dibbell-Hope 2000). A randomized control trial showed that ten sessions of DMT group intervention significantly reduced stress and improved stress management (Bräuninger 2012a) and quality of life (Bräuninger 2012b) in the short term and long term.

Cognitive functioning in elderly patients with moderate to severe dementia (Hamill et al. 2011; Van de Winckel et al. 2003) and late-stage Alzheimer's disease (Dayanim 2009) improved significantly through DMT, as well as participants' general wellbeing and mood, and communication with others (Hamill et al. 2011). A Cochrane protocol outlined criteria for considering studies for a review on DMT for dementia (Karkou and Meekums 2014). The review, which will include published or unpublished randomized controlled trials, will evaluate the effects of DMT on the behavioural, social, cognitive, and emotional problems of people with dementia. The effects will be compared to no treatment (waiting list), standard care, other treatment, and different DMT approaches. An intervention study in women with chronic fatigue syndrome revealed that physical and psychological wellbeing improved in women after the four-month DMT programme (Blázquez et al. 2010). In sum, reviews, randomized control trials, and intervention studies suggest that DMT is effective in improving health and wellbeing, and improvements last over time.

DMT is offered for handling anxiety and supporting relaxation in pain, preparing patients for procedures, including family members in care, and supporting end-of-life-care and clinical staff, for example, in burnout prevention (Goodill 2010; 2005). Dance movement therapists accompany clients in creating their personal choreographic story—a process that supports an integrated sense of identity. Spontaneous and unconscious movements are an expression of the inner world of the mover. Each movement reflects psychological and relational ways of being and communicating with the environment.

The research evidence therefore indicates that DMT is effective in improving health, quality of life, and wellbeing, and reduces symptoms, in particular in the cases of depression, dementia, stress, cancer, and chronic fatigue syndrome. In the next section we explore how DMT works in preventive, curative, rehabilitative, and promotional healthcare, and present assessment and intervention tools.

Preventive Dance Movement Therapy

Preventive DMT intends to identify people at risk. It deals with healthy or non-diagnosed individuals, and differs from other services because it uses movement analysis as a diagnostic tool and body, and as a protective intervention against the disease. Its treatment goals are to foster reparative capacities, coping mechanisms, recovery, and resilience. It is applied in violence prevention and empowerment, physical activity, healthy diet, mental health, addictive behaviour, and dementia prevention.

DMT aggression prevention programmes have been installed in various settings. The PEACE programme directed at elementary-school children aimed at reducing aggressive behaviour and bullying (Koshland et al. 2004), and the Disarming the Playground programme with secondary-school children has been successful in decreasing incidences of aggression and increasing levels of empathy (Kornblum 2002; Hervey and Kornblum 2006). The Dinka Initiative to Empower and Restore (DIER) offered primary prevention for African refugee adolescent torture survivors living in the United States that included a set of traditional dancing and drumming events, strengthened group cohesion, and reinforced preventive and reparative capacities and traditional coping mechanisms (Harris 2007). Another programme with former child combatant adolescents in a post-war zone in Sierra Leone taught skills to reduce hyper-arousal, manage difficult emotions, and integrate extreme traumatic histories through improvisational dancing and revitalizing psychosocial support (Harris 2007). Beyond Words in Israel (Gordon-Giles and Zidan 2009) integrated therapeutic movement work into an education programme for Arab and Jewish kindergarten teachers working with young children to promote tolerance, prevent aggression, empower women, and enhance empathy. Research revealed significant changes in attitudes towards sex roles as a result of participating in the programme (Gordon-Giles 2011).[1]

Dementia is another important area of preventive DMT. Dementia is a chronic degenerative illness with a prevalence growing fast and rapidly worldwide (Alzheimer Europe 2009); it is a key health issue and a major cause of disability in people aged over 60. Dancing is identified as one of several protective factors and as an effective prevention against dementia in a five-year follow-up study on leisure activities and the risk of dementia (Verghese et al. 2003). In a randomized control study, dancing was shown to improve cognitive functioning in those with moderate to severe dementia, compared to those who participated in talking therapies (Van de Winckel et al. 2003). A movement programme significantly decreased aphasia and/or agnosia in late-stage Alzheimer disease patients in the pre-test/post-test comparison (Dayanim 2009). DMT intervention exerted favourable effects on language abilities in patients with moderate to severe Alzheimer's disease (Hokkanen et al. 2008), thereby preventing further decrease in cognitive and self-care abilities.

DMT also strengthens coping mechanisms and resilience in clients with eating disorders (Kleinman 2009), and promotes awareness for body sensations and emotional needs (Pratt 2004). A DMT group for obese women with emotional eating was found to be more successful in increasing body-image satisfaction and decreasing psychological and body-image distress than exercise or a non-exercise alternatives (Vaverniece et al. 2012). The focus on tension and relaxation as a DMT intervention was found effective in improving body image, stress management, and self-awareness in clients with eating disorders (DuBose 2001). DMT should become a standard treatment when working on issues related to eating disorders, nutrition, and diet.

DMT includes traditional activities with therapeutic components in violence prevention, and empowerment work with children war refugees (Bräuninger 2009; Harris 2007). It combines cross-cultural notions with interventions that are 'congruent with alleged not dividing of psyche and soma in non-Western countries' (Jordans et al.

2009: 11)—an integration that it is especially valuable when working with refugees and torture survivors (Callaghan 1998; Gray 2001; Koch and Weidinger-von der Recke 2009; van Keuk 2006). Moreover, talking therapy is often uncommon in many countries. Working with other venues of expression, therefore, can be less frightening and more acceptable, as it is associated with sports, celebrations, and joyful events (Callaghan 1998), as the following case vignette demonstrates.

Similar to two other children in a primary school in London, a third boy also caught the attention of the dance therapist because of his held upper posture (Bräuninger 2009). Two session excerpts with Richard (pseudonym)—an eleven-year old boy from Afghanistan—illustrates the DMT. His chest was also extremely rigid, bound and held in a convex way with shoulders pulled back, reminiscent of a shield. Could the child's posture be a reaction to extreme stressful events? The class teachers confirmed that Richard, like the other two children, had experienced war and were recent refugee arrivals in the host country. Richard's aggressive acting-out in the classroom led to his referral for DMT. He reported in one of the first sessions that his best friend had been killed during the war, and that people had told him to be thankful for being alive. In the fifth session, he changed a balloon game suddenly into a 'sword fight', with the balloons representing swords. During the fight, Richard expressed that he would feel tired, but had to continue fighting despite his injuries and pain. His stance was wide, front leg bent, shoulders pulled back, and his chest extremely bound in an open, arched and convex position. Only when he pretended to get 'an arm cut off' and 'bowels exposed' did he give up his held upper-body posture and bend over in pain. In the eighth session he talked about two English children who had recently been killed by a bomb. 'Why do they kill all these children?' he asked. The sword fight theme re-emerged in that session as a fight for justice, revenge—'You have killed my brother/sister'—and punishment—'I am cutting off your head'. His bound chest melted briefly into a curved, concave shape representing the outcome of symbolic injuries, but he immediately lengthened his spine again, ready to fight and defend himself bravely. During the DMT session, Richard expressed feelings of threat, loss, anger, and sadness, shared his traumatic experiences, and created a solution—'fight for justice'—while he kept control of the pace, direction, and process. His held upper-body posture served as a protective shield against overwhelming feelings and enabled him to cope with stressful memories in the present.

The case of Richard illustrates how the use of movement analysis served as a specific DMT diagnostic tool to identify children at risk. The focus on movement, dance, and creative expression may enable access to their emotional needs.

Research suggesting that DMT prevents the onset of aggression in war-traumatized children is confirmed in Richard's case. Research also suggests that DMT protects against the onset of dementia and stabilizes cognitive functions in secondary dementia and memory recall of patients with late-stage Alzheimer's disease. It further strengthens the coping mechanism against eating disorders. Hence, DMT protects against disease or slows its progression, and reinforces preventive capacities and resilience.

CURATIVE AND REHABILITATIVE DANCE MOVEMENT THERAPY

The improvement of symptoms and cure of a patient's problems or disease are at the core of DMT. Rehabilitative DMT is the follow-up care aiming at strengthening clients' satisfaction towards their overall treatment and improvement of quality of life. DMT is more effective in the treatment for depression (Heimbeck and Hölter 2011; Koch et al. 2007). As mentioned previously, a randomized control trial showed that body-oriented psychotherapy significantly reduced negative symptoms in schizophrenia, compared to group supportive counselling plus standard care intervention (Röhricht and Priebe 2006). Conversely, a systematic literature review on DMT for schizophrenia revealed that results were inconclusive due to the lack of randomized single blind studies, and no evidence exists to support or refute its effectiveness (Ren and Xia 2013; Xia and Grant 2009). However, the National Institute for Health and Clinical Excellence (NICE) in the United Kingdom recommends DMT as a core intervention in the treatment of schizophrenia in adults in primary and secondary care, particularly in people with negative symptoms (NICE 2009). Results of a clinical DMT study showed in the pre-test/post-test comparison an increase in happiness and in alpha EEG activity in psychotic patients' awake resting state (Margariti et al. 2012).

Another systematic literature review (Bradt et al. 2011) and two outcome studies with a pre-test/post-test design (Ho 2005; Mannheim and Weis 2006) showed that DMT with cancer patients played an important role in the improvement of quality of life (Bradt et al. 2011; Mannheim and Weis 2006). Furthermore, DMT would improve self-image and reduce anxiety, depression (Mannheim and Weis 2006), fatigue (Bradt et al. 2011), and stress (Ho 2005). DMT may also feel patients psychologically at ease in the healthcare setting (Aktas and Ogce 2005; Ho 2005). Findings are not conclusive regarding mood, distress, and mental health (Bradt et al. 2011). In palliative care, DMT could expand problem-solving skills in participants (Selman et al. 2012).

DMT can enable participants to relate to others and to communicate confusing and scary experiences, thereby being seen and accepted by others (Sandel et al. 1993), which is of particular importance in psychiatry. DMT has been utilized in the treatment of various disorders: depression (Heimbeck and Hölter 2011; Koch et al. 2007; Pylvänäinen 2010), anxiety (Bräuninger 2000), psychosis (Margariti et al. 2012), schizophrenia (Röhricht and Priebe 2006; Ren and Xia 2013; Xia and Grant 2009), addictions (Bräuninger 2000), and trauma (Eberhard-Kaechele 2012; Koch and Harvey 2012; van Keuk 2006). DMT can be utilized at every stage of illness; for example, with a disorganized, aggressive, acute psychotic patient on the ward. The therapist approaches the client by adapting his own body language to the needs of the client, takes on the breathing rhythm, and builds up a mutual, embodied empathetic relationship that has a soothing and calming effect. The sessions can continue on the ward or in the therapy room.

Research has revealed that DMT improved both physical and psychological wellbeing in patients with fibromyalgia (Bojner Horwitz et al. 2003) and chronic fatigue syndrome

(Blázquez et al. 2010). In neurology, DMT is conducted to rehabilitate patients with brain trauma (Berrol 2009; Bräuninger and Züger 2007), and in geriatrics, in the case of dementia (Hill 2009). Treatment goals are to reduce depressive symptoms and increase self-efficacy and self-image (Bräuninger and Züger 2007). A study of older adults with sustained neurological insult confirmed that DMT improved cognitive performance, social interaction, and physical wellbeing (Berrol et al. 1997).

The following case vignette illustrates the curative and rehabilitative capacity of DMT in a depressed client who had been an inpatient in a psychiatric clinic.

Mr Stuck—a divorced man whose son regularly visited him and who had been downgraded at his working place—was severely depressed and presented suicidal ideas. At the beginning of a course of twelve DMT sessions over two months, he mentioned that he had lost all sense of self-worth and interest and did not have any energy to get up in the morning or look after his son. He only sat on the floor without moving. Movement qualities were predominantly in passive, non-animated neutral weight, while he reported in a monotonous voice that he had to change his apartment, which further stressed him. Treatment goals were to improve his stress management capacities and stabilize him. After some relaxation and breathing exercises at the beginning of sessions, guided imagery was introduced. Mr Stuck was invited to actively imagine his old apartment as a way of appreciating the past and present. Embodied exercises helped him to visualize and feel the new apartment. He started to outline the new apartment's walls with ropes on the therapy floor, and to walk along them and explore the space. With a direct hand gesture he imaginatively opened a door and invited his son in. As the process unfolded, Mr Stuck's role changed from a passive–receptive non-mover to an upright standing person, better grounded on the floor in the vertical plane. His movements became more activated and direct, and he seemed more self-confident and emotionally stable. At the end of the treatment he reported that his despair had largely vanished, that his interest in his son and in other contacts had returned, and that he would be able to plan effectively.

As shown in Mr Stuck's example, kinaesthetic enacting and experiencing can clarify and provide solutions, because 'cognition is embodied action' (Koch and Fischman 2011: 63). It further illustrates how curative and rehabilitative DMT helps to reduce symptoms and improve self-efficacy, self-image, cognitive functioning, social interaction, and physical and psychological wellbeing.

Promotional Dance Movement Therapy

Promotional DMT aims to improve health and resilience, and promotes physical, psychological, and spiritual wellbeing. It is participatory, interdisciplinary, and integrative. Interventions promote self-regulated health behaviour and a healthy lifestyle in order to maintain and improve health (Chakarova and Gatev 2010). It is provided in private practice, as well as in schools, hospitals, communities, and workplaces on an individual, group, organizational, and public health level.

Research overlaps with other healthcare fields. Previously mentioned positive DMT results for depression with school pupils and university students also apply in the field of promotional DMT (Akandere and Demir 2011; Jeong et al. 2005). DMT reduces psychological distress and improves stress management, quality of life, physical and emotional wellbeing, and social interaction (Bräuninger 2006, 2012a, 2012b). Parkinson's disease patients improved on all measures of balance, falls, and gait through the therapeutic use of tango dance, but not through exercise interventions (Earhard 2009; Hackney et al. 2007). Ballroom dance with the elderly builds a culture of inclusion that may improve understanding and acceptance among participants and increase quality of life (Lima and Pedreira Vieira 2007). A systematic review of DMT on therapeutic ballroom dances intervention revealed that DMT increased quality of life in patients with breast cancer and reduced psychological distress in patients with depression. It further showed that tango dance improved coordination and balance in patients with Parkinson's disease and heart failure (Kiepe et al. 2012). An intervention study on a DMT programme with pre-testing and post-testing revealed that body image and psychosocial aspects improved in obese patients ($N = 18$) after a thirty-six-week programme (Muller-Pinget et al. 2012).

Promotional DMT is on the rise: 40% of dance movement therapists in the UK work in an educational setting in promotional mental healthcare (Karkou et al. 2010). 'One great advantage of providing DMT in the school is that for many children it is their only access to therapy' (Kornblum and Lending Halsten 2006, p. 146). As children express themselves through their movement and bodies, the integration of DMT in the pre-school (Thom 2010) and school curriculum (Karkou et al. 2010) contributes to address children's socioemotional development and strengthens their emotional, social, and cognitive self. Furthermore, DMT raises awareness amongst teaching staff on children's mental health issues (Karkou et al. 2010).

In sum, promotional DMT can be successfully integrated in schools to address children's needs on all levels. Creative expression in DMT promotes self-awareness, self-reflection, wellness, and relaxation (Goodill 2010), and strengthens physical, psychological, and spiritual wellbeing and health in patients with cancer, depression, heart failure, obesity, and Parkinson's disease. Promotional dance therapy is on the rise, and its full potential unfolds as more therapists develop new programmes. Besides healthcare services, a potential area for DMT to expand may be in the community in the form of mental health promotion.

Dance Movement Therapy Assessment, Treatment Documentation, and Evaluation

DMT assessment integrates the resource-oriented cognitive process of movement analysis as in diagnosing and the embodied empathetic understanding of a person's movement profile through the therapist—a synthesis unique to DMT. Documentation records the client's health status at the beginning, the development and changes during the intervention, and the wellbeing at the end, and it can be process-goal, resource-goal, and/or treatment-goal oriented. Therapists usually develop their distinctive DMT treatment protocols and adapt them to the documentation system of the health institution. The DMT movement profile assessment focuses on phenomenological aspects of the client's movement repertoire and resources. Therapists additionally apply validated and reliable standardized psychological questionnaires to evaluate treatment outcomes.

DMT assessments document healthy and dysfunctional movement patterns in clients, of which the most common are Effort-Shape Analysis (Laban 1988; Lamb 1965), mostly used in Europe, and its offspring, Laban Movement Analysis (LMA) (Bartenieff and Lewis 1980), mainly used in the United States. A complex instrument for describing, assessing, and interpreting non-verbal behaviour and conducting research is the Kestenberg Movement Profile (KMP), which integrates principles from Effort-Shape Analysis with a developmentally based outline (Kestenberg-Amighi et al. 1999). The Movement Psychodiagnostic Inventory (MPI) documents movement patterns with diagnostic potential and is also Laban-based (Cruz 2009; Davis et al. 2007). The reliability (Cruz and Koch 2004) of Effort-Shape Analysis has recently been confirmed in a study on movement characteristics associated with positive and negative emotions experienced during walking, where it was more sensitive to differentiate emotions than the kinaematic assessment (Gross et al. 2012). This result is significant, considering that the first client contact often includes movement observation and analysis.

Movement analysis also assesses emotional wellbeing and contributes to the diagnostic process, especially when clients show reduced mobility and inhibition in verbally expressing feelings, thoughts, and inner states. Complex assessment systems should show good inter-rater reliability, and this has been partly confirmed for some KMP diagrams (Koch 1999) and the MPI, which has been able to distinguish personality disorders from those within the schizophrenia spectrum disorders (Cruz 2009).

DMT clinicians complete movement-coding sheets (Davis et al. 2007) and documentation reports. The majority of therapists use Laban-based DMT assessment tools (Cruz 2006; Powell 2008). The highly individualized practice and lack of standardized assessment procedures, however, pose the danger of generating a certain vagueness, which makes it difficult for DMT to be recognized in its full potential. And yet efforts are intensified to develop standardized DMT research tools. The movement diagnostic test, with scales for diagnosis and therapy evaluation in DMT, has been applied for use in psychosomatics (Lausberg 1997). Dance Movement Assessment (DMA) is another movement test consisting of five standardized movement exercises. It can be applied easily as a pre-test and post-test treatment evaluation in neurology, psychiatry, psychosomatics, psychotherapy, somatic medicine, and so on (Bräuninger and Züger 2014; Bräuninger and Züger 2007). Based on DMA, an additional version is currently being developed as pre-therapeutic assessment for people with empathy dysfunction, as in the autism spectrum (Behrends et al. 2012).

This section presents examples of DMT tools. Dance therapists apply movement analysis and observation tools that assess, evaluate, and report movement patterns while focusing on clients' movement resources. The necessity to become more visible as a profession has stimulated preliminary investigations that provide standardized tools for movement assessments (Bräuninger and Züger 2014; Bräuninger and Züger 2007; Lausberg 1997). DMT measures show validity (Cruz 2009) and reliability (Gross et al. 2012; Koch 1999). Still, the field needs standardized DMT tools that are more time-saving, integrate a qualitative view of the individual, and show reliability and validity.

Conclusion

This chapter focuses on the application of DMT in healthcare. It presents the main characteristics and research results, and provides an overview with some case vignettes—how DMT is applied as preventive, curative, rehabilitative, and promotional therapy. The most relevant applications underline DMT's preventive role to address violence, aggression, and chronic illnesses. These results are of particular importance, as violence and aggression in minors and chronic illnesses in the adult population are on the rise. DMT raises the awareness in the interdisciplinary team towards children's needs, and is an important intervention when searching for new strategies to prevent violence in the playground, school, and neighbourhood communities. The case of Richard's expression of aggression suggests some venues in which DMT could be particularly meaningful in addressing the prevention of violent behaviour. DMT seems to protect against the onset of dementia, stabilizes cognitive functions in dementia and memory recall in patients with late-stage Alzheimer's disease, and strengthens resilience against eating disorders. If the quality of life and health status of an increasingly larger elderly population can be ameliorated through DMT, the value of an expressive intervention in preventing and/or delaying the onset of dementia could increase. Healthcare policies, therefore, could be much more supportive of having DMT be as a cornerstone of the ward floor, making the ward floor a site for effective prevention and treatment.

What are the implications for DMT's future? The cost of caring for chronic illness are becoming a substantial burden, and the need for holistic low cost treatments are indispensable. The role of DMT could be extensive in providing effective care for patients in need, while also reducing the burden on society. The types of illness that affect more people are areas where research has proven DMT's highest success. It is in the case of anxiety, dementia, depression, and cancer treatment where the evidence is strong for the application of DMT that coincide with the accelerated reversal of prevalence of chronic versus acute illness. This is an epidemiological shift that includes a larger life expectancy. In Europe, the number of people with dementia is expected to increase from about 10 million today to about 14 million in 2030, and the budget in healthcare would increase by about 43% between 2008 and 2030 (Alzheimer Europe 2009) to keep pace with the demographic changes. Other chronic illnesses are also part of this equation.

Depression is the leading cause of years lost due to disability, with a 50% higher risk factor for women (WHO 2009). Cancer also becomes commonplace, with 3.2 million Europeans diagnosed with cancer every year. In 2006 the number of new cases was about 2.3 million, with more than 1 million deaths due to cancer in the former EU25 (European Commission 2012). The role of DMT in anxiety, depression, dementia, and cancer treatment should therefore expand and be intensified because of DMT's strong evidence of efficacy in these fields.

It is of substantial benefit that preventive, curative, rehabilitative, and promotional DMT appears to be more effective in reducing symptoms and increasing cognitive performance, empathy, physical and psychological wellbeing, self-efficacy, self image, social interaction, and tolerance in complex illnesses such as cancer, cardiovascular disorders, chronic fatigue syndrome, dementia, depression, Parkinson's disease, post-traumatic stress disorders, schizophrenia, and stress. Moreover, through DMT, patients may experience hope, joy, and self-worth. This is crucial when aiming to achieve patients' satisfaction and cooperation in the overall treatment goal, and to improve quality of life and restore a sense of wholeness.

So far, DMT has been applied marginally in somatic medicine. Integrating DMT as a treatment has great potential, as movement is known to be one of the most important factors in preventing cardiovascular diseases (Krebsinformationsdienst 2012), which cause the highest overall cost of treatment and remain the leading cause of death in men and women, and 'often lead to a premature death under age 70 in a significant loss of (potential) years of life' (Gesundheitsberichterstattung des Bundes 2012). DMT could be applied on all levels: as a movement-based primary and secondary prevention to foster recovery, and as a curative and rehabilitative intervention to strengthen the physical health. Violence prevention programmes have been successful, and could be introduced more widely and further developed in pre-schools, schools, and leisure facilities. Because DMT can promote self-regulated health behaviour and a healthy lifestyle in patients in order to maintain and improve one's health in the long run, it may also have an important role in public health in schools. Research that examines effectiveness should evaluate systematically the outcomes associated with these interventions.

DMT can therefore play a much more significant role in healthcare and in addressing core societal challenges such as the rise of chronic diseases. It may be that DMT is seen as an alternative in the present healthcare environment. The question is, therefore, not whether we can dance across the ward floor, but whether we can afford not to. In other words, mainstreaming DMT could contribute to resolving some of the daunting problems the healthcare system already has, and to meaningfully and holistically address the needs of the wave of patients who are living longer, want to live productive lives while taking care of their chronic illness, and are not able to afford expensive medical procedures. DMT contributes to a redefinition of health from cure to care, a movement that requires strengthening clients' resources and coping mechanisms, and fostering physical activities in a supportive social context. The ability to adapt and face social, physical, and emotional challenges is, we strongly believe, best achieved through an expressive medium such as DMT.

NOTE

1. The programme continues with Arabic, Jewish, and Palestinian women: http://www.beyon-dwords.org.il

REFERENCES

Akandere, M. and Demir, B. (2011). 'The effect of dance over depression', *Collegium Antropologicum*, 35: 651–6.

Aktas, G. and Ogce, F. (2005). 'Dance as a therapy for cancer prevention', *Asian Pacific Journal of Cancer Prevention*, 6: 408–11.

Alzheimer Europe (2009). 'Cost of illness and burden of dementia in Europe: Prognosis to 2030.' <http://www.alzheimer-europe.org/%20%20%20%20EN/Research/European-Collaboration-on-Dementia/Cost-of-dementia/Prognosis-to-2030> (accessed 20 October 2014).

Bartenieff, I., and Lewis, D. (1980). *Body Movement: Coping with the Environment*. New York, NY: Gordon and Breach Science.

Behrends, A., Müller, S., and Dziobek, I. (2012). 'Moving in and out of synchrony: A concept for a new intervention fostering empathy through interactional movement and dance', *The Arts in Psychotherapy*, 39: 107–16. doi:10.1016/j.aip.2012.02.003

Berrol, C. F. (2009). 'Dance/movement therapy and acquired brain trauma rehabilitation', in S. Chaiklin and H. Wengrower (eds.), *The Art and Science of Dance/Movement Therapy: Life is Dance*. New York, NY: Routledge, pp. 195–216.

Berrol, F., Ooi, W. L., and Katz, S. (1997). 'Dance/movement therapy with older adults who have sustained neurological insult: A demonstration project', *American Journal of Dance Therapy*, 19: 135–60. doi:10.1023/A:1022316102961

Blázquez, A., Guillamó, E., and Javierre, C. (2010). 'Preliminary experience with dance movement therapy in patients with chronic fatigue syndrome', *The Arts in Psychotherapy*, 37: 285–92. doi:10.1016/j.aip.2010.05.003

Bojner Horwitz, E., Theorell, T., and Anderberg, U. M. (2003). 'Dance/movement therapy and changes in stress-related hormones: A study of fibromyalgia patients with video-interpretation', *The Arts in Psychotherapy*, 30: 255–64. doi:10.1016/j.aip.2003.07.001

Bradt, J., Goodill, S., Dileo, C. (2011), 'Dance/movement therapy for improving psychological and physical outcomes in cancer patients', *Cochrane Database of Systematic Reviews Online*, 10, Cd007103. doi:10.1002/14651858.CD007103.pub2

Bräuninger, I (2000). 'Tanztherapie mit Menschen in der zweiten Lebenshälfte: Möglichkeiten der Angst- und Suchtbewältigung [Dance therapy with clients in their second part of life: Possibilities in the treatment of anxiety and substance abuse disorders]', in P. Bäuerle, H. Radebold, R. D. Hirsch, K. Studer, U. Schmid-Furstoss, and B. Struwe (eds.), *Klinische Psychotherapie mit älteren Menschen. Grundlagen und Praxis*. Bern: Hans Huber, pp. 136–41.

Bräuninger, I. (2006). *Tanztherapie [Dance Therapy]*. Weinheim: Beltz PVU.

Bräuninger, I. (2009). 'Tanztherapie mit kriegstraumatisierten Kindern [Dance movement therapy with war-traumatized children]', in C. Moore and U. Stammermann (eds.), *Bewegung aus dem Trauma. Traumazentrierte Tanz- und Bewegungspsychotherapie*. Stuttgart: Schattauer, pp. 144–61.

Bräuninger, I. (2012a). 'Dance movement therapy group intervention in stress treatment: A randomized controlled trial (RCT)', *The Arts in Psychotherapy*, 39: 443–50. doi:10.1016/j.aip.2012.07.002

Bräuninger, I. (2012b). 'The efficacy of dance movement therapy group on improvement of quality of life: A randomized controlled trial', *The Arts in Psychotherapy*, 39: 293–303. doi:1016/j.aip.2012.03.008

Bräuninger, I. and Züger, B. (2007). 'Filmbasierte Bewegungsanalyse zur Behandlungs-evaluation von Tanz- und Bewegungstherapie [Film-based movement analysis in evalu-ating dance movement therapy treatment outcome]', in S. C. Koch and S. Bender (eds.), *Movement analysis: Bewegungsanalyse: The Legacy of Laban, Bartenieff, Lamb and Kestenberg*. Berlin: Logos, pp. 213–23.

Bräuninger, I. and Züger, B. (2014). 'The Dance Movement Assessment (DMA): A movement-based creative evaluation to detect changes through dance movement therapy', in H. Panhofer and A. Ratés (eds.) (2014), *Encontrar–Compartir–Aprender*. Barcelona: Universitat Autònoma de Barcelona, pp. 55–68. <https://ddd.uab.cat/pub/llibres/2014/117258/encco-mapr_a2014.pdf> (accessed 20 October 2014).

Callaghan K. (1998). 'In limbo: Movement psychotherapy with refugees and asylum seek-ers', in D. Dokter (ed.), *Arts Therapists, Refugees and Migrants: Reaching Across Borders*. London: Jessica Kingsley, pp 25–40.

Chakarova, L. and Gatev, S. (2010). 'The health promotive skills as an element of the sustainable development of public health', *Trakia Journal of Sciences*, 8, 440–3.

Cruz, R. F. (2006). 'Assessment in dance/movement therapy', in S. L. Brooke (ed.), *Creative Arts Therapies Manual: A Guide to the History, Theoretical Approaches, Assessment, and Work with Special Populations of Art, Play, Dance, Music, Dramas, and Poetry Therapies*. Springfield, IL: Charles C. Thomas, pp. 133–43.

Cruz, R. F. (2009). 'Validity of the movement psychodiagnostic inventory: A pilot study', *American Journal of Dance Therapy*, 31: 122–35. doi: 10.1007/s10465-009-9072-4

Cruz, R. F. and Koch, S. C. (2004). 'Issues of validity and reliability in the use of movement observations and scales', in R. F. Cruz and C. F. Berrol (eds.), *Dance/Movement Therapists in Action. A Working Guide to Research Options*. Springfield, IL: Charles C. Thomas, pp. 45–68.

Davis, M., Lausberg, H., Cruz, R. F., and Roskin Berger, M. (2007). 'The Movement Psychodiagnostic Inventory (MPI)', in S. C. Koch and S. Bender (eds.), *Movement Analysis, Bewegungsanalyse: The Legacy of Laban, Bartenieff, Lamb and Kestenberg*. Berlin: Logos, pp. 119–32.

Dayanim, S. (2009). 'The acute effects of a specialized movement program on the verbal abili-ties of patients with late-stage dementia', *Alzheimer's Care Today*, 10: 93–8. doi:10.1097/ACQ.0b013e3181a410ab

Dibbell-Hope, S. (2000). 'The use of dance/movement therapy in psychological adaptation to breast cancer', *The Arts in Psychotherapy*, 27: 51–68. doi:10.1016/S0197-4556(99)00032-5

DuBose, L. R. (2001). 'Dance/movement treatment perspectives', in J. J. Robert-McComb (ed.), *Eating Disorders in Women and Children: Prevention, Stress Management, and Treatment*. Boca-Raton, FL: CRC Press, pp. 373–85.

Earhard, G. M. (2009). 'Dance as therapy for individuals with Parkinson disease', *European Journal of Physical and Rehabilitation Medicine*, 45: 231–8.

Eberhard-Kaechele, E. (2012). 'Memory, metaphor, and mirroring in movement therapy with trauma patients', in S. C. Koch, T. Fuchs, M. Summa, and C. Müller (eds.), *Body Memory, Metaphor and Movement*. Amsterdam: Benjamin Franklin, pp. 267–87.

European Association Dance Movement Therapy (EADMT) (2012). *What is Dance Movement Therapy*. <http://www.eadmt.com/?action=article&id=22> (accessed 20 October 2014).

European Commission (2012). <http://ec.europa.eu/health-eu/health_problems/cancer/index_de.htm> (accessed 20 October 2014).

Gesundheitsberichterstattung des Bundes (2012). <http://www.gbe-bund.de/>

Gordon-Giles, N. (2011). 'Stories from Beyond Words', *American Journal of Dance Therapy*, 33: 73–7. doi:10.1007/s10465-010-9088-9

Gordon-Giles, N. and Zidan, W. (2009). 'Assessing the Beyond Words educational model for empowering women, decreasing prejudice and enhancing empathy', *American Journal of Dance Therapy*, 31: 20–52. doi:10.1007/s10465-009-9069-z

Goodill, S. (2010). 'The creative arts therapies: Making health care whole', *Clinical and Health Affairs*. <http://www.minnesotamedicine.com/Default.aspx?tabid=3497> (accessed 20 October 2014).

Goodill, S. (2005). *An Introduction to Medical Dance/Movement Therapy: Health Care in Motion*. London: Jessica Kingsley.

Gray, A. E. L. (2001). 'The body remembers: Dance movement therapy with an adult survivor of torture', *American Journal of Dance Therapy*, 23: 29–43. doi:10.1023/A:1010780306585

Gross, M. M., Crane, E. A., and Fredrickson, B. L. (2012). 'Effort-shape and kinematic assessment of bodily expression of emotion during gait', *Human Movement Science*, 31: 202–21. doi:10.1016/j.humov.2011.05.001

Hackney, M. E., Kantorovich, S., Levin, R., and Earhart, G. M. (2007). 'Effects of tango on functional mobility in Parkinson's disease: A preliminary study', *Journal of Neurologic Physical Therapy*, 31: 173–9. doi:10.1097/NPT.0b013e31815ce78b

Hamill, M., Smith, L., and Röhricht, F. (2011). 'Dancing down memory lane: Circle dancing as a psychotherapeutic intervention in dementia—a pilot study', *Dementia*, first published on 13 September. doi:10.1177/1471301211420509

Harris, D. A. (2007). 'Dance/movement therapy approaches to fostering resilience and recovery among African adolescent torture survivors', *Torture*, 17: 134–55.

Heimbeck, A., and Hölter, G. (2011). 'Bewegungstherapie und Depression: Evaluationsstudie zu einer unspezifischen und einer störungsorientierten bewegungstherapeutischen Förderung im klinischen Kontext', *Psychotherapie Psychosomatik Medizinische Psychologie*, 61: 200–7. doi:10.1055/s-0030-1267999.

Hervey, L. and Kornblum, R. (2006). 'An evaluation of Kornblum's body-based violence prevention curriculum for children', *The Arts in Psychotherapy*, 33: 113–29. doi:10.1016/j.aip.2005.08.001

Hill, H. (2009). 'Dancing with hope: Dance therapy with people with dementia', in. S. Chaiklin and H. Wengrower (eds.), *The Art and Science of Dance/Movement Therapy: Life is Dance*. New York, NY: Routledge, pp. 181–94.

Ho, R. T. H. (2005). 'Effects of dance movement therapy on Chinese cancer patients: A pilot study in Hong Kong', *The Arts in Psychotherapy*, 32: 337–45. doi:10.1016/j.aip.2005.04.005

Hokkanen, L., Rantala, L, Remes, A., Härkönen, B., Viramo, P., and Winblad, I. (2008). 'Dance and movement therapeutic methods in management of dementia: A randomized, controlled study', *Journal of the American Geriatrics Society*, 56, 771–2. doi:10.1111/j.1532-5415.2008.01611.x

Huber, M., Knottnerus, J. A., Green, L., van der Horst, H., Jadad, A. J., Kromhout, D., Leonard, B., Lorig, K., Loureiro, M. I., van der Meer, J. W. M., Schnabel, P., Smith, R., van Weel, C., and Smid, H. (2011). 'How should we define health?', *British Medical Journal*, 343: 1–3. doi:10.1136/bmj.d4163

Jeong, Y.-J., Hong, S.-C., Lee, M., Park, M.-C., Kim, Y.-K., and Suh, C.-M. (2005). 'Dance move-ment therapy improves emotional responses and modulates neurohormones in adolescents with mild depression', *The International Journal of Neuroscience*, 115: 1711–20. doi:10.1080/00207450590958574

Jordans, M. J. D., Tol, M. A., Komproe, I. H., and de Jong, J. V. T. M. (2009). 'Systematic review of evidence and treatment approaches: Psychosocial and mental health care for children in war', *Child and Adolescent Mental Health*, 14: 2–14. doi:10.1111/j.1475-3588.2008.00515.x

Karkou, V., Fullarton, A., and Scarth, S. (2010). 'Finding a way out on the labyrinth through dance movement psychotherapy: Collaborative work in mental health promotion pro-gramme for secondary schools', In V. Karkou (ed.), *Arts Therapies in Schools: Research and Practice*. London: Jessica Kingsley, pp. 59–84.

Karkou, V. and Meekums, B. (2014). 'Dance movement therapy for dementia', *The Cochrane Library*. doi:10.1002/14651858.CD011022

Kestenberg-Amighi, J., Loman, S., Lewis, P., and Sossin, M. (1999). *The Meaning of Movement Developmental and Clinical Perspectives of the Kestenberg Movement Profile*. Amsterdam: Nordon and Breach.

Kiepe, M.-S., Stöckigt, B., and Keil, T. (2012). 'Effects of dance therapy and ballroom dances on physical and mental illnesses: A systematic review', *The Arts in Psychotherapy*, 5: 404–11. doi:10.1016/j.aip.2012.06.001.

Kleinman, S. (2009). 'Becoming whole again: Dance/movement therapy for those who suffer from eating disorder', in. S. Chaiklin and H. Wengrower (eds.), *The Art and Science of Dance/Movement Therapy: Life is Dance*. New York, NY: Routledge, pp. 125–44.

Koch, S. C. (1999). *The Kestenberg Movement Profile. Reliability of Novice Raters*. Stuttgart: Ibidem.

Koch, S. C. and Fischman, D. (2011). 'Embodied enactive dance/movement therapy', *American Journal of Dance Therapy*, 33: 57–72. doi:10.1007/s10465-011-9108-4

Koch, S. C. and Harvey, S. (2012). 'Dance/movement therapy with traumatized dissociative patients', in S. C. Koch, T. Fuchs, M. Summa, and C. Müller (eds.), *Body Memory, Metaphor and Movement*. Amsterdam: Benjamin Franklin, pp. 369–85.

Koch, S. C., Kunz, T., Lykou, S., and Cruz, R. F. (2014). 'Effects of dance movement ther-apy and dance on health-related psychological outcomes: A meta-analysis', *The Arts in Psychotherapy*, 41: 46–64. doi:10.1016/j.aip.2013.10.004

Koch, S. C., Morlinghaus, K., and Fuchs, T. (2007). 'The joy dance: Specific effects of a sin-gle dance intervention on psychiatric patients with depression', *The Arts in Psychotherapy*, 34: 340–9. doi:10.1016/j.aip.2007.07.001

Koch, S. C. and Weidinger-von der Recke, B. (2009). 'Traumatised refugees: An integrated dance and verbal therapy approach', *The Arts in Psychotherapy*, 36: 289–96. doi:10.1016/j.aip.2009.07.002

Kornblum, R. (2002). *Disarming the Playground: Violence Prevention Through Movement and Pro-Social Skills*. Oklahoma City, OK: Wood and Barnes.

Kornblum, R. and Lending Halsten, R. (2006). 'In-school dance/movement therapy for trau-matized children', in S. L. Brooke (ed.), *Creative Arts Therapies Manual. A Guide to the History, Theoretical Approaches, Assessment, and Work with Special Populations of Art, Play, Sance, Music, Drama, and Poetry Therapies*. Springfield, IL: Charles C. Thomas, pp. 144–55.

Koshland, L., Wilson, J., and Wittaker, B. (2004). 'PEACE through dance/move-ment: Evaluating a violence prevention program', *American Journal of Dance Therapy*, 26: 69–90. doi:10.1007/s10465-004-0786-z

Krebsinformationsdienst (2012). <http://www.krebsinformationsdienst.de/grundlagen/krebsregister.php> (accessed 20 October 2014).

Laban, R. v. (1988). *Modern Educational Dance*. Plymouth: Macdonald and Evans.

Lamb, W. (1965). *Posture and Gesture: An Introduction to the Study of Physical Behaviour*. London: Gerald Duckworth.

Lausberg H. (1997). 'Bewegungsdiagnosetest mit Bewertungsskalen für Diagnostik und Therapieevaluation in der Tanztherapie [Movement diagnostic test with scales for diagnosis and therapy evaluation in dance therapy]', *Zeitschrift für Tanztherapie* 7: 35–42.

Lima, M. M. S. and Pedreira Vieira, A. (2007). 'Ballroom dance as therapy for the elderly in Brazil', *American Journal of Dance Therapy*, 29: 129–42. doi:10.1007/s10465-007-9040-9

Mala, A., Karkou, V. and Meekums, B. (2012). 'Dance/movement therapy (D/MT) for depression: A scoping review', *The Arts in Psychotherapy*, 39: 287–95. doi: 10.1016/j.aip.2012.04.002

Mannheim, E. and Weis, J. (2006). 'Dance/movement therapy with cancer inpatients: Evaluation of process and outcome parameters', in S. C. Koch, and I. Bräuninger (eds.), *Advances in Dance/Movement Therapy: Theoretical Perspectives and Empirical Findings*. Berlin: Logos, pp. 61–72.

Margariti, A., Ktonas, P., Hondraki, P., Daskalopoulou, E., Kyriakopoulos, G., Economou, N.-T., Tsekou, H., Paparrigopoulos, T., Barbousi, V., and Vaslamatzis, G. (2012). 'An application of the primitive expression form of dance therapy in a psychiatric population', *The Arts in Psychotherapy*, 39: 95–101. doi:10.1016/j.aip.2012.01.001

Meekums, B., Karkou, V., and Nelson, E. A. (2012). *Dance Movement Therapy for Depression*. The Cochrane Library.

Muller-Pinget, S., Carrard, I., Ybarra, J., and Golay, A. (2012). 'Dance therapy improves self-body image among obese patients', *Patient Education and Counseling*, 89: 525–8. doi:10.1016/j.pec.2012.07.008

NICE (2009). 'Schizophrenia. Core interventions in the treatment and management of schizophrenia in adults in primary and secondary care (updated edition). *NICE Clinical Guideline 82*. London: NICE.

Powell, M. A. (2008). *Assessment in Dance/Movement Therapy Practice: A State of the Field Survey*. Unpublished Master's thesis. <https://idea.library.drexel.edu/islandora/object/idea%3A2944 > (accessed 20 October 2014).

Pratt, R. R. (2004). 'Art, dance, and music therapy', *Physical Medicine and Rehabilitation Clinics of North America*, 15: 827–41. doi:10.1016/j.pmr.2004.03.004

Pylvänäinen, P. (2010). 'The dance/movement therapy group in a psychiatric outpatient clinic: Explorations in body image and interaction', *Body, Movement and Dance in Psychotherapy*, 5: 219–30. doi:10.1080/17432979.2010.518016

Quiroga Murcia, C. and Kreutz, G. (2012). 'Dance and health: Exploring interactions and implications', in R. MacDonald, G. Kreutz, and L. Mitchell (eds.), *Music, Health, and Wellbeing*. Oxford: Oxford University Press, pp. 125–35.

Ren J. and Xia J. (2013). 'Dance therapy for schizophrenia', *Cochrane Database of Systematic Reviews*, 10, Art. No.: CD006868. doi:10.1002/14651858.CD006868.pub3

Röhricht, F., Papadopoulos, N., and Priebe, S. (2013). 'An exploratory randomized controlled trial of body psychotherapy for patients with chronic depression', *Journal of Affective Disorders*, 151: 85–91. doi:10.1016/j.jad.2013.05.056

Röhricht, F. and Priebe, S. (2006). 'Effect of body-oriented psychological therapy on negative symptoms in schizophrenia: A randomized controlled trial', *Psychological Medicine*, 36: 669–78. doi:10.1017/S0033291706007161

9

Sandel, S., Chaiklin, S., and Lohn, A. (eds.) (1993). *Foundations of Dance/Movement Therapy: The Life and Work of Marian Chace (S. 98-111)*. Columbia, MD: The Marian Chace Memorial Fund of the American Dance Therapy Association.

Sandel, S. L., Judge, J. O., Landry, N., Faria, L., Ouellette, R., and Majczak, M. (2005). 'Dance and movement program improves quality-of-life measures in breast cancer survivors', *Cancer Nursing*, 28: 301–9.

Selman, L. E., Williams, J., and Simms, V. (2012). 'A mixed-methods evaluation of complementary therapy services in palliative care: Yoga and dance therapy', *European Journal of Cancer Care*, 21: 87–97. doi: 10.1111/j.1365-2354.2011.01285.x

Thom, L. (2010). 'From simple line to expressive movement: The use of creative movement to enhance socio-emotional development in the preschool curriculum', *American Journal of Dance Therapy*, 32(2): 100–12.

Van de Winckel, A., Feys, H., and De Weerdt, W. (2003). 'Cognitive and behavioural effects of music-based exercises in patients with dementia', *Clinical Rehabilitation*, 18: 253–60.

van Keuk, E. (2006). 'Tanz- und Bewegungstherapie bei Posttraumatischer Belastungsstörung am Beispiel traumatisierter Flüchtlinge [Dance movement therapy of post traumatic stress disorder as for example with traumatized refugees]', in A. Maercker and R. Rosner (eds.), *Psychotherapie der posttraumatischen Belastungsstörungen. Krankheitsmdoelle und Therapiepraxis–störungsspezifisch und schulenübergreifend*. Stuttgart: Thieme, pp. 174–91.

Vaverniece, I., Majore-Dusele, I., Meekums, B., and Rasnacs, O. (2012). 'Dance movement therapy for obese women with emotional eating: A controlled pilot study', *The Arts in Psychotherapy*, 39: 126–33.

Verghese, J., Lipton, R. B., Katz, M. J., Hall, C. B., Derby, C. A., Kuslansky, G., Ambrose, A. F., Sliwinski, M., and Buschke, H. (2003). 'Leisure activities and the risk of dementia in the elderly', *The New England Journal of Medicine*, 348: 2508–16.

World Health Organization (WHO) (1946). *Preamble to the Constitution of the World Health Organization as adopted by the International Health Conference, New York, 19 June–22 July 1946; signed on 22 July 1946 by the representatives of 61 States (Official Records of the World Health Organization, no. 2, p. 100) and entered into force on 7 April 1948*. <http://www.who.int/suggestions/faq/en/index.html> (accessed 20 October 2014).

World Health Organization (WHO) (2007). *Everybody Business: Strengthening Health Systems to Improve Health Outcomes: WHO's Framework for Action*. <http://www.who.int/healthsystems/strategy/everybodys_business.pdf> (accessed 20 October 2014).

World Health Organization (WHO) (2009). *Global Health Risks: Mortality and the Burden of Disease Attributable to Selected Major Risks*. <http://www.who.int/healthinfo/global_burden_disease/GlobalHealthRisks_report_full.pdf> (accessed 20 October 2014).

World Health Organization (WHO) (2012). *Primary Health Care*. <http://www.who.int/topics/primary_health_care/en/> (accessed 20 October 2014).

Xia, J. and Grant, T. J. (2009). 'Dance therapy for schizophrenia', *Cochrane Database of Systematic Reviews*, 2009 1, Art. No.: CD0068e68. doi:10.1002/14651858.CD006868.pub2

CHAPTER 41

DANCE AS ART IN HOSPITALS

DIANE AMANS

INTRODUCTION

WHAT are dancers actually doing when they come into hospitals? What kind of dance? If it is not therapy, what is its purpose? Joe Moran (2012) is artistic director of Dance Art Foundation, an organization that has considerable experience of delivering dance projects in hospitals. He states:

> We believe that any kind of movement can create playful and exciting dances. Sometimes our dance may be almost imperceptible; perhaps simply eyes blinking, breath moving, or tiny dances with fingers. At other times, we may move our whole bodies, direct others to dance our choreography, or simply enjoy the dance of our moving, shifting perceptions.
>
> We believe we can all, whatever our condition, experience the benefits of dancing and moving creatively: discovery, play, expression, connection, physical replenishment, inquiry, choice. We believe that these dancing experiences nurture our wellbeing and can make profound contributions to our lives. (Moran 2012)

As dance artists we are creating the conditions for change. Dance as art in hospital settings shifts the focus from illness and treatment to creative engagement that frees the participants to see themselves in a different light. Dance artists aim to offer experiences rather than working towards specific clinical outcomes. Nikki Crane, Head of Arts and Strategy at Guy's and St Thomas' Charity, argues:

> Arts have intrinsic value—we don't go in with a particular issue or outcome in mind. If we have a focus on the outcome then we lose something of the process. (Crane 2012)

Sometimes dance artists work alongside hospital staff to support the health profession-als' functional objectives. In other contexts, dancers deliver one-off workshops, demon-strations, or performances, and have little contact with hospital staff. Engagement with dance as art may well support clinical outcomes, and some of the dance activities are similar to those used by therapists.

This chapter offers:

- Examples of work by dance artists in hospitals.
- Discussion of relevant literature.
- Exploration of similarities and differences between dance artists and dance move-ment psychotherapists.
- Arguments for the contribution that such work can make to the concept of wellbeing.

In this context, wellbeing refers to a sense of vitality, as individuals are engaged in activ-ities which are meaningful to them and help develop their resilience in challenging circumstances.

Dance Artists: Methods
and Approaches

Although dance practitioners working in participatory arts come from very diverse backgrounds there are some significant common factors in the approach to dance work in hospital settings. Often we know very little about the participants before we meet them, and need to be able to facilitate creative movement interactions in the moment. For example, I offer a creative stimulus, observe the responses, and find a way of con-necting with people through dance. This may be to mirror their movement, respond with a different movement, or reach out my hands and see if they want to hold them in a partner dance. This initial informal assessment provides me with useful feedback and helps me to find a starting point for meaningful interaction.

Reflexivity is a key to deepening the understanding and the connection between practitioner and dancer. There is a growing body of research on kinaesthetic empa-thy and mirror neurons (Bläsing et al. 2010; Jola et al. 2012). In a dance session in which communication is as much non-verbal as verbal, the practitioner can often 'read' subtext through kinaesthetic empathy (Tortora 2005; Oliver 2010) to acquire 'empathetic knowledge' (Löytönen 2004, p. 135) about how the dancer feels. In order to make meaningful interpretations of the dancer's movements, the practitioner will draw on her/his own experience(s) as a basis for understanding. Oliver (2010) illustrates this with reference to an audience watching a dance performance: they can feel the movement without actually moving, by drawing on synaptic knowl-edge which is already present in their bodies, provided they have already had that experience. On a simpler level, if I see someone fall I know how it will feel because I myself have fallen. MacLeod (2001) states that 'true knowing involves embracing the subjective dimension of experience' (p. 122): it becomes something shared. However, later studies (Jola 2015) have found that mirror neurons, responsible for kinaesthetic empathy, can be activated irrespective of the spectator's experience of doing the observed action.

As a reflexive practitioner I observe posture, movement, facial expression, and verbal communication. I also check in with *my* feelings and responses—noticing my spontaneous responses and evaluating the extent to which these are appropriate and helpful. According to Tufnell (2010), this approach to dance still maintains the quality of the art form, but is

> concerned with spontaneous, non-stylized movement—with tuning in to inner sensation and to our surroundings, and allowing movement to evolve, moment by moment. Whereas the traditional conception of dance is associated with learning steps and a set style, this other dance emerges from the inside out and draws upon our interior lives. (Tufnell 2010, p. 17)

Miranda Tufnell is a dance artist, Alexander technique teacher, and craniosacral therapist who believes that 'movement offers a way of listening to and sensing the body as more than its symptoms and illnesses, and a way of exploring with imagination what is going on' (Tufnell 2010, p. 17). Catherine Hawkins—a dance artist who works at Alder Hey children's hospital—also highlights the importance of listening:

> I'm often asked what I do on the Oncology ward, and I have begun to answer that I listen and that enables me to offer a response that can include touch, play, movement, creativity, dancing, and more. (Hawkins 2010, cited in Tuffnell 2010, p. 82)

Several of the artists interviewed for this chapter referred to the notion of artists 'holding the creative space' (McNiff 2004) and being 'creatively alert', for that special moment when the individual shows readiness to respond and interact (Warren 2008). The artist who is 'creatively alert' adopts very different methods and preparation compared to an artist leading a dance class with set steps. The leadership style is one of leading from alongside or even leading by following. The artist needs to be able to draw on a range of behaviours to deal with different people in different situations and have the judgement to use these effectively. The work is about getting 'the fit' right—recognizing individual need and being available to support individuals in their own creative expression, perhaps by introducing a new activity or a different stimulus.

It is often the case that dance artists working in hospitals offer opportunities for patients to engage with others and find their own creative voice. Often, patients are supported to become artists and take part in mini-performances. The following case study illustrates how one hospital project managed to create opportunities for a constantly changing group of children to perform for an audience of parents, children, and hospital staff.

CASE STUDY 1: STRICTLY BED. . .VROOM, EVELINA HOSPITAL SCHOOL, LONDON

In 2008, Lauderdale House—an arts and education centre—commissioned choreographer Luca Silvestrini and the Protein Dance Company to run a dance project in the Evelina Children's Hospital at Guy's and St Thomas' Hospital. It was a two-week project with the following aims:

- To make children more aware of their bodies and how movement can be used to communicate and transform reality.
- To engage children in the creation of dance as an art form for the purposes of performance.

During the project, children (and adults) came to see how their bodies could be used to communicate and change mood, feeling, and meaning through movement. Hospital equipment and furniture were used as props, taking on new 'character' roles; for example, a dividing bed screen became a shadow puppet theatre with the aid of a lamp. Wheelchairs and beds were transformed into moving machines as children used arms and legs and high and low positions to run, crawl, roll, and leap through a tunnel of waves generated by a transparent blue-green cloth.

> The Strictly Bed. . .vroom project was highly successful in motivating children to engage both on the wards and in group workshops . . . The choreographer and dance team were particularly keen for children to develop a 'sense of audience' for their performance and to 'be a reflective audience'. With children performing one-to-one by the bedside and others performing in the atrium away from bedside view, giving live performances with audience participation was clearly going to be difficult. In addition, with a constant stream of children joining and leaving the project throughout the two-week period, it was clear there could be no 'gala performance'. (Naish and Beste 2009, p. 25)

They decided to involve a film-maker to record the project and give the children an opportunity to both perform and review their performances. Thus the children experienced the roles of artist, spectator, and critic, rather than being the passive recipients of care.

DANCE ARTIST: ROLES AND FUNCTIONS

In Case Study 1, the dancers' brief was clear: they were expected to develop work as dance artists, not as entertainers or therapists. In setting up projects in hospital it is important to clarify roles and occupational boundaries, particularly when this work is a new initiative and the dance artist is something of an unknown element. What do artists and hospital staff expect from each other? In my experience the dance artist often needs to be proactive in managing expectations about roles and about developing collaborative working.

One way to promote effective teamwork and positive relationships between artists and hospital staff is for the artist to offer continuing professional development opportunities for hospital staff as part of the Dance as Art project. These sessions are often a valuable way to ensure that all those involved are clear about their respective roles and functions. In my NHS[1] work in Stockport I ran staff development sessions with therapy support workers prior to the start of an eight-week project. Staff participants had the opportunity to experience some of the creative activities I planned to introduce as starting points for making dance together. I was also able to discuss with staff the extent to which patients needed to be 'assisted' in order to make a contribution. I supported them in developing a less interventionist approach during the dance sessions so that people were given the time and space to choose when and how (and if) they wanted to join the dance. Throughout the project I met weekly with the department manager and therapy staff so that we could discuss their observations. These review meetings resulted in a deeper, shared understanding of respective roles.

Green Candle is a UK-based community and education dance company that has delivered many dance projects in hospital settings, and their work often incorporates continuing professional development opportunities for staff. As part of their *forWard motion!* project they delivered a training session at Southampton General Hospital. Staff feedback revealed that initial apprehension was replaced by enjoyment and enthusiasm. Another significant outcome was that staff had a heightened awareness of the importance of creativity. The external evaluator noted that the participants understood the benefits of this type of creative activity because they had experienced it personally, and so would be more inclined to promote them in the future (Bax 2001).

The interface between dance artists and other staff in hospital is interesting. Where roles are clearly understood and time is allowed for reflecting on the practice from different perspectives, there are considerable benefits from collaborative working (Charnock 2008). On the other hand, if the artist is viewed as an entertainer and used as a holding activity whilst staff are engaged elsewhere, there are missed opportunities for integration and for developing cross-disciplinary relationships.

It is unusual for hospital staff not to be present when dance artists are working with patients, but it does happen, even when there has been a prior agreement that staff will work alongside artists. In dance sessions there needs to be present a member of the hospital staff who understands the needs of the patients so that health and safety risks are managed and the artist can focus on the dance work and take on responsibility for creative leadership, as in the following case study.

CASE STUDY 2: GROUP SESSION IN AN NHS FACILITY FOR PEOPLE LIVING WITH DEMENTIA

The following example illustrates my role and function as a creative leader. Here I describe a session that I led at the invitation of a member of the community mental health team. I was a guest artist working with a group that usually takes part in a weekly dance session run by a technical instructor (therapy assistant). There were twelve of us altogether: six in-patients, two day-hospital participants, a technical instructor, a staff nurse, and an NHS volunteer. From time to time, other members of staff and a relative joined us.

Jane[2] arrived at the day hospital with her husband, who usually leaves her for a few hours whilst he has a break. This is a session for people living with dementia, and participants are a mixture of people attending the day hospital and in-patients on the continuing care and assessment wards. Hospital staff accompanied patients into the lounge, and day patients arrived with their carers.

Jane was quite angry. She grumbled about her husband, did not want to take her coat off, and was quite belligerent with staff members who tried to engage her in conversation. As the other participants were arriving I played some music: George Formby's 'When I'm Cleaning Windows'. I watched Jane, who stopped complaining and caught my eye with a slight smile. I began to move to the music, and Jane stood up, took hold of my hands, and led me in a jive. Soon she was beaming and twirling me under her arm. 'You now', she said with a lively smile. She looked like she could carry on for some time, but other people were ready to begin and I was concerned to make sure Jane did not over-exert herself. I lowered the volume of the music, and Jane sat down again.

Colourful props engaged interest and drew the group together. I introduced a giant velvet-covered elastic band that we all held together and used to support movement. When an individual initiated a new way of moving, we copied or responded with moves of our own.

Other activities used in this session included mirroring a partner's dance using brightly coloured scarves and improvising with a range of other props. During the one-hour session Jane watched the other participants dancing, and joined in from time to time. When I brought out some dressing-up clothes Jane snatched a bright pink feather boa and initiated a partner dance with me. Others joined in with their partners. Peter's wife arrived and she was eager to take part.

After the impromptu 'Strictly Ballroom' session we ended with a gentle shoulder rub and a chat.

Immediately after the dance session, staff members and the volunteer recorded comments made by participants. Day patient Peter said that it made him 'feel alive'. He and his wife had danced together, as they used to. On returning to the assessment ward, Malik told the staff nurse that he had enjoyed it because 'people really noticed me'. Both of these participants had experienced an hour during which they took part in activities that had nothing to do with the medical world and where they were able to relate to others as equals.

Moira—the hospital staff member who usually leads this group—observed that the session felt more fluid than a traditional dance-class structure, which has a beginning, middle, and end. There were warm-up activities, creative dance, and closure, but they 'flowed into one another—it had a playful quality'. There is increasing acknowledgment of the importance of 'playfulness' in participatory arts work (Amans 2012), and occupational therapists Perrin, May and Anderson (2000) have written about the links between wellbeing and 'playful encounter'. Their description of a 'playful practitioner' incorporates many of the elements of creative leadership: being present, receptive, and available for spontaneous interaction. These aspects appear to be closely connected with the work of dance movement psychotherapists. However, there are also a number of substantial differences, as I argue in the following section.

DANCE ARTISTS AND DANCE MOVEMENT PSYCHOTHERAPISTS: COMPARING CORE VALUES AND CODES OF CONDUCT

The methods and approaches described previously reflect some of the values that are central to the work of community and hospital dance practitioners. For many years, dance artists, like other participatory arts workers, did not articulate their core beliefs and professional practices. Although there was an implicit commitment to provide quality practice, the principles and beliefs were not clear. Therapists have different professional bodies that provide validation and registration, but artists working in participatory arts are not regulated in the same way.

However, there is now a growing interest in developing guidelines for good practice as arts in health work continues to evolve (White 2010). The Foundation for Community Dance (2010)—more recently renamed People Dancing[3]—has set out the core values of community dance work in a professional code of conduct. Dance artists who have professional membership of People Dancing are required to sign up for this code of conduct, which gives them access to benefits such as civil liability insurance protection. It includes the following beliefs:

- Everybody has the capacity to dance, express themselves, and make meaning through dance, and that by engaging with it every individual has a creative and powerful contribution to make to their communities in a safe, supportive environment.

- To operate as artists do—with an artist's questions, perspectives, intuitions, feelings, and responses, to make sense of and create meaning in the world—is of itself a positive, empowering, and humanizing activity for people to engage in.
- Connecting people to dance experiences over which they have ownership, and through which they achieve a sense of belonging, individual's lives and their experiences of being in a community can be changed for the better.
- Dance can contribute to the personal and social development, and the health and wellbeing, of individuals in society.

The code of conduct goes on to describe how community dance avails the dancer with opportunities to engage in artistic and aesthetic exploration in a safe environment. The document illustrates the shared values that inform and guide practice such as the hospital dance work described in this chapter, and while the wellbeing of the dancer is explicit in the code there is also clear regard for the art of dance as a goal.

By contrast, the Code of Ethics and Professional Practice (2013), which governs dance movement psychotherapy, is more specifically client-centred, and is aimed at treatment 'for a range of neurological, psychological, relationship, and social problems' (Association of Dance Movement Psychotherapists 2013: 1), with special regard for the therapist–client relationship.

Many of the values embodied in the descriptors for the code of conduct will be familiar to dance movement psychotherapists, who also seek to offer opportunities for creative engagement in a safe supportive environment. Both professions accept the responsibility for the welfare and protection of the dancer, whether he/she is a patient or a community participant. It is clear from their governing codes that both practices regard wellbeing as a holistic state in which mental, emotional, and physical harmony are the aim. However, where the two professions differ is in the focus of the work; dance artists are not working towards therapeutic goals. Their focus is on the aesthetic aspects of the dance work, rather than its potential as a diagnostic tool, though artists often work in partnership with other health professionals to achieve positive outcomes for patients. The two roles can be complementary (Senior and Croall 1993).

On reflecting on the difference between dance as art and dance as therapy I decided to look more closely at some of the activities which are common to both of them. For example, as I illustrate in Case Study 2, I often use activities such as mirroring and 'pass the leadership' in my work (Bläsing et al. 2010; Jola et al. 2012). These activities are also used by many therapists, so what makes one art and the other therapy? I believe the answer lies in the intent and the desired outcomes. As an artist I aim to foster an environment in which people will make active creative contributions.

The 'follow the leader' activity changes the energy in the room, and that change helps create the ideal conditions for dance making. Participants begin to tune in to the movement of others, just as they do in a more intimate way with mirroring. These activities can develop into dance that has a particular aesthetic quality as dancers focus on the movement of others. The interventions I choose to make are based on helping people to extend their movement vocabulary and find the artist inside them.

I asked dance artist Lisa Dowler why she believes it is important to have dance artists in hospitals:

> As artists who offer improvised somatic dance and play, primarily we offer choice and an opportunity for the participant to be creative in their own way. As skilled improvisers we respond sensitively and hold the space for them, making movement and dance that is light-hearted and not goal orientated.
>
> We believe that everyone has a right to participate in art activity, and just because an individual may have a life threatening or life limiting condition they do not forgo this. In a structured clinical environment where one intervention follows another, we have found unstructured person-centred movement practice to be a welcome outlet, where individuals can express themselves without assessment or measurement. It is valued by patients, parents, and clinical staff for this very reason. It is not another therapy; it offers something different. (Dowler 2012)

CHALLENGES AND ISSUES

As arts interventions often have a different focus from healthcare interventions, the evaluation methods are usually different. In gathering evidence and agreeing on definitions of success, partners need to be prepared to view the work 'through different spectacles' and share the findings. Here is an example from my practice:

> Towards the end of a lively session in a day hospital for older adults, we danced with coloured ribbons whilst a live band played a jig. Most of the participants were seated but they joined in with enthusiasm, except for John. Whilst the rest of the group waved their ribbons energetically, John sat motionless, holding his ribbon and gazing into space. The arts and health coordinator, who had commissioned the event and was responsible for evaluation, commented that the activity had worked well. 'Everyone really enjoyed that—apart from John. It's a shame, but he didn't get much out of it.'
>
> As I collected the ribbons, John held onto his and looked at me. 'Takes you back,' he said, 'takes you back to the maypole dancing on the village green. And that music—I haven't heard Irish music for ages. My dad was Irish, you know ...'
>
> John was smiling as he shared his memories.

Viewed from a different perspective there is evidence of a very positive outcome for John. He had been engaged in an activity that connected him to enjoyable memories, and was still savouring the moment long after the ribbons had been packed away. The dance session had indirectly promoted at least two of the Five Ways to Wellbeing,[4]—these being Learn and Give. The Five Ways to Wellbeing framework (Aked and Thompson 2011) is being incorporated into a range of strategies for evaluating the impact of participatory arts. Merseyside Dance Initiative (MDI), for example, is using it as part of their three-year dance and health project.

The MDI project is a long-term programme of activity, and its concern has involved evaluation. Questions such as the following become relevant. How do we measure the impact of a one-off session? Is it worth going into a hospital to deliver just one short dance event? As an artist who is sometimes invited to deliver very short projects, I have questioned their value, particularly when hospital staff seem unsure what they are hoping for. Nikki Crane (2012) provides reassurance on this point: "A one-off workshop can be powerful—something shifts—the arts act as ignition." I know what she means, though it is difficult to communicate this to stakeholders who are considering setting up a dance project in hospital and have yet to witness the transformative moments of surprise and delight that so often occur in these projects.

Conclusion

As dance artists, we need to be prepared to articulate what we do and promote discussion with each other and with our partners in other professions. However, it can often be challenging to find the appropriate language to analyse or describe our practice. Dance practitioners Manny Emslie and Sue Akroyd have written about these difficulties:

> It feels like an impossible task to be able to offer arguments that are decisive or well reasoned. We are passionate about our beliefs and practice and yet when faced with the need to contextualize and confirm their impact we resort to the emotive and generalized use of language . . . It seems that language cannot do justice to the substance of what we do, how we do it, and why we do it. (Emslie and Akroyd 2004, p. 23).

And yet if we can broaden the language of dance and find ways of promoting interdisciplinary dialogue, this will enhance our understanding of creative engagement and help us measure the impact and value of the work. Different partners will place different emphasis and value on different aspects of a project, but open discussion will help us grow the field of dance in health settings. The challenge for artists is to nurture effective collaborations in order to maintain the quality of the art form whilst delivering this in the context of the hospital environment.

Hopefully this chapter will have provided the reader with an understanding of the ways in which dance artists approach work in hospitals and how dance can contribute to wellbeing through freeing creative expression. Dance as art is not a therapy, but it can be therapeutic, and it complements the work of other professionals in healthcare settings.

NOTES

1. The National Health Service (NHS) is the UK's publicly funded health service
2. Names have been changed to protect identity.
3. The Foundation for Community Dance was renamed People Dancing in November 2014.
4. The Five Ways to Wellbeing is a set of evidence-based public mental health messages developed by the New Economics Foundation (NEF). It is aimed at improving the mental health and wellbeing of the whole population. The five ways to wellbeing are Connect, Be Active, Take Notice, Keep Learning, and Give.

REFERENCES

Aked, J. and Thompson, S. (2011). *Five Ways to Wellbeing: New Applications, New Ways of Thinking.* London: New Economics Foundation.

Amans, D. (2012). *Age and Dancing: Older People and Community Dance Practice.* Palgrave Macmillan.

Association of Dance Movement Psychotherapists (2013). *Code of Ethics and Professional Practice.* <http://www.admt.org.uk/dance-movement-psychotherapy/code-of-professional-practice/> (accessed 19 October 2014).

Bax, A. (2001) *forWard motion!: Evaluation Report,* Green Candle Dance Company, Autumn Tour.

Bläsing, B., Puttke, M., and Schack, T. (eds.) (2010). *The Neurocognition of Dance: Mind, Movement and Motor Skills.* London: Psychology Press.

Charnock, V. (2008) *Cultural Champions: Evaluation Report.* Alder Hey Children's NHS Foundation Trust

Crane, N. (2012). Interview for this chapter, 12 August.

Dowler, L. (2012). Interview for this chapter, 23 August.

Emslie, M. and Akroyd, S. (2004). *The Secret Life of the Creative Self.* Animated. Foundation for Community Dance, 22–23.

Foundation for Community Dance. (2010). *Professional Code of Conduct.* <http://www.communitydance.org.uk/about-community-dance/> (accessed 19 October 2014).

Hawkins, C. (2010). In Tufnell, *Dance Health and Wellbeing.* Foundation for Community Dance, 82.

Jola, C., Ehrenberg, S., Reynolds, D. (2012). 'The experience of watching dance: phenomenological-neuroscience duets', *Phenomenology and the Cognitive Sciences,* 11(1): 17–37.

Jola, C. (2015). 'Dancing queen', in V. Karkou, S. Oliver, and S. Lycouris (eds.), *The Oxford Handbook of Dance and Wellbeing.* New York: Oxford University Press.

Löytönen, T. (2004). 'Art, emotion and morals in the everyday life of a dance school', in L. Rouhaniainin, E. Anttila, S. Hämäläinen, and T. Löytönen (eds.) *The Same Difference? Ethical and Political Perspectives on Dance.* Helsinki: Theatre Academy, pp. 133–53.

Moran, J. (2012). Dance Art Foundation. <http://www.danceartfoundation.com> (accessed 20 August 2012).

Macleod, J. (2001). *Qualitative Research in Counselling and Psychotherapy.* London: Sage.

McNiff, S. (2004). *Art Heals: How Creativity Cures the Soul.* Boston, MA: Shambala.

Naish, C. and Beste, M. (2009). *Strictly Bed. . .vroom.* Animated. Winter, 25–27. <http://www.communitydance.org.uk>

Oliver, S. (2010). *Creative Dance for Adolescents, and Their Social Wellbeing.* Saarbrücken: VDM Verlag Dr Müller, Aktiengesellschaft and Co. KG.

Perrin, T., May, H., and Anderson, E. (2000). *Wellbeing in Dementia. An Occupational Approach for Therapists.* Philadelphia: Churchill Livingston Elsevier.

Senior, P. and Croall, J. (1993). 'Helping to heal: The arts in health care. London: Calouste Gulbenkian Foundation, in Jones, P. (2005). *The Arts Therapies.* Sussex: Brunner-Routledge.

Tortora, S. (2005). *The Dancing Dialogue: Using the Communicative Power of Movement with Young Children.* St Paul, MN: Redleaf Press.

Tufnell, M. (2010). *Dance Health and Wellbeing.* Foundation for Community Dance.

Warren, B. (ed.) (2008). *Using the Creative Arts in Therapy.* Sussex: Routledge.

White, M. (2010). 'Developing guidelines for good practice in participatory arts-in-health-care contexts', *Journal of Applied Arts and Health*, 1(2): 139–55.

....

CHAPTER 42

THE BODYMIND APPROACH

Supporting the Wellbeing of Patients with Chronic Medically Unexplained Symptoms in Primary Healthcare in England

....

HELEN PAYNE

INTRODUCTION

....

THIS chapter provides an overview of the theoretical underpinnings and rationale for an innovative intervention derived from dance movement psychotherapy called The BodyMind Approach™ (TBMA).[1] Following research studies (Payne 2009; Payne and Stott 2010), this innovative intervention has been designed specifically to promote wellbeing and self-managed care for patients with chronic medically unexplained symptoms (MUS),[2] previously known as psychosomatic conditions. This patient population and the problem of their frequent use of the health service in primary and secondary care are described. The patients can often suffer from insecure attachment and alexithymia. The relevance of these conditions to MUS is considered in the light of using this embodied, enactive, non-verbal intervention methodology, within a specified design, for delivery in the National Health Service (NHS) in England, though since MUS is a worldwide problem it is not exclusive to England. The role of creative expression, symbolism, mindful movement, and practices derived from dance are also presented.

The chapter begins with an introduction to MUS, leading to a discussion of attachment style and somatization as they relate to patients with MUS. There follows an overview of TBMA and an insight into alexithymia as it connects to patients with MUS. Two case vignettes are presented to illustrate the types of patient and the way the intervention supports them to self-manage their symptoms.

Wellbeing is defined as a state in which every individual realizes their own potential, can cope with the usual stresses of life, and can work productively and fruitfully to make a contribution to the community. The World Health Organisation (2010) defines health as a state of physical, mental, and social wellbeing, and not merely an absence of disease or infirmity. For the purposes of this chapter this holistic definition is proposed. Wellbeing is intrinsically associated with health.

MEDICALLY UNEXPLAINED SYMPTOMS

When Edwards et al. (2010: 209) defined MUS as a 'clinical and social predicament that includes a broad spectrum of presentations where there is difficulty in accounting for symptoms based on known pathology', then the problem of having either an organic or a psychological explanation for MUS is obviated. An all-inclusive, biopsychosocial treatment that addresses both types of predicament simultaneously can be provided instead.

These patients are worldwide and are high health utilizers with no pathway to support them to address their problems and achieve an acceptable level of wellbeing. Bermingham et al. (2010) found that around £3 billion was spent on these patients in 2008 on medication, referrals, secondary care appointments, and so on. In secondary care, three out of four complaints were unexplained medically (Kroenke and Mangelsdorff 1989).

In a study by Barsky and Borus (1995) there was a diagnosis of no serious medical cause in 25–50% of all primary care visits. In another study only 10–15% of the fourteen common physical symptoms seen in half of general physician (GP) consultations over twelve months were found to be caused by an organic illness (Morriss et al. 2007).

Lipsitt (1996) showed that eight of the common physical complaints (fatigue, backache, headache, dizziness, chest pain, abdominal pain, and physical effects of anxiety such as palpitations and breathing problems) accounted for 80 million GP visits annually in the USA, but that an organic cause was found for less than 25% of these symptoms. Furthermore, other studies have confirmed that 25–50% of primary care patients experience MUS, making this the most common category of complaints in primary care (Katon et al. 1999; Kroenke 2007; Kirmayer and Tailefer 1997).

There are two types of patient with MUS. There are those who have the capacity for self-examination, self-reflection, introspection, and personal insight, including the ability to recognize meanings that underlie words and actions. They usually appreciate emotional nuance and complexity, recognize links between past and present, and have insight into their own and others' motives and intentions. Most importantly, however, TBMA also appeals to those who have less than the average capacity to reflect on their own and others' behaviour, understand the motivation and behaviour of themselves and others, notice connections among thoughts, feelings, and actions, or recognize meaning beneath experiences and behaviours. These types of patient with MUS can be termed psychologically-minded and psychologically-resistant respectively.

The majority of patients with MUS are 'psychologically resistant'—often due to the stigma of mental health services and the fact that they have a bodily symptom which they explain as physical and not mental ill health. Consequently, they frequently do not complete a referral to mental health services (Gonzalez et al. 2005). Therefore, the burden of care rests with GPs. For busy GPs both the identification and the treatment of patients with MUS can be challenging and frustrating. Patient and GP capacities to promote wellbeing are severely impaired. Moderate to severe anxiety and/or depression is common in these patients (Burton et al. 2011), ranging from 25–54% (de Waal et al. 2004; Löwe et al. 2008). Negative results from repeated secondary care referrals also exacerbate patients' feelings of anxiety and depression.

According to Rasmussen et al. (2008), GPs show a high degree of accuracy in identifying MUS subjectively, without the aid of standardized assessments. Cohen (2010) proposes that perhaps the best test for identifying patients with MUS is whether the GP feels dissatisfaction or not in the consultation. Consequently, although MUS are very common in primary care, accounting for as many as one in five new consultations (Bridges and Goldberg 1985), GPs do not have a suitable pathway to support these patients' wellbeing. Patients present frequently for over six months with persistent physical symptom(s) which do not appear to have an organic (physiological) cause and do not appear to respond to treatment. They are more likely to take sick leave or be unemployed. There is a comparable, or greater, impairment of physical function as that found with a solely organic diagnosis. Patients, in addition, may have a disability/diagnosis of an illness which is unconnected to the MUS.

Many people suffering from chronic (more than six months) MUS, when compared to other chronically ill patients, report a lower quality of life, impaired functionality, poorer general health, and worse mental health (Smith, Monson, and Ray 1986). Research also demonstrates an associated lowered affect regulation—specifically alexithymia (a difficulty in identifying feelings, distinguishing between feelings and bodily sensations, or describing feelings and with an external locus of control) (Mattila et al. 2008; De Gucht and Heiser 2003).

These patients tend to take additional time in GP appointments, which are also more frequent (more than five visits per annum), according to Barsky et al. (2001). Furthermore, medication is prescribed for long durations—mostly for anxiety, pain, and depression. Patients require more emotional support (Kirmayer and Robbins 1996), though if a referral is made to mental health (such as CBT), many find it unacceptable (Raine et al. 2002), as they are reluctant to have a psychiatric diagnosis (Kroenke et al. 2007). Consequently, either referrals are not made, or if they are, 50–80% of patients do not attend even first appointments (Allen and Woolfolk 2010). This is probably as a result of the stigma attached to psychological illness, together with the patient's explanatory model of their symptoms as being entirely physical.

Often there is past/current family dysfunction and/or a history of neglect, sexual or physical trauma (Drossman et al. 1995; Kirmayer and Robbins 1996; Waitzkin and Magana 1997), and a correlation has been found between child sexual abuse in women and MUS (Waldinger, Schulz, Barsky, and Ahern 2006).

These patients have higher healthcare costs in primary/secondary care due to the frequent and longer GP visits, medication prescriptions, and the many secondary care referrals for tests and scans (Edwards et al. 2010). Thus, people with MUS have poor wellbeing, appear as fairly needy, complex with long-lasting symptoms. Unfortunately they appear to frustrate GPs and take up much of the NHS resources. Clearly, a pathway to promote day-to-day wellbeing and to help them self-manage is much needed.

ATTACHMENT STYLE AND SOMATIZATION

Research has shown that early insecure attachment patterns are more common in patients with MUS. For example, early exposure to illness increases the likelihood of anxious attachment to adult interpersonal interaction styles, including to caregivers such as GPs. A rejection–abandonment cycle may result (Stuart and Noyes 1999). Symptoms can be related to threats to attachment and thus to the self (fragility). Bowlby (1969) states that the interactions between caregiver and infant lays down the pattern for adult-seeking/receiving care from those on whom they are dependent. Patterns persist throughout life, and can influence the expectations brought to relations with others whose role is to care for the patient. In other words, the GP may attract the patient's transferential material and become, to the patient, 'the inadequate carer'. Studies demonstrating the association between insecure attachment style and MUS include Spertus et al. (2003), Taylor et al. (2000), Ciechanowski et al. (2002), and Noyes et al. (2003).

Childhood trauma and adult MUS have also been related. A study by Stalker and Davies (1995) found a correlation between sexual abuse survivors and preoccupied/insecure attachment. Other studies found connections between child trauma and somatization (Waldinger et al. 2006), child trauma and attachment (Sansone et al. 2001), and attachment and somatization (Stuart and Noyes 1999). Therefore, it can be hypothesized that in adults with MUS, some may be manifesting their somatization due to insecure attachment which in turn may be as a result of childhood trauma; that is, the body holds the anxiety. It might be helpful to understand the bodily symptoms as a form of somatization (the manifestation of psychological distress by the presentation of bodily symptoms). MUS is sometimes referred to as a 'somatization disorder' within the mental health field. In addition, somatization has been linked to insecure attachment. People with an insecure attachment style may have an expectation of others not meeting their needs. In this type of patient there is an increased emphasis on, and reporting of, somatic concerns which may be a way to seek help from carers who are then expected by the patient to be unresponsive to their emotional distress.

Waldinger et al. (2006) used a community setting sample to study any links between childhood trauma and somatization in adults not seeking healthcare (physical or mental). Results showed that insecure attachment style facilitated a link between childhood trauma and adult somatization in the women in the sample. The correlation was strongest for the aspect termed 'fearful' attachment in particular. Fearful attachment refers to when a child is abused or neglected by a significant adult caregiver. They may be more prone to develop a self-image as unworthy of support from others, and of caregivers as unreliable or even dangerous—beliefs that form the basis of a fearful attachment style. In the context of GP consultations, the mixture of caregiver and patient experience may create a pattern of misunderstanding and frustration. Thus there is often reduced doctor–patient relationship and less than best practice care. The patient may sense that their emotional neediness might drive others away and/or may trigger insufficient effect, leading to a compensatory focus on bodily sensations, and care-seeking for unexplained medical complaints. For the men in this study, insecure attachment did not mediate any connection between childhood trauma and somatization. Depression was found to be present in both genders, alongside somatization. The authors did not propose that all children who are traumatized develop insecure attachment or that all insecurely attached adults report higher levels of somatic symptoms. They acknowledge that genetically-based temperamental factors and adult experiences also influence the way that individuals respond to early life stressors. Resilience is derived from different factors.

Similarly, people with a 'dismissing' type of attachment style may also bring the expectation that they will receive inadequate attention or care from others. They may be especially worried about their symptoms and not being believed or taken seriously by healthcare providers.

By contrast, those with a 'preoccupied' attachment style may be more concerned about losing the relationship with a healthcare provider once diagnostic testing is complete and no more treatment is indicated. They may become anxious that this relationship will have to end, so they become overly dependent and preoccupied with it. Bodily symptoms engage both parties in the relationship; the patient visits with more symptoms and becomes very needy of the GP's attention.

Consequently, TBMA as an intervention has been designed with this research on insecure attachment style in mind. It honours the symptoms and provides structured ongoing contact even after face-to-face treatment has concluded, both of which appear to reduce patients' concerns about whether they have a fearful, dismissing, or preoccupied attachment style. Furthermore, the research findings on insecure attachment has also helped inform the structure and content of this clinical intervention (TBMA) which addresses some of the particular anxieties that people with MUS bring, so as, for example, to reduce their fear, preventing the repetition of dysfunctional patterns affecting the continuity of care to sustain recovery.

Similarly, people who are fearfully attached may avoid long-term care situations both because of concerns about greater intimacy with providers and due to an assumption that they will be given insufficient care. Patient's fears about caregiver dependability promotes GP shopping—visiting each GP in a practice and/or changing practices frequently—and a fragmentation of care. These patients are likely to be experienced by the caregiver as inadequate, fragile, needy, and difficult to reassure. Greater outreach may be required to help these patients maintain ongoing relationships with providers rather than seeking care only in emergency settings. Hence the TBMA programme has developed a design over a twelve-month duration, divided into two phases to support patients in the longer term, sustaining the relationship. It has been found that the intervention dose of twelve face-to-face group workshop sessions over eight weeks is just about manageable and bearable for the fearfully attached patient. However, the follow-up phase omit over a further six months via text, emails, letters, and telephone calls appears to sustain and empower them to self-manage and even continue to improve in their overall wellbeing. Their anxiety reduces, and they no longer appear to need to visit their GP.

THE BODYMIND APPROACH

TBMA uses a mindful, kinetic practice—a model derived from dance movement psycho-therapy (Payne 1992, 2006a, 2006b), mindfulness, experiential learning through exper-imentation/exploration, group analysis, and theories (see Video 42.1 on the Companion Website ⊙). Some practices used derive from Authentic Movement—a particular approach to dance movement psychotherapy, a body-based psychotherapy that aims to integrate body and mind. TBMA is framed as experiential learning to patients whereby the facilitator enables access to perceptions of symptoms through coaching embodied mindful practices involving, for example, body awareness, sensory experiences, symbol-ism, and metaphor. TBMA honours and engages with the patient's relationship to, and perception of, their bodily symptoms. It is biopsychosocial, focusing on the whole person holistically.

Aspects of dance, presented as gentle mindful movement, can promote wellbeing in the healthcare of patients with MUS. For example, by using creative movement expres-sion, stressing the relationship between movement and the mind, and focusing on mindfulness, body awareness, and witnessing within group work, a setting can be pro-vided within which the patient can explore and symbolize the sensory experience of their symptom. From this, they are coached to learn about their symptoms—a process which empowers them to manage them more effectively day to day. Dancing the symp-toms can bridge the gap between mental and physical health.

In some forms of dance, whether this is practiced in artistic, social, or cultural contexts, symbolism is crucial to expression and to experiencing feelings conveyed by dancer to audience to give an implicit embodied knowing, beyond words. Dancing together pro-motes a sense of belonging to a group and can be a way of defining the individual. For example, Maree (2008) shows dance as both a binding and divisive force in South Africa; and in Brazil, the dyadic 'against' dance-game of capoeira promotes a feeling of social con-nectedness through its symbolic content (Reis 2005). The use of symbolism in dance is one tool amongst many others in which artistic work of all types communicates mean-ing to an audience or group of participants. In dance as a performance art, the extent to which meaning symbolized by a dancer's action is accurately perceived and understood by the audience might be entirely dependent on their shared knowledge and understanding (Cohen Bull 1997; Best 1999; Oliver 2009), and in the context of dance movement psy-chotherapy, dance, and symbolic movement in particular, is one way of communicating meaning amongst participants and between therapist and client (Payne 1992; Karkou and Sanderson 2006). Symptoms can become symbolic and invested by the patient with all sorts of meaning. The movement emerging from the body language can become representative of aspects of the symptom; for example, the sensory experience such as pain. As an example, in a practice exercise in twos, when I close my eyes with my headache in mind I begin to move from the sensation of the pain in my head. My hands move up and outwards, coming slowly down in front of me. My hands feel like claws, tense, and with long sharp talons they scratch at the air, up and down in front of me. This movement is seen by my witness, and afterwards, when invited, she speaks of her experience in the presence of my moving hands imagining an angry bear with claws outstretched, wanting to hurt. As I hear these words I begin to relate to the hand gesture as symbolic of the conflict I have with a person close to me, I want to hurt her, punish her. I am the angry, the clawing bear experiencing the pain of conflict in my head. I recognize that my anger needs to be integrated so that I can feel resolved with that conflictual relationship being held in my aching head. Hence, symbolism is a useful approach in the context of patients with MUS.

The concept of symbolic movement as gateways to meaning-making for patients with medically unexplained bodily symptoms is part of the bedrock of this approach towards recovery. For example, symbols give meanings or significance to objects, events, or relationships. Essentially, a symbol communicates through the senses to the unconscious or spirit. The affect bound to a bodily symptom (the body-felt sense) can be used to discover how the symptom has become symbolic for 'something' in a patient's life. If this 'something' becomes attached to a symbol and as a consequence is distanced from the patient, then she/he can take advantage of this distance with the support of the coach/ facilitator and/or the group, to understand their issue through exploring that symbol. The patient is then able to reassociate to their body from which they were disassociated previously due to the sensory distress caused by the symptom.

Through a series of sessions using TBMA as a learning approach, patients can uncover the symbol to find meaning, which arises from the depths of the unconscious, through their imagination (or that of another acting as witness), which pours out when a patient moves naturally (doing what I will call a 'small' dance) in the presence of a witness. When speaking about her/his experience and listening to the witness speaking about their experience in the presence of the movement, it becomes apparent that patients start to unpack symbolic meanings and link them with the symptom. This meaning-making helps empower patients to self-manage and consider change in small aspects of their life in order to cope better with their symptoms, so, as one participant said, 'the bad days are not so bad any more'. These aspects of dance can kick-start the process of change in lifestyle, reducing symptom distress and increasing wellbeing for this difficult-to-reach patient population

Called a Symptoms Group to patients, TBMA differs from Cognitive Behavioural Therapy (CBT), psychotherapy, or counselling in that it focuses on the physical symptom and any emerging verbal communication from bodily responses to the practices. Instead of a counsellor or psychotherapist there is a group coach or facilitator. There is no explicit discussion of psychological, biographic, or causal relationship with the symptoms unless the patient makes such connections themselves, nor are psychoeducative components involved in this intervention. There is an evidence base for the use of CBT with some specific conditions included in the MUS category, such as IBS or fibromyalgia. TBMA can, however, address a range of symptoms for a number of patients in the same group.

Body-oriented psychotherapy methods such as Focusing, developed by Gendlin (1996), and the Hakomi Method (Kurtz 1990) give full appreciation to the role and importance of acceptance in a mindfulness-based process (Weiss, Harrer, and Dietz 2010). Mindfulness practice is similar to the moving meditation process and witnessing state found in Authentic Movement practices (Whitehouse 1999; Adler 2002; Chodorow 1991; Payne 2006a), which is used in an adapted form in TBMA.

The patient enters a process of becoming engaged in a state of inner mindfulness, as she/he moves in the presence of a witness/facilitator. Weiss (2009) refers to this dialogic practice as assisted meditation. The facilitator guides the patient from everyday consciousness into mindfulness whilst attending to their sense of wellbeing. The patient directs her/his attention to embodied, inner experiences of self, actively reflecting and commenting on bodily sensations as they are raised into awareness. Gradually, participants become more connected to their embodied, direct experience of self and may then be able to act as their own witness and as a witness for others. Embodied, experiential learning exercises which the patient can practice between sessions form an integral part of the intervention, such as correct breathing methods.

The facilitator coaches patients who are requested to 'suspend their judgements' with kindness through explorations relating to their symptoms, modelling attitudes towards recovery simultaneously. Afterwards, patient responses to the practices are reviewed verbally and then reported by them in their journals.

The facilitator's approach to mindfulness will influence the process as well as the patient outcomes. An accepting, empathic, and compassionate style has been claimed to be the most effective (Hubble et al. 1999). The facilitator becomes attuned to herself and the group, whereby a non-directive stance can be employed.

The facilitator will have immersed her/himself in the practices during training, thus the concept is not an add-on technique. She/he uses her/his internal witness to guide interventions and model to the patient this form of self-witnessing. Initially the facilitator monitors the patient's state of consciousness noticing, any identification with a feeling state, sensory experience, or thought, gently coaching the patient to notice their inner witness. In this way there is a coregulation of attention processes by an external interactive regulator (Schore, 1994). The formative experiences leave imprints in the implicit (body) memory which can organize unconsciously everyday behaviours.

TBMA is presented as Symptoms Groups to patients because they are preoccupied with their symptoms. It is very accessible for this population because it is not framed as a psychological therapy or explicitly associated with mental health as in psycho-education, counselling or psychotherapy, or CBT; therefore the patient is non-stigmatised. Commitment is thus high, and patients on average attend all but one or two sessions. Furthermore, accessibility is enhanced by the venue, which is in a suitable community location, rather than a mental health setting or GP surgery/medical centre/hospital.

TBMA identifies and embraces aspects which are healthy in life, reduces isolation, and installs hope for change—seeing small changes as positive. The relationship of the symptom to life experience is examined whereby the patient is encouraged to set and review goals. Towards the end, an action plan is created based on their learning outlining what small change is to be made and practiced in the future. This is monitored with the patient for a further six months.

TBMA works subtly to change perceptions and thus experiences of symptoms by, for example, increasing understanding of the symptom's nature and purpose. Moreover, it raises awareness of the body, its cues/signals, and its needs and the nature of relationship with the body, leading to a positive reassociation with it, attributing new elements to any explanation of symptoms.

The recovery model, with its aim of sustainable self-management of care, is integrated into the design of the TBMA programme. By practising new habits over time in a supportive setting, it is demonstrated experientially to the patient that she/he can self-manage. The support gained from the group setting and the knowledge that they are not alone adds value to her/his experience.

By being encouraged to explore, and for some patients acknowledge the payoffs in having symptoms which may perpetuate the symptom's presence, patients realize that they have a conscious choice to change behaviour. The way patients relate to their symptoms and caregivers is explored. The hidden parts of themselves emerge, and with their increased embodied knowing and understanding a new perception of their symptom develops which challenges beliefs and assumptions about caregivers, health, and wellbeing (see Video 42.2 on the Companion Website ⏵).

Mindfulness and The BodyMind Approach™

Patients with MUS often have accompanying depression and/or anxiety. There is evidence that mindfulness can reduce depression and anxiety (Hofmann et al. 2010), and that it can have a moderate effect on some MUS (Grossman et al. 2004). Segal, Williams, and Teasdale (2002) demonstrate an association between lack of mindful self-awareness and depression. The lack of self-awareness results in poor recognition and reflection on bodily cues/signals such as pain, fatigue, destructive patterns, negative thoughts/feelings, anxiety, or tension.

Mindfulness has gained significance in the literature on therapeutic change since Kabat-Zinn (2003). A 'mindful attitude' relates to a state of absolute presence moment to moment, achieved through intentionally directed attention which at the same time allows internal and external stimuli to come into awareness and leave it without judgement or classification. A mindful state is not dissociation but participation as an empathic observer. It has an intrapsychic aspect, and is significant for interpersonal communication at an emotional level. As a state of metacognition (Weiss, Harrer, and Dietz 2010), there is a refraining from automatic reactions and identifying with the person or object observed (Kabat-Zinn 1994). An accepting, non-judgemental, and detached attitude, as promoted and cultivated through practices in TBMA, makes it possible to experience more intensely the self and relationships.

Studies by Ma and Teasdale (2004), Segal et al. (2002), Teasdale et al. (2000), and Williams and Kuyken (2012) showed the effectiveness of mindfulness-based CBT in preventing the recurrence of depression. The effects of mindfulness include physiological changes (Siegel 2007) and, as Schwartz (1996) showed, systematic changes in brain synaptic activity patterns. The relationship between left-sided and right-sided prefrontal neural activity may correlate with aspects of mood. Davidson et al. (2003) found that meditating Tibetan monks had enhanced activity in the left prefrontal cortex—an area which maintains emotional regulation, a general positive mood, and heightened attention. By contrast, depressed individuals with an overall negative mood showed more activity in the right frontal lobe (Davidson and Coleman 1974; Davidson et al. 1976; Davidson et al. 2003).

Weiss (2009) names mechanisms of mindfulness practice in the context of body oriented psychotherapy:

- Activation of the observer state makes it possible to sense inner somatic processes, allowing them to come to awareness.
- Simple regulation of attentional processes takes place, which in turn makes it possible to examine unconscious processes in a slow but direct manner.
- Non-judgemental self-examination is facilitated, creating a benevolent, accepting attitude towards dissociated parts of the self.
- Establishing an inner observer through repeated practice has in itself an aspect of transformation whereby the observer facilitates a process of disidentification with automated, self-limiting ways of being such as can emerge in states of depression.

When included in TBMA, this process of becoming mindfully aware of body, feelings, and thoughts, practised with an empathic, non-judgemental attitude can help to change, in a deeply embodied way, perspectives on symptoms and the sense of self.

Body awareness practice involves a focus on internal body cues/sensations, and these are the subjective aspect of proprioception which can be raised to conscious awareness. Processes such as attention, interpretation, appraisal, beliefs, memories, conditioning, attitudes, and affect can be adjusted through such practices (Mehling et al. 2011). Bodily aspects distinct from thoughts and external stimuli can be employed to help develop a deeper experience of the body–mind connection. Communication through movement or metaphor is helpful when words fail to express feeling.

Affective neurobiologists understand emotions as physiologically-based, and feelings as the mind's subjective interpretation of somatic cues (Damasio 1994, 1999; Schore 2003). Neuroscience research found observable connections between the body and the functioning of the mind (Damasio 1994, 1999; Hart 2008; Porges 2009). Emotions are body-based, involving the processing of responses to the environment, influencing the perception of experience, although the impact of the body on the experience of emotion is implicit rather than consciously registered in the moment (Schore 2003). The mind's interpretation of emotions is formed from somatic cues such as hormonal levels, blood flow, dimensions of cellular metabolism, neurotransmitters, and digestion. Physiological processes which relate to emotion can be triggered by movement, which can be noticed by the one who is moving or by their witness/coach. This can result in the emotion becoming available to the conscious mind. By mindful witnessing of the experience in the body, feeling states can be tracked. Homann (2010) claims that by sensing and responding through movement, capacities for emotional regulation and/or containment can be shaped. Using the functioning of the psyche in this way—that is, through the body/movement—resilience and recovery is possible.

In TBMA, patients learn to associate somatic cues in the movement process with primary feeling states such as sadness, rage, or joy. These 'here and now' (Stern 2004) feelings, thoughts, sensations, and images triggered by somatic cues become connected to the implicit emotional memory and right brain, through TBMA techniques. This unconscious state gains an embodied knowing through repetitive experiences stored in the body's tissue (Damasio, 1999). The empathic witnessing of movement by another may facilitate the development of the limbic system, including the capacity to track and read facial expressions and engage in relational interactions (Homann 2010). As more conscious associations are made between body and mind, verbal descriptions may develop, which in turn may lead to a reduction in the bodily symptom as its purpose is disrupted.

Furthermore, mirroring dance movement in pairs or synchronous movement in a group activates the mirror neurons, resulting in affective attunement, increasing participants feeling of being emotionally connected to each other, and thus reducing the sense of isolation which so many of these patients experience.

Consequently, the use of mindfulness-informed body awareness and mindful movement interventions can aid the recovery process in people with MUS as they enable feelings to be felt, understood and expressed, choices to be identified, strengths acknowledged, coping skills augmented, limitations accepted, and emotional regulation/relaxation learned. Through an improved integration of body with mind, preverbal/childhood experiences (such as childhood sexual abuse in women and/or trauma/dysfunction in the family of origin) and the associated emotions/conflicts can be processed. This embodied learning can lead to a stronger sense of self whereby patients may begin to relate to their bodily symptoms in a different way, learning to live well with them and promoting less distressing consequences and a sense of wellbeing.

ALEXITHYMIA

Emotional intelligence is crucial for adaption to life and encompasses the intention to attend to one's emotions, a lucidity of emotional state, and the ability to repair or regulate emotions (Salovey et al. 1995). Emotional intelligence is connected to mentalization (the imaginative ability to understand one's own and others' mental states, which is said to underlie overt behaviour), with its central focus on emotional expression, understanding and regulation, as well as the self and other (Fonagy et al. 2002). Waller and Scheidt (2006) consider somatization to be mainly a disorder of affect regulation.

Alexithymia is common in patients with MUS (Rasmussen et al. 2008). It is considered as a dispositional deficit in the intrapersonal and interpersonal processing of emotions constituting a negative mirror image of emotional intelligence (Velasco, Fernandez, Paez, and Campos 2006). Emotional competence is thus more limited. Hart (2008) states that verbal psychotherapy begins with language and then moves towards influencing perceptual processing including more emotionally engaged exploration, reflecting on memories and self-states. Alexithymic patients often have reduced self-reflection and the capacity to learn new emotional behaviour from language-based interventions.

Duddu et al. (2003), when reviewing somatization, somatosensory amplification, attribution styles, and illness behaviour, concluded that there was some evidence that anxiety, depression, neuroticism, and alexithymia have an influence on somatizing states.

Therapists may become annoyed by the patient's apparent lack of cooperation, and patients may feel stuck when they are requested to make use of reflexivity, emotional engagement, or symbolic/verbal communication. Therefore, therapeutic techniques need to adapt to the patient's non-reflective/-symbolic style (Vanheule, Verhaeghe, and Desmet 2011). Most forms of verbal psychotherapy require self-reflection, interest in internal events, and access to feelings—the very capacities/skills that people with alexithymia lack, so are viewed as poor candidates for insight-oriented psychotherapies (Krystal 1982).

Emotions are felt due to bodily reactions. Individuals who perceive bodily signals with a high degree of sensitivity may experience emotions more forcefully. People with alexithymia have limited ability to regulate and describe their emotions. Interoceptive sensitivity is the extent to which an individual is sensitive to bodily signals, considered essential in the theory of emotions proposed by Damasio (1999). People with high levels of alexithymia have significant difficulties in expressing their feelings/emotions, so they tend to have body language (such as somatization) as a substitute for verbalization. They often experience somatic intensification and observe/check their bodily functions frequently. They may have reduced motor expression and/or increased muscular tone and tension. Because of the difficulty in verbal expression, non-verbal methods such as mindful movement with body awareness, as used in TBMA, can be an accessible method for recovery.

These patients frequently suffer from isolation due to their symptoms, and a group provides social support. Studies have shown the benefits of group therapy for alexithymic patients (Zonneveld et al. 2012; Beresnevaite 2000; Grabe et al. 2008), though it was found that highly alexithymic patients did not benefit as much as non-alexithymic patients from different forms of group therapy (McCallum et al. 2003).

Case Vignette: Richard

Richard is 26 years old, he is one of two brothers, he is living at home with his parents, and he works full time. He was referred to the Symptoms Group by his GP, whom he was visiting every week. He attended eleven of the twelve sessions, and seemed to be very committed (he missed one session because he had flu).

The most prominent symptoms that Richard was aware of were concerned with his eyes. In his description he saw bright white light, he had static vision, and had vision blink. He suffered this for more than a year in which he had almost all medical tests (three secondary care referrals) available, but nothing was found. He was given medication to attend to his pain. Richard was worried that he might have some incurable illness or the start of some psychological impairment. He continued to be affected by these symptoms. He went to work, but his condition prevented him from doing sports or socializing. He became depressed and socially isolated. He was anxious and preoccupied that his eyesight would diminish and that he might have something more serious. No one, despite repeated investigations and tests, could find any explanation for these symptoms.

Richard was suffering from MUS. He had appeared withdrawn and tense ever since his first individual intake meeting with his group facilitator and during the group sessions. His answers to queries about how he was feeling were brief and concise. Everything was matter-of-fact. Inquiring into his feelings and emotions was rather difficult for him. He seemed to have no words for feelings often saying that he did not know what was meant and 'I don't feel anything'.

The group welcomed Richard warmly. He experimented with the various activities that he called 'strange things', he listened to the others, and although he did not seem to be able to empathize, he seemed attentive and interested. He said that he was not expecting anything from this group, but as he had never done anything like it he was curious. He was a good listener, and the group offered him an opportunity to learn from others. He was taken into consideration by other group members and given kind attention.

After a while, Richard seemed to relax in the group. In one session he told the group that he had joined a fencing course and that he enjoyed it. He was invited to show the group the fencing technique. He used it for his improvised movement from his symptom—it looked like a dance. The facilitator felt a great pleasure to see him looking at ease and free in his body. Perhaps he could be free of his symptom too. After a little while he was teaching the group the fencing movements. He was offering something to the group. He seemed pleased, but although everyone was overjoyed he remained undemonstrative.

Post-intervention TBMA group outcomes for Richard included reduction in symptom distress levels, medication, a decrease in anxiety and depression (which had previously been severe), improvement in social support, activity levels, and general health, and no further visits to the GP or secondary care for his symptoms. Richard's wellbeing was supported and sustained for up to six months after the TBMA intervention.

Case Vignette: Lyn

At our first meeting, Lyn looked very tense, a bundle of nerves. Her main symptoms were muscular cramps, insomnia, migraine, and depression. Some traumatic events in her past seemed to signify the beginning of her symptoms, and with it her frequent visits to her GP.

Lyn attended every session possible for her, being absent on only two occasions. Since the first session, when she was following verbal instructions to optimize her breathing pattern, she realized that there was something different in the way she was breathing. She was puzzled, as she described that she was contracting her tummy muscles when inhaling whilst relaxing, and expanding her tummy muscles when exhaling. Too much carbon dioxide was stored in her body, and not enough oxygen was circulating throughout her body, but instead was trapped in her chest and stomach. It appeared that Lyn was breathing in the way people breathe when they are in shock. Given the particular pattern of breathing, her body was suffering.

In everyday life when stressful situations occurred, Lyn became extremely anxious and had panic attacks which made her unable to function. She was unable to sleep well, and found it difficult going to work, as she felt tired and could not concentrate. Like a vicious circle, one thing affected the other, and life was difficult for Lyn.

As she discovered the right way of breathing she began to integrate/let go of the stress. She practised the new breathing pattern between and in sessions. Each week she reported an amazing recovery. She looked happier, and seemed more energized. She said that she slept better and even enjoyed work, taking some stressful situations in her stride, finding them perfectly manageable. Lyn told the group that the new breathing pattern was second nature to her now.

Another aspect of Lyn's new wellbeing was her increased self-confidence. Through the movement work she discovered that she was well coordinated and gracious in her movement, had a good sense of rhythm, and that actually she could dance! Her distorted idea that she could not dance (left over from a childhood memory of a cruel teacher telling her this) vanished. She enjoyed the movement in the group, and confessed that she enjoyed dancing in her kitchen!

CONCLUSIONS

TBMA appeals to both psychologically-minded and psychologically-resistant patients with MUS. It can be delivered anywhere in the NHS. Early indications suggest that it appears to provide the following benefits for patients: self-managed care, improved wellbeing and functioning, and reduced anxiety/depression/symptom distress, though these conclusions are very tentative and cautious (Payne 2014, 2015, 2016). For the health service it is possible that it can provide immediate cost savings, increasing year on year, increasing patient and GP choice, and helping GP practices in England to meet their quality outcomes framework targets.

The MUS clinic acts as a gateway for patients with MUS, enabling access to the psychological therapies if required, and complementing and enhancing the effects of other approaches to MUS. TBMA is affordable and effective and in these times of austerity it delivers much needed savings in both primary and secondary care.

NOTES

1. For more information about TBMA, see <http://www.pathways2wellbeing.com>, or email info@pathways2wellbeing.com.
2. The new term, somatic symptom disorder (SSD), has replaced MUS in the new dsm-5.

REFERENCES

Adler, J. (2002). *Offering from the Conscious Body*. Rochester, VT: Inner Traditions.

Allen, L. A., &and Woolfolk, R.L. (2010). 'Cognitive behavioral therapy for somatoform disorders', *Psychiatric Clinics of North America*, 33: 579–593. doi: 10.1016/j.psc.2010.04.014.

Barsky, A. J., Ettner, S. L., Horsky, J., and Bates, D. W. (2001). 'Resource utilization of patients with hypochondriacal health anxiety and somatization', *Medical Care*; 39: 705–15.

Barsky, A. J., and Borus, J. F. (1995). 'Somatization and medicalization in the era of managed care', JAMA, 274(24): 1931–4.

Bermingham, S., Cohen, A., Hague, J. and Parsonage, M. (2010). 'The cost of somatisation among the working-age population in England for the year 2008–09', *Mental Health in Family Medicine*, 7: 71–84.

Beresnevaite, M. (2000). 'Exploring the benefits of group psychotherapy alexithymia in coronary heart disease patients: A preliminary study', *Psychotherapy and Psychosomatics*, 69: 117–22.

Best, D. (1999). 'Dance before you think', in G. McFee (ed.). *Dance, Education and Philosophy*. Oxford: Meyer and Meyer Sport, pp. 101–22.

Bowlby, J. (1969). *Attachment and Loss, Vol. 1: Attachment*. New York, NY: Basic Books.

Bridges, K. and Goldberg, D. (1985). Somatic Presentation of DSM-III Psychiatric Disorders in Primary Care', *Journal of Psychosomatic Research*, 29: 563–9.

Burton, C. (2003). 'Beyond somatisation: A review of the understanding and treatment of medically unexplained physical symptoms (MUPS)', *British Journal of General Practice*, 53: 233–41.

Burton, C., McGorm, K., Weller, D., and Sharpe, M. (2011). 'Depression and anxiety in patients repeatedly referred to secondary care with medically unexplained symptoms: a case-control study', *Psychological Medicine*, 41(3): 555–63. doi:10.1017/S0033291710001017.

Chodorow, J. (1991). *Dance Therapy and Depth Psychology: The Moving Imagination*. London: Routledge.

Ciechanowski, P. S., Walker, A. E., Katon, W. J., and Russo, J. E. (2002). 'Attachment theory: A model for health care utilization and somatization', *Psychosomatic Medicine*, 64: 660–7.

Cohen, A. (2010). 'Not yet explained symptoms', *Mental Health Family Medicine*, 7(4): 189–90.

Cohen Bull, C. J. (1997). 'Sense, meaning and perception in three dance cultures', in J. Desmond (ed.), *Meaning in Motion: New Cultural Studies in Dance*. London: Duke University Press, pp. 269–88.

Damasio, A. R. (1999). *The Feeling of What Happens*. New York, NY: Harcourt Brace and Company.

Damasio, A. R. (1994). *Descartes' Error: Emotion, Reason, and the Human Brain*. New York, NY: Grosset/Putnam.

Davidson, R. J., and Coleman D. J. (1974). 'The role of attention in meditation and hypnosis: a psychobiological perspective on transformation of consciousness', *International Journal of Clinical and Experimental Hypnosis*, 4: 291–308.

Davidson, R. J., Schwartz, G. E., and Rothman, L. P. (1976). 'Attention style and self-regulation of mode-specific attention: An electroencephalographic study. *Journal of Abnormal Psychology*, 85: 235–8.

Davidson, R. J., Kabat-Zinn, J., Schumacher, J., Rosenkranz, M., Muller, D. and Santorelli, S. F. (2003). 'Alterations in brain and immune function produced by mindfulness meditation', *Journal of Psychosomatic Medicine*, 65: 564–70.

De Gucht, V. and Heiser, W. (2003). 'Alexithymia and somatisation: A quantitative review of the literature', *Journal of Psychosomatic Research*, 54: 425–34.

de Waal, M. W. M., Arnold, I. A., Eekhof, J. A. H., Van Hemert, A. M. (2004). 'Somatoform disorders in general practice: prevalence, functional impairment and comorbidity with anxiety and depressive disorders', *British Journal of Psychiatry*, 184: 470–6. doi: 10.1192/bjp.184.6.470

Drossman, D. A., Talley, N. J., Leserman, J. J., Olden, K. W., and Barreiro, M. A. (1995). 'Sexual and physical abuse and gastrointestinal illness: Review and recommendations', *Annals of Internal Medicine*, 123: 782–94.

Duddu, V., Isaac, M. K., Chaturvedi, S. K. (2003). 'Alexithymia in somatoform and depressive disorders, *Journal of Psychosomatic Research*, 54: 435–8.

Edwards, T., Stern, A., Clarke, D., Ivbijaro, G., and Kasney, L. M. (2010). 'The treatment of patients with medically unexplained symptoms in primary care: A review of the literature', *Medical Mental Health Family Medicine*, 7(4): 209–21.

Fonagy, P., Gergely, G., Jurist, E., and Target, M. (2002). *Affect Regulation, Mentalization, and the Development of the Self*. New York, NY: Other Press.

Gendlin, E. T. (1996). *Focusing-Oriented Psychotherapy: A Manual of the Experiential Method*. New York, NY: Guilford Press.

Gonzalez, J., Williams, J. W., Noel, P. H., and Lee, S. (2005). 'Adherence to mental health treatment in a primary care clinic', *Journal of the American Board of Family Practice*, 18: 87–96.

Grossman, P., Niemann, L., Schmid, S., and Walach, H. (2004). 'Mindfulness-based stress reduction and health benefits: A meta-analysis', *Journal of Psychosomatic Research*, 57: 35–43.

Grabe, S., Ward, M. L., and Hyde, J. S. (2008). 'The role of the media in body image concerns among women: A meta-analysis of experimental and correlational studies', *Psychological Bulletin*, 134(3): 460–6.

Hart, S. (2008). *Brain, Attachment, Personality: An Introduction to Neuroaffective Development*. London: Karnac Books.

Hofmann, S. G., Sawyer, A. T., Witt, A. A., and Oh, D. (2010). 'The effect of mindfulness-based therapy on anxiety and depression: A meta-analytic review', *Journal of Consult Clinical Psychology*, 78(2): 169–83. doi: 10.1037/a0018555

Homann, K. (2010). 'Embodied concepts of neurobiology in dance movement therapy practice', *American Journal of Dance Therapy*, 32: 80–99.

Hubble, M. A., Duncan, B. L., and Miller, S. C. (1999). *The Heart and Soul of Change*. Washington, DC: American Psychological Association.

Kabat-Zinn, J. (1994). *Full Catastrophe Living: Using the Wisdom of Your Body and Mind to Face Stress, Pain and Illness*. New York, NY: Random House.

Kabat-Zinn, J. (2003). Mindfulness-based interventions in context: past, present and future', *Clinical Psychology: Science and Practice*, 10(2): 133–56.

Karkou, V. and Sanderson, P. (2006) *Arts Therapies: A Research-Based Map of the Field*. Edinburgh: Elsevier.

Katon, W., Von Korff, M., Lin, E., et al. (1999). 'Stepped collaborative care for primary care patients with persistent symptoms of depression: a randomized trial', *Archives of General Psychiatry*, 56(12), 1109–15.

Kirmayer, L. J., and Tailefer, S. (1997). 'Somatoform disorders', in S. M. Turner and M. Hersen (eds.), *Adult Psychopathology and Diagnosis*, 3rd edn. New York: Wiley, pp. 333–83.

Kirmayer, L. J. and Robbins, J. M. (1996). 'Patients who somatize in primary care: A longitudinal study of cognitive and social characteristics', *Psychological Medicine*, 26: 937–51.

Kroenke, K. (2007). 'Efficacy of treatment for somatoform disorders: A review of randomized controlled trials', *Psychosomatic Medicine*; 69: 881–8.

Kroenke, K. and Mangelsdorff, A. D. (1989). 'Common symptoms in ambulatory care: Incidence, evaluation, therapy and outcome', *American Journal of Medicine*, 86: 262–6.

Kroenke, K., Sharpe, M., and Sykes, R. (2007). 'Revising the classification of somatoform disorders: Key questions and preliminary recommendations', *Psychosomatics: Journal of Consultation and Liaison Psychiatry* 48: 277–85. doi:10.1176/appi.psy.48.4.277.

Krystal, H. (1982). Alexithymia and the effectiveness of psychoanalytic treatment', *International Journal of Psychoanalytic Psychotherapy*, 9: 353–88.

Kurtz, R. (1990). *Body-Centered Psychotherapy: The Hakomi Method*. Mendocino, CA: LifeRhythm.

Lipsitt, D. R. (1996). 'Primary care of the somatizing patient: A collaborative model', *Hospital Practice*, 31: 77–88.

Löwe, B., Spitzer, R. L., Williams, J. B. W., Mussell, M., Schellberg, D., and Kroenke, K. (2008). 'Depression, anxiety and somatization in primary care: Syndrome overlap and functional impairment', *General Hospital Psychiatry*, 30: 191–9. doi:10.1016/j.genhosppsych.2008.01.001.

Ma, S. H. and Teasdale, J. (2004). 'Mindfulness-based cognitive therapy for depression: Replication and exploration of differential relapse prevention effects', *Journal of Consulting and Clinical Psychology*, 72(1): 31–40.

Maree, L. (2008). 'Acts of love under a southern moon', in S. Shapiro (ed.), *Dance in a World of Change: Reflections on Globalization and Cultural Difference*. Champaign, IL: Human Kinetics, pp. 117–35.

Mattila, A. K., Kronholm, E., Jula, A., Salminen, J. K., Koivisto, A. M., and Mielonen, R. L. (2008). 'Alexithymia and somatization in general population', *Psychosomatic Medicine*, 70(6): 716–22.

McCallum, M., Piper, W. E., Ogrodniczuk, J. S., and Joyce, A. S. (2003). 'Relationships among psychological mindedness, alexithymia and outcome in four forms of short-term psychotherapy', *Psychology and Psychotherapy* 76(Pt 2): 133–44.

Mehling, W. E., Wrubel, J., Daubenmier, J. J., Price, C. J., Kerr, C. E., Silow, T., Gopisetty, V., and Stewart, A. L. (2011). 'Body awareness: A phenomenological inquiry into the common ground of mind-body therapies', *Philosophy, Ethics, and Humanities in Medicine*, 6: 6. doi:10.1186/1747-5341-6-6

Morriss, R., Dowrick, C., and Salmon, P. (2007). 'Cluster randomised controlled trial of training practices in reattribution for medically unexplained symptoms', *British Journal of Psychiatry*, 191: 536–42.

Noyes, R. J., Stuart, S. P., Langbehn, D. R., Happel, R. L., Longley, S. L., Muller, B. A., Yagla, S. J. (2003). 'Test of an interpersonal model of hypochondriasis', *Psychosomatic Medicine*, 65: 292–300.

Oliver, S. (2009). *Community-Based Creative Dance for Adolescents and their Feelings of Social Wellbeing*. PhD thesis, Queen Margaret University, Edinburgh.

Payne, H. (ed.) (1992). *Dance Movement Therapy: Theory and Practice*. London and New York: Routledge. First edition.

Payne, H. (2006a). 'The body as container and expresser: Authentic Movement groups in the development of wellbeing in our bodymindspirit', in J. Corrigall, H. Payne, and H. Wilkinson (eds.), *About a Body: Working with the Embodied Mind in Psychotherapy*. London: Routledge. pp. 162–80.

Payne, H. (ed.) (2006b). *Dance Movement Therapy: Theory, Research and Practice*. London and New York: Routledge. Second, revised edition.

Payne, H. (2009). 'Pilot study to evaluate Dance Movement Psychotherapy (The BodyMind Approach) with patients with medically unexplained symptoms: Participant and facilitator perceptions and a summary discussion', *International Journal for Body, Movement and Dance in Psychotherapy*. 5(2): 95–106.

Payne, H. (2015). 'The body speaks its mind: The BodyMind Approach® for patients with medically unexplained symptoms in the UK primary care health system', *The Arts in Psychotherapy*, 42: 19–27.

Payne, H. (2016). Clinical outcomes from The BodyMind Approach™ in the treatment of patients with medically unexplained symptoms in the English primary care setting: practice-based evidence', *The Arts in Psychotherapy*, 47: 55–65.

Payne, H. and Stott, D. (2010). 'Change in the moving bodymind: Quantitative results from a pilot study on the BodyMind Approach (BMA) to group work for patients with medically unexplained symptoms (MUS)', *Counselling and Psychotherapy Research*, 10(4): 295–307.

Porges, S. W. (2009). 'Reciprocal influences between body and brain in the perception and expression of affect: A polyvagal perspective', in D. Fosha and D. J. Siegel (eds.), *The Healing Power of Emotion: Affective Neuroscience, Development and Clinical Practice*. New York, NY: W. W. Norton, pp. 27–54.

Rasmussen, N. H., Agerter, D. C., Colligan, R. C., Baird, A. M., Yunghans, C. E., and Cha, S. S. (2008). 'Somatization and alexithymia in patients with high use of medical care and medically unexplained symptoms', *Mental Health in Family Medicine*, 5: 139–48.

Raine, R., Haines, A., Sensky, T., Hutchings, A., Larkin, K., and Black, N. (2002). 'Systematic review of mental health interventions for patients with common somatic symptoms: Can research evidence from secondary care be extrapolated to primary care?', *British Medical Journal*, 325: 1082–92. doi: 10.1136/bmj.325.7372.1082

Reis, A. (2005). *Capoeira: Health and Social Wellbeing*. Brasilia: Thesaurus.

Salovey, P., Mayer, J. D., Goldman, S. L., Turvey, C., and Palfai, T. P. (1995). 'Emotional attention, clarity and repair: Exploring emotional intelligence using the trait meta-mood scale', in J. Pennebaker (ed.), *Emotion, Disclosure and Health*. Washington, DC: American Psychological Association, pp. 125–54.

Sansone, R. A., Wiederman, M., and Sansone, L.(2001). 'Adult somatic preoccupation and its relationship to childhood trauma', *Violence Victims*; 16: 39–47.

Schore, A. (1994). *Affect Regulation and the Repair of the Self*. New York: Norton Series on Interpersonal Neurobiology.

Schwartz, J. M. (1996). 'Systematic changes in cerebral glucose metabolic rate after successful behavior treatment of obsessive-compulsive disorder', *Archives of General Psychiatry*, 53: 109–13.

Segal, Z. V., Williams, J. M. G., and Teasdale, J. D. (2002). *Mindfulness-Based Cognitive Therapy for Depression: A New Approach to Preventing Relapse*. New York, NY: Guilford Press.

Siegel, D. J. (2007). *The Mindful Brain: Reflection and Attunement in the Cultivation of Wellbeing*. New York, NY: W. W. Norton.

Smith, G. R., Monson, R. A., and Ray, D. C. (1986). 'Patients with multiple unexplained symptoms: Their characteristics, functional health, and health care utilization', *Archives of Internal Medicine*; 146: 69–72.

Spertus, I., Yehuda, R., Wong, C., Halligan, S., Seremetis, S. (2003). 'Childhood emotional abuse and neglect as predictors of psychological and physical symptoms in women presenting to a primary care practice', *Child Abuse Neglect*, 27: 1247–58.

Stalker, C. A. and Davies, F. (1995). 'Attachment organization and adaptation in sexually abused women', *Canadian Journal of Psychiatry*, 40: 234–40.

Stern, D. N. (2004). *The Present Moment in Psychotherapy and in Everyday Life*. New York, NY: W. W. Norton.

Stuart, S. and Noyes, R. J. (1999). 'Attachment and interpersonal communication in somatization', *Psychosomatic Journal of Consulting Liaison Psychiatry*, 40: 34–43.

Taylor, R. E., Mann, A. H., White, N. J., and Goldberg, D. P. (2000). 'Attachment style in patients with unexplained physical complaints', *Psychological Medicine*, 30: 931– 41.

Teasdale, J. D., Segal, Z. V., Williams, J. M., Ridgeway, V. A., Soulsby, J. M., and Lau, M. A. (2000). 'Prevention of relapse/recurrence in major depression by mindfulness-based cognitive', *Journal of Consulting and Clinical Psychology*, 68(4): 615–23.

Vanheule, S., Verhaeghe, P., and Desmet, M. (2011). 'In search of a framework for the treatment of alexithymia', *Psychology and Psychotherapy: Theory, Research and Practice*, 84: 84–97.

Velasco, C., Fernandez, I., Paez, D., and Campos M. (2006). 'Perceived emotional intelligence, alexithymia, coping and emotional regulation', *Psicothema*, 18: 89–94.

Waldinger, R. J., Schulz, M. S., Barsky, A. J., and Ahern, D. K. (2006). 'Mapping the road from childhood trauma to adult somatization: The role of attachment', *Psychosomatic Medicine* 68: 129–35.

Waller, E. and Scheidt, C.E. (2006). 'Somatoform disorders as disorders of affect regulation: A development perspective', *International Review of Psychiatry*; 18: 13–24.

Waitzkin, H., and Magana, H. (1997). 'The black box in somatization: Unexplained physical symptoms, culture, and narratives of trauma', *Social Science and Medicine*; 45: 811–25.

Weiss, H., Harrer, M., and Dietz, T. (2010). *The Mindfulness Book*. Stuttgardt: Klett-Cotta.

Weiss, H. (2009). 'The use of mindfulness in psychodynamic and body oriented psychotherapy', *Body, Movement and Dance in Psychotherapy*, 4(1): 5–16.

Williams, J. M., and Kuyken, W. (2012). 'Mindfulness-based cognitive therapy: A promising new approach to preventing depressive relapse', *British Journal of Psychiatry*, 200(5): 359–60.

Whitehouse, M. S. (1999). 'Reflections on a metamorphosis', in P. Pallero (ed.), *Authentic Movement: Essays by Mary Starkes Whitehouse, Janet Adler and Joan Chodorow*. London: Jessica Kingsley, pp. 58–62.

World Health Organization (2010) 'Mental health: Strengthening our response'. *Fact Sheet No. 220*, September.

Zonneveld, L. N. L., van Rood, Y. R., Timman, R., Kooiman, C., Spijker, A., Busschbach, J. J. V. (2012). 'Effective group training for patients with unexplained physical symptoms: A randomized controlled trial with a non-randomized one-year follow-up', *PLoS ONE*, 7(8): e42629. doi:10.1371/journal.pone.0042629

CHAPTER 43

....

DANCE THERAPY

Primitive Expression Contributes to Wellbeing

....

ALEXIA MARGARITI, PERIKLIS KTONAS,
THOMAS PAPARRIGOPOULOS,
AND GRIGORIS VASLAMATZIS

INTRODUCTION

....

IN the last ten years, much has been said about one's psychological condition, with the main quest being the positive mood of individuals. This, of course, relates to their wellbeing. Creative, growth-oriented societies are concerned about the wellbeing of their members, which, by contributing to the health, functionality, and productivity of the members, enables the societies to pursue the aim of growth more easily and at a lower cost.

Over the centuries, dance has been 'used' to promote the wellbeing of the individual: to assuage human fears towards nature, to promote socialization among the members of a group–community–society, to entertain, to turn tough living conditions into something more positive, more encouraging, and more creative. Examples abound: warriors who danced before the battle to empower themselves; shamans who healed through dance; the ecstasy achieved through dancing in ancient Greece, leading to fulfilment. Many examples can be produced to show that dance has been used for its therapeutic properties. Research has expanded our knowledge of the therapeutic effects of dance, and has uncovered encouraging new evidence that places dance in a psychotherapeutic context.

Dance therapy, while exhibiting various differentiations in approach and technique, is a single approach to the standard objective of enhancing the participants' psychological, physical, and mental health. Several research projects have attempted a systematic study of the therapeutic effects of dance therapy on various disorders, as well as on the quality of life. Indicatively, the randomized controlled trial completed in Germany by Bräuninger (2012) showed that dance therapy with patients suffering from stress has a short-term as well as long-term positive effect on quality of life (Bräuninger 2012). Another example—a study that explored the use of dance therapy with psychotic outpatients—focused on variables relating to social adjustment and quality of life. The study showed a marked improvement in the quality of life of participants (Lee et al. 2008).

An approach to dance therapy is that of Primitive Expression—a form of dance therapy based on anthropological and psychoanalytic principles, providing physical and neuropsychological benefits. It involves ethologically and socially-based forms which are supplied for re-enactment, as well as an incentive for successful performance and a challenge to 'transcend'. In Primitive Expression, play, rhythm, dance and song work on a symbolic level. The aim is to alert the participants to act and to express themselves, while orienting their drives in a positive way. Preliminary results of a Primitive Expression-based therapy protocol with a small group of psychiatric patients (psychotic and depressive disorders) are presented in this chapter. It will be shown that a relatively short duration of this treatment led to observable changes in psychological state, behaviour, and brain physiology.

More specifically, this chapter present (1) an overview of the therapeutic aspects of dance, (2) an overview of the history of dance therapy in the West, including a detailed explanation of the tools used by dance therapy–Primitive Expression, and (3) findings of a recent research project involving the use of dance therapy–Primitive Expression with psychiatric patients.

Dance and Therapeutic Aspects of Dance

Dance

From the beginning of humanity, people assigned great importance to dance, and made it an integral part of mythology and religion (Lawler 1984; Tsilimigra 1983, pp. 14–25). Over the years, dance has been examined by many disciplines and from various perspectives: historical, anthropological, phenomenological, and medical. It is, therefore, hard to provide a clear definition of dance, but perhaps the 1937 interpretation of dance by Sachs (1937), as the most comprehensive art that expresses simultaneously one's mental, spiritual, and physical world, is the most apposite. The certain thing is that dance has been around for as long as humanity, always exerting a fascination on human beings and, in certain cultures, becoming an integral part of mythology and religion, as the next section shows.

Therapeutic Aspects of Dance

For the ancient Greeks, Terpsichore was considered to be the muse of dance. Her name, denoting 'pleasure from dance', expresses the importance of that human activity and its links with wellbeing. Plato, in the *Laws*, mentions the relationship of pleasure (*chara*) and dance (*choros*)—the latter being regarded as a gift from the Greek gods Apollo and Dionysus and from the Muses (Lawler 1984, p. 14).

Anthropological studies demonstrate people's necessity to use dance in order to meet functional needs of a magical–religious nature, as well as for healing purposes (Tsilimigra 1983, pp. 18–20). One such example is shamanism, which expressed the hopes and fears of our hunting forefathers and opened the gates to another, supernatural reality that people obviously needed. A shaman 'travelled' in other 'worlds' to meet spirits and ancestors, to 'convey' them symbolically and to become the mediator between the sick mortal and the hereafter. He used dance to lead patients into rituals aimed at their cure (Eliade 1978).

On the other hand, in ancient Greece, warriors would dance before the battle to empower themselves (Tsilimigra 1983, pp. 18–20). Indeed, the ancient Greeks believed that a correlation existed among mind, body, music, and medicine. The god Orpheus provided relief with his soothing, therapeutic music. Plato claims in *Laws* (Lawler 1984, p. 14) that participation in the offerings to gods through sacrificial rituals complete with rhythm and accompanied by the flute led people to equilibrium, through a certain state (ecstasy?). As Peterson Royce (2005) reports, dance had the power to initiate one in cathartic experiences (p. 98). Aristotle also asserted that Bacchic singing and dancing treated bouts of depression (Schott-Billmann 1997, p. 15). In southern Italy, women were 'cured' of the poisonous sting of spiders by dancing the Tarantella for three days and nights, imitating the movements of the spider.

Examples of the therapeutic aspects of dance abound through the centuries, as dance has been used for these purposes at various points in human history. Therefore, what we call 'dance therapy' today is a familiar therapeutic practice with deep roots in the memory of the collective past of the human species. The human body is the centre of accumulation of positive and negative experiences, and dance is the 'medium of expression' for all of these.

DANCE THERAPY AND PRIMITIVE EXPRESSION

General Observations

The foundations of dance therapy date from the twentieth century, when modern dance was looking for new values such as spontaneity, authenticity, and personal expression. The two world wars and the development of psychoanalytical theories and psychotherapeutic approaches contributed to the birth of dance therapy in the West. The term 'dance therapy' was used mainly after World War II, and the field evolved as a separate discipline. Many of the pioneer American dance therapists, such as B. Evan, M. Chase, M. Whitehouse, T. Schoop, and others were trained in contemporary dance. They also used the theories of European choreographer Rudolph Laban, who developed a system of observing, recording, and analyzing movement based on its key factors: space, time, dynamics, flow, and their interactions (Savrami 1990). The system of dance therapy that was developed in the United States was called dance/movement therapy (Levy 1998).

Primitive Expression, born almost at the same time, was a technique initiated by Katherine Dunham (dancer, choreographer, and educator) in the United States during the 1950s. She named it 'modern primitive', and it was based on anthropological studies of ritualistic dances that she conducted in the Caribbean while working on her doctorate in anthropology, during which time she examined the dance rhythms particular to Jamaica, Martinique, Trinidad, and Haiti. (Encyclopedia of World Biographies 2007). Based on her work, France Schott-Billmann, in France, developed the Primitive Expression technique further, utilizing ethnopsychoanalytical principles (Schott-Billmann 1977, 1985, 1997). The work of Schott- Billmann has utilized, among others, a therapeutic tool which Levi-Strauss (1958) calls 'symbolic effectiveness'.

Contemporary human beings, trapped in the modern way of life with little physical activity, are constantly at war with their inner and outer self. The struggle to meet the demands of family, work, and financial adversity, as well as to find balance within themselves, often leads to depression, panic attacks, or even total disruption of one's life. Dance therapy can have an effect by empowering people and helping them to arrive at solutions and ways out of the problems in a positive way. Can dance therapy, therefore, promote wellbeing? Several research studies are in progress in order to examine possible positive effects on quality of life (QoL) (Bräuninger 2012) which should relate to wellbeing.

The various aspects of the human condition —biological, psychological, cognitive, spiritual, social— are in constant interaction with one another, and affecting one of them will have an impact on the others. Through movement, we gain access to everything that concerns the pre-verbal stages of development and maturation (we move before we can talk). Every individual has his/her own personal movement, his/her own movement vocabulary. Furthermore, one's movement and body are mirrors of one's personal history, personality, and emotional state.

The body is the key tool which, guided by the dance therapist, discovers the spontaneous and authentic movement, one's personal rhythm as well as that of the group, one's own movement vocabulary. Over time, this vocabulary acquires shape and meaning, shedding light on the thoughts and emotions that come to the surface. Person–dancer retrieves his/her personal and collective memories and experiences, finds again the joy of the 'living' body, overcomes his/her initial inhibitions, and discovers a range of new options which enable him/her to affect desired changes (Margariti 2012). Dance therapy–Primitive Expression, with its appropriate tools, provides some powerful support in this process.

Primitive Expression

Primitive Expression is a body activity which provides physical and neuropsychological benefits. There is an epigenetic interaction of ethologically and socially-based forms which are supplied for re-enactment, as well as an incentive for successful performance and a challenge to 'transcend'. The individual undergoing Primitive Expression therapy finds himself/herself involved in dynamics which push himself/herself to go even further, to exceed each time his/her previous output, to go beyond limits. The atmosphere of play, which exists in the therapeutic procedure, reinforces the possibility of permissible excess. In Primitive Expression, with the use of percussion, roles are played just as children do, and figures of myth are enacted: warrior, hunter, thief, tribal leader, real or imaginary animals. This provides opportunities, and justifications, for satisfying the most varied desires, for exploring new behaviours, for trying out unfamiliar stances, and for expressing a wide range of feelings such as power, anger, pride, fear, and tenderness, leading to a therapeutic experience. The combination of rhythm, dance, and song works on a symbolic level. If a person utilizes symbolism—as in art, for example—it is because his/her desires are suppressed by society. He/she feels obliged to defer, by giving a ceremonial form to his/her needs, utilizing speech, writing, movement, and music.

Thus, the aim through symbolic movements in Primitive Expression is to alert the participants to act and express themselves, while orienting their drives in a positive way. In this manner they experience the truth and the beauty of movement through exceeding the limits of their personality, in a warm, secure, and playful environment.

The Tools of Primitive Expression

(a) The Force of Rhythm

In all its modalities, rhythm has a definite force. From the first hearing experience of the mother's heartbeat, to the everyday experience of breathing and the change from day to night, a rhythm can make an individual relax, and feel calm and secure. Paradoxically, however, it can also give him/her strength and lead him/her to action by activating related neurophysiological mechanisms (Hanna 2006; Schott-Billmann 1989).

(b) The Sound of Percussion

The sound of percussion is a reminder of the human heartbeat—the strong rhythm that the baby hears while a foetus. This experience has a maternal as well as a paternal component, relating to calmness (security) and excitement (independence) respectively (Schott-Billmann 1997).

(c) The Use of Voice

The human species needs to communicate. One means is the human voice. The baby matures by listening to his/her mother's voice. In Primitive Expression, the use of voice is very important. The technique uses melodies or *phonimata* (a Greek word meaning 'phonetic forms') in order to engage the participant in a communication process reminiscent of the one he/she was involved with as a baby, while in his/her mother's lap. Singing, along with all the others in the group, he/she uses the voice in a completely acceptable way. Through his/her voice, he/she expresses his/her own personal feelings, consciously or subconsciously.

(d) *The Simplicity of Movements*

The dancer engages in the Primitive Expression session by copying the simple movement provided by the therapist. Usually, an individual may not have a movement vocabulary. In other words, he/she may have no preconceived notion concerning a dance output. The simplicity of movement tool helps the dancer to copy effectively the movement that is given from the therapist, even if he/she may not have a good relation with his/her body, providing the possibility for the dancer to impart his/her own meaning to the movement. So, finally, by using the rhythm and the simplicity of movements as catalysts, the participant starts moving and dancing.

(e) *The Repetition Process*

Through this tool, the dancer is made to 'give a bit more' with each repetition of a given movement. It is as if, by moving rhythmically in a specific place in space, with repetitive movements, the dancer may be 'putting things in order'.

(f) *The Importance of the Group*

The Primitive Expression experience is a group process which provides the dancers with a maternal substitute. In other words, being part of the group provides the experience of a *mother–child* relation and prepares for the experience of a *me–Other* relation. The mover–dancer can see the group as a reflection of his/her self, and can be encouraged to experience the above dynamics. This provides a feeling of calmness and safety.

(g) *The Relation to the Ground*

The Primitive Expression technique requires the dancers to be barefoot, since the relation to the ground is very important for wellbeing (a sense of grounding). The feeling of the ground under the feet contributes to the sense of support and safety. Given that, the whole body feels free to act, by moving and dancing.

(h) *The Use of Play*

It is in the experience of play that the individual, whether child or adult, is able to become creative and to use his/her personality effectively. Also, since laughing can occur during play, it enables the experience of joy. Engaged in the creative process mentioned previously, the Primitive Expression dancer is dancing roles—as if he/she were a warrior or an animal, aggressor or victim, seducing or being seduced. He/she improvises ceremonies influenced by nature. He/she plays and dances roles from his/her own life, and expresses them effortlessly without the criticism of anyone, because he/she is in a play. In this way, he/she also minimizes paying attention to himself/herself, contributing to the ensuing sublimation.

(i) *The Duality*

Duality is everywhere. Human beings have to struggle with biphasic conditions (for example, positive–negative, life–death, male–female) which are inherent in everyday life. This Primitive Expression tool relates to the above by proposing exercises which involve antitheses and sequences thereof.

Through the combination of all these tools, the dancer may feel more free to overcome the super-ego, the possible limits expressed in restricted movements, and may experience sublimation, enabling the feeling of enthusiasm (a word of Greek origin meaning 'God within you'). Freud (1930) wrote:

> Sublimation of instinct is an especially conspicuous feature of cultural development; it is what makes it possible for higher physical activities, scientific, artistic, or ideological, to play such an important part in civilized life. If one were to yield to a first impression, one would say that sublimation is a vicissitude which has been forced upon the instincts entirely by civilization.

This state of sublimation can lead to the ultimate Primitive Expression objective which is transcendence (Schott-Billmann 1997). By this is meant a quest for beauty in the participant's movements, independent of social or other conventions. As a result, the participant empowers himself/herself, exceeds his/her limits, and experiences a sense of fulfilment and, eventually, happiness. A state facilitating this process may be that of trance, which can lead to transcendence by engaging powerful dynamics within the individual. Such dynamics have been described from a psychoanalytical as well as anthropological perspective (Schott-Billmann 1985). Primitive Expression, by engaging the participant in a complex physical–cognitive–affective process of recollecting and releasing repressed emotions and tensions, enables him/her to come to terms with them through the goal of transcendence (e.g. Hanna 2006).

There is a video accompanying this chapter, showcasing a short session of dance therapy–Primitive Expression, during which the specific tools of the Expression approach are highlighted Primitive (see Video 43.1 on the Companion Website ▶).

An Example of the Use of Primitive Expression Therapy with Psychiatric Patients

Severe mental disorders—psychotic disorders in particular, for example—are characterized by a disintegration of thought processes, most commonly manifesting as delusional/paranoid ideas, auditory hallucinations, and disorganized thinking, as well as by disturbed emotional responsiveness. In addition, the cardinal feature of depressive disorders is the occurrence of low mood, which pervades all aspects of life and severely impacts wellbeing and everyday functioning. These symptoms are expressed with increased psychic tension, anxiety, and aggression, and reduce the capacity for interpersonal communication and pleasure. Primitive Expression therapy may produce improvements through the engagement and encouragement of such patients to express themselves, relate to others, and increase self-awareness in a secure environment. Above all, however, it may help them discover joy through their body.

The use of Primitive Expression therapy with a small group of psychiatric patients (psychotic and depressive disorders) showed that a relatively short duration of this treatment led to observable changes in psychological state, behaviour, and brain physiology. In what follows, we present an overview of this study, and further information can be found in Margariti et al. (2012). For this study, by "wellbeing" is meant "happiness".

Participants

The place of the study was the University of Athens Psychiatric Clinic in the Aiginiteion Hospital. The participants were eleven live-in psychiatric patients chosen randomly with the same diagnostic criteria. The group included six patients with psychotic disorders, one with an obsessive compulsive disorder, and four with depressive disorder. There were six females and five males, with an age range of 21–64. The patients were under appropriate pharmacotherapy (mostly atypical antipsychotics and antidepressants), and there were twelve Primitive Expression sessions, twice a week for six weeks. The study conformed to the Helsinki declaration on human experimentation, and was approved by the ethics committee of the Aiginiteion Hospital. Written informed consent was obtained from all participants.

Data Collection and Analysis

(a) Questionnaires

Two questionnaires were utilized in this study: a Greek version of the Oxford Happiness Questionnaire (OHQ), which assesses the happiness level of the patients (Hills and Argyle 2002), and a questionnaire about word associations (WA) concerning the patient experience/response with the Primitive Expression sessions. Included in the WA questionnaire were questions asking the patients to indicate which words came to their mind related to, for example, 'dance therapy', 'sound of percussion', 'dance group', and others. In this work we present results concerning WA with 'dance therapy' only. OHQ was administered before the first session and after the fifth and eleventh sessions. WA was administered after the first, fifth, and eleventh sessions by the investigators.

(b) Electroencephalogram

Electroencephalography (EEG) was performed in the awake, resting state with eyes closed, for about three minutes, before and after the fifth and the eleventh sessions, in five patients with psychotic disorders, in order to have a clinically homogeneous EEG group. Electrodes were applied at the frontal, central, and occipital scalp areas in both hemispheres. The presence of alpha EEG activity was quantified with visual analysis, since EEG activity in the alpha range (8–12 Hz) is typical of a state of relaxed wakefulness in healthy adults (Spehlmann 1981).

Results

(a) *Questionnaires*

Analysis of the OHQ data indicated that as the Primitive Expression therapy sessions progressed there was a statistically significant gradual increase in happiness level for the patient group, on the average (ANOVA for repeated measures and post hoc t-tests; $p < 0.05$; see Table 43.1).

Analysis of the WA data indicated that after the first as well as after the fifth therapy session, the word group 'movement, dance, sound, music' was considered by the patients as the most important description of 'dance therapy'. However, after the eleventh therapy session, this word group was replaced by the group 'joy, happiness, laughter', implying that the patients could have reached the objective of their therapy process, which was an improvement in their happiness (for more details see Margariti et al. 2012).

(b) *Electroencephalogram*

There was more alpha EEG activity incidence after the fifth therapy session than before the fifth session in two of the five patients monitored for EEG; and there was more alpha activity incidence after the eleventh therapy session than before the eleventh session in three of four patients. These results indicate a possible acute effect of Primitive Expression therapy on the alpha EEG activity; that is, immediately after a dance therapy session. There was more alpha activity incidence after the eleventh therapy session than after the fifth session in four of five patients, indicating a possible long-term effect as well; that is, throughout a period of several sessions (for more details see Margariti et al. 2012).

Table 43.1. Average happiness level scores.

	Average Happiness Level Score	Std. Deviation
Before the first session	2.76	0.46
After the fifth session	3.04	0.44
After the eleventh session	3.25	0.58

(Credit: Margariti.)

DISCUSSION

This example presents encouraging results of using a Primitive Expression-based dance therapy protocol with a small group of psychiatric patients in order to improve their happiness/wellbeing. It was shown that a relatively short duration of Primitive Expression treatment lasting for about 1½ months led to changes in patient psychological state, behaviour, and, to some extent, brain physiology. Specifically, it was shown that the patients 1) experienced throughout the Primitive Expression process a progressive increase in their happiness level as measured by the OHQ, 2) expressed a positive attitude to the Primitive Expression process by utilizing appropriate WA which related to the tools of the Primitive Expression process, and 3) exhibited (in a subset of five patients with psychotic disorders) a relative increase in alpha EEG activity (indicative of a relaxed awake state in healthy adults) both in an acute fashion (immediately after a Primitive Expression session) as well as in a long-term fashion (throughout a period of several Primitive Expression sessions). Furthermore, the patients became happier, more functional, and more social, as attested by evidence provided by the nursing personnel and the families of the patients (the specific data are not presented in this chapter).

Since it has been known that there is decreased alpha EEG activity in the awake resting state in schizophrenia (Dierks et al. 1989; Fenton et al. 1980; Itil 1977; Koukkou 1982), these results indicate that Primitive Expression therapy might have 'normalized' the alpha activity level in these patients. Furthermore, given the fact that alpha EEG activity is typical of a state of relaxed wakefulness in healthy adults (Spehlmann 1981), it is of interest to hypothesize that this EEG change might have related to the happiness level improvement in this patient group. A similar Primitive Expression-based dance therapy protocol involving a group of nine psychotic patients led to similar results as far as happiness level improvement and alpha EEG activity enhancement were concerned (Margariti 2012). Furthermore, a detailed mathematical analysis of the EEG in that patient group revealed changes in the intra- and interhemispheric brain connectivity as a result of the therapeutic process. Since these changes are apparently commensurate with an improvement in patient status, the results presented make the Primitive Expression form of dance therapy a promising therapeutic tool for this mental disorder (Ventouras et al. 2015). It is tempting to speculate that changes in the psychological state of the patients (an increased happiness level), possibly related to the Primitive Expression process, seem to be accompanied by 'appropriate' changes in the brain physiology of the patients.

According to the results of the study, after the first Primitive Expression session the word group 'movement, dance, sound, music' was considered by the patients as the most important description of the therapeutic process. This could be explained by the fact that the structure of a Primitive Expression session is characterized to a large extent by these components, which, apparently, impressed the patients and were reflected in their words. On the other hand, after the eleventh Primitive Expression session a different word group, 'joy, happiness, laughter', was the most important for the description of the process. This word group summarizes the ultimate objective of the Primitive Expression therapeutic process—quest of transcendence through sublimation—which, apparently, was achieved by the patients. Interestingly, the words 'joy' and 'happiness' were mentioned as patient responses to their therapeutic experience in a previous Primitive Expression study conducted in the Psychiatric Hospital of Attica, with patients suffering from drug addiction (Margariti 1994).

It may be of interest to investigate how specific Primitive Expression tools might have led to the WA results. The following are some of the Primitive Expression tools, with related WA used by the patients indicated in parentheses:

- the force of rhythm (sound, music)
- the sound of percussion (sound, music)
- the use of voice (sound)
- the simplicity of movements (movement)
- the use of play (laughter)

These indicate that although the patients did not know beforehand the methodology to be followed in the Primitive Expression procedure, the tools of this technique were sufficiently powerful to modify the disposition of the patients, which they expressed in words commensurate with the objectives of the tools, and to eventually lead them to respond that dance therapy for them is joy, happiness, laughter.

Conclusion

The more a society develops, the more creative, strong, and growth-oriented it becomes, having healthy and happy members who are functional and productive. However, in order for this to happen, the wellbeing of the people needs to be at an appropriate level. Throughout the centuries, dance has contributed to wellbeing, serving several purposes, one of which has been therapeutic. There are many examples of the therapeutic dimension of dance in human history. During the twentieth century in the West, it was called 'dance therapy'.

Primitive Expression is an approach to dance therapy, aiming at the release of tension and the creation of joy through psychodynamic mechanisms. The emergence of the unconscious at the conscious level through symbolic movements, as well as the interconnection of the physical, mental, and spiritual parts of human nature through appropriate tools, render dance therapy–Primitive Expression a very promising method that is straightforward in its implementation. Its tools enable the participants to easily reach the essence of their human existence and to change 'negative' to 'positive', which must be very important for wellbeing. Besides, the uncomplicated and playful structure of the procedure accommodates populations with a very limited movement vocabulary.

This example of applying dance therapy–Primitive Expression to a psychiatric population showed encouraging results concerning the happiness/wellbeing of the patients. Specifically, although the patients did not have any a priori knowledge concerning the tools of this procedure, the questionnaire and EEG results indicated that these tools are sufficiently effective to lead to positive changes in the psychological state, behaviour, and brain physiology of the patients. Furthermore, the patients became happier, more functional, and more social, as attested by evidence provided by the nursing personnel and the families of the patients (the specific data are not presented here). Although the patient sample was limited, and long-term effects after the termination of the sessions were not measured, the study offers some promising results for the value of dance therapy–Primitive Expression as a tool towards happiness/wellbeing. Therefore, Primitive Expression can be added to the other dance therapy methodologies which have been shown to be promising therapeutic approaches for these patient populations.

It appears that there is an emerging interest in applying neuroscience-based approaches in dance therapy applications in order to investigate specific brain functions during this therapeutic process (see, for example, the work of Jeong et al. 2005, who report that dance therapy modulates hormonal and neurotransmitter release, which may be involved in the therapeutic process). The dance therapy–Primitive Expression application discussed in this chapter may be one of very few dance therapy applications which utilize in their protocol the assessment of possible neurophysiological changes (such as EEG changes) as a result of the dance therapy process.

In the more than twenty-five-year experience of the authors in dance therapy–Primitive Expression, the application of this procedure to "normal neurotics" has produced positive results concerning the wellbeing of the participants. After years of the dance therapy–Primitive Expression experience, they mention that they have learned how to 'listen' to their body and be aware of their feelings. In this way, they have learned to manage their problems and find a solution for them through the happiness resulting from the dance therapy experience. Furthermore, they know how to use the process in their own lives. It is as if the knowledge obtained from such sessions has been incorporated into their everyday life, so that they can use it whenever it is needed. This offers a strong argument that the Primitive Expression approach to dance therapy contributes to happiness/wellbeing.

ACKNOWLEDGEMENTS

We would like to thank the Psychiatric Clinic of the University of Athens Medical School in the Aiginiteion Hospital, Athens, Greece, for providing the patients and for overall encouragement for the studies described in this chapter. Professors C. Soldatos and G. Papadimitriou were especially helpful in establishing the proper arrangements for the realization of the studies. The nursing personnel of the Psychiatric Clinic, especially P. Hondraki and associated social workers, are thanked for their important contribution to these studies.

References

Bräuninger, I. (2012). 'The efficacy of dance movement therapy, group on improvement of quality of life: A randomized controlled trial', *The Arts in Psychotherapy*, 39: 296–303.

Dierks, T., Maurer, K., Ihl, R., and Schmidtke, A. (1989). 'Evaluation and interpretation of topographic EEG data in schizophrenic patients', in K. Maurer (ed.), *Topographic Brain Mapping of EEG and Evoked Potentials*. Berlin: Springer, pp. 507–517.

Fenton, G. W., Fenwick, P. B., and Dollimore, J. (1980). 'EEG spectral analysis in schizophrenia', *British Journal of Psychiatry*, 136: 445–55.

Eliade, M. (1978). *Le Chamanisme et les Techniques Archaiques de l'Extase* (Greek translation). Athens: Editions Chadjinikoli.

Encyclopedia of World Biographies (2007). <http://www.notablebiographies.com/newsmakers2/2007-Co-Lh/Dunham-Katherine.html>

Freud, S. (1930). *Civilisation and its Discontents*. <http://203.200.22.249:8080/jspui/bitstream/2014/9419/1/Civilization-and-its-discontent.pdf >

Hanna, J. L. (2006). *Dancing for Health*. Lanham, MD: Altamira Press.

Hills, P. and Argyle, M. (2002). 'The Oxford Happiness Questionnaire: A compact scale for the measurement of psychological well-being', *Personality and Individual Differences*, 33: 1073–82.

Itil, T. M. (1977). 'Qualitative and quantitative EEG findings in schizophrenia', *Schizophrenia Bulletin*, 3: 61–79.

Jeong, Y. J., Hong, S. C., Lee, M., Park, M. C., Kim, Y. K., and Suh, C. M. (2005). 'Dance/movement therapy improves emotional responses and modulates neurohormones in adolescents with mild depression', *International Journal of Neuroscience*, 115(12): 1711–20.

Koukkou, M. (1982). 'EEG states of the brain, information processing, and schizophrenic primary symptoms', *Psychiatry Research*, 6: 235–44.

Lawler, L. B. (1984). *Dance in Ancient Greece* (Greek translation). Athens: Cultural Association of Greek Dances, Traditional Dance Center.

Lee, J., Park, S., Kim, H. S., and Kim, C. Y. (2008). 'Clinical application of dance therapy in psychiatric outpatients with schizophrenia', *Journal of Korean Neuropsychiatric Association*, 47(3): 279–85.

Levy, F. (1988). *Dance Movement Therapy: A Healing Art*. New York, NY: National Dance Association, American Alliance for Health, Physical Education, Recreation and Dance.

Levi-Strauss, J. (1958). *Anthropologie Structurale*. Paris: Plon.

Margariti, A. (1994). 'The application of dance therapy in the case of a drug addicts group.' 3rd European Conference for Arts Therapies-Ecarte. Ferrara, Italy.

Margariti, A., Ktonas, P., Hondraki, P., Daskalopoulou, E., Kyriakopoulos, G., Economou, N. T., Tsekou, H., Paparrigopoulos, T., Barbousi, V., and Vaslamatzis, G. (2012). 'An application of the Primitive Expression form of dance therapy in a psychiatric population', *The Arts in Psychotherapy*, 39: 95–101.

Margariti, A. (2012). *Results of the Primitive Expression form of Dance Therapy in a Psychiatric Population*. PhD thesis, University of Peloponnese, Nafplion, Greece.

Peterson Royce, A. (2005). *The Anthropology of Dance* (Greek translation). Athens: Nisos.

Sachs, C., (1937). *World History of the Dance*. New York, NY: W. W. Norton.

Savrami, K. (1990). *Kinisiographica*. Athens.

Schott-Billmann, F. (1977). *Corps et Possession*. Paris: Gauthier-Villars.

Schott-Billmann, F. (1985). *Possession, Danse et Therapie*. Paris: Sand.

Schott-Billmann, F. (1989). *Le Primitivisme en Danse*. Paris: Chiron.

Schott-Billmann, F. (1997). *Quand la Danse Guerit*. Paris: La Recherche en Danse.

Spehlmann, R. (1981). *EEG Primer*. Amsterdam: Elsevier/North-Holland Biomedical Press.

Tsilimigra, K. (1983). *Dance* (in Greek). Athens: Melissa.

Ventouras, E. C., Margariti, A., Chondraki, P., Kalatzis, I., Economou, N.T., Tsekou H., Paparrigopoulos, T., and Ktonas, P. (2015). 'EEG-based investigation of brain connectivity changes in psychotic patients undergoing the Primitive Expression form of dance therapy: A methodological pilot study', *Cognitive Neurodynamics*, 9: 231–48.

CHAPTER 44

DANCE MOVEMENT THERAPY

An Aesthetic Experience to Foster Wellbeing for Vulnerable Mothers and Infants

ELIZABETH LOUGHLIN

INTRODUCTION

BABIES can be full of awe and wonder, and vividly aware of everything that goes on around them; they attend, riveted, to a new or unexpected event for a surprisingly long time, and have more neural pathways available than do adults, with less inhibiting action (Gopnik 2009). As Trevarthen (1997) claims, the baby from birth possesses motives for companionship that are specially adapted to perceive, respond to, attract, and influence how other people feel and act. The infant develops these capacities within the love, devoted care, and ongoing sensitive responsiveness of the mother, supported by father or other family.

However, for an estimated 14% of mothers (Buist et al. 2004) the advent of the infant is a biologically and emotionally stressful event to the extent that the mother develops postnatal depression (PND) or anxiety.[1] While some mothers with PND can maintain their relationship with their infant, for many who may have extra risk factors—for example, past history of depression, lack of social support, prior miscarriage, or a history of childhood abuse (Milgrom et al. 2010)—the experience of PND is debilitating and does not easily remit. A very small percentage of mothers develop a more severe condition, postpartum psychosis, requiring immediate hospitalization.

The physical and emotional symptoms of depression (American Psychiatric Association 2013) can dampen or alter the mother's wish to love and care for her baby. A mother may not understand why she is so tired, feeling tearful, low in confidence, or losing her joy about her baby (Fettling and Tune 2005). If her mental health deteriorates further, the mother may be confused about her care for her baby. It has been argued by Tronick and Weinberg (1997) that the infant himself/herself notices the mother's 'still face' and lack of responsiveness, and looks away, self-comforts, and disengages from mother. Where there has been severe disruption in the relationship, the infant may withdraw from social interaction (Guedeney 2007).

Studies show that even when the mother is treated for PND and infant behaviour problems, the mother–infant interactions do not necessarily improve beyond the short term (Murray et al. 2003). In these families, infant and mother need thoughtful planned opportunities within the health system[2] for the infant with mother to regain the natural and necessary 'liveness of the intercommunication' (Winnicott 1988, p. 99).

Key concepts in clinical infant observation or observational research (Winnicott 1960; Stern 1985, 1995) inform dance movement therapy (DMT) for the hospital mother–infant population. Winnicott's concept of 'primary maternal preoccupation' (Davis and Wallbridge 1981) describes the ordinary mother's identification with her new baby, her interest and absorption in her infant, and her reliable handling and secure holding of her infant over the first months. The infant's cross-modal capacities to perceive and respond in different sense modalities (Stern 1985) allows the infant of a few months to be open to a range of 'toy' objects, and mother's varying expressive responses. The multimodal mother–infant interactions are termed by Stern (2010) 'vitality forms', of which movement is the most salient. Kestenberg and Buelte (1977), Kestenberg (1992), and Loman (2014) offer a method for the dance therapist to observe the developmental issues and the therapeutic changes in the mother–infant interaction, while the Kestenberg Movement Profile (KMP) (Loman and Sossin 2009) provides a quantitative methodology for research.

The next section refers to DMT research for depression, and outlines documented DMT programmes in the hospital and community setting that aim to ameliorate the effects of PND on mother–infant interaction.

DANCE MOVEMENT THERAPY
FOR DEPRESSION

In the review of DMT evidence-based practice for depression (Mala et al. 2011), the experimental study by Koch et al. (2007) of DMT intervention for psychiatric adult patients diagnosed with depression underlines the value of vitality in DMT for mothers with PND. Koch et al. (2007) used pre- and post-measures of a single intervention of a traditional circle 'joy' dance, with small vertical jumps, in a two-one factorial design: dance versus music, and dance versus movement/machine trainer. Patients in the dance-only group showed significant less depression compared to the music-only and movement/trainer-only, and a significant increase in vitality compared to the music-only group.

Hospital Models of Mother–Infant DMT

In the mother–baby inpatient psychiatric unit, the Move and Play group (Albiston 1992) integrated movement with education on play and baby care to enhance wellbeing.

Batcup (2004) adapted a Chacian model of guided movement experiences for mothers to access feelings about motherhood, their own infant, and their stay in the psychiatric unit.

In the hospital outpatient clinic, Coulter and Loughlin (1999) found that the synergy of group creative DMT and individual psychoanalytic psychotherapy clinically improved the mother–infant interactions. Again in the outpatient clinic, a sequential group model of psychological therapies, followed by Intuitive Mothering—an eight-week programme of DMT and verbal closure—for approximately five mothers with infants of ages 7–9 months, further developed the team collaborative approach (Milgrom et al. 2001). Two outreach hospital models include a fourteen-week programme of therapeutic play and dance in the community, (Women & Children's Hospital Foundation (2013) *Therapeutic Arts, Acorn Project. http://www.wchfoundation.org.au/therapeutic-arts*) and a ten-week therapeutic playgroup with a hospital-authored manual of contrasting paradigms of psychoeducation/parenting strategies, interwoven with creative play/dance, designed for disadvantaged communities (Milgrom et al. 2008).

Study Outcomes of Mother–Infant DMT

In contrast to the number of evaluated mother–infant health and welfare therapeutic programmes (Zeanah, 1993; Cichetti et al. 2000; Poobalan et al. 2007), published systematic studies in hospital mother–infant DMT are few. A hospital ethics-approved phenomenological study 'The experience of dancing with my baby' of five mothers from the community or clinic (Loughlin 1997) reviewed their experience in video feedback and reflection twelve months later. One mother was referred to group DMT with an anxiety disorder and concern about bonding with her 18-month-old infant. She perceived the change in herself in her increasingly lively dance as 'a new freedom' that gave her 'confidence, and improved self-esteem . . . and assertiveness', as well as a new 'closeness' with her infant in their dancing together (Loughlin 1997, p. 217).

DMT studies have made use of the KMP to measure specific aspects of mother–infant relational behaviour. In a German mother–infant psychiatric ward, videotapes of 3–5 minutes of mother–infant interactions in play situations were coded by a KMP trained rater on four mother–infant pairs (Lier-Schehl 2003). The results revealed significant differences in shape flow between mother and infant. Depressed mothers were observed as often under-involved in movement, especially in shape flow, while mothers with psychosis were over-involved and disorganized (Lier-Schehl 2003).[3]

Depression may be present in families with a history of abuse or trauma. In a community family service unit, Meekums (1992) studied the outcome of a twenty-week DMT programme of movement games and improvisation for four mothers and their children, aged 2–3 years, who were considered at risk of abuse. One mother and her son were described with depressed body attitude. The programme was evaluated with dance movement therapist/researcher observation and maternal report. Included in the outcomes of DMT was a rise in physical interaction through molding and shaping of the mother and child bodies to each other. This interaction modality was found to be defensively avoided at times by the mothers, even when the child approached its mother (Meekums 1992).

In a different approach to DMT, a case study by Ostroburski (2009) describes a twenty-four-month programme of creative dance and play interventions for mother and child, within a dance psychotherapy model in a family support agency. Play objects were used as metaphors that allowed the 2-year-old child to find her expressive movement pathway through her traumatic experience of the loss of her older sibling in a road accident, and also to contribute towards the repair of her disrupted relationship with her grieving mother.

The literature accounts of DMT with the depressed mother and her infant/young child demonstrate differing DMT interventions and varying methodology for evaluation of programmes. The range of DMT practices documented suggests that there is a need for examining a DMT approach that may continue in the health setting over the long term. A need is also seen for dance movement therapists to be involved with evaluation and research measures which are familiar to mainstream hospital clinical staff, in order to ensure professional DMT development and employment.

This chapter focuses on one type of dance arts intervention, linked with psychodynamic concepts (Coulter and Loughlin 1999; Ostroburski 2009), that has developed over time, named here as the 'aesthetic approach'. The background of the aesthetic processes in DMT and the contribution of arts philosophy is considered, and a description of the aesthetic 'tools' or interventions, with accompanying vignettes, illustrate DMT with mother–infant in the hospital setting. A summary of research outcomes of a three-part treatment programme for mother–infant, which includes DMT with the aesthetic approach (Loughlin, 2009; Milgrom et al. 2010) is presented later in the chapter.

THE AESTHETIC APPROACH

Professional dancers and dance teachers brought aesthetic elements of dance to early DMT with hospital psychiatric populations (Levy 1988). Marian Chace started her session with the spatial form of the circle and the dance form of the waltz as a safe way to draw her patients into movement with others (Chaiklin 2009). Trudi Schoop drew on humour inherent in her earlier dance and mime performance career to engage her patients in movement and dance expression (Levy 1988).

Decades later, Bruno (1990) called for dance movement therapists to maintain the integrity of their original medium of dance as 'health-inspiring, force-awakening, nurturing, and guiding the individual's expressive energies into meaningful form' (112), while applying a psychological perspective. More recently, dance movement therapy writers remind us of the action of metaphor in DMT as a healing agent (Meekums 2000), and that DMT is one of the arts psychotherapy modalities 'that base their theories and practices on the potential for change and healing inherent to the creative processes and artistic endeavor' (Wengrower 2009, p. 14).

In the area of arts philosophy, de Botton and Armstrong (2013) argue that art is a therapeutic 'tool' for our psychological frailties. They examine how the communication power of the art object or design provides the function of Remembering; Hope; Sorrow; Rebalancing; Self-understanding; Growth; and Appreciation (de Botton and Armstrong 2013). Arts philosopher Suzanne Langer (1953) wrote about the dance arts owning a vital power; the dancer has an experience of volition and free agency. She argues that in the dance arts there is a rightness of form for the patterns of feeling expressed. In DMT, forming brings clarity of expression, allowing maladaptive patterns to be released and new behaviours to be developed (Leventhal 1993). Psychoanalyst Bollas (1987) refers to the 'aesthetic moment'—fundamentally, a wordless moment of form and feeling which reflects the mother's idiom of care and her infant's experience of that care.

According to the *Concise English Dictionary* (Annadale *c.*1918–30), aesthetic is defined as pertaining to the science and sense of beauty, from the Greek word *aesthetikos*, which is derived from *aesthanomai*, to perceive by the senses (p. 13). This early definition presages Stern's (1985) finding of the infant's cross-modal sense perception and responses, and of Bollas' (1987) 'aesthetic moment' of play with the mother.

Another way of thinking about the change process in DMT is Bion's (1983) psychoanalytic concept of 'dreaming'. Grotstein (2009), in his preface to Pistiner de Cortinas' commentary on Bion, explains that the Alpha function or 'dreaming' intercepts the sense impressions of our emotional experiences and transforms them into the creative as well as the more tolerable renditions of the original emotional truth. The process of 'dreaming' what the infant brings to the mother or what the infant and mother show the therapist, also depends on the dance movement therapist's 'being with' in the unstructured 'dreaming' of the mother and baby, yet with a thinking mind to anticipate the qualities to be encouraged in the infant–mother interaction.

AESTHETIC TOOLS

Tool: Liminal Space

Both the outpatient and inpatient settings for DMT offer a liminal space, a space in between (Turner 1979), set apart from the usual expectations of hospital clinic and ward. In both the larger space in the outpatient clinic and the smaller space of the inpatient psychiatric unit, carpeted floors, minimal furniture, and natural light create an open, pleasant, safe, and predictable environment for each session. At the same time, a different aesthetic form of one type of play object, for example, upturned colourful small buckets on the floor, or a blue and silver patterned silk material hanging from a corner of the space, arouses surprise and holds the mother–infant curiosity to initiate a cycle of interest, feeling, engagement, play, gesture, and dance together.

Tool: the Expressive 'Toy' Objects

The selection and use of play 'toy' objects in the DMT follow the infant's interactive social development stages (Murray 1989; Stern 1995; Trevarthen 1987, 2004). The stages range from approximately 0–10/12 weeks, where the sense impressions of the movement of a transparent cloth, light reflected off soft silver paper, or the sound of small bells, elicit the infant's attention and response. The mother in the inpatient DMT notices her infant's response, and sometimes says 'I didn't know this was playing'.

The next stage, from approximately 3/4–8/9 months, the infant initiates play with the 'toy' object; for example, waving a coloured plastic fly swat and noticing when mother mirrors the game with her swat, to bring about what Stern (1974) observes as shared humour. The more mobile infant of 9–12 months enjoys moving across the floor to investigate and roll brightly coloured stubby cylinders, and references mother to watch or join in the action.

The 'toy' object can represent a means of connecting the mother-and-infant pair,[4] who, following mother's PND, has not found the pleasure of face-to-face 'talk'.

> A cane hoop with amber cellophane over the internal space is held vertically by the mother. Sean, her 10-month infant, peers through the cellophane at his mother, who is filtered by the colour. The infant smiles and grabs one side of the hoop and laughs, pleased to look at his mother in the game, as she is pleased to see his smiling face. Both draw closer, their faces coming together in a cellophane kiss.

The hoop acts as a metaphor (Meekums 2000) for a filtered gaze that allows a new communication for both mother and infant, and the action represents 'Hope' (de Botton and Armstrong 2013) for mother in their future relationship.

In the Intuitive Mothering group, a mother may say of the DMT space, 'There is always something new for us here. Where do you find these things?' While in the psychiatric unit a mother may look in to say 'What have you brought in today?' or 'Is there time for me this afternoon?' With this expression of interest, mothers begin their engagement in shared play with their infants. After the first session they may report on the objects they have 'Remembered' (de Botton and Armstrong 2013) and found at home after the group, or on their weekend leave—a preloved scarf, bubbles, or a newly bought rattle.

Tool: Form of Dyadic Space

The dance movement therapist works directly with the dyadic space in which the quality of the interaction between mother and infant can be seen. Do the infant and mother look harmoniously at each other, or in opposite directions? Can the mother show a clear bodily intent (Merleau-Ponty 1962) and lean her upper body towards her infant, or broaden her face (Kestenberg, 1992) into a smile as her young infant turns to her. Kestenberg and Buelte (1977) describe these moving dyadic shapes as rhythms of shape flow, growing and shrinking, that represent trust. Kestenberg advises direct education of the mother–infant mutual holding in the upright position: 'Mother's embracing arms supports the child's pelvis; the child's embracing arm holds the mother's neck or shoulder; together they form a holding unit' (Kestenberg and Buelte 1977: 358). In the following vignette I structure the dyadic intervention through gradual increase of space and rhythmical music to encourage the mother–infant habitual holding pattern into more communicative contours.

> In the first session of the outpatient DMT group the mother's depression has improved after CBT, but her flat appearance is a residue of that depression, and remains in her interaction with her baby. Eight-month-old infant Helena is quiet in her mother's arms, with no squirming around to see the others in the group. The mother's upper body is still. Mother says she finds her infant heavy to carry. There are no ongoing muscular flow adjustments between the pair. In spite of interesting wooden chimes hanging from the ceiling, both mother and Helena look in opposite directions. In the following session, as mother moves to the regular rhythm of a Baroque lute she accepts my suggestion to support her infant's pelvis from underneath and lift her infant higher, so she can easily see around. In the next session the mother intuitively lifts her daughter up so the infant no longer is caught on her mother's chest. By the end of the eight-week programme, Helena is holding on to her mother's shoulder and shaping to her mother's movement flow as mother steps out confidently, both smiling and rising and sinking to the joyous African music.[5]

Molding and shape-flow rhythms are foremost in other reported DMT outcomes (Meekums 1992; Lier-Schehl 2003). The focus on holding patterns for Helena and her mother contributes to improved shape flow. This 'Rebalancing' (de Botton and Armstrong 2013) is a visual sign of their happier relationship.

Tool: Aliveness

Dance, by its essential quality, animates the dancer and the viewer through its kinaesthetic feel (Sheets-Johnstone 2010). The action of movement experience objectifies vitality (Langer 1953). In the next vignette the infant's energetic responses to the 'toy' object and the music spurs her mother to 'vitalization' (Schmais 1985).

> Terrie, a depressed mother in the inpatient unit, was referred to individual DMT, as mother was not happy with her infant. She says she is not a good mother, and that she is not sure what to do with her baby. 'She doesn't like me' is her projection of her own worry. The 8-month-old infant is noting her mother but not looking at her directly; the infant is interested in the 'toy' objects on the floor, but leaves her mother out of this baby game. After the second session, Terrie says she only comes in because her baby likes coming to play. In the third session, after trying to engage her infant,

Terrie watches her baby crawling faster, pushing a small pretty bell ball forward with the music, and then collecting it, very busy. Terrie suddenly gathers her energy and breaks out in a crawling movement around her infant, who is so surprised by her mother's initiative and intensity that the infant straightaway looks at mother and joins with her in her game, and there are moments of shared bright sounds.

The atmosphere and the energy of her baby's engagement in the moving play arouses an implicit non-conscious memory (Bebe et al. 2005) in Terrie, and an 'Appreciation' (de Botton and Armstrong 2013) of her infant's aliveness with the bell ball. Mother finds her own initiative and energetic crawling movement—a form of vitality (Stern 2010) to match her infant's enthusiasm. A brief joy is experienced (Koch et al. 2007). Mother said: 'I know I can play with my baby now.'

A similar process of enlivenment occurs in a more unwell mother.

Mimi, from Africa, has experienced a psychotic disorder. She and her infant are admitted to the inpatient unit. Mimi has suffered from much trauma in various cycles of fleeing from her own country and resettling. It is hard for Mimi to remember to look after her infant. In the DMT room, her 10-month infant looks at me but not at his mother. He holds the egg maracas, and hearing the rhythmical syncopated music, he bobs his sitting body and shakes the maracas. In the next weekly session, the infant's engagement draws mother into his movement play. She smiles, and gradually enlivens her body to the rhythms. She asks a relative to bring in her music. By the fourth session she is dancing, holding her infant on her hip, and he enjoys her dynamic movement and its closeness. In the last session before discharge, she takes the bubbles and blows with soft intent, holding her infant's gaze with her smile.

Mimi sees Hope (de Botton and Armstrong 2013) in her son's bobbing dance to the maracas sound. She draws on her cultural life to literally regain an aliveness that is a natural part of her heritage. She offers a 'repair' (Tronick and Weinberg 1997) of her earlier low interest and is seen differently by her son, who has a new expectation that she is there for him in both the lively and quiet moments.

Tool: Dance Pathways for Intentionality

In the outpatient dance group, the use of group movement in directions draws on Laban's action drive of space, time, and weight, and includes the attentional and intentional functions of the self (Goodill 2005). Direction in planes and shaping movement in space (Dell 1977) allows mother to use her moving body as a bridge to the world (Merleau-Ponty 1962). I often gather the mothers, holding their babies, into a circle to swoop forward at a walking pace to the centre of the circle and out, or we may line up in a horizontal form along one wall to step in one direction together across the room, supported by the energy of each other's bodies.

Rosie, a hesitant mother in the Intuitive Mothering outpatient group, could not cross the room for many weeks. She and her 10-month-old infant stayed close together in the space. Her seated posture was still, and she bent over her baby as if to control her infant's movement. In the sixth session, the other dancing mothers and my assistant and I built up a dance dynamic in the space. Suddenly trying out the scarf to Dvořák's music, Rosie was on her feet, twirling her scarf around her sitting infant son, dancing in all directions away and back to her baby. Her infant looked at her new movement gestures with pleasure. In a final movement, Rosie swept diagonally across the room with the other adults while the delighted sitting infants watched.

Rosie's habitual movement reflects the findings of Michalak, Troj, Schulte, and Heidenreich (2006) in their conference presentation, reported in Koch et al. (2007), that currently depressed patients showed more pronounced lateral and reduced sagittal and vertical movements and also a bowed posture. Video and clinical observation showed that Rosie's walking pattern was limited in its sagittal direction and her sitting posture habitually bowed, until her sudden attention to space showed a confident vitality to her infant.

Tool: Triadic Pathway

In the smaller inpatient space, dance pathways are shorter. The infants ages are in the range 3–52 weeks. At first I indicate, through my slight movement to a classical berceuse, that mother may rock her 5-month-old daughter from side to side to become more comfortable with the closeness of her infant. Then the mother, holding her baby, and I may encircle the blanket on the floor with stops and turns; or we stand on opposite sides of the space, and to a lilting tune, move towards each other to meet with a gentle 'boo' greeting. In these various dances over the weeks of her inpatient stay, the mother is adapting to her increasingly engaged infant and experiencing adjustments herself in her own expressive movement. It is not easy for many of the inpatient mothers, who often have been very unwell to reflect on the experience, but I ask 'What did your baby like best? How was it to come in with your baby today?'—a short verbal exchange to metabolize the bodily shifts (Coulter and Loughlin 1999) into a memory.

Tool: Physical Support of Floor Movement

Mothers can develop PND through trauma in childbirth.

Mary was referred specifically for individual DMT in the outpatient clinic, following an unexpected traumatic birth with her son, now 7 months old. She had rejected her infant Claude from birth. He was born with a difficult prognosis, but at 5 months he had physically recovered. In the first DMT session, Claude began to touch a textured ball on the floor, and Mary, as if from an implicit memory (Bebe et al. 2005), intuitively mirrored his rolling and reaching movement with her own ball. After ten sessions of largely floor-based movement games, the relationship was healthier. Mary said in a simple verbal summary of her 'self-understanding' (de Botton and Armstrong 2013): 'I got my bonding back.'

Mary tried out the play objects for her own sake in a physical way that mirrored her son's movements. She became more interested and gradually absorbed (Winnicott 1960) in his play investigations, and began to see him as a competent, not damaged, infant. She identified with him as her son.

Dance Movement Therapist in Relationship: Processes of Change

An important element is the aesthetic or idiom (Bollas 1987) of the dance movement therapist herself, attuned (Stern 1985) to the progress of the mother and infant in their connection. The therapist's own gestures and subtly alive movement is neurally mirrored (Gallese 2003; Tortora 2011). Shifts which occur in the mother's physical self are felt and remembered in her body (Leventhal 2014). The new patterns of expressiveness in movement together is part of the psychological change process through evoking accompanying emotional arousal (Greenberg and Safran 1987), which allows meanings to emerge. The new meanings become part of the mother's intent towards wellness.

A Study of Outpatient Hospital Treatment for PND

Methodology

The aesthetic approach to DMT described here was evaluated in a pre- and post-testing study—the Intuitive Mothering Intervention study (Loughlin 2009)—which was part of the tertiary hospital Parent–Infant Research Institute ongoing outpatient psychological research into the treatment of PND. The Intuitive Mothering programme—the name of the eight-week aesthetic approach to DMT—was formally added, with ethics approval, to expand the mother–infant focus of an existing two-part group treatment programme, 'Getting ahead of postnatal depression' (Milgrom et al. 1999). This latter programme consisted of twelve weeks of cognitive behaviour therapy (CBT) for parents, and three weeks of psychoeducation of mother–infant behaviour (Happiness,

Understanding, Giving, Sharing: HUGS) for mother–infants, and with the addition of the eight weeks of Intuitive Mothering (IM-Dance), became a twenty-three-week programme for treating PND.

The study investigated the outcome of parenting stress, mood, and mother–infant interaction for the patients who attended the enlarged three-part programme of CBT, HUGS, and IM-Dance. Evaluation was carried out at baseline assessment and after the three treatment programmes, with self-report instruments: Parenting Stress Index (PSI) (Abidin1986); Beck Depression Inventory (BDI) (Beck et al. 1961; Beck and Steer 1987); Beck Anxiety Inventory (BAI) (Beck et al. 1988), and an observation measure of mother–infant interaction, the Infant Caregiver Behavioural Measures (ICBM) (Milgrom and Burn 1988) of separate videoed play segments. Qualitative data were not systematically collected as part of this study.

Results

Significant reductions (improvements) occurred as measured by the PSI in the PSI Total Scores (p = 0.005) and the PSI Parent Domain Scores (p = 0.001) (Loughlin 2009) over the whole three-part programme to demonstrate improved parenting function. Following the third intervention (IM-Dance), the scores on the PSI had reduced (further improved) to the top level of the normative range (Loughlin 2009).

Reductions (improvements) occurred on mood as measured by the scores in the BDI and the BAI over the whole three-part programme. Following the third intervention (IM-Dance), the scores had reduced to below or near the minimal threshold scores for depression and anxiety (Loughlin 2009).

The Intuitive Mothering DMT intervention targeted the mother–infant interaction. Following IM-Dance, nineteen of the twenty-five subscales of the full observation measures (ICBM) improved in the predicted favourable direction, p <0.05 (Loughlin 2009). The scores on the ICBM post-IM-Dance showed improvement in particular in the four Joint subscales: Connectedness, Joy, Reciprocity/synchronicity, Mutual attention, and in five of the six Infant subscales: Attend to mother, Fuss/cry, Smile/excite, Explore, Clarity of cues (see Figure 44.1).

COMMENT

The effect on the IM-Dance treatment of the previous CBT for PND and the HUGS mother–infant focus are not controlled. Possible changes through time itself (twenty-three weeks) are not known. Nevertheless, the outcome measures highlight the relevance of the Intuitive Mothering study (Loughlin 2009). Positive outcomes were found progressively for the three sequential therapies: cognitive behavior therapy,

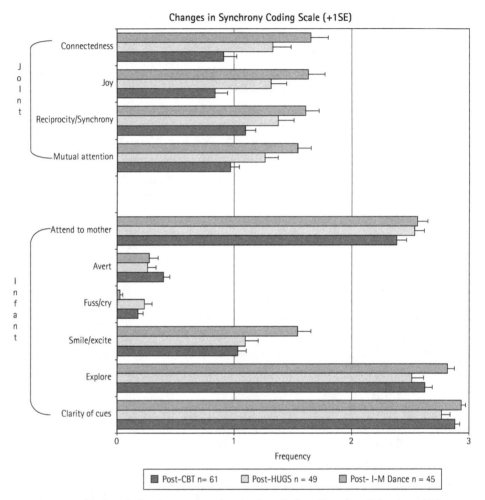

FIGURE 44.1. Mother–infant interaction observations: Infant-Caregiver Behavioural Measures (ICBM) showing changes in joint and infant subscales post-CBT, post-HUGS, and post-IM-Dance. (Credit: © 2009 Dance therapy Association of Australia; adapted from the full ICBM chart (Loughlin 2009, p. 79) with permission.)

psychoeducation of mother–infant behaviour, and experiential Intuitive Mothering DMT. The contribution of IM-Dance to improved measures on the ICBM reflects the positive shifts in mother–infant interaction, seen earlier in the chapter's clinical vignettes. The treatment outcomes of the programme demonstrate the viability of the model of DMT with psychological therapies, within the context of interdisciplinary collaboration.

The positive outcomes post-IM-Dance for parent stress, depression, and anxiety, with measures reduced (improved) to or towards the normative range, raise the issue of what may be the specific contribution of DMT to improvement in parenting stress and in PND, and anxiety for vulnerable mothers and their infants.

Murray and Cooper (1997) pose the question of whether the maternal depression, or the mother–infant relationship, or social adversity, or other factors, is the primary cause in parental impairments. Should the treatment start with mother or infant, or both infant and mother, or all three? This chapter argues that helping the infant regain the 'liveness of the intercommunication between mother and baby' (Winnicott 1988, p. 99) through the aesthetic processes of dance is the pressing guide for treatment for vulnerable mother and infant, within the team supports that the hospital setting can offer.

ACKNOWLEDGEMENTS

I thank Professor Jeannette Milgrom, of the University of Melbourne, and Director of the Parent–Infant Research Institute, for research design, and for the use of outcome data from a larger study in the treatment of PND, in order to evaluate the three-part Intuitive Mothering Intervention study. Drs Alan Gemmill and Chris Holt for manipulation of study data, I also thank participant parents and infants in the DMT programmes of the outpatient clinic and the inpatient psychiatric unit.

NOTES

1. PND and anxiety are closely linked.
2. Mother–infant psychological problems are treated in the hospital clinic with infants of 0–24 months, and in the inpatient setting with infants of 0–12 months.
3. Full unread study in Lier-Schehl (2008). *Movement Dialogues in Mother-and-Child Relationship, Movement Patterns of Relationship Disorders Postpartum and Their Infants Sick in an Inpatient Psychiatric Mother-and-Child Clinic.* Hamburg: Verlag Dr Kovac. (English translation of the title; published in German only.)
4. Vignettes are deidentified.
5. Classical and world music support the therapeutic intentions of the dance interventions.

REFERENCES

Abidin. R. (1986). *Parenting Stress Index Manual*, 2nd edn. Charlotsville. VA: Pediatric Psychology Press.

Albiston, D. (1992). 'Mothers with post-partum depression and their babies', in R. Rawson and E. Loughlin (eds.), *Dance Therapy Collections Number One*. Australia: Australia Dance Council, pp. 7–9.

American Psychiatric Association (2013). *Diagnostic and Statistical Manual of Mental Disorders (DSM- V)*, 5th edn. Washington DC: American Psychiatric Association.

Annadale, C. (c.1918–30). *The Concise English Dictionary*. London and Glasgow: Blackie and Son.

Batcup, D. (2004). 'Dance movement therapy with mothers and babies'. *e-motion*, xiv, 6, 5–12.

Beck, A., Ward, C., Mendelson, M., Mark, J., and Erbaugh, J. (1961). 'An inventory for measuring depression', *Archives of General Psychiatry*, 4: 561–71.

816   ELIZABETH LOUGHLIN

Beck, A. and Steer, R. (1987). *Manual for the Revised Beck Depression Inventory*. San Antonio, TX: The Psychological Corporation.

Beck, A., Epstein, N., Brown, G., and Steer, R. (1988). 'An inventory for measuring clinical anxiety: Psychometric properties', *Journal of Consulting and Clinical Psychology*, 56: 893–7.

Bion, W. R. (1983). *Learning from Experience*. London: Jason Aronson.

Bebe, B., Knoblauch, S., Rustin, J., and Sorter, D. (2005). *Forms of Intersubjectivity in Infant Research and Adult Treatment*. New York, NY: Other Press.

Bollas, C. B. (1987). *The Shadow of the Object: Psychoanalysis of the Unknown Thought*. London: Free Association Books.

Buist, A., Minto, B., Szego, K., Samhuel, M., Shawyer, L., and O'Connor, L. (2004). Mother-baby psychiatric units in Australia: the Victorian experience', *Archives of Women's Health*, 7: 81–7.

Bruno, C. (1990). 'Maintaining a concept of the dance in dance/movement therapy', *American Journal of Dance Therapy*, 12(2):101–13.

Chaiklin, S (2009). 'We dance from the moment our feet touch the earth', in S. Chailkin and H. Wengrower (eds.), *The Art and Science of Dance/Movement Therapy*. New York, NY: Routledge, pp. 3–11.

Cichetti, D., Rogosch, F., and Toth, S. (2000). 'The efficacy of toddler–parent psychotherapy for fostering cognitive development in offspring of depressed mothers', *Journal of Abnormal Child Psychology*, 28(2): 135–48.

Coulter, H. and Loughlin, E. (1999). 'Synergy of verbal and non-verbal therapies in the treatment of mother–infant relationships', *British Journal of Psychotherapy*, 16(1): 59–73.

Davis, M. and Wallbridge, D. (1981). *Boundary and Space: An Introduction to the Work of D. W. Winnicott*. Melbourne: Penguin Books.

de Botton, A. and Armstrong, J. (2013). *Art as Therapy*. London and New York: Phaidon Press.

Dell, C. (1977). *A Primer for Movement Description, Using Effort–Shape and Supplementary Concepts*. New York, NY: Dance Notation Bureau.

Fettling, L. and Tune, B. (2005). *Women's Experience of Postnatal Depression*. Hawthorn, Australia: IP Communications.

Gallese, V. (2003). 'The roots of empathy: The shared manifold hypotheses and the neural basis of intersubjectivity', *Pathology*, 36: 171–80.

Goodill, S. (2005). *An Introduction to Medical Dance/Movement therapy*. London and Philadelphia: Jessica Kingsley.

Gopnik, A. (2009). *The Philosophical Baby*. New York, NY: Picador.

Greenberg, L. and Safran, J. (1987). *Emotion in Psychotherapy: Affect, Cognition, and the Process of Change*. New York, NY: Guilford Press.

Grotstein, J. 'Preface', in Pistiner de Cortinas, L. (2009). *The Aesthetic Dimension of the Mind: Variations on a Theme of Bion*. London: Karnac Books.

Guedeney, A. (2007). 'Withdrawal behavior and depression in infancy', *Infant Mental Health Journal*, 28(4): 393–408.

Kestenberg, J. (1992). 'The use of expressive arts in prevention: Facilitating the construction of objects', in S. Loman (ed.), *The Body–Mind Connection on Human Movement Analysis*. Antioch, NH: Antioch New England Graduate School, pp. 55–92.

Kestenberg, J. and Buelte, A. (1977). 'Prevention, infant therapy, and the treatment of adults 1. Towards understanding mutuality', *International Journal of Psychoanalytic Psychotherapy*, 6: 339–67.

Koch, S., Morlinghaus. K., and Fuchs, T. (2007). 'The "joy dance": Specific effects of a single dance intervention on psychiatric patients with depression', *The Arts in Psychotherapy*, 34: 340–9.

Langer, S. K. (1953). *Feeling and Form*. London: Routledge and Kegan.

Leventhal, M. B. (1993). *Moving towards Health: Stages of Therapeutic Unfolding in Dance Movement. Current Researches in Arts Medicine*. Chicago, IL: A Cappella Books, pp. 257–61.

Leventhal, M. B. (2014). *The Embodied Moment and the Role of the Conscious Healing Dance in Growth, Transformation and Healing*. Paper presented at the 37th World Congress on Dance Research, Athens, Greece.

Levy, F. (1988*). Dance Movement Therapy: A Healing Art*. Reston, VA: American Alliance for Health, Physical Education, Recreation and Dance.

Lier-Schehl, H. (2003). Abstract: 'Identification of early relationship from the analysis of movement patterns in mother–infant interaction observed in an inpatient psychiatric wards', Research poster session abstracts, American Dance Therapy Association Conference 2003. *American Journal of Dance Therapy*, 26: 52–3.

Loman, S. and Sossin, K. (2009). 'Applying the Kestenberg Movement Profile in dance/movement therapy: An introduction', in S. Chaiklin and H. Wengrower (eds.), *The Art and Science of Dance/Movement Therapy*. London and New York: Routledge, pp. 237–64.

Loman, S. (2014). 'Collaboration through movement: KMP movement patterns underlying mutuality and disconnection', *Moving On. DTAA*, 11(1–2): 52–4.

Loughlin, E. (1997). 'Mother and infant dance as a health program for community and clinic', *The Call of Forests and Lakes: Proceedings of the 7th International Dance and the Child 1997 Conference*. Kuopio, Finland: Dance and the Child International, pp. 293–319.

Loughlin, E. (2009). 'Intuitive mothering: Developing and evaluating a dance therapy model for mothers with postnatal depression and their vulnerable infants', in K. Dunphy, J. Guthrie, and E. Loughlin (eds.), *Dance Therapy Collections, Number Three*. Australia: Dance Movement Therapy Association of Australia, pp. 70–85.

Mala, A., Karkou, V., and Meekums, B. (2011). 'Dance/movement therapy (DMT) for depression: Scoping review', *The Arts in Psychotherapy*, 39(4): 287–95.

Meekums, B. (1992). 'The love bugs: Dance movement therapy in a family service unit', in H. Payne (ed.), *Dance/Movement Therapy: Theory and Practice*. London: Routledge, pp. 18–38.

Meekums. B. (2000). *Dance Movement Therapy*. London: Sage.

Merleau-Ponty, M. (1962). *The Phenomenology of Perception*. London: Routledge and Kegan Paul.

Michalak, J., Troj, N., Schulte, P. and Heidenreich, T. (2006, September) Mindful walking. The association between depression, mindfulness and gait patterns. Paper presented at the Congress of the European Association of Behavioural and Cognitive therapies EABCT), Paris, France.

Milgrom, J. and Burn, J. (1988). *Synchrony Coding Scale in Maternal Perceptions of Infant Temperament, Maternal Competence, Mothering Style and Later Mother–Infant Synchrony*. Unpublished Master's thesis, Melbourne College of Advanced Education (revised 2003).

Milgrom, J., Dubow, H., and Ericksen, J. (2010). 'Postnatal depression and mother–infant attachment', *Advances in Psychology Research*, 62: 185–213.

Milgrom, J., Ericksen, J., De Paola, C., McCarthy, R. and Loughlin, E. (2001). *Is it Enough to use Depression Improvements as an Outcome with PND Treatment? The Parent-Infant*

Interaction. Abstract. Marcé Society, Australasian Conference, Christchurch, New Zealand. September 2001. <http://www.marcesociety.com/marce/abstracts/abstract0138.html>

Milgrom, J., Ericksen, J., Loughlin, E., Leigh, B., Andrew, M., Schembri, C., Lawry, V., and Reich, C. (2008). Poster: *Community Hugs: A Specialized Playgroup Focusing on the Interaction Between Mother and Infant Following Postnatal Depression*. Austin Research Week.

Milgrom, J., Martin, P., and Negri, L. (1999). *Treating Postnatal Depression*. Chichester: Wiley and Sons.

Murray, L. (1989). 'Winnicott and the developmental psychology of infancy', *British Journal of Psychotherapy*, 5(3): 333–48.

Murray, L. and Cooper P. J. (1997). 'The role of infant and maternal factors in postpartum depression, mother–infant interactions, and infant outcomes', in L. Murray and P. J. Cooper (eds.), *Postpartum Depression and Child Development*. New York, NY: Guilford Press, pp. 111–35.

Murray, L., Cooper, P. J., Wilson, A., and Romaniuk, H. (2003). 'Controlled trial of the short and long term effect of psychological treatment of post-partum depression. 2. Impact on the mother–child relationship and child outcome', *British Journal of Psychiatry*, 182: 420–7.

Ostroburski, F. (2009). 'Dance movement psychotherapy as primary treatment: A case study', in K. Dunphy, J. Guthrie, and E. Loughlin (eds.), *Dance Therapy Collections, Number Three*. Australia: Dance Movement Therapy Association of Australia, pp. 151–7.

Poobalan, A., Aucett, L., Ross, L., Smith, W., Helus, P. and Williams, J. (2007). 'Effect of treating postnatal depression on mother–infant interaction and child development: Systematic review', *British Journal of Psychiatry*, 191: 378–86. doi:10.1192/bjp.bp.106.032789

Schmais, C. (1985). 'Healing processes in group dance therapy', *American Journal of Dance Therapy*, 8(1): 17–36.

Sheets-Johnstone, M. (2010). 'Why is movement therapeutic?', *American Journal of Dance Therapy*, 32: 2–15.

Stern, D. N. (1974). 'The goal and structure of mother–infant play', *Journal of the American Academy of Child Psychiatry*, 13: 402–21.

Stern, D. N. (1985). *The Interpersonal World of the Infant*. New York, NY: Basic Books.

Stern, D. N. (1995). *The Motherhood Constellation*. New York, NY: Basic Books.

Stern, D. N. (2010). *Forms of Vitality*. Oxford: Oxford University Press.

Tortora, S. (2011). 'The need to be seen: From Winnicott to the mirror neuron system: Dance/movement therapy comes of age', *American Journal of Dance Therapy*, 33: 4–17. doi: 10.1007/s10465-011-9107-5

Turner, V. (1979). *Process, Performance and Pilgrimage and a Study of Comparative Symbology*. New Delhi: Concept Publishing.

Trevarthen, C. (1987). 'Sharing makes sense: Infant subjectivity and the making of an infant's meaning', in R. Steele and T. Threadgold (eds.), *Language Topics: Essays in Honor of Michael Halliday*. Amsterdam and Philadelphia: John Benjamins, pp. 177–99.

Trevarthen C. (1997). 'The nature of motives for human consciousness', *The Journal of the Hellenic Psychological Society*. 4(3): 187–221.

Trevarthen C. (2004). 'Learning about ourselves, from children: Why a growing human brain needs interesting companions', *Research and Clinical Centre for Child Development, Annual Report 2002-2003, 26*. Graduate School of Education, Hokkaido University, pp. 9–44.

Tronick, E. and Weinberg, M. (1997). 'Depressed mothers and infants: Failure to form dyadic states of consciousness', in L. Murray and P. J. Cooper (eds.), *Postpartum Depression and Child Development*. New York, NY: Guilford Press, pp. 54–84.

Wengrower, H. (2009). 'The creative–artistic process in dance/movement therapy', in S. Chailkin and H. Wengrower (eds.), *The Art and Science of Dance/Movement Therapy*. New York, NY: Routledge, pp. 13–32.

Winnicott, D. W. (1960). 'The theory of the parent–infant relationship', in D. W. Winnicott (1965). *The Maturational Processes and the Facilitating Environment*. London: Karnac Books, pp. 37–55.

Winnicott, D. W. (1988). 'Communication between infant and mother, and mother and infant compared and contrasted', in D. W. Winnicott, *Babies and Their Mothers*. London: Free Association Press, pp. 89–103.

Zeanah, C. (1993). *Handbook of Infant Mental Health*. New York, NY: Guilford Press.

....

CHAPTER 45

DANCE MOVEMENT THERAPY AND THE POSSIBILITY OF WELLBEING FOR PEOPLE WITH DEMENTIA

....

HEATHER HILL

INTRODUCTION

DEMENTIA and wellbeing—were there ever two words that seemed so inherently opposed to each other? From a biomedical perspective, dementia[1] is seen to result from irreversible pathological processes in the brain. The person with dementia progressively loses function and ultimately 'self'. 'The light is on, but no one's home', 'dissolution of self', 'living death' are some of the expressions which have been used to describe the state of the person with dementia. Within our current scientific knowledge, there is no cure. Formal care of the person focuses on carrying out the physical tasks of care and managing symptoms to ensure the safety of the person and others. While this pure biomedical stance has been softened by the introduction of more activities and therapies, the priorities of care remain medical and physical.

Wellbeing from this perspective, then, has mainly to do with having the physical essentials of life attended to. In a context where cure is the hallmark of health and wellbeing, the situation of the person with dementia is necessarily one lacking in hope. Where cure is impossible, there is little staff can do, and descent into oblivion is inevitable. Anxiety, restlessness, and distress are viewed as 'behaviours', symptoms to be managed, mainly through medication. In essence, the biomedical model of dementia offers a rather minimalist version of wellbeing.

However, since the 1980s the biomedical model has been challenged by the person-centred movement, and I believe this offers a far more robust, positive outlook for people with dementia. I therefore discuss in some depth person-centred care as the context in which wellbeing is possible for people with dementia. Understanding dementia from a person-centred perspective will lead us first to an understanding of the concept of wellbeing in dementia and later to an understanding of the role that dance movement therapy may play in promoting wellbeing for people with dementia.

PERSON-CENTRED APPROACHES
TO WELLBEING

Kitwood's Person-Centred Care

In the 1980s the late Tom Kitwood, of Bradford University in the UK, developed the approach to dementia care called 'person-centred care' (Kitwood 1997). The experience of dementia, he suggested, was not only about pathological processes in the brain, but was influenced by many factors, including the person's life history, personal coping style, and environmental and relational factors. This took the emphasis away from pure disease processes back to the person; rather than the 'person *with dementia*', we should focus on the '*person* with dementia' (Kitwood 1997, p. 7). This is a radical change of focus from the biomedical perspective, and one which implies a different view of the person's behaviour and how we should interact with him or her. No longer is behaviour considered a 'symptom'; rather, it is an expression of unmet needs. No longer are staff mere bystanders to a pathological process; rather, care staff may have a significant impact on the person's experience of dementia and quality of life.

The Person with Dementia

For Kitwood, people with dementia retained the same basic psychological needs as all human beings. He represented these as a cluster of interrelated needs—identity, comfort, attachment, inclusion, and occupation—held together by the absolutely core human need, the need for love. By 'love', he meant not romantic love, but 'a generous, forgiving, and unconditional acceptance, a wholehearted emotional giving, without any expectation of direct reward' (Kitwood 1997, p. 81). To this, Kasayka (2001) adds: '. . . the love needed is practical love. This is love that makes the space safe and stands by the individual no matter what the situation, no matter what the confusion, no matter what the emotion' (p. 12).

Kitwood's call to take the person with dementia seriously, to relate to the person as a full human being with needs, desires, weaknesses, strengths, and the potential for growth, is, I believe, his greatest gift to the field and to people with dementia. Years later, Richard Taylor—a powerful voice for people with dementia and who himself was living with dementia—echoed this call for the recognition of personhood: '*I am a whole person*, dammit. I am not half full. I am not half empty. I am a *whole person*' (DVD: 'Be with me now').

Maintaining the Person through Relationship

To Kitwood, a key psychological task of dementia care was the maintenance of person-hood (Kitwood and Bredin 1992). He challenged the notion that cognition and individual autonomy were central to personhood, instead defining personhood as 'a standing or status that is bestowed upon one human being by others, in the context of relationship and social being. It implies recognition, respect, and trust' (p. 8).

For Kitwood, relationship lay at the heart of care, and he highlighted a particular type of relationship which was nourishing of the person, drawing on Buber's concept of an I–Thou rather than I–It relationship. The latter 'implies coolness, detachment, instrumentality. It is a way of maintaining a safe distance, of avoiding risks' (Kitwood 1997, p. 10). Such relationships 'can never rise above the banal and trivial' (p. 10). In contrast, I–Thou 'implies going out towards the other; self-disclosure, spontaneity—a journey into uncharted territory' (p. 10). Buber wrote: 'So long as the heaven of Thou is spread out over me, the wind of causality cowers at my heels and the whirlwind of fates stays its course' (quoted in Kitwood 199, p. 11). These words suggest that this kind of I–Thou relationship opens up possibilities well beyond the narrow confines of the so-called 'real world' of diagnoses and pathology.

'Malignant social psychology' (Kitwood 1997, p. 45) (such as disempowerment, infantilization, labelling) would reinforce pathology and add to the fragmentation of self. In contrast, 'positive person work' (such as recognition, engagement, collaboration) (Kitwood 1997, p. 89) could actively maintain and build self. Care was very much a relational process rather than a disease treatment or symptom management process.

Wellbeing

Rather than an unmitigated process of misery and loss, as they slid downhill towards death, people with dementia could experience 'relative wellbeing'. Kitwood identified four global states of wellbeing

- Sense of personal worth.
- Sense of agency.
- Feeling of being at ease with others, of being able to move toward them, of having something to offer them.
- Hope: basic trust that things will be okay (Kitwood and Bredin 1992, p. 283)

While initially talking of *relative* wellbeing (Kitwood and Bredin 1992), Kitwood came later to talk simply of wellbeing (Kitwood 1997).

Enhanced Lifestyle through Optimal Stimulus (ELTOS)

The work of Australian researchers Garratt and Hamilton-Smith (1995), which was being carried out around the same time as the work of Kitwood, mirrors much of the above but gives prominence to some additional aspects. For instance, they emphasized the need for particular kinds of environment—environments which were not fragmented or confusing, where stimulus was 'optimal' (p. 38). They also emphasized the need for the person to find meaning in his/her current life, and that this required carers to enter the person's reality and work with the person to create a life that felt meaningful. Some of this work was influenced by Csikszentmihalyi's (1990) concept of optimal experience and Antonovsky's (1987) work on wellness, both of which are discussed in this chapter. Garratt and Hamilton-Smith (1995) also addressed staff and organizational issues, which I will not discuss here. These are, however, important components of a person-centred culture which focuses not just on carer/cared for relationships but on relationships throughout the whole organization.

Through their practical research, Garratt and Hamilton-Smith (1995) demonstrated the possibilities of achieving wellbeing in dementia. It is important to note, however, that wellbeing needs to be understood within the lived world of the person with dementia, not in terms of our expectations within our reality.

In summary, the work of Kitwood (1997) and Garratt and Hamilton-Smith (1995) highlights the following elements important to wellbeing in dementia:

- Reinforcing the person's sense of self (identity, control, belonging).
- Relationship.
- Meaningful, appropriate occupation.
- Meaning/making sense/coherence.
- All of these within a framework of entering the person's current reality and being with the person as he or she is now.

In the years that have followed this work, person-centred care has continued to evolve with more developed and nuanced understandings of relationship, environment, and personal meaning/coherence. However, the basics were already spelt out in the work of these pioneers.

Non-Dementia Writings Relevant to Wellbeing in Dementia

It is also worthwhile looking at writings outside the field of dementia on the topic of wellbeing. As I have emphasized previously, people with dementia remain people and therefore share the same basic needs. The following writings address the core ingredients of wellbeing for all, which may then offer some guidance as to those aspects which will be most helpful in promoting wellbeing for people with dementia.

Wellness and the Sense of Coherence (Antonovsky)

In the field of health, Antonovsky (1987) moved away from the traditional medical focus on pathology—what makes people ill—to an examination of what keeps people well (salutogenesis). His interest was in examining why some people remain healthy, despite experiencing stresses similar to others who do not. He linked this to differences in what he called the Sense of Coherence (SOC). He suggested that a strong SOC tended to be linked to wellness. The SOC incorporates three aspects (Antonovsky 1987):

- Comprehensibility (what happens in life seems to make sense in some way).
- Meaningfulness ('being a participant in the processes shaping one's destiny as well as one's daily experience' (p. 128).
- Manageability: one has the resources to cope with what one encounters.

The three elements of SOC are the very aspects which break down in dementia, and there would seem to be a degree of overlap between SOC and Kitwood's global states of wellbeing discussed previously—in particular, in relation to making sense of one's world and being able to cope with and act upon one's world.

Resilience (Grotberg)

From a different field, Grotberg (1995), in writing about resilience in children, suggested that resilience was underwritten by 'I have', 'I am', 'I can' (p. 15). These relate, respectively, to

- External supports and resources, especially having people who love me (I have).
- Internal, personal strengths, beliefs, feeling of being worthwhile, and that life is okay (I am).
- Being able to cope with life's challenges (I can).

The relational aspects ('I have') of the resilient self seem more evident in Grotberg's framework than in Antonovsky's. Indeed, Grotberg (1995) noted that relationship precedes personal abilities and skills:

> Before the child is aware of who she is ('I am') or what she can do (I can'), she needs external supports and resources to develop the feelings of safety and security that lay the foundation, that are the core, for developing resilience. These supports continue to be important throughout childhood. (p. 15)

Here, Grotberg shares with Kitwood an emphasis on the importance of relationship in maintaining and growing the self.

The Relational Self (Gergen)

Kitwood placed emphasis on the role of relationship in supporting the self and 'holding' the personhood of the person with dementia. This, however, is not particular to dementia. While, of course, additional support is needed for the person with dementia, the writings of psychologist Kenneth Gergen (2009) suggest that we, in our Western culture, are wrong to hold up the ideal of the autonomous, individuated self who needs no one. Rather, we all need people; we are all selves in and through relationship.

Gergen (2009) has some interesting thoughts on therapy which bear upon the discussion of wellbeing. Therapy for him is about 'relational recovery'. 'From a relational standpoint, therapy is not so much about altering the mind as it is about enhancing resources for viable relationships' (p. 307). In terms of the therapist's role, Gergen invites us to 'view the therapist and client as engaged in a subtle and complex dance of co-action, a dance in which meaning is continuously in motion and the outcomes of which may transform the relational life of the client' (p. 282). This suggests that client wellbeing—a sense of 'ease' rather than 'dis-ease'—lies within the relational realm.

Flow and Wellbeing

Csickszentmihalyi's studies on the concept of 'flow' shed further light on the topic of wellbeing and the kinds of experience that may promote it. He was led by his interest in 'optimal experiences'. He observed, time and time again, people passionately engaged in certain activities, which could be difficult or had little financial or material reward. He concluded that there must be something about the quality of those experiences that kept people engaged. He called these optimal experiences 'flow', and identified several of its characteristics: activities carried out simply for their own sake, where participants became totally involved (no separation between mind, body, feeling, and action; lack of self-consciousness), and where the demands were not so great as to create anxiety, nor so small as to create boredom. This may be likened to the tennis player's experience of 'being in the zone'. Every dancer will recognize those moments when the will disappears and everything comes together in a flow of mind–body–feeling action.

These flow experiences are optimal moments of aliveness. In the course of his many studies (1975, 1990, 1994) Csickszentmihalyi came to link flow activities to happiness, to feelings of self-efficacy, and to the growth of self. His concept of flow highlights a state of ease, wholeness, and integration which, of course, are those very aspects the person with dementia struggles to maintain. Applied to the person with dementia, then, Csickszentmihalyi's work on flow offers some insight into the kinds of experience which might promote these feelings of ease and wholeness.

WELLBEING IN DEMENTIA

Dementia is a state in which the person's very core sense of self is attacked and fragmented. Abilities, activities, personal characteristics, and, importantly, memory—
all of which provide a sense of being oneself—may begin to dissolve. Alongside this,
and contributing to the losses, is disruption of relationships. Even one's closest family and friends can be daunted by the dementia label, confused by the changes, and
find it difficult to relate to the person. Richard Taylor (quoted previously) has talked
of how, following his diagnosis, friends stopped telephoning him. When asked why,
they explained that they did not know what to say to him. His reply: 'How about saying
hello?' Yet even this simple communication can appear difficult. The label becomes a
huge barrier to everyday interactions, and often leads family and friends to assume that
every response and action of the person with dementia is a 'symptom'. This fragmentation in one's experience of the world, disruption of relationships, and multiple assaults
on all that gives the person his/her identity and lends meaning to life, creates a state of
dis-ease. Sacks (1991) describes the huge contrast between ease and dis-ease in a patient
'awakened' from their dis-eased state through the L-dopa drug. 'Where, previously, he
felt ill at ease, uncomfortable, unnatural, and strained, he now feels at ease, and at one
with the world . . . The stream of being, no longer clogged or congealed, flows with an
effortless, unforced ease' (p. 241)

So, how might we understand 'wellbeing' in dementia, given the realities of the ongoing changes occurring in the person's life world? To do so, we may need to let go of some
long-held and culturally entrenched preconceptions.

We need to free ourselves from the assumption that without cognition wellbeing is
impossible. Wellbeing 'is not dependent on cognitive or functional ability' (Power 2010,
p. 85). We do not need to be able to reflect on or analyse a Mozart aria; it is enough to feel
the emotion, feel the resonance.

We also need to see beyond the diagnostic label and recognize the person with
dementia as a fellow human being who shares many of the same needs and desires as the
rest of humanity (Kitwood 1997).

We need to expand the concept of wellbeing in dementia beyond the physical. Of
course, it is necessary to do as much as possible to ensure that physical needs are met,
and to respond to pain (which can often be easily overlooked because of the person's
expressive difficulties or the caregiver's lack of observation or skills). However, this is
not nearly enough. Furthermore, I would suggest that to separate out different aspects
of wellbeing is, I believe, to make false distinctions. Wellbeing is about all aspects of the
person—physical, functional, social, emotional, spiritual.

Finally, as Garratt and Hamilton-Smith (1995) have argued, we need to enter and
work with the person's reality in order to support them in making sense of their experience, his world. For all of us, but especially for people with dementia, personhood and
wellbeing are relational rather than individual enterprises.

Common themes in the literature discussed earlier point to the importance of self-worth, agency, and (existential) meaning for human wellbeing. I suggest that the following may be seen as core parameters for wellbeing in dementia:

- Feeling in some way intact and feeling good about oneself, at ease, safe (which does not depend on cognition)—closely intertwined, indeed inseparable from the next point.
- Having satisfying relationships: being acknowledged, included, accepted for who one is, listened to.
- Being able to engage in activities (or even non-activities of simply 'being') which seem meaningful.
- Finding meaning, feeling that there is some meaning in one's current life. This does not need to be a cognitive understanding, but merely a sense that life is good and that it is worthwhile getting up in the morning. Retaining a sense of hope.

Drawing on Sacks's concept of ease (vs dis-ease), one might frame the concept of wellbeing in terms of having an overall sense of ease—with oneself, one's relationships, and with one's life.

The work of enhancing wellbeing requires caregivers with certain personal and professional qualities who can engage creatively with the person with dementia in an ever-unfolding relational process. And who better than a dance therapist to use 'creativity and collaboration to create a life worth living for people with dementia'?! (Power 2010, p. 85).

Dance Movement Therapy and People with Dementia

> Dance movement therapy is the therapeutic use of movement to further the emotional, cognitive, physical, and social integration of the individual, based on the empirically supported premise that the body, mind, and spirit are interconnected.
>
> (DTAA 2015)

This definition makes clear that dance therapists reject the dualist view of human beings which separates mind and body and assigns overriding importance to the cognitive/verbal aspects of human functioning. They recognize (as does more recent neuroscientific research, such as Damasio 1996) that people are not disembodied minds loosely associated with the body, but are a complex, integrated, mind–body–feeling systems. Human beings are *embodied* beings. In working with the body, then, dance therapists are working with the whole person—mind, body, feeling, spirit. In the context of dementia, this means that they do not view communication, expression, and the capacity for relationship as limited to people with sharp minds and verbal skills. There is also an underlying respect for the capacity of people to change and grow. Dance therapists, by working and building upon strengths and abilities, contribute to reinforcing and maintaining the personhood of people with dementia (Newman-Bluestein and Hill 2010).

The practice of dance movement therapy requires the ability to be present and attuned to clients, to be able to respond in the moment, and to work relationally through multiple modes of interaction, but in particular through body movement and dance. Dance movement therapists must also be attuned to the quality of the space (environment) and to the aesthetic dimensions of experience (Fischman 2009).

At the heart of dance movement therapy practice is 'dance', but not in the narrow sense of a particular technique. Exiner and Kelynack (1994), in explaining the nature of dance (vs movement), quote W. B. Yeats' (1928/1997) poem:

> O body swayed to music, O brightening glance,
> How can we know the dancer from the dance?

They further discuss definitions of 'dance' from various dancers and dance theorists: 'inside the movement with all your faculties' (Leah), coming from within (Laban), non-utilitarian (Barbara Mettler), transformative (Boas) (Exiner and Kelynack 1994, p. 14). These would seem to connect to many of the qualities which Csickszentmihali attributes to 'flow'. Indeed, he considered dance to be one of the flow activities, par excellence.

Exiner and Kelynack (1994) conclude their discussion of 'dance' with their definition of dance as 'movement carried out with sensitivity, mindfulness, and imagination' (p. 15). They further add 'transformation'. The qualities of sensitivity, mindfulness, and imagination—and indeed, transformation—are closely linked to the aesthetic, which Fraleigh (1987) suggests is founded in subjectivity and the 'felt life . . . the sentient life' (p. 44). Exiner and Kelynack (1994) describe the transformational quality of dance. It represents 'a change, an entry into another dimension of experience. A new way of knowing is encountered. We have entered the dance mode which transports us into the domain of aesthetics . . . It elates, expands, excites, and fulfils' (p. 15).

In many respects, doing dance movement therapy with a group of people with dementia is not that different from working with any group, but of course, certain aspects become more important, and are emphasized to meet the needs of the individuals and the group. These are as follows.

Environment

Environment refers to the physical, social, and emotional space. For people whose world is fragmenting and becoming difficult to understand, there is a need to have an environment which 'holds' them (Shustik and Thompson 2002). It needs to have some coherence, to make sense, to have focus. The dance therapist works to create this environment of safety, trust, and acceptance (Newman-Bluestein and Hill 2010). At the end of one dance movement therapy session, a resident said to me 'that little [dance] room gave us a whole lot of room to be ourselves'. In this space, the person's difficulties are accommodated, but they do not define the person. This leaves space for the person to be themselves and perhaps to grow, to become more than themselves.

Presence/Responding in the Moment

The present moment is where the person with dementia lives. The capacity to be fully present, to be able to respond to the subtleties of non-verbal interactions, and to be able to work with whatever comes up in that moment, is essential, and this is something dance therapists do well (Levy 2005).

Working Beyond Cognition/Embodiment

As embodied beings, our first way of being in the world and learning about ourselves and the world was through our bodies (Koch 2006; Coaten 2009; Coaten and Newman-Bluestein 2013). While we give primacy to the 'higher functions' of cognition, we continue throughout our lives to experience through our bodies. 'It is our organic flesh and blood, our structural bones, the ancient rhythms of our internal organs, and the pulsing flow of our emotions that give us whatever meaning we can find and that shape our very thinking' (Johnson 2007, p. 3).

Over time, cognitive function and ability to express oneself verbally declines for the person with dementia. However, by meeting the person in this most basic of mediums—the body—the dance therapist may enter the reality of the person, which is within the affective realm. (Indeed, Gibson (1998) suggests that the affective domain becomes more acute in dementia.) Words and rational thought may diminish, but communication, expression, and human interaction are still possible—through the body!

Relationship

We are embodied beings, and we are also beings who are embedded in a relational context (Gergen 2009; Karkou and Sanderson 2006). For people with dementia, struggling to make sense of a fragmenting world, relationship becomes even more crucial in supporting their efforts to make sense of their world and in helping them reconnect to life.

Dance

The dance of dance movement therapy, as described previously, and in contrast to mechanical movement, brings a richness and quality of experience so much needed by people with dementia (Halprin 2008; Hill 2003, 2009). I have seen in my own sessions the transformations that can happen: the withdrawn person suddenly having eye contact; the confused, fragmented person finding focus as they work with a partner; the 'I can't and won't do anything' person who leaps up to dance in the circle.

DANCE MOVEMENT THERAPY AND ITS RELATIONSHIP TO WELLBEING IN DEMENTIA

How do these aspects of dance movement therapy relate to the concept of wellbeing in dementia? Perhaps the following example, from a research study, will help to illuminate this relationship.

Out of the Cupboard . . . to the Brightness

Having worked for several years with people with dementia, and having already carried out one research project, I undertook a study focused on the meaning which the person himself or herself attributed to the experience of dance movement therapy. For questions of subjective meaning, a quantitative methodology would have been quite inappropriate. Instead, I adapted Giorgi's (1985) phenomenological methodology with a focus on bracketing out prior theory, on broad description, with further reflection and progressive reduction to essence, with the aim of staying as close to the 'raw' experience as possible. It was only after I had completed this process that I turned to the literature to provide context to, and further illuminate, what the material had revealed.

I carried out a series of four individual dance movement therapy sessions with Elsie, a patient in a psychiatric hospital, who had moderate dementia. The sessions were completely improvised, with the process directed by the moment-to-moment interactions. The music, performed by a music therapist on a keyboard, was also completely improvised. The only instruction given to the music therapist was to focus on the interaction: namely, what Elsie and I were creating between us in movement. Of course, as with all such improvisations, the division of roles was not a neat one, and the roles of leader and follower were exchanged among the three of us. At times there were quite magic moments of total synchrony when participants, music, and movement all came together.

In order to open a space for the possibility of some verbal feedback from Elsie, she and I would view the videotapes of our dance, a few hours after each session. This viewing session was also videotaped in the hope of gaining verbal or non-verbal responses from Elsie. With a person with dementia, it was unlikely that a post-session interview would necessarily produce meaningful, if any, information, so I hoped that watching the session would in some way reimmerse Elsie in the experience and allow her to feed back her immediate responses to what she was seeing. And this is indeed what happened.

I then carried out a phenomenological process with this verbal material, in a similar fashion to the non-verbal, observational material.

The data which formed the basis of my conclusions about Elsie's experience came, then, from my observations and from Elsie's feedback, with input from the music therapist and from Elsie's daughter (Hill 1995).

Each of the four sessions with Elsie was quite different in mood and dynamic, and was very much of the moment. At one level, one cannot talk of a progression because there was so much variation from session to session. Yet there was a sense of a growing relational connection which continued regardless of the level of movement. This relationship was tested—literally, physically—by pushing and pulling each other, by hanging around when the other did not feel like moving, by playful challenging each other, and by simply being together. This latter was perhaps most vividly displayed at the end of the first session, when Elsie and I sat together at rest after all our 'struggles' in testing our relationship. We moved a little, but basically we were just there comfortably together, as old friends can be, without a need to talk nor to do anything.

I carried out an in-depth study of session 1, and out of that focused on three 'significant moments'. The nature of these significant moments was not defined in advance: I selected them intuitively from a practitioner perspective as 'high points' of the session. From my study, they emerged as moments when there appeared to be total involvement and focus, as well as a more defined quality of movement (see 'Sensitivity, mindfulness and imagination', in Exiner and Kelynack 1994)—what I would call 'dance'. These were moments when the dancer and the dance become one, akin to Csickszentmihalyi's 'flow' experience, and, from a dance movement therapy perspective, moments of transformation. In such moments, Elsie seemed to emerge from being a shadowy 'patient with dementia' to the dynamic, strong, and humorous person at the core of who she was. She became an equal partner in the dance; indeed, at times she took control. Her personal qualities came shining through, and it was a delight to behold. These were moments which lifted all three of us (Elsie, the music therapist, and myself) into a different space where we went beyond our individual limitations and where the dance became more than its individual parts.

The visible transformation of Elsie and the connections experienced among us three participants suggested that in that session, and particularly in those significant moments, Elsie was feeling good, and was at ease with us and with herself. Furthermore, thanks to the opportunity to hear Elsie's words, I came to understand her experience at a deeper level, and to perceive possibilities that the sense of wellbeing could persist even beyond the sessions.

The first thing I noticed when I looked at the transcripts of her words was that it took until part way through the second session viewing for her to talk about 'I' rather than 'she'. Elsie could not at first believe that that person who was actively engaged in moving was herself. As she came to own that strong, active person with a good sense of humour and play, she began to connect it to herself, to her family, and to family stories. The dance reinforced who she was. When her daughter viewed the video she could identify actions which were 'typically my mother' (Hill 1995, p. 88).

Those qualities which she had always had (and probably thought she had lost) she was able to re-experience and live out in the world. Hill (1995) reports that she felt she had 'got together again' (p. 196). She felt she was re-emerging from a dark place: 'It's brought the dullness out from me . . . to the brightness' (p. 195), 'So that's brought me out of my cupboard' (p. 193).

Even when she did not feel good, coming to the sessions made her feel better: 'I've been as dull as ditch this morning. I'm tired I think. I get worried. I shouldn't do this and I shouldn't do that, and I don't know why they picked me, and then after, I feel good' (p. 197).

In reconnecting to herself, she seemed to regain a more positive sense of herself and her life generally. She commented on successes in the games on the ward, and she offered a more optimistic view of the worth of her life: 'I often get a remark . . . on how old I am and they say that they can't believe it and they think I look, you know, young. And they won't believe it and somebody else will say it and I think I must look good . . . But eh, I'm glad I'm alive' (p. 196)

Figure 45.1 demonstrates some links between the framework of wellbeing in dementia described previously as important aspects of the reviewed literature and Elsie's experience based on the research study.

My work with Elsie was intense, and it is rare to have the opportunity to do such concentrated one-to-one work. However, within the group context, all those aspects of wellbeing to do with acknowledgement, relationship, and meaningful engagement still hold. Participants can feel, not only at ease with themselves and others, but feel elated, on high, excited. They may surprise themselves, as well as others. Transformation can happen in these moments of dance.

There are, of course, limits to what a weekly session of dance movement therapy can achieve, and the more ongoing, universal sense of wellbeing will only be possible if the whole care organization embraces a person-centred approach. However, for people with dementia, who experience an ever-changing fragmented lifeworld, the moment is the unit of value; this is all they have. In increasing those positive moments to their lives, we can hope to build towards a life that is still worth living.

The good feelings may also reach beyond the dance session and impact on the participants' larger life world. In an article written jointly with American dance therapist Donna Newman-Bluestein (Newman-Bluestein and Hill 2010), we note that the dance movement therapy session can also reach out to, and draw in, staff, thereby changing their perceptions of, and attitude towards, the people in their care, as well as developing their relational skills. This may then flow on into their interactions with their residents/patients outside the dance session. Given the importance of relationship and the fact that care staff have the most contact hours with residents (they are often the residents' whole world), changes in staff attitudes can have a major ongoing impact on the wellbeing of residents. At one nursing home where I worked, a staff member who had attended some dance movement therapy sessions noted that through his contact with a particular resident in the dance sessions, that resident had come to trust him. Whereas previously, the resident had felt very suspicious of, and resistant to, the nurse's efforts to give him

---

ELSIE'S EXPERIENCE IN RELATION TO WELLBEING

SENSE OF SELF/SELF WORTH/AGENCY

- Elsie was able to reconnect to the qualities of her "old" self and was able to live (embody) that self in the dance session.
- She identified with a very positive quality "strength", which also happened to be a particular characteristic she attributed to herself and her family generally.
- She was an equal partner in the dance, and many times took control and led the action.
- She felt good about herself and wanted others to see how she was in the sessions. "Would be good fun for my daughters to see me like that" (Hill, 1995, p.172). She was delighted to be on television. "Good Lord, I can't believe me on television". (p.181) "I never in my life thought, I never thought I'd get on the movies." (p.186)
- She felt good that she had been "chosen" to participate in the research and was aware of the importance of her contribution to the research study

RELATIONSHIP

- The relationship between Elsie and me was the strong thread that persisted throughout, regardless of how Elsie might feel on a particular day.
- The relationship continued even months after the sessions finished and Elsie moved to a nursing home.
- Elsie was aware that she was playing an important part in my research and was keen to do her best to help.
  "I hope I don't fail you" (p.185).
- The benefits flowed out to the family relationships. The video of Elsie dancing enabled her daughters to see her in a different light. It also offered an opportunity to share the experience by sitting together to watch the video. Elsie was obviously proud she could show this to her daughters.

MEANINGFUL ACTIVITY

- Dance and play acting were things Elsie had enjoyed in the past and she clearly responded to the play and humour in the dance.
- The experience reconnected her to important memories, memories very much linked to who she was as a person.
- During the dance session, she could be the strong person she had always been (but had seemingly "lost" in dementia).

MEANING/HOPE

- Elsie expressed more positive thoughts about her current life.

FIGURE 45.1. Elsie's experience in relation to wellbeing. (Credit: H. Hill.)

medication, he now was quite relaxed and cooperative. This was not just a matter of making things easier for staff, but would have had a profound impact on the resident's sense of wellbeing, as he felt able to trust his carer.

CONCLUSION

In this chapter I have suggested that, viewed from a person-centred perspective, well-being is indeed possible for people with dementia, and that it is a relational enterprise which is creative and ongoing. Wellbeing, as I have defined for this population, is not so very different from wellbeing for all of us, especially in its dependence on relationship. Certainly, wellbeing becomes more challenging for the person with dementia to attain, because of the attacks on the self and the disruption of relationships. However, as clinical experience and research studies suggest, it remains very possible.

Dance, along with other art forms, has particular strengths in making connections between and among people, and in reaching out to include people of all ages, cultures, and abilities. For this reason, it is a particularly apt modality to engage with people with dementia and to contribute to their sense of wellbeing through meeting those basic needs, identified by Kitwood, of identity, comfort, attachment, inclusion, and (meaningful) occupation, all in a context of relationship.

Finally, having advocated thus far the possibility of wellbeing, I find myself drawn to move beyond this concept. Wellbeing can seem to denote a rather passive state. More attractive to me is the concept of 'flourishing', by which I mean a much more active, alive, and growing state. People engaged in person-centred care are beginning to recognize that wellbeing is the minimum aim, and that flourishing is the direction we should be working towards. People with dementia have the capacity to learn new things, to experience highs, to be creative. Dance movement therapy offers one of the spaces where the person with dementia can feel not only at ease, but supremely alive.

NOTE

1. For the purposes of this chapter I use the generic term 'dementia' in discussing the state of being which is usually associated with Alzheimer's disease and signifies an irreversible pathological process in the brain. However, there are more than sixty varieties of dementia with different origins—vascular dementia, for example—types of progression, and different outcomes (some are reversible), Alzheimer's disease being the most common.

REFERENCES

Antonovsky, A. (1987). *Unravelling the Mystery of Health: How People Manage Stress and Stay Well*. San Francisco, CA: Jossey-Bass.

Buber, M. (1965). *The Knowledge of Man: A Philosophy of the Interhuman*. New York, NY: Harper & Row.

Coaten, R. (2009). *Building Bridges of Understanding: The Use of Embodied Practices with Older People with Dementia and their Care Staff as Mediated by Dance Movement Psychotherapy*, PhD thesis, University of Roehampton, London.

Coaten, R. and Newman-Bluestein, D. (2013). 'Embodiment and dementia: Dance movement therapists respond', *Dementia*, 12(6): 677–81.

Csikszentmihalyi, M. (1975). *Beyond Boredom and Anxiety: Experiencing Flow in Work and Play*. San Francisco, CA: Jossey-Bass.

Csikszentmihalyi, M. (1990). *Flow: The Psychology of Optimal Experience*. New York, NY: Harper & Row.

Csikszentmihalyi, M. (1994). *The Evolving Self*. New York, NY: Harper Perennial.

Damasio, A. (1996). *Descartes' Error: Emotion, Reason and the Human Brain*. London: Papermac.

Dance Movement Therapy Association of Australasia (DTAA) (2015) 'What is Dance Movement Therapy?' <http://dtaa.org.au/therapy/>

Exiner, H. and Kelynack, D. (1994). *Dance Therapy Redefined: A Body Approach to Therapeutic Dance*. Springfield, IL: Charles C. Thomas.

Fischman, D. (2009). 'Therapeutic relationships and kinaesthetic empathy', in S. Chaiklin and H. Wengrower, *The Art and Science of Dance/Movement Therapy: Dance is Life*. New York: Routledge, pp. 33–53.

Fraleigh, S. H. (1987). *Dance and the Lived Body*. Pittsburgh, PA: University of Pittsburgh Press.

Garratt, S. and Hamilton-Smith, E. (eds.). (1995). *Rethinking Dementia: An Australian Approach*. Melbourne: Ausmed Publications.

Gergen, K. (2009). *Relational Being: Beyond Self and Community*. New York, NY: Oxford University Press.

Gibson, F. (1998). 'Unmasking dementia', *Community Connections*, October–November: 6–7.

Giorgi, A. (1985). *Phenomenology and Psychological Research*. Pittsburgh, PA: Duquesne University Press.

Grotberg, E. (1995). 'A guide to promoting resilience in children: Strengthening the human spirit', *Early Childhood Development: Practice and Reflections Number 8*. The Hague: Bernard van Leer Foundation.

Halprin, D. (2008). *The Expressive Body in Life, Art, and Therapy: Working with Movement, Metaphor and Meaning*. London: Jessica Kingsley.

Hill, H. (1995). *An Attempt to Describe and Understand Moments of Experiential Meaning Within the Dance Therapy Process for a Patient with Dementia*. Unpublished Master's thesis, Latrobe University, Australia. <http://arrow.latrobe.edu.au:8080/vital/access/manager/Repository/latrobe:19713;jsessionid=1DD7C6FD8A48C5EEF3AD3F74694AD100> (accessed 26 February 2015).

Hill, H. (2009). *Invitation to the Dance*, 2nd edn. Stirling: University of Stirling. <http://www.dtaa.org.au/publications>

Hill, H. (2003). 'A space to be myself', *Signpost to Older People and Mental Health Matters*, 7(3): 37–39.

Johnson, M. (2007). *The Meaning of the Body: Aesthetics of Human Understanding*. Chicago, IL: University of Chicago Press.

Karkou, V. and Sanderson, P. (2006). *Arts Therapies: A Research-Based Map of the Field*. Edinburgh: Elsevier.

Kasayka, R. E. (2001). 'Introduction', in A. Innes and K. Hatfield (eds.), *Healing Arts Therapies and Person-Centered Dementia Care*. London: Jessica Kingsley, pp. 9–17.

Kitwood, T. (1997). *Dementia Reconsidered: The Person Comes First*. Buckingham: Open University Press.

Kitwood, T. and Bredin, K. (1992). 'Towards a theory of dementia care: Personhood and well-being', *Ageing and Society*, 12: 269–87.

Koch, S. (2006). 'Interdisciplinary embodiment approaches: Implications for creative arts therapies', in S. C. Koch and I. Brauninger (eds.), *Advances in Dance/Movement Therapy: Theoretical Perspectives and Empirical Findings*. Berlin: Logos, pp.17–28.

Levy, F. (2005). *Dance Movement Therapy: A Healing Art*, revised edn. Reston, VA: National Dance Association/AAHPERD.

Newman-Bluestein, D. and Hill, H. (2010) 'Movement as the medium for connection, empathy, playfulness', *Journal of Dementia Care* 18(5): 24–7.

Power, G. A. (2010). *Dementia Beyond Drugs: Changing the Culture of Care*. Baltimore, MD: Health Professions Press.

Sacks, O. (1991). *Awakenings*. New York: Picador.

Shustik, L. R. and Thompson, T. (2002). 'Dance/movement therapy: Partners in personhood', in A. Innes and K. Hatfield (eds.), *Healing Arts Therapies and Person-Centered Dementia Care*. London: Jessica Kingsley, pp. 49–78.

Taylor, R. 'Be with me today' (DVD). <https://dementiaresources.org.au/2015/08/21/richard-taylor-collected-works/>

Yeats, W. B. (1928/1997). 'Among school children', in E. Larrissy (ed.), *W. B. Yeats: The Major Works*. Oxford: Oxford University Press.

CHAPTER 46

EMOTIONS IN MOTION

Depression in Dance-Movement and Dance-Movement in Treatment of Depression

MARKO PUNKANEN, SUVI SAARIKALLIO,
OUTI LEINONEN, ANITA FORSBLOM,
KRISTO KAARLO MATIAS KULJU,
AND GEOFF LUCK

INTRODUCTION

DEPRESSION is a disabling medical illness characterized by persistent and all-encompassing feelings of sadness, loss of interest or pleasure in normally enjoyable activities, and low self-esteem (Sobocki et al. 2006). Onset of depression frequently occurs during adolescence (Leinonen 2013), and depressed individuals have difficulty in identifying, expressing, and regulating emotions, especially negative ones such as anger (Joormann and Gotlib 2010). Depression affects about 121 million people worldwide, and is predicted to become the second most disabling illness in the world after ischemic heart disease within the next ten years (WHO 2010). Medication, sometimes in combination with verbal psychotherapy or counselling, is the predominant method of treatment for depression, but there is good evidence to suggest that movement- and body-based interventions such as interactive dance movement therapy can reduce depression (Stewart et al. 1994; Jeong et al. 2005; Koch et al. 2007; Mala et al. 2012; Meekums et al. 2015). By better understanding relationships between interactive dance movement therapy and both expression of emotional states in general and depression in particular, we can take a step towards understanding and improving the wellbeing of society as a whole.

In this chapter we introduce the central role of body and dance-movement in expression and regulation of emotional states, consider motion capture technology as a method for studying dance-movement, and provide a short overview of related studies. We also present recent findings concerning the effect of depression on a person's movement expression, as well as possibilities of using dance/movement therapy (D/MT) as a therapy intervention for depression. Finally, we give a voice to one of the clients with depression who participated in our D/MT study. A mixed-method case study based on her diary during the therapy process provides us with a unique possibility to take a detailed look at depression and D/MT from a client's perspective.

DANCE-MOVEMENT AS EXPRESSION OF EMOTIONAL STATES

Body movement is a fundamental form of emotional expression (Darwin 1872/1965; Coulson 2004; Wallbott 1998). Movement to music is a great illustration of this, and it has been shown that people efficiently identify emotional content expressed through the body movements of dancers and instrumentalists (Aronoff et al. 1992; Camurri et al. 2003; Castellano et al. 2008; Dahl and Friberg 2007; Thompson and Luck 2008). Our movements also inherently tell something about our inner states: body postures and movements have been shown to be reflective of both short-term mood states (Amaya et al. 1996; Castellano et al. 2007; Crane and Gross 2007; Paterson et al. 2000; Pollick et al. 2001; Troje 2008; Wallbott 1998), as well as of more long-term affective phenomena such as personality (Ball and Breese 2000; Kluft et al. 2006; Koppensteiner and Grammer 2010) and depression (Lemke et al. 2000).

It was Charles Darwin who first proposed that joy boosts, but fear hinders movement in animals (Darwin 1872/1965). In a broad sense, the overall increase or decrease of movement can be linked to a major theoretical distinction regarding emotional behaviour: approach motivation (positive emotionality, extraversion, behavioural activation system) relates to increased behavioural activation towards a desired goal, while avoidance motivation (negative emotionality, neuroticism, behavioural inhibition system) relates to decreased behavioural activation generated by an undesired event or goal (Gray 1970; Elliot and Thrash 2002; James 1890; Watson et al. 1988). A variety of recent studies have indeed confirmed that emotions that contain high arousal and positive valence (reflective of approach motivation) are reflected in faster and broader movement, while emotions that contain low arousal and negative valence (reflective of avoidance motivation) tend to be reflected through decreased movement (Amaya et al. 1996; Paterson et al. 2000; Pollick et al. 2001; Wallbott 1998).

There is some indication that arousal level in particular is reflected in the speed of movement: anger, joy, and excitement all relate to fast movement, while sadness and tiredness relate to slow movement (Amaya et al. 1996; Castellano et al. 2007; Paterson et al. 2000; Pollick et al. 2001; Wallbott 1998). Meanwhile, valence may be particularly reflected in posture: open and upright postures relate to positive emotional states, while forward-leaning and closed postures relate to sadness, shame, and boredom (Ball and

Breese 2000; Castellano et al. 2007; Coulson 2004; De Silva and Bianchi-Berthouze 2004; Schouwstra and Hoogstraten 1995; Wallbott 1998).

As regards dance-movement, the results of the first pioneering studies are in line with the previous descriptions. The personality trait of extraversion appears to be reflected in faster and more accelerated dance-movement as well as of greater use of space and hand distance. Conversely, neuroticism relates negatively to these components; that is, generally to less movement while dancing (Luck et al. 2010). Furthermore, current mood state reflective of approach motivation (positive, energetic state) has been shown to relate to faster dance-movement, more spread-out posture of hands, and more complex movement patterns (Saarikallio et al. 2013).

DEPRESSION AS AN EMOTION REGULATION DISORDER

Depression is one of the leading causes of disability, affecting approximately 121 million people worldwide (WHO 2010). The estimated prevalence of depression in Finland is 5–6.5% of the population, and lifetime prevalence is 20% of the population (Tuulari et al. 2007), which is similar to lifetime prevalence estimates in The Netherlands, Australia (Kruijshaar et al. 2005) and the United States (Kessler et al. 1994). Because of the high prevalence of this disorder and its effects on a person's ability to work, depression has huge economic effects on our society. In Finland, for example, 4,600 people received a new disability pension in 2007 because of depression (Depressio: Käypä hoito-suositus 2013).

According to the American Psychiatric Association (2000), depression is seen as a mood disorder characterized by sad mood, anhedonia, and changes in psychomotor, sleeping, and eating patterns. It is most commonly described as a disorder that affects a person's ability to represent and regulate mood and emotion (Davidson et al. 2002). There are different kinds of symptoms related to depression. It can manifest itself through hopelessness, loss of mood reactivity, inability to experience pleasure, suicidal thoughts, and psychosis (Kalia 2005; Sobocki et al. 2006). These are symptoms that cause a lot of suffering for both the patients with depression and their families. However, impaired emotion regulation remains the essence of depression.

Theorists have suggested that the difference between vulnerable and non-vulnerable people to depression is not in their initial response to a negative event, but in their ability to recover from it (Teasdale 1988). This leads us to different emotion-regulation strategies. Previous studies have shown that the level of depression symptoms correlates with more frequent use of strategies, such as expressive suppression, thought suppression, rumination and catastrophising, and less frequent use of strategies such as reappraisal and self-disclosure (Campbell-Sills et al. 2006; Garnefski and Kraaij 2007; Gross and John 2003).

As regards how depression is reflected in the body, both postural and kinematic (such as speed and fluidity) features are relevant aspects for study. Pioneering research has demonstrated that patients with depression show significantly lower gait velocity than healthy controls (Lemke et al. 2000). Tilted postures that minimize size are also being perceived to reflect submissive characteristics of a person (Ball and Breese 2000). Furthermore, body postures actually influence our behaviour: Riskind and Gotay (1982) showed that subjects who had temporarily been placed in a slumped posture demonstrated higher learned helplessness and lower persistence in a following behavioural task in comparison to subjects who had been placed in an expansive, upright posture. However, no effect of posture on self-report ratings of emotional states was observed in that study.

In a more recent study about the benefit of power posing before a high-stakes social evaluation (mock job interview), the researchers found that high-power posers (expansive and open postures) performed better and were more likely to be chosen for hire (Cuddy et al. 2012). In another study on the effect of two minutes posing it was found that high-power posers (both male and female) experienced elevations in testosterone, decreases in cortisol, and increased feelings of power and tolerance for risk, while low-power posers (closed and contractive postures) exhibited the opposite pattern (Carney et al. 2010). These findings suggest that embodiment causes changes at psychological, physiological, and behavioural levels.

Motion Capture Technology in Movement Studies: from Posed Postures to Spontaneous Movement

The majority of research on body movement as a form of emotional expression has focused on posed expression using settings where participants (such as actors) are purposefully asked to express certain emotions. This may lead to exaggerated gestures, not particularly illustrative of everyday expression of inner states, which are typically subtle and sometimes even purposefully inhibited. Much of the research has also used static postures instead of continuous movement, which omit the measurement of a range of kinematic qualities of movement, such as speed and fluidity, that may be highly relevant to the subtle, spontaneous expression of personal emotional state.

An alternative to examining static poses is to record fluid motion. To do so, there are two main possibilities: video camera or motion capture. The main advantages of using a video camera are relatively low cost, ease of set-up and use, and inclusion of the context in which the movements are made. In contrast, motion-capture systems tend to be relatively expensive, complicated to set up and operate, and record only the specific movements specified by the researcher, providing no information about the context in which the movements were made. However, motion capture offers much higher temporal and spatial resolution, as well as recording in three dimensions. Moreover, motion-capture data are considerably more amenable to computational analysis, and allow the researcher to focus purely on the characteristics of the motion itself. Thus, motion capture might be considered as the optimal method of examining continuous, spontaneous movement of the type of interest to those studying the effects of depression on body movement.

Study 1: Depression in Dance-Movement

This section describes a study that investigated how depression affects the expression of basic emotions through spontaneous bodily movement. The results are based on a thesis entitled 'Movement analysis of depressed and non-depressed persons expressing emotions through spontaneous movement to music' (Leinonen 2013). This study, as well as the two related studies (Study 2 and Study 3) described in later parts of this chapter, was conducted as part of a project entitled 'Emotions in Motion' that was carried out at the Finnish Centre of Excellence in Interdisciplinary Music Research, University of Jyväskylä. Given the topic of the project and the involvement of participants who were diagnosed with depression, approval was sought and consequently gained by the Ethical Board of the Central Finland Health Care District.

The overall aim of the 'Emotions in Motion' project was to increase our understanding of relationships between music and movement-based emotional expression and regulation, and how these are associated with depression and mental wellbeing. Moreover, it was hoped that this research would advance our understanding of mechanisms underlying the effects of D/MT, further clarify depression-related emotional skills, and highlight the potential of music as a welfare-improving tool in everyday life.

Methodology

Participants

Data were collected from two groups of participants: An *experimental* group consisting of twenty-one individuals diagnosed with clinical depression, including three men and eighteen women aged 21–58 (mean age = 40, SD of age = 13), and a *control* group consisting of nineteen participants with no clinical diagnosis, including four men and fifteen women aged 19–57 (mean age = 30, SD of age = 10). The control group was chosen to match the experimental group as closely as possible in relation to age and sex.

Apparatus and Procedure

Data collection began with completion of psychometric measures and a background questionnaire. Participants' level of depression was evaluated with the Beck Depression Inventory (BDI) (Beck et al 1961), and other psychometric measures were also administered. In the background questionnaire, participants answered questions concerning their background in music, dance, and sports.

Following this, movement data were collected from each participant individually. For this, participants wore a tight-fitting motion-capture suit equipped with twenty-eight reflective markers, the locations of which are shown in Figure 46.1.

Each session began with a warm-up, during which the therapist offered some movement possibilities to the participant and explained the participant's task. After the warm-up, participants were presented with fifteen short (60-second) music excerpts. Each excerpt represented one of five basic emotions (happiness, sadness, anger, fear, and tenderness), and there were three excerpts for each emotion. Participants were instructed to express the emotion conveyed in the music through their body movement.

The three-dimensional position of each marker was tracked by an eight-camera optical motion-capture system (Qualisys ProReflex) at 120 frames per second. Music stimuli were played back via a pair of Genelec 8030A loudspeakers, and the ambient room sound was recorded with two overhead microphones positioned at a height of 2.5 metres. The microphone input, the direct audio signal of the playback, and the TTL1 pulse transmitted by the Qualisys cameras when recording, were recorded using Pro Tools software in order to facilitate synchronization of the motion-capture data with the

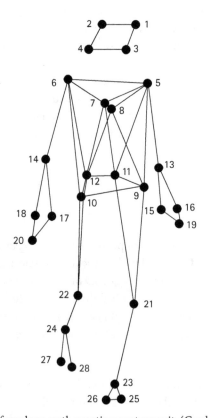

FIGURE 46.1. Location of markers on the motion capture suit. (Credit: Punkanen et al.)

music stimuli. In addition to the motion capture system, sessions were recorded with three Sony video cameras.

In all, 171 movement features were computationally extracted from the movement data using MATLAB Motion Capture (MoCap) Toolbox (Toiviainen and Burger 2011) software. In this study we examined a subset of these movement features. Specifically, we examined the speed and acceleration of the torso (mean and SD for both), the distance between the hands (mean and SD), the distance between the feet (mean and SD), the sum of the total distance travelled by all body parts, and the size of the floor area within which each participant moved. Technical descriptions of these features can be found in Saarikallio et al. (2013).

The effect of Depression (people with depression vs. people with no depression) and Felt Emotion (happiness, sadness, anger, fear, and tenderness) on the movement features was investigated by Multivariate Analysis of Variance (MANOVA) using Wilks' Lambda. The post hoc comparisons were made with Bonferroni correction. SPSS 2.0 was used to run all statistical analyses.

Stimuli

All participants were presented with short (60-second) excerpts taken from the fifteen pieces shown in Table 46.1. Each excerpts represented one of five basic emotions (happiness, sadness, anger, fear, and tenderness). The pieces were classified according to the emotion represented in the Table.

Results

The MANOVA revealed that there was a significant main effect of Felt Emotion, $F_{(52, 1795.302)} = 6.237$, $p = 0.000$, on Torso Speed mean, Torso Speed SD, Torso Acceleration

Table 46.1. Music excerpts used in the study classified according to the emotion they represented.

Anger	Fear	Joy	Sadness	Tenderness
High Energy: The Box	David Julyan: The Bone Dam	ABBA: Dancing Queen	A Fine Frenzy: Almost Lover	Bob McFerrin: Common Threads
Marilyn Mazur: Unbound	Mussorgsky: Night on a Bare Mountain	Earth, Wind and Fire: Boogie Wonderland	Glen Hansard and Marketa Irglova: If You Want Me	Gabriela Anders: Fire of Love
Rage Against the Machine: Wake Up	Bernard Herrmann: Theme for Psycho (Prelude)	Marvin Gaye: Pride and Joy	Jukka Leppilampi: Black Iris	Sade: Is It a Crime?

(Credit: Punkanen et al.)

Table 46.2. Significant main effects of felt emotion on movement features.

	Emotion										
	1. Joy		2. Sadness		3. Anger		4. Tenderness		5. Fear		Bonferroni
Movement feature	m.	std.	m.	std.	m.	std.	m.	std.	m.	std.	
Torso Speed mean	0.442	0.078	-0.434	0.094	0.285	0.106	0-0.157	0.089	0.248	0.095	1 > 2***, 4*** 2 < 3***, 4*** 4 < 5*
Torso Speed SD.	0.205	0.079	-0.256	0.095	0.209	0.107	-0.094	0.090	0.560	0.097	1 > 2**, 1 < 5** 2 < 3*, 5*** 3 < 5* 4 < 5***
Torso Acceleration mean	0.692	0.075	-0.507	0.089	0.632	0.101	-0.273	0.085	-0.036	0.091	1, 3 > 2***, 4***, 5*** 2 < 5***
Torso Acceleration SD	0.518	0.083	-0.311	0.099	0.489	0.112	-0.232	0.094	0.230	0.101	1, 3 > 2***, 4*** 2 < 5*** 4 < 5***
Size of the floor area SD	0.049	0.084	-0.138	0.101	0.018	0.114	-0.154	0.096	0.368	0.103	5 > 2***, 4***
Total distance travelled	0.362	0.080	-0.405	0.095	0.346	0.108	-0.110	0.091	0.190	0.097	1 > 2***, 4* 2 < 3***, 5***

(Credit: Punkanen et al.)

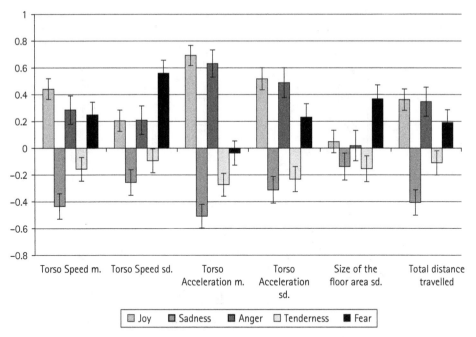

FIGURE 46.2. Standardized means of movement features when expressing basic emotions. (Credit: Punkanen et al.)

mean, Torso Acceleration SD, Size of the floor area SD, and Total distance travelled. In addition, a significant main effect of Depression, $F(13,463) = 15.148$, $p = 0.000$, on Torso Speed mean, Torso Speed SD, Torso Acceleration mean, Torso Acceleration SD, Hand Distance mean, Hand Distance SD, Feet Distance mean, Feet Distance SD, Size of the floor area SD, and Total distance travelled, was revealed. The main effect of Felt Emotion on participant's movement is shown in Table 46.2 and Figure 46.2, and the main effect of Depression on participant's movement is shown in Figure 46.3 and Table 46.3. A statistically significant Depression x Felt Emotion interaction effect was also found: $F(52, 1795.302) = 2.253$, $p = 0.000$. Significant Depression x Felt Emotion interaction effects are shown in Figure 46.4.

Main Effects of Felt Emotion on Participants' Movement

Post hoc comparisons with Bonferroni correction revealed that torso mean speed was significantly lower for sadness and tenderness compared to joy and anger. This same movement feature was also significantly lower for sadness compared to fear. Torso SD was significantly higher for fear compared to all the other emotions, and significantly higher for joy and anger compared to sadness and tenderness.

Mean Torso Acceleration was lower for sadness, tenderness, and fear compared to joy and anger, and lower for sadness compared to fear. This same feature was also lower for sadness and tenderness compared to joy, anger, and fear.

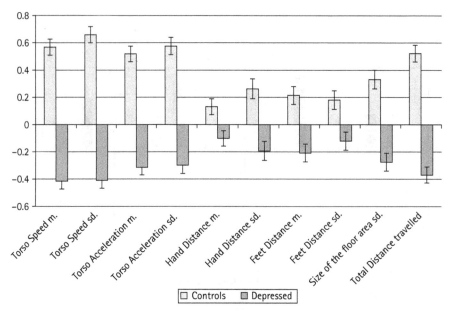

FIGURE 46.3. Movement features of both depressed and controls, standardized values. (Credit: Punkanen et al.)

Table 46.3. Significant main effects of depression on participants' movement.

Movement feature	F	df	P
Torso Speed mean	140.555	1.475	0.000
Torso Speed SD	161.566	1.475	0.000
Torso Acceleration m	110.834	1.475	0.000
Torso Acceleration SD	98.493	1.475	0.000
Hand Distance m	5.206	1.475	0.023
Hand Distance SD	23.452	1.475	0.000
Feet Distance m	20.019	1.475	0.000
Feet Distance S.	10.035	1.475	0.002
Size of the floor area SD	46.018	1.475	0.000
Total distance travelled	110.6	1.475	0.000

(Credit: Punkanen et al.)

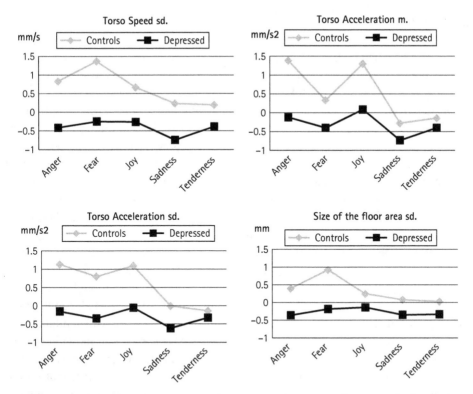

FIGURE 46.4. Significant Depression x Felt Emotion interaction effects. Standardized values. (Credit: Punkanen et al.)

The size of the floor area within which participants moved was significantly lower for sadness and tenderness compared to fear. Finally, Total distance travelled was lower for sadness and tenderness compared to joy and anger, and lower for sadness compared to fear. The standardized means of movement features when expressing different emotions are shown in Figure 46.2.

Main Effects of Depression on Participants' Movement

Depression had a significant main effect on all movement features except the size of the floor area within which participants moved. Participants with depression moved slower, with lower acceleration, in more closed position, and less overall than the controls. The standardized means of movement features are shown in Figure 46.3 (see also Video 46.1 on Companion Website ▶).

Depression: Felt Emotion Interaction Effects

A significant interaction effect was found for the SD of Torso Speed, $F_{(4,475)} = 4.250$, $p = 0.002$, mean, $F_{(4,475)} = 8.591$, $p = 0.000$, and SD, $F_{(4,475)} = 5.765$, $p = 0.000$, Torso Acceleration, and the size of the area within which they moved, $F_{(4,475)} = 2.627$, $p = 0.034$.

Discussion

We found that participants with diagnosis of depression moved less, slower, with slow acceleration, and in more closed positions, and additionally changed the way they moved only slightly when expressing different emotions, compared to participants in the control group. According to these results, depression affects emotional expression through movement by reducing the expressivity of the movement. Loss of interest, passiveness, steadiness, and psychomotor retardation induced by depression seem to affect emotional expression through movement as well as the completion of the participant's task. This study suggests that the difficulties patients with depression have in expressing emotions (Joormann and Gotlib 2010) extend to emotional expression through movement.

The groups differed especially in expression of anger, happiness, and fear. Anger and happiness are categorized as high-arousal emotions, and are expressed through fast, accelerated, wide, and sharp movements (Dahl and Friberg 2007; Gross et al. 2012; Pollick et al. 2001; Sawada et al. 2003). In this study, fear was also expressed through fast and accelerated movements such as anger and happiness, even though it is categorized as low-arousal emotion (Barrett and Russell 1998; Castellano et al. 2007). These emotions require more energy when expressed through movement, which might cause the difference between the groups. Previous studies have shown that individuals with depression tend to suppress negative emotions in particular (Beblo et al. 2012; Joormann and Gotlib 2010), but according to this result, people with depression might also have difficulties expressing positive high-arousal emotions, such as joy, through movement.

Previous work has shown that affective states are reflected in dance movements to music (Saarikallio et al. 2013), but there has been no previous work on how mental disorders affect expressions through movement. Study 1 shows that the ability to express emotions through movement relates to mental health.

STUDY 2: DANCE-MOVEMENT THERAPY IN THE TREATMENT OF DEPRESSION

Study 1, then, revealed that depression is clearly visible in the dance-movement of participants with depression. Consequently, we decided to examine the possibilities of using a dance-movement-based intervention in the treatment of depression (Punkanen et al. 2014). Depression has been closely related to problems expressing and regulating negative emotions, such as anger. Early psychoanalytic theories suggested that depression was caused by the suppression of anger, and a turning of those feelings against the self (Blatt 1998). The tendency of patients with depression to suppress anger has been shown in many studies (Riley et al. 1989; Goldman and Haaga 1995). In many cases, depression causes a lot of problems in emotion-regulation skill, which includes awareness of emotions (especially at the sensorimotor level), ability to identify emotions (one's own and those of others), and flexible strategies to manage emotions. We expected that the dance-movement intervention would reduce depressive symptoms and improve the overall emotional functioning of the participants.

Methodology

Participants

Participants from the experimental group in Study 1 were invited to participate in Study 2. Thus, twenty-one individuals diagnosed with clinical depression, including three men and eighteen women aged 21–58 (mean age = 40, SD of age = 13) took part. Inclusion criteria required that participants' primary diagnosis was depression, F32 or F33, according to ICD–10 classification (WHO 1992). Participants' depression was assessed by the BDI (score of 10 or more) before inclusion. At the beginning of the study, three participants (14.3%) had mild depression (BDI scores 10–16), fifteen participants (71.4%) had moderate depression (BDI scores 17–29), and three participants (14.3%) had severe depression (BDI scores 30–63). Because of the frequent comorbidity of depression and anxiety (Aina and Susman 2006; Cassidy et al. 2005), many participants also suffered from anxiety (72% of them were diagnosed as suffering from mild, moderate, or severe anxiety).

Outcome Measures

The primary outcome measure of the study was the BDI (Beck et al 1961). This self-completed questionnaire consists of twenty-one items, and the total score can vary from 0 to 63. Additionally, we used several secondary outcome measurements for anxiety, personality, life satisfaction, alexithymia, and adult attachment style.

Intervention

D/MT is a psychotherapeutic use of body awareness, movement, and dance founded on the principle of motion and emotion being inextricably entwined. It is a form of psychotherapy in which creative use of movement and dance plays a fundamental role within the therapeutic alliance. In Study 2 we investigated short-term (twenty biweekly sessions) group form D/MT intervention in the treatment of depression among working-age people. In group form D/MT, participants are able to receive peer support and learn new skills from other group members. In the D/MT context, a person is seen as a whole with different levels of experience, including thoughts, emotions, sensations, and motor behaviour.

The main D/MT methods in this study were dance-movement improvisations, body awareness exercises, and reflection through drawing/painting, writing, and verbalizing. Each therapy session was structured through three phases: warm-up, thematic work, and closure. The group techniques employed were space orientation and body awareness, interaction in pairs, and interaction with the whole group.

Themes of the therapy process were mainly chosen beforehand based on previous clinical experiences with this client group. Additionally, the participants' personal themes and aims were included in the therapy process. Some examples of the themes were exploration of boundaries, somatic resources (core and periphery of the body), symbols, pleasant and unpleasant emotions, mindfulness and body awareness, enriched movement experiences, safety, and touch. Development of emotion regulation skill was a specific focus of the D/MT intervention in Study 2.

Results

Study 2 revealed that short-term group form D/MT intervention can indeed help people with mild, moderate, or severe depression in terms of reducing their levels of both depression and comorbid anxiety. The mean score of the BDI dropped notably from pre- (M = 21.67, SD 5.26) to post-measurement (M =10.50, SD = 5.50), and the difference was statistically significant, t(17) = 10.40, p <0.001. It is also notable that BDI scores were reduced for every participant. Study 2 also showed that D/MT decreases participants' features of neuroticism, and increases their features of extraversion, secure attachment style, and satisfaction of life. Significant, positive changes were also measured in participants' ability to identify their feelings.

Discussion

It was relatively common during the therapy process that participants felt that anger was something they were not allowed to feel and express. Expression of anger led very easily to feelings of guilt. In these situations, symbolic distance offered in creative dance-movement activity enabled expression of this 'forbidden' emotion in a safe and tolerable way. This aspect of active doing is a rather unique property of D/MT, and seems to be a meaningful dimension for dealing with difficult emotions such as anger. The special role of anger is also linked to its destructive aspect. People often forget that anger also has many positive aspects related to defending oneself and fighting for one's rights and justice. Through D/MT, many depressed participants learnt that anger was a justified feeling and an important power for change in their lives, and that it was possible to express it in a non-destructive way. Denial of anger requires an amazing amount of energy, and can finally lead to severe depression and anxiety. It became obvious that one important aim of the therapy process was to help participants express their anger in a safe way. This helped them to release tension related to the prolonged control of anger. Dance-movement improvisation offered a safe, creative, and playful medium for anger expression, and the therapist could support it by mirroring, or modelling it to the participant when necessary. After improvisations, there was often a clear change in participants' level of emotion and energy. The change could be seen in their posture, facial expression, breathing pattern, and more open verbal expression. It was very important to make participants realize that there were changes in their verbal and non-verbal expressions, and to become aware of changed sensations and emotions.

In D/MT with clients with depression, it appears important to give special attention to the activation of clients' 'action systems' of social engagement (Van der Hart et al. 2006), exploring, and play, and in that way diminish the role of defensive systems. In the literature, different terms have been used to describe concepts similar to action systems. For example, attachment theorists have used the term 'behavioural systems' (e.g. Bowlby 1982; Cassidy and Shaver 1999), but motivational systems (e.g. Gould 1982; Lichtenberg and Kindler 1994), functional systems (Fanselow and Lester 1988), and emotional operating systems (Panksepp 1998) have also been used. Van der Hart et al. (2006) chose to use the term 'action systems' because the engagement of each system stimulates particular physical actions, such as body sensations and movements, as well as corresponding mental actions such as thoughts and emotions.

Depression affects a person's action systems so that the defence action system dominates that person's perception about her/himself and the outer world. The defence system activates when a person experiences insecurity, discomfort, or danger.

According to Panksepp (1998), the exploration action system 'fills the mind with interest and motivates organisms to move their bodies effortlessly in search of the things they need, crave, and desire' (pp. 53, 145). Activities of exploration often lead to play, and play can lead to new ideas and increased exploration. This beautiful and gradually strengthened interaction between exploration and play was clearly visible in D/MT sessions among participants with depression. Improvisation in D/MT offers a safe and motivating playground for exploration and play. Spontaneous movements stimulate to create more movements, and sooner or later the client is in a creative process. In that process, the action system of defence is deactivated, and enjoyment of interactive play with the group members and the therapist takes over.

STUDY 3: CASE STUDY OF A 21-YEAR-OLD WOMAN'S EXPERIENCES OF D/MT GROUP THERAPY

We shall now give a voice to one of the clients who participated in Study 2. A mixed method case study based on her diary during the therapy process will provide us with a unique possibility to take a detailed look at a client's perspective on depression and D/MT.

Life History

The female subject of the study, Tiina (name changed), was 21 years old at the time of the therapeutic intervention. In the appendix of her diary, she describes her background.

Tiina is the youngest of three children, and experienced the divorce of her parents when she was 3 years old, after which, the mother acted as the primary caretaker of children. She describes her childhood home environments as 'mentally oppressed', and having a culture of non-communication, especially concerning 'negative' emotions. As a child, sports and dance used to be her 'whole life'. However, due to ankle and knee problems she could not exercise for five years during her adolescence. In addition to the pain and depressive thoughts caused by this, she lived in fear caused by her mentally unstable older sister. These difficult issues were never discussed in the family.

One and a half years before the D/MT intervention, Tiina moved to another city to begin studies. Starting an independent life proved to be difficult for her, as she realized she depended on her mother. The following autumn her mother was diagnosed with cancer, which escalated Tiina's depression and anxiety. At the beginning of the therapeutic intervention, her mother was still in a life-threatening condition.

Methodology

Tiina wrote a diary during her group D/MT process, and voluntarily submitted it for research purposes. She participated in seventeen of twenty therapy sessions, and wrote diary entries about thirteen of those sessions. The diary also included a *reflection* written soon after the intervention, and an *appendix* describing her background (as already noted). The diary was the primary datasource, and was analyzed using a phenomenological framework. The focus of this case study was to observe the client's significant experiences during the D/MT intervention. The diary was first read through by the researchers to obtain an overall sense of the client's process and experiences during the therapy. Following this, two independent researchers highlighted sentences that appeared to be significant for the client. These sentences were formed into 'meaning units' (Giorgi 1984, p. 19). These meaning units were further formed into broader categories, and these categories finally formed one broad theme.

Two years after the therapy was completed, Tiina was asked again to write about her experiences of taking part in the therapy group, and this later reflection was then compared to her previous diary information.

Results and Discussion

All the positive changes identified as significant in the analysis of group results can be seen in Tiina's scores as well. In this respect she can be said to be representative of the group. In particular, her BDI score (our primary outcome measurement) decreased from 21 to 7; that is, from moderate depression to no depression.

During the qualitative data analysis of Tiina's diary, the unifying theme that appeared was the meaning of relationships. On an interpersonal level it was seen in connection with the therapist and with the therapy group. Throughout the diary, she expressed distrust toward the therapist. For example:

> I was most nervous about the instructor [the therapist]. I always find instructors having huge impact on me, as they are someone I should trust and follow . . . She seemed like she was trying to please everyone and create a relaxed ambiance. It felt artificial. [Session 1]
>
> The therapist annoys me, I think she is not honest. [Session 4]

Relationships to others were significant and important for Tiina, and raised questions and emotions about relationships from the group to the therapist and to family members too.

> It feels like I'm sharing my goal with another person who is supporting me. [Session 2, doing a mirroring exercise with a partner]
>
> I placed my stone in the middle of other stones. I was surrounded by others. There was safety in every direction. [Session 8, using pebbles in symbolic work]

Although Tiina writes about her inability to trust people and show her "inner self", gradually she gains more trust towards the group and the therapist, and she is able to open up and share more about herself and the hidden feelings of fear, sorrow, and anger.

> She [a group member] said my movements were so smooth and beautiful to watch. Wow. I thanked her and was very grateful for that. That comment still warms my heart. Dancing and putting my soul into that are my great fears. I always observe if I stand out from the crowd or if I'm accepted by others. [Session 5, concerning the warm up dance]
>
> I was telling how during the Christmas I had felt enormous hate towards my family and friends. I couldn't stand them. At some point I realized that the hate was just one form of fear. I was afraid of losing them." [Session 10, induced by other group member telling about her anger]
>
> Moving was extremely easy. Even if I didn't see the therapist's eyes or her reaction, I didn't panic . . . I felt quite neutral. Peaceful and positive." [Session 15, while improvising dance with the therapist as partner]

The diary documents Tiina gaining *support* and *acceptance* from the group in various ways. Another theme that has been meaningful is the relationship to oneself. Gaining self-confidence and growing as a human being has been something that Tiina found very important. Depression seemed to affect her thinking of herself badly. In group therapy she discovered that she was not alone with her problems.

> I know my resources that are always available but I am not using them. They exist but don't exist. [Session 5]
>
> I'm growing all the time. My thinking has evolved. I see more clearly that I am not the only one who suffers in this world. [Session 8]

> *Although I see the chaos, I have taken time for myself. I really have started to realize the value of my life and how everything depends on me.* [Session 10]

Also, a process of empowerment can be seen, as Tiina experiments with taking 'risky' decisions of her own, and trying out the roles of non-conformist and/or innovator instead of more familiar roles of conformist or retreatist (Schmais 1998). And she learned that she was still accepted and appreciated by the group:

> *So far, for almost my whole life, I have surrendered to the lead of an instructor, listened to and tried by all means to please, always showing my best side. Now I managed to keep my head and travel the way from beginning to end without completely losing my hope.* [Reflection]

The diary documents how many of Tiina's insights stem from non-verbal exercises and communication; that is, from body-based and creative modes of being and doing typical for D/MT and other art therapies. These include movement improvisation and also symbolic work through images and objects. Because emotions reside in the body (Nummenmaa et al. 2014), we believe that D/MT methods allowed Tiina to have more integrated experiences of being seen and being connected to others. And for people with depression, moving one's body can lead to movement in stagnant mental processes as well.

> *I already beforehand knew that movement is very important for me. It's the factor which, as if unnoticed, drives the process forward.* [Session 15]

In the reflections written two years after the intervention, Tiina still thinks very positively about the therapy, and points out that the main benefit from group therapy was in making contact with people, being seen, and being accepted by them.

From her final reflection:

> *I feel like D/MT had a huge impact on my life. It was an incredible kickstart to a new beginning. During that I got to feel like I am part of something, I am significant, important and accepted. As I got depressed I lost the deeper connection with people . . . As I lost the connection with others, I lost myself as well. I couldn't see anything good in myself, and there was no one who could have reflected the good part of me. In therapy I got to feel like a part of the group . . . in retrospect I can see these meetings as an enormous resource. I also got good tools to offload my feelings and try to feel good. Those tools are music listening, moving, drawing, writing my thoughts down and holding on to my social contacts.*

These words demonstrate unique and meaningful ways in which we could further understand the client's experience in the context of participating in D/MT.

We have very briefly described one woman's journey through depression. She found her therapy process very helpful, and also the group work meaningful. It is possible that D/MT could be a potentially useful mode of therapy for other clients too.

CONCLUSION

In this chapter we have seen that body movement and the perception and production of emotion are closely intertwined. Moreover, we have seen how a therapy process that focuses on body movement and emotional expression can help alleviate symptoms of depression, and reduce levels of depression as shown in psychometric measures. For these reasons, we suggest that D/MT be taken under consideration in future approaches and methods utilized in the diagnosis and treatment of depression.

Through the use of motion-capture methodology we were able to study clients' movement very precisely, and in Study 1 we found clear and significant differences in spontaneous dance-movement expression of basic emotions of participants with and without depression. This might offer additional, valuable information for clinicians about a client's state of depression by using dance-movement evaluation. Traditionally, depression is diagnosed by using depression scales such as the BDI or the Montgomery-Åsberg Depression Rating Scale (MADRS), in both of which the client self-evaluates his/her life situation based on different statements. This is a rather subjective method of evaluating a person's clinical state. The assessment of spontaneous dance-movement could work as a more objective tool in diagnostic work, because it is not grounded solely in the cognitive domain. Of course, there is a need for further research before this kind of movement-based method could be used for diagnostic purposes.

In the treatment of depression, a bottom-up approach, in which we focus on sensorimotor processing through body and movement, seems to be a promising and effective way of treatment based upon the results of Study 2 and other previous work (Jeong et al. 2005; Koch et al. 2007; Mala et al. 2012; Stewart et al. 1994; Meekums et al. 2015).

When working with clients with depression, emotion regulation plays a central role. It is not enough to enable clients to externalize anger and other feelings. They also need support to tolerate and regulate those feelings. It is possible that the dance/movement therapist is invited to become an interactive psychobiological regulator for depressed clients' deregulated emotional states.

From Schore's (2003) perspective, 'affect regulation is not just the reduction of affective intensity, the dampening of negative emotion. It also involves an amplification, an intensification of positive emotion, a condition necessary for more complex self-organization' (p. 78). Schore (1994) has divided self-regulation capacity into autoregulation and interactive regulation. Autoregulation is defined as the ability to self-regulate without the help of another; that is, the ability to calm down when emotions are becoming overwhelmed and the person is hyperaroused, and also self-stimulate when arousal drops too low. Autoregulation is often impaired in patients with depression, and they are not able to regulate their emotional states in a sufficient way. They easily go out of their 'window of tolerance' (optimal arousal zone) and become hyperaroused (experiencing 'too much' activation) or hypoaroused (experiencing 'too little' activation). Keeping clients within their 'window of tolerance' enables them to integrate the information they receive from both internal and external environments during the therapy session. Interactive regulation involves the ability to calm down or to increase arousal by interactions with others. By using interactive emotion-regulation strategies, the therapist helps the client to gradually increase her abilities for emotional autoregulation and interactive regulation with people other than the therapist.

With clients with depression, as well as with other emotional problems, it is very important to systematically and gradually increase and develop clients' self-regulation capacity, and in that way widen their 'window of tolerance' related to arousal level and intensity of emotions (Siegel 1999; Punkanen 2006). Tiina's case demonstrates beautifully how she was able to find a sufficiently safe way of expressing her emotions through dance-movement improvisation, while at the same time she learned to use interactive regulation by the group members and the therapist.

We believe that the three studies described in this chapter provide crucial evidence that D/MT is indeed a valid therapeutic tool in the treatment of depression and emotional functioning. Further research on the use of body movement and dance-related interventions would be of great benefit to more clearly elucidate the precise mechanisms at work, and to make a substantial contribution to the treatment of depression.

References

Aina, Y. and Susman, J. L. (2006). 'Understanding comorbidity with depression and anxiety disorders', *The Journal of the American Osteopathic Association*, 106 (5 Suppl. 2): S9–S14.

Amaya, K., Bruderlin, A., and Calvert, T. (1996). 'Emotion from motion', in *Proceedings of the Graphics Interface Conference*. Toronto, pp. 228–229

American Psychiatric Association. (2000). *Diagnostic and Statistical Manual of Mental Disorders*, 4th edn. Washington, DC: Author.

Aronoff, J., Woike, B. A., and Hyman, L. M. (1992). 'Which are the stimuli in facial displays of anger and happiness? Configurational bases of emotion recognition', *Journal of Personality and Social Psychology*, 62: 1050–66.

Ball, G. and Breese, J. (2000). 'Relating personality and behavior: Posture and gestures', in *Affective Interactions. Lecture Notes in Computer Science, 1814*. Berlin: Springer, pp. 196–203.

Barrett, L. F. and Russell, J. A. (1998). 'Independence and bipolarity in the structure of current affect. *Journal of Personality and Social Psychology*, 74(4): 967–84.

Beblo, T., Fernando, S., Klocke, S., Griepenstroh, J., Ascehenbrenner, S., and Driessen, M. (2012). 'Increased suppression of negative and positive emotions in major depression', *Journal of Affective Disorders*, 141(2–3): 474–9.

Beck, A. T., Ward, C. H., Mendelson, M. M., Mock, J. J., and Erbaugh, J. J. (1961). 'An inventory for measuring depression', *Archives of General Psychiatry*, 4(6): 561–71.

Blatt, S. J. (1998). 'Contributions of psychoanalysis to the understanding and treatment of depression', *Journal of the American Psychoanalytic Association*, 46(3): 723–52.

Bowlby, J. (1982). *Attachment*, 2nd edn. New York, NY: Basic Books.

Camurri, A., Lagerlof, I., and Volpe, G. (2003). 'Recognizing emotion from dance movement: Comparison of spectator recognition and automated techniques', *International Journal of Human-Computer Studies*, 59: 213–25.

Campbell-Sills, L., Barlow, D., Brown, T., and Hofmann, S. (2006). 'Acceptability and suppression of negative emotion in anxiety and mood disorders', *Emotion*, 6: 587–95.

Carney, D. R., Cuddy, A. J. C., and Yap, A. J. (2010). 'Power posing: Brief nonverbal displays affect neuroendocrine levels and risk tolerance', *Psychological Science*, 21(10): 1363–8.

Cassidy, J. and Shaver, P. (1999). *Handbook of Attachment: Theory, Research, and Clinical Applications*. New York, NY: Guilford Press.

Cassidy, E. L., Lauderdale, S., and Sheikh, J. I. (2005). 'Mixed anxiety and depression in older adults: Clinical characteristics and management', *Journal of Geriatric Psychiatry and Neurology*, 18: 83–8.

Castellano, G., Villalba, S. D., and Camurri, A. (2007). 'Recognising human emotions from body movement and gesture dynamics', in *Affective Computing and Intelligent Interaction: Book Series Lecture Notes in Computer Science, 4738*. Berlin: Springer, pp. 71–82.

Castellano, G., Mortillaro, M., Camurri, A., Volpe, G., and Scherer, K. R. (2008). 'Automated analysis of body movement in emotionally expressive piano performances', *Music Perception*, 26: 103–19.

Coulson, M. (2004). 'Attributing emotion to static body postures: Recognition accuracy, confusions, and viewpoint dependence', *Journal of Nonverbal Behavior*, 28: 117–39.

Crane, E. and Gross, M. (2007). 'Motion capture and emotion: Affect detection in whole body movement', in *Affective Computing and Intelligent Interaction: Lecture Notes in Computer Science, 4738*. Berlin: Springer, pp. 95–101.

Cuddy, A. J. C., Wilmuth, C. A., and Carney, D. R. (2012). 'The benefit of power posing before a high-stakes social evaluation.' Harvard Business School Working Paper, No. 13-027. <http://nrs.harvard.edu/urn-3:HUL.InstRepos:9547823>

Dahl, S. and Friberg, A. (2007). 'Visual perception of expressiveness in musician's body movements', *Music Perception*, 24: 433–54.

Darwin, C. (1965). *The Expression of the Emotions in Man and Animals*. Chicago: University of Chicago Press. Originally published in 1872.

De Silva, P. R. and Bianchi-Berthouze, N. (2004). 'Modeling human affective postures: An information theoretic characterization of posture features', *Computer Animation and Virtual Worlds*, 15: 269–76.

Davidson, R. J., Pizzagalli, D., Nitschke, J. B., and Putnam, K. (2002). 'Depression: Perspectives from affective neuroscience', *Annual Review of Psychology*, 53: 545–74.

Depressio: Käypä hoito-suositus (2013). <http://www.kaypahoito.fi/web/kh/suositukset/suositus?id=hoi50023>

Elliot, A. J. and Thrash, T. M. (2002). 'Approach-avoidance motivation in personality: Approach and avoidance temperaments and goals', *Journal of Personality and Social Psychology*, 82: 804–18.

Fanselow, M. and Lester, L. (1988). 'A functional behavioristic approach to aversively motivated behavior: Predatory imminence as a determinant of the topography of defensive behavior', in R. Bolles and M. Beecher (eds.), *Evolution and Learning*. Hillsdale, NJ: Erlbaum, pp. 185–212.

Garnefski, N. and Kraaij, V. (2007). 'The cognitive emotion regulation questionnaire: Psychometric features and prospective relationships with depression and anxiety in adults', *European Journal of Psychological Assessment*, 23: 141–49.

Giorgi, A. (1984). 'A phenomenological psychological analysis of the artistic process', in J. G. Gilbert (ed.), *Qualitative Evaluation in the Arts, II*. New York, NY: New York University School of Education, Health, Nursing and Arts Professions.

Goldman, L. and Haaga, D. A. (1995). 'Depression and the experience and expression of anger in marital and other relationships', *The Journal of Nervous and Mental Disease*, 183(8): 505–9.

Gould, J. (1982). *Ethology: The Mechanisms and Evolution of Behavior*. New York, NY: W. W. Norton.

Gray, J. A. (1970). 'The psychophysiological basis of introversion–extroversion', *Behavior Research and Therapy*, 8: 249–66.

Gross, M. M., Crane, E. A., and Fredrickson, B. L. (2012). 'Effort-shape and kinematic assessment of bodily expression of emotion during gait', *Human Movement Science*, 31(1): 202–21.

Gross, J. J. and John, O. P. (2003). 'Individual differences in two emotion regulation processes: Implications for affect, relationships, and well-being. *Journal of Personality and Social Psychology*, 85(2): 348–62.

James, W. (1890). *The Principles of Psychology*, vol. 2. New York, NY: Holt.

Jeong, Y. J., Hong, S. C., Lee, M. S., and Park, M. (2005). 'Dance movement therapy improves emotional responses and modulates neurohormones in adolescents with mild depression', *International Journal of Neuroscience*, 115: 1711–20.

Joormann, J. and Gotlib, I. H. (2010). 'Emotion regulation in depression: Relation to cognitive inhibition', *Cognition and Emotion*, 24(2): 281–98.

Kalia, M. (2005). 'Neurobiological basis of depression: An update', *Metabolism Clinical and Experimental*, 54: 24–7.

Kessler, R. C., McGonagle, K. A., Zhao, S., Nelson, C. B., Hughes, M., Eshleman, S., Wittchen, H-U., and Kendler, K. S. (1994). 'Lifetime and 12-month prevalence of DSM-III-R psychiatric disorders in the United States: Results from the National Comorbidity Survey', *Archives of General Psychiatry*, 51(1): 8–19.

Kluft, E. S., Poteat, J., and Kluft, R. P. (2006). 'Movement observations in multiple personality disorder: A preliminary report', *American Journal of Dance Therapy*, 9: 31–46.

Koch, S., Morlinghaus, K., and Fuchs, T. (2007). 'The joy dance: Specific effects of a single dance intervention on psychiatric patients with depression', *The Arts in Psychotherapy*, 34: 340–9.

Koppensteiner, M. and Grammer, K. (2010). 'Motion patterns in political speech and their influence on personality ratings', *Journal of Research in Personality*, 44: 374–9.

Kruijshaar, M. E., Barendregt, J., Vos, T., de Graaf, R., Spijker, J., and Andrews, G. (2005). 'Lifetime prevalence estimates of major depression: An indirect estimation method and a quantification of recall bias', *European Journal of Epidemiology*, 20: 103–11.

Leinonen, O. (2013). 'Liikeanalyysi masentuneiden ja ei-masentuneiden musiikista havaitsemien perustunteiden ilmaisusta liikkeessä' ('Movement analysis of depressed and non-depressed persons expressing emotions through spontaneous movement to music'). Master's thesis, University of Jyväskylä.

Lemke, M. R., Wendorff, T., Mieth, B., Buhl, K., and Linnemann, M. (2000). 'Spatiotemporal gait patterns during over ground locomotion in major depression compared with healthy controls', *Journal of Psychiatric Research*, 34: 277–83.

Lichtenberg, J. D. and Kindler, A. R. (1994). 'A motivational systems approach to the clinical experience', *Journal of the American Psychoanalytic Association*, 42: 405–20.

Luck, G., Saarikallio, S., Burger, B., Thompson, M. R., and Toiviainen, P. (2010). 'Effects of the Big Five and musical genre on music-induced movement', *Journal of Research in Personality*, 44: 714–20.

Mala, A., Karkou, V., and Meekums, B. (2012). 'Dance/movement therapy (D/MT) for depression: A scoping review', *The Arts in Psychotherapy*, 39: 287–95.

Meekums, B., Karkou, V., Nelson, E. A. (2015) 'Dance movement therapy for depression. *Cochrane Database of Systematic Reviews*, Issue 2, Art. No: CD009895. doi:0.1002/14651858. CD009895.pub2

Nummenmaa, L., Glerean, E., Hari, R., and Hietanen, J. K. (2014). 'Bodily maps of emotions', *Proceedings of the National Academy of Sciences of the United States of America*, 111(2): 646–51.

Panksepp, J. (1998). *Affective Neuroscience: The Foundations of Human and Animal Emotions*. New York, NY: Oxford University Press.

Paterson, H. M., Pollick, F. E., and Sanford, A. J. (2000). 'The role of velocity in affect discrimination', in J. D. Moore and K. Stenning (eds.) *Proceedings of the Twenty-third Annual Conference of the Cognitive Science Society*, pp. 756–61.

Pollick, F. E., Paterson, H. M., Bruderlin, A., and Sanford, A. J. (2001). 'Perceiving affect from arm movement', *Cognition*, 82: B51–B61.

Punkanen, M. (2006). 'On a journey to somatic memory: Theoretical and clinical approaches for the treatment of traumatic memories in music therapy-based drug rehabilitation', in D. Aldridge and J. Fachner (eds.), *Music and Altered States: Consciousness, Transcendence, Therapy and Addiction*. London: Jessica Kingsley Publishers, pp. 140–54.

Punkanen, M., Saarikallio, S., and Luck, G. (2014). 'Emotions in motion: Short-term group form dance/movement therapy in the treatment of depression: A pilot study', *The Arts in Psychotherapy*. doi:10.1016/j.aip.2014.07.001

Riley, W. T., Treiber, F. A., and Woods, M. G. (1989). 'Anger and hostility in depression', *The Journal of Nervous and Mental Disease*, 177(11): 668–75.

Riskind, J. H. and Gotay, C. C. (1982). 'Physical posture: Could it have regulatory or feedback effects on motivation and emotion?', *Motivation and Emotion*, 6: 273–98.

Saarikallio, S., Luck, G., Burger, B., Thompson, M., and Toiviainen, P. (2013). 'Dance moves reflect current affective state illustrative of approach-avoidance motivation', *Psychology of Aesthetics, Creativity, and the Arts*, 7(3): 296–305.

Sawada, M., Suda, K., and Ishii, M. (2003). 'Expression of emotions in dance: Relation between arm movement characteristics and emotion', *Perceptual and Motor Skills*, 97(3): 697–708.

Schmais, C. (1998). 'Understanding the dance/movement therapy group', *American Journal of Dance Therapy*, 20(1): 23–5.

Schore, A. N. (1994). *Affect Regulation and the Origin of the Self: The Neurobiology of Emotional Development*. Hillsdale, NJ: Erlbaum.

Schore, A. N. (2003). *Affect Regulation and the Repair of the Self*. New York and London: W. W. Norton.

Schouwstra, S. J. and Hoogstraten, J. (1995). 'Head position and spinal position as determinants of perceived emotional state', *Perceptual and Motor Skills*, 81: 673–4.

Siegel, D. (1999). *The Developing Mind*. New York, NY: Guilford Press.

Sobocki, P., Jönsson, B., Angst, J., and Rehnberg, C. (2006). 'Cost of depression in Europe', *The Journal of Mental Health Policy and Economics*, 9: 87–98.

Stewart, N. J., McMullen, L. M., and Rubin, L. D. (1994). 'Movement therapy with depressed inpatients: A randomized multiple single case design;', *Archives of Psychiatric Nursing*, 8(1): 22–9.

Teasdale, J. D. (1988). 'Cognitive vulnerability to persistent depression', *Cognition and Emotion*, 2: 247–74.

Thompson, M. R., and Luck, G. (2008). 'Effect of pianists' expressive intention on amount and type of body movement', in S. W. Yi (ed.), *Proceedings of the 10th International Conference on Music Perception and Cognition*. Sapporo, Japan, pp. 540–4.

Toiviainen, P. and Burger, B. (2011). *MoCap toolbox manual.* Jyväskylän yliopisto. <https://www.jyu.fi/hum/laitokset/musiikki/en/research/coe/materials/mocaptoolbox/MCTmanual> (accessed 17 January 2013).

Troje, N. F. (2008). 'Retrieving information from human movement patterns', in T. F. Shipley and J. M. Zacks (eds). *Understanding Events: From Perception to Action.* Oxford University Press: New York.

Tuulari, J., Aromaa, E., Herberts, K., and Wahlbeck, K. (2007). 'Pohjalainen masennus ja hakeutuminen hoitoon. *Suomen Lääkärilehti,* 62(8): 790–1.

Van der Hart, O., Nijenhuis, E., and Steele, K. (2006). *The Haunted Self: Structural Dissociation and the Treatment of Chronic Traumatization.* New York, NY: W. W. Norton.

Wallbott, N. (1998). 'Bodily expression of emotion', *European Journal of Social Psychology,* 28: 879–96.

Watson, D., Clark, L. A., and Tellegen, A. (1988). 'Development and validation of brief measures of positive and negative affect: The PANAS scale', *Journal of Personality and Social Psychology,* 54: 1063–70.

World Health Organization. (1992). *The ICD-10 Classification of Mental and Behavioural Disorders: Clinical Descriptions and Diagnostic Guidelines.* Geneva: World Health Organization.

World Health Organization (WHO) (2010). *Depression.* <http://www.who.int/topics/depression/en//> (accessed 15 February 2013).

CHAPTER 47

(DIS-)EMBODIMENT IN SCHIZOPHRENIA

Effects of Mirroring on Self-Experience, Empathy, and Wellbeing

SABINE C. KOCH, JANNA KELBEL,
ASTRID KOLTER, HERIBERT SATTEL,
AND THOMAS FUCHS

INTRODUCTION

DANCE movement therapy (DMT) is defined as 'the psychotherapeutic use of movement to further the emotional, cognitive, physical, and social integration of the individual' (American Dance Therapy Association 2017). But how does it help people with severe psychological disorders, such as patients with schizophrenia—one of the most serious and long-term mental health conditions? Does it improve their wellbeing? Does it increase their empathy? Studies on the effectiveness of DMT interventions in the broader context of body-oriented psychotherapy for schizophrenia have found that they strengthen body- and self-awareness and reduce anxiety and negative symptoms, such as flat affect and motor retardation (Röhricht and Priebe 2006). Most findings in the area of DMT stem from qualitative studies, and as such do not provide hard evidence on the effectiveness of the intervention in the same way as do studies with experimental designs such as randomized controlled trials. This study mainly worked towards the extension of quantitative approaches and manualized DMT interventions. Apart from this, we collected descriptive data on metaphors in movement.

The theoretical basis of our work derives from the recently developed embodiment approaches (e.g. Koch and Fuchs 2011; Fuchs and De Jaegher 2009; Gallagher 2005; Gallese 2001), which offer an alternative explanatory base to the classical Theory of Mind (ToM) approaches in psychology and psychopathology (e.g. Frith, 1992) with regard to an explanation of schizophrenia. Embodiment approaches emphasize the role of the body in affective and cognitive functioning and wellbeing, and are here focused upon in the context of clinical work and psychopathology (e.g. Fuchs and Koch 2014; Fuchs and Schlimme 2009; Koch 2006). Moreover, our approach integrates specific aspects of developmental mirroring theories, developed by Eberhard-Kaechele (2009, 2012). Specific operationalizations of Eberhard-Kaechele's mirroring theory have been selected and integrated into the movement observations of this study.

The goal of our work was to investigate how a DMT mirroring intervention (for a detailed description see Koch, Mehl, et al. 2015) contributes to the improvement of self-experience and interaction skills of patients with schizophrenia. In particular, we looked at the effects of DMT on body awareness, self–other awareness, empathy, social skills, and wellbeing. Wellbeing is here defined as the positive mood or affect of a client measured with the Heidelberger State Inventory (HSI) with the subdimensions of positive affect, depressed affect, tension, anxiety, vitality, and coping before and after the intervention. Of course, more broadly defined, other measures in this study, such as positive changes in body and self-awareness, empathy, and social skills, also account for wellbeing focusing on the body-based, self-related, and social aspects of the construct.

UNDERSTANDING SCHIZOPHRENIA

Schizophrenia is a severe mental health disorder with a heterogeneous clinical picture and a widely differing prognosis. While schizophrenia in its acute form in an everyday language is the classical full-blown madness, a homogenous clinical picture does not exist (Rey 2006). The disorder is characterized by profound changes in perception, cognition, and consciousness, including the feeling of disembodiment, lost body boundaries, lost agency, and determination by external forces. According to ICD 10 (World Health Organization 1992) the basic symptoms of schizophrenia are disturbances mainly of cognition (content and form of thought, perception, sense of self versus external world, volition) and psychomotor function. Schizophrenia (F20.0) is subcategorized into 'paranoid schizophrenia' (F20.0), 'disorganized schizophrenia' (F20.1), 'catatonic schizophrenia' (F20.2), 'undifferentiated schizophrenia' (F20.3), and 'residual schizophrenia' (F.20.5).

Symptoms of schizophrenia are differentiated into *positive symptoms* (abundance of perceptual, emotional, and cognitive experiences, such as visual or auditory hallucinations, associational break-down, or bizarre expressive behaviours) and *negative symptoms* (flat affect, apathy, lack of motivation, poor speech, and motor retardation). On the basis of their severity, medical research, for a long time, focused almost exclusively on the treatment of positive symptoms. Nowadays, positive symptoms can be effectively regulated by neuroleptic medication. Negative symptoms, however, are not improved by existing medication, are often irreversible, and are rarely addressed in research. One such exception is the above-mentioned randomized control trial by Röhricht and Priebe

(2006), which found that body-oriented psychotherapy improved negative symptoms in patients with schizophrenia.

Embodiment Approaches Versus Theory of Mind

Embodiment (*Leiblichkeit*) is a recent interdisciplinary research paradigm that offers an explanation different from classical cognitive approaches such as ToM (Frith 1992). ToM assumes that social interaction requires the competence to differentiate between one's own and others' thoughts, feelings, and actions and to interpret them according to a common sense of social exchange. ToM is about the competence to take on another person's perspective. This skill helps us in social situations to interpret actions, utterances, and signals of others in an adequate, coherent way, and to react accordingly (that is, to contribute to a successful social interaction). Psychopathologies with severely restricted social or intersubjective functioning such as autism or schizophrenia can, from this perspective, be explained with an impaired ToM. The Frith model (Frith 1992; Frith and Corcoran 1996) emphasizes the under-mentalizing of patients with schizophrenia in some areas (negative symptoms) and the over-mentalizing in other areas (positive symptoms). Frith (1992) thinks that patients with schizophrenia can understand others' mental states but that they attribute them wrongly. DMT, in light of recent *embodiment* approaches, would assume that 'outer simulation'—the corporeal taking-on—is also an important aspect of perspective taking. In fact, simulation and theory building are always grounded in a primary embodied experience (Koch and Fischman 2011; Koch and Fuchs 2011).

Embodiment approaches have developed in anthropology, robotics, linguistics, neurosciences, psychology, and psychotherapy (Koch 2006) on the basis of cognitive neuroscience and phenomenology—particularly Merleau-Ponty's 'phenomenology of perception' (1962). Merleau-Ponty describes the body as an experiential platform on which consciousness is grounded and which offers direct and communicative access to the world. He also postulates (1962) that we experience ourselves by experiencing our world, which is accomplished via movement; we have acquired a movement when the living body has understood it. He distinguishes the living body or subjective body (*corps vivante, Leib*), and the objective material body (*corps propre, Körper*; that is, the physical body such as in medicine or the sciences). The objective body is mostly not consciously perceived. It becomes more conscious when we are; for example, exhausted or in pain (Gallagher 2005). On the other hand, the subject, or living body is the entity through which people experience their world; it is thus central to who we are. The body in Merleau-Ponty's (1962) understanding offers a direct access to consciousness. Our living body becomes the mediating force between body and mind, and the mind itself becomes an 'embodied' entity.

Usually, our body is in the background of our experience. However, Sheets-Johnstone (1999) argues that we experience our bodies more in the foreground in dance and non-goal-related movement. Through our bodies, we experience existential feelings and thoughts such as a sense of belonging to the world, of reality, of feeling at home, of connectedness to others, which all help us to experience our world in an integrated way. In a recent definition, embodiment is defined as a field of research, in which the reciprocal influence of the *body* and *mind* is investigated with respect to their expressive and impressive functions (Koch and Fuchs 2011). Expressive functions are the motor expressions (transported on efferent pathways) from the mind to the body, while impressive functions are proprioceptive body feedback functions (transported on afferent pathways) from the body to the mind. Both body and mind form the living, animate, sensing, and moving *Leib* as conceptualized in phenomenology (Meleau-Ponty 1962).

Disembodiment and Impairment of Empathic Intersubjectivity in Schizophrenia

Through our body we gain access to our world. Through our bodies we interactively develop our social cognition and our understanding of the world (Burns 2006).

In schizophrenia, however, we see the loss of the implicitness of 'being in the world':

> . . . a disembodiment of self in the sense of losing one's implicit body functioning, and with it the pre-reflective, questionless being-in-the-world that is mediated by the body. As the sense of self is bound up with the sense of others, disembodiment of self and disturbance of intercorporeality mutually influence each other, resulting in a 'loss of natural self-evidence', a lack of tacit attunement to other people and situations. (Fuchs and Schlimme 2009: 572)

Patients with schizophrenia suffer from a fundamental impairment of the embodied self (De Haan and Fuchs 2010; Stanghellini 2009). They experience their body or parts of it as alien, their outer world as alien, and themselves as separate from it. Due to this condition there is no true contact with others, resulting in blurred boundaries between self and others. This fundamental impairment of the embodied self includes the perception of objects without understanding the meaning related to them; the perception of too great or too little detail, and the sensation of being a spectator of one's own perceptual processes. Moreover, patients with schizophrenia often experience a disruption of formerly automated actions (for example, walking can lose its implicitness and disintegrate into fragments of actions of which each part needs to be executed separately). This can also lead to the experience of being controlled by some external force.

The Role of Empathy

Necessary for a successful interaction is the ability to empathize with the interlocutor. Empathy is the ability to understand the other from a self-similar position, yet deliberately differentiating oneself from the other (Gallese 2003). The lack of empathy in schizophrenia has been demonstrated in a recent study by Haker and Rössler (2009). These authors studied the resonance of patients with schizophrenia compared to participants with no mental health problem (non-clinical). Resonance was defined as the unconscious mirroring of the movements of the interlocutor. Resonance, as the basis of sharing perceptual and emotional states, is an important predecessor of empathy. Haker and Rössler (2009) found that patients with schizophrenia had a diminished resonance compared to the control group, possibly evolving into a lack of empathy. Functional imaging studies support these findings, highlighting deficits in emotional and mirror-neuron brain area activity in patients with schizophrenia (Burns 2006).

In sum, embodiment approaches are based on the assumption that individuals are in constant contact with the environment through their bodies; when interacting they experience intercorporeality in a joint experiential space. In this space, empathic skills develop (kinaesthetic empathy, emotional empathy, cognitive empathy) to form the foundations of social skills and altruistic behaviour, and the base of one's integrated self-experience.

DANCE MOVEMENT THERAPY

DMT can offer patients with schizophrenia (1) a complete form of self-experience, (2) integrative ways of experiencing their bodies, (3) ways to express their emotions, (4) ways to enter into contact with others, and (5) ways to experience their own and the others' boundaries in a more realistic way.

DMT assumes the unity between body and mind, and their reciprocal influence; for example, emotional and cognitive states can manifest in body attitudes, and body attitudes can also influence emotional and cognitive states (e.g. Riskind 1984). If we walk around with the head sunk on the chest and hanging shoulders, it will be difficult for us to experience joy. Within DMT there have been early publications on mirroring in movement (e.g. Sandel et al. 1993; Schmais and Schmais 1983) that now fall on the fertile ground of basic research in neuroscience and embodiment research.

DMT is closely connected to human development. It assumes that movement from birth on has a central influence not only on motor functions but also on the development of body image, self-concept, cognition, emotion, and relational and attachment competencies. An appropriate motor stimulation, as well as a fitting cross-modal relating (the selective use of different sense modalities to communicate and provide feedback), are relevant to infants' development of communicative and social skills.

In the same way, as we grow up, we use these primary non-verbal skills for cognitive and social attunement with our interlocutors, and gradually acquire the skills to form healthy and functional relations (Duggan 1987; Trautmann-Voigt 2003). It is therefore possible that DMT can be a suitable non-verbal approach to work with patients with social-cognitive difficulties, for whom a complex verbal approach might not be useful. There is evidence that DMT helps patients to develop body- and self-awareness and healthy body boundaries (Koch, Mehl, et al. 2015), and increases their sense of well-being and quality of life, as evidenced in a recent meta-analysis on the effects of DMT (Koch, Kunz, et al. 2014). DMT furthers the expression of inner impulses in a contained and structured way, the expression and regulation of feelings, the integration of body and mind, of self- and world-experience, and the development of relational skills (e.g. Hartshorn et al. 2001; Meekums et al. 2012; Sandel et al. 2005) and improves clinical outcomes such as depression and anxiety (Koch, Kunz, et al. 2014). Joint movement creates a feeling of closeness and belonging among group members and within the therapeutic relationship and helps to decrease social isolation. Finally, DMT follows the goal of developing a sense of one's own body boundaries and the boundaries between self and others in the group (Duggan 1987; Eberhard and Lausberg 1999), for example, by varying deliberately between complete and partial attunement (Kestenberg 1975).

In two previous meta-analyses, DMT was found to be effective with various populations (such as children and adolescents, patients suffering from trauma, psycho-oncological patients) and clinical conditions (such as anxiety, depression, and so on) (Ritter and Low 1996; Koch, Kunz, et al. 2014); leading to an overall effect size of Cohen's $d > 0.60$ (Cruz and Sabers 1998) or SMD's > 0.30 (Koch, Kunz, et al. 2014). In a Cochrane review of studies on DMT for schizophrenia, Xia and Grant (2009) were not able to make clear recommendations in favour of or against the use of DMT for patients with schizophrenia, since only one clinical study fulfilled the criteria to enter into the review (Röhricht and Priebe 2006). The specific study found that DMT significantly decreased the negative symptoms of flat affect and motor retardation of this client group. Our pilot study aims to generate feasibility data for further quantitative evidence in the area of DMT and schizophrenia.

MIRRORING IN MOVEMENT

Mirroring in movement is applied in both individual and group DMT (Koch, Mehl, et al. 2015; Sandel et al. 1993). In a mirroring process, the therapist initiates the contact with the patient by reflecting his/her movements, amplifying or reducing certain aspects of them. This encourages the patients—in a non-intrusive way—to vary, expand, or reflect on their movement repertoire. Similarly to the person-centred approach (Rogers 1951), the therapist's reflections, acceptance, and unconditional positive regard of the patient's movement open a possibility of empathic understanding between patient and therapist, and yield insights into the patient's emotional world for both of them (Duggan 1987; Trautmann-Voigt 2003).

Research on *mirror neurons* (Rizzolatti et al. 1996; Gallese 2001) provides a neurobiological basis of the mirroring method in DMT. Mirror neurons enable us to understand actions, action goals, and emotions of other people (Buccino et al. 2001), since they fire in our own sensory and motor brain areas when we observe the actions of others. They even fire when the observed action is incomplete or a mere fragment, and allow us to internally complete the action. An infant needs lots of opportunities to use his/her mirror neurons in order to built implicit relational skills and predict the actions of others. This skill is what we know as 'intuition'—to be able to predict approximately what is going to happen in the course of an action or interaction. Such predictability enables us to adapt our behaviour in a functional way, and makes smooth interaction possible.

Eberhard-Kaechele (2009, 2012) created a developmental system of mirroring stages and related them to the development of the mentalization stages (Fonagy et al. 2004). According to this system, mirroring processes always start with an imitation of an action that can be mirrored in different ways. Eberhard-Kaechele (2009, 2012) assumes that therapist and patient coregulate on a neurological level when involved in a mirroring activity, and that successful mirroring leads to increased resonance, attunement, empathy, social skills, the perception of boundaries between the patient and other group members, self-efficacy; and—as Gallese (2003) notes—to improved self-perception and identity.

RESEARCH QUESTION AND HYPOTHESIS

The main research question of this study was whether the application of 'mirroring in movement'—a manualized DMT intervention (see Koch, Mehl et al. 2015)—leads to improved body awareness (H1), self–other distinction (H2), wellbeing (H3), empathy (H4), and social competence (H5) in patients with schizophrenia, compared to a control group receiving no treatment.

Method

Sample

The study included fourteen patients with schizophrenia (five women and nine men, with a mean age of M = 36.64, SD = 8.9, age range, 26–54) from the Psychiatric University Hospital in Heidelberg. Seven of them (two women and five men) participated in the treatment group, and seven in the control group. All patients in the *treatment group* were diagnosed with paranoid schizophrenia (F20.0): two of low, three of medium, and two of severe degree at the beginning of treatment. Five patients in the *control group* were also diagnosed with paranoid schizophrenia (F20.0): two of low, four of medium—one with an additional depressive episode—and two of severe degree. The degree of disorder (1 = low, 2 = medium, 3 = severe) did not systematically influence the outcome. Originally, twenty-five patients had completed the pre-test questionnaire. Many could not follow up with the post-test due to releases, ward changes, or participation in less than half of the therapy sessions. Three patients completed six of the seven sessions, three patients four of the seven sessions, and one patient five of the seven sessions. A drop-out analysis was not performed. On the basis of an outlier analysis of the first data set with $n = 16$ participants, two participants of the control group needed to be excluded because they were identified as extreme outliers.

Patients had received information about the study via their medical doctors. The treatment group consisted of two existing movement therapy groups (two settings), for which the study took on the vacation replacement of the regular ward therapists. The members of the control group were recruited from the same wards as the members of the treatment group; control group patients were not participating in the regular movement therapy group and were matched in severity of diagnosis. A randomized allocation was not possible, since the therapies took place in already established groups conducted as a vacation replacement for their main therapist. Patients spent at least six weeks on the wards. The intervention was provided to two actual treatment groups (two settings) for a total of eight sessions, twice a week for 45 minutes. The groups were facilitated by a dance movement therapist (Koch, the first author of this chapter), supported by a co-therapist (Jenny Jünger), and a number of student assistants. The regular ward therapists were present in the groups at least for the first session of the study and then again for the last session of the study. The first treatment group consisted of inpatients (patients residing in the hospital), and the second of outpatients (patients residing at home but spending their entire day in the hospital's day programme)—the latter including four patients with a different diagnosis (depression and bipolar disorder), who participated in the sessions but not in the study.

Inclusion criteria for the study were: age >18 years, a diagnosis of the schizophrenic spectrum following ICD 10, no acute psychosis, and the ability and bodily fitness to move standing for 45 minutes. Exclusion criteria were: pronounced language barriers, but patients with such barriers were able to participate in the therapy sessions without participating in the study ($n = 2$).

Design

The study was conducted as a quasi-experimental pre-post control group design. Independent variables were condition (treatment group vs control group) and time (pre-test vs post-test). Dependent variables were body awareness, self–other distinction, empathy, social competence, and wellbeing. Control variables were sex, age, and degree of disorder. The study was conceptualized as a pilot study, and thus had an explorative character. One of the main goals was to test the manualized mirroring intervention (Koch, Mehl, et al. 2015) that was helpful in the treatment of adults with autism spectrum disorder.

Procedure and Intervention

One week before the beginning of the study, participants received an information sheet about the study from their regular movement therapist in the ward. If they agreed to participate and fulfilled the inclusion criteria, they were invited, an hour before their second-to-next movement therapy session, to complete the pre-test. The intervention was conducted replacing their regular movement therapy sessions (by their movement therapist who was on vacation). All participants who completed the pre-test, firstly signed the consent form and then received the questionnaire with the dependent measures. The duration of the intervention was five weeks. The control group was tested one-to-one on the ward within the same time frame. The physician additionally rated the degree of disorder on three levels (1 = low, 2 = medium, 3 = severe) for all participants.

The intervention followed the same format each time, and consisted of four parts:

(a) *Warm-up*. In the Chace circle (Sandel et al. 1993), named after dance therapy pioneer Marian Chace, who worked at St Elizabeth's Hospital in Washington, the therapist picked up movements from each of the participants, structured, strengthened, and modified them, and thus encouraged the participants to try innovative forms of movement while adapting them to their own abilities and limitations. The Chace circle served to increase group awareness, create a pleasant atmosphere, establish the basis of trust, and let the group theme emerge, which are crucial aspects for the remainder of a successful therapy process (Sandel 1993). Verbalization also was important, particularly for the facilitation of emerging thoughts and feelings. The co-therapist facilitated these connections by offering their own verbal associations (about 5–10 minutes).

(b) *Dyadic mirroring* (Eberhard-Kaechele 2012). This format was developed based upon turn-taking in leading and following. Upon the request of the therapist, participants chose a partner. To the first song, participants led the non-verbal mirroring while therapists and assistants followed, to the second song they stayed in the same dyad and the therapist or assistants led while the participant followed, and to the third song, both danced in a free manner and were merely asked to 'stay connected, even when on opposite sides of the room'. In the initial instruction it was emphasized that the mirroring should reflect the quality of the movement (dynamic qualities such as efforts, rhythms, vitality affects, and so on) rather than the shape (about 15 minutes).

(c) *Baum circle* (Koch and Harvey 2012): In the third part of the session, one or two of the participants had the chance to do a free improvisation (modelled by the therapist in the first session), following a self-chosen piece of music that was meaningful to them and being followed by the entire group (Baum circle). This format was chosen to establish rapport and empathy in the participants via kinesthetic resonance, attunement, and emotional contagion. To be mirrored as a single person by the entire group was intended to convey acceptance, respect, and a feeling of unity. In most of the sessions, two participants were able to initiate the improvisation, and the therapists then joined the group in following the initiating participant. Sometimes—particularly when there was no volunteer—initiation was done by the assistants. In the very first session, initiation was modelled by the therapist to demonstrate the focus on one's own authentic expression while improvising (about 15 minutes).

(d) *Verbal processing*: The last step of the intervention was the verbal processing which served for the emotional, cognitive, and social integration of the experience. Patients who had initiated the improvisation in the Baum circle were first asked to talk about their improvisation. The rest were then asked for their feedback on how it felt to move with this particular person, before the rest of the session was processed (about 5–10 minutes).

After each session, participants received a process questionnaire containing items on the boundary differentiation and the self in relation to the group. For more qualitative data on their self-experience, the experience of the intervention, mirroring, memory, and metaphoricity, four of the patients took part in an extra short interview and an individual movement improvisation after the sessions. In these interviews they were asked about preferences in the sessions, metaphors for their disorder, and images and memories resulting from the DMT sessions. The analysis of these three aspects is not part of this chapter; however, a case description of the movement part of such a follow-up session is provided in the Appendix.

Material

Main dependent variables

Psychological wellbeing. For measuring psychological wellbeing we used the unipolar twenty-four-item version of the HSI (Koch et al. 2007), with a range from 1 (does not apply at all) to 6 (applies exactly) containing the dimensions of tension, anxiety, coping, positive affect, depressed affect, and vitality. The HSI was constructed for use in DMT (Goodill 2006) with clinical patients, and has been tested and factor-analyzed in clinical and forensic studies (e.g. Koch et al. 2007). Since it is of major importance in this chapter, we analyzed the single subdimensions here. The internal consistency of the entire scale in previous studies was in the range of Cronbach's $\alpha = 0.63–0.91$, while in this study it was 0.65–0.95 for the single subscales (all internal consistencies were computed for post-test values).

Body awareness. For measuring this specific dependent variable we used the subscale body awareness of the bipolar fifteen-item Movement Therapy Questionnaire (FTT; Gunther and Koch 2010). This scale consists of seven bipolar items with a range from 1 (does not apply at all) to 6 (applies exactly). All seven items describe the ability to be aware of one's body, relevant affects, and the interaction of both of these aspects. The scale was developed for measuring the effect of DMT, and has been tested and factor-analyzed in previous studies with bigger samples. Sample items are 'I am able to recognize my own needs and to express and enforce them appropriately', or 'I feel able to accept closeness to others'. The internal consistency of the body awareness scale in our sample was Cronbach's $\alpha = 0.85$ (in a previous study with an autistic sample it was 0.64).

Empathy. We used the subscale 'empathy' (SPF-E) from the *Saarbrückener Persönlichkeitsfragebogen* (*SPF*) (Paulus 2009)—a German short form of the Interpersonal Reactivity Index (IRI) by Davis (1980), with four out of sixteen items that ranged from 1 (does not apply at all) to 5 (applies exactly), addressing feelings of compassion or worry about other people. Sample items are 'I often have warm feelings for people that are worse off than I am', or 'When I observe how someone is exploited, I feel the need to protect that person'. In addition, a fifth item of the same format was introduced on a missing aspect: 'When listening to someone, it is easy for me to understand and reproduce what my interlocutor in essence wants to say.' The internal consistency of the entire scale of the SPF is Cronbach's α = 0.78. The internal consistency of the SPF-E subscale is in the range of Cronbach's α = 0.66–0.71. The internal consistency in our study was an acceptable Cronbach's α = 0.65.

Social skills/social competence. For the measurement of social skills we used the subscale of the FTT (Gunther and Koch 2010) described previously. Equivalent to the scale of body awareness, the scale of social skills had been tested and factor-analyzed in previous studies with bigger samples (patients with depression vs non-clinical controls). Sample items are 'I am able to behave appropriately in interpersonal situations', 'I am able to accept criticism directed to me', and 'I am able to trust others'. The internal consistency in our study was Cronbach's α = 0.88 (in a previous study with an autistic sample it was 0.83).

Data Analysis

For the data analysis we computed a Mann–Whitney U test (non-parametrical test) with an α level of 0.05. We computed the means of items on the outcome dimensions and a difference score, subtracting the pre-test value of each dimension from the corresponding post-test value. The analysis used condition (treatment group vs control group) as the independent variable, and the difference scores of the outcome variables as the dependent variables, in order to analyze how the treatment affected the outcomes regarding wellbeing, body awareness, social competence, and empathy.

In addition to the *p* values, the effect size *d* was computed—an estimator of the degree of departure from the null hypothesis (Cohen 1969), whereby *d* = 0.2 indicates a small effect size, *d* = 0.5 a medium effect size, and *d* = 0.8 a large effect size.

Results

Since we tested two-sided, but had directional hypotheses, we corrected the *p* value by dividing it by 2. This results section reports the uncorrected values where not otherwise specified. The data on the outcome variables were normally distributed, and the values of the group differences on the main dependent variables are provided in Table 47.1.

A significant improvement of the treatment group compared to the control group was found for empathy U = 4.5, *p* = 0.007, and *d* = 1.81. Participants of the treatment group showed greater self-reported empathy (see Table 47.2) after the intervention—compared to before the intervention—than the control group. The analysis was performed on the SPF (German short version of the IRI; Davis 1980) including the fifth self-constructed item.

Table 47.1. Descriptive statistics of the main dependent variables.

		Pre-test		Post-test		Difference		
		M	SD	M-P	SD-P	Delta M	Delta SD	N
Body Awareness	CG	4.17	0.58	4.15	0.50	−0.02	0.32	7
	EG	4.22	0.62	4.29	0.80	0.06	0.35	7
Wellbeing	CG	3.49	0.26	3.46	0.22	−0.04	0.22	7
	EG	3.40	0.14	3.56	0.35	0.15	0.45	7
Empathy	CG	4.04	0.57	3.68	0.77	−0.36	0.43	7
	EG	3.07	0.83	3.46	0.86	0.39	0.40	7
Social skills	CG	4.55	0.40	4.54	0.28	−0.02	0.26	7
	EG	4.45	0.62	4.38	0.84	−0.07	0.48	7

Note: EG = Experimental Group; CG = Control Group.
(Credit: Sabine Koch/Janna Kelbel, 2014.)

Table 47.2. Descriptive statistics of the well–being subscales (HSI).

		Pretest		Posttest		Difference		
		M	SD	M-P	SD-P	Delta M	Delta SD	N
Tension	CG	3,46	0,83	3,57	0,57	0,11	0,48	7
	EG	3,25	1,07	3,96	0,42	0,71	1,28	7
Positive Affect	CG	4,21	0,60	3,57	0,87	−0,64	0,52	7
	EG	3,36	1,53	4,29	0,85	0,93	1,72	7
Depres. Affect	CG	2,68	0,91	3,18	1,30	0,50	0,87	7
	EG	3,46	1,68	2,68	0,66	−0,79	1,73	7
Coping	CG	3,71	0,70	3,21	0,87	−0,50	0,41	7
	EG	3,43	1,28	4,07	0,97	0,64	1,48	7
Anxiety	CG	3,61	0,89	3,89	1,18	0,29	1,19	7
	EG	3,39	1,42	2,61	0,75	−0,79	1,33	7
Vitality	CG	3,29	0,71	3,32	0,83	0,04	0,60	7
	EG	3,54	0,51	3,75	1,09	0,21	1,11	7

Note: EG = Experimental Group, CG = Control Group.
(Credit: Sabine Koch/Janna Kelbel, 2014.)

There were no significant differences on the total value of *wellbeing* (HSI), U = 11, $p = 0.097$, $d = 0.54$; *body awareness*, U = 21.5, $p = 0.710$, $d = 0.24$; or *social skills*, U = 21, $p = 0.710$, $d = 0.13$ (see Table 47.2). Since we had data on perception of self–other differences from the treatment group only, this dimension was excluded from the analysis of variance (ANOVA).

When dividing *p* by 2, five subdimensions of *wellbeing* showed effects as well as tendencies in the hypothesized direction: *coping* increased, U = 14, $p = 0.209$, $d = 1.05$ (after correction, $p = 0.105$); *anxiety* decreased, U = 15, $p = 0.259$, $d = 0.86$ (after correction, $p = 0.130$); *positive affect* increased, U = 7, $p = 0.026$, $d = 1.24$ (after correction, $p = 0.013$); *depressed affect* decreased, U = 12.5, $p = 0.128$, $d = 0.94$ (after correction, $p = 0.064$); and *tension* decreased, U = 19, $p = 0.535$; $d = 0.62$ (after correction, $p = 0.268$), in the treatment group compared to the control group. *Vitality* did not change, U = 22.5, $p = 0.805$, $d = 0.19$ (after correction, $p = 0.403$). The descriptive values of the group differences on the subscales of the HSI are provided in Table 47.2.

In sum, on the wellbeing subdimensions, positive affect increased significantly. Coping, anxiety, and depressed affect showed a hypothesized (but non-significant) difference in means, resulting in positive assumptions for future testing with larger samples.

Discussion

The study investigated the influence of a DMT mirroring intervention on patients with schizophrenia. There was a significant increase of empathy (as measured with the SPF-E by Paulus 2009, a modified German translation of the IRI by Davis 1980) and of positive affect, as a self-report measure of wellbeing measured with the HSI (Koch et al. 2007), in the treatment group compared to the control group. The increase in self-reported positive affect can be carefully interpreted as an increase in subjective wellbeing. Furthermore, descriptive difference on the other variables all pointed in the hypothesized direction, particularly on the following subdimensions of wellbeing: positive affect, depressed affect, anxiety, and coping. Results suggest that DMT mirroring interventions for schizophrenic populations could lead to improved empathy and wellbeing in line with the assumptions of Eberhard-Kaechele (2009, 2012) and Koch, Mehl et al. (2015). Limitations and future directions are discussed subsequently.

Limitations

The most important limitation is the small sample size. Increasing the sample to $n = 60$ would yield the necessary power to compute an ANOVA and, possibly result in more significant results. To avoid high drop-out rates in future studies, the programme offered should be yet more centrally integrated into the therapeutic treatment plan.

A second limitation was the small number of therapy sessions; patients received only eight sessions. A longer intervention could have probably led to stronger effects. In future studies it would be indicated to investigate the effectiveness of such an intervention as a function of its duration (in order to identify minimum treatment duration, and so on).

The intervention type was a further limitation. During the sessions we noticed that the dyadic mirroring was often too close and anxiety-provoking for the patients; they avoided eye-contact with the mirroring partner and seemed to be relieved when this part of the session was over. It is important, therefore, to improve the intervention in this respect. Group mirroring worked well for the patients and can be elaborated upon. The introduction of props (balls, scarfs, and so on) in the work with patients with schizophrenia can reduce their anxiety in dyads (Röhricht and Priebe 2006; Röhricht et al. 2011), because the presence of an object is suited to mediate the direct interactional contact.

Another important limitation was the application of foremost self-report measures. It is unclear as to how far the patients were able to introspect, to reflect on self-related questions, or to take on a metaperspective of themselves due to their impairment. In future studies, triangulation methods should be enabled by having the outcome measures also rated by the carers of the patients (or at least by the therapists of the study), to be able to compare them to the self-ratings.

A final limitation was that many of the questionnaires applied in this study have not yet been standardized. Thus, their psychometric quality is unclear. Tests of internal consistency of the scales, however, showed good to acceptable values. An advantage of the scales was that they were particularly targeted for DMT interventions and have been proven useful in a number of studies in the field (e.g. Koch et al. 2007; Koch, Mehl, et al. 2015). Regarding the measurement of empathy, the addition of the extra item to the SPF-E scale did not compromise the reliability of the scale, and can thus be accepted in the context of this study. Future studies should replicate results with these scales and standardization of the instruments needs to be attained.

IMPLICATIONS FOR FUTURE RESEARCH

Future research should replicate this study with a bigger sample, a randomized allocation of participants, and a longer duration of the intervention. Dyadic mirroring should be replaced by less threatening formats of mirroring, such as group mirroring in the format of the Chace circle. Moreover, to address diagnosis-related motivational problems, patients in future studies need some form of extrinsic reward system in addition to strong support from the treatment team to comply with the treatment. Questionnaires should be cut down to the most necessary dimensions. Self-constructed measures need to be further validated, and ratings from carers and therapists also need to be integrated.

Future research should additionally explore outcome measures related closer to intersubjectivity and translational resources. Such outcomes would, for example, be *body self-efficacy* and *embodied intersubjectivity* (see Fuchs and Koch 2014). The improvement of such variables through DMT and the reduction of negative symptoms through this method need to be shown in a more targeted way.

The study was a first trial to apply a manualized DMT-mirroring technique to patients with schizophrenia. It piloted the investigation of effects of mirroring on self-experience and intersubjectivity in schizophrenia. Results suggest improvement on the intersubjective aspect of empathy and on the positive affect aspect of wellbeing. In line with recent neuroscientific findings on mirror neurons and their functions (Buccino et al. 2001; Gallese 2003), and developmental mirroring taxonomies from DMT (Eberhard-Kaechele 2009; 2012), the study was able to point out the value of DMT-mirroring interventions for the increase in empathy and wellbeing in patients with schizophrenia.

ACKNOWLEDGEMENTS

We would like to thank Jenny Jünger for her Master Thesis upon which the first draft of the empirical part of this chapter was built. Parts of this work was based on the Bachelor-Thesis of Jenny Jünger: Jünger, J. (2011). Pilotstudie zu Embodiment: Der Einfluss bewegungstherapeutischer Spiegelmethodik auf das Selbsterleben schizophrener Patienten. Heidelberg: Unpublished Bachelor Thesis.

We would like to thank the BMBF for the research grant 01UB0390A to Sabine Koch and Thomas Fuchs in the project 'Body Language of Dance and Movement'. (Further information is available at <http://www.psychologie.uni-heidelberg.de/projekte/bewegung/projektbeschreibung.shtml>). Thanks are also extended to S. Lykou for formatting this chapter, to the participating patients and their movement therapists and physicians, and to our families for their support.

APPENDIX

METAPHORICITY IN MOVEMENT: THE EXAMPLE OF MR P.

Mr P. is a 51-year-old inpatient diagnosed with paranoid schizophrenia (F20.0) in an open ward at the Psychiatric University Hospital of Heidelberg. The patient had been asked to develop some aspect of his life in movement, and once he found something fitting, to verbalize what this aspect is about.

The patient is moving in the movement therapy room (of approximately 12 square metres) in direct paths, from one wall to the other along the walls (about 1.5 metres), at a quite rapid pace. The therapist is sitting on the floor, and observes him. After three of four minutes of observing him walking, the therapist asks: 'How is that for you? What does your movement express?'. He answers: 'It is calming'. Then he starts describing the contrast this offers to just having been 'outside': 'Outside . . . in the supermarket, I was standing at the cashier and I saw her gesticulate to the prior client saying "That is also one of those . . .", with reference to me.' Therapist: 'That's not nice'. Mr. P.: 'No'. He continues walking. Mr. P.: 'Walking is calming. Here it is different.' Therapist: '. . . here you have some space . . . some secure space.'

Mr P. continues to walk. Therapist: 'What else comes up for you when you continue to move like this?' Mr. P.: '. . . waiting for the *execution*' (he speaks this last word very clearly, pronouncing every syllable). Therapist: 'That is a strong image.' Mr. P.: 'Yes, a strong image.'

Mr P. continues walking, and at the end of each path, right before the wall, he starts to perform a slight-kick. He comes into a clear rhythm with this step, emphasizing the void before the kick. After approximately one or two minutes of the new movement, the therapist asks: 'You are always doing this step at the end of each pathway'. He replies 'Yes . . . like an *animal in a cage*.' Therapist: 'Just as in the poem of the panther by Rielke . . . do you know that poem?' Mr. P.: 'No.' Therapist: 'I can bring it with me next time I see you . . . Are there any other images or memories that emerge with the movement?' Mr. P.: 'It is calming to walk' (the patient continues walking for another minute, then the interview part follows).

When later the therapist brought the poem to the patient, he was able to accept it as a metaphor for his situation.

The Panther.

His gaze has grown so weary from the passing
Of bars that there is nothing it may hold.
There seem to be a thousand bars about him
And, out beyond a thousand bars, no world.

The mellowed stride of sleekly powered footsteps
Revolving in the smallest circeling
Just like a dance of strength about a center
Wherein a mighty will stands paralyzed.

Only at times the pupil's soundless curtain
Is reeled away, —letting an image pass
Through the taut silence of his sinews
Right to the heart—and ceases there to be.

Rainer Maria Rilke
(transl. A. Z. Foreman and S. C. Koch)

Der Panther.

Sein Blick ist vom Vorübergehen der Stäbe
so müd geworden, dass er nichts mehr hält.
Ihm ist, als ob es tausend Stäbe gäbe
und hinter tausend Stäben keine Welt.

Der weiche Gang geschmeidig starker Schritte,
der sich im allerkleinsten Kreise dreht,
ist wie ein Tanz von Kraft um eine Mitte,
in der betäubt ein großer Wille steht.

Nur manchmal schiebt der Vorhang der Pupille
sich lautlos auf—dann geht ein Bild hinein,
geht durch der Glieder angespannte Stille—
und hört im Herzen auf zu sein.

Rainer Maria Rilke

FIGURE 47.1. Panther. (Copyright-free.)

References

American Dance Therapy Association (ADTA, 2017). What is Dance/Movement Therapy? https://adta.org/faqs/ (accessed 23 March 2017).

Burns, J. (2006). 'The social brain hypothesis of schizophrenia', *World Psychiatry: Special Article*, 5(2): 77–81.

Buccino, G., Binkofski, F., Fink, G. R., Fadiga, L., Fogassi, L., Gallese, V., Seitz, R. J., Zilles, K., Rizzolatti, G., and Freund, H. J. (2001). 'Action observation activates premotor and parietal areas in a somatotopic manner: An fMRI study', *European Journal of Neuroscience*, 13; 400–4.

Cohen, J. (1969). *Statistical Power Analysis for the Behavioral Sciences*. New York, NY: Academic Press.

Cruz, R. F. and Sabers, D. L. (1998). 'Dance/movement therapy is more effective than previously reported', *The Arts in Psychotherapy*, 25(2): 101–4.

Davis, M. (1980). 'A multidimensional approach to individual differences in empathy', *JSAS Catalog of Selected Documents in Psychology*, 10(4): 1–17.

De Haan, S. and Fuchs, T. (2010). 'The ghost in the machine: Disembodiment in schizophrenia, two case studies. *Psychopathology*, 43(5): 327–33.

Duggan, D. (1987). 'Tanztherapie', in R. J. Corsini (ed.), *Handbuch der Psychotherapie*, vol. 2, 2nd edn. Weinheim: Psychologie Verlags Union, pp. 1256–70.

Eberhard, M. and Lausberg, H. (1999). 'Therapieziele in der Tanztherapie', in H. Ambühl and B. Strauß (eds.), *Therapieziele*. Göttingen: Hogrefe, pp. 277–91.

Eberhard-Kaechele, M. (2009). 'Von der Ko-Regulation zur Selbstregulation: Spiegelungsphä nomene in der Tanz- und Ausdruckstherapie', in M. Thielen (ed.), *Körper–Gefühl–Denken. Körperpsychotherapie und Selbstregulation*. Gießen: Psychosozial, pp. 251–64.

Eberhard-Kaechele, M. (2012). 'Memory, metaphor, and mirroring in movement therapy with trauma patients', in S. C. Koch, T. Fuchs, M. Summa, and C. Müller (eds.), *Memory, Metaphor, and Movement*. Philadelphia, PA: John Benjamins.

Fonagy, P., Gergely, G., Jurist, E., and Target, M. (2004). *Affect Regulation, Mentalization and the Development of the Self*. Stuttgart: Klett-Cotta.

Frith, C. D. (1992). *The Cognitive Neuropsychology of Schizophrenia*. Hove: Lawrence Erlbaum Associates.

Frith, C. D. and Corcoran, R. (1996). 'Exploring "theory of mind" in people with schizophrenia', *Psychological Medicine*, 26(3): 521–30.

Fuchs, T. and De Jaegher, H. (2009). 'Enactive intersubjectivity: Participatory sense-making and mutual incorporation', *Phenomenology and the Cognitive Sciences*, 8: 465–86.

Fuchs, T. and Koch, S. C. (2014). 'Embodied affectivity: On moving and being moved', *Frontiers in Psychology*, 5(508). <http://journal.frontiersin.org/Journal/10.3389/fpsyg.2014.00508/full>

Fuchs, T. and Schlimme, J. E. (2009). 'Embodiment and psychopathology: A phenomenological perspective', *Current Opinion in Psychiatry*, 22: 570–5.

Gallese, V., Fadiga, L., Fogassi, L., and Rizzolatti, G. (1996). 'Action recognition in the premotor cortex', *Brain*, 119: 593–609.

Gallese, V. (2001). 'The "shared manifold" hypothesis: From mirror neurons to empathy', *Journal of Consciousness Studies*, 8: 33–50.

Gallese, V. (2003). 'The roots of empathy: The shared manifold hypothesis and the neural basis of intersubjectivity', *Psychopathology*, 36: 171–80.

Goodill, S., W. (2006). 'Dance/movement therapy for people living with medical illness', in S. C. Koch and I. Bräuninger (eds.), *Advances in Dance Movement Therapy: Theoretical Perspectives and Empirical Findings.* Berlin: Logos.

Gunther, C. and Koch, S. C. (2010). *Fragebogen zur Tanztherapie (FTT).* Unpublished document.

Haker, H. and Rössler, W. (2009). 'Empathy in schizophrenia: impaired resonance', *European Archives of Psychiatry and Clinical Neurosciences,* 259: 352–61.

Hartshorn, K., Olds, L., Field, T., Delage, J., Cullen, C., and Escalona, A. (2001). 'Creative movement therapy benefits children with autism', *Early Child Development and Care,* 166: 1–5.

Kestenberg, J. S. (1975). *Parents and Children.* Northvale, NJ: Jason Aronson.

Koch, S. C. (2006). 'Interdisciplinary embodiment approaches: Implications for creative arts therapies', in S. C. Koch, and I. Bräuninger (eds.), *Advances in Dance/Movement Therapy: Theoretical Perspectives and Empirical Findings.* Berlin: Logos, pp. 17–28.

Koch, S. C. and Fischman, D. (2011). 'Embodied enactive dance movement therapy', *American Journal of Dance Therapy,* 33(1): 57–72.

Koch, S. C. and Fuchs, T. (2011). 'Embodied arts therapies', *The Arts in Psychotherapy,* 38: 276–80.

Koch, S. C. and Harvey, S. (2012). 'Dance therapy with traumatized dissociative patients', in S. C. Koch, T. Fuchs, M. Summa, and C. Müller (eds.), *Body Memory, Metaphor, and Movement.* Philadelphia, PA: John Benjamins, pp. 369–85.

Koch, S. C., Kunz, T., Lykou, S., and Cruz, R. (2014). 'Effects of dance and dance movement therapy on health-related psychological outcomes: A meta-analysis', *The Arts in Psychotherapy,* 41(1): 46–64.

Koch, S. C., Mehl, L., Sobanski, E., Sieber, M., and Fuchs, T. (2015). 'Fixing the mirrors: Effects of dance therapy on young adults with autism spectrum disorder', *Autism,* 24 February 2014 (E-publication ahead of print), PMID: 24566716.

Koch, S. C., Morlinghaus, K., and Fuchs, T. (2007). 'The joy dance: Specific effects of a single dance intervention on psychiatric patients with depression', *The Arts in Psychotherapy,* 34: 340–9.

Meekums, B., Vaverniece, I., Majore-Dusele, I., and Rasnacs, O. (2012). 'Dance movement therapy for obese women with emotional eating: A controlled pilot study', *The Arts in Psychotherapy,* 39(2): 126–33.

Merleau-Ponty, M. (1962). *Phenomenology of Perception.* New York: Routledge.

Paulus, C. (2009). *Der Saarbrücker Persönlichkeitsfragebogen SPF (IRI) zur Messung von Empathie: Psychometrische Evaluation der deutschen Version des Interpersonal Reactivity Index.* <http://psydok.sulb.uni-saarland.de/volltexte/2009/2363/>

Rey, E. R. (2006). 'Psychotische Störungen und Schizophrenie', in J. Hoyer, and H. U. Wittchen (eds.), *Klinische Psychologie und Psychotherapie.* Heidelberg: Springer, pp. 675–725.

Riskind, J. (1984). 'They stoop to conquer: Guiding and self-regulatory functions of physical posture after success and failure', *Journal of Personality and Social Psychology,* 47: 479–93.

Ritter, M., and Low, K. (1996). 'Effects of dance/movement therapy: A meta-analysis', *The Arts in Psychotherapy,* 23(3): 249–60.

Rizzolatti, G., Fadiga, L., Gallese, V., and Fogassi, L. (1996). 'Premotor cortex and the recognition of motor actions', *Cognitive Brain Research,* 3: 131–41.

Rogers, C. R. (1951). *Client-Centered Therapy: Its Current Practice, Implications and Theory.* London: Constable.

Röhricht, F. and Priebe, S. (2006). 'Effect of body-oriented psychological therapy on negative symptoms in schizophrenia: a randomized controlled trial', *Psychological Medicine*, 36: 669–78. (Complete Manual unpublished, available from the authors.)

Röhricht, F., Papadopoulos, N., Holden, S., Clarke, T. and Priebe, S. (2011). 'Clinical effectiveness and therapeutic processes of body psychotherapy in chronic schizophrenia: An open clinical trial', *The Arts in Psychotherapy*, 38: 196–203.

Sandel, S. L. (1993). 'The process of empathic reflexion in dance therapy', in S. L. Sandel, S. Chaiklin, and A. Lohn (eds.), *Foundations of Dance/Movement Therapy: The life and work of Marian Chace*. Columbia, MD: American Dance Therapy Association.

Sandel, S. L., Chaiklin, S., and Lohn, A. (eds.) (1993). *Foundations of Dance/Movement Therapy: The Life and Work of Marian Chace*. Columbia, MD: American Dance Therapy Association.

Sandel, S. L., Judge, J. O., Landry, N., Faria, L., Quellette, R., and Majczak, M. (2005). 'Dance and movement program improves quality-of-life measures in breast cancer survivors', *Cancer Nursing*, 28(4): 301–9.

Schmais, C., and Schmais, A. (1983). 'Reflecting emotions: The movement-mirroring test', *Journal of Nonverbal Behavior*, 8: 42–54.

Sheets-Johnstone M. (1999). *The Primacy of Movement*. Amsterdam /Philadelphia: John Benjamins.

Stanghellini, G. (2009). 'Embodiment and schizophrenia', *World Psychiatry*, 8(1): 56–9.

Trautmann-Voigt, S. (2003). ,Tanztherapie: Zum aktuellen Diskussionsstand in Deutschland', *Psychotherapeut*, 48; 215–29.

World Health Organization (1992). *ICD-10 Classification of Mental and Behavioural. Disorders: Clinical Descriptions and Diagnostic Guidelines*. Geneva: World Health Organization.

Xia, J. and Grant, T. J. (2009). 'Dance therapy for schizophrenia', *Cochrane Database of Systematic Reviews, 2009(1)*. Art. No: CD006868. Oxford: Wiley.

....

CHAPTER 48

DANCE/MOVEMENT THERAPY AND BREAST CANCER CARE

A Wellbeing Approach

....

ILENE A. SERLIN, NANCY GOLDOV,
AND ERIKA HANSEN

INTRODUCTION

....

BREAST cancer causes the second highest mortality rate for any type of cancer, and will affect approximately one in eight US women over the course of their lifetime (US Breast Cancer Statistics 2014). Due to new treatments and research, as of 2008 there were more than 2.6 million breast cancer survivors in the US alive ten years after diagnosis (Cancer Facts and Figures 2012). Because cancer survival is a transition through a difficult period of time that can cause severe anxiety, distress, and impaired quality of life, many women must sort through a confusing array of physical and emotional therapies (Lethborg et al. 2000).

Medical dance/movement therapy (MDMT)—a subspecialty of dance/movement therapy (DMT)—is a holistic therapeutic method uniquely suited to working with women with breast cancer. It aims to support the development of personal resources by creating a safe and supportive environment that encourages creativity (Serlin 2007), and enhances physical, cognitive, and spiritual functioning (Serlin 2000; Stockley 1992). The literature suggests that MDMT brings positive changes for patients coping with severe illnesses (Cohen and Walco 1999; Palo-Bengtsson et al. 1998; Yang et al. 2005), increases positive social skills (Aktas and Ogce 2005; Webster et al. 2005), and utilizes archetypal dimensions (Ayres 1973). Recent discoveries in neuroscience (Schore 2012; Siegel 2012; Marks-Tarlow 2012; Wright 2009) provide further support of the power of mind–body approaches to healing; the connection between mind and body is indeed a core component of DMT and MDMT practice.

Cancer treatments can cause extreme fatigue, loss of physical functioning or disfigurement (Dimeo 2001; Jereczek-Fossa et al. 2002), and emotional distress. These include feelings of helplessness, uncertainty, anxiety, depression, loss of identity and meaning, and feeling betrayed by one's body (Clark et al. 2003). MDMT addresses these issues 'primarily as a psychosocial support intervention, complementary to conventional and standard medical treatments' (Goodill 2005, p. 17). Interventions of MDMT intersect with the psycho, social, and spiritual dimensions of women's lives at a time when their life trajectory has been interrupted, forcing them into a new assumptive world (Fawzy et al. 1995). Resuming their forward life trajectory (Fawzy et al. 1995), constructing new meaning making systems (Brown 2008), and experiencing wellbeing—all goals of MDMT—originate with the simplest instruction: to move.

This chapter engages in an extensive review of the literature by exploring ways in which this particular approach will support women struggling with issues around breast cancer revisit their sense of self, and create new stories about who they are in themselves and in the world.

BREAST CANCER, WELLBEING, AND MDMT

The experience of breast cancer radically diminishes the person's sense of wellbeing, and MDMT is an approach that supports wellbeing. The word 'wellbeing' is essential for this chapter and for the entire book, and has been defined in different ways across cultures. Our definition of wellbeing is essentially holistic, including physical, emotional, and social dimensions. For example, Prilletensky and Fox (2007) defined wellness as 'achieved by the balanced and synergistic satisfaction of personal, relational, and collective needs, which, in turn, are dependent on how much justice people experience in each domain' (793). Five domains of wellness criteria can diminish one's sense of justice: (a) affective or emotional responses, (b) polarized or cognitive, (c) acquired or educational, (d) situational or historical, and (e) invested or political (Prilletensky and Fox 2007). Assessments of wellbeing use self-report and socially constructed terms to observe social relationships, work, physical health, and other demographic variables. Interpersonal relationships can affect happiness and wellbeing, increasing quality of life, confidence, and success (Diener and Ryan 2009). Living with breast cancer can also negatively impacts intimate relationships, creating problems of self-confidence and communication (Fletcher et al. 2010).

Wellbeing is also associated positively with creativity, as shown in recent studies of the role of creativity in health and healing. The creative process involves novelty, learning, and the reduction of stress, which can promote mental wellbeing (Evans 2007; Hanna 2006), and in which 'each individual has the opportunity to enjoy and benefit from that which is rightfully his [sic] possession—the power to create' (Hawkins 1988, p. 8).

Wellbeing approaches are traceable to psychological, medical, aesthetic, and spiritual roots because they are based in a philosophical vision that recognizes individual and collective strengths and meaning in experience (Christopher 1999). However, wellbeing for women with breast cancer can also be very unique due to the value a woman attaches to the breast, the severity, results and side-effects of the treatment, the impact on intimate relationships, and body image issues (Hopwood et al. 2001; Hormes et al. 2008; White 2002). Some argue that wellbeing can simply be associated with normal, 'good day' activities such as sleeping well, taking care of personal needs, and doing the normal things one did 'before you got cancer' (J. Cohen, personal communication, 26 July 2009).

DANCE AND WELLBEING

Relevant literature suggests that dance has numerous health benefits (Arcangeli 2000; Bremer 2007; Cannon 1967; Hanna 2006). Hanna (1987), for example, argues that dance is a cultural necessity that has been implanted in 'emotional expression, play, work, duty, union with the sacred, theater, ceremonials of authority, and art" (p. 13). It can show and mirror important dimensions of human existence: transcendental practices in religion, and individual and group self-exertion, education, and induction in secular society. It echoes practices of ancient healing rituals (Kiev 1964), while reproducing sociocultural patterns and politics as a vehicle for imparting information, maintaining cultural customs, and beliefs (Kraus 1969).

It is our belief that the arts speak to our souls in a time of increasing speed and mechanism. Ancient traditions in the arts have provided restoration in times of imbalance. Sometimes they have helped us articulate our pain, while at other times they help us transcend our pain and lift us into a larger dimension. We believe that through the arts, people can express their experience of having the illness, explore their own imagery and resources for healing, and decrease loneliness by deeply sharing rhythmic and non-verbal connectedness. Martha Graham tapped into the 'collective unconscious' to discover symbols of renewal and regeneration in her dancing. Armitage (1978) quoted Graham:

> It is the affirmation of life through movement . . . to impart the sensation of living, to energize the spectator into keener awareness of the vigor, of the mystery, the humor, the variety and the wonder of life; to send the spectator away with a fuller sense of his own potentialities and the power of realizing them, whatever the medium of his activity. (pp. 102–3)

DANCE/MOVEMENT THERAPY

DMT was established in 1966 as 'the psychotherapeutic use of movement to further the emotional, cognitive, physical, and social integration of the individual (American Dance Therapy Association 2013). Dance/movement therapists use movement for diagnosis and treatment, as movement reflects patterns of coping, defences, memories, inner states, and relational patterns which are concretized as qualities in relation to space, time, weight, and flow. The direct use of the body as a tool allows dance therapists to explore body image and its distortions, as well as to discover unfamiliar or disowned parts of the psyche (Chaiklin 1969; Serlin 1999). This very specific understanding of the language of the body is a key element in working with the physical and psychological changes accompanying breast cancer. There are a number of approaches within DMT, one of which is MDMT, which highlights the need to address the person as a whole.

MDMT: A WHOLE-PERSON PERSPECTIVE

A whole-person approach does not focus on symptom reduction, but considers the person in the context of his or her world (Serlin 2007). This approach seeks to understand the meaning of symptoms, as well as their biological and behavioural causes. In a whole-person approach, mind and body are interrelated (Rossi 1986). Candace Pert's (1997) groundbreaking work on psychoneuroimmunology demonstrated that the processing of emotions often affects physical illnesses and the ability to heal. Research on healthy humans, as well cancer and HIV-positive patients, has shown that significant increases in immune function and positive health outcomes correlate with constructive emotional expression (Pert 1997).

Within MDMT a whole-person perspective is often associated with a wellbeing approach that embodies humanistic values such as positive strengths, meaning, resiliency, creativity, and self-actualization (Engler 2003). The humanistic approach to trauma encourages us to confront our death anxiety; for example, discover new meaning and identity, and move from beyond prior levels of functioning to transcendence (Calhoun and Tedeschi 1998; Epel et al. 1998; Parapully et al. 2002; Serlin and Cannon 2004; Updegraff and Taylor 2000). It is not only positive, however, but also encourages us to learn from life's struggles and value growth through adversity (Joseph and Linley 2008). Telling the story of the disruption and the reconstruction of a meaningful life can provide a narrative to deal with the existential loss and help recover meaning, faith, and courage (Epting and Leitner 1992, Feinstein and Krippner 1988; Howard 1991).

KinAesthetic Imagining is a method of MDMT which is 'a theory and an experiential process . . . a dynamic embodied form of imagination in which participants as artists compose themselves and transform their lives. KinAesthetic Imagining is both a theo-retical understanding and a process of an embodied aesthetic psychology' in which 'the imagery and material arise from the participants and the group itself' (Serlin 1996: 32). It has three parts: 1) check-in and warm-up, consisting of meditation, verbal sharing, grounding, breathwork, and simple movements; 2) amplifying the themes through repetitive movements, imagery, metaphors, and archetypal themes; and (c) cool-down movements, reflection, and sharing (Serlin 2000). Through the expressive, creative, movement of DMT, participants can find kinaesthetic images on which they can focus which act as support for their healing (Ganahl 1995). It is then possible to find ways to explore aspects of themselves and reconnect positively with themselves despite the pain of their lives (see Video 48.1 on the Companion Website ▶).

EFFECTS OF MEDICAL DANCE MOVEMENT THERAPY AND CANCER CARE

Individual and group MDMT services for women with breast cancer can be found in hospitals, outpatient clinics, rehabilitation centres, and many other settings where psychosocial support interventions are provided to breast cancer patients, survivors, caregivers, and family members. MDMT for women with breast cancer, along with pediatric oncology, has seen the most growth and expansion within cancer-specific applications of MDMT. According to Goodill (2005), 'it is an interdisciplinary field: a hybrid of the art of dance and the science of psychology adapted to human serv-ice. The field has a history of embracing theories and findings from various other fields' (p. 21). Hock et al. (2006) conducted a survey of ninety women with a diag-nosis of cancer to explore each participant's preferences for an exercise outlet. The participants, with an average age of 52.4 years, ranked different forms of exercise on an ordinal scale with five positions indicating interest, from very interested to not interested. They ranked dance/movement among the second most popular forms of exercise.

The effectiveness of MDMT for outpatient psychosocial cancer rehabilitation has been documented for children (Cohen and Walco 1999; Goodill and Morningstar 1993; Mendelsohn 1999) and adults (Dibble-Hope 2000; Ho 2005; Mannheim and Weis 2006; Sandel et al. 2005; Serlin et al. 2000). Furthermore, the literature suggests that MDMT can enable breast cancer patients to cope with pain and ease depression by increasing vitality and supporting development of a healthier body image (Dibbell-Hope 2000; Goodill 2005; Goldov 2011; Lacour et al. 1983; Mannheim and Weis 2006; Serlin 2000; Serlin 2006). Dietrich's (1990) preliminary and descriptive multimodal Master's the-sis introduced a teaching-tool video to promote mind–body integration with cancer clients. Results from the subjective reports of participants indicate that an integrative approach using DMT can be a valuable method for increasing wellbeing and aid the healing process during a stressful time.

Serlin's (1996) pilot study measured the effectiveness of movement therapy with women with breast cancer. The measures included the Profile of Mood Scale, the Body Cathexis Scale, the Mizes Anorectic Cognitions questionnaire, a spiritual inventory, and semistructured interviews. 70% percent of the variance on the Body Cathexis Scale was predicted by the helplessness/hopelessness, coping, depression, confusion, and anxiety subscales, while 74% of the variance of total mood disturbance was predicted by vigour, confusion, fatigue, anger, tension, fighting spirit, helplessness/hopelessness, body cathexis, and spiritual belief inventory. Qualitative analysis of the interviews pointed to shifts from perceiving the body as enemy to friend, from a distant to a close relationship with the body, from a feeling of unreality and inauthenticity about the body to feelings of reality and authenticity. Although the study pointed to promising trends, it was possible that the scales did not accurately reflect the profound disturbances and changes in a woman's perception of her body during cancer.

The second phase of the study, therefore, focused on developing a body awareness inventory which drew from the women's own words to investigate changes in body awareness and image, since the available assessments of body image were normed on women with eating disorders and measured external or concrete evaluations of the body (questions such as 'Do you feel fat?'), and did not address the 'mutilating and desexualizing experiences of undergoing treatments for breast cancer' (Serlin et al. 2000: 130). The Serlin Kinaesthetic Imagining Profile (SKIP) (Serlin 1999) was developed to assess the subjective, symbolic, and qualitative inner experience of bodily change over time. The items began with and stayed true to the women's own words, and captured the layers of emotional and spiritual shifts. Statements from participants held metaphoric and symbolic content: ('When I started the group I felt like my body betrayed me, when I ended the group I felt like my body was my friend'). Section I of the SKIP was based on interviews asking for the subjective experience of change, and Section II was a Laban-based observational system.

Pilarski (2008) conducted a multiple case study on the effects of DMT using a nested concurrent, mixed-methods design involving two participants. The objective of this study was to gain a better understanding of the effects of DMT on women living with breast cancer. After two sessions of DMT that focused on issues of body image and sexuality, the participants' experience was explored using the SKIP, participants' journal entries, and the researchers' field notes. Findings showed mixed results, suggesting further exploration of the relationship between body-image disturbance and the results of the SKIP.

In Goldov's research (2011), the effectiveness of individual MDMT to decrease body image problems in women with breast cancer was observed in a Cohen's d analysis, comparing means to examine the strength of a phenomenon (Cohen 1988; Goldov 2011). Goldov's study used a mixed-method, quasi-experimental, nonequivalent control group, A–B–A design, and three cancer-specific body image measures including the SKIP (Serlin 1999). The study examined the effects of a manualized intervention of five sessions of MDMT, with a dyadic rhythmic component. In the study, the researcher provided the sessions for each woman in the experimental group, individually, within two weeks, according to each woman's schedule. Following the manualized intervention, each participant engaged in a creative improvisation beginning with a warm up, transitioned to moving more dynamically with rhythmicity as the researcher played a percussion instrument, and ended with slowing down, internalizing the experience, and reflecting on its meaning.

Remaining within the domain of oncology-specific measures, a cancer-specific body-image construct (White 2002) was utilized in Goldov's (2011) study to evaluate the strength of the MDMT intervention. White's (2002) heuristic cognitive behavioural body-image model for cancer patients integrates multiple dimensions of body-image problems into a dynamic understanding that ignores the illusory bidirectionality of body-image problems which commonly accompany discourses on body image. Terms such as 'good' or 'positive' body image and 'bad' or 'negative' body image are avoided in this model. The body-image dimensions in the model are self-schema, body image schema, investment in changed body features, self/ideal self-discrepancy, appearance assumptions, automatic thoughts and images, body-image emotions, and compensatory behaviours (White 2002).

This heuristic model of important body-image dimensions explains body-image problems as stemming from a self/ideal self-discrepancy between a woman's actual and/or perceived appearance and function of discrete bodily attribute(s), and her investment in the ideals concerning that bodily attribute(s). Investments in body ideals are maintained by one's self, one's thoughts of what others think they ought to look like, and from standpoints of actual others. The system of self/ideal self-discrepancies fosters beliefs that are disparate from who one is, and interferes with one's capacities for maintaining good feelings. As part of this model, situation-specific automatic thoughts and images can determine the primary emotional consequences and compensatory behaviours. Women with perceived or actual appearance changes, accompanied by the presence of a threat to their ideal selves, may experience negative appearance-related assumptions, thoughts, images, emotions, and behaviours if their self/ideal self-discrepancy relates to a physical attribute in which they have had significant personal investment. Self/ideal self-discrepancies adjudicate body-image problems, and negative emotional and behavioural consequences, which interfere significantly with normal routine, occupational functioning, social functioning, and/or relationship quality (White 2002).

In Goldov's (2002) study, three cancer-specific Likert-scale questionnaires and written responses to questions were employed to provide the quantitative and qualitative data. The Likert-scale measures were the Body Image Scale (BIS) (Hopwood et al. 2001), the SKIP (Serlin 1999), and the Body Image and Relationship Scale (BIRS) (Hormes et al. 2008). The items on the BIS addressed interpersonal dimensions of body image relating to features of attractiveness from an outerpersonal perspective on the body-image dimensions of self-schema, self/ideal self-discrepancy, appearance assumptions, and compensatory behaviours. Items on the SKIP encompassed women's intrapersonal experiences about bodily changes during and after cancer treatments, and addressed the dimensions of self-schema, body image schema, self/ideal self-discrepancy, and body-image emotions. The items on the BIRS captured experiences related to appearance, health, physical strength, sexuality, relationships, and social functioning on the body-image dimensions of self-schema, body-image schema, and compensatory behaviours. For ease of comparison the scales were converted to numbers, with higher numbers representing higher levels of body-image problems across all assessments. When the means of the three Likert-scale measures were compared over the phases of the study, reductions in body-image problems for women in the experimental group were observed in a Cohen's *d* analysis, compared to women in the control group (Christensen 2004; Cohen 1988). The Cohen's *d* analysis revealed medium and large effect sizes immediately at the end of all five MDMT sessions, and then again two weeks later.

The writings of experimental-group women collected throughout the study, and then two weeks after their last MDMT session, confirmed the medium and large effect sizes. Comments such as 'I am taking responsibility for my body image', 'I feel good about my body', and 'I have a stronger connection to my emotions' were evidence of the changes taking place within the women who experienced MDMT (Goldov 2011). The writings by patient number 2 exemplifies the changes that took place in the majority of women who danced. Patient number 2 wrote: 'I feel strength in discovering various aspects of my body', 'I see my knees as weak, yet they do quite well with this movement', and 'I think that movement changes my mood' (see vignette number 1). Additionally, the majority of the women who danced described feeling able to take time to rebuild a better level of health and wellness. They also described new plans to maintain their body-image gains, such as joining a gym, taking a walk, and engaging in new behaviours, whereas the writings by women in the control group indicated that they were still struggling with body-image problems and self-discrepancies. Contained in their written responses were comments such as 'I believe that I don't really have a very good body image', 'I am embarrassed and miserable', 'I am more aware of the disjointedness of my body', 'I am dreading having my picture taken', and 'there is more work to do' (Goldov 2011). In addition to experiencing gains in body-image wellness after MDMT, women in the experimental group had reduced resistance to making other changes. They indicated their intentions to continue maintaining their body-image wellbeing by making plans and taking action. Prochaska and Norcross's (2003) integrative, biopsychosocial model of change describes planning to take action in the immediate future as the preparation state, and making modifications in one's lifestyle as the action stage. In contrast, the comments by women in the control group appeared to be in the pre-contemplation stage of change. They were learning to cope and unaware of what to change, with no actions planned for the foreseeable future (Goldov 2011; Prochaska and Norcross 2003). These results point to possible value for MDMT as a worthwhile intervention for improving body-image wellness in women with breast cancer.

Anna Halprin—choreographer, dancer, and movement teacher—was a pioneer in the field of dance as a healing art, beginning in 1980 (Halprin 2000). As she struggled with cancer, she knew how to engage people with life-threatening illnesses in sensory awareness exercise and expressive movement and dance to help participants 'begin the journey into the body's endless mysteries' (p. 49) and 'act out the drama of the immune system in relation to the cancer cells' (p. 109).

Dibble-Hope (2000), using a form of DMT called Authentic Movement, looked at body-image, self-concept, mood state, and levels of distress using the Profile of Moods States, Symptom Checklist 90-Revised, the Berscheid-Walster, Bohrnstedt Image Scale, and also semistructured interviews and written evaluations. Results showed significantly greater improvements in physical wellbeing and vigour, reduction in fatigue and somatization, and greater body appreciation, acceptance, the benefit of social support, and positive feelings about participants' bodies.

Dance/movement therapist Susan Sandel used the Lebed Method (Sandel et al. 2005) to assess change in shoulder function and quality of life. The self-report measures used to establish outcome data were the Functional Assessment of Cancer Therapy-Breast (FACT-B), the BIS, the SF-36 Health Survey, shoulder range of motion measures, and a physical examination. The results of the BIS showed that both groups improved their body image after the movement intervention. On the FACT-B, the improvement in the intervention group was statistically and clinically significant as well (Sandel et al. 2005).

Rainbow Ho's pilot study (2005) using the Perceived Stress Scale (Cohen 1988) and the Rosenberg Scale (Rosenberg 1965) found that DMT reduced stress and increased self-esteem in Chinese cancer patients. In this study, the significantly lowered perceived stress scores and the improvement in self-esteem scores indicated that the programme was effective (Ho 2005). People reported that the programme helped them express their feelings and emotions more openly, increase their confidence, and obtain support. A content analysis of their evaluations identified the personal themes of relaxation, mind–body interaction, personal growth, and spirituality.

A multimodal pilot study conducted by Klagsbrun et al. (2005) assessed the utility of focusing and expressive arts therapies on the quality of life of women with breast cancer using The Experiencing Scale, Clearing a Space Checklist, the Grindler Body Attitudes Scale, the FACT-B Scale, the Functional Assessment of Chronic Illness Therapy–Spiritual Wellbeing Scale, and observations, interviews, and written responses to specific questions. One randomly selected individual participated in a case study and took part in a follow-up interview. The Grindler Body Attitudes Scale assessed how well she kept a positive attitude toward her body and evaluated to what extent her body was perceived as being able to heal itself. Klagsbrun designed the study to 'help motivate women with breast cancer to care for their bodies more effectively, and participate in activities that enhance wellness' (Klagsbrun et al. 2005: 117).

Mannheim and Weis (2006) conducted a three-year pilot study to observe how MDMT improved physical and emotional wellbeing and impacted variables of health, anxiety, depression, and self-esteem. They used the Dortmund Questionnaire on Movement Therapy, the Quality of Life Questionnaire, the Hospital Anxiety and Depression Scale, and four subscales from the Frankfurt Self-Image Concept scales. They also gathered data from written responses to open-ended questions, Laban/Bartenieff Movement Notation observations, and movement analysis write-ups about three participants in the dance therapy sessions. Mannheim and Weis (2006) found that participants reported significant improvements in physical functioning, a decrease in fatigue, and significant improvements in self-esteem.

VIGNETTES

The following vignettes illustrate the use of MDMT with individual, group, and healing rituals.

1: Individual MDMT

This example demonstrates the impact of MDMT on one of the six women who, as part of Goldov's (2011) study, received five individual MDMT sessions within a period of two weeks. In each session, the patient began with a warm-up and then moved according to her feelings and needs, improvising in movement, while being rhythmically accompanied by the dance/movement therapist playing a rhythmic instrument of the patient's choosing. Each participant was assessed using the three oncology-specific body-image measures, before the individual MDMT sessions, after the conclusion of the last MDMT session at the end of two weeks, and then one more time, two weeks post-treatment.

P2, a 55-year-old Caucasian female, was diagnosed with Stage I breast cancer, and had a lumpectomy and then radiation treatment. Her score means on the quantitative measures of the SKIP and the BIRS, before receiving the manualized MDMT intervention, were 2.73 and 3.53 respectively. Two weeks after taking part in her last MDMT session her score means on these measures decreased to 2.33 and 3.03 respectively. These score decreases represent a reduction in body-image problems (White 2002), as higher scores signify higher levels of body-image problems (Goldov 2011).

P2 joined the study approximately three months after her diagnosis. The data from her written responses to questions revealed that before her first MDMT session she was initially 'a bit apprehensive' and 'not certain what it might involve'. But after moving in her first MDMT session she wrote 'I was surprised at my ability to move' and 'I believe that this opened up my mind to various parts of my body that are reacting to the stress of treatment. She added: 'I discovered that I have more creative movement that I had thought.' She also wrote 'I felt the stress in my back—which I was not very aware of', and she visualized herself 'in the clouds moving freely—then in the water splashing up as though to cleanse my entire body and spirit.' She wrote that she was 'fighting off the cancer in movement (kind of like Pac-Man) and 'moving through the cancer', commenting that 'my body is stronger and I am more flexible than I thought.' P2 also wrote: 'I am a bit self-conscious but I found that you were very supportive and I appreciated the instruction that helped me move through the exercise and transition beyond various stages to explore further.' After the second session, she stated: 'I find this process interesting as

I open myself up to the concept and let go of the thoughts of programmed exercise.' She noticed how various elements of her body work together, saying that 'the sensation is that of connectedness.' She reported feeling different after MDMT saying: 'I feel strength in discovering various aspects of my body as they move. I found it interesting that I see my knees as weak—yet they do quite well with this movement.'

After the third session, P2 felt 'less inhibited', and realized 'how painful movement can be when you haven't utilized your body fully.' She remarked: 'My strength comes from inner being', and 'from knowing that I am taking steps to help my body become well.' At the fourth session, P2 wrote that she 'took a risk in self directing myself this time', and found that 'it was interesting growing in the freedom of movement.' After the fifth session, P2 wrote that the 'musical instrument helped to take me deeper into how my body is moving.' She also noted that 'I believe that I am healing' and 'I think that movement changes my mood' and 'centres me more'.

Two weeks after the last MDMT session, P2 reported that she 'began to listen to meditation tapes to get in touch with my emotions and regain physical strength.' She began 'walking for 30 minutes during the day . . . to reduce the stress in my work life', noting that she 'found freedom in just moving.' She stated: 'I always thought that you needed to have an exercise tape or something of that nature and didn't value the fact that you just got up and moved.' She wrote about her body image:

> I am working on taking responsibility for my body image. I have a different view of what I want to be and I am taking pride in the baby steps I am taking to better my body to respond to the things I want to do in life, which is different than just sitting on the sidelines and thinking I just can't do that anymore.

This patient's experience with MDMT began with her feeling apprehensive and self-conscious during the first session. With the presence of the dance/movement therapist who supported her mood, mirrored her rhythm, and played a percussion instrument while she danced, P2 was able to take risks, direct her own movement, and give herself experiences of personal empowerment. Her written comments, tracking her positive and varied experiences, are a testimony to the potential of MDMT to satisfy and balance personal and relational needs (Prilletensky and Fox 2007), increase quality of life, confidence, and success (Diener and Ryan 2009), reduce human suffering through creativity (Evans 2007), reduce body-image problems (White 2002; Goldov 2011), and promote health and mental wellbeing (Evans 2007; Hanna 2006).

2: Group MDMT

During the twelve-week session at the California Pacific's Institute of Health and Healing (Serlin 2000), women used movement to discover unfamiliar parts of themselves, including new discoveries of creativity, resourcefulness, and humour. Some found anger that energized their will to live, and used art to release normally socially unacceptable parts of themselves. One woman, who had spent her life being a 'good girl' helped create a group 'bad girl' dance, and said:

> Oh, the Halloween and the Bad Girl. One of the things for me that happened as a result which was tremendously impactful for me is that, well, it started with the dance when we were dancing with the scarves on that one day I was in there and what I got in touch with was how when I was a young girl, I kind of shut down, I think, to my femininity . . . and I got really back in touch with that in the group, in the going back and remembering even when I was in first grade . . . about how I . . . loved to dance and I was in this recital and, for some reason, something happened in the recital that I somehow remember my father saying I was fat or something like that, that I would never dance again and in the group I got in touch with that pain through some kind of movement that we did . . . and then afterwards you said why don't you take this scarf and have the people hold it . . . and dance behind it . . . and so what happened to me was I felt really protected . . . with the scarf there, very safe with the people in the room and then danced my dance and out of that it freed up really in me the desire to dance and move, the fun that I had doing it, the joy and the love that comes into my life from it and also the essential woman that has been there that is . . . really afraid to come out because . . . it was always bad to be that way and bad to be interested in sensuality and sexuality . . . and so, as a result of that, the Halloween thing was we were supposed to come as our bad girl . . . so I came all dressed in black, black leather jacket, black top, black bottoms and just really felt I could be my awful self or the other self, that's in there that's part of me as well. And in doing that it just freed up really who I am because now I'm so much more embracing of all that part of me and none of that is bad and it's more fun . . . We've all been good girls . . . and I've never looked at it that way. It seemed like all of us in the group had that bad girl that we were really thrilled at allowing to get in touch with and to let out and that we always felt . . . that we had to be good girls all our lives.

From this dance, she drew a figure (see Figure 48.1) and called it Sultry Jet. Reflecting on her experience, she understood more about the meaning of her illness: 'Well, what is cancer? Cancer is a cell that's lost. Its nucleus takes over, right? And it goes out of control. Well, I think that what's happening is that as people we're out of control. We do not connect.'

3: Creating Healing Rituals

Rituals are dramatized symbolic enactments which help individuals move from one stage of life to another, and can help women prepare for treatments, mourn losses, and so on. While traditional rituals are passed down from generation to generation, constructed rituals are built on modern symbols and vocabulary. Victor Turner and Barbara Myerhoff argue that 'applied anthropology' allows us to give communal meaning to modern crises (Turner 1982, p. 25), and that today's lack of ritual makes these 'constructions of performance' essential. Such constructions can help women who are facing

FIGURE 48.1. The Sultry Jet. 'This is me [points] the sultry jet. I don't remember much about growing up except one time I was dancing as the Jet—it was anti-feminine. Black leather. smoke-filled room, sultry poetry, silence. Hey Mom, I'm a beatnik and I wanna dance Sultry Jet.' (Photo credit: I. Serlin.)

breast cancer alone feel part of a group, reduce fear and isolation, and express and share feelings in a common symbolic structure. In fact, taking the initiative to construct a ritual with a trusted group can bring out courage and creativity in a participant and help her move from passivity to empowerment.

In the MDMT group, boundaries were different from those in a usual support group. For example, the group became involved in some activist activities in the community that took us outside the therapy or clinic room. One such example of work in the community is the annual Race for the Cure, sponsored by the Komen Foundation as part of Breast Cancer Awareness month in San Francisco's Golden Gate Park and attended by approximately 8,000 participants. An Opening Invocation led by Ilene Serlin began the race at 7.30 am on 19 October 1997. Emerging out of four years of working together, eight women who are trainees and/or ex-group members led participants in the meadow in a special choreography called a Movement Choir. Movement Choirs were created in the early 1900s by Rudolf von Laban, a Hungarian architect, visionary, and grandfather of modern dance (Laban 1971). Based on simple forms like notes, accompanied by live drumming, and combined into structures like chords, ritualistically repeated patterns create vibrations and resonances which unite the participants in an attitude of harmonious reverence (Bartenieff 1974). A contemporary use of the Movement Choir in Golden Gate Park is shown in Figure 48.2.

Another kind of healing ritual grows organically from the movement and the group's creativity. One woman was going through bone marrow transplant in the spring, and she was forbidden to work in her garden. So our support group decided to offer help, and organized a Garden Party to which we took a picnic lunch. She organized shovels and equipment to plant her precious rose bushes, and the group planted, sang, and ate lunch together. A month later, the group returned to check on the plants, and weed. This ritual gave them support in a tangible yet symbolic way. While the ritual was reminiscent of old-fashioned traditions such as neighborhood barn-raising, this one grew naturally from our group work in creating a sense of safety, trust, and collaboration.

FIGURE 48.2. Race for the Cure. Leading the Opening Invocation with a Movement Choir for the annual Race for the Cure, Golden Gate Park, San Francisco, 15 October 2000. (Photo credit: I. Serlin.)

Conclusion

A life-threatening illness confronts patients with the reality of their mortality. A diagnosis and treatment of cancer can have a profound effect on one's experience of self. The shock of the diagnosis, the confusing choices about medical treatment, and a radically altered body leaves many patients with the difficult task of having to integrate these changes into their self-concept.

MDMT makes possible changes in women's experiences of themselves through expressive creative movement. Movement helps them uncover and explore the meaning of their illness both verbally and non-verbally. Existential fears such as the confrontation with mortality and spiritual fears, such as loss of meaning or hope, call for a therapy that addresses mind, body, and spirit in a framework of a whole-person, wellness perspective. Through MDMT, patients can express loss and fears symbolically, find new images for themselves, and reconstruct new lives and wellbeing.

References

American Dance Therapy Association (2013). *About Dance Movement Therapy.* <https://adta.org/faqs/ >

Aktas, G. and Ogce, F. (2005). 'Dance as a therapy for cancer prevention', *Asian Pacific Journal of Cancer Prevention*, 6b: 408–11.

Arcangeli, A. (2000). 'Dance and health: The renaissance physicians' view', *Dance Research*, 18(1): 3.

Armitage, M. (ed.). (1978). *Martha Graham: The Early Years.* New York, NY: Dacapo Press. First published in 1937.

Ayres, A. J., (1973). *Sensory Integration and Learning Disorders.* Los Angeles, CA: Western Psychological Services.

Bartenieff, I. (1974). 'Exploring interaction through ritual structure. Therapeutic process: movement as integration', *Proceedings of the Ninth Annual Conference.* Columbia, MD: American Dance Therapy Association, pp. 118–23.

Bremer, Z. (2007). 'Dance as a form of exercise', *British Journal of General Practice*, 57(535): 166

Brown, L. (2008). *Cultural Competence in Trauma Therapy: Beyond the Flashback.* Washington, DC: American Psychological Association.

Cancer Facts and Figures (2012). <http://uacc.arizona.edu/sites/default/files/acs_2012.pdf>

Calhoun, L. G. and Tedeschi, R. G. (1998). 'Posttraumatic growth: Future directions', in R. Tedeschi and L. Calhoun (eds.), *Posttraumatic Growth: Positive Changes in the Aftermath of Crisis.* Mahwah, NJ: Lawrence Earlbaum Associates, pp. 215–40.

Cannon, W. (1967). *The Wisdom of the Body.* New York, NY: The Norton Library.

Cohen, J. (1988). *Statistical Power Analysis for the Behavioral Sciences*, 2nd edn. Hillsdale, NJ: Lawrence Earlbaum Associates.

Cohen, S. (1988). 'Perceived stress in a probability sample of the United States', in S. Spacapan and S. Oskamp (eds.), *The Social Psychology of Health: The Claremont Symposium on Applied Social Psychology.* Thousand Oaks, CA: Sage Publications, pp. 31–67.

Chaiklin, S. (1969). 'Dance therapy', in *American Dance Therapy Association Proceedings. Fourth Annual Conference*. Columbia, MD: American Dance Therapy Association, pp. 25–32.

Christensen, L. B. (2004). *Experimental Methodology*. Boston, MA: Pearson.

Christopher, J. C. (1999). 'Situating psychological wellbeing: Exploring the cultural roots of its theory and research', *Journal of Counseling and Development*, 22(2): 141–52.

Clark, M. M., Bostwick, J. M., and Rummans, T. A. (2003). 'Group and individual treatment strategies for distress in cancer participants', *Mayo Clinic Proceedings*, 78: 1538–43.

Cohen, S. O. and Walco, G. A. (1999). 'Dance/movement therapy for children and adolescents with cancer', *Cancer Practice*, 7(1): 34–42.

Dibble-Hope, S. (2000). 'The use of dance/movement therapy in psychological adaptation to breast cancer', *The Arts in Psychotherapy*, 27(1): 51–68.

Diener, E. and Ryan, K. (2009). 'Subjective well-being: A general overview', *South African Journal of Psychology*, 39(4): 391–406.

Dietrich, H. (1990). *The Art of healing: A Multimodal Treatment Approach to Cancer using Dance/Movement Therapy and Imagery*. Unpublished Master's thesis, California State University.

Dimeo, F. C. (2001). 'Effects of exercise on cancer-related fatigue', *Cancer*, 92(6): 1689–93.

Engler, B. (2003). *Personality Theories: An Introduction*, 6th edn. New York, NY: Houghton Mifflin Company.

Epel, E. S., McEwen, B. S., and Ickovics, J. R. (1998). 'Embodying psychological thriving: Physical thriving in response to stress', *Journal of Social Issues*, 54: 301–22.

Epting, F. R. and Leitner, L. M. (1992). 'Humanistic psychology and personal construct theory', *Humanistic Psychologist*, 20: 243–59.

Evans, J. E. (2007). 'The science of creativity and health', in I. Serlin (ed.), *Whole Person Healthcare*. Westport, CT: Praeger, pp. 87–105.

Fawzy, F. I., Fawzy, N. W., Arndt, L. A., and Pasnau, R. O. (1995). 'Critical review of psychosocial interventions in cancer care. *Archives of General Psychiatry*, 52: 100–13

Feinstein, D. and Krippner, S. (1988). *Personal Mythology*. Los Angeles, CA: Jeremy P. Tarcher.

Fletcher, K. A., Lewis, F. M., and Haberman, M. R. (2010). 'Cancer-related concerns of spouses of women with breast cancer', *Psycho-oncology*, 19(10): 1094–101.

Ganahl, J. (1995). *San Francisco Chronicle*, 31 October.

Goldov, N. B. (2011). *The effects of individualized brief medical dance/movement therapy on body image in women with breast cancer* (Order N. 3515650, Argosy University/Seattle). *Proquest Dissertations and Theses*, 266. <http://search.proquest.com/docview/1021376710?accountid=131239> (1021376710)

Goodill, S. W. and Morningstar, D. M. (1993). 'The role of dance/movement therapy with medically involved children', *International Journal of Arts Medicine*, 2(2): 24–7.

Goodill, S. W. (2005). *An Introduction to Medical Dance/Movement Therapy*. Philadelphia, PA: Jessica Kingsley.

Halprin, A. (2000). *Dance as a Healing Art*. Mendocino, CA: LifeRhythm.

Hanna, J. L. (1987). *To Dance is Human: A Theory of Nonverbal Communication*. Chicago, IL: University Of Chicago Press.

Hanna, J. L. (2006). *Dancing for Health: Conquering and Preventing Stress*. New York, NY: Rowman and Littlefield.

Hawkins, A. (1988). *Creating Through Dance*. Pennington, NJ: Princeton Book Company.

Ho, R. T. H. (2005). 'Effects of dance movement therapy on Chinese cancer participants: A pilot study in Hong Kong', *The Arts in Psychotherapy*, 32(5): 337–45.

Hock, K., Leffler, J., Schmitt, P., Brown, S., and Eggleston, V. (2006). 'Assessment of female cancer participants' interest in an exercise program', *Rehabilitation Oncology*, 24(3): 3–5.

Hopwood, P., Fletcher, I., Lee, A., and Ghazal, S. A. (2001). 'A body image scale for use with cancer patients', *European Journal of Cancer*, 37: 189–97.

Hormes, J. M., Lytle, L. A., Gross, C. R., Ahmed, R. L., Troxel, A. B., and Schmitz, K. H. (2008). 'The body image and relationships scale: Development and validation of a measure of body image in female breast cancer survivors', *Journal of Clinical Oncology: Official Journal of the American Society of Clinical Oncology*, 26(8): 1269–74.

Howard, G. (1991). 'Culture tales: A narrative approach to thinking, cross-cultural psychology, and psychotherapy', *American Psychologist*, 46: 187–97.

Joseph, S. and Linley, P.A. (2008). 'Psychological assessment of growth following adversity', in S. Joseph and P. A. Linley (eds.), *Trauma, Recovery, and Growth: Positive Psychological Perspectives on Posttraumatic Stress*. Hoboken, NJ: John Wiley and Sons, pp. 21–38.

Jereczek-Fossa, B. A., Marsiglia, H. R., and Orecchia, R. (2002). 'Radiotherapy-related fatigue', *Critical Reviews in Oncology/Hematology*, 41: 317–25.

Kiev, A. (1964). *Magic, Faith and Healing: Studies in Primitive Psychiatry Today*. London: The Free Press of Glencoe.

Klagsbrun, J., Rappaport, L., Speiser, V. M., Post, P., Byers, J., Stepakoff, S., and Karman, S. (2005). 'Focusing and expressive arts therapy as a complementary treatment for women with breast cancer', *Journal of Creativity in Mental Health*, 1(1): 107–37.

Kraus, R. (1969). *History of the Dance*. Englewood Cliffs, NJ: Prentice-Hall.

Laban, R. (1971). *The Mastery of Movement*, 3rd edn. Boston, MA: Plays Inc.

Lacour, J., Le, M., Caceres, E., Koszarowski, T., Veronesi, U., and Hill, C. (1983). 'Radical mastectomy versus radical mastectomy plus internal mammary dissection: Ten-year results of an international cooperative trial in breast cancer', *Cancer*, 51: 1941–3. doi: 10.1002/1097-0142(19830515)51:10<1941:: AID-CNCR2820511032>3.0.CO;2-T.

Lethborg, C. E., Kissane, D., Burns, W. I., and Snyder, R. (2000). ' "Cast adrift": The experience of completing treatment among women with early stage breast cancer', *Journal of Psychosocial Oncology*, 18(4): 73–90.

Marks-Tarlow, T. (2012). *Clinical Intuition in Psychotherapy: The Neurobiology of Embodied Response*. New York, NY: W. W. Norton.

Mannheim, E. and Weis, J. (2006). 'Dance/movement therapy with cancer participants: Evaluation of process and outcome parameters', in S. Koch, and I. Brauninger (eds.), *Advances in Dance/Movement Therapy*. Berlin: Logos Verlag Berlin, pp. 61–72.

Mendelsohn, J. (1999). 'Dance/movement therapy with hospitalized children', *American Journal of Dance Therapy*, 21(2): 65–80.

Palo-Bengtsson, L. P., Winblad, B., and Ekman, S. L. (1998). 'Social dancing: A way to support intellectual, emotional and motor functions in persons with dementia', *Journal of Psychiatric and Mental Health Nursing*, 5(6): 545–54. doi:10.1046/J.1365-2850.1998.560545.X

Parapully, J., Rosenbaum, R., van den Daele, L., and Nzewi, E. (2002). 'Thriving after trauma: The experience of parents of murdered children', *Journal of Humanistic Psychology*, 42(1): 33–71.

Pert, C. B. (1997). *Molecules of Emotion: Why You Feel the Way You Feel*. New York, NY: Touchstone.

Pilarski, D. L. (2008). *The experience of younger women diagnosed with breast cancer involved in dance/movement therapy with regards to body image and sexuality*. Unpublished Master's thesis, Drexel University, Philadelphia.

Prilletensky, I. and Fox, D. R. (2007). 'Psychopolitical literacy for wellness and justice', *Journal of Community Psychology*, 35(6): 793–805. doi:10.1002/Jcop.20179

Prochaska, J. O. and Norcross, J. C. (2003). *Systems of Psychotherapy: A Transtheoretical Analysis*. Pacific Grove, CA: Brooks/Cole.

Rosenberg, M. (1965). *Society and the Adolescent Self-Image*. Princeton, NJ: Princeton University Press.

Rossi, E. L. (1986). *The Psychobiology of Mind–Body Healing*. New York, NY: W. W. Norton.

Sandel, S. L., Judge, J. O., Landry, N., Faria, L., Ouellette, R., and Majczak, M. (2005). 'Dance and movement program improves quality-of-life measures in breast cancer survivors', *Cancer Nursing*, 28(4): 301–9.

Schore, A. N. (2012). *The Science of the Art of Psychotherapy*. New York, NY: W. W. Norton.

Serlin, I. A. (1996). 'The power of the whole: Exploring new ways to heal', *A Quarterly Community Service Publication of Sutter/CHS-Sacramento County*, 10(3): 5–7.

Serlin, I. A. (1999). 'Serlin KinAesthetic Imagining Profile for women with breast cancer.' Unpublished manuscript.

Serlin, I. A. (2000). 'Supportive/expressive psychotherapy groups for women with breast cancer: Incorporating imagery and movement as arts medicine', *The California Psychologist*, 33(3): 26.

Serlin, I. A. (2006). 'Expressive therapies', in M. Micozzi (ed.), *Complementary and Integrative Medicine in Cancer Care and Prevention*. New York, NY: Springer, pp. 81–94.

Serlin, I. A. (ed.) (2007). *Whole Person Healthcare*, 3 vols. Westport, CT: Praeger.

Serlin, I. A. and Cannon, J. (2004). 'A humanistic approach to the psychology of trauma', in D. Knafo (ed.), *Living with Terror, Working with Trauma: A Clinician's Handbook*. Northvale, NJ: Jason Aronson, pp. 313–31.

Serlin, I. A., Classen, C., Frances, B., and Angell, K. (2000). 'Symposium. Support groups for women with breast cancer: Traditional and alternative expressive approaches', *The Arts in Psychotherapy*, 27(2): 123–38.

Siegel, D. (2012). *The Developing Mind: How Relationships and the Brain Interact to Shape Who We Are*, 2nd edn. New York, NY: Guilford Press.

Stockley, S. (1992). 'Older lives, older dances: Dance movement therapy with older people', in H. Payne (ed.), *Dance Movement Therapy: Theory and Practice*. London: Tavistock/Routledge.

Turner, V. (1982). *From Ritual to Theater: The Human Seriousness of Play*. New York, NY: PAJ Publications.

Updegraff, J. A. and Taylor, S. E. (2000). 'From vulnerability to growth: The positive and negative effects of stressful life events', in J. Harvey and E. Miller (eds.), *Loss and Trauma*. Philadelphia, PA: Taylor and Francis.

US Breast Cancer Statistics (2014). <http://www.breastcancer.org/symptoms/understand_bc/statistics.jsp>

Webster, S., Clare, A., and Collier, E. (2005). 'Creative solutions: Innovative arts of the arts in mental health settings', *Journal Psychosocial Nursing Mental Health Services*, 43(5): 42–9. <http://www.ncbi.nlm.nih.gov/pubmed/15960034>

White, C. A. (2002). 'Body images in oncology', in T. Cash and T. Pruzinsky (eds.), *Body Image: A Handbook of Theory, Research, and Clinical Practice*. New York, NY: The Guilford Press, pp. 379–86.

Wright, K. (2009). *Mirroring and Attunement: Self-Realization in Psychoanalysis and Art*. New York, NY: Routledge.

Yang, K. H., Kim, Y. H., and Lee, M. S. (2005). 'Efficacy of QI-therapy (external Qigong) for elderly people with chronic pain', *International Journal Neuroscience*, 115(7): 949–63.

CHAPTER 49

ATTENDING TO THE HEARTBEAT IN DANCE MOVEMENT PSYCHOTHERAPY

Improvements in Mood and Quality of Life for Patients with Coronary Heart Disease

MARIAM MCHITARIAN, JOSEPH MOUTIRIS, AND VICKY KARKOU

INTRODUCTION

DESPITE the consistent growth of the field of medicine, coronary heart disease (CHD) remains a serious and life-threatening clinical condition. It is a major cause of mortality around the globe, and can be described as an umbrella term that contains a number of other pathophysiological and clinical events (Goodill 2005), such as unstable angina and myocardial infarction. According to the World Health Organization (2003), 16.7 million people die of cardiovascular disease (CVD) each year, worldwide, and by 2020 this number will increase to 25 million.

People with CHD often suffer from severe distress due to diagnosis, hospitalization, surgical procedures, worries about progress in recovery, fear of dying, uncertainty of outcome, loss of control, and helplessness (Barnason et al. 1995; Bolwerk 1990; Guzzetta 1989; Malan 1992). Stress is likely to stimulate the release of endogenous substances, known as catecholamines, which cause an increase in heart rate, respiratory rate, and blood pressure. As a result, anxiety and myocardial oxygen consumption increase. These adverse effects put the cardiac patient at greater risk of complications, including sudden cardiac death (White 1999). Consequently, it is of crucial importance that the care of patients with CHD focuses not just on medical care, as psychological needs to be considered next to physiological needs.

Clinicians and other professionals who work with cardiac patients direct their efforts in meeting the above needs. Among the therapeutic modalities applied, dance movement psychotherapy (DMP) is a fairly new intervention with a potentially important role to play in the psychological support of patients with CHD. In DMP a combination of verbal and non-verbal techniques are used. DMP engages unique creative movements which are a function of natural biological rhythms and are hence close to natural human expression. It has been argued that since CHD patients need long-term management, DMP can be considered as a valuable adjunctive therapeutic tool, especially for 'worried and depressed patients (Seides 1986: 88).

This chapter discusses the role of DMP in patients with established CHD through the review of relevant literature and findings from two relatively small studies.

Coronary Heart Disease (CHD)

The heart is often associated with life. Life is seen as continuing for as long as the heart is beating; a silent heart means death. From a sentimental point of view, the heart is often seen as the metaphor of love, caring, and emotions (Goodill 2005). Furthermore, Yu (2002) claims that the heart is 'the only organ linked to all emotions' (360). Garbin (1981) explains that the heart symbolizes life itself, while Maguire and Parkers (1998, cited in Thompson 2002, p. 154) similarly defined the heart as the symbol and source of life and as an internal clock that ticks our life away, until it stops. Because of the physical and emotional importance of the heart, cardiac illness (especially CHD) signifies a risk for the individual's life and thus often propels a patient into a crisis (Garbin 1981).

Medically, a cardiac emergency condition, such as acute myocardial infraction, is life threatening, and is associated with much stress for the patient, who feels that his/her life is in danger. The risk for serious complication is high. Myocardial infarction is usually treated through catheter-guided balloon angioplasty and stenting of the infarct-related artery, or sometimes with bypass surgery. (See Figures 49.1 and 49.2.)

Psychologically, following the initial shock, it is very common for patients to feel that the unpleasant event has changed them completely—especially their quality of life and their wellbeing (Seides 1986). They may feel a significant difference in their daily life, their role within the family, their work, and their finances.

CHD patients often understand that the management of their disease is life-long and the consequences and complications are largely unknown. They may also continue to face problems, not purely physical in nature but also psychological and social, for the rest of their lives. Patients' negative feelings such as stress, anger, anxiety, fear, depression, and loss of self-esteem are a usual and predictable accompaniment to the disease (Thompson et al. 2004).

Stress commonly accompanies the cardiac patient. This may be because CHD can be experienced as an imminent threat to their lives. Seyle (1976) describes stress as 'the non-specific response of the body to any demand made upon it' (p. 1). Some psychological

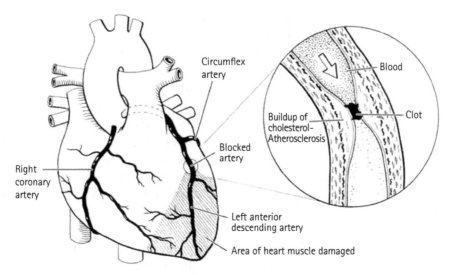

FIGURE 49.1. Myocardial infarction. (Credit: M. Mchitarian and J. Moutiris.)

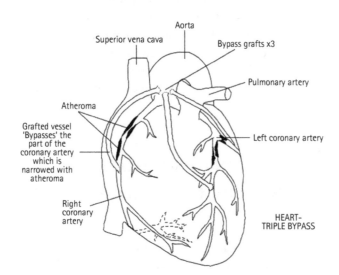

FIGURE 49.2. Catheter-guided ballon angioplasty. Myocardial infarction is usually treated through catheter-guided balloon angioplasty and stenting of the infarct-related artery. (Credit: M. Mchitarian and J. Moutiris.)

stressors for the coronary patient comprise loss of health, frustration, confusion, and changes in lifestyle. In addition, anger occurs very frequently and can be passive, active, or self-directed (Rozanski et al. 1999).

Furthermore, anxiety and fear tend to be very prevalent among CHD patients. According to Hackett and Cassem (1984, p. 437), 'anxiety is a state resembling fear, the sufferer being apprehensive and hyperalert, with signs of heightened autonomic activity.' The main reason for anxiety and fear is not the threat of sudden death but, more usually, the threat that the illness poses to their lifestyle.

If anxiety persists for some time, then this could lead the patients down the road to depression. There is a large body of evidence to suggest that depression is an important primary and secondary risk factor for CHD (Glassman and Shapiro 1998; Carney and Freedland 2003; van Melle et al. 2004; Blumenthal 2008). It is relatively frequent among CHD patients: 20% of patients have subclinical or minor depression, and 14% of patients have moderate to severe depression (Blumenthal 2008). Depression can be so severe as to turn into an 'invisible killer' (Jiang 2008, p. s20). However, many cases are undiagnosed and untreated due to the fact that depression may be masked by anxiety (Ahto et al. 1997; Thompson et al. 2004). Furthermore, depression may be triggered by the psychological trauma associated with CHD, by the disease itself, which suggests that one may be getting older, alongside feelings of weakness, fatigue, and a decreased ego strength (Cassem and Hackett 1973).

The experience of loss, real or imaginary, is also common amongst patients with CHD; for example, the loss of what they were before the heart condition changed their lives, loss of status, interests, and role within the family and the community. Besides, CHD patients experience loss of their self-esteem. As early as 1977, Cassem and Hackett claimed that myocardial infarction produces an 'ego infarction' (713).

The ultimate loss is, of course, death (Katz 2002). Fear of death is often a very real concern for the cardiac patients and their families. Patients consider death as the most direct threat to their existence. The increased awareness of the connection of CHD to morbidity and mortality makes patients link their illness with death. Therefore, what CHD patients may need in addition to their medical treatment is somatic and psychological mobilization.

DANCE MOVEMENT PSYCHOTHERAPY (DMP) AND CORONARY HEART DISEASE (CHD)

Through DMP, CHD patients have the opportunity to explore their changed world by looking at the changes in their lives in a safe environment (Seides 1986). An environment that is accepting and non-judgemental, alongside the development of trust, may enable patients to feel the freedom to be within the restrictions of their own capabilities (Sandel and Hollander 1995). In this environment, heart patients can integrate words, experiences, and actions, and they can be supported to discover new and alternative avenues of expression as gratifying ways of dealing with changes in their lives.

Furthermore, DMP may support patients to externalize their feelings and thoughts; if these are not externalized, they can cause tension and lead to physical manifestation of psychosomatics symptoms (Seides 1986). DMP can provide, through dance and movement, structures to express what is difficult to express and offer opportunities for people to explore difficult emotions associated with their losses, such as their anxiety and anger.

In addition, within DMP, patients may attempt to discover sources of support, external and internal; they may become more aware of their inner sensations and of the messages their bodies give; they may find their internal strength and agency and thus become more able to take charge of their lives (Seides 1986).

In CHD patients, vitality may return in a slow manner in a way that they feel comfortable with changes in their lifestyles following the disease. Furthermore, the majority of the patients experience invasive interventions, such as bypass surgery, in which their hearts and their chests have been opened and manipulated. As a result, they may feel that they are 'coming apart' and that their bodies are not familiar to them any more. Through dance and movement, developing a realistic new image of their bodies that is positive and healthy may be achieved through activating different parts of the body and through gradually integrating whole body movements (Seides 1986).

Group work may be of particular value for CHD patients because of the support they may receive from peers for their individual struggles, pain, and emotions. Moreover, group DMP may enable patients to deal with unhealthy coping mechanisms such as withdrawal and hypochondriasis. Within a group context, patients may encourage one another and develop openness for new learning and self-acceptance, and they become more aware of, and responsive to, others (Seides 1986). It is possible that the realization that others experience similar struggles may enable people to feel less isolated in their journey towards health.

EXISTENTIAL THEORY AND DMP

The body can be seen as a vehicle of expression: human beings communicate through their bodies long before they learn to talk; the language of the body is, in essence, our native language. Merleau-Ponty described 'le corps phenomenal' (the phenomenal body) as 'the body as I live it, as I experience it, and as it shapes my experience . . . the body is the primary self' (Strasser and Strasser 2002, p. 87).

Movement and breath indicate the start of life, the start of human existence (Chaiklin 2009). Existential theory deals with the 'science of being' and the 'examination of how humans intersubjectively understand themselves in the midst of their lived experiences' (Strasser and Strasser 2002, p. 8).

Many of the most difficult issues faced by CHD patients can be seen as existential. For example, the four ultimate concerns outlined by Yalom (1980) become relevant:

- Responsibility and freedom: we are free to make our lives what we want, and we bear full responsibility for our choices.
- Meaningless: our life has no inherent, prearranged meaning.
- Loneliness: we are ultimately alone.
- Death: we are all going to die.

According to Yalom (1980) these 'givens' are an unavoidable part of human existence in the world. In normal circumstances, people tend to push these to the back of their mind, until something triggers them and brings them to the foreground. After a serious illness, distances may seem longer, objects may become out of reach, time may feel more precious or come to a standstill. For the bereaved, a loss that occurred ten years earlier may seem as if it occurred yesterday (Barnett 2009). In the case of CHD patients, the trigger for them is the illness and all the anxious thoughts associated with this illness. Patients surviving an acute cardiac event feel that the meaning of their lives is to maintain their health and to avoid any harmful situations which would put their life at risk again.

The fear of death becomes particularly prominent. For example, from our experiences in cardiac rehabilitation units, the majority of the cardiac patients talk about a permanent fear of death which is 'shadowing' their lives. However, existentialists will argue that 'to be mindful of death is to be mindful of freedom' (Montaigne 1946, cited in Barnett 2009, p. 1). The integration of the awareness of death saves us from, rather than sentences us to, an existence of terror or bleak pessimism. According to Yalom (1998), being aware of our death can act as a catalyst to drop us into more authentic life modes, and it enhances our pleasure in the living of life.

The concept of death may be explored within the therapeutic space without turning therapy into a space that is doom and gloom (Barnett 2009). Oblique opportunities such as the use of symbolism and metaphor, offered in DMP, can enable explorations of difficult feelings such as the fear of death. Karkou and Sanderson (2006) argue that symbolic work and abstract movement may allow for profound explorations to take place that are bearable and can lead to therapeutic change without having to name things that are difficult to name. It can create an aesthetic distance that enables people to delve into deep and difficult issues, and at the same time manage with overwhelming feelings. Furthermore, symbolic work can support communication of these feelings to others, offer itself to multiple, and potentially new, readings, and open up possibilities for creative solutions.

Karkou and Sanderson (2006) also attach similar value to the role of metaphor, while Meekums (2002) argues that within DMP the body is the metaphor of all that is happening in one's life. Concepts such as creativity and creative play, associated with a democratic definition of dance as a simple, pedestrian movement, that may or may not have a rhythmical form, allow for people with no prior dance training and certainly with no training or talent to benefit by participating in DMP sessions (Meekums, Karkou and Nelson 2015). However, one of the most important ingredients in this discipline—one that can certainly enable patients with CHD to create trust, share thoughts and feelings freely, and work non-verbally on difficult emotional material—is the relationship between the client and therapist and between the group members (Karkou and Sanderson 2006; Meekums et al. 2015). Within an existential frame this relationship tends to take the form of a 'real' relationship (Clarkson 1994), which often takes place in the 'here and now'. It entails mutual participation with the therapist fully present, and empathetic and warm, while there is an acknowledgement that there is a mutual influence between the therapist and the client. In DMP practice, Karkou and Sanderson (2006) argue that the 'real' relationship may take the form of an 'active' relationship in which both client and therapist move together, exploring issues that the client brings to the sessions, within a warm and supportive environment.

Since the mid-1980s, reports have emerged concerning the inclusion of DMP as a psychosocial support service for people with primary medical illness (Goodill 2005). DMP is considered to be beneficial for CHD patients, according to a few sources of 'qualitative and anecdotal evidence' (Goodill 2005 p. 98). There is therefore a need to explore the potential contribution of DMP to this client population through empirical research. The two small case studies presented here attempt to address this need.

METHODOLOGY

The two empirical studies reported here took place on two different occasions, among two groups of cardiac patients. In both cases, a mixed-method pre- and post-case study research design was adopted to study the effect of DMP on participants' quality of life and level of depression. The first group (the Paphos DMP Study) included patients within days of an acute cardiac event, and the second group (the Edinburgh DMP Study) included patients who had had a cardiac event 8–10 years before enrolment. The first study, involving twelve patients for one month, was conducted in a public hospital in Cyprus in 2010, and the second study, involving seven patients for three months, took place in a rehabilitation centre at a private hospital in Scotland in 2011.

Inclusion criteria for both groups were: a) the occurrence of at least one acute cardiac event, such as acute myocardial infarction (MI), percutaneous coronary intervention (PCI), or coronary artery bypass graft (CABG) surgery; and b) ages between 50 and 82 years old. Exclusion criteria were: a) age less than 50 and more than 82 years; and b) co-existence of other chronic disease such as malignancy.

Previous contact with DMP sessions was not a prerequisite for inclusion. The content of DMP and its purpose was described to the patients—the potential candidates for the study. Understanding the therapeutic goals of DMP was considered essential for entry.

DATA COLLECTION

Multiple techniques can be used in a case study, so that the rich information gathered allows a detailed and multiperspective analysis of a given subject. This is known as 'triangulating the data' (Robson 2002). According to Chaiklin and Chaiklin (2004), 'simple, complete, and consistent data collection instruments should be used' (p. 81). Numerous research data were employed during the collection period in both studies, such as observation, interviews, questionnaires, and inventory scales. The therapist included general gathering information from participants, and note-taking (clinical notes), which were used as a reflective tool. Movement observation was achieved by using concepts influenced by Laban Movement Analysis—a movement system that was developed by Laban (1960) and is extensively used within DMP practice (Karkou and Sanderson 2006).

The therapist also conducted some interviews with the participants before and after the DMP sessions. Interviews can be a valuable tool of data collection regarding information on personal characteristics, attitudes, behaviours, values, and perspectives of the study participants (Robson 2002). The type of the interview used was semi-structured, in which the therapist/interviewer asked some predetermined questions relevant to participants' experience of DMP while allowing interviewees to respond to these questions fairly freely. The order of the questions was adapted based on therapist/interviewer's perception of what seemed more appropriate (Robson 2002). The interviews were held before starting and after finishing DMP sessions.

Goodill (2005) suggests that the quality of life can be included as an outcome measure to a medical DMP clinical study. Thus the contribution of DMP towards quality of life can be compared to other health modalities. In the studies presented here, the researcher/therapist used a questionnaire named 'Quality of Life Index, Cardiac Version- IV', which has been developed to measure the quality of life in ill individuals within four domains: health-functioning, socioeconomic, psychological–spiritual, and family. The scale has two parts, each of thirty-five questions, and measures the level of satisfaction (part 1) and importance (part 2) (Smith et al. 2000).

Beck's depression inventory scale was used to measure the patients' depression. This is a twenty-one-question multiple-choice self-report inventory, and is one of the most commonly used scales for measuring presence and severity of depression (Beck et al. 1996). All data gathered from participant observation and interviews helped to explore the value of DMP with acute and chronic CHD patients.

DATA ANALYSIS

According to Yin (2009): 'The analysis of case study evidence is one of the least developed and most difficult aspects of doing case studies' (p. 127). The studies discussed here used thematic analysis for the qualitative data gathered, and statistical analysis for the quantitative data.

In the thematic analysis, data were grouped into themes. After thoroughly studying the data, the therapist/researcher identified core ideas and concepts that were formulated as themes, and the frequency with which each theme was mentioned was recorded and compared to all other themes (Pope and Mays 2006). As part of the analysis, categories were identified and labelled, so that all the different aspects of the data were, if possible, included. Looking into the interconnection of emerging themes was important as a way of strengthening the analysis (Pope and Mays 2006).

Quantitative data collected from the Quality of Life Index, Cardiac Version- IV questionnaire (Ferrans and Powers 1985) and Beck's depression inventory scale (Beck et al. 1996) was entered in an SPSS file for analysis. Analysis was carried out for each parameter between baseline and final results, using the Wilcoxon test—a test used for nonparametric data that can accommodate for small samples.

The Paphos Study of DMP

Twelve patients treated for MI in the Cardiology Department of Paphos General Hospital—a district public hospital in Cyprus—were studied for one month. Written approval for the study was obtained from the Director of the Cardiology Department, and a consent form was signed by each participant. Beck's Depressions Inventory (Beck et al. 1996) and a QoL questionnaire (Ferrans and Powers 1985) were completed for each patient on the day of enrolment and one month later. Interviews took place before and after the DMP sessions. Four DMP sessions were provided individually to each patient, at regular intervals, during the thirty-day study period. The patients had never experienced any therapy nor any counselling before, and some of them were facing negatively any psychological or psychotherapeutic interventions.

The mean age of the participants was 65 ± 9 (range 54–81). Two of them were women, and ten were men. All of them had MI. They all received thrombolytic and other medical therapy, and they were waiting for further invasive treatment such as PCI or CABG surgery.

DMP Intervention

DMP sessions included discussions, relaxation and breathing techniques, and minor movements—mostly facial expressions and hand movements—which better described the patients' feelings about the disease. In this stage the acute cardiac event acted as an obstacle for major motility. The policy of the Cardiology Department suggests mainly bed rest of patients on the first few days of the infarction. DMP sessions had a client-led character.

Results

Changes in Scores on QoL Cardiac Version-IV Questionnaire (Ferrans and Powers 1985)

The satisfaction and importance of the four domains of this test (health-functioning, socioeconomic, psychological–spiritual, and family) were measured through a six-point Likert scale, ranging from 'very satisfied' to 'very unsatisfied' and from 'very important' to 'very unimportant'. The higher the score, the higher the satisfaction (see Table 49.1 and Figure 49.3).

As Table 49.1 suggests, an improvement of 46% in overall QoL was demonstrated after each DMP sessions. All parameters defining QoL also showed significant improvement. The highest positive change was observed in the health-functioning parameter in which participating in DMP was associated with a 91% improvement. Socioeconomic parameters showed 43%, whereas the psychological–spiritual domain showed a 29% improvement and the family domain a 17% improvement.

Table 49.1. The Paphos DMP Study: QoL index cardiac version: IV score.

	Before DMP	After DMP	Change (absolute/percentage)
Overall QoL	14.75	21.69	+6.8 (46%)
Health/function	9.20	17.60	+8.4 (91%)
Socioeconomic	17.29	24.79	+7.5 (43%)
Psych/spiritual	19.21	24.86	+3.6 (29%)
Family	21.60	25.20	+3.6 (17%)

(Credit: M. Mchitarian.)

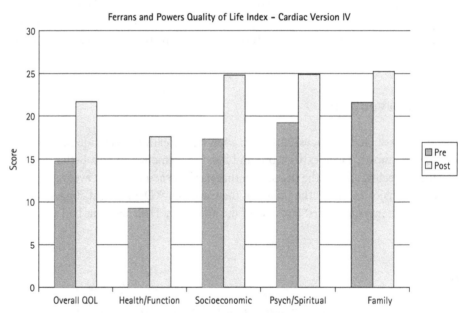

FIGURE 49.3. Paphos DMP study. Changes of scores of QoL before and after DMP. (Credit: M. Mchitarian.)

Changes in Scores on Beck's Depression Inventory Scale (Beck et al. 1996)

There was an overall improvement in the depression scale following four individual sessions. Before enrolment, one patient was found to have severe depression, three patients had a moderate degree of depression, four patients had a mild degree of depression, and four had no depression. There was a shift towards lower degrees of depression at the end of the study. The results are shown in Table 49.2 and Figure 49.4.

Table 49.2. The Paphos DMP Study: classification of the degree of depression of the study group according to Beck's depression inventory scale.

Patients	Before DMP	After DMP	Change
1	0	0	0
2	2	1	1
3	1	0	1
4	1	0	1
5	2	1	1
6	0	0	0
7	1	1	0
8	2	2	0
9	0	0	0
10	3	2	1
11	1	0	1
12	0	0	0

0: no depression; 1: mild depression; 2: moderate depression; 3: severe depression

12	Non depressed	Non depressed

Credits: M. Mchitarian

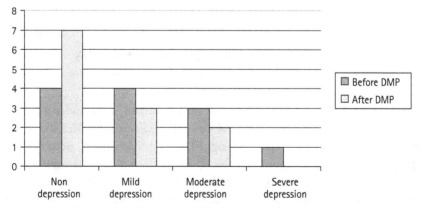

FIGURE 49.4. Paphos DMP study. Changes of scores of Beck's Depression Inventory before and after DMP. (Credit: M. Mchitarian.)

Scores on Beck's depression inventory scale were changed from before to after DMP sessions, as indicated in Table 49.2 and Figure 49.4. Before starting DMP sessions, four (4) patients had no depression, four (4) patients were found to have mild depression, three (3) had moderate depression and one (1) patient had severe depression. After four individual sessions of DMP, seven (7) patients were found to have no depression, three (3) patients had mild depression and only two (2) had moderate depression. In fact, levels of depression were reduced in all cases.

Key Themes from Interviews and Clinical Notes

In the thematic analysis of interviews and clinical notes, two main themes were identified: physiological explorations and psychological explorations.

1: Physiological Explorations in DMP

In sessions, patients were exploring mostly their physiological needs. This was because of the fact that their acute cardiac event had taken place soon before DMP was offered to them. Patients commonly worried about their treatment and medications, which were expected to be lifelong. Furthermore, they were concerned about the future invasive procedures they would have to undertake, and worried about the outcome. One of the patients said 'I do worry very much about the effectiveness of medicines', and another said 'I am not sure whether the grafts last long enough.'

2: Psychological Explorations in DMP

Due to the recent cardiac event, patients had the need to explore their feelings related to the disease. They all tried to find reasons that caused the illness, and they usually related it to problems at work or in the family. One patient said 'My work was so hard that it almost killed me' and a second patient said "Stress at work and at home created all my health problems".

Similar design was followed and results were found in the Edinburgh study.

THE EDINBURGH DMP STUDY

Seven patients with a history of myocardial infarction and angina were studied for a period of three months. Written approval was obtained from the Director of Cardiac Rehabilitation, and a consent form was signed by each participant. Beck's depression inventory scale (Beck et al. 1996) and the Quality of Life (QoL) questionnaire from Ferrans and Powers (1985) were completed for each patient on the day of enrolment and three months later. Interviews took place before and after the DMP sessions, and the sessions were provided once a week for three months to the two groups.

The age of the patients ranged from 61 to 82. The mean age was 72 (72.4 ± 6.8). Four of them were women and three of them men.

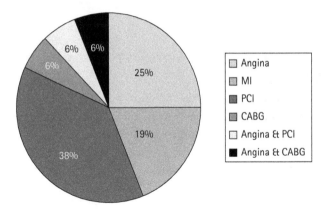

FIGURE 49.5. Edinburgh DMP study; group diagnosis. Changes of scores of QoL before and after DMP. (Credit: M. Mchitarian.)

Figure 49.5 shows the basic cardiac diagnosis (angina, MI) and the revascularization (PCI, CABG) treatment provided, of the participants. A quarter of them had a history of angina, and 19% had a history of myocardial infarction (MI). Of the surgical treatment provided, 38% underwent PCI and 6% underwent coronary bypass surgery (CABG). A further 6% had their angina treated by PCI, and another 6% had their angina treated by CABG.

DMP Intervention

Focusing on the 'here and now' was an important principle of practice in DMP sessions. The therapist's intention was for the work to be largely client-led. This was done with varying degrees of structure introduced and determined by the patients. As highlighted by them at the end of the DMP sessions, their own culture prevented them from expressing inner thoughts and feelings, and the presence of structure was therefore seen as a useful way of managing moderate expressions of emotions. Gradually, and as the sessions progressed, patients began sharing their feelings more readily, with a consequent result in the development of less structured sessions.

Different interventions were introduced, such as playful and rhythmical tasks. Playing was seen as a health-promoting activity for CHD patients, essential for people who need to reclaim this natural facility, particularly during periods of serious illness (Graham-Pole 2000). Rhythmical activities included clapping, tapping, singing, and moving, and participants were encouraged to follow their inner rhythms in their bodies as a metaphor of existing and being alive.

Results

Changes in scores on QoL Cardiac Version-IV questionnaire (Ferrans and Powers 1985)

The Wilcoxon test was also used in the Edinburgh DMP Study, which tested differences before and after the DMP intervention on the QoL and on the depression status of patients with chronic CHD. The results are presented in Table 49.3 and Figure 49.6.

Improvement in overall QoL scores of 3.31% was observed at the end of the study period. All parameters defined as QoL showed improvement apart from the domain

Table 49.3. The Edinburgh Study: improvement of QoL cardiac version IV questionnaire.

	Before DMP	After DMP	Change
Overall QoL	23.23	24	+0.87 (3.31%)
Health/function	21.93	22.39	+0.46 (2.10%)
Socioeconomic	25.03	26.35	+1.32 (5.27%)
Psych/spiritual	22.29	23.88	+1.69 (7.13%)
Family	26.07	25.85	−0.22 (0.84%)

(Credit: M. Mchitarian.)

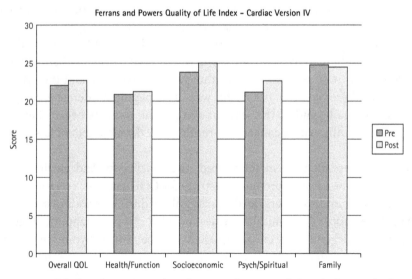

FIGURE 49.6. Edinburgh DMP study. Changes of scores of QoL before and after DMP. (Credit: M. Mchitarian.)

'Family', which showed a non-significant 0.84% reduction in the satisfaction and importance scale. The highest positive change was observed in the psychological–spiritual parameter with a 7.3% improvement. Socioeconomic parameters showed a 5.70% improvement, whereas in the health/function domain there was 2.2% improvement.

Changes in Scores on Beck's Depression Inventory Scale (Beck et al. 1996)

Scores from the pre-post measurements on depression are presented in Table 49.4 and Figure 49.7. Before the DMP group, three (3) patients were found to have mild depression, three (3) patients had moderate depression, and one (1) had no depression. After thirteen sessions of DMP, four (4) patients were found to have no depression, two (2) patients had mild depression, and one (1) had moderate depression. In fact, the degree of depression improved in all but one patient, who was absent from seven of the thirteen sessions. His absences might be a reason for not observing any improvement on the depression scale.

Key Themes from Interviews and Clinical Notes

In the thematic analysis of clinical notes, arts-based engagement, the relationships in the group and with the therapist, and opportunities for physiological exploration and psychological exploration appeared to be important themes.

Table 49.4. The Edinburgh DMP Study: classification of degree of depression of study group, according to Beck's depression inventory.

Patients	Before DMP	After DMP	Change
1	2	1	1
2	1	0	1
3	0	0	0
4	1	0	1
5	1	0	1
6	2	2	0
7	2	1	1

0: no depression; 1: mild depression; 2: moderate depression; 3: severe depression

(Credit: M. Mchitarian.)

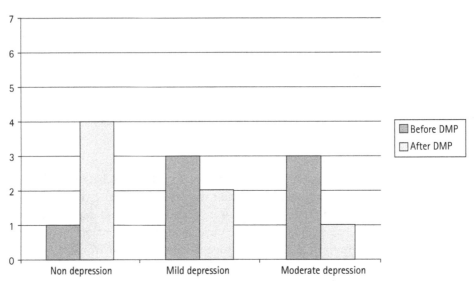

FIGURE 49.7. Edinburgh DMP Study. The effect of DMP on the degree of depression. (Credit: M. Mchitarian.)

1: Arts as a Valuable Tool in DMP

Movement, role-playing, and music were used extensively during DMP sessions. Initial scepticism and hesitation were replaced by openness, as patients began to express thoughts and feelings, showing how deeply they were affected by the sessions.

Comments such as the following were made:

> I was surprised at what came up through the arts.

> Arts have a magic element: you draw something quickly and then what have you drawn connects totally with your life.

> The instruments and the movement helped me to express difficult feelings.

> It was like my movement had been memorized to my body, and I continued exploring it back home.

2: The Relationships in the Group

None of the seven patients had previous experience of DMP, so the sessions were a challenge for both the therapist and the patients. Nevertheless, most participants attended most sessions, and those who were absent expressed sadness for not being able to attend. In general, mutual attachment between patient and therapist was strong, and was maintained throughout the sessions.

Interestingly, patients also built up a good relationship between them. Gradual trust and openness was created and initial hesitation was quickly overcome. Participants shared their experiences and expressed their opinions on related matters and on aspects of their life influenced by the disease.

During the sessions they made statements such as:

> I liked the group work we did, especially the fact that I could exchange my experience with other people with approximately the same conditions.

> I enjoyed the togetherness of the group, and I trusted my peers enough to reveal my difficulties.

> I valued the togetherness of the group.

> I valued the group camaraderie and I felt we all gelled together.

3: Physiological Explorations in DMP

Problems, such as bad control of diabetes or modification of their medical treatment, were producing much stress in the patients. They felt freedom in discussing these matters, externalized their concerns, and shared the latest developments in their medical condition with the group and with the therapist. During sessions they reported things such as:

> My consultant said that I have to normalize my weight.

> I am waiting for the next appointment with my doctor; he is going to change my medication.

> I have to do a blood test to check my cholesterol.

4: Psychological Exploration in DMP

Participants had the need to explore feelings such as loss and fear of recurrence of disease or of death. By encouraging dialogue they expressed these negative feelings deeply and shared them with the other participants, relieving much of the stress they had and better exploring their psychological needs. Some made claims such as 'I am the best doctor of myself', while jokingly they would 'rendezvous' each other: "if our hearts are still beating, we will see you next Tuesday"

DISCUSSION

The two studies were undertaken to explore the value of DMP and to explore any tentative associations between group DMP interventions and positive changes on quality of life and levels of depression amongst acute and chronic CHD patients. In both studies, all patients who engaged in the process of therapy continued with their attendance throughout the duration of the study. High acceptability of the particular intervention was therefore demonstrated. Furthermore, there were some interesting changes in quality of life and depression amongst patients with established CHD. Quality of life was improved, whilst levels of depression were reduced in both groups. It is interesting that in the second study that took place with participants who had had heart attacks some time previously, the quality of life did not improve as much as for the first study involving participants still in acute states of recovery. This is possibly a consequence of the fact that participants in the second study had already scored highly on this measure prior to the commencement of the group. It is possible that participants had already reached a plateau effect of how much they could improve in terms of quality of life.

Goodill (2005) and Serlin (2007) discussed the importance of creative arts and expressive therapies as powerful tools for potential healing of medical patients, which can happen in the medical department or within interdisciplinary treatment teams in rehabilitation centres. The creative arts therapies also stress the importance of affective experiencing in psychotherapy (Chaiklin 1975; Head 1975). Zwerling (1979) supported the importance of the arts therapies by stating that 'the creative arts therapies evoke responses, precisely at the level at which psychotherapists seek to engage their patients, more directly and more immediately than do any of the more traditional verbal therapies' (843). Qualitative data collected in the second study suggests that participants understood the importance of using the arts and dance movement in particular, and acknowledged this in their comments about their experience. It is possible that as the literature suggests (Berrol 2000; Meekums 2002, Meekums et al. 2015), when they drew a picture or executed a movement, they acquired a particular memory in their body. Even if sometimes they did not actually move but just looked at the prompts and at other people's movements, they had a sensory input which was processed via mirror neurons (Berrol 2000). Thus, they were acquiring an experience of the movement and the arts in their inner worlds.

Participants were also given opportunities to externalize their feelings and thoughts through verbal or non-verbal explorations. As the literature suggests, if these feelings are not externalized they can cause tension and physical manifestation of psychosomatic symptoms (Seides 1986). At the same time, it is important to externalize these feelings to feel emotional discharge. The patients explored these difficulties through the movement metaphor associated with the embodied experience of movement, the projected symbolism through the use of props, the iconic imagery, and the verbalization (Meekums 2002). According to Meekums(2002), metaphor, 'because of its capacity both for holding many layers of complex meaning and for mutation of these meanings, is an ideal medium for exploration in therapy. (p. 25). It is possible that participants experienced the use of metaphor as not only a useful medium for exploration, but also as a safe way of dealing with complex and difficult issues.

Yalom (2005) highlights the importance of the client–therapist relationship for some clients and some groups. He states: 'A strong therapeutic relationship may not guarantee a positive outcome, but a poor therapeutic relationship will certainly not result in an effective treatment' (p. 61). In the existential perspective highlighted in the work discussed here, the therapist aimed to develop an 'active' (Karkou and Sanderson 2006) but 'real' relationship (Clarkson 1994). Furthermore, as Rogers (1961) has argued, within such a real relationship the therapist has to be 'authentic' to himself/herself and at the same time keep this authenticity with the client. Empathy, warmth, congruence, and positive regard were part of the intention of the therapist and created a particular culture in the group that was valued by the participants, as suggested in some of the qualitative results.

Furthermore, participants explored similarities and differences amongst themselves. As they began to bond with each other they acquired a sense of being understood and being supported in both practical and emotional ways. It is possible that this enabled them to relieve some of the feelings of isolation. Yalom's (2005) therapeutic factors, such as altruism, group cohesiveness, universality, interpersonal learning input and output, and guidance, seemed to be present in the groups' life, and these factors helped the patients to enhance their relationships amongst themselves. Finally, working in the here and now was highly important. Katz (2002) argues that this is particularly relevant when one is faced with an ongoing and very present fear of death.

Interestingly, towards the end of the group, participants did not seem to want to part from each other. They arranged further meetings, and gave the impression that they wanted to keep their relationships continuing for much longer.

Conclusions

It is often discussed that the medical profession serves the physiological aspects of the body, while often excluding the emotional needs of the individual. Participants in the DMP groups themselves highlighted the importance of having psychological support along with physiological support, and they stressed the need to include such therapies in the NHS services.

Furthermore, although the pre–post design adopted in both studies and the very small sample do not allow us to draw conclusions regarding the effectiveness of the intervention, these first studies could be an indication that this is an area worthy of further investigation. The presence of a control group, randomization, the use of larger samples, and a larger team of researchers could all become important ingredients of future studies. The time when an intervention could take place—for example, soon after an operation or at later stages of the rehabilitation process—is another important factor that needs to be considered for future studies. This would inevitably have consequences on the type of intervention used, and the measures adopted in order to have meaningful outcomes. Combining such designs with thorough and in-depth qualitative studies that capture the experiences of participants could also be of particular value, and could enhance our understanding of ways in which DMP with this population could be developed further.

References

Ahto, M., Isoaho, R., Puolijoki, H., Laippala, P., Romo, M., and Kivela, S. L. (1997). 'Coronary heart disease and depression in the elderly-a population-based study', *Family Practice*, 14: 436–45.

Barnason, S., Zimmerman, L., and Nieveen, J. (1995). 'The effects of music interventions on anxiety in the patient after coronary artery bypass grafting', *Heart and Lung* 24(2): 124–32.

Barnett, L. (2009). *When Death Enters the Therapeutic Space: Existential Perspectives in Psychotherapy and Counselling*. London: Routledge.

Beck, A. T., Steer, R. A., and Brown, G. K. (1996). *BDI-II Manual*, 2nd edn. San Antonio, TX: Pearson.

Berrol, C. F. (2000). 'The spectrum of research options in dance/movement therapy', *American Journal of Dance Therapy*, 22(1): 29–46.

Blumenthal, J. A. (2008). 'Depression and coronary heart disease: Association and implications for treatment', *Clevelant Clinic Journal of Medicine*, 75(2): S48–53.

Bolwerk, C. A. (1990). 'Effects of relaxing music on state anxiety in myocardial infarction patients', *Critical Care Nursing Quarterly*, 13(2): 63–72.

Carney, R. M., and Freedland, K. E. (2003). 'Depression, mortality, and medical morbidity in patients with coronary heart disease', *Biological Psychiatry*, 54: 241–47.

Cassem, N. M. and Hackett, T.P. (1973). 'Psychological rehabilitation and myocardial infarction patients in the acute phase', *Heart Lung*, 2: 382–88.

Cassem, N. M. and Hackett, T. P. (1977). 'Psychological aspects of myocardial infarction', *Medical Clinics of North America*, 61: 711–21.

Chaiklin, H. (1975). *Marian Chace: Her Papers*. Columbia, MD: American Dance Therapy Association.

Chaiklin, H., and Chaiklin, S. (2004). 'The case study', in R. F. Cruz and C. F. Berrol (eds.), *Dance/Movement Therapists In Action: A Working Guide to Research Option*. Springfield: Charles C. Thomas, pp. 69–85.

Chaiklin, S. (2009). 'We dance from the moment our feet touch the earth', in S. Chaiklin and H. Wengrower (eds.), *The Art and Science of Dance/Movement Therapy Life is Dance*. New York, NY: Routledge, pp. 3–11.

Clarkson, P. (1994). 'The psychotherapeutic relationship', in P. Clarkson and M. Pokorny (eds.), *The Handbook of Psychotherapy*. London: Routledge, pp. 28–48.

Ferrans, C. and Powers, M. (1985). 'Quality of life index: Development and psychometric properties', *Advances in Nursing Science*, 8: 15–24.

Garbin, M. (1981). 'Principles of mental health applied to the care of people with cardiac problems', in W. C. McGurn (ed.), *People with Cardiac Problems: Nursing Concepts*. Pennsylvania, PA: J. B. Lippincott Company, pp. 123–44.

Glassman, A. H. and Shapiro, P. A. (1998). 'Depression and the course of coronary artery disease', *American Journal of Psychiatry*, 155: 4–11.

Goodill, S. W. (2005). *An Introduction to Medical Dance/Movement Therapy*. London: Jessica Kingsley.

Graham-Pole, J. (2000). *Illness and the Art of Creative Self-Expression; Stories and Exercises from the Arts for Those with Chronic Illness*. Oakland, CA: New Harbinger Publications.

Guzzetta, C. E. (1989). 'Effects of relaxation and music therapy on patients in a coronary care unit with presumptive acute myocardial infarction', *Heart and Lung*, 18(6): 609–16.

Hackett, T. P. and Cassem, N. H. (1984). 'Psychologic aspects of rehabilitation after myocardial infarction and coronary artery bypass surgery', in N. K. Wenger and H. K. Hellerstein (eds.), *Rehabilitation of the Coronary Patient*. New York, NY: John Wiley and Sons, pp. 437–51.

Head, V. B. (1975). 'Experiences with art therapy in short term groups of day clinic addicted patients', *Ontario Psychologist*, 7(4): 42–9.

Jiang, W. (2008). 'Impacts of depression and emotional distress on cardiac disease', *Cleveland Clinic Journal of Medicine*, 75(2): S20–5.

Karkou, V. and Sanderson, P. (2006). *Arts Therapies: A Research Based Map of the Field*. Edinburgh: Elsevier.

Katz, J. (2002). 'Ill-health', in N. Thompson (ed.). *Loss and Grief: A Guide for Human Services Practitioners*. New York: Palgrave, pp. 149–61.

Laban, R. (1960). *Mastery of Movement*. London: MacDonald and Evans.

Malan, S. S. (1992). 'Psychological adjustment following MI: Current views and nursing implications', *Journal of Cardiovascular Nursing*, 6: 57–70.

Meekums, B. (2002). *Dance Movement Psychotherapy: A Creative Psychotherapeutic Approach*. London: Sage.

Meekums, B., Karkou, V., and Nelson, E. A. (2015). 'Dance movement therapy for depression', *Cochrane Database of Systematic Reviews*, Issue 2, Art. No. CD009895. doi: 10.1002/14651858.CD009895.pub2. <http://onlinelibrary.wiley.com/doi/10.1002/14651858.CD009895.pub2/abstract>

Pope, C. and Mays, N. (2006). 'Qualitative methods in health research', in C. Pope and N. Mays (eds.), *Qualitative Research in Health Care*, 3rd edn. Massachusetts, Oxford and Victoria: Blackwell, pp. 1–11.

Robson, C. (2002). *Real World Research*, 2nd edn. Oxford: Blackwell.

Rogers, C. (1961). *A Therapist's View of Psychotherapy on Becoming a Person*. London: Constable and Company.

Rozanski, A., Blumenthal, J. A., and Kaplan, J. (1999). 'Impact of psychological factors on the pathogenesis of cardiovascular disease and implications for therapy', *Circulation*, 99(16): 2192–217.

Sandel, L. S. and Hollander, A. S. (1995). 'Dance/movement therapy with aging populations', in F. J. Levy, J. P. Fried, and F. Leventhal, *Dance and Other Expressive Art Therapies: When Words are Not Enough*. London: Routledge, pp. 133–43.

Seides, M. R. (1986). 'Dance/movement therapy as a modality in the treatment of the psychosocial complications of heart disease', *American Journal of Dance Therapy*, 9: 83–101.

Serlin, I. A. (2007). 'The arts therapies: Whole person integrative approaches to healthcare.' <http://www.union-street-health-associates.com/articles/arts_therapies.pdf> (accessed 28 April 2011).

Seyle, H. (1976). *The Stress of Life*. New York, NY: McGraw-Hill.

Smith, H. J., Taylor, R., and Mitchell, A. (2000). 'A comparison of four quality of life instruments in cardiac patients: SF-36, QLI, QLMI and SEIQoL', *Heart*, 84(4): 390–4.

Strasser, F. and Strasser, A. (2002). *Existential Time-Limited Therapy: The Wheel of Existence*, 3rd edn. Chichester: John Wiley and Sons.

Thompson, N. (2002). *Loss and Grief: A Guide for Human Services Practitioners*. New York, NY: Palgrave.

Thompson, D. R., Webster, R.T., and Quinn, T. (2004). *Caring for the Coronary Patient*, 2nd edn. Edinburgh: Elsevier.

van Melle, J. P., de Jonge, P., Spijjkerman, T. A., Tijssen, J. G., Ormel, J., van Veldhuisen D. J., van den Bring, R. H., and van den Berg, M. P. (2004). 'Prognostic association of depression following myocardial infarction with mortality and cardiovascular events: A meta-analysis', *Psychosomatic Medicine*, 71: 253–9.

White, J. M. (1999). 'Effects of relaxing music on cardiac autonomic balance and anxiety after acute myocardial infarction', *American Journal of Critical Care*, 8(4): 220–30.

World Health Organization (2003). *World Health Report 2003: Shaping the Future*. Geneva: World Health Organization.

Yalom, I. D. (1980). *Existential Psychotherapy*. New York, NY: Basic Books.

Yalom, I. D. (1998). *The Yalom Reader: Selections from the Work of a Mastery Therapist and Storyteller*. New York, NY: Basic Books.

Yalom, I. D. (2005). *The Theory and Practice of Group Psychotherapy*, 5th edn. New York, NY: Basic Books.

Yin, R. K. (2009). *Case Study Research Design and Methods*, 4th edn. London: Sage.

Yu, N. (2002). 'Body and emotion: Body parts in Chinese expression of emotions', *Pragmatics and Cognition*, 10(1): 341–67.

Zwerling, I. (1979). 'The creative arts therapies as "real therapies"', *Hospital and Community Psychiatry*, 30(12): 841–4.

CONCLUSION

VICKY KARKOU AND SUE OLIVER

In compiling this collection of chapters on the many aspects of dance which impinge on human wellbeing, we have striven to tap into expertise from many parts of the world, to present to the readers multiple perspectives with a truly international flavour. We have been fortunate to have found contributors who are pioneers in their fields as scientists, artists, somatic practitioners, educators, community dancers, or therapists. From their respective specialties they offer glimpses of how their work breaks new ground in the application of dance as a vehicle for promoting feelings of wellbeing in adults and children, those with learning and/or physical disabilities, those with mental health and/or medical conditions, and often individuals, groups, and communities with no urgent health needs. And yet we know that the study of dance and wellbeing is a growth area; even in this large volume we have only managed to scratch the surface of this topic.

The diverse contributions included in the book cover physiological, social, emotional, and spiritual aspects of dance, and sit—sometimes comfortably, other times less so—within the different parts in which we have placed them. Similar to how dance practitioners may or may not sit with ease within professional contexts, in this book the contributors have been offered an opportunity to voice their position, debate and challenge prevailing ideas and norms, and attempt to shape new ones. Current debates in education, community, and health, for example, are noted in the different parts of the book. Discussing educational policies and conceptualizing dance practice as contributing, either directly or indirectly, towards learning outcomes and towards an improved learning experience are certainly apparent in Part III: Dance in Education. Activism, community engagement, resolution of societal conflict, and alleviation of personal trauma are clearly part of Part IV: Dance in the Community. Evidence, outcomes, and effectiveness are concepts explored in the last part of the book which refers to dance in healthcare contexts.

These diverse cultures captured, recreated, and partly created anew in this book have a number of interwoven threads that run through all parts. In each part the art form is kept alive, further enhanced by the addition of online video material. These are not simply add-ons. In some cases they constitute the main contribution made with the text, simply following the dance experience (see, for example, the work by Andrea Olsen in Part I, many of the contributions in Part II, and projects briefly described in some of the introductions). Furthermore, the inclusion of video material on the companion website enable readers to appreciate fully the extent to which this visual art form has become entrenched in diverse cultural settings worldwide, and allows flexibility for further development.

Readers will also find that there is a vein of dance movement psychotherapy running through the book. The techniques which are encompassed in that discipline lend themselves to educational and community settings, health and care settings, and professional dance contexts alike, shaped and reshaped every time to reflect diverse contexts, philosophical assumptions, and client needs. The inclusion of dance movement psychotherapy, therefore, is another unifying agent among the disparate sections of the book. Furthermore, in some cases the distinction between therapy and art is not as easy to make as it is the case with the different types of interventions described in this book and the numerous examples of therapeutic dance included.

From the beginning of this project we set out to explore the contribution of dance to wellbeing. The different chapters of this book make compelling cases for their perspectives. They also argue that certain aspects of dance may be responsible for effects upon positive experiences; they may constitute the 'active ingredients' in the process towards enhancing different types of wellbeing.

Karkou and Sanderson (2006) argue that (i) the nature of the art form in itself, (ii) creativity and its capacity to create new meaning, (iii) imagination, symbolism, and metaphor, (iv) the use of non-verbal communication, both inner as well as outer, and (v) the relationship, are important explanatory factors as to why dance may be important in 'generating wellness'. This relationship within, but also outside, a clear therapeutic context and therapeutic approach, may offer the conditions needed to address what is essentially a core human need to relate with other human beings. This is about humans as mammals being essentially social beings who need to breath, move, eat and sleep—even die—in the presence of another or others, as social psychologists and child psychotherapists have argued (Stern 2005; Trevarthen 1998).

Furthermore, the diverse chapters covered here provide support to our belief that dance is an ideal catalyst in multidisciplinary contexts: it offers the opportunity for a multifaceted understanding of the body, a means of communication between performers and spectators or among participants, creating a social 'bridge' between groups. This is evident from the disparate range of professions represented among the authors. For example, the authorship of the chapter by Grosbras et al. in Part I encompasses the disciplines of psychology, theatre, dance, performance, and IT. In Part V there are also a number of examples from multidisciplinary work. Margariti, for example, a Greek dance therapist, works alongside a team of scientists and physicians at the Department of Psychiatry in Athens, while Koch, a German psychologist and dance therapist, works closely with Fuchs, a German psychiatrist and philosopher. Furthermore, as promised in the Introduction in this book, the contributors include medical professionals, therapists, school teachers, lecturers, choreographers, sports professionals, and community dance artists. We claim that dance, in its various applications, can serve as a link across subjects in school curricula, and a medium for people with health problems to explore their feelings and promote a sense of wellbeing at a time when they are perhaps at their most vulnerable. It allows cultural links to thrive across the globe, so we can find, for example, Butoh classes in Edinburgh and Capoeira in Warsaw. Dancers are not just learning a particular genre of dance, but are catching a glimpse of other cultures, which might entice them to explore these cultures further. It is possible that looking at dance from diverse cultural perspectives—and moreover, *doing* it—could be an effective way of uniting our fragmented world.

However, the degree to which these assumptions are indeed founded in empirical research and scientific evidence remains unclear. Although there is a growing number of empirical studies that look at the effectiveness of dance and dance movement psychotherapy (see, for example, Koch et al. 2014; Meekums et al. 2015; Kiepe et al. 2012), and several chapters in this book certainly contribute to this growth, this area still needs further development. Furthermore, to look at this topic only through a positivistic perspective would be highly inappropriate for a topic so highly complex. For this reason, both qualitative and quantitative research examples are included throughout the whole of the book, next to practice-based and arts-based studies. From chapters with personal and subjective focus to chapters that make claims for objective and generalizable results, all contributions make a particular yet considered contribution to the topic.

We hope that this range of perspectives will have stimulated thoughts, feelings, and somatic responses to the subject of dance and wellbeing, and kindled desires to contribute more to the body of (and embodied) knowledge. At different points, we as editors have also asked questions as a way of contributing to the debate. The intention was never to present the subject as a finished entity but as fertile ground in which others will feel inspired to nurture their practice and contribute further. We therefore hope that 'plants' of all sorts will find this ground hospitable to deepen their roots and expand their branches in ways that, as Heather Hill referred to in her contribution to this book, are not just well, but can also 'flourish'.

References

Karkou, V. and Sanderson, P. (2006). *Arts Therapies: A Research-Based Map of the Field*. Edinburgh: Elsevier.

Kiepe, M.-S., Stöckigt, B., and Keil, T. (2012). 'Effects of dance therapy and ballroom dances on physical and mental illnesses: A systematic review', *The Arts in Psychotherapy*, 39(5): 404–11.

Koch, S., Kunz, T., Lykou, S., and Cruz, R. (2014). 'Effects of dance movement therapy and dance on health-related psychological outcomes: A meta-analysis', *The Arts in Psychotherapy*, 41: 46–64.

Meekums, B., Karkou, V., Nelson, E. A. (2015). 'Dance movement therapy for depression', *Cochrane Database of Systematic Reviews, Issue 2. Art. No.: CD009895.* doi:10.1002/14651858. CD009895.pub2.   <http://onlinelibrary.wiley.com/doi/10.1002/14651858.CD009895.pub2/abstract>

Stern, D. N. (2005) 'Intersubjectivity', in Person, E. S., Cooper, A. M., and Gobbard, G. O. (eds.), *Textbook of Psychoanalysis.* Washington, DC: American Psychiatric Publishing, pp. 77–92.

Trevarthen, C. (1998). 'The concept and foundations of infant intersubjectivity', in S. Bråten (ed.), *Intersubjective Communication and Emotion in Early Ontogeny.* Cambridge: Cambridge University Press, pp. 15–46.

Index

Note: Page references followed by a "*t*" indicate table; "*f*" indicate figure.

CPSIA information can be obtained
at www.ICGtesting.com
Printed in the USA
BVHW080401190520
579768BV00002B/2

9 780197 526330